BUSINESS MATH

Tenth Edition

CHERYL CLEAVES
Southwest Tennessee Community College

MARGIE HOBBS
Southwest Tennessee Community College

JEFFREY NOBLE
Madison College

PEARSON

Boston   Columbus   Indianapolis   New York   San Francisco   Upper Saddle River
Amsterdam   Cape Town   Dubai   London   Madrid   Milan   Munich   Paris   Montreal   Toronto
Delhi   Mexico City   São Paulo   Sydney   Hong Kong   Seoul   Singapore   Taipei   Tokyo

Editorial Director: Vernon R. Anthony
Acquisitions Editor: Sara Eilert
Editor, Digital Projects: Nichole Caldwell
Editorial Assistant: Doug Greive
Director of Marketing: David Gesell
Marketing Manager: Stacey Martinez
Senior Marketing Coordinator: Alicia Wozniak
Senior Marketing Assistant: Les Roberts
Senior Managing Editor: JoEllen Gohr
Senior Project Manager: Rex Davidson
Senior Operations Supervisor: Pat Tonneman

Creative Director: Andrea Nix
Art Director: Diane Y. Ernsberger
Cover Designer: Wanda Espana
Media Project Manager: Christina Maestri
Full-Service Project Management: Kelly Ricci/ Aptara®, Inc.
Composition: Aptara®, Inc.
Printer/Binder: R. R. Donnelley & Sons
Cover Printer: Lehigh/Phoenix Color Hagerstown
Text Font: Times Roman

Credits and acknowledgments for materials borrowed from other sources and reproduced, with permission, in this textbook appear on the credits page.

Library of Congress Cataloging-in-Publication Data

Cleaves, Cheryl S.

Business math/Cheryl Cleaves, Margie Hobbs, Jeffrey Noble.—10th ed.
    p. cm.
  Includes bibliographical references and index.
  ISBN 978-0-13-301120-3 (alk. paper)
  1. Business mathematics. I. Hobbs, Margie J. II. Noble, Jeffrey J. III. Title.

HF5691.C53 2014
650.01′513—dc23   2012040057

10 9 8 7 6 5 4 3 2 1

ISBN 10:   0-13-301120-8
ISBN 13: 978-0-13-301120-3

PREFACE

From the Authors: About the 10th Edition of Business Math

Does just opening this text increase your stress level? What can be more stressful than managing your own money or the finances of a small business? Well, we hope you will be pleasantly surprised as you work through this text.

This text is designed to empower individuals and small business owners with the skills they need to handle their personal and business finances. For too long, too many of us have avoided the topics presented in this text. We either thought that we couldn't learn them because they involved math or that we didn't need them because we had a good background in more advanced mathematical concepts. *Business Math* deals with money, and everyone needs to understand how to manage money.

In this text you will review some basic math that you may have forgotten; even if you haven't, the basic math will relate to the world in which you live. All the applied problems are designed to simulate instances in real life where you would need these math skills.

You will learn about banking, interest, consumer credit, mortgages, investments, insurance, taxes, and many more topics that you will encounter no matter what career you pursue. You will examine some common business practices such as payroll, markup, markdown, trade discounts, cash discounts, and business statistics that will be beneficial whether you are a consumer, employee, or owner of a small business.

For those more involved with the recordkeeping of a small business, you will find topics such as depreciation, inventory, and financial statements to be very informative, especially if you plan to take some accounting courses. Recordkeeping requirements that we encounter from government agencies, lending agencies, and investors can be overwhelming if we don't have a basic understanding of these concepts.

Why is this text special? We have tried to use a conversational writing style and to incorporate interesting but relevant examples, applications, and case studies. All three of us have families, business interests, educational experiences, and many business contacts that we have drawn on when writing this text. Above all, we care about our students. We want our students to enjoy learning new things while they get beyond some of the anxieties and dislikes that are commonly associated with these topics. While we all take pride in our work, we also make it fun. One of our main objectives is to make it fun for you, too.

We hope you enjoy your journey through the text. If you have questions or suggestions, we would love to hear from you.

Cheryl Cleaves
ccleaves@bellsouth.net

Margie Hobbs
margiehobbs@bellsouth.net

Jeffrey Noble
JNoble@madisoncollege.edu

What's New in the 10th Edition
Complete and Brief (Ch. 1–16) Editions

Focus on Facilitating Learning

- Stop and Check Exercises and Section Exercises have been mapped to Examples.
- Calculator assistance has been expanded to include more calculator options.
- MyMathLab resources have been significantly enhanced.

New Trends and New Laws Incorporated

- Banking chapter reflects the increase in electronic banking.
- Payroll, Consumer Credit, and Taxes chapters reflect new laws and procedures.
- Investment and insurance topics reflect recent changes in the marketplace.

Updated to Enhance Real-World Relevancy

- Examples and exercises have been updated to reflect current products and prices.
- Chapter openers and case studies have been updated to reflect relevant data.
- New chapter openers and case studies have been added.

Revision to Chapter on Financial Statements

- Discussion of shareholder ratios and their impact on company stock evaluation.
- Examples and exercises have been added to help determine if the price of a company's stock is reasonable from the basis of its financial position.
- Emphasis is placed on the importance of solvency and financial responsibility in financial statement reporting.

TIME-TESTED PEDAGOGY AIDS STUDENT LEARNING

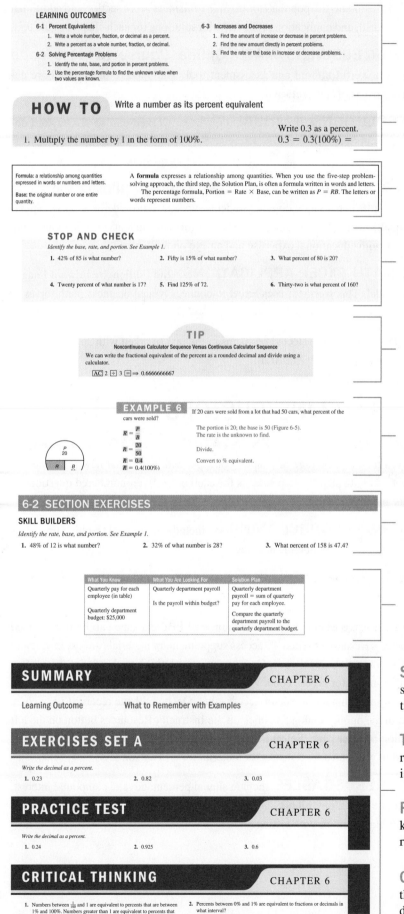

LEARNING OUTCOMES

6-1 Percent Equivalents
1. Write a whole number, fraction, or decimal as a percent.
2. Write a percent as a whole number, fraction, or decimal.

6-2 Solving Percentage Problems
1. Identify the rate, base, and portion in percent problems.
2. Use the percentage formula to find the unknown value when two values are known.

6-3 Increases and Decreases
1. Find the amount of increase or decrease in percent problems.
2. Find the new amount directly in percent problems.
3. Find the rate or the base in increase or decrease problems.

HOW TO Write a number as its percent equivalent

1. Multiply the number by 1 in the form of 100%.

Write 0.3 as a percent.
0.3 = 0.3(100%) =

Formula: a relationship among quantities expressed in words or numbers and letters.

Base: the original number or one entire quantity.

A **formula** expresses a relationship among quantities. When you use the five-step problem-solving approach, the third step, the Solution Plan, is often a formula written in words and letters. The percentage formula, Portion = Rate × Base, can be written as $P = RB$. The letters or words represent numbers.

STOP AND CHECK

Identify the base, rate, and portion. See Example 1.

1. 42% of 85 is what number?
2. Fifty is 15% of what number?
3. What percent of 80 is 20?
4. Twenty percent of what number is 17?
5. Find 125% of 72.
6. Thirty-two is what percent of 160?

TIP

Noncontinuous Calculator Sequence Versus Continuous Calculator Sequence
We can write the fractional equivalent of the percent as a rounded decimal and divide using a calculator.
AC 2 ÷ 3 = ⟹ 0.6666666667

EXAMPLE 6 If 20 cars were sold from a lot that had 50 cars, what percent of the cars were sold?

$R = \dfrac{P}{B}$ The portion is 20; the base is 50 (Figure 6-5). The rate is the unknown to find.

$R = \dfrac{20}{50}$ Divide.

$R = 0.4$ Convert to % equivalent.

$R = 0.4(100\%)$

6-2 SECTION EXERCISES

SKILL BUILDERS

Identify the rate, base, and portion. See Example 1.
1. 48% of 12 is what number?
2. 32% of what number is 28?
3. What percent of 158 is 47.4?

What You Know	What You Are Looking For	Solution Plan
Quarterly pay for each employee (in table)	Quarterly department payroll	Quarterly department payroll = sum of quarterly pay for each employee.
Quarterly department budget: $25,000	Is the payroll within budget?	Compare the quarterly department payroll to the quarterly department budget.

SUMMARY CHAPTER 6

Learning Outcome	What to Remember with Examples

EXERCISES SET A CHAPTER 6

Write the decimal as a percent.
1. 0.23
2. 0.82
3. 0.03

PRACTICE TEST CHAPTER 6

Write the decimal as a percent.
1. 0.24
2. 0.925
3. 0.6

CRITICAL THINKING CHAPTER 6

1. Numbers between $\frac{1}{100}$ and 1 are equivalent to percents that are between 1% and 100%. Numbers greater than 1 are equivalent to percents that
2. Percents between 0% and 1% are equivalent to fractions or decimals in what interval?

LEARNING OUTCOMES are outlined at the beginning of each chapter, repeated throughout the chapter, and reviewed in the Summary to keep students focused on important concepts.

HOW TO feature takes students through the steps to solve different business applications.

KEY TERMS are highlighted in bold in the text and called out in the margin with their definitions.

STOP AND CHECK exercises give students practice so they can master every outcome. Exercises are coded to Examples. Solutions are in an appendix at the end of the text.

TIP AND DID YOU KNOW? boxes give students alternate strategies for solving problems, point out common mistakes to avoid, and give instruction on using calculators.

EXAMPLES show all the steps and use annotations and color to highlight the concepts.

SKILL BUILDERS AND APPLICATIONS are the two types of section exercises that are included to help students first master basic concepts and then apply them.

FIVE-STEP PROBLEM-SOLVING STRATEGY gives students an efficient and effective way to approach problem solving and gives them a strategy for good decision making.

SUMMARY at the end of each chapter functions as a mini study-review with learning outcomes and step-by-step instructions and examples.

TWO PROBLEM SETS (A & B) are provided on perforated pages for easy removal. Ample space for students' work is provided, so these can be assigned as hand-in homework.

PRACTICE TEST gives students a chance to gauge their knowledge of the chapter material and see where they need to review.

CRITICAL THINKING questions ask the students to apply their knowledge to more complex questions and build their decision-making skills.

RESOURCES FOR STUDENTS

- **STUDY GUIDE** contains the popular *How to Study Business Math* section and additional sets of vocabulary, drill, and application problems with solutions for each chapter in the text.

- **MATHXL® FOR BUSINESS MATH Online Course (access code required)** is a powerful tutorial and assessment tool. The features of this tool are described later in the pages of this preface.

- **STUDENT SOLUTIONS MANUAL** includes worked-out solutions to odd-numbered problems in Section Exercises, Exercise Sets A and B, and to all Practice Test questions.

- **MYMATHLAB® Online Course (access code required)** MyMathLab delivers **proven results** in helping individual students succeed. It provides **engaging experiences** that personalize, stimulate, and measure learning for each student. And, it comes from a **trusted partner** with educational expertise and an eye on the future.

- **BUSINESS MATH EXCEL APPLICATIONS,** 2nd Edition, by Edward Laughbaum and Ken Seidel. This worktext uses Excel to connect typical business math topics to real-world applications.

- **EXCEL TEMPLATES** for selected problems in the text (marked with an Excel icon in the margin) are available with **MyMathLab.**

RESOURCES FOR INSTRUCTORS

- **POWERPOINT® LECTURE PRESENTATION PACKAGE** has been revised and augmented to include coverage of chapter concepts with additional new problems not found in the text and with step-by-step screens for each of the even-numbered questions in the exercise sets and practice test.

- **INSTRUCTOR'S RESOURCE MANUAL** includes additional teaching tips, class presentation outlines, and reproducible activities.

- **TEST GENERATOR** now features a mix of over 1,800 algorithmically generated computational questions and static concept questions.

The Instructor's Resource Manual, Test Generator, and PPT Package can be downloaded from our Instructor's Resource Center. To access supplementary materials online, instructors need to request an instructor access code. Go to **www.pearsonhighered.com/irc,** where you can register for an instructor access code. Within 48 hours of registering you will receive a confirming e-mail including an instructor access code. Once you have received your code, locate your text in the online catalog and click on the Instructor Resources button on the left side of the catalog product page. Select a supplement and a log-in page will appear. Once you have logged in, you can access instructor material for all Pearson texts.

- **QUICK REFERENCE TABLES** include annual percentage rate, compound interest, present value, future value, payroll tax, and income tax tables, which are available to adopters for use in the classroom or with testing.

PROVEN TO DRAMATICALLY IMPROVE STUDENT PERFORMANCE!

MyMathLab MyMathLab® Business Math Online Course (access code required)

MyMathLab delivers **proven results** in helping individual students succeed.

- MyMathLab has a consistently positive impact on the quality of learning in higher education math instruction. MyMathLab can be successfully implemented in any environment—lab-based, hybrid, fully online, traditional—and demonstrates the quantifiable difference that integrated usage has on student retention, subsequent success, and overall achievement.

- MyMathLab's comprehensive online gradebook automatically tracks your students' results on tests, quizzes, homework, and in the study plan. You can use the gradebook to quickly intervene if your students have trouble, or to provide positive feedback on a job well done. The data within MyMathLab is easily exported to a variety of spreadsheet programs, such as Microsoft Excel. You can determine which points of data you want to export, and then analyze the results to determine success.

MyMathLab provides **engaging experiences** that personalize, stimulate, and measure learning for each student.

- EXERCISES: The homework and practice exercises in MyMathLab are correlated to the exercises in the text, and they regenerate algorithmically to give students unlimited opportunity for practice and mastery. The software offers immediate, helpful feedback when students enter incorrect answers.

- MULTIMEDIA LEARNING AIDS: Exercises include guided solutions, sample problems, animations, videos, and eText clips for extra help at point-of-use.

- EXPERT TUTORING: Although many students describe the whole of MyMathLab as "like having your own personal tutor," students using MyMathLab do have access to live tutoring from Pearson from qualified math and statistics instructors.

And MyMathLab comes from a **trusted partner** with educational expertise and an eye on the future.

- Knowing that you are using a Pearson product means knowing that you are using quality content. That means that our eTexts are accurate and our assessment tools work. Whether you are just getting started with MyMathLab, or have a question along the way, we're here to help you learn about our technologies and how to incorporate them into your course.

To learn more about how MyMathLab combines proven learning applications with powerful assessment, visit **www.mymathlab.com** or contact your Pearson representative.

MathXL MathXL® Business Math Online Course (access code required)

MathXL® is the homework and assessment engine that runs MyMathLab. (MyMathLab is MathXL plus a learning management system.)

With MathXL, instructors can:

- Create, edit, and assign online homework and tests using algorithmically generated exercises correlated at the objective level to the text.
- Create and assign their own online exercises and import TestGen tests for added flexibility.
- Maintain records of all student work tracked in MathXL's online gradebook.

With MathXL, students can:

- Take chapter tests in MathXL and receive personalized study plans and/or personalized homework assignments based on their test results.
- Use the study plan and/or the homework to link directly to tutorial exercises for the objectives they need to study.
- Access supplemental animations and video clips directly from selected exercises.

MathXL is available to qualified adopters. For more information, visit our web site at www.mathxl.com, or contact your Pearson representative.

MyCourse   MyCourse for Business Math

MyCourse is an innovative combination of two of Pearson's award-winning digital solutions: the powerful assessment and media content of MyMathLab and the instructional content and full course design of CourseConnect. The result is a premium courseware solution that includes the best of Pearson's digital content in a fully scoped and sequenced course solution designed to be used in online or blended classes, with a single sign-on. For more information and a demonstration, please contact your local representative.

VALUE PACKAGING OPTIONS: WHICH PACKAGE IS RIGHT FOR YOUR PROGRAM?

10th Edition packaging options provide you with a variety of levels of involvement with electronic tools beyond classroom teaching. Here are a few notes to help you identify the best package to fit your needs. Please contact your Pearson representative to learn more about our tools and packaging options.

Traditional classroom with online homework and quizzes that automatically feed an Instructor gradebook:

MathXL MATHXL® ONLINE packaged with the Student Text and the printed Study Guide is ideal for this setting. MathXL Online for Business Math allows you to set up homework assignments and quizzes for students and easily monitor student performance at any time.

Fully online or traditional classroom course with a need for a full range of classroom management and assessment tools including an interactive ebook:

MyMathLab MYMATHLAB® packaged with the Student Text and the printed Study Guide is ideal for this setting. MyMathLab provides you with all of the content, classroom management tools, and diagnosis and assessment options you might need in this course. Order package (Complete Edition ISBN: 0-13-340229-0. Brief Edition ISBN: 0-13-340230-4)

MyCourse MYCOURSE packaged with the Student Text and the printed Study Guide delivers all of the MyMathLab content and facilities along with robust interactive learning modules that enrich the learning experience. Your local representative will set up a custom ISBN for this package for your school.

The *PRINTED STUDENT SOLUTIONS MANUAL* (Complete and Brief Edition ISBN: 0-13-335538-1) and the *QUICK REFERENCE TABLES* (ISBN: 0-13-302737-6) can be packaged with any of these options on demand.

VIDEO CASES HELP YOU BRING THE REAL WORLD OF BUSINESS MATH INTO THE CLASSROOM

BUSINESS MATH CASE VIDEOS: Ten video case scenarios, focusing on business issues encountered by Charlie Cleaves and his employees at The 7th Inning Sports Memorabilia Company, require the use of business math. Charlie got his start in the memorabilia business collecting, trading, and selling sports cards. His business has grown to include five specialized departments: sports and historical memorabilia, trading cards and collectible supplies, custom framing, trophy and engraving, and a barbecue restaurant. The videos focus on business and personal finance issues that Charlie and his staff encounter on the job and when making consumer decisions.

Video Topics:

　　Video 1—The Real World: Introduction to The 7th Inning Business and Personnel

　　Video 2—Which Bank Account Is Best?

　　Video 3—How Many Hamburgers?

　　Video 4—How Many Baseball Cards?

　　Video 5—An All-Star Signing!

　　Video 6—Should I Buy New Equipment Now?

　　Video 7—Which Credit Card Deal Is Best?

　　Video 8—Should I Buy or Lease a Car?

　　Video 9—Should I Invest in Elvis?

　　Video 10—Should I Buy a House?

The videos are designed for in-class use and are accompanied by worksheets that aid in classroom discussion and in calculating the solution to the scenario. Annotated worksheets and teaching notes are in the Online Instructor's Video Cases Toolkit. Students can view the videos and download the worksheets from MyMathLab.

ACKNOWLEDGMENTS

We especially thank the students and faculty who used the previous editions for their thoughtful suggestions for improving this book. We also appreciate and thank the long list of reviewers who have contributed their ideas for improving the text. Colleagues who reviewed the ninth edition and provided ideas and suggestions for improving edition ten are:

Marylynne Abbott, Ozarks Technical Community College
Dawn Addington, Albuquerque TVI
Susan Baker, Lanier Technical College
Roxane Barrows, Hocking Tech College
Mildred Battle, Marshall Community and Technical College
Susan Bennet, Wake Technical Community College
Mary Lou Bertrand, Jefferson Community College, Watertown
Tom Bilyeu, Southwestern Illinois College
Sylvia Brown, East Tennessee State University
Angelic Cole, St. Louis Community College System
Ronald Deaton, Grays Harbor College
Kathleen DiNisco, Erie Community College
Douglas Dorsey, Manchester Community College
John Falls, North Central Technical College
John Fielding, University of Northwestern Ohio
Beverly Hallmon, Suffolk Community College
Mike Haynes, Arkansas State University, Beebe
Roy Iraggi, New York City College of Technology
Jenna Johannpeter, Southwestern Illinois College
Douglas Kearnaghan, Chicago State University
Lawrence Lichter, Waukesha County Technical College

Jean McArthur, Joliet Junior College
Mary McClelland, Texas Southern University
Sharon Meyer, Pikes Peak Community College
Rick Michaelsen, Mid Plains Community College
Brian Mom, St. Mary's College
Karen S. Mozingo, Pitt Community College
Kathleen Offenholley, City University of New York
Roy Peterson, Northeast Wisconsin Technical College
Jodee Phillips, Central Oregon Community College
Lana Powell, Valencia Community College
Nimisha Rival, Central Georgia Technical College
Sandra Robertson, Thomas Nelson Community College
Lisa Rombes, Washtenaw Community College
Barbara Schlachter, Baker College, Auburn Hills
Denise Schoenherr, Kaplan College—Online
Kimberly D. Smith, County College of Morris
Scott States, University of Northwestern Ohio
Pamela Walker, Northwestern Business College—Chicago
Louis Watanabe, Loyola Marymont University
Thomas Watkins, Solano Community College
Joe Westfall, Carl Albert State College
Andrea Williams, Shasta College

The Pearson Education team has been outstanding. The key players are listed on the copyright page and we want to thank all of them for the role they played in this project. Our team leader, Sara Eilert, had the daunting task of keeping all the balls bouncing. With the magnitude of this project, this is no small task. Rex Davidson, our project manager, made sure the production process was accomplished in a timely manner and that a quality product was generated. We thank Ellen and Albert Sawyer for accuracy checking the manuscript, and working the examples and exercises.

We also thank Tamra Davis, Tulsa Community College; Sally Proffitt, Tarrant County College; Cheryl Fetterman, Cape Fear Community College; Joyce Walsh-Portillo, Broward Community College; Blane Franckowiak, Tarrant County College; Anne Cremarosa, Reedley College; Alton Evans, Tarrant County College; and Beverly Vance, Southwest Tennessee Community College who all contributed to various aspects of this or previous editions and Rod Stairs of Running Pony Productions, Memphis, Tennessee, who produced the *Business Math in the Real World* videos and the learning outcome videos.

As the manuscript for this edition was developed, we consulted with numerous business professionals so that we could reflect current business practices in the examples and exercises. We thank all of our consultants for so graciously sharing their expertise. It was a pleasure to work with Kelly Ricci at Aptara®, Inc., throughout the production process.

All of us want to thank our families for their continued support. Without them we couldn't get this done, and it wouldn't be nearly as much fun.

CHERYL CLEAVES, MARGIE HOBBS, AND JEFFREY NOBLE

BRIEF CONTENTS

PHOTO CREDITS

CONTENTS

CHAPTER 3 DECIMALS 80

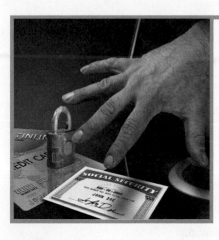

CHAPTER 4 BANKING 108

CHAPTER 5   EQUATIONS   148

CHAPTER 6   PERCENTS   184

CHAPTER 7   BUSINESS STATISTICS   216

CHAPTER 8   TRADE AND CASH DISCOUNTS   262

CHAPTER 12   CONSUMER CREDIT   426

CHAPTER 13   COMPOUND INTEREST, FUTURE VALUE, AND PRESENT VALUE   458

CHAPTER 14 ANNUITIES AND SINKING FUNDS   496

CHAPTER 15 BUILDING WEALTH THROUGH INVESTMENTS   540

CHAPTER 16 MORTGAGES 574

CHAPTER 17 DEPRECIATION 602

CHAPTER 18   INVENTORY   634

CHAPTER 19   INSURANCE   672

Virtual Gaming in a Virtual World, or How Much Is Your Degree Worth?

With revenues approaching $10 billion annually, online gaming has become more popular than ever. In fact, today worldwide estimates report that over one billion people play simple online games, such as checkers, bridge, or mahjong. A typical Friday afternoon may find upwards of 50,000 people playing pool on Yahoo! alone. The incredible numbers of online gamers have led to soaring revenues, making online advertising one of the fastest growing business sectors in the world today. Google, for example, has seen annual revenues skyrocket to over $35,000,000,000 ($35 billion)—that number has nine 0's in it!

But while checkers or pool may be popular with more people, committed gamers have a number of alternatives to choose from. One of the longest running is EverQuest, one of several role-playing games that have been around since the 1990s. The virtual world inside EverQuest is called Norrath, and it took six years and $28 million to create. To date, more than 500,000 people have subscribed to the virtual world, and at any given time there could be 30,000 people from over 100 countries playing simultaneously. EverQuest represents an entire world with its own diverse species, economic systems, alliances, and politics. There are more than 40,000 unique items for players to discover, create, or buy within the game, which has had 18 expansions since its original release.

But what does playing EverQuest have to do with whole numbers or with studying math in general? Research by U.S. economist Edward Castronova showed that EverQuest players earned an average of more than $3 for every hour spent playing the game, by trading skills and possessions with other players. But does doing math homework (or any other subject) have an economic value as well? The answer, of course, is yes. The average college student will spend approximately 150 hours per course, while studying or attending class, or 3,000 hours total for an associate's degree (AD). Increased earnings for AD graduates will total nearly $312,000 more over a career, when compared to high school graduates' earnings. For every hour you spend studying or attending class, you will get over $100 back! So before you get started gaming, make sure your business math homework is finished!

LEARNING OUTCOMES

1-1 Place Value and Our Number System

1. Read whole numbers.
2. Write whole numbers.
3. Round whole numbers.
4. Read and round integers.

1-2 Operations with Whole Numbers and Integers

1. Add and subtract whole numbers.
2. Add and subtract integers.
3. Multiply integers.
4. Divide integers.
5. Apply the standard order of operations to a series of operations.

This text will prepare you to enter the business world with mathematical tools for a variety of career paths. The chapters on business topics build on your knowledge of mathematics, so it is important to begin the course with a review of the mathematics and problem-solving skills you will need in the chapters to come.

In most businesses, arithmetic computations are done on a calculator or computer. Even so, every businessperson needs a thorough understanding of mathematical concepts and a basic number sense to make the best use of a calculator. A machine will do only what you tell it to do. Pressing a wrong key or performing the wrong operations on a calculator will result in a rapid but incorrect answer. If you understand the mathematics and know how to make reasonable estimates, you can catch and correct many errors.

1-1 PLACE VALUE AND OUR NUMBER SYSTEM

LEARNING OUTCOMES

1 Read whole numbers.
2 Write whole numbers.
3 Round whole numbers.
4 Read and round integers.

Digit: one of the ten symbols used in the decimal-number system: 0, 1, 2, 3, 4, 5, 6, 7, 8, 9.

Whole number: a number from the set of numbers including zero and the counting or natural numbers: 0, 1, 2, 3, 4, ...

Mathematical operations: calculations with numbers. The four operations that are often called basic operations are addition, subtraction, multiplication, and division.

Our system of numbers, the decimal-number system, uses ten symbols called **digits:** 0, 1, 2, 3, 4, 5, 6, 7, 8, 9. Numbers in the decimal system can have one or more digits. Each digit in a number that contains two or more digits must be arranged in a specific order to have the value we intend for the number to have. One set of numbers in the decimal system is the set of **whole numbers:** 0, 1, 2, 3, 4, ...

Most business calculations involving whole numbers include one or more of four basic **mathematical operations:** addition, subtraction, multiplication, and division.

1 Read whole numbers.

Period: a group of three place values in the decimal-number system.

Place-value system: a number system that determines the value of a digit by its position in a number.

What business situations require that we read and write whole numbers? Communication is one of the most important skills of successful businesspersons. Both the giver and the receiver of communications must have the same interpretation for the communication to be effective. That is why understanding terminology and the meanings of symbolic representations is an important skill.

Beginning with the ones place on the right, the place values are grouped in groups of three places. Each group of three place values is called a **period.** Each period has a name and a ones place, a tens place, and a hundreds place. In a number, the first period from the left may have less than three digits. In many cultures the periods are separated with commas.

Reading numbers is based on an understanding of the **place-value system** that is part of our decimal-number system. The chart in Figure 1-1 shows that system applied to the number 381,345,287,369,021.

To apply the place-value chart to any number, follow the steps given in the HOW TO feature. You'll find this feature, and examples illustrating its use, throughout this text.

Trillions			Billions			Millions			Thousands			Units		
Hundred trillions (100,000,000,000,000)	Ten trillions (10,000,000,000,000)	Trillions (1,000,000,000,000)	Hundred billions (100,000,000,000)	Ten billions (10,000,000,000)	Billions (1,000,000,000)	Hundred millions (100,000,000)	Ten millions (10,000,000)	Millions (1,000,000)	Hundred thousands (100,000)	Ten thousands (10,000)	Thousands (1,000)	Hundreds (100)	Tens (10)	Ones (1)
3	8	1	3	4	5	2	8	7	3	6	9	0	2	1
381 trillion,			345 billion,			287 million,			369 thousand,			21		

FIGURE 1-1
Place-Value Chart for Whole Numbers

HOW TO   Read a whole number

1. Separate the number into periods beginning with the rightmost digit and moving to the left.

Read the number 4,693,107.

2. Identify the period name of the leftmost period.

million

3. For each period, beginning with the leftmost period:
   (a) Read the three-digit number from left to right.
   (b) Name the period.

four *million,* six hundred ninety-three *thousand,* one hundred seven

4. Note these exceptions:
   (a) Do not read or name a period that is all zeros.
   (b) Do not name the units period.

EXAMPLE 1

The annual operating budget for a major corporation is $3,007,047,203. Show how you would read this number.

3 007 047 203
3 billion, 007 million, 047 thousand, 203

Identify each period name.
Read the words for the numbers in each period. Name each period except the units period.

Three billion, seven million, forty-seven thousand, two hundred three.

TIP

Points to Remember in Reading Whole Numbers

1. Commas separating periods are inserted from right to left between groups of three numbers. The leftmost period may have fewer than three digits.
2. The period name will be read at each comma.
3. Period names are read in the singular: *million* instead of *millions,* for example.
4. Because no comma follows the units period, that will serve as your reminder that the period name *units* is not read.
5. *Hundreds* is NOT a period name.
6. Every period has a ones, tens, and hundreds *place.*
7. The word *and* is NOT used when reading whole numbers.
8. Commas ordinarily do not appear in calculator displays.
9. If a number has more than four digits, but no commas, such as you see on a calculator display, insert commas when you write the number. The comma is optional in numbers with four digits.

STOP AND CHECK

Write the words used to read the number. See Example 1.

1. New Balance Shoes has sold 7,352,496 pairs of running shoes.

2. An investor has net assets of $4,023,508.

3. A large international corporation has an annual operating budget of $62,805,000,927.

4. At one time the U.S. national debt was $587,000,000,912.

2 Write whole numbers.

Suppose you are in a sales meeting and the marketing manager presents a report of the sales for the previous quarter, the projected sales for the current quarter, and the projected sales for the entire year. How would you record these figures in the notes you are taking for the meeting? You will need to have a mental picture of the place-value structure of our numbering system.

HOW TO   Write a whole number

1. Begin recording digits from left to right.
2. Insert a comma at each period name.
3. Every period after the first period must have three digits. Insert zeros as necessary.

EXAMPLE 2   In a sales presentation, Marty reported that the gross sales for the month were five hundred forty-two million, six hundred sixty-two thousand, five hundred thirty-eight. The gross sales for the previous year were fifteen billion, five hundred thousand, twenty-nine. Write these numbers in digits.

(a) Five hundred forty-two million, six hundred sixty-two thousand, five hundred thirty-eight
(b) Fifteen billion, five hundred thousand, twenty-nine

(a) 542, __ __ , __ __ __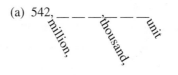
       million,   _thousand,_   _unit_

Record the first digits followed by a comma when the period name *million* is heard (or read). Then anticipate the periods to follow (thousand and unit).

542,662,538

Fill in each remaining period as the digits and period names are heard (or read).

The number is 542,662,538.

(b) 15, __ __ , __ __ __ , __ __ __
    billion,   _million,_   _thousand,_   _unit_

Record the first period and anticipate the periods to follow (million, thousand, and unit).

15, __ __ __ , 500, __ __ __

The next period name you hear (or read) is *thousand*, so you place the 500 in the thousand period, leaving space to place three zeros in the million period.

15,000,500,029

Place three zeros in the *million* period and listen for (read) the last three digits. You hear (read) *twenty-nine*, which is a two-digit number. Thus, a 0 is placed in the hundreds place.

The number is 15,000,500,029.

STOP AND CHECK

Write the number. See Example 2.

1. A Fortune 500 company reported gross sales of eighteen billion, seventy-eight million, three hundred ninety-seven thousand, two hundred three dollars.

2. Jason's annual net salary is thirty-six thousand, seventeen dollars.

3. Krispy Kreme had profits of nine hundred thirty-two thousand, eight hundred six dollars. Write the profit in numbers.

4. Jet Blue, one of the nation's most profitable airlines, sold fifty-two thousand, eight hundred ninety-six tickets. Write the number.

3 Round whole numbers.

Rounded number: an approximate number that is obtained from rounding an exact amount.

Approximate number: a rounded amount.

Exact numbers are not always necessary or desirable. For example, the board of directors does not want to know to the penny how much was spent on office supplies (although the accounting staff should know). Approximate or rounded numbers are often used. A **rounded number** does not represent an exact amount. It is instead an **approximate number**. You round a number to a specified place, which may be the first digit from the left in a number.

HOW TO   Round a whole number to a specified place

	Round 2,748 to the nearest hundred.
1. Find the digit in the specified place.	2,748
2. Look at the next digit to the right.	2,748
(a) If this digit is less than 5, replace it and all digits to its right with zeros.	2,700
(b) If this digit is 5 or more, add 1 to the digit in the specified place, and replace all digits to the right of the specified place with zeros.	

EXAMPLE 3

After the sales presentation, Marty's supervisor suggested that in future presentations, Marty use approximate numbers to illustrate the company's progress. Look at the two sales amounts in Example 2 on page 6. What are appropriate place values for rounding these numbers? Round each number to an appropriate place value.

Appropriate Rounding Places:

Large numbers are often rounded to a period place like nearest million, nearest billion, and so on.
Round the monthly sales amount to the nearest million.
Round the annual sales amount to the nearest billion.

(a) Round 542,662,538 to the nearest million.   2 is in the millions place.
542,662,538   The digit to the right is 6.
543,000,000   6 is 5 or more, so step 2b applies. Add 1 to 2 to get 3 and replace all digits to the right with zeros.

(b) Round 15,000,500,029 to the nearest billion.   5 is in the billions place.
15,000,500,029   The digit to the right is 0.
15,000,000,000   0 is less than 5, so step 2a applies. Leave 5 and replace all digits to the right with zeros.

EXAMPLE 4

In making estimations it is common to round a number to the first digit from the left. Round 27,389,092 to the first digit.

27,389,092   The first digit on the left is 2.
27,389,092   The next digit to the right is 7.
30,000,000   7 is 5 or more, so step 2b applies. Increase 2 by 1 to get 3 and replace all digits to the right of 3 with zeros.

STOP AND CHECK

See Example 3.

1. Round 3,784,921 to the nearest thousand.

2. Round 6,098 to the nearest ten.

3. Round 52,973 to the nearest hundred.

4. Round 17,439 to the first digit. *See Example 4.*

5. Southwest Airlines, one of the largest in the United States, sold 584,917 tickets. Write this as a number rounded to the first digit.

6. The two-year-average median household income for Maryland in a recent year was $57,265. Round to the nearest thousand dollars. *See Example 3.*

4 Read and round integers.

Negative number: a number that is less than zero.

Integers: the set of numbers that includes the positive whole numbers, the negatives of whole numbers, and zero.

In the business world and in real-life situations we sometimes want to express numbers that are smaller than 0. These numbers are **negative numbers.** If the temperature is lower than 0, the temperature is a negative amount. If you write a check for more than the amount of money in your bank account, your balance will be a negative number. Some business terms that often imply negative amounts are *loss* and *debt*.

The set of whole numbers is expanded by including negatives of whole numbers. This new set of numbers that includes whole numbers and negatives of whole numbers is called the set of **integers.** Figure 1-2 shows how the set of whole numbers is extended to include all integers. Numbers get larger as you move to the right and smaller as you move to the left. The arrows at the ends of the number line indicate that the numbers continue indefinitely in *both* directions.

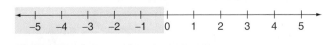

FIGURE 1-2
Integers

Negative sign, −: a symbol that is written before a number to show that it is a negative number. In business applications negative numbers are sometimes enclosed in parentheses, as (5) for −5.

In reading and rounding negative numbers, the same rules apply. The negative number is preceded by a **negative sign, −,** or enclosed in parentheses. In business reports negative five may be written as −5 or (5).

> **DID YOU KNOW?**
> The symbol $\approx$ is often used to indicate a rounded value.

HOW TO   Read and round integers

1. For reading integers, the rules are the same as for reading whole numbers. State the word *negative* or *minus* as you begin to read a number that is less than zero. Other words such as *loss* or *debt* may be used to indicate a negative amount.
2. For rounding integers, the rules are the same as for rounding whole numbers.

EXAMPLE 5 The U.S. national debt is estimated on many different web sites. On a recent electronic counter, the national debt was given as −$11,936,042,802,503. Show how you would read this number.

| −$11,936,042,802,503 | Identify each period name. |
| Negative 11 trillion, 936 billion, 42 million, 802 thousand, 503 | Read the words for the numbers in each period. Name each period except the units period. |

Negative eleven trillion, nine hundred thirty-six billion, forty-two million, eight hundred two thousand, five hundred three dollars.

EXAMPLE 6 Round the U.S. national debt given in Example 5 to the nearest trillion.

−$11,936,042,802,503	The trillions digit is 1.
−$11,936,042,802,503	The digit to the right of the trillions digit is 9.
−$12,000,000,000,000	9 is more than 5, so increase 1 by 1 to get 2 and replace all digits to the right of 2 with zeros.
−$12 trillion	Sometimes in business the period name is used instead of showing all the zeros.

−$11,936,042,802,503 rounded to the nearest trillion is −$12,000,000,000,000 or −$12 trillion.

STOP AND CHECK

See Example 5.

1. The public debt for the state of California was recently given as −$94,002,052,157. Show how you would read this number.

2. Recently the U.S. paid −$19,812,486,187 in interest on its public debt. Show how you would read this number to indicate it is being *paid out* of the national treasury.

See Example 6.

3. A recent study showed that citizens of New Hampshire had the highest overall debt in the nation, with an average per person debt of −$16,845. Round the average per person debt to the nearest ten thousand.

4. Citizens in Oklahoma had the lowest average debt in the country, −$8,823 per person. Round the average debt to the nearest thousand.

1-1 SECTION EXERCISES

SKILL BUILDERS

Write the words used to read the number. See Example 1.

1. 22,356,027

2. 106,357,291,582

3. 730,531,968

4. 21,000,017

5. 523,800,007,190

6. 713,205,538

Write as numbers. See Example 2.

7. Fourteen thousand, nine hundred eighty-five.

8. Thirty-two million, nine hundred forty-three thousand, six hundred eight.

9. Seventeen billion, eight hundred three thousand, seventy-five.

10. Fifty million, six hundred twelve thousand, seventy-eight.

11. Three hundred six thousand, five hundred forty-one.

12. Three hundred million, seven hundred sixty thousand, five hundred twelve.

See Examples 3–4.

13. Round 483 to tens.

14. Round 3,762 to hundreds.

15. Round 298,596 to ten-thousands.

16. Round 57,802 to the first digit.

APPLICATIONS

17. Cisco, the world's largest Internet equipment maker, recorded earnings of about $3,585,000,000. Write the words used to read Cisco's earnings.

18. Net income at Levi Strauss, the world's biggest maker of branded clothing, was expected to be twenty-five million, nine hundred seventy-two thousand, eight hundred dollars. Write as a number.

19. McDonald's produced 86,347,582 Big Macs. How many Big Macs were produced to the nearest million?

20. Oslo, Hong Kong, Tokyo, and New York City are the four most expensive cities in the world, according to one source. Workers in Oslo work 1,582 hours per year on average. Round the number of hours to the first digit.

21. According to Experian, a credit-reporting agency, the average debt for people living in Connecticut recently was −$15,314, second highest of any state. Show how this number would be read.

22. Experian reported that the average debt for people living in Mississippi was the second lowest for all states at −$8,420. Show how this number would be read.

See Example 5.

23. Experian reported that people in the age range of 18 to 29 had the second lowest average debt of all age groups with −$8,636 per person. Show how you would read this number.

24. Experian recently reported that people in the 50 to 69 age range carried the highest debt of all age groups. The average debt per person was −$20,157. Show how you would read this number.

See Example 6.

25. Horizon Lines, a company that provides shipping services recently had a debt of −$516,120,235. Round the amount of company debt to the nearest ten-million.

26. KB Home, a company that builds homes recently reported a debt of −$1,780,038,503. Report the debt of KB Home rounded to the nearest hundred-million.

1-2 OPERATIONS WITH WHOLE NUMBERS AND INTEGERS

LEARNING OUTCOMES

1 Add and subtract whole numbers.
2 Add and subtract integers.
3 Multiply integers.
4 Divide integers.
5 Apply the standard order of operations to a series of operations.

The operation of addition is used to find the total of two or more quantities. At Dollar General you purchase two toys, three bottles of cleaning products, and four types of cosmetic products. We use addition to find the total number of items purchased.

1 Add and subtract whole numbers.

If you purchase more than one item, you do not ordinarily pay for each item separately. Instead, the prices of all items are added together and you pay the total amount.

Addends: numbers being added.

Numbers being added are called **addends.** The answer, or result, of addition is called the **sum** or **total.**

Sum or total: the answer or result of addition.

$$6 + 7 = 13$$

addends   sum or total

Commutative property of addition: two numbers can be added in either order without changing the sum.

Only two numbers are added at a time. These two numbers can be added in either order without changing the sum. This property is called the **commutative property of addition.** It is casually referred to as the *order property of addition.*

$$4 + 8 = 12 \qquad 8 + 4 = 12$$

Associative property of addition: when more than two numbers are added, the addends can be grouped two at a time in any way.

When more than two numbers are added, two are grouped and added first. Then, the sum of these two numbers is added to another number. The addends can be grouped two at a time in any way. This property is called the **associative property of addition** and is casually referred to as the *grouping property of addition.*

$$(2 + 3) + 4 = \qquad 2 + (3 + 4) =$$
$$5 + 4 = 9 \qquad 2 + 7 = 9$$

Businesses normally use a personal calculator, a desktop calculator, or a spreadsheet like Excel® to make calculations. It is a good practice to always **estimate** your sum before making the calculations for the exact sum. The estimated sum is an **approximate number.**

HOW TO   Add whole numbers

1. Estimate the sum by rounding each addend to the first digit and adding the rounded addends.
2. Find the exact sum by adding the numbers by hand or by using a calculator.
3. Compare the estimate and the exact sum to see if the exact sum is reasonable.
4. Check the exact sum by adding the numbers a second time.

EXAMPLE 1

In the month of March, Speedy Printers ordered paper from three different suppliers. The orders were for 472, 83, and 3,255 reams of paper. How many reams of paper were ordered in March?

Estimate:

$472 + 83 + 3,255$	Round each addend to the first digit.
$500 + 80 + 3,000$	Add the rounded addends.
3,580	

Exact sum:

$472 + 83 + 3,255$	Add the numbers by hand or using a calculator.
3,810	The estimate and exact sum are reasonably close.

Check by adding the numbers again.

Subtraction is the opposite of addition. We use subtraction to find a *part* when we know a total amount and one of two *parts*. We may need to know the amount of change when a price has increased to a higher price. If we do not have enough material to complete a job, we may need to know how much more material is needed.

When subtracting one number from another, the number subtracted from is called the **minuend**. The number being subtracted is called the **subtrahend**. The result of subtraction is called the **difference**.

$$135 \rightarrow \text{minuend}$$
$$\underline{-72} \rightarrow \text{subtrahend}$$
$$63 \rightarrow \text{difference}$$

The order of the numbers in a subtraction problem *is* important. That is, subtraction is *not* commutative. For example, $5 - 3 = 2$, but $3 - 5$ does not equal 2.

Grouping in subtraction *is* important. That is, subtraction is *not* associative. For example, $(8 - 3) - 1 = 5 - 1 = 4$, but $8 - (3 - 1) = 8 - 2 = 6$.

HOW TO   Subtract whole numbers

1. Estimate the difference by rounding the minuend (number subtracted from) and subtrahend (number being subtracted) to the first digit and subtracting the rounded amounts.
2. Find the exact difference by subtracting the numbers by hand or by using a calculator. Be sure to put the minuend on top or enter it first on the calculator.
3. Compare the estimate and the exact difference to see if the exact difference is reasonable.
4. Check the exact difference by adding the difference and the subtrahend. The sum should equal the minuend.

EXAMPLE 2

Mario sold \$34,356 worth of clothing in September and \$53,943 in October. How much more were his sales in October than in September?

Estimate difference:

\$53,943 is the number subtracted from (minuend).	\$34,356 is the number being subtracted (subtrahend).

$53,943 − $34,356	Round each amount to the first digit.	
$50,000 − $30,000	Subtract rounded amounts.	
$20,000	Estimated difference in sales.	

Exact difference:

$53,943 − $34,356	Subtract the number by hand or by using a calculator.
$19,587	The estimate and the exact differences are reasonably close.

Check:

$19,587 + $34,356 = $53,943   Add the difference and the subtrahend to equal the minuend.

When we perform calculations with a calculator or computer software, it is important to estimate and to check the reasonableness of our answer. There are many different types of calculators, and each type may operate slightly differently. You can teach yourself how to use your calculator using some helpful learning strategies.

TIP

Test Your Calculator by Entering a Problem That You Can Do Mentally

Add 3 + 5 on your calculator. Some options are

3 $+$ 5 $=$

3 $+$ 5 $+$ $\boxed{T}$ $\boxed{T}$ represents Total.

3 $+$ 5 $\boxed{ENTER}$ $\boxed{EXE}$ is equivalent to $\boxed{ENTER}$ or $\boxed{=}$ on some calculators.

When adding more than two numbers, does your calculator accumulate the total in the display as you enter numbers? Or does your calculator give the total after the $\boxed{ENTER}$, $\boxed{T}$, or $\boxed{=}$ key is pressed?

In general, we will provide calculator steps for a business or scientific calculator. To show the result of a calculation that appears in the display of the calculator, we will precede the result with the symbol $\Rightarrow$.

Five-Step Problem-Solving Strategy   Decision making or problem solving is an important skill for the successful businessperson. The decision-making process can be applied by either individuals or action teams. Many strategies have been developed to enable individuals and teams to *organize* the information given and to *develop* a plan for finding the information needed to make effective business decisions or to solve business-related problems.

The plan we use is a five-step process. This feature will be highlighted throughout the text. The key words to identify each of the five steps are:

What You Know	What You Are Looking For	Solution Plan
What relevant facts are known or given?	What amounts do you need to find?	How are the known and unknown facts related? What formulas or definitions are used to establish a model? In what sequence should the operations be performed?

Solution

Perform the operations identified in the solution plan.

Conclusion

What does the solution represent within the context of the problem?

EXAMPLE 3   Holly Hobbs supervises the shipping department at AH Transportation and must schedule her employees to handle all shipping requests within a specified time frame while keeping the payroll amount within the amount budgeted. Complete the payroll report (Table 1-1) for the first quarter and decide if Holly has kept the payroll within the quarterly department payroll budget of $25,000.

TABLE 1-1
Quarterly Payroll Report for the Shipping Department

Employee	Quarterly Payroll
Doroshonko, Nataliya	$ 5,389
Campbell, Karen	5,781
Linebarger, Lydia	6,463
Ores, Vincent	5,389
Department Total	$23,022

What You Know	What You Are Looking For	Solution Plan
Quarterly pay for each employee (in table) Quarterly department budget: $25,000	Quarterly department payroll Is the payroll within budget?	Quarterly department payroll = sum of quarterly pay for each employee. Compare the quarterly department payroll to the quarterly department budget.

Solution

Find the quarterly department payroll.

Using a calculator:

5389 ⊞ 5781 ⊞ 6463 ⊞ 5389 ⊟ ⟹ 23022

The quarterly department payroll is $23,022, which is less than the budgeted amount of $25,000.

Conclusion

Holly's department payroll for the quarter *is* within the amount budgeted for the department.

TIP

Alternative Method for Estimating Addition

A reasonable estimate for the preceding example may be a range of values that you expect the exact value to fall within. All values are at least $5,000. All values except one are also less than $6,000.

$$\$5,000 + \$5,000 + \$5,000 + \$5,000 = \$20,000$$
$$\$6,000 + \$6,000 + \$6,000 + \$6,000 = \$24,000$$

Therefore, the exact amount is probably between $20,000 and $24,000.

Because one amount is over $6,000, if the other amounts were close to $6,000, the sum could possibly be slightly over $24,000. That is not the case in this example.

STOP AND CHECK

Mentally estimate the sum by rounding to the first digit. Compare the estimate with the exact sum. See Example 1.

1. 372 + 583 + 697

2. 9,823 + 7,516 + 8,205

3. $618 + $736 + $107

4. $1,809 + $3,521

For each subtraction, mentally estimate by rounding to the first digit; then find the exact difference. See Example 2.

5. Subtract 96 from 138.

6. Subtract: 1,352 − 787

7. Subtract: $3,807 − $2,689

8. Subtract 5,897 from 10,523.

See Example 3.

9. Hales Shipping Company is projecting revenue of $1,200,000. At the end of the year Hales had revenue of $789,000 from its ten largest clients and $342,000 from its other clients. Did the company reach its projection?

10. Marie's Costume Shop projected annual revenue of $2,500,000. Revenue for each quarter was $492,568; $648,942; $703,840; and $683,491. Did the shop achieve its revenue goal?

11. Jet Blue sold 2,196,512 tickets and Southwest Airlines sold 1,993,813 tickets. How many more tickets did Jet Blue sell?

12. According to the Bureau of Labor Statistics, the number of U.S. firms with 1 to 4 employees was 2,734,133 and the number of firms with 5 to 9 employees was 1,025,497. How many more firms had 1 to 4 employees?

2 Add and subtract integers.

Because we deal with negative amounts in business, we will need to perform operations with these numbers. For example, if you have $1,275 of credit card debt (−$1,275) and you charge $25 (represented as −$25) more, your debt has increased. That is, −$1,275 + (−$25) = −$1,300.

On the other hand, if you have $1,300 in credit card debt (−$1,300) and make a $50 payment (+$50), your debt has decreased. That is, −$1,300 + (+$50) = −$1,250.

Using your intuitive number sense, you can follow the discussion without additional rules. As we put in more numbers and the numbers are harder to work with mentally, rules will help us maintain our systematic thinking.

Integers include both positives and negatives of whole numbers and zero. Positive integers do not require that we put a positive sign in front of the number. $50 and +$50 mean exactly the same thing. Adding two positive integers is what we have been doing all along with addition. What does it mean to add two negative numbers?

As in the illustration, if you consider debt to be a negative value and you add more debt, another negative value, you are still in debt and the amount of your debt has increased.

HOW TO   Add two negative integers

1. Add the numbers without regard to the signs.
2. Assign a negative to the sum.

EXAMPLE 4   Last year Murphy's Used Car Company lost approximately $23,000. This year they incurred another loss of approximately $16,000. What is the approximate loss for the two years?

A loss is translated as a negative value.

A second loss increases the total loss for the two years.

−$23,000 + (−$16,000) = −$39,000

Add the amounts without regard to the signs. Assign a negative to the sum.

The two-year loss is −$39,000.

HOW TO   Add a positive and a negative integer

1. Subtract the numbers without regard to the signs.
2. Look at the numbers without the signs. Choose the larger of these numbers. Assign the sum the sign that is in front of the larger of these numbers.

Do we mean that to add two integers, we sometimes subtract? Yes. Look at the illustration given when we first introduced adding and subtracting integers. If you have a debt and make a payment, the new amount of debt is smaller than the original debt.

EXAMPLE 5

Jeremy has a bank balance of $47. He writes a check for his utility bill for $89. What is his new balance after the check clears? If a fee of $30 is charged when an account goes into a negative balance, what would be the new balance after the fee is charged? Translate the numbers into integers. The original balance is +$47 (the + sign is not required). The check is −$89. The fee is −$30.

First add +$47 and −$89.	One integer is positive and the other is negative. Subtract 47 from 89. We see that 89 is the larger value and it has a negative sign in front, so the difference will be negative.
$47 + (−$89) = −$42	The balance after the check clears is −$42. Because this is a negative balance, a $30 fee is charged.
−$42 + (−$30) = −$72	Both integers are negative, so use the rule for adding two negative numbers. The sum is negative.

The final balance after the check is processed and the fee is charged is −$72.

DID YOU KNOW?

It is common to use parentheses to separate two signs that are side by side with no number between them. For example, 14 + −9 = 5 can be written as 14 + (−9) = 5.

If we subtract to find the sum of a positive and negative number, what do we do when we subtract signed numbers? The most common approach is to translate a subtraction problem as an equivalent addition problem.

What is 9 subtracted from 14? 14 − 9 = what number? We know from past experience that it is 5. That is, 14 − 9 = 5. Now, what is −9 added to 14? Applying the rule for adding a positive number and a negative number, we subtract and keep the sign of 14. The result is also 5. That is, 14 + (−9) = 5. The relationship between addition and subtraction is that a subtraction problem is equivalent to adding the minuend and the *opposite* of the subtrahend.

HOW TO   Change a subtraction problem to an equivalent addition problem

1. Rewrite the problem as adding the minuend and the *opposite* of the subtrahend.
2. Apply the appropriate rule for adding integers.

This process is used mostly when making symbolic manipulations, as you will see more of in Chapter 5 on Equations.

EXAMPLE 6

Perform the indicated operations by first changing all subtractions to equivalent additions.

(a) −23 − 15 =   (b) 37 − (−4)   (c) −41 − (−8)

(a) −23 − 15 =	Rewrite the subtraction as an equivalent addition.
−23 + (−15) =	The opposite of 15 is −15. Apply the rule for adding two negative integers.
−23 + (−15) = **−38**	
(b) 37 − (−4) =	Rewrite the subtraction as an equivalent addition.
37 + 4 =	The opposite of −4 is 4. Both numbers are now positive.
37 + 4 = **41**	
(c) −41 − (−8) =	Rewrite the subtraction as an equivalent addition.
−41 + 8 =	The opposite of −8 is 8. Apply the rule for adding a positive and a negative integer.
−41 + 8 = **−33**	

How does a calculator deal with negative numbers? Most scientific or graphing calculators have a *negative key*. It often looks like this: (−). You press this key *before* entering the number.

(−) 41 − (−) 8 =   Display shows −33.

Most basic business or financial calculators have a *change sign key*. If often looks like this: +/−. You press this key *after* entering the number.

41 +/− − 8 +/− =   Display shows −33.

STOP AND CHECK

See Example 4.

1. Thurston Peyton had a Visa® card debt of $7,217 and purchased a 14K gold ring for $2,314. What is his credit card balance?

2. Last year Triple M Motors lost $137,942. This year the company lost $38,457. Find the two-year loss for Triple M Motors.

See Example 5.

3. In a recent year Valero Energy had revenue of $118,298 million and a loss of −$1,131 million. If Expenses = Revenue − Profit, find the expenses for Valero Energy for the year where the "profit" is a loss.

4. Ethan had a credit card debt of $4,815 and paid $928 on the account. What was his credit card debt after the payment?

Perform the indicated operations by first changing all subtractions to equivalent additions. See Example 6.

5. 48 − (−21)

6. −18 − 14

3   Multiply integers.

Multiplication is a shortcut for repeated addition.

The Krispy Kreme donut store at London-based Harrods sent 3 dozen (36) donuts each to 75 neighboring merchants to celebrate the grand opening of its first European location. We can multiply to get the total number of Krispy Kreme donuts sampled.

When multiplying one number by another, the number being multiplied is called the **multiplicand.** The number we multiply by is called the **multiplier.** Each number can also be called a **factor.** The result of multiplication is called the **product.** Numbers can be multiplied in any order without changing the product. When the multiplier has more than one digit, the product of each digit and the multiplicand is called a **partial product.**

Multiplicand: the number being multiplied.

Multiplier: the number multiplied by.

Factor: each number involved in multiplication.

Product: the answer or result of multiplication.

Partial product: the product of one digit of the multiplier and the entire multiplicand.

$$
\begin{array}{r}
75 \\
\times\ 36 \\
\hline
450 \\
2\ 25 \\
\hline
2{,}700
\end{array}
$$

← multiplicand ⎫ ← factors
← multiplier ⎭

← partial products

← product

HOW TO   Multiply whole numbers

1. Write the numbers in a vertical column, aligning digits according to their places.
2. For each *place* of the multiplier in turn, beginning with the ones place:
   (a) Multiply the multiplicand by the *place* digit of the multiplier.
   (b) Write the partial product directly below the multiplier (or the last partial product), aligning the ones digit of the partial product with the *place* digit of the multiplier (and aligning all other digits to the left accordingly).
3. Add the partial products.

EXAMPLE 7

Multiply 127 by 53.

```
    127    ← multiplicand
×    53    ← multiplier
    381    ← first partial product: 3 × 127 = 381; 1 in 381 aligns with 3 in 53.
  6 35     ← second partial product: 5 × 127 = 635; 5 in 635 aligns with 5 in 53.
  6,731    ← product: add the partial products.
```

The product of 127 and 53 is 6,731.

TIP

Placing Partial Products Properly

When you multiply numbers that contain two or more digits, it is crucial to *place the partial products* properly. A common mistake in multiplying is to forget to "indent" the partial products that follow the first partial product.

```
    265
×    23
    795       We get the second partial product, 530, by multiplying
  5 30        265 × 2. Therefore, the 0 in 530 should be directly
  6,095       below the 2 in 23.
```

CORRECT

```
    265
×    23
    795
    530
  1,325
```

INCORRECT

Most calculations in the business world are performed using an electronic device. For multiplication all calculators have a multiplication key that looks like $\boxed{\times}$. When entering calculations as formulas on an electronic spreadsheet like Excel®, the asterisk (*), which is the upper case of the number 8 on a standard keyboard, is used to indicate multiplication.

HOW TO   Multiply whole numbers with a calculator

1. Estimate the product by rounding each factor to the first digit and multiplying the rounded factors.
2. Find the exact product by multiplying the numbers using a calculator.
3. Compare the estimate and the exact product to see if the exact product is reasonable.
4. Check the exact product by multiplying the numbers a second time.

DID YOU KNOW?

Parentheses are also used to show multiplication and some calculators do not require the times sign to be entered if parentheses are used. Test your calculator to see how it works.

Multiplication, like addition, is **commutative** and **associative.** That is, in multiplication order and grouping do not matter.

$$3 \times 4 = 12 \qquad 4 \times 3 = 12 \qquad 2 \times (3 \times 4) = (2 \times 3) \times 4$$
$$2 \times 12 = 6 \times 4$$
$$24 = 24$$

Commutative Property of Multiplication   Associative Property of Multiplication

EXAMPLE 8

Ethan Thomas is purchasing 48 shares of FedEx stock that is selling for $85 a share. What is the cost of the stock?

Estimate:

48 × $85	Round each number to the first digit.
50 × $90	Multiply the rounded amounts.
$4,500	Estimate.

Exact product:

On a calculator enter 48 $\boxed{\times}$ 85 $\boxed{=}$	Display shows 4080.
48 × $85 = $4,080	Interpret result within context of the problem.
	Exact amount is reasonably close to the estimate of $4,500.

The total cost of the stock is $4,080.

As in addition, you can improve your multiplication accuracy by recalculating manually, by recalculating using a calculator, and by estimating the product.

Zeros are used in many helpful shortcuts to multiplying. When one or both of the numbers being multiplied has ending zeros, you can use a shortcut to find the product.

HOW TO   Multiply when numbers end in zero

1. Mentally eliminate zeros from the end of each number.
2. Multiply the new numbers.
3. Attach to the end of the product the total number of zeros mentally eliminated in step 1.

EXAMPLE 9   Multiply 50 times 90 mentally by applying the rule about ending zeros.

$5 \times 9 = 45$	Multiply.
$50 \times 90 = 4500$	Attach two zeros.

50 times 90 is 4,500.

EXAMPLE 10   Max Wertheimer is processing store orders at McDonald's warehouse totaling 45,000 sixteen-ounce cups. He found 303 packages of sixteen-ounce cups. Each package contains a gross of cups. Does Max need to order more cups from the manufacturer to fill the store orders if one gross is 144 items?

What You Know	What You Are Looking For	Solution Plan
Store orders: 45,000 cups	Total quantity of cups on hand	Total quantity of cups on hand = packages of cups on hand $\times$ cups per package
Packages of cups on hand: 303	Should more cups be ordered?	
Cups per package: 1 gross, or 144		Compare the total quantity of cups on hand with 45,000 cups.

Solution

Using a calculator:

$303 \boxed{\times} 144 \boxed{=} \Rightarrow 43632$

Conclusion

There are 43,632 cups in the warehouse, but store orders total 45,000. **Max needs to order more cups from the manufacturer to fill all the store orders.**

Anthony's Art Shop bought too many of a decorative picture frame. He needs to get what he can from them and plans to sell each frame at a $2 loss (−$2). If he has 87 frames to sell, what will be his total loss? This brings up a situation in which a negative integer and a positive integer are multiplied.

HOW TO   Multiply a negative and a positive integer

1. Multiply the two integers without regard to the signs.
2. Assign a negative sign to the product.

EXAMPLE 11   In the situation above with Anthony's Art Shop, what will be the total loss from selling the 87 frames each for $2 below cost?

$87 \times (-\$2) =$	Multiply 87 times 2. $87 \times 2 = 174$. Attach a negative sign to the product.
$87 \times (-\$2) = -\$174$	Interpret the result.

The total loss from the sale of the frames will be −$174.

Occasionally in manipulating equations (Chapter 5) you will multiply two negative numbers.

> **HOW TO** Multiply two negative integers or two positive integers
>
> 1. Multiply the two integers without regard to the signs.
> 2. The product is positive.

EXAMPLE 12 Perform the following multiplications.

(a) $(-16)(-3)$ (b) $(-6)(-5)(-2)$ (c) $(-4)(7)(-2)$

(a) $(-16)(-3) =$ **48**   Multiply 16×3. Product is positive.

(b) $(-6)(-5)(-2)$ First, multiply $6 \times 5 = 30$. The product is positive.
$(30)(-2) =$ **-60**   Next, multiply 30×2. The product is negative.

(c) $(-4)(7)(-2)$ First, multiply $4 \times 7 = 28$. The product is negative.
$(-28)(-2) =$ **56**   Next, multiply 28×2. The product is positive.

DID YOU KNOW?

When multiplying more than two factors, an *even* number of negative factors will result in a positive product. An odd number of negative factors will result in a negative product.

STOP AND CHECK

Mentally estimate the product by rounding to the first digit. Find the exact product. See Example 7.

1. 317×52

2. $6,723 \times 87$

See Example 9.

3. $4,600 \times 70$

4. $538,000 \times 420$

Perform the multiplications. See Example 12.

5. $(-21)(-15)$

6. $(-8)(-12)(-9)$

See Example 8.

7. A plastic film machine can produce 75 rolls of plastic in an hour. How many rolls of plastic can be produced by the machine in a 24-hour period? Arcaro Plastics has 15 of these machines. How many rolls of plastic can be produced if all 15 machines operate for 24 hours?

See Example 10.

8. Malina Kodama creates 48 pottery coffee cups and 72 pottery bowls in a day. How many can be produced in a 22-day month? If 809 coffee cups and 1,242 bowls were sold in the same 22-day month, how many of each item remained in inventory?

See Example 11.

9. Hasan's Electronic Shop is overstocked with 456 USB cables and sells them to a discount house at a $4 loss ($-$4). What is his total loss on the sale?

10. Dante sold 976 shares of stock at a $9 loss ($-$9) per share. What was his total loss on the stock?

4 Divide integers.

Dividend: the number being divided or the total quantity available.

Divisor: the number the dividend is divided by.

Quotient: the answer or result of division.

Whole-number part of quotient: the quotient without regard to the remainder.

Remainder of quotient: a number that is smaller than the divisor that remains after the division is complete.

Christine Shott received a price quote by fax for a limited quantity of discontinued portable telephones. The fax copy was not completely readable, but Christine could read that the total bill, including shipping, was $905 and each telephone costs $35. How many telephones were available and how much was the shipping cost? Division is used to find the number of equal parts a total quantity can be separated into.

When dividing one number by another, the number being divided (total quantity) is called the **dividend.** The number the dividend is divided by is called the **divisor.** The result of division is called the **quotient.** When the quotient is not a whole number, the quotient has a **whole-number part** and a **remainder.** When a dividend has more digits than a divisor, parts of the

Partial dividend: the part of the dividend that is being considered at a given step of the process.

Partial quotient: the quotient of the partial dividend and the divisor.

dividend are called **partial dividends,** and the quotient of a partial dividend and the divisor is called a **partial quotient.**

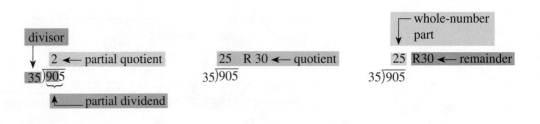

Christine now knows that 25 telephones are available. What does the remainder represent? The dividend, $905, is in dollars, so the remainder also represents dollars. The remainder of $30 is the shipping cost.

HOW TO   Divide whole numbers

1. Beginning with its leftmost digit, identify the first group of digits of the dividend that is larger than or equal to the divisor. This group of digits is the first *partial dividend*.
2. For each partial dividend in turn, beginning with the first:
   (a) Divide the partial dividend by the divisor. Write this partial quotient above the rightmost digit of the partial dividend.
   (b) Multiply the partial quotient by the divisor. Write the product below the partial dividend, aligning places.
   (c) Subtract the product from the partial dividend. Write the difference below the product, aligning places. The difference must be less than the divisor.
   (d) After the difference, bring down the next digit of the dividend. This is the new partial dividend.
3. When all the digits of the dividend have been used, write the final difference in step 2c as the remainder (unless the remainder is 0). The whole-number part of the quotient is the number written above the dividend.
4. To check, multiply the quotient by the divisor and add the remainder to the product. This sum equals the dividend.

$$905 \div 35$$

$$35\overline{)905}$$

$$\begin{array}{r} 25 \\ 35\overline{)905} \\ 70 \\ \hline 205 \\ 175 \\ \hline 30 \end{array}$$

Check:
$$\begin{array}{r} 25 \\ \times\ 35 \\ \hline 125 \\ 75 \\ \hline 875 \end{array} \qquad \begin{array}{r} 875 \\ +\ 30 \\ \hline 905 \end{array}$$

TIP

What Types of Situations Require Division?

Two types of common business situations require division. Both types involve distributing items equally into groups.

1. Distribute a specified total quantity of items so that each group gets a specific equal share. Division determines the number of groups.

   For example, you need to ship 78 crystal vases. With appropriate packaging to avoid breakage, only 5 vases fit in each box. How many boxes are required? You divide the total quantity of vases by the quantity of vases that will fit into one box to determine how many boxes are required.

2. Distribute a specified total quantity so that we have a specific number of groups. Division determines each group's equal share.

   For example, how many ounces will each of four cups contain if a carafe of coffee containing 32 ounces is poured equally into the cups? The capacity of the carafe is divided by the number of coffee cups: 32 ounces ÷ 4 coffee cups = 8 ounces. Eight ounces of coffee are contained in each of the four cups.

EXAMPLE 13

Tuesday Morning Discount Store needs to ship 78 crystal vases. With standard packing to avoid damage, 5 vases fit in each box. How many boxes will be needed to ship the 78 vases? Does the Tuesday Morning shipping clerk need to arrange for extra packing or will each box contain exactly 5 vases?

What You Know	What You Are Looking For	Solution Plan
Total quantity of vases to be shipped: 78 Quantity of vases per box without the extra packing: 5	How many boxes are required to ship the vases? Is extra packing required?	Quantity of boxes needed = total quantity of vases ÷ quantity of vases per box Quantity of boxes needed = 78 ÷ 5

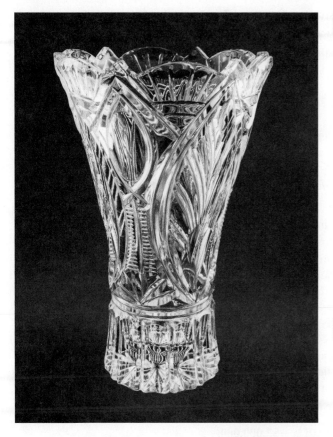

Solution

$$\begin{array}{r} 15 \text{ R}3 \\ 5\overline{)78} \\ \underline{5} \\ 28 \\ \underline{25} \\ 3 \end{array}$$

Divide 78 by 5. The whole-number part of the quotient is 15; the remainder is 3.

Check:

Multiply the whole-number part of the quotient, 15, by the divisor, 5. Then add the remainder. The sum should equal the dividend, 78.

$$\begin{array}{r} 15 \\ \times\ 5 \\ \hline 75 \end{array} \qquad \begin{array}{r} 75 \\ +\ 3 \\ \hline 78 \end{array}$$
The result checks.

The quantity of boxes needed is 15 boxes containing 5 vases and 1 box containing 3 vases.

Conclusion

Fifteen boxes will have 5 vases each, needing no extra packing. One additional box is required to ship the remaining 3 vases for a total of **16 boxes needed. Extra packing is needed to fill the additional box.**

TIP

Using Guess and Check to Solve Problems

An effective strategy for solving problems involves guessing. Make a guess that you think might be reasonable and check to see if the answer is correct. If your guess is not correct, decide if it is too high or too low. Make another guess based on what you learned from your first guess. Continue until you find the correct answer.

Let's try guessing in the previous example. Estimating, we find that we can pack 70 vases in 14 boxes ($14 \times 5 = 70$). As we need to pack 78 vases, how many vases can we pack with 15 boxes? $15 \times 5 = 75$. Still not enough. Therefore, we will need 16 boxes, but the last box will not be full.

HOW TO   Divide whole numbers using a calculator

1. Estimate the quotient by rounding the divisor to the first digit and find the first partial quotient. Place zeros over the remaining digits in the dividend.
2. Find the exact quotient by dividing the numbers by using a calculator.
3. Compare the estimate and the exact quotient to see if the exact quotient is reasonable.
4. Check the exact quotient by multiplying the quotient times the divisor and adding any remainder. The result should equal the original dividend.

How does a calculator handle division? If the quotient is not a whole number, the calculator will continue the division to decimal places. We will look more at decimal places in Chapter 3. For now, we want to convert the decimal portion of the quotient to a remainder.

HOW TO   Convert a decimal portion of a quotient to a remainder

1. Perform a division on a calculator.
2. If there is a decimal portion in the quotient, subtract the whole-number part of the quotient from the quotient showing in the display.
3. Multiply the result of step 2 by the original divisor to get the whole-number value of the remainder.

EXAMPLE 14   Perform the division from Example 13 on a calculator and convert the decimal portion of the quotient to a whole number.

78 ÷ 5 = 15.6	Subtract whole-number part of quotient.
− 15 = .6	Do not clear calculator. Continue with the subtract symbol and 15.
× 5 = 3	Do not clear calculator and multiply by the original divisor of 5. Interpret the result.

The quotient is 15 with a remainder of 3.

The division rules for integers are very similar to the multiplication rules for integers.

HOW TO   Divide by integers

1. Divide the numbers without regard to the signs.
2. If both numbers are positive or both are negative, the quotient is positive.
3. If one number is positive and the other is negative, the quotient is negative.

EXAMPLE 15   Adams-Duke Realty Company estimates that its losses for this year will be $36,000,000. What is the average loss per month? There are 12 months in a year. Divide the estimated loss for the year by 12.

(−) $36,000,000 ÷ 12 = −$3,000,000   Interpret the result.

The estimated average loss per month is −$3,000,000.

As with multiplication, dividing numbers that end in zeros can use a shortcut.

HOW TO   Divide numbers ending in zero by place-value numbers like 10, 100, 1,000

1. Mentally eliminate the same number of ending zeros from both the divisor and the dividend.
2. Divide the new numbers.

EXAMPLE 16   Divide the following: (a) 531,000 ÷ 300   (b) 63,500,000 ÷ 1,000

(a) 531,000 ÷ 300   Eliminate two ending zeros from both numbers.

5,310 ÷ 3   Divide.

$$\begin{array}{r} 1,770 \\ 3)\overline{5,310} \end{array}$$

531,000 ÷ 300 = 1,770

(b) 63,500,000 ÷ 1,000   Eliminate three ending zeros from both numbers.

63,500 ÷ 1 = 63,500   Divide.

STOP AND CHECK

Divide. See Example 14.

1. 2,772 ÷ 6

2. 6,744 ÷ 24

3. 14,305 ÷ 47

4. 1,263 ÷ 15

See Example 13.

5. The Gap purchased 5,184 pairs of blue jeans to be distributed evenly among 324 stores. How many pairs were sent to each store?

6. Auto Zone purchased 26,560 cans of car wax on a special manufacturer's offer. It distributed a case of 64 cans to each store. How many stores got the special offer?

See Example 15.

7. Citigroup reported an annual loss of −$27,684 million. What is the average loss for each of the 12 months in the year?

8. ConocoPhillips reported an annual loss of −$16,998,000,000. What is the average loss for each of the 12 months in the year?

Divide. See Example 16.

9. 834,000 ÷ 600

10. 14,560,000 ÷ 7,000

5 Apply the standard order of operations to a series of operations.

Chain (chn) calculation method: calculator mode that performs operations in the order they are entered.

When a series of operations is performed, there is a specified order for making those calculations. For the basic calculator, you will have to apply the appropriate order of operations as you enter the calculations. For a financial or business calculator, you may have to choose the calculation method. The **chain (chn) calculation method** will perform the operations in the order in which you enter them. This is the default setting (factory setting) for most financial calculators. For example, if you enter 2 $\boxed{+}$ 3 $\boxed{\times}$ 4 $\boxed{=}$, the result will be 20. That is, 2 + 3 = 5 and 5 × 4 = 20. **Note this result is not correct!** To work the problem correctly you must enter the numbers and operations according to the standard rules for the order of operations. 3 $\boxed{\times}$ 4 $\boxed{+}$ 2 $\boxed{=}$ ⇒ 4.

Algebraic operating system method (AOS): calculator mode that performs operations according to the standard rules for the order of operations.

For scientific calculators and electronic spreadsheet formulas like Excel®, the default setting is generally the **algebraic operating system method (AOS).** This applies the standard rules for the order of operations.

HOW TO   Apply the standard order of operations to a series of operations

1. Perform all operations that are inside grouping symbols, such as parentheses.
2* Perform all multiplications and divisions as they appear from left to right.
3. Perform all additions and subtractions as they appear from left to right.

*Later another step will be added here for exponents and roots.

If 2 $\boxed{+}$ 3 $\boxed{\times}$ 4 $\boxed{=}$ is entered for a calculator or device that uses the AOS method, the result will be 14. The multiplication will be performed first, and then the addition.

$$3 \times 4 = 12 \text{ then } 2 + 12 = 14.$$

If you are not sure which method your calculator or device uses, do a test problem like the one above to see which method your calculator or device uses. On a financial calculator the mode can be changed to the AOS method.

EXAMPLE 17   Perform the following operations applying the standard order of operations for a series of calculations.

(a) 15 − (4 + 7) =

(b) (75 + 50 + 35 + 90) ÷ 5 =

(c) 45 − 4 × 9 =

(a) 15 − (4 + 7) =   Perform the calculation in parentheses first.

  15 − 11 = **4**   Subtract.

(b) $(75 + 50 + 35 + 90) \div 5 =$ Perform the calculations in parentheses first.

$$250 \div 5 = \mathbf{50} \quad \text{Divide.}$$

(c) $45 - 4 \times 9 =$ Multiply first.

$$45 - 36 = \mathbf{9} \quad \text{Subtract.}$$

STOP AND CHECK

Apply the standard order of operations for a series of calculations to perform the indicated operations. See Example 17.

1. $38 - (5 + 12)$
2. $(42 + 38 + 26 + 86) \div 12$
3. $42 - 26 + 13 \times 3$
4. $38 + 12 \div (-3)$

1-2 SECTION EXERCISES

SKILL BUILDERS

Mentally estimate the sum by rounding to the first digit, then add to get the exact answer. See Example 1.

1.
$$\begin{array}{r} 328 \\ 583 \\ +726 \\ \hline \end{array}$$

2.
$$\begin{array}{r} 671 \\ 982 \\ +\ 57 \\ \hline \end{array}$$

3. $791 + 1{,}000 + 52$

4. $5{,}784 + 21{,}872 + 26{,}215$

Add the integers. See Examples 4–5.

5. $-42 + 36$

6. $-283 + 375$

7. $-4{,}216 + (-3{,}972)$

Subtract and check the difference. See Example 2.

8.
$$\begin{array}{r} 5\ 5 \\ -\ 3\ 6 \\ \hline \end{array}$$

9.
$$\begin{array}{r} 3\ 0\ 8 \\ -2\ 7\ 5 \\ \hline \end{array}$$

10. $5{,}409 - 2{,}176$

Subtract the integers. See Example 6.

11. $18 - (-3)$

12. $-12 - (5)$

13. $-5 - (-17)$

14. $37 - 41$

Multiply and check the product. See Examples 7–9.

15.
$$\begin{array}{r} 730 \\ \times\ \ \ 60 \\ \hline \end{array}$$

16.
$$\begin{array}{r} 904 \\ \times\ \ \ 24 \\ \hline \end{array}$$

17. $1{,}005$ by 89

Multiply the integers. See Examples 11–12.

18. $(-3)(46)$

19. $(32)(-15)$

20. $(-64)(-83)$

21. $(-\$82{,}916)(7)$

Divide and check the quotient. See Examples 13–14.

22. $96 \div 6$

23. $13{,}838 \div 34$

24. $17\overline{)4{,}424}$

Divide the integers. See Example 15.

25. $72 \div (-9)$

26. $(-56) \div (-8)$

27. $-672 \div 16$

28. $-\$13{,}623 \div 57$

Perform the operations by applying the standard order of operations for a series of calculations. See Example 17.

29. $28 - (9 + 15)$

30. $(\$38 + \$46 + \$72 + \$48) \div 4$

31. $82 - 7 \times 8$

32. $(46 + 38) \times 2 - 385$

Divide the following. See Example 16.

33. $2{,}950 \div 50$

34. $689{,}100 \div 30$

35. $57{,}800{,}000 \div 2{,}000$

36. $5{,}730{,}000 \div 300$

APPLICATIONS

37. *See Example 3.* The menswear department of the Gap has a sales goal of $1,384,000 for its Spring sale. Complete the worksheet (Table 1-2) for the sales totals by region and by day. Decide if the goal was reached. What is the difference between the goal and the actual total sales amount?

TABLE 1-2						
Region	**W**	**Th**	**F**	**S**	**Su**	**Region Totals**
Eastern	$ 72,492	$ 81,948	$ 32,307	$ 24,301	$ 32,589	
Southern	81,897	59,421	48,598	61,025	21,897	
Central	71,708	22,096	23,222	21,507	42,801	
Western	61,723	71,687	52,196	41,737	22,186	
Daily Sales Total						

38. Atkinson's Candy Company manufactures seven types of hard candy for its Family Favorites mixed candy. The bulk candy is repackaged from 84 containers that each contain 25 pounds of candy. The bulk candy is bagged in 3-pound bags and then packed in boxes for shipping. Each box contains 12 bags of mixed candy. Wilma Jackson-Randle reports that she currently has 1,000 3-pound bags on hand and 100 boxes of the size that will be used to ship the candy. Decide if enough materials are in inventory to complete the mixing and packaging process.

39. University Trailer Sales Company sold 352 utility trailers during a recent year. If the gross annual sales for the company was $324,800, what was the average selling price for each trailer?

40. An acre of ground is equivalent to a square piece of land that is 210 feet on each of the four equal sides. Fencing can be purchased in 50-foot rolls for $49 per roll. You are making a bid to install the fencing of a square plot of ground that is an acre at a cost of $1 per foot of fencing plus the cost of materials. If the customer has bids of $1,700, $2,500, and $2,340 in addition to your bid, decide if your bid is the low bid for the job to determine if you will likely get the business.

41. If you are paying three employees $9 per hour and the fence installation in Exercise 40 requires 21 hours when all three employees are working, determine how much you will be required to pay in wages. What will be your gross profit on the job?

42. The 7th Inning buys baseball cards from eight vendors. In the month of November the company purchased 8,832 boxes of cards. If an equal number of boxes were purchased from each vendor, how many boxes of cards were supplied by each vendor?

43. If you have 348 packages of holiday candy to rebox for shipment to a discount store and you can pack 12 packages in each box, how many boxes will you need?

44. Bio Fach, Germany's biggest ecologically sound consumer goods trade fair, had 21,960 visitors. This figure was up from 18,090 the previous year and 16,300 two years earlier. What is the increase in visitors to Bio Fach from two years earlier to the present?

45. The "communication revolution" has given us prepaid phone calling cards. These cards are used to make long-distance phone calls from any phone. In a recent year the industry posted sales of $500,000. Three years later the sales figure had risen to $200,000,000. What is the increase in sales over the three-year period?

46. *See Example 16.* Strategic Telecomm Systems, Inc. (STS), in Knoxville, Tennessee, made one of the largest single purchases of long-distance telephone time in history. STS purchased 42 million minutes. If STS paid 2 cents per minute, how much did they pay for the purchase? To convert cents to dollars, divide by 100.

47. In Exercise 46, if STS resells the phone time at an average of 6 cents per minute, how much profit will it make on the purchase?

48. American Communications Network (ACN) of Troy, Michigan, also markets prepaid phone cards, which it refers to as "equity calling cards." If ACN employs 214,302 persons in 32 locations, on the average, how many employees work at each location?

49. Last year Wilmington Motors lost $39,583. This year the company lost $23,486. Find the two-year loss for Wilmington Motors.

50. Brentwood Fashions posted a net loss of $32,871 last year and a net profit of $29,783 for this year. Find the two-year profit or loss.

51. Lisle Building Supplies sold 291 rolls of damaged insulation at a $3 loss (−$3) per roll. What was the total loss?

52. *See Example 15.* Kent Realty Company had an annual loss of $63,408. What was the average loss per month?

53. *See Example 10.* Angela is at the Office Depot warehouse processing store orders for 15,000 reams of copy paper. She found 1,358 cases of paper. Each case contains 10 reams. Does Angela need to order more paper from the wholesaler to have enough to complete the store orders?

54. *See Example 11.* Maria's Plant Nursery has 487 trees that will be sold to a landscape design firm at a loss of $12 each. What total loss will result from the sale?

Learning Outcomes

Section 1-1

What to Remember with Examples

1 Read whole numbers. (p. 4)

1. Separate the number into periods beginning with the rightmost digit and moving to the left.
2. Identify the period name of the leftmost period.
3. For each period, beginning with the leftmost period:
    (a) Read the three-digit number from left to right.
    (b) Name the period.
4. Note these exceptions:
    (a) Do not read or name a period that is all zeros.
    (b) Do not name the units period.
    (c) The word *and* is never part of the word name for a whole number.

574 is read *five hundred seventy-four.*
3,804,321 is read *three million, eight hundred four thousand, three hundred twenty-one.*

2 Write whole numbers. (p. 6)

1. Begin recording digits from left to right.
2. Insert a comma at each period name.
3. Every period after the first period must have three digits. Insert zeros as necessary.

Write the number: twenty billion, fifteen million, two hundred four.

20, _ _ _, _ _ _, _ _ _   Record the first digits and anticipate the periods
   billion   *million*   *thousand*   to follow.

20, _ 15,_ _ _, 204   Fill in the remaining periods, using zeros as
                        necessary.

20,015,000,204

3 Round whole numbers. (p. 7)

1. Find the digit in the specified place.
2. Look at the next digit to the right.
    (a) If this digit is less than 5, replace it and all digits to its right with zeros.
    (b) If this digit is 5 or more, add 1 to the digit in the specified place, and replace all digits to the right of the specified place with zeros.

4,860 rounded to the nearest hundred is 4,900.
7,439 rounded to the nearest thousand is 7,000.
4,095 rounded to the first digit is 4,000.

4 Read and round integers. (p. 8)

1. For reading integers, the rules are the same as for reading whole numbers. State the word *negative* or *minus* as you begin to read a number that is less than zero. Other words such as *loss* or *debt* may be used to indicate a negative amount.
2. For rounding integers, the rules are the same as for rounding whole numbers.

−$3,493,209 rounded to the first digit is −$3,000,000. It can be read as negative three million dollars or as a loss of three million dollars.

Section 1-2

1 Add and subtract whole numbers. (p. 10)

Add whole numbers.

1. Estimate the sum by rounding each addend to the first digit and adding the rounded addends.
2. Find the exact sum by adding the numbers by hand or by using a calculator.
3. Compare the estimate and the exact sum to see if the exact sum is reasonable.
4. Check the exact sum by adding the numbers a second time.

Add: 2,074 + 485 + 12,592	
Estimate: 2,000 + 500 + 10,000 = 12,500	Round each addend to the first digit and add the rounded addends.
2074 $+$ 485 $+$ 12592 $=$ $\Rightarrow$ 15151	Enter the addends in the calculator.
15,151	Insert commas as appropriate.
	The estimate and exact sum are reasonably close.

Subtract whole numbers.

1. Estimate the difference by rounding the minuend (number subtracted from) and subtrahend (number being subtracted) to the first digit and subtracting the rounded amounts.
2. Find the exact difference by subtracting the numbers by hand or by using a calculator. Be sure to put the minuend on top or enter it first on the calculator.
3. Compare the estimate and the exact difference to see if the exact difference is reasonable.
4. Check the exact difference by adding the difference and the subtrahend. The sum should equal the minuend.

Subtract 34,315 from 112,396.	
112,396 − 34,315	The number being subtracted (subtrahend) goes second.
Estimate:	
100,000 − 30,000 = 70,000	Round each amount to the first digit and subtract the rounded amounts.
112396 $-$ 34315 $=$ $\Rightarrow$ 78081	Enter the numbers in the calculator.
78,081	Insert commas as appropriate.

2 Add and subtract integers. (p. 14)

Add two negative integers.

1. Add the numbers without regard to the signs.
2. Assign a negative to the sum.

−25 + (−8) = −33	Add without regard to the signs. The sum is negative.
Calculator options:	
$(-)$ 25 $+$ $(-)$ 8 ENTER $\Rightarrow$ −33	Steps for scientific or graphing calculator.
25 $+/-$ $+$ 8 $+/-$ $=$ $\Rightarrow$ −33	Steps for basic or financial calculator.

Add a positive and a negative integer.

1. Subtract the numbers without regard to the signs.
2. Look at the numbers without the signs. Choose the larger of these numbers. Assign the sum the sign that was in front of the larger of the numbers.

−15 + 7 = −8	15 − 7 = 8. The sum is negative because 15 is negative in the original problem.
$(-)$ 15 $+$ 7 ENTER $\Rightarrow$ −8	Steps for scientific or graphing calculator.
15 $+/-$ $+$ 7 $=$ $\Rightarrow$ −8	Steps for basic or financial calculator.
16 + (−7) = 9	16 − 7 = 9. The sum is positive because 16 is positive.
16 $+$ $(-)$ 7 ENTER $\Rightarrow$ 9	Steps for scientific or graphing calculator.
16 $+$ 7 $+/-$ $=$ $\Rightarrow$ 9	Steps for basic or financial calculator.

Subtract two integers.

Change a subtraction problem to an equivalent addition problem.

1. Rewrite the problem as adding the minuend and the opposite of the subtrahend.
2. Apply the appropriate rule for adding integers.

$-32 - 8$	Change to an equivalent addition problem.
$-32 + (-8)$	Apply the rule for adding two negative integers.
$-32 + (-8) = -40$	Add; sum is negative.
$\boxed{(-)}\,32\,\boxed{-}\,8\,\boxed{\text{ENTER}} \Rightarrow -40$	Steps for scientific or graphing calculator.
$32\,\boxed{+/-}\,\boxed{-}\,8\,\boxed{=} \Rightarrow -40$	Steps for basic or financial calculator.
$-32 - (-8)$	Change to an equivalent addition problem.
$-32 + 8$	Apply the rule for adding a positive and negative integer.
$-32 + 8 = -24$	Subtract; sum is negative.
$\boxed{(-)}\,32\,\boxed{-}\,\boxed{(-)}\,8\,\boxed{\text{ENTER}} \Rightarrow -24$	Steps for scientific or graphing calculator.
$32\,\boxed{+/-}\,\boxed{-}\,8\,\boxed{+/-}\,\boxed{=} \Rightarrow -24$	Steps for basic or financial calculator.

3   Multiply integers. (p. 16)

Multiply whole numbers.

1. Write the numbers in a vertical column, aligning digits according to their places.
2. For each *place* of the multiplier in turn, beginning with the ones place:
   (a) Multiply the multiplicand by the *place* digit of the multiplier.
   (b) Write this partial product directly below the multiplier (or the last partial product), aligning the ones digit of the partial product with the *place* digit of the multiplier (and aligning all other digits to the left accordingly).
3. Add the partial products.

$$
\begin{array}{r}
543 \\
\times \;\; 32 \\
\hline
1\,086 \\
16\,29 \\
\hline
17{,}376
\end{array}
\qquad
\begin{array}{r}
509 \\
\times \;\; 87 \\
\hline
3\,563 \\
40\,72 \\
\hline
44{,}283
\end{array}
$$

Multiply whole numbers using a calculator.

1. Estimate the product by rounding each factor to the first digit and multiplying the rounded factors.
2. Find the exact product by multiplying the numbers using a calculator.
3. Compare the estimate and the exact product to see if the exact product is reasonable.
4. Check the exact product by multiplying the numbers a second time.

Multiply: 543×32	
Estimate:	
$500 \times 30 = 15{,}000$	Round each factor to the first digit and multiply rounded factors.
$543\,\boxed{\times}\,32\,\boxed{=} \Rightarrow 17376$	Enter the numbers into the calculator.
17,376	Insert commas as appropriate.

Multiply when numbers end in zero.

1. Mentally eliminate zeros from the end of each number.
2. Multiply the new numbers.
3. Attach to the end of the product the total number of zeros mentally eliminated in step 1.

$$
\begin{array}{r}
8{,}1\!\mid\!00 \\
\times \;\; 3\!\mid\!00 \\
\hline
2{,}4\,3\!\mid\!0{,}000
\end{array}
\qquad
\begin{array}{l}
18 \times 10 = 180 \\
18 \times 100 = 1{,}800 \\
18 \times 1{,}000 = 18{,}000
\end{array}
$$

Multiply a negative and a positive integer.

1. Multiply the integers without regard to the signs.
2. Assign a negative sign to the product.

$23 \times (-15) = -345$		Multiply the integers without regard to signs. The product is negative.
$23\boxed{\times}\boxed{(-)}15\boxed{\text{ENTER}} \Rightarrow -345$		Steps for scientific or graphing calculator.
$23\boxed{\times}15\boxed{+/-}\boxed{=} \Rightarrow -345$		Steps for basic or financial calculator.
-345		Insert commas as appropriate.

Multiply two negative integers.

1. Multiply the integers with regard to the signs.
2. The product is positive.

$(-273) \times (-35) =$	Multiply integers without regard to signs. Product is positive.
$\boxed{(-)}273\boxed{\times}\boxed{(-)}35\boxed{\text{ENTER}} \Rightarrow 9555$	Steps for scientific or graphing calculator.
$\boxed{273}\boxed{+/-}\boxed{\times}35\boxed{+/-}\boxed{=} \Rightarrow 9555$	Steps for basic or financial calculator.
$9{,}555$	Insert commas as appropriate.

4   Divide integers. (p. 19)

Divide whole numbers.

1. Beginning with its leftmost digit, identify the first group of digits of the dividend that is larger than or equal to the divisor. This group of digits is the first *partial dividend.*
2. For each partial dividend in turn, beginning with the first:
   (a) *Divide* the partial dividend by the divisor. Write this partial quotient above the rightmost digit of the partial dividend.
   (b) *Multiply* the partial quotient by the divisor. Write the product below the partial dividend, aligning places.
   (c) *Subtract* the product from the partial dividend. Write the difference below the product, aligning places. The difference must be less than the divisor.
   (d) After the difference, *bring down* the next digit of the dividend. This is the new partial dividend.
3. When all the digits of the dividend have been used, *write* the final difference in step 2c as the remainder (unless the remainder is 0). The whole-number part of the quotient is the number written above the dividend.
4. To check, multiply the quotient by the divisor and add the remainder to the product. This sum will equal the dividend.

$$
\begin{array}{r}
287\,\text{R}1 \\
3\overline{)862} \\
\underline{6} \\
26 \\
\underline{24} \\
22 \\
\underline{21} \\
1
\end{array}
\qquad
\begin{array}{r}
804 \\
56\overline{)45{,}024} \\
\underline{44\ 8} \\
22 \\
\underline{0} \\
224 \\
\underline{224}
\end{array}
$$

$21{,}000 \div 10 = 2{,}100$

$21{,}000 \div 100 = 210$

$21{,}000 \div 1{,}000 = 21$

Divide whole numbers using a calculator.

1. Estimate the quotient by rounding the divisor to the first digit and find the first partial quotient. Place zeros over the remaining digits in the dividend.
2. Find the exact quotient by dividing the numbers using a calculator.
3. Compare the estimate and the exact quotient to see if the exact quotient is reasonable.
4. Check the exact quotient by multiplying the quotient times the divisor and adding any remainder. The result should equal the original dividend.

Divide 1,614,060 by 5,124.	
$1{,}614{,}060 \div 5{,}124 =$	
Estimate:	
$2{,}000{,}000 \div 5{,}000 = 400$	Round each number to the first digit and divide rounded amounts.
$1614060\boxed{\div}5124\boxed{=}315$	Enter amounts into a calculator.
	Compare results with the estimate. It is reasonable.
$1{,}614{,}060 \div 5{,}124 = \mathbf{315}$	

Convert a decimal portion of a quotient to a remainder.

1. Perform a division on a calculator.
2. If there is a decimal portion in the quotient, subtract the whole-number part of the quotient from the quotient showing in the calculator display.
3. Multiply the result of step 2 by the original divisor to get the whole-number value of the remainder.

What is the remainder when 3,054 is divided by 23?	
3054 $\div$ 23 $=$ $\Rightarrow$ 132.7826087	Enter the amounts into a calculator as a division.
$-$ 132 $=$ $\Rightarrow$ 0.7826086957	Continue the operations in the calculator or use the feature of the calculator to enter the previous answer.
$\times$ 23 $=$ $\Rightarrow$ 18	This is the remainder of the division.
3,054 $\div$ 23 $=$ **132 R18**	

Divide by integers.

1. Divide the numbers without regard to the signs.
2. If both numbers are positive or both are negative, the quotient is positive.
3. If one number is positive and the other is negative, the quotient is negative.

Divide -45 by -5.	
$-45 \div (-5) = $ **9**	Divide without regard to the signs. The quotient is positive as both signs are negative.
$(-)$ 45 $\div$ $(-)$ 5 ENTER $\Rightarrow$ 9	Steps for scientific or graphing calculator
45 $+/-$ $\div$ 5 $+/-$ $=$ $\Rightarrow$ 9	Steps for basic or business calculator
Divide -45 by 5.	
$-45 \div 5 = $ **-9**	Divide without regard to the signs. The quotient is negative as one sign is negative and one is positive.
$(-)$ 45 $\div$ 5 ENTER $\Rightarrow$ -9	Steps for scientific or graphing calculator
45 $+/-$ $\div$ 5 $=$ $\Rightarrow$ -9	Steps for basic or business calculator

Divide numbers ending in zero by place-value numbers such as 10, 100, 1,000.

1. Mentally eliminate the same number of ending zeros from both the divisor and the dividend.
2. Divide the new numbers.

Divide 483,000 $\div$ 200	
483,000 $\div$ 200	Eliminate two ending zeros from both numbers.
4830 $\div$ 2	Divide.
$\begin{array}{r} 2415 \\ 2\overline{)4830} \end{array}$	
483,000 $\div$ 200 = 2,415	

5 Apply the standard order of operations to a series of operations. (p. 23)

1. Perform all operations that are inside grouping symbols such as parentheses.
2.* Perform all multiplications and divisions as they appear from left to right.
3. Perform all additions and subtractions as they appear from left to right.

*Later another step will be added here for exponents and roots.

Perform the operations according to the standard order of operations.

(a) $(6 + 8) \div 2$ **(b)** $6 + 8 \div 2$ **(c)** $2 + (-5) \times 6$

(a) $(6 + 8) \div 2$	Work inside the parentheses first.
$14 \div 2 = \mathbf{7}$	Divide.
(b) $6 + 8 \div 2$	Divide first.
$6 + 4 = \mathbf{10}$	Add.
(c) $2 + (-5) \times 6$	Multiply first.
$2 + (-30)$	Add.
$\mathbf{-28}$	

1. According to a major auto manufacturer, the company invested more than $7 billion in manufacturing, research, and design. Use digits to write this number.

2. An automobile manufacturer claims to create more than twenty thousand direct jobs. Use digits to write this number.

Write the word name for the number.

3. In a recent year Ford Motor Company had a loss of −$14,672,000,000. Show how you would read this number.

4. LVMH had a gain of $30,860,000,000 in a recent year. Show how you would read this number.

Round Exercises 5 through 7 to the specified place.

5. 378 (nearest hundred)

6. 9,374 (nearest thousand)

7. −834 (nearest ten)

8. A color video surveillance system with eight cameras is priced at $3,899. Round this price to the nearest thousand dollars.

9. Fiber-optic cable capacity for communications such as telephones grew from 265,472 miles to 6,316,436 miles in a six-year period. Round each of these numbers of miles to the nearest hundred thousand.

Round to the first digit.

10. 3,784,809

Round to the first digit.

11. 5,178

Add.

12. 47 + 385 + 87 + 439 + 874

Add.

13. 32,948 + 6,804 + 15,695 + 415 + 7,739

Mentally estimate the sum by rounding each number to the first digit. Then find the exact sum.

14.
74,374
82,849
72,494
+ 89,219

15.
3,748
9,409
3,577
+ 4,601

Mentally estimate the sum in Exercise 16 by rounding each number to the nearest hundred. Then find the exact sum.

16.
747
854
324
+ 687

17. Mary Luciana bought 48 pencils, 96 pens, 36 DVDs, and 50 printer cartridges. How many items did she buy?

18. Kiesha had the following test scores: 92, 87, 96, 85, 72, 84, 57, 98. What is the student's total number of points?

Estimate the difference by rounding each number to the first digit in Exercises 19 through 21. Then find the exact difference.

19.
9,748
−5,676

20.
83,748,194
−27,209,104

21.
84,378
−28,746

22. Sam Andrews has 42 packages of hamburger buns on hand but expects to use 130 packages. How many must he order?

23. An inventory shows 596 fan belts on hand. If the normal in-stock count is 840, how many should be ordered?

Add or subtract the integers as indicated.

24. $(-32) + (-27)$

25. $\$21 + (-\$47)$

26. $14 - (-12)$

27. $-36 - (-18)$

Multiply and check the product.

28. $\begin{array}{r} 5,931 \\ \times\ \ \ 835 \\ \hline \end{array}$

29. $\begin{array}{r} 1,987 \\ \times\ \ \ 394 \\ \hline \end{array}$

30. 33×500

31. $7,870 \times 6,000$

Mentally estimate the product in Exercise 32 by rounding each number to the first digit. Then find the exact product.

32. $\begin{array}{r} 7,489 \\ \times\ \ \ 34 \\ \hline \end{array}$

Mentally estimate the product in Exercise 33 by rounding each number to the nearest hundred. Then find the exact product.

33. $\begin{array}{r} 3,128 \\ \times\ \ \ 478 \\ \hline \end{array}$

34. A day-care center has 28 children. If each child eats one piece of fruit each day, how many pieces of fruit are required for a week (five days)?

35. Industrialized nations have 2,017 radios per thousand people. This is six times the number of radios per thousand people as there are in the underdeveloped nations. What is the number of radios per thousand people for the underdeveloped nations?

Divide and check the quotient.

36. $1,232 \div 16$

Estimate the quotient in Exercise 37 by rounding each number. Then find the exact quotient.

37. $85\overline{)748,431}$

Divide.

38. $483,000 \div 3,000$

39. $73,460,000 \div 10,000$

40. A parts dealer has 2,988 washers. The washers are packaged with 12 in each package. How many packages can be made?

41. If 127 employees earn $2,032 in one hour, what is the average hourly wage per employee?

42. Carissa's Fashions sold 138 jackets at a loss of $7 (−$7) each. What was her total loss?

43. Chantal's Sound Shop had an annual loss of −$69,708. What was her average monthly loss for each of the 12 months?

Perform the operations according to the standard order of operations.

44. $34 - 3 \times 7$

45. $(\$32 - \$17 + \$57) \div 9$

46. $(-3)(-12) - 5$

EXERCISES SET B

1. Local people build Toyota vehicles in twenty-six countries around the world. Use digits to write this number.

2. By its own claim, HFS, Inc., is the world's largest hotel franchising organization. It claims to have five thousand, four hundred hotels with four hundred ninety-five thousand rooms in over seventy countries, and more than twenty percent of the franchises are minority-owned. Use digits to write each of the numbers.

Write the word name for the number.

3. Citigroup had a loss of −$27,684,000,000 in a recent year. Show how you would read this number.

4. Delta Airlines had an annual loss of −$8,922,000,000 in a recent year. Show how you would read this number.

Round Exercises 5 through 7 to the specified place.

5. 8,248 (nearest hundred)

6. 348,218 (nearest ten-thousand)

7. 29,712 (nearest thousand)

8. A black-and-white video surveillance system with eight cameras is priced at $2,499. What is the price to the nearest hundred dollars?

9. The industrialized nations of the world have six times the number of radios per thousand people as the underdeveloped nations. The industrialized nations have 2,017 radios per thousand people. Round the number of radios to the nearest thousand.

Round to the first digit.

10. 2,063,948

Round to the first digit.

11. 17,295,183,109

Add.

12. $72 + 385 + 29 + 523 + 816$

Add.

13. $46,867 + 7,083 + 723 + 5,209$

Mentally estimate the sum by rounding each number to the first digit. Then find the exact sum.

14.
```
   374
   847
   521
   873
+  482
```

15.
```
  3,470
    843
  3,872
+   574
```

Mentally estimate the sum in Exercise 16 by rounding each number to the nearest hundred. Then find the exact sum.

16.
```
  4,274
    643
  1,274
+    97
```

17. Jorge Englade has 57 baseball cards from 1978, 43 cards from 1979, 104 cards from 1980, 210 cards from 1983, and 309 cards from 1987. How many cards does he have in all?

18. A furniture manufacturing plant had the following labor-hours in one week: Monday, 483; Tuesday, 472; Wednesday, 497; Thursday, 486; Friday, 464; Saturday, 146; Sunday, 87. Find the total labor-hours worked during the week.

Mentally estimate the difference by rounding each number to the first digit in Exercises 19 through 21. Then find the exact difference.

19.
```
  370,408
 −187,506
```

20.
```
  12,748
 − 5,438
```

21.
```
  109,849
 − 35,464
```

22. Frieda Salla had 148 tickets to sell for a baseball show. If she has sold 75 tickets, how many does she still have to sell?

23. Veronica McCulley weighed 132 pounds before she began a weight-loss program. After eight weeks, she weighed 119 pounds. How many pounds did she lose?

Add or subtract the integers as indicated.

24. $46 + (-58)$

25. $\$35 + (-\$52)$

26. $37 - (-21)$

27. $72 - (-42)$

Multiply and check the product.

28. $\begin{array}{r} 5,565 \\ \times\ \ 839 \end{array}$

29. $\begin{array}{r} 78,626 \\ \times\ \ \ \ 87 \end{array}$

30. $283 \times 3,000$

31. 405×400

Mentally estimate the product in Exercise 32 by rounding each number to the first digit. Then find the exact product.

32. $\begin{array}{r} 378 \\ \times\ \ 72 \end{array}$

Mentally estimate the product in Exercise 33 by rounding each number to the nearest hundred. Then find the exact product.

33. $\begin{array}{r} 378 \\ \times 546 \end{array}$

34. Auto Zone has a special on fuel filters. Normally, the price of one filter is $15, but with this sale, you can purchase two filters for only $27. How much can you save by purchasing two filters at the sale price?

35. Industrialized nations have 793 TV sets per thousand people. If this is nine times as many TVs per thousand people as there are in the underdeveloped nations, what is the number of TVs per thousand people in the underdeveloped nations?

Divide and check the quotient.

36. $4,020 \div 12$

Estimate the quotient in Exercise 37 by rounding the divisor to the first digit. Then find the exact quotient.

37. $346\overline{)174,891}$

Divide.

38. $835,000 \div 5,000$

39. $68,650,000 \div 10,000$

40. A stack of countertops measures 238 inches. If each countertop is 2 inches thick, how many are in the stack?

41. Sequoia Brown has 15 New Zealand coins, 32 Canadian coins, 18 British coins, and 12 Australian coins in her British Commonwealth collection. How many coins does she have in this collection?

42. Soledad's Tamale Shop had an annual loss of −$10,152. What was her average quarterly loss for each of the four quarters in the year?

43. Julio's Video Store sold 219 videos at a loss of $3 (−$3) each. What was his total loss?

Perform the operations according to the standard order of operations.

44. $63 + 126 \div 7$

45. $(\$72 + \$38 - \$21 + \$32) \times 3$

46. $(-5)(-11) - 18$

Review of Whole Numbers and Integers

BUSINESS MATH

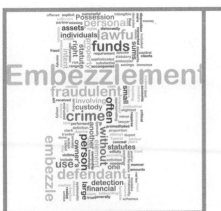

PRACTICE TEST

Write the word name for the number.

1. 503

2. 12,056,039

Round to the specified place.

3. 84,321 (nearest hundred)

4. 58,967 (nearest thousand)

5. 80,235 (first digit)

6. 587,213 (first digit)

Write the number.

7. Five billion, seventeen million, one hundred thirty-five thousand, six hundred thirty-two.

8. Seventeen million, five hundred thousand, six hundred eight.

9. Delta Airlines had revenues of $22,697,000,000 in a recent year. Show how you would read the revenue.

10. CVS Caremark Drugs had revenues of $87,471,900,000 in a recent year. Show how you would read the revenue.

11. New York Life Insurance, a Fortune 500 company, had a loss of −$949,700,000 in a recent year. Show how you would read the loss.

12. Macy's Department Store had an annual loss of −$4,803,000,000 in a recent year. Show how you would read the loss.

Estimate by rounding to hundreds. Then find the exact result.

13. 863 + 983 + 271

14. 987 − 346

Estimate by rounding to the first digit. Then find the exact result.

15. 892 × 46

16. $53\overline{)4{,}021}$

17. An inventory clerk counted the following items: 438 rings, 72 watches, and 643 pen-and-pencil sets. How many items were counted?

18. A section of a warehouse is 31 feet high. Boxes that are each two feet high are to be stacked in the warehouse. How many boxes can be stacked one on top of the other?

19. A parts dealer has 2,988 washers. The washers are packaged with 12 in each package. How many packages can be made?

20. Baker's Department Store sold 23 pairs of ladies' leather shoes. If the store's original inventory was 43 pairs of the shoes, how many pairs remain in inventory?

21. Galina makes $680 a week. If she works 40 hours a week, what is her hourly pay rate?

22. A day-care center has 28 children. If each child eats two pieces of fruit each day, how many pieces of fruit are required for a week (five days)?

23. An oral communication textbook contains three pages of review at the end of each of its 16 chapters. What is the total number of pages devoted to review?

24. John Chang ordered 48 paperback novels for his bookstore. When he received the shipment, he learned that 11 were on back order. How many novels did he receive?

25. McDonald's® had revenues of $23,522,400,000 and profits of $4,313,200,000 in a recent year. If Expenses = Revenues − Profits, find the expenses for the year.

26. Ingram Micro in Santa Ana, California, recently had annual revenues of $34,362,200,000 and losses of −$394,900,000. Find their annual expenses. (Expenses = Revenues − Profits)

27. Karoline's Sports Equipment Store sold 186 exercise mats at a loss of $11 (−$11) each. What was the total loss?

28. Lifecycle Fitness Center had an annual loss of −$26,136. What was the average loss for each of the twelve months?

Perform the operations according to the standard order of operations.

29. $133 \div 7 \times (-4) + 26$

30. $(\$68 + \$52 - \$71 + \$32) \times 9$

1. Addition and subtraction are inverse operations. Write the following addition problem as a subtraction problem and find the value of the letter n.

   $12 + n = 17$

2. Multiplication and division are inverse operations. Write the following multiplication problem as a division problem and find the value of the letter n.

   $5 \times n = 45$

3. Give an example illustrating that the associative property does NOT apply to subtraction.

4. Give an example illustrating that the commutative property does NOT apply to division.

5. Describe a problem you have encountered that required you to add whole numbers.

6. Describe a problem you have encountered that required you to multiply whole numbers.

7. What operation is a shortcut for repeated addition? Give an example to illustrate your answer.

8. If you know a total amount and all the parts but one, explain what operations you would use to find the missing part.

9. What operation enables you to find the cost per item if you know the total cost of a certain number of items and you know each item has the same price?

10. Find and explain the error in the following. Rework the problem correctly.

$$
\begin{array}{r}
59 \\
12\overline{)6{,}108} \\
6\,0 \\
\hline
108 \\
108 \\
\hline
\end{array}
$$

Find and explain the error in the following. Rework the problem correctly.

11. $5 + 3(8) - 12 =$

    $8(8) - 12 =$

    $64 - 12 =$

    $\qquad 52$

12. $25 - 12 + 7 =$

    $25 - 22 =$

    $\qquad 3$

Challenge Problem

Sales Quotas. A sales quota establishes a minimum amount of sales expected during a given period for a salesperson in some businesses, such as selling cars or houses. In setting sales quotas, sales managers take certain factors into consideration, such as the nature of the sales representative's territory and the experience of the salesperson. Such sales quotas enable a company to forecast the sales and future growth of the company for budget and profit purposes.

Try the following quota problem:

A sales representative for a time-sharing company has a monthly sales quota of 500 units. The representative sold 120 units during the first week, 135 units during the second week, and 165 units during the third week of the month. How many units must be sold before the end of the month if the salesperson is to meet the quota?

CASE STUDIES

1-1 Take the Limo Liner

At Graphics Express, Inc., Bob is planning to take three managers to a weekly meeting in New York. Traveling from Boston to New York for meetings has been part of the normal course of doing business at Graphics Express for several years, and the travel expenses and wasted time represent a considerable cost to the company. Normally, Bob's managers set up travel arrangements individually and get a reimbursement from the company. Desiring to cut costs and increase productivity, Bob decides to investigate alternative modes of making this weekly trip. He discovered that Amtrak Acela Express costs $242 for the round trip from Boston to New York. A taxi from the train station to the meeting costs about $40. The managers live in different parts of Boston, so carpooling in one car has not worked well; however, if two of the managers drive the 440-mile round-trip drive and each takes one of the other managers, the process might be manageable, and the cost is only the mileage reimbursement of $244 plus $125 parking for each car. A round trip airline ticket is $443 if purchased in advance. Although the flight is only about one hour in duration, the total travel time when flying from home to the New York office is about the same as when driving—the trip takes between three and four hours depending on traffic. The taxi from the airport to the meeting costs about $40. A service called Limo Liner, a sort of bus with upgrades, advertises that round-trip cost is about $60 less than an Amtrak ticket, and they offer extra services including a kitchen, TVs, restrooms, and a conference table that can be reserved. A taxi from the Limo Liner terminal to the meeting will cost around $20. In the past, most of the managers have flown to the meeting—citing the ability to work en route as a productivity advantage. The idea of using the Limo Liner intrigues Bob. He likes the idea that he and his managers could work together while they travel but wonders if this feature is worth the expense.

1. What is the cost of Bob and his three managers traveling by each method: by Amtrak with two taxi fares in New York, in individual cars including parking, carpooling in two cars including parking, by airplane with two taxi fares in New York, and by Limo Liner with two taxi fares in New York?

2. In the past, costs for the trip have totaled around $1,140 per trip for the group of four people using different methods of traveling to New York. Bob thinks he and his managers should probably drive in two cars to save the most money, but he is still intrigued by the possibility of conducting a meeting on the Limo Liner while traveling to New York. How much will the company save with either of these options? Which method of travel might yield the most productivity increase?

3. Each year Bob and his managers attend 12 weekly meetings in New York. How much will the cost savings be in a year over past average cost if the group travels regularly by Limo Liner?

1-2 Leaky Roof? Sanderson Roofing Can Help

Rick Sanderson owns a residential roofing business near Memphis. Rick has a small crew of three employees, and he does all of the measuring and calculations for the roofing jobs his company bids. Rick does all of his materials calculations based on the number of "squares" in a roof—one of the most commonly used terms in the roofing industry. One roofing square = 100 square feet. It does not matter how you arrive at 100 square feet: 10 feet × 10 feet = 100 square feet, or 1 roofing square, is the same as 5 feet × 20 feet, and so on. Although roofs come in many shapes and sizes, one of the most common is a gable roof. This is a type of roof containing sloping planes of the same pitch on each side of the ridge or peak, where the upper portion of the sidewall forms a triangle.

1. Rick just finished measuring a gable roof for a detached garage, and needs help with his materials calculations. Each of the two sides of the roof measured 45 feet (ft) $\times$ 20 feet (ft). How many square feet (ft^2) would this be in total? How many roofing squares would this equal?

2. Rick knows that for each roofing square he needs 4 bundles of 40-year composition shingles, which he can buy at $14 per bundle. He also uses 15-pound (lb) roofing felt as a base under the shingles, and each roll costs $9 and covers 3 squares. Given your answers to Exercise 1, how many bundles of shingles will he need? How many rolls of roofing felt? What are the costs for each?

3. To finish the job, Rick needs roofing nails and drip edge. A four-pound box of one-inch roofing nails will cover 3 squares and cost $5. Drip edge comes only in 10-foot lengths, costs $3 per length, and is attached only to the horizontal edges of the roof. How many pounds of 1-inch roofing nails will the job require, and what is the cost? How many 10-foot lengths of drip edge will finish the job, and at what cost? Finally, what is the total materials cost of the entire roofing project?

1-3 The Cost of Giving

United Way is a nonprofit organization working with nearly 1,300 local chapters that raise resources and mobilize care units for communities in need. With over $4 billion of annual revenue, United Way continues its status as one of the nation's largest charities. A substantial portion of those funds was raised through annual campaigns and corporate sponsorships. Alaina has been asked to coordinate her company's United Way fund drive. Because she has seen some of the projects United Way has supported in her own community, Alaina is excited to help her company try to reach its goal of raising $100,000 this year. Alaina will be distributing pledge cards to each of the company's employees to request donations. There are 150 people working on the first shift, 75 people working on the second shift, and a crew of 25 people working on the third shift.

1. If each person were to make a one-time donation, how much would each person need to donate for the company to reach its goal of raising $100,000?

2. Alaina feels that very few people can contribute this amount in one lump sum, so she is offering to divide this amount over 10 months. If the employees agree to this arrangement, how much will be deducted from each person's monthly paycheck?

3. Two weeks have passed and Alaina has collected the pledge cards from each of the employees with the following results:

- First Shift: 100 employees agreed to have $40 a month deducted for 10 months; 25 employees agreed to make a one-time contribution of $100; 15 employees agreed to make a one-time contribution of $50. The remaining employees agreed to have $20 per month withheld for the next 10 months.
- Second Shift: 25 people agreed to a one-time contribution of $150; 25 people agreed to have $40 a month deducted for 10 months; and the remaining employees agreed to a one-time contribution that averaged about $35 each.
- Third Shift: All 25 people agreed to double the $40 contribution and have it deducted over the next 10 months.

   How much was pledged or contributed on each shift?

4. Has Alaina met the company's goal of raising $100,000 for the year? By how much is she over or short?

5. If Alaina's company were to match the employee's contributions with $2 for every $1 the employees contributed, how much would the company contribute? What would be the total contribution to the United Way?

Top Chef

Even for adult students, fractions can be a difficult concept to grasp. The problem is that fractions are not always presented in a recognizable manner, though they are literally everywhere: in the mall when a store advertises "half off"; when we order a quarter-pound hamburger with cheese; or with most household projects, such as woodworking, curtain hanging, or painting. Perhaps the most familiar place where fractions are used is in the kitchen. Cooking utilizes fractions because it requires very precise measurements. In fact, every ingredient in a cake recipe is a fraction of something: $\frac{1}{4}$ cup of milk, $\frac{1}{2}$ teaspoon of salt, $1\frac{1}{3}$ cups of flour, and even a stick of butter $= \frac{1}{2}$ cup.

Many Americans are fascinated by cooking, and today cooking shows have become more popular than ever. One of Bravo's top-rated television series is *Top Chef*, an American reality competition show in which chefs compete against each other in a variety of culinary challenges. The hour-long episodes of *Top Chef* have it all: high-stakes culinary throw-downs; gorgeous food; likable (and not so likable) characters; awesomely talented judges; and nonstop drama.

Each episode of *Top Chef*, save for the finale, typically has two challenges. In the Quickfire Challenge, each chef is asked to cook a dish with certain requirements, such as using specific ingredients like $\frac{1}{4}$ cup of sherry or $\frac{3}{4}$ pound of beef tenderloin; or to inspire a certain taste or participate in a culinary-related challenge, such as a taste test. They are often given only a fraction of an hour, sometimes as little as 10 minutes or $\frac{1}{6}$ of an hour, to complete these tasks. A guest judge selects one or more chefs as the best in the challenge. Early in the season the winning chef(s) are granted immunity from the following Elimination Challenge.

In the Elimination Challenge, the chefs have to prepare one or more dishes to meet the challenge requirements. Many of these are individual challenges and may require several courses, although some instances require teams to complete the challenge. In one example two different four-member teams were to prepare a four-course meal consisting of scallops, lobster, duck, and beef. Teams were given 30 minutes of shopping time, with a budget of only $200, and two hours of cooking time.

A challenge of this nature required very precise planning and, of course, the use of fractions. Decisions had to be made regarding shopping and cooking, such as what portion of the budget to spend on each dish, the types and amounts of spices to be used, and the cooking times. For example, if the lobster cost $\frac{2}{5}$ of the $200 budget, how much would that be? And if it required $\frac{1}{4}$ hour to boil the water and $\frac{1}{3}$ hour of cooking time, how much time would a chef have left to prepare any side dishes? Answers to questions like this require a thorough understanding of fractions. So just like on the show, it's time to get cooking—with fractions!

LEARNING OUTCOMES

2-1 Fractions

1. Identify types of fractions.
2. Convert an improper fraction to a whole or mixed number.
3. Convert a whole or mixed number to an improper fraction.
4. Reduce a fraction to lowest terms.
5. Raise a fraction to higher terms.

2-2 Adding and Subtracting Fractions

1. Add fractions with like (common) denominators.
2. Find the least common denominator for two or more fractions.
3. Add fractions and mixed numbers.
4. Subtract fractions and mixed numbers.

2-3 Multiplying and Dividing Fractions

1. Multiply fractions and mixed numbers.
2. Divide fractions and mixed numbers.

LEARNING OUTCOMES

1 Identify types of fractions.
2 Convert an improper fraction to a whole or mixed number.
3 Convert a whole or mixed number to an improper fraction.
4 Reduce a fraction to lowest terms.
5 Raise a fraction to higher terms.

Fraction: a part of a whole amount. It is also a notation for showing division.

Denominator: the number of a fraction that shows how many parts one whole quantity is equally divided into. It is also the divisor of the indicated division.

Numerator: the number of a fraction that shows how many parts are considered. It is also the dividend of the indicated division.

Fraction line: the line that separates the numerator and denominator. It is also the division symbol.

Proper fraction: a fraction with a value that is less than 1. The numerator is smaller than the denominator.

Improper fraction: a fraction with a value that is equal to or greater than 1. The numerator is the same as or greater than the denominator.

Fractions are used to represent parts of whole items. Often fractions are implied in the narrative portion of reports and news articles. For example, a news article may claim that three out of four voters are in favor of a proposed change in a city ordinance.

1 Identify types of fractions.

We use fractions as a way to represent parts of whole numbers. If one whole quantity has four equal parts, then one of the four parts is represented by the fraction $\frac{1}{4}$ (Figure 2-1).

FIGURE 2-1
One part out of four parts is $\frac{1}{4}$ of the whole.

In the fraction $\frac{1}{4}$, 4 represents the number of equal parts contained in one whole quantity and is called the **denominator.** The 1 in the fraction $\frac{1}{4}$ represents the number of parts under consideration and is called the **numerator.**

The line separating the numerator and denominator may be written as a horizontal line (—) or as a slash (/) and is called the **fraction line.**

A fraction that has a value less than 1 is called a **proper fraction.** The numerator is smaller than the denominator. A fraction that has a value equal to or greater than 1 is called an **improper fraction.** The numerator is the same as or greater than the denominator.

> **DID YOU KNOW?**
>
> Fractions also show division. The fraction ¼ can be interpreted as 1 divided by 4 or 1 ÷ 4.
>
> $$\frac{\text{numerator}}{\text{denominator}} \qquad \frac{\text{dividend}}{\text{divisor}}$$
>
> The fraction line is interpreted as the division symbol.

EXAMPLE 1 Write the fraction that is illustrated and indicate if the fraction is proper or improper.

(a) In Figure 2-2 the whole quantity has been divided into nine (9) equal parts so the denominator of the fraction is 9. Four of the parts are shaded so the numerator is 4. **The fraction represented is $\frac{4}{9}$.** Since the numerator is smaller than the denominator, the fraction is less than 1 and is a **proper fraction.**

FIGURE 2-2

(b) In Figure 2-3 *two* whole quantities have been divided into four parts each so the denominator of the fraction is 4. Five parts are shaded so the numerator is 5. **The fraction represented is $\frac{5}{4}$.** Since the numerator is larger than the denominator, the fraction is an **improper fraction.**

FIGURE 2-3

EXAMPLE 2 Visualize the fraction to identify whether it is a proper or improper fraction. Describe the relationship between the numerator and denominator. Is the fraction proper or improper?

(a) $\frac{2}{5}$ (b) $\frac{3}{2}$ (c) $\frac{4}{4}$

(a) Figure 2-4 represents $\frac{2}{5}$ or two parts out of five equal parts.

FIGURE 2-4

The fraction $\frac{2}{5}$ is a proper fraction, because it is less than one whole quantity. The numerator is smaller than the denominator. The fraction is proper.

(b) Figure 2-5 represents $\frac{3}{2}$ or three parts when the one whole quantity contains two equal parts.

FIGURE 2-5

The fraction $\frac{3}{2}$ is more than one whole quantity. It is an improper fraction, because the numerator is greater than the denominator. The fraction is improper.

(c) Figure 2-6 represents $\frac{4}{4}$ or four parts when the one whole quantity contains four equal parts.

FIGURE 2-6

The fraction $\frac{4}{4}$ represents one whole quantity. It is an improper fraction, because the numerator and the denominator are equal. The fraction is improper.

STOP AND CHECK

Write the fraction that is illustrated. Indicate if the fraction is proper or improper. See Example 1.

1.

2.

Visualize the fraction to identify it as proper or improper. See Example 2.

3. $\dfrac{3}{7}$ **4.** $\dfrac{12}{5}$ **5.** $\dfrac{16}{16}$ **6.** $\dfrac{5}{9}$

2   Convert an improper fraction to a whole or mixed number.

In Figure 2-5, the fraction $\frac{3}{2}$ was shown as one whole quantity and $\frac{1}{2}$ of a second whole quantity. This amount, $\frac{3}{2}$, can also be written as $1\frac{1}{2}$. An amount written as a combination of an integer and a fraction is called a **mixed number.** Every mixed number can also be written as an improper fraction.

Mixed number: an amount that is a combination of an integer and a fraction.

To interpret the meaning of an improper fraction, we use its whole number or mixed number form. Thus, it is important to be able to convert between improper fractions and mixed numbers.

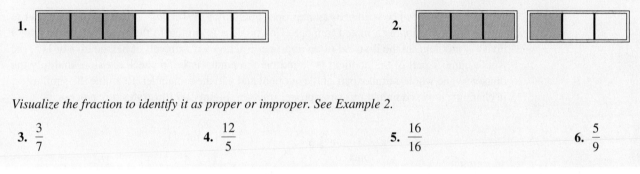

HOW TO   Write an improper fraction as a whole or mixed number

Write $\frac{12}{3}$ and $\frac{13}{3}$ as whole or mixed numbers.

1. Divide the numerator of the improper fraction by the denominator.

$$\begin{array}{r} 4 \\ 3\overline{)12} \end{array} \qquad \begin{array}{r} 4\,\text{R}1 \\ 3\overline{)13} \end{array}$$

2. Examine the remainder.
   (a) If the remainder is 0, the quotient is a whole number. The improper fraction is equivalent to this whole number.

$$\frac{12}{3} = 4$$

   (b) If the remainder is not 0, the quotient is not a whole number. The improper fraction is equivalent to a mixed number. The whole-number part of this mixed number is the whole-number part of the quotient. The fraction part of the mixed number has a numerator and a denominator. The numerator is the remainder; the denominator is the divisor (the denominator of the improper fraction).

$$\frac{13}{3} = 4\frac{1}{3}$$

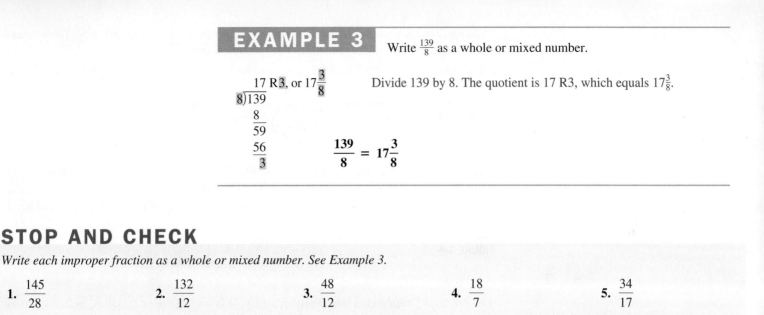

EXAMPLE 3

Write $\frac{139}{8}$ as a whole or mixed number.

$$
\begin{array}{r}
17 \text{ R}3, \text{ or } 17\frac{3}{8} \\
8)\overline{139} \\
\underline{8} \\
59 \\
\underline{56} \\
3
\end{array}
$$

Divide 139 by 8. The quotient is 17 R3, which equals $17\frac{3}{8}$.

$$\frac{139}{8} = 17\frac{3}{8}$$

STOP AND CHECK

Write each improper fraction as a whole or mixed number. See Example 3.

1. $\frac{145}{28}$ **2.** $\frac{132}{12}$ **3.** $\frac{48}{12}$ **4.** $\frac{18}{7}$ **5.** $\frac{34}{17}$

3 Convert a whole or mixed number to an improper fraction.

A mixed number can be written as an improper fraction by "reversing" the steps you use to write an improper fraction as a mixed number. This process is similar to the process for checking a division problem. In the division of an improper fraction with a result of $3\frac{1}{5}$, the divisor is 5, the whole-number part of the quotient is 3, and the remainder is 1. To check division, multiply the divisor by the whole-number part of the quotient and add the remainder. Examine the similarities in changing a mixed number to an improper fraction. Figure 2-7 illustrates this process.

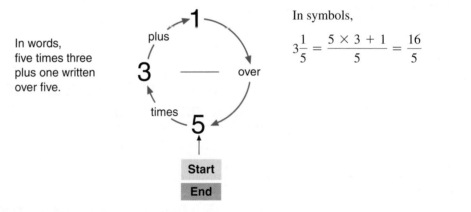

In words,
five times three
plus one written
over five.

In symbols,

$$3\frac{1}{5} = \frac{5 \times 3 + 1}{5} = \frac{16}{5}$$

FIGURE 2-7
$3\frac{1}{5}$ written as an improper fraction.

HOW TO	Write a mixed number or whole number as an improper fraction

Mixed number:

1. Find the numerator of the improper fraction.
   (a) Multiply the denominator of the mixed number by the whole-number part.
   (b) Add the product from step 1a to the numerator of the mixed number.
2. For the denominator of the improper fraction use the denominator of the mixed number.

Write $1\frac{2}{5}$ and 9 as improper fractions.
$(5 \times 1) + 2 = 7$

$\dfrac{7}{5}$

Whole number:

1. Write the whole number as the numerator.
2. Write 1 as the denominator.

9

$\dfrac{9}{1}$

EXAMPLE 4

Write $2\frac{3}{4}$ and 8 as improper fractions.

$$2\frac{3}{4} = \frac{(4 \times 2) + 3}{4} = \frac{11}{4}$$ For the numerator, multiply 4 times 2 and add 3.

$$8 = \frac{8}{1}$$ Write the whole number as the numerator and 1 as the denominator.

$$2\frac{3}{4} = \frac{11}{4} \text{ and } 8 = \frac{8}{1}.$$

STOP AND CHECK

Write as an improper fraction. See Example 4.

1. $3\frac{1}{4}$

2. $7\frac{2}{3}$

3. $5\frac{7}{8}$

4. 3

5. 2

4   Reduce a fraction to lowest terms.

Equivalent fractions: fractions that indicate the same portion of the whole amount.

Lowest terms: the form of a fraction when its numerator and denominator cannot be evenly divided by the same whole number except 1.

Many fractions represent the same portion of a whole. Such fractions are called **equivalent fractions.** For example, $\frac{1}{2}$, $\frac{2}{4}$, and $\frac{4}{8}$ are equivalent fractions (Figure 2-8).

To be able to recognize equivalent fractions, we often reduce fractions to lowest terms. Reducing a fraction to lowest terms is also called *simplifying* the fraction. A fraction in **lowest terms** has a numerator and denominator that cannot be evenly divided by the same whole number except 1.

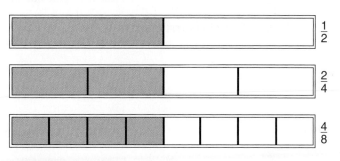

FIGURE 2-8
Equivalent fractions

HOW TO   Reduce a fraction to lowest terms

1. Inspect the numerator and denominator to find any whole number that both can be evenly divided by.
2. Divide both the numerator and the denominator by that number and inspect the new fraction to find any other number that the numerator and denominator can be evenly divided by.
3. Repeat steps 1 and 2 until 1 is the only number that the numerator and denominator can be evenly divided by.

Reduce $\frac{8}{10}$ to lowest terms.

8 and 10 are divisible by 2.

$$\frac{8 \div 2}{10 \div 2} = \frac{4}{5}$$

DID YOU KNOW?

Reducing a fraction and *writing an improper fraction as a whole or mixed number* are two different procedures. The use of correct terminology is illustrated here.

Writing an improper fraction as a mixed number:

$$\frac{5}{3} = 1\frac{2}{3}$$

Reducing or simplifying a fraction:

$$\frac{18}{12} = \frac{18 \div 6}{12 \div 6} = \frac{3}{2}$$

Note that $\frac{18}{12}$ is an improper fraction; when it is reduced to $\frac{3}{2}$, it is still an improper fraction that we can write as the mixed number $1\frac{1}{2}$.

EXAMPLE 5

Reduce $\frac{30}{36}$ to lowest terms by inspection.

$$\frac{30}{36} = \frac{30 \div 2}{36 \div 2} = \frac{15}{18}$$ Both the numerator and the denominator can be evenly divided by 2.

$$\frac{15}{18} = \frac{15 \div 3}{18 \div 3} = \frac{5}{6}$$ Both the numerator and the denominator of the new fraction can be evenly divided by 3.

$\frac{30}{36}$ is reduced to $\frac{5}{6}$.   Now 1 is the only number that both the numerator and the denominator can be evenly divided by. The fraction is now in lowest terms.

The most direct way to reduce a fraction to lowest terms is to divide the numerator and denominator by the **greatest common divisor (GCD).** The GCD is the greatest number by which both parts of a fraction can be evenly divided. The GCD often can be found **by inspection.** Otherwise, a systematic process can be used.

HOW TO   Find the greatest common divisor of the two numbers of a proper fraction

1. Use the numerator as the first divisor and the denominator as the dividend.
2. Divide.
3. Divide the first divisor from step 2 by the remainder from step 2.
4. Divide the divisor from step 3 by the remainder from step 3.
5. Continue this division process until the remainder is 0. The last divisor is the greatest common divisor.

EXAMPLE 6   Find the greatest common divisor (GCD) of 30 and 36. Then simplify the fraction $\frac{30}{36}$.

$$\overset{1\,R\,6}{30\overline{)36}}$$ Use the numerator as the first divisor and the denominator as the dividend.

$$\overset{5\,R\,0}{6\overline{)30}}$$ Divide the first divisor, 30, by the first remainder, 6.

GCD = 6.   The remainder is 0, so the last divisor is the GCD.

Reduce using the GCD.

$$\frac{30}{36} = \frac{30 \div 6}{36 \div 6} = \frac{5}{6}$$ Divide the numerator and denominator by the GCD.

$\frac{30}{36}$ **reduced to lowest terms is** $\frac{5}{6}$**.**

STOP AND CHECK

See Example 5.

1. Reduce $\frac{18}{24}$ to lowest terms by inspection.

2. Reduce $\frac{12}{36}$ to lowest terms by inspection.

3. Recent data shows the number of personal computers (PCs) per 1,000 people in the United States is 932. Express the fraction of U.S. people that have PCs in lowest terms.

4. The United Arab Emirates has the highest rate of cellular phones in the world. The United Sates ranks 72nd in countries of the world in cellular phone use with approximately 850 phones per 1,000 people. Express the fraction of U.S. people that have phones in lowest terms.

See Example 6.

5. Find the greatest common divisor (GCD) of 16 and 24. Then, reduce the fraction $\frac{16}{24}$ to lowest terms.

6. Find the GCD of 39 and 51. Then, reduce the fraction $\frac{39}{51}$ to lowest terms.

7. Find the GCD of 12 and 28. Then, reduce the fraction $\frac{12}{28}$ to lowest terms.

8. Find the GCD of 21 and 24. Then, reduce the fraction $\frac{21}{24}$ to lowest terms.

5   Raise a fraction to higher terms.

Just as you can reduce a fraction to lowest terms by dividing the numerator and denominator by the same number, you can write a fraction in *higher* terms by *multiplying* the numerator and denominator by the same number. This process is used in addition and subtraction of fractions.

HOW TO   Write a fraction in higher terms given the new denominator

Change $\frac{1}{2}$ to eighths, or $\frac{1}{2} = \frac{?}{8}$.

1. Divide the *new* denominator by the *old* denominator.

$$\begin{array}{r} 4 \\ 2\overline{)8} \end{array}$$

2. Multiply *both* the old numerator and the old denominator by the quotient from step 1.

$$\frac{1}{2} = \frac{1 \times 4}{2 \times 4} = \frac{4}{8}$$

EXAMPLE 7   Rewrite $\frac{5}{8}$ as a fraction with a denominator of 72.

$$\frac{5}{8} = \frac{?}{72}$$

Write the problem symbolically.

$$\begin{array}{r} 9 \\ 8\overline{)72} \end{array}$$

Divide the new denominator (72) by the old denominator (8) to find the number by which the old numerator and the old denominator must be multiplied. That number is 9.

$$\frac{5}{8} = \frac{5 \times 9}{8 \times 9} = \frac{45}{72}$$

Multiply the numerator and denominator by 9 to get the new fraction with a denominator of 72.

$$\frac{5}{8} = \frac{45}{72}$$

STOP AND CHECK

See Example 7.

1. Write $\frac{7}{12}$ as a fraction with a denominator of 36.

2. Write $\frac{3}{4}$ as a fraction with a denominator of 32.

Change the fraction to an equivalent fraction with the given denominator. *See Example 7.*

3. $\frac{1}{2}, \frac{}{18}$

4. $\frac{3}{5}, \frac{}{25}$

5. $\frac{5}{12}, \frac{}{36}$

6. $\frac{7}{8}, \frac{}{24}$

2-1 SECTION EXERCISES

SKILL BUILDERS

Classify the fractions as proper or improper. See Examples 1–2.

1. $\frac{5}{9}$

2. $\frac{12}{7}$

3. $\frac{7}{7}$

4. $\frac{1}{12}$

5. $\frac{12}{15}$

6. $\frac{21}{20}$

Write the fraction as a whole or mixed number. See Example 3.

7. $\frac{12}{7}$

8. $\frac{21}{20}$

9. $\frac{18}{18}$

10. $\frac{17}{7}$

11. $\frac{16}{8}$

12. $\frac{387}{16}$

13. The Czech Republic has approximately 1,300 cellular phones per 1,000 people. Express the number of phones per person as a whole or mixed number.

14. Hong Kong reported approximately 1,500 cellular phones per 1,000 people. Express the number of phones per person as a whole or mixed number.

Write the whole or mixed number as an improper fraction. See Example 4.

15. $6\dfrac{1}{4}$

16. $27\dfrac{2}{5}$

17. $2\dfrac{1}{3}$

18. $3\dfrac{4}{5}$

19. $1\dfrac{5}{8}$

20. $6\dfrac{2}{3}$

Reduce to lowest terms. See Example 5.

21. $\dfrac{12}{15}$

22. $\dfrac{12}{20}$

23. $\dfrac{20}{24}$

24. $\dfrac{18}{36}$

25. $\dfrac{24}{36}$

26. $\dfrac{13}{39}$

27. GameStop® reported profits of approximately $400 million with approximately $9,000 million in revenues. Compare the profit to revenue by writing as a fraction in lowest terms.

28. McDonald's® reported profits of approximately $4,000 million and revenues of approximately $24,000 million. Compare the profit to revenue by writing as a fraction in lowest terms.

Find the greatest common divisor (GCD) for the following then simplify the fraction. See Example 6.

29. $\dfrac{21}{36}$

30. $\dfrac{15}{24}$

31. $\dfrac{18}{48}$

32. $\dfrac{15}{40}$

Change the fraction to an equivalent fraction with the given denominator. See Example 7.

33. $\dfrac{3}{8}, \dfrac{}{16}$ **34.** $\dfrac{4}{5}, \dfrac{}{20}$ **35.** $\dfrac{3}{8}, \dfrac{}{32}$ **36.** $\dfrac{5}{9}, \dfrac{}{27}$ **37.** $\dfrac{1}{3}, \dfrac{}{15}$ **38.** $\dfrac{3}{5}, \dfrac{}{15}$

2-2 ADDING AND SUBTRACTING FRACTIONS

LEARNING OUTCOMES

1 Add fractions with like (common) denominators.
2 Find the least common denominator for two or more fractions.
3 Add fractions and mixed numbers.
4 Subtract fractions and mixed numbers.

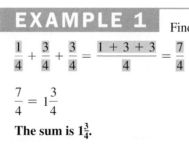

1 Add fractions with like (common) denominators.

The statement that three calculators plus four fax machines is the same as seven calculators is not true. The reason this is not true is that calculators and fax machines are *unlike* items, and we can only add *like* terms. It is true that three calculators plus four fax machines are the same as seven office machines. What we have done is to *rename* calculators and fax machines using a like term. Calculators and fax machines are both office machines. In the same way, to add fractions that have different denominators, we must rename the fractions using a like, or common, denominator. When fractions have like denominators, we can write their sum as a single fraction.

HOW TO   Add fractions with like (common) denominators

Add $\dfrac{2}{9} + \dfrac{1}{9}$.

1. Find the numerator of the sum: Add the numerators of the addends.

$$2 + 1 = 3$$

2. Find the denominator of the sum: Use the like denominator of the addends.

$$\dfrac{2}{9} + \dfrac{1}{9} = \dfrac{3}{9}$$

3. Reduce the sum to lowest terms and/or write as a whole or mixed number.

$$\dfrac{3}{9} = \dfrac{3 \div 3}{9 \div 3} = \dfrac{1}{3}$$

EXAMPLE 1   Find the sum: $\dfrac{1}{4} + \dfrac{3}{4} + \dfrac{3}{4}$. Write the sum as a mixed number.

$$\dfrac{1}{4} + \dfrac{3}{4} + \dfrac{3}{4} = \dfrac{1 + 3 + 3}{4} = \dfrac{7}{4}$$

The sum of the numerators is the numerator of the sum. The original like (common) denominator is the denominator of the sum.

$$\dfrac{7}{4} = 1\dfrac{3}{4}$$

Convert the improper fraction to a whole or mixed number.

The sum is $1\dfrac{3}{4}$.

STOP AND CHECK

Add. Reduce or write as a whole or mixed number if appropriate. See Example 1.

1. $\dfrac{3}{4} + \dfrac{1}{4} + \dfrac{1}{4}$ **2.** $\dfrac{3}{8} + \dfrac{7}{8} + \dfrac{1}{8}$ **3.** $\dfrac{1}{5} + \dfrac{2}{5} + \dfrac{2}{5}$ **4.** $\dfrac{5}{8} + \dfrac{3}{8} + \dfrac{1}{8}$ **5.** $\dfrac{5}{12} + \dfrac{7}{12} + \dfrac{11}{12}$

2 Find the least common denominator for two or more fractions.

Least common denominator (LCD): the smallest number that can be divided evenly by each original denominator.

To add fractions with different denominators, the fractions must first be changed to equivalent fractions with a common denominator. It is desirable to use the **least common denominator (LCD)**—the smallest number that can be evenly divided by each original denominator.

The common denominator can sometimes be found by inspection—that is, mentally selecting a number that can be evenly divided by each denominator. However, there are several systematic processes for finding the least common denominator. One way to find the least common denominator is to use prime numbers.

Prime number: A number greater than 1 that can be divided evenly only by itself and 1.

A **prime number** is a number greater than 1 that can be evenly divided only by itself and 1. The first ten prime numbers are 2, 3, 5, 7, 11, 13, 17, 19, 23, and 29.

HOW TO   Find the least common denominator for two or more fractions

Find the LCD of $\frac{7}{12}$ and $\frac{11}{30}$.

1. Write the denominators in a row and divide each one by the smallest prime number that any of the numbers can be evenly divided by.

$2)\underline{12 \quad 30}$ $12 \div 2 = 6$
                           $30 \div 2 = 15$

2. Write a new row of numbers using the quotients from step 1 and any numbers in the first row that cannot be evenly divided by the first prime number. Divide by the smallest prime number that any of the numbers can be evenly divided by.

$2)\underline{6 \quad 15}$ $6 \div 2 = 3$
                          Bring down 15.

3. Continue this process until you have a row of 1s.

$3)\underline{3 \quad 15}$ $3 \div 3 = 1; 15 \div 3 = 5$
$5)\underline{1 \quad 5}$ $5 \div 5 = 1;$ bring down 1.
     $1 \quad 1$

4. Multiply all the prime numbers you used to divide the denominators. The product is the least common denominator.

$\text{LCD} = 2 \times 2 \times 3 \times 5 = 60$

EXAMPLE 2   Find the least common denominator (LCD) of $\frac{5}{6}$, $\frac{5}{8}$, and $\frac{1}{12}$.

$2)\underline{6 \quad 8 \quad 12}$ Write the denominators in a row and divide by 2, the smallest prime divisor.
                                     $6 \div 2 = 3; 8 \div 2 = 4; 12 \div 2 = 6$

$2)\underline{3 \quad 4 \quad 6}$ Divide by 2 again.
                                    Bring down 3; $4 \div 2 = 2; 6 \div 2 = 3$.

$2)\underline{3 \quad 2 \quad 3}$ Divide by 2 again. Bring down both 3s.
                                    $2 \div 2 = 1$.

$3)\underline{3 \quad 1 \quad 3}$ Divide by 3.
     $1 \quad 1 \quad 1$ $3 \div 3 = 1$. Bring down 1.

$2 \times 2 \times 2 \times 3 = 24$ The LCD is the product of all the divisors.

The LCD is 24.

STOP AND CHECK

Find the LCD. See Example 2.

1. $\frac{1}{6}, \frac{5}{12}$ **2.** $\frac{15}{24}, \frac{37}{48}$ **3.** $\frac{1}{2}, \frac{5}{8}$ **4.** $\frac{8}{11}, \frac{3}{7}$ **5.** $\frac{5}{42}, \frac{7}{30}, \frac{9}{35}$

3 Add fractions and mixed numbers.

We can use the procedure for finding a least common denominator to add fractions with different denominators.

HOW TO — Add fractions with different denominators

1. Find the LCD.
2. Change each fraction to an equivalent fraction using the LCD.

3. Add the new fractions with like (common) denominators.
4. Reduce to lowest terms and write as a whole or mixed number if appropriate.

Add $\frac{2}{3} + \frac{3}{4}$.

LCD $= 12$ by inspection

$$\frac{2}{3} = \frac{2 \times 4}{3 \times 4} = \frac{8}{12}$$

$$\frac{3}{4} = \frac{3 \times 3}{4 \times 3} = \frac{9}{12}$$

$$\frac{8}{12} + \frac{9}{12} = \frac{17}{12}$$

$$\frac{17}{12} = 1\frac{5}{12}$$

EXAMPLE 3 Find the sum of $\frac{5}{6}$, $\frac{5}{8}$, and $\frac{1}{12}$.

LCD $= 24$ From Example 2 above.

$$\frac{5}{6} = \frac{5 \times 4}{6 \times 4} = \frac{20}{24}$$

Change each fraction to an equivalent fraction.

$$\frac{5}{8} = \frac{5 \times 3}{8 \times 3} = \frac{15}{24}$$

$$\frac{1}{12} = \frac{1 \times 2}{12 \times 2} = \frac{2}{24}$$

Add the numerators and use the common denominator.

$$\frac{37}{24} = 1\frac{13}{24}$$

Write the improper fraction as a mixed number.

The sum is $1\frac{13}{24}$.

HOW TO — Add mixed numbers

1. Add the whole-number parts.
2. Add the fraction parts and reduce to lowest terms.
3. Change improper fractions to whole or mixed numbers.
4. Add the whole-number parts.

EXAMPLE 4 Add $3\frac{2}{5} + 10\frac{3}{10} + 4\frac{7}{15}$.

Find the LCD.

$2)\overline{5\ \ 10\ \ 15}$ Divide by 2; $10 \div 2 = 5$.
Bring down 5 and 15.

$3)\overline{5\ \ 5\ \ 15}$ Divide by 3; $15 \div 3 = 5$.
Bring down both 5s.

$5)\overline{5\ \ 5\ \ 5}$
$\quad\ 1\ \ \ 1\ \ \ 1$ Divide by 5; $5 \div 5 = 1$.

$2 \times 3 \times 5 = 30$ LCD

$$3\frac{2}{5} = 3\frac{2 \times 6}{5 \times 6} = 3\frac{12}{30}$$

Change fraction parts to equivalent fractions with LCD.

$$10\frac{3}{10} = 10\frac{3 \times 3}{10 \times 3} = 10\frac{9}{30}$$

$$4\frac{7}{15} = 4\frac{7 \times 2}{15 \times 2} = 4\frac{14}{30}$$

Add whole numbers. Add fractions.

$$17\frac{35}{30}$$

Reduce the fraction and change the improper fraction to a mixed number.

$$\frac{35}{30} = \frac{7}{6} = 1\frac{1}{6}$$

$$17 + 1 + \frac{1}{6} = 18\frac{1}{6}$$

Add the whole numbers.

The sum is $18\frac{1}{6}$.

TIP
Estimate Sum of Mixed Numbers Using an Interval Method

A quick way to estimate the sum of mixed numbers is to add only the whole number parts. This estimate is smaller than the exact sum of the mixed numbers. To find an estimate that is larger than the exact sum, add 1 to the low estimate for each mixed number addend. Do not add 1 for whole number addends. Apply this estimation process to Example 4.

$3 + 10 + 4 = 17$ low estimate

$17 + 1 + 1 + 1 = 20$
            high estimate

The exact sum is between 17 and 20. Refer to Example 4 to see that the exact sum is $18\frac{1}{6}$, which is in the interval of the estimate.

EXAMPLE 5 If an employee works the following overtime hours each day, find his total overtime for the week: $1\frac{3}{4}$ hours on Monday, $2\frac{1}{2}$ hours on Tuesday, $1\frac{1}{4}$ hours on Wednesday, $2\frac{1}{4}$ hours on Thursday, and $1\frac{3}{4}$ hours on Friday.

$$1\frac{3}{4} = 1\frac{3}{4} \qquad \text{LCD is 4.}$$

$$2\frac{1}{2} = 2\frac{2}{4} \qquad \text{Change } 2\frac{1}{2} \text{ to } 2\frac{2}{4}.$$

$$1\frac{1}{4} = 1\frac{1}{4}$$

$$2\frac{1}{4} = 2\frac{1}{4}$$

$$1\frac{3}{4} = 1\frac{3}{4} \qquad \text{Add fractions. Add whole numbers.}$$

$$= 7\frac{10}{4} \qquad\qquad \frac{10}{4} = \frac{5}{2} = 2\frac{1}{2}$$

$$= 9\frac{1}{2} \qquad\qquad 7 + 2\frac{1}{2} = 9\frac{1}{2}$$

The total overtime is $9\frac{1}{2}$ hours.

STOP AND CHECK

Add. See Examples 3–4.

1. $4\frac{3}{8} + 5\frac{5}{8} + 3\frac{7}{8}$ **2.** $\frac{5}{12} + \frac{3}{4} + \frac{2}{3}$ **3.** $4\frac{3}{5} + 5\frac{7}{10} + 3\frac{4}{15}$ **4.** $23\frac{5}{14} + 37\frac{9}{10}$

5. *See Example 5.* A decorator determines that $25\frac{3}{8}$ yards of fabric are needed as window covering and decides to order an additional $6\frac{3}{4}$ yards of the same fabric for a tablecloth. How many yards of fabric are needed for windows and table?

6. A decorator used $32\frac{5}{8}$ yards of fabric for window treatments and $8\frac{3}{4}$ yards for chair covering. How many yards of fabric were used?

4   Subtract fractions and mixed numbers.

In subtracting fractions, just as in adding fractions, you need to find a common denominator.

HOW TO   Subtract fractions

With like denominators   Subtract $\frac{5}{12} - \frac{1}{12}$.

$5 - 1 = 4$

1. Find the numerator of the difference:
   Subtract the numerators of the fractions. $\dfrac{5}{12} - \dfrac{1}{12} = \dfrac{4}{12}$
2. Find the denominator of the difference:
   Use the like denominator of the fractions. $\dfrac{4}{12} = \dfrac{1}{3}$
3. Reduce to lowest terms.

With different denominators   Subtract $\frac{5}{12} - \frac{1}{3}$.

$\text{LCD} = 12$

1. Find the LCD.
2. Change each fraction to an equivalent fraction using the LCD. $\dfrac{1}{3} = \dfrac{1 \times 4}{3 \times 4} = \dfrac{4}{12}$
3. Subtract the new fractions with like (common) denominators. $\dfrac{5}{12} - \dfrac{4}{12} = \dfrac{1}{12}$
4. Reduce to lowest terms.

EXAMPLE 6

Subtract and simplify: $\frac{5}{12} - \frac{4}{15}$.

Find the LCD.

$$
\begin{array}{r}
2)\underline{12\ \ 15} \\
2)\underline{\ \ 6\ \ 15} \\
3)\underline{\ \ 3\ \ 15} \\
5)\underline{\ \ 1\ \ \ 5} \\
\ \ 1\ \ \ 1
\end{array}
$$

Divide by 2; $12 \div 2 = 6$. Bring down 15.

Divide by 2; $6 \div 2 = 3$. Bring down 15.

Divide by 3; $3 \div 3 = 1$; $15 \div 3 = 5$.

Divide by 5; $5 \div 5 = 1$. Bring down 1.

$2 \times 2 \times 3 \times 5 = 60$

$$\frac{5}{12} = \frac{5 \times 5}{12 \times 5} = \frac{25}{60}$$

$$-\frac{4}{15} = -\frac{4 \times 4}{15 \times 4} = -\frac{16}{60}$$

$$\frac{9}{60} = \frac{3}{20}$$

LCD = 60

Change to equivalent fractions.

Subtract fractions.

Reduce.

The difference is $\frac{3}{20}$.

HOW TO   Subtract mixed numbers

1. If the fractions have different denominators, find the LCD and change the fractions to equivalent fractions using the LCD.
2. If necessary, regroup by subtracting 1 from the whole number in the minuend and add 1 (in the form of LCD/LCD) to the fraction in the minuend.
3. Subtract the fractions and the whole numbers.
4. Reduce to lowest terms.

Subtract $2\frac{1}{3} - 1\frac{1}{2}$.

$$
\begin{array}{rcl}
2\frac{1}{3} &=& 2\frac{2}{6} = 1 + \frac{6}{6} + \frac{2}{6} = 1\frac{8}{6} \\
-1\frac{1}{2} &=& -1\frac{3}{6} \qquad\qquad\quad = -1\frac{3}{6} \\
\hline
&& \qquad\qquad\qquad\qquad\quad \frac{5}{6}
\end{array}
$$

EXAMPLE 7

Subtract $10\frac{1}{3} - 7\frac{3}{5}$.

$$10\frac{1}{3} = 10\frac{5}{15} = 9 + \frac{15}{15} + \frac{5}{15} = 9\frac{20}{15}$$

$$-7\frac{3}{5} \qquad\qquad\qquad\qquad = -7\frac{9}{15}$$

$$\qquad\qquad\qquad\qquad\qquad\quad 2\frac{11}{15}$$

Change fractions to equivalent fractions with the same LCD. Regroup in the minuend.

Subtract fractions. Subtract whole numbers.

The fraction is already in lowest terms, so it is not reducable.

The difference is $2\frac{11}{15}$.

TIP

Regroup or Borrow

Regrouping is also referred to as borrowing. The original form of the number has the same value as the new form of the number. Reexamine the previous example.

$$10\frac{5}{15} = (10 - 1) + \left(1 + \frac{5}{15}\right) = 9 + \left(1 + \frac{5}{15}\right)$$

$$= 9 + \left(\frac{15}{15} + \frac{5}{15}\right)$$

$$= 9\frac{20}{15}$$

EXAMPLE 8

An interior designer had 65 yards of fabric wall covering on hand and used $35\frac{3}{8}$ yards for a client's sunroom. How many yards of fabric remain?

$$65 = 64\frac{8}{8}$$ Regroup by subtracting 1 from 65. Add 1 as $\frac{8}{8}$.

$$-35\frac{3}{8} = -35\frac{3}{8}$$ Subtract fractions. Subtract whole numbers.

$$29\frac{5}{8}$$

$29\frac{5}{8}$ yards of fabric remain.

Some problems require both addition and subtraction. For example, if we know the total of several parts and we know all the parts but one, we can add the parts we know and subtract the sum from the total to find the unknown part.

EXAMPLE 9

Dee Wallace bought ten 12-inch pizzas for a business meeting of four focus groups. Group 1 ate $1\frac{3}{8}$ pizzas, Group 2 ate $2\frac{5}{8}$ pizzas, and Group 3 ate $3\frac{3}{4}$ pizzas. How many pizzas were left for Group 4?

$$1\frac{3}{8} + 2\frac{5}{8} + 3\frac{3}{4} =$$ Add the pizzas eaten by Groups 1, 2, and 3. Write all fractions with a common denominator.

$$1\frac{3}{8} + 2\frac{5}{8} + 3\frac{6}{8} =$$ Add the whole number parts. Add the numerators of the fractions.

$$6\frac{14}{8} =$$ Simplify the mixed number.

$$6 + \frac{8}{8} + \frac{6}{8} =$$

$$7\frac{6}{8} = 7\frac{3}{4}$$

$$10 - 7\frac{3}{4} =$$ To find the amount of pizza Group 4 ate, subtract the total number of pizzas eaten by the first three groups from the total number of pizzas ordered.

$$9\frac{4}{4} - 7\frac{3}{4} = 2\frac{1}{4}$$ Regroup to create a fraction in the minuend (first number), then subtract.

Group 4 ate $2\frac{1}{4}$ pizzas.

STOP AND CHECK

Subtract. See Examples 6–7.

1. $\frac{7}{8} - \frac{3}{8}$

2. $\frac{5}{8} - \frac{1}{12}$

3. $12\frac{5}{8} - 3\frac{7}{8}$

4. $15\frac{11}{12} - 7\frac{5}{18}$

5. $32 - 14\frac{5}{12}$

6. $27\frac{4}{15} - 14\frac{7}{12}$

See Example 8.

7. Top Chef winner Gale Simmons started with 50 pounds of cheddar cheese and used $38\frac{3}{4}$ pounds for a catering function. How many pounds of cheese were left for other uses?

8. Atlanta Granite Company is installing a countertop $3\frac{3}{4}$ feet long that is cut from a granite slab that measures $9\frac{1}{4}$ feet long. How long is the remaining piece of granite?

See Example 9.

9. Marcus Johnson, a real estate broker, owns 100 acres of land. During the year he purchased additional tracts of $12\frac{3}{4}$ acres, $23\frac{2}{3}$ acres, and $5\frac{1}{8}$ acres. If he sold a total of $65\frac{2}{3}$ acres during the year, how many acres does he still own?

10. To make a picture frame, two pieces $10\frac{3}{4}$ inches and two pieces $12\frac{5}{8}$ inches are cut from 60 inches of frame material. How much frame material remains?

2-2 SECTION EXERCISES

SKILL BUILDERS

Perform the indicated operations. Write the sum as a fraction, whole number, or mixed number in lowest terms. See Examples 1–3.

1. $\frac{1}{9} + \frac{2}{9} + \frac{5}{9}$

2. $\frac{7}{8} + \frac{5}{8}$

3. $\frac{5}{6} + \frac{7}{15}$

4. $\frac{5}{8} + \frac{7}{12}$

See Example 4.

5. $4\frac{5}{6} + 7\frac{1}{2}$

6. $23\frac{5}{12} + 48\frac{7}{16}$

7. $51\frac{5}{18} + 86\frac{9}{24}$

8. $5\frac{7}{12} + 3\frac{1}{4} + 2\frac{2}{3}$

9. $\frac{7}{8} + 2\frac{3}{24} + 6\frac{1}{6}$

10. $3\frac{5}{9} + 5\frac{1}{12} + 2\frac{2}{3}$

Find the difference. Write the difference in lowest terms. See Examples 6–7.

11. $\dfrac{7}{8} - \dfrac{3}{8}$

12. $\dfrac{8}{9} - \dfrac{2}{9}$

13. $\dfrac{3}{4} - \dfrac{5}{7}$

14. $9\dfrac{2}{3} - 6\dfrac{1}{2}$

15. $15 - 12\dfrac{7}{9}$

16. $21\dfrac{3}{5} - 12\dfrac{7}{10}$

17. $15\dfrac{8}{15} - 7\dfrac{5}{12}$

18. $23\dfrac{1}{8} - \dfrac{7}{12}$

19. $8\dfrac{1}{3} - 5$

20. $12\dfrac{1}{5} - 7\dfrac{4}{5}$

APPLICATIONS

See Example 5.

21. Loretta McBride is determining the amount of fabric required for window treatments. A single window requires $11\dfrac{3}{4}$ yards and a double window requires $18\dfrac{5}{8}$ yards of fabric. If she has two single windows and one double window, how much fabric is required?

22. Marveen McCready, a commercial space designer, has taken these measurements for an office in which she plans to install a wallpaper border around the ceiling: $42\dfrac{3}{8}$ feet, $37\dfrac{5}{8}$ feet, $12\dfrac{3}{8}$ feet, and $23\dfrac{3}{4}$ feet. How much paper does she need for the job?

23. Rob Farinelli is building a gazebo and plans to use for the floor two boards that are $10\dfrac{3}{4}$ feet, four boards that are $12\dfrac{5}{8}$ feet, and two boards that are $8\dfrac{1}{2}$ feet. Find the total number of feet in all the boards.

24. Tenisha Gist cuts brass plates for an engraving job. From a sheet of brass, three pieces $4\dfrac{4}{5}$ inches wide and two pieces $7\dfrac{3}{8}$ inches wide are cut. What is the smallest sheet of brass required to cut all five plates?

See Example 8.

25. The fabric Loretta McBride has selected for the window treatment in Exercise 21 has only 45 yards on the only roll available. Will she be able to use the fabric or must she make an alternate selection?

26. Rob Farinelli purchased two boards that are 12 feet and will cut them to make $10\frac{3}{4}$-foot boards for the gazebo he is building. How much must be removed from each board?

27. Rob Farinelli purchased four boards that he expected to be each 14 feet to make $12\frac{5}{8}$-foot boards for his gazebo. Upon measuring, he finds they are $13\frac{15}{16}$ feet, $14\frac{1}{8}$ feet, 14 feet, and $13\frac{13}{16}$ feet. How much must be removed from each board to get $12\frac{5}{8}$-foot boards?

28. Charlie Carr has a sheet of brass that is 36 inches wide and cuts two pieces that are each $8\frac{3}{4}$ inches wide. What is the width of the leftover brass?

2-3 MULTIPLYING AND DIVIDING FRACTIONS

LEARNING OUTCOMES

1 Multiply fractions and mixed numbers.
2 Divide fractions and mixed numbers.

1 Multiply fractions and mixed numbers.

Alexa May has three Pizza Hut restaurants. Her distributor shipped only $\frac{3}{4}$ of a cheese order that Alexa had expected to distribute equally among her three restaurants. What fractional part of the original order will each restaurant receive?

Each restaurant will receive $\frac{1}{3}$ of the *shipment,* but the shipment is only $\frac{3}{4}$ of the *original order.* Each restaurant, then, will receive only $\frac{1}{3}$ of $\frac{3}{4}$ of the original order. Finding $\frac{1}{3}$ of $\frac{3}{4}$ illustrates the use of multiplying fractions just as "2 boxes **of** 3 cans each" amounts to 2 × 3, or 6 cans. Similarly, $\frac{1}{3}$ **of** $\frac{3}{4}$ amounts to $\frac{1}{3} \times \frac{3}{4}$.

We can visualize $\frac{1}{3} \times \frac{3}{4}$, or $\frac{1}{3}$ **of** $\frac{3}{4}$, by first visualizing $\frac{3}{4}$ of a whole (Figure 2-9).

FIGURE 2-9
3 parts out of 4 parts $= \frac{3}{4}$ of a whole.

Now visualize $\frac{1}{3}$ of $\frac{3}{4}$ of a whole (Figure 2-10).

FIGURE 2-10
1 part out of 3 parts in $\frac{3}{4}$ of a whole $=$ 1 part out of 4 parts or $\frac{1}{4}$ of a whole.

> ### TIP
> **Part of a Part**
> A part of a part is a smaller part.
> The product of two proper fractions is a proper fraction. That is, its value is less than 1.

$$\frac{1}{3} \text{ of } \frac{3}{4} \text{ is } \frac{1}{4}$$
$$\frac{1}{3} \times \frac{3}{4} = \frac{1}{4}$$

Multiply fractions

	Multiply $\frac{1}{2} \times \frac{7}{8}$.
1. Find the numerator of the product: Multiply the numerators of the fractions.	$1 \times 7 = 7$
2. Find the denominator of the product: Multiply the denominators of the fractions.	$2 \times 8 = 16$
3. Reduce to lowest terms.	$\frac{1}{2} \times \frac{7}{8} = \frac{1 \times 7}{2 \times 8} = \frac{7}{16}$

DID YOU KNOW?

A common denominator is *not* needed when multiplying fractions.

EXAMPLE 1

What fraction of the original cheese order will each of Alexa's three restaurants receive equally if $\frac{9}{10}$ of the original order is shipped?

What You Know	What You Are Looking For	Solution Plan
Fraction of shipment each restaurant can receive: $\frac{1}{3}$ Fraction of original order received for all the restaurants: $\frac{9}{10}$	Fraction of original order that each restaurant will receive equally.	Fraction of original order that each restaurant will receive = fraction of shipment each restaurant can receive $\times$ fraction of original order received.

Solution

$\dfrac{1}{3} \times \dfrac{9}{10} = \dfrac{1 \times 9}{3 \times 10} = \dfrac{9}{30}$ Multiply numerators; multiply denominators.

$\dfrac{9}{30} = \dfrac{3}{10}$ Reduce to lowest terms.

Conclusion

Each restaurant will receive $\frac{3}{10}$ of the original order.

TIP

Reduce Before Multiplying

When you multiply fractions, you save time by reducing fractions *before* you multiply. If *any* numerator and *any* denominator can be divided evenly by the same number, divide both the numerator and the denominator by that number. You can then multiply the reduced numbers with greater accuracy than you could multiply the larger numbers.

$\dfrac{1}{\overset{}{\underset{1}{3}}} \times \dfrac{\overset{1}{3}}{4} = \dfrac{1}{4}$ $\dfrac{1}{\overset{}{\underset{1}{3}}} \times \dfrac{\overset{3}{9}}{10} = \dfrac{3}{10}$ A numerator and a denominator can be divided evenly by 3 in both examples.

HOW TO   Multiply mixed numbers and whole numbers

1. Write the mixed numbers and whole numbers as improper fractions.
2. Reduce numerators and denominators as appropriate.
3. Multiply the fractions.
4. Reduce to lowest terms and write as a whole or mixed number if appropriate.

EXAMPLE 2

Multiply $2\frac{1}{3} \times 3\frac{3}{4}$.

$$2\frac{1}{3} \times 3\frac{3}{4} = \frac{(3 \times 2) + 1}{3} \times \frac{(4 \times 3) + 3}{4}$$

Write the mixed numbers as improper fractions.

$$= \frac{7}{\cancel{3}_1} \times \frac{\cancel{15}^5}{4}$$

Divide both 3 and 15 by 3, reducing to 1 and 5. Multiply the numerators and denominators.

$$= \frac{35}{4} = 8\frac{3}{4}$$

Write as a mixed number.

The product is $8\frac{3}{4}$.

TIP

Are Products Always Larger Than Their Factors?

A product is not always greater than the factors being multiplied.

When the *multiplier* is a proper fraction, the product is *less than* the *multiplicand*. This is true whether the *multiplicand* is a whole number, fraction, or mixed number.

$5 \times \dfrac{3}{5} = 3$ Product 3 is less than factor 5.

$\dfrac{3}{4} \times \dfrac{4}{9} = \dfrac{1}{3}$ Product $\frac{1}{3}$ is less than factor $\frac{3}{4}$.

$2\dfrac{1}{2} \times \dfrac{1}{2} = \dfrac{5}{2} \times \dfrac{1}{2} = \dfrac{5}{4} = 1\dfrac{1}{4}$ Product $1\frac{1}{4}$ is less than factor $2\frac{1}{2}$.

STOP AND CHECK

Multiply. Write products as proper fractions or mixed numbers in lowest terms. See Examples 1–2.

1. $\dfrac{3}{7} \times \dfrac{5}{8}$

2. $\dfrac{4}{9} \times \dfrac{3}{8}$

3. $3\dfrac{1}{4} \times 1\dfrac{5}{13}$

4. $1\dfrac{1}{9} \times 3$

5. $2\dfrac{2}{5} \times \dfrac{15}{21}$

6. The outside width of a boxed cooktop is $2\frac{3}{8}$ feet, and a shipment of boxed cooktops is placed in a 45-foot trailer. How many feet will 16 cooktop boxes require?

7. Computer boxes are $2\frac{1}{3}$ feet high. How high is a stack of 14 computer boxes?

2 Divide fractions and mixed numbers.

Division of fractions is related to multiplication.

Total amount = number of units of a specified size times ($\times$) the specified size. If you know the total amount and the number of equal units, you can find the size of each unit by dividing the total amount by the number of equal units. If you know the total amount and the specified size, you can find the number of equal units by dividing the total amount by the specified size.

Home Depot has a stack of plywood that is 32 inches high. If each sheet of plywood is $\frac{1}{2}$ inch, how many sheets of plywood are in the stack? How many equal units of plywood are contained in the total stack? Divide the height of the stack (total amount) by the thickness of each sheet (specified size).

$32 \div \dfrac{1}{2}$ Total thickness divided by thickness of one sheet of plywood

Another way of approaching the problem is to think of the number of sheets of plywood in 1 inch of thickness. If each sheet of plywood is $\frac{1}{2}$ inch, then two sheets of plywood are 1 inch thick. If there are two sheets of plywood for each inch, there will be 64 pieces of plywood in the 32-inch stack.

$$32 \div \frac{1}{2} = 32 \times \frac{2}{1} = 64$$

The relationship between multiplying and dividing fractions involves a concept called **reciprocals**. Two numbers are reciprocals if their product is 1. Thus, $\frac{2}{3}$ and $\frac{3}{2}$ are reciprocals ($\frac{2}{3} \times \frac{3}{2} = 1$) and $\frac{7}{8}$ and $\frac{8}{7}$ are reciprocals ($\frac{7}{8} \times \frac{8}{7} = 1$).

Reciprocals: two numbers are reciprocals if their product is 1. $\frac{4}{5}$ and $\frac{5}{4}$ are reciprocals.

HOW TO   Find the reciprocal of a number

Write the reciprocal of 3.

1. Write the number as a fraction.

$$\frac{3}{1}$$

2. Interchange the numerator and denominator.

$$\frac{1}{3}$$

EXAMPLE 3   Find the reciprocal of (a) $\frac{7}{9}$; (b) 5; (c) $4\frac{1}{2}$.

(a) The reciprocal of $\frac{7}{9}$ is $\frac{9}{7}$.   The reciprocal can be stated as $1\frac{2}{7}$.

(b) The reciprocal of $\frac{5}{1}$ is $\frac{1}{5}$.   Write 5 as the fraction $\frac{5}{1}$.

(c) The reciprocal of $4\frac{1}{2}$ is $\frac{2}{9}$.   Write $4\frac{1}{2}$ as the fraction $\frac{9}{2}$.

In the Home Depot discussion, we reasoned that $32 \div \frac{1}{2}$ is the same as 32×2. $\frac{1}{2}$ and 2 are reciprocals. So, to divide by a fraction, we *multiply* by the *reciprocal* of the divisor.

HOW TO   Divide fractions or mixed numbers

Divide $\frac{3}{4}$ by 5.

1. Write the numbers as fractions.
2. Find the reciprocal of the divisor.
3. Multiply the dividend by the reciprocal of the divisor.
4. Reduce to lowest terms and write as a whole or mixed number if appropriate.

$$\frac{3}{4} \div \frac{5}{1} \quad \text{The reciprocal of 5 is } \frac{1}{5}.$$

$$\frac{3}{4} \times \frac{1}{5} = \frac{3}{20}$$

$$\frac{3}{20} \text{ (lowest terms)}$$

EXAMPLE 4   Madison Duke makes appliqués from brocade fabric. A customer has ordered five appliqués. Can Madison fill the order without buying more fabric? She has $\frac{3}{4}$ yard of fabric and each appliqué requires $\frac{1}{6}$ of a yard.

What You Know	What You Are Looking For	Solution Plan
Total length of fabric: $\frac{3}{4}$ yard Length of fabric needed for each appliqué: $\frac{1}{6}$ yard	The number of appliqués that can be made from the fabric. Can Madison fill the order?	Number of appliqués that can be made = total length of fabric ÷ length of fabric needed for each appliqué

Number of appliqués $= \dfrac{3}{4} \div \dfrac{1}{6}$	Total fabric ÷ fabric in 1 appliqué Multiply by the reciprocal of the divisor.
$= \dfrac{3}{\overset{2}{\cancel{4}}} \times \dfrac{\overset{3}{\cancel{6}}}{1}$	Reduce and multiply.
$= \dfrac{9}{2} = 4\dfrac{1}{2}$	Change the improper fraction to a mixed number.

Conclusion

Madison can make four appliqués from the $\frac{3}{4}$ yard of fabric.

Because the order is five appliqués, Madison cannot fill the order without buying more fabric.

EXAMPLE 5   Find the quotient: $5\frac{1}{2} \div 7\frac{1}{3}$.

$5\dfrac{1}{2} \div 7\dfrac{1}{3} =$	Write the numbers as improper fractions.
$\dfrac{11}{2} \div \dfrac{22}{3} =$	Multiply $\frac{11}{2}$ by the reciprocal of the divisor, $\frac{3}{22}$.
$\dfrac{\overset{1}{\cancel{11}}}{2} \times \dfrac{3}{\underset{2}{\cancel{22}}} = \dfrac{1 \times 3}{2 \times 2} = \dfrac{3}{4}$	Reduce and multiply.

The quotient is $\frac{3}{4}$.

STOP AND CHECK

Find the reciprocal. See Example 3.

1. $\dfrac{5}{12}$

2. 32

3. $7\dfrac{1}{8}$

Divide. Write the quotient as a proper fraction or mixed number in lowest terms. See Examples 4–5.

4. $\dfrac{7}{8} \div \dfrac{3}{4}$

5. $2\dfrac{2}{5} \div 2\dfrac{1}{10}$

6. $3\dfrac{3}{8} \div 9$

7. *See Example 4.* Kisha stacks lumber in a storage bin that is 72 inches in height. If she stores $\frac{3}{4}$-inch-thick plywood in the bin, how many sheets can she expect to fit in the bin?

SKILL BUILDERS

Find the product. See Examples 1–2.

1. $\dfrac{3}{8} \times \dfrac{4}{5}$

2. $\dfrac{5}{7} \times \dfrac{1}{6}$

3. $5\dfrac{3}{4} \times 3\dfrac{8}{9}$

4. $\dfrac{3}{8} \times 24$

Find the reciprocal. See Example 3.

5. $\dfrac{7}{12}$ **6.** $\dfrac{3}{5}$ **7.** 9   **8.** 12   **9.** $5\dfrac{4}{7}$ **10.** $3\dfrac{3}{8}$

Find the quotient. See Examples 4–5.

11. $\dfrac{5}{8} \div \dfrac{3}{4}$

12. $\dfrac{3}{5} \div \dfrac{9}{10}$

13. $2\dfrac{2}{5} \div 1\dfrac{1}{7}$

14. $5\dfrac{1}{4} \div 2\dfrac{2}{3}$

APPLICATIONS

For Exercises 15–19, see Example 4. For Exercises 20–22, see Examples 1–2.

15. Pierre Hugo is handling the estate of a prominent businesswoman. The will states that the surviving spouse is to receive $\frac{1}{4}$ of the estate and the remaining $\frac{3}{4}$ of the estate will be divided equally among five surviving children. What fraction of the estate does each child receive?

16. Ty Jones is estimating the number of plywood sheets in a 75-inch-tall stack. If each sheet of plywood is $1\frac{1}{8}$ inch thick, how many sheets should he expect?

17. A roll of carpet that contains 200 yards of carpet will cover how many rooms if each room requires $9\frac{3}{4}$ yards of carpet?

18. A box of kitty litter is $8\frac{3}{4}$ inches tall. How many boxes of kitty litter can be stored on a warehouse shelf that can accommodate boxes up to a height of 40 inches?

19. Carl Heinz is placing filing cabinets on an office wall. Each cabinet is $3\frac{1}{2}$ feet wide and the wall is 21 feet long. How many cabinets can be placed on the wall?

20. Each of the four walls of a room measures $18\frac{5}{8}$ feet. How much chair rail must be purchased to install the chair rail on all four walls? Disregard any openings.

21. Four office desks that are $4\frac{1}{8}$ feet long are to be placed together on a wall that is $16\frac{5}{8}$ feet long. Will they fit on the wall?

22. Ariana Pope is making 28 trophies and each requires a brass plate that is $3\frac{1}{4}$ inches long and 1 inch wide. What size sheet of brass is required to make the plates if the plates are aligned with two plates per horizontal line?

Learning Outcomes

Section 2-1

1   Identify types of fractions. (p. 44)

What to Remember with Examples

The denominator of a fraction shows how many parts make up one whole quantity. The numerator shows how many parts are being considered. A proper fraction has a value less than 1. An improper fraction has a value equal to or greater than 1.

Write the fraction illustrated by the shaded parts.

$$\frac{3}{7}$$

Identify the fraction as proper or improper.

$\frac{5}{8}$ proper   less than 1

$\frac{8}{8}$ improper   equal to 1

$\frac{11}{8}$ improper   greater than 1

2   Convert an improper fraction to a whole or mixed number. (p. 45)

1. Divide the numerator of the improper fraction by the denominator.
2. Examine the remainder.
   (a) If the remainder is 0, the quotient is a whole number. The improper fraction is equivalent to this whole number.
   (b) If the remainder is not 0, the quotient is not a whole number. The improper fraction is equivalent to a mixed number. The whole-number part of this mixed number is the whole-number part of the quotient. The fraction part of the mixed number has a numerator and a denominator. The numerator is the remainder; the denominator is the divisor (the denominator of the improper fraction).

Write each improper fraction as a whole or mixed number.

$$\frac{150}{3} \qquad 3)\overline{150} \;\; 50\,R0 \qquad \frac{150}{3} = 50; \qquad \frac{152}{3} \qquad 3)\overline{152} \;\; 50\,R2 \qquad \frac{152}{3} = 50\frac{2}{3}$$

3   Convert a whole or mixed number to an improper fraction. (p. 46)

1. Find the numerator of the improper fraction.
   (a) Multiply the denominator of the mixed number by the whole-number part.
   (b) Add the product from step 1a to the numerator of the mixed number.
2. For the denominator of the improper fraction use the denominator of the mixed number.
3. For a whole number write the whole number as the numerator and 1 as the denominator.

Write each whole or mixed number as an improper fraction.

$$5\frac{5}{8} = \frac{(8 \times 5) + 5}{8} = \frac{40 + 5}{8} = \frac{45}{8} \qquad \text{Mixed number as improper fraction}$$

$$7 = \frac{7}{1} \qquad \text{Whole number as improper fraction}$$

4   Reduce a fraction to lowest terms. (p. 47)

1. Inspect the numerator and denominator to find any whole number that both can be evenly divided by.
2. Divide both the numerator and the denominator by that number and inspect the new fraction to find any other number that the numerator and denominator can be evenly divided by.
3. Repeat steps 1 and 2 until 1 is the only number that the numerator and denominator can be evenly divided by.

Write each fraction in lowest terms.

$$\frac{12}{36} = \frac{12 \div 2}{36 \div 2} = \frac{6}{18} \quad \text{or} \quad \frac{12 \div 12}{36 \div 12} = \frac{1}{3}; \qquad \frac{100}{250} = \frac{100 \div 50}{250 \div 50} = \frac{2}{5}$$

$$= \frac{6 \div 2}{18 \div 2} = \frac{3}{9}$$

$$= \frac{3 \div 3}{9 \div 3} = \frac{1}{3}$$

Find the greatest common divisor (GCD) of the two numbers of a proper fraction.

1. Use the numerator as the first divisor and the denominator as the dividend.
2. Divide.
3. Divide the first divisor from step 2 by the remainder from step 2.
4. Divide the divisor from step 3 by the remainder from step 3.
5. Continue this division process until the remainder is 0. The last divisor is the greatest common divisor.

Find the GCD of 27 and 36 or the fraction $\frac{27}{36}$.

$$\begin{array}{r} 1\,R9 \\ 27\overline{)36} \\ 27 \\ \hline 9 \end{array} \qquad \begin{array}{r} 3 \\ 9\overline{)27} \\ 27 \\ \hline 0 \end{array}$$

The GCD is 9.

Find the GCD of 28 and 15 or the fraction $\frac{15}{28}$.

$$\begin{array}{r} 1\,R13 \\ 15\overline{)28} \\ 15 \\ \hline 13 \end{array} \qquad \begin{array}{r} 1\,R2 \\ 13\overline{)15} \\ 13 \\ \hline 2 \end{array} \qquad \begin{array}{r} 6\,R1 \\ 2\overline{)13} \\ 12 \\ \hline 1 \end{array} \qquad \begin{array}{r} 2 \\ 1\overline{)2} \\ 2 \\ \hline 0 \end{array}$$

The GCD is 1.

5 Raise a fraction to higher terms. (p. 48)

1. Divide the *new* denominator by the *old* denominator.
2. Multiply both the old numerator and the old denominator by the quotient from step 1.

$$\frac{3}{4} = \frac{?}{20} \qquad\qquad\qquad \frac{2}{3} = \frac{?}{60}$$

$$\begin{array}{r} 5 \\ 4\overline{)20} \end{array} \qquad\qquad\qquad \begin{array}{r} 20 \\ 3\overline{)60} \end{array}$$

$$\frac{3}{4} = \frac{3}{4} \times \frac{5}{5} = \frac{15}{20} \qquad \frac{2}{3} \times \frac{20}{20} = \frac{40}{60}$$

Section 2-2

1 Add fractions with like (common) denominators. (p. 51)

1. Find the numerator of the sum: Add the numerators of the addends.
2. Find the denominator of the sum: Use the like denominator of the addends.
3. Reduce to lowest terms and/or write as a whole or mixed number.

$$\frac{3}{5} + \frac{7}{5} + \frac{5}{5} = \frac{15}{5} = 3 \qquad \frac{82}{109} + \frac{13}{109} = \frac{95}{109}$$

2 Find the least common denominator (LCD) for two or more fractions. (p. 52)

1. Write the denominators in a row and divide each one by the smallest prime number that any of the numbers can be evenly divided by.
2. Write a new row of numbers using the quotients from step 1 and any numbers in the first row that cannot be evenly divided by the first prime number. Divide by the smallest prime number that any of the numbers can be evenly divided by.
3. Continue this process until you have a row of 1s.
4. Multiply all the prime numbers you used to divide the denominators. The product is the LCD.

Find the LCD

$\dfrac{5}{6}, \dfrac{6}{15},$ and $\dfrac{7}{20}.$

```
2)6  15  20
2)3  15  10
3)3  15   5
5)1   5   5
   1   1   1
```

LCD $= 2 \times 2 \times 3 \times 5 = 60$

Find the LCD

of $\dfrac{4}{5}, \dfrac{3}{10},$ and $\dfrac{1}{6}.$

```
2)5  10  6
3)5   5  3
5)5   5  1
   1   1  1
```

LCD $= 2 \times 3 \times 5 = 30$

3 Add fractions and mixed numbers. (p. 52)

Add fractions with different denominators.

1. Find the LCD.
2. Change each fraction to an equivalent fraction using the LCD.
3. Add the new fractions with like (common) denominators.
4. Reduce to lowest terms and write as a whole or mixed number if appropriate.

Add $\dfrac{5}{6} + \dfrac{6}{15} + \dfrac{7}{20}.$

The LCD is 60.

$\dfrac{5}{6} = \dfrac{5}{6} \times \dfrac{10}{10} = \dfrac{50}{60}$

$\dfrac{6}{15} = \dfrac{6}{15} \times \dfrac{4}{4} = \dfrac{24}{60}$

$\dfrac{7}{20} = \dfrac{7}{20} \times \dfrac{3}{3} = \dfrac{21}{60}$

$\dfrac{5}{6} + \dfrac{6}{15} + \dfrac{7}{20} = \dfrac{50}{60} + \dfrac{24}{60} + \dfrac{21}{60} =$

$\dfrac{95}{60} = \dfrac{19}{12} = 1\dfrac{7}{12}$

Add $\dfrac{4}{5} + \dfrac{3}{10} + \dfrac{1}{6}.$

The LCD is 30.

$\dfrac{4}{5} \times \dfrac{6}{6} = \dfrac{24}{30}$

$\dfrac{3}{10} \times \dfrac{3}{3} = \dfrac{9}{30}$

$\dfrac{1}{6} \times \dfrac{5}{5} = \dfrac{5}{30}$

$\dfrac{4}{5} + \dfrac{3}{10} + \dfrac{1}{6} = \dfrac{24}{30} + \dfrac{9}{30} + \dfrac{5}{30} =$

$\dfrac{38}{30} = \dfrac{19}{15} = 1\dfrac{4}{15}$

Add mixed numbers.

1. Add the whole-number parts.
2. Add the fraction parts and reduce to lowest terms.
3. Change improper fractions to whole or mixed numbers.
4. Add the whole-number parts.

Add $2\dfrac{1}{2} + 5\dfrac{2}{3} + 4.$

The LCD is 6.

$2\dfrac{1}{2} = 2\dfrac{3}{6}$

$5\dfrac{2}{3} = 5\dfrac{4}{6}$

$4 = 4$

$11\dfrac{7}{6}; \dfrac{7}{6} = 1\dfrac{1}{6}$

$11 + 1\dfrac{1}{6} = 12\dfrac{1}{6}$

4 Subtract fractions and mixed numbers. (p. 54)

Subtract fractions with like denominators.

1. Find the numerator of the difference: Subtract the numerators of the fractions.
2. Find the denominator of the difference: Use the like denominator of the fractions.
3. Reduce to lowest terms.

Subtract fractions with different denominators.

1. Find the LCD.
2. Change each fraction to an equivalent fraction using the LCD.
3. Subtract the new fractions with like (common) denominators.
4. Reduce to lowest terms.

$$\frac{10}{81} - \frac{7}{81} = \frac{3}{81} = \frac{1}{27} \qquad \frac{7}{8} - \frac{1}{3} = \frac{21}{24} - \frac{8}{24} = \frac{13}{24}$$

Subtract mixed numbers.

1. If the fractions have different denominators, find the LCD and change the fractions to equivalent fractions using the LCD.
2. If necessary, regroup by subtracting 1 from the whole number in the minuend and add 1 (in the form of LCD/LCD) to the fraction in the minuend.
3. Subtract the fractions and the whole numbers.
4. Reduce to lowest terms.

$$
\begin{array}{ll}
24\frac{1}{2} = 24\frac{2}{4} = 23\frac{6}{4} & \qquad 53 = 53\frac{0}{5} = 52\frac{5}{5} \\
\underline{-11\frac{3}{4} = -11\frac{3}{4} = -11\frac{3}{4}} & \qquad \underline{-37\frac{4}{5} = -37\frac{4}{5} = -37\frac{4}{5}} \\
\phantom{24\frac{1}{2} = 24\frac{2}{4} = }12\frac{3}{4} & \qquad \phantom{53 = 53\frac{0}{5} = }15\frac{1}{5}
\end{array}
$$

Section 2-3

1 Multiply fractions and mixed numbers. (p. 59)

Multiply fractions.

1. Find the numerator of the product: Multiply the numerators of the fractions.
2. Find the denominator of the product: Multiply the denominators of the fractions.
3. Reduce to lowest terms.

$$\frac{3}{2} \times \frac{12}{17} = \frac{36}{34} = 1\frac{2}{34} = 1\frac{1}{17}; \qquad \frac{7}{9} \times \frac{15}{28} = \frac{5}{12}$$

or

$$\frac{3}{2} \times \frac{12}{17} = \frac{18}{17} = 1\frac{1}{17}$$

Multiply mixed numbers and whole numbers.

1. Write the mixed numbers and whole numbers as improper fractions.
2. Reduce numerators and denominators as appropriate.
3. Multiply the fractions.
4. Reduce to lowest terms and write as a whole or mixed number if appropriate.

$$3\frac{3}{4} \times 3\frac{2}{3} = \frac{15}{4} \times \frac{11}{3} = \frac{165}{12} = \frac{55}{4} = 13\frac{3}{4}; \qquad 5\frac{7}{8} \times 3 = \frac{47}{8} \times \frac{3}{1} = \frac{141}{8} = 17\frac{5}{8}$$

or

$$\frac{\cancel{15}}{4} \times \frac{11}{\cancel{3}} = \frac{55}{4} = 13\frac{3}{4}$$

2 Divide fractions and mixed numbers. (p. 61)

Find the reciprocal of a number.

1. Write the number as a fraction.
2. Interchange the numerator and denominator.

The reciprocal of $\frac{2}{3}$ is $\frac{3}{2}$ or $1\frac{1}{2}$.

The reciprocal of 6 is $\frac{1}{6}$. $6 = \frac{6}{1}$.

The reciprocal of $1\frac{1}{2}$ is $\frac{2}{3}$. $1\frac{1}{2} = \frac{3}{2}$.

Divide fractions or mixed numbers.

1. Write the numbers as fractions.
2. Find the reciprocal of the divisor.
3. Multiply the dividend by the reciprocal of the divisor.
4. Reduce to lowest terms and write as a whole or mixed number if appropriate.

$$\frac{55}{68} \div \frac{11}{17} = \frac{55}{68} \times \frac{17}{11} = \frac{5}{4} = 1\frac{1}{4};$$

$$3\frac{1}{4} \div 1\frac{1}{2} = \frac{13}{4} \div \frac{3}{2}$$

$$= \frac{13}{4} \times \frac{2}{3} = \frac{13}{6} = 2\frac{1}{6}$$

EXERCISES SET A

1. Give five examples of fractions whose value is less than 1. What are these fractions called?

2. Give five examples of fractions whose value is greater than or equal to 1. What are these fractions called?

Write the improper fraction as a whole or mixed number.

3. $\dfrac{124}{6}$

4. $\dfrac{84}{12}$

5. $\dfrac{17}{2}$

Write the mixed number as an improper fraction.

6. $5\dfrac{5}{6}$

7. $4\dfrac{1}{3}$

8. $33\dfrac{1}{3}$

Reduce to lowest terms. Try to use the greatest common divisor (GCD).

9. $\dfrac{15}{18}$

10. $\dfrac{20}{30}$

11. $\dfrac{30}{48}$

Rewrite as a fraction with the indicated denominator.

12. $\dfrac{5}{6} = \dfrac{}{12}$

13. $\dfrac{5}{8} = \dfrac{}{32}$

14. $\dfrac{9}{11} = \dfrac{}{143}$

15. A company employed 105 people. If 15 of the employees left the company in a three-month period, what fractional part of the employees left?

Find the least common denominator (LCD) for these fractions.

16. $\dfrac{1}{4}, \dfrac{1}{12}, \dfrac{11}{16}$

17. $\dfrac{5}{56}, \dfrac{7}{24}, \dfrac{7}{12}, \dfrac{5}{42}$

18. $\dfrac{2}{1}, \dfrac{1}{5}, \dfrac{1}{10}, \dfrac{5}{6}$

Add. Reduce to lowest terms and write as whole or mixed numbers if appropriate.

19. $\dfrac{3}{5} + \dfrac{4}{5}$

20. $\dfrac{2}{5} + \dfrac{2}{3}$

21. $7\dfrac{1}{2} + 4\dfrac{3}{8}$

22. $11\dfrac{5}{6} + 8\dfrac{2}{3}$

23. Two types of fabric are needed for curtains. The lining requires $12\dfrac{3}{8}$ yards and the curtain fabric needed is $16\dfrac{5}{8}$ yards. How many yards of fabric are needed?

Subtract. Borrow when necessary. Reduce the difference to lowest terms (simplify).

24. $\dfrac{5}{12} - \dfrac{1}{4}$

25. $7\dfrac{4}{5} - 4\dfrac{1}{2}$

26. $5 - 3\dfrac{2}{5}$

27. $4\dfrac{5}{6} - 3\dfrac{1}{3}$

28. A board $3\dfrac{5}{8}$ feet long must be sawed from a 6-foot board. How long is the remaining piece?

Multiply. Reduce to lowest terms and write as whole or mixed numbers if appropriate.

29. $\dfrac{5}{6} \times \dfrac{1}{3}$

30. $5 \times \dfrac{2}{3}$

31. $6\dfrac{2}{9} \times 4\dfrac{1}{2}$

Find the reciprocal of the numbers.

32. $\dfrac{5}{8}$

33. $\dfrac{1}{4}$

34. $3\dfrac{1}{4}$

Divide. Reduce to lowest terms and write as whole or mixed numbers if appropriate.

35. $\dfrac{3}{4} \div \dfrac{1}{4}$

36. $7\dfrac{1}{2} \div 2$

37. $3\dfrac{1}{7} \div 5\dfrac{1}{2}$

38. A board 244 inches long is cut into pieces that are each $7\dfrac{5}{8}$ inches long. How many pieces can be cut?

39. Bill New placed a piece of $\dfrac{5}{8}$-inch plywood and a piece of $\dfrac{3}{4}$-inch plywood on top of one another to create a spacer between two 2 by 4s, but the spacer was $\dfrac{1}{8}$ inch too thick. How thick should the spacer be?

40. Certain financial aid students must pass $\dfrac{2}{3}$ of their courses each term in order to continue their aid. If a student is taking 18 hours, how many hours must be passed?

41. Sol's Hardware and Appliance Store is selling electric clothes dryers for $\dfrac{1}{3}$ off the regular price of $288. What is the sale price of the dryer?

EXERCISES SET B

Write the improper fraction as a whole or mixed number.

1. $\dfrac{52}{15}$

2. $\dfrac{83}{4}$

3. $\dfrac{77}{11}$

4. $\dfrac{19}{10}$

Write the mixed number as an improper fraction.

5. $7\dfrac{3}{8}$

6. $10\dfrac{1}{5}$

Reduce to lowest terms. Try to use the greatest common divisor (GCD).

7. $\dfrac{18}{20}$

8. $\dfrac{27}{36}$

9. $\dfrac{18}{63}$

10. $\dfrac{78}{96}$

Rewrite as a fraction with the indicated denominator.

11. $\dfrac{7}{9} = \dfrac{}{81}$

12. $\dfrac{4}{7} = \dfrac{}{49}$

13. If 8 students in a class of 30 earned grades of A, what fractional part of the class earned A's?

Find the least common denominator (LCD) for these fractions.

14. $\dfrac{7}{8}, \dfrac{1}{20}, \dfrac{13}{16}$

15. $\dfrac{1}{8}, \dfrac{5}{9}, \dfrac{7}{12}, \dfrac{9}{24}$

16. $\dfrac{5}{12}, \dfrac{3}{15}$

Add. Reduce to lowest terms and write as whole or mixed numbers if appropriate.

17. $\dfrac{7}{8} + \dfrac{1}{8}$

18. $\dfrac{1}{4} + \dfrac{11}{12} + \dfrac{7}{16}$

19. $3\dfrac{1}{4} + 2\dfrac{1}{3} + 3\dfrac{5}{6}$

20. Three pieces of lumber measure $5\dfrac{3}{8}$ feet, $7\dfrac{1}{2}$ feet, and $9\dfrac{3}{4}$ feet. What is the total length of the lumber?

Subtract. Borrow when necessary. Reduce the difference to lowest terms (simplify).

21. $\dfrac{6}{7} - \dfrac{5}{14}$

22. $4\dfrac{1}{2} - 3\dfrac{6}{7}$

23. $12 - 4\dfrac{1}{8}$

24. $4\dfrac{1}{5} - 2\dfrac{3}{10}$

25. George Mackie worked the following hours during a week: $7\dfrac{3}{4}, 5\dfrac{1}{2}, 6\dfrac{1}{4}, 9\dfrac{1}{4}$, and $8\dfrac{3}{4}$. Maxine Ford worked 40 hours. Who worked the most hours? How many more?

Multiply. Reduce to lowest terms and write as whole or mixed numbers if appropriate.

26. $\dfrac{9}{10} \times \dfrac{3}{4}$

27. $\dfrac{3}{7} \times 8$

28. $\dfrac{9}{10} \times \dfrac{2}{5} \times \dfrac{5}{9} \times \dfrac{3}{7}$

29. $10\dfrac{1}{2} \times 1\dfrac{5}{7}$

30. After a family reunion, $10\dfrac{2}{3}$ cakes were left. If Shirley McCool took $\dfrac{3}{8}$ of these cakes, how many did she take?

Find the reciprocal of the numbers.

31. $\dfrac{2}{3}$

32. 8

33. $2\dfrac{3}{8}$

34. $5\dfrac{1}{12}$

Divide. Reduce to lowest terms and write as whole or mixed numbers if appropriate.

35. $\dfrac{5}{6} \div \dfrac{1}{8}$

36. $15 \div \dfrac{3}{4}$

37. $7\dfrac{1}{2} \div 1\dfrac{2}{3}$

38. A stack of $1\dfrac{5}{8}$-inch plywood measures 91 inches. How many pieces of plywood are in the stack?

39. Sue Parsons has three lengths of $\dfrac{3}{4}$-inch polyvinyl chloride (PVC) pipe: $1\dfrac{1}{5}$ feet, $2\dfrac{3}{4}$ feet, and $1\dfrac{1}{2}$ feet. What is the total length of pipe?

40. Brienne Smith must trim $2\dfrac{3}{16}$ feet from a board 8 feet long. How long will the board be after it is cut?

41. Eight boxes that are each $1\dfrac{5}{8}$ feet high are stacked. Find the height of the stack.

PRACTICE TEST

Write the reciprocal.

1. 5

2. $\dfrac{3}{5}$

3. $1\dfrac{3}{5}$

Reduce by using the greatest common divisor (GCD).

4. $\dfrac{12}{15}$

5. $\dfrac{15}{35}$

6. $\dfrac{21}{51}$

Write as an improper fraction.

7. $2\dfrac{5}{8}$

8. $3\dfrac{1}{12}$

Write as a mixed number or whole number.

9. $\dfrac{21}{9}$

10. $\dfrac{56}{13}$

Perform the indicated operation. Reduce results to lowest terms and write as whole or mixed numbers if appropriate.

11. $\dfrac{5}{6} - \dfrac{4}{6}$

12. $\dfrac{5}{8} + \dfrac{9}{10}$

13. $\dfrac{5}{8} \times \dfrac{7}{10}$

14. $\dfrac{5}{6} \div \dfrac{3}{4}$

15. $10\dfrac{1}{2} \div 5\dfrac{3}{4}$

16. $56 \times 32\dfrac{6}{7}$

17. $2\dfrac{1}{2} + 3\dfrac{1}{3}$

18. $137 - 89\dfrac{4}{5}$

19. Dale Burton ordered $\frac{3}{4}$ truckload of merchandise. If approximately $\frac{1}{3}$ of the $\frac{3}{4}$ truckload of merchandise has been unloaded, how much remains to be unloaded?

20. A company that employs 580 people expects to lay off 87 workers. What fractional part of the workers are expected to be laid off?

21. Wallboard measuring $\frac{5}{8}$ inch thick makes a stack $62\frac{1}{2}$ inches high. How many sheets of wallboard are there?

22. If city sales tax is $5\frac{1}{2}\%$ and state sales tax is $2\frac{1}{4}\%$, what is the total sales tax rate for purchases made in the city?

23. Stephen Asprinio, competing in *Top Chef*, the television series, is given a $200 budget to prepare a five-course meal. If the main course costs $80 to prepare, what fraction of the budget was used for the main course?

24. The top-rated television series *Cupcake Wars* requires the two finalists to use their cupcake recipes to create a display for a large event. Lindsey Morton's Cinnamon Sugar Graham cupcake recipe for 36 cupcakes requires $1\frac{1}{4}$ cup of sugar. How much sugar is required for 900 cupcakes for her display?

1. What two operations require a common denominator?

2. What number (except 0) can be written as any fraction that has the same numerator and denominator? Give an example of a fraction that equals the number.

3. What is the product of any number and its reciprocal? Give an example to illustrate your answer.

4. What operation requires the use of the reciprocal of a fraction? Write an example of this operation and perform the operation.

5. What operations must be used to solve an applied problem if all of the parts but one are given and the total of all the parts is given? Write an example.

6. What steps must be followed to find the reciprocal of a mixed number? Give an example of a mixed number and its reciprocal.

7. Under what conditions are two fractions equivalent? Give an example to illustrate your answer.

8. Write three examples of dividing a whole number by a proper fraction.

9. Explain why the quotient of a whole number and a proper fraction is *more* than the whole number.

10. Explain the difference between a proper fraction and an improper fraction.

11. Explain the error in each problem, then work the problem correctly.

$$12\frac{1}{4}$$
$$-7\frac{3}{4}$$
$$5\frac{2}{4} = 5\frac{1}{2}$$

$$\frac{4}{9} \div 2\frac{1}{4} =$$

$$\frac{4}{9} \times \frac{9}{4} = \frac{36}{36} = 1$$

Challenge Problem

A room is $25\frac{1}{2}$ feet by $32\frac{3}{4}$ feet. How much will it cost to cover the floor with carpet costing \$12 a square yard (9 square feet), if 4 extra square yards are needed for matching? If a portion of a square yard is needed, an entire square yard must be purchased. Area = length × width.

2-1 Bitsie's Pastry Sensations

It was the grand opening of Elizabeth's pastry business, and she wanted to make something extra special. As a tribute to her Grandma Gertrude—who had helped pay for culinary school (and incidentally nicknamed her Bitsie), she had decided to make her grandmother's favorite recipe, apple crisp. Although she thought she remembered the recipe by heart, she decided she had better write it down just to make sure.

Apple Crisp

4 cups tart apples	Peel, core, and slice.
$\frac{1}{2}$ cup brown sugar	
$\frac{1}{2}$ tsp ground cinnamon	Add to apples and mix.
$\frac{1}{4}$ tsp ground nutmeg	Pour into a buttered
$\frac{1}{4}$ tsp ground cloves	9×13-inch glass
2 tsp lemon juice	baking dish.
$\frac{2}{3}$ cup granulated sugar	
$\frac{1}{8}$ tsp salt	Blend until crumbly.
$\frac{3}{4}$ cup unbleached white flour	
$\frac{1}{3}$ cup butter	
$\frac{1}{4}$ cup chopped walnuts, pecans, or raisins	Add to the sugar/flour mixture and sprinkle over apples.

Heat oven to 375°F. Bake until topping is golden brown and apples are tender, approximately 30 minutes.

1. Elizabeth planned to make 6 pans of apple crisp for the day, using extra tart Granny Smith apples—just like her grandmother had. But after peeling, coring, and slicing she had a major problem: she had 10 cups of apple slices. It was getting late and she needed to get some pans of apple crisp into the oven. She knew that 10 cups of apples was $2\frac{1}{2}$ times as much as the 4 cups she needed, so she decided to use multiplication to figure out $2\frac{1}{2}$ batches. Based on her hasty decision, how much of each ingredient will she need?

2. After looking at her math, Elizabeth realized her dilemma. She didn't have a pan that she could use for half a batch, and her math seemed too complicated anyway. She decided she would just make a double batch for now, because then she wouldn't need to multiply. Using addition, how much of each ingredient would she need for a double batch?

3. The two pans of apple crisp were just starting to brown when Elizabeth returned from the store with more apples. But instead of tart apples, the store had only honeycrisp, a much sweeter variety. After preparing 14 more cups of apples, she could make 3 batches using the honeycrisp (12 cups) and the fourth and final batch using both kinds of apples. Her concern, however, was the sweetness of the

apples. For the batches using the honeycrisp only, if the brown sugar and granulated sugar were reduced by $\frac{1}{2}$, how much sugar should she use for each batch? How much for all 3 batches?

2-2 Greenscape Designs

Travon returned from a meeting with his client, the City of Orlando, to begin preparing his bid for a new park project that the city was planning for the upcoming year. As a landscape architect, it is Travon's job to make areas such as parks, malls, and golf courses beautiful and useful. For this project, he would decide where the playground equipment and walkways would go, and how the flower gardens and trees should be arranged. For now, his most important task was to estimate costs based on the park specifications that he had received from the city, for which $240,000 had been budgeted.

1. Travon knows from experience that a typical bid for a landscaping job consists of $\frac{1}{2}$ for the materials, $\frac{1}{3}$ for the labor, and the remainder for the anticipated profit margin. Using the city's budgeted figure of $240,000, what dollar amount is expected for materials? For labor? And finally, what amount is the anticipated profit margin and what fraction of the cost does this amount represent?

2. The dimensions for the park are 400 × 400 feet square, and the specifications require 40,000 ft^2 (square feet) of flower/tree gardens; 5,000 ft^2 for a playground equipment area; 10,000 ft^2 in walkways; and at least 80,000 ft^2 of open green space. On a fractional basis, what portion of the park will be covered by each of these designated components?

3. Travon hopes to use any additional space for the creation of a water garden. What portion of the park, if any, remains for the creation of a water garden?

CHAPTER
3
Decimals

NASCAR

The National Association for Stock Car Auto Racing (NAS-CAR) claims as many as 75 million fans responsible for over $2.5 billion in licensed product sales annually. The NASCAR season begins in February in Daytona and runs through late November before finishing at the Homestead-Miami Speedway. The Daytona 500 is regarded by many as the most important and prestigious race on the NASCAR calendar, carrying by far the largest purse, with the winner receiving over $1.5 million. The event serves as the final event of Speedweeks and is sometimes referred to as "The Great American Race" or the "Super Bowl of Stock Car Racing." It is also the series' first race of the year; this phenomenon is virtually unique in sports, which tend to have championships or other major events at the end of the season rather than the start. The Daytona 500 is 500 miles (804.7 km) long and is run on a 2.5-mile tri-oval track. How many laps would that be?

The 2012 champion, Matt Kenseth, posted an average speed after the final restart of 188.269 miles per hour on his way to claiming the first prize of nearly $1.59 million, though rain delays meant an unprecedented Monday night start. Since 1995, U.S. television ratings for the Daytona 500 have been the highest for any auto race of the year, surpassing the traditional leader, the Indianapolis 500, which in turn greatly surpasses the Daytona 500 in in-track attendance and international viewing. According to Nielsen Media Research, the 2012 Daytona 500 attracted more than 36.5 million American viewers. With a total U.S. population of over 313 million, that means 0.1166 or at least 1 out of 10 people watched the Daytona 500—a lot of committed NASCAR fans!

The final race of the NASCAR season is the Ford 400 at the 1.5-mile oval Homestead-Miami Speedway. How many laps would that be? A shorter track like this often leads to more action during the race. During recent years, a typical Homestead race had 17.8 lead changes, 8.6 cautions for 45.5 laps, and an average green-flag run of 23.1 laps. In 2011, Tony Stewart won his third NASCAR championship with an epic victory over Carl Edwards in the Ford 400. The win put Stewart in the NASCAR annals with legendary names such as Cale Yarborough and Darrell Waltrip as three-time champions. With 2011 yearly earnings totaling $12.67 million, Stewart also became the first owner-driver since Alan Kulwicki to win the Cup Series championship, ending Jimmie Johnson's streak of consecutive championships at five. Congratulations, Tony, and here's to another great NASCAR season!

LEARNING OUTCOMES

3-1 Decimals and the Place-Value System

1. Read and write decimals.
2. Round decimals.

3-2 Operations with Decimals

1. Add and subtract decimals.
2. Multiply decimals.
3. Divide decimals.

3-3 Decimal and Fraction Conversions

1. Convert a decimal to a fraction.
2. Convert a fraction to a decimal.

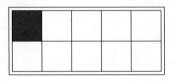

Decimal system: a place-value number system based on 10.

Decimals are another way to write fractions. We use decimals in some form or another every day—even our money system is based on decimals. Calculators use decimals, and decimals are the basis of percentages, interest, markups, and markdowns.

1 Read and write decimals.

Our money system, which is based on the dollar, uses the **decimal system.** In the decimal system, as you move right to left from one digit to the next, the place value of the digit increases by 10 times (multiply by 10). As you move left to right from one digit to the next, the place value of the digit gets 10 times smaller (divide by 10). The place value of the digit to the right of the ones place is 1 divided by 10.

There are several ways of indicating 1 divided by 10. In the decimal system, we write 1 divided by 10 as 0.1.

FIGURE 3-1
1 whole divided into 10 parts. The shaded part is 0.1.

How much is 0.1? How much is 1 divided by 10? It is one part of a 10-part whole (Figure 3-1). We read 0.1 as one-tenth. Using decimal notation, we can extend our place-value chart to the right of the ones place and express quantities that are not whole numbers. When extending to the right of the ones place, a period called a **decimal point** separates the **whole-number part** from the **decimal part.**

The names of the places to the right of the decimal are tenths, hundredths, thousandths, and so on. These place names are similar to the place names for whole numbers, but they all end in *ths.* In Figure 3-2, we show the place names for the digits in the number 2,315.627432.

DID YOU KNOW?

Some countries, such as France, Mexico, and South Africa, use a comma instead of a dot to separate the whole-number part of a number from the decimal part. They use a space to separate groups of three, called the periods, in the whole-number part.

15,396.7 is written as 15 396,7

Millions			Thousands			Units											
Hundred millions (100,000,000)	Ten millions (10,000,000)	Millions (1,000,000)	Hundred thousands (100,000)	Ten thousands (10,000)	Thousands (1,000)	Hundreds (100)	Tens (10)	Ones (1)	Decimal point	Tenths 0.1	Hundredths 0.01	Thousandths 0.001	Ten-thousandths 0.0001	Hundred-thousandths 0.00001	Millionths 0.000001	Ten-millionths 0.0000001	Hundred-millionths 0.00000001
					2	3	1	5	.	6	2	7	4	3	2		

FIGURE 3-2
Place-Value Chart for Decimals

Decimal point: the notation that separates the whole-number part of a number from the decimal part.

Whole-number part: the digits to the left of the decimal point.

Decimal part: the digits to the right of the decimal point.

HOW TO   Read or write a decimal

	Read 3.12.
1. Read or write the whole-number part (to the left of the decimal point) as you would read or write a whole number.	Three
2. Use the word *and* for the decimal point.	and
3. Read or write the decimal part (to the right of the decimal point) as you would read or write a whole number.	twelve
4. Read or write the place name of the rightmost digit.	hundredths

TIP

Informal Use of the Word *Point*

Informally, the decimal point is sometimes read as *point*. Thus, 3.6 is read *three point six*. The decimal 0.209 can be read as *zero point two zero nine*. This informal process is often used in communication to ensure that numbers are not mis-communicated. However, without hearing the place value, it is more difficult to get a sense of the size of the number.

EXAMPLE 1 Write the word name for these decimals: (a) 3.6, (b) 0.209, (c) $234.93.

(a) three and six-tenths
(b) two hundred nine thousandths
(c) two hundred thirty-four dollars and ninety-three cents

3 is the whole-number part; 6 is the decimal part.
The whole-number part, 0, is not written.
The whole-number part is dollars. The decimal part is cents.

TIP

Reading Decimals as Money Amounts

When reading decimal numbers that represent money amounts:

Read whole numbers as *dollars*.
Decimal amounts are read as *cents*. In the number $234.93, the decimal part is read ninety-three *cents* rather than ninety-three *hundredths of a dollar*. Because 1 cent is one hundredth of a dollar, the words *cent* and *hundredth* have the same meaning.

EXAMPLE 2 The fraction three-eighths has the same value as the decimal three hundred seventy-five thousandths. Write the decimal as a number.

The thousandths place is the third place to the right of the decimal.

0._ _ _   Write 375 thousandths.

0.375

STOP AND CHECK

See Example 1.

1. Write 5.8 in words.

2. Write 0.721 in words.

3. Recent statistics show that France had 789.48 cellular phones for each 1,000 people. Express the number of phones in words.

4. Recent statistics show that Italy had 1,341.466 cellular phones for each 1,000 people. Express the number of phones in words.

See Example 2.

5. Write three thousand five hundred forty-eight ten-thousandths as a number.

6. Write four dollars and eighty-seven cents as a number.

2 Round decimals.

As with whole numbers, we often need only an approximate amount. The process for rounding decimals is similar to rounding whole numbers.

TIP

When Do I Round?

In making a series of calculations, only round the result of the *final* calculation.

When making estimates, round the numbers of the problem *before* calculations are made.

HOW TO   Round to a specified decimal place

	Round to hundredths:
	17.3754
1. Find the digit in the specified place.	17.3754
2. Look at the next digit to the right.	17.3754
(a) If this digit is less than 5, eliminate it and all digits to its right.	
(b) If this digit is 5 or more, add 1 to the digit in the specified place, and eliminate all digits to its right.	17.38

EXAMPLE 3 Round the number to the specified place: (a) $193.48 to the nearest dollar, (b) $28.465 to the nearest cent.

(a) $19**3**.48   Rounding to the nearest dollar means rounding to the ones place. The digit in the ones place is 3.

$193.**4**8   The digit to the right of 3 is 4. Because 4 is less than 5, step 2a applies; eliminate 4 and all digits to its right.

$19**3**

$193.48 rounded to the nearest dollar is $193.

(b) $28.4**6**5   Rounding to the nearest cent means rounding to the nearest hundredth. The digit in the hundredths place is 6.

$28.46**5**   The digit to the right of 6 is 5. Because 5 is 5 or more, step 2b applies.

$28.4**7**

$28.465 rounded to the nearest cent is $28.47.

DID YOU KNOW?

To round to the *nearest dollar* is to round to the *ones place*.

To round to the *nearest cent* is to round to the *hundredths place*.

STOP AND CHECK

See Example 3.

1. Round 14.342 to the nearest tenth.

2. Round 48.7965 to the nearest hundredth.

3. Round $768.57 to the nearest dollar.

4. Round $54.834 to the nearest cent.

3-1 SECTION EXERCISES

SKILL BUILDERS

Write the word name for the decimal. See Example 1.

1. 0.582   **2.** 0.21   **3.** 1.0009   **4.** 2.83   **5.** 782.07

Write the number that represents the decimal. See Example 2.

6. Thirty-five hundredths   **7.** Three hundred twelve thousandths   **8.** Sixty and twenty-eight thousandths   **9.** Five and three hundredths

Round to the nearest dollar. See Example 3b.

10. $493.91   **11.** $785.03   **12.** $19.80   **13.** $1,823.37

Round to the nearest cent. See Example 3a.

14. $0.5239   **15.** $0.3962   **16.** $21.09734   **17.** $32,048.87219

Round to the nearest tenth.

18. 42.3784   **19.** 17.03752   **20.** 4.293

APPLICATIONS

21. Tel-Sales, Inc., a prepaid phone card company in Oklahoma City, sells phone cards for $19.89. Write the card cost in words.

22. Destiny Telecom of Oakland, California, introduced a Braille prepaid phone card that costs fourteen dollars and seventy cents. Write the digits to show Destiny's sales figure.

23. GameStop® reported a quarterly gross margin of 839.18 dollars in millions of dollars. Write the reported gross margin in millions of dollars in words.

24. Gannett Company reported a quarterly income before tax of negative five thousand, three hundred eighty-seven and twenty-four hundredths dollars in millions of dollars. Write the reported gross margin in millions of dollars in words.

3-2 OPERATIONS WITH DECIMALS

LEARNING OUTCOMES
1 Add and subtract decimals.
2 Multiply decimals.
3 Divide decimals.

1 Add and subtract decimals.

Some math skills are used more often than others. Adding and subtracting decimal numbers are regularly used in transactions involving money. To increase your awareness of the use of decimals, refer to your paycheck stub, grocery store receipt, fast-food ticket, odometer on your car, bills you receive each month, and checking account statement balance.

HOW TO   Add or subtract decimals

Add 32 + 2.55 + 8.85 + 0.625.

1. Write the numbers in a vertical column, aligning digits according to their place values.
2. Attach extra zeros to the right end of each decimal number so that each number has the same quantity of digits to the right of the decimal point. It is also accept-able to assume blank places to be zero.
3. Add or subtract as though the numbers are whole numbers.
4. Place the decimal point in the sum or difference to align with the decimal point in the addends or subtrahend and minuend.

```
   32
    2.55
    8.85
    0.625
   44.025
```

TIP

Unwritten Decimals

When we write whole numbers using numerals, we usually omit the decimal point; the decimal point is understood to be at the right end of the whole number. Therefore, any whole number, such as 32, can be written without a decimal (32) or with a decimal (32.).

TIP

Aligning Decimals in Addition or Subtraction

A common mistake in adding decimals is to misalign the digits or decimal points.

32	All digits and decimal	32	← not aligned correctly
2.55	points are aligned	2.55	
8.85	correctly.	8.85	
0.625		0.625	
44.025		1.797	← not aligned correctly
CORRECT		**INCORRECT**	

EXAMPLE 1

Subtract 26.3 − 15.84.

$$\begin{array}{r} {}^{5\ \ 12\,10}\\ 26.3\,0 \\ -\ 15.8\,4 \\ \hline 10.4\,6 \end{array}$$

Write the numbers so that the digits align according to their place values. Subtract the numbers, regrouping as you would in whole-number subtraction.

The difference of 26.3 and 15.84 is 10.46.

STOP AND CHECK

See How To Example, p. 85

1. Add: 67 + 4.38 + 0.291

2. Add: 57.5 + 13.4 + 5.238

See Example 1.

3. Subtract: 17.53 − 12.17

4. Subtract: 542.83 − 219.593

5. Garza Humada purchased a shirt for $18.97 and paid with a $20 bill. What was his change?

6. The stock of FedEx Corporation had a high for the day of $120.01 and a low of $95.79, closing at $117.58. By how much did the stock price change during the day?

2 Multiply decimals.

Suppose you want to calculate the amount of tip to add to a restaurant bill. A typical tip in the United States is 20 cents per dollar, which is 0.20 or 0.2 per dollar. To calculate the tip on a bill of $28.73 we multiply 28.73 × 0.2.

We multiply decimals as though they are whole numbers. Then we place the decimal point according to the quantity of digits in the decimal parts of the factors.

HOW TO Multiply decimals

1. Multiply the decimal numbers as though they are whole numbers.
2. Count the digits in the decimal parts of both decimal numbers.
3. Place the decimal point in the product so that there are as many digits in its decimal part as there are digits you counted in step 2. If necessary, attach zeros on the left end of the product so that you can place the decimal point accurately.

Multiply 3.5 × 0.3

$$\begin{array}{r} 3.5 \quad \text{one place}\\ \times\ 0.3 \quad \text{one place}\\ \hline 1.0\,5 \quad \text{two places} \end{array}$$

EXAMPLE 2

Multiply 2.35 × 0.015.

$$\begin{array}{r} 2.35 \quad \text{two decimal places}\\ \times\ 0.015 \quad \text{three decimal places}\\ \hline 1175 \\ 235 \\ \hline 0.03525 \quad \text{five decimal places.} \end{array}$$

One 0 is attached on the left to accurately place the decimal point.

The product of 2.35 and 0.015 is 0.03525.

HOW TO — Multiply by place-value numbers such as 10, 100, and 1,000

1. Determine the number of zeros in the multiplier.
2. Move the decimal in the multiplicand to the right the same number of places as there are zeros in the multiplier. Insert zeros as necessary.

EXAMPLE 3

Multiply 36.56 by (a) 10, (b) 100, and (c) 1,000.

(a) 36.56(10) = 365.6   Move the decimal one place to the right.

(b) 36.56(100) = 3,656   Move the decimal two places to the right.

(c) 36.56(1,000) = 36,560   Move the decimal three places to the right. Insert a zero to have enough places.

TIP

Round Money Amount to Cents

When working with money, we often round answers to the nearest cent. In Example 4 the amount $5.746 is rounded to $5.75.

EXAMPLE 4

Find the amount of tip you would pay on a restaurant bill of $28.73 if you tip 20 cents on the dollar (0.20, or 0.2) for the bill.

What You Know	What You Are Looking For	Solution Plan
Restaurant bill: $28.73 Rate of tip: 0.2 (20 cents on the dollar) of the bill	Amount of tip	Amount of tip = restaurant bill times rate of tip Amount of tip = 28.73(0.2)

Solution

$28.73 \boxed{\times} .2 \boxed{=} \Rightarrow 5.746$ Round to the nearest cent.

Conclusion

The tip is $5.75 when rounded to the nearest cent.

STOP AND CHECK

Multiply. See Example 2.

1. 4.35(0.27)

2. 7.03(0.035)

3. 5.32(15)

4. $8.31(4)

See Example 3.

5. 18.38(10)

6. 5.241(100)

7. 125.6(1,000)

8. A dinner for 500 guests costs $27.42 per person. What is the total cost of the dinner? *See Example 4.*

9. Tromane Mohaned purchased 1,000 shares of IBM stock at a price of $94.05. How much did the stock cost? *See Example 3.*

10. Marty Webb wants to tip her taxi driver at the rate of 20 cents on the dollar. How much would the tip be for a fare of $38.50? *See Example 4.*

3 Divide decimals.

Division of decimals has many uses in the business world. A common use is to determine how much one item costs if the cost of several items is known. Also, to compare the best buy of similar products that are packaged differently, we find the cost per common unit. A 12-ounce package and a 1-pound package of bacon can be compared by finding the cost per ounce of each package.

HOW TO   Divide a decimal by a whole number

Divide 95.2 by 14.

$$14\overline{)95.2}$$

1. Place a decimal point for the quotient directly above the decimal point in the dividend.
2. Divide as though the decimal numbers are whole numbers.
3. If the division does not come out evenly, attach zeros as necessary and carry the division one place past the desired place of the quotient.
4. Round to the desired place.

$$\begin{array}{r} 6.8 \\ 14\overline{)95.2} \\ \underline{84} \\ 11\ 2 \\ \underline{11\ 2} \\ 0 \end{array}$$

EXAMPLE 5   Divide 5.95 by 17.

$$\begin{array}{r} 0.35 \\ 17\overline{)5.95} \\ \underline{5\ 1} \\ 85 \\ \underline{85} \\ 0 \end{array}$$

Place a decimal point for the quotient directly above the decimal point in the dividend.

The quotient of 5.95 and 17 is 0.35.

EXAMPLE 6   Find the quotient of 37.4 ÷ 24 to the nearest hundredth.

$$\begin{array}{r} 1.558 \\ 24\overline{)37.400} \\ \underline{24} \\ 13\ 4 \\ \underline{12\ 0} \\ 1\ 40 \\ \underline{1\ 20} \\ 200 \\ \underline{192} \\ 8 \end{array}$$

rounds to 1.56

Carry the division to the thousandths place, and then round to hundredths. Attach two zeros to the right of 4 in the dividend.

The quotient is 1.56 to the nearest hundredth.

HOW TO   Divide by place-value numbers such as 10, 100, and 1,000

1. Determine the number of zeros in the divisor.
2. Move the decimal in the dividend to the left the same number of places as there are zeros in the divisor. Insert zeros as necessary.

EXAMPLE 7   Divide 23.71 by (a) 10, (b) 100, and (c) 1,000.

(a) 23.71 ÷ 10 = 2.371   Move the decimal one place to the left.

(b) 23.71 ÷ 100 = 0.2371   Move the decimal two places to the left. It is preferable to write a zero in front of the decimal point.

(c) 23.71 ÷ 1,000 = 0.02371   Move the decimal three places to the left. Insert a zero to have enough places.

If the divisor is a decimal rather than a whole number, we use an important fact: Multiplying both the divisor and the dividend by the same factor does not change the quotient.

We can see this by writing a division as a fraction.

$$10 \div 5 = \frac{10}{5} = 2$$

$$\frac{10}{5} \times \frac{10}{10} = \frac{100}{50} = 2$$

$$\frac{100}{50} \times \frac{10}{10} = \frac{1,000}{500} = 2$$

We've multiplied both the divisor and the dividend by a factor of 10, and then by a factor of 10 again. The quotient is always 2.

HOW TO   Divide by a decimal

Divide 3.4776 by 0.72.

$$0.72_\wedge \overline{)3.4776}$$

1. Change the divisor to a whole number by moving the decimal point to the right, counting the places as you go. Use a caret (^) to show the new position of the decimal point.

2. Move the decimal point in the dividend to the right as many places as you moved the decimal point in the divisor.

$$0.72_\wedge \overline{)3.47_\wedge 76}$$

3. Place the decimal point for the quotient directly above the *new* decimal point in the dividend.

$$0.72_\wedge \overline{)3.47_\wedge 76}$$

4. Divide as you would divide by a whole number. Carry the division one place past the desired place of the quotient. Round to the desired place.

```
          4. 83
0.72 ∧)3.47∧76
          2 88
           59  7
           57  6
            2  16
            2  16
               0
```

EXAMPLE 8   Find the quotient of 59.9 ÷ 0.39 to the nearest hundredth.

```
0.39)59.90     39∧)5,990∧
```

Move the decimal point two places to the right in both the divisor and the dividend.

```
         .
39)5,990∧
```

Place the decimal point for the quotient directly above the new decimal point in the dividend.

```
        153.589  ≈ 153.59 (rounded)
39)5,990.000
   3 9
   2 09
   1 95
     140
     117 .
      23 0
      19 5
       3 50
       3 12
         380
         351
          29
```

Divide, carrying out the division to the thousandths place. Attach three zeros to the right of the decimal point.

The quotient is 153.59 to the nearest hundredth.

Unit price or unit cost: price for 1 unit of a product.

EXAMPLE 9

Alicia Toliver is comparing the price of bacon to find the better buy. A 12-oz package costs $2.49 and a 16-oz package costs $2.99. Which package has the cheaper cost per ounce (often called **unit price**)?

What You Know	What You Are Looking For	Solution Plan
Price for 12-oz package = $2.49	Cost per ounce for each package	Price per ounce = $\dfrac{\text{Cost of 12-oz package}}{12}$
Price for 16-oz package = $2.99	Which package has the cheaper price per ounce?	Price per ounce = $\dfrac{\text{Cost of 16-oz package}}{16}$ Compare the prices per ounce.

Solution

Price per ounce = $2.49 \;\boxed{\div}\; 12 \;\boxed{=}\; \Rightarrow 0.2075$ 12-oz package

Price per ounce = $2.99 \;\boxed{\div}\; 16 \;\boxed{=}\; \Rightarrow 0.186875$ 16-oz package

Rounding to the nearest cent, $0.2075 rounds to $0.21 and $0.186875 rounds to $0.19. $0.19 is less than $0.21.

Conclusion

The 16-oz package of bacon has the cheaper unit price.

STOP AND CHECK

Divide.

See Example 5.

1. $100.80 \div 15$

See Example 6.

2. Round the quotient to tenths: $358.26 \div 23$

See Example 7.

3. $78 \div 100$

See Example 8.

4. Round the quotient to tenths: $12.97 \div 3.8$

5. Round the quotient to hundredths: $103.07 \div 5.9$

6. Gwen Hilton's gross weekly pay is $716.32 and her hourly pay is $19.36. How many hours did she work in the week?

7. *The Denver Post* reported that Wal-Mart would sell 42-inch Hitachi plasma televisions in a 4-day online special for $1,198 each. If Wal-Mart had paid $648,000,000 for a million units, how much did each unit cost Wal-Mart? *See Example 9.*

3-2 SECTION EXERCISES

SKILL BUILDERS

See How to Example, p. 85.

1. $6.005 + 0.03 + 924 + 3.9$

2. $82 + 5,000.1 + 101.703$

3. $21.13 + $42.78 + $16.39

4. $203.87 + $1,986.65 + $3,047.38

Subtract. See Example 1.

5. 407.96 − 298.39

6. 500.7 from 8,097.125

7. $468.39 − $223.54

8. $21.65 − $15.96

9. $52,982.97 − $45,712.49

10. $38,517 − $21,837.46

Multiply. See Examples 2–4.

11. 19.7

12. 0.0321 × 10

13. 73.7 × 0.02

14. 43.7 × 1.23

15. 5.03 × 0.073

16. 642 × $12.98

Divide and round to the nearest hundredth if necessary. See Examples 5–8.

17. 123.72 ÷ 12

18. 35)589.06

19. 0.35)0.0084

20. 1,482.97 ÷ 1.7

21. 32.73 ÷ 10

22. 0.014 ÷ 100

23. 483 ÷ 10

24. 315.7 ÷ 1,000

APPLICATIONS

25. Kathy Mowers purchased items costing $14.97, $28.14, $19.52, and $23.18. How much do her purchases total?

26. Jim Roznowski submitted a travel claim for meals, $138.42; hotel, $549.78; and airfare, $381.50. Total his expenses.

27. Joe Gallegos purchased a calculator for $12.48 and paid with a $20 bill. How much change did he get?

28. Martisha Jones purchased a jacket for $49.95 and a shirt for $18.50. She paid with a $100 bill. How much change did she receive?

29. Laura Voight earns $8.43 per hour as a telemarketing employee. One week she worked 28 hours. What was her gross pay before any deductions?

30. Cassie James works a 26-hour week at a part-time job while attending classes at Southwest Tennessee Community College. Her weekly gross pay is $213.46. What is her hourly rate of pay?

31. Calculate the cost of 1,000 gallons of gasoline if it costs $2.47 per gallon. *See Example 3.*

32. A buyer purchased 2,000 umbrellas for $4.62 each. What is the total cost?

33. All the employees in your department are splitting the cost of a celebratory lunch, catered at a cost of $142.14. If your department has 23 employees, will each employee be able to pay an equal share? How should the catering cost be divided?

34. AT&T offers a prepaid phone card for $5. The card provides 20 minutes of long-distance phone service. Find the cost per minute. *See Example 9.*

3-3 DECIMAL AND FRACTION CONVERSIONS

LEARNING OUTCOMES

1 Convert a decimal to a fraction.
2 Convert a fraction to a decimal.

1 Convert a decimal to a fraction.

Decimals represent parts of a whole, just as fractions can. We can write a decimal as a fraction, or a fraction as a decimal.

HOW TO Convert a decimal to a fraction

Write 0.8 as a fraction.

1. Find the denominator: Write 1 followed by as many zeros as there are places to the right of the decimal point.

Denominator = 10

2. Find the numerator: Use the digits without the decimal point.

$\dfrac{8}{10}$

3. Reduce to lowest terms and write as a whole or mixed number if appropriate.

$\dfrac{4}{5}$

EXAMPLE 1

Change 0.38 to a fraction.

$$0.38 = \frac{38}{100}$$

The digits without the decimal point form the numerator.

There are two places to the right of the decimal point, so the denominator is 1 followed by two zeros.

$$\frac{38}{100} = \frac{19}{50}$$

Reduce the fraction to lowest terms.

0.38 written as a fraction is $\frac{19}{50}$.

EXAMPLE 2

Change 2.43 to a mixed number.

$$2.43 = 2\frac{43}{100}$$

The whole-number part of the decimal stays as the whole-number part of the mixed number.

2.43 is $2\frac{43}{100}$ as a mixed number.

STOP AND CHECK

Write as a fraction or mixed number, and write in simplest form.

See Example 1.

1. 0.7   **2.** 0.32   **3.** 0.07

See Example 2.

4. 2.087   **5.** 23.41

2 Convert a fraction to a decimal.

Fractions indicate division. Therefore, to write a fraction as a decimal, perform the division. Divide the numerator by the denominator, as you would divide decimals.

HOW TO   Write a fraction as a decimal

1. Write the numerator as the dividend and the denominator as the divisor.
2. Divide the numerator by the denominator. Carry the division as many decimal places as necessary or desirable.
3. For repeating decimals:
   (a) Write the remainder as the numerator of a fraction and the divisor as the denominator.
   or
   (b) Carry the division one place past the desired place and round.

TIP

Divide by Which Number?

An aid to help remember which number in the fraction is the divisor: Divide by the bottom number. Both *by* and *bottom* start with the letter *b*.

In the preceding example, $\frac{1}{4}$ was converted to a decimal by dividing by 4, the bottom number.

EXAMPLE 3

Change $\frac{1}{4}$ to a decimal number.

```
   0.25
4)1.00
   8
   20
   20
```

Divide the numerator by the denominator, attaching zeros to the right of the decimal point as needed.

The decimal equivalent of $\frac{1}{4}$ is 0.25.

When the division comes out even (there is no remainder), we say the division terminates, and the quotient is called a **terminating decimal.** If, however, the division *never* comes out even (there is always a remainder), we call the number a **nonterminating** or **repeating decimal.** If the quotient is a repeating decimal, either write the remainder as a fraction or round to a specified place.

EXAMPLE 4

Write $\frac{2}{3}$ as a decimal number in hundredths (a) with the remainder expressed as a fraction and (b) with the decimal rounded to hundredths.

(a)
$$
\begin{array}{r}
0.66\frac{2}{3} \\
3\overline{)2.00} \\
\underline{1\,8} \\
20 \\
\underline{18} \\
2
\end{array}
$$

(b)
$$
\begin{array}{r}
0.666 \approx 0.67 \\
3\overline{)2.000} \\
\underline{1\,8} \\
20 \\
\underline{18} \\
20 \\
\underline{18} \\
2
\end{array}
$$

$\frac{2}{3} = 0.66\frac{2}{3}$ **or** $\frac{2}{3} \approx 0.67.$

EXAMPLE 5

Write $3\frac{1}{4}$ as a decimal.

$3\frac{1}{4} = 3.25$

The whole-number part of the mixed number stays as the whole-number part of the decimal number.

$3\frac{1}{4}$ **is 3.25 as a decimal number.**

STOP AND CHECK

Change to decimal numbers. Round to hundredths if necessary.

See Example 3.

1. $\frac{3}{5}$

2. $\frac{7}{8}$

See Example 4.

3. $\frac{5}{12}$

4. Write $\frac{5}{6}$ as a decimal in hundredths with the remainder expressed as a fraction.

See Example 5.

5. $7\frac{4}{5}$

6. $8\frac{4}{7}$

3-3 SECTION EXERCISES

SKILL BUILDERS

Write as a fraction or mixed number and write in simplest form. See Examples 1–2.

1. 0.6

2. 0.58

3. 0.625

4. 0.1875   **5.** 7.3125   **6.** 28.875

Change to a decimal. Round to hundredths if necessary. See Examples 3–5.

7. $\dfrac{7}{10}$ **8.** $\dfrac{3}{8}$

Write the following fractions as decimals in hundredths with the remainder expressed as a fraction.

9. $\dfrac{1}{6}$ **10.** $\dfrac{5}{12}$ **11.** $\dfrac{7}{12}$

12. $\dfrac{7}{16}$ **13.** $2\dfrac{1}{8}$ **14.** $21\dfrac{11}{12}$

Learning Outcomes

What to Remember with Examples

Section 3-1

1 Read and write decimals. (p. 82)

Read or write a decimal.

1. Read or write the whole number part (to the left of the decimal point) as you would read or write a whole number.
2. Use the word *and* for the decimal point.
3. Read or write the decimal part (to the right of the decimal point) as you would read or write a whole number.
4. Read or write the place of the rightmost digit.

> Write the decimal in words.
>
> 0.3869 is read *three thousand, eight-hundred sixty-nine ten-thousandths.*

2 Round decimals. (p. 83)

Round to a specified decimal place.

1. Find the digit in the specified place.
2. Look at the next digit to the right.
   (a) If this digit is less than 5, eliminate it and all digits to its right.
   (b) If this digit is 5 or more, add 1 to the digit in the specified place, and eliminate all digits to its right.

> Round to the specified place.
>
> 37.357 rounded to the nearest tenth is 37.4.
> 3.4819 rounded to the first digit is 3.

Section 3-2

1 Add and subtract decimals. (p. 85)

1. Write the numbers in a vertical column, aligning digits according to their places.
2. Attach extra zeros to the right end of each decimal number so that each number has the same quantity of digits to the right of the decimal point (optional). It is also acceptable to assume blank spaces to be zero.
3. Add or subtract as though the numbers are whole numbers.
4. Place the decimal point in the sum or difference to align with the decimal point in the addends or subtrahend and minuend.

> Add: $32.68 + 3.31 + 49$
>
> $$\begin{array}{r} 32.68 \\ 3.31 \\ +\ 49. \\ \hline 84.99 \end{array}$$
>
> Subtract: $24.7 - 18.25$
>
> $$\begin{array}{r} 24.70 \\ -18.25 \\ \hline 6.45 \end{array}$$

2 Multiply decimals. (p. 86)

Multiply decimals.

1. Multiply the decimal numbers as though they are whole numbers.
2. Count the digits in the decimal parts of both decimal numbers.
3. Place the decimal point in the product so that there are as many digits in its decimal part as there are digits you counted in step 2. If necessary, attach zeros on the left end of the product so that you can place the decimal point accurately.

> Multiply: 36.48×2.52
>
> $$\begin{array}{r} 36.48 \\ \times\ 2.52 \\ \hline 72\ 96 \\ 18\ 24\ 0 \\ 72\ 96 \\ \hline 91.92\ 96 \end{array}$$
>
> Multiply: 2.03×0.036
>
> $$\begin{array}{r} 2.03 \\ \times\ 0.0\ 36 \\ \hline 1\ 2\ 18 \\ 6\ 09 \\ \hline 0.07\ 3\ 08 \end{array}$$

Multiply by place-value numbers such as 10, 100, and 1,000.

1. Determine the number of zeros in the multiplier.
2. Move the decimal in the multiplicand to the right the same number of places as there are zeros in the multiplier. Insert zeros as necessary on the right.

Multiply: 4.52(1,000)

4.52(1,000) = 4,520   Move the decimal three places to the right. Insert a zero to have enough places.

3 Divide decimals. (p. 88)

Divide a decimal by a whole number.

1. Place a decimal point for the quotient directly above the decimal point in the dividend.
2. Divide as though the decimal numbers are whole numbers.
3. If the division does not come out evenly, attach zeros as necessary and carry the division one place past the desired place of the quotient.
4. Round to the desired place.

Divide: 58.5 ÷ 45

$$
\begin{array}{r}
1.3 \\
45\overline{)58.5} \\
45 \\
\overline{13\,5} \\
13\,5 \\
\overline{0}
\end{array}
$$

Divide by place-value numbers such as 10, 100, and 1,000.

1. Determine the number of zeros in the divisor.
2. Move the decimal in the dividend to the left the same number of places as there are zeros in the divisor. Insert zeros as necessary on the left.

Divide: 4.52 ÷ 100

4.52 ÷ 100 = 0.0452   Move the decimal two places to the left. Insert a zero to have enough places. It is preferable to write a zero in front of the decimal.

Divide by a decimal.

1. Change the divisor to a whole number by moving the decimal point to the right, counting the places as you go. Use a caret ($_\wedge$) to show the new position of the decimal point.
2. Move the decimal point in the dividend to the right as many places as you moved the decimal point in the divisor.
3. Place the decimal point for the quotient directly above the *new* decimal point in the dividend.
4. Divide as you would divide by a whole number. Carry the division one place past the desired place of the quotient. Round to the desired place.

Divide: 0.770 ÷ 3.5

$$
\begin{array}{r}
0.\,22 \\
3.5_\wedge\overline{)0.7_\wedge70} \\
7\;\;0 \\
\overline{70} \\
70 \\
\overline{0}
\end{array}
$$

Divide: 0.485 ÷ 0.24
Round to the nearest tenth.

$$
\begin{array}{r}
2.\,02 \approx 2.0\ \text{rounded} \\
0.24_\wedge\overline{)0.48_\wedge50} \\
48 \\
\overline{50} \\
48 \\
\overline{2}
\end{array}
$$

1   Convert a decimal to a fraction.
(p. 92)

1. Find the denominator: Write 1 followed by as many zeros as there are places to the right of the decimal point.
2. Find the numerator: Use the digits without the decimal point.
3. Reduce to lowest terms and write as a whole or mixed number if appropriate.

Write each decimal as a fraction in lowest terms.

$$0.05 = \frac{5}{100} \div \frac{5}{5} = \frac{1}{20} \qquad 0.584 = \frac{584}{1,000} \div \frac{8}{8} = \frac{73}{125}$$

2   Convert a fraction to a decimal.
(p. 93)

1. Write the numerator as the dividend and the denominator as the divisor.
2. Divide the numerator by the denominator. Carry the division as many decimal places as necessary or desirable.
3. For repeating decimals:
   (a) Write the remainder as the numerator of a fraction and the divisor as the denominator.
   or
   (b) Carry the division one place past the desired place and round.

Write each fraction as a decimal.

$$\frac{5}{8} = 8)\overline{5.000} \qquad \frac{1}{6} = 6)\overline{1.000} \approx 0.17 \text{ (Rounded to hundredths)}$$

```
        0.625                          0.166  ≈   0.17 (Rounded to hundredths)
   5
   - = 8)5.000                 1
   8                           - = 6)1.000
        4 8                    6
          20                         6
          16                         40
          40                         36
          40                         40
                                     36
                                      4
```

EXERCISES SET A

Write the word name for the decimal.

1. 0.5

2. 0.108

3. 0.00275

4. 17.8

5. 128.23

6. 500.0007

Write the number that represents the decimal.

7. Seventy-eight thousandths

8. Eighteen and forty-seven ten-thousandths

Round to the specified place.

9. 0.1345 (nearest thousandth) **10.** 384.73 (nearest ten) **11.** 1,745.376 (nearest hundred) **12.** $175.24 (nearest dollar)

Add.

13. 0.3 + 0.05 + 0.266 + 0.63

14. 78.87 + 54 + 32.9569 + 0.0043

15. $5.13 + $8.96 + $14.73

16. $283.17 + $58.73 + $96.92

Subtract.

17. 500.05 − 123.31 **18.** 125.35 − 67.8975 **19.** 423 − 287.4 **20.** 482.073 − 62.97

Multiply.

21. 27.63
   ×   7

22. 6.42
   × 7.8

23. 75.84
   × 0.28

24. 27.58 × 10

Divide. Round to hundredths if necessary.

25. $34\overline{)291.48}$ 　　　　**26.** $2.8\overline{)94.546}$ 　　　　**27.** $296.36 \div 0.19$ 　　　　**28.** $41,285 \div 0.68$

$$\begin{array}{r} 1{,}5\,59\,.789 \approx 1{,}559.79 \\ 0.19\,\overline{)296.36\,000} \end{array}$$

Write as fractions or mixed numbers in simplest form.

29. 0.55 　　　　　　　　　　　　　　　　　　**30.** 191.82

Write as decimals. Round to hundredths if necessary.

31. $\dfrac{17}{20}$ 　　　　　　　　　　　　　　　**32.** $\dfrac{13}{16}$

33. A shopper purchased a cake pan for $8.95, a bath mat for $9.59, and a bottle of shampoo for $2.39. Find the total cost of the purchases.

34. Leon Treadwell's checking account had a balance of $196.82 before he wrote checks for $21.75 and $82.46. What was his balance after he wrote the checks?

35. Four tires that retailed for $486.95 are on sale for $397.99. By how much are the tires reduced?

36. If 100 gallons of gasoline cost $342.90, what is the cost per gallon?

37. What is the cost of 5.5 pounds of chicken breasts if they cost $3.49 per pound?

38. A. G. Edwards is purchasing 100 cell phones for $189.95. How much is the total purchase?

EXERCISES SET B

Write the word name for the decimal.

1. 0.27

2. 0.013

3. 0.120704

4. 3.04

5. 3,000.003

6. 184.271

Write the number that represents the decimal.

7. Two thousand seventeen hundred-thousandths

8. Thirty and one hundred twenty-seven ten-thousandths

Round to the specified place.

9. 384.72 (nearest tenth)

10. 1,745.376 (nearest hundredth)

11. 32.57 (nearest whole number)

12. $5.333 (nearest cent)

Add.

13. 31.005 + 5.36 + 0.708 + 4.16

14. 9.004 + 0.07 + 723 + 8.7

15. $7.19 + $5.78 + $21.96

16. $596.16 + $47.35 + $72.58

Subtract.

17. 815.01 − 335.6

18. 404.04 − 135.8716

19. 807.38 − 529.79

20. 5,003.02 − 689.23

Multiply.

21. $\begin{array}{r} 3\,84 \\ \times\ 3.51 \\ \hline \end{array}$

22. $\begin{array}{r} 0.0015 \\ \times\ 6.003 \\ \hline \end{array}$

23. $\begin{array}{r} 73.41 \\ \times\ 15 \\ \hline \end{array}$

24. 1.394 × 100

Divide. Round to the nearest hundredth if division does not terminate.

25. $27\overline{)365.04}$ **26.** $74\overline{)85.486}$ **27.** $923.19 \div 0.541$ **28.** $363.45 \div 2.5$

Write as fractions or mixed numbers in simplest form.

29. 0.75 **30.** 17.5

Write as decimals. Round to hundredths if necessary.

31. $\dfrac{1}{20}$ **32.** $3\dfrac{7}{20}$

33. Rob McNab ordered 18.3 square meters of carpet for his halls, 123.5 square meters for the bedrooms, 28.7 square meters for the family room, and 12.9 square meters for the playroom. Find the total amount of carpet he ordered.

34. Janet Morris weighed 149.3 pounds before she began a weight-loss program. After eight weeks she weighed 129.7 pounds. How much did she lose?

35. Ernie Jones worked 37.5 hours at the rate of $14.80 per hour. Calculate his earnings.

36. If sugar costs $2.87 for 80 ounces, what is the cost per ounce, rounded to the nearest cent?

37. If two lengths of metal sheeting measuring 12.5 inches and 15.36 inches are cut from a roll of metal measuring 240 inches, how much remains on the roll?

38. If 1,000 gallons of gasoline cost $3,589, what is the cost of 45 gallons?

PRACTICE TEST

1. Round 42.876 to tenths.

2. Round 30.5375 to one nonzero digit.

3. Write the word name for 24.1007.

4. Write the number for three and twenty-eight thousandths.

Perform the indicated operation.

5. $39.17 - 15.078$

6. 27.418×100

7. $0.387 + 3.17 + 17 + 204.3$

8. $28.34 \div 50$ (nearest hundredth)

9.
$$\begin{array}{r} 324 \\ \times\, 1.38 \\ \hline \end{array}$$

10. $0.138 \div 10$

11. $128 - 38.18$

12.
$$\begin{array}{r} 17.75 \\ \times\ 0.325 \\ \hline \end{array}$$

13. $2.347 + 0.178 + 3.5 + 28.341$

14. $91.25 \div 12.5$

15. $317.24 - 138$

16. 374.17×100

17. A patient's chart showed a temperature reading of 101.2 degrees Fahrenheit at 3 P.M. and 99.5 degrees Fahrenheit at 10 P.M. What was the drop in temperature?

18. Eastman Kodak's stock changed from $26.14 a share to $22.15 a share. Peter Carp owned 2,000 shares of stock. By how much did his stock decrease?

19. Stephen Lewis owns 100 shares of PepsiCo at $47.40; 50 shares of Alcoa at $27.19; and 200 shares of McDonald's at $24.72. What is the total stock value?

20. What is the average price per share of the 350 shares of stock held by Stephen Lewis if the total value is $11,043.50?

1. Explain why numbers are aligned on the decimal point when they are added or subtracted.

2. Describe the process for placing the decimal point in the product of two decimal numbers.

3. Explain the process of changing a fraction to a decimal number.

4. Explain the process of changing a decimal number to a fraction.

Identify the error and describe what caused the error. Then work the example correctly.

5. Change $\frac{5}{12}$ to a decimal number.

$$\begin{array}{r} 2.4 \\ 5\overline{)12.0} \\ 10 \\ \hline 2\ 0 \end{array} \qquad \frac{5}{12} = 2.4$$

6. Add: $3.72 + 6 + 12.5 + 82.63$

$$\begin{array}{r} 3.72 \\ 6 \\ 12.5 \\ 82.63 \\ \hline 87.66 \end{array}$$

7. Multiply: 4.37×2.1

$$\begin{array}{r} 4.37 \\ \times\ 2.1 \\ \hline 4\ 37 \\ 87\ 4 \\ \hline 91.77 \end{array}$$

$$\begin{array}{r} 4.3\ 7 \\ \times\ \ 2.1 \\ \hline 4\ 3\ 7 \\ 8\ 7\ 4 \\ \hline 9.1\ 7\ 7 \end{array}$$

8. Divide: $18.27 \div 54$. Round to tenths.

$$\begin{array}{r} 2.95 \approx 3.0 \\ 18.27\overline{)54.00\ 00} \\ 36\ 54 \\ \hline 17\ 460 \\ 16\ 443 \\ \hline 1\ 0170 \\ 9135 \\ \hline 1035 \end{array}$$

Challenge Problem

Net income for Hershey Foods for the third quarter is $143,600,000 or $1.09 a share. This is compared with net income of $123,100,000 or $0.89 a share for the same quarter a year ago. What was the increase or decrease in the number of shares of stock?

CASE STUDIES

3-1 Pricing Stock Shares

Shantell recognized the stationery, and looked forward to another of her Aunt Mildred's letters. Inside, though, were a number of documents along with a short note. The note read: "Shantell, your Uncle William and I are so proud of you. You are the first female college graduate in our family. Your parents would have been so proud as well. Please accept these stocks as a gift toward the fulfillment of starting your new business. Cash them in or keep them for later, it's up to you! With love, Aunt Millie." Shantell didn't know how to react. Finishing college had been very difficult for her financially. Having to work two jobs meant little time for studying and a nonexistent social life. But this she never expected. With dreams of opening her own floral shop, any money would be a godsend. She opened each certificate and found the following information: Alcoa—35 shares at 15 3/8; Coca Cola—150 shares at 24 5/8; IBM—80 shares at 40 11/16; and AT&T—50 shares at 35 1/8.

1. Shantell knew the certificates were old, because stocks do not trade using fractions anymore. What would the stock prices be for each company if they were converted from fractions to decimals?

2. Using your answers with decimals from Exercise 1, find the total value of each company's stock. What is the total value from all four companies?

3. Shantell couldn't believe her eyes. The total she came up with was over $9,000! Suddenly, though, she realized that the amounts she used could not possibly be the current stock prices. After 30 minutes online, she was confident she had the current prices: Alcoa: 35 shares at $10.43; Coca Cola: 150 shares at $69.18; IBM: 80 shares at $197.76; and AT&T: 50 shares at $30.34. Using the current prices, what would be the total value of each company's stock? What would be the total value for all of the stocks? Given the answer, would you cash the stocks in now or hold on to them to see if they increased in value?

3-2 JK Manufacturing Demographics

Carl has just started his new job as a human resource management assistant for JK Manufacturing. His first project is to gather demographic information on the personnel at their three locations in El Paso, San Diego, and Chicago. Carl studied some of the demographics collected by the Bureau of Labor Statistics (www.stats.bls.gov) in one of his human resource classes and decided to collect similar data. Primarily, he wants to know the gender, level of education, and ethnic/racial backgrounds of JK Manufacturing's workforce. He designs a survey using categories he found at the Bureau of Labor Statistics web site.

Employees at each of the locations completed Carl's survey and reported the following information:

El Paso: 140 women, 310 men; 95 had a bachelor's degree or higher, 124 had some college or an associate's degree, 200 were high school graduates, and the rest had less than a high school diploma; 200 employees were white non-Hispanic, 200 were Hispanic or Latino, 20 were black or African American, 15 were Asian, and the rest were "other."

San Diego: 525 women, 375 men; 150 had a bachelor's degree or higher, 95 had some college or an associate's degree, 500 were high school graduates, and the rest had less than a high school diploma; 600 employees were Hispanic or Latino, 200 were black or African American, 50 were white non-Hispanic, 25 were Asian, and the rest were "other."

Chicago: 75 women, 100 men; 20 had a bachelor's degree or higher, 75 had some college or an associate's degree, 75 were high school graduates, and the rest had less than a high school diploma; 100 employees were white non-Hispanic, 50 were black or African American, 25 were Hispanic or Latino, there were no Asians or "other" at the facility.

1. Carl's supervisor asked him to summarize the information and convert the raw data to a decimal part of the total for each location. Carl designed the following chart to organize the data. To complete the chart, write a fraction with the number of employees in each category as the numerator and the total number of employees in each city as the denominator. Then convert the fraction to a decimal rounded to the nearest hundredth. Enter the decimal in the chart. To check your calculations, the total of the decimal equivalents for each city should equal 1 or close to 1 because of rounding discrepancies.

Gender	El Paso		San Diego		Chicago	
Men	310		375		100	
Women	140		525		75	
Total	450		900		175	

Education	El Paso		San Diego		Chicago	
Bachelor's degree or higher	95		150		20	
Some college or an associate's degree	124		95		75	
High school (HS) graduate	200		500		75	
Less than a HS diploma	31		155		5	
Total	450		900		175	

Race/Ethnicity	El Paso		San Diego		Chicago	
White/non-Hispanic	200		50		100	
Black/African American	20		200		50	
Hispanic/Latino	200		600		25	
Asian	15		25			
Other	15		25			
Total	450		900		175	

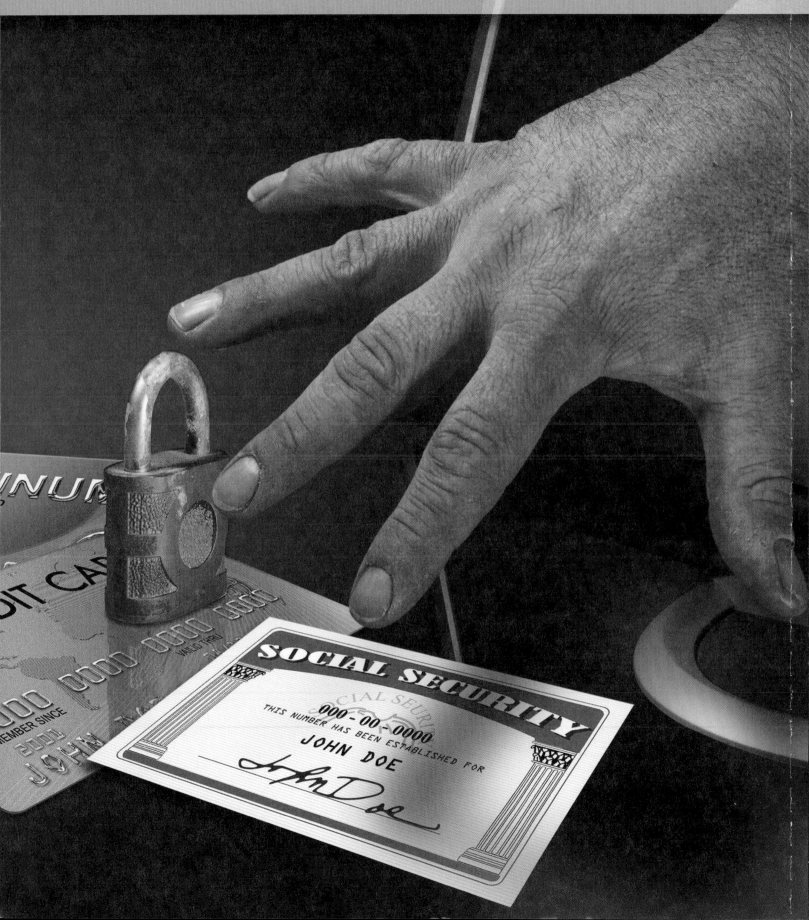

Record Keeping: Identity Fraud

In 2010, the research company Javelin Strategy & Research released a report showing that 11.1 million U.S. adults were victims of identity fraud in 2010, a marked decline over the past year. This great news is a testament to the significant efforts businesses, the financial services industry, and government agencies are making to educate consumers, protect data, and prevent and resolve identity fraud. One of the significant trends in the report, though, is that "friendly fraud"—fraud perpetrated by people known to the victim such as a relative or roommate—is on the rise. Consumers between the ages of 25 and 34 are most likely to be victims of this type of fraud and are most likely to have their Social Security number (SSN) stolen.

To reduce or minimize the risk of becoming a victim of identity theft or fraud, you can take these basic steps:

- Keep a list of all your credit, debit, and bank accounts in a secure place, so you can quickly call the issuers to inform them about missing or stolen cards. Include account numbers, expiration dates, and telephone numbers of customer service and fraud departments.
- Shred and destroy unwanted documents that contain personal information including credit, debit, and ATM card receipts and preapproved credit offers. Use a cross-cut shredder.
- Never permit your credit card number to be written on your checks.
- Take credit and debit card receipts with you. Never toss them into a public trash container.
- Never respond to "phishing" email messages. These messages may appear to be from your bank, eBay, or PayPal. They instruct you to visit their web site, which looks just like the real thing. They ask you for your financial account numbers and Social Security number, but the request is a scam and will result in identity theft.

- Do not carry extra credit or debit cards, Social Security card, birth certificate, or passport in your wallet or purse except when necessary.
- When shopping online, use only a credit card. Debit cards do not provide as much protection from fraud as credit cards.
- Order your credit report each year. You can obtain your credit report free of charge from each of the three credit bureaus once a year: Equifax, Experian, and TransUnion or from annualcreditreport.com. If you are a victim of identity theft, your credit report will contain the telltale signs of activity.
- Ask your financial institutions to add extra security protection to your account. Add a strong password to each account.
- Install virus and spyware detection software and a firewall on your computer and keep them updated.
- Deposit mail in U.S. Postal Service collection boxes. Do not leave mail in your mailbox overnight or on weekends.

If you think you are a victim of identity theft, follow these guidelines:

- Contact the fraud department of each one of the three credit reporting companies to place a fraud alert on your credit report. A fraud alert tells creditors to follow certain procedures before opening any new accounts.
- For the greatest protection, establish a security freeze with the three credit bureaus.
- Order your credit report to learn of any new credit accounts opened fraudulently in your name.
- Close the accounts that you know or believe have been tampered with or opened fraudulently.
- File an ID theft affidavit with the Federal Trade Commission, found on its web site. You may print a copy of your affidavit to provide important standardized information for your police report.
- File a report with your local police or police in the community where the identity theft took place.

Source: ID theft/fraud tips are reprinted with consent of the Privacy Rights Clearinghouse, http://www.privacyrights.org.

LEARNING OUTCOMES

4-1 Checking Account Transactions

1. Make account transactions.
2. Record account transactions.

4-2 Bank Statements

1. Reconcile a bank statement with an account register.

Most businesses and many individuals use computer software and online banking for making, recording, and reconciling transactions for a bank account. All of the processes discussed in this chapter are similar to the processes used with a computer. It is important to use banking forms correctly, to keep accurate records, and to track financial transactions carefully.

4-1 CHECKING ACCOUNT TRANSACTIONS

LEARNING OUTCOMES

1 Make account transactions.
2 Record account transactions.

Checking account: a bank account for managing the flow of money into and out of the account.

Financial institutions such as banks and credit unions provide a variety of services for both individual and business customers. One of these services is a **checking account**. This account holds your money and disburses it according to the policies and procedures of the bank and to your instructions. Various checking account forms or records are needed to maintain a checking account for your personal or business financial matters. The bank must be able to account for all funds that flow into and out of your account, and written evidence of changes in your account is necessary.

1 Make account transactions.

Transaction: a banking activity that changes the amount of money in a bank account.

Deposit: a transaction that increases a checking account balance; this transaction is also called a credit.

Credit: a transaction that increases a checking account balance.

Deposit slip: a banking form for recording the details of a deposit.

Any activity that changes the amount of money in a bank account is called a **transaction**.

When money is put into a checking account, the transaction is called a **deposit**. The bank refers to this transaction as a **credit**. A deposit or credit *increases* the amount of the checking account. One bank record for deposits made by the account holder is called the **deposit slip**. Figure 4-1 shows a sample deposit slip for a personal account. Figure 4-2 shows a sample deposit ticket for a business account. Deposit slips are available to the person opening an account along with a set of preprinted checks. The bank's account number and the customer's account number are written at the bottom of the ticket in magnetic ink using specially designed characters and symbols to facilitate machine processing. The bank also has generic forms that can be used for deposits by writing in the account information.

HOW TO   Make an account deposit on the appropriate deposit form

1. Record the date.
2. Enter the amount of currency or coins being deposited.
3. List the amount of each check to be deposited. Include an identifying name or company.
4. Add the amounts of currency, coins, and checks.
5. If the deposit is to a personal account and you want to receive some of the money in cash, enter the amount on the line "less cash received" and sign on the appropriate line.
6. Subtract the amount of cash received from the total for the net deposit.

EXAMPLE 1   Complete a deposit slip for Lee Wilson. The deposit on May 29, 2013, will include $392 in currency, $0.90 in coins, a $373.73 check from Nichols, and a tax refund check from the IRS for $438.25. Lee wants to get $100 in cash from the transaction.

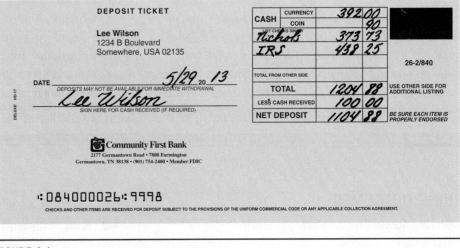

FIGURE 4-1
Deposit Slip for a Personal Account

Businesses generally will have several checks in each deposit. A different type of deposit ticket allows more checks to be entered on one side of the deposit ticket, and a copy of the ticket is kept by the business. When depositing to a business account, you do not have the option of receiving a portion of the deposit in cash.

EXAMPLE 2

Macon Florist makes a deposit on August 19, 2013, that includes the checks shown in Table 4-1. Complete the deposit ticket (Figure 4-2).

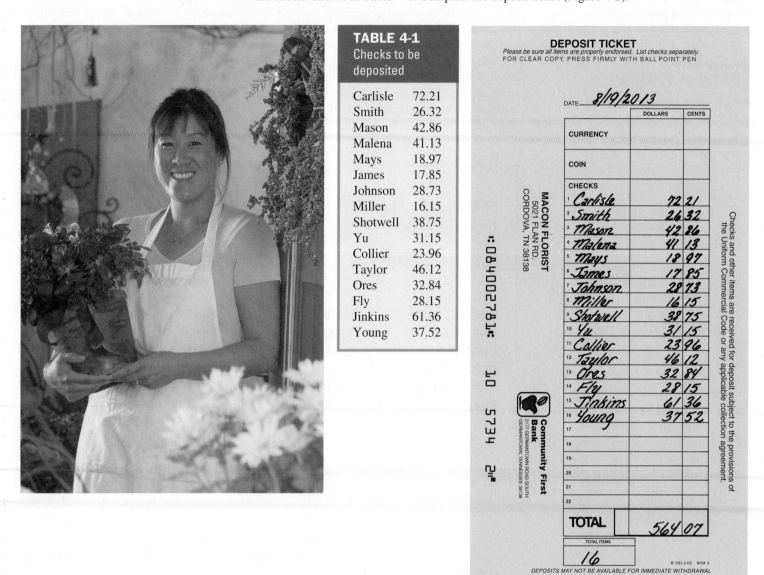

TABLE 4-1
Checks to be deposited

Carlisle	72.21
Smith	26.32
Mason	42.86
Malena	41.13
Mays	18.97
James	17.85
Johnson	28.73
Miller	16.15
Shotwell	38.75
Yu	31.15
Collier	23.96
Taylor	46.12
Ores	32.84
Fly	28.15
Jinkins	61.36
Young	37.52

DEPOSIT TICKET
Please be sure all items are properly endorsed. List checks separately.
FOR CLEAR COPY, PRESS FIRMLY WITH BALL POINT PEN

MACON FLORIST
5021 FLAN RD.
CORDOVA, TN 38138

DATE 8/19/2013

	DOLLARS	CENTS
CURRENCY		
COIN		
CHECKS		
1 Carlisle	72	21
2 Smith	26	32
3 Mason	42	86
4 Malena	41	13
5 Mays	18	97
6 James	17	85
7 Johnson	28	73
8 Miller	16	15
9 Shotwell	38	75
10 Yu	31	15
11 Collier	23	96
12 Taylor	46	12
13 Ores	32	84
14 Fly	28	15
15 Jinkins	61	36
16 Young	37	52
17		
18		
19		
20		
21		
22		
TOTAL	564	07
TOTAL ITEMS		
16		

Community First Bank
2177 GERMANTOWN ROAD SOUTH
GERMANTOWN, TENNESSEE 38138

© DELUXE 8DM-3

DEPOSITS MAY NOT BE AVAILABLE FOR IMMEDIATE WITHDRAWAL

Checks and other items are received for deposit subject to the provisions of the Uniform Commercial Code or any applicable collection agreement.

⑈08400278⑈ 10 5734 2⑈

FIGURE 4-2
Complete Deposit Ticket for Macon Florist

TIP

Personal Checking Account Versus Business Checking Account

Bank policies for a personal checking account are often different from the policies for a business checking account. Some of the most common differences are:

Personal	Business
Sometimes banking forms are provided free. Preprinted checks and deposit slips come together.	All banking forms have to be purchased. Preprinted deposit slips are purchased separately.
A separate check register is provided with the checks and deposit slips.	No check register is provided and preprinted checks have stubs.
A deposit slip can specify that a portion of the transaction can be received in cash.	There is no option for receiving a portion of a deposit back as cash.

Bank memo: a notification of a transaction error.

Credit memo: a notification of an error that increases the checking account balance.

Debit memo: a notification of an error that decreases the checking account balance.

Automatic teller machine (ATM): an electronic banking station that accepts deposits and disburses cash when you use an authorized ATM card, a debit card, or some

Electronic deposit: a deposit that is made by an electronic transfer of funds.

Point-of-sale transaction: electronic transfer of funds when a sale is made.

Electronic funds transfer (EFT): a transaction that transfers funds electronically.

Withdrawal: a transaction that decreases a checking account balance; this transaction is also called a debit.

Debit: a transaction that decreases a checking account balance.

Check or bank draft: a banking form for recording the details of a withdrawal.

Payee: the one to whom the amount of money written on a check is paid.

Payor: the bank or institution that pays the amount of the check to the payee.

Maker: the one who is authorizing the payment of the check.

If the bank discovers an error in the deposit transaction, it will notify you of the correction through a **bank memo**. If the error correction increases your balance, the bank memo is called a **credit memo**. If the error correction decreases your balance, the bank memo is called a **debit memo**.

Deposits to bank accounts can be made electronically. Individuals or businesses may make deposits using a debit card or an **automatic teller machine (ATM)** card (Figure 4-3). Individuals may also request their employer to deposit their paychecks directly to their bank account by completing a form that gives the banking information, including the account number. Government agencies encourage recipients of Social Security and other government funds to have these funds **electronically deposited**. Businesses that permit customers to use credit cards to charge merchandise or subscribe to an automatic check processing service ordinarily receive payment through electronic deposit from the credit card or check processing company. These transactions are sometimes called **point-of-sale transactions**, because the money is transferred electronically when the sale is made. VISA, MasterCard, American Express, and Discover are examples of major credit card companies that electronically transmit funds to business accounts. Transactions made electronically are called **electronic funds transfers (EFTs)**.

02/25/13	14:08:30	0826
1845 KIRBY PARKWAY		
XXXXXXXXXXXXXX4143		
DEPOSIT 8202		$583.21
CHECKING		XXXXXX4293
CURRENT		$2,314.32
RESERVE AVAIL		$200.00
CREDITS TODAY		$583.21
AVAILABLE		$3,097.53

FIGURE 4-3
ATM Receipt Showing Deposited Funds

When money is taken from a checking account, this transaction is called a **withdrawal**. The bank refers to this transaction as a **debit**. A withdrawal or debit *decreases* the amount of the checking account. One bank record for withdrawals made by the account holder is called a **check or bank draft**. Figure 4-4 shows the basic features of a check.

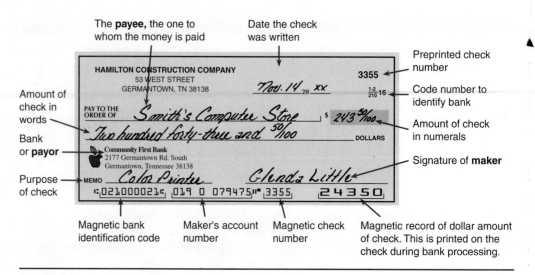

FIGURE 4-4
Bank Check

1. Enter the date of the check.
2. Enter the name of the payee.
3. Enter the amount of the check in numerals.
4. Write the amount of the check in words. Cents can be written as a fraction of a dollar or by using decimal notation.
5. Explain the purpose of the check.
6. Sign the check.

EXAMPLE 3   Write a check dated April 8, 20XX, to Disk-O-Mania in the amount of $84.97 for DVDs.

Enter the date: 4/8/20XX.
Write the name of the payee: Disk-O-Mania.
Enter the amount of the check in numerals: 84.97.
Enter the amount of the check in words. Note the fraction $\frac{97}{100}$ showing cents, or hundredths of a dollar: eighty-four and $\frac{97}{100}$.
Write the purpose of the check on the memo line: DVDs.
Sign your name.
The completed check is shown in Figure 4-5.

FIGURE 4-5
Completed Check

Signature card: a document that a bank keeps on file to verify the signatures of persons authorized to write checks on an account.

When a checking account is opened, those persons authorized to write checks on the account must sign a **signature card**, which is kept on file at the bank. Whenever a question arises regarding whether a person is authorized to write checks on an account, the bank refers to the signature card to resolve the question.

Automatic drafts: periodic withdrawals that the owner of an account authorizes to be made electronically.

Withdrawals from personal and business bank accounts can also be made electronically. Many persons elect to have regular monthly bills, such as their mortgage payment, rent, utilities, and insurance, paid electronically through **automatic drafts** from their bank account. The amount of the debit is shown on the bank statement. One-time electronic checks can be authorized when a company accepts an electronic check over the telephone. When this service is used, the bank routing number, your bank account number, and the amount of the check are given over the phone. Generally the customer is given a confirmation number to use if there is any dispute over the transaction. **Online banking services** are becoming more and more popular. These services allow you to pay bills and manage your account using the Internet. Accounts are accessible 24 hours a day, seven days a week. Bank statements are posted online and account holders can file them electronically or print paper copies.

Online banking services: a variety of services and transaction options that can be made through Internet banking.

Debit card: a card that can be used like a credit card but the amount of debit (purchase or withdrawal) is deducted immediately from the checking account.

Individuals may also use a **debit card** to pay for services and goods. A debit card looks very similar to a credit card and often even includes a credit card name and logo such as Visa. The debit card works just like a check except the transaction is handled electronically at the time the transaction is made. Debit card transactions generally require a **personal identification number (PIN)** to authorize the transaction. ATM/debit cards can be used to make deposits to checking or savings accounts, get cash withdrawals from checking or savings accounts, transfer funds between checking and savings accounts, make payments on bank loan accounts, and to get checking and savings account information. Debit cards can be used to make purchases in person, by phone, or by computer. Debit cards can also be used to get cash from merchants who permit it.

Personal identification number (PIN): a private code that is used to authorize a transaction on a debit card or ATM card.

Don't toss those ATM or debit card receipts! Customers are issued receipts when they deposit or withdraw money from an ATM. Use these receipts to update your account register and to verify your next bank statement. When you are certain the transaction has been properly posted by your bank, dispose of the receipts by shredding or by some other means to maintain the security of your banking record.

STOP AND CHECK

1. Complete the deposit ticket for Camryn Pastner (Figure 4-6). The deposit includes $987 in cash, $41.93 in coins, and three checks in the amounts of $48.17, $153.92, and $105.18. The deposit was made on July 5, 20XX. *See Example 1.*

FIGURE 4-6
Deposit Ticket

2. Complete the deposit ticket for SellIt.com (Figure 4-7). The deposit is made on April 11, 20XX, and includes the following items: cash: $821; and checks: Olson, $18.15; Drewrey, $38.15; Tinkler, $82.15; Brannon, $17.19; McCready, $38.57; Mowers, $132.86; Lee, $15.21; and Wang, $38.00. *See Example 2.*

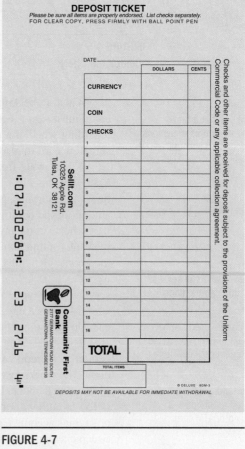

FIGURE 4-7
Deposit Ticket

See Example 3 for Exercises 3 and 4.

3. Write a check (Figure 4-8) dated October 18, 20XX, to Frances Johnson in the amount of $583.17 for a tool chest. Albert Adkins is the maker.

ABC Plumbing		4359
408 Jefferson		
Rexburg, ID 00000	_____ 20 _____	87-278/840
PAY TO THE ORDER OF _____	$	
_____		DOLLARS
First National Bank		
400 Washington		
Rexburg, ID 00000		
MEMO _____	_____	
⑈044503279⑈		

FIGURE 4-8
Check Number 4359

4. Max Murphy wrote a check dated August 18, 20XX, to Harley Davidson, Inc., for motorcycle parts. The amount of the check is $2,872.15. Complete the check in Figure 4-9 to show this transaction.

5. Describe some advantages of online banking.

Max's Motorcycle Shop		5887
1280 State Street		
Tulsa, OK 00000	_____ 20 _____	87-278/840
PAY TO THE ORDER OF _____	$	
_____		DOLLARS
Tulsa State Bank		
295 Adams Street		
Tulsa, OK 00000		
MEMO _____	_____	
⑈584325911⑈		

FIGURE 4-9
Check Number 5887

2 Record account transactions.

Businesses and individuals who have banking accounts must record all transactions made to the account.

Check-writing supplies are available for handwritten, typed, or computer-generated checks. One type of checkbook has a **check stub** for each check. The check stub is used to record account transactions; computer-generated checks also produce a check stub. Another form for recording transactions is an **account or transaction register**. The account register is separate from the check but includes the same information as a check stub. Electronic money management systems generally produce a check stub and keep an account register automatically from the information entered on the check.

Check stub: a form attached to a check for recording checking account transactions that shows the account balance.

Account or transaction register: a separate form for recording all checking account transactions. It also shows the account balance.

TIP

Stub versus Register

The check-stub method for recording account transactions works well when you only make withdrawals using checks. If withdrawals are made with a debit card, an ATM card, or with online or electronic checks, there is no place to record these transactions on the normal check stub. A check register allows you to record all different types of transactions.

HOW TO   Record account transactions on a check stub or an account register

For checks and other debits:

1. Make an entry for every account transaction.
2. Enter the date, the amount of the check or debit, the person or company that will receive the check or debit, and the purpose of the check or debit.
3. Subtract the amount of the check or debit from the previous balance to obtain the new balance.
4. For handwritten checks with stubs, carry the new balance forward to the next stub.

For deposits or other credits:

1. Make an entry for every account transaction.
2. Enter the date, the amount of the deposit or credit, and a brief explanation of the deposit or credit.
3. Add the amount of the deposit or credit to the previous balance to obtain the new balance.

On an electronic money management system:

1. Enter the appropriate details for producing a check.
2. Record other debits and all deposits and credits. The account register is maintained by the system automatically.
3. For business accounts or personal accounts that are used for tracking expenses, record the type of expense or budget account number.

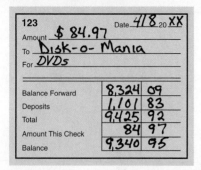

FIGURE 4-10
Completed Stub

TIP

Keep Accurate, Up-to-Date Account Records

The key to maintaining control of your banking account balance is to record and track every transaction. In today's busy world, it is easy to use a debit card or online banking to make many charges in a short time. Recording every transaction *when it is made* will help you keep track of your balance.

EXAMPLE 4   Complete the stub (Figure 4-10) for the check written in the preceding example. The balance forward is $8,324.09. Deposits of $325, $694.30, and $82.53 were made after the previous check was written.

The check number, 123, is preprinted in this case.
Enter the date: 4/8/20XX.
Enter the amount of this check: $84.97.
Enter the payee: Disk-O-Mania.
Enter the purpose: DVDs.
Enter the balance forward if it has not already been entered: $8,324.09
Enter the total of the deposits: $1,101.83.
Add the balance forward and the deposits to find the total: $9,425.92.
Enter the amount of this check: $84.97.
Subtract the amount of the check from the total to find the balance: $9,340.95.

The completed stub is shown in Figure 4-10. Carry the balance to the next stub as the Balance Forward.

Account registers for individual account holders are generally supplied with an order of personalized checks. Most banks also supply an account register upon request. Account registers can be set up in Excel® or accounting software such as Quickbooks® to maintain banking records electronically.

EXAMPLE 5   Complete the account register in Figure 4-11 to record a tax refund deposit on March 31 for $325, a paycheck deposit on April 3 for $694.30, a travel reimbursement deposit on April 5 for $82.53, and check #123 written to Disk-O-Mania on April 8 in the amount of $84.97.

		RECORD ALL TRANSACTIONS THAT AFFECT YOUR ACCOUNT							
NUMBER	DATE	DESCRIPTION OF TRANSACTION	DEBIT (−)	√ T	FEE (IF ANY) (−)	CREDIT (+)		BALANCE	
								8,324	09
	3/31	Deposit				325	00	+325	00
		tax refund						8,649	09
	4/3	Deposit				694	30	+694	30
		paycheck						9,343	39
	4/5	Deposit				82	53	+82	53
		travel reimbursement						9,425	92
123	4/8	Disk-O-Mania	84	97				−84	97
		DVDs						9,340	95

FIGURE 4-11
Check Register

TIP

I'll Do It Later

The details of a check or debit should be recorded in the account register as soon as the transaction is made. Write checks in numerical order to make it easier to verify that all checks have been recorded in the account register or on the check stub.

Detaching checks from the checkbook and using them out of order creates a greater risk for errors and oversights.

For transactions made with a debit card, keep the receipts in a specified place. Make handwritten notes on these receipts as appropriate. Your checkbook or account register wallet is a good temporary place to keep receipts until the transactions have been properly recorded.

As banking becomes increasingly complex and more electronic and the penalty for overdrawing bank accounts escalates, it becomes more important to carefully maintain an account register of all transactions. Debit cards are very common as a substitute for checks. With the increased use of electronic transactions, it becomes more important to keep systematic records of all account transactions. Thus, the account register can be used to record transactions made while away from your computer. Then the computer can be used to calculate balances as new transactions are entered.

Before a check can be cashed, it must be **endorsed**. That is, the payee must sign or stamp the check on the back. There are several ways to endorse a check. The simplest way is for the payee to sign the back of the check exactly as the payee's name is written on the front of the check. Banks generally cash checks drawn on their own bank or checks presented by payees who are account holders. A bank cashing checks drawn on its own bank normally requires the payees to present appropriate identification if they are not account holders at that bank. Banks will cash checks drawn on a different bank for payees who are account holders and require the payee's account number to be written below the signature. The payee's account will be debited if the check is returned unpaid.

Appropriate identification is required for receiving cash from an account or for cashing a check. This identification is also required for opening an account. The Patriot Act of 2001 now requires financial institutions to follow specific identification procedures. Most banks require two forms of identification (ID), with at least one being a primary form of identification. An acceptable primary ID must include a photo and be issued by a government agency. Some examples are a state driver's license or ID, a military ID, or a passport or visa. Some secondary forms of identification are a credit card, utility bill, property tax bill, or employer ID.

Although banking procedures are designed to prevent misuse of checks, it is a good idea to use a **restricted endorsement** for signing checks. One type of restricted endorsement changes the payee of the check. The original payee writes "pay to the order of," lists the name of the new payee, and then signs the check. This choice would be used when you want to assign the check to someone else. Another type of restricted endorsement is used for depositing the check into the payee's bank account. The payee writes "for deposit only," lists the account number, and then endorses the check. Most banking practices only allow checks to be deposited to a business account if they have a business listed as the payee. That is, they do not allow cash to be received for a check made out to a business. For greater security most businesses endorse checks as soon as they are received. Many businesses imprint the endorsement on checks using an electronic cash register or an ink stamp.

The Federal Reserve Board regulates the way endorsements can be placed on checks. As Figure 4-12 shows, the endorsement must be placed within $1\frac{1}{2}$ inches of the left edge of the check. The rest of the back of the check is reserved for bank endorsements. Many check-printing companies now mark this space and provide lines for endorsements.

Electronic checks do not require the same type of endorsement. PINs and knowledge of bank routing numbers and account numbers are used to maintain security with electronic transactions.

Endorsement: a signature, stamp, or electronic imprint on the back of a check that authorizes payment in cash or directs payment to a third party or account.

Restricted endorsement: a type of endorsement that reassigns the check to a different payee or directs the check to be deposited to a specified account.

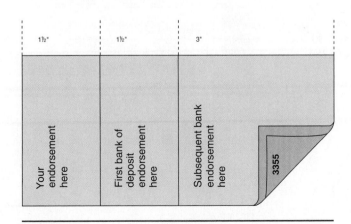

FIGURE 4-12
The Back of a Check Showing Areas for Endorsements

STOP AND CHECK

See Example 4 for Exercises 1 and 2.

1. Examine the check stub in Figure 4-13 to answer these questions.
   a. How much is check 1492 written for?

   b. What was the account balance from the previous transaction?

   c. What is the new balance?

1492		Date Mar 15 20 XX
Amount $152.87		
To Brown's Shoes		
For Shoes		
Balance Forward	2,896	15
Deposits	+800	00
Total	3,696	15
Amount This Check	−152	87
Balance	3,543	28

FIGURE 4-13
Check Stub Number 1492

2. Complete the check stub for check 4359 (Figure 4-14) written to Frances Johnson on October 18, 20XX, in the amount of $583.17 for a tool chest.

4359		Date_____20____
Amount _____		
To _____		
For _____		
Balance Forward	5,902	08
Deposits		
Total		
Amount This Check		
Balance		

FIGURE 4-14
Check Stub Number 4359

See Example 5 for Exercises 3 and 4.

3. Complete the account register in Figure 4-15 to record check 5887 written on August 18, 20XX, to Harley Davidson, Inc., for motorcycle parts that cost $2,872.15. Also record a debit card entry of $498.31 made on August 20, 20XX, to Remmie Raynor for pool services.

RECORD ALL TRANSACTIONS THAT AFFECT YOUR ACCOUNT

NUMBER	DATE	DESCRIPTION OF TRANSACTION	DEBIT (−)	√T	FEE (IF ANY) (−)	CREDIT (+)	BALANCE	

FIGURE 4-15
Account Register

4. Complete the account register in Figure 4-16 to show the purchase of a tool chest for $583.17 using check number 4359 written to Frances Johnson on October 8, 20XX. Also record an ATM withdrawal of $250 on October 8, 20XX.

RECORD ALL TRANSACTIONS THAT AFFECT YOUR ACCOUNT

NUMBER	DATE	DESCRIPTION OF TRANSACTION	DEBIT (−)	√T	FEE (IF ANY) (−)	CREDIT (+)	BALANCE	
							5,108	31
4358	10/6	Quesha Blunt	49 80				−49	80
		Cleaning Service					5,058	51
Dep	10/6	Deposit				843 57	+843	57
		travel reimb.					5,902	08

FIGURE 4-16
Account Register

4-1 SECTION EXERCISES

SKILL BUILDERS

1. On April 29, 20XX, Mr. Yan Yu deposited $850.00 in cash, $8.63 in coins, and two checks, one in the amount of $157.38, the other in the amount of $32.49. Fill out Mr. Yu's deposit ticket for April 29, 20XX (Figure 4-17). *See Example 1.*

DEPOSIT TICKET

Yan Yu
1428 Central Ave.
Germantown, TN 38138

DATE ______________ 20____
DEPOSITS MAY NOT BE AVAILABLE FOR IMMEDIATE WITHDRAWAL

SIGN HERE FOR CASH RECEIVED (IF REQUIRED)

CASH	CURRENCY		
	COIN		
LIST CHECKS SINGLY			
TOTAL FROM OTHER SIDE			
TOTAL			
LESS CASH RECEIVED			
NET DEPOSIT			

26-2/840

USE OTHER SIDE FOR ADDITIONAL LISTING

BE SURE EACH ITEM IS PROPERLY ENDORSED

DELUXE HD-17

Community First Bank
2177 Germantown Road • 7808 Farmington
Germantown, TN 38138 • (901) 754-2400 • Member FDIC

⑆084000063⑆ 1579⑈ 5

CHECKS AND OTHER ITEMS ARE RECEIVED FOR DEPOSIT SUBJECT TO THE PROVISIONS OF THE UNIFORM COMMERCIAL CODE OR ANY APPLICABLE COLLECTION AGREEMENT.

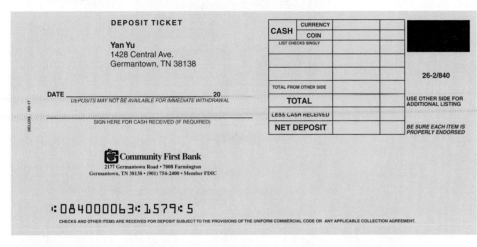

FIGURE 4-17
Deposit Ticket for Yan Yu

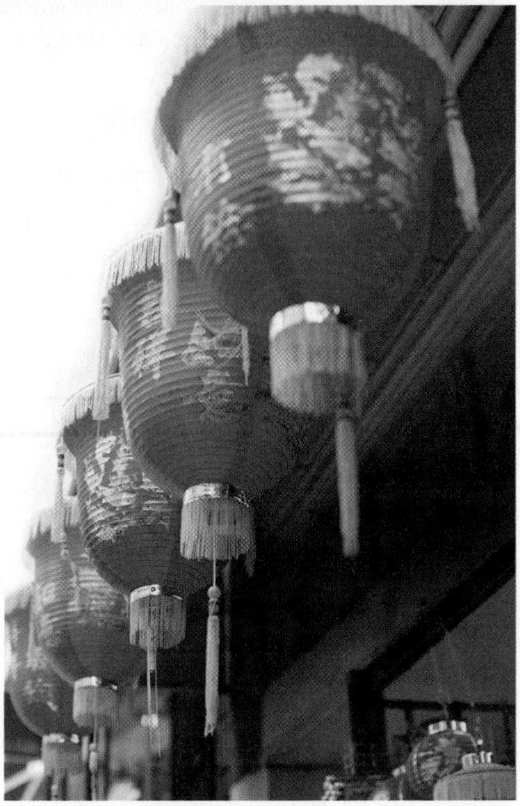

2. Complete the deposit ticket for Delectables Candies in Figure 4-18. The deposit is made on March 31, 20XX, and includes the following items: cash: $196.00; and checks: Cavanaugh, $14.72; Bryan, $31.18; Wossum, $16.97; Wright, $28.46; Howell, $17.21; Coe, $32.17; Beulke, $17.84; Palinchak, $31.96; and Paszel, $19.16. *See Example 2.*

DEPOSIT TICKET
Please be sure all items are properly endorsed. List checks separately.
FOR CLEAR COPY, PRESS FIRMLY WITH BALL POINT PEN

DATE ______________

	DOLLARS	CENTS
CURRENCY		
COIN		
CHECKS		
1		
2		
3		
4		
5		
6		
7		
8		
9		
10		
11		
12		
13		
14		
15		
16		
17		
18		
19		
20		
TOTAL		

TOTAL ITEMS

DELECTABLES CANDIES
5981 POPLAR AVE.
MEMPHIS, TN 38121

87-278/840

Community First Bank
2177 GERMANTOWN ROAD SOUTH
GERMANTOWN, TENNESSEE 38138

Checks and other items are received for deposit subject to the provisions of the Uniform Commercial Code or any applicable collection agreement.

© DELUXE

DEPOSITS MAY NOT BE AVAILABLE FOR IMMEDIATE WITHDRAWAL

⑆084002781⑆ 11 2118 3⑈

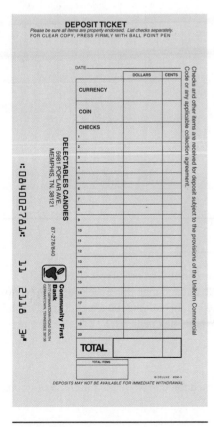

FIGURE 4-18
Deposit Ticket for Delectables Candies

See Example 3 for Exercises 3 and 4.

3. On April 29, 20XX, after Mr. Yu made his deposit (see Exercise 1), he wrote a check to Green Harvest in the amount of $155.30 for fresh vegetables. Write a check (Figure 4-19) as Mr. Yu wrote it.

Park's Oriental Shop
1428 Central Ave.
Germantown, TN 38138

456

______________ 20 ______ 87-278/840

PAY TO THE ORDER OF ______________________________ $

______________________________ DOLLARS

Community First Bank
2177 Germantown Rd. South
Germantown, Tennessee 38138

MEMO ______________ ______________

⑆084002781⑆

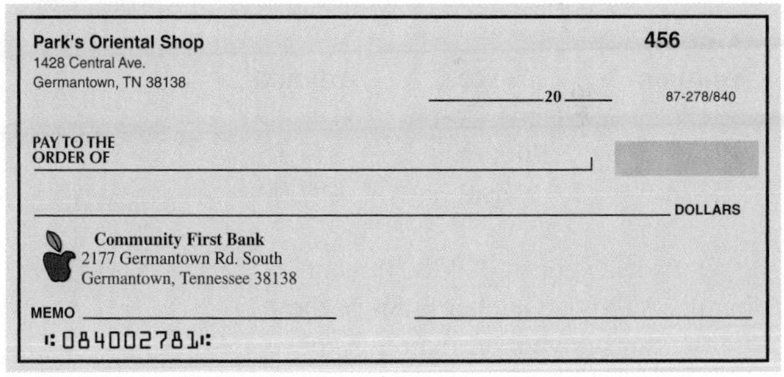

FIGURE 4-19
Check Number 456

4. Write a check dated June 20, 20XX, to Ronald H. Cox Realty in the amount of $596.13 for house repairs (Figure 4-20).

Your Name
5983 Macon Cove
Yellville, TX 00000

3215

______________ 20 ______ 87-278/840

PAY TO THE ORDER OF ______________________________ $

______________________________ DOLLARS

Community First Bank
2177 Germantown Rd. South
Germantown, Tennessee 38138

MEMO ______________ ______________

⑆084003218⑆

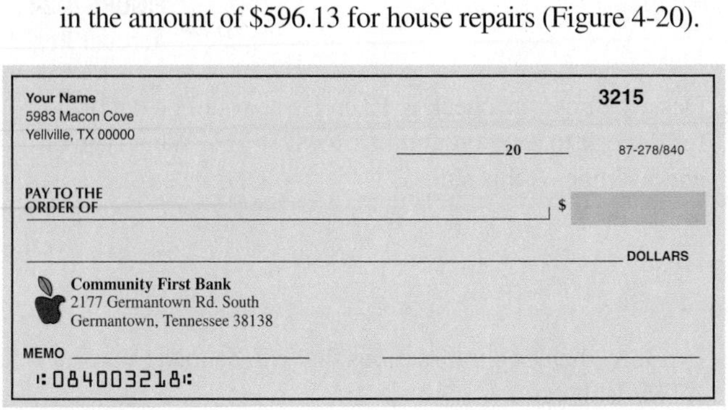

FIGURE 4-20
Check Number 3215

See Example 4 for Exercises 5 and 6.

5. Before Mr. Yu made his deposit (see Exercise 1), the balance in the account was $7,869.40. Complete the check stub for the deposit made in Exercise 1 and the check he wrote in Exercise 3 (Figure 4-21).

456	Date _____ 20 ____
Amount _____	
To _____	
For _____	
Balance Forward	
Deposits	
Total	
Amount This Check	
Balance	

FIGURE 4-21
Check Stub Number 456

6. Complete the check stub for the check you wrote in Exercise 4 if the balance brought forward is $2,213.56 (Figure 4-22).

3215	Date _____ 20 ____
Amount _____	
To _____	
For _____	
Balance Forward	
Deposits	
Total	
Amount This Check	
Balance	

FIGURE 4-22
Check Stub Number 3215

See Example 5 for Exercises 7 and 8.

7. Enter in the account register in Figure 4-23 all the transactions described in Exercises 1, 3, and 5 and find the ending balance.

RECORD ALL TRANSACTIONS THAT AFFECT YOUR ACCOUNT

NUMBER	DATE	DESCRIPTION OF TRANSACTION	DEBIT	√	FEE	CREDIT	BALANCE
			$			$	

FIGURE 4-23
Account Register

8. On September 30 you deposited your payroll check of $932.15. You then wrote the following checks on the same day:

Check Number	Payee	Amount
3176	Electric Co-op.	$107.13
3177	Pilot Oil	$47.15
3178	Visa	$97.00

You made a deposit of $280 at your bank's ATM on October 3. Show these transactions in your account register in Figure 4-24, and show the ending balance if your beginning balance was $435.97.

RECORD ALL TRANSACTIONS THAT AFFECT YOUR ACCOUNT

NUMBER	DATE	DESCRIPTION OF TRANSACTION	DEBIT (−)	√ T	FEE (IF ANY) (−)	CREDIT (+)	BALANCE

FIGURE 4-24
Account Register

9. Describe how the check in Exercise 4 would be endorsed for deposit to account number 26-8224021. What type of endorsement is this called?

10. If you were the owner of Green Harvest (Exercise 3), would you be able to exchange this check for cash? If so, describe how you would endorse the check. If not, explain how you could handle the check.

11. List three banking transactions that can be made with an ATM/debit card.

12. How can you use a debit card to make purchase of goods?

LEARNING OUTCOME

1 Reconcile a bank statement with an account register.

Financial institutions provide account statements to their checking account customers to enable account holders to reconcile any differences between that statement and the customer's own account register. These statements are either mailed or provided online.

Many persons or businesses monitor their bank transactions on a daily basis through online access to their accounts. They still use the monthly statements as documentation of their transactions.

1   Reconcile a bank statement with an account register.

Bank statement: an account record periodically provided by the bank for matching your records with the bank's records.

The primary tool for reconciling an account is the **bank statement**, a listing of all transactions that take place in the customer's account. It includes checks and other debits and deposits and other credits.

Most bank statements explain the various letter codes and symbols contained in the statement. One of the first steps to take when you receive a bank statement is to check this explanatory section for any terms that you do not understand in the statement.

Service charge: a fee the bank charges for maintaining the checking account or for other banking services.

One of the items that may appear on a bank statement is a **service charge**. This is a fee the bank charges for maintaining the checking account; it may be a standard monthly fee, a charge for each check or transaction, or some combination.

Returned check: a deposited check that was returned because the maker's account did not have sufficient funds.

Returned check fee: a fee the bank charges the depositor for returned checks.

Nonsufficient funds (NSF) fee: a fee charged to the account holder when a check is written for which there are not sufficient funds.

Another type of bank charge appearing on a bank statement is for checks that "bounce" (are not backed by sufficient funds). Suppose Joe writes you a check and you cash the check or deposit it. Later your bank is notified that Joe does not have enough money in his bank account to cover the check. So Joe's bank returns the check to your bank. Such a check is called a **returned check**. Your bank will deduct the amount of the returned check from your account. Your bank may also deduct a **returned check fee** from your account to cover the cost of handling this transaction. If you write a check for which you do not have sufficient funds in your account, your bank will charge you a **nonsufficient funds (NSF) fee**. The bank notifies you through a debit memo of the decrease in your account balance.

It has become standard procedure for many companies and businesses, as an added employee benefit, to have their employees' paychecks or earnings automatically deposited into the employees' bank accounts. This is called an electronic funds transfer (EFT). Your bank statement also reflects electronic funds transfers such as withdrawals and deposits made using an **automatic teller machine (ATM)**, debit cards, wire transfers, online transfers, and authorized electronic withdrawals and deposits.

Outstanding checks: checks and debits that have been written and given to the payee but have not been processed at the bank or presented for payment.

What does *not* appear on the bank statement is the amount of any check you wrote or deposit you made that reaches the bank *after* the statement is printed. Such transactions may be called **outstanding checks** or **deposits**. This is one reason the balance shown on your bank statement and your account register may not agree initially.

Outstanding deposits: deposits and credits that have been made but have not yet been posted to the maker's account. They may also be called *deposits in transit*.

When a bank statement and an account register do not agree initially, you need to take steps to make them agree. The process of making the bank statement agree with the account register is called reconciling a bank statement or **bank reconciliation**.

Bank reconciliation: the process of making the account register agree with the bank statement.

Bank statements are not always issued on a calendar month basis. Most business bank statements are compiled as of the end of the month. Personal bank statements cover a month's transactions, but may begin and end on any day. For instance, a statement may cover May 18 through June 17 for one month. You may review your account transactions at any time using Internet online access or telephone access to your account. This service allows you to reconcile your account at any time.

The first thing to do when you receive a bank statement or review your account online is to go over it and compare its contents with your account register. You can check off all the checks and deposits listed on the statement by using the ✓ column in the account register (refer to Figure 4-11) or by marking the check stub.

There are several methods for reconciling your banking records. We will use a method that uses an account reconciliation form. Figure 4-25 shows a sample bank statement reconciliation form. A reconciliation form is often printed on the back of the bank statement. The bank's form leads you through a reconciliation process that may be slightly different from the one given in this book, but the result is the same: a reconciled statement.

	BALANCE AS SHOWN ON BANK STATEMENT		BALANCE AS SHOWN IN YOUR REGISTER	$
$				
	ADD TOTAL OF OUTSTANDING DEPOSITS		SUBTRACT AMOUNT OF SERVICE CHARGE	
	NEW TOTAL		NEW TOTAL	
	SUBTRACT TOTAL OF OUTSTANDING CHECKS		ADJUSTMENTS IF ANY	
	YOUR ADJUSTED STATEMENT BALANCE	SHOULD EQUAL	YOUR ADJUSTED REGISTER BALANCE	

Outstanding Deposits (Credits)			Outstanding Checks (Debits)		
Date	Amount		Check Number	Date	Amount
	$				$
Total	$			Total	$

FIGURE 4-25
Account Reconciliation Form

HOW TO   Reconcile a bank statement

1. Check off all matching transactions appearing on both the bank statement and the account register.
2. Enter into the register the transactions appearing on the bank statement that have not been checked off. Check off these transactions in the register as they are entered. Update the register balance accordingly. This is the **adjusted register balance.**
3. Make a list of all the checks and other debits appearing in the register that have not been checked off. Add the amounts on the list to find the *total outstanding debits*. Use Figure 4-25 as a guide.
4. Make a list of all the deposits and other credits appearing in the register that have not been checked off in step 1. Add the amounts on the list to find the *total outstanding credits*. Use Figure 4-25 as a guide.
5. Calculate the *adjusted statement balance* by adding the statement balance and the total outstanding deposits and other credits, and then subtracting the total outstanding checks and other debits: **Adjusted statement balance = statement balance + total outstanding credits − total outstanding debits.**
6. Compare the adjusted statement balance with the adjusted register balance. These amounts should be equal.
7. If the adjusted statement balance does not equal the register balance, locate the cause of the discrepancy and correct the register or notify the bank accordingly.
8. Write *statement reconciled* on the next blank line in the account register and record the statement date.

TIP

Finding Discrepancies

When your adjusted statement balance does not equal your account register balance, you need to locate the cause of the discrepancy and correct the register accordingly.

To do so, first be sure you have calculated the adjusted statement balance accurately. Double-check, for instance, that the list of outstanding debits is complete and their sum is accurate. Double-check the list of outstanding credits, too. Double-check that you correctly added the total outstanding credits and subtracted the total outstanding debits from the statement balance. If you are sure you have carried out all the reconciliation steps correctly, the discrepancy may be from an error that you made in the account register or from an error made by the bank. Here are some common errors and strategies to locate them.

Error: You entered a transaction in the register, but you did not update the account register balance.

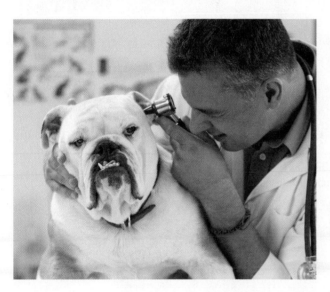

When using software programs to keep banking records, the user enters transaction amounts into the computer, and the program updates the register balance. At reconciliation time, the user enters information from the bank statement into the computer, and the program reconciles the bank statement with the account register.

These programs can also be useful for budgeting and tax purposes. Transactions can be categorized and tracked according to the user's specifications. Monthly and yearly budgets can be prepared accordingly, for both individuals and businesses. At tax time, these programs may even be used to generate tax forms.

EXAMPLE 1 Pope Animal Clinic regularly transfers money from its checking account to a special account used for one-time expenditures such as equipment. The decision to transfer is made each month when the bank statement is reconciled. Money is transferred only if the adjusted statement balance exceeds $2,500; all the excess is transferred. The bank statement is shown in Figure 4-27, and the register is shown in Figure 4-28. Should money be transferred? If so, how much?

What You Know	What You Are Looking For	Solution Plan
Bank statement transactions (Figure 4-27) and register transactions (Figure 4-28)	The adjusted statement balance and the adjusted checkbook balance.	Adjusted statement balance = statement balance + total outstanding credits − total outstanding debits. (Figure 4-26).
Balance in excess of $2,500 is transferred.	Should money be transferred? If so, how much?	Transfer any amount that is more than $2,500.

Solution

Check off all matching transactions appearing on both the statement and the register (Figures 4-27 and 4-28).

Now enter into the register the transactions appearing on the bank statement that have not been checked off. The service fee is the only transaction not checked off. As you enter it into the register, check it off the bank statement and the register. Now use the account reconciliation form (Figure 4-26) to list the outstanding credits and debits: transactions appearing on the register that have not been checked off.

The adjusted statement balance is more than $2,500.

Money should be transferred. Because the excess over $2,500 should be transferred, **the amount to be transferred is** $3,167.85 − $2,500, or **$667.85.**

FIGURE 4-26
Account Reconciliation Form

FIGURE 4-27
Matching Transactions Checked Off the Bank Statement

TIP

Make Your Own Checklist on a Bank Statement

Although the bank statement does not have a ✓ column, it is helpful to verify that every transaction is recorded in the account register by checking each item on the bank statement as it is checked in the register.

The check method on both the bank statement and the account register makes it easier to identify errors, omissions, and outstanding transactions.

FIGURE 4-28
Reconciled Account Register

STOP AND CHECK

The bank statement for Katherine Adam's Apparel Shop is shown in Figure 4-29. See Example 1.

1. How many deposits were made during the month?

2. What amount of interest was earned?

3. How much were the total deposits?

4. How many checks appear on the bank statement?

5. What is the balance at the beginning of the statement period?

6. What is the balance at the end of the statement period?

7. What is the amount of check 8214?

8. On what date did check 8219 clear the bank?

9. Kroger Stores permit customers to get cash with a debit card. Lindy Rascoe has an ATM/debit card from her bank in Illinois. Can she use the card to get $200 cash at the Kroger checkout counter in her college town of Fresno, California?

10. The account register for Katherine Adam's Apparel Shop is shown in Figure 4-30. Update the register and reconcile the bank statement (see Figure 4-29) with the account register using the account reconciliation form in Figure 4-31.

Community First Bank

2177 Germantown Rd. South • Germantown, Tennessee 38138 • (901) 555-2400 • Member FDIC

KATHERINE ADAM'S APPAREL SHOP
1396 MALL OF AMERICA
MINNEAPOLIS, MN

ACCOUNT NUMBER   12-324134523
FEDERAL ID NUMBER   XX-XXXX2445   DATE 6/30/20XX   PAGE 1

		BALANCE OF YOUR FUNDS
PREVIOUS BALANCE -----		700.81
4	DEPOSITS TOTALING	8,218.00
5	WITHDRAWALS TOTALING	5,433.08
NEW BALANCE -----------		3,485.73

ACCOUNT TRANSACTIONS FOR THE PERIOD FROM 6/1/20XX THROUGH 6/30/20XX

DATE	AMOUNT	DESCRIPTION
6/1	1,830.00	DEPOSIT
6/5	2,583.00	DEPOSIT
6/15	3,800.00	DEPOSIT
6/30	5.00	INTEREST EARNED

DATE	CHECK #	AMOUNT	DATE	CHECK #	AMOUNT
6/2	8213	647.93	6/12	8217*	416.83
6/3	8214	490.00	6/20	8219*	3,150.00
6/5	8215	728.32			

CHECKING DAILY BALANCE SUMMARY

DATE	BALANCE OF YOUR FUNDS	DATE	BALANCE OF YOUR FUNDS
6/1	2,530.81	6/12	2,830.73
6/2	1,882.88	6/15	6,630.73
6/3	1,392.88	6/20	3,480.73
6/5	3,247.56	6/30	3,485.73

FIGURE 4-29
Bank Statement for Katherine Adam's Apparel Shop

RECORD ALL TRANSACTIONS THAT AFFECT YOUR ACCOUNT

NUMBER	DATE	DESCRIPTION OF TRANSACTION	DEBIT (-)	√ T	FEE (IF ANY) (-)	CREDIT (+)	BALANCE	
							700	81
8213	5/28	Lands End	647 93				-647	93
							52	88
Deposit	6/1	Receipts				1,830 00	+1,830	00
							1,882	88
8214	6/1	Collier Management Co.	490 00				-490	00
							1,392	88
8215	6/3	Jinkins Wholesale	728 32				-728	32
							664	56
Deposit	6/5	Receipts				2583 00	+2,583	00
							3,247	56
8216	6/15	Minneapolis Utility Co.	257 13				-257	13
							2,990	43
8217	6/10	State of MN	416 83				-416	83
							2573	60
Deposit	6/15	Receipts				3,800 00	+3,800	00
							6,373	60
8218	6/15	Tracie Burke Salary	2,000 00				-2,000	00
							4,373	60
8219	6/20	Brown's Wholesale	3,150 00				-3,150	00
							1,223	60
Deposit	7/2	Receipts				1,720 00	+1,720	00
							2943	60

FIGURE 4-30
Account Register for Katherine Adam's Apparel Shop

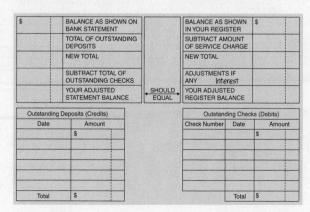

$	BALANCE AS SHOWN ON BANK STATEMENT	BALANCE AS SHOWN IN YOUR REGISTER	$
	TOTAL OF OUTSTANDING DEPOSITS	SUBTRACT AMOUNT OF SERVICE CHARGE	
	NEW TOTAL	NEW TOTAL	
	SUBTRACT TOTAL OF OUTSTANDING CHECKS	ADJUSTMENTS IF ANY Interest	
	YOUR ADJUSTED STATEMENT BALANCE	YOUR ADJUSTED REGISTER BALANCE	

SHOULD EQUAL

Outstanding Deposits (Credits)	
Date	Amount
	$
Total	$

Outstanding Checks (Debits)		
Check Number	Date	Amount
		$
	Total	$

FIGURE 4-31
Account Reconciliation Form

SKILL BUILDERS

Use Tom Deskin's bank statement (Figure 4-32) for Exercises 1 to 3.

1. Does Tom pay bills through EFT? If so, which ones?

2. Did Tom use the ATM during the month? If so, what transactions were made and for what amounts?

3. What were the lowest and highest daily bank balances for the month?

4. A bank statement shows a balance of $12.32. The service charge for the month was $2.95. The account register shows deposits of $300, $100, and $250 that do not appear on the statement. Outstanding checks are in the amount of $36.52, $205.16, $18.92, $25.93, and $200. The register balance is $178.74. Find the adjusted statement balance and the adjusted register balance. Use one of the account reconciliation forms in Figure 4-34. *See Example 1.*

5. Tom Deskin's account register is shown in Figure 4-33. Use one of the account reconciliation forms in Figure 4-34 to reconcile the bank statement in Figure 4-32 with the account register.

Community First Bank

2177 Germantown Rd. South • Germantown, Tennessee 38138 • (901) 555-2400 • Member FDIC

Tom Deskin
1234 South Street
Germantown, TN 38138

ACCOUNT NUMBER   13-2882139
SOCIAL SECURITY NUMBER   SECURED   DATE 9-29-20XX   PAGE 1

		BALANCE OF YOUR FUNDS
PREVIOUS BALANCE -----		$2,472.86
3	DEPOSITS TOTALING	4,812.12
15	WITHDRAWALS TOTALING	4,684.40
NEW BALANCE -----------		$2,600.58

ACCOUNT TRANSACTIONS FOR THE PERIOD FROM 8-28-20XX THROUGH 9-27-20XX

DATE	AMOUNT	DESCRIPTION
9/1	2,401.32	DEPOSIT - SCHERING-PLOUGH PAYROLL 213446688
9/1	942.18	WITHDRAWAL - LEADER FEDERAL MTG PMT 314123
9/4	217.17	WITHDRAWAL - LG&W PMT 21814
9/15	2,401.32	DEPOSIT - SCHERING-PLOUGH PAYROLL 213446688
9/20	60.00	WITHDRAWAL - ATM KIRBY WOODS
9/27	9.48	INTEREST EARNED

DATE	CHECK #	AMOUNT	DATE	CHECK #	AMOUNT	DATE	CHECK #	AMOUNT
8/31	1094	42.37	9/10	1099	583.21	9/25	1106*	1,238.42
9/2	1095	12.96	9/16	1100	283.21	9/25	1107	500.00
9/5	1096	36.01	9/18	1102*	48.23			
9/5	1097	178.13	9/21	1103	71.16			
9/5	1098	458.60	9/23	1104	12.75			

CHECKING DAILY BALANCE SUMMARY

DATE	BALANCE OF YOUR FUNDS	DATE	BALANCE OF YOUR FUNDS
8/28	2,472.86	9/15	4,804.87
8/31	2,430.49	9/16	4,521.66
9/1	3,889.63	9/18	4,473.43
9/2	3,876.67	9/20	4,413.43
9/4	3,659.50	9/21	4,342.27
9/5	2,986.76	9/23	4,329.52
9/10	2,403.55	9/25	2,591.10
		9/27	2,600.58

FIGURE 4-32
Tom Deskin's Bank Statement

RECORD ALL TRANSACTIONS THAT AFFECT YOUR ACCOUNT

NUMBER	DATE	DESCRIPTION OF TRANSACTION	DEBIT (−)	√T	FEE (IF ANY) (−)	CREDIT (+)	BALANCE
							2,472 86
1094	8/28	K-mart	42 37				−42 37
							2,430 49
1095	8/28	Walgreen's	12 96				−12 96
							2,417 53
Deposit	9/1	Payroll Schering-Plough				2,401 32	+2,401 32
							4,818 85
AW	9/1	Leader Federal	942 18				−942 18
							3,876 67
AW	9/1	LG & W	217 17				−217 17
							3,659 50
1096	9/1	Kroger	36 01				−36 01
							3,623 49
1097	9/1	Texaco	178 13				−178 13
							3,445 36
1098	9/1	Univ. of Memphis	458 60				−458 60
							2,986 76
1099	9/5	GMAC Credit Corp	583 21				−583 21
							2,403 55
1100	9/8	Visa	283 21				−283 21
							2,120 34
1101	9/10	Radio Shack	189 37				−189 37
							1,930 97
1102	9/10	Auto Zone	48 23				−48 23
							1,882 74
Deposit	9/15	Payroll - Schering Plough				2,401 32	+2,401 32
							4,284 06

REMEMBER TO RECORD AUTOMATIC PAYMENTS/DEPOSITS ON DATE AUTHORIZED.

RECORD ALL TRANSACTIONS THAT AFFECT YOUR ACCOUNT

NUMBER	DATE	DESCRIPTION OF TRANSACTION	DEBIT (−)	√T	FEE (IF ANY) (−)	CREDIT (+)	BALANCE
							4,284 06
1103	9/15	Geoffrey Beane	71 16				−71 16
							4,212 90
1104	9/14	Heaven Scent Flowers	12 75				−12 75
							4,200 15
1105	9/20	Kroger	87 75				−87 75
							4,112 40
ATM	9/20	Kirby Woods	60 00				−60 00
							4,052 40
1106	9/21	Traveler's Insurance	1,238 42				−1,238 42
							2,813 98
1107	9/23	Nation's Bank - Savings	500 00				−500 00
							2,313 98

FIGURE 4-33
Tom Deskin's Account Register

Exercise 4

$	BALANCE AS SHOWN ON BANK STATEMENT		BALANCE AS SHOWN IN YOUR REGISTER	$
	TOTAL OF OUTSTANDING DEPOSITS		SUBTRACT AMOUNT OF SERVICE CHARGE	
	NEW TOTAL		NEW TOTAL	
	SUBTRACT TOTAL OF OUTSTANDING CHECKS		ADJUSTMENTS IF ANY Interest	
	YOUR ADJUSTED STATEMENT BALANCE	=	YOUR ADJUSTED REGISTER BALANCE	

Outstanding Deposits (Credits)	
Date	Amount
	$
Total	$

Outstanding Checks (Debits)		
Check Number	Date	Amount
		$
	Total	$

Exercise 5

$	BALANCE AS SHOWN ON BANK STATEMENT		BALANCE AS SHOWN IN YOUR REGISTER	$
	TOTAL OF OUTSTANDING DEPOSITS		SUBTRACT AMOUNT OF SERVICE CHARGE	
	NEW TOTAL		NEW TOTAL	
	SUBTRACT TOTAL OF OUTSTANDING CHECKS		ADJUSTMENTS IF ANY Interest	
	YOUR ADJUSTED STATEMENT BALANCE	=	YOUR ADJUSTED REGISTER BALANCE	

Outstanding Deposits (Credits)	
Date	Amount
	$
Total	$

Outstanding Checks (Debits)		
Check Number	Date	Amount
		$
	Total	$

FIGURE 4-34
Tom Deskin's Reconciliation Form

Learning Outcome

Section 4-1

1 Make account transactions. (p. 110)

What to Remember with Examples

To make account deposits, on the appropriate deposit form (Figures 4-35 and 4-36):

1. Record the date.
2. Enter the amount of currency or coins being deposited.
3. List the amount of each check to be deposited. Include an identifying name or company.
4. Add the amounts of currency, coins, and checks.
5. If the deposit is to a personal account and you want to receive some of the money in cash, enter the amount on the line "less cash received" and sign on the appropriate line.
6. Subtract the amount of cash received from the total for the net deposit.

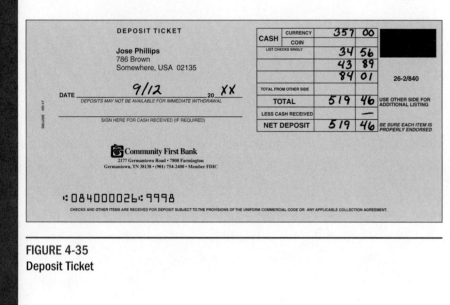

FIGURE 4-35
Deposit Ticket

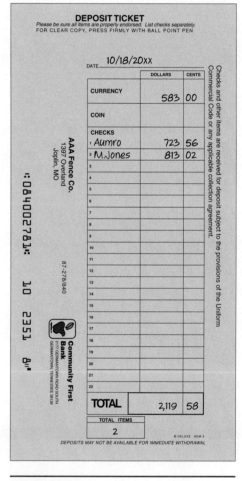

FIGURE 4-36
Deposit Ticket

To make a withdrawal using a check:

1. Enter the date of the check.
2. Enter the name of the payee.
3. Enter the amount of the check in numerals.
4. Write the amount of the check in words. Cents can be written as a fraction of a dollar or by using decimal notation.
5. Explain the purpose of the check.
6. Sign the check.

2 Record account transactions. (p. 115)

On a check stub or an account register (Figures 4-37 and 4-38):

For checks and other debits:

1. Make an entry for every account transaction.
2. Enter the date, the amount of the check or debit, the person or company that will receive the check or debit, and the purpose of the check or debit.
3. Subtract the amount of the check or debit from the previous balance to obtain the new balance.
4. For handwritten checks with stubs, carry the new balance forward to the next stub.

For deposits or other credits:

1. Make an entry for every account transaction.
2. Enter the date, the amount of the deposit or credit, and a brief explanation of the deposit or credit.
3. Add the amount of the deposit or credit to the previous balance to obtain the new balance.

On an electronic money management system:

1. Enter the appropriate details for producing a check.
2. Record other debits and all deposits and credits. The account register is maintained by the system automatically.
3. For business accounts or personal accounts that are used for tracking expenses, record the type of expense or budget account number.

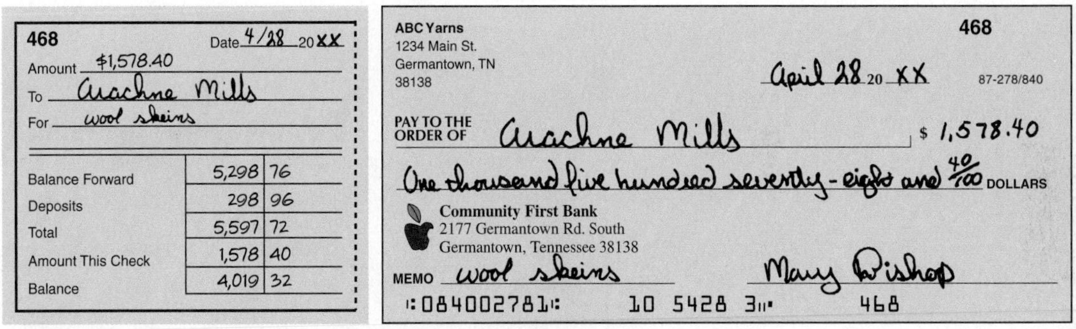

FIGURE 4-37
Business Check and Stub

RECORD ALL TRANSACTIONS THAT AFFECT YOUR ACCOUNT

NUMBER	DATE	DESCRIPTION OF TRANSACTION	DEBIT	√	FEE	CREDIT	BALANCE
							5,298 76
	4/21	Deposit				298 96	+298 96
							5,597 72
468	4/28	Arachne Mills	1,578 40				-1,578 40
							4,019 32

FIGURE 4-38
Account Register

Section 4-2

1 Reconcile a bank statement with an account register. (p. 121)

1. Check off all matching transactions appearing on both the bank statement and the account register.
2. Enter into the register the transactions appearing on the bank statement that have not been checked off. Check off these transactions in the register as they are entered. Update the register balance accordingly. This is the adjusted register balance.
3. Make a list of all the checks and other debits appearing in the register that have not been checked off. Add the amounts on the list to find the *total outstanding debits*.
4. Make a list of all the deposits and other credits appearing in the register that have not been checked off in step 1. Add the amounts on the list to find the *total outstanding credits.*
5. Calculate the *adjusted statement balance* by adding the statement balance and the total outstanding deposits and other credits, and then subtracting the total outstanding checks and other debits: Adjusted statement balance = statement balance + total outstanding credits − total outstanding debits (Figure 4-40).
6. Compare the adjusted statement balance with the register balance. These amounts should be equal.

7. If the adjusted statement balance does not equal the register balance, locate the cause of the discrepancy and correct the register accordingly.
8. Write *statement reconciled* on the next blank line in the account register and record the statement date.

Figure 4-39 shows the bank statement for Eiland's Information Services. Steps 1 and 2 of the reconciliation process have been carried out: matching transactions have been checked off and all transactions appearing on the bank statement have been entered in the register and checked off, including the service charge of $0.72 and interest earned of $14.32. The updated register balance is $18,020.36.

Now we complete the account reconciliation form in Figure 4-40 by recording the total outstanding debits and the total outstanding credits—transactions in the register that do not appear on the bank statement. Note: Even though all transactions seemed to match, a mistake was not noted.

The adjusted statement balance does not equal the register balance. To locate the error, first find the difference of the two amounts: 19,304.72 − 18,020.36 = 1,284.36. This amount does not match any transaction exactly. So, divide the difference by 2: 1,284.36 ÷ 2 = 642.18. This amount matches a deposit made on 6/15. The deposit was subtracted from the balance when it should have been added. Make an entry in the account register to offset the error: deposit $1,284.36, which is the amount that was subtracted in error plus the amount of the 6/15 deposit. Figure 4-41 shows the reconciled register. Notice the entry "statement reconciled" dated 7/2.

Community First Bank

2177 Germantown Rd. South • Germantown, Tennessee 38138 • (901) 555-2400 • Member FDIC

EILAND'S INFORMATION SERVICES
314 ROSAMOND ST
DRUMMONDS, TN 38072

ACCOUNT NUMBER   21-4658321
FEDERAL ID NUMBER   XX-XXX7214   DATE 7/2/20XX   PAGE 1

		BALANCE OF YOUR FUNDS
PREVIOUS BALANCE -----		$3,472.16
3	DEPOSITS TOTALING	2,498.50
7	WITHDRAWALS TOTALING	1,647.55
NEW BALANCE -----------		$4,323.11

ACCOUNT TRANSACTIONS FOR THE PERIOD FROM 6/3/20XX THROUGH 7/2/20XX

DATE	AMOUNT	DESCRIPTION
6/15	642.18 ✓	DEPOSIT
6/20	1,842.00 ✓	DEPOSIT
7/2	.72 ✓	SERVICE CHARGE
7/2	14.32 ✓	INTEREST EARNED

DATE	CHECK #	AMOUNT	DATE	CHECK #	AMOUNT
6/15	5832	200.00 ✓	6/17	5835	82.37 ✓
6/16	5833	225.00 ✓	7/2	5837*	175.00 ✓
6/17	5834	72.00 ✓	7/2	5839*	892.46 ✓

CHECKING DAILY BALANCE SUMMARY

DATE	BALANCE OF YOUR FUNDS	DATE	BALANCE OF YOUR FUNDS
6/3	3,472.16	6/17	3,534.97
6/15	3,914.34	6/20	5,376.97
6/16	3,689.34	7/2	4,323.11

FIGURE 4-39
Bank Statement

$ 4,323 11	BALANCE AS SHOWN ON BANK STATEMENT		BALANCE AS SHOWN IN YOUR REGISTER	$ 18,006 76
20,000 00	TOTAL OF OUTSTANDING DEPOSITS		SUBTRACT AMOUNT OF SERVICE CHARGE	– 72
24,323 11	NEW TOTAL		NEW TOTAL	18,006 04
5,018 39	SUBTRACT TOTAL OF OUTSTANDING CHECKS		ADJUSTMENTS IF ANY	+14 32 + 1,284 36
$19,304 72	YOUR ADJUSTED STATEMENT BALANCE	SHOULD EQUAL →	YOUR ADJUSTED REGISTER BALANCE	$19,304 72

Outstanding Deposits (Credits)			Outstanding Checks (Debits)		
Date	Amount		Check Number	Date	Amount
6/25	$ 20,000 00		5836		$ 42 18
			5838		4,976 21
Total	$ 20,000 00		Total		$ 5,018 39

FIGURE 4-40
Account Reconciliation Form

		RECORD ALL TRANSACTIONS THAT AFFECT YOUR ACCOUNT					BALANCE	
NUMBER	DATE	DESCRIPTION OF TRANSACTION	DEBIT (–)	√T	FEE (IF ANY) (–)	CREDIT (+)	3472	16
5832	6/13	City of Chicago	200 00	√			–200	00
							3,272	16
5833	6/13	City of Phoenix	225 00	√			–225	00
							3,047	16
5834	6/14	City of Fresno	72 00	√			–72	00
							2975	16
5835	6/15	Hardware house	82 37	√			–82	37
							2892	79
Deposit	6/15	Can Com, Inc. *	642 18	√			–642	18
							2250	61
5836	6/18	Office Max	42 18				–42	18
		copies					2,208	43
5837	6/20	City of New Orleans	175 00	√			–175	00
							2,033	43
Deposit	6/20	List Purchases		√		1842 00	+1842	00
							3,875	43
Deposit	6/25	Federal Credit Union				20,000 00	+20,000	00
		Small business loan					23,875	43
5838	6/30	Hardware house	4976 21				–4976	21
		computer					18,899	22
5839	6/30	Wade office Furniture	892 46	√			–892	46
		Desk chair, file cabinet					18006	76
	7/2	Service Charge		√	72		–72	
							18,006	04
	7/2	Interest earned		√		14 32	+14	32
							18,020	36

REMEMBER TO RECORD AUTOMATIC PAYMENTS/DEPOSITS ON DATE AUTHORIZED.

* Posting error (should be in deposit column)

		RECORD ALL TRANSACTIONS THAT AFFECT YOUR ACCOUNT					BALANCE	
NUMBER	DATE	DESCRIPTION OF TRANSACTION	DEBIT (–)	√T	FEE (IF ANY) (–)	CREDIT (+)	18,020	36
	7/4	Correction to deposit on 6/15		√		1284 36	+1,284	36
							19,304	72
	7/2	Statement Reconciled		√				

FIGURE 4-41
Account Register

EXERCISES SET A

1. Write a check (Figure 4-42) dated June 13, 20XX, to Byron Johnson in the amount of $296.83 for a washing machine. Complete the check stub.

456	Date_____20____
Amount _____	
To _____	
For _____	

Balance Forward	$4,307	21
Deposits		
Total		
Amount This Check		
Balance		

KRA, INC.   456
2596 Jason Blvd.
Kansas City, KS 00000
_____20____   87-278/840

PAY TO THE
ORDER OF _____ $

_____ DOLLARS

Community First Bank
2177 Germantown Rd. South
Germantown, Tennessee 38138

MEMO _____ _____

⑆084000456⑆

FIGURE 4-42
Check Number 456

2. Write a check (Figure 4-43) dated June 12, 20XX, to Alpine Industries in the amount of $85.50 for building supplies. Complete the check stub.

8212	Date_____20____
Amount _____	
To _____	
For _____	

Balance Forward	$2,087	05
Deposits	+1,500	00
Total		
Amount This Check		
Balance		

Barter Home Repair   8212
302 Cannon Dr.
Germantown, TN 38138
_____20____   87-278/840

PAY TO THE
ORDER OF _____ $

_____ DOLLARS

Community First Bank
2177 Germantown Rd. South
Germantown, Tennessee 38138

MEMO _____ _____

⑆035008212⑆

FIGURE 4-43
Check Number 8212

3. Complete a deposit slip (Figure 4-44) to deposit checks in the amounts of $136.00 and $278.96, and $480 cash on May 8, 20XX.

DEPOSIT TICKET

S & R Consulting Co.
PO Box 921
Flint, MI 00000

CASH	CURRENCY		
	COIN		
LIST CHECKS SINGLY			
			26-2/840
TOTAL FROM OTHER SIDE			
TOTAL			USE OTHER SIDE FOR ADDITIONAL LISTING
LESS CASH RECEIVED			
NET DEPOSIT			BE SURE EACH ITEM IS PROPERLY ENDORSED

DATE _____20____
DEPOSITS MAY NOT BE AVAILABLE FOR IMMEDIATE WITHDRAWAL

SIGN HERE FOR CASH RECEIVED (IF REQUIRED)

Community First Bank
2177 Germantown Road • 7808 Farmington
Germantown, TN 38138 • (901) 754-2400 • Member FDIC

⑆084000026⑆ 9998

CHECKS AND OTHER ITEMS ARE RECEIVED FOR DEPOSIT SUBJECT TO THE PROVISIONS OF THE UNIFORM COMMERCIAL CODE OR ANY APPLICABLE COLLECTION AGREEMENT.

FIGURE 4-44
Deposit Ticket for S & R Consulting Co.

4. Enter the following information and transactions in the check register for Happy Center Day Care (Figure 4-45). On July 10, 20XX, with an account balance of $983.47, the account debit card was used at Linens, Inc., for $220 for laundry services, and check 1214 was written to Bugs Away for $65 for extermination services. On July 11, $80 was withdrawn from an ATM, and on July 12, checks in the amounts of $123.86, $123.86, and $67.52 were deposited. Show the balance after these transactions.

		RECORD ALL TRANSACTIONS THAT AFFECT YOUR ACCOUNT					BALANCE	
NUMBER	DATE	DESCRIPTION OF TRANSACTION	DEBIT (−)	√ T	FEE (IF ANY) (−)	CREDIT (+)		

FIGURE 4-45
Check Register

Tree Top Landscape Service's bank statement is shown in Figure 4-46.

5. How many deposits were cleared during the month?

6. What amount of service charge was paid?

7. What was the amount of the largest check written?

8. How many checks appear on the bank statement?

9. What is the balance at the beginning of the statement period?

10. What is the balance at the end of the statement period?

11. What is the amount of check 718?

12. On what date did check 717 clear the bank?

Community First Bank

2177 Germantown Rd. South • Germantown, Tennessee 38138 • (901) 555-2400 • Member FDIC

Tree Top Landscape Service
31125 Forest Hill-Irene Rd
Collierville, TN 38017

ACCOUNT NUMBER   25-39042
FEDERAL ID NUMBER   XX-XXX6387   DATE 8/2/20XX   PAGE 1

	BALANCE OF YOUR FUNDS
PREVIOUS BALANCE -----	$4,782.96
DEPOSITS TOTALING	425.00
WITHDRAWALS TOTALING	532.46
NEW BALANCE -----------	$4,675.50

ACCOUNT TRANSACTIONS FOR THE PERIOD FROM 7/3/20XX THROUGH 8/2/20XX

DATE	AMOUNT	DESCRIPTION
7/3	200.00	Deposit
7/5	175.00	Deposit
7/9	50.00	Deposit
7/20	80.00	Withdrawal - ATM
		5172 Poplar Ave
7/22	30.92	Debit Card
7/25	21.17	Check Order

DATE	CHECK #	AMOUNT	DATE	CHECK #	AMOUNT
7/5	716	90.23	7/15	719	238.00
7/7	717	42.78			
7/12	718	29.36			

CHECKING DAILY BALANCE SUMMARY

DATE	BALANCE OF YOUR FUNDS	DATE	BALANCE OF YOUR FUNDS
7/3	4,982.96	7/15	4,807.59
7/5	5,067.73	7/20	4,727.59
7/7	5,024.95	7/22	4,696.67
7/9	5,074.95	7/25	4,675.50
7/12	5,045.59	8/2	4,675.50

FIGURE 4-46
Bank Statement for Tree Top Landscape Service

13. Tree Top Landscape Service's account register is shown in Figure 4-47 and its bank statement in Figure 4-46. Update the account register and use the reconciliation form in Figure 4-48 to reconcile the bank statement with the account register.

RECORD ALL TRANSACTIONS THAT AFFECT YOUR ACCOUNT

NUMBER	DATE	DESCRIPTION OF TRANSACTION	DEBIT (−)	√ T	FEE (IF ANY) (−)	CREDIT (+)	BALANCE	
							4,782	96
716	7/1	Dabney Nursery	90 23				4,692	73
717	7/1	office Max	42 78				4,649	95
Deposit	7/3	Louis Lechleiter				200 00	4,849	95
Deposit	7/5	Tony Trim				175 00	5,024	95
Deposit	7/9	Dale Crosby				50 00	5,074	95
718	7/10	Texaco Gas	29 36				5,045	59
719	7/10	Nation's Bank	238 00				4,807	59
Deposit	7/15	Bobby Cornelius				300 00	5,107	59
ATM	7/20	Withdrawl Branch	80 00				5,027	59
Debit card	7/20	AT&T	30 92				4,996	67
720	7/20	Visa	172 83				4,823	84

REMEMBER TO RECORD AUTOMATIC PAYMENTS/DEPOSITS ON DATE AUTHORIZED.

FIGURE 4-47
Account Register for Tree Top Landscape Service

$	BALANCE AS SHOWN ON BANK STATEMENT		BALANCE AS SHOWN IN YOUR REGISTER	$
	TOTAL OF OUTSTANDING DEPOSITS		SUBTRACT AMOUNT OF SERVICE CHARGE	
	NEW TOTAL		NEW TOTAL	
	SUBTRACT TOTAL OF OUTSTANDING CHECKS		ADJUSTMENTS IF ANY	
	YOUR ADJUSTED STATEMENT BALANCE	SHOULD EQUAL	YOUR ADJUSTED REGISTER BALANCE	

Outstanding Deposits (Credits)			Outstanding Checks (Debits)		
Date	Amount		Check Number	Date	Amount
	$				$
Total	$			Total	$

FIGURE 4-48
Account Reconciliation Form

14. The July bank statement for A & H Iron Works shows a balance of $37.94 and a service charge of $8.00. The account register shows deposits of $650 and $375.56 that do not appear on the statement. Checks in the amounts of $217.45, $57.82, $17.45, and $58.62 are outstanding. The register balance before reconciliation is $720.16. Reconcile the bank statement with the account register using the form in Figure 4-49.

$		BALANCE AS SHOWN ON BANK STATEMENT		BALANCE AS SHOWN IN YOUR REGISTER	$	
		TOTAL OF OUTSTANDING DEPOSITS		SUBTRACT AMOUNT OF SERVICE CHARGE		
		NEW TOTAL		NEW TOTAL		
		SUBTRACT TOTAL OF OUTSTANDING CHECKS		ADJUSTMENTS IF ANY		
		YOUR ADJUSTED STATEMENT BALANCE	SHOULD EQUAL	YOUR ADJUSTED REGISTER BALANCE		

Outstanding Deposits (Credits)			Outstanding Checks (Debits)		
Date	Amount		Check Number	Date	Amount
	$				$
Total	$			Total	$

FIGURE 4-49
Account Reconciliation Form

15. The September bank statement for Dixon Fence Company shows a balance of $275.25 and a service charge of $7.50. The account register shows deposits of $120.43 and $625.56 that do not appear on the statement. Checks in the amounts of $144.24, $154.48, $24.17, and $18.22 are outstanding. A $100 ATM withdrawal does not appear on the statement. The register balance before reconciliation is $587.63. Reconcile the bank statement with the account register using the form in Figure 4-50.

$		BALANCE AS SHOWN ON BANK STATEMENT		BALANCE AS SHOWN IN YOUR REGISTER	$	
		TOTAL OF OUTSTANDING DEPOSITS		SUBTRACT AMOUNT OF SERVICE CHARGE		
		NEW TOTAL		NEW TOTAL		
		SUBTRACT TOTAL OF OUTSTANDING CHECKS		ADJUSTMENTS IF ANY		
		YOUR ADJUSTED STATEMENT BALANCE	SHOULD EQUAL	YOUR ADJUSTED REGISTER BALANCE		

Outstanding Deposits (Credits)			Outstanding Checks (Debits)		
Date	Amount		Check Number	Date	Amount
	$				$
Total	$			Total	$

FIGURE 4-50
Account Reconciliation Form

EXCEL

EXERCISES SET B

1. Write a check dated August 18, 20XX (Figure 4-51), to Valley Electric Co-op in the amount of $189.32 for utilities. Complete the check stub in Figure 4-51.

789	Date_____20____
Amount _____	
To _____	
For _____	

Balance Forward	$1,037 | 15
Deposits	—
Total	
Amount This Check	
Balance	

Fileclip, Co.
10003 Lapolma Av.
Radcliff, NH 00000

789

_____20____   87-278/840

PAY TO THE
ORDER OF _____ $ ▒▒▒▒

_____ DOLLARS

Neshoba Bank
1518 S. Bramlett
Radcliff, NH 00000

MEMO _____ _____

⑈084000789⑈

FIGURE 4-51
Check Number 789

2. Write a check dated December 28, 20XX (Figure 4-52), to Lundy Daniel in the amount of $450.00 for legal services. James Ludwig is the maker. Complete the check stub.

1599	Date_____20____
Amount _____	
To _____	
For _____	

Balance Forward	$8,917 | 22
Deposits	6,525 | 00
Total	
Amount This Check	
Balance	

Ludwig's Towing Service
4837 Brentwood Cl
Pulaski, TN 00000

1599

_____20____   87-278/840

PAY TO THE
ORDER OF _____ $ ▒▒▒▒

_____ DOLLARS

Community Bank
2177 Germantown Rd. South
Germantown, Tennessee 38138

MEMO _____ _____

⑈035001599⑈

FIGURE 4-52
Check Number 1599

3. Complete a deposit slip on November 11, 20XX (Figure 4-53), to show the deposit of $100 in cash, checks in the amounts of $87.83, $42.97, and $106.32, with a $472.13 total from the other side of the deposit slip.

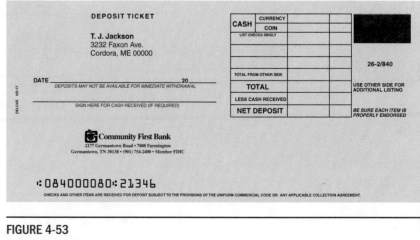

FIGURE 4-53
Deposit Ticket for T. J. Jackson

4. Enter the following information and transactions in the check register for Sloan's Tree Service (Figure 4-54). On May 3, 20XX, with an account balance of $876.54, check 234 was written to Organic Materials for $175 for fertilizer and check 235 was written to Klean Kuts in the amount of $524.82 for a chain saw. On May 5, checks in the amounts of $147.63 and $324.76 were deposited at the bank ATM. Show the balance after these transactions.

RECORD ALL TRANSACTIONS THAT AFFECT YOUR ACCOUNT								
NUMBER	DATE	DESCRIPTION OF TRANSACTION	DEBIT (−)	√ T	FEE (IF ANY) (−)	CREDIT (+)	BALANCE	

FIGURE 4-54
Account Register

Enrique Anglade's bank statement is shown in Figure 4-55.

5. How many deposits were made during the month?

6. What amount of service charge was paid?

7. What was the amount of the smallest check written?

8. How many checks appear on the bank statement?

9. What is the balance at the beginning of the statement period?

10. What is the balance at the end of the statement period?

11. What is the amount of check 5375?

12. On what date did check 5376 clear the bank?

Community First Bank
2177 Germantown Rd. South • Germantown, Tennessee 38138 • (901) 555-2400 • Member FDIC

Enrique Anglade
1901 Jones Drive
Miami, FL 33017

ACCOUNT NUMBER   32-123-32
SOCIAL SECURITY NUMBER   XXX-XX-5634   DATE 4/30/20XX   PAGE 1

		BALANCE OF YOUR FUNDS
PREVIOUS BALANCE -----		1,034.10
3	DEPOSITS TOTALING	2,500.00
4	WITHDRAWALS TOTALING	962.73
NEW BALANCE -----------		2,571.37

ACCOUNT TRANSACTIONS FOR THE PERIOD FROM 4/1/20XX THROUGH 4/30/20XX

DATE	AMOUNT	DESCRIPTION
4/1	850.00	Deposit - Walgreens 237875
4/3	800.00	Deposit - Walgreens 237875
4/15	850.00	Deposit - Walgreens 237875
4/30	12.50	Service Fee

DATE	CHECK #	AMOUNT
4/5	5374	647.53
4/5	5375	82.75
4/8	5376	219.95

CHECKING DAILY BALANCE SUMMARY

DATE	BALANCE OF YOUR FUNDS	DATE	BALANCE OF YOUR FUNDS
4/1	1,884.10	4/8	1,733.87
4/3	2,684.10	4/15	2,583.87
4/5	1,953.82	4/30	2,571.37

FIGURE 4-55
Bank Statement for Enrique Anglade

13. Enrique Anglade's account register is shown in Figure 4-56. Update the account register and reconcile the bank statement (see Figure 4-55) with the account register by using the reconciliation form in Figure 4-57.

RECORD ALL TRANSACTIONS THAT AFFECT YOUR ACCOUNT

NUMBER	DATE	DESCRIPTION OF TRANSACTION	DEBIT (−)	√T	FEE (IF ANY) (−)	CREDIT (+)	BALANCE
Deposit	4/1	Payroll				850 00	1,034 10
							+850 00
							1,884 10
Deposit	4/3	Payroll − Bonus				800 00	+800 00
							2,684 10
5374	4/3	First Union Mortgage Co.	647 53				−647 53
							2,036 57
5375	4/3	South Florida Utility	82 75				−82 75
							1,953 82
5376	4/5	First Federal Credit Union	219 95				−219 95
							1,733 87
5377	4/15	Banc Boston	510 48				−510 48
							1,223 39
Deposit	4/15	Payroll				850 00	+850 00
							2,073 39
5378	4/20	Northwest Air lines	403 21				−403 21
							1,670 18
5379	4/26	Auto Zone	18 97				−18 97
							1,651 21
ATM	5/4	Cordova Branch	100 00				−100 00
							1,551 21

REMEMBER TO RECORD AUTOMATIC PAYMENTS/DEPOSITS ON DATE AUTHORIZED.

FIGURE 4-56
Account Register for Enrique Anglade

$	BALANCE AS SHOWN ON BANK STATEMENT		BALANCE AS SHOWN IN YOUR REGISTER	$
	TOTAL OF OUTSTANDING DEPOSITS		SUBTRACT AMOUNT OF SERVICE CHARGE	
	NEW TOTAL		NEW TOTAL	
	SUBTRACT TOTAL OF OUTSTANDING CHECKS		ADJUSTMENTS IF ANY	
	YOUR ADJUSTED STATEMENT BALANCE	SHOULD ↔ EQUAL	YOUR ADJUSTED REGISTER BALANCE	

Outstanding Deposits (Credits)	
Date	Amount
	$
Total	$

Outstanding Checks (Debits)		
Check Number	Date	Amount
		$
Total		$

FIGURE 4-57
Account Reconciliation Form

14. Taylor Flowers' bank statement shows a balance of $135.42 and a service charge of $8.00. The account register shows deposits of $112.88 and $235.45 that do not appear on the statement. The register shows outstanding checks in the amounts of $17.42 and $67.90 and two cleared checks recorded in the account register as $145.69 and $18.22. The two cleared checks actually were written for and are shown on the statement as $145.96 and $18.22. The register balance before reconciliation is $406.70. Reconcile the bank statement with the account register using the form in Figure 4-58.

$		BALANCE AS SHOWN ON BANK STATEMENT		BALANCE AS SHOWN IN YOUR REGISTER	$	
		TOTAL OF OUTSTANDING DEPOSITS		SUBTRACT AMOUNT OF SERVICE CHARGE		
		NEW TOTAL		NEW TOTAL		
		SUBTRACT TOTAL OF OUTSTANDING CHECKS		ADJUSTMENTS IF ANY		
		YOUR ADJUSTED STATEMENT BALANCE	SHOULD EQUAL	YOUR ADJUSTED REGISTER BALANCE		

Outstanding Deposits (Credits)			Outstanding Checks (Debits)		
Date	Amount		Check Number	Date	Amount
	$				$
Total	$			Total	$

FIGURE 4-58
Account Reconciliation Form

15. The bank statement for Randazzo's Market shows a balance of $1,102.35 and a service charge of $6.50. The account register shows a deposit of $265.49 that does not appear on the statement. The account register shows outstanding checks in the amounts of $617.23 and $456.60 and two cleared checks recorded as $45.71 and $348.70. The two cleared checks actually were written for $45.71 and $384.70. The register balance before reconciliation is $336.51. Reconcile the bank statement with the account register using the form in Figure 4-59.

$		BALANCE AS SHOWN ON BANK STATEMENT		BALANCE AS SHOWN IN YOUR REGISTER	$	
		TOTAL OF OUTSTANDING DEPOSITS		SUBTRACT AMOUNT OF SERVICE CHARGE		
		NEW TOTAL		NEW TOTAL		
		SUBTRACT TOTAL OF OUTSTANDING CHECKS		ADJUSTMENTS IF ANY		
		YOUR ADJUSTED STATEMENT BALANCE	SHOULD EQUAL	YOUR ADJUSTED REGISTER BALANCE		

Outstanding Deposits (Credits)			Outstanding Checks (Debits)		
Date	Amount		Check Number	Date	Amount
	$				$
Total	$			Total	$

FIGURE 4-59
Account Reconciliation Form

PRACTICE TEST

CHAPTER 4

1. Write the check and fill out the check stub provided in Figure 4-60. The balance brought forward is $2,301.42, deposits were made for $200 on May 12 and $83.17 on May 20, and check 195 was written on May 25 to Lon Associates for $152.50 for supplies. The check was signed by Lonnie Branch.

```
┌──────────────────────────┐   ┌────────────────────────────────────────────────┐
│ 195          Date____20__ │   │ Khayat Cleaners                          195     │
│ Amount _____ │   │ 2438 Broad St.                                   │
│ To _____ │   │ Oklahoma City, OK 00000                          │
│ For _____ │   │                          _____ 20 ___ 87 278/040│
│ _____ │   │ PAY TO THE                                       │
│ Balance Forward │   │   │   │ ORDER OF _____ $ _____  │
│ Deposits        │   │   │   │                                        ___ DOLLARS │
│ Total           │   │   │   │   First State Bank                               │
│ Amount This Check│  │   │   │   1543 S. Main                                    │
│ Balance         │   │   │   │   Oklahoma City, OK 00000                         │
│                          │   │ MEMO _____  _____          │
│                          │   │ ⑆074200195⑆                                      │
└──────────────────────────┘   └────────────────────────────────────────────────┘
```

FIGURE 4-60
Check Number 195

D. G. Hernandez Equipment's bank statement is shown in Figure 4-61.

2. What is the balance at the beginning of the statement period?

3. How many checks cleared the bank during the statement period?

4. What was the service charge for the statement period?

5. Check 3786 was written for what amount?

6. On what date did check 3788 clear the account?

7. What was the total of the deposits?

8. What was the balance at the end of the statement period?

9. What was the total amount for all checks written during the period?

Community First Bank
2177 Germantown Rd. South • Germantown, Tennessee 38138 • (901) 555-2400 • Member FDIC

D. G. Hernandez Equipment
25 Santa Rosa Dr.
Piperton, TN 38027

ACCOUNT NUMBER 8-523145
FEDERAL ID NUMBER XX-XXXX5135   DATE 3/31/20XX   PAGE 1

		BALANCE OF YOUR FUNDS
PREVIOUS BALANCE -----		5,283.17
2	DEPOSITS TOTALING	3,600.00
6	WITHDRAWALS TOTALING	1,900.49
NEW BALANCE ----------		6,982.68

ACCOUNT TRANSACTIONS FOR THE PERIOD FROM 3/1/20xx THROUGH 3/31/20xx

DATE	AMOUNT	DESCRIPTION
3/15	1,600.00	Deposit
3/17	19.00	Returned Check Charge
3/31	2,000.00	Deposit

DATE	CHECK #	AMOUNT	DATE	CHECK #	AMOUNT
3/2	3784	96.03	3/15	3788	973.12
3/7	3786*	142.38	3/31	3792*	182.03
3/12	3787	487.93			

CHECKING DAILY BALANCE SUMMARY

DATE	BALANCE OF YOUR FUNDS	DATE	BALANCE OF YOUR FUNDS
3/2	5,187.14	3/15	5,183.71
3/7	5,044.76	3/17	5,164.71
3/12	4,556.83	3/31	6,982.68

FIGURE 4-61
Bank Statement for D. G. Hernandez Equipment

10. D. G. Hernandez Equipment's account register is shown in Figure 4-62. Reconcile the bank statement in Figure 4-61 with the account register in Figure 4-62. Use the account reconciliation form in Figure 4-63.

RECORD ALL TRANSACTIONS THAT AFFECT YOUR ACCOUNT

NUMBER	DATE	DESCRIPTION OF TRANSACTION	DEBIT (−)	√ T	FEE (IF ANY) (−)	CREDIT (+)	BALANCE
							5,283 17
3784	2/27		96 03				−96 03
							5,187 14
3785	3/5		346 18				−346 18
							4840 96
3786	3/5		142 38				−142 38
							4698 58
3787	3/11		487 93				−487 93
							4,210 65
3788	3/11		973 12				−973 12
							3,237 53
3789	3/15		72 83				−72 83
							3,164 70
Dep.	3/15					1,600 00	+1,600 00
							4,764 70
3790	3/17		146 17				−146 17
							4,618 53
3791	3/20		152 03				−152 03
							4,466 50
3792	3/31	*	182 08				−182 08
							4,284 42
Deposit	3/31					2,000 00	+2,000 00
							6,284 42

REMEMBER TO RECORD AUTOMATIC PAYMENTS/DEPOSITS ON DATE AUTHORIZED.

FIGURE 4-62
Account Register

$	BALANCE AS SHOWN ON BANK STATEMENT		BALANCE AS SHOWN IN YOUR REGISTER	$
	TOTAL OF OUTSTANDING DEPOSITS		SUBTRACT AMOUNT OF SERVICE CHARGE	
	NEW TOTAL		NEW TOTAL	
	SUBTRACT TOTAL OF OUTSTANDING CHECKS		ADJUSTMENTS IF ANY	
	YOUR ADJUSTED STATEMENT BALANCE	SHOULD EQUAL	YOUR ADJUSTED REGISTER BALANCE	

Outstanding Deposits (Credits)	
Date	Amount
	$
Total	$

Outstanding Checks (Debits)		
Check Number	Date	Amount
		$
	Total	$

FIGURE 4-63
Account Reconciliation Form

11. Before reconciliation, an account register balance is $1,817.93. The bank statement balance is $860.21. A service fee of $15 and one returned item of $213.83 were charged against the account. Deposits in the amounts of $800 and $412.13 are outstanding. Checks written for $243.17, $167.18, $13.97, $42.12, and $16.80 are outstanding. Complete the account reconciliation form in Figure 4-64 to reconcile the bank statement with the account register.

$	BALANCE AS SHOWN ON BANK STATEMENT		BALANCE AS SHOWN IN YOUR REGISTER	$
	TOTAL OF OUTSTANDING DEPOSITS		SUBTRACT AMOUNT OF SERVICE CHARGE	
	NEW TOTAL		NEW TOTAL	
	SUBTRACT TOTAL OF OUTSTANDING CHECKS		ADJUSTMENTS IF ANY	
	YOUR ADJUSTED STATEMENT BALANCE	SHOULD EQUAL	YOUR ADJUSTED REGISTER BALANCE	

Outstanding Deposits (Credits)	
Date	Amount
	$
Total	$

Outstanding Checks (Debits)		
Check Number	Date	Amount
		$
	Total	$

FIGURE 4-64
Account Reconciliation Form

1. If adjacent digits of an account register entry have been transposed, the error will produce a difference that is divisible by 9. Give an example of a two-digit number and the number formed by transposing the digits, and show that the difference is divisible by 9.

2. Give an example of a three-digit number and the number formed by transposing two adjacent digits. Show that the difference is divisible by 9.

3. Give an example of a four-digit number and a number formed by transposing any two adjacent digits. Show that the difference is divisible by 9.

4. Will the difference be divisible by 9 if two digits that are not adjacent are interchanged to form a new number? Illustrate your answer.

5. What if more than two digits are interchanged? Will the difference still be divisible by 9? Illustrate your answer.

6. When you receive your bank statement, you should first identify any items on the statement that are not listed in your account register. Discuss some items you may find on a bank statement and explain what should be done with them.

7. Explain the various types of endorsements for checks.

8. Explain why you would not want to use a deposit ticket that had someone else's name printed on it to make a deposit for your account even if you cross out the account number and name and enter your own.

9. Discuss the advantages and disadvantages of online banking.

10. Discuss at least three advantages for a business of having a checking account.

Challenge Problem

Terry Kelly was discussing her checking and savings accounts with her bank officer when the officer suggested that she talk with the bank's investment counselor. Terry was advised by the investment counselor to calculate her current net worth and to project her 2014 net worth to determine if her 2014 projections would accomplish her objective of increasing her net worth. She listed the following assets and liabilities for 2013. To calculate her net worth, she found the difference between total assets and total liabilities.

Terry's home appreciated (increased) in value by 0.04 times the 2013 value while her car depreciated (decreased) in value by 0.125 times the 2013 value. Her car loan decreased by $2,100 while her home mortgage balance decreased by $887. Terry plans to pay her personal loan in full by the end of 2014. Of her $2,000 planned investment, she will place $1,000 in savings and $1,000 in stocks and bonds. She also plans to reinvest the interest income of $141 (in savings) and the dividend income of $364 (in stocks and bonds) earned in 2013. She projects her checking account balance will be $1,500 at yearend for 2014.

Calculate Terry's total assets and total liabilities for 2013. Then calculate her net worth for 2013. Use the information given to project Terry's assets and liabilities for 2014. Then project her 2014 net worth. How much does Terry expect her net worth to increase (or decrease) from 2013 to 2014?

ASSETS:	
Checking account	2,099
Savings account	2,821
Auto	10,500
Home and furnishings	65,000
Stocks and bonds	4,017
Other personal property	3,200
Total assets	
LIABILITIES:	
Car loan	8,752
Home mortgage	54,879
Personal loan	1,791
Total liabilities	

CASE STUDIES

4-1 Mark's First Checking Account

During his first year in college, Mark Sutherland opened a checking account at the First National Bank of Arlington, Texas. His account does not have a minimum balance requirement, but he does pay a monthly service charge of $3.00. Mark has just received his first monthly bank statement and notices that the end-of-month balance on the statement is quite different from the end-of-month balance he shows in his check register. The bank statement and Mark's check register are summarized below.

Bank Statement of Activity This Month				
ACCOUNT: Mark J. Sutherland ACCOUNT # 43967			PERIOD: January 3, 2014 through January 31, 2014	
Beginning Balance 300.00		Total Deposits and Other Credits to Your Account 300.00	Total Checks and Other Charges to Your Account 206.25	Ending Balance 93.75
Date	Transaction			
03	Deposit	300.00		
05	100		16.50	
07	101		20.00	
09	Debit card transaction		17.45	
12	103		42.96	
14	104		16.87	
17	105		5.00	
17	106		11.43	
17	ATM withdrawal		25.00	
19	107		25.00	
24	108		14.04	
28	109		9.00	
31	Service charge		3.00	

Mark's Check Register					
Date	No.	Payee	For	Amount	Balance
1/3		Deposit		300.00	300.00
1/3	100	Harmon Foods	Food	16.50	283.50
1/4	101	Cash		20.00	263.50
1/5	102	VOID			
1/7	103	Mel's Sporting Goods	Gym shoes	42.96	220.54
1/10	104	Valley Cleaners	Dry cleaning	18.67	201.87
1/13	105	Sharon Mackey	Birthday present	5.00	196.87
1/14	106	University Bookstore	Supplies	11.43	190.44
1/14	107	Cash		25.00	175.44
1/19	108	Harmon Foods	Food	14.04	161.40
1/24	109	Mom	Repay loan	9.00	152.40
1/25	110	Poindexter's Café	Sharon's birthday party	20.00	132.40
1/26		Deposit		50.00	182.40
1/28	111	Exxon	Monthly statement	12.96	169.44

1. What are the steps Mark needs to include when reconciling his account register with the bank's statement?

2. Reconcile Mark's register with the bank statement using the steps listed in the previous answer.

3. Why are there differences between Mark's records and the bank's statement? What could Mark do during the next month to make the month-end reconciliation easier?

4. Suppose Mark finds a $100 deposit in his bank statement that he knows he did not make. What should he do?

4-2 Expressions Dance Studio

It was the end of a very long first month in her sole proprietorship, and Kara Noble was exhausted. Between moving into a new apartment and teaching dance classes five nights a week, there was not much downtime. Consequently, the mail had started to pile up. After sorting through a few bills and way too much junk mail, Kara spotted her first bank statement from U.S. Bank. The format was different from what she was used to, and she was startled to see the ending balance of only $506.18, less than the balance she thought she had. Kara went to find her business checkbook, which along with the bank statement is summarized below:

		FINANCIAL SUMMARY: 08/25/13 to 09/25/13		
ACCOUNT: Expressions Dance ACCOUNT #: 1007508279		ENDING BALANCE: $506.18		
Date	Activity	Deposits/Other Additions	Withdrawals/Other Deductions	Ending Balance
9/1/2013	Deposit	2,475.00		2,475.00
9/7/2013	1001		110.00	2,365.00
9/7/2013	1000		900.00	1,465.00
9/14/2013	1003		156.00	1,309.00
9/14/2013	1002		29.49	1,279.51
9/20/2013	Deposit	336.19		1,615.70
9/24/2013	Debit		93.50	1,522.20
9/24/2013	Debit		25.75	1,496.45
9/24/2013	Debit		4.79	1,491.66
9/25/2013	1005		900.00	591.66
9/25/2013	Service charge		3.00	588.66
9/25/2013	Check printing		82.48	506.18

Check #	Date	Pay to	Memo	Amount	Balance
Deposit	9/1/2013	Deposit	Business Loan	$2,475.00	$2,475.00
1000	9/1/2013	Stephens Properties	Sept. Studio Rent	$900.00	$1,575.00
1001	9/5/2013	Renae Peterson	Refund	$110.00	$1,685.00
1002	9/10/2013	Gannett Newspapers	Ad Bill	$29.49	$1,655.51
1003	9/12/2013	Liturgical Publications	Ad Bill	$156.00	$1,499.51
Deposit	9/20/2013	Deposit	Students	$336.19	$1,835.70
1004	9/21/2013	Wisconsin Dance	Repay loan to Kara	$133.62	$1,702.08
1005	9/22/2013	Stephens Properties	Oct. Studio Rent	$900.00	$802.08
Debit card	9/23/2013	Pom Express	Poms	$39.50	$762.58
Debit card	9/23/2013	Gas	Gas	$25.75	$736.83
Deposit	9/27/2013	Deposit	Students	$319.71	$1,056.45
Deposit	9/29/2013	Deposit	Studio rentalfee	$200.00	$1,256.54
1006	9/30/2013	VOID	Mistake	$	$1,256.54
1007	9/30/2013	Cintas Fire Protection	Extinguisher Replace	$36.93	$1,219.61
1008	9/30/2013	Besberg Realty	October Apt. Rent	$570.00	$649.61

1. What steps should Kara take to reconcile her bank statement? (Hint: they are listed in your text.)

2. Reconcile Kara's register for Expressions Dance with the bank statement following the steps you provided in your answer to question 1.

3. What are some ways that Kara can avoid discrepancies in the future?

4. The last entry in Kara's Expressions Dance checkbook register is for check 1008 written to Besberg Realty for her personal apartment rent. Is it legal to write checks for personal expenses out of a business account? Even if it is legal, is it a good idea?

Equations

Bungee Jumping: How High Should You Go?

Bungee jumping has quite an old origin. The idea comes from ancient "vine jumping" performed in the island nation of Vanuatu, off the coast of Australia. This practice later transformed into a tribal ritual for proving manhood during the fig-harvesting festival. The era of modern bungee jumping actually started on April 1, 1979, when a group from the Oxford University Dangerous Sport Club, impressed by a film about the Vanuatu "vine jumpers," jumped from the 245-foot Clifton Suspension Bridge in Bristol, England. Using nylon-braided, rubber shock cord instead of vines, and dressed in their customary top hat and tails, they performed a simultaneous jump. The enthusiasts were promptly arrested, but the new adrenaline mania had been started.

The first commercial jump site opened in early 1988 in New Zealand. Since that time bungee jumping, like many extreme sports, has become increasingly popular. There are few things quite as exhilarating as seeing the ground come rushing at you—only to be yanked back skyward in the nick of time. But did you know that bungee jumping safety is based on applied math equations?

Tim does, and he is opening a new business, Extreme Bungee Jumping. His primary concern, of course, is with the safety of the jumpers. One mistake and the results could be catastrophic! He has been reviewing the math equation used in the computer program that came with the bungee jump cord he purchased, and realizes there are five variables: the height of the platform, the length of the cord, the elasticity or spring of the cord, the weight of the individual, and an appropriate safety margin. Because the jump will take place over water that is 12-feet deep, Tim knows that a safety margin of 2 meters is acceptable. He knows the length and spring of the cord, as stated by the manufacturer.

Tim wants to try out his new bungee jumping equipment, but is unsure how tall the tower must be to ensure a safe jump. For Tim to complete the calculations, he must know his weight, which is 165 lb or about 75 kg. He uses 75 kg, and gets the following results:

$$\text{height} = 47.285 \text{ meters} + 2 \text{ meters (added for safety)}$$
$$= 49.285 \text{ m}$$

(based on solving a complex quadratic equation)

The tower must be at least 49.285 m tall to accommodate jumpers who are 165 lb or less. Tim was glad that the computer did the calculations for him. The good news was that he could now bungee jump safely. Luckily for you, the equations in this chapter are much easier to follow. So, it is time to jump in!

LEARNING OUTCOMES

5-1 Equations

1. Solve equations using multiplication or division.
2. Solve equations using addition or subtraction.
3. Solve equations using more than one operation.
4. Solve equations containing multiple unknown terms.
5. Solve equations containing parentheses.
6. Solve equations that are proportions.

5-2 Using Equations to Solve Problems

1. Use the problem-solving approach to analyze and solve word problems.

5-3 Formulas

1. Evaluate a formula.
2. Find an equivalent formula by rearranging the formula.

LEARNING OUTCOMES

1 Solve equations using multiplication or division.
2 Solve equations using addition or subtraction.
3 Solve equations using more than one operation.
4 Solve equations containing multiple unknown terms.
5 Solve equations containing parentheses.
6 Solve equations that are proportions.

Equation: a mathematical statement in which two quantities are equal.

Unknown or variable: the unknown amount or amounts that are represented as letters in an equation.

Known or given value: the known amounts or numbers in an equation.

Solve: find the value of the unknown or variable that makes the equation true.

Isolate: perform systematic operations to both sides of the equation so that the unknown or variable is alone on one side of the equation. Its value is given on the other side of the equation.

An **equation** is a mathematical statement in which two quantities are equal. Equations are represented by mathematical shorthand that uses numbers, letters, and operational symbols. The letters represent unknown amounts and are called **unknowns or variables.** The numbers are called **known** or **given values.** The numbers, letters, and mathematical symbols show how the knowns and unknowns are related. To **solve** an equation like $10 = 2(B)$ means finding the value of B so that 2 times this value is the same as 10. We accomplish this by performing systematic operations so that the unknown value is **isolated.** That is, the letter representing the unknown or variable stands alone on one side of the equation and the value of the unknown is given on the other side of the equation.

1 Solve equations using multiplication or division.

To begin our examination of equations, we look at equations that involve multiplication or division and one unknown value.

TIP

Multiplication Notation

If there is no sign of operation between a number and a letter, a number and a parenthesis, or two letters, it means multiplication. So $2A$ means $2 \times A$, $2(9)$ means 2×9, and AB means $A \times B$. In equations, multiplication is usually indicated without the $\times$ sign.

DID YOU KNOW?

In the example in the How To box, notice that $\frac{5N}{5}$ is expressed in the next line as N. The fraction $\frac{5}{5}$ equals 1 and $1(N) = N$. It is not necessary to write the factor of 1 in front of a variable.

HOW TO   Solve an equation with multiplication or division

Solve the equation
$5N = 20$

1. Isolate the unknown value or variable:
   (a) If the equation contains the *product* of the unknown factor and a known factor, then *divide* both sides of the equation by the known factor.
   $$\frac{5N}{5} = \frac{20}{5}$$
   (b) If the equation contains the *quotient* of the unknown value and the divisor, then *multiply* both sides of the equation by the divisor.
2. Identify the solution: The solution is the number on the side opposite the isolated unknown value.
   $$N = 4$$
3. Check the solution: In the original equation, replace the unknown-value letter with the solution; perform the indicated operations; and verify that both sides of the equation are the same number.
   $$5(4) \stackrel{?}{=} 20$$
   $$20 = 20$$

TIP

What Does $\stackrel{?}{=}$ Mean?

The symbol $\stackrel{?}{=}$ is used when checking a solution until the solution is verified. $2(9) \stackrel{?}{=} 18$ can be read as *Does 2 times 9 equal 18?*

EXAMPLE 1   Solve the equation $2A = 18$. (A number multiplied by 2 is 18.)

$2A = 18$ The product and one factor are known.

$\dfrac{2A}{2} = \dfrac{18}{2}$ Divide by the known factor on both sides of the equation. $\frac{2}{2} = 1$, $1(A) = A$.

$A = \boxed{9}$ The solution is 9.

Check:

$2A = 18$ Replace A with the solution 9 and see if both sides are equal.
$2(9) \stackrel{?}{=} 18$
$18 = 18$

The solution of the equation is 9.

EXAMPLE 2 Find the value of A if $\dfrac{A}{4} = 5$. (A number divided by 4 is 5.)

$\dfrac{A}{4} = 5$ The quotient and divisor are known. The dividend is unknown.

$4\left(\dfrac{A}{4}\right) = 5(4)$ Multiply both sides of the equation by the divisor, 4.

$A = \boxed{20}$ The solution is 20.

Check:

$\dfrac{A}{4} = 5$ Replace A with the solution 20 and see if both sides are equal.

$\dfrac{20}{4} \overset{?}{=} 5$

$5 = 5$

The solution of the equation is 20.

STOP AND CHECK

See Example 1.

1. Solve for A: $3A = 24$ **2.** Solve for N: $5N = 30$

See Example 2.

3. Solve for B: $8 = \dfrac{B}{6}$ **4.** Solve for M: $\dfrac{M}{5} = 7$ **5.** Solve for K: $\dfrac{K}{2} = 3$ **6.** Solve for A: $7 = \dfrac{A}{3}$

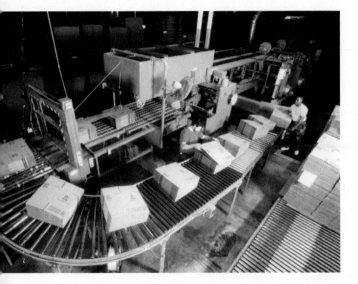

2 Solve equations using addition or subtraction.

Suppose 15 of the 25 people who work at Carton Manufacturers work on the day shift. How many people work there in the evening? You know that 15 people work there during the day, that 25 people work there in all, and that some unknown number of people work there in the evening. Assign the letter N to the unknown number of night-shift workers. The information from the problem can then be written in words as "the night-shift workers plus the day-shift workers equals 25" and in symbols: $N + 15 = 25$. This equation is one that can be solved with subtraction.

HOW TO   Solve an equation with addition or subtraction

	Solve the equation
	$B + 2 = 8$

1. Isolate the unknown value or variable:
   (a) If the equation contains the *sum* of an unknown value and a known value, then *subtract* the known value from both sides of the equation.

$$\begin{aligned} B + 2 &= 8 \\ -2 &= -2 \end{aligned}$$

   (b) If the equation contains the *difference* of an unknown value and a known value, then *add* the known value to both sides of the equation.

$$B = 6$$

2. Identify the solution: The solution is the number on the side opposite the isolated unknown-value letter.

$$\begin{aligned} 6 + 2 &\overset{?}{=} 8 \\ 8 &= 8 \end{aligned}$$

3. Check the solution: In the original equation, replace the unknown-value letter with the solution; perform the indicated operations; and verify that both sides of the equation are the same number.

EXAMPLE 3 Suppose 15 of the 25 people who work at Carton Manufacturers work on the day shift. How many people work there on the night shift?

N = the number of night-shift workers

$$
\begin{array}{ll}
N + 15 = 25 & \text{The sum of the night-shift workers and the day-shift workers is 25.} \\
\underline{ - 15 \quad -15} & \text{Subtract the known value, 15, from both sides.} \\
N = 10 \\
 N = \boxed{10} & \text{The solution is 10.}
\end{array}
$$

Check:

$$
\begin{array}{ll}
N + 15 = 25 & \text{Replace } N \text{ with the solution, 10, and see if both sides are equal.} \\
\boxed{10} + 15 \stackrel{?}{=} 25 \\
25 = 25
\end{array}
$$

The number of night-shift workers is 10.

EXAMPLE 4 Find the value of A if $A - 5 = 8$. (A number decreased by 5 is 8.)

$$
\begin{array}{ll}
A - 5 = 8 & \text{The difference and the number being subtracted, 5, are known.} \\
\underline{ + 5 \quad +5} & \text{Add 5 to both sides.} \\
A = \boxed{13} & \text{The solution is 13.}
\end{array}
$$

Check:

$$
\begin{array}{ll}
A - 5 = 8 & \text{Replace } A \text{ with the solution, 13, and see if both sides are equal.} \\
\boxed{13} - 5 \stackrel{?}{=} 8 \\
8 = 8
\end{array}
$$

The solution is 13.

TIP

Solve by Undoing

In general, unknowns are isolated in an equation by "undoing" all operations associated with the unknown.

- Use addition to undo subtraction.
- Use subtraction to undo addition.
- Use multiplication to undo division.
- Use division to undo multiplication.

To keep the equation in balance, we perform the same operation on both sides of the equation.

STOP AND CHECK

Solve for the variable.

See Example 3.

1. $A + 12 = 20$

2. $A + 5 = 28$

3. $15 = A + 3$

See Example 4.

4. $N - 5 = 11$

5. $N - 7 = 10$

6. $28 = M - 5$

3 Solve equations using more than one operation.

Many business equations contain more than one operation. To solve such equations, we undo each operation in turn. We first undo all additions or subtractions and then undo all multiplications or divisions. Our goal is still to isolate the unknown.

HOW TO Solve an equation with more than one operation

Solve the equation
$$3N - 1 = 14$$

1. Isolate the unknown value or variable:
   (a) Add or subtract as necessary *first*.

   $$3N - 1 = 14$$
   $$\underline{ + 1 \quad + 1}$$
   $$3N \quad = 15$$

   (b) Multiply or divide as necessary *second*.

   $$\frac{3N}{3} = \frac{15}{3}$$

2. Identify the solution: The solution is the number on the side opposite the isolated unknown value.

   $$N = 5$$

3. Check the solution: In the original equation, replace the unknown-value letter with the solution and perform the indicated operations.

   $$3(5) - 1 \overset{?}{=} 14$$
   $$15 - 1 \overset{?}{=} 14$$
   $$14 = 14$$

Order of Operations: the specific order in which calculations must be performed to evaluate a series of calculations.

TIP

Order of Operations Versus Steps for Solving Equations

Recall that when two or more calculations are written symbolically, the operations are performed in a specified order.

1. Perform multiplication and division as they appear from left to right.
2. Perform addition and subtraction as they appear from left to right.

To solve an equation, we *undo* the operations, so we work in reverse order.

1. Undo addition or subtraction.
2. Undo multiplication or division.

In the example in the preceding How To box, examine the sequence of steps.

To solve: Undo subtraction.   To check: Multiply first.
               Undo multiplication.   Subtract.

EXAMPLE 5

Find A if $2A + 1 = 15$. (Two times a number increased by 1 is 15.)

The equation contains both addition and multiplication. Undo addition first, and then undo multiplication.

$$2A + 1 = 15$$ Undo addition.
$$\underline{ - 1 \quad -1}$$
$$2A \quad = 14$$ Undo multiplication.
$$2A = 14$$
$$\frac{2A}{2} = \frac{14}{2}$$
$$A = \boxed{7}$$ Solution.

Check:

$$2A + 1 = 15$$ Replace A with 7 in the original equation and see if both sides are equal.
$$2(7) + 1 \overset{?}{=} 15$$ Multiply first.
$$14 + 1 \overset{?}{=} 15$$ Add.
$$15 = 15$$

The solution is 7.

 **EXAMPLE 6** Solve the equation $\dfrac{A}{5} - 3 = 1$. (A number divided by 5 and decreased by 3 is 1.)

The equation contains both subtraction and division: Undo subtraction first, and then undo division.

$$\dfrac{A}{5} - 3 = 1 \qquad \text{Undo subtraction.}$$

$$\dfrac{\;\;\;+3\quad +3\;\;\;}{\dfrac{A}{5} \quad = \quad 4} \qquad \text{Undo division.}$$

$$\cancel{5}\left(\dfrac{A}{\cancel{5}}\right) = 4(5)$$

$$A = \boxed{20} \qquad \text{Solution.}$$

Check:

$$\dfrac{A}{5} - 3 = 1 \qquad \text{Replace } A \text{ with 20 in the original equation and see if both sides are equal.}$$

$$\dfrac{20}{5} - 3 \overset{?}{=} 1 \qquad \text{Divide first.}$$

$$4 - 3 \overset{?}{=} 1 \qquad \text{Subtract.}$$

$$1 = 1$$

The solution is 20.

STOP AND CHECK

Solve.
See Example 5.

1. $3N + 4 = 16$

2. $5N - 7 = 13$

See Example 6.

3. $\dfrac{B}{8} - 2 = 2$

4. $\dfrac{M}{3} + 2 = 5$

5. $\dfrac{S}{6} - 3 = 4$

6. $12 = \dfrac{A}{5} - 8$

4 Solve equations containing multiple unknown terms.

In some equations, the unknown value may occur more than once. The simplest instance is when the unknown value occurs in two addends. We solve such equations by first combining these addends. Remember that $5A$, for instance, means 5 times A, or $A + A + A + A + A$. To combine $2A + 3A$, we add 2 and 3, to get 5, and then multiply 5 by A, to get $5A$. Thus, $2A + 3A$ is the same as $5A$.

| **HOW TO** | Solve an equation when the unknown value occurs in two or more addends |

Find A if $2A + 3A = 10$

1. Combine the unknown-value addends when the addends are on the same side of the equal sign:
   (a) Add the numbers in each addend. $\qquad (2 + 3)A = 10$
   (b) Represent the multiplication of their sum $\qquad 5A = 10$
       by the unknown value.
2. Solve the resulting equation. $\qquad \dfrac{5A}{5} = \dfrac{10}{5}$

$$A = 2$$

EXAMPLE 7

Find A if $A + 3A - 2 = 14$.

$A + 3A - 2 = 14$	First, combine the unknown-value addends. Note that A is the same as $1A$, so $A + 3A = (1 + 3) A = 4A$.
$4A - 2 = 14$	Undo subtraction.

$$
\begin{array}{r}
4A - 2 = 14 \\
\underline{+\ 2 \qquad +\ 2} \\
4A \quad = \quad 16
\end{array}
$$

$$\dfrac{4A}{4} = \dfrac{16}{4} \qquad \text{Undo multiplication.}$$

$$A = \boxed{4} \qquad \text{Solution.}$$

Check:

$A + 3A - 2 = 14$	Replace A with 4 and see if both sides are the same.
$4 + 3(4) - 2 \overset{?}{=} 14$	Multiply first.
$4 + 12 - 2 \overset{?}{=} 14$	Add.
$16 - 2 \overset{?}{=} 14$	Subtract.
$14 = 14$	

The solution is 4.

STOP AND CHECK

Solve.
See Example 7.

1. $B + 3B - 5 = 19$ **2.** $6B - 2B - 7 = 13$ **3.** $7 + 3B + 2B = 17$

4. $5A - 3 + 2A = 18.$ **5.** $3C - C = 16$ **6.** $12 = 8C - 5C$

5 Solve equations containing parentheses.

To solve an equation containing parentheses, we first write the equation in a form that contains no parentheses.

HOW TO Solve an equation containing parentheses

Find A if $2(3A + 1) = 14$

1. Eliminate the parentheses:
   (a) Multiply the number just outside the parentheses by each addend inside the parentheses.
   (b) Show the resulting products as addition or subtraction as indicated.
2. Solve the resulting equation.

$$2(3A + 1) = 14$$

$$6A + 2 = 14$$

$$
\begin{array}{r}
6A + 2 = 14 \\
\underline{-\ 2 \qquad -\ 2} \\
6A \quad = \quad 12
\end{array}
$$

$$\dfrac{6A}{6} = \dfrac{12}{6}$$

$$A = 2$$

EXAMPLE 8 Solve the equation $5(A + 3) = 25$.

$5(A + 3) = 25$	First eliminate the parentheses. Multiply 5 by A, multiply 5 by 3, and
$5A + 15 = 25$	then show the products as addition.
$5A + 15 = \quad 25$	Undo addition.
$\quad\; - 15 \quad - 15$	
$5A \qquad = \quad 10$	Undo multiplication.
$\dfrac{5A}{5} = \dfrac{10}{5}$	
$A = \boxed{2}$	Solution.

Check:

$5(A + 3) = 25$	Replace A with 2 and see if both sides are equal.
$5(\boxed{2} + 3) \overset{?}{=} 25$	Add inside parentheses.
$5(5) \overset{?}{=} 25$	Multiply.
$25 = 25$	

The solution is 2.

TIP

Dealing With Parentheses in the Order of Operations and Solving Equations

Order of Operations

To perform a series of calculations:

1. Perform the operations inside the parentheses or eliminate the parentheses by multiplying.
2. Perform multiplication and division as they appear from left to right.
3. Perform addition and subtraction as they appear from left to right.

Solving Equations

To solve an equation:

1. Eliminate parentheses by multiplying each addend inside the parentheses by the factor outside the parentheses.
2. Undo addition or subtraction.
3. Undo multiplication or division.

In the preceding example, examine the sequence of steps.

To solve:	Eliminate parentheses.
	Undo addition.
	Undo multiplication.
To check:	Add inside parentheses.
	Multiply.

STOP AND CHECK

Solve.
See Example 8.

1. $2(N + 4) = 26$

2. $3(N - 30) = 45$

3. $4(R - 3) = 8$

4. $7(2R - 3) = 21$

5. $5(3R + 2) = 40$

6. $30 = 6(2A + 3)$

6 Solve equations that are proportions.

Ratio: the comparison of two numbers through division. Ratios are most often written as fractions.

Proportion: two fractions or ratios that are equal.

A proportion is based on two pairs of related quantities. The most common way to write proportions is to use fraction notation. A number written in fraction notation is also called a **ratio.** A ratio is the comparison of two numbers through division. When two fractions or ratios are equal, they form a **proportion.**

Cross product: the product of the numerator of one fraction times the denominator of the other fraction of a proportion.

An important property of proportions is that the cross products are equal. A **cross product** is the product of the numerator of one fraction times the denominator of another fraction of a proportion. In the proportion $\frac{1}{2} = \frac{2}{4}$, one cross product is 1×4 and the other cross product is 2×2. Notice that the two cross products are both equal to 4. Let's look at other proportions.

$$\frac{3}{6} = \frac{5}{10}$$
$$3(10) = 6(5)$$
$$30 = 30$$

$$\frac{2}{4} = \frac{5}{10}$$
$$2(10) = 4(5)$$
$$20 = 20$$

$$\frac{4}{8} = \frac{6}{12}$$
$$4(12) = 8(6)$$
$$48 = 48$$

HOW TO — Verify that two fractions form a proportion

1. Find the two cross products.
2. Compare the two cross products.
3. If the cross products are equal, the two fractions form a proportion.

Do $\frac{4}{12}$ and $\frac{6}{18}$ form a proportion?
$4(18) = 72 \quad 12(6) = 72$
Cross products are equal. $72 = 72$
Fractions form a proportion.

EXAMPLE 9

Of the fractions $\frac{2}{3}$ and $\frac{3}{4}$, which one is proportional to $\frac{12}{16}$?

Are $\frac{2}{3}$ and $\frac{12}{16}$ proportional?

$$\frac{2}{3} \overset{?}{=} \frac{12}{16}$$ Find the cross products.

$$2(16) \overset{?}{=} 3(12)$$ Multiply.
$$32 \overset{?}{=} 36$$ Not equal, not a proportion.

Are $\frac{3}{4}$ and $\frac{12}{16}$ proportional?

$$\frac{3}{4} \overset{?}{=} \frac{12}{16}$$ Find the cross products.

$$3(16) \overset{?}{=} 4(12)$$ Multiply.
$$48 \overset{?}{=} 48$$ Equal, proportional.

$\frac{3}{4}$ **is proportional to** $\frac{12}{16}$.

HOW TO — Solve a proportion

1. Find the cross products.
2. Isolate the unknown by undoing the multiplication.

EXAMPLE 10

Solve: $\frac{3}{8} = \frac{21}{N}$

$$\frac{3}{8} = \frac{21}{N}$$ Find the cross products.

$$3N = 8(21)$$ Multiply.
$$3N = 168$$ Undo multiplication by dividing both sides by 3.
$$\frac{3N}{3} = \frac{168}{3}$$ Divide.

$$N = 56$$

STOP AND CHECK

See Example 9.

1. Which of the fractions $\frac{5}{7}$ or $\frac{3}{4}$ is proportional to $\frac{20}{28}$?

2. Which of the fractions $\frac{1}{2}$ or $\frac{2}{3}$ is proportional to $\frac{12}{18}$?

See Example 10.

3. Solve: $\frac{3}{4} = \frac{N}{8}$

4. Solve: $\frac{5}{N} = \frac{4}{12}$

5. Solve: $\frac{N}{4} = \frac{9}{6}$

6. Solve: $\frac{5}{12} = \frac{15}{N}$

SKILL BUILDERS

Solve for the unknown in each equation.

See Example 1.
1. $5A = 20$

See Example 2.
2. $4M = 48$

3. $7C = 56$

4. $\dfrac{B}{7} = 4$

5. $\dfrac{R}{12} = 3$

6. $\dfrac{P}{5} = 8$

See Example 3.
7. $B + 7 = 12$

See Example 4.
8. $R + 7 = 28$

9. $C + 5 = 21$

10. $A - 9 = 15$

11. $A - 16 = 3$

12. $X - 48 = 36$

See Example 5.
13. $4A + 3 = 27$

14. $3B - 1 = 11$

15. $7B - 1 = 6$

16. $8A - 1 = 19$

See Example 6.
17. $\dfrac{B}{3} + 2 = 7$

18. $\dfrac{K}{4} - 5 = 3$

19. $\dfrac{K}{2} + 3 = 5$

20. $\dfrac{C}{2} - 1 = 9$

See Example 7.
21. $2A + 5A = 35$

22. $B + 2B = 27$

23. $5K - 3K = 40$

24. $8K - 2K = 42$

25. $3J + J = 28$ **26.** $2J - J = 21$ **27.** $3B + 2B - 6 = 9$ **28.** $8C - C + 6 = 48$

See Example 8.

29. $2(X - 3) = 6$ **30.** $4(A + 3) = 16$ **31.** $3(B - 1) = 21$ **32.** $6(B + 2) = 30$

Solve each proportion for N. *See Example 10.*

33. $\dfrac{N}{5} = \dfrac{9}{15}$ **34.** $\dfrac{3}{N} = \dfrac{4}{12}$ **35.** $\dfrac{2}{5} = \dfrac{N}{20}$ **36.** $\dfrac{2}{4} = \dfrac{9}{N}$

See Example 9.

37. Which of the fractions $\dfrac{5}{8}$ or $\dfrac{3}{5}$ is proportional to $\dfrac{24}{40}$?   **38.** Which of the fractions $\dfrac{5}{12}$ or $\dfrac{3}{8}$ is proportional to $\dfrac{10}{24}$?

5-2 USING EQUATIONS TO SOLVE PROBLEMS

LEARNING OUTCOME

1 Use the problem-solving approach to analyze and solve word problems.

Equations are powerful business tools because equations use mathematical shorthand for expressing relationships. As we know from our problem-solving strategies, developing a solution plan is a critical step.

1 Use the problem-solving approach to analyze and solve word problems.

Certain key words in a problem give you clues as to whether a certain quantity is added to, subtracted from, or multiplied or divided by another quantity. For example, if a word problem tells you that Carol's salary in 2011 *exceeds* her 2010 salary by $2,500, you know that you should *add* $2,500 to her 2010 salary to find her 2011 salary. Many times, when you see the word *of* in a problem, the problem involves multiplication. Table 5-1 summarizes important key words and what they generally imply when they are used in a word problem. This list should help you analyze the information in word problems and write the information in symbols.

TABLE 5-1
Key Words and What They Generally Imply in Word Problems

Addition	Subtraction	Multiplication	Division	Equality
The sum of	Less than	Times	Divide(s)	Equals
Plus/total	Decreased by	Multiplied by	Divided by	Is/was/are
Increased by	Subtracted from	Of	Divided into	Is equal to
More/more than	Difference between	The product of	Half of (divided by two)	The result is
Added to	Diminished by	Twice (two times)	Third of (divided by three)	What is left
Exceeds	Take away	Double (two times)	Per	What remains
Expands	Reduced by	Triple (three times)		The same as
Greater than	Less/minus	Half of ($\frac{1}{2}$ times)		Gives/giving
Gain/profit	Loss	Third of ($\frac{1}{3}$ times)		Makes
Longer	Shorter			Leaves

We can relate the steps in our five-step problem-solving approach to writing and solving equations.

What You Know	Known or given facts
What You Are Looking For	Unknown amounts (Assign a letter to represent an unknown amount. Other unknown amounts are written related to the assigned letter.)
Solution Plan	Equation or relationship among the known and unknown facts
Solution	Solving the equation
Conclusion	Solution interpreted within the context of the problem

EXAMPLE 1

Full-time employees at Charlie's Steakhouse work more hours per day than part-time employees. If the difference of working hours is 4 hours per day, and if part-timers work 6 hours per day, how many hours per day do full-timers work?

What You Know	What You Are Looking For	Solution Plan
Hours per day that part-timers work: 6	Hours per day that full-timers work: N	The word *difference* implies subtraction.
Difference between hours worked by full-timers and hours worked by part-timers: 4		Full-time hours $-$ part-time hours $=$ difference of hours $N - 6 = 4$

Solution

$$N - 6 = 4 \qquad \text{Undo subtraction.}$$
$$\underline{+6 \quad +6}$$
$$N = 10 \qquad \text{The solution is 10.}$$

Check:

$$10 - 6 \stackrel{?}{=} 4 \qquad \text{Replace } N \text{ with 10. Subtract.}$$
$$4 = 4 \qquad \text{The sides are equal.}$$

Conclusion

The hours per day that full-timers work is 10.

EXAMPLE 2

Wanda plans to save $\frac{1}{10}$ of her salary each week. If her weekly salary is $350, how much will she save each week?

What You Know	What You Are Looking For	Solution Plan
Salary = $350 Rate of saving: $\frac{1}{10}$	Amount to be saved: S	The word *of* implies multiplication. $$\text{Amount to be saved} = \frac{\text{rate of saving}}{} \times \text{salary}$$ $$S = \frac{1}{10}(\$350)$$

Solution

$S = \frac{1}{\cancel{10}}(\$\cancel{350}^{35})$ Reduce and multiply.

$S = \$35$ The solution is 35.

Check:

$\$35 \overset{?}{=} \frac{1}{\cancel{10}}(\$\cancel{350}^{35})$ Replace S with $35 and see if the sides are equal.

$\$35 = \$35$

Conclusion

Wanda will save $35 per week.

Many times a problem requires finding more than one unknown value. Our strategy will be to choose a letter to represent one unknown value. Using known facts, we can then express all other unknown values *in terms of* the one letter. For instance, if we know that twice as many men as women attended a conference, then we might represent the number of women as W and the number of men as $2W$, twice as many as W.

EXAMPLE 3

In planning for a conference on Successful Small Business Practices, the organizers are anticipating that twice as many men as women will attend the conference. If they are expecting 600 to attend the conference, how many men and how many women are likely to attend?

What You Know	What You Are Looking For	Solution Plan
Total expected attendees: 600 Twice as many men as women are expected.	Both the number of men and women are unknown. We can choose to represent the number of women expected to attend as W. Then, the number of men expected to attend is *twice* as many or $2W$. Women: W Men: $2W$	Men + Women = Total Attendees $2W + W = 600$

Continued on next page

$$2W + W = 600$$ Combine addends.

$$3W = 600$$

$$\frac{3W}{3} = \frac{600}{3}$$ Divide both sides by 3.

$$W = 200$$ Number of women expected

$$2W = 2(200)$$

$$= 400$$ Number of men expected

Check:

$$\text{Men} + \text{Women} = 600$$ Substitute 400 for men and 200 for women.

$$400 + 200 = 600$$

$$600 = 600$$

Conclusion

The organizers expect 400 men and 200 women to attend the conference.

Many problems give a *total* number of two types of items. You want to know the number of each of the two types of items. The next example illustrates this type of problem.

EXAMPLE 4   Diane's Card Shop spent a total of $950 ordering 600 cards from Wit's End Co., whose humorous cards cost $1.75 each and whose nature cards cost $1.50 each. How many of each style of card did the card shop order?

What You Know

Total cost of cards: $950   Cost per humorous card: $1.75
Total number of cards: 600   Cost per nature card: $1.50

What You Are Looking For

There are two unknown facts, but we choose one—the number of humorous cards—to be represented by a letter, H.
Number of humorous cards: H
Knowing that the total number of cards is 600, we represent the number of nature cards as 600 minus the number of humorous cards, or $600 - H$.

Solution Plan

Total cost = (cost per humorous card)(number of humorous cards)
           + (cost per nature card)(number of nature cards)
$$950 = (1.75)(H) + (1.50)(600 - H)$$

Solution

$$950 = 1.75H + 1.50(600 - H)$$ Eliminate parentheses that show grouping.

$$950 = 1.75H + (1.50)(600) - 1.50H$$ Multiply 1.50(600).

$$950 = 1.75H + 900 - 1.50H$$ Combine letter terms.

$$950 = 0.25H + 900$$

$$-900 \qquad\qquad -900$$ Subtract 900 from both sides.

$$50 = 0.25H$$

$$\frac{50}{0.25} = \frac{0.25H}{0.25}$$ Divide both sides by 0.25.

$$200 = H$$ The solution is 200, which represents the number of humorous cards.

$$600 - H = 600 - 200$$ Subtract 200 from 600 to find $600 - H$.

$$= 400$$ or 400, the number of nature cards.

Check:

$$950 \stackrel{?}{=} (1.75)(200) + (1.50)(600 - 200)$$ Substitute 200 in place of H. Then perform

$$950 \stackrel{?}{=} (1.75)(200) + (1.50)(400)$$ calculations using the order of operations.

$$950 \stackrel{?}{=} 350 + 600$$ Subtract inside parentheses first.

$$950 = 950$$

Conclusion

The card shop ordered 200 humorous cards and 400 nature cards.

Many problems encountered daily involve proportions.

EXAMPLE 5
Your car gets 23 miles to a gallon of gas. How far can you go on 16 gallons of gas?

What You Know	What You Are Looking For	Solution Plan
Distance traveled using 1 gallon: 23 miles (Pair 1)	Distance traveled using 16 gallons: M miles (Pair 2)	Miles traveled per 16 gallons is proportional to miles traveled for each 1 gallon. $$\frac{1 \text{ gallon}}{23 \text{ miles}} = \frac{16 \text{ gallons}}{M \text{ miles}}$$ Pair 1 Pair 2

Solution

$$\frac{1}{23} = \frac{16}{M}$$ Cross multiply.

$$1M = (16)(23)$$ Multiply.

$$M = 368$$

Check:

$$\frac{1}{23} \overset{?}{=} \frac{16}{368}$$ Substitute 368 for M and cross multiply.

$$(1)(368) \overset{?}{=} (23)(16)$$ Multiply.

$$368 = 368$$

Conclusion

You can travel 368 miles using 16 gallons of gas.

TIP

Arranging the Proportion

Many business-related problems that involve pairs of numbers that are proportional are *direct proportions*. That means an increase in one amount causes an increase in the number that pairs with it. Or, a decrease in one amount causes a decrease in the second amount.

In Example 6, for every 2 gallons of water, 3 ounces of weed killer are needed. It is a direct proportion: more water means more weed killer needed.

The pairs of values in a direct proportion can be arranged in other ways. Another way to arrange the pairs from the preceding example is *across* the equal sign. Each fraction will have the same units of measure.

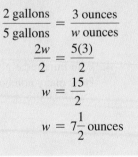

$$\frac{2 \text{ gallons}}{5 \text{ gallons}} = \frac{3 \text{ ounces}}{w \text{ ounces}}$$ pair 1   pair 2

$$\frac{2w}{2} = \frac{5(3)}{2}$$ Cross multiply, then divide.

$$w = \frac{15}{2}$$

$$w = 7\frac{1}{2} \text{ ounces}$$

EXAMPLE 6
The label on a container of concentrated weed killer gives directions to mix 3 ounces of weed killer with every 2 gallons of water. For 5 gallons of water, how many ounces of weed killer should you use?

What You Know	What You Are Looking For	Solution Plan
Amount of weed killer for 2 gallons of water: 3 ounces (Pair 1)	Amount of weed killer for 5 gallons of water: W ounces (Pair 2)	Amount of weed killer per 5 gallons is proportional to the amount of weed killer for each 2 gallons. $$\frac{2 \text{ gallons}}{3 \text{ ounces}} = \frac{5 \text{ gallons}}{W \text{ ounces}}$$ Pair 1 Pair 2

Solution

$$\frac{2}{3} = \frac{5}{W}$$ Cross multiply.

$2W = (3)(5)$ Multiply.

$2W = 15$ Divide both sides by 2.

$$\frac{2W}{2} = \frac{15}{2}$$

$$W = 7\frac{1}{2}$$ The solution is $7\frac{1}{2}$.

Check: $$\frac{2}{3} \stackrel{?}{=} \frac{5}{7\frac{1}{2}}$$ Substitute $7\frac{1}{2}$ for W and divide the right side.

$$\frac{2}{3} \stackrel{?}{=} 5 \div 7\frac{1}{2}$$

$$\frac{2}{3} \stackrel{?}{=} 5 \div \frac{15}{2}$$

$$\frac{2}{3} \stackrel{?}{=} 5\left(\frac{2}{15}\right)$$

$$\frac{2}{3} = \frac{2}{3}$$

Conclusion

You should use $7\frac{1}{2}$ ounces of weed killer for 5 gallons of water.

STOP AND CHECK

1. Marcus James purchased 2,500 pounds of produce. Records indicate he purchased 800 pounds of potatoes, 150 pounds of broccoli, and 390 pounds of tomatoes. He also purchased apples. How many pounds of apples did he purchase? *See Example 1.*

2. Carrie McConnell spends $\frac{1}{6}$ of her weekly earnings on groceries. What are her weekly earnings if she spends $117.50 on groceries each week? *See Example 2.*

3. Hilton Hotel has 8 times as many nonsmoking rooms as it has smoking rooms. If the hotel has 873 rooms in its inventory, how many are smoking rooms? *See Example 3.*

4. Four hundred eighty notebooks can be purchased for $1,656. How many notebooks can be purchased for $2,242.50? *See Example 5 or 6.*

See Example 4.

5. DFS spent a total of $131,263 ordering 5,280 units of two different beauty products from Chanel®. Each unit of face cream costs $18.20 and each unit of perfume costs $32.10. How many units of each product were ordered?

APPLICATIONS

1. The difference in hours between full-timers and the part-timers who work 5 hours a day is 4 hours. How long do full-timers work? *See Example 1.*

2. Manny plans to save $\frac{1}{12}$ of his salary each week. If his weekly salary is $372, find the amount he will save each week. *See Example 2.*

See Example 3.

3. Last week at the Sunshine Valley Rock Festival, Joel sold 3 times as many tie-dyed T-shirts as silk-screened shirts. He sold a total of 176 shirts. How many tie-dyed shirts did he sell?

4. Elaine sold 3 times as many magazine subscriptions as Ron did. Ron sold 16 fewer subscriptions than Elaine did. How many subscriptions did each sell?

See Example 4.

5. Will ordered 2 times as many boxes of ballpoint pens as boxes of felt-tip pens. Ballpoint pens cost $3.50 per box, and felt-tip pens cost $4.50. If Will's order of pens totaled $46, how many boxes of each type of pen did he buy?

6. A real estate salesperson bought promotional calendars and date books to give to her customers at the end of the year. The calendars cost $0.75 each, and the date books cost $0.50 each. She ordered a total of 500 promotional items and spent $300. How many of each item did she order?

Use proportions to solve each problem. See Example 5 or 6.

7. Hershey Foods stock earned $151,000,000. If these earnings represent $1.15 per share, how many shares of stock are there?

8. A scale drawing of an office building is not labeled, but indicates $\frac{1}{4}$ inch = 5 feet. On the drawing, one wall measures 2 inches. How long is the actual wall?

9. A recipe uses 3 cups of flour to $1\frac{1}{4}$ cups of milk. If you have 2 cups of flour, how much milk should you use?

10. For 32 hours of work, you are paid $241.60. How much would you receive for 37 hours?

11. The annual real estate tax on a duplex house is $2,321 and the owner sells the house after 9 months of the tax year. How much of the annual tax will the seller pay? How much will the buyer pay?

12. A wholesale price list shows that 18 dozen headlights cost $702. If 16 dozen can be bought at the same rate, how much will they cost?

13. Two part-time employees share one full-time job. Charris works Mondays, Wednesdays, and Fridays, and Chloe works Tuesdays and Thursdays. The job pays an annual salary of $28,592. What annual salary does each employee earn?

14. A car that leases for $5,400 annually is leased for 8 months of the year. How much will it cost to lease the car for the 8 months?

15. If 1.0000 U.S. dollar is equivalent to 0.1273 Chinese yuan, convert $12,000 to yuan.

16. Asunta's Candle Store ordered 750 candles at a total wholesale cost of $8,660.34. The soy candles cost $12.83 each and the specialty candles cost $10.72 each. How many of each type of candle were ordered? *See Example 4.*

LEARNING OUTCOMES

1 Evaluate a formula.
2 Find an equivalent formula by rearranging the formula.

1 Evaluate a formula.

Formula: a procedure that has been used so frequently to solve certain types of problems that it has become the accepted means of solving the problems.

Variables: letters used to represent unknown numbers.

Evaluate a formula: a process to substitute known values for appropriate letters of the formula and perform the indicated operations to find the unknown value.

Formulas are procedures that have been used so frequently to solve certain types of problems that they have become the accepted means of solving these problems. Formulas are composed of numbers, letters or **variables** that are used to represent unknown numbers, and operations that relate these known and unknown values. To **evaluate a formula** is to substitute known values for the appropriate letters of the formula and perform the indicated operations to find the unknown value. Sometimes the equation must be solved to isolate the unknown value in the formula.

HOW TO   Evaluate a formula

1. Write the formula.
2. Rewrite the formula substituting known values for the letters of the formula.
3. Solve the equation for the unknown letter or perform the indicated operations, applying the order of operations.
4. Interpret the solution within the context of the formula.

EXAMPLE 1
Wal-Mart purchases a Sony plasma television for $875 and marks it up $400. What is the selling price of the television? Use the formula $S = C + M$, where S is the selling price, C is the cost, and M is the markup.

$S = C + M$ Write the formula. Substitute known values for C and M.
$S = \$875 + \$400$ Add.
$S = \$1{,}275$

The selling price for the television is $1,275.

In some instances, the missing value is not the value that is isolated in the formula. After the known values are substituted into the formula, use the techniques for solving equations to find the missing value.

EXAMPLE 2
A DVD player that costs $85 sells for $129. What is the markup on the player? Use the formula $S = C + M$, where S is the selling price, C is the cost, and M is the markup.

$S = C + M$ Write the formula. Substitute known values for C and S.
$\$129 = \quad \$85 + M$ Subtract $85 from each side of the equation.
$\underline{-85 \quad\quad -85}$
$\$44 = M$

The markup for the DVD player is $44.

TIP

Interchanging the Sides of an Equation

In Example 2, the solved equation was $\$44 = M$. Because equations show equality, it is allowable to interchange the sides of the equation. The equation can also be written as $M = \$44$.

EXAMPLE 3
Greg Jackson earned $960 in a 40-hour week. Use the formula $P = RH$, where P is the amount of pay, R is the rate per hour, and H is the number of hours worked to find his hourly rate.

$P = RH$
$\$960 = R(40)$
$\dfrac{\$960}{40} = \dfrac{R(40)}{40}$
$\$24 = R$

Greg's hourly rate is $24 per hour.

STOP AND CHECK

1. Office Depot purchased an office chair for $317 and marked it up $250. Find the selling price of the chair. Use the formula $S = C + M$. *See Example 1.*

2. Office Max purchased a computer workstation for $463 and marked its retail (selling) price at $629. Use the formula $S = C + M$ to find the markup on the workstation. *See Example 2.*

See Example 3.

3. Trios Mixon worked 40 hours at $19.26 per hour. Find his pay. Use the formula $P = RH$, where P is the pay, R is the rate per hour, and H is the number of hours worked.

4. Luis Pardo earned $612 for a 40-hour week. Use the formula $P = RH$ to find his hourly rate.

2 Find an equivalent formula by rearranging the formula.

A formula can have as many variations as there are letters or variables in the formula. Using the techniques for solving equations, any missing number can be found no matter where it appears in the formula. Variations of formulas are desirable when the variation is used frequently. Also, in using an electronic spreadsheet, the missing number should be isolated on the left side of the equation. To **isolate** a variable is to **solve for** that variable.

Isolate a variable: to solve a formula for a desired variable.

HOW TO   Find an equivalent formula by rearranging the formula

1. Determine which variable of the formula is to be isolated (solved for).
2. Highlight or mentally locate all instances of the variable to be isolated.
3. Treat all other variables of the formula as you would treat a number in an equation, and perform normal steps for solving an equation.
4. If the isolated variable is on the right side of the equation, interchange the sides so that it appears on the left side.

EXAMPLE 4

Solve the formula $S = C + M$ for C.

$S = C + M$	Isolate C. Subtract M from both sides of the equation.
$S - M = C + M - M$	Simplify. $M - M = 0$. $C + 0 = C$.
$S - M = C$	Interchange the sides of the equation.
$C = S - M$	Formula variation

The unit price of a product is used when comparing prices of a product available in different quantities. The formula for finding the **unit price** is $U = \frac{P}{N}$, where U is the unit price of a specified amount of a product, P is the total price of the product, and N is the number of specified units contained in the product. The specified unit can be identified in many ways. The unit could be any measuring unit such as pounds (lb) or ounces (oz) or the number of items such as an individual snack cake in a package of cakes.

Unit price: the price of a specified amount of a product.

EXAMPLE 5

Find a variation of the formula $U = \dfrac{P}{N}$ that is solved for P.

$U = \dfrac{P}{N}$	Isolate P. Multiply both sides of the equation by N.
$N(U) = \left(\dfrac{P}{N}\right)N$	Simplify. $\dfrac{N}{N} = 1$. $P(1) = P$.
$NU = P$	Interchange the sides of the equation.
$P = NU$	Formula variation

STOP AND CHECK

See Example 4.

1. Solve the formula $S = C + M$ for M.

2. Solve the formula $M = S - N$ for S.

See Example 5.

3. Solve the formula $U = \dfrac{P}{N}$ for N.

4. The unit depreciation formula, Unit depreciation $= \dfrac{\text{depreciable Value}}{\text{units Produced during expected life}}$ can be written in symbols as $U = \dfrac{V}{P}$. Solve the formula to find V, the depreciable value.

5-3 SECTION EXERCISES

SKILL BUILDERS

1. Sears purchased 10,000 pairs of men's slacks for $18.46 a pair and marked them up $21.53. What was the selling price of each pair of slacks? Use the formula $S = C + M$. *See Example 1.*

2. K-Mart had 896 swimsuits that were marked to sell at $49.99 per unit. Each suit was marked down $18.95. Find the reduced price of each unit using the formula $N = S - M$, where M is the markdown, S is the original selling price, and N is the reduced price. *See Example 1.*

3. Home Depot sold bird feeders for $69.99 and had marked them up $36.12. What was the cost of the feeders? Use the formula $S = C + M$. *See Example 2.*

4. Dollar General sold garden hoses at a reduced price of $7.64 and took an end-of-season markdown of $12.35. What was the original selling price of each hose? Use the formula $M = S - N$ (Markdown = selling price − reduced price). *See Example 2.*

5. Jacob borrowed $30,000 to start up his consulting business. The loan had a simple interest rate of 6.2% for 3 years. Use the formula $I = prt$ to find the amount of interest he will pay on the loan. $I = $ interest; $p = $ principal; $r = $ rate (expressed as a decimal 0.062); $t = $ time in years. *See Example 3.*

6. Jordan purchased a new copy machine and financed it for one year. The installment price was $4,235.50 and the cash price was $3,940. Find the amount of finance charge using the formula: Finance charge = Installment price − Cash price. *See Example 1.*

7. The formula Total cost = Cost + Shipping + Installation is used to find the total cost of a business asset when setting up a depreciation schedule for the asset. The formula can be written in symbols as $T = C + S + I$. Solve the formula for C, the cost of the asset. *See Example 4.*

8. The formula depreciable Value = total Cost − Salvage value is used to set up a depreciation schedule for an asset. The formula can be written in symbols as $V = C - S$. Solve the formula for C. *See Example 4.*

9. The formula Yearly depreciation $= \dfrac{\text{depreciable Value}}{\text{years of expected Life}}$ is used to find yearly depreciation using the straight line depreciation method. The formula can be written in symbols as $Y = \dfrac{V}{L}$. Solve the formula for V. *See Example 5.*

10. Solve the formula $Y = \dfrac{V}{L}$ for L. *See Example 5.*

11. The formula Amount financed $=$ Cash price $-$ Down payment is used to find the amount financed on a purchase that is paid in monthly payments. The formula can be written in symbols as $A = C - D$. Solve the formula for D, the down payment. *See Example 4.*

12. The formula Finance charge $=$ unpaid Balance $\times$ monthly Rate is sometimes used to calculate the monthly finance charge on a credit card. The formula can be written in symbols as $F = B \times R$. Solve the formula for B, the unpaid balance. *See Example 5.*

Learning Outcomes

What to Remember with Examples

Section 5-1

1 Solve equations using multiplication or division. (p. 150)

1. Isolate the unknown value or variable:
   (a) If the equation contains the *product* of the unknown value and a number, then *divide* both sides of the equation by the number.
   (b) If the equation contains the *quotient* of the unknown value and the divisor, then *multiply* both sides of the equation by the divisor.
2. Identify the solution: The solution is the number on the side opposite the isolated unknown-value letter.
3. Check the solution: In the original equation, replace the unknown-value letter with the solution; perform the indicated operations; and verify that both sides of the equation are the same number.

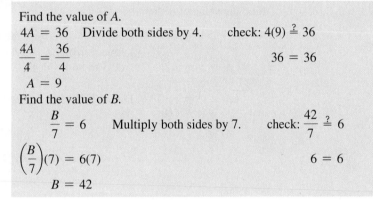

Find the value of A.

$4A = 36$ Divide both sides by 4.   check: $4(9) \stackrel{?}{=} 36$

$$\frac{4A}{4} = \frac{36}{4}$$

$$36 = 36$$

$$A = 9$$

Find the value of B.

$$\frac{B}{7} = 6$$ Multiply both sides by 7.   check: $\frac{42}{7} \stackrel{?}{=} 6$

$$\left(\frac{B}{7}\right)(7) = 6(7)$$

$$6 = 6$$

$$B = 42$$

2 Solve equations using addition or subtraction. (p. 151)

1. Isolate the unknown value or variable:
   (a) If the equation contains the *sum* of the unknown value and a known value, then *subtract* the known value from both sides of the equation.
   (b) If the equation contains the *difference* of the unknown value and a known value, then *add* the known value to both sides of the equation.
2. Identify the solution: The solution is the number on the side opposite the isolated unknown-value letter.
3. Check the solution: In the original equation, replace the unknown-value letter with the solution; perform the indicated operations; and verify that both sides of the equation are the same number.

Find the value of A.

$A - 7 = 12$ Add 7 to both sides.

$\underline{ + 7 \quad + 7}$

$A \quad\;= 19$

Find the value of B.

$B + 5 = 32$ Subtract 5 from both sides.

$\underline{ - 5 \quad - 5}$

$B \quad\;= 27$

3 Solve equations using more than one operation. (p. 152)

1. Isolate the unknown value or variable:
   (a) Add or subtract as necessary *first*.
   (b) Multiply or divide as necessary *second*.
2. Identify the solution: The solution is the number on the side opposite the isolated unknown-value letter.
3. Check the solution: In the original equation, replace the unknown-value letter with the solution and perform the indicated operations.

Find the value of *A*.

$4A + 4 = 20$ Undo addition first.
$\underline{ -4 \quad -4}$
$4A = 16$ Undo multiplication.
$\dfrac{4A}{4} = \dfrac{16}{4}$
$A = 4$

Find the value of *B*.

$\dfrac{B}{3} - 5 = 12$ Undo subtraction first.
$\underline{\phantom{\dfrac{B}{3}} +5 \quad +5}$
$\dfrac{B}{3} = 17$ Undo division.
$\left(\dfrac{B}{3}\right)(3) = 17(3)$
$B = 51$

---

4   Solve equations containing multiple unknown terms. (p. 154)

Solve an equation when the unknown value occurs in two or more addends.

1. Combine the unknown-value addends when the addends are on the same side of the equal sign:
   (a) Add the numbers in each addend.
   (b) Represent the multiplication of their sum by the unknown value.
2. Solve the resulting equation.

Find the value of *A*.

$A - 5 + 5A = 25$ Combine addends on the same side of the equal sign that have unknown factors. $A + 5A = 6A$
$6A - 5 = 25$ Add 5 to both sides.
$\underline{ +5 \quad +5}$
$6A = 30$ Divide both sides by 6.
$\dfrac{6A}{6} = \dfrac{30}{6}$
$A = 5$

---

5   Solve equations containing parentheses. (p. 155)

1. Eliminate the parentheses:
   (a) Multiply the number just outside the parentheses by each addend inside the parentheses.
   (b) Show the resulting products as addition or subtraction as indicated.
2. Solve the resulting equation.

Find the value of *A*.

$3(A + 4) = 27$ Eliminate parentheses first. $3(A) = 3A$; $3(4) = 12$
$3A + 12 = 27$ Subtract 12 from both sides.
$\underline{ -12 \quad -12}$
$3A = 15$ Divide both sides by 3.
$\dfrac{3A}{3} = \dfrac{15}{3}$
$A = 5$

---

6   Solve equations that are proportions. (p. 156)

Verify that two fractions form a proportion.

1. Find the two cross products.
2. Compare the two cross products.
3. If the cross products are equal, the two fractions form a proportion.

Verify that $\dfrac{5}{12} = \dfrac{15}{36}$ is a proportion.

$5(36) \overset{?}{=} 12(15)$ Find the cross products.

$180 = 180$ Since the cross products are equal $\dfrac{5}{12} = \dfrac{15}{36}$ is a proportion.

Solve a proportion.

1. Find the cross products.
2. Isolate the unknown by undoing the multiplication.

Solve the proportion $\dfrac{5}{x} = \dfrac{7}{12}$.

$\dfrac{5}{x} = \dfrac{7}{12}$ Cross multiply.

$7x = 5(12)$ Multiply.

$7x = 60$ Divide.

$\dfrac{7x}{7} = \dfrac{60}{7}$ Convert $\dfrac{60}{7}$ to a mixed number.

$x = 8\dfrac{4}{7}$

Section 5-2

1 Use the problem-solving approach to analyze and solve word problems. (p. 160)

Keywords and what they generally imply in word problems.

Addition	Subtraction	Multiplication	Division	Equality
The sum of	Less than	Times	Divide(s)	Equals
Plus/total	Decreased by	Multiplied by	Divided by	Is/was/are
Increased by	Subtracted from	Of	Divided into	Is equal to
More/more than	Difference between	The product of	Half of (divided by two)	The result is
Added to	Diminished by	Twice (two times)	Third of (divide by 3)	What is left
Exceeds	Take away	Double (two times)	Per	What remains
Expands	Reduced by	Triple (three times)		The same as
Greater than	Less/minus	Half of ($\frac{1}{2}$ times)		Gives/giving
Gain/profit	Loss	Third of ($\frac{1}{3}$ times)		Makes
Longer	Lower			Leaves
Older	Shrinks			
Heavier	Smaller than			
Wider	Younger			
Taller	Slower			

Use the five-step problem-solving approach.

What You Know	Known or given facts
What You Are Looking For	Unknown or missing amounts
Solution Plan	Equation or relationship among the known and unknown facts
Solution	Solving the equation
Conclusion	Solution interpreted within the context of the problem

If 4 printer cartridges cost $56.80, how much would 7 cartridges cost?

What You Know	What You Are Looking For	Solution Plan
4 cartridges cost $56.80 Pair 1	7 cartridges cost $N Pair 2	$\dfrac{4 \text{ cartridges}}{\$56.80} = \dfrac{7 \text{ cartridges}}{\$N}$ Pair 1 Pair 2

Solution

$\dfrac{4}{\$56.80} = \dfrac{7}{N}$ Cross multiply.

$4N = \$56.80(7)$ Multiply.

$4N = \$397.60$ Divide.

$\dfrac{4N}{4} = \dfrac{\$397.60}{4}$

$N = \$99.40$

Conclusion

7 cartridges cost $99.40.

1 Evaluate a formula. (p. 167)

1. Write the formula.
2. Rewrite the formula substituting known values for the letters of the formula.
3. Solve the equation for the unknown letter or perform the indicated operations, applying the order of operations.
4. Interpret the solution within the context of the formula.

Find the unit price of a snack cake that is available in a package of 6 cakes for $1.98. Use the formula $U = \frac{P}{N}$, where U is the unit price of a specified amount of a product, P is the total price of the product, and N is the number of specified units contained in the product.

$$U = \frac{P}{N}$$ Substitute known values.

$$U = \frac{\$1.98}{6}$$ Divide.

$$U = \$0.33$$ Cost per cake

---

2 Find an equivalent formula by rearranging the formula. (p. 168)

1. Determine which variable of the formula is to be isolated (solved for).
2. Highlight or mentally locate all instances of the variable to be isolated.
3. Treat all other variables of the formula as you would treat a number in an equation, and perform the normal steps for solving an equation.
4. If the isolated variable is on the right side of the equation, interchange the sides so that it appears on the left side.

The distance formula is $D = RT$, where D is the distance traveled, R is the rate or speed traveled, and T is the time traveled. Find a variation of the distance formula that is solved for the time traveled.

$$D = RT$$ Isolate T. Divide both sides of the equation by R.

$$\frac{D}{R} = \frac{RT}{R}$$ Simplify. $\frac{R}{R} = 1$; $1(T) = T$.

$$\frac{D}{R} = T$$ Interchange the sides of the equation.

$$T = \frac{D}{R}$$ Formula variation.

EXERCISES SET A

Find the value of the variable:

1. $5N = 35$

2. $\dfrac{A}{6} = 2$

3. $N - 5 = 12$

4. $2N + 4 = 12$

5. $\dfrac{A}{3} + 4 = 12$

6. $2(x - 3) = 8$

7. $3(x - 1) = 30$

8. $8A - 3A = 40$

9. $4X - X = 21$

10. $12N + 5 - 7N = 45$

11. Solve the proportion for N:
$$\dfrac{5}{12} = \dfrac{35}{N}$$

12. Solve the proportion for N:
$$\dfrac{7}{18} = \dfrac{N}{9}$$

13. Ace Motors sold a total of 15 cars and trucks during one promotion sale. Six of the vehicles sold were trucks. What is the number of cars that were sold?

14. Bottletree Bakery and Card Shop ordered an equal number of 12 different cards. If a total of 60 cards were ordered, how many of each type of card were ordered?

15. An electrician pays $\frac{2}{5}$ of the amount he charges for a job for supplies. If he was paid $240 for a certain job, how much did he spend on supplies?

16. An inventory clerk is expected to have 2,000 fan belts in stock. If the current count is 1,584 fan belts, how many more should be ordered?

17. Shaquita Davis earns $350 for working 40 hours. How much does she make for each hour of work?

18. Wallpaper costs $12.97 per roll and a kitchen requires 9 rolls. What is the cost of the wallpaper needed to paper the kitchen?

19. Bright Ideas purchased 1,000 lightbulbs. Headlight bulbs cost $13.95 each, and taillight bulbs cost $7.55 each. If Bright Ideas spent $9,342 on lightbulb stock, how many headlights and how many taillights did it get? What was the dollar value of the headlights ordered? What was the dollar value of the taillights ordered?

20. If 5 dozen roses can be purchased for $62.50, how much will 8 dozen cost?

21. For an installment loan, a formula is used to find the total amount of installment payments. The formula is Total installment payments = installment Price − Down payment. The formula can be written in symbols as $T = P - D$. Find the total installment payments if $P = \$6,508.72$ and $D = \$2,250$.

22. In the formula $T = P - D$, T represents total installment payments, P represents installment price, and D represents down payment amount. Find the installment price if the total of installment payments is $15,892.65 and the down payment is $3,973.16.

23. To find the amount of each installment payment for a loan, use the formula $p = \frac{T}{N}$, where p is the installment payment, T is the total of installment payments, and N is the number of payments. Solve the formula to find the total of installment payments.

24. Solve the installment payment formula $p = \frac{T}{N}$ for N.

EXERCISES SET B

Solve.

1. $3N = 27$

2. $\dfrac{A}{2} = 3$

3. $N + 8 = 20$

4. $3N - 5 = 10$

5. $\dfrac{A}{2} - 5 = 1$

6. $5A - 45 = 10$

7. $7B - 14 = 21$

8. $3A = 3$

9. $5X - 4 = 11$

10. $5(2A - 3) = 15$

11. Solve the proportion for N:
$$\dfrac{N}{4} = \dfrac{24}{32}$$

12. Solve the proportion for N:
$$\dfrac{14}{N} = \dfrac{7}{9}$$

13. Edna's Book Carousel ordered several cookbooks and received 12. The shipping invoice indicated that 6 books would be shipped later. What was the original number of books ordered?

14. The Stork Club is a chain of baby clothing stores. The owner of the chain divided a number of bonnets equally among the 7 stores in the chain. If each store got 9 bonnets, what was the number of bonnets distributed by the owner of the chain?

15. Liz Bliss spends 18 hours on a project and estimates that she has completed $\frac{2}{3}$ of the project. How many hours does she expect the project to take?

16. A personal computer costs $4,000 and a printer costs $1,500. What is the total cost of the equipment?

17. A purse that sells for $68.99 is reduced by $25.50. What is the price of the purse after the reduction?

18. Wilson's Auto, Inc., has 37 employees and a weekly payroll of $10,878. If each employee makes the same amount, how much does each make?

19. An imprint machine makes 22,764 imprints in 12 hours. How many imprints can be made in 1 hour?

20. If a delivery van travels 252 miles on 12 gallons of gasoline, how many gallons are needed to travel 378 miles?

21. Financial statements use the formula working Capital = current Assets − current Liabilities. This formula can be written in symbols as $C = A − L$. Find the working capital if current assets are $483,596 and current liabilities are $346,087.

22. In the formula $C = A − L$, C represents working capital, A represents current assets, and L represents current liabilities. Find the current assets of Premier Travel Company if working capital is $1,803,516 and current liabilities are $483,948.

23. Financial ratios are used to evaluate the performance of a business. One ratio is expressed by the formula

Current ratio $= \dfrac{\text{current Assets}}{\text{current Liabilities}}$. The formula can be written

in symbols as $C = \dfrac{A}{L}$. Solve the formula for A.

24. Solve the current ratio formula $C = \dfrac{A}{L}$ for L.

PRACTICE TEST

Solve.

1. $N + 7 = 18$

2. $\frac{A}{3} = 6$

3. $3A - 5 = 10$

4. $2(N + 1) = 14$

5. $4A = 48$

6. $3R + 5 - R = 7$

7. $5N = 45$

8. $B - 8 = 7$

9. $5A + 8 = 33$

10. $5A + A = 30$

11. An employee who was earning $249 weekly received a raise of $36. How much is the new salary?

12. A container of oil holds 585 gallons. How many containers each holding 4.5 gallons will be needed if all the oil is to be transferred to the smaller containers?

13. A discount store sold plastic cups for $3.50 each and ceramic cups for $4 each. If 400 cups were sold for a total of $1,458, how many cups of each type were sold? What was the dollar value of each type of cup sold?

14. Find the cost of 200 suits if 75 suits cost $10,200.

15. Lashonna Harris is a buyer for Plough. She can purchase 100 pounds of chemicals for $97. At this same rate, how much would 2,000 pounds of the chemical cost?

16. From the currency exchange rate table shown in Table 5-2, 1.0000 EUR (euro) is equivalent to 0.7338 USD (U.S. dollars). Use a proportion to convert $2,500 to EUR.

17. From Table 5-2, 1.0000 USD is equivalent to 0.011126 JPY. Use a proportion to convert 250 USD to the equivalent amount of JPY currency.

TABLE 5-2
Currency Exchange Rate Table

Currency names	British Pound (GBP)	Canadian Dollar (CAD)	Euro (EUR)	Japanese Yen (JPY)	U.S. Dollar (USD)	Chinese Yuan Renminbi (CNY)
British pound	1.0000	0.6069	0.8687	0.007088	0.6371	0.09323
Canadian dollar	1.6504	1.0000	1.4331	0.011691	1.0508	0.1538
Euro	1.1524	0.6990	1.0000	0.00816	0.7338	0.1074
Japanese yen	141.2860	85.7113	122.6500	1.0000	89.9832	13.1678
U.S. dollar	1.5706	0.9525	1.3638	0.011126	1.0000	0.1463
Chinese yuan renminbi	10.7352	6.5106	9.3216	0.07604	6.8351	1.0000

Source: Currency Exchange Rates provided by OANDA, the currency site.

18. The formula for the installment price of an item purchased with financing is Installment price = Total of installment payments + Down payment. The formula can be written in symbols as $I = T + D$. Find the installment price I if $T = \$24,846.38$ and $D = \$2,500$.

19. In the formula $I = T + D$, the letter I represents installment price, T represents total of installment payments, and D represents the amount of down payment. Find the down payment for an installment loan if the installment price is $13,846.76 and the total of installment payments is $10,673.26.

20. Rearrange the formula $I = T + D$ to solve for D.

1. Give some instances when it would be desirable to have more than one version of a formula. For example,

$$P = R \times B, R = \frac{P}{B}, B = \frac{P}{R}.$$

2. Explain why $1.2 + n = 1.7$ and $1.7 - 1.2 = n$ will give the same result for n.

3. Explain why $5n = 4.5$ and $n = \frac{4.5}{5}$ give the same result for n.

4. Either of these two formulas, $P = 2l + 2w$ or $P = 2(l + w)$, can be used to find the perimeter of a rectangle. Explain why.

5. Test both of the formulas $P = s + s + s + s$ and $P = 4s$ to see if each formula gives the same perimeter for a square of your choosing. If each formula gives the same result, explain why.

6. Find and explain the error. Then rework the problem correctly.
$$10 + 7(8 + 4) =$$
$$17(8 + 4) =$$
$$17(12) = 204$$

7. If the wholesale cost of 36 printer cartridges is $188, explain how a proportion can be used to find the cost of one cartridge.

Challenge Problem

Solve $\frac{5}{8}X + \frac{3}{5} = 8$

CASE STUDIES

5-1 Shiver Me Timbers

Cape Fear Riverwood is a lumber company that specializes in recovering, cutting, and selling wood from trees discarded long ago, even those that have been underwater or buried in the ground for more than 100 years! Historically, the logging industry used rafts made of wood to transport cut trees to logging pens along the Cape Fear River in North Carolina. Some of the heavier trees sank during transportation. Other trees were intentionally dumped in the river for disposal after being bled for turpentine. The company used side-scan penetrating radar to find large quantities of logs in 30 locations in and around the river. The first two sites the company salvaged contained heart pine and river pine. A more recent site contained a treasure trove of perfectly preserved 38,000-year-old cypress trees buried 30 feet in a sand pit. Scientists have identified these as trees that became extinct more than 20,000 years ago.

1. The cypress trees are 60 to 80 feet long. If there are 14,285 trees at an average length of 70 feet, how many feet of wood will the company have?

2. If the cypress is worth $80 per foot, what are the 14,285 trees worth?

3. If the cost to recover the 60- to 70-foot cypress trees is $375.00 each and the cost to harvest the larger trees is $500.00, how much would it cost to recover all of the trees if $\frac{2}{5}$ of the trees are more than 70 feet long?

4. Because the harvested lumber depletes the total amount of natural resources available to the citizens of North Carolina, the state of North Carolina places an excise tax of $\frac{1}{20}$ of all profits earned by lumber companies within the state. If the harvested cypress wood is worth approximately $80,000,000 and the only expense of obtaining the wood is the recovery cost, how much excise tax is owed to North Carolina?

Source: Rachel Wimberly, "Shiver Me Timbers," *Wilmington Star-News*, November 2, 2003, p. El.

5-2 Artist's Performance Royalties

Performance rights organizations track and pay royalties to song writers, publishers, and musicians for use of their works. Royalties are paid to an artist based on a complicated credit system using a formula with weights assigned for a variety of factors, including the following:

- **Use:** weight based on the type of song or performance (theme, underscore, or promotional).
- **Licensee:** weight based on the station's licensing fee, which is determined by the size of the licensee's markets and number of stations carrying its broadcast signal.
- **Time-of-Day:** weight assigned according to whether the performances are broadcast during peak viewing or listening times.
- **Follow-the-Dollar:** factor based on the medium from which the money came (radio play, live performance, TV performance, and so on).
- **General Licensing Allocation:** based on fees collected from bars, hotels, and other nonbroadcast licensees.

These amounts are multiplied together, and then a **radio feature premium** is added, if applicable, to arrive at a total number of credits for the particular artist, or his or her **credit total** for a particular reporting period. Royalties are usually split among the writer, the publisher, and possibly a performer if the writer does not perform his or her own work. The proportion that each party receives is called the **share value**. All of the money collected for the reporting period divided by the total number of credits for all performers is called the **credit value**. An artist who wants to figure out what money he or she will receive for a period has to multiply the three factors; credit total, share value, and credit value.

1. Nicole wants to know how much her royalty will be for a song she has written. How will it be calculated? Write the steps or the formulas that will be used to calculate her royalty payment.

2. Nicole has written a popular song entitled "Going There," which has been recorded by a well-known performer. She recently received a royalty check for $7,000. If Nicole gets a 0.5 share of the royalties and the credit value is $3.50, what was the credit total that her song earned? Write out the problem in the form of an equation and solve it.

3. Nicole quickly published another song, "Take Me There," that is played even more often than "Going There." If her first song earns 4,000 credits and her second song earns 6,000 credits, what will the royalty payment be from the two songs if the credit value remains at $3.50?

4. Nicole is considering an offer to perform her own songs on a CD to be titled "Waiting There." In the past she has written, but not performed, her music. If Nicole's royalty is 0.12 of the suggested retail price of $15.00 for the CD, but 0.25 of the retail price is deducted for packaging before Nicole's royalty is calculated, how much will she receive for sale of the CD? Write your answer in the form of an equation and solve it.

Source: http://entertainment.howstuffworks.com/music-royalties.htm

5-3 Educational Consultant

Jerome Erickson is a retired school district administrator who now works as a consultant specializing in hiring administrators for school districts. Jerome used to charge a flat fee of $5,000 for each administrator hired, but decided to develop a new pricing structure due to some inherent problems with his previous approach. The new structure is as follows:

Due at signing:	$1,500
Contract review:	$125/hour capped at 8 hours
Contract formulation:	$125/hour capped at 12 hours
Applicant screening:	$25 per applicant
Preliminary interviews:	$125 per interview
Final interviews:	$175 per interview

Carol Ferguson is an overworked accounting clerk in a small school district. She sits at her desk, reviewing the pricing structure in the brochure from Erickson Consulting. She knows that Mr. Erickson is one of the most highly regarded educational consultants in the state, but is not sure that the district can afford him. The school board had voted to budget $5,000 for the district administrator search, based on Carol's recommendation.

1. Write a formula reflecting the pricing structure for Erickson Consulting.

2. Carol presumes that there will be approximately 90 applicants, 10 preliminary interviews, and 3 final interviews. Using her numbers, what is the maximum that the district will have to pay Mr. Erickson?

3. Presuming that Carol is correct about the number of applicants, what are some ways that Carol can reduce her costs? What would you recommend?

4. Why do you think Jerome Erickson changed his pricing structure? What were some of those inherent problems? What are the benefits of the current pricing structure?

Source: http://entertainment.howstuffworks.com/music-royalties.htm

World Series of Poker: Do You Have What It Takes?

Chances are that if you are a sports fan, you've heard of the World Series of Poker. Texas Hold 'em is the name of the game, with fame and considerable fortune on the line. With as many as 8,773 players participating in the main event, at an entry fee of $10,000 each and a first prize of $12 million, the stakes are incredibly high. But does the average player stand a chance? Statistically you do, but the probability of winning first place is 0.0001139, or 0.01139%. Unfortunately, most players who enter lose their entry fee; tournament rules state that only 1 in 10, or 10%, will finish in the money. Based on 8,773 entries, how many players would that be?

To answer that question, you need to know how to use percents. Knowing percents will also help you to know how to play your cards. Probability is a huge factor in Texas Hold 'em. Players use odds or percentages—the focus of this chapter—to determine their actions. For example, say you are playing for free online with some of your Facebook friends in a $1/$2 Texas Hold 'em game. You have J♥ 10♠, with only one opponent left in the hand. So far, the following cards have been turned up: 2♠ 5♦ 9♣ Q♥. You have an outside straight draw, and only one card left (called the river) to make it. Any 8 or any King will finish this straight for you (8-9-10-J-Q or 9-10-J-Q-K), so you have 8 chances (four 8's: 8♠ 8♦ 8♣ 8♥ and four K's: K♠ K♦ K♣ K♥ left in the deck) with 46 unseen cards left.

By computing your percentages, you realize that 8/46 (or 17.4%) is close to a 1 in 6 (or 16.7%) chance of making it. Your sole opponent bets the maximum, $2. If you take the $2 bet and call, you could win the current pot of $40. The fraction $40/$2 is a 20 to 1 ratio, so you stand to make 20 times more if you call. If your chances to win the hand were only 1 in 20 (or 5%), there wouldn't be much incentive to call the bet. But as your percentages are higher than 1/20 at 1/6 or 17%, calling (making the bet) might not be a bad idea.

So whether you're playing in Las Vegas, with friends on a Saturday night, or for free online, knowledge of percentages will make you a better poker player. If you pay special attention studying percents in this chapter, then who knows—maybe someday you could be a Texas Hold 'em champion wearing the World Series of Poker bracelet. But with the probability of becoming a champion just slightly over 1/100 of 1 percent, you should expect a significantly higher probability of success in the career you are considering—while studying business mathematics.

LEARNING OUTCOMES

6-1 Percent Equivalents

1. Write a whole number, fraction, or decimal as a percent.
2. Write a percent as a whole number, fraction, or decimal.

6-2 Solving Percentage Problems

1. Identify the rate, base, and portion in percent problems.
2. Use the percentage formula to find the unknown value when two values are known.

6-3 Increases and Decreases

1. Find the amount of increase or decrease in percent problems.
2. Find the new amount directly in percent problems.
3. Find the rate or the base in increase or decrease problems. .

LEARNING OUTCOMES

1 Write a whole number, fraction, or decimal as a percent.
2 Write a percent as a whole number, fraction, or decimal.

Percent: a standardized way of expressing quantities in relation to a standard unit of 100 (hundredth, per 100, out of 100, over 100).

With fractions and decimals, we compare only like quantities, that is, fractions with common denominators and decimals with the same number of decimal places. We can standardize our representation of quantities so that they can be more easily compared. We standardize by expressing quantities in relation to a standard unit of 100. This relationship, called a **percent**, is used to solve many different types of business problems.

The word *percent* means *hundredths* or *out of 100* or *per 100* or *over 100* (in a fraction). That is, 44 percent means 44 hundredths, or 44 out of 100, or 44 per 100, or 44 over 100. We can write 44 hundredths as 0.44 or $\frac{44}{100}$.

The symbol for *percent* is %. You can write 44 percent using the percent symbol: 44%; using fractional notation: $\frac{44}{100}$; or using decimal notation: 0.44.

$$44\% = 44 \text{ percent} = 44 \text{ hundredths} = \tfrac{44}{100} = 0.44$$

Mixed percents: percents with mixed numbers or mixed decimals.

Percents can contain whole numbers, decimals, fractions, mixed numbers, or mixed decimals. Percents with mixed numbers and mixed decimals are often referred to as **mixed percents.** Examples are $33\frac{1}{3}\%$, $0.05\frac{3}{4}\%$, and $0.23\frac{1}{3}\%$.

1 Write a whole number, fraction, or decimal as a percent.

The businessperson must be able to write whole numbers, decimals, or fractions as percents, and to write percents as whole numbers, decimals, or fractions. First we examine writing whole numbers, decimals, and fractions as percents.

Hundredths and percent have the same meaning: per hundred. Just as 100 cents is the same as 1 dollar, 100 percent is the same as 1 whole quantity.

$$100\% = 1$$

This fact is used to write percent equivalents of numbers and to write numerical equivalents of percents. It is also used to calculate markups, markdowns, discounts, and numerous other business applications.

When we multiply a number by 1, the product has the same value as the original number. $N \times 1 = N$. We have used this concept to change a fraction to an equivalent fraction with a higher denominator. For example,

$$1 = \frac{2}{2} \quad \text{and} \quad \frac{1}{2}\left(\frac{2}{2}\right) = \frac{2}{4}$$

We can also use the fact that $N \times 1 = N$ to change numbers to equivalent percents.

$$1 = 100\% \qquad \frac{1}{2} = \frac{1}{2}(100\%) = \frac{1}{2}\left(\frac{100\%}{1}\right) = 50\%$$

$$0.5 = 0.5(100\%) = 050.\% = 50\%$$

In each case when we multiply by 1 in some form, the value of the product is equivalent to the value of the original number even though the product *looks different.*

HOW TO   Write a number as its percent equivalent

1. Multiply the number by 1 in the form of 100%.
2. The product has a % symbol.

Write 0.3 as a percent.
0.3 = 0.3(100%) =
030.% = 30%

EXAMPLE 1

Write the decimal or whole number as a percent.

(a) 0.27   (b) 0.875   (c) 1.73   (d) 0.004   (e) 2

(a) $0.27 = 0.27(100\%) = 027.\% = 27\%$ Multiply 0.27 by 100% (move the decimal point two places to the right).
0.27 as a percent is 27%.

(b) $0.875 = 0.875(100\%) = 087.5\% = 87.5\%$ Multiply 0.875 by 100% (move the decimal point two places to the right).
0.875 as a percent is 87.5%.

(c) $1.73 = 1.73(100\%) = 173.\% = 173\%$ Multiply 1.73 by 100% (move the decimal point two places to the right).
1.73 as a percent is 173%.

(d) $0.004 = 0.004(100\%) = 000.4\% = 0.4\%$ Multiply 0.004 by 100% (move the decimal point two places to the right).
0.004 as a percent is 0.4%

(e) $2 = 2(100\%) = 200.\% = 200\%$ Multiply 2 by 100% (move the decimal point two places to the right).
2 as a percent is 200%.

As you can see, the procedure is the same regardless of the number of decimal places in the number and regardless of whether the number is greater than, equal to, or less than 1.

EXAMPLE 2

Write the fraction as a percent.

(a) $\frac{67}{100}$ (b) $\frac{1}{4}$ (c) $3\frac{1}{2}$ (d) $\frac{7}{4}$ (e) $\frac{2}{3}$

(a) $\frac{67}{100} = \frac{67}{100}\left(\frac{100\%}{1}\right) = \mathbf{67\%}$ Reduce and multiply.

(b) $\frac{1}{4} = \frac{1}{4}\left(\frac{100\%}{1}\right) = \mathbf{25\%}$ Reduce and multiply.

(c) $3\frac{1}{2} = 3\frac{1}{2}\left(\frac{100\%}{1}\right) = \frac{7}{2}\left(\frac{100\%}{1}\right) = \mathbf{350\%}$ Change to an improper fraction, reduce, and multiply.

(d) $\frac{7}{4} = \frac{7}{4}\left(\frac{100\%}{1}\right) = \mathbf{175\%}$ Reduce and multiply.

(e) $\frac{2}{3} = \frac{2}{3}\left(\frac{100\%}{1}\right) = \frac{200\%}{3} = \mathbf{66\frac{2}{3}\%}$ Multiply.

STOP AND CHECK

Write the decimal or whole number as a percent. See Example 1.

1. 0.82   **2.** 3.45   **3.** 0.0007   **4.** 5

5. From a recent U.S. Census Bureau report, the portion of the U.S. population under 18 years old was 0.273. What percent of the population was under 18 years old?

6. A recent consumer expenditures survey showed that the portion of total expenditures for telephone services that was spent on cellular phone service for persons under 25 was 0.752. What percent of this age group's total expenditures on telephone service was spent for cellular phone services?

Write the fraction or mixed number as a percent. See Example 2.

7. $\frac{43}{100}$ **8.** $\frac{3}{10}$ **9.** $8\frac{1}{4}$ **10.** $\frac{1}{6}$

11. The report, Global Video Game Market Forecast, projects that online game revenues will account for approximately $\frac{2}{5}$ of total software revenue in the next three years. What percent of the total software revenue will online game revenues be within three years?

12. According to recent data from the U.S. Census Bureau, approximately $\frac{9}{10}$ of the U.S. population was less than 65 years of age. What percent of the population was less than 65?

2   Write a percent as a whole number, fraction, or decimal.

When a number is divided by 1, the quotient has the same value as the original number. $N \div 1 = N$ or $\frac{N}{1} = N$. We have used this concept to reduce fractions. For example,

$$1 = \frac{2}{2} \qquad \frac{2}{4} \div \frac{2}{2} = \frac{1}{2}$$

We can also use the fact that $N \div 1 = N$ or $\frac{N}{1} = N$ to change percents to numerical equivalents.

$$50\% \div 100\% = \frac{50\%}{100\%} = \frac{50}{100} = \frac{1}{2}$$

$$50\% \div 100\% = 50 \div 100 = 0.50 = 0.5$$

HOW TO   Write a percent as a number

1. Divide the number by 1 in the form of 100% or multiply by $\frac{1}{100\%}$.
2. The quotient does not have a % symbol.

EXAMPLE 3   Write the percent as a decimal.

(a) 37%   (b) 26.5%   (c) 127%   (d) 7%   (e) 0.9%   (f) $2\frac{19}{20}\%$ (g) $167\frac{1}{3}\%$

(a) $37\% = 37\% \div 100\% = 0.37 = \mathbf{0.37}$ Divide by 100 mentally.

(b) $26.5\% = 26.5\% \div 100\% = 0.265 = \mathbf{0.265}$ Divide by 100 mentally.

(c) $127\% = 127\% \div 100\% = 1.27 = \mathbf{1.27}$ Divide by 100 mentally.

(d) $7\% = 7\% \div 100\% = 0.07 = \mathbf{0.07}$ Divide by 100 mentally.

(e) $0.9\% = 0.9\% \div 100\% = 0.009 = \mathbf{0.009}$ Divide by 100 mentally.

(f) $2\frac{19}{20}\% = 2.95\% \div 100\% = 0.0295 = \mathbf{0.0295}$ Write the mixed number in front of the percent symbol as a mixed decimal before dividing by 100%.

(g) $167\frac{1}{3}\% = 167.3\overline{3}\% \div 100\%$
$$= 1.673\overline{3} = \mathbf{1.673\overline{3}} \textbf{ or } \mathbf{1.673} \textbf{ (rounded)}$$
Write the mixed number in front of the percent symbol as a repeating decimal before dividing by 100.

EXAMPLE 4   Write the percent as a fraction or mixed number.

(a) 65%   (b) $\frac{1}{4}\%$ (c) 250%   (d) $83\frac{1}{3}\%$ (e) 12.5%

(a) $65\% = 65\% \div 100\% = \frac{65\%}{1}\left(\frac{1}{100\%}\right) = \mathbf{\frac{13}{20}}$ Convert division to multiplication.

(b) $\frac{1}{4}\% = \frac{1}{4}\% \div 100\% = \frac{1\%}{4}\left(\frac{1}{100\%}\right) = \mathbf{\frac{1}{400}}$

(c) $250\% = 250\% \div 100\% = \frac{250\%}{1}\left(\frac{1}{100\%}\right) = \frac{5}{2} = \mathbf{2\frac{1}{2}}$

(d) $83\frac{1}{3}\% = 83\frac{1}{3}\% \div 100\% = \frac{250\%}{3}\left(\frac{1}{100\%}\right) = \frac{5}{6}$ Convert to improper fraction.

(e) $12.5\% = 12\frac{1}{2}\% = 12\frac{1}{2}\% \div 100\% = \frac{25\%}{2}\left(\frac{1}{100\%}\right) = \frac{1}{8}$ Convert mixed decimal to mixed number.

STOP AND CHECK

Write the percent as a decimal. See Example 3.

1. 52%

2. 38.5%

3. 143%

4. 0.72%

5. A recent consumer expenditures survey showed that 54.8% of all expenditures in the United States for annual telephone services was allocated to cellular phone service. Write the percent as a decimal.

6. Recent statistics showed that 25.7% of California's population was under 18 years old and 0.4% of the state's population was Native Hawaiian or Other Pacific Islander. Express these two percents as decimals.

Write the percent as a fraction or mixed number. See Example 3.

7. 72%

8. $\frac{1}{8}\%$

9. 325%

10. $16\frac{2}{3}\%$

11. Statistics from FedStats, a governmental web site, showed that approximately 30% of firms in California were owned by women and 15% were owned by Hispanics. Express each percent as a fraction.

12. Statistics from FedStats, a governmental web site, showed that approximately 0.5% of Florida's population was American Indian or Alaskan Native. Express the percent as a fraction.

6-1 SECTION EXERCISES

SKILL BUILDERS

Write the decimal as a percent. See Example 1.

1. 0.39

2. 0.693

3. 0.75

4. 0.2

5. 2.92

6. 0.0007

7. Data collected from those who reported their credit card debt showed that Arkansas had the lowest average annual percentage rate (APR) on its credit cards at 0.0721. Represent this as a percent.

8. One study reported that of all Americans, 0.86 gambled legally at least some of the time. What percent of Americans gamble?

Write the fraction and mixed number as a percent. See Example 2.

9. $\frac{39}{100}$

10. $\frac{3}{4}$

11. $3\frac{2}{5}$

12. $5\dfrac{1}{4}$

13. $\dfrac{9}{4}$

14. $\dfrac{7}{5}$

15. $\dfrac{2}{300}$

16. $\dfrac{3}{8}$

17. $\dfrac{4}{5}$

18. Approximately 23 of every 50 legal-aged adults gambled in casinos. What percent gambled in casinos?

19. According to one study, an average payout for slot machines is 90 cents on each dollar. What is the percent return on every dollar spent in playing slots?

Write the percent as a decimal. Round to the nearest thousandth if the division does not terminate. See Example 3.

20. $15\dfrac{1}{2}\%$

21. $\dfrac{1}{8}\%$

22. 45%

23. 150%

24. $125\dfrac{1}{3}\%$

25. $\dfrac{3}{7}\%$

26. In a recent year, $9\dfrac{9}{10}\%$ of American children had no health insurance. Write this percent as a decimal.

27. A recent report indicated that Hawaii had the lowest percent of residents with no health insurance at $8\dfrac{3}{5}\%$. Express the percent as a decimal.

Write the percent as a fraction or mixed number. See Example 4.

28. 45%

29. 60%

30. 250%

31. 180%

32. $\frac{3}{4}\%$

33. $33\frac{1}{3}\%$

34. A recent report indicated that 16% of South Carolina residents had no health insurance. What is the fraction of South Carolina residents with no health insurance?

35. A recent report indicated that $12\frac{1}{2}\%$ of all residents in Washington state did not have health insurance. What fraction of Washington residents were uninsured?

6-2 SOLVING PERCENTAGE PROBLEMS

LEARNING OUTCOMES

1 Identify the rate, base, and portion in percent problems.
2 Use the percentage formula to find the unknown value when two values are known.

1 Identify the rate, base, and portion in percent problems.

Formula: a relationship among quantities expressed in words or numbers and letters.

Base: the original number or one entire quantity.

Portion: part of the base.

Rate: the rate of the portion to the base expressed as a percent.

A **formula** expresses a relationship among quantities. When you use the five-step problem-solving approach, the third step, the Solution Plan, is often a formula written in words and letters.

The percentage formula, Portion = Rate × Base, can be written as $P = RB$. The letters or words represent numbers.

In the formula $P = RB$, the **base** (B) represents the original number or one entire quantity. The **portion** (P) represents a part of the base. The **rate** (R) is a percent that tells us how the base and portion are related. In the statement "50 is 20% of 250," 250 is the base (the entire quantity), 50 is the portion (part), and 20% is the rate (percent).

> **HOW TO**   Identify the rate, base, and portion
>
> 1. Identify the rate. *Rate* is usually written as a percent, but it may be a decimal or fraction.
> 2. Identify the base. *Base* is the total amount, original amount, or entire amount. The base often follows the preposition *of*.
> 3. Identify the portion. *Portion* can refer to the part, partial amount, amount of increase or decrease, or amount of change. It is a portion of the *base*. The portion often follows a form of the verb *is*.

> **EXAMPLE 1**   Identify the given and missing elements for each example.
>
> (a) 20% of 75 is what number?
> (b) What percent of 50 is 30?
> (c) Eight is 10% of what number?
>
>   *R*   *B*   *P*
> (a) 20% of 75 is what number?
>   Percent   Total   Part
>
>   *R*   *B*   *P*
> (b) What percent of 50 is 30?
>   Percent   Total   Part
>
>   *P*   *R*   *B*
> (c) Eight is 10% of what number?
>   Part   Percent   Total

Use the identifying key words for rate (*percent* or %), base (*total, original*, associated with the word *of*), and portion (*part*, associated with the word *is*).

STOP AND CHECK

Identify the base, rate, and portion. See Example 1.

1. 42% of 85 is what number?

2. Fifty is 15% of what number?

3. What percent of 80 is 20?

4. Twenty percent of what number is 17?

5. Find 125% of 72.

6. Thirty-two is what percent of 160?

7. According to the American Association of Community Colleges, the United States has 1,195 community colleges. Of these, 987 are public institutions. What percent are public institutions? Identify the base, rate, and portion.

8. Of the 1,195 community colleges in the United States, 2.6% are tribal colleges. How many U.S. colleges are tribal colleges? Identify the base, rate, and portion.

2 Use the percentage formula to find the unknown value when two values are known.

The percentage formula, Portion = Rate × Base, can be written as $P = RB$. When the numbers are put in place of the letters, the formula guides you through the calculations.

The three forms of the percentage formula are

Portion = Rate × Base	$P = RB$	For finding the portion.
Base = $\dfrac{\text{Portion}}{\text{Rate}}$	$B = \dfrac{P}{R}$	For finding the base.
Rate = $\dfrac{\text{Portion}}{\text{Base}}$	$R = \dfrac{P}{B}$	For finding the rate.

Circles can help us visualize these formulas. The shaded part of each circle in Figure 6-1 represents the missing amount. The unshaded parts represent the known amounts. If the unshaded parts are *side by side, multiply* their corresponding numbers to find the unknown number. If the unshaded parts are *one on top of the other, divide* the corresponding numbers, top divide by bottom, to find the unknown number.

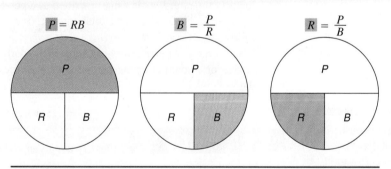

FIGURE 6-1
Forms of the Percentage Formula

HOW TO Use the percentage formula to solve percentage problems

1. Identify and classify the two known values and the one unknown value.
2. Choose the appropriate percentage formula for finding the unknown value.
3. Substitute the known values into the formula. For the rate, use the decimal or fractional equivalent of the percent.
4. Perform the calculation indicated by the formula.
5. Interpret the result. If finding the rate, convert decimal or fractional equivalents of the rate to a percent.

EXAMPLE 2

Solve the problems.

(a) 20% of 400 is what number?
(b) 20% of what number is 80?
(c) 80 is what percent of 400?

(a) 20% = Rate — Identify known values and unknown value.
400 = Base
Portion is unknown
$P = RB$ — Choose the appropriate formula.
$P = 0.2(400)$ — Substitute values using the decimal equivalent of 20%.
$P = \mathbf{80}$ — Perform calculation.
20% of 400 is 80. — Interpret result.

(b) 20% = Rate — Identify known values and unknown value.
80 = Portion
Base is unknown
$B = \dfrac{P}{R}$ — Choose the appropriate formula.

$B = \dfrac{80}{0.2}$ — Substitute values. Perform calculation.

$B = \mathbf{400}$
20% of 400 is 80. — Interpret result.

(c) 80 = Portion — Identify known values and unknown value.
400 = Base
Rate is unknown

$R = \dfrac{P}{B}$ — Choose the appropriate formula.

$R = \dfrac{80}{400}$ — Substitute values. Perform calculation.

$R = 0.2$ or **20%**
80 is 20% of 400. — Interpret result. $0.2 = 20\%$.

Very few percentage problems that you encounter in business tell you the values of P, R, and B directly. Percentage problems are usually written in words that must be interpreted before you can tell which form of the percentage formula you should use.

EXAMPLE 3

During a special one-day sale, 600 customers bought the on-sale pizza. Of these customers, 20% used coupons. The manager will run the sale again the next day if more than 100 coupons were used. Should she run the sale again?

What You Know	What You Are Looking For	Solution Plan
Total customers: 600 Coupon-using customers as a percent of total customers: 20%	Quantity of coupon-using customers Should the manager run the sale again?	The quantity of coupon-using customers is a *portion* of the *base* of total customers, at a *rate* of 20% (Figure 6-2). $P = RB$ Quantity of coupon-using customers = RB

Solution

$P = RB$ — P is unknown; $R = 20\%$; $B = 600$
$P = 20\% (600)$ — Substitute known values. Change % to decimal equivalent.
$P = 0.2 (600)$ — Multiply.
$P = 120$

Conclusion

The quantity of coupon-using customers is 120.
Because 120 is more than 100, the manager should run the sale again.

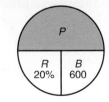

FIGURE 6-2

EXAMPLE 4

If $66\frac{2}{3}\%$ of the 900 employees in a company choose the Preferred Provider insurance plan, how many people from that company are enrolled in the plan?

First, identify the terms. The rate is the percent, and the base is the total number of employees. The portion is the quantity of employees enrolled in the plan.

$P = RB$	The portion is the unknown value (Figure 6-3).
$P = 66\frac{2}{3}\%(900)$	The rate is $66\frac{2}{3}\%$; the base is 900. Write $66\frac{2}{3}\%$ as a fraction.
$P = \frac{2}{3}\left(\frac{900}{1}\right) = 600$	Multiply.

The Preferred Provider plan has 600 people enrolled.

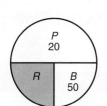

FIGURE 6-3

TIP

Noncontinuous Calculator Sequence Versus Continuous Calculator Sequence

We can write the fractional equivalent of the percent as a rounded decimal and divide using a calculator.

$$\boxed{AC}\ 2\ \boxed{\div}\ 3\ \boxed{=} \Rightarrow 0.6666666667$$
$$\boxed{AC}\ 900\ \boxed{\times}\ .6666666667\ \boxed{=} \Rightarrow 599.9999994$$

As one continuous sequence, enter

$$\boxed{AC}\ 2\ \boxed{\div}\ 3\ \boxed{\times}\ 900\ \boxed{=} \Rightarrow 600$$

Note slight discrepancies from rounding when using two separate calculations. The answer obtained by using a continuous sequence of steps is more accurate.

EXAMPLE 5

Stan sets aside 15% of his weekly income for rent. If he sets aside $150 each week, what is his weekly income?

Identify the terms: The rate is the number written as a percent, 15%. The portion is given, $150; it is a portion of his weekly income, the unknown base.

$B = \dfrac{P}{R}$	The rate is 15% and the portion is $150 (Figure 6-4). The base is the weekly income to be found.
$B = \dfrac{\$150}{15\%}$	Convert 15% to a decimal equivalent.
$B = \dfrac{150}{0.15}$	Divide.
$B = \$1,000$	

Stan's weekly income is $1,000.

FIGURE 6-4

EXAMPLE 6

If 20 cars were sold from a lot that had 50 cars, what percent of the cars were sold?

$R = \dfrac{P}{B}$	The portion is 20; the base is 50 (Figure 6-5). The rate is the unknown to find.
$R = \dfrac{20}{50}$	Divide.
$R = 0.4$	Convert to % equivalent.
$R = 0.4(100\%)$	
$R = 40\%$	

Of the cars on the lot, 40% were sold.

FIGURE 6-5

Many students mistakenly think that the portion can never be larger than the base. The portion (percentage) is smaller than the base only when the rate is less than 100%. The portion is larger than the base when the rate is greater than 100%.

EXAMPLE 7   48 is what percent of 24?

$$R = \frac{P}{B}$$ The rate is unknown. The portion is 48. The base is 24.

$$R = \frac{48}{24}$$ Divide.

$R = 2$ Rate written as a whole number.

$\boldsymbol{R = 200\%}$ Rate written as a percent.

STOP AND CHECK

See Example 2.

1. 15% of 200 is what number?

2. 25% of what number is 120?

3. 150 is what percent of 750?

4. Find $33\frac{1}{3}\%$ of 72. *See Example 4.*

5. $16\frac{2}{3}\%$ of 81 is what number?

See Example 4.

6. What percent of 45 is 180?
See Example 7.

7. Seventy-five percent of students in a class of 40 passed the first test. How many passed? *See Example 3.*

8. The projected population of the United States in 2050 is 419,854,000 people with 33,588,320 Asians alone. What percent of the population is projected to be Asians alone in 2050? *See Example 6.*

9. Poker tournament rules state that 10% of those who pay the entry fee will finish in the money. If 877 players finish in the money for a recent tournament, how many paid the entry fee? *See Example 5.*

6-2 SECTION EXERCISES

SKILL BUILDERS

Identify the rate, base, and portion. See Example 1.

1. 48% of 12 is what number?

2. 32% of what number is 28?

3. What percent of 158 is 47.4?

4. What number is 130% of 149?

5. 15% of what number is 80?

6. 48% of what number is 120?

Use the appropriate form of the percentage formula. Round division to the nearest hundredth if necessary. See Example 2.

7. Find P if $R = 25\%$ and $B = 300$.

8. Find 40% of 160.

9. What number is 154% of 30?
See Example 4.

10. What number is $33\frac{1}{3}\%$ of 150?

11. Find B if $P = 36$ and $R = 66\frac{2}{3}\%$

12. Find P if $B = 75$ and $R = 16\frac{2}{3}\%$.

See Example 2.

13. 40% of 30 is what number?

14. 52% of 17.8 is what number?

15. 30% of what number is 21?

16. 17.5% of what number is 18? Round to hundredths.

17. What percent of 16 is 4?

18. What percent of 50 is 30?

19. 172% of 50 is what number?

20. 0.8% of 50 is what number?

21. What percent of 15.2 is 12.7? Round to the nearest hundredth of a percent.

See Example 7.

22. What percent of 73 is 120? Round to the nearest hundredth of a percent.

23. 325 is what percent of 260?

24. 532 is what percent of 350?

APPLICATIONS

See Example 3.

25. At the Evans Formal Wear department store, all suits are reduced 20% from the retail price. If Charles Stewart purchased a suit that originally retailed for $258.30, how much did he save?

26. Joe Passarelli earns $8.67 per hour working for Dracken International. If Joe earns a merit raise of 12%, how much is his raise?

27. An ice cream truck began its daily route with 95 gallons of ice cream. The truck driver sold 78% of the ice cream. How many whole gallons of ice cream were sold?

28. Lars Pacheco earns $132,500 annually. He received a 52% bonus on sales and stock management. How much was his annual bonus?

See Example 5.

29. Nancy Botano expects to receive $18,000 in bonuses for managing the media center at the Olympic Games. If the bonus is 24% of her annual salary, what is her annual salary?

30. Stacy Bauer sold 80% of the tie-dyed T-shirts she took to the Green Valley Music Festival. If she sold 42 shirts, how many shirts did she take?

31. A stockholder sold her shares and made a profit of $1,466. If this is a profit of 23%, how much were the shares worth when she originally purchased them?

32. The Drammelonnie Department Store sold 30% of its shirts in stock. If the department store sold 267 shirts, how many shirts did the store have in stock?

See Example 6.

33. Ali gave correct answers to 23 of the 25 questions on the driving test. What percent of the questions did he get correct?

34. A soccer stadium in Manchester, England, has a capacity of 78,753 seats. If 67,388 seats were filled, what percent of the stadium seats were vacant? Round to the nearest hundredth of a percent.

35. Holly Hobbs purchased a magazine at the Atlanta airport for $2.99. The tax on the purchase was $0.18. What is the tax rate at the Atlanta airport? Round to the nearest percent.

36. A receipt from Wal-Mart in Memphis showed $4.69 tax on a subtotal of $53.63. What is the tax rate? Round to the nearest hundredth percent.

6-3 INCREASES AND DECREASES

LEARNING OUTCOMES

1 Find the amount of increase or decrease in percent problems.
2 Find the new amount directly in percent problems.
3 Find the rate or the base in increase or decrease problems.

New amount: the ending amount after an amount has changed (increased or decreased).

In many business applications an original amount is increased or decreased to give a **new amount.** Some examples of increases are the sales tax on a purchase, the raise in a salary, and the markup on a wholesale price. Some examples of decreases are the deductions on your paycheck and the markdown or the discount on an item for sale.

1 Find the amount of increase or decrease in percent problems.

The amount of increase or decrease is the amount that an original number changes. Subtraction is used to find the amount of change when the beginning and ending (or new) amounts are known.

Find the amount of increase or decrease from the beginning and ending amounts

1. To find the amount of increase (when new amount is larger than beginning amount):

   Amount of increase = new amount − beginning amount

2. To find the amount of decrease (when new amount is smaller than beginning amount):

   Amount of decrease = beginning amount − new amount

EXAMPLE 1

David Spear's salary increased from $58,240 to $63,190. What is the amount of increase?

Beginning amount = $58,240
New amount = $63,190
Increase = new amount − beginning amount
= $63,190 − $58,240
= $4,950

David's salary increase was $4,950.

EXAMPLE 2

A coat was marked down from $98 to $79. What is the amount of markdown?

Beginning amount = $98
New amount = $79
Decrease = beginning amount − new amount
= $98 − $79
= $19

The coat was marked down $19.

DID YOU KNOW?

Using signed numbers you can combine the two previous rules into one rule for finding the amount of change.

To find the amount of change:

1. Subtract the beginning amount from the new amount.

   Amount of change = New amount − Beginning amount

2. A positive result represents an increase.
3. A negative result represents a decrease.
   Look at Example 2 again.

   Amount of change = New amount − Beginning amount
   = $79 − $98
   = −$19

The negative result means that the change was a decrease.

Percent of change: the percent by which a beginning amount has changed (increased or decreased).

A change in a value is often expressed as a **percent of change.** The amount of change is a percent of the original or beginning amount.

HOW TO Find the amount of change (increase or decrease) from a percent of change

1. Identify the original or beginning amount and the percent or rate of change.
2. Multiply the decimal or fractional equivalent of the rate of change times the original or beginning amount.

   Amount of change = percent of change × original amount

EXAMPLE 3

Your company has announced that you will receive a 3.2% raise. If your current salary is $42,560, how much will your raise be?

What You Know	What You Are Looking For
Current salary = $42,560 Rate of change = 3.2%	Amount of raise

Solution Plan

$$\begin{matrix} \text{Amount} \\ \text{of raise} \end{matrix} = \begin{pmatrix} \text{percent of} \\ \text{change} \end{pmatrix} \begin{pmatrix} \text{original} \\ \text{amount} \end{pmatrix}$$

Solution

$$\begin{aligned} \text{Amount of raise} &= \text{percent of change} \times \text{original amount} \\ &= 3.2\%(\$42,560) \\ &= 0.032(\$42,560) \qquad\qquad \text{Multiply.} \\ &= \$1,361.92 \end{aligned}$$

Conclusion

The raise will be $1,361.92.

STOP AND CHECK

See Example 1.

1. The price of a new Lexus is $53,444. The previous year's model cost $51,989. What is the amount of increase?

See Example 2.

2. In trading on the New York Stock Exchange, Bank of America fell to $73.57. The stock had sold for $81.99. What is the amount of decrease in the stock price per share?

See Example 3.

3. Marilyn Bauer earns $62,870 and gets a 4.3% raise. How much is her raise?

4. International Paper reported third-quarter earnings were down 16% from $145 million. What was the amount of decrease?

5. Zack weighed 230 pounds before experiencing a 12% weight loss. How many pounds did he lose?

6. The number of active registered nurses is currently 2,249,000. A 20.3% increase by 2020 will be needed. How many nurses will need to be added to the existing workforce?

2   Find the new amount directly in percent problems.

Often in increase or decrease problems we are more interested in the new amount than the amount of change. We can find the new amount directly by adding or subtracting percents first. The original or beginning amount is always considered to be our *base* and is represented by 100%.

HOW TO   Find the new amount directly in a percent problem

1. Find the rate of the new amount.

   For increase: 100% + rate of increase

   For decrease: 100% − rate of decrease

2. Find the new amount.

   $$P = RB$$

   New amount = rate of new amount × original amount

EXAMPLE 4

Medical assistants are to receive a 9% increase in wages per hour. If they were making $15.25 an hour, what is the *new wage per hour* to the nearest cent?

Rate of new amount = 100% + rate of increase
$$= 100\% + 9\%$$
$$= 109\%$$

New amount = rate of new amount × original amount
$$= 109\%(\$15.25) \quad \text{Change \% to its decimal equivalent.}$$
$$= 1.09(\$15.25) \quad \text{Multiply.}$$
$$= \$16.6225 \quad \text{New amount}$$
$$= \$16.62 \quad \text{Nearest cent}$$

The new hourly wage is $16.62.

EXAMPLE 5

A pair of jeans that originally cost $49.99 now is advertised as 70% off. What is the sale price of the jeans?

Rate of new amount = 100% − rate of decrease
$$= 100\% - 70\%$$
$$= 30\%$$

New amount = rate of new amount × original amount
$$= 30\%(\$49.99) \quad \text{Change \% to its decimal equivalent.}$$
$$= 0.3(\$49.99) \quad \text{Multiply.}$$
$$= \$14.997 \quad \text{New amount}$$
$$= \$15.00 \quad \text{Nearest cent}$$

The sale price of the jeans is $15.

STOP AND CHECK

See Example 4.

1. Marilyn Bauer earns $62,870 and gets a 4.3% raise. How much is her new salary?

See Example 5.

2. International Paper reported third-quarter earnings were down 16% from $145 million. Find the third-quarter earnings.

See Example 5.

3. Zack weighed 230 pounds before experiencing a 12% weight loss. How many pounds does he now weigh?

See Example 4.

4. Over the next ten years Stacy Bauer plans to increase her investment of $9,500 by 250%. How much will she have invested altogether?

See Example 4.

5. Shares of McDonald's, the world's largest hamburger restaurant chain, rose 51% this year. Find the new share price if the stock sold for $24.25 last year.

See Example 4.

6. The number of registered nurses is currently 2,249,000. If a 20.3% increase in this number is projected for 2020, how many nurses will be needed by 2020?

3 Find the rate or the base in increase or decrease problems.

Many kinds of increase or decrease problems involve finding either the rate or the base.

The rate is the *percent of change* or the *percent of increase or decrease.* The base is still the *original amount.*

HOW TO   Find the rate or the base in increase or decrease problems

1. Identify or find the amount of change (increase or decrease).

2. To find the rate of increase or decrease, use the percentage formula $R = \dfrac{P}{B}$.

$$R = \frac{\text{amount of change}}{\text{original amount}}$$

3. To find the base or original amount, use the percentage formula $B = \dfrac{P}{R}$.

$$B = \frac{\text{amount of change}}{\text{rate of change}}$$

EXAMPLE 6   During the month of May, a graphic artist made a profit of $1,525. In June she made a profit of $1,708. What is the percent of increase in profit?

What You Know	What You Are Looking For
Original amount = $1,525 New amount = $1,708	Percent of increase in profit

Solution Plan
Amount of increase = new amount − original amount Percent of increase = $\dfrac{\text{amount of increase}}{\text{original amount}}$

Solution

$$
\begin{aligned}
\text{Amount of increase} &= \$1,708 - \$1,525 \quad \text{Subtract.}\\
&= \$183
\end{aligned}
$$

$$
\begin{aligned}
\text{Percent of increase} &= \frac{\$183}{\$1,525} \quad &&\text{Divide.}\\
&= 0.12 \quad &&\text{Convert to \% equivalent.}\\
&= 0.12(100\%)\\
&= 12\%
\end{aligned}
$$

Conclusion

The percent of increase in profit is 12%.

In some cases you may not have enough information to determine the amount of increase or decrease with the previous procedure. Then we must match the rate with the information we are given.

EXAMPLE 7   At Best Buy the price of a DVD player dropped by 20% to $179. What was the original price to the nearest dollar?

What You Know	What You Are Looking For
Reduced price = new amount = $179 Rate of decrease = 20%	Original price

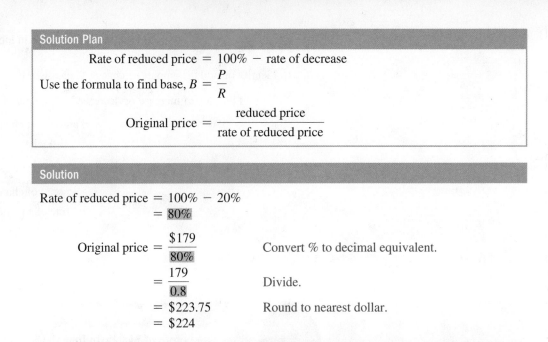

Solution Plan

Rate of reduced price = 100% − rate of decrease

Use the formula to find base, $B = \dfrac{P}{R}$

$$\text{Original price} = \dfrac{\text{reduced price}}{\text{rate of reduced price}}$$

Solution

Rate of reduced price = 100% − 20%
$$= 80\%$$

Original price $= \dfrac{\$179}{80\%}$ Convert % to decimal equivalent.

$$= \dfrac{179}{0.8}$$ Divide.

$$= \$223.75$$ Round to nearest dollar.

$$= \$224$$

Conclusion

The original price of the DVD player was $224.

TIP

Be Sure to Use the Correct Rate

When using the percentage formula, the description for the rate must match the description of the portion.

	Example 7 above **DVD Problem**	**Example 5** **Jeans Problem**
Form of percentage formula	$B = \dfrac{P}{R}$	$P = RB$
Description of rate	Rate of *reduced price*	Rate of *new amount*
Description of portion	*Reduced price*	*New amount*

STOP AND CHECK

See Example 6.

1. Emily Sien reported sales of $23,583,000 for the third quarter and $38,792,000 for the fourth quarter. What is the percent of increase in profit? Round to the nearest tenth of a percent.

See Example 6.

2. Ken Sien reduced his college spending from $9,524 in the fall semester to $8,756 in the spring semester. What percent was the decrease? Round to the nearest percent.

See Example 7.

3. Sydney Sien showed a house that was advertised as a 10% decrease on the original price. The sale price was $148,500. What was the original price?

See Example 7.

4. You know that a DVD is reduced 25% and the amount of reduction is $6.25. Find the original price and the discounted price of the movie.

See Example 6.

5. A used truck is reduced by 48% of its new price. You know the used price is $14,799. Find the new price to the nearest dollar.

6. The average NFL ticket price was $113.17 for 2011 and for 2007 it was $72.20. What was the percent increase in ticket price? Round to the nearest tenth percent.

SKILL BUILDERS

See Examples 1–2.

1. A number increased from 5,286 to 7,595. Find the amount of increase.

2. A number decreased from 486 to 104. Find the amount of decrease.

See Example 3.

3. Find the amount of increase if 432 is increased by 25%.

4. Find the amount of decrease if 68 is decreased by 15%.

See Examples 4–5.

5. If 135 is decreased by 75%, what is the new amount?

6. If 78 is increased by 40%, what is the new amount?

See Example 6.

7. A number increased from 224 to 336. Find the percent of increase.

8. A number decreased from 250 to 195. Find the rate of decrease.

See Example 7.

9. A number is decreased by 40% to 525. What is the original amount?

10. A number is increased by 15% to 43.7. Find the original amount.

APPLICATIONS

See Example 6.

11. The cost of a pound of nails increased from $2.36 to $2.53. What is the percent of increase to the nearest whole-number percent?

12. Wrigley announced the first increase in 16 years in the price of a five-stick pack of gum. The price was raised by 5 cents to 30 cents. Find the percent of increase. Round to the nearest percent.

See Example 3.

13. Bret Davis is getting a 4.5% raise. His current salary is $38,950. How much will his raise be?

14. Kewanna Johns plans to lose 12% of her weight in the next 12 weeks. She currently weighs 218 pounds. How much does she expect to lose?

See Example 4.

15. DeMarco Jones makes $13.95 per hour but is getting a 5.5% increase. What is his new wage per hour to the nearest cent?

See Example 5.

16. Carol Wynne bought a silver tray that originally cost $195 and was advertised at 65% off. What was the sale price of the tray?

See Example 6.

17. A laptop computer that was originally priced at $2,400 now sells for $2,700. What is the percent of increase?

See Example 7.

18. Federated Department Stores dropped the price of a winter coat by 15% to $149. What was the original price to the nearest cent?

Learning Outcome	What to Remember with Examples

Section 6-1

1 Write a whole number, fraction, or decimal as a percent. (p. 186)

1. Multiply the number by 1 in the form of 100%.
2. The product has a % symbol.

$$6 = 6(100\%) = 600\% \qquad \frac{3}{5} = \frac{3}{5}\left(\frac{100}{1}\%\right) = 60\%$$

$$0.075 = 0.075(100\%) = 7.5\%$$

2 Write a percent as a whole number, fraction, or decimal. (p. 188)

1. Divide by 1 in the form of 100% or multiply by $\frac{1}{100\%}$.
2. The quotient does not have a % symbol.

$$48\% = 48\% \div 100\% = 0.48 \qquad 20\% = 20\% \div 100\% = \frac{20}{100} = \frac{1}{5}$$

$$157\% = 157\% \div 100\% = 1.57 \qquad 33\frac{1}{3}\% = 33\frac{1}{3}\% \div 100\% = 0.33\frac{1}{3} \text{ or } \frac{1}{3} \text{ or } 0.3\overline{3}$$

Section 6-2

1 Identify the rate, base, and portion in percent problems. (p. 191)

1. *Rate* is usually written as a percent, but may be converted to a decimal or fraction.
2. *Base* is the total amount, original amount, or entire amount. The base often follows the preposition *of*.
3. *Portion* can refer to the part, partial amount, amount of increase or decrease, or amount of change. It is a portion of the *base*. The portion often follows a form of the verb *is*.

Identify the rate, base, and portion.
42% of 18 is what number?
42% is the rate.
18 is the base.
The missing number is the portion.

2 Use the percentage formula to find the unknown value when two values are known. (p. 192)

1. Identify and classify the two known values and the one unknown value.
2. Choose the appropriate percentage formula for finding the unknown value.
3. Substitute the known values into the formula. For the rate, use the decimal or fractional equivalent of the percent.
4. Perform the calculation indicated by the formula.
5. Interpret the result. If finding the rate, convert decimal or fractional equivalents of the rate to a percent.

Find P if $B = 20$ and $R = 15\%$.

$$P = RB$$

$$P = 15\%(20) = 0.15(20)$$

$$P = 3$$

Find B if $P = 20$ and $R = 9\%$.

$$B = \frac{P}{R}$$

$$B = \frac{36}{9\%} = \frac{36}{0.09}$$

$$B = 400$$

Section 6-3

1 Find the amount of increase or decrease in percent problems. (p. 197)

1. To find the amount of increase (when new amount is larger than beginning amount):

   Amount of increase = new amount − beginning amount

2. To find the amount of decrease (when new amount is smaller than beginning amount):

   Amount of decrease = beginning amount − new amount

A truck odometer increased from 37,580.3 to 42,719.6. What was the increase?

$42{,}719.6 - 37{,}580.3 = 5{,}139.3$

A truck carrying 62,980 pounds of food delivered 36,520 pounds. What was the amount of food (in pounds) remaining on the truck?

$62{,}980 - 36{,}520 = 26{,}460$ pounds

To find the amount of change (increase or decrease) from a percent of change:

1. Identify the original or beginning amount and the percent or rate of change.
2. Multiply the decimal or fractional equivalent of the rate of change times the original or beginning amount.

   Amount of change = percent of change × original amount

Laura Daily received a 4.7% raise. If her original salary is $52,318, how much was her raise?

Amount of raise = percent of change × original amount
$$= 4.7\%(\$52{,}318)$$
$$= 0.047(\$52{,}318)$$
$$\approx \$2{,}458.95 \quad \text{(rounded)}$$

2 Find the new amount directly in percent problems. (p. 199)

1. Find the rate of the new amount.

   For increase: 100% + rate of increase
   For decrease: 100% − rate of decrease

2. Find the new amount.

   $P = RB$
   New amount = rate of new amount × original amount

Emily Denly works 30 hours a week but plans to increase her work hours by 20%. How many hours will she be working after the increase?

For increase: 100% + 20% = 120%
$P = RB$
$P = 120\%(30 \text{ hours})$
$\quad = 1.20(30)$
$\quad = 36 \text{ hours}$

3 Find the rate or the base in increase or decrease problems. (p. 200)

1. Identify or find the amount of change (increase or decrease).
2. To find the rate of increase or decrease, use the percentage formula $R = \dfrac{P}{B}$.

   $$R = \frac{\text{amount of change}}{\text{original amount}}$$

3. To find the base or original amount, use the percentage formula $B = \dfrac{P}{R}$.

   $$B = \frac{\text{amount of change}}{\text{rate of change}}$$

Tancia Brown made a profit of $5,896 in June and a profit of $6,265 in July. What is the percent of increase? Round to tenths of a percent.

Amount of increase = $6,265 − $5,896 = $369
$$R = \frac{\text{amount of change}}{\text{original amount}}$$
$$= \frac{\$369}{\$5{,}896}$$
$$= 0.0625848033(100\%)$$
$$= 6.3\% \quad \text{(rounded)}$$

EXERCISES SET A

Write the decimal as a percent.

1. 0.23

2. 0.82

3. 0.03

4. 0.34

5. 0.601

6. 1

7. 3

8. 0.37

9. 0.2

10. 4

Write the fraction or mixed number as a percent. Round to the nearest hundredth of a percent if necessary.

11. $\dfrac{17}{100}$

12. $\dfrac{6}{100}$

13. $\dfrac{52}{100}$

14. $\dfrac{1}{10}$

15. $\dfrac{5}{4}$

16. $2\dfrac{3}{5}$

Write the percent as a decimal.

17. 0.25%

18. 98%

19. 256%

20. 91.7%

21. 0.5%

22. 6%

Write the percent as a whole number, mixed number, or fraction, reduced to lowest terms.

23. 10%   **24.** 6%   **25.** 89%   **26.** 45%   **27.** 225%

Percent	Fraction	Decimal
28. $33\dfrac{1}{3}\%$	_____	_____
29. _____	_____	0.125
30. _____	_____	0.8

Find P, R, or B using the percentage formula or one of its forms. Round decimals to the nearest hundredth and percents to the nearest whole number percent.

31. $B = 300$, $R = 27\%$ **32.** $P = 25$, $B = 100$ **33.** $P = \$600$, $R = 5\%$ **34.** $P = \$835$, $R = 3.2\%$

35. $P = 125$, $B = 50$ **36.** Find 30% of 80.   **37.** 90% of what number is 27?   **38.** 51.52 is what percent of 2,576?

39. Jaime McMahan received a 7% pay increase. If he was earning $2,418 per month, what was the amount of the pay increase?

40. Eighty percent of one store's customers paid with credit cards. Forty customers came in that day. How many customers paid for their purchases with credit cards?

41. Seventy percent of a town's population voted in an election. If 1,589 people voted, what is the population of the town?

42. Thirty-seven of 50 shareholders attended a meeting. What percent of the shareholders attended the meeting?

43. The financial officer allows $3,400 for supplies in the annual budget. After three months, $898.32 has been spent on supplies. Is this figure within 25% of the annual budget?

44. Chloe Denley's rent of $940 per month was increased by 8%. What is her new monthly rent?

45. The price of a wireless phone increased by 14% to $165. What was the original price to the nearest dollar?

EXCEL

46. Global wind energy had a record growth in a recent year, achieving a level of 159,213 megawatts. Some in the industry project the global wind capacity to be 1,900,000 megawatts in 2020. What is the percent increase in additional megawatts projected for the global market? Round to the nearest tenth percent.

EXERCISES SET B

Write the decimal as a percent.

1. 0.675

2. 2.63

3. 0.007

4. 3.741

5. 0.0004

6. 0.6

7. 0.242

8. 0.811

Write the fraction or mixed number as a percent. Round to the nearest hundredth of a percent if necessary.

9. $\dfrac{99}{100}$

10. $\dfrac{20}{100}$

11. $\dfrac{13}{20}$

12. $3\dfrac{2}{5}$

13. $\dfrac{2}{5}$

14. $2\dfrac{3}{4}$

Write the percent as a decimal.

15. 328.4%

16. 84.6%

17. 52%

18. 3%

19. 0.02%

20. 274%

Write the percent as a whole number, mixed number, or fraction, reduced to lowest terms.

21. 20%

22. 170%

23. 361%

24. 25%

25. $12\dfrac{1}{2}\%$

	Percent	Fraction	Decimal
26.	_____	$\dfrac{2}{5}$	_____
27.	50%	_____	_____
28.	$87\dfrac{1}{2}\%$	_____	_____
29.	_____	_____	0.45

Find P, R, or B using the percentage formula or one of its forms.

30. $B = \$1,900, R = 106\%$

31. $P = 170, B = 85$

32. $P = \$15.50, R = 7.75\%$

Round decimals to the nearest hundredth and percents to the nearest whole number percent.

33. $P = 68, B = 85$

34. $R = 72\%, B = 16$

35. $P = 52, R = 17\%$

Use the percentage formula or one of its forms.

36. Find 150% of 20.

37. 82% of what number is 94.3?

38. 27 is what percent of 9?

39. Ernestine Monahan draws $1,800 monthly retirement. On January 1, she received a 3% cost of living increase. How much was the increase?

40. If a picture frame costs $30 and the tax on the frame is 6% of the cost, how much is the tax on the picture frame?

41. Five percent of a batch of fuses were found to be faulty during an inspection. If 27 fuses were faulty, how many fuses were inspected?

42. The United Way expects to raise $63 million in its current drive. The chairperson projects that 60% of the funds will be raised in the first 12 weeks. How many dollars are expected to be raised in the first 12 weeks?

43. An accountant who is currently earning $42,380 annually expects a 6.5% raise. What is the amount of the expected raise?

44. Last year Docie Johnson had net sales of $582,496. This year her sales decreased by 12%. What were her net sales this year?

45. The price of Internet service decreased by 7% to $52. What was the original price to the nearest dollar?

PRACTICE TEST

Write the decimal as a percent.

1. 0.24

2. 0.925

3. 0.6

4. According to a recent Cone Business in Social Media study, 0.93 of Americans believe a company should have a presence on social media sites. Express the decimal as a percent.

5. The Cone Business in Social Media study revealed that 0.43 of consumers expect companies to use social networks to solve consumer's problems. What percent of consumers had this expectation?

Write the fraction as a percent.

6. $\dfrac{21}{100}$

7. $\dfrac{3}{8}$

8. Write $\dfrac{1}{4}\%$ as a fraction.

9. A recent report from Istrategylabs showed a 276.4% growth rate in Facebook accounts for the 35- to 54-year-old group. Express the growth rate as a decimal.

10. Recent data about Facebook usage shows that 40.8% of account holders are age 18–24. Represent this percent as a fraction.

Use the percentage formula or one of its forms.

11. Find 30% of $240.

12. 50 is what percent of 20?

13. What percent of 8 is 7?

14. What is the sales tax on an item that costs $42 if the tax rate is 6%?

15. If 100% of 22 rooms are full, how many rooms are full?

16. Twelve employees at a meat packing plant were sick on Monday. If the plant employs 360 people, what percent to the nearest whole percent of the employees was sick on Monday?

17. A department store had 15% turnover in personnel last year. If the store employs 600 people, how many employees were replaced last year?

18. The Lawson family left a 15% tip for a restaurant check. If the check totaled $19.47, find the amount of the tip. What was the total cost of the meal, including the tip?

19. A certain make and model of automobile was projected to have a 3% rate of defective autos. If the number of defective automobiles was projected to be 1,698, how many automobiles were to be produced?

20. The recent estimated total expenditure on a child by husband–wife families with an average income of $76,520 was $221,190, and $69,660 was projected for the child's housing cost. What percent of the total expenditure was projected for housing? Round to the nearest tenth percent.

21. The recent estimated total expenditure on a child by husband–wife families with an average income of $36,380 was $159,870, and $29,250 was projected for the child's food cost. What percent of the total expenditure was projected for food? Round to the nearest tenth percent.

22. Of the 26 questions on this practice test, 17 are word problems. What percent of the problems are word problems? (Round to the nearest whole number percent.)

23. Frances Johnson received a 6.2% increase in earnings. She was earning $86,900 annually. What is her new annual earnings?

24. Byron Johnson took a pay cut of 5%. He was earning $148,200 annually. What is his new annual salary?

25. Sylvia Williams bought a microwave oven that had been reduced by 30% to $340. What was the original price of the oven? Round to the nearest dollar.

26. Sony decided to increase the wholesale price of its DVD players by 18% to $320. What was the original price rounded to the nearest cent?

1. Numbers between $\frac{1}{100}$ and 1 are equivalent to percents that are between 1% and 100%. Numbers greater than 1 are equivalent to percents that are _____.

2. Percents between 0% and 1% are equivalent to fractions or decimals in what interval?

3. Explain why any number can be multiplied by 100% without changing the value of the number.

4. Can any number be divided by 100% without changing the value of the number? Explain.

5. A complement of a percent is the difference of 100% and the given percent. What is the conjugate percent of 48%?

6. Finding which one of the three elements of the percentage formula requires multiplication?

7. If the cost of an item increases by 100%, what is the effect of the increase on the original amount? Give an example to illustrate your point.

8. Describe two ways to find the new amount when a given number is increased by a given percent.

Explain the error in each problem, then work the problem correctly.

9. Cathy Woolfrey is buying a new home. Her realtor tells her that the home she is buying has increased in price by 10% since it was last sold. If the current price of the home is $220,000, what was the price the last time it was sold?

$P = RB$
$P = 10\%(\$220,000)$ The home sold for $198,000 the last time it sold.
$P = 0.1(\$220,000)$
$P = \$198,000$

10. Annette Cook has stocks currently valued at $16,250. Her stock value has decreased by 8.5% over the last three years. Find the value of her stock three years ago.

$P = RB$
$P = 8.5\%(\$16,250)$ $\$16,250 + \$1,381.25 = \$17,631.25$
$P = 0.085(\$16,250)$
$P = \$1,381.25$
The stock was valued at $17,631.25 three years ago.

Challenge Problem

Brian Sangean has been offered a job in which he will be paid strictly on a commission basis. He expects to receive a 4% commission on all sales of computer hardware he closes. Brian's goal for a gross yearly salary is $60,000. How much computer hardware must Brian sell to meet his target salary?

6-1 Wasting Money or Shaping Up?

Sarah belongs to an upscale gym and health spa and pays $90 a month for membership. Sarah works out three times a week regularly. One day, one of the club's personal trainers came by to talk and offered to plan a routine for Sarah. The trainer had noticed that Sarah came in regularly, and commented that most members don't have the self-control to do that. In fact, she explained that there was a study of 8,000 members in Boston-area gyms showing that members went to the gym only about five times per month. The study also found that people who choose a pay-per-visit membership spend less money than people who choose a monthly or annual membership fee.

1. At Sarah's club the pay-per-visit fee is $5 per day. Would Sarah save money paying per visit? Assume that a month has 4.3 weeks. What percent of her monthly $90 fee would she spend if she paid on a per-visit basis?

2. If Sarah goes to the gym three times per week, what percent of days of the year does she use the gym? Round to the nearest percent.

3. If Sarah went to the gym every day, how much would she pay per day on the monthly payment plan? Assume 30 days in a month. If she went every day and paid $5 per day, how much would she be spending per month? What percent more is this compared to the $90 monthly rate rounded to the nearest percent?

6-2 Customer Relationship Management

Minh Phan is going over the numbers one more time. He is about to make the most important sales presentation of his young career to Media Systems, Inc., a leading media and communications organization. Media Systems' primary challenge is how to effectively manage its diverse customer base. It has 70,000 publication subscribers, 58,000 advertisers, 30,000 telephone services customers, and 18,000 ISP (Internet service provider) customers. The company had little information about who its customers truly were, which products they were using, and how satisfied they were with the service they received. That's where Minh and his company, Customer Solution Technologies, LLC, come in. Through the use of customer relationship management software, Minh believed Media Systems would be able to substantially improve its ability to cross-sell and up-sell multiple media and communications services to customers, while substantially reducing customer complaints.

1. What percentage of the total does each of the four customer groups represent? Round to the nearest hundredth of a percent.

2. Minh's data shows that on average, only 4.6% of customers were purchasing complementary services available within Media Systems. By using his company's services, Minh was projecting that these percentages would triple across all user groups within one year. How many customers would that equate to in total for each group? What would be the difference compared to current levels?

3. Customer complaint data showed that within the last year, complaints by category were as follows: publication subscribers, 1,174; advertisers, 423; telephone service customers, 4,411; and ISP customers 823. What percentage of customers (round to two decimal places) complained within the last year in each category? If the CRM software were able to reduce complaints by 50% each year over the next two years, how many complaints would there be by category at the end of that time period? What would the number of complaints at the end of two years represent on a percentage basis?

6-3 Carpeting a New Home

Knowing that home ownership is a good step toward a sound financial future, Jeremy and Catherine are excited about buying their first home. The mortgage payments on their new home fit well within their budget, but after making a $20,000 down payment, they want to make certain they can afford any necessary improvements as well.

Their first-priority improvement is to replace the carpeting. Jeremy and Catherine recognized that their house was priced below market because the sellers knew the carpeting would need to be replaced. Their plan is to recarpet the three bedrooms, the living room, and the hallway. The area of each room is found by multiplying length by width. The result is "square feet" and is written ft^2. The dimensions of the rooms are as follows:

Room	Dimensions	Area in Square Feet	Cost to Carpet	% of total cost by Room
Master bedroom	16 ft by 18 ft			
Bedroom #1	12 ft by 13 ft			
Bedroom #2	10 ft by 12 ft			
Hallway	10 ft by 3 ft			
Living room	15 ft by 20 ft			
Total Cost				

1. Find the area of each room and record your results in the chart above.

2. Although they have not yet decided on a color, the grade of carpet Jeremy and Catherine are interested in costs $36 a square yard. How much does it cost per square foot? Hint: There are 9 square feet in a square yard.

3. How much will it cost to carpet the areas listed above, and what percentage of the total cost does each room represent? Report your answers by room in the chart above; determine the total cost, and the percentage of total cost for each room. Round to one-tenth of one percent.

4. Lowe's is offering Jeremy and Catherine a 10% discount if they carpet the whole area with the same color carpet. How much will they save if they decide to do this?

5. Jeremy and Catherine feel they can pay $2,000 in cash for carpeting right now. How many square feet of carpet can they afford to buy with the cash they have? How much would they need to borrow if they decide to carpet all the areas listed above with the same color carpet?

6. How much would it cost to carpet only the bedrooms (assume no 10% discount)? How much would it cost to carpet only the living room and hallway (again, assume no discount)?

7. Jeremy would prefer to carpet the whole area at once with the same color carpeting rather than doing it room by room; however, he is hesitant to take out another loan because they will be taking out a mortgage at the same time. He would prefer to save the full amount so that they can pay cash for their entire purchase. How long would it take for them to have enough money if they can save $300 each month if the discount still applies? Remember, they already have $2,000 to put toward their purchase.

Big Business in the NFL

The sports business means many different things to different people. This is truly a global industry, and sports stir up deep passion within spectators and players alike in countries around the world. To athletes, sports may lead to high levels of personal achievement; to professionals, sports can bring fame and fortune. To businesspeople, sports provide a lucrative and continually growing marketplace worthy of immense investment.

When the astonishing variety of sports-related sectors are considered, a significant number of workers in developed nations such as the United States, the United Kingdom, Australia, and Japan rely on the sports industry for their livelihoods. Official U.S. Bureau of Labor Statistics figures state that 130,000 people work in U.S. spectator sports alone (including about 8,700 professional athletes), while 500,000 work in fitness or recreation centers, about 70,000 work in snow skiing facilities, and about 300,000 work at country clubs or golf courses. In total, well over 1,000,000 Americans work directly in the amusement and recreation sectors.

Amazingly, an average of nearly 1,000 people work in each of the National Football League stadiums around the country, and nowhere is the impact of sports-related marketing as prevalent as in the NFL. Experts say that the marketing of top stars has played a big role in driving the NFL's business to new heights, which has benefited everyone. Today's $1.9 million average salary is more than double the level in 1994. A look at NFL MVP salaries over the past 25 years shows that, overall, they made 3.3 times the average league salary during the 1980s, a ratio that rose to 5.3 in the 1990s, and to 6.2 times the average in the 2000s. By comparison, reigning NFL MVP Aaron Rodger's $11.15 million salary in 2012 was a bargain at less than seven times the $1.9 million average. While that is still a lot of money, the NFL's new 10-year labor agreement and increased TV rights deals are the reasons that NFL teams are worth—on average—a staggering $1.04 billion!

Coinciding with the birth of the NFL salary cap in the mid-1990s, of course, was the high-tech age. In the new media world, one that demands involving fans interactively through games and online fantasy leagues in addition to television, football's "top down" star system is working. Business is booming in the NFL, with both television revenue and player salaries at record levels. Fantasy football and Madden games, which help drive TV viewership, surely wouldn't be what they are without identifiable names like Eli Manning, Aaron Rodgers, and Drew Brees.

LEARNING OUTCOMES

7-1 Graphs and Charts

1. Interpret and draw a bar graph.
2. Interpret and draw a line graph.
3. Interpret and draw a circle graph.

7-2 Measures of Central Tendency

1. Find the mean.
2. Find the median.
3. Find the mode.
4. Make and interpret a frequency distribution.
5. Find the mean of grouped data.

7-3 Measures of Dispersion

1. Find the range.
2. Find the standard deviation.

Galileo once said that mathematics is the language of science. In the 21st century, he might have said that mathematics is also the language of business. Through numbers, businesspeople communicate their business history, status, and goals. Statistics, tables, and graphs are three important tools with which to do so.

7-1 GRAPHS AND CHARTS

LEARNING OUTCOMES

1 Interpret and draw a bar graph.
2 Interpret and draw a line graph.
3 Interpret and draw a circle graph.

Data set: a collection of values or measurements that have a common characteristic.

Scan a newspaper, a magazine, or a business report, and you are likely to see graphs. Graphs do more than present sets of data. They visually represent the relationship between the sets. The relationship between **data sets** might be visualized by a bar graph, a line graph, or a circle graph. By data set we mean a collection of values or measurements that have a common characteristic. Depending on "what you want to see," one of these forms helps you to see the relationship more meaningfully.

In today's fast-paced society, a person is given a limited amount of time to *sell* his or her idea or to *show* his or her data. Graphs and charts tell a story in pictures.

1 Interpret and draw a bar graph.

Bar graph: a graph that uses horizontal or vertical bars to show how values compare to each other.

Bar graphs are used to visually represent the relationship between data. As its name implies, a bar graph uses horizontal or vertical bars to show relative quantities. The data are grouped into categories or classes, and each category is represented by a bar. The length of the bars for horizontal bars or the height of the bars for vertical bars shows the number of items in each category. Suppose an instructor wants to see a visual representation of the scores that 25 students made on an exam. Table 7-1 gives the data in table form. Instead of graphing individual scores, the data are grouped into intervals of scores. Figure 7-1 shows a bar graph of this data.

Figure 7-1 demonstrates why bar graphs are so useful: We can easily compare the scores for grade intervals at a glance.

TABLE 7-1
Distribution of 25 Exam Scores

Grade Intervals	Frequency of Scores
60–64	1
65–69	1
70–74	2
75–79	6
80–84	3
85–89	5
90–94	5
95–99	2

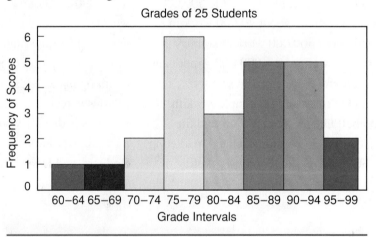

FIGURE 7-1
Bar Graph of 25 Exam Scores

EXAMPLE 1 Answer the questions using the data represented in Figure 7-1.

(a) Which grade interval(s) had the highest number of scores?
(b) Which grade interval(s) had the lowest number of scores?
(c) If 90–99 is a grade of A, how many As were there?

(a) Which grade interval(s) had the highest number of scores?

The interval 75–79 had the highest number of scores, 6.

(b) Which grade interval(s) had the lowest number of scores?

The intervals 60–64 and 65–69 had the lowest number of scores, 1.

(c) If 90–99 is a grade of A, how many A's were there?

There are 5 scores in the 90–94 interval and 2 scores in the 95–99 interval. **There are 5 + 2 or 7 scores that are A's.**

A **histogram** is a special type of bar graph that represents the data from a frequency distribution. The procedure for making a frequency distribution is given in Section 7-2. Figure 7-1 is a histogram. Because there are no gaps in the intervals, the bars in a histogram are drawn with no space between them. In contrast, the bars on a standard bar graph describe categories, and they are drawn with gaps between the bars.

HOW TO   Draw a bar graph

1. Write an appropriate title.
2. Make appropriate labels for the bars and scale. The intervals on the scale should be equally spaced and include the smallest and largest values.
3. Draw bars to represent the data. Bars should be of uniform width and should not touch.
4. Make additional notes as appropriate. For example, "Amounts in Thousands of Dollars" allows values such as $30,000 to be represented as 30.

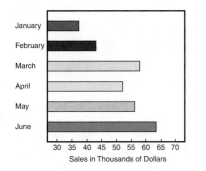

FIGURE 7-2
Horizontal Bar Graph Showing Corky's Barbecue Restaurant Sales, January–June

EXAMPLE 2

The investors of Corky's Barbecue Restaurant have asked to see a semiannual report of sales. The data show Corky's Barbecue Restaurant sales during January through June. Draw a bar graph that represents the data.

January	$37,734	April	$52,175
February	$43,284	May	$56,394
March	$58,107	June	$63,784

The title of the graph is "Corky's Barbecue Restaurant Sales, January–June."

The smallest value is $37,734 and the largest value is $63,784. Therefore, the graph should show values from $30,000 to $70,000. To avoid using very large numbers, indicate on the graph that the numbers represent dollars in thousands. Therefore, 65 on the graph would represent $65,000. The bars can be either horizontal or vertical. In Figure 7-2 we make the bars horizontal. Months are labeled along the vertical line, and the dollar scale is labeled along the horizontal line. For each month, the length of the bar corresponds to the sales for the month.

Figure 7-3 interchanges the labeling of the scales, and the bars are drawn vertically.

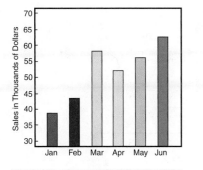

FIGURE 7-3
Vertical Bar Graph Showing Corky's Barbecue Restaurant Sales, January–June

Standard bar graph: bar graph with just one variable.

Bar graphs may illustrate relationships among more than one variable. A **standard bar graph** illustrates the change in magnitude of just one variable. Figure 7-2 is a standard horizontal bar graph. Figure 7-3 shows the same data as a standard vertical bar graph.

In many instances it is important for a business to see how data compares from one time period to another. For example, The 7th Inning wants to compare annual sales by department for the past four years. Look at the data that is shown in Table 7-2.

TABLE 7-2

Department	2011 Sales	2012 Sales	2013 Sales	2014 Sales
Memorabilia	$ 74,778	$ 93,923	$ 79,013	$ 80,422
Engraving	$ 42,285	$ 49,209	$ 63,548	$ 73,846
Framing	$ 20,125	$ 21,798	$ 38,243	$ 36,898
Restaurant	$ 26,285	$ 27,881	$ 31,745	$ 29,006
Total Sales	$163,473	$192,811	$212,549	$220,172

Comparative bar graph: bar graph with two or more variables.

A **comparative bar graph** is used to illustrate two or more related variables. The bars representing each variable are shaded or colored differently so that visual comparisons can be made more easily. Figure 7-4 shows a comparative bar graph for the annual sales for The 7th Inning from 2011 through 2014.

Component bar graph: bar graph with each bar having more than one component.

A **component bar graph** is used to show that each bar is the total of various components. The components are stacked immediately on top of each other and shaded or colored differently. Figure 7-5 is a component bar graph that shows the total annual sales for The 7th Inning as well as the sales by department.

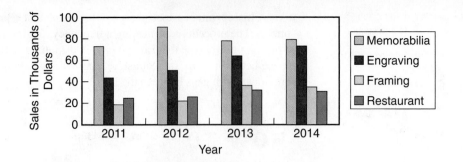

FIGURE 7-4

Comparative bar graph showing The 7th Inning Sales by Department

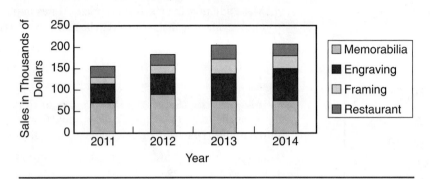

FIGURE 7-5

Component bar graph showing The 7th Inning Annual Sales

STOP AND CHECK

Fifty business students were given a project to complete. The bar graph in Figure 7-6 shows the number of days it took the students to complete the assignment. See Example 1.

1. How many students took 4 days to complete the assignment?

2. How many students completed the project in 3 days or less?

3. What percent of students completed the project in 3 days or less?

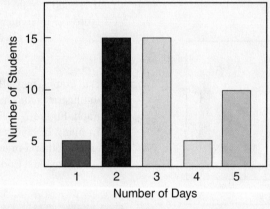

FIGURE 7-6

See Example 2.

4. The staff at Tulsa Community College have accumulated the following number of vacation days: 11 have accumulated 0–19 days; 12 have accumulated 20–39 days; 5 have accumulated 40–59 days; 5 have accumulated 60–79 days; and 3 have accumulated 80–89 days. Make a histogram to illustrate these data.

5. From the graph, identify the number of vacation days (interval) that 12 staff members have.

2 Interpret and draw a line graph.

Line graph: line segments that connect points on a graph to show the rising and falling trends of a data set.

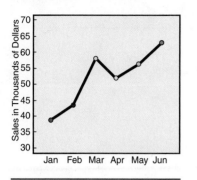

FIGURE 7-7
Line Graph Showing Corky's Barbecue
Restaurant Sales, January–June

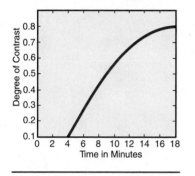

FIGURE 7-8
Developing Time Required for
Degrees of Contrast

Line graphs are very similar to vertical bar graphs. The difference is that a line graph uses a single dot to represent height, rather than a whole bar. When the dots are in place, they are connected by a line. Line graphs make even more apparent the rising and falling trends of the data. Figure 7-7 is a line graph representing the data given in Example 2 for the January to June sales for Corky's Barbecue Restaurant.

Line graphs may have enough points that connecting them yields a curve rather than angles. Figure 7-8 shows such a line graph, relating the time film is developed to the degree of contrast achieved in the developed film. To read the graph, we locate a specific degree of contrast on the vertical scale, and then move horizontally until we intersect the curve. From that point, we move down to locate the corresponding number of minutes on the horizontal scale.

EXAMPLE 3 Use Figure 7-9 to answer the following questions:

(a) If the film is to be developed to a contrast of 0.5, how long must it be developed?
(b) If the film is developed for 13 minutes, what is its degree of contrast?

(a) Find 0.5 on the vertical scale, and then move horizontally until you intersect the curve. From the point of intersection, move down to locate the corresponding number of minutes on the horizontal scale. **Figure 7-9 shows the minutes are 9.**
(b) Find 13 minutes on the horizontal scale, and move up until you intersect the curve. From the point of intersection, move across to locate the corresponding degree of contrast. **Figure 7-9 shows the degree of contrast is 0.7.**

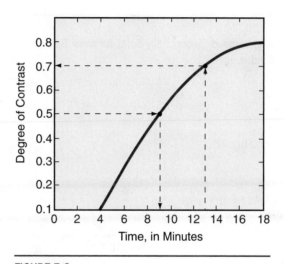

FIGURE 7-9
Reading a Line Graph

As in drawing bar graphs, drawing line graphs often means using approximations of the given data.

HOW TO Draw a line graph

1. Write an appropriate title.
2. Make and label appropriate horizontal and vertical scales, each with equally spaced intervals. Often, the horizontal scale represents time.
3. Use points to locate data on the graph.
4. Connect data points with line segments or a smooth curve.

TABLE 7-3
Neighborhood Grocery Daily
Sales for Week Beginning Monday,
June 21

Monday	$1,567
Tuesday	1,323
Wednesday	1,237
Thursday	1,435
Friday	1,848
Saturday	1,984

EXAMPLE 4 Draw a line graph to represent the data in Table 7-3.

The smallest and largest values in the table are $1,237 and $1,984, respectively, so the graph may go from $1,000 to $2,000 in $100 increments. Do not label every increment. This would crowd the side of the graph and make it hard to read. The purpose of any graph is to give information that is quick and easy to understand and interpret.

The horizontal side of the graph will show the days of the week, and the vertical side will show the daily sales. Plot each day's sales by placing a dot directly above the appropriate day of the week across from the approximate value. For example, the sales for Monday totaled $1,567. Place the dot above Monday between $1,500 and $1,600. After each amount has been plotted, connect the dots with straight lines.

Figure 7-10 shows the resulting graph.

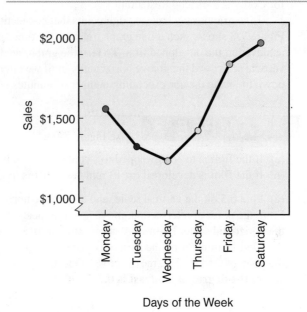

FIGURE 7-10
Neighborhood Grocery Daily Sales for Week Beginning Monday, June 21

STOP AND CHECK

See Example 3.

1. Is the graph in Figure 7-11 increasing, decreasing, or fluctuating?

2. Find the monthly average number of CDs sold by House of Music for the 6-month period January–June.

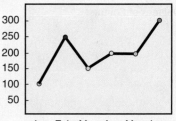

CDs sold by House of Music

See Example 4.

3. Draw a line graph to represent the data in Table 7-4.

TABLE 7-4	
Personal Income for June 2009–December 2009 (Billions of Dollars)	
June 2009	$12,029.7
July 2009	$12,050.6
August 2009	$12,084.5
September 2009	$12,116.5
October 2009	$12,147.5
November 2009	$12,208.6
December 2009	$12,253.1

Source: Bureau of Economic Analysis, an agency of the U.S. Department of Commerce.

4. Is the graph in Exercise 3 increasing, decreasing, or fluctuating?

5. Which month showed the highest personal income?

FIGURE 7-11

3 Interpret and draw a circle graph.

Circle graph: a circle that is divided into parts to show how a whole quantity is being divided.

A **circle graph** is a circle divided into sections to give a visual picture of *how some whole quantity* (represented by the whole circle) *is being divided*. Each section represents a portion of the total amount. Figure 7-12 shows a circle graph illustrating how different portions of a family's total take-home income are spent on nine categories of expenses: food, housing, contributions, savings, clothing, insurance, education, personal items, and miscellaneous items.

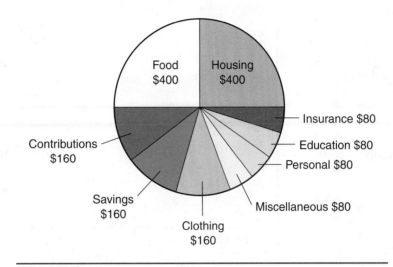

FIGURE 7-12
Distribution of Family Monthly Take-Home Pay

Circle graphs are relatively easy to read, and they make it easy to visually compare categories. Constructing a circle graph requires that you make several calculations and use a measuring device called a **protractor** that measures angles. Each value in the data set should be represented as a fraction of the sum of all the values. We calculate these fractions, then calculate the number of degrees needed for each sector, and then draw the graph.

Protractor: a measuring device that measures angles.

Sector: portion or wedge of a circle identified by two lines from the center to the outer edge of the circle.

Compass: a tool for drawing circles.

HOW TO   Draw a circle graph

1. Write an appropriate title.
2. Find the sum of the values in the data set.
3. Represent each value as a fractional or decimal part of the sum of values. Total of all parts equal 1.
4. For each fraction or decimal, find the number of degrees in the **sector** of the circle to be represented by the fraction or decimal: Multiply the fraction or decimal by 360 degrees. The sum of the degrees for all sectors should be 360 degrees.
5. Use a **compass** (a tool for drawing circles) to draw a circle. Indicate the center of the circle and a starting point on the circle.
6. For each degree value, draw a sector: Use a protractor (a measuring instrument for angles) to measure the number of degrees for the sector of the circle that represents the value. Where the first sector ends, the next sector begins. The last sector should end at the starting point.
7. Label each sector of the circle and make additional explanatory notes as necessary.

EXAMPLE 5   Construct a circle graph showing the budgeted operating expenses for one month for Silver's Spa: salary, $25,000; rent, $8,500; depreciation, $2,500; miscellaneous, $2,000; taxes and insurance, $10,000; utilities, $2,000; advertising, $3,000. The title of the graph is "Silver's Spa Monthly Budgeted Operating Expenses."

Because several calculations are required, it is helpful to organize the calculation results in a chart (Table 7-5).

Computer software such as *Microsoft Word* and *Excel* has built-in features that can be used to construct many different types of graphs, called *charts*. Data are organized in a table format and the software builds the chart and guides you through the process of giving the chart a title, labeling the scales or *axes*, and identifying other information about the data through *legends* and *notes*.

Knowing how a graph is constructed helps in reading the graph and analyzing the data of the graph. In reality, you will probably use computer software in making graphs for business presentations.

In *Word*, you will find the graphing options under the *Insert* tab, *Illustrations*, and *Chart*. In *Excel*, the graphing options are under the *Insert* tab and *Charts*. Some of the types of graphing options included are *Column* (vertical bar graph), *Line*, *Pie* (circle graph), and *Bar* (horizontal bar graph). Selecting one of these options will give you several pictorial choices including options for comparative and component graphs. You will make a selection based on the characteristics of the data you wish to display.

TABLE 7-5
Silver's Spa Monthly Budgeted Operating Expenses

Type of Expense	Amount of Expense	Expense as Fraction of Total Expenses	Degrees in Sector: Fraction × 360
Salary	$25,000	$\frac{25,000}{53,000}$ or $\frac{25}{53}$	$\frac{25}{53}(360)$, or 170
Rent	8,500	$\frac{8,500}{53,000}$ or $\frac{17}{106}$	$\frac{17}{106}(360)$, or 58
Depreciation	2,500	$\frac{2,500}{53,000}$ or $\frac{5}{106}$	$\frac{5}{106}(360)$, or 17
Miscellaneous	2,000	$\frac{2,000}{53,000}$ or $\frac{2}{53}$	$\frac{2}{53}(360)$, or 14
Taxes and insurance	10,000	$\frac{10,000}{53,000}$ or $\frac{10}{53}$	$\frac{10}{53}(360)$, or 68
Utilities	2,000	$\frac{2,000}{53,000}$ or $\frac{2}{53}$	$\frac{2}{53}(360)$, or 14
Advertising	3,000	$\frac{3,000}{53,000}$ or $\frac{3}{53}$	$\frac{3}{53}(360)$, or 20
Total	$53,000	1	**361***

*Extra degree due to rounding.

Decimal equivalents can be used instead of fractions of total expenses. The sum of the fractions or decimal equivalents is 1. To the nearest thousandth, the decimal equivalents are 0.472, 0.160, 0.047, 0.038, 0.189, 0.038, and 0.057. The sum is 1.001. Rounding causes the sum to be slightly more than 1, just as the sum of the degrees is slightly more than 360°.

Use a compass to draw a circle. Measure the sectors of the circle with a protractor, using the calculations you just made. **The finished circle graph is shown in Figure 7-13.**

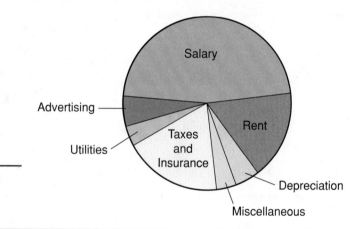

FIGURE 7-13
Monthly Budgeted Operating Expenses for Silver's Spa

STOP AND CHECK

See Example 5.

1. Construct a circle graph showing the distribution of market share using data in Table 7-6.

TABLE 7-6
Percent Dollar Market Share of Comics and Magazine Sales for September (Rounded to the Nearest Whole Percent)

Publisher	Market Share
Marvel Comics	35%
DC Comics	32%
Image Comics	5%
Dark Horse Comics	4%
Dreamweave Productions	4%
All others	20%

2. What percent of market share is held by the largest three companies?

3. If the total market had $80,000,000 in comics and magazine sales for September, what were the sales for Marvel Comics?

4. What was Image Comics' sales for September if the total market was $80,000,000?

7-1 SECTION EXERCISES

APPLICATIONS

Use Table 7-7 for Exercises 1 through 4.

TABLE 7-7
Sales by Each Salesperson at Happy's Gift Shoppe

| Salesperson | Sales | | | | | | |
	Mon.	Tues.	Wed.	Thurs.	Fri.	Sat.	Total
Brown	Off	$110.25	$114.52	$186.42	$126.81	$315.60	$ 853.60
Jackson	$121.68	Off	$118.29	Off	$125.42	Off	$ 365.39
Ulster	$112.26	$119.40	$122.35	$174.51	$116.78	Off	$ 645.30
Young	Off	$122.90	Off	$181.25	Off	$296.17	$ 600.32
Totals	**$233.94**	**$352.55**	**$355.16**	**$542.18**	**$369.01**	**$611.77**	**$2,464.61**

1. Construct a bar graph showing total sales by salesperson for Happy's Gift Shoppe in Table 7-7. *See Example 2.*

2. Construct a line graph showing total sales by the days of the week for Happy's Gift Shoppe in Table 7-7. *See Example 4.*

3. What day of the week had the highest amount in sales? What day had the lowest amount in sales? *See Example 3.*

4. Which salesperson made the most sales for the week? Which salesperson made the second highest amount in sales? *See Example 1.*

Use Figure 7-14 for Exercises 5 through 7. See Example 1.

5. Which quarter had the highest dollar volume?

6. What percent of the yearly sales were the sales for October–December?

7. What was the percent of increase in sales from the first to the second quarter?

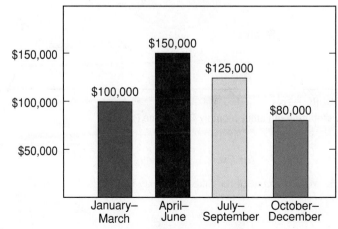

FIGURE 7-14
Quarterly Dollar Volume of Batesville Tire Company

8. Draw a bar graph comparing the quarterly sales of the Oxford Company: January–March, $280,000; April–June, $310,000; July–September, $250,000; October–December, $400,000. *See Example 2.*

Use Figure 7-15 for Exercises 9 through 12. See Example 3.

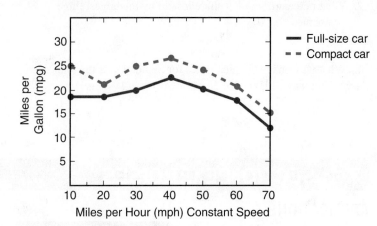

FIGURE 7-15
Automobile Gasoline Mileage Comparisons

9. What speed gave the highest gasoline mileage for both types of automobiles?

10. What speed gave the lowest gasoline mileage for both types of automobiles?

11. At what speed did the first noticeable decrease in gasoline mileage occur? Which car showed this decrease?

12. Identify factors other than gasoline mileage that should be considered when deciding which type of car to purchase, full size or compact.

See Example 5.

13. The family budget is illustrated in Figure 7-16. What is the total take-home pay and what percent is allocated for transportation?

14. Match the dollar values with the names in the circle graph of Figure 7-17: $192, $144, $96, $72, $72.

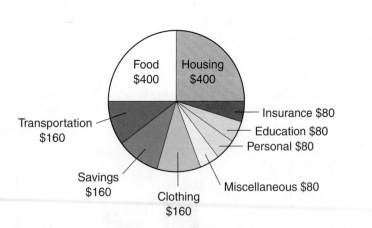

FIGURE 7-16
Distribution of Family Monthly Take-Home Pay

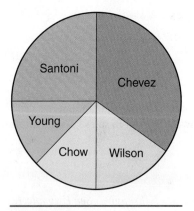

FIGURE 7-17
Daily Sales by Salesperson

Use Figure 7-16 for Exercises 15 through 17.

15. What percent of the take-home pay is allocated for food?

16. What percent of take-home pay is spent for education?

17. What percent of take-home pay is spent for education if education, savings, and miscellaneous funds are used for education?

Use Figure 7-18 for Exercises 18 through 21. Round to the nearest tenth of a percent.

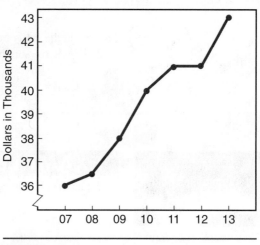

FIGURE 7-18
Dale Crosby's Salary History

18. What is the percent of increase in Dale's salary from 2008 to 2009?

19. Calculate the amount and percent of increase in Dale's salary from 2010 to 2011.

20. Calculate the amount and percent of increase in Dale's salary from 2012 to 2013.

21. If the cost-of-living increase was 10% from 2007 to 2013, determine if Dale's salary for this period of time kept pace with inflation.

7-2 MEASURES OF CENTRAL TENDENCY

LEARNING OUTCOMES

1 Find the mean.
2 Find the median.
3 Find the mode.
4 Make and interpret a frequency distribution.
5 Find the mean of grouped data.

All through the year, a business records its daily sales. At the end of the year, 365 values—one for each day—are on record. These values are a data set. With this data set, and using the right *statistical* methods, we may calculate manageable and meaningful information; this information is called **statistics.** By using the statistics, we should be able to reconstruct—well enough—the original data set or make predictions about a future data set.

Statistic: a standardized, meaningful measure of a set of data that reveals a certain feature or characteristic of the data.

1 Find the mean.

One common statistic we may calculate for a data set is its mean. The **mean** is the statistical term for the ordinary arithmetic average. To find the mean, or arithmetic average, we divide the sum of the values by the total number of values.

Mean: the arithmetic average of a set of data or the sum of the values divided by the number of values.

HOW TO   Find the mean of a data set

1. Find the sum of the values.
2. Divide the sum by the total number of values.

$$\text{Mean} = \frac{\text{sum of values}}{\text{number of values}}$$

Find the mean for these scores:
96, 86, 95, 89, 92.
$96 + 86 + 95 + 89 + 92 = 458$

$$\text{Mean} = \frac{458}{5} = 91.6$$

TABLE 7-8
Prices of Used Automobiles Sold in Tyreville over the Weekend of May 1–2

$7,850	$ 9,600
6,300	6,100
9,600	7,800
6,750	9,400
8,800	11,500
8,200	15,450

EXAMPLE 1   Find the mean used car price for the prices in Table 7-8. Round to the nearest ten dollars.

First find the sum of the values.

$$
\begin{array}{r}
\$ \quad 7,850 \\
6,300 \\
9,600 \\
6,750 \\
8,800 \\
8,200 \\
9,600 \\
6,100 \\
7,800 \\
9,400 \\
11,500 \\
+ \ 15,450 \\
\hline
\$107,350
\end{array}
$$

Add all the prices.

$\$107,350 \div 12 = \$8,945.8\overline{3}$ There are 12 prices listed, so find the mean by dividing the sum of the values by 12.

The mean price is $8,950, rounded to the nearest 10 dollars.

STOP AND CHECK

See Example 1.

1. Find the mean salary to the nearest dollar: $37,500; $32,000; $28,800; $35,750; $29,500; $47,300.

2. Find the mean number of hours for the life of a lightbulb to the nearest whole hour: 2,400; 2,100; 1,800; 2,800; 3,450.

3. Find the mean number of days a patient stays in the hospital rounded to the nearest whole day: 2 days; 15 days; 7 days; 3 days; 1 day; 3 days; 5 days; 2 days; 4 days; 1 day; 2 days; 6 days; 4 days; 2 days.

4. Find the mean number of CDs purchased per month by a group of college students: 12, 7, 5, 2, 1, 8, 0, 3, 1, 2, 7, 5, 30, 5, 2.

5. Find the mean for the Internal Revenue gross collection of estate taxes for a recent 10-year period: $23,627,320,000; $25,289,663,000; $25,532,186,000; $25,618,377,000; $20,887,883,000; $24,130,143,000; $23,565,164,000; $26,717,493,000; $24,557,815,000; $26,543,433,000 (*Source: IRS Data Book FY 2008, Publication 55b*)

6. Find the mean for the Internal Revenue gross collection of gift taxes for a recent 10-year period: $4,758,287,000; $4,103,243,000; $3,958,253,000; $1,709,329,000; $1,939,025,000; $1,449,319,000; $2,040,367,000; $1,970,032,000; $2,420,138,000; $3,280,502,000. (*Source: IRS Data Book FY 2008, Publication 55b*)

---

2   Find the median.

Median: the middle value of a data set when the values are arranged in order of size.

A second kind of average is a statistic called the **median.** To find the median of a data set, we arrange the values in order from the smallest to the largest or from the largest to the smallest and select the value in the middle.

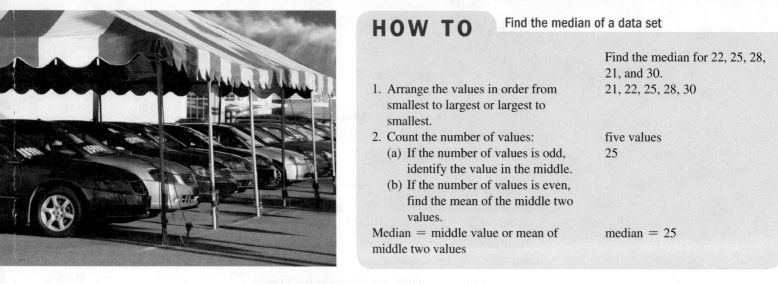

Find the median for 22, 25, 28, 21, and 30.

1. Arrange the values in order from smallest to largest or largest to smallest.

21, 22, 25, 28, 30

2. Count the number of values:

five values

(a) If the number of values is odd, identify the value in the middle.

25

(b) If the number of values is even, find the mean of the middle two values.

Median = middle value or mean of middle two values

median = 25

EXAMPLE 2   Find the median price of the used cars in Table 7-8.

$15,450

Arrange the values from largest to smallest. There are 12 prices, an even number, so there are two "middle" prices.

11,500

9,600

9,600

9,400

8,800 ←

These two are the "middle" values. Five values are above and 5 values are below these two values.

8,200 ←

7,850

7,800

6,750

6,300

6,100

$$\frac{8,800 + 8,200}{2} = \frac{17,000}{2} = 8,500$$ Find the mean of the two middle values.

The median price is $8,500.

STOP AND CHECK

See Example 2.

1. Find the median salary: $37,500; $32,000; $28,800; $35,750; $29,500; $47,300.

2. Find the median number of hours for the life of a lightbulb: 2,400; 2,100; 1,800; 2,800; 3,450.

3. Find the median number of days a patient stays in the hospital: 2 days; 15 days; 7 days; 3 days; 1 day; 3 days; 5 days; 2 days; 4 days; 1 day; 2 days; 6 days; 4 days; 2 days.

4. Find the median number of CDs purchased per month by college students: 12, 7, 5, 2, 1, 8, 0, 3, 1, 2, 7, 5, 30, 5, 2.

5. Find the median Internal Revenue gross collection of estate taxes for a recent 10-year period: $23,627,320,000; $25,289,663,000; $25,532,186,000; $25,618,377,000; $20,887,883,000; $24,130,143,000; $23,565,164,000; $26,717,493,000; $24,557,815,000; $26,543,433,000 (*Source: IRS Data Book FY 2008*, Publication 55b)

6. Find the median for the Internal Revenue gross collection of gift taxes for a recent 10-year period: $4,758,287,000; $4,103,243,000; $3,958,253,000; $1,709,329,000; $1,939,025,000; $1,449,319,000; $2,040,367,000; $1,970,032,000; $2,420,138,000; $3,280,502,000. (*Source: IRS Data Book FY 2008*, Publication 55b)

---

3   Find the mode.

Mode: the value or values that occur most frequently in a data set.

A third kind of average is the **mode.** The mode is the value or values that occur most frequently in a data set. If no value occurs most frequently, then there is no mode for that data set. In Table 7-8 there are two cars priced at $9,600. The mode for that set of prices is $9,600.

Find the mode(s) of a data set

1. For each value, count the number of times the value occurs.

2. Identify the value or values that occur most frequently.

    Mode = most frequent value(s)

Find the mode(s) for 95, 96, 98, 72, 96, 95, 96.
95 occurs twice.
96 occurs three times.
All others occur only once.
96 occurs most frequently.

96 is the mode.

EXAMPLE 3 Find the mode(s) for this set of test grades in a business class: 76, 83, 94, 76, 53, 83, 74, 76, 97, 83, 65, 77, 76, 83.

The grade of 76 occurs four times. The grade of 83 also occurs four times. All other grades occur only once. Therefore, both 76 and 83 occur the same number of times and are modes.

Both 76 and 83 are modes for this set of test grades.

Measures of central tendency: statistical measurements such as the mean, median, or mode that indicate how data group toward the center.

The mean, median, and mode may each be called an *average*. These statistics are **measures of central tendency.** They indicate how data group toward the center. Taken together, the mean, median, and mode describe the tendencies of a data set to cluster between the smallest and largest values. Sometimes it is useful to know all three of these statistical averages, since each represents a different way of describing the data set. It is like looking at the same thing from three different points of view.

Looking at just one statistic for a set of numbers often distorts the total picture. It is advisable to find the mean, median, and mode of a data set and then analyze the results.

EXAMPLE 4 A real estate agent told a prospective buyer that the average cost of a home in Tyreville was $171,000 during the past three months. The agent based this statement on this list of selling prices: $270,000, $250,000, $150,000, $150,000, $150,000, $150,000, $149,000, $145,000, $125,000.

Which statistic—the mean, the median, or the mode—gives the most realistic picture of how much a home in Tyreville is likely to cost?

What You Know	What You Are Looking For	Solution Plan
Houses sold during the period: 9 Prices of these houses: $270,000, $250,000, $150,000, $150,000, $150,000, $150,000, $149,000, $145,000, and $125,000	Which statistic gives the most realistic picture of how much a home in Tyreville is likely to cost? Find the mean, median, and mode.	Mean = sum of values ÷ number of values Median = middle value when values are arranged in order Mode = most frequent value

Solution

Mean = sum of values ÷ number of values
    = $1,539,000 ÷ 9
    = $171,000

The values are listed in order from largest to smallest, and the middle value is $150,000.
Median = middle value = $150,000
Mode = most frequent amount = $150,000

The mean is $171,000. The median is $150,000. The mode is $150,000.

Conclusion

Because two values are significantly different from the other values, the mean is probably not the most useful statistic.

The median and mode give a more realistic picture of how much a home is likely to cost—about $150,000.

See Example 3.

1. From Table 7-9 find the mode score for vacation days.

2. State sales tax rates are given in Table 7-10. What is the mode?

TABLE 7-9
Number of Vacation Days Accumulated by Staff at Tulsa Community College

2	62	7	23	32	48	32	92	48
56	17	0	12	19	21	9	17	32
32	86	73	74	18	32	18	66	6
38	62	32	48	32	48	83	32	23

TABLE 7-10
State Sales Tax Rates

State	Tax Rate	State	Tax Rate	State	Tax Rate
Alabama	4%	Louisiana	4%	Ohio	5.5%
Alaska	0%	Maine	5%	Oklahoma	4.5%
Arizona	5.6%	Maryland	6%	Oregon	0%
Arkansas	6%	Massachusetts	6.25%	Pennsylvania	6%
California	8.25%	Michigan	6%	Rhode Island	7%
Colorado	2.9%	Minnesota	6.875%	South Carolina	6%
Connecticut	6%	Mississippi	7%	South Dakota	4%
Delaware	0%	Missouri	4.225%	Tennessee	7%
Florida	6%	Montana	0%	Texas	6.25%
Georgia	4%	Nebraska	5.5%	Utah	4.7%
Hawaii	4%	Nevada	6.85%	Vermont	6%
Idaho	6%	New Hampshire	0%	Virginia	4%
Illinois	6.25%	New Jersey	7%	Washington	6.5%
Indiana	7%	New Mexico	5%	West Virginia	6%
Iowa	6%	New York	4%	Wisconsin	5%
Kansas	5.3%	North Carolina	5.75%	Wyoming	4%
Kentucky	6%	North Dakota	5%		

Compiled by Federation of Tax Administrators from various sources.

3. Michelle Baragona recorded the test scores on a biology exam. Find the mode score: 98, 92, 76, 48, 97, 83, 42, 86, 79, 100.

4. What is the mode score for number of points scored by players in the season-opening basketball game?

Baragona 11	Guest 12	Pounds 0
Byrd 8	Kennedy 7	Ramsey 11
Freese 2	Nock 22	

See Example 4.

5. What is the mean, median, and mode weight of soccer players? 148, 172, 158, 160, 170, 158, 170, 165, 162, 173, 155, 161

6. Write a statement about the data set in Exercise 5 based on your findings.

4 Make and interpret a frequency distribution.

In Section 7-1, Graphs and Charts, we constructed graphs of data that were already organized in categories. Now, examine some processes for organizing data. Table 7-1 shows the result of organizing 25 exam scores. Let's look at the individual scores that were used to build this table.

76	91	71	83	97	87	77	88	93	77	93	81	63
79	74	77	76	97	87	89	68	90	84	88	91	

It is difficult to make sense of all these numbers as they appear here. But the instructor can arrange the scores into several smaller groups, called **class intervals.** The word *class* means a special category.

These scores can be grouped into class intervals of 5, such as 60–64, 65–69, 70–74, 75–79, 80–84, 85–89, 90–94, and 95–99. Each class interval has an odd number of scores.

Class intervals: special categories for grouping the values in a data set.

The instructor can now **tally** the number of scores that fall into each class interval to get a **class frequency,** the number of scores in each class interval.

A compilation of class intervals, tallies, and class frequencies is called a **grouped frequency distribution.**

HOW TO   Make a frequency distribution

1. Identify appropriate intervals for the data.
2. Tally the data for the intervals.
3. Count the tallies in each interval.

TABLE 7-11
Frequency Distribution of 25 Exam Scores

Class Interval	Exam Tally	Class Frequency
60–64	/	1
65–69	/	1
70–74	//	2
75–79	ЦН /	6
80–84	///	3
85–89	ЦН	5
90–94	ЦН	5
95–99	//	2
		25

EXAMPLE 5   Make a grouped frequency distribution of the 25 math exam scores given in Table 7-1 on page 218. Prepare a table with a title and class intervals and tally the data to determine the class frequencies (Table 7-11). Examine the grouped frequency distribution in Table 7-11 to answer questions *a–e*.

(a) How many students scored 70 or above?

$2 + 6 + 3 + 5 + 5 + 2 = 23$ Add the frequencies for class intervals with scores 70 or higher.

23 students scored 70 or above.

(b) How many students made A's (90 or higher)?

$5 + 2 = 7$ Add the frequencies for class intervals 90–94 and 95–99.

7 students made A's (90 or higher).

(c) What percent of the total grades were A's (90's)?

$$\frac{7 \text{ A's}}{25 \text{ total}} = \frac{7}{25} = 0.28 = 28\% \text{ A's}$$ The portion or part is 7 and the base or total is 25.

(d) Were the students prepared for the test or was the test too difficult?
The relatively high number of 90's (7) compared to the relatively low number of 60's (2) suggests that **in general, most students were prepared for the test.**

(e) What is the ratio of A's (90's) to F's (60's)?

$$\frac{7 \text{ A's}}{2 \text{ F's}} = \frac{7}{2}$$

The ratio is $\frac{7}{2}$.

Sometimes you want more information about how data are distributed. For instance, you may want to know how each class interval of a frequency distribution relates to the whole set of data. This information is called a relative frequency distribution. A **relative frequency distribution** is a distribution that shows the percent that each class interval of a frequency distribution is of the whole.

HOW TO   Make a relative frequency distribution

1. Make the frequency distribution.
2. Calculate the percent that the frequency of each class interval is of the total number of data items in the set. These percents make up the relative frequency distribution.

$$\text{Relative frequency of a class interval} = \frac{\text{class interval frequency}}{\text{total number in the data set}} \times 100\%$$

EXAMPLE 6 Make a relative frequency distribution of the data in Table 7-11.

Class Interval	Class Frequency	Calculations	Relative Frequency
60–64	1	$\frac{1}{25}(100\%) = \frac{100\%}{25} = 4\%$	4%
65–69	1	$\frac{1}{25}(100\%) = \frac{100\%}{25} = 4\%$	4%
70–74	2	$\frac{2}{25}(100\%) = \frac{200\%}{25} = 8\%$	8%
75–79	6	$\frac{6}{25}(100\%) = \frac{600\%}{25} = 24\%$	24%
80–84	3	$\frac{3}{25}(100\%) = \frac{300\%}{25} = 12\%$	12%
85–89	5	$\frac{5}{25}(100\%) = \frac{500\%}{25} = 20\%$	20%
90–94	5	$\frac{5}{25}(100\%) = \frac{500\%}{25} = 20\%$	20%
95–99	2	$\frac{2}{25}(100\%) = \frac{200\%}{25} = 8\%$	8%

STOP AND CHECK

See Example 5.

1. Make a frequency distribution for the number of vacation days accumulated by staff at Tulsa Community College (Table 7-9, page 231). Use intervals 0–19, 20–39, 40–59, 60–79, and 80–99.

Use the frequency distribution from Exercise 1 to answer questions 2–5.

2. How many staff have more than 39 vacation days?

3. How many staff have fewer than 40 vacation days?

4. What percent of the staff have 80 or more vacation days? Round to the nearest tenth of a percent.

5. What percent of the staff have 20 to 59 vacation days? Round to the nearest tenth of a percent.

6. Make a relative frequency distribution of the data in Table 7-9 on page 231. Round percents to the nearest tenth percent. *See Example 6.*

5 Find the mean of grouped data.

When data are grouped, it may be desirable to find the mean of the grouped data. To do this, we extend our frequency distribution.

HOW TO   Find the mean of grouped data

1. Make a frequency distribution.
2. Find the midpoint of each class interval by averaging the beginning and ending points.

$$\text{Midpoint} = \frac{\text{beginning point} + \text{ending point}}{2}$$

3. For each interval in step 1, find the products of the midpoint of the interval and the frequency.
4. Find the sum of the class frequencies.
5. Find the sum of the products from step 2.
6. Divide the sum of the products (from step 4) by the sum of the class frequencies (from step 3).

$$\text{Mean of grouped data} = \frac{\text{sum of the products of the midpoints and the class frequencies}}{\text{sum of the class frequencies}}$$

EXAMPLE 7   Find the grouped mean of the scores in Table 7-11 on p. 232.

Find the midpoint of each class interval:

$$\frac{60 + 64}{2} = \frac{124}{2} = 62 \qquad \frac{65 + 69}{2} = \frac{134}{2} = 67 \qquad \frac{70 + 74}{2} = \frac{144}{2} = 72$$

$$\frac{75 + 79}{2} = \frac{154}{2} = 77 \qquad \frac{80 + 84}{2} = \frac{164}{2} = 82 \qquad \frac{85 + 89}{2} = \frac{174}{2} = 87$$

$$\frac{90 + 94}{2} = \frac{184}{2} = 92 \qquad \frac{95 + 99}{2} = \frac{194}{2} = 97$$

Class interval	Class frequency	Midpoint	Product of midpoint and frequency
60–64	1	62	62
65–69	1	67	67
70–74	2	72	144
75–79	6	77	462
80–84	3	82	246
85–89	5	87	435
90–94	5	92	460
95–99	2	97	194
Total	25		2,070

$$\text{Mean of grouped data} = \frac{\text{sum of the products of the midpoints and the class frequencies}}{\text{sum of the class frequencies}}$$

$$= \frac{2,070}{25}$$

$$= 82.8$$

The grouped mean of the scores is 82.8.

TIP

Is the Mean of Grouped Data Exact?

No. The mean of grouped data is based on the assumption that all the data in an interval have a mean that is exactly equal to the midpoint of the interval. Because this is usually not the case, the mean of grouped data is a reasonable approximation for the mean of the data set.

STOP AND CHECK

See Example 7.

1. Find the grouped mean of the data in Exercise 4 on page 220. Round to tenths.

2. Use the grouped frequency distribution in Table 7-12 to find the grouped mean. Round to hundredths.

3. Find the grouped mean to the nearest whole number of the data in the frequency distribution in Table 7-13. Round to hundredths.

TABLE 7-12		
Frequency Distribution of 25 Scores		
Class interval	**Class frequency**	**Midpoint**
60–64	6	
65–69	8	
70–74	12	
75–79	22	
80–84	18	
85–89	9	

TABLE 7-13		
Frequency Distribution of Credit-Hour Loads		
Class interval	**Class frequency**	**Midpoint**
0–4	3	
5–9	7	
10–14	4	
15–19	2	
Total	16	

7-2 SECTION EXERCISES

SKILL BUILDERS

See Example 1.

1. Find the mean for the scores: 3,850; 5,300; 8,550; 4,300; 5,350.

2. Find the mean for the amounts: 92, 68, 72, 83, 72, 95, 88, 76, 72, 89, 89, 96, 74, 72. Round to the nearest whole number.

3. Find the mean for the amounts: $17,485; $14,978; $13,592; $14,500; $18,540; $14,978. Round to the nearest dollar.

See Example 2.

4. Find the median for the scores: 3,850; 5,300; 8,550; 4,300; 5,350.

5. Find the median for the scores: 92, 68, 72, 83, 72, 95, 88, 76, 72, 89, 89, 96, 74, 72.

See Example 3.

6. Find the median for the amounts: $17,485; $14,978; $13,592; $14,500; $18,540; $14,978.

7. Find the mode for the scores: 3,850; 5,300; 8,550; 4,300; 5,350.

8. Find the mode for the scores: 92, 68, 72, 83, 72, 95, 88, 76, 72, 89, 89, 96, 74, 72.

9. Find the mode for the amounts: $17,485; $14,978; $13,592; $14,500; $18,540; $14,978.

APPLICATIONS

See Example 4.

10. Weekly expenses of students taking a business mathematics class are shown in Table 7-14.
    a. Find the mean rounded to the nearest whole number.
    b. Find the median.
    c. Find the mode.
    d. Write a statement about the data set based on your findings.

TABLE 7-14 Weekly Expenses of Students												
89	42	78	156	67	85	92	80	55	75	85	99	88
90	85	95	100	95	79	93	56	78	81	84	105	77

11. Salaries for the research and development department of Richman Chemical are given as $48,397; $27,982; $42,591; $19,522; $32,400; and $37,582.
    a. Find the mean rounded to the nearest dollar.
    b. Find the median.
    c. Find the mode.
    d. Write a statement about the data set based on your findings.

12. Sales in thousands of dollars for men's suits at a Macy's department store for a 12-month period were $127; $215; $135; $842; $687; $512; $687; $742; $984; $752; $984; $1,992.
    a. Find the mean rounded to the nearest whole thousand.
    b. Find the median.
    c. Find the mode.
    d. Write a statement about the data set based on your findings.

13. Accountants often use the median when studying salaries for various jobs. What is the median of the following salary list: $32,084; $21,983; $27,596; $43,702; $38,840; $25,997?

14. Weather forecasters sometimes give the average (mean) temperature for a particular city. The following temperatures were recorded as highs on June 30 of the last 10 years in a certain city: 89°, 88°, 90°, 92°, 95°, 89°, 93°, 98°, 93°, 97°. What is the mean high temperature for June 30 for the last 10 years?

See Example 5.

15. The following grades were earned by students on a midterm business math exam:

75	82	63	88	94
81	90	72	84	87
98	93	85	68	91
78	86	91	83	92

Make a frequency distribution of the data using the intervals 60–69, 70–79, 80–89, and 90–99.

16. What percent of the students in Exercise 15 earned a grade that was below 80?

See Example 6.

17. The 7th Inning wants to group a collection of autographed photos by price ranges. Make a relative frequency distribution of the prices using the intervals $0–$9.99, $10–$19.99, $20–$29.99, $30–$39.99, and $40–$49.99.

$2.50	$3.75	$1.25	$21.50	$43.00	$15.00
$26.00	$14.50	$12.75	$35.00	$37.50	$48.00
$7.50	$6.50	$7.50	$8.00	$12.50	$15.00
$9.50	$8.25	$14.00	$25.00	$18.50	$45.00
32.50	$20.00	$10.00	$17.50	$6.75	$28.50

18. In Exercise 17, what percent to the nearest whole percent of the collection is priced below $20?

19. In Exercise 17, what percent of the collection is priced $40 or over?

20. Use the given hourly rates (rounded to the nearest whole dollar) for 35 support employees in a private college to complete the frequency distribution and find the grouped mean rounded to the nearest cent. *See Example 7.*

$14	$16	$9	$10	$12	$13	$15
$11	$12	$16	$17	$22	$19	$28
$18	$16	$12	$9	$11	$12	$17
$26	$16	$18	$21	$18	$16	$14
$10	$13	$12	$15	$12	$12	$9

LEARNING OUTCOMES

1 Find the range.
2 Find the standard deviation.

The mean, the median, and the mode are measures of central tendency. Another group of statistical measures is **measures of variation or dispersion.** The variation or dispersion of a set of data may also be referred to as the **spread.**

Measures of variation or dispersion: statistical measurements such as the range and standard deviation that indicate how data are dispersed or spread.

Spread: the variation or dispersion of a set of data.

Range: the difference between the highest and lowest values in a data set.

1 Find the range.

One measure of dispersion of a set of data is the **range**. The range is the difference between the highest value and the lowest value in a set of data.

DID YOU KNOW?

In *Excel* there is no function for finding the range, but you can use the functions *MAX* and *MIN* to identify the highest and lowest values in a set of data.

HOW TO   Find the range

1. Find the highest and lowest values.
2. Find the difference between the highest and lowest values.

$$\text{Range} = \text{highest value} - \text{lowest value}$$

EXAMPLE 1

Find the range for the data in Table 7-8 in the example on page 228 for prices of used automobiles sold over the weekend.

The high value is $15,450. The low value is $6,100.
Range = $15,450 − $6,100 = **$9,350.**

TIP

Use More Than One Statistical Measure

A common mistake when making conclusions or inferences from statistical measures is to examine only one statistic, such as the range. To obtain a complete picture of the data requires looking at more than one statistic.

STOP AND CHECK

See Example 1.

1. Find the range for salary: $37,500; $32,000; $28,800; $35,750; $29,500; $47,300.

2. Find the range for the number of hours for the life of a lightbulb: 2,400; 2,100; 1,800; 2,800; 3,450.

3. Find the range for the number of days a patient stays in the hospital: 2 days; 15 days; 7 days; 3 days; 1 day; 3 days; 5 days; 2 days; 4 days; 1 day; 2 days; 6 days; 4 days; 2 days.

4. Find the range for the number of CDs purchased per month by college students: 12, 7, 5, 2, 1, 8, 0, 3, 1, 2, 7, 5, 30, 5, 2.

5. Find the range for the Internal Revenue gross collection of estate taxes for a recent 10-year period: $23,627,320,000; $25,289,663,000; $25,532,186,000; $25,618,377,000; $20,887,883,000; $24,130,143,000; $23,565,164,000; $26,717,493,000; $24,557,815,000; $26,543,433,000 (*Source: IRS Data Book FY 2008,* Publication 55b)

6. Find the range for the Internal Revenue gross collection of gift taxes for a recent 10-year period: $4,758,287,000; $4,103,243,000; $3,958,253,000; $1,709,329,000; $1,939,025,000; $1,449,319,000; $2,040,367,000; $1,970,032,000; $2,420,138,000; $3,280,502,000. (*Source: IRS Data Book FY 2008,* Publication 55b)

2 Find the standard deviation.

Outlier: a data point that is outside the overall pattern of the distribution of the data.

Deviation from the mean: the difference between a value of a data set and the mean.

Although the range gives us some information about dispersion, it does not tell us whether the highest or lowest values are typical values or extreme outliers. An **outlier** is a data point that is outside the overall pattern of the distribution of the data. We can get a clearer picture of the data set by examining how much each data point *differs* or *deviates* from the mean.

The **deviation from the mean** of a data value is the difference between the value and the mean.

HOW TO   Find the deviation from the mean

Data set: 38, 43, 45, 44.

1. Find the mean of the set of data.

$$\text{Mean} = \frac{\text{sum of data values}}{\text{number of values}}$$

$$\frac{38 + 43 + 45 + 44}{4} = \frac{170}{4} = 42.5$$

2. Find the amount by which each data value deviates or is different from the mean.

   Deviation from the mean = data value − mean

   $38 - 42.5 = -4.5$ (below the mean)
   $43 - 42.5 = 0.5$ (above the mean)
   $45 - 42.5 = 2.5$ (above the mean)
   $44 - 42.5 = 1.5$ (above the mean)

When the value is smaller than the mean, the difference is represented by a *negative* number, indicating the value is *below* or less than the mean. When the value is larger than the mean, the difference is represented by a positive number, indicating the value is *above* or greater than the mean. In the example in the How To feature, only one value is below the mean, and its deviation is -4.5. Three values are above the mean, and the sum of these deviations is $0.5 + 2.5 + 1.5 = 4.5$. Note that *the sum of all deviations from the mean is zero*. This is true for all sets of data.

EXAMPLE 2   Find the deviations from the mean for the set of data 45, 63, 87, and 91. Show that the sum of the deviations from the mean is zero.

$$\text{Mean} = \frac{\text{Sum of values}}{\text{Number of values}} = \frac{45 + 63 + 87 + 91}{4} = \frac{286}{4} = 71.5$$

To find the deviation from the mean, subtract the mean from each value. We arrange these values in a table.

Data Values	Deviations (Data Value − Mean)
45	$45 - 71.5 = \mathbf{-26.5}$
63	$63 - 71.5 = \mathbf{-8.5}$
87	$87 - 71.5 = \mathbf{15.5}$
91	$91 - 71.5 = \mathbf{19.5}$

The sum of deviations are found as follows:

Opposites: a positive and negative number that represent the same distance from 0 but in opposite directions.

$-26.5 + -8.5 = -35$ The sum of two negative numbers is negative.
$15.5 + 19.5 = 35$ The sum of two positive numbers is positive.
$-35 + 35 = 0$ -35 and 35 are **opposites.** The sum of opposites is 0.

We have not gained any statistical insight or new information by analyzing the sum of the deviations from the mean or even by analyzing the average of the deviations.

$$\text{Average deviation} = \frac{\text{sum of deviations}}{\text{number of values}} = \frac{0}{n} = 0$$

Standard deviation: a statistical measurement that shows how data are spread above and below the mean.

Variance: a statistical measurement that is the average of the squared deviations of data from the mean. The square root of the variance is the standard deviation.

To compensate for this situation, we use a statistical measure called the **standard deviation,** which uses the square of each deviation from the mean. The square of a negative value is always positive. The squared deviations are averaged (mean), and the result is called the **variance.**

The square root of the variance is taken so that the result can be interpreted within the context of the problem. Various formulas exist for finding the standard deviation of a set of values, but we will use only one formula, the formula for a sample of data or a small data set. This formula averages the values by dividing by 1 less than the number of values ($n - 1$). Several calculations are necessary and are best organized in a table.

HOW TO · Find the standard deviation of a sample of a set of data

1. Find the mean of the sample data set.

$$\text{Mean} = \frac{\text{sum of values}}{\text{number of values}}$$

2. Find the deviation of each value from the mean.
3. Square each deviation.

Deviation = data value − mean
Deviation squared = deviation × deviation

4. Find the sum of the squared deviations.
5. Divide the sum of the squared deviations by 1 *less than* the number of values in the data set. This amount is called the *variance*.

$$\text{Variance} = \frac{\text{sum of squared deviations}}{n - 1}$$

6. Find the standard deviation by taking the square root of the variance found in step 5.

$$\text{Standard deviation} = \sqrt{\text{variance}}$$

EXAMPLE 3

Find the standard deviation for the values 45, 63, 87, and 91. From Example 2, the mean is 71.5 and the number of values is 4.

Data Values	Deviations from the Mean: Data Value − Mean	Squares of the Deviations from the Mean
45	$45 - 71.5 = -26.5$	$(-26.5)(-26.5) = 702.25$
63	$63 - 71.5 = -8.5$	$(-8.5)(-8.5) = 72.25$
87	$87 - 71.5 = 15.5$	$(15.5)(15.5) = 240.25$
91	$91 - 71.5 = 19.5$	$(19.5)(19.5) = 380.25$
	Sum of Deviations $= 0$	Sum of Squared Deviations $= 1,395$

$$\text{Variance} = \frac{\text{sum of squared deviations}}{n-1} = \frac{1,395}{4-1} = \frac{1,395}{3} = 465$$

$$\text{Standard deviation} = \text{square root of variance} = \sqrt{465}$$
$$= 21.56385865 \text{ or } \mathbf{21.6} \quad \text{rounded}$$

A small standard deviation indicates that the mean is a typical value in the data set. A large standard deviation indicates that the mean is not typical, and other statistical measures should be examined to better understand the characteristics of the data set.

Examine the various statistics for the data set on a number line (Figure 7-19). We can confirm visually that the dispersion of the data is broad and the mean is not a typical value in the data set.

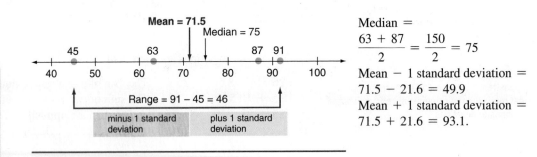

Median $=$
$$\frac{63 + 87}{2} = \frac{150}{2} = 75$$

Mean − 1 standard deviation =
$71.5 - 21.6 = 49.9$
Mean + 1 standard deviation =
$71.5 + 21.6 = 93.1$.

FIGURE 7-19
Dispersion of Data Using a Number Line

Another interpretation of the standard deviation is in its relationship to the **normal distribution**. Many data sets are normally distributed, and the graph of a normal distribution is a bell-shaped curve, as in Figure 7-20. The curve is **symmetrical**; that is, if folded at the highest point of the curve, the two halves would match. The mean of the data set is at the highest point or fold line. Then, half the data (50%) are to the left or *below* the mean and half the data (50%) are to the right or *above* the mean. Other characteristics of the normal distribution are:

68.3% of the data are within **1** standard deviation of the mean.
95.4% of the data are within **2** standard deviations of the mean.
99.7% of the data are within **3** standard deviations of the mean.

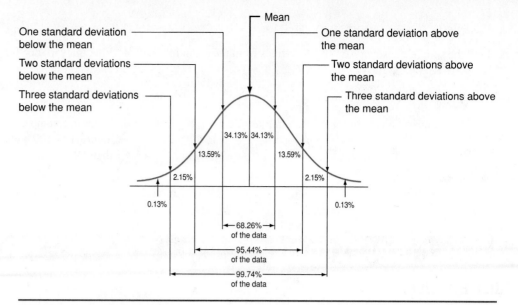

FIGURE 7-20
The Normal Distribution

EXAMPLE 4 An Auto Zone Duralast Gold automobile battery has an expected mean life of 46 months with a standard deviation of 4 months. In an order of 100 batteries, how many do you expect to last 54 months? Round to the nearest battery.

54 months is 8 months above the mean.
4 months is 1 standard deviation.
8 months is 2 standard deviations.
Visualize the facts (Figure 7-21).
50% + 34.13% + 13.59% = 97.72%

54 months − 46 months = 8 months
$\dfrac{8 \text{ months}}{4 \text{ months}} = 2$ standard deviations
Sum of percents

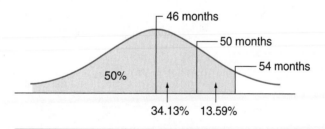

FIGURE 7-21
Mean Life for Automotive Batteries

97.72% of the batteries should last *less* than 54 months.

100% − 97.72% = 2.28%   Complement of 97.72%

2.28% of the batteries should last 54 months or longer.

2.28% × 100 batteries = 0.0228(100) = 2.28 batteries

2 batteries (rounded) of the 100 batteries should last 54 months or longer.

STOP AND CHECK

1. Find the deviations from the mean for the set of data: 72, 75, 68, 73, 69. *See Example 1.*

2. Show that the sum of the deviations from the mean in Exercise 1 is 0. *See Example 2.*

3. Find the sum of the squares of the deviations from the mean in Exercise 1.

4. Find the variance for the data in Exercise 1.

5. Find the standard deviation for the data in Exercise 1.

6. Refer to Example 4 on Auto Zone Duralast Gold batteries. In an order of 100 batteries, how many do you expect to last less than 50 months?

7-3 SECTION EXERCISES

SKILL BUILDERS

Use the sample ACT test scores 24, 30, 17, 22, 22 for Exercises 1 through 7.

1. Find the range. *See Example 1.*

2. Find the mean.

See Example 3.

3. Find the deviations from the mean. *See Example 2.*

4. Find the sum of squares of the deviations from the mean.

5. Find the variance.

6. Find the standard deviation.

7. In a set of 100 ACT scores that are normally distributed and with a mean of 23 and standard deviation of 4.69, (a) how many scores are expected to be lower than 18.31 (one standard deviation below the mean)? (b) How many of the 100 scores are expected to be below 32.38 (two standard deviations above the mean)? *See Example 4.*

APPLICATIONS

The data shows the total number of employee medical leave days taken for on-the-job accidents in the first six months of the year: 12, 6, 15, 9, 18, 12. Use the data for Exercises 8 through 14.

8. Find the range of days taken for medical leave for each month. *See Example 1.*

9. Find the mean number of days taken for medical leave each month.

10. Find the deviations from the mean. *See Example 2.*

See Example 3.

11. Find the sum of squares of the deviations from the mean.

12. Find the variance.

13. Find the standard deviation.

14. In a set of 36 months of data for medical leave that has a mean of 12 days per month and a standard deviation of 4.24, how many months are expected to have fewer than 16.24 days per month reported medical leave (one standard deviation above the mean)? *See Example 4.*

Learning Outcomes

Section 7-1

1 Interpret and draw a bar graph. (p. 218)

What to Remember with Examples

Draw a bar graph.

1. Write an appropriate title.
2. Make appropriate labels for the bars and scale. The intervals on the scale should be equally spaced and include the smallest and largest values.
3. Draw bars to represent the data. Bars should be of uniform width and should not touch.
4. Make additional notes as appropriate. For example, "Amounts in Thousands of Dollars" allows values such as $30,000 to be represented by 30.

Draw a bar graph to represent daily sales for the week.

Monday: $18,000
Tuesday: $30,000
Wednesday: $50,000
Thursday: $29,000
Friday: $40,000
Saturday: $32,000
Sunday: $8,000

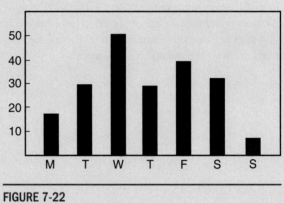

FIGURE 7-22
Daily Sales in Thousands of Dollars

2 Interpret and draw a line graph. (p. 221)

Draw a line graph.

1. Write an appropriate title.
2. Make and label appropriate horizontal and vertical scales, each with equally spaced intervals. Often, the horizontal scale represents time.
3. Use points to locate data on the graph.
4. Connect data points with line segments or a smooth curve.

Draw a line graph to show temperature changes: 12 A.M., 62°; 4 A.M., 65°; 8 A.M., 68°; 12 P.M., 73°; 4 P.M., 76°; 8 P.M., 72°; 12 A.M., 59°.

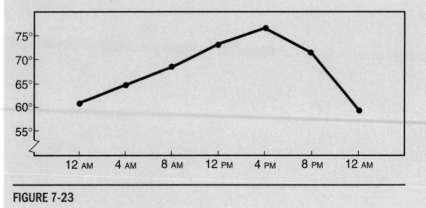

FIGURE 7-23
Temperature for a 24-Hour Period

3 Interpret and draw a circle graph. (p. 223)

Draw a circle graph.

1. Write an appropriate title.
2. Find the sum of the values in the data set.
3. Represent each value as a fractional or decimal part of the sum of values.

4. For each fraction or decimal, find the number of degrees in the sector of the circle to be represented by the fraction or decimal: Multiply the fraction or decimal by 360 degrees. The sum of the degrees for all sectors should be 360 degrees.

5. Use a compass (a tool for drawing circles) to draw a circle. Indicate the center of the circle and a starting point on the circle.

6. For each degree value, draw a sector: Use a protractor (a measuring instrument for angles) to measure the number of degrees for the sector of the circle that represents the value. Where the first sector ends, the next sector begins. The last sector should end at the starting point.

7. Label each sector of the circle and make additional explanatory notes as necessary.

Draw a circle graph to represent the expenditures of a family with an annual income of $42,000:

Annual income: $42,000
Housing: $12,000
Food: $9,000
Clothing: $1,500
Transportation: $3,000
Taxes: $7,500
Insurance: $2,700
Utilities: $1,800
Savings: $4,500

Housing: $\dfrac{\$12,000}{\$42,000}(360°) = 103°$

Food: $\dfrac{\$9,000}{\$42,000}(360°) = 77°$

Clothing: $\dfrac{\$1,500}{\$42,000}(360°) = 13°$

Transportation: $\dfrac{\$3,000}{\$42,000}(360°) = 26°$

Taxes: $\dfrac{\$7,500}{\$42,000}(360°) = 64°$

Insurance: $\dfrac{\$2,700}{\$42,000}(360°) = 23°$

Utilities: $\dfrac{\$1,800}{\$42,000}(360°) = 15°$

Savings: $\dfrac{\$4,500}{\$42,000}(360°) = 39°$

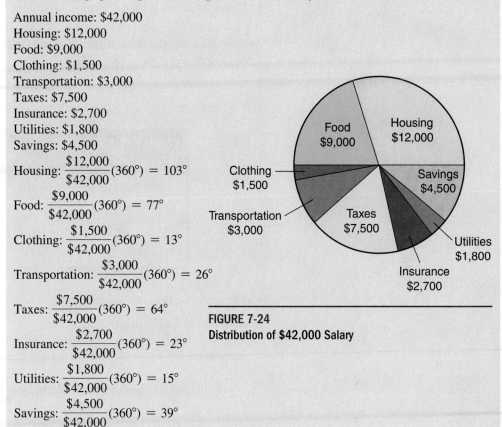

FIGURE 7-24
Distribution of $42,000 Salary

Section 7-2

1 Find the mean. (p. 227)

1. Find the sum of the values.
2. Divide the sum by the total number of values.

$$\text{Mean} = \frac{\text{sum of values}}{\text{number of values}}$$

Find the mean price of the printers: $435, $398, $429, $479, $435, $495, $435

$\text{Mean} = \dfrac{\text{sum of values}}{\text{number of values}}$

$= \$435 + \$398 + \$429 + \$479 + \$435 + \$495 + \$435 = \dfrac{\$3,106}{7}$

$= \$443.71$ (rounded)

2 Find the median. (p. 228)

1. Arrange the values in order from smallest to largest or largest to smallest.
2. Count the number of values:
   (a) If the number of values is odd, identify the value in the middle.
   (b) If the number of values is even, find the mean of the middle two values.

$$\text{Median} = \text{middle value or mean of middle two values}$$

Find the median price of the printers: $495, $479, $435, $435, $435, $429, $398

Arrange the values from smallest to largest

Median = middle value of $398, $429, $435, **$435**, $435, $479, $495
= $435

| 3 | Find the mode. (p. 229) | 1. For each value, count the number of times the value occurs. |
| | | 2. Identify the value or values that occur most frequently. |

$$\text{Mode} = \text{most frequent value(s)}$$

Find the mode price of the printers for the prices: $495, $479, $435, $435, $435, $429, $398.
Mode = most frequent value
     = $435

4	Make and interpret a frequency distribution. (p. 231)	1. Identify appropriate intervals for classifying the data.
		2. Tally the data for the intervals.
		3. Count the tallies in each interval.

Make a frequency distribution with the following data, indicating leave days for State College employees (see Table 7-15).

| 2 | 2 | 4 | 4 | 4 | 5 | 5 | 6 | 6 | 8 |
| 8 | 8 | 9 | 12 | 12 | 12 | 14 | 15 | 20 | 20 |

TABLE 7-15
Annual Leave Days of 20 State College Employees

Class Interval	Tally	Class Frequency
16–20	//	2
11–15	LH1	5
6–10	LH1 /	6
1–5	LH1 //	7

To make a relative frequency distribution:

1. Make the frequency distribution.
2. Calculate the percent that the frequency of each class interval is of the total number of data items in the set.

$$\text{Relative frequency of a class interval} = \frac{\text{class interval frequency}}{\text{total number in the data set}} \times 100\%$$

Make a relative frequency distribution for the leave days for State College employees. (Table 7-15).

Class interval	Class frequency	Relative frequency
16–20	2	$\frac{2}{20}(100\%) = \frac{200\%}{20} = 10\%$
11–15	5	$\frac{5}{20}(100\%) = \frac{500\%}{20} = 25\%$
6–10	6	$\frac{6}{20}(100\%) = \frac{600\%}{20} = 30\%$
1–5	7	$\frac{7}{20}(100\%) = \frac{700\%}{20} = 35\%$
Total	20	100%

| 5 | Find the mean of grouped data. (p. 234) | 1. Make a frequency distribution. |
| | | 2. Find the midpoint of each class interval by averaging the beginning and ending points. |

$$\text{Midpoint} = \frac{\text{beginning point} + \text{ending point}}{2}$$

3. For each interval in step 1, find the products of the midpoint of the interval and the class frequency.
4. Find the sum of the class frequencies.
5. Find the sum of the products from step 3.
6. Divide the sum of the products (from step 5) by the sum of the class frequencies (from step 4).

$$\text{Mean of grouped data} = \frac{\text{Sum of the products of the midpoints and the class frequencies}}{\text{sum of the class frequencies}}$$

Find the grouped mean of the number of leave days taken by the State College employees (see Table 7-15).

Find the midpoint of each class interval:

$$\frac{16 + 20}{2} = \frac{36}{2} = 18 \qquad \frac{11 + 15}{2} = \frac{26}{2} = 13$$

$$\frac{6 + 10}{2} = \frac{16}{2} = 8 \qquad \frac{1 + 5}{2} = \frac{6}{2} = 3$$

	Class frequency	Midpoint	Product of midpoint and class frequency
16–20	2	18	36
11–15	5	13	65
6–10	6	8	48
1–5	7	3	21
Total	20		170

$$\text{mean of grouped data} = \frac{170}{20}$$
$$= 8.5$$

Section 7-3

1 Find the range. (p. 238)

1. Find the highest and lowest values.
2. Find the difference between the highest and lowest values.

$$\text{Range} = \text{highest value} - \text{lowest value}$$

A survey of computer stores in a large city shows that a certain printer was sold for the following prices: $435, $398, $429, $479, $435, $495, and $435. Find the range.

$$\text{Range} = \text{highest value} - \text{lowest value} = \$495 - \$398 = \$97$$

Find the deviations from the mean.

2 Find the standard deviation. (p. 239)

1. Find the mean of the set of data.

$$\text{Mean} = \frac{\text{sum of data values}}{\text{number of values}}$$

2. Find the amount by which each data value deviates or is different from the mean.

$$\text{Deviation from the mean} = \text{data value} - \text{mean}$$

Find the deviation from the mean for each test score: 97, 82, 93, 86, 74

$$\text{Mean} = \frac{97 + 82 + 93 + 86 + 74}{5} = \frac{432}{5} = 86.4$$

Deviations

$$97 - 86.4 = 10.6$$
$$82 - 86.4 = -4.4$$
$$93 - 86.4 = 6.6$$
$$86 - 86.4 = -0.4$$
$$74 - 86.4 = -12.4$$

Find the standard deviations.

1. Find the mean of the sample data set. Mean = $\dfrac{\text{sum of data values}}{\text{number of values}}$

2. Find the deviation of each value from the mean. Deviation = data value − mean
3. Square each deviation. Deviation squared = deviation × deviation
4. Find the sum of the squared deviations.
5. Divide the sum of the squared deviations by 1 *less than* the number of values in the data set. This amount is called the *variance*.

$$\text{Variance} = \frac{\text{sum of squared deviations}}{n - 1}$$

6. Find the standard deviation by taking the square root of the *variance* found in step 5.

Find the standard deviation of these test scores: 68, 76, 76, 86, 87, 88, 93.

$$\text{Mean} = \frac{68 + 76 + 76 + 86 + 87 + 88 + 93}{7} = \frac{574}{7} = 82$$

Deviations	Squared Deviations
68 − 82 = −14	196
76 − 82 = −6	36
76 − 82 = −6	36
86 − 82 = 4	16
87 − 82 = 5	25
88 − 82 = 6	36
93 − 82 = 11	121
	466 Sum of squared deviations

$$\text{Variance} = \frac{\text{sum of squared deviations}}{n - 1} = \frac{466}{6} = 77.66666667$$

Standard deviation = $\sqrt{\text{variance}} = \sqrt{77.66666667} = 8.812869378 = 8.8$ rounded

EXERCISES SET A

Find the range, mean, median, and mode for the following. Round to the nearest hundredth if necessary.

1. New car mileages

17 mi/gal	16 mi/gal
25 mi/gal	22 mi/gal
30 mi/gal	

2. Sandwiches

$0.95	$1.65
$1.27	$1.97
$1.65	$1.15

3. Find the range, mean, median, and mode of the hourly pay rates for the employees. Write a statement about the data set based on your findings.

Thompson	$13.95	Cleveland	$ 5.25
Chang	$ 5.80	Gandolfo	$ 4.90
Jackson	$ 4.68	DuBois	$13.95
Smith	$ 4.90	Serpas	$13.95

4. During the past year, Piazza's Clothiers sold a certain sweater at different prices: $42.95, $36.50, $40.75, $38.25, and $43.25. Find the range, mean, median, and mode of the selling prices. Write a statement about the data set based on your findings.

Use Table 7-16 for Exercises 5 through 9.

TABLE 7-16

Class Enrollment by Period and Days of the First Week for the Second Semester

Period		Mon.	Tues.	Wed.	Thur.	Fri.
1.	7:00–7:50 A.M.	277	374	259	340	207
2.	7:55–8:45 A.M.	653	728	593	691	453
3.	8:50–9:40 A.M.	908	863	824	798	604
4.	9:45–10:35 A.M.	962	782	849	795	561
5.	10:40–11:30 A.M.	914	858	795	927	510
6.	11:35–12:25 P.M.	711	773	375	816	527
7.	12:30–1:20 P.M.	686	734	696	733	348
8.	1:25–2:15 P.M.	638	647	659	627	349
9.	2:20–3:10 P.M.	341	313	325	351	136
10.	3:15–4:05 P.M.	110	149	151	160	45

5. Find the mean number of students for each period in Table 7-16. Round to the nearest whole number.

6. Which period had the highest average enrollment?

7. Which period had the lowest average enrollment?

8. Draw a bar graph representing the mean enrollment for each period.

9. Identify enrollment trends for the 10 periods from the bar graph in Exercise 8.

Use Table 7-17 for Exercises 10 through 13.

10. What is the least value for 2012 sales? For 2013 sales?

11. What is the greatest value for 2012 sales? For 2013 sales?

TABLE 7-17

Sales for The Family Store, 2012–2013

	2012	2013
Girls' clothing	$ 74,675	$ 81,534
Boys' clothing	65,153	68,324
Women's clothing	125,115	137,340
Men's clothing	83,895	96,315

12. Using the values in Table 7-17, which of the following interval sizes would be more appropriate in making a bar graph? Why?
   a. $1,000 intervals ($60,000, $61,000, $62,000, . . .)
   b. $10,000 intervals ($60,000, $70,000, $80,000, . . .)

13. Draw a comparative bar graph to show both the 2012 and 2013 values for The Family Store (see Table 7-17). Be sure to include a title, explanation of the scales, and any additional information needed.

Use Figure 7-25 for Exercises 14 and 15.

14. What three-month period maintained a fairly constant sales record?

15. What month showed a dramatic drop in sales?

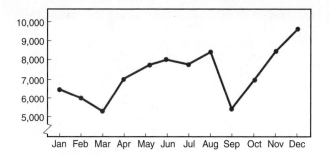

FIGURE 7-25
Monthly Sales for 7th Inning Sports Memorabilia

Use Figure 7-26 for Exercises 16 through 19.

16. What percent of the gross pay goes into savings? (Round to tenths.)

17. What percent of the gross pay is federal income tax? (Round to tenths.)

18. What percent of the gross pay is the take-home pay? (Round to tenths.)

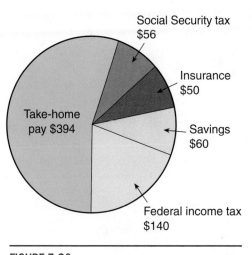

FIGURE 7-26
Distribution of Gross Pay ($700)

19. What are the total deductions for this payroll check?

20. Find the range for the data set: 90, 89, 82, 87, 93, 92, 98, 79, 81, 80.

21. Find the mean, median, and mode for the data set: 90, 89, 82, 87, 93, 92, 98, 79, 81, 80.

22. Find the variance for the scores in the following data set: 90, 89, 82, 87, 93, 92, 98, 79, 81, 80. Show that the sum of the deviations is zero.

23. Find the standard deviation from the variance in Exercise 22.

24. Use the test scores of 24 students taking Marketing 235 to complete the frequency distribution and find the grouped mean rounded to the nearest whole number:

57	91	76	89	82	59	72	88
76	84	67	59	77	66	56	76
77	84	85	79	69	88	75	58

25. Use the frequency distribution for Exercise 24 to make a relative frequency distribution. Round to the nearest tenth percent.

26. Home Depot sells compact fluorescent lamps (CFLs) that have a mean life of 10,000 hours with a standard deviation of 1,000 hours. In an order of 8,000 lamps, how many can be expected to last 11,000 hours or longer?

EXERCISES SET B

Find the range, mean, median, and mode for the following. Round to the nearest hundredth if necessary.

1. Test scores

61	72
63	70
93	87

2. Credit hours

16	12
18	15
16	12
12	

3. Find the range, mean, median, and mode of the weights of the metal castings after being milled. Write a statement about the data set based on your findings.

Casting A	1.08 kg	Casting D	1.1 kg
Casting B	1.15 kg	Casting E	1.25 kg
Casting C	1.19 kg	Casting F	1.1 kg

Use Figure 7-27 for Exercises 4 through 7.

4. What expenditure is expected to be the same next year as this year?

5. What two expenditures are expected to increase next year?

6. What two expenditures are expected to decrease next year?

7. What expenditure was greatest both years?

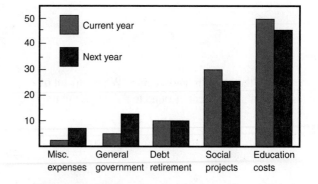

FIGURE 7-27
Distribution of Tax Dollars

Use the following information for Exercises 8 through 11. The temperatures were recorded at two-hour intervals on June 24.

12 A.M.	76°	8 A.M.	70°	2 P.M.	84°	8 P.M.	82°
2 A.M.	75°	10 A.M.	76°	4 P.M.	90°	10 P.M.	79°
4 A.M.	72°	12 P.M.	81°	6 P.M.	90°	12 A.M.	77°
6 A.M.	70°						

8. What is the smallest value?

9. What is the greatest value?

10. Which interval size is most appropriate when making a line graph for the data? Why?
  a. 1°
  b. 5°
  c. 50°
  d. 100°

11. Draw a line graph representing the data. Be sure to include the title, explanation of the scales, and any additional information needed.

12. Which of the following terms would describe the line graph in Exercise 11.
  a. Continually increasing
  b. Continually decreasing
  c. Fluctuating

Use Figure 7-28 for Exercises 13 through 15.

13. What percent of the overall cost does the lot represent? (Round to the nearest tenth.)

14. What is the cost of the lot with landscaping? What percent of the total cost does this represent? Round to the nearest tenth.

15. What is the cost of the house with furnishings? What percent of the total cost does this represent? Round to the nearest tenth.

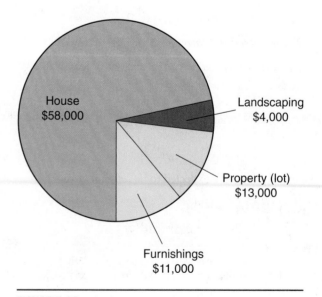

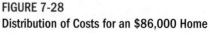

FIGURE 7-28
Distribution of Costs for an $86,000 Home

Use Table 7-18 for Exercises 16 through 19.

TABLE 7-18
Automobile Dealership's New and Repeat Business

Customer	Cars Sold
New	920
Repeat	278

16. What was the total number of cars sold?

17. How many degrees should be used to represent the new car business on a circle (to the nearest whole degree)?

18. How many degrees should be used to represent the repeat business on the circle graph (to the nearest whole degree)?

19. Construct a circle graph for the data in Table 7-18. Label the parts of the graph as "New" and "Repeat." Be sure to include a title and any additional information needed.

Use Table 7-19 for Exercises 20 and 21.

TABLE 7-19

First Semester Fall			Second Semester Spring			Third Semester Fall			Fourth Semester Spring		
Course	Cr. Hr.	Gr.	Course	Cr. Hr.	Gr.	Course	Cr. Hr.	Gr.	Course	Cr. Hr.	Gr.
BUS MATH	4	90	SOC	3	92	FUNS	4	88	CAL I	4	89
ACC I	4	89	PSYC	3	91	ACC II	4	89	ACC IV	4	90
ENG I	3	91	ENG II	3	90	ENG III	3	95	ENG IV	3	96
HISTORY	3	92	ACC II	4	88	PURCH	3	96	ADV	3	93
ECON	5	85	ECON II	4	86	MGMT I	5	84	MGMT II	5	83

20. Give the range and mode of grades for each semester.

21. Give the range and mode of grades for the entire two-year program.

22. Find the mean, variance, and standard deviation for the scores: 82, 60, 78, 81, 65, 72, 72, 78. Show that the sum of the deviations is zero.

23. Use the test scores of 32 students taking Business 205 to complete the frequency distribution and find the grouped mean rounded to the nearest whole number.

88	91	68	83	72	69	82	94
86	94	69	59	75	66	62	66
87	88	95	92	95	90	89	60
92	83	79	78	74	70	79	68

24. Use the frequency distribution for Exercise 23 to make a relative frequency distribution. Round to the nearest tenth percent.

25. A group of 85 executives has an average annual salary of $80,000 and a standard deviation of $2,000. How many executives are expected to have an annual salary of $84,000 or more?

PRACTICE TEST

1. Use the data to find the statistical measures.

   42 86 92 15 32 67 48 19 87 63
   15 19 21 17 53 27 21 15 82 15

   a. What is the range?   b. What is the mean?   c. What is the median?   d. What is the mode?

The costs of producing a piece of luggage at ACME Luggage Company are labor, $45; materials, $40; overhead, $35. Use this information for Exercises 2 through 7.

2. What is the total cost of producing a piece of luggage?

3. What percent of the total cost is attributed to labor?

4. What percent of the total cost is attributed to materials?

5. What percent of the total cost is attributed to overhead?

6. Compute the number of degrees for labor, materials, and overhead needed for a circle graph. Round to whole degrees.

7. Construct a circle graph for the cost of producing a piece of luggage.

Katz Florist recorded the sales for a six-month period for fresh and silk flowers in Table 7-20. Use the table for Exercises 8 through 11.

8. What is the greatest value of fresh flowers? Of silk flowers?

TABLE 7-20
Sales for Katz Florist, January–June

	January	February	March	April	May	June
Fresh	$11,520	$22,873	$10,380	$12,562	$23,712	$15,816
Silk	$ 8,460	$14,952	$ 5,829	$10,621	$17,892	$ 7,583

9. What is the smallest value of fresh flowers? Of silk flowers?

10. What interval size would be most appropriate when making a bar graph? Why?

   a. $100

   b. $1,000

   c. $5,000

   d. $10,000

11. Construct a bar graph for the sales at Katz Florist.

Use the following data for Exercises 12 and 13. The totals of the number of laser printers sold in the years 2008 through 2013 by Smart Brothers Computer Store are as follows:

2008	2009	2010	2011	2012	2013
983	1,052	1,117	615	250	400

12. What is the smallest value? The greatest value?

13. Draw a line graph representing the data. Use an interval of 250. Be sure to include a title and explanation of the scales.

14. Find the mean, variation, and standard deviation for the set of average prices for NFL tickets using Table 7-21.

15. A dusk-to-dawn outdoor lightbulb has an expected (mean) life of 8,000 hours with a standard deviation of 250 hours. How many bulbs in a batch of 500 can be expected to last no longer than 7,500 hours?

TABLE 7-21

Year	2004	2005	2006	2007	2008	2009
Average Ticket Price	$54.75	$59.05	$62.38	$67.11	$72.20	$74.99

Average price of NFL tickets 2004–2009

1. What type of information does a circle graph show?

2. Give a situation in which it would be appropriate to organize the data in a circle graph.

3. What type of information does a bar graph show?

4. Give a situation in which it would be appropriate to organize the data in a bar graph.

5. What type of information does a line graph show?

6. Give a situation in which it would be appropriate to organize the data in a line graph.

7. Explain the differences among the three types of averages: the mean, the median, and the mode.

8. What can we say about the mean for a data set with a large range?

9. What can we say about the mean for a data set with a small range?

10. What components of a graph enable us to analyze and interpret the data given in the graph?

Challenge Problem

Have the computers made a mistake? You have been attending Northeastern State College (which follows a percentage grading system) for two years. You have received good grades, but after four semesters you have not made the dean's list, which requires an overall average of 90% for all accumulated credits or 90% for any given semester. Your grade reports are shown in Table 7-22.

TABLE 7-22

First Semester Fall			Second Semester Spring			Third Semester Fall			Fourth Semester Spring		
Course	Cr. Hr.	Gr.	Course	Cr. Hr.	Gr.	Course	Cr. Hr.	Gr.	Course	Cr. Hr.	Gr.
BUS MATH	4	90	SOC	3	92	FUNS	4	88	CAL I	4	89
ACC I	4	89	PSYC	3	91	ACC II	4	89	ACC IV	4	90
ENG I	3	91	ENG II	3	90	ENG III	3	95	ENG IV	3	96
HISTORY	3	92	ACC II	4	88	PURCH	3	96	ADV	3	93
ECON	5	85	ECON II	4	86	MGMT I	5	84	MGMT II	5	83

To find the grade point average for a semester, multiply each grade by the credit hours. Add the products and then divide by the total number of credit hours for the semester. To calculate the overall grade point average, proceed similarly, but divide the sum of the products for all semesters by the total accumulated credit hours. Find the grade point average for each semester and the overall grade point average. Round to tenths.

7-1 Progeny Plastics Inc.

A small plastics manufacturing company specializes in making accessories for cell phones, particularly plastic covers. The company currently utilizes a single shift of production workers, and in total employs 13 people with the following annual salaries:

$125,000 President $100,000 Vice president
$ 75,000 Financial manager $ 65,000 Sales manager
$ 54,000 Production manager $ 48,400 Production supervisor
$ 42,000 Warehouse supervisor $ 27,600 Six assembly line workers

1. Calculate the mean, median, and mode for the salaries rounded up to the nearest thousand.

2. The statistic most often used to describe company salaries is the median or the mean. For this company, does the mean give an accurate description of the salaries? Why or why not?

3. Progeny decides to add a second shift of six more assembly line workers at $27,600 each, along with one additional production supervisor at $48,400. Calculate the mean, median, and mode including the seven additional salaries rounded up to the nearest thousand.

4. Which statistic would this company's labor union representative be most likely to cite during contract negotiations and why? Which statistic would the company president most likely report at the annual shareholders' meeting and why?

5. Name another situation in which it would be beneficial to report the highest average salary, and name another situation where it would be beneficial to use the lowest average salary.

7-2 Ink Hombre: Tattoos and Piercing

At 42 years of age, Enrique Chavez was starting to think more and more about retirement. After 17 years of running one of the Bay Area's most popular tattoo parlors, Ink Hombre, he decided to take on a partner—his 21-year-old bilingual niece Diana. Her words still echoed in his head—the same words she repeated every time someone left his shop to go elsewhere: "*Tío, debe ofrecer la perforación del cuerpo*: You should offer body piercing." She would go on to say, "Piercing gives people the opportunity to express their identity, just like a tattoo." She was right, of course. After she got her piercing certification, Diana came to work with Enrique full-time. But she didn't come cheaply. Between her salary and benefits, she was costing the business $1,000 per month! Enrique kept very detailed records, and her first month's sales were a bit disappointing. Piercings were offered as Category I, II, or III, and cost $35, $55, and $75 for stainless steel jewelry, respectively, and $55, $85, and $120 for gold. Diana sold five Category I, two Category II, and three Category III in stainless, and one each of categories I, II, and III in gold.

1. Find the mean, median, and mode for Diana's first month of sales.

2. Given the total sales value for Diana's first month, how long will it take for her to break even with her salary and benefits, assuming a 10 percent increase in sales value each month? Is the increase more likely to come from increased number of sales or a higher average sales value?

3. Diana's second month results show that she made six sales at $35, two at $55, three at $75, three at $85, and two at $120. Calculate the standard deviation for this data set. Does your answer for the standard deviation indicate that this is a normal distribution? If not, what are the implications?

4. Month 3 was a breakthrough for Diana, as she made seven sales at $35, four at $55, five at $75, two at $85, and three at $120. Enrique also saw a marked increase in his tattoo business due to direct referrals from Diana, and he decided to pay Diana a 15% referral fee. If Enrique had new tattoo business of $1,200 from Diana's referrals, what were her total earnings for the month?

Trade and Cash Discounts

Wisconsin Dells: Mount Olympus Tickets

Wisconsin Dells is known as "The Waterpark Capital of the World." One of the newer attractions, Mount Olympus Water and Theme Park, is the Dells's first "mega park," and has a theme of Greek mythology. The park has 37 water slides, numerous kiddie rides, 8 go-cart tracks, 6 rollercoasters, a wave pool, indoor and outdoor water play areas, and much more.

One of the main attractions is a wooden roller coaster named Hades. With a 65-degree drop, the world's longest underground tunnel, and speeds up to 70 mph, it was voted "Best New Ride" by *Amusement Today* when it first opened. Slowly you scale the 160-foot height of Hades, then with heart-pounding speed, reach the bottom of the first 140-foot drop, make a 90-degree turn underground in complete darkness, then blast into daylight to dip, spin around, and do it again. You won't forget the experience of riding Hades, the master of the Underworld!

How do you get tickets to Mount Olympus, or one of over 70 other Wisconsin Dells attractions? More importantly, how can you get the best discounts available? One of the best places to start is www.wisdells.com, where you can find a number of vacation packages offering substantial discounts. There are waterpark packages, a Comedy Club package, and even a Girlfriends Get-A-Way package. Some packages offer discounts of $100 or more per day.

Recently, Angela was organizing a youth trip for her church, and decided to check out ticket prices at the Mount Olympus web site at: www.mtolympuspark.com. There she learned she could receive a $5 discount off the regular price of $40 on an all-day unlimited pass for tickets purchased using an online coupon. She also discovered the discount could be as much as $15 per person for a group of 15 or more. Although Angela wasn't sure yet which would be the best deal, she knew that she wanted to save her church group as much as possible—in this case it could be $225 or more. Either way, Angela, enjoy the rides and hang on to your hat.

Sources: wisdells.com; mtolympuspark.com

LEARNING OUTCOMES

8-1 Single Trade Discounts

1. Find the trade discount using a single trade discount rate; find the net price using the trade discount.
2. Find the net price using the complement of the single trade discount rate.

8-2 Trade Discount Series

1. Find the net price applying a trade discount series and using the net decimal equivalent.
2. Find the trade discount applying a trade discount series and using the single discount equivalent.

8-3 Cash Discounts and Sales Terms

1. Find the cash discount and the net amount using ordinary dating terms.
2. Interpret and apply end-of-month (EOM) terms.
3. Interpret and apply receipt-of-goods (ROG) terms.
4. Find the amount credited and the outstanding balance from partial payments.
5. Interpret freight terms.

A discount is an amount deducted from the list price. Manufacturers and distributors give retailers *trade discounts* as incentives for a sale and *cash discounts* as incentives for paying promptly. Discounts are usually established by *discount rates,* given in percent or decimal form, based on the money owed. The discount, then, is a percentage of the list price.

8-1 SINGLE TRADE DISCOUNTS

LEARNING OUTCOMES

1 Find the trade discount using a single trade discount rate; find the net price using the trade discount.
2 Find the net price using the complement of the single trade discount rate.

Most products go from the manufacturer to the consumer by way of the wholesale merchant (wholesaler or distributor) and the retail merchant (retailer).

Product flow

Manufacturer *:* Wholesaler *:* Retailer *:* Consumer

Price flow

Consumer	→ Retailer	→ Wholesaler	→ Manufacturer
List price	Net price	Net price	Cost
	Discount off list	Discount off list	
$80	$56	$40	$20
	30% off list	50% off list	

Manufacturers often describe each of their products in a book or catalog that is made available to wholesalers or retailers. In such catalogs, manufacturers suggest a price at which each product should be sold to the consumer. This price is called the **suggested retail price,** the **catalog price,** or, most commonly, the **list price.**

When a manufacturer sells an item to the wholesaler, the manufacturer deducts a certain amount from the list price of the item. The amount deducted is called the **trade discount.** The wholesaler pays the **net price,** which is the difference between the list price and the trade discount. Likewise, the wholesaler discounts the list price when selling to the retailer. The discount rate that the wholesaler gives the retailer is smaller than the discount rate that the manufacturer gives the wholesaler. The consumer pays the list price.

The trade discount is not usually stated in the published catalog. Instead, the wholesaler or retailer calculates it using the list price and the **discount rate.** The discount rate is a *percent* of the list price.

The manufacturer makes available lists of discount rates for all items in the catalog. The discount rates vary considerably depending on such factors as the wholesaler's and retailer's purchasing history, the season, the condition of the economy, whether a product is being discontinued, and the manufacturer's efforts to encourage volume purchases. Each time the discount rate changes, the manufacturer updates the listing. Each new discount rate applies to the original list price in the catalog.

Suggested retail price, catalog price, list price: three common terms for the price at which the manufacturer suggests an item should be sold to the consumer.

Trade discount: the amount of discount that the wholesaler or retailer receives off the list price, or the difference between the list price and the net price.

Net price: the price the wholesaler or retailer pays or the list price minus the trade discount.

Discount rate: a percent of the list price.

1 Find the trade discount using a single trade discount rate; find the net price using the trade discount.

List prices and discounts apply the percentage formula.

$$\text{Portion (part)} = \text{rate (percent)} \times \text{base (whole)}$$

The portion is the trade discount T, the rate is the single trade discount rate R, and the base is the list price L.

$$P = RB$$
$$T = RL$$

HOW TO Find the trade discount using a single trade discount rate

1. Identify the single discount rate and the list price.
2. Multiply the list price by the decimal equivalent of the single trade discount rate.

$$\text{Trade discount} = \text{single trade discount rate} \times \text{list price}$$
$$T = RL$$

Because the trade discount is deducted from the list price to get the net price, once you know the trade discount, you can calculate the net price.

> **HOW TO** Find the net price using the trade discount
>
> 1. Identify the list price and the trade discount.
> 2. Subtract the trade discount from the list price.
>
> $$\text{Net price} = \text{list price} - \text{trade discount}$$
> $$N = L - T$$

EXAMPLE 1 The list price of a refrigerator is $1,200. Young's Appliance Store can buy the refrigerator at the list price less 20%. (a) Find the trade discount. (b) Find the net price of the refrigerator.

(a) Trade discount = single trade discount rate × list price

$T = RL$	Discount rate is 20%; list price is
$T = 20\%(\$1,200)$	$1,200. Change the percent to a
$T = 0.2(\$1,200)$	decimal equivalent. Multiply.
$T = \boxed{\$240}$	

The trade discount is $240.

(b) Net price = list price − trade discount   List price is $1,200; trade

$N = L - T$	discount is $240. Subtract.
$N = \$1,200 - \boxed{\$240}$	
$N = \$960$	

The net price is $960.

> **DID YOU KNOW?**
>
> In theory, the consumer is always expected to pay the list price. Trade discounts are discounts from the list price that determine what a retailer or wholesaler pays. The difference between the net price that the retailer and wholesaler pay and the list price that the consumer pays has to cover the retailer or wholesaler's expenses and the profits they make. Therefore, the more hands that a product passes through, the greater the difference between the amount that the manufacturer receives and the amount the consumer pays.
>
> In reality, competition causes large-volume retailers to negotiate larger trade discounts, which allow them to offer a product below the list price. Another strategy that they might use is to decrease their amount of profit per item as much as possible to increase sales. Retailers will make a smaller profit on each sale but have more sales. That is why small-volume retailers rely more on strategies like personal attention, convenience, and shopper loyalty to compete with the large-volume retailers.

STOP AND CHECK

See Example 1.

1. The list price of an NSX-T Acura is $89,765. Shavells Automobiles can buy the car at the list price less 12%.
   a. Find the trade discount.

   b. Find the net price of the car.

2. Find the trade discount and net price of an electric VeloBinder that has a retail price of $124 and a trade discount of 32%.

3. Direct Safes offers a Depository Safe for $425 with an 8% trade discount. Find the amount of the trade discount and the net price.

4. PlumbingStore.com buys one model of tankless water heater that has a list price of $395. The trade discount is 18%. What is the trade discount and net price of the heater?

5. The *Generation Money Book* has a suggested list price of $21.00 and ECampus.com can get a 24% trade discount on each copy of the book. Find the trade discount and net price.

6. Duty Free Stores purchased handbags, wallets, and key fobs for a total of $20,588.24 from Gucci, the manufacturer. The order has a trade discount of 15%. Find the amount of trade discount and find the net price of the goods.

2 Find the net price using the complement of the single trade discount rate.

Complement of a percent: the difference between 100% and the given percent.

Another method for calculating the net price uses the *complement* of a percent. The **complement of a percent** is the difference between 100% and the given percent. For example, the complement of 35% is 65%, as 100% − 35% = 65%. The complement of 20% is 80% because 100% − 20% = 80%.

The complement of the single trade discount rate can be used to find the net price. Observe the relationships among the rates for the list price, discount, and net price.

List price	Discount (amount off list)	Net price (amount paid)
100%	25% of list price	75% of list price
100%	20% of list price	80% of list price
100%	40% of list price	60% of list price
100%	50% of list price	50% of list price

Net price rate: the complement of the trade discount rate.

Because the complement is a percent, it is a rate. The complement of the trade discount rate is the **net price rate.** The single trade discount rate is used to calculate the amount the retailer *does not* pay: the trade discount. The net price rate is used to calculate the amount the retailer *does* pay: the net price.

HOW TO   Find the net price using the complement of the single trade discount rate

Find the net price of a computer that lists for $3,200 with a trade discount of 35%.

1. Find the net price rate: Subtract the single trade discount rate from 100%.

$$100\% - 35\% = 65\%$$

2. Multiply the decimal equivalent of the net price rate by the list price.

$$\text{Net price} = 0.65(\$3,200)$$
$$= \$2,080$$

$$\text{Net price} = \text{net price rate} \times \text{list price}$$

or

$$\text{Net price} = (100\% - \text{single trade discount rate}) \times \text{list price}$$

TIP

To Summarize the Concept of Trade Discounts

Trade discount = amount list price is reduced

= part of list price you *do not* pay

Net price = part of list price you *do* pay

EXAMPLE 2   Mays' Stationery Store orders 300 pens that list for $0.30 each, 200 pads that list for $0.60 each, and 100 boxes of paper clips that list for $0.90 each. The single trade discount rate for the order is 12%. Find the net price of the order.

300($0.30) = $ 90	Find the total list price of the pens.
200($0.60) = $120	Find the total list price of the legal pads.
100($0.90) = $ 90	Find the total list price of the paper clips.
$300	Add to find the total list price of the entire order.

$$\text{Net price} = (100\% - \text{single trade discount rate}) \times \text{list price}$$

$$= (100\% - 12\%)(\$300)$$

$$= 88\%(\$300)$$
$$= 0.88(\$300)$$
$$= \$264$$

The single trade discount rate is 12%; the list price is $300. The complement of 12% is 88%. Write 88% as a decimal. Multiply.

The net price of the order is $264.

STOP AND CHECK

See Example 2.

1. Find the net price of the PC software SystemWorks that lists for $70 and has a discount rate of 12%.

2. The InFocus LP 120 projector lists for $3,200 and has a trade discount rate of 15%. Find the net price.

3. Canon has a fancy new digital camera that lists for $1,299 and has a trade discount of 18%. What is the net price?

4. Find the net price of 100 sheets of display board that list for $3.99 each, 40 pairs of scissors that list for $1.89 each, and 20 boxes of push pins that list for $3.99 if a 22% trade discount is allowed.

8-1 SECTION EXERCISES

SKILL BUILDERS

See Example 1.

1. Find the trade discount on a computer that lists for $400 if a discount rate of 30% is offered.

2. Find the net price of the computer in Exercise 1.

3. Calculate the trade discount for 20 boxes of computer paper if the unit price is $14.67 and a single trade discount rate of 20% is allowed.

4. Calculate the trade discount for 30 cases of antifreeze coolant if each case contains 6 one-gallon units that cost $2.18 per gallon and a single trade discount rate of 18% is allowed.

5. Calculate the net price for the 20 boxes of computer paper in Exercise 3.

6. Calculate the net price for the 30 cases of antifreeze coolant in Exercise 4.

See Example 2.

7. Use the net price rate to calculate the net price for the 20 boxes of computer paper in Exercise 3. Compare this net price with the net price found in Exercise 5.

8. Use the net price rate to calculate the net price for the 30 cases of antifreeze coolant in Exercise 4. Compare this net price with the net price found in Exercise 6.

9. Which method of calculating net price do you prefer? Why?

10. EXCEL If you were writing a spreadsheet program to calculate the net price for several items and you were not interested in showing the trade discount, which method would you be likely to use? Why?

11. Complete the following invoice No. 2501, finding the net price using the single trade discount rate.

Qty.	Item	Unit price	List price
	Invoice No. 2501		
	October 15, 20XX		
15	Notebooks	$1.50	
10	Looseleaf paper	0.89	
30	Ballpoint pens	0.79	
	Total list price		
	40% trade discount		
	Net price		

12. Verify that the net price calculated in Exercise 11 is correct by recalculating the net price using the net price rate.

13. Best Buy Company, Inc., purchased video and digital cameras from Sony for its new store in Shanghai, China, with a total of $148,287. The order has a trade discount of 28%. Use the net price rate to find the net price of the merchandise.

8-2 TRADE DISCOUNT SERIES

LEARNING OUTCOMES

1 Find the net price applying a trade discount series and using the net decimal equivalent.
2 Find the trade discount applying a trade discount series and using the single discount equivalent.

Trade discount series (chain discount): more than one discount deducted one after another from the list price. This series of discounts can also be called **successive discounts** or **multiple discounts.**

Sometimes a manufacturer wants to promote a particular item or encourage additional business from a buyer. Also, buyers may be entitled to additional discounts as a result of buying large quantities. In such cases, the manufacturer may offer additional discounts that are deducted one after another from the list price. Such discounts are called a **trade discount series, chain discounts** or **successive discounts.** An example of a discount series is $400 (list price) with a discount series of 20/10/5 (discount rates). That is, a discount of 20% is allowed on the list price, a discount of 10% is allowed on the amount that was left after the first discount, and a discount of 5% is allowed on the amount that was left after the second discount. It *does not* mean a total discount of 35% is allowed on the original list price.

One way to calculate the net price is to make a series of calculations:

$400(0.2) = $80	$400 − $80 = $320	The first discount is taken on the list price of $400, which leaves $320.
$320(0.1) = $32	$320 − $32 = $288	The second discount is taken on $320, which leaves $288.
$288(0.05) = $14.40	$288 − $14.40 = $273.60	The third discount is taken on $288, which leaves the net price of $273.60.

Thus, the net price of a $400 order with a discount series of 20/10/5 is $273.60.

It is time-consuming to calculate a trade discount series this way. The business world uses a faster way of calculating the net price of a purchase when a series of discounts are taken.

1 Find the net price applying a trade discount series and using the net decimal equivalent.

Complements are used to find net prices directly. For the $400 purchase with discounts of 20/10/5, the net price after the first discount is 80% of $400 since 100% − 20% = 80%.

$$0.8(400) = $320$$

The net price after the second discount is 90% of $320.

$$0.9($320) = $288$$

The net price after the third discount is 95% of $288.

$$0.95(\$288) = \$273.60$$

To condense this process, the decimal equivalents of the complements of the discount rates can be multiplied in a continuous sequence in any order.

$$(0.8)(0.9)(0.95)(\$400) = 0.684(\$400) = \$273.60$$

The product of the decimal equivalents of the complements of the discount rates in a series is the **net decimal equivalent** of the net price rate.

Net decimal equivalent: the decimal equivalent of the net price rate for a series of trade discounts.

HOW TO   Find net price using the net decimal equivalent of a trade discount series

Find the net price of a copy machine if the list price is $1,830 with a series discount of 10/10.

1. Find the net decimal equivalent: Multiply the decimal form of the complement of each trade discount rate in the series.

   $0.9(0.9) = 0.81$

2. Multiply the net decimal equivalent by the list price.

   Net price = $0.81(\$1,830)$
   Net price = $\$1,482.30$

Net price = net decimal equivalent $\times$ list price

EXAMPLE 1

Stone Powell found a set of surround-sound speakers for his bistro that lists for $600 and a trade discount series of 15/10/5. What is the net price that Stone will pay?

$100\% - 15\% = 85\% = 0.85$ Find the complement of each discount rate and write it as
$100\% - 10\% = 90\% = 0.9$ an equivalent decimal.
$100\% - 5\% = 95\% = 0.95$
$0.85(0.9)(0.95) = 0.72675$ Multiply the complements to find the net decimal equivalent.

Net price = net decimal equivalent $\times$ list price
$= 0.72675(\$600)$ The net decimal equivalent is 0.72675;
$= \$436.05$ the list price is $600.

The net price for a $600 set of surround-sound speakers with a trade discount series of 15/10/5 is $436.05.

TIP

A Trade Discount Series Does Not Add Up!

The trade discount series of 15/10/5 is *not* equivalent to the single discount rate of 30% (which is the *sum* of 15%, 10%, and 5%). Look at Example 1 worked incorrectly.

Net price = net decimal equivalent $\times$ list price
$= (100\% - 30\%) \times \text{list price}$
$= 0.70(\$600)$
$= \$420$

INCORRECT

To add the discount rates implies that all the discounts are taken from the list price. In a series of discounts, each successive discount is taken from the remaining price.

EXAMPLE 2

One manufacturer lists a desk at $700 with a discount series of 20/10/10. A second manufacturer lists the same desk at $650 with a discount series of 10/10/10. Which is the better deal?

What You Know	What You Are Looking For	Solution Plan
List price for first deal: $700	Net price for the first deal	Net price = net decimal equivalent × list price
Discount series for first deal: 20/10/10	Net price for the second deal	
List price for second deal: $650	Which deal on the desk is better?	
Discount series for second deal: 10/10/10		

Solution

Decimal equivalents of complements of 20%, 10%, and 10% are 0.8, 0.9, and 0.9, respectively.

$$\text{Net decimal equivalent} = 0.8(0.9)(0.9) \qquad \text{Deal 1}$$
$$= 0.648$$
$$\text{Net price for first deal} = (0.648)\$700$$
$$= \$453.60$$

Decimal equivalents of complements of 10%, 10%, and 10% are 0.9, 0.9, and 0.9, respectively.

$$\text{Net decimal equivalent} = 0.9(0.9)(0.9) \qquad \text{Deal 2}$$
$$= 0.729$$
$$\text{Net price for second deal} = (0.729)\$650$$
$$= \$473.85$$

Conclusion

The net price for the first deal is $20.25 less than the net price for the second deal ($473.85 − $453.60 = $20.25).

The first deal—the $700 desk with the 20/10/10 discount series—is the better deal.

STOP AND CHECK

See Example 1.

1. Find the net price of a piano that has a list price of $4,800 and a trade discount series of 10/5.

2. The web site www.Mobile-Tronics.com offers a three-deck instrument cart at a retail (list) price of $535 and a trade discount series of 12/6. What is the net price?

3. A five-shelf Instrument Cart that lists for $600 has a trade discount series of 15/10. What is the net price?

4. A Tuffy Utility Cart listing for $219 has a chain discount of 10/6/5. What is the net price?

See Example 2.

5. One manufacturer lists a stand-up workstation for $448 with a chain discount of 10/6/4. Another manufacturer lists a station of similar quality for $550 with a discount series of 15/10/10. Which is the better deal?

6. Home Depot can purchase gas grills from one manufacturer for $695 with a 5/10/10 discount. Another manufacturer offers a similar grill for $705 with a 6/10/12 discount. Which is the better deal?

2 Find the trade discount applying a trade discount series and using the single discount equivalent.

If you want to know how much less than the list price you pay (trade discount) by using a discount series, you can calculate the savings—the trade discount—the long way, by finding the net price and then subtracting the net price from the list price. Or you can apply another, quicker complement method. In percent form, the complement of the net decimal equivalent is the **single discount equivalent.**

Single discount equivalent: the complement of net decimal equivalent. It is the decimal equivalent of a single discount rate that is equal to the series of discount rates.

Total amount of a series of discounts = single discount equivalent × list price

Net amount you pay after a series of discounts = net decimal equivalent × list price

1. Find the single discount equivalent: Subtract the net decimal equivalent from 1.

$$\text{Single discount equivalent} = 1 - \text{net decimal equivalent}$$

2. Multiply the single discount equivalent by the list price.

$$\text{Trade discount} = \text{single discount equivalent} \times \text{list price}$$

EXAMPLE 3

Ethan Thomas found an oval mat cutter that he wants to purchase and use in framing pictures. It lists for $1,500 and has a trade discount series of 30/20/10. What is the single discount equivalent? Use the single discount equivalent to find the trade discount.

The single discount equivalent is the complement of the net decimal equivalent. So first find the net decimal equivalent.

$100\% - 30\% = 70\% = 0.7$	Find the complement of each discount rate and write it as an equivalent decimal.
$100\% - 20\% = 80\% = 0.8$	
$100\% - 10\% = 90\% = 0.9$	
$0.7(0.8)(0.9) = 0.504$	Net decimal equivalent
$1.000 - 0.504 = 0.496$	Subtract the net decimal equivalent from 1 to find the single discount equivalent.

Thus, the single discount equivalent for the trade discount series 30/20/10 is 0.496, or 49.6%.

$\text{Trade discount} = \text{single discount equivalent} \times \text{list price}$	The single discount equivalent is 0.496; the list price is $1,500.
$= 0.496(\$1,500)$	
$= \$744$	

The trade discount on the $1,500 oval mat cutter with a trade discount series of 30/20/10 is $744.

TIP

Perform Some Steps Mentally

Even using a calculator, it is still desirable to make some calculations mentally. This makes calculations with the calculator less cumbersome. If the complements of each discount rate can be found mentally, then the remaining calculations will be multiplication steps that can be made using the calculator: Multiply the complements to find the net decimal equivalent, then multiply by the list price. Because the order and grouping of factors does not matter, they can be entered in various ways. Try each of the following sequences from the previous example.

Mentally:
$1 - 0.3 = 0.7$
$1 - 0.2 = 0.8$
$1 - 0.1 = 0.9$

To find the single discount equivalent and trade discount:

$\boxed{AC}\,.7\boxed{\times}.8\boxed{\times}.9\boxed{=} \Rightarrow 0.504$	net decimal equivalent
$1\boxed{-}.504\boxed{=} \Rightarrow 0.496$	single discount equivalent
(do not clear) $\boxed{\times}\,1500 \Rightarrow 744$	trade discount

We strongly encourage you to develop calculator proficiency by performing mentally as many steps as possible.

Some calculators have a key labeled $\boxed{ANS}$, which allows you to enter the answer from the last calculation. To find the single discount equivalent and the trade discount using the $\boxed{ANS}$ key and parentheses:

$\boxed{AC}\,1-\boxed{(}.7\boxed{\times}.8\boxed{\times}.9\boxed{)}\boxed{=} \Rightarrow 0.496$

$\boxed{ANS}\boxed{\times}1500\boxed{=} \Rightarrow 744$

STOP AND CHECK

See Example 3.

1. Use the single discount equivalent to find the trade discount on a wood desk that lists for $504 and has a trade discount series of 12/10/5.

2. A child's adjustable computer workstation lists for $317 and has a chain discount of 10/5. What is the discount amount?

3. A children's chair lists for $24.00 with a chain discount of 10/5/3. Find the amount of discount.

4. What is the discount amount of a toddler's work desk that lists for $74 with discounts of 12/8/6?

5. Tots Room offers a play-a-round table and chairs at a list price of $289.95 with a chain discount of 8/6/5. What is the trade discount?

6. If you want to know how much you have *saved* by using a discount series, would you use the net decimal equivalent or the single discount equivalent? Explain the reason for your choice.

8-2 SECTION EXERCISES

SKILL BUILDERS

See Example 1.

1. Guadalupe Mesa manages an electronic equipment store and has ordered 100 LED TVs for a special sale. The list price for each TV is $815 with a trade discount series of 7/10/5. Find the net price of the order by using the net decimal equivalent.

2. Tim Warren purchased computers for his computer store. Find the net price of the order of 36 computers if each one has a list price of $1,599 and a trade discount series of 5/5/10 is offered by the distributor.

3. Donna McAnally needs to calculate the net price of an order with a list price of $800 and a trade discount series of 12/10/6. Use the net decimal equivalent to find the net price.

See Example 3.

4. Payten Pastner is responsible for Cummins Appliance Store's accounts payable department and has an invoice that shows a list price of $2,200 with a trade discount series of 25/15/10. Use the single discount equivalent to calculate the trade discount on the purchase.

5. Mary Harrington is calculating the trade discount on a dog kennel with a list price of $269 and a trade discount series of 10/10/10. What is the trade discount? What is the net price for the kennel?

6. Braxton Sebastian manages a computer software distributorship and offers a desktop publishing software package for $395 with a trade discount series of 5/5/8. What is the trade discount on this package?

APPLICATIONS

See Example 2.

7. One distributor lists Ogio Kingpin II® golf bags for $189.97 with a trade discount series of 5/5/10. Another distributor lists the same brand of golf bag at $210 with a trade discount series of 5/10/10. Which is the better deal if all other aspects of the deal, such as shipping, time of availability, and warranty are the same or equivalent?

8. Two distributors offer the same brand and model PC computer. One distributor lists the computer at $1,899 with a trade discount series of 8/8/5 and free shipping. The other distributor offers the computer at $2,000 with a trade discount series of 10/5/5 and $50 shipping cost added to the net price. Which computer is the better deal?

9. Dylan Murphy currently receives a trade discount series of 5/10/10 on merchandise purchased from a furniture company. He is negotiating with another furniture manufacturer to purchase similar furniture of the same quality. The first company lists a dining room table and six chairs for $1,899. The other company lists a similar set for $1,800 and a trade discount series of 5/5/10. Which deal is better?

10. We have seen that the trade discount series 20/10/5 is *not* equal to a single trade discount rate of 35%. Does the trade discount series 20/10/5 equal the trade discount series 5/10/20? Use an item with a list price of $1,000 and calculate the trade discount for both series to justify your answer.

11. One distributor lists a printer at $460 with a trade discount series of 15/12/5. Another distributor lists the same printer at $410 with a trade discount series of 10/10/5. Which is the better deal?

12. A Nintendo Wii Console has a list price of $289 and a trade discount series of 8/8. Find the net price and trade discount.

LEARNING OUTCOMES

1 Find the cash discount and the net amount using ordinary dating terms.
2 Interpret and apply end-of-month (EOM) terms.
3 Interpret and apply receipt-of-goods (ROG) terms.
4 Find the amount credited and the outstanding balance from partial payments.
5 Interpret freight terms.

1 Find the cash discount and the net amount using ordinary dating terms.

Cash discount: a discount on the amount due on an invoice that is given for prompt payment.

To encourage prompt payment, many manufacturers and wholesalers allow buyers to take a **cash discount,** a reduction of the amount due on an invoice. The cash discount is a specified percentage of the price of the goods. Customers who pay their bills within a certain time receive a cash discount. Many companies use computerized billing systems to compute the exact amount of a cash discount and show it on the invoice, so the customer does not need to calculate the discount and resulting net price. But the customer still determines when the bill must be paid to receive the discount.

Bills are often due within 30 days from the date of the invoice. To determine the exact day of the month the payment is due, you have to know how many days are in the month, 30, 31, 28, or 29 in the case of February. There are two ways to help remember which months have 31 days and which have 30 or fewer days. The first method, shown in Figure 8-1, is called the *knuckle method*. Each knuckle represents a month with 31 days and each space between knuckles represents a month with 30 days (except February, which has 28 days except in a leap year, when it has 29).

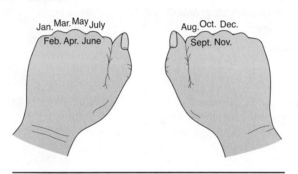

FIGURE 8-1
The knuckle months (Jan., Mar., May, July, Aug., Oct., and Dec.) have 31 days. The other months have 30 or fewer days.

Another way to remember which months have 30 days and which months have 31 is the following rhyme:

Thirty days has September,

April, June, and November.

All the rest have 31,

'cept February has 28 alone.

And leap year, that's the time

when February has 29.

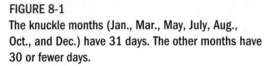

HOW TO Find the ending date of an interval of time

1. Add the beginning date and the number of days in the interval.
2. If the sum exceeds the number of days in the month, subtract the number of days in the month from the sum.
3. The result of step 2 will be the ending date in the next month of the interval.

EXAMPLE 1 If Marie Husne has an invoice that is dated March 19, what is the date (a) 10 days later and (b) 15 days later?

(a) $19 + 10 = 29$

Ten days later is March 29.

(b) $19 + 15 = 34$ March has 31 days.
    $34 - 31 = 3$

Fifteen days later is April 3.

With this in mind, let's look at one of the most common credit terms and dating methods.

Many firms offer credit terms 2/10, n/30 (read *two ten, net thirty*). The 2/10 means a 2% cash discount rate may be applied if the bill is paid within 10 days of the invoice date. The n/30 means that the full amount or net amount of the bill is due within 30 days. After the 30th day, the bill is overdue, and the buyer may have to pay interest charges or late fees.

For example, say an invoice is dated January 4 with credit terms of 2/10, n/30. If the buyer pays on or before January 14, then a 2% cash discount rate is applied. If the buyer pays on or after January 15, no cash discount is allowed. Finally, because 30 days from January 4 is February 3, if the buyer pays on or after February 4, interest charges or a late fee may be added to the bill.

HOW TO   Find the cash discount

1. Identify the cash discount rate and the net price.
2. Multiply the cash discount rate by the net price.

$$\text{Cash discount} = \text{cash discount rate} \times \text{net price}$$

EXAMPLE 2 Tommye Adams received an invoice dated July 27 from Webb Printing Services that shows a net price of $450 with the terms 2/10, n/30. (a) Find the latest date the cash discount is allowed. (b) Find the cash discount.

(a) The cash discount is allowed up to and including 10 days from the invoice date, July 27.

27th of July	Invoice date
+ 10 days	Days allowed according to terms 2/10
" 37th of July"	If July had 37 days . . .
− 31 days in July	July has 31 days.
6th of August	Latest date allowed

August 6 is the latest date the cash discount is allowed.

(b) Cash discount = Cash discount rate × net price
Cash discount = 2%($450)
$\qquad\quad = 0.02(\$450)$
$\qquad\quad = \$9.00$

The cash discount is $9.00.

Once a cash discount is deducted from a net price, the amount remaining is called the **net amount.** The net amount is the amount the buyer actually pays. Like the net price, there are two ways to calculate the net amount.

Because we attempt to use terms that are commonly used in the business world, the terms *net price* and *net amount* can be confusing. The list price is the suggested retail price, the net price is the price a retailer pays to the distributor or manufacturer for the merchandise, and the net amount is the net price minus any additional discount for paying the bill promptly.

Net amount: the amount you owe if a cash discount is applied.

Find the net amount

Using the cash discount:
1. Identify the net price and the cash discount.
2. Subtract the cash discount from the net price.

$$\text{Net amount} = \text{net price} - \text{cash discount}$$

Using the complement of the cash discount rate:
1. Identify the net price and the complement of the cash discount rate.
2. Multiply the complement of the cash discount rate by the net price.

$$\text{Net amount} = \text{complement of cash discount rate} \times \text{net price}$$

EXAMPLE 3 Find the net amount for the invoice in Example 2.

Using the cash discount:

$$\begin{aligned}
\text{Net amount} &= \text{net price} - \text{cash discount} \\
&= \$450 - \$9 \\
&= \$441
\end{aligned}$$

Using the complement of cash discount rate:

$$\begin{aligned}
\text{Net amount} &= \text{complement of cash discount rate} \times \text{net price} \\
&= (100\% - 2\%)(\$450) \\
&= 0.98(\$450) \\
&= \$441
\end{aligned}$$

The net amount is $441.

Another common set of discount terms is 2/10, 1/15, n/30. These terms are read *two ten, one fifteen, net thirty*. A 2% cash discount is allowed if the bill is paid within 10 days after the invoice date, a 1% cash discount is allowed if the bill is paid during the 11th through 15th days, and no discount is allowed during the 16th through 30th days. Interest charges or late fees may accrue if the bill is paid after the 30th day from the date of the invoice.

EXAMPLE 4 Charming Shoppes received a $1,248 invoice for computer supplies, dated September 2, with sales terms 2/10, 1/15, n/30. A 5% late fee is charged for payment after 30 days. Find the amount due if the bill is paid (a) on or before September 12; (b) on or between September 13 and September 17; (c) on or between September 18 and October 2; and (d) on or after October 3.

(a) If the bill is paid on or before September 12 (within 10 days), the 2% discount applies:

$$\begin{aligned}
\text{Cash discount} &= 2\%(\$1,248) = 0.02(\$1,248) = \boxed{\$24.96} \\
\text{Net amount} &= \$1,248 - \boxed{\$24.96} = \$1,223.04
\end{aligned}$$

The net amount due on or before September 12 is $1,223.04.

(b) If the bill is paid on or between September 13 and September 17 (within 15 days), the 1% discount applies:

$$\begin{aligned}
\text{Cash discount} &= 1\%(\$1,248) = 0.01(\$1,248) = \boxed{\$12.48} \\
\text{Net amount} &= \$1,248 - \boxed{\$12.48} = \$1,235.52
\end{aligned}$$

The net amount due on or between September 13 and September 17 is $1,235.52.

(c) If the bill is paid on or between September 18 and October 2, no cash discount applies.

The net price of $1,248 is due.

(d) If the bill is paid on or after October 3, a 5% late fee is added:

$$\begin{aligned}
\text{Late fee} &= 5\%(\$1,248) = 0.05(\$1,248) = \boxed{\$62.40} \\
\text{Net amount} &= \$1,248 + \boxed{\$62.40} = \$1,310.40
\end{aligned}$$

The net amount due on or after October 3 is $1,310.40.

STOP AND CHECK

1. The Gap has an invoice dated August 20 with terms 3/15, n/30. It must be paid by what date to get the discount? *See Example 1.*

2. VPGames.com received an invoice for $286,917 that was dated October 12 with terms of 2/10, 1/15, n/30. By what date must the invoice be paid to receive a 2% discount? What is the amount of the discount if the invoice is paid on October 25? *See Examples 1 and 2.*

3. An invoice received by Best Buy and dated March 15 has a net price of $985 with terms 2/15, n/30. Find the latest date a cash discount is allowed and find the cash discount. Find the net amount. *See Examples 2 and 3.*

4. Federated Department Stores received an invoice dated April 18 that shows a billing for $3,848.96 with terms 2/10, 1/15, n/30. Find the cash discount and net amount if the invoice is paid within 15 days but after 10 days. *See Examples 2 and 3.*

5. Office Depot has an invoice for $3,814 dated May 8, with terms of 3/10, 2/15, n/30. The invoice also has a 1% penalty per month for payment after 30 days. *See Example 4.*
   a. What amount is due if paid on May 12?
   b. What amount is due if paid on May 25?
   c. What amount is due if paid on June 7?
   d. What amount is due if paid on June 13?

2 Interpret and apply end-of-month (EOM) terms.

End-of-month (EOM) terms: a discount is applied if the bill is paid within the specified days after the end of the month. An exception occurs when an invoice is dated on or after the 26th of a month.

Another type of sales terms is **end-of-month (EOM) terms.** For example, the terms might be 2/10 EOM, meaning that a 2% discount is allowed if the bill is paid during the first 10 days of the month *after* the month in the date of the invoice. Thus, if a bill is dated November 19, a 2% discount is allowed as long as the bill is paid on or before December 10.

An exception to the EOM rule occurs when the invoice is dated *on or after the 26th of the month*. When this happens, the discount is allowed if the bill is paid during the first 10 days of the month after the next month. If an invoice is dated May 28 with terms 2/10 EOM, a 2% discount is allowed as long as the bill is paid on or before *July* 10. This exception allows retailers adequate time to receive and pay the invoice.

HOW TO   Apply EOM terms

To an invoice dated **before the 26th** day of the month:

1. A cash discount is allowed when the bill is paid by the specified day of the *next month*.
2. To find the net amount, multiply the invoice amount times the complement of the discount rate.

To an invoice dated **on or after the 26th day** of the month:

1. A cash discount is allowed when the bill is paid by the specified day of the *month after the next month*.
2. To find the net amount, multiply the invoice amount times the complement of the discount rate.

EXAMPLE 5

Newman, Inc., received a bill for cleaning services dated September 17 for $5,000 with terms 2/10 EOM. The invoice was paid on October 9. How much did Newman, Inc., pay?

Because the bill was paid within the first 10 days of the next month, a 2% discount was allowed. The complement of 2% is 98%. Thus, 98% is the rate that is paid.

$$\text{Net amount} = 98\%(\$5,000) = 0.98(\$5,000) = \$4,900$$

The net amount paid on October 9 is $4,900.

EXAMPLE 6 H-E-B of San Antonio received a $200 bill for copying services dated April 27. The terms on the invoice were 3/10 EOM. The firm paid the bill on June 2. How much did it pay?

Because the bill was paid within the first 10 days of the second month after the month on the invoice, a 3% discount was allowed. The complement of 3% is 97%.

$$\text{Net amount} = 97\%(\$200) = 0.97(\$200) = \$194$$

The net amount paid was $194.

STOP AND CHECK

See Examples 5 and 6.

1. AutoZone received an invoice dated November 2 for $2,697 with terms 3/15 EOM and paid it on November 14. How much was paid?

2. McDonald's received an invoice dated December 1 for $598.46 with terms 2/10 EOM. The invoice must be paid by what date to get a cash discount? How much is the cash discount?

3. Domino's Pizza received an invoice dated April 29 with terms 2/10 EOM. What is the latest date the invoice can be paid at a discount? What percent of the invoice must be paid if the discount applies?

4. Find the net amount to be paid on an invoice for $1,096.82 dated May 26 with terms of 1/10 EOM if the invoice is paid on July 7.

5. Find the net amount required on an invoice for $187.17 with terms of 2/10 EOM if it is dated February 15 and paid March 12.

6. Target Stores received an invoice for $84,896 dated July 28 with terms 3/15 EOM. If the invoice is paid on September 10, what is the net amount due?

3 Interpret and apply receipt-of-goods (ROG) terms.

Receipt-of-goods (ROG) terms: a discount applied if the bill is paid within the specified number of days of the receipt of the goods.

Sometimes sales terms apply to the day the *goods are received* instead of the invoice date. For example, the terms may be written 1/10 ROG, where **ROG** stands for **receipt of goods.** The terms 1/10 ROG mean that a 1% discount is allowed on the bill if it is paid within 10 days of the receipt of goods.

An invoice is dated September 6 but the goods do not arrive until the 14th. If the sales terms are 2/15 ROG, then a 2% discount is allowed if the bill is paid on any date up to and including September 29.

HOW TO Apply ROG terms

1. A cash discount is allowed when the bill is paid within the specified number of days from the **receipt of goods,** not from the date of the invoice.
2. To find the net amount, multiply the invoice amount times the complement of the discount rate.

EXAMPLE 7 Jim Riddle Heating and Air receives an invoice for machine parts for $400 that is dated November 9 and has sales terms 2/10 ROG. The machine parts arrive November 13.

(a) If the bill is paid on November 21, what is the net amount due?
(b) If the bill is paid on December 2, what is the net amount due?

(a) Because the bill is being paid within 10 days of the receipt of goods, a 2% discount is allowed. The complement of 2% is 98%.

$$\text{Net amount} = 98\%(\$400) = 0.98(\$400) = \$392$$

The net amount due is $392.

(b) No discount is allowed because the bill is not being paid within 10 days of the receipt of goods.

Thus, $400 is due.

See Example 7.

1. Curves Fitness Center received an invoice for $3,097.15 that was dated September 8 with terms of 3/15 ROG. The goods being invoiced arrived on September 12. By what date must the invoice be paid to get the cash discount? How much should be paid?

2. Johnson's Furniture purchased furniture that totaled $8,917.48 and received the furniture on March 12. The invoice dated March 5 arrived on March 15 and had discount terms of 2/10, n/30, ROG. Explain the discount terms. How much is paid if the invoice is paid on March 20?

3. Columbus Fitness Center received three new weight machines on May 15 and the invoice in the amount of $1,215 for these goods arrived on May 1 with discount terms of 2/15, n/30, ROG. How much must be paid if the invoice is paid on May 28? June 14?

4. Tracy Burford purchased two new dryers for Fashion Flair Beauty Salon at a cost of $797. The dryers were delivered on June 17 and the invoice arrived on June 13 with cash terms of 3/15, n/30, ROG. Tracy decided to pay the invoice on July 12. How much did she pay?

Partial payment: a payment that does not equal the full amount of the invoice less any cash discount.

Partial cash discount: a cash discount applied only to the amount of the partial payment.

Amount credited: the sum of the partial payment and the partial discount.

Outstanding balance: the invoice amount minus the amount credited.

4 Find the amount credited and the outstanding balance from partial payments.

A company sometimes cannot pay the full amount due in time to take advantage of cash discount terms. Most sellers allow buyers to make a **partial payment** and still get a **partial cash discount** off the net price if the partial payment is made within the time specified in the credit terms. The **amount credited** to the account, then, is the partial payment plus this partial cash discount. The **outstanding balance** is the amount still owed and is expected to be paid within the time specified by the sales terms.

> **HOW TO** Find the amount credited and the outstanding balance from partial payments
>
> 1. Find the amount credited to the account: Divide the partial payment by the complement of the cash discount rate.
>
> $$\text{Amount credited} = \frac{\text{partial payment}}{\text{complement of cash discount rate}}$$
>
> 2. Find the outstanding balance: Subtract the amount credited from the net price.
>
> $$\text{Outstanding balance} = \text{net price} - \text{amount credited}$$

EXAMPLE 8 The Semmes Corporation received an $875 invoice for cardboard cartons with terms of 3/10, n/30. The firm could not pay the entire bill within 10 days but sent a check for $500. What amount was credited to Semmes' account? What was the outstanding balance?

$$\text{Amount credited} = \frac{\text{partial payment}}{\text{complement of rate}}$$
$$= \frac{\$500}{0.97}$$
$$= \$515.46$$

Divide the amount of the partial payment by the complement of the discount rate to find the amount credited.

Outstanding balance = $875 − $515.46 = $359.54   Subtract the amount credited from the net price to find the outstanding balance.

A \$515.46 payment was credited to the account, and the outstanding balance was \$359.54.

TIP

Get Proper Credit for Partial Payments

Remember to find the *complement* of the discount rate and then divide the partial payment by this complement. Students sometimes just multiply the discount rate times the partial payment, which does not allow the proper credit.

From Example 8,

$$\frac{\$500}{0.97} = \$515.46$$

$$\$875 − \$515.46 = \$359.54$$

CORRECT

From Example 8,

$$\$500(0.03) = \$15$$
$$\$500 + \$15 = \$515$$
$$\$875 − \$515 = \$360$$

INCORRECT

STOP AND CHECK

See Example 8.

1. Coach of New York sold DFS in San Francisco $340,800 in leather goods with terms of 3/10, n/30. DFS decided to make a partial payment of $200,000 within 10 days. What amount was credited to DFS's invoice?

2. DFS purchased handbags from Burberry in the amount of $2,840,000 with terms of 2/10, n/30, ROG. If the goods arrived on November 12 and DFS made a partial payment of $1,900,000 on November 15, how much should be credited to the DFS account?

3. Office Max purchased office furniture in the amount of $89,517 and was invoiced with terms of 2/10, n/30. Cash strapped at the time, Office Max decided to make a partial payment of $50,000 within 10 days. How much should be credited to its account?

4. Cellular Services sold 6,000 new phones to AT&T Wireless for $79 each. The invoice arrived with terms of 3/10, n/30, and AT&T paid $400,000 immediately. How much should be credited to AT&T Wireless's account? How much was still to be paid on the invoice?

---

5   Interpret freight terms.

Bill of lading: shipping document that includes a description of the merchandise, number of pieces, weight, name of consignee (sender), destination, and method of payment of freight charges.

FOB shipping point: free on board at the shipping point. The buyer pays the shipping when the shipment is received.

Freight collect: The buyer pays the shipping when the shipment is received.

FOB destination: free on board at the destination point. The seller pays the shipping when the merchandise is shipped.

Freight paid: the seller pays the shipping when the merchandise is shipped.

Prepay and add: the seller pays the shipping when the merchandise is shipped, but the shipping costs are added to the invoice for the buyer to pay.

Manufacturers rely on a wide variety of carriers (truck, rail, ship, plane, and the like) to distribute their goods. The terms of freight shipment are indicated on a document called a **bill of lading** that is attached to each shipment. This document includes a description of the merchandise, number of pieces, weight, name of consignee, destination, and method of payment of freight charges. Freight payment terms are usually specified on the *manufacturer's price list* so that purchasers clearly understand who is responsible for freight charges and under what circumstances before purchases are made. The cost of shipping may be paid by the buyer or seller. If the freight is paid by the buyer, the bill of lading is marked **FOB shipping point**—meaning "free on board" at the shipping point—or **freight collect.** For example, CCC Industries located in Tulsa purchased parts from Rawhide in Chicago. Rawhide ships FOB Chicago, so CCC Industries must pay the freight from Chicago to Tulsa. The freight company then collects freight charges from CCC upon delivery of the goods.

If the freight is paid by the seller, the bill of lading may be marked **FOB destination**—meaning "free on board" at the destination point—or **freight paid.** If Rawhide paid the freight in the preceding example, the term *FOB Tulsa* could also have been used. Many manufacturers pay shipping charges for shipments above some minimum dollar value. Some shipments of very small items may be marked **prepay and add.** That is, the seller pays the shipping charge and adds it to the invoice, so the buyer pays the shipping charge to the seller rather than to the freight company. **Cash discounts do *not* apply to freight or shipping charges** nor to handling or bookkeeping charges.

EXAMPLE 9 Susan Duke Photography orders customized business forms. Calculate the cash discount and the net amount paid for the $800 order of business forms with sales terms of 3/10, 1/15, n/30 if the cost of shipping was $40 (which is included in the $800). The invoice was dated June 13, marked *freight prepay and add*, and paid June 24.

Net price of merchandise

Apply the cash discount rate *only* to the net amount of the merchandise.

= total invoice − shipping fee

= $800 − $40 = $760

The net price is $760.

Cash discount

= $760(0.01) = $7.60

The bill was paid after 10 days but within 15 days, so the 1% discount applies.

Net amount

= $800 − $7.60 = $792.40

Discount is taken from total bill.

The cash discount was $7.60 and the net amount paid was $792.40, which included the shipping fee.

TIP

Who Pays and When

The chart below summarizes the most common shipping terms.

Term	Who Pays	When	Who Doesn't Pay
FOB-shipping	Buyer	On receipt	Seller
Freight collect	Buyer	On receipt	Seller
FOB-destination	Seller	When shipped	Buyer
Freight paid	Seller	When shipped	Buyer
Prepay and add	Both	Seller pays when shipped; buyer pays with invoice payment	Seller gets reimbursed for shipping

STOP AND CHECK

See Example 9.

1. Windshield Rescue received a shipment of glass on May 3 marked *freight prepay and add*. The invoice dated April 25 showed the cost of the glass to be $2,896 and the freight to be $72. The invoice also showed sales terms of 2/10, n/30. Find the cash discount and the net amount if the invoice is paid within the discount period. Find the total amount to be paid within the discount period.

2. Stout's Carpet, Inc., in Oxford, Mississippi, received a shipment of carpet from Nortex Mills in Dalton, Georgia, delivered by M.S. Carriers truck line. The shipment was marked *FOB destination*. Who is responsible for paying shipping costs?

3. Dee's Discount Tires received a shipment from Cooper Tires in Novi, Michigan, that was marked *Freight collect* $215. The invoice Dee received was dated March 21 with terms 2/10, 1/15, n/30. Find the total amount paid for the tires if the invoice showed a balance of $7,925 before discounts and the invoice was paid 7 days after it was dated.

4. Memphis Hardwood Lumber in Memphis, Tennessee, shipped 10 teak boards $6'' \times 24'' \times \frac{1}{2}''$ that cost $26.50 per board and 25 mahogany boards $6'' \times 24'' \times \frac{1}{2}''$ that cost $7.95 per board. High Point Furniture received the shipment marked *Prepay and add*. The invoice showed $65 for freight and was dated July 15 with terms 3/10, n/30. The invoice was paid on July 23. How much was paid?

SKILL BUILDERS

Ken Bennett received an invoice dated March 9, with terms 2/10, n/30, amounting to $540. He paid the bill on March 12.

1. How much was the cash discount? *See Examples 1 and 2.*

2. What is the net amount Ken will pay? *See Example 3.*

Isabella Riddle gets an invoice for $450 with terms 4/10, 1/15, n/30. See Example 4.

3. How much would Isabella pay 7 days after the invoice date?

4. How much would Isabella pay 15 days after the invoice date?

5. How much would Isabella pay 25 days after the invoice date?

Alexa May, director of accounts, received a bill for $648, dated April 6, with sales terms 2/10, 1/15, n/30. A 3% penalty is charged for payment after 30 days. See Example 4.

6. Find the amount due if the bill is paid on or before April 16.

7. What amount is due if the bill is paid on or between April 17 and April 21?

8. What amount is due if Alexa pays on or between April 22 and May 6?

9. If Alexa pays on or after May 7, how much must she pay?

Chloe Duke is an accounts payable officer for her company and must calculate cash discounts before paying invoices. She is paying bills on June 18 and has an invoice dated June 12 with terms 3/10, n/30. See Examples 1 through 3.

10. If the net price of the invoice is $1,296.45, how much cash discount can Chloe take?

11. What is the net amount Chloe will need to pay?

See Examples 5 and 6.

12. Charlene Watson received a bill for $800 dated July 5, with sales terms of 2/10 EOM. She paid the bill on August 8. How much did Charlene pay?

13. An invoice for a camcorder that cost $1,250 is dated August 1, with sales terms of 2/10 EOM. If the bill is paid on September 8, how much is due?

14. Ruby Wossum received an invoice for $798.53 dated February 27 with sales terms of 3/10 EOM. How much should she pay if she pays the bill on April 15?

15. Zack Willis received an invoice for a leaf blower for $493 dated April 15 with sales terms of 3/10 EOM. How much should he pay if he pays the bill on May 4?

An invoice for $900 is dated October 15 and has sales terms of 2/10 ROG. The merchandise arrives October 21. See Example 7.

16. How much is due if the bill is paid October 27?

17. How much is due if the bill is paid on November 3?

18. Sharron Smith is paying an invoice showing a total of $5,835 and dated June 2. The invoice shows sales terms of 2/10 ROG. The merchandise delivery slip shows a receiving date of 6/5. How much is due if the bill for the merchandise is paid on June 12?

19. Kariem Salaam is directing the accounts payable office and is training a new accounts payable associate. They are processing an invoice for a credenza that is dated August 19 in the amount of $392.34. The delivery ticket for the credenza is dated August 23. If the sales terms indicated on the invoice are 3/10 ROG, how much needs to be paid if the bill is paid on September 5?

See Example 8.

20. Clordia Patterson-Nathanial handles all accounts payable for her company. She has a bill for $730 and plans to make a partial payment of $400 within the discount period. If the terms of the transaction were 3/10, n/30, find the amount credited to the account and find the outstanding balance.

21. David Wimberly has an invoice for a complete computer system for $3,982.48. The invoice shows terms of 3/10, 2/15, n/30. He can afford to pay $2,000 within 10 days of the date on the invoice and the remainder within the 30-day period. How much should be credited to the account for the $2,000 payment, and how much is still due?

22. Lacy Dodd has been directed to pay all invoices in time to receive any discounts offered by vendors. However, she has an invoice with terms of 2/10, n/30 for $2,983 and the fund for accounts payable has a balance of $2,196.83. So she elects to pay $2,000 on the invoice within the 10-day discount period and the remainder within the 30-day period. How much should be credited to the account for the $2,000 payment and how much remains to be paid?

See Example 9.

23. Dorothy Rogers' Bicycle Shop received a shipment of bicycles via truck from Better Bilt Bicycles. The bill of lading was marked FOB destination. Who paid the freight? To whom was the freight paid?

24. Joseph Denatti is negotiating the freight payment for a large shipment of office furniture and will take a discount on the invoice offered by the vendor as the freight terms are FOB shipping point. Who is to pay the freight?

25. Charlotte Oakley receives a shipment with the bill of lading marked "prepay and add." Who is responsible for freight charges? Who pays the freight company?

26. Explain the difference in the freight terms *FOB shipping point* and *prepay and add*.

Learning Outcomes

What to Remember with Examples

Section 8-1

1 Find the trade discount using a single trade discount rate; find the net price using the trade discount. (p. 264)

Find the trade discount using a single trade discount rate.

1. Identify the single discount rate and the list price.
2. Multiply the list price by the decimal equivalent of the single trade discount rate.

$$\text{Trade discount} = \text{single trade discount rate} \times \text{list price}$$
$$T = RL$$

> The list price of a laminating machine is $76 and the single trade discount rate is 25%. Find the trade discount.
>
> $$\begin{aligned} \text{Trade discount} &= 25\%(\$76) \\ &= 0.25(76) \\ &= \$19 \end{aligned}$$

Find the net price using the trade discount.

1. Identify the list price and the trade discount.
2. Subtract the trade discount from the list price.

$$\text{Net price} = \text{list price} - \text{trade discount}$$
$$N = L - T$$

> Find the net price when the list price is $76 and the trade discount is $19.
>
> $$\begin{aligned} \text{Net price} &= \$76 - \$19 \\ &= \$57 \end{aligned}$$

2 Find the net price using the complement of the single trade discount rate. (p. 266)

1. Find the net price rate: Subtract the single trade discount rate from 100%.
2. Multiply the decimal equivalent of the net price rate by the list price.

$$\text{Net price} = \text{net price rate} \times \text{list price}$$

or

$$\text{Net price} = (100\% - \text{single trade discount rate}) \times \text{list price}$$

> The list price is $480 and the single trade discount rate is 15%. Find the net price.
>
> $$\begin{aligned} \text{Net price} &= (100\% - 15\%)(\$480) \\ &= 0.85(\$480) \\ &= \$408 \end{aligned}$$

Section 8-2

1 Find the net price, applying a trade discount series and using the net decimal equivalent. (p. 268)

1. Find the net decimal equivalent: Multiply the complement of each trade discount rate, in decimal form, in the series.
2. Multiply the net decimal equivalent by the list price.

$$\text{Net price} = \text{net decimal equivalent} \times \text{list price}$$

> The list price is $960 and the discount series is 10/5/2. Find the net price.
>
> $$\text{Net decimal equivalent} = (0.9)(0.95)(0.98) = 0.8379$$
> $$\begin{aligned} \text{Net price} &= (0.8379)(\$960) \\ &= \$804.38 \end{aligned}$$

2 Find the trade discount, applying a trade discount series and using the single discount equivalent. (p. 270)

1. Find the single discount equivalent: Subtract the net decimal equivalent from 1.

$$\text{Single discount equivalent} = 1 - \text{net decimal equivalent}$$

2. Multiply the single discount equivalent by the list price.

$$\text{Trade discount} = \text{single discount equivalent} \times \text{list price}$$

The list price is $2,800 and the discount series is 25/15/10. Find the trade discount.

Net decimal equivalent = (0.75)(0.85)(0.9) = 0.57375
Single decimal equivalent = 1 − 0.57375 = 0.42625
Trade discount = (0.42625)($2,800)
= $1,193.50

Section 8-3

1 Find the cash discount and the net amount using ordinary dating terms. (p. 274)

Find the ending date of an interval of time:

1. Add the beginning date and the number of days in the interval.
2. If the sum exceeds the number of days in the month, subtract the number of days in the month from the sum.
3. The result of step 2 will be the ending date in the next month of the interval.

Interpret ordinary dating terms:

To find the last day to receive a discount, add to the invoice date the number of days specified in the terms. If this sum is greater than the number of days in the month the invoice is dated, subtract from the sum the number of days in the month the invoice is dated. The result is the last date the cash discount is allowed in the next month. Use the knuckle method to remember how many days are in each month or use the days-in-a-month rhyme.

By what date must an invoice dated July 10 be paid if it is due in 10 days?

July 10 + 10 days = July 20

By what date must an invoice dated May 15 be paid if it is due in 30 days?

May 15 + 30 = "May 45"

May is a "knuckle" month, so it has 31 days.

"May 45" − 31 days in May = June 14

The invoice must be paid on or before June 14.

1. Find the cash discount: Multiply the cash discount rate by the net price.

Cash discount = cash discount rate × net price

2. Find the net amount using the cash discount: Subtract the cash discount from the net price.

Net amount = net price − cash discount

3. Find the net amount using the complement of the cash discount rate: Multiply the complement of the cash discount rate by the net price.

Net amount = complement of cash discount rate × net price

An invoice is dated July 17 with terms 2/10, n/30 on a $2,500 net price. What is the latest date a cash discount is allowed? What is the net amount due on that date? On what date may interest begin accruing? What is the net amount due one day earlier?

The sale terms 2/10, n/30 mean the buyer takes a 2% cash discount if he or she pays within 10 days of the invoice date; interest may accrue after the 30th day.

Latest discount date = July 17 + 10 days = July 27

Net amount = (100% − 2%)($2,500)
= (0.98)($2,500)
= $2,450

Latest no-interest date = July 17 + 30 = "July 47"

"July 47" − 31 days in July = August 16

Interest begins accruing August 17. On August 16 the amount due is the net price of $2,500.

2 Interpret and apply end-of-month (EOM) terms. (p. 277)

Apply EOM terms:

To an invoice dated *before the 26th* day of the month:

1. A cash discount is allowed when the bill is paid by the specified day of the *next month*.
2. To find the net amount, multiply the invoice amount times the complement of the discount rate.

To an invoice dated *on or after the 26th day* of the month:

1. A cash discount is allowed when the bill is paid by the specified day of the *month after the next month*.
2. To find the net amount, multiply the invoice amount times the complement of the discount rate.

An invoice dated November 5 shows terms of 2/10 EOM on an $880 net price. By what date does the invoice have to be paid in order to get the cash discount? What is the net amount due on that date?

Sale terms 2/10 EOM for an invoice dated before the 26th day of a month mean that a 2% cash discount is allowed if the invoice is paid on or before the 10th day of the next month.

Latest discount day = December 10
Net amount = $(100\% - 2\%)(\$880)$
= $(0.98)(\$880)$
= $862.40

3 Interpret and apply receipt-of-goods (ROG) terms. (p. 278)

1. A cash discount is allowed when the bill is paid within the specified number of days from the *receipt of goods*, not from the date of the invoice.
2. To find the net amount, multiply the invoice amount times the complement of the discount rate.

What is the net amount due on April 8 for an invoice dated March 28 with terms of 1/10 ROG on a net price of $500? The shipment arrived April 1.

Sales terms 1/10 ROG mean that a 1% cash discount is allowed if the invoice is paid within 10 days of the receipt of goods.

April 8 is within 10 days of April 1, the date the shipment is received, so the cash discount is allowed.

Net amount = $(100\% - 1\%)(\$500)$
= $(0.99)(\$500)$
= $495

4 Find the amount credited and the outstanding balance from partial payments. (p. 279)

1. Find the amount credited to the account: Divide the partial payment by the complement of the cash discount rate.

$$\text{Amount credited} = \frac{\text{partial payment}}{\text{complement of cash discount rate}}$$

2. Find the outstanding balance: Subtract the amount credited from the net price.

$$\text{Outstanding balance} = \text{net price} - \text{amount credited}$$

Estrada's Restaurant purchased carpet for $1,568 with sales terms of 3/10, n/30 and paid $1,000 on the bill within the 10 days specified. How much was credited to Estrada's account and what balance remained?

Amount credited to account = $1,000 ÷ 0.97 = $1,030.93
Outstanding balance = $1,568 − $1,030.93 = $537.07

5 Interpret freight terms. (p. 280)

If the bill of lading is marked FOB (free on board) *shipping point,* or *freight collect,* the buyer is responsible for paying freight expenses directly to the freight company. If the bill of lading is marked *FOB destination* or *freight paid,* the shipper is responsible for paying freight expenses directly to the freight company. If the bill of lading is marked *prepay and add,* the buyer is responsible for paying the freight expenses to the seller, who has paid the freight company. Cash discounts do not apply to freight charges.

A shipment is sent from a manufacturer in Boston to a wholesaler in Dallas and is marked FOB destination. Who is responsible for the freight cost?

The manufacturer is responsible and pays the freight company.

EXERCISES SET A

SKILL BUILDERS

Find the trade discount. Round to the nearest cent.

Item	List price	Single discount rate	Trade discount
1. Water heater	$300	15%	_____
2. Mountain bike	$149.50	20%	_____
3. Sun Unicycle	$49.97	12%	_____

Find the net price. Round to the nearest cent.

Item	List price	Trade discount	Net price
4. Home gym	$279	$49	_____
5. Dagger Kayak	$399	$91.77	_____

Find the trade discount and net price. Round to the nearest cent.

Item	List price	Single discount rate	Trade discount	Net price
6. Spaulding golf club	$25	5%	_____	_____
7. Minolta camera	$199.95	2%	_____	_____
8. Jeep radio	$100	17%	_____	_____

Find the complement of the single trade discount rate and net price. Round the net price to the nearest cent.

Item	List price	Single discount rate	Net price rate	Net price
9. Casio camera watch	$329	4%	_____	_____
10. MP3 player	$399.98	6%	_____	_____
11. Teslar watch	$1,595	11%	_____	_____

Find the decimal equivalents of complements, net decimal equivalent, and net price. Round the net price to the nearest cent.

Item	List price	Trade discount series	Decimal equivalents of complements	Net decimal equivalent	Net price
12. Ralph sunglasses	$200	20/10	_____	_____	_____
13. HDTV monitor	$1,399.99	10/15/10	_____	_____	_____
14. Nintendo Wii	$99.99	15/5	_____	_____	_____

Round to the nearest hundredth of a percent when necessary.

Net decimal equivalent	Net decimal equivalent in percent form	Single discount equivalent in percent form
15. 0.765	_____	_____
16. 0.6835	_____	_____
17. 0.7434	_____	_____

Find the single discount equivalent in percent form for the discount series.

18. 20/10   **19.** 10%, 5%, 2%   **20.** 10/5

APPLICATIONS

21. Find the trade discount on a conference table listed at $1,025 less 10% (single discount rate).

22. Find the trade discount on a suit listed for $165 less 12%.

23. Find the trade discount on an order of 30 lamps listed at $35 each less 9%.

24. The list price on slacks is $22, and the list price on jumpers is $37. If Petit's Clothing Store orders 30 pairs of slacks and 40 jumpers at a discount rate of 11%, what is the trade discount on the purchase?

25. A trade discount series of 10/5 was given on ladies' scarves listed at $4. Find the net price of each scarf.

26. A trade discount series of 10/5/5 is offered on a printer, which is listed at $800. Also, a trade discount series of 5/10/5 is offered on a desk chair listed at $250. Find the total net price for the printer and the chair. Round to the nearest cent.

27. One manufacturer lists an aquarium for $58.95 with a trade discount of $5.90. Another manufacturer lists the same aquarium for $60 with a trade discount of $9.45. Which is the better deal?

28. Beverly Vance received a bill dated March 1 with sales terms of 3/10, n/30. What percent discount will she receive if she pays the bill on March 5?

29. Find the cash discount on an invoice for $270 dated April 17 with terms of 2/10, n/30 if the bill was paid April 22.

30. Christy Hunsucker received an invoice for $650 dated January 26. The sales terms in the invoice were 2/10 EOM. She paid the bill on March 4. How much did Christy pay?

31. An invoice for $5,298 has terms of 3/10 ROG and is dated March 15. The merchandise is received on March 20. How much should be paid if the invoice is paid on March 25?

32. An invoice for $1,200 is dated on June 3, and terms of 3/10, n/30 are offered. A payment of $800 is made on June 12, and the remainder is paid on July 12. Find the amount remitted on July 12 and the total amount paid.

EXERCISES SET B

SKILL BUILDERS

Find the trade discount or net price as indicated. Round to the nearest cent.

	List price	Single discount rate	Trade discount		List price	Trade discount	Net price
1.	$48	10%	_____	4.	$24.62	$5.93	_____
2.	$100	12%	_____	5.	$0.89	$0.12	_____
3.	$425	15%	_____				

Find the net price. Round to the nearest cent.

	List price	Single discount rate	Trade discount	Net price		List price	Single discount rate	Complement	Net price
6.	$1,263	12%	_____	_____	9.	$421	5%	_____	_____
7.	$27.50	3%	_____	_____	10.	$721.18	3%	_____	_____
8.	$8,952	18%	_____	_____	11.	$3,983.00	8%	_____	_____

Find the decimal equivalents of complements, net decimal equivalent, and net price. Round to the nearest cent.

	List price	Trade discount series	Decimal equivalents of complements	Net decimal equivalent	Net price
12.	$50	10/7/5	_____	_____	_____
13.	$35	20/15/5	_____	_____	_____
14.	$2,834	5/10/10	_____	_____	_____

Round to the nearest hundredth of a percent when necessary.

	Net decimal equivalent	Net decimal equivalent in percent form	Single discount equivalent in percent form
15.	0.82	_____	_____

Net decimal equivalent	Net decimal equivalent in percent form	Single discount equivalent in percent form
16. 0.6502	_____	_____
17. 0.758	_____	_____

Find the single discount equivalent.

18. 30/20/5

19. 10%, 10%, 5%

20. 20/15

APPLICATIONS

21. The list price for velvet at Harris Fabrics is $6.25 per yard less 6%. What is the trade discount?

22. Rocha Bros. offered a $12\frac{1}{2}\%$ trade discount on a tractor listed at $10,851. What was the trade discount?

23. The list price for a big-screen TV is $1,480 and the trade discount is $301. What is the net price?

24. A stationery shop bought 10 boxes of writing paper listed at $5 each and 200 greeting cards listed at $3.00 each. If the single discount rate for the purchase is 15%, find the trade discount.

25. Find the net price of an item listed at $800 with a trade discount series of 25/10/5.

26. Five desks are listed at $400 each, with a trade discount series of 20/10/10. Also, 10 bookcases are listed at $200 each, discounted 10/20/10. Find the total net price for the desks and bookcases.

27. One manufacturer lists a table at $200 less 12%. Another manufacturer lists the same table at $190 less 10%. Which is the better deal?

28. Chris Merillat received a bill dated September 3 with sales terms of 2/10, n/30. Did she receive a discount if she paid the bill on September 15?

29. Find the cash discount on an invoice for $50 dated May 3 with terms 1/15, n/30 if the bill was paid May 14.

30. How much would have to be paid on an invoice for $328 with terms of 2/10 ROG if the merchandise invoice is dated January 3, the merchandise arrives January 8, and the invoice is paid (a) January 11; (b) January 25?

31. Find the amount credited and the outstanding balance on an invoice dated August 19 if a partial payment of $500 is paid on August 25 and has terms of 3/10, 1/15, n/30. The amount of the invoice is $826.

PRACTICE TEST

1. The list price of a refrigerator is $550. The retailer can buy the refrigerator at the list price minus 20%. Find the trade discount.

2. The list price of a television is $560. The trade discount is $27.50. What is the net price?

3. A retailer can buy a lamp that is listed at $36.55 for 20% less than the list price. How much does the retailer have to pay for the lamp?

4. One distributor lists a chair for $250 less 20%. Another distributor lists the same chair at $240 less 10%. Which distributor offers the better deal?

5. Find the net price if a discount series of 20/10/5 is deducted from $70.

6. Find the single discount equivalent for the discount series 20/20/10.

7. Find the net decimal equivalent of the series 20/10/5.

8. What is the complement of 15%?

9. A retailer buys 20 boxes of stationery at $4 each and 400 greeting cards at $0.50 each. The discount rate for the order is 15%. Find the trade discount.

10. A retailer buys 30 electric frying pans listed at $40 each for 10% less than the list price. How much does the retailer have to pay for the frying pans?

11. Domingo Castro received an invoice for $200 dated March 6 with sales terms 1/10, n/30. He paid the bill on March 9. What was his cash discount?

12. Shareesh Raz received a bill dated September 1 with sales terms of 3/10, 1/15, n/30. What percent discount will she receive if she pays the bill on September 6?

13. An invoice for $400 dated December 7 has sales terms of 2/10 ROG. The merchandise arrived December 11. If the bill is paid on December 18, what is the amount due?

14. Gladys Quaweay received a bill for $300 dated April 7. The sales terms on the invoice were 2/10 EOM. If she paid the bill on May 2, how much did she pay?

15. If the bill in Exercise 13 is paid on January 2, what is the amount due?

16. Zing Manufacturing lists artificial flower arrangements at $30 less 10% and 10%. Another manufacturer lists the same flower arrangements at $31 less 10%, 10%, and 5%. Which is the better deal?

17. A trade discount series of 10% and 20% is offered on 20 dartboards that are listed at $14 each. Also, a trade discount series of 20% and 10% is offered on 10 bowling balls that are listed at $40 each. Find the total net price for the dartboards and bowling balls.

18. Campbell Sales purchased merchandise worth $745 and made a partial payment of $300 on day 13. If the sales terms were 2/15, n/30, how much was credited to the account? What was the outstanding balance?

EXCEL

19. The Gurney Corporation received an invoice for $5,893.21 for carbon-neutral printing supplies. The invoice had terms of 2/15, n/30. The firm decided to make a partial payment of $3,500 within the 15-day discount period. How much was credited to the Gurney Corp. account? Find the outstanding balance after the partial payment was made.

20. The monogrammed items purchased by Dean Specialty Company are shipped by rail from the manufacturer. The bill of lading is marked "FOB destination." Who is responsible for paying freight expenses?

1. Who generally pays the list price? Who generally pays the net price?

2. Use an example to illustrate that a trade discount series of 20/10 is not the same as a discount of 30%. Why are the discounts not the same?

3. The net price can be found by first finding the trade discount as discussed in Outcome 1 in Section 8.1, then subtracting to get the net price. When is it advantageous to use the complement of the discount rate for finding the net price directly?

4. To find the amount credited for a partial payment, we must find the complement of the discount rate and then divide the partial payment by this complement. Explain why we cannot multiply the payment by the discount rate and then add the product to the payment to find the amount to be credited to the account balance.

5. If the single discount rate is 20%, the complement is 80%. What does the complement represent?

6. Describe a procedure for mentally finding a 1% discount on an invoice. Illustrate with an example.

7. Describe the calculations used to project a due date of 60 days from a date of purchase, assuming the 60 days are within the same year.

8. Expand the mental process for using a 1% discount on an invoice to find a 2% discount. Illustrate with an example.

9. Develop a process for estimating a cash discount on an invoice. Illustrate with an example.

10. Why is it important to estimate the discount amount on an invoice?

Challenge Problems

1. Swift's Dairy Mart receives a shipment of refrigeration units totaling $2,386.50 including a shipping charge of $32. Swift's returns $350 worth of the units. Terms of the purchase are 2/10, n/30. If Swift's takes advantage of the discount, what is the net amount payable?

2. An important part of owning a business is the purchasing of equipment and supplies to run the office. Before paying an invoice, all items must be checked and amounts refigured before writing the check for payment. At this time the terms of the invoice can be applied.

   Using the information on the invoice in Figure 8-2, fill in the extended amount for each line, the merchandise total, the tax amount, and the total invoice amount. Locate the terms of the invoice and find what you would write on a check to pay Harper on each of the following dates: Discounts are applied before sales tax is calculated.

   March 5, 20XX
   March 12, 20XX
   March 25, 20XX

INVOICE DATE	TERMS	DATE OF ORDER	ORDERED BY		PHONE NO.	REMIT TO ▶	HARPER General Accounting Office	
02/27/XX	2/10, 1/15, n/30	02/27/XX			803-000-4488			

LINE NO.	MANUFACTURER PRODUCT NUMBER	QTY. ORD.	QTY. B.O.	QTY. SHP.	U/M	DESCRIPTION	UNIT PRICE		EXTENDED AMOUNT
001	REMYY370/02253	3	0	3	EA	TONER, F/ROYAL TA210 COP 1	11.90		
002	Sk 1230M402	5	2	3	PK	CORRECTABLE FILM RIBBON	10.95		
003	JRLM01023	10	0	10	PK	COVER-UP CORRECTION TAPE	9.90		
004	rTu123456	9	0	9	CS	PAPER, BOND, WHITE 8 1/2 x 11	58.23		

DATE REC'D._____	01460900001		5%		$0.00	TOTAL INVOICE AMOUNT ▶	
	OUR ORDER NO.	MDSE. TOTAL	TAX RATE	TAX AMOUNT	FREIGHT AMOUNT		

FIGURE 8-2
Harper Invoice

CASE STUDIES

8-1 Image Manufacturing's Rebate Offer

Misuse and abuse of trade discounts infringe on fair trade laws and can cost companies stiff fines and legal fees. One way to avoid misuse is to establish the same discount for everyone and give rebates based solely on volume. Image Manufacturing, Inc., uses this policy for equipment sales to companies that develop photographs. For example, one developing machine component, a special hinge, sells for about $3 to a company buying 15,000 pieces per month. In an effort to run more cost-efficient large jobs and capture market share, Image Manufacturing will give an incentive for higher volume. It offers a 5% rebate on orders of 20,000 pieces per month, or a 17–18 cents apiece rebate for orders of at least 22,000 pieces per month. The increased volume needed for a rebate is determined by market research that tells Image Manufacturing factors such as the volume a customer is capable of ordering per month and the volume and cost of the same part a customer currently buys from other suppliers. The rebate amount is determined by Image Manufacturing's profit margin and the company's ability to acquire sufficient raw materials to produce larger volumes without raising production costs. In some industries this is called a bill-back because the buyer receives credit toward the next order rather than a rebate check.

1. Suppose Photo Magic currently orders 15,000 hinges per month from Image Manufacturing at $3 each, which is about half of what they buy each month from other suppliers. If they move 5,000 pieces per month from another company to Image Manufacturing, what will be their rebate on the total order? What will be the discounted cost per piece?

2. If Photo Magic increases its order to 22,000 pieces per month and negotiates an 18 cents-per-piece trade discount, what will be the rebate? What is the percent of the discount?

3. In addition to the 18 cent-per-piece trade discount, Photo Magic also receives a $\frac{1}{2}$% cash discount (10 days, net 30). Calculate the rebate and cash discount on a 30,000-piece-per-month order, and then find the net price. Cash discount of $\frac{1}{2}$% is taken after the rebate is applied.

4. Another company currently orders about 6,000 hinges per month from Image Manufacturing at $3 each. Image Manufacturing's marketing manager believes this company is capable of expanding its business to 8,000 pieces per month and recommends a rebate of 17 cents per piece if they do so. Rounded to the nearest tenth, what is the rebate percentage? Do you think this trade discount violates fair trade laws? Why or why not?

8-2 McMillan Oil & Propane, LLC

Rob McMillan finished reading the article in the local paper, "Fuel Prices Expected to Increase into Summer." The article cited major factors in the crude oil spike such as Iran's nuclear program and overall Mideast instability. Rob, an independent fuel oil and propane distributor in rural Virginia, thought this wasn't good news. It had been a moderate winter, but wholesale fuel prices were higher than normal. Rob grabbed the last invoice from his supplier and saw that fuel oil was priced at $3.353 per gallon, with trade discounts of 7/5/2.5 available. It seemed like those discounts were not as good as in the past. McMillan Oil offers its own customers credit terms of 2/15, net/30, with a 1% service charge on late payments. Of the $25,000 in average fuel oil sales per month, normally half of Rob's sales are paid within the discount period, and only 5% incur the monthly service charge. Rob is concerned because a number of his fuel oil customers are behind in their payments, and he is considering some changes.

1. Using the starting price of $3.353 per gallon, what is Rob's net price after applying the 7/5/2.5 trade discount series using the net decimal equivalent?

2. Rob is considering purchasing his fuel oil from a new supplier offering fuel oil at $3.561 per gallon, but with a better trade discount series of 10/7/4. Compared to your answers in Exercise 1, which supplier would be a better deal for his company?

3. Using the average monthly sales of $25,000, what is the total savings enjoyed by those fuel oil customers who normally pay within the discount period? What is the total penalty paid by those that are delinquent over 30 days?

4. Currently, only 25% of the sales volume is paid by customers who are taking advantage of the discount, and 20% of the sales are over 30 days. Using these figures, how does that change your results from Exercise 3 above? Because your answers show that Rob is presently making more money (at least he should), why should he be concerned about the current situation? What suggestions do you have?

8-3 The Artist's Palette

The Artist's Palette sells high-end art supplies to the art students at three regional art and design schools in Philadelphia, Washington, D.C., and Baltimore. It carries paints, brushes, drawing pads, frames, charcoal, pastels, and other supplies used in a variety of artistic media. Because its clientele is very discriminating, The Artist's Palette tends to carry only the top lines in its inventory and it is known for having the best selection on hand. It is rare that an item is out of stock. Artists can visit the store, purchase from The Artist's Palette catalog, or buy from the secure web site.

1. The Artist's Palette purchases its inventory from a number of suppliers and each supplier offers different purchasing discounts. The manager of The Artist's Palette, Marty Parma, is currently comparing two offers for purchasing modeling clay and supplies. The first company offers a chain discount of 20/10/5, and the second company offers a chain discount of 18/12/7 as long as the total purchases are $300 or more. Assuming Parma purchases $300

worth of supplies, what is the net price from supplier 1? From supplier 2? From which supplier would you recommend Parma purchase her modeling clay and supplies?

2. What is the net decimal equivalent for supplier 1? For supplier 2?

3. What is the trade discount from supplier 1? From supplier 2?

4. The Artist's Palette recognizes that students may purchase supplies at the beginning of the term to cover all of their art class needs. Because this could represent a fairly substantial outlay, The Artist's Palette offers discounts to those students who pay sooner than required. Assume that if students buy more than $250 of art supplies in one visit, they may put it on a student account with terms of 2/10, n/30. If a student purchases $250 of supplies on September 16, what amount is due by September 26? How much would the student save by paying early?

5. Assume that if students buy more than $250 of art supplies in one visit, they may put the charge on a student account with terms of 2/10 EOM. If a student makes the purchase on September 16, on what day does the 2% discount expire? If the purchase is made on September 26, on what day does the 2% discount expire? If you were an art student, which method would you prefer: 2/10, n/30, or 2/10 EOM?

Markup and Markdown

Hip Hop Clothing

Kendra and Mikala are excited about opening their own hip hop clothing store, 'Nue Rhythm. 'Nue is short for Avenue, and they want their clothing to capture the "rhythm of the street." They know that the urban clothing market is one of the most exciting and fastest growing markets for today's consumers. Urban wear has increased in popularity as the number of new, musical hip hop artists has increased. This style of baggy pants, baseball caps worn backwards (NBA, NFL, or successful university teams), oversized rugby or polo shirts, and expensive tennis shoes, although still very popular, is being replaced in some areas with a trend toward tighter hipster-inspired items such as polo shirts, sports coats, large ornamental belt buckles, and tighter jeans. But what really concerns Kendra and Mikala is pricing their new hip hop clothing lines. While typical markups on clothing and accessories can be 30–85%, they know from research that the markup for hip hop clothing is often 100–200% or more.

Pricing a new clothing line can be especially difficult for new business owners, and depends on a number of factors. Among the considerations for Kendra and Mikala were mate-rial costs, typically provided by suppliers; a study of labor rates in the area; industry manufacturers' prices; and perhaps most important, research on competitors' prices. Armed with this information, Kendra and Mikala had a well-educated "guess" on which to base their pricing.

For now, 'Nue Rhythm is strictly a retail operation; however, the owners have hopes of introducing their own retail line, "Hip Hop Tops," in the future. Kendra and Mikala feel they are on the right track and decide to take a seasonal approach to pricing. For the peak shopping months during the summer and leading up to Christmas, they will institute markups of 150% across the board on all lines. In order to draw customers into the store, a specific designer or line will be marked down as much as 50% off the normal price and will still be profitable for them. During the rest of the year, 10–50% markdowns will be taken to generate interest among shoppers or to move obsolete inventory. With this approach their focus will be creating competitive prices for truly unique hip hop clothing pieces that hopefully, their customers will not be able to resist.

LEARNING OUTCOMES

9-1 Markup Based on Cost

1. Find the cost, markup, or selling price when any two of the three are known.
2. Find the cost, markup, selling price, or percent of markup when the percent of markup is based on the cost.

9-2 Markup Based on Selling Price and Markup Comparisons

1. Find the cost, markup, selling price, or percent of markup when the percent of markup is based on the selling price.
2. Compare the markup based on the cost with the markup based on the selling price.

9-3 Markdown, Series of Markdowns, and Perishables

1. Find the amount of markdown, the reduced (new) price, and the percent of markdown.
2. Find the final selling price for a series of markups and markdowns.
3. Find the selling price for a desired profit on perishable and seasonal goods.

Cost: price at which a business purchases merchandise.

Selling price (retail price): price at which a business sells merchandise.

Markup (gross margin): difference between the selling price and the cost.

Net profit: difference between gross margin and operating expenses and overhead.

Markdown: amount the original selling price is reduced.

Chapter 8 introduced the mathematics associated with buying for a small business. This chapter will focus on the mathematics of selling. Any successful business must keep prices low enough to attract customers, yet high enough to pay expenses and make a profit.

The price at which a retail business purchases merchandise is called the **cost.** The merchandise is then sold at a higher price called the **selling price** or the **retail price.** The difference between the selling price and the cost is the **markup.** The markup is also called the **gross margin.** The gross margin includes operating expenses and the overhead. The difference between the gross margin and the expenses and overhead is the **net profit.** In Chapter 20 we will look at these concepts. For now, we will only consider the gross margin or markup.

Merchandise may also be reduced from the original selling price. The amount the original selling price is reduced is the **markdown.**

9-1 MARKUP BASED ON COST

LEARNING OUTCOMES

1 Find the cost, markup, or selling price when any two of the three are known.
2 Find the cost, markup, selling price, or percent of markup when the percent of markup is based on the cost.

In business situations it is common to need to find missing information. The cost, markup, and selling price are related so that when any two amounts are known, the third amount can be found.

1 Find the cost, markup, or selling price when any two of the three are known.

Visualize the relationships among the cost, markup, and the selling price. The basic relationship can be written as the formula

$$\text{Selling price} = \text{cost} + \text{markup}$$
$$S = C + M$$

Relate this to the concept that two parts add together to get a sum or total. Then we can develop variations of the formula using the concept that the sum or total minus one part gives the other part.

$$\text{Cost} = \text{selling price} - \text{markup}$$
$$C = S - M$$

$$\text{Markup} = \text{selling price} - \text{cost}$$
$$M = S - C$$

HOW TO Find the cost, markup, or selling price when any two of the three are known

1. Identify the two known amounts.
2. Identify the missing amount.
3. Select the appropriate formula.
4. Substitute the known amounts into the formula.
5. Evaluate the formula.

EXAMPLE 1  What is the selling price of a media charging station if the cost is $28.35 and the markup is $5.64?

What You Know	What You Are Looking For	Solution Plan
Cost = $28.35 Markup = $5.64	Selling price	Selling price = cost + markup

1. Charlie Cook bought a light fixture that cost $32 and marked it up $40. Find the selling price. *See Example 1.*

2. Margaret Davis sells a key fob for $12.95 and it costs $7. Find the markup. *See Example 2.*

3. Sylvia Knight bought a printer cartridge and marked it up $18 and set the selling price at $34.95. Find the cost. *See Example 3.*

4. Berlin Jones introduced a new veggie sandwich at Subway, the sandwich shop. He determines that each sandwich costs $3 and plans to sell each sandwich for $5.25, which is 175% of the cost. Find the markup. *See Example 2.*

2 Find the cost, markup, selling price, or percent of markup when the percent of markup is based on the cost.

When the markup is based on cost, the cost is the base in the basic percentage formula shown in Figure 9-1.

$$P = RB$$

We can apply the percentage formula to markup to get the formula

Markup = rate of markup × cost   or $M = M\%(C)$

Then, we can find variations of the formula by solving the equation for each variable.

Solve for $M\%$.

$M = M\%(C)$	Divide both sides by C.
$\dfrac{M}{C} = \dfrac{M\%(C)}{C}$	Reduce.
$\dfrac{M}{C} = M\%$	Write the isolated variable on the left.

$$M\% = \frac{M}{C}$$

Solve for C.

$M = M\%(C)$	Divide both sides by $M\%$.
$\dfrac{M}{M\%} = \dfrac{M\%(C)}{M\%}$	Reduce.
$\dfrac{M}{M\%} = C$	Write the isolated variable on the left.

$$C = \frac{M}{M\%}$$

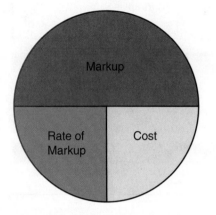

FIGURE 9-1
Markup Based on Cost

HOW TO   Find the rate of markup based on the cost, the cost, or the markup when any two of the three are known

1. Identify the known and unknown amounts.
2. Select the formula variation that has the unknown on the left of the equation.

$M = M\%(C)$	Use the decimal equivalent of $M\%$.
$M\% = \dfrac{M}{C}(100\%)$	Change to a percent by multiplying by 100%.
$C = \dfrac{M}{M\%}$	Use the decimal equivalent of $M\%$.

3. Substitute the known amounts into the formula.
4. Solve for the missing amount.

EXAMPLE 4   Duke's Photography pays $9 for a 5 in.-by-7 in. photograph. If the photograph is sold for $15, what is the percent of markup based on cost? Round to the nearest tenth of a percent.

What You Know	What You Are Looking For	Solution Plan
Cost = $9 Cost% = 100% Selling price = $15	Rate of markup	Markup = selling price − cost $M\% = \dfrac{M}{C}(100\%)$

Solution

Find the amount of markup:

$M = S - C$	Substitute known values into the formula.
$M = \$15 - \$9$	Subtract.
$M = \$6$	Amount of markup

Find the rate of markup:

$M\% = \dfrac{M}{C}(100\%)$	Substitute known values into the formula.
$M\% = \dfrac{\$6}{\$9}(100\%)$	Divide.
$M\% = 0.667(100\%)$	Rounded to thousandths. Change to percent equivalent.
$M\% = 66.7\%$	Rate or percent of markup

Conclusion

The percent of markup based on cost of the photograph is 66.7%.

EXAMPLE 5 A boutique pays $68 a pair for handmade earrings and sells them at an 80% markup rate based on cost. Find the selling price of the earrings.

What You Know	What You Are Looking For	Solution Plan
Cost = $68 Markup % = 80%	Amount of markup Selling price	$M = M\%(C)$ $S = C + M$

Solution

Find the amount of markup.

$M = M\%(C)$	Substitute known amounts.
$M = 80\%(\$68)$	Change the percent to its decimal equivalent.
$M = 0.8(\$68)$	Multiply.
$M = \$54.40$	

Find the selling price.

$S = C + M$	Substitute known amounts.
$S = \$68 + \$54.40$	Add.
$S = \$122.40$	

Conclusion

The selling price of the earrings is $122.40.

EXAMPLE 6 A DVD movie was marked up $6.50, which was a 40% markup based on cost. What was the cost of the DVD? What was the selling price?

What You Know	What You Are Looking For	Solution Plan
Markup = $6.50 $M\% = 40\%$	Cost	$C = \dfrac{M}{M\%}$

Find the cost:

$$C = \frac{M}{M\%}$$ Substitute known amounts.

$$C = \frac{\$6.50}{40\%}$$ Change percent to its decimal equivalent.

$$C = \frac{\$6.50}{0.4}$$ Divide.

$$C = \$16.25$$

Find the selling price:

$$S = C + M$$
$$S = \$16.25 + \$6.50$$
$$S = \$22.75$$

The cost of the DVD movie was \$16.25 and the selling price was \$22.75.

If the markup is based on cost, the cost percent is 100% and the selling price percent is 100% + the markup percent.

HOW TO   Find the cost when the selling price and the percent of markup based on the cost are known

1. Find the rate of selling price.

Rate of selling price = rate of cost + rate of markup based on cost
$$S\% = 100\% + M\%$$

2. Find the cost using the formula

$$\text{Cost} = \frac{\text{selling price}}{\text{rate of selling price based on cost}} \qquad C = \frac{S}{S\%}$$

3. Change the rate of selling price to a numerical equivalent and divide.

EXAMPLE 7   A camera sells for \$439. The markup rate is 60% of the cost. Find the cost of the camera and the markup. Round to the nearest cent.

What You Know	What You Are Looking For	Solution Plan
Selling price = \$439 $M\% = 60\%$ $C\% = 100\%$	Cost Markup	$S\% = 100\% + M\%$ $C = \dfrac{S}{S\%}$ $M = S - C$

Find the selling price rate:

$$S\% = 100\% + M\%$$ Substitute known amounts.
$$S\% = 100\% + 60\%$$ Add.
$$S\% = 160\%$$

Find the cost:

$$C = \frac{S}{S\%}$$ Substitute known amounts.

$$C = \frac{\$439}{160\%}$$ Change the percent to its decimal equivalent.

$$C = \frac{\$439}{1.6}$$ Divide.

$$C = \$274.38$$ Rounded to the nearest cent

Find the markup:

$M = S - C$ Substitute known amounts.
$M = \$439 - \$274.38$ Subtract.
$M = \$164.62$

Conclusion

The cost of the camera is $274.38 and the markup is $164.62.

STOP AND CHECK

Round to the nearest tenth of a percent or to the nearest cent as appropriate. See Example 4.

1. Find the percent of markup based on cost for a table that costs $220 and sells for $599. Round to the nearest tenth of a percent.

2. A file cabinet costs $145 and sells for $197.20. Find the percent of markup based on cost.

3. A bicycle costs $245 and sells for $395. Find the percent of markup based on cost. Round to the nearest tenth percent.

4. A motorcycle costs $690 and sells for $1,420. Find the percent of markup based on cost. Round to the nearest tenth percent.

5. A patio lounger costs $89 and is sold for $249. What is the percent of markup based on cost? Round to the nearest tenth percent.

6. Lowe's can purchase a KitchenAid Energy Star dishwasher for $738. Find the percent of markup based on cost if the dishwasher sells for $1,048.00. Round to the nearest tenth percent.

See Example 5.

7. Ed's Camera Shop pays $218 for a camera and sells it at a 78% markup based on cost. What is the selling price of the camera?

8. Holly's Leather Shop pays $87.50 for a Coach bag and sells it at a 95% markup based on cost. What is the selling price of the bag rounded to the nearest cent?

9. Wimberly Computers buys computers for $465 and sells them at an 80% markup based on cost. What will the computers sell for?

10. The National Parks Conservation Association purchases calendars for $0.86 and sells them at a 365% markup based on cost. What will the calendars sell for rounded to the nearest cent?

11. A 4-oz bottle of Vanilla Bean Panache lotion is purchased for $0.45 and sells at a 110% markup based on cost. What is the selling price of the lotion?

12. J. C. Penney buys Casio watches for $58.82 and sells them at a 70% markup based on cost. Find the selling price of the watches.

See Example 6.

13. A pair of New Balance running shoes is marked up $38, which is a 62% markup based on cost. Find the cost of the shoes.

14. Bradley's Sound Shop marks up a music system $650 and sells it at a 92% markup based on cost. What is the cost of the system? Round to the nearest cent.

15. Wiggins Clock Shop marked up an order of marble clocks $358 each and sells them at a 65% markup based on cost. What is the cost of each clock? Round to the nearest cent.

16. EnviroTote can purchase laundry bags in large quantities and mark them up $4.14 each. What is the cost of each bag if it is marked up 125% of cost? Round to the nearest cent.

17. EnviroTote can purchase a 10-oz Organic Barrel Bag with 25″ handles and mark it up $7.82. What is the cost of each bag if it is marked up 80% of cost? Round to the nearest cent.

18. Kroger marks up Armour chili $0.24 and sells it at a 32% markup based on cost. What is the cost of each can of chili?

See Example 7.

19. A paper cutter sells for $39. The markup rate is 60% of the cost. Find the cost of the paper cutter and find the markup.

20. A leather jacket sells for $149. The markup rate is 110% of the cost. Find the cost of the jacket and find the markup.

21. Find the cost and markup of a box of cereal that sells for $4.65 and has a markup rate of 85% based on the cost.

22. A model train engine sells for $595 and has a markup rate of 165% based on the cost. What is the cost and markup of the engine?

23. Charlie at the 7th Inning sells Topps baseball cards for $65 a box and has a markup rate of 45% based on cost. Find the cost and markup of each box of cards.

24. AutoZone sells Anco windshield wiper blades for $9.99 and has a markup rate of 62% based on cost. What is the cost and markup for the wiper blades?

SKILL BUILDERS

Round amounts to the nearest cent and percents to the nearest whole percent.

1. Cost = $30; markup = $20. Find the selling price.
   See Example 1.

2. Selling price = $75; cost = $50. Find the markup.
   See Example 2.

3. Selling price = $36.99; markup = $12.99. Find the cost.
   See Example 3.

4. Cost = $40; rate of markup based on cost = 35%.
   See Example 5.
   a. Find the markup.

   b. Find the selling price.

5. Markup = $70; rate of markup based on cost = 83%.
   See Example 6.
   a. Find the cost.

   b. Find the selling price.

6. Selling price = $148.27; rate of markup based on cost = 40%. *See Example 7.*
   a. Find the cost.

   b. Find the markup.

7. Cost = $60; selling price = $150. *See Example 4.*
   a. Find the markup.

   b. Find the rate of markup based on cost.

8. Cost = $82; markup = $46. *See Example 4.*
   a. Find the rate of markup based on cost.

   b. Find the selling price.

APPLICATIONS

9. Mugs cost $2 each and sell for $6 each. Find the markup.

10. Belts cost $4 and sell with a markup of $2.40. Find the selling price of the belts.

11. A compact disc player sells for $300. The cost is $86. Find the markup of the CD player.

12. Twenty decorative enamel balls cost $12.75 each and are marked up $9.56.
    a. Find the selling price for each one.

    b. Find the total amount of margin or markup for the 20 balls.

13. A DVD costs $4 and sells for $12. Find the amount of markup.

14. Find the cost if a hard hat is marked up $5 and has a selling price of $12.50.

15. Find the cost of a magazine that sells for $3.50 and is marked up $1.75.

16. Find the selling price if a case of photocopier paper costs $8 and is marked up $14.

17. A sofa costs $398 and sells for $716.40, which is 180% of the cost.
   a. Find the rate of markup.

   b. Find the markup.

18. An audio system sells for $2,980, which is 160% of the cost. The cost is $1,862.50.
   a. What is the rate of markup?

   b. What is the markup?

19. A lamp costs $32 and is marked up based on cost. If the lamp sold for $72, what was the percent of markup?

20. A TV that costs $1,899 sells for a 63% markup based on the cost. What is the selling price of the TV?

21. A computer desk costs $196 and sells for $395. What is the percent of markup based on cost? Round to the nearest tenth percent.

22. Battery-powered massagers cost $8.50 if they are purchased in lots of 36 or more. The Gift Horse Shoppe purchased 48 and sells them at a 45% markup based on cost. Find the selling price of each massager.

23. What is the cost of a sink that is marked up $188 if the markup rate is 70% based on cost?

24. A wristwatch sells for $289. The markup rate is 250% of cost.
   a. Find the cost of the watch.

   b. Find the markup.

25. A wallet is marked up $12, which is an 80% markup based on cost. What is the cost of the wallet?

26. Tombo Mono Correction Tape sells for $3.29. The markup rate is 65% of the cost.
   a. What is the cost?

   b. What is the markup of the tape?

27. A Vizio® Razor 23″ LED HDTV sells for $349 and has a 48% markup based on cost. Find the cost and markup.

Find the cost.

28. A DreamGear Wii® Lady Fitness Workout Kit sells for $70.19 on a popular web site. The kit has a 62% markup based on cost. Find the cost and markup.

Find the cost.

Find the markup.

Find the markup.

9-2 MARKUP BASED ON SELLING PRICE AND MARKUP COMPARISONS

LEARNING OUTCOMES

1 Find the cost, markup, selling price, or percent of markup when the percent of markup is based on the selling price.
2 Compare the markup based on the cost with the markup based on the selling price.

The markup can be calculated as a portion of either the cost or the selling price of an item. Most manufacturers and distributors calculate markup as a portion of *cost,* because they typically keep their records in terms of cost. Some wholesalers and a few retailers also use this method. Many retailers, however, use the *selling price* or *retail price* as a base in computing markup because they keep most of their records in terms of selling price.

1 Find the cost, markup, selling price, or percent of markup when the percent of markup is based on the selling price.

When the markup is based on selling price, the rate of the selling price is known and is 100%. The amount of the selling price is the base in the basic percentage formulas $P = RB$.

We can apply the percentage formula to markup to get the formula shown in Figure 9-2.

$$\text{Markup} = \text{rate of markup} \times \text{selling price} \quad \text{or} \quad M = M\%(S)$$

Then, we can find variations of the formula by solving the equation for each variable.

Solve for $M\%$.

$M = M\%(S)$	Divide both sides by S.
$\dfrac{M}{S} = \dfrac{M\%(S)}{S}$	Simplify.
$\dfrac{M}{S} = M\%$	Write the isolated variable on the left.
$M\% = \dfrac{M}{S}$	$M\%$ is expressed as a decimal.

FIGURE 9-2
Markup Based on Selling Price

Solve for S.

$$M = M\%(S)$$ Divide both sides by M% in decimal form.

$$\frac{M}{M\%} = \frac{M\%(S)}{M\%}$$ Simplify.

$$\frac{M}{M\%} = S$$ Write the isolated variable on the left.

$$S = \frac{M}{M\%}$$

HOW TO

Find the rate of markup based on the selling price, the selling price, or the markup when any two of the three are known.

1. Identify the known and unknown amounts.
2. Select the formula variation that has the unknown on the left side of the equation.

$$M = M\%(S)$$ Use the decimal equivalent of M%.

$$M\% = \frac{M}{S}(100\%)$$ Change to a percent by multiplying by 100%.

$$S = \frac{M}{M\%}$$ Use the decimal equivalent of M%.

3. Substitute the known amounts into the formula.
4. Solve for the missing amount.

EXAMPLE 1

A calculator costs $4 and sells for $10. Find the rate of markup based on the selling price.

What You Know	What You Are Looking For	Solution Plan
Cost = $4	Amount of markup	Markup = selling price − cost
Selling price = $10	Rate of markup based on the selling price	$M\% = \dfrac{M}{S}(100\%)$

Solution

Find the markup:

$M = S - C$ Substitute known values into the formula.

$M = \$10 - \$4$ Subtract.

$M = \$6$ Amount of markup

Find the rate of markup:

$M\% = \dfrac{M}{S}(100\%)$ Substitute known values into the formula.

$M\% = \dfrac{\$6}{\$10}(100\%)$ Divide.

$M\% = 0.6(100\%)$ Change to percent equivalent.

$M\% = 60\%$ Rate or percent of markup

Conclusion

The rate of markup for the calculator is 60%.

EXAMPLE 2

Find the cost and selling price if a handbag is marked up $5 with a 20% markup rate based on the selling price.

What You Know	What You Are Looking For	Solution Plan
Markup = $5	Selling price	$S = \dfrac{M}{M\%}$
M% based on selling price = 20%	Cost	$C = S - M$

Find the selling price:

$$S = \frac{M}{M\%}$$ Substitute known amounts.

$$S = \frac{\$5}{20\%}$$ Change percent to its decimal equivalent.

$$S = \frac{\$5}{0.2}$$ Divide.

$$S = \$25$$ Selling price

Find the cost:

$$C = S - M$$ Substitute known amounts.

$$C = \$25 - \$5$$ Subtract.

$$C = \$20$$ Cost

Conclusion

The selling price of the handbag is $25 and the cost is $20.

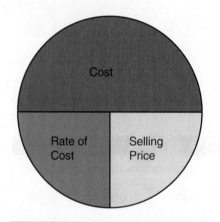

FIGURE 9-3
Cost When Markup is Based on Selling Price

In the percentage formula the portion and the rate must correspond to the base. When we use the markup formulas, if we know the cost, then the rate should be the rate of the cost. If we know the markup, then the rate should be the rate of the markup. If we know the selling price, the rate should be the rate of the selling price. The rates are related just like the amounts or portions are related.

$$S = C + M$$

$$S\% = C\% + M\%$$

When the markup is based on the cost, we have $S\% = 100\% + M\%$.

When the markup is based on the selling price, we have $100\% = C\% + M\%$ or $C\% = 100\% - M\%$.

A variation of the formula $C = C\%(S)$ can be used to relate the cost and selling price when the markup is based on the selling price to get the relationship $S = \frac{C}{C\%}$, where $C\% = 100\% - M\%$.

The percentage formula can be used to get the formula shown in Figure 9-3.

$$\text{Cost} = \text{Rate of Cost} \times \text{Selling Price or } C = C\%(S)$$

Then, we can find the selling price formula by solving the equation for S.

Solve for S.

$$C = C\%(S)$$ Divide both sides by $C\%$.

$$\frac{M}{C\%} = \frac{C\%(S)}{C\%}$$ Simplify.

$$\frac{M}{C\%} = S$$ Write the isolated variable on the left.

$$S = \frac{M}{C\%}$$

EXAMPLE 3 Find the selling price and markup for a pair of jeans that costs the retailer $28 and is marked up 30% of the selling price.

What You Know	What You Are Looking For	Solution Plan
Cost = $28	Rate of cost	$C\% = 100\% - M\%$
M% based on selling price = 30%	Selling price	$S = \frac{C}{C\%}$
	Markup	$M = S - C$

Find the rate of cost:

$C\% = 100\% - M\%$	Substitute known amounts.
$C\% = 100\% - 30\%$	Subtract.
$C\% = 70\%$	Rate of cost

Find the selling price:

$S = \dfrac{C}{C\%}$	Substitute known amounts.
$S = \dfrac{\$28}{70\%}$	Change percent to its decimal equivalent.
$S = \dfrac{\$28}{0.7}$	Divide.
$S = \$40$	Selling price

Find the markup:

$M = S - C$	Substitute known amounts.
$M = \$40 - \$28$	Subtract.
$M = \$12$	Markup

Conclusion

The selling price is \$40 and the markup is \$12.

EXAMPLE 4 Find the markup and cost of a box of pencils that sells for \$2.99 and is marked up 25% of the selling price.

What You Know	What You Are Looking For	Solution Plan
Selling price = \$2.99 $S\% = 100\%$ $M\% = 25\%$	Markup Cost	$M = M\%(S)$ $C = S - M$

Solution

Find the markup:

$M = M\%(S)$	Substitute known amounts.
$M = 25\%(\$2.99)$	Change the percent to its decimal equivalent.
$M = 0.25(\$2.99)$	Multiply.
$M = \$0.75$	Markup rounded to the nearest cent

Find the cost:

$C = S - M$	Substitute known amounts.
$C = \$2.99 - \$0.75$	Subtract.
$C = \$2.24$	Cost

Conclusion

The cost of the box of pencils is \$2.24 and the markup is \$0.75.

To summarize the concepts we have presented in this chapter to this point, all markup problems are solved in basically the same way. One key point is that one rate is known when you know if the markup is based on the *cost* or the *selling price*. When the markup is based on *cost,* the rate of the *cost* is 100%. When the markup is based on *selling price,* the rate of the *selling price* is 100%.

In markup problems there are three amounts and three percents (rates). If three of the six parts are known and at least one known part is an amount and another is whether the markup as based on the cost or the selling price, the other three parts can be determined.

To organize the known and unknown parts, we can use a chart. This chart can guide you in selecting the appropriate formula.

HOW TO

Find all the missing parts if three parts are known and at least one part is an amount and it is known whether the markup is based on the cost or the selling price

1. Place the three known parts into the chart.

	$	%
C		
M		
S		

If the $ column has two entries:

2. Add or subtract as appropriate to find the third amount.

3. Find a second percent by using the formula $R = \dfrac{P}{B}$.

4. Find the third percent by adding or subtracting as appropriate.

If the % column has two entries:

Add or subtract as appropriate to find the third percent.

Find an additional amount by using the formula $P = RB$ or $B = \dfrac{P}{R}$.

Find the third amount by adding or subtracting as appropriate.

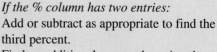

EXAMPLE 5 Wal-Mart plans to mark up a package of 8 AA batteries $3.50 over cost. This will be a 50% markup based on cost. Find the cost and selling price of the batteries and the rate of the selling price.

What You Know	What You Are Looking For	Solution Plan
$C\% = 100\%$ $M\% = 50\%$ $M = \$3.50$	$S\%$, C, and S	$S\% = C\% + M\%$ $B = \dfrac{P}{R}$ or $C = \dfrac{M}{M\%}$ $S = C + M$

	$	%
C		100
M	3.50	50
S		

Solution

Find the rate of the selling price: Two percents are known.

$S\% = C\% + M\%$ Substitute known percents.

$S\% = 100\% + 50\%$ Add.

$S\% = 150\%$ Rate of selling price

Find the cost:

$C = \dfrac{M}{M\%}$ Substitute known amounts.

$C = \dfrac{\$3.50}{50\%}$ Change percent to its decimal equivalent.

$C = \dfrac{\$3.50}{0.5}$ Divide.

$C = \$7.00$ Cost

Find the selling price:

$S = C + M$ Substitute known amounts.

$S = \$7.00 + \$3.50$ Add.

$S = \$10.50$ Selling price

	$	%
C	7.00	100
M	3.50	50
S	10.50	150

Conclusion

The rate of the selling price is 150%, the cost is $7.00, and the selling price is $10.50.

When so many formulas can be used in a process, it is important to have a sense of the reasonableness of an answer.

Markup based on cost:
$C\% = 100\%$
$S\% = $ more than 100%
$M\% = S\% - 100\%$

Markup based on selling price:
$S\% = 100\%$
$C\% = $ less than 100%
$M\% = 100\% - C\%$

STOP AND CHECK

Round to the nearest tenth percent. See Example 1.

1. A textbook costs $58 and sells for $70. Find the rate of markup based on the selling price.

2. The manufacturer's suggested retail price for a refrigerator is $1,499 and it costs $385. What is the rate of markup based on the suggested retail price?

3. Hale's Trailers purchases 16-ft trailers for $395 and sells them for $795. What is the rate of markup based on the selling price?

4. Martha's Birding Society purchases hummingbird feeders for $2.40 and sells them for $6.00. Find the rate of markup based on the selling price.

5. AutoZone purchases tire cleaner for $0.84 and sells it for $2.39. What is the rate of markup based on the selling price?

6. Federated Department Stores purchased men's shoes for $132 and sells them for $229. What is the rate of markup based on selling price?

Round to the nearest cent. See Example 2.

7. Find the cost and selling price if a handbag is marked up $195 with a 60% markup rate based on selling price.

8. Find the cost and selling price of a baseball that is marked up $21 with an 80% markup based on the selling price.

9. The 7th Inning marks a soccer trophy up $14, a 75% markup based on the selling price. What is the cost and selling price of the trophy?

10. Wolf Camera marks a camera up 25% of the selling price. If the markup is $145, what is the cost and selling price of the camera?

11. Shekenna's Dress Shop marks up a business suit $38. This represents a 70% markup based on the selling price. What is the cost and selling price of the suit?

12. May Department Store marks one stock keeping unit (SKU) of its Coach handbags up $70.08 or 32% of the selling price. Find the cost and selling price of the handbags.

See Example 3.

13. Dollar General Stores buys detergent from the manufacturer for $2.99 and marks it up 25% of the selling price. Find the selling price and markup for the detergent.

14. Best Buy buys a digital camera for $187 and marks it up 38% of the selling price. Find the selling price and markup for the camera.

15. Lucinda Gallegos buys scissors for $3.84 and sells them with a 27% markup based on selling price. What is the selling price and markup for the scissors?

16. A Singer sewing machine costs $127.59 and the Fabric Center marks it up 23% of the selling price. What is the selling price and markup for the machine?

17. The Fabric Center pays $1.92 per yard for bridal satin, then marks it up 65% of the selling price. What is the selling price and markup for the fabric?

18. IZZE sparkling grapefruit soda costs $32.49 per case and Trader Joe's marks it up 35% of the selling price. Find the selling price and markup per case.

See Example 4.

19. Find the markup and cost of a fishing lure that sells for $18.99 and is marked up 38% of the selling price.

See Example 5.

20. Al's Golf Supply plans to mark up its persimmon wood drivers by 60% based on cost, or $135. Find the rate of the selling price, the cost and selling price for the drivers.

See Example 4.

21. What is the cost and markup of a chair that sells for $349 and is marked up 58% of the selling price?

22. Ronin Copies marks up signs that sell for $49. The markup is 80% based on the selling price. What is the cost and the amount of markup of a sign?

See Example 3.

23. A scanner that is marked up 46% of the selling price sells for $675. Find the cost and the amount of markup of the scanner.

24. A Canon copier is marked up 38% of the selling price. It costs $3,034.90. Find the selling price and markup of the copier.

2 Compare the markup based on the cost with the markup based on the selling price.

If a store manager tells you that the standard markup rate is 25%, you don't know if that means markup based on cost or on selling price. What's the difference?

TIP

Using Subscripts

It is a common notation to use subscripts to distinguish between similar amounts. $M\%_{cost}$ means the markup rate based on the cost. $M\%_{selling\ price}$ means the markup rate based on the selling price.

EXAMPLE 6 Find the rate of markup based on cost and based on selling price of a computer that costs $1,500 and sells for $2,000.

What You Know	What You Are Looking For	Solution Plan
$C = \$1,500$ $S = \$2,000$	$M\%$ based on cost $M\%$ based on selling price	$M = S - C$ $M\%_{cost} = \dfrac{M}{C}(100\%)$ $M\%_{selling\ price} = \dfrac{M}{S}(100\%)$

Solution

Find the markup:

$M = S - C$	Substitute known amounts.
$M = \$2,000 - \$1,500$	Subtract.
$M = \$500$	Amount of markup

Find the rate of markup based on cost:

$M\%_{cost} = \dfrac{M}{C}(100\%)$	Substitute known amounts.
$M\%_{cost} = \dfrac{\$500}{\$1,500}(100\%)$	Divide and write percent equivalent.
$M\%_{cost} = 33\dfrac{1}{3}\%$	Markup rate based on cost

Find the rate of markup based on selling price:

$M\%_{selling\ price} = \dfrac{M}{S}(100\%)$	Substitute known amounts.
$M\%_{selling\ price} = \dfrac{\$500}{\$2,000}(100\%)$	Divide and write percent equivalent.
$M\%_{selling\ price} = 25\%$	Markup rate based on selling price

Conclusion

The markup rate based on cost is $33\frac{1}{3}\%$ and the markup rate based on selling price is 25%.

Sometimes it is necessary to switch from a markup based on selling price to a markup based on cost, or vice versa.

HOW TO Convert a markup rate based on selling price to a markup rate based on cost

1. Find the complement of the markup rate based on the selling price. That is, subtract the markup rate from 100%.
2. Divide the decimal equivalent of the markup rate based on the selling price by the decimal equivalent of the complement of the rate.

$$M\%_{\text{cost}} = \frac{M\%_{\text{selling price}}}{100\% - M\%_{\text{selling price}}}(100\%)$$

EXAMPLE 7

A desk is marked up 30% based on selling price. What is the equivalent markup rate based on the cost?

What You Know	What You Are Looking For	Solution Plan
$M\%_{\text{selling price}} = 30\%$	$M\%_{\text{cost}}$	$M\%_{\text{cost}} = \dfrac{M\%_{\text{selling price}}}{100\% - M\%_{\text{selling price}}}(100\%)$

Solution

$M\%_{\text{cost}} = \dfrac{M\%_{\text{selling price}}}{100\% - M\%_{\text{selling price}}}(100\%)$	Substitute known amounts.
$M\%_{\text{cost}} = \dfrac{30\%}{100\% - 30\%}(100\%)$	Subtract in denominator.
$M\%_{\text{cost}} = \dfrac{30\%}{70\%}(100\%)$	Change percents to decimal equivalents.
$M\%_{\text{cost}} = \dfrac{0.3}{0.7}(100\%)$	Divide and round to hundredths.
$M\%_{\text{cost}} = 0.43(100\%)$	Change to percent equivalent rounded to
$M\%_{\text{cost}} = 43\%$	the nearest whole-number percent.

Conclusion

A 30% markup based on selling price is equivalent to a 43% markup based on cost.

HOW TO Convert a markup rate based on cost to a markup rate based on selling price

1. Add 100% to the markup rate based on the cost.
2. Divide the decimal equivalent of the markup rate based on the cost by the decimal equivalent of the sum found in step 1.

$$M\%_{\text{selling price}} = \frac{M\%_{\text{cost}}}{100\% + M\%_{\text{cost}}}(100\%)$$

EXAMPLE 8

A DVD player is marked up 40% based on cost. What is the markup rate based on selling price?

What You Know	What You Are Looking For	Solution Plan
$M\%_{\text{cost}} = 40\%$	$M\%_{\text{selling price}}$	$M\%_{\text{selling price}} = \dfrac{M\%_{\text{cost}}}{100\% + M\%_{\text{cost}}}(100\%)$

$$M\%_{\text{selling price}} = \frac{M\%_{\text{cost}}}{100\% + M\%_{\text{cost}}}(100\%)$$ Substitute known amounts.

$$M\%_{\text{selling price}} = \frac{40\%_{\text{cost}}}{100\% + 40\%_{\text{cost}}}(100\%)$$ Add in denominator.

$$M\%_{\text{selling price}} = \frac{40\%}{140\%}(100\%)$$ Change percents to decimal equivalents.

$$M\%_{\text{selling price}} = \frac{0.4}{1.4}(100\%)$$ Divide and round to hundredths.

$$M\%_{\text{selling price}} = 0.29(100\%)$$ Change to percent equivalent rounded to
$$M\%_{\text{selling price}} = 29\%$$ the nearest whole-number percent.

Conclusion

A 40% markup based on cost is equivalent to a 29% markup based on selling price.

TIP

Estimating Markup Equivalencies

Known	Unknown	Estimate
$M\%_{\text{cost}}$	$M\%_{\text{selling price}}$	$M\%_{\text{selling price}}$ will be smaller
$M\%_{\text{selling price}}$	$M\%_{\text{cost}}$	$M\%_{\text{cost}}$ will be larger

STOP AND CHECK

Round to the nearest tenth percent. See Example 6.

1. Find the rate of markup based on cost and based on selling price of a blanket that costs $12.50 and sells for $38.

2. Find the rate of markup based on cost and based on selling price of a copy machine that costs $12,500 and sells for $18,900.

See Example 7.

3. A diamond ring is marked up 75% based on selling price. Find the equivalent markup based on cost.

See Example 7.

4. A stroller is marked up 40% based on selling price. What is the equivalent markup based on cost?

See Example 8.

5. A DVD is marked up 120% of cost. What is the equivalent rate of markup based on selling price?

See Example 8.

6. A wallet is marked up 60% of cost. What is the equivalent rate of markup on selling price?

9-2 SECTION EXERCISES

SKILL BUILDERS

Round to the nearest cent or tenth of a percent.

1. Cost = $32; selling price = $40. Find the rate of markup based on the selling price. *See Example 1.*

2. Markup = $75; markup rate of 60% based on the selling price.
   a. Find the selling price.　　　b. Find the cost.

3. Selling price = $1,980; cost = $795. Find the rate of markup based on the selling price. *See Example 1.*

4. Markup = $2,050; markup rate is 42% of the selling price. *See Example 2.*
   a. Find the selling price. b. Find the cost.

5. Markup rate based on selling price = 15%; markup = $250. Find the selling price and cost. *See Example 2.*

6. Find the selling price and markup for an item that costs $792 and is marked up 42% of the selling price. *See Example 3.*
   a. Find the cost rate.

   b. Find the selling price. c. Find the markup.

7. Zagg, Inc. plans to mark up a folio $66 over cost. This will be a 32% markup based on cost. Find the cost and selling price of the folio and the rate of the selling price. *See Example 5.*

8. Selling price = $1.98; markup is 48% of the selling price.
   a. What is the markup?

   b. What is the cost?

9. An item sells for $5,980 and costs $3,420. What is the rate of markup based on selling price? *See Example 1.*

10. The selling price of an item is $18.50 and the markup rate is 86% of the selling price. *See Example 4.*
   a. Find the markup.

   b. Find the cost.

11. An item has a 30% markup based on selling price. The markup is $100.
   a. Find the selling price.

   b. Find the cost.

12. An item costs $20 and sells for $50. *See Example 6.*
   a. Find the rate of markup based on cost.

   b. Find the rate of markup based on selling price.

13. An item has a 60% markup based on selling price. What is the equivalent markup percent based on the cost? *See Example 7.*

14. A 40% markup based on cost is equivalent to what percent based on selling price (retail)? *See Example 8.*

APPLICATIONS

15. An air compressor costs $350 and sells for $695. Find the rate of markup based on the selling price. *See Example 1.*

16. A lateral file is marked up $140, which represents a 28% markup based on the selling price. *See Example 2.*
   a. Find the selling price.

   b. Find the cost.

17. A lawn tractor that costs the retailer $599 is marked up 36% of the selling price.
   a. Find the selling price.

   b. Find the markup.

18. A recliner chair that sells for $1,499 is marked up 60% of the selling price. *See Example 4.*
   a. What is the markup?

   b. What is the cost?

19. Lowe's plans to sell its best-quality floor tiles for $15 each. This is a 48% markup based on selling price.
   a. Find the cost.

   b. Find the markup.

20. A serving tray costs $1,400 and sells for $2,015. *See Example 6.*
   a. Find the rate of markup based on cost.

   b. Find the rate of markup based on selling price.

21. What is the equivalent markup based on cost of a water fountain that is marked up 63% based on the selling price? *See Example 7.*

22. A box of Acco paper clips is marked up 46% based on cost. What is the markup based on selling price? *See Example 8.*

9-3 MARKDOWN, SERIES OF MARKDOWNS, AND PERISHABLES

LEARNING OUTCOMES

1 Find the amount of markdown, the reduced (new) price, and the percent of markdown.
2 Find the final selling price for a series of markups and markdowns.
3 Find the selling price for a desired profit on perishable and seasonal goods.

Markdown: amount by which an original selling price is reduced.

Perishable: an item for sale that has a relatively short time during which the quality of the item is acceptable for sale.

Merchants often have to reduce the price of merchandise from the price at which it was originally sold. The amount by which the original selling price is reduced is called the **markdown.**

There are many reasons for making markdowns. Sometimes merchandise is marked too high to begin with. Sometimes it gets worn or dirty or goes out of style. Flowers, fruits, vegetables, and baked goods are called **perishables** and are sold for less when the quality of the item is not as good as the original quality. Competition from other stores may also require that a retailer mark prices down.

1 Find the amount of markdown, the reduced (new) price, and the percent of markdown.

Markdowns are generally based on the original selling price. That is, the original selling price is the base in the percentage formulas and the rate of the selling price is 100%.

HOW TO

Find the amount of markdown, the reduced (new) price, and the percent of markdown

1. Place the known values into the chart:

	$	%
Original Selling Price (S)		100%
Markdown (M)		
Reduced (New) Price (N)		

2. Select the appropriate formula based on the known values:

$$\text{Markdown} = \text{original selling price} - \text{reduced price} \quad M = S - N$$

$$\text{Reduced price} = \text{original selling price} - \text{markdown} \quad N = S - M$$

$$\text{Rate of markdown} = \frac{\text{amount of markdown}}{\text{original selling price}} \times 100\% \quad M\% = \frac{M}{S}(100\%)$$

EXAMPLE 1

A lamp originally sold for $36 and was marked down to sell for $30. Find the markdown and the rate of markdown based on the selling price (to the nearest hundredth).

What You Know	What You Are Looking For	Solution Plan
$S = \$36$ $N = \$30$	Markdown Rate of markdown	(see below)

Solution Plan chart:

	$	%
S	36	100%
M		
N	30	

$$M = S - N$$
$$M\% = \frac{M}{S}(100\%)$$

Solution

Find the markdown:

$M = S - N$	Substitute known values.
$M = \$36 - \$30$	Subtract.
$M = \$6$	Markdown

Find the rate of markdown:

$M\% = \dfrac{M}{S}(100\%)$	Substitute known values.
$M\% = \dfrac{\$6}{\$36}(100\%)$	Perform calculations.
$M\% = 0.1666666667(100\%)$	Rate of markdown
$M\% = 16.7\%$	Rounded

Conclusion

The markdown is $6 and the rate of markdown is 16.7%.

TIP

Making Connections between Markup and Markdown

Some business processes use the same or similar terminology in different contexts. Examine the terms *original price* and *new price* when associated with markup and markdown.

Markup
Original price = cost (C)
Upward change = markup (M)
New price = selling price (S)
$S = C + M$

Markdown
Original price = selling price (S)
Downward change = markdown (M)
New price = reduced or sale price (N)
$N = S - M$

EXAMPLE 2
A wallet was originally priced at $12 and was reduced by 25%. Find the markdown and the sale (new) price.

What You Know	What You Are Looking For	Solution Plan
$S = \$12$ $M\% = 25\%$	Markdown Sale price	(see table below)

	$	%
S	12	100%
M		25%
N		

$M = M\%(S)$
$N = S - M$

Solution

Find the markdown:

$M = M\% (S)$	Substitute known values.
$M = 25\%(\$12)$	Change percent to its decimal equivalent.
$M = 0.25(\$12)$	Multiply.
$M = \$3$	Markdown

Find the sale (new) price:

$N = S - M$	Substitute known values.
$N = \$12 - \$3$	Subtract.
$N = \$9$	Sale price

Conclusion

The markdown is $3 and the sale price is $9.

STOP AND CHECK

See Example 1.

1. A purse originally sold for $135 and was marked down to sell for $75. Find the markdown and the rate of markdown (to the nearest tenth).

2. An umbrella originally sold for $15 and was marked down to sell for $8. Find the markdown and rate of markdown rounded to the nearest tenth of a percent.

See Example 2.

3. A ladder was originally priced to sell for $249 and was reduced by 35%. Find the amount of markdown and the reduced price.

4. A book bag is priced to sell for $38.99. If the bag was reduced 25%, find the amount of markdown and the reduced price.

5. A corkboard was originally priced to sell at $85 and was reduced by 40%. Find the amount of markdown and the reduced price.

6. Lowe's reduced a Maytag dishwasher 12.563%. If the dishwasher was priced at $398, find the amount of markdown and the reduced price.

2 Find the final selling price for a series of markups and markdowns.

Prices are in a continuous state of flux in the business world. Markups are made to cover increased costs. Markdowns are made to move merchandise more rapidly, to move dated or perishable merchandise, or to draw customers into a store.

Sometimes prices are marked down several times or marked up between markdowns before the merchandise is sold. In calculating each stage of prices, markups, markdowns, and rates, we use exactly the same markup/markdown formulas and procedures as before. To apply these formulas and procedures, we agree that both the markup and the markdown are based on the *previous selling price* in the series.

1. Find the first selling price using the given facts and markup procedures in Sections 9-1 and 9-2.
2. For each remaining stage in the series:
   (a) If the stage requires a *markdown*, identify the previous selling price as the *original selling price S* for this stage. Find the *reduced price N*. This reduced price is the new selling price for this stage.
   (b) If the stage requires a *markup*, identify the previous selling price as the *cost C* for this stage. Find the *selling price S*. This price is the new selling price for this stage.
3. Identify the selling price for the last stage as the *final selling price*.

EXAMPLE 3   Belinda's China Shop paid a wholesale price of $800 for a set of imported china. On August 8, Belinda marked up the china 50% based on the cost. On October 1, she marked the china down 25% for a special 10-day promotion. On October 11, she marked the china up 15%. The china was again marked down 30% for a preholiday sale. What was the final selling price of the china?

What You Know	What You Are Looking For	Solution Plan
Cost = $800	Selling price for stage 1 (S_1)	Find the selling price for each stage using the formulas:
Stage 1: markup of 50% based on cost	Selling price for stage 2 (N_2)	
Stage 2: markdown of 25% based on selling price	Selling price for stage 3 (S_3)	$S\% = C\% + M\%$ $N\% = S\% - M\%$ $S = S\%(C)$ $N = N\%(S)$
Stage 3: markup of 15% based on new selling price	Selling price for stage 4 (N_4)	
Stage 4: markdown of 30% based on new selling price		

Solution

Stage 1: August 8

Find the first selling price (S_1), which is a markup, based on cost:

	$	%
C	800	100
M		50
S	1,200	150

$S_1\% = C\% + M\%$
$S_1\% = 100\% + 50\%$
$S_1\% = 150\%$

$S_1 = S_1\%(C)$
$S_1 = 150\%(\$800)$
$S_1 = 1.5(\$800)$
$S_1 = \$1,200$

Stage 2: October 1

Find the second selling price (N_2), which is a markdown, using S_1 as the original selling price:

	$	%
S_1	1,200	100
M		25
N_2	900	75

$N_2\% = S\% - M\%$
$N_2\% = 100\% - 25\%$
$N_2\% = 75\%$

$N_2 = N\%(S_1)$
$N_2 = 75\%(\$1,200)$
$N_2 = 0.75(\$1,200)$
$N_2 = \$900$

Stage 3: October 11

Find the third selling price (S_3), which is a markup, using N_2 as the cost:

	$	%
N_2	900	100
M		15
S_3	1,035	115

$S_3\% = N_2\% + M\%$
$S_3\% = 100\% + 15\%$
$S_3\% = 115\%$

$S_3 = S_3\%(N_2)$
$S_3 = 115\%(\$900)$
$S_3 = 1.15(\$900)$
$S_3 = \$1,035$

Stage 4: Final markdown

Find the final selling price (N_4), which is a markup, using S_3 as the selling price:

	$	%
S_3	1,035	100
M		30
N_4	724.50	70

$N_4\% = S\% - M\%$

$N_4\% = 100\% - 30\%$

$N_4\% = 70\%$

$N_4 = N_4\%(S_3)$

$N_4 = 70\%(\$1,035)$

$N_4 = 0.7(\$1,035)$

$N_4 = \$724.50$

Conclusion

The final price of the china in the series is $724.50.

Sometimes in retail marketing all changes in the series are markdowns. We can adapt our procedure for finding the net price after applying a trade discount series, which was discussed in Chapter 8. Repricing individual items can be very time-consuming, and many department stores have chosen to use a single sign on an entire table or rack to indicate the same percent markdown on a variety of items. Also, as a further incentive to buy, they may publish a coupon that entitles customers to "take an extra 10% off already reduced prices." This is a situation that can model the procedure for finding the net price after applying a trade discount series.

Net decimal equivalent = product of decimal equivalents of the complements of each discount rate

Net price = net decimal equivalent × original price

Total rate of reduction = (1 − net decimal equivalent)(100%)

EXAMPLE 4

Burdines' has various sales racks throughout the store. Chloe Duke finds a coat from a rack labeled 40% off. She also has a newspaper coupon that reads "Take an additional 10% off any already reduced price." How much will she pay for a coat (net price) that was originally priced at $145? What is the total rate of reduction?

What You Know	What You Are Looking For	Solution Plan
Original price = $145 Discount rates are 40% and 10%.	Final reduced price Total percent of reduction	Find the net decimal equivalent of the rate you pay: Net price = net decimal equivalent × original price Total rate of reduction = (1 − net decimal equivalent) × 100%

Solution

Find the net decimal equivalent:

$0.6(0.9) = 0.54$ Multiply the complements of each rate.

Find the final reduced price:

$(0.54)(\$145) = \$78.30$ Multiply the net decimal equivalent times the original price.

Find the total rate of reduction:

$1 - 0.54 = 0.46$ The complement of the net decimal equivalent is the decimal equivalent of the total rate of reduction.

$0.46(100\%) = 46\%$ Percent equivalent

Conclusion

The final reduced price is $78.30 and the total percent of reduction is 46%.

STOP AND CHECK

See Example 3.

1. Holly's Interior Design Shoppe paid $189 for a fern stand and marked it up 60% based on the cost. Holly included it in a special promotional markdown of 30%. The stand was damaged during the sale and was marked down an additional 40%. What was the final selling price of the stand?

See Example 4.

2. Johnson's Furniture bought a table for $262 and marked it up 85% based on the cost. For a special promotion, it was marked down 25%. Store management decided to mark it down an additional 30%. What was the final reduced price?

3. Rich's placed a "10% off" coupon in a newspaper for a holiday sale. Becca selected shoes from the sale rack that were marked 30% off and also used the coupon. How much will Becca pay for the shoes if they were originally priced at $128? What is the total percent reduction?

4. Neilson's Department Store placed a "15% off" coupon in the newspaper for an after-Thanksgiving sale. Lakisha purchased a formal dress that was marked 40% off and used the coupon. The dress was originally priced at $249. How much did Lakisha pay for the dress? What is the total rate of reduction?

3 Find the selling price for a desired profit on perishable and seasonal goods.

Most businesses anticipate that some seasonal merchandise will not sell at the original selling price. Stores that sell perishable or strictly seasonal items (fresh fruits, vegetables, swimsuits, or coats, for example) usually know from past experience how much merchandise will be marked down or discarded because of spoilage or merchandise out of date. For example, most retail stores mark down holiday items to 50% of the original price the day after the holiday. Thus, merchants set the original markup of such items to obtain the desired profit level based on the projected number of items sold at "full price" (the original selling price).

HOW TO   Find the selling price to achieve a desired profit

1. Establish the rate of profit (markup)—based on cost—desired on the sale of the merchandise.
2. Find the total cost of the merchandise by multiplying the unit cost by the quantity of merchandise. Add in additional charges such as shipping.
3. Find the total desired profit (markup) based on cost by multiplying the rate of profit (markup) by the total cost.
4. Find the total selling price by adding the total cost and the total desired profit.
5. Establish the quantity expected to sell.
6. Divide the total selling price (step 4) by the expect-to-sell quantity (step 5).

$$\text{Selling price per item to achieve desired profit (markup)} = \frac{\text{total selling price}}{\text{expect-to-sell quantity}}$$

EXAMPLE 5   Green's Grocery specializes in fresh fruits and vegetables. Merchandise is priced for quick sale and some must be discarded because of spoilage. Hardy Green, the owner, receives 400 pounds of bananas, for which he pays $0.15 per pound. On average, 8% of the bananas will spoil. Find the selling price per pound to obtain a 175% markup on cost.

What You Know	What You Are Looking For
400 lb of bananas at $0.15 per pound	Selling price per pound
175% markup on cost (desired profit)	
8% expected spoilage	

Solution Plan
Total cost = cost per pound × number of pounds   Markup = $M\%(C)$
Total selling price = $C + M$
Pounds expected to sell = 92%(400)
Selling price per pound = $\dfrac{\text{total selling price}}{\text{pounds expected to sell}}$

$C = \$0.15(400) = \$60$ Find the total cost of the bananas.

$M = 1.75(\$60) = \$105$ $175\% = 1.75$. Find the desired profit (markup).

$S = C + M = \$60 + \$105 = \boxed{\$165}$ Find the total selling price.

Hardy must receive \$165 for the bananas he expects to sell. He expects 8% not to sell, or 92% to sell.

$0.92(400) = \boxed{368}$ Establish how many pounds he can expect to sell.

He can expect to sell 368 pounds of bananas.

$$\text{Selling price per pound} = \frac{\text{total selling price}}{\text{pounds expected to sell}}$$

$$= \frac{\$165}{368} = \$0.4483695652 \text{ or } \$0.45$$

Conclusion

Hardy must sell the bananas for \$0.45 per pound to receive the profit he desires. If he sells more than 92% of the bananas, he will receive additional profit.

STOP AND CHECK

See Example 5.

1. Drewrey's Market pays \$0.30 per pound for 300 pounds of peaches. On average, 5% of the peaches will spoil before they sell. Find the selling price per pound needed to obtain a 180% markup on cost.

2. Cozort's Produce pays \$0.35 per pound for 500 pounds of apples. On average, 8% of the apples will spoil before they sell. Find the selling price per pound needed to obtain a 175% markup on cost.

3. Wesson Grocery buys tomatoes for \$0.27 per pound. On average, 4% of the tomatoes must be discarded. Find the selling price per pound needed to obtain a 160% markup on cost for 2,000 pounds.

4. EZ Way Produce pays \$0.92 per pound for 1,000 lb of mushrooms. On average, 10% of the mushrooms will spoil before they sell. Find the selling price per pound needed to obtain a 180% markup based on cost.

9-3 SECTION EXERCISES

SKILL BUILDERS

Round dollar amounts to the nearest cent, and percents to the nearest tenth percent.

See Example 1.

1. An item sells for \$48 and is reduced to sell for \$30. Find the markdown amount and the rate of markdown.

2. An item is reduced from \$585 to sell for \$499. What is the markdown amount and the rate of markdown?

3. Selling price = $850; reduced (new) price = $500. Find the markdown amount and the rate of markdown.

4. Selling price = $795; reduced price = $650. Find the markdown amount and the rate of markdown.

See Example 4.

5. An item is originally priced to sell for $75 and is marked down 40%. A customer has a coupon for an additional 15%. What is the total percent reduction and the final selling price?

See Examples 3–4.

6. An item costs $400 and is marked up 60% based on the cost. The first markdown rate is 20% and the second markdown rate is 30%. What is the final selling price?

APPLICATIONS

See Example 5.

7. Jung's Grocery received 1,000 pounds of onions at $0.12 per pound. On the average, 4% of the onions will spoil before they are sold. Find the selling price per pound to obtain a markup rate of 200% based on cost.

See Example 1.

8. Deron marks down pillows at the end of the season. They sell for $35 and are reduced to $20. What is the markdown and the rate of markdown?

See Example 2.

9. Desmond found a bicycle with an original price tag of $349 but it had been reduced by 45%. What is the amount of markdown and the sale price?

See Example 1.

10. Julia purchased a sweatshirt that was reduced from $42 to sell for $26. How much was her markdown? What was the markdown and the rate of markdown?

11. A ladies' suit selling for $135 is marked down 25% for a special promotion. It is later marked down 15% of the sale price. Because the suit still hasn't sold, it is marked down to a price that is 75% off the original selling price. What are the two sale prices of the suit? What is the final selling price of the suit?

12. The Swim Shop paid a wholesale price of $24 each for Le Paris swimsuits. On May 5 it marked up the suits 50% of the cost. On June 15 the swimsuits were marked down 15% for a two-day sale, and on June 17 they were marked up again to the original selling price. On August 30, the shop sold all remaining swimsuits for 40% off the original selling price. What was the May 5 price, the June 15 price, and the final selling price of a Le Paris swimsuit?

13. Tancia Boone ordered 600 pounds of Red Delicious apples for the produce section of the supermarket. She paid $0.32 per pound for the apples and expected 15% of them to spoil. If the store wants to make a profit of 90% on the cost, what should be the per-pound selling price?

14. Drewrey's fruit stand sells fresh fruits and vegetables. Becky Drewrey, the manager, must mark the selling price of incoming produce high enough to make the desired profit while taking expected markdowns and spoilage into account. Becky paid $0.35 per pound for 300 pounds of grapes. On average, 12% of the grapes will spoil. Find the selling price per pound needed to achieve a 175% markup on cost.

15. The 7th Inning is buying Ohio State T-shirts. The cost of the shirts, which includes permission fees paid to Ohio State, will be $10.90 each if 1,000 shirts are purchased. Charlie sells 800 shirts before the football season begins at a 50% markup based on cost. What is the gross margin (markup) if Charlie sells the remaining 200 shirts at a 25% reduction from the selling price?

Learning Outcomes

Section 9-1

What to Remember with Examples

1 Find the cost, markup, or selling price when any two of the three are known. (p. 300)

1. Identify the two known amounts.
2. Identify the missing amount.
3. Select the appropriate formula.
4. Substitute the known amounts into the formula.
5. Evaluate the formula.

Find the markup based on a cost of $38 if the selling price is $95.

$M = S - C$
$M = \$95 - \$38$
$M = \$57$

Find the rate of markup based on the cost, the cost, or the markup when any two of the three are known:

2 Find the cost, markup, selling price, or percent of markup when the percent of markup is based on the cost. (p. 302)

1. Identify the known and unknown amounts.
2. Select the formula variation that has the unknown on the left of the equation.

$$M = M\%(C) \qquad \text{Use the decimal equivalent of } M\%.$$

$$M\% = \frac{M}{C}(100\%) \qquad \text{Change to a percent by multiplying by } 100\%.$$

$$C = \frac{M}{M\%} \qquad \text{Use the decimal equivalent of } M\%.$$

3. Substitute the known amounts into the formula.
4. Solve for the missing amount.

Find the percent of markup based on a cost of $86 if the selling price is $124.70.

$M = S - C$
$M = \$124.70 - \$86$
$M = \$38.70$
$M\% = \dfrac{\$38.70}{\$86}(100\%)$
$M\% = 45\%$

An item that costs $70 has a 40% markup based on cost. Find the selling price.

$S\% = C\% + M\%$
$S\% = 100\% + 40\%$
$S\% = 140\%$
$S = S\%(C)$
$S = 140\%(\$70)$
$S = 1.4(\$70)$
$S = \$98$

Find the cost of an item that is marked up $140 and has a markup of 35% of the cost.

$C = \dfrac{M}{M\%}$
$C = \dfrac{\$140}{35\%}$
$C = \dfrac{\$140}{0.35}$
$C = \$400$

Find the cost when the selling price and the percent of markup based on the cost are known:

1. Find the rate of selling price.

$$S\% = 100\% + M\%$$

2. Find the cost using the formula

$$C = \frac{S}{S\%}$$

3. Change the rate of selling price to a numerical equivalent and divide.

An item that sells for $5,950 has a 42% markup based on cost. Find the cost.

$$S\% = C\% + M\%$$
$$S\% = 100\% + 42\%$$
$$S\% = 142\%$$

$$C = \frac{S}{S\%}$$
$$C = \frac{\$5,950}{142\%}$$
$$C = \frac{\$5,950}{1.42}$$
$$C = \$4,190.14 \text{ rounded}$$

Section 9-2

1 Find the cost, markup, selling price, or percent of markup when the percent of markup is based on the selling price. (p. 308)

1. Identify the known and unknown amounts.
2. Select the formula variation that has the unknown on the left side of the equation.

$M = M\%(S)$	Use the decimal equivalent of $M\%$.
$M\% = \dfrac{M}{S}(100\%)$	Change to a percent by multiplying by 100%.
$S = \dfrac{M}{M\%}$	Use the decimal equivalent of $M\%$.
$S = \dfrac{C}{C\%}$	Use the decimal equivalent of $C\%$.
$C = C\%(S)$	Use the decimal equivalent of $C\%$.

3. Substitute the known amounts into the formula.
4. Solve for the missing amount.

Find the amount of markup and the percent of markup based on the selling price if an item costs $40 and sells for $100.

$$M = S - C$$
$$M = \$100 - \$40$$
$$M = \$60$$

$$M\% = \frac{M}{S}(100\%)$$
$$M\% = \frac{\$60}{\$100}(100\%)$$
$$M\% = 60\%$$

Find the selling price of an item that is marked up $68 when the percent of markup based on the selling price is 54%.

$$S = \frac{M}{M\%}$$
$$S = \frac{\$68}{54\%}$$
$$S = \frac{\$68}{0.54}$$
$$S = \$125.93 \text{ rounded}$$

Find the selling price of an item that costs $40 and is marked up 35% based on selling price.

$$C\% = 100\% - M\%$$
$$C\% = 100\% - 35\%$$
$$C\% = 65\%$$

$$S = \frac{C}{C\%}$$
$$S = \frac{\$40}{65\%}$$
$$S = \frac{\$40}{0.65}$$
$$S = \$61.54 \text{ rounded}$$

An item sells for $85 and is marked up 60% based on the selling price. Find the cost.

$$C\% = 100\% - 60\%$$
$$C\% = 40\%$$

$$C = C\%(S)$$
$$C = 40\%(\$85)$$
$$C = 0.4(\$85)$$
$$C = \$34$$

To find all the missing parts if three parts are known and at least one part is an amount and it is known whether the markup is based on the cost or the selling price:

1. Place the three known parts into the chart.

	$	%
C		
M		
S		

If the $ column has two entries:

2. Add or subtract as appropriate to find the third amount.
3. Find a second percent by using the formula $R = \dfrac{P}{B}$.
4. Find the third percent by adding or subtracting as appropriate.

If the % column has two entries:

Add or subtract as appropriate to find the third percent.
Find an additional amount using the formula $P = RB$ or $B = \dfrac{P}{R}$.
Find the third amount by adding or subtracting as appropriate.

Find the rate of markup of an item based on the cost of $38 if the selling price is $76.

$$M = S - C$$
$$M = \$76 - \$38$$
$$M = \$38$$

$$M\% = \frac{M}{C}(100\%)$$
$$M\% = \frac{\$38}{\$38}(100\%)$$
$$M\% = 100\%$$

2 Compare the markup based on the cost with the markup based on the selling price. (p. 314)

To convert a markup rate based on selling price to a markup rate based on cost:

1. Find the complement of the markup rate based on the selling price. That is, subtract the markup rate from 100%.
2. Divide the decimal equivalent of the markup rate based on the selling price by the decimal equivalent of the complement of the rate.

$$M\%_{\text{cost}} = \frac{M\%_{\text{selling price}}}{100\% - M\%_{\text{selling price}}}(100\%)$$

A fax machine is marked up 30% based on selling price. What is the rate of markup based on cost?

$$M\%_{\text{cost}} = \frac{M\%_{\text{selling price}}}{100\% - M\%_{\text{selling price}}}(100\%)$$ Substitute known values.

$$M\%_{\text{cost}} = \frac{30\%}{100\% - 30\%}(100\%)$$ Change percent to its decimal equivalent.

$$M\%_{\text{cost}} = \frac{0.3}{1 - 0.3}(100\%)$$ Subtract in the denominator.

$$M\%_{\text{cost}} = \frac{0.3}{0.7}(100\%)$$ Divide. Round to thousandths.

$$M\%_{\text{cost}} = 0.4285714286(100\%)$$ Change to the percent equivalent.
$$M\%_{\text{cost}} = 42.9\%$$ Rounded

To convert a markup rate based on cost to a markup rate based on selling price:

1. Add 100% to the markup rate based on the cost.
2. Divide the decimal equivalent of the markup rate based on the cost by the decimal equivalent of the sum found in step 1.

$$M\%_{\text{selling price}} = \frac{M\%_{\text{cost}}}{100\% + M\%_{\text{cost}}}(100\%)$$

A DVD player is marked up 80% based on cost. What is the rate of markup based on selling price?

$$M\%_{\text{selling price}} = \frac{M\%_{\text{cost}}}{100\% + M\%_{\text{cost}}}(100\%)$$ Substitute known values.

$$M\%_{\text{selling price}} = \frac{80\%}{100\% + 80\%}(100\%)$$ Change percent to its decimal equivalent.

$$M\%_{\text{selling price}} = \frac{0.8}{1 + 0.8}(100\%)$$ Add in denominator.

$$M\%_{\text{selling price}} = \frac{0.8}{1.8}(100\%)$$ Divide. Round to thousandths.

$$M\%_{\text{selling price}} = 0.4444444444(100\%)$$ Change to the percent equivalent.
$$M\%_{\text{selling price}} = 44.4\%$$ Rounded

Section 9-3

1 Find the amount of markdown, the reduced (new) price, and the percent of markdown. (p. 318)

1. Place the known values into the chart.

	$	%
Original Selling Price (S)		100
Markdown (M)		
Reduced (New) Price (N)		

2. Select the appropriate formula based on the known values.

Markdown = original selling price − reduced price $M = S - N$
Reduced price = original selling price − markdown $N = S - M$

Rate of markdown = $\dfrac{\text{amount of markdown}}{\text{original selling price}}(100\%)$ $M\% = \dfrac{M}{S}(100\%)$

Find the markdown and rate of markdown if the original selling price is $4.50 and the sale (new) price is $3.

$M = S - N$
$M = \$4.50 - \$3$
$M = \$1.50$

$M\% = \dfrac{M}{S}(100\%)$

$M\% = \dfrac{\$1.50}{\$4.50}(100\%)$

$M\% = 0.3333333333(100\%)$
$M\% = 33.3\%$ Rounded

	$	%
S	4.50	100
M		
N	3.00	

2 Find the final selling price for a series of markups and markdowns. (p. 320)

1. Find the first selling price using the given facts and markup procedures in Sections 9-1 and 9-2.
2. For each remaining stage in the series:
   (a) If the stage requires a *markdown,* identify the previous selling price as the *original selling price S* for this stage. Find the *reduced price N.* This reduced price is the new selling price for this stage.
   (b) If the stage requires a *markup,* identify the previous selling price as the *cost C* for this stage. Find the *selling price S.* This price is the new selling price for this stage.
3. Identify the selling price for the last stage as the *final selling price.*

An item costing $7 was marked up 70% on cost, then marked down 20%, marked up 10%, and finally marked down 20%. What was the final selling price?

First stage:	$S\% = C\% + M\%$	$S_1 = S\%(C)$
Markup	$S\% = 100\% + 70\%$	$S_1 = 170\%(\$7)$
	$S\% = 170\%$	$S_1 = 1.7(\$7)$
		$S_1 = \$11.90$

Second stage:	$N\% = 100\% - M\%$	$N_2 = N\%(S_1)$
Markdown	$N\% = 100\% - 20\%$	$N_2 = 80\%(\$11.90)$
$S_1 = S$	$N\% = 80\%$	$N_2 = 0.8(\$11.90)$
		$N_2 = \$9.52$

Third stage:	$S\% = C\% + M\%$	$S_3 = S\%(N_2)$
Markup	$S\% = 100\% + 10\%$	$S_3 = 110\%(\$9.52)$
$N_2 = C$	$S\% = 110\%$	$S_3 = 1.1(\$9.52)$
		$S_3 = \$10.47$

Final stage:	$N\% = 100\% - M\%$	$N_4 = N\%(S_3)$
Markdown	$N\% = 100\% - 20\%$	$N_4 = 80\%(\$10.47)$
$S_3 = S$	$N\% = 80\%$	$N_4 = 0.8(\$10.47)$
		$N_4 = \$8.38$

The final selling price was $8.38.

---

3 Find the selling price for a desired profit on perishable and seasonal goods. (p. 323)

1. Establish the rate of profit (markup)—based on cost—desired on the sale of the merchandise.
2. Find the total cost of the merchandise by multiplying the unit cost by the quantity of merchandise. Add in additional charges such as shipping.
3. Find the total desired profit (markup) based on cost by multiplying the rate of profit (markup) by the total cost.
4. Find the total selling price by adding the total cost and the total desired profit.
5. Establish the quantity expected to sell.
6. Divide the total selling price (step 4) by the expect-to-sell quantity (step 5).

$$\text{Selling price per item to achieve desired profit (markup)} = \frac{\text{total selling price}}{\text{expect-to-sell quantity}}$$

At a total cost of $25, 25% of 400 lemons are expected to spoil before being sold. A 75% rate of profit (markup) on cost is needed. At what selling price must each lemon be sold to achieve the needed profit?

C = total cost of lemons = $25
$M\%$ = rate of profit (markup) = 75%

$M = M\%(C)$	$S = C + M$
$M = 75\%(\$25)$	$S = \$25 + \$18.75$
$M = 0.75(\$25)$	$S = \$43.75$
$M = \$18.75$	

$$\begin{aligned}\text{Quantity expected to sell} &= (100\% - 25\%)(400) \\ &= (75\%)(400) \\ &= 0.75(400) \\ &= 300 \text{ lemons}\end{aligned}$$

$$\begin{aligned}\text{Selling price per item} &= \frac{\$43.75}{300 \text{ lemons}} \\ &= \$0.15 \text{ per lemon (rounded)}\end{aligned}$$

1. Find the selling price of a Casio® calculator if the cost is $12.74 and the markup is $9.25.

2. Peacock's Jewelry buys a pair of stylish earrings for $52 and sells them for $129. What is the markup?

3. AmeriMark® sells ladies' patent sandals for $56.99 and marks them up $26.22. What is the cost of the sandals?

4. Old Towne Hardware pays $12.15 for lightbulbs that have a 35,000-hour life. The bulbs sell for $29.99. What is the percent of markup based on cost? Round to the nearest tenth of a percent.

5. Beach Glass Bingo® Jewelry makes handcrafted bracelets and marks them up 175% based on cost. The cost of making one bracelet is $26. Find the selling price of the bracelets.

6. A computer table sells for $198.50 and costs $158.70.
   a. Find the markup.

   b. Find the rate of markup based on the cost.

7. A flower arrangement is marked up $12, which is 50% of the cost.
   a. Find the cost.

   b. Find the selling price.

8. Paradise Solar Lights marked up each box of four-color changing LED solar accent lights $8.25. The 60% markup of $8.25 was based on cost. Find the cost and selling price of each box of lights.

9. Jenny's Electronics sells a camera for $1,399. The markup rate is 72% of the cost. Find the cost and markup for the camera.

10. A hole punch costs $40 and sells for $58.50.
    a. Find the markup.

    b. Find the rate of markup based on selling price.

11. Find the selling price and cost if an over-the-range microwave oven is marked up $182 with a 65% markup rate based on the selling price.

12. A briefcase is marked up $15.30, which is 30% of the selling price.
    a. Find the selling price of the briefcase.

    b. Find the cost.

13. Find the selling price and markup for a pair of Orvis sensor gloves that costs the retailer $20.40 if the markup is 60% of the selling price.

14. A desk organizer sells for $35, which includes a markup rate of 60% based on the selling price.
    a. Find the markup based on selling price.   b. Find the cost.

15. Nordstrom plans to mark up a Brahmin Croc Embossed Laptop Case $130.50 over cost, which is a 58% markup based on the cost. Find the cost, the selling price, and the rate of the selling price. Round to the nearest tenth percent.

16. A reclaimed T-shirt scarf sells for $32.00 and costs $20.00. Find the rate of markup based on cost and based on selling price. Round to the nearest tenth of a percent.

17. Find the rate of markup based on cost of a textbook that is marked up 20% based on the selling price.

18. A chest is marked up 63% based on cost. What is the rate of markup based on selling price?

19. A fiberglass shower originally sold for $379.98 and was marked down to sell for $341.98.
    a. Find the markdown.

    b. Find the rate of markdown based on selling price.

20. A portable DVD player was originally priced at $249.99 and was reduced by 20%.
    a. Find the markdown.

    b. Find the sale (new) price.

21. Crystal stemware originally marked to sell for $49.50 was reduced 20% for a special promotion. The stemware was then reduced an additional 30% to turn inventory. What were the markdown and the sale price for each reduction?

22. Michelle Dockter has selected a Sonic® electric toothbrush that is on sale for 25% off. She also has a store coupon that reads "Take 15% off any already reduced price." How much will she pay for the toothbrush if it was originally priced at $79.99? What is the rate of reduction?

23. James McDonnell purchases 800 pounds of potatoes at a cost of $0.18 per pound. If he anticipates a spoilage rate of 20% of the potatoes and wishes to make a profit of 140% of the cost, for how much must he sell the potatoes per pound?

EXERCISES SET B

1. Find the selling price of a Men's Stainless Steel Black Detail money clip if the cost is $42.25 and the markup is $84.40.

2. A Waterford® Marquis ballpoint pen costs $22.50 and sells for $50.99. What is the markup?

3. A set of stainless steel tableware sells for $159.99 and has a markup of $83.59. What is the cost of the tableware?

4. Wolfe Camera Shop pays $78.50 for a Panasonic® 16.1 MP digital camera. The camera sells for $179.99. What is the percent of markup based on cost? Round to the nearest tenth of a percent.

5. A Fujifilm digital camera with software is marked up 67% based on cost. The cost of the camera is $167.45. Find the selling price of the camera.

6. Macy's Department Store marked up a Cuisinart® blender 38% based on cost. If the markup was $53.20, find the cost and selling price of each blender.

7. Lenox® sells a serving platter for $359. The markup rate is 110% of the cost. Find the cost and markup for the platter.

8. A Canon® black-and-white multifunction laser printer costs $49 and sells for $119.99. Find the rate of markup based on the selling price.

9. Find the selling price and cost if a tennis table is marked up $279.99 with a 56% markup rate based on the selling price.

10. Find the selling price and markup for a case of Newman's Own® special blend coffee that costs the retailer $35.87 if the markup is 22% of the selling price.

11. A toaster sells for $28.70 and has a markup rate of 50% based on selling price.
   a. Find the markup.

12. May Department Stores plans to mark up a Cuisinart Single Serve® brewing system $82.25 over cost, which is a 72% markup based on the cost. Find the cost, the selling price, and the rate of the selling price.

   b. Find the cost.

13. Costco sells a set of Velox® custom vehicle wheels for $529.00. They cost $278.00. Find the rate of markup based on cost and based on selling price. Round to the nearest tenth of a percent.

14. A dining room suite is marked up 45% based on cost. What is the rate of markup based on selling price? Round to the nearest tenth percent.

15. A desk has an 84% markup based on selling price. What is the rate of markup based on cost?

16. A down comforter was originally priced to sell at $280 and was reduced by 65%. Find the markdown and the sale price.

17. A three-speed fan originally sold for $29.98 and was reduced to sell for $25.40. Find the markdown and the rate of markdown. Round to the nearest tenth percent.

18. Bolivia's Gifts paid a wholesale price of $625 for a set of imported hand-cut crystal and marked the crystal up 82% based on cost. On April 1, the crystal was marked down 30% for a special promotion. On April 15, the crystal was marked up 15% of its marked-down price. On September 12, the crystal was marked down 35% for a clearance sale. What was the final selling price of the crystal?

19. Keven Dockter has selected a Garmin® portable GPS that is on sale for 20% off. He also has a store coupon that reads "Take 10% off any already reduced price." How much will he pay for the portable GPS if it was originally priced at $279.99? What is the rate of reduction?

20. Hampton's Organic Market specializes in organic produce. Merchandise is priced for quick sale and some is expected to be discarded because of spoilage. The market receives 500 pounds of apples that cost $0.62 per pound. On average 6.3% of the apples will spoil. Find the selling price per pound to obtain a 210% markup on cost.

PRACTICE TEST

1. A calculator sells for $23.99 and costs $16.83. What is the markup?

2. A mixer sells for $109.98 and has a markup of $36.18. Find the cost.

3. A cookbook has a 34% markup rate based on cost. If the markup is $5.27, find the cost of the cookbook. Find the selling price.

4. A computer stand sells for $385. What is the markup if it is 45% of the selling price? What is the cost?

5. A box of printer paper sells for $22.68. Find the cost and markup if there is a 35% markup rate based on cost.

6. The reduced price of a dress is $54.99. Find the original selling price if a reduction of 40% has been taken.

7. A coffeemaker that originally sold for $86.90 was marked down to sell for $60.30. What is the markdown?

8. What is the rate of markdown of the coffeemaker in Exercise 7?

9. If a television costs $498.15 and was marked up $300, what is the selling price?

10. A refrigerator that costs $489.99 was marked up $100. What is the selling price?

11. What is the rate of markdown based on the selling price of a scanner that sells for $498 and is marked down $142? Round to the nearest tenth percent.

12. A wallet was originally priced at $49.99 and was reduced by 30%. Find the markdown and the sale price.

13. A lamp costs $88. What is the selling price and markup if the markup is 45% of the selling price?

14. A file cabinet originally sold for $215 but was damaged and had to be reduced. If the reduced cabinet sold for $129, what was the rate of markdown based on the original selling price?

15. A desk that originally sold for $589 was marked down 25%. During the sale it was scratched and had to be reduced an additional 25% of the original price. What was the final selling price of the desk?

16. Brenda Wimberly calculates the selling price for all produce at Quick Stop Produce. If 400 pounds of potatoes were purchased for $0.13 per pound and 18% of the potatoes were expected to spoil before being sold, determine the price per pound that the potatoes must sell for if a profit of 120% of the purchase price is desired.

17. A rugby shirt that was originally priced at $89.95 is marked down 35%. Madison has a coupon for 15% off the reduced price. How much will Madison pay for the shirt? What is the total rate of reduction?

18. A CD costs $0.90 and sells for $1.50. Find the rate of markup based on selling price. Round to the nearest whole percent.

19. A radio is marked up 65% of the selling price. Find the equivalent markup rate based on the cost. Round to the nearest tenth of a percent.

20. Becky Drewery purchased a small refrigerator for her dorm room for $159. The refrigerator costs $127. Find the rate of markup based on cost and based on the selling price. Round the rate to the nearest tenth of a percent.

21. A Yamaha® 88 Portable Grand Keyboard has a cost of $345.58 and is marked up 63% based on cost. Find the selling price and cost of the keyboard.

22. A 10-ream case of printer paper sells for $39.99 and has a 47% markup based on the selling price. Find the markup and cost of one case of paper.

23. One big box store sells a Toshiba® notebook computer for $549.99. Each computer has a 57% markup based on selling price. What is the markup and cost of each computer?

24. A copy machine is marked up 82.2% based on the cost. Find the markup rate based on selling price. Round to the nearest tenth percent.

25. Find the selling price and cost of an Amana® portable room air conditioner that is marked up $220 with a 55% markup rate based on selling price.

26. A stainless steel patio heater is marked up $87 over cost. The markup rate of 48% is based on cost. Find the cost and selling price of the heater. Find the rate of the selling price.

1. Will the series markdown of 25% and 30% be more than or less than 55%? Explain why.

2. Explain why taking a series of markdowns of 25% and 30% is not the same as taking a single markdown of 55%. Illustrate your answer with a specific example.

3. Under what circumstances would you be likely to base the markup of an item on the selling price?

4. Under what circumstances would you be likely to base the markup for an item on cost?

5. What clues do you look for to determine whether the cost or selling price represents 100% in a markup problem?

6. If you were a retailer, would you prefer to base your markup on selling price or cost? Why? Give an example to illustrate your preference.

7. When given the rate of markup, describe at least one situation that leads to adding the rate to 100%. Describe at least one situation that leads to subtracting the rate from 100%.

8. Show by giving an example that the final reduced price in a series markdown can be found by doing a series of computations or by using the net decimal equivalent.

9. An item is marked up 60% based on a selling price of $400. What is the cost of the item? Find and correct the error in the solution.

$$C\% = S\% - M\%$$
$$C\% = 100\% - 60\%$$
$$C\% = 40\%$$

$$C = \frac{S}{S\%}$$
$$C = \frac{\$400}{100\%}$$
$$C = \frac{\$400}{1}$$
$$C = \$400$$

10. Explain why the percent of markup based on selling price cannot be greater than 100%.

Challenge Problems

1. Pro Peds, a local athletic shoe manufacturer, makes a training shoe at a cost of $22 per pair. This cost includes raw materials and labor only. A check of previous factory runs indicates that 10% of the training shoes will be defective and must be sold to Odd Tops, Inc., as irregulars for $32 per pair. If Pro Peds produces 1,000 pairs of the training shoes and desires a markup of 100% on cost, find the selling price per pair of the regular shoes to the nearest cent.

2. A business estimates its operating expenses at 35% and its net profit at 20%, *based on the selling price*. For what price must an item costing $457.89 be sold to cover both the operating expenses and net profit?

CASE STUDIES

9-1 Acupuncture, Tea, and Rice-Filled Heating Pads

Karen is an acupuncturist with a busy practice. In addition to acupuncture services, Karen sells teas, herbal supplements, and rice-filled heating pads. Because Karen's primary income is from acupuncture, she feels that she is providing the other items simply to fill a need and not as an important source of profits. As a matter of fact, the rice-filled heating pads are made by a patient who receives acupuncture for them instead of paying cash. The rice-filled pads cost Karen $5.00, $8.00, and $12.00, respectively, for small, medium, and large sizes. The ginger tea, relaxing tea, cold & flu tea, and detox tea cost her $2.59 per box plus $5.00 shipping and handling for 24 boxes. Karen uses a cost plus markup method, whereby she adds the same set amount to each box of tea. She figures that each box costs $2.59 plus $0.21 shipping and handling, which totals $2.80, then she adds $0.70 profit to each box and sells it for $3.50. Do you think this is a good pricing strategy? How would it compare to marking up by a percentage of the cost?

1. What is the markup percent for a box of ginger tea?

2. If the rice-filled heating pads sell for $7.00, $10.00, and $15.00 for small, medium, and large, respectively, what is the markup percent on each one?

3. Karen wants to compare using the cost plus method to the percent markup method. If she sells 2 small rice pads, 4 medium rice pads, 2 large rice pads, and 20 boxes of $3.50 tea in a month, how much profit does she accumulate? What markup percent based on cost would she have to use to make the same amount of profit on this month's sales?

4. What prices should Karen charge (using the markup percent) to obtain the same amount of profit as she did with the cost plus method? Do not include shipping.

9-2 Carolina Crystals

Carolina Crystals, a midrange jewelry store located at Harbor Village in San Diego, serves two clienteles: regular customers who purchase gifts and special-occasion jewelry year-round, and tourists visiting the city. Although tourism is high in San Diego most months of the year, the proprietor of Carolina Crystals, Amanda, knows that her regular customers tend to purchase more jewelry during November and December for Christmas presents; in late January and early February for Valentine's Day; and in late April and May for summer weddings. Typically, jewelry is marked up 100% based on cost, but Amanda adjusts her pricing throughout the year to reflect seasonal needs. Amanda always carries a selection of diamond engagement and eternity rings, a wide array of gold charms that appeal to tourists, both regular and baroque pearl strands, and other types of jewelry.

1. If Amanda purchases diamond rings at $1,200 each, what would be the regular selling price to her customers, assuming a 100% markup on cost?

2. If Amanda thinks that an 85% markup on cost is more appropriate for gold charms, what would be the selling price on a gold sailboat charm Amanda purchases for $135?

Source: Cape Fear Community College web site, North Carolina

3. Amanda also sells gold bracelets on which the charms can be mounted. She runs a special all year that allows a customer to purchase a gold charm bracelet at 50% off if the customer also buys three gold charms at the same time. If a 7″ gold bracelet costs Amanda $125, what would be the price if the customer bought only the bracelet (without the charms) at a regular 100% markup on cost?

4. What would be the total price of the purchase if a customer purchased 3 charms and the bracelet, assuming the first charm cost Amanda $150, the second $185, and the third $125, and were marked up 85% based on cost?

5. Amanda often suggests to her male customers who buy diamond engagement rings that they also purchase a pearl necklace as a wedding gift for their bride. As a courtesy to men purchasing diamond engagement rings, Amanda discounts pearl strands 18″ and shorter by 35% and pearl strands longer than 18″ by 45%. If the diamond rings have a 100% markup on cost and the pearl necklaces have a 60% markup on cost, what would be Amanda's cost for a ring selling at $4,500 and a 22″ pearl necklace selling for $1,500?

6. If a customer purchases both the diamond ring for $4,500 and the 22″ pearl strand for $1,500 and receives the 45% discount on the pearl strand, what would be the total purchase price? How much did the customer save by purchasing the ring and necklace together?

9-3 Deer Valley Organics, LLC

With an original goal of selling fresh apples from the family orchard at a roadside stand, Deer Valley Organics has become a unique operation featuring a wide variety of locally grown organic produce and farm products that include their own fruit as well as products from the area's finest growers. A number of different products are available, including apples, strawberries, and raspberries as either prepackaged or pick your own; assorted fresh vegetables; ciders, jams, and jellies; and organic fresh eggs and free-range chicken whole fryers. Prepackaged apples are still the mainstay of the business, and after adding all production and labor costs, Deer Valley determined that the cost of these apples was 84 cents per pound.

1. What would be the selling price per pound for the prepackaged apples using a 30% markup based on cost? A 40% markup? A 50% markup?

2. Based on the national average for apples sold on a retail basis, Deer Creek sets a target price of $1.49 per pound for the prepackaged apples. Using this selling price, compute the percent of markup **based on cost** for the prepackaged apples. Then, compute the percent of markup **based on selling price.**

3. Deer Valley allows customers to pick their own apples for $10.50 a bag, which works out to approximately 62 cents per pound. How is that possible given the cost data in the introductory paragraph? Would the orchard be losing money? Explain.

4. Deer Valley receives a delivery of 1,250 lb of tomatoes from a local supplier, for which they pay 58 cents per pound. Normally, 6% of the tomatoes will be discarded because of appearance or spoilage. Find the selling price needed per pound to obtain a 120% markup based on cost.

Your First Job: Understanding Your Paycheck

"My paycheck isn't right!" Kenee can't believe it: $461.69? He's supposed to be paid $600 each week! That's the salary he was quoted when he was hired.

Many people, when they receive their first paycheck, are surprised at the amount of money that is deducted from it before they get paid. These are payroll taxes. There's a big difference between gross income, salary or hourly rate times the number of hours; and net income, or take-home pay.

In Kenee's case, his tax withholding status is single with zero exemptions. His withholding is calculated using state tax tables and IRS information. The deductions from his pay are:

- Federal withholding, money sent to the IRS to pay federal income taxes. Federal taxes pay for many programs such as national defense, foreign affairs, law enforcement, education, and transportation.
- Social Security, money set aside for a federal program that provides monthly benefits to retired and disabled workers, their dependents, and their survivors.

- Medicare, money to provide health care coverage for older Americans and people with disabilities.
- State withholding, money sent to a person's state of residence to pay state income taxes. State taxes pay for state programs such as education, health, welfare, public safety, and the state court justice system. Some states may require additional deductions for state disability insurance and local taxes.
- Additional items, such as health and life insurance premiums and retirement plan contributions, may also be deducted from a person's paycheck.

Always check your pay stub. It should include your identification information and the pay period (dates you worked for this check). It also lists your gross income, all your deductions, and most importantly your net income, which is the amount you get to keep!

LEARNING OUTCOMES

10-1 Gross Pay

1. Find the gross pay per paycheck based on salary.
2. Find the gross pay per weekly paycheck based on hourly wage.
3. Find the gross pay per paycheck based on piecework wage.
4. Find the gross pay per paycheck based on commission.

10-2 Payroll Deductions

1. Find federal tax withholding per paycheck using IRS tax tables.
2. Find federal tax withholding per paycheck using the IRS percentage method.
3. Find Social Security tax and Medicare tax per paycheck.
4. Find net earnings per paycheck.

10-3 The Employer's Payroll Taxes

1. Find an employer's total deposit for withholding tax, Social Security tax, and Medicare tax per pay period.
2. Find an employer's SUTA tax and FUTA tax due for a quarter.

Gross earnings (gross pay): the amount earned before deductions.

Net earnings (net pay) or **(take-home pay):** the amount of your paycheck.

Wages: earnings based on an hourly rate of pay and the number of hours worked.

Salary: an agreed-upon amount of pay that is not based on the number of hours worked.

Pay is an important concern of employees and employers alike. If you have worked and received a paycheck, you know that part of your earnings is taken out of your paycheck before you ever see it. Your employer *withholds* (deducts) taxes, union dues, medical insurance payments, and so on. Thus, there is a difference between **gross earnings (gross pay),** the amount earned before deductions, and **net earnings (net pay)** or **take-home pay**—the amount of your paycheck.

Employers have the option of paying their employees in salary or in wages and of distributing these earnings at various time intervals. **Wages** are based on an hourly rate of pay and the number of hours worked. **Salary** is most often stated as a certain amount of money paid each year.

10-1 GROSS PAY

LEARNING OUTCOMES

1 Find the gross pay per paycheck based on salary.
2 Find the gross pay per weekly paycheck based on hourly wage.
3 Find the gross pay per paycheck based on piecework wage.
4 Find the gross pay per paycheck based on commission.

Employees may be paid according to a salary, an hourly wage, a piecework rate, or a commission rate. Employers are required to withhold taxes from employee paychecks and forward these taxes to federal, state, and local governments.

1 Find the gross pay per paycheck based on salary.

Weekly: once a week or 52 times a year.

Biweekly: every two weeks or 26 times a year.

Semimonthly: twice a month or 24 times a year.

Monthly: once a month or 12 times a year.

Companies differ in how often they pay salaried employees, which determines how many paychecks an employee receives in a year. If employees are paid **weekly,** they receive 52 paychecks a year; if they are paid **biweekly** (every two weeks), they receive 26 paychecks a year. **Semimonthly** (twice a month) paychecks are issued 24 times a year, and **monthly** paychecks come 12 times a year.

> **HOW TO** Find the gross pay per paycheck based on annual salary
>
> 1. Identify the number of pay periods per year:
>   Monthly—12 pay periods per year
>   Semimonthly—24 pay periods per year
>   Biweekly—26 pay periods per year
>   Weekly—52 pay periods per year
> 2. Divide the annual salary by the number of pay periods per year. Round to the nearest cent.

EXAMPLE 1 Charles Demetriou earns a salary of $60,000 a year.

(a) If Charles is paid biweekly, how much is his gross pay per pay period before taxes are taken out?
(b) If Charles is paid semimonthly, how much is his gross pay per pay period?

(a) $60,000 ÷ 26 = $2,307.69   Biweekly paychecks are issued 26 times a year,
Charles earns $2,307.69 biweekly   so divide Charles's salary by 26.
before deductions.

(b) $60,000 ÷ 24 = $2,500   Semimonthly paychecks are issued 24 times a
Charles earns $2,500 semimonthly   year, so divide Charles's salary by 24.
before deductions.

EXAMPLE 2 Anetha Brown earns $3,068 per pay period and is paid biweekly. What is her annual gross pay?

$3,068(26) = $79,768   Biweekly pay checks are issued 26 times per year.

Anetha's annual gross pay is $79,768.

STOP AND CHECK

See Example 1.

1. Ryan Thomas earns $42,822 a year. What is his biweekly gross pay?

2. Jaswant Jain earns $32,928 annually and is paid semimonthly. Find his earnings per pay period.

See Example 2.

3. Alison Bishay earns $1,872 each pay period and is paid weekly. Find her annual gross pay.

4. Annette Ford earns $3,315 monthly. What is her gross annual pay?

2 Find the gross pay per weekly paycheck based on hourly wage.

Hourly rate or **hourly wage:** the amount of pay per hour worked based on a standard 40-hour work week.

Overtime rate: the rate of pay for hours worked that are more than 40 hours in a week.

Time and a half: standard overtime rate that is $1\frac{1}{2}$ (or 1.5) times the hourly rate.

Regular pay: earnings based on hourly rate of pay.

Overtime pay: earnings based on overtime rate of pay.

Many jobs pay according to an *hourly wage*. The **hourly rate,** or **hourly wage,** is the amount of money paid for each hour the employee works in a standard 40-hour work week. The Fair Labor Standards Act (FLSA) of 1938 set the standard work week at 40 hours. When hourly employees work more than 40 hours in a week, they earn the hourly wage for the first 40 hours, and they earn an **overtime rate** for the remaining hours. The standard overtime rate is often called **time and a half.** By law, it must be at least 1.5 (one and one-half) times the hourly wage. Earnings based on the hourly wage are called **regular pay.** Earnings based on the overtime rate are called **overtime pay.** An hourly employee's gross pay for a pay period is the sum of his or her regular pay and his or her overtime pay.

HOW TO   Find the gross pay per week based on hourly wages

1. Find the regular pay:
   (a) If the hours worked in the week are 40 or fewer, multiply the hours worked by the hourly wage.
   (b) If the hours worked are more than 40, multiply 40 hours by the hourly wage.
2. Find the overtime pay:
   (a) If the hours worked are 40 or fewer, the overtime pay is $0.
   (b) If the hours worked are more than 40, subtract 40 from the hours worked and multiply the difference by the overtime rate.
3. Add the regular pay and the overtime pay.

When Does the Week Start? Even if an employee is paid biweekly, overtime pay is still based on the 40-hour standard work week. So overtime pay for each week in the pay period must be calculated separately. Also, each employer establishes the formal work week. For example, an employer's work week may begin at 12:01 A.M. Thursday and end at 12:00 midnight on Wednesday of the following week, allowing the payroll department to process payroll checks for distribution on Friday. Another employer may begin the work week at 11:01 P.M. on Sunday evening and end at 11:00 P.M. on Sunday the following week so that the new week coincides with the beginning of the 11 P.M.–7 A.M. shift on Sunday.

EXAMPLE 3   Marcia Scott, whose hourly wage is $10.25, worked 46 hours last week. Find her gross pay for last week if she earns time and a half for overtime.

40($10.25) = $410	Find the regular pay for 40 hours of work at the hourly wage.
46 − 40 = 6	Find the overtime hours.
$\underbrace{6(\$10.25)(1.5)}_{\text{overtime rate}}$ = $92.25	Find the overtime pay by multiplying the overtime hours by the overtime rate, which is the hourly wage times 1.5. Round to the nearest cent.
$410 + $92.25 = $502.25	Add the regular pay and the overtime pay to find Marcia's total gross earnings.

Marcia's gross pay is $502.25.

Some salaried employees do earn overtime pay for hours worked above 40 hours per week. A common misconception is that salaried employees do not earn overtime. An employee that is *nonexempt* from FLSA is entitled to overtime. To be exempt from FLSA, an employee must meet the test for exempt status as defined by federal and state laws.

If an employee is salaried and nonexempt, the overtime pay rate is calculated by applying the following process:

1. If the salary is defined as a monthly salary, multiply the monthly salary by 12 months to get the annual salary.
2. Divide the annual salary by 52 (weeks) to get a weekly salary.
3. Divide the weekly salary by the maximum number of hours in a regular work week (40) to get the regular hourly pay rate.
4. Multiply the regular hourly pay rate by 1.5 to get the overtime hourly pay rate.

EXAMPLE 4

Ann Glover earns a monthly salary of $3,600 and is nonexempt from FLSA. Last week she worked 56 hours. What are her overtime earnings for the week?

$3,600(12) = $43,200	Annual salary
$43,200 ÷ 52 = $830.77	Weekly pay rate
$830.77 ÷ 40 = $20.77	Hourly pay rate
$20.77(1.5) = $31.16	Overtime pay rate
56 − 40 = 16	Hours of overtime worked
16($31.16) = $498.56	Overtime pay

Ann Glover earned $498.56 in overtime pay for the week.

STOP AND CHECK

See Example 3.

1. Shekenna Chapman earns $15.83 per hour and worked 48 hours in a week. Overtime is paid at 1.5 times hourly pay. What is her gross pay?

2. McDonald's pays Kelyn Blackburn 1.5 times her hourly pay for overtime. She worked 52 hours one week and her hourly pay is $13.56. Find her gross pay for the week.

3. Mark Kozlowski earns $14.27 per hour and worked 55 hours in one weekly pay period. What is his gross pay?

4. Marc Showalter earns $22.75 per hour with time and a half for regular overtime and double time on holidays. He worked 62 hours the week of July 4th and 8 of those hours were on July 4th. Find his gross pay.

See Example 4.

5. Jamila Long earns a monthly salary of $3,224 and is nonexempt from FLSA. Last week she worked 61 hours. What are her overtime earnings for the week?

6. Bogdan Zcesky earns a monthly salary of $4,472 and is nonexempt from FLSA. Last week he worked 48 hours. What are his overtime earnings for the week?

3 Find the gross pay per paycheck based on piecework wage.

Piecework rate: amount of pay for each acceptable item produced.

Straight piecework rate: piecework rate where the pay is the same per item no matter how many items are produced.

Differential piece rate (escalating piece rate): piecework rate that increases as more items are produced.

Many employers motivate employees to produce more by paying according to the quantity of acceptable work done. Such **piecework rates** are typically offered in production or manufacturing jobs. Garment makers and some other types of factory workers, agricultural workers, and employees who perform repetitive tasks such as stuffing envelopes or packaging parts may be paid by this method. In the simplest cases, the gross earnings of such workers are calculated by multiplying the number of items produced by the **straight piecework rate.**

Sometimes employees earn wages at a **differential piece rate,** also called an **escalating piece rate.** As the number of items produced by the worker increases, so does the pay per item. This method of paying wages offers employees an even greater incentive to complete more pieces of work in a given period of time.

HOW TO Find the gross pay per paycheck based on piecework wage

1. If a *straight piecework rate* is used, multiply the number of items completed by the straight piecework rate.
2. If a *differential piecework rate* is used:
   (a) For each rate category, multiply the number of items produced for the category by the rate for the category.
   (b) Add the pay for all rate categories.

EXAMPLE 5

A shirt manufacturer pays a worker a straight piecework rate of $0.47 for each acceptable shirt inspected under the prescribed job description. If the worker had the following work record, find the gross earnings for the week: Monday, 250 shirts; Tuesday, 300 shirts; Wednesday, 178 shirts; Thursday, 326 shirts; Friday, 296 shirts.

250 + 300 + 178 + 326 + 296   Find the total number of shirts inspected.
= 1,350 shirts
1,350($0.47) = $634.50   Multiply the number of shirts by the piecework rate.

The weekly gross earnings are $634.50.

EXAMPLE 6

Last week, Jorge Sanchez assembled 317 game boards. Find Jorge's gross earnings for the week if the manufacturer pays at the following differential piece rate:

Boards assembled per week	Pay per board
First 100	$1.82
Next 200	$1.92
Over 300	$2.08

Find how many boards were completed at each pay rate, multiply the number of boards by the rate, and add the amounts.

First 100 items: 100($1.82) = $182.00
Next 200 items: 200($1.92) = $384.00
Last 17 items: 17($2.08)   = $ 35.36
                                $601.36

Jorge's gross earnings were $601.36.

STOP AND CHECK

See Example 5.

1. JR Tinkler and Co. employs pear and peach pickers on a piecework basis. Paul Larson picks enough pears to fill 12 bins in the 40-hour work week. He is paid at the rate of $70 per bin. What is his pay for the week?

2. A rubber worker is paid $5.50 for each finished tire. In a given week, Dennis Swartz completed 21 tires on Monday, 27 tires on Tuesday, 18 tires on Wednesday, 29 tires on Thursday, and 24 tires on Friday. How much were his gross weekly earnings?

See Example 6.

3. A tool assembly company pays differential piecework wages:

Units Assembled	Pay per Unit
1–200	$1.18
201–400	$1.35
401 and over	$1.55

Find Virginia March's gross pay if she assembled 535 units in one week.

4. Thai Notebaert assembles computer keyboards according to this differential piecework scale on a weekly basis:

Units Assembled	Pay per Unit
1–50	$2.95
51–150	$3.10
Over 150	$3.35

He assembled 37 keyboards on Monday, 42 on Tuesday, 40 on Wednesday, 46 on Thursday, and 52 on Friday. What is his gross pay for the week?

4 Find the gross pay per paycheck based on commission.

Commission: earnings based on sales.

Straight commission: entire pay based on sales.

Salary-plus-commission: a set amount of pay plus an additional amount based on sales.

Commission rate: the percent used to calculate the commission based on sales.

Quota: a minimum amount of sales that is required before a commission is applicable.

Many salespeople earn a **commission,** a percentage based on sales. Those whose entire pay is commission are said to work on **straight commission.** Those who receive a salary in addition to a commission are said to work on a **salary-plus-commission** basis. A **commission rate** can be a percent of total sales or a percent of sales greater than a specified **quota** of sales.

> ## HOW TO Find the gross pay per paycheck based on commission
>
> 1. Find the commission:
>   (a) If the commission is *commission based on total sales,* multiply the commission rate by the total sales for the pay period.
>   (b) If the commission is *commission based on quota,* subtract the quota from the total sales and multiply the difference by the commission rate.
> 2. Find the salary:
>   (a) If the wage is *straight commission,* the salary is $0.
>   (b) If the wage is *commission-plus-salary,* determine the gross pay based on salary.
> 3. Add the commission and the salary.

EXAMPLE 7 Shirley Garcia is a restaurant supplies salesperson and receives 8% of her total sales as commission. Her sales totaled $15,000 during a given week. Find her commission.

Use the percentage formula $P = RB$.

$P = 0.08(\$15,000) = \$1,200$ Change the rate of 8% to an equivalent decimal and multiply it times the base of $15,000.

Shirley's commission is $1,200.

EXAMPLE 8 Matthew Darling receives 1.3% of sales plus $2.50 for each book he lists for sale at Internet bookstores through Darling Book Listing Services, Inc. In May he listed 827 items and had sales that totaled $21,715. What were his gross earnings?

Earnings for book listings = $2.50(827) = \$2,067.50$
Earnings for commission sales = $1.3\%(\$21,715) = 0.013(\$21,715) = \$282.30$
Gross earnings = $\$2,067.50 + \$282.30 = \$2,349.80$

EXAMPLE 9 Eloise Brown is paid on a salary-plus-commission basis. She receives $450 weekly in salary and 3% of all sales over $8,000. If she sold $15,000 worth of goods, find her gross earnings.

$\$15,000 - \$8,000 = \$7,000$ Subtract the quota from total sales to find the sales on which commission is paid.

$P = RB$ Change the rate of 3% to an equivalent decimal.

$P = 0.03(\$7,000)$ Multiply the rate by the base of $7,000.

$P = \$210$ (commission)
$\$210 + \$450 = \$660$ Add the commission and salary to find gross pay.

Eloise Brown's gross earnings were $660.

STOP AND CHECK

1. Reyna Mata sells furniture and is paid 6% of her total sales as commission. One week her sales totaled $17,945. What are her gross earnings? *See Example 7.*

2. Keith Strawn receives 1% of eBay sales plus $4.00 for each item he lists through his eBay listing service. One month he listed 547 items that sold for a total of $30,248. Find his gross earnings. *See Example 8.*

See Example 9.

3. Kate Citrino is paid $200 weekly plus 2% of her sales above $3,000. One week she sold $26,572 in merchandise. Find her gross pay. Find her estimated annual gross pay.

4. Arita Hannus earns $275 biweekly and 4% of her sales. In one pay period her sales were $32,017. Find her gross pay. At this same rate, find her estimated annual gross pay.

10-1 SECTION EXERCISES

SKILL BUILDERS

See Example 1.

1. If Timothy Oaks earns a salary of $35,204 a year and is paid weekly, how much is his weekly paycheck before taxes?

2. If Nita McMillan earns a salary of $31,107.96 a year and is paid biweekly, how much is her biweekly paycheck before taxes are taken out?

See Example 2.

3. Gregory Maksi earns a salary of $52,980 annually and is paid monthly. How much is his gross monthly income?

4. Amelia Mattix is an accountant and is paid semimonthly. Her annual salary is $38,184. How much is her gross pay per period?

For Exercises 5–7, see Example 3.

5. William Melton worked 47 hours in one week. His regular pay was $7.60 per hour with time and a half for overtime. Find his gross earnings for the week.

6. Bethany Colangelo, whose regular rate of pay is $8.25 per hour, with time and a half for overtime, worked 44 hours last week. Find her gross pay for the week.

For Exercises 8–9, see Example 4.

7. Carlos Espinosa earns $15.90 per hour with time and a half for overtime and worked 47 hours during a recent week. Find his gross pay for the week.

8. Lacy Dodd earns a monthly salary of $2,988 and is nonexempt from FLSA. Last week she worked 52 hours. What are her overtime earnings for the week?

9. Drew Darling earns a monthly salary of $2,756 and is nonexempt from FLSA. Last week he worked 58 hours. What are his overtime earnings for the week?

10. A belt manufacturer pays a worker $0.84 for each buckle she correctly attaches to a belt. If Yolanda Jackson had the following work record, find the gross earnings for the week: Monday, 132 buckles; Tuesday, 134 buckles; Wednesday, 138 buckles; Thursday, 134 buckles; Friday, 130 buckles. *See Example 5.*

APPLICATIONS

11. Last week, Laurie Golson packaged 289 boxes of Holiday Cheese Assortment. Find her gross weekly earnings if she is paid at the following differential piece rate. *See Example 6.*

   Cheese boxes
packaged per week	Pay per package
1–100	$1.88
101–300	$2.08
301 and over	$2.18

12. Joe Thweatt makes icons for a major distributor. He is paid $9.13 for each icon and records the following number of completed icons: Monday, 14; Tuesday, 11; Wednesday, 10; Thursday, 12; Friday, 12. How much will he be paid for his work for the week? *See Example 5.*

See Example 7.

13. Mark Moses is a paper mill sales representative who receives 6% of his total sales as commission. His sales last week totaled $8,972. Find his gross earnings for the week.

14. Mary Lee Strode is paid a straight commission on sales as a real estate salesperson. In one pay period she had a total of $452,493 in sales. What is her gross pay if the commission rate is $3\frac{1}{2}\%$?

See Example 8.

15. Molly Strawn receives 1.5% of eBay sales plus $2.15 for each item she lists through her eBay listing service. In August she listed 342 items that sold for a total of $18,206. What were her gross earnings?

16. Kay Darling receives 2% of eBay sales plus $1.85 for each item she lists through her eBay listing service. In February she listed 198 items that sold for a total of $15,981. What were her gross earnings?

See Example 9.

17. Dwayne Moody is paid on a salary-plus-commission basis. He receives $275 weekly in salary and a commission based on 5% of all weekly sales over $2,000. If he sold $7,821 in merchandise in one week, find his gross earnings for the week.

18. Vincent Ores sells equipment to receive satellite signals. He earns a 3% commission on monthly sales above $2,000. One month his sales totaled $145,938. What is his commission for the month?

10-2 PAYROLL DEDUCTIONS

LEARNING OUTCOMES

1 Find federal tax withholding per paycheck using IRS tax tables.
2 Find federal tax withholding per paycheck using the IRS percentage method.
3 Find Social Security tax and Medicare tax per paycheck.
4 Find net earnings per paycheck.

As anyone who has ever drawn a paycheck knows, many deductions may be subtracted from gross pay. Deductions may include federal, state, and local income or payroll taxes, Social Security and Medicare taxes, union dues, medical insurance payments, credit union payments, and a host of others. By law, employers are responsible for withholding and paying their employee's payroll taxes.

MARRIED Persons—WEEKLY Payroll Period
(For Wages Paid through December 2012)

And the wages are–		And the number of withholding allowances claimed is—										
At least	But less than	0	1	2	3	4	5	6	7	8	9	10
		The amount of income tax to be withheld is—										
$ 0	$160	$0	$0	$0	$0	$0	$0	$0	$0	$0	$0	$0
160	165	1	0	0	0	0	0	0	0	0	0	0
165	170	1	0	0	0	0	0	0	0	0	0	0
170	175	2	0	0	0	0	0	0	0	0	0	0
175	180	2	0	0	0	0	0	0	0	0	0	0
180	185	3	0	0	0	0	0	0	0	0	0	0
185	190	3	0	0	0	0	0	0	0	0	0	0
190	195	4	0	0	0	0	0	0	0	0	0	0
195	200	4	0	0	0	0	0	0	0	0	0	0
200	210	5	0	0	0	0	0	0	0	0	0	0
210	220	6	0	0	0	0	0	0	0	0	0	0
220	230	7	0	0	0	0	0	0	0	0	0	0
230	240	8	1	0	0	0	0	0	0	0	0	0
240	250	9	2	0	0	0	0	0	0	0	0	0
250	260	10	3	0	0	0	0	0	0	0	0	0
260	270	11	4	0	0	0	0	0	0	0	0	0
270	280	12	5	0	0	0	0	0	0	0	0	0
280	290	13	6	0	0	0	0	0	0	0	0	0
290	300	14	7	0	0	0	0	0	0	0	0	0
300	310	15	8	0	0	0	0	0	0	0	0	0
310	320	16	9	1	0	0	0	0	0	0	0	0
320	330	17	10	2	0	0	0	0	0	0	0	0
330	340	18	11	3	0	0	0	0	0	0	0	0
340	350	19	12	4	0	0	0	0	0	0	0	0
350	360	20	13	5	0	0	0	0	0	0	0	0
360	370	21	14	6	0	0	0	0	0	0	0	0
370	380	22	15	7	0	0	0	0	0	0	0	0
380	390	23	16	8	1	0	0	0	0	0	0	0
390	400	24	17	9	2	0	0	0	0	0	0	0
400	410	25	18	10	3	0	0	0	0	0	0	0
410	420	26	19	11	4	0	0	0	0	0	0	0
420	430	27	20	12	5	0	0	0	0	0	0	0
430	440	28	21	13	6	0	0	0	0	0	0	0
440	450	29	22	14	7	0	0	0	0	0	0	0
450	460	30	23	15	8	1	0	0	0	0	0	0
460	470	31	24	16	9	2	0	0	0	0	0	0
470	480	32	25	17	10	3	0	0	0	0	0	0
480	490	33	26	18	11	4	0	0	0	0	0	0
490	500	34	27	19	12	5	0	0	0	0	0	0
500	510	36	28	20	13	6	0	0	0	0	0	0
510	520	37	29	21	14	7	0	0	0	0	0	0
520	530	39	30	22	15	8	0	0	0	0	0	0
530	540	40	31	23	16	9	1	0	0	0	0	0
540	550	42	32	24	17	10	2	0	0	0	0	0
550	560	43	33	25	18	11	3	0	0	0	0	0
560	570	45	34	26	19	12	4	0	0	0	0	0
570	580	46	35	27	20	13	5	0	0	0	0	0
580	590	48	37	28	21	14	6	0	0	0	0	0
590	600	49	38	29	22	15	7	0	0	0	0	0
600	610	51	40	30	23	16	8	1	0	0	0	0
610	620	52	41	31	24	17	9	2	0	0	0	0
620	630	54	43	32	25	18	10	3	0	0	0	0
630	640	55	44	33	26	19	11	4	0	0	0	0
640	650	57	46	35	27	20	12	5	0	0	0	0
650	660	58	47	36	28	21	13	6	0	0	0	0
660	670	60	49	38	29	22	14	7	0	0	0	0
670	680	61	50	39	30	23	15	8	1	0	0	0
680	690	63	52	41	31	24	16	9	2	0	0	0
690	700	64	53	42	32	25	17	10	3	0	0	0
700	710	66	55	44	33	26	18	11	4	0	0	0
710	720	67	56	45	34	27	19	12	5	0	0	0
720	730	69	58	47	36	28	20	13	6	0	0	0
730	740	70	59	48	37	29	21	14	7	0	0	0
740	750	72	61	50	39	30	22	15	8	0	0	0
750	760	73	62	51	40	31	23	16	9	1	0	0
760	770	75	64	53	42	32	24	17	10	2	0	0
770	780	76	65	54	43	33	25	18	11	3	0	0
780	790	78	67	56	45	34	26	19	12	4	0	0
790	800	79	68	57	46	35	27	20	13	5	0	0

FIGURE 10-3

Portion of IRS Withholding Table for Married Persons Paid Weekly

MARRIED Persons—WEEKLY Payroll Period
(For Wages Paid through December 2012)

And the wages are—		And the number of withholding allowances claimed is—										
At least	But less than	0	1	2	3	4	5	6	7	8	9	10
		The amount of income tax to be withheld is—										
$800	$810	$81	$70	$59	$48	$37	$28	$21	$14	$6	$0	$0
810	820	82	71	60	49	38	29	22	15	7	0	0
820	830	84	73	62	51	40	30	23	16	8	1	0
830	840	85	74	63	52	41	31	24	17	9	2	0
840	850	87	76	65	54	43	32	25	18	10	3	0
850	860	88	77	66	55	44	33	26	19	11	4	0
860	870	90	79	68	57	46	35	27	20	12	5	0
870	880	91	80	69	58	47	36	28	21	13	6	0
880	890	93	82	71	60	49	38	29	22	14	7	0
890	900	94	83	72	61	50	39	30	23	15	8	1
900	910	96	85	74	63	52	41	31	24	16	9	2
910	920	97	86	75	64	53	42	32	25	17	10	3
920	930	99	88	77	66	55	44	33	26	18	11	4
930	940	100	89	78	67	56	45	34	27	19	12	5
940	950	102	91	80	69	58	47	36	28	20	13	6
950	960	103	92	81	70	59	48	37	29	21	14	7
960	970	105	94	83	72	61	50	39	30	22	15	8
970	980	106	95	84	73	62	51	40	31	23	16	9
980	990	108	97	86	75	64	53	42	32	24	17	10
990	1,000	109	98	87	76	65	54	43	33	25	18	11
1,000	1,010	111	100	89	78	67	56	45	34	26	19	12
1,010	1,020	112	101	90	79	68	57	46	35	27	20	13
1,020	1,030	114	103	92	81	70	59	48	37	28	21	14
1,030	1,040	115	104	93	82	71	60	49	38	29	22	15
1,040	1,050	117	106	95	84	73	62	51	40	30	23	16
1,050	1,060	118	107	96	85	74	63	52	41	31	24	17
1,060	1,070	120	109	98	87	76	65	54	43	32	25	18
1,070	1,080	121	110	99	88	77	66	55	44	33	26	19
1,080	1,090	123	112	101	90	79	68	57	46	35	27	20
1,090	1,100	124	113	102	91	80	69	58	47	36	28	21
1,100	1,110	126	115	104	93	82	71	60	49	38	29	22
1,110	1,120	127	116	105	94	83	72	61	50	39	30	23
1,120	1,130	129	118	107	96	85	74	63	52	41	31	24
1,130	1,140	130	119	108	97	86	75	64	53	42	32	25
1,140	1,150	132	121	110	99	88	77	66	55	44	33	26
1,150	1,160	133	122	111	100	89	78	67	56	45	35	27
1,160	1,170	135	124	113	102	91	80	69	58	47	36	28
1,170	1,180	136	125	114	103	92	81	70	59	48	38	29
1,180	1,190	138	127	116	105	94	83	72	61	50	39	30
1,190	1,200	139	128	117	106	95	84	73	62	51	41	31
1,200	1,210	141	130	119	108	97	86	75	64	53	42	32
1,210	1,220	142	131	120	109	98	87	76	65	54	44	33
1,220	1,230	144	133	122	111	100	89	78	67	56	45	34
1,230	1,240	145	134	123	112	101	90	79	68	57	47	36
1,240	1,250	147	136	125	114	103	92	81	70	59	48	37
1,250	1,260	148	137	126	115	104	93	82	71	60	50	39
1,260	1,270	150	139	128	117	106	95	84	73	62	51	40
1,270	1,280	151	140	129	118	107	96	85	74	63	53	42
1,280	1,290	153	142	131	120	109	98	87	76	65	54	43
1,290	1,300	154	143	132	121	110	99	88	77	66	56	45
1,300	1,310	156	145	134	123	112	101	90	79	68	57	46
1,310	1,320	157	146	135	124	113	102	91	80	69	59	48
1,320	1,330	159	148	137	126	115	104	93	82	71	60	49
1,330	1,340	160	149	138	127	116	105	94	83	72	62	51
1,340	1,350	162	151	140	129	118	107	96	85	74	63	52
1,350	1,360	163	152	141	130	119	108	97	86	75	65	54
1,360	1,370	165	154	143	132	121	110	99	88	77	66	55
1,370	1,380	166	155	144	133	122	111	100	89	78	68	57
1,380	1,390	168	157	146	135	124	113	102	91	80	69	58
1,390	1,400	169	158	147	136	125	114	103	92	81	71	60

$1,400 and over	Use Table 1(b) for a **MARRIED person** on page 36. Also see the instructions on page 35.

FIGURE 10-3
Continued

EXAMPLE 2

Barry Strawn is married, has a gross weekly salary of $1,367, claims three withholding allowances, and has no allowable adjustments. Find the amount of withholding tax to be deducted from his gross salary.

Use Figure 10-3.	Select appropriate tax table for a married person who is paid weekly.
Use the row for interval "At least 1,360 but less than 1,370."	$1,367 is in the selected interval.
Use the column for three withholding allowances.	Find the intersection of the row and column.

The withholding tax is $132.

EXAMPLE 3

Haruna Jing is married, has a gross weekly salary of $615, claims two withholding allowances, and has allowable adjustments of $30. Find the amount of withholding tax to be deducted from her gross salary.

Find taxable earnings: $615 − $30 = $585

Use Figure 10-3.	Select appropriate tax table for a married person who is paid weekly.
Use the row for interval "At least $580 but less than $590."	$585 is in the selected interval.
Use the column for two withholding allowances.	Find the intersection of the row and column.

The withholding tax is $28.

STOP AND CHECK

See Example 1.

1. W. F. Kenoyer is single, claims two withholding allowances, has no allowable adjustments, and has a gross semimonthly income of $1,685. Find the amount of withholding tax to be deducted.

2. Dot Strawn is single, has no allowable adjustments, and claims one exemption for herself. Her semimonthly earnings are $2,020. How much withholding tax will be deducted?

See Example 2.

3. Kiyoshi Maruyama is married, has a weekly gross salary of $705, and has no allowable adjustments. He claims four withholding allowances. How much withholding tax will be deducted?

See Example 3.

4. D. M. Park earns $1,128 weekly and has allowable adjustments of $20. Find his withholding tax if he is married and claims seven withholding allowances.

2 Find federal tax withholding per paycheck using the IRS percentage method.

Percentage method income: the result of subtracting the appropriate withholding allowances when using the percentage method of withholding.

Percentage method of withholding: an alternative method to the tax tables for calculating employees' withholding taxes.

Instead of using the tax tables, many companies calculate federal tax withholding using software such as QuickBooks or Peachtree Accounting that uses the tax rates. Before using tax rates, the employer must deduct from the employee's adjusted gross income a tax-exempt amount based on the number of withholding allowances the employee claims. The resulting amount is sometimes called the **percentage method income.**

Figure 10-4 shows how much of an employee's adjusted gross income is exempt for each withholding allowance claimed, according to the type of pay period—weekly, biweekly, and so on. The table in Figure 10-4 is available from the IRS and is one of the tables used for calculating employees' withholding taxes. This method is called the **percentage method of withholding.**

Payroll Period	One Withholding Allowance
Weekly	$ 73.08
Biweekly	146.15
Semimonthly	158.33
Monthly	316.67
Quarterly	950.00
Semiannually	1,900.00
Annually	3,800.00
Daily or miscellaneous (each day of the payroll period)	14.62

FIGURE 10-4

2012 IRS Table for Figuring Withholding Allowance According to the Percentage Method

HOW TO   Find the percentage method income per paycheck

1. Find the exempt-per-allowance amount: From the withholding allowance table (Figure 10-4), identify the amount exempt for one withholding allowance according to the type of pay period.
2. Find the total exempt amount: Multiply the number of withholding allowances the employee claims by the exempt-per-allowance amount.
3. Subtract the total exempt amount from the employee's adjusted gross income for the pay period.

EXAMPLE 4   Find the percentage method income on Macy Strawn's biweekly gross earnings of $3,150. She has no adjustments to income, is single, and claims two withholding allowances on her W-4 form.

Because Macy has no adjustments to income, her gross earnings of $3,150 is her adjusted gross income. From the table in Figure 10-4, the amount exempt for one withholding allowance in a biweekly pay period is $146.15.

$2(\$146.15) = \$292.30$ Multiply the number of withholding allowances by the exempt-per-allowance amount.

$\$3,150 - \$292.30 = \$2,857.70$ Subtract the total exempt amount from the adjusted gross income.

The percentage method income is $2,857.70.

Once an employee's percentage method income is found, the employer consults the percentage method tables, also available from the IRS, to know how much of this income should be withheld (taxed at the appropriate tax rate), according to the employee's marital status and the type of pay period. Figure 10-5 shows the IRS percentage method tables.

HOW TO   Find federal tax withholding per paycheck using the IRS percentage method tables

1. Select the appropriate table in Figure 10-5 according to the employee's filing status and the type of pay period.
2. Find the income row: In the columns labeled "If the amount of wages (after subtracting withholding allowances) is:" select the "Over—" and "But not over—" interval that includes the employee's percentage method income for the pay period.
3. Find the cell where the income row and the column labeled "of excess over—" intersect, and subtract the amount given in this cell from the employee's percentage method income for the pay period.
4. Multiply the difference from step 3 by the percent given in the income row.
5. Add the product from step 4 to the amount given with the *percent* in the income row and "The amount of income tax to withhold is:" column.

Percentage Method Tables for Income Tax Withholding
(For Wages Paid in 2012)

TABLE 1—WEEKLY Payroll Period

(a) SINGLE person (including head of household)—

If the amount of wages (after subtracting withholding allowances) is:

The amount of income tax to withhold is:

Not over $41 . . . . $0

Over—	But not over—		of excess over—
$41	—$209	. . . . $0.00 plus 10%	—$41
$209	—$721	. . . . $16.80 plus 15%	—$209
$721	—$1,688	. . . . $93.60 plus 25%	—$721
$1,688	—$3,477	. . . . $335.35 plus 28%	—$1,688
$3,477	—$7,510	. . . . $836.27 plus 33%	—$3,477
$7,510	. . . .	$2,167.16 plus 35%	—$7,510

(b) MARRIED person—

If the amount of wages (after subtracting withholding allowances) is:

The amount of income tax to withhold is:

Not over $156 . . . . $0

Over—	But not over—		of excess over—
$156	—$490	. . . . $0.00 plus 10%	—$156
$490	—$1,515	. . . . $33.40 plus 15%	—$490
$1,515	—$2,900	. . . . $187.15 plus 25%	—$1,515
$2,900	—$4,338	. . . . $533.40 plus 28%	—$2,900
$4,338	—$7,624	. . . . $936.04 plus 33%	—$4,338
$7,624	. . . .	$2,020.42 plus 35%	—$7,624

[handwritten: test]

TABLE 2—BIWEEKLY Payroll Period

(a) SINGLE person (including head of household)—

If the amount of wages (after subtracting withholding allowances) is:

The amount of income tax to withhold is:

Not over $83 . . . . $0

Over—	But not over—		of excess over—
$83	—$417	. . . . $0.00 plus 10%	—$83
$417	—$1,442	. . . . $33.40 plus 15%	—$417
$1,442	—$3,377	. . . . $187.15 plus 25%	—$1,442
$3,377	—$6,954	. . . . $670.90 plus 28%	—$3,377
$6,954	—$15,019	. . . . $1,672.46 plus 33%	—$6,954
$15,019	. . . .	$4,333.91 plus 35%	—$15,019

[handwritten: Macy]

(b) MARRIED person—

If the amount of wages (after subtracting withholding allowances) is:

The amount of income tax to withhold is:

Not over $312 . . . . $0

Over—	But not over—		of excess over—
$312	—$981	. . . . $0.00 plus 10%	—$312
$981	—$3,031	. . . . $66.90 plus 15%	—$981
$3,031	—$5,800	. . . . $374.40 plus 25%	—$3,031
$5,800	—$8,675	. . . . $1,066.65 plus 28%	—$5,800
$8,675	—$15,248	. . . . $1,871.65 plus 33%	—$8,675
$15,248	. . . .	$4,040.74 plus 35%	—$15,248

TABLE 3—SEMIMONTHLY Payroll Period

(a) SINGLE person (including head of household)—

If the amount of wages (after subtracting withholding allowances) is:

The amount of income tax to withhold is:

Not over $90 . . . . $0

Over—	But not over—		of excess over—
$90	—$452	. . . . $0.00 plus 10%	—$90
$452	—$1,563	. . . . $36.20 plus 15%	—$452
$1,563	—$3,658	. . . . $202.85 plus 25%	—$1,563
$3,658	—$7,533	. . . . $726.60 plus 28%	—$3,658
$7,533	—$16,271	. . . . $1,811.60 plus 33%	—$7,533
$16,271	. . . .	$4,695.14 plus 35%	—$16,271

(b) MARRIED person—

If the amount of wages (after subtracting withholding allowances) is:

The amount of income tax to withhold is:

Not over $338 . . . . $0

Over—	But not over—		of excess over—
$338	—$1,063	. . . . $0.00 plus 10%	—$338
$1,063	—$3,283	. . . . $72.50 plus 15%	—$1,063
$3,283	—$6,283	. . . . $405.50 plus 25%	—$3,283
$6,283	—$9,398	. . . . $1,155.50 plus 28%	—$6,283
$9,398	—$16,519	. . . . $2,027.70 plus 33%	—$9,398
$16,519	. . . .	$4,377.63 plus 35%	—$16,519

TABLE 4—MONTHLY Payroll Period

(a) SINGLE person (including head of household)—

If the amount of wages (after subtracting withholding allowances) is:

The amount of income tax to withhold is:

Not over $179 . . . . $0

Over—	But not over—		of excess over—
$179	—$904	. . . . $0.00 plus 10%	—$179
$904	—$3,125	. . . . $72.50 plus 15%	—$904
$3,125	—$7,317	. . . . $405.65 plus 25%	—$3,125
$7,317	—$15,067	. . . . $1,453.65 plus 28%	—$7,317
$15,067	—$32,542	. . . . $3,623.65 plus 33%	—$15,067
$32,542	. . . .	$9,390.40 plus 35%	—$32,542

(b) MARRIED person—

If the amount of wages (after subtracting withholding allowances) is:

The amount of income tax to withhold is:

Not over $675 . . . . $0

Over—	But not over—		of excess over—
$675	—$2,125	. . . . $0.00 plus 10%	—$675
$2,125	—$6,567	. . . . $145.00 plus 15%	—$2,125
$6,567	—$12,567	. . . . $811.30 plus 25%	—$6,567
$12,567	—$18,796	. . . . $2,311.30 plus 28%	—$12,567
$18,796	—$33,038	. . . . $4,055.42 plus 33%	—$18,796
$33,038	. . . .	$8,755.28 plus 35%	—$33,038

FIGURE 10-5

IRS Tables for Percentage Method of Withholding

EXAMPLE 5 Find the federal withholding tax to be deducted from Macy's income in Example 4.

From Figure 10-5 select Table 2(a) for single employees paid biweekly. We found Macy's percentage method income to be $2,857.70 for the pay period. Table 2(a) tells us that the tax for that income is $187.15 plus 25% of the income in excess of $1,442.

$2,857.70 − $1,442 = $1,415.70 — Subtract $1,442 from the percentage method income to find the amount in excess of $1,442.

[handwritten: test — 3284.25 - 2900 = 384.25]

$1,415.70(0.25) = $353.93 — Find 25% of the income in excess of $1,442.

[handwritten: 384.25(0.28) = 107.59]

$187.15 + $353.93 = $541.08 — Add $353.93 to $187.15 to find the withholding tax.

[handwritten: 533.40 + 107.59 = 640.99]

The federal tax withholding is $541.08 for the pay period.

The withholding tax calculated by the percentage method may differ slightly from the withholding tax given in the tax table. The tax table uses $20 income intervals and tax amounts are rounded to the nearest dollar.

See Example 4.

1. Use the percentage method to find the total withholding allowance for weekly gross earnings of $850 with no adjustments if the wage earner is single and claims three withholding allowances.

2. Find the adjusted income after withholding allowances for the wage earner in Exercise 1.

See Example 5.

3. Find the amount of income tax to withhold for the wage earner in Exercise 1.

4. Emily Harrington earns $4,700 semimonthly and claims four withholding allowances and no other income adjustments. Emily is married. Find the amount of income tax to be withheld each pay period.

3 Find Social Security tax and Medicare tax per paycheck.

Two other amounts withheld from an employee's paycheck are the deductions for Social Security and Medicare taxes. The Federal Insurance Contribution Act (FICA) was established by Congress during the Depression of the 1930s. Prior to 1991, funds collected under the Social Security tax act were used for both Social Security and Medicare benefits. Beginning in 1991, funds were collected separately for these two programs.

The Social Security tax rate and the income subject to Social Security tax change periodically as Congress passes new legislation. In 2012, Congress enacted the Middle Class Tax Relief and Job Creation Act of 2012, which extended the Social Security tax withholding rate of 4.2% for employees that had been in effect for all of 2011. For 2012, the Social Security tax applies to the first $110,100 of wages for employees. The act extended the reduced rate for all of 2012. Updates can be found at www.irs.gov/pub15.

This means that after a person has earned $110,100 in a year, no Social Security tax will be withheld on any additional money he or she earns during that year. A person who earns $150,000 in a year pays exactly the same Social Security tax as a person who earns $110,100. In a recent year, the rate for Medicare was 1.45% (0.0145). All wages earned are subject to Medicare tax, unless the employee participates in a flexible benefits plan that is exempt from Medicare tax and under certain other conditions specified in the Internal Revenue Code. These plans are written to provide employees with a choice or "menu" of benefits such as health insurance, child care, and so on. In some instances, the wages used to pay for these benefits are subtracted from gross earnings to give an adjusted gross income that is used as the basis for withholding tax, Social Security tax, and Medicare tax.

Employers also pay a share of Social Security and Medicare taxes: Employers still pay a Social Security withholding tax rate of 6.2% for each employee on the first $110,100 of wages. Employers contribute the same amount as the employee contributes to that employee's Medicare account.

HOW TO   Find the amount of Social Security and Medicare tax to be paid by an employee

Social Security tax:
1. Determine the amount of the earnings subject to tax.
   (a) If the year-to-date earnings for the previous pay period exceeded $110,100, no additional Social Security tax is to be paid in this year.
   (b) If the year-to-date earnings exceed $110,100 for the first time this pay period, subtract the year-to-date earnings of the previous pay period from $110,100. This gives the untaxed part.
   (c) If the year-to-date earnings for this period are less than $110,100, the entire earnings for this period are subject to tax.
2. Multiply the earnings to be taxed by 4.2% (0.042). Round to the nearest cent.

Medicare tax:
Multiply the earnings to be taxed, which is all the current period earnings, by 1.45% (0.0145). Round to the nearest cent.

Use the same steps to find the amount of Social Security tax to be paid by the employer, but multiply by 6.2% rather than 4.2%. The employer pays the same amount of Medicare tax as the employee pays.

EXAMPLE 6 Mickey Beloate has a gross weekly income of $967. How much Social Security tax and Medicare tax should be withheld?

$967(52) = \$50,284$	The salary for the entire year will not exceed $110,100. The entire salary is to be taxed.
$967(0.042) = \$40.61$	Social Security tax on $967
$967(0.0145) = \$14.02$	Medicare tax on $967

The Social Security tax withheld per week should be $40.61, and the Medicare tax withheld should be $14.02.

EXAMPLE 7 John Friedlander, vice president of marketing for Golden Sun Enterprises, earns $118,300 annually, or $2,275 per week. Find the amount of Social Security and Medicare taxes that should be withheld for the 49th week.

At the end of the 49th week, John will have earned a total gross salary for the year of $111,475. The year-to-date earnings on the 48th week was $109,200 from $4 \times \$2,275$. Since Social Security tax is withheld on the first $110,100 annually, he needs to pay Social Security tax on $900 for the remainder of the year ($110,100 − $109,200 = $900).

$900(0.042) = \$37.80$ Multiply $900 by the 4.2% tax rate to find the Social Security tax for the 49th week.

Since Medicare tax is paid on the entire salary, John must pay the Medicare tax on the full week's salary of $2,275.

$$\$2,275(0.0145) = \$32.99$$

The Social Security tax for the 49th week is $37.80 and the Medicare tax is $32.99.

A person who is self-employed must also pay Social Security tax and Medicare tax. Because there is no employer involved to make matching contributions, the self-employed person must pay the equivalent of both amounts. The self-employment rates for 2012 are 10.4% Social Security and 2.9% Medicare tax for a total of 13.3%. For 2012, the maximum income for paying Social Security tax for persons who are self-employed is $110,100. The tax is called the **self-employment (SE) tax.** However, one-half of the self-employment tax can be deducted as an adjustment to income when finding the adjusted income for paying income tax. Self-employed persons report and pay taxes differently from people who receive a W-2.

Self-employment (SE) tax: the equivalent of both the employee's and the employer's tax for both Social Security and Medicare.

STOP AND CHECK

See Example 6.

1. Lars Pacheco has a gross biweekly income of $1,730. How much Social Security tax and Medicare tax should be withheld?

2. Jim Smith earns $6,230 monthly. How much Social Security tax and Medicare tax should be withheld from his monthly pay?

See Example 7.

3. Sarah Grafe earns $112,200 annually or $4,675 semimonthly. How much Social Security tax and Medicare tax should be withheld from her 24th paycheck of the year?

4. Ajala Lewis earns $112,112 annually or $2,156 per week. How much Social Security tax and Medicare tax should be withheld for the 47th week?

4 Find net earnings per paycheck.

In addition to federal taxes, a number of other deductions may be made from an employee's paycheck. Often, state and local income taxes must also be withheld by the employer. Other deductions are made at the employee's request, such as insurance payments or union dues. Some retirement plans and insurance plans are tax exempt; others are not. When all these deductions have been made, the amount left is called net earnings, net pay, or take-home pay.

HOW TO   Find net earnings per paycheck

1. Find the gross pay for the pay period.
2. Find the adjustments-to-income deductions, such as tax-exempt retirement, tax-exempt medical insurance, and so on.
3. Find the Social Security tax and Medicare tax based on the adjusted gross income.
4. Find the federal tax withholding based on (a) or (b):
   (a) Adjusted gross income (gross pay minus adjustments to income) using IRS tax tables.
   (b) Percentage method income (adjusted gross income minus amount exempt for withholding allowances) using IRS percentage method tables.
5. Find other withholding taxes, such as local or state taxes.
6. Find other deductions, such as insurance payments or union dues.
7. Find the sum of all deductions from steps 2–6, and subtract the sum from the gross pay.

EXAMPLE 8
Jeanetta Grandberry's gross weekly earnings are $976. She is married and claims two withholding allowances. Five percent of her gross earnings is deducted for her nonexempt retirement fund and $25.83 is deducted for nonexempt insurance. Find her net earnings.

Income tax withholding: $84	In Figure 10-3, find the amount of income tax to be withheld.
Social Security tax withholding: $976(0.042) = $40.99	Find the Social Security tax by the percentage method.
Medicare tax withholding: $976(0.0145) = $14.15	Find the Medicare tax by the percentage method.
Retirement fund withholding: 0.05($976) = $48.80	Use the formula $P = R \times B$. Multiply rate (5% = 0.05) by base (gross pay of $976).
Total deductions	Add all deductions including the nonexempt insurance.

= withholding tax + Social Security tax + Medicare tax + retirement fund + insurance
= $84.00   + $40.99   + $14.15   + $48.80   + $25.83 = $213.77

Net earnings:
Gross earnings − total deductions
  $976   − $213.77   = $762.23   Subtract total deductions from the gross earnings.

The net earnings are $762.23.

STOP AND CHECK

See Example 8.

1. Olena Koduri earns $1,032 weekly. She is married and claims three withholding allowances. $110.15 is deducted for nonexempt insurance and 6% of her gross earnings is deducted for nonexempt retirement. Find the amount deducted for retirement and Social Security and Medicare taxes.

2. Find the amount of withholding tax deducted.

3. Find the total deductions.

4. Find the net pay for Olena.

See Example 2.

1. Khalid Khouri is married, has a gross weekly salary of $686 (all of which is taxable), and claims three withholding allowances. Use the tax tables to find the federal tax withholding to be deducted from his weekly salary.

See Example 3.

2. Mae Swift is married and has a gross weekly salary of $783. She has $32 in adjustments to income for tax-exempt health insurance and claims two withholding allowances. Use the tax tables to find the federal tax withholding to be deducted from her weekly salary.

See Example 1.

3. Jacob Drewrey is paid semimonthly an adjusted gross income of $1,431. He is single and claims two withholding allowances. Use the tax tables to find the federal withholding tax to be deducted from his salary.

See Example 4.

4. Find the percentage method income on Darcie Love's weekly gross earnings of $2,985. She has no adjustments to income, is married, and claims four withholding allowances on her W-4 form.

See Example 5.

5. Find the federal withholding tax to be deducted from Darcie's income in Exercise 4.

See Examples 2 and 3.

6. Dieter Tillman earns a semimonthly salary of $1,698. He has a $100 adjustment-to-income flexible benefits package, is single, and claims three withholding allowances. Find the federal tax withholding to be deducted from his salary using the percentage method tables.

See Examples 2 and 3.

7. Carter Manning has a weekly adjusted gross income of $980, is single, and claims one withholding allowance. Find the federal tax withholding to be deducted from his weekly paycheck using the percentage method tables.

8. Margie Young is an associate professor at a major research university and earns $6,598 monthly with no adjustments to income. She is married and claims one withholding allowance. Find the federal tax withholding that is deducted from her monthly paycheck using the percentage method tables.

See Example 6.

9. Dr. Josef Young earns an adjusted gross weekly income of $2,583. How much Social Security tax should be withheld the first week of the year? How much Medicare tax should be withheld?

10. Dierdri Williams earns a gross biweekly income of $1,020 and has no adjustments to income. How much Social Security tax should be withheld? How much Medicare tax should be withheld?

See Example 7.

11. Rodney Whitaker earns $116,904 annually and is paid monthly. How much Social Security tax will be deducted from his December earnings? How much Medicare tax will be deducted from his December earnings?

See Example 8.

12. Pam Trim earns $5,291 monthly, is married, and claims four withholding allowances. Her company pays her retirement, but she pays $52.83 each month for nonexempt insurance premiums. Find her net pay.

See Example 8

13. Shirley Riddle earns $2,319 biweekly. She is single and claims no withholding allowances. She saves 2% of her salary for retirement and pays $22.80 in nonexempt insurance premiums each pay period. What are her net earnings for each pay period?

14. Donna Wood's gross weekly earnings are $715. Three percent of her gross earnings is deducted for her nonexempt retirement fund and $25.97 is deducted for nonexempt insurance. Find the net earnings if Donna is married and claims two withholding allowances.

10-3 THE EMPLOYER'S PAYROLL TAXES

LEARNING OUTCOMES

1 Find an employer's total deposit for withholding tax, Social Security tax, and Medicare tax per pay period.
2 Find an employer's SUTA tax and FUTA tax due for a quarter.

1 Find an employer's total deposit for withholding tax, Social Security tax, and Medicare tax per pay period.

The employer must pay to the Internal Revenue Service the income tax withheld and both the employees' and employer's Social Security and Medicare taxes. This payment is made by making a deposit at an authorized financial institution or Federal Reserve bank. If the employer's

An employee can request that additional income tax be withheld from each pay check.

accumulated tax is less than $500 for the quarter, this payment may be made with the tax return (generally Form 941, Employer's Quarterly Federal Tax Return). Other circumstances create a different employer's deposit schedule. This schedule varies depending on the amount of tax liability and other criteria. IRS Publication 15 (Circular E, Employer's Tax Guide) and Publication 334 (Tax Guide for Small Business) give the criteria for depositing and reporting these taxes.

HOW TO Find an employer's total deposit for withholding tax, Social Security tax, and Medicare tax per pay period

1. Find the withholding tax deposit: From employee payroll records, find the total withholding tax for all employees for the period.
2. Find the Social Security tax deposit: Find the total Social Security tax paid by all employees for the pay period. Find the employee's Social Security tax for each employee by multiplying the gross earnings that are below the $110,100 maximum times 4.2%. Add the employee's total and the employer's total for the amount of the Social Security tax deposit for this period.
3. Find the Medicare tax deposit: Find the total Medicare tax paid by all employees for the pay period and multiply the total by 2 to include the employer's matching tax.
4. Add the withholding tax deposit, Social Security tax deposit, and Medicare tax deposit.

EXAMPLE 1
Determine the employer's total deposit of withholding tax, Social Security tax, and Medicare tax for the payroll register.

Payroll for June 1 through June 15, 2012

Employee	Gross earnings	Withholding	Employee Social Security	Employer Social Security	Medicare	Net earnings
Plumlee, C.	$1,050.00	$ 52	$44.10	$ 65.10	$15.23	$ 938.67
Powell, M.	2,085.00	220.03	87.57	129.27	30.23	1,747.17
Randle, M.	1,995.00	182.42	83.79	123.69	28.93	1,699.86
Robinson, J.	2,089.00	427.17	87.74	129.52	30.29	1,543.80

Total withholding = $52 + $220.03 + $182.42 + $427.17 = $881.62
Employee's Social Security = $44.10 + $87.57 + $83.79 + $87.74 = $303.20
Employer's Social Security = $65.10 + $129.27 + $123.69 + $129.52 = $447.58
Employee's Medicare = $15.23 + $30.23 + $28.93 + $30.29 = $104.68
Employer's Medicare = $104.68
Total employer's deposit = $881.62 + $303.20 + $447.58 + $104.68 + $104.68 = $1,841.76

The total amount of the employer's deposit for this payroll is $1,841.76.

Bookkeeping software will compile payroll records and generate a report of tax liability for a month, quarter, or any selected time interval.

STOP AND CHECK

Use the following weekly payroll register for Exercises 1–4. See Example 1.

Weekly Payroll Register

Employee	Gross earnings	Withholding	Employee Social Security	Employer Social Security	Medicare	Net earnings
Cohen, P.	$740	$61	$31.08	$45.88	$10.73	$637.19
Faneca, T.	867	90	36.41	53.75	12.57	728.02
Gex, M.	630	33	26.46	39.06	9.14	561.40
Hasan, F.	695	53	29.19	43.09	10.08	602.73

1. Find the total withholding tax for the employer payroll register.
2. Find the total Social Security tax withheld from employees' pay.
3. Find the total Medicare tax withheld from employees' pay.
4. Find the employer's total deposit for the payroll register.

2 Find an employer's SUTA tax and FUTA tax due for a quarter.

The major employee-related taxes paid by employers are the employer's share of the Social Security and Medicare taxes, which we already have discussed, and federal and state unemployment taxes. Federal and state unemployment taxes do not affect the paycheck of the employee. They are paid entirely by the employer. Under the Federal Unemployment Tax Act (FUTA) most employers pay a federal unemployment tax. This tax, along with state unemployment tax, provides for payment of unemployment compensation to workers who have lost their job under certain conditions. **Federal unemployment (FUTA) tax** is currently 6.2% of the first $7,000 earned by an employee.

According to IRS Publication *Instructions for Form 940*, Employer's Annual Federal Unemployment (FUTA) Tax Return, employers "are entitled to the maximum credit if [they] paid all state unemployment tax by the due date of [their] Form 940 or if [they] are not required to pay state unemployment tax during the calendar year due to [their] state experience rate." The FUTA tax rate for an employer receiving the maximum credit against FUTA taxes is 0.8% of the first $7,000 of each employee's annual wages. **State Unemployment Tax (SUTA)** is a state tax required of most employers that provides funds for payments of unemployment compensation to workers who have lost their jobs under certain conditions. The SUTA tax rate varies from state to state and employer to employer depending on the employer's experience rate and is paid to each state separately from FUTA tax. SUTA tax guidelines vary from state to state. For our examples, we will use 5.4% of the first $7,000 of each employee's annual wages.

Federal unemployment (FUTA) tax: a federal tax required of most employers. The tax provides for payment of unemployment compensation to certain workers who have lost their jobs.

State unemployment (SUTA) tax: a state tax required of most employers. The tax also provides payment of unemployment compensation to certain workers who have lost their jobs.

HOW TO   Find the SUTA tax due for a quarter

1. For each employee, multiply 5.4% or the employer's appropriate rate by the employee's cumulative earnings for the quarter (up to $7,000 annually).
2. Add the SUTA tax owed on all employees.

According to the IRS, "If [employers] were not required to pay state unemployment tax because all of the wages [employers] paid were excluded from state unemployment tax, [employers] must pay FUTA tax at the 6.2% (0.062) rate." FUTA tax is accumulated by the employer for all employees and is deposited quarterly if the amount exceeds $500. Amounts less than $500 are paid with the annual tax return that is due January 31 of the following year.

HOW TO   Find the FUTA tax due for a quarter

1. For each employee:
   (a) If no SUTA tax is required, multiply 6.2% by the employee's cumulative earnings for the quarter (up to $7,000 annually).
   (b) If SUTA tax is required and paid by the due date, multiply 0.8% by the employee's cumulative earnings for the quarter (up to $7,000 annually).
2. Add the FUTA tax owed on all employees' wages for the quarter.
3. If the total from step 2 is less than $500, no FUTA tax is due for the quarter, but the total from step 2 must be added to the amount due for the next quarter.

EXAMPLE 2
Melanie McFarren earned $32,500 last year and over $7,000 in the first quarter of this year. If the SUTA tax rate for her employer is 5.4% of the first $7,000 earned in a year, how much SUTA tax must Melanie's employer pay on her behalf? Also, how much FUTA must be paid?

SUTA = tax rate × taxable wages $7,000 is subject to SUTA tax in the first quarter.
SUTA = 5.4%($7,000)
SUTA = 0.054($7,000) = $378
FUTA = 0.8% × taxable wages $7,000 is subject to FUTA tax in the first quarter.
          0.008($7,000) = $56

SUTA tax is $378 and FUTA tax is $56.

EXAMPLE 3 Leak Busters has two employees who are paid semimonthly. One employee earns $1,040 per pay period and the other earns $985 per pay period. Based on the SUTA tax rate of 5.4%, the FUTA tax rate is 0.8% of the first $7,000 of each employee's annual gross pay. At the end of which quarter should the FUTA tax first be deposited?

What You Know	What You Are Looking For
Employee 1 pay = $1,040 Employee 2 pay = $985 Semimonthly pay period FUTA rate = 0.8% of 1st $7,000 FUTA deposit not required until accumulated amount is more than $500.	First FUTA deposit should be made at the end of which quarter?

Solution Plan

Find the FUTA tax for each employee for each pay period and total the tax by quarters.

Solution

Pay period	Employee 1 salary	Accumulated salary subject to FUTA tax	FUTA tax	Employee 2 salary	Accumulated salary subject to FUTA tax	FUTA tax
Jan. 15	$1,040	$1,040	$8.32	$985	$ 985	$7.88
Jan. 31	1,040	2,080	8.32	985	1,970	7.88
Feb. 15	1,040	3,120	8.32	985	2,955	7.88
Feb. 28	1,040	4,160	8.32	985	3,940	7.88
Mar. 15	1,040	5,200	8.32	985	4,925	7.88
Mar. 31	1,040	6,240	8.32	985	5,910	7.88

First quarter FUTA tax totals: $8.32(6) + $7.88(6) = 49.92 + 47.28 = $97.20
$97.20 is less than $500.00, so no deposit should be made at the end of the first quarter.

Pay period	Employee 1 salary	Accumulated salary subject to FUTA tax	FUTA tax	Employee 2 salary	Accumulated salary subject to FUTA tax	FUTA tax
Apr. 15	$1,040	$7,000	$6.08*	$985	$6,895	$7.88
Apr. 30	1,040			985	7,000	0.84**
May 15	1,040			985		
May 31	1,040			985		
Jun. 15	1,040			985		
Jun. 30	1,040			985		

*$7,000 − $6,240 = $760; $760(0.008) = $6.08
**$7,000 − $6,895 = $105; $105(0.008) = $0.84

Second quarter FUTA tax totals: $6.08 + $7.88 + $0.84 = $14.80
Total FUTA tax for first two quarters = $97.20 + $14.80 = $112.00

Conclusion

Because both employees have reached the $7,000 accumulated salary subject to FUTA tax, and the accumulated FUTA tax is less than $500, the amount of $112.00 should be deposited by the end of the month following the fourth quarter, or by January 31 of the following year.

STOP AND CHECK

See Example 2.

1. Kumar Konde earned $35,200 last year and over $7,000 in the first quarter of this year. State unemployment tax for Kumar's employer is 5.4% of the first $7,000 earned in a year. How much SUTA tax must Kumar's employer pay on his behalf?

2. In Exercise 1, how much FUTA tax must Kumar's employer pay on his behalf?

See Example 3.

3. Powell's Lumber Company has two employees who are paid semimonthly. One employee earns $1,320 and the other earns $1,275 per pay period. At the end of which quarter must the first FUTA tax be deposited for the year if the company's SUTA rate is 5.4% of the first $7,000 earnings for each employee?

4. In Exercise 3, how much FUTA tax should be deposited by Powell's Lumber Company with the first payment of the year?

10-3 SECTION EXERCISES

SKILL BUILDERS

See Example 1.

1. Carolyn Luttrell owns Just the Right Thing, a small antiques shop with four employees. For one payroll period the total withholding tax for all employees was $1,633. The total employees' Social Security tax was $163, and the total employer's Social Security tax was $241. The total employees' Medicare tax was $113. How much tax must Carolyn deposit as the employer's share of Social Security tax and Medicare tax? What is the total tax that must be deposited?

2. Hughes' Trailer Manufacturer makes utility trailers and has seven employees who are paid weekly. For one payroll period the withholding tax for all employees was $1,661. The total Social Security tax withheld from employees' paychecks was $412, the employer's share of Social Security tax was $608, and the total Medicare tax withheld was $142. What is the total tax that must be deposited by Hughes?

3. Determine the employer's deposit of withholding Social Security, and Medicare for the payroll register.

Employee	Gross earnings	Withholding	Employee's Social Security	Medicare	Net earnings	Employer's Social Security
Paszel, J.	$1,905	$160	$80.01	$27.62	$1,637.37	$118.11
Thomas, P.	1,598	159	67.12	23.17	1,348.71	99.08
Tillman, D.	1,431	88	60.10	20.75	1,262.15	88.72

4. Heaven Sent Gifts, a small business that provides custom meals, flowers, and other specialty gifts, has three employees who are paid weekly. One employee earns $875 per week, is single, and claims one withholding allowance. Another employee earns $850 per week, is married, and claims two withholding allowances. The manager earns $940 per week, is married, and claims one withholding allowance. Calculate the amount of withholding tax, Social Security tax, and Medicare tax that will need to be deposited by Heaven Sent Gifts.

APPLICATIONS

Bruce Young earned $30,418 last year. His employer's SUTA tax rate is 5.4% of the first $7,000. See Example 2.

5. How much SUTA tax must Bruce's employer pay for him?

6. How much FUTA tax must Bruce's company pay for him?

7. Bailey Plyler has three employees in his carpet cleaning business. The payroll is semimonthly and the employees earn $745, $780, and $1,030 per pay period. Calculate when and in what amounts FUTA tax payments are to be made for the year. *See Example 3.*

SUMMARY

Learning Outcomes

Section 10-1

What to Remember with Examples

1 Find the gross pay per paycheck based on salary. (p. 344)

1. Identify the number of pay periods per year: monthly, 12; semimonthly, 24; biweekly, 26; weekly, 52.
2. Divide the annual salary by the number of pay periods per year. Round to the nearest cent.

> If Barbara earns $23,500 per year, how much is her weekly gross pay?
>
> $$\frac{\$23,500}{52} = \$451.92$$
>
> Clemetee earns $32,808 annually and is paid twice a month. What is her gross pay per pay period?
>
> $$\frac{\$32,808}{24} = \$1,367$$

2 Find the gross pay per weekly paycheck based on hourly wage. (p. 345)

1. Find the regular pay:
   (a) If the hours worked in the week are 40 or fewer, multiply the hours worked by the hourly wage.
   (b) If the hours worked are more than 40, multiply 40 hours by the hourly wage.
2. Find the overtime pay:
   (a) If the hours worked are 40 or fewer, the overtime pay is $0.
   (b) If the hours worked are more than 40, subtract 40 from the hours worked and multiply the difference by the overtime rate.
3. Add the regular pay and the overtime pay.

> Aldo earns $10.25 per hour. He worked 38 hours this week. What is his gross pay?
>
> $38(\$10.25) = \$389.50$
>
> Belinda worked 44 hours one week. Her regular pay was $7.75 per hour and time and a half for overtime. Find her gross earnings.
>
> $$40(\$7.75) = \$310$$
> $$4(\$7.75)(1.5) = \$46.50$$
> $$\$310 + \$46.50 = \$356.50$$

3 Find the gross pay per paycheck based on piecework wage. (p. 346)

1. If a *straight piecework rate* is used, multiply the number of items completed by the straight piecework rate.
2. If a *differential piecework rate* is used:
   (a) For each rate category, multiply the number of items produced for the category by the rate for the category.
   (b) Add the pay for all rate categories.

> Willy earns $0.53 for each widget he twists. He twisted 1,224 widgets last week. Find his gross earnings.
>
> $1,224(\$0.53) = \$648.72$
>
> Nadine does piecework for a jeweler and earns $0.65 per piece for finishing 1 to 25 pins, $0.70 per piece for 26 to 50 pins, and $0.75 per piece for pins over 50. Yesterday she finished 130 pins. How much did she earn?
>
> $$25(\$0.65) + 25(\$0.70) + 80(\$0.75) =$$
> $$\$16.25 + \quad \$17.50 + \quad \$60 \quad = \$93.75$$

4 Find the gross pay per paycheck based on commission. (p. 348)

1. Find the commission:
   (a) If the commission is *commission based on total sales,* multiply the commission rate by the total sales for the pay period.
   (b) If the commission is *commission based on quota,* subtract the quota from the total sales and multiply the difference by the commission rate.

2. Find the salary:
   (a) If the wage is *straight commission,* the salary is $0.
   (b) If the wage is *commission-plus-salary,* determine the gross pay based on salary.
3. Add the commission and the salary.

Bart earns a 4% commission on the appliances he sells. His sales last week totaled $18,000. Find his gross earnings.

$$0.04(\$18,000) = \$720$$

Elaine earns $250 weekly plus 6% of all sales over $1,500. Last week she had $9,500 worth of sales. Find her gross earnings.

$$\$9,500 - \$1,500 = \$8,000$$
$$\text{Commission} = 0.06(\$8,000) = \$480$$
$$\$250 + \$480 = \$730$$

Section 10-2

1 Find federal tax withholding per paycheck using IRS tax tables. (p. 351)

1. Find the adjusted gross income by subtracting the total allowable adjustments from the gross pay per pay period. Select the appropriate table according to the employee's filing status (single, married, or head of household) and according to the type of pay period (weekly, biweekly, and so on).
2. Find the income row: In the columns labeled "If the wages are—," select the "At least" and "But less than" interval that includes the employee's adjusted gross income for the pay period.
3. Find the allowances column: In the columns labeled "And the number of withholding allowances claimed is—," select the number of allowances the employee claims.
4. Find the cell where the income row and allowance column intersect. The correct tax is given in this cell.

Archy is married, has a gross weekly salary of $680, and claims two withholding allowances. Find his withholding tax.

Look in the first two columns of Figure 10-3 to find the range for $680. Move across to the column for two withholding allowances. The amount of federal tax to be withheld is $41.

Lexie Lagen is married and has a gross weekly salary of $855. He claims three withholding allowances and has $20 deducted weekly from his paycheck for a flexible benefits plan, which is exempted from federal income taxes. Find the amount of his withholding tax.

$$\text{Adjusted gross income} = \$855 - \$20 = \$835$$

Find the range for $835 and three withholding allowances in Figure 10-3. The tax is $52.

---

2 Find federal tax withholding per paycheck using the IRS percentage method. (p. 357)

Find the percentage method income per paycheck.

1. Find the exempt-per-allowance amount: From the withholding allowance table (Figure 10-4), identify the amount exempt for one withholding allowance according to the type of pay period.
2. Find the total exempt amount: Multiply the number of withholding allowances the employee claims by the exempt-per-allowance amount.
3. Subtract the total exempt amount from the employee's adjusted gross income for the pay period.

Edith Sailor has weekly gross earnings of $1,590. Find her percentage method income tax if she has no adjustments to income, is married, and claims three withholding allowances.

Use Figure 10-4 to find one withholding allowance for a weekly payroll period. Multiply by 3.

$$\$73.08(3) = \$219.24$$

Percentage method income = $1,590.00 - $219.24 = $1,370.76.

Find the federal tax withholding per paycheck using the IRS percentage method tables.

1. Select the appropriate table in Figure 10-5 according to the employee's filing status and the type of pay period.
2. Find the income row: In the columns labeled "If the amount of wages (after subtracting withholding allowances) is:" select the "Over—" and "But not over—" interval that includes the employee's percentage method income for the pay period.

3. Find the cell where the income row and the column labeled "of excess over—" intersect, and subtract the amount given in this cell from the employee's percentage method income for the pay period.
4. Multiply the difference from step 3 by the percent given in the income row.
5. Add the product from step 4 to the amount given with the *percent* in the income row and "The amount of income tax to withhold is:" column.

Find the federal withholding tax on Ruth's monthly income of $3,938. She is single and claims one exemption.

1 exemption = $316.67   (Figure 10-4)
$3,938 − $316.67 = $3,621.33
$3,621.33 is in the $3,125 to $7,317 range (Figure 10-5, Table 4a), so the amount of withholding tax is $405.66 plus 25% of the amount over $3,125.

$3,621.33 − $3,125 = $496.33
$496.33(0.25) = $124.08
$405.65 + $124.08 = $529.73

3 Find Social Security tax and Medicare tax per paycheck. (p. 360)

Social Security tax:
1. Determine the amount of the employee earnings subject to tax.
   (a) If the year-to-date earnings for the previous pay period exceed $110,100, no additional Social Security tax is to be paid.
   (b) If the year-to-date earnings exceed $110,100 for the first time this pay period, subtract the year-to-date earnings of the previous pay period from $110,100 to get the untaxed excess.
   (c) If the year-to-date earnings for this period are less than $110,100, the entire earnings for this period are subject to tax.
2. Multiply the earnings to be taxed by 4.2% (0.042). Round to the nearest cent.

Medicare tax:
   Multiply all the current period earnings by 1.45% (0.0145). Round to the nearest cent.

Find the Social Security and Medicare taxes for Abbas Laknahour, who earns $938 every two weeks.

Social Security = $938(0.042) = $39.40
Medicare = $938(0.0145) = $13.60

Donna Shroyer earns $9,870 monthly. Find the Social Security and Medicare taxes that will be deducted from her December paycheck.

Pay for first 11 months = $9,870(11) = $108,570
December pay subject to Social Security = $110,100 − $108,570 = $1,530
Social Security tax = $1,530(0.042) = $64.26
Medicare tax = $9,870(0.0145) = $143.12

4 Find net earnings per paycheck. (p. 362)

1. Find the gross pay for the pay period.
2. Find the adjustments-to-income deductions, such as tax exempt retirement, tax exempt medical insurance, and so on.
3. Find the Social Security tax and Medicare tax based on the adjusted gross income.
4. Find the federal tax withholding based on (a) or (b):
   (a) Adjusted gross income (gross pay minus adjustments to income) using IRS tax tables;
   (b) Percentage method income (adjusted gross income minus amount exempt for withholding allowances) using IRS percentage method tables.
5. Find other withholding taxes, such as local or state taxes.
6. Find other deductions, such as insurance payments or union dues.
7. Find the sum of all deductions from steps 2–6, and subtract the sum from the gross pay.

Beth Cooley's gross weekly earnings are $788. Four percent of her gross earnings is deducted for her nonexempt retirement fund and $27.48 is deducted for nonexempt insurance. Find her net earnings if Beth is married and claims three withholding allowances.

Retirement fund = $788(0.04) = $31.52
Withholding tax = $45.00 (from Figure 10-3)
Social Security = $788(0.042) = $33.10
Medicare = $788(0.0145) = $11.43
Total deductions = $31.52 + $27.48 + $45.00 + $33.10 + $11.43 = $148.53
Net earnings = $788 − $148.53 = $639.47

Section 10-3

1 Find an employer's total deposit for withholding tax, Social Security tax, and Medicare tax per pay period. (p. 364)

1. Find the withholding tax deposit: From employee payroll records, find the total withholding tax for all employees for the pay period.
2. Find the Social Security tax deposit: Find the total Social Security tax paid by all employees for the pay period and find the total Social Security tax paid by the employer for all employees. Add the two amounts.
3. Find the Medicare tax deposit: Find the total Medicare tax paid by all employees for the pay period and multiply this total by 2 to include the employer's matching tax.
4. Add the withholding tax deposit, Social Security tax deposit, and Medicare tax deposit.

Determine the employer's total deposit.

Employee	Gross earnings	Withholding	Employees' Social Security	Employees' Medicare	Net earnings
Davis, T.	$ 985.00	$ 24	$ 41.37	$14.28	$ 905.35
Dobbins, L.	832.00	41	34.94	12.06	744.00
Harris, M.	790.00	46	33.18	11.46	699.36
Totals	$2,607.00	$111	$109.49	$37.80	$2,348.71

Employer's Social Security tax = $985(0.062) + $832(0.062) + $790(0.062) =
$61.07 + $51.58 + $48.98 = $161.63
Employer's tax deposit = $111 + $109.49 + $37.80 + $161.63 + $37.80 = $457.72

2 Find an employer's SUTA tax and FUTA tax due for a quarter. (p. 366)

Find the SUTA tax due for a quarter.
1. For each employee, multiply 5.4% or the appropriate rate by the employee's cumulative earnings for the quarter (up to $7,000 annually).
2. Add the SUTA tax owed on all employees.

Kim Brown has three employees who each earn $8,250 in the first three months of the year. How much SUTA tax should Kim pay for the first quarter if the SUTA rate is 5.4% of the first $7,000 earnings for each employee?

$7,000(0.054)(3) = $1,134

Kim should pay $1,134 in SUTA tax for the first quarter since the amount is more than $500.

Find the FUTA tax due for a quarter.
1. For each employee:
   (a) If no SUTA tax is required, multiply 6.2% by the employee's cumulative earnings for the quarter (up to $7,000 annually).
   (b) If SUTA tax is required and paid by the due date, multiply 0.8% by the employee's cumulative earnings for the quarter (up to $7,000 annually).
2. Add the FUTA tax owed on all employees' wages for the quarter.
3. If the total from step 2 is less than $500, no FUTA tax is due for the quarter, but the total from step 2 must be added to the amount due for the next quarter.

How much FUTA tax should Kim pay for the three employees?

$7,000(0.008)(3) = $168; to be paid in a future quarter

EXERCISES SET A

CHAPTER 10

SKILL BUILDERS

Find the gross earnings for each employee in Table 10-1. A regular week is 40 hours and the overtime rate is 1.5 times the regular rate.

TABLE 10-1

Employee	M	T	W	T	F	S	S	Hourly wage	Regular hours	Regular pay	Overtime hours	Overtime pay	Gross pay
1. Allen, H.	8	9	8	7	10	4	0	$ 9.86					
2. Pick, J.	8	8	8	8	8	4	0	$11.35					
3. Lovett, L.	8	8	8	8	0	0	0	$14.15					
4. Mitze, A.	8	8	8	8	8	2	4	$12.00					

5. Brian Williams is a salaried employee who earns $95,256 and is paid monthly. What is his pay each payroll period?

6. Varonia Reed is paid a weekly salary of $1,036. What is her annual salary?

7. Melanie Michael has a salaried and exempt job. She earns $825 a week. One week she worked 46 hours. Find her gross weekly earnings.

8. Glenda Chaille worked 27 hours in one week at $12.45 per hour. Find her gross earnings.

9. Susan Wood worked 52 hours in a week. She was paid at the hourly rate of $12.45 with time and a half for overtime. Find her gross earnings.

10. Ronald James is paid 1.5 times his hourly wage for all hours worked in a week exceeding 40. His hourly pay is $18.55 and he worked 52 hours in a week. Calculate his gross pay.

11. For sewing buttons on shirts, employees are paid $0.28 a shirt. Marty Hughes completes an average of 500 shirts a day. Find her average gross weekly earnings for a five-day week.

12. Patsy Hilliard is paid 5% commission on sales of $18,200. Find her gross pay.

13. Vincent Ores is paid a salary of $400 plus 8% of sales. Calculate his gross income if his sales total $9,890 in the current pay period.

14. Find the gross earnings if Juanita Wilson earns $275 plus 4% of all sales over $3,000 and the sales for a week are $18,756.

Use Figure 10-3 to find the amount of federal tax withholding for the gross earnings of the following married persons who are paid weekly and have the indicated number of withholding allowances.

15. $525, two allowances

16. $682, zero allowances

17. $1,495, three allowances

18. $1,348, five allowances

Use Figures 10-4 and 10-5, the percentage method tables, to find the amount of federal income tax to be withheld from the gross earnings of married persons who are paid weekly and have the indicated number of withholding allowances in Exercises 19 and 20.

19. $755, five allowances

20. $2,215, two allowances

Find the employee's Social Security and Medicare taxes deducted for each pay period in Exercises 21–24.

21. Weekly gross income of $842

22. Yearly gross income of $24,000

23. Semimonthly gross income of $1,856

24. Biweekly gross income of $1,426

APPLICATIONS

25. Irene Gamble earns $675 weekly and is married with 1 withholding allowance. She has a deduction for nonexempt insurance of $12.45. A 5% deduction is made for retirement. Find her total deductions including Social Security and Medicare taxes and find her net earnings.

26. Vince Bremaldi earned $32,876 last year. The state unemployment tax paid by his employer is 5.4% of the first $7,000 earned in a year. How much SUTA tax must Vince's employer pay for him? How much FUTA tax must Vince's employer pay?

27. Media Services, Inc. has a payroll in which the total employee withholding is $765.26; the total employee Social Security tax is $185.56; the total employer Social Security tax is $273.92; the total employee Medicare tax is $64.06. How much Medicare taxes must the employer pay for this payroll? What is the total amount of taxes that must be sent to IRS for the payroll?

EXERCISES SET B

SKILL BUILDERS

Find the gross earnings for each employee in Table 10-2. A regular week is 40 hours and the overtime rate is 1.5 times the regular rate.

TABLE 10-2

Employee	M	T	W	T	F	S	S	Hourly wage	Regular hours	Regular pay	Overtime hours	Overtime pay	Gross pay
1. Brown, J.	4	6	8	9	9	5	0	$10.43					
2. Sayer, C.	9	10	8	9	11	9	0	$18.45					
3. Lovett, L.	8	8	8	8	0	0	0	$19.95					
4. James, M.	8	8	4	8	8	8	0	$11.10					

5. Arsella Gallagher earns a salary of $63,552 and is paid semi-monthly. What is her gross salary for each payroll period?

6. John Edmonds is paid a biweekly salary of $1,398. What is his annual salary?

7. Fran Coley earns $1,896 biweekly on a salaried and exempt job. If she works 89 hours in one pay period, how much does she earn?

8. Robert Stout worked 40 hours at $21 per hour. Find his gross earnings for the week.

9. Leslie Jinkins worked a total of 58 hours in one week. Eight hours were paid at 1.5 times his hourly wage and 10 hours were paid at the holiday rate of 2 times his hourly wage. Find his gross earnings for the week if his hourly wage is $14.95.

10. Mike Kelly earns $21.30 per hour as a chemical technician. One week he works 38 hours. What is his gross pay for the week?

11. Employees are paid $3.50 per piece for a certain job. In a week's time, Maria Sanchez produced a total of 218 pieces. Find her gross earnings for the week.

12. Ada Shotwell is paid 4% commission on all computer sales. If she needs a monthly income of $2,500, find the monthly sales volume she must meet.

13. Cassie Lyons earns $350 plus 7% commission on all sales over $2,000. What are the gross earnings if sales for a week are $15,276?

14. Dieter Tillman is paid $2,000 plus 5% of the total sales volume. If he sold $3,000 in merchandise, find the gross earnings.

Use Figure 10-3 to find the amount of federal tax withholding for the gross earnings of the following married persons who are paid weekly and have the indicated number of withholding allowances.

15. $724, two allowances

16. $695, three allowances

17. $928, three allowances

18. $1,394, zero allowances

Use Figures 10-4 and 10-5, the percentage method tables, to find the amount of federal income tax to be withheld from the gross earnings of married persons who are paid weekly and have the indicated number of withholding allowances.

19. $620, eight allowances

20. $7,290, four allowances

Find the employee's Social Security and Medicare taxes deducted for each pay period for Exercises 21–24.

21. Monthly gross income of $3,500

22. Yearly gross income of $78,500

23. Semimonthly gross income of $1,226

24. Biweekly gross income of $1,684

APPLICATIONS

25. Anita Loyd earns $1,775 semimonthly. She is single and claims two withholding allowances. She also pays $12.83 each pay period for nonexempt health insurance. What is her net pay?

26. Elisa Marus has three employees who earn $2,500, $2,980, and $3,200 monthly. How much SUTA tax will she need to pay at the end of the first quarter if the SUTA tax rate is 5.4% of the first $7,000 for each employee?

27. Computer Solutions, Inc. has a payroll in which the total employee withholding is $1,250.37; the total employee Social Security tax is $267.96; the total employer Social Security tax is $395.56; the total employee Medicare tax is $92.51. How much Social Security and Medicare taxes must the employer pay for this payroll? What is the total amount of taxes that must be sent to the IRS for the payroll?

PRACTICE TEST

1. Cheryl Douglas works 43 hours in a week for an exempt salary of $1,827 per week. What are Cheryl's gross weekly earnings?

2. June Jackson earns $18.59 an hour. Find her gross earnings if she worked 46 hours (time and a half for overtime over 40 hours).

3. Willy Bell checks wrappers on cans in a cannery. He receives $0.15 for each case of cans. If he checks 1,400 cases on an average day, find his gross weekly salary. (A work week is five days.)

4. Stacey Ellis is paid at the following differential piece rate: 1–100, $2.58; 101–250, $2.72; 251 and up, $3.15. Find her gross earnings for completing 475 pieces.

5. Dorothy Ford, who sells restaurant supplies, works on 6% commission. If her sales for a week are $18,200, find her gross earnings.

6. Carlo Mason works on 5% commission. If he sells $17,500 in merchandise, find his gross earnings.

7. Find the gross earnings of Sallie Johnson who receives a 9% commission and whose sales totaled $7,852.

8. Find the Social Security tax (at 4.2%) and the Medicare tax (at 1.45%) for Anna Jones, whose gross earnings are $513.86. Round to the nearest cent.

9. Find the Social Security and Medicare taxes for Michele Cottrell, whose gross earnings are $861.25.

10. How much income tax should be withheld for Terry McLean, a married employee who earns $686 weekly and claims two allowances? (Use Figure 10-3.)

11. Use Figure 10-3 to find the federal income tax paid by Charlotte Jordan, who is married with four withholding allowances, if her weekly gross earnings are $776.

12. If LaQuita White had net earnings of $877.58 and total deductions of $261.32, find her gross earnings.

13. Peggy Lovern is single, earns $1,987 weekly, and claims 3 withholding allowances. By how much must her gross earnings be reduced to find her gross taxable earnings?

14. Amiee Dodd is married, earns $3,521 biweekly, and claims four withholding allowances. By how much must her gross earnings be reduced?

15. Edmond Van Dorn is married and earns $1,017 weekly. How much federal income tax will be withheld from his check if he claims two withholding allowances?

16. Emilee Houston is single and is paid semimonthly. She earns $1,682 each pay period and claims zero withholding allowances. How much federal income tax is withheld from her paycheck?

Complete the weekly register for married employees in Table 10-3. The number of each person's allowances is listed after each name. Round to the nearest cent. Use Figure 10-3.

TABLE 10-3

Employee (allowances)	Gross earnings	Employee Social Security tax	Medicare tax	Withholding tax	Other nonexempt deductions	Net earnings
17. Jackson (0)	$735.00				$25.12	
18. Love (1)	$673.80				$12.87	
19. Chow (2)	$892.17				0	
20. Ferrante (3)	$577.15				$ 4.88	
21. Towns (4)	$610.13				0	

22. How much SUTA tax must Anaston, Inc., pay to the state for a part-time employee who earns $5,290? The SUTA tax rate is 5.4% of the wages.

23. How much SUTA tax must University Dry Cleaners pay to the state for an employee who earns $38,200?

24. How much FUTA tax must University Dry Cleaners pay for the employee in Exercise 23? The FUTA tax rate is 0.08% of the first $7,000.

25. Use Figures 10-4 and 10-5 to find the amount of federal income tax to be withheld from Joey Surrette's gross biweekly earnings of $2,555 if Joey is married and claims 3 withholding allowances.

SINGLE Persons—SEMIMONTHLY Payroll Period
(For Wages Paid through December 2012)

And the wages are—		And the number of withholding allowances claimed is—										
At least	But less than	0	1	2	3	4	5	6	7	8	9	10
		The amount of income tax to be withheld is—										
$800	$820	$90	$66	$42	$25	$9	$0	$0	$0	$0	$0	$0
820	840	93	69	45	27	11	0	0	0	0	0	0
840	860	96	72	48	29	13	0	0	0	0	0	0
860	880	99	75	51	31	15	0	0	0	0	0	0
880	900	102	78	54	33	17	1	0	0	0	0	0
900	920	105	81	57	35	19	3	0	0	0	0	0
920	940	108	84	60	37	21	5	0	0	0	0	0
940	960	111	87	63	40	23	7	0	0	0	0	0
960	980	114	90	66	43	25	9	0	0	0	0	0
980	1,000	117	93	69	46	27	11	0	0	0	0	0
1,000	1,020	120	96	72	49	29	13	0	0	0	0	0
1,020	1,040	123	99	75	52	31	15	0	0	0	0	0
1,040	1,060	126	102	78	55	33	17	1	0	0	0	0
1,060	1,080	129	105	81	58	35	19	3	0	0	0	0
1,080	1,100	132	108	84	61	37	21	5	0	0	0	0
1,100	1,120	135	111	87	64	40	23	7	0	0	0	0
1,120	1,140	138	114	90	67	43	25	9	0	0	0	0
1,140	1,160	141	117	93	70	46	27	11	0	0	0	0
1,160	1,180	144	120	96	73	49	29	13	0	0	0	0
1,180	1,200	147	123	99	76	52	31	15	0	0	0	0
1,200	1,220	150	126	102	79	55	33	17	1	0	0	0
1,220	1,240	153	129	105	82	58	35	19	3	0	0	0
1,240	1,260	156	132	108	85	61	37	21	5	0	0	0
1,260	1,280	159	135	111	88	64	40	23	7	0	0	0
1,280	1,300	162	138	114	91	67	43	25	9	0	0	0
1,300	1,320	165	141	117	94	70	46	27	11	0	0	0
1,320	1,340	168	144	120	97	73	49	29	13	0	0	0
1,340	1,360	171	147	123	100	76	52	31	15	0	0	0
1,360	1,380	174	150	126	103	79	55	33	17	1	0	0
1,380	1,400	177	153	129	106	82	58	35	19	3	0	0
1,400	1,420	180	156	132	109	85	61	37	21	5	0	0
1,420	1,440	183	159	135	112	88	64	40	23	7	0	0
1,440	1,460	186	162	138	115	91	67	43	25	9	0	0
1,460	1,480	189	165	141	118	94	70	46	27	11	0	0
1,480	1,500	192	168	144	121	97	73	49	29	13	0	0
1,500	1,520	195	171	147	124	100	76	52	31	15	0	0
1,520	1,540	198	174	150	127	103	79	55	33	17	2	0
1,540	1,560	201	177	153	130	106	82	58	35	19	4	0
1,560	1,580	205	180	156	133	109	85	61	38	21	6	0
1,580	1,600	210	183	159	136	112	88	64	41	23	8	0
1,600	1,620	215	186	162	139	115	91	67	44	25	10	0
1,620	1,640	220	189	165	142	118	94	70	47	27	12	0
1,640	1,660	225	192	168	145	121	97	73	50	29	14	0
1,660	1,680	230	195	171	148	124	100	76	53	31	16	0
1,680	1,700	235	198	174	151	127	103	79	56	33	18	2
1,700	1,720	240	201	177	154	130	106	82	59	35	20	4
1,720	1,740	245	205	180	157	133	109	85	62	38	22	6
1,740	1,760	250	210	183	160	136	112	88	65	41	24	8
1,760	1,780	255	215	186	163	139	115	91	68	44	26	10
1,780	1,800	260	220	189	166	142	118	94	71	47	28	12
1,800	1,820	265	225	192	169	145	121	97	74	50	30	14
1,820	1,840	270	230	195	172	148	124	100	77	53	32	16
1,840	1,860	275	235	198	175	151	127	103	80	56	34	18
1,860	1,880	280	240	201	178	154	130	106	83	59	36	20
1,880	1,900	285	245	206	181	157	133	109	86	62	38	22
1,900	1,920	290	250	211	184	160	136	112	89	65	41	24
1,920	1,940	295	255	216	187	163	139	115	92	68	44	26
1,940	1,960	300	260	221	190	166	142	118	95	71	47	28
1,960	1,980	305	265	226	193	169	145	121	98	74	50	30
1,980	2,000	310	270	231	196	172	148	124	101	77	53	32
2,000	2,020	315	275	236	199	175	151	127	104	80	56	34
2,020	2,040	320	280	241	202	178	154	130	107	83	59	36
2,040	2,060	325	285	246	206	181	157	133	110	86	62	38
2,060	2,080	330	290	251	211	184	160	136	113	89	65	41
2,080	2,100	335	295	256	216	187	163	139	116	92	68	44
2,100	2,120	340	300	261	221	190	166	142	119	95	71	47
2,120	2,140	345	305	266	226	193	169	145	122	98	74	50

$2,140 and over		Use Table 3(a) for a **SINGLE person** on page 36. Also see the instructions on page 35.

FIGURE 10-2
Continued

SINGLE Persons—SEMIMONTHLY Payroll Period
(For Wages Paid through December 2012)

And the wages are—		And the number of withholding allowances claimed is—										
At least	But less than	0	1	2	3	4	5	6	7	8	9	10
		The amount of income tax to be withheld is—										
$ 0	$115	$0	$0	$0	$0	$0	$0	$0	$0	$0	$0	$
115	120	3	0	0	0	0	0	0	0	0	0	
120	125	3	0	0	0	0	0	0	0	0	0	
125	130	4	0	0	0	0	0	0	0	0	0	
130	135	4	0	0	0	0	0	0	0	0	0	
135	140	5	0	0	0	0	0	0	0	0	0	
140	145	5	0	0	0	0	0	0	0	0	0	
145	150	6	0	0	0	0	0	0	0	0	0	
150	155	6	0	0	0	0	0	0	0	0	0	
155	160	7	0	0	0	0	0	0	0	0	0	
160	165	7	0	0	0	0	0	0	0	0	0	
165	170	8	0	0	0	0	0	0	0	0	0	
170	175	8	0	0	0	0	0	0	0	0	0	
175	180	9	0	0	0	0	0	0	0	0	0	
180	185	9	0	0	0	0	0	0	0	0	0	
185	190	10	0	0	0	0	0	0	0	0	0	
190	195	10	0	0	0	0	0	0	0	0	0	
195	200	11	0	0	0	0	0	0	0	0	0	
200	205	11	0	0	0	0	0	0	0	0	0	
205	210	12	0	0	0	0	0	0	0	0	0	
210	215	12	0	0	0	0	0	0	0	0	0	
215	220	13	0	0	0	0	0	0	0	0	0	
220	225	13	0	0	0	0	0	0	0	0	0	
225	230	14	0	0	0	0	0	0	0	0	0	
230	235	14	0	0	0	0	0	0	0	0	0	
235	240	15	0	0	0	0	0	0	0	0	0	
240	245	15	0	0	0	0	0	0	0	0	0	
245	250	16	0	0	0	0	0	0	0	0	0	
250	260	17	1	0	0	0	0	0	0	0	0	
260	270	18	2	0	0	0	0	0	0	0	0	
270	280	19	3	0	0	0	0	0	0	0	0	
280	290	20	4	0	0	0	0	0	0	0	0	
290	300	21	5	0	0	0	0	0	0	0	0	
300	310	22	6	0	0	0	0	0	0	0	0	
310	320	23	7	0	0	0	0	0	0	0	0	
320	330	24	8	0	0	0	0	0	0	0	0	
330	340	25	9	0	0	0	0	0	0	0	0	
340	350	26	10	0	0	0	0	0	0	0	0	
350	360	27	11	0	0	0	0	0	0	0	0	
360	370	28	12	0	0	0	0	0	0	0	0	
370	380	29	13	0	0	0	0	0	0	0	0	
380	390	30	14	0	0	0	0	0	0	0	0	
390	400	31	15	0	0	0	0	0	0	0	0	
400	410	32	16	0	0	0	0	0	0	0	0	
410	420	33	17	1	0	0	0	0	0	0	0	
420	430	34	18	2	0	0	0	0	0	0	0	
430	440	35	19	3	0	0	0	0	0	0	0	
440	450	36	20	4	0	0	0	0	0	0	0	
450	460	37	21	5	0	0	0	0	0	0	0	
460	470	38	22	6	0	0	0	0	0	0	0	
470	480	40	23	7	0	0	0	0	0	0	0	
480	490	41	24	8	0	0	0	0	0	0	0	
490	500	43	25	9	0	0	0	0	0	0	0	
500	520	45	26	10	0	0	0	0	0	0	0	
520	540	48	28	12	0	0	0	0	0	0	0	
540	560	51	30	14	0	0	0	0	0	0	0	
560	580	54	32	16	1	0	0	0	0	0	0	
580	600	57	34	18	3	0	0	0	0	0	0	
600	620	60	36	20	5	0	0	0	0	0	0	
620	640	63	39	22	7	0	0	0	0	0	0	
640	660	66	42	24	9	0	0	0	0	0	0	
660	680	69	45	26	11	0	0	0	0	0	0	
680	700	72	48	28	13	0	0	0	0	0	0	
700	720	75	51	30	15	0	0	0	0	0	0	
720	740	78	54	32	17	1	0	0	0	0	0	
740	760	81	57	34	19	3	0	0	0	0	0	
760	780	84	60	36	21	5	0	0	0	0	0	
780	800	87	63	39	23	7	0	0	0	0	0	

FIGURE 10-2

Portion of IRS Withholding Table for Single Persons Paid Semimonthly

Form W-4 (2012)

Purpose. Complete Form W-4 so that your employer can withhold the correct federal income tax from your pay. Consider completing a new Form W-4 each year and when your personal or financial situation changes.

Exemption from withholding. If you are exempt, complete **only** lines 1, 2, 3, 4, and 7 and sign the form to validate it. Your exemption for 2012 expires February 18, 2013. See Pub. 505, Tax Withholding and Estimated Tax.

Note. If another person can claim you as a dependent on his or her tax return, You cannot claim exemption from withholding if your income exceeds $950 and includes more than $300 of unearned income(for example, interest and dividends)

Basic instructions. If you are not exempt, complete the **Personal Allowances Worksheet** below. The worksheets on page 2 further adjust your withholding allowances based on itemized deductions, certain credits, adjustments to income, or two-earners/multiple jobs situations. Complete all worksheets that apply. However, you may claim fewer (or zero) allowances. For regular wages, withholding must be based on allowances you claimed and may not be a flat amount or percentage of wages.

Head of household. Generally, you may claim head of household filing status on your tax return only if you are unmarried and pay more than 50% of the costs of keeping up a home for yourself and your dependent(s) or other qualifying individuals. See Pub. 501, Exemptions, Standard Deduction, and Filing Information, for information.

Tax credits. You can take projected tax credits into account in figuring your allowable number of withholding allowances. Credits for child or dependent care expenses and the child tax credit may be claimed using the **Personal Allowances Worksheet** below. See Pub. 505, for information on converting your other credits into withholding allowances.

Nonwage income. If you have a large amount of nonwage income, such as interest or dividends, consider making estimated tax payments using Form 1040-ES, Estimated Tax for Individuals. Otherwise, you may owe additional tax. If you have pension or annuity income, see Pub. 505 to find out if you should adjust your withholding on Form W-4 or W-4P.

Two earners or multiple jobs. If you have a working spouse or more than one job, figure the total number of allowances you are entitled to claim on all jobs using worksheets from only one Form W-4. Your withholding usually will be most accurate when all allowances are claimed on the Form W-4 for the highest paying job and zero allowances are claimed on the others. See Pub. 505 for details.

Nonresident alien. If you are a nonresident alien, see Notice 1392, Supplemental Form W-4 Instructions for Nonresident Aliens, before completing this form.

Check your withholding. After your Form W-4 takes effect, use Pub. 505 to see how the amount you are having withheld compares to your projected total tax for 2012. See Pub. 505, especially if your earnings exceed $130,000 (Single) or $180,000 (Married).

Future developments The IRS has created a page on IRS.gov for information about the form W-4, at www.irs.gov/w4. information about any future developments affecting Form W-4 (such as legislation enacted after we release it) will be posted on that page

---

Personal Allowances Worksheet (Keep for your records.)

A   Enter "1" for **yourself** if no one else can claim you as a dependent . . . . **A** _____

B   Enter "1" if:
- You are single and have only one job; or
- You are married, have only one job, and your spouse does not work; or
- Your wages from a second job or your spouse's wages (or the total of both) are $1,500 or less.

  . . **B** _____

C   Enter "1" for your **spouse.** But, you may choose to enter "-0-" if you are married and have either a working spouse or more than one job. (Entering "-0-" may help you avoid having too little tax withheld.) . . . . **C** _____

D   Enter number of **dependents** (other than your spouse or yourself) you will claim on your tax return . . . . . . **D** _____

E   Enter "1" if you will file as **head of household** on your tax return (see conditions under **Head of household** above) . **E** _____

F   Enter "1" if you have at least $1,900 of **child or dependent care expenses** for which you plan to claim a credit . . **F** _____

    (**Note.** Do **not** include child support payments. See Pub. 503, Child and Dependent Care Expenses, for details.)

G   **Child Tax Credit** (including additional child tax credit). See Pub. 972, Child Tax Credit, for more information.
- If your total income will be less than $61,000 ($90,000 if married), enter "2" for each eligible child; then less"1" if you have three to seven eligible children or less "2" if you have eight or more eligible children.
- If your total income will be between $61,000 and $84,000 ($90,000 and $119,000 if married), enter "1" for each eligible child plus . . . . **G** _____

H   Add lines A through G and enter total here. (**Note.** This may be different from the number of exemptions you claim on your tax return.) ▶ **H** _____

For accuracy, complete all worksheets that apply.
- If you plan to **itemize or claim adjustments to income** and want to reduce your withholding, see the **Deductions and Adjustments Worksheet** on page 2.
- If you are **single or more than one job** or are **married and you and your spouse both work** and the combined earnings from all jobs exceeds $40,000 ($10,000 if married), see the **Two-Earners/Multiple Jobs Worksheet** on page 2 to avoid having too little tax withheld.
- If **neither** of the above situations applies, **stop here** and enter the number from line H on line 5 of Form W-4 below.

- - - - - - - - - - - - Cut here and give Form W-4 to your employer. Keep the top part for your records. - - - - - - - - - - - -

Form W-4

Department of the Treasury
Internal Revenue Service

Employee's Withholding Allowance Certificate

▶ Whether you are entitled to claim a certain number of allowances or exemption from withholding is subject to review by the IRS. Your employer may be required to send a copy of this form to the IRS.

OMB No. 1545-0074

2012

1 Type or print your first name and middle initial.	Last name	2 Your social security number
Home address (number and street or rural route)	3 ☐ Single ☐ Married ☐ Married, but withhold at higher Single rate. **Note.** If married, but legally separated, or spouse is a nonresident alien, check the "Single" box.	
City or town, state, and ZIP code	4 If your last name differs from that shown on your social security card, check here. You must call 1-800-772-1213 for a replacement card. ▶ ☐	

5   Total number of allowances you are claiming (from line **H** above **or** from the applicable worksheet on page 2)   **5** |_____

6   Additional amount, if any, you want withheld from each paycheck . . . . **6** $ |_____

7   I claim exemption from withholding for 2012, and I certify that I meet **both** of the following conditions for exemption.
- Last year I had a right to a refund of **all** federal income tax withheld because I had **no** tax liability **and**
- This year I expect a refund of **all** federal income tax withheld because I expect to have **no** tax liability.

If you meet both conditions, write "Exempt" here . . . . ▶ **7** |_____

Under penalties of perjury, I declare that I have examined this certificate and to the best of my knowledge and belief, it is true, correct, and complete.

Employee's signature
(Form is not valid unless you sign it.) ▶ _____   Date ▶ _____

8 Employer's name and address (Employer: Complete lines 8 and 10 only if sending to the IRS.)	9 Office code (optional)	10 Employer identification number (EIN)

For Privacy Act and Paperwork Reduction Act Notice, see page 2.   Cat. No. 10220Q   Form **W-4** (2012)

FIGURE 10-1

Employee's Withholding Allowance Certificate

Income tax: local, state, or federal tax paid on one's income.

Federal tax withholding: the amount required to be withheld from a person's pay and paid to the federal government.

Tax-filing status: status based on whether the employee is married, single, or a head of household that determines the tax rate.

Withholding allowance (exemption): a portion of gross earnings that is not subject to tax.

W-4 form: form required to be held by the employer for determining the amount of federal tax to be withheld for an employee.

Adjustment: amount that can be subtracted from the gross income, such as qualifying IRAs, tax-sheltered annuities, 401Ks, or employer-sponsored child care or medical plans.

Adjusted gross income: the income that remains after allowable adjustments have been made.

One of the largest deductions from an employee's paycheck usually comes in the form of **income tax.** The tax paid to the federal government is called **federal tax withholding.** The tax withheld is based on three things: the employee's gross earnings, the employee's **tax-filing status,** and the number of *withholding allowances* the person claims.

The employee's filing status is determined by marital status and eligibility to be classified as a head of household. A **withholding allowance,** called an **exemption,** is a portion of gross earnings that is not subject to tax. Each employee is permitted one withholding allowance for himself or herself, one for a spouse, and one for each eligible dependent (such as a child or elderly parent). A detailed discussion on eligibility for various allowances can be found in several IRS publications, such as Publication 15 (Circular E, Employer's Tax Guide), Publication 505 (Tax Withholding and Estimated Tax), and Publication 17 (Your Federal Income Tax for Individuals).

There are several ways to figure the withholding tax for an employee. The most common methods use tax tables and tax rates. These and other methods are referenced in IRS Publication 15 (Circular E, Employer's Tax Guide).

1 Find federal tax withholding per paycheck using IRS tax tables.

To calculate federal withholding tax using IRS tax tables, an employer must know the employee's filing status (single, married, or head of household), the number of withholding allowances the employee claims, the type of pay period (weekly, biweekly, and so on), and the employee's *adjusted gross income.* When an employee is hired for a job, he or she is asked for payroll purposes to complete a federal **W-4 form.** Figure 10-1 shows a 2012 W-4 form. On this form an employee must indicate tax-filing status and number of exemptions claimed. This information is necessary to compute the amount of federal income tax to be withheld from the employee's earnings.

In many cases, adjusted gross income is the same as gross pay. However, earnings contributed to funds such as qualifying IRAs, tax-sheltered annuities, 401ks, or some employer-sponsored child care and medical plans are called **adjustments** to income and are subtracted from gross pay to determine the **adjusted gross income.**

Figures 10-2 and 10-3 show a portion of two IRS tax tables.

HOW TO Find federal tax withholding per paycheck using the IRS tax tables

1. Find the adjusted gross income by subtracting the total *allowable* adjustments from the gross pay per pay period. Select the appropriate table according to the employee's filing status (single, married, or head of household) and according to the type of pay period (weekly, biweekly, and so on).
2. Find the income row: In the columns labeled "And the wages are—," select the "At least" and "But less than" interval that includes the employee's adjusted gross income for the pay period.
3. Find the allowances column: In the columns labeled "And the number of withholding allowances claimed is—," select the number of allowances the employee claims.
4. Find the cell where the income row and allowance column intersect. The correct tax is given in this cell.

EXAMPLE 1 Charlie Strawn has a gross semimonthly income of $1,240, is single, claims three withholding allowances, and has no allowable adjustments. Find the amount of federal tax withholding to be deducted from his gross earnings.

Use Figure 10-2.

Use row for interval "At least $1,240 but less than $1,260."
Use the column for three withholding allowances.

The withholding tax is $85.

Select appropriate tax table for a single person who is paid semimonthly.
$1,240 is in the selected interval.

Find the intersection of the row and column.

1. Anita Loyd works 45 hours in one week, is paid $18.98 per hour, and earns 1.5 times her hourly wage for all hours worked over 40 in a given week. Calculate Anita's gross pay using the method described in the chapter.

2. Calculate Anita Loyd's gross pay by multiplying the total number of hours worked by the hourly rate and multiplying the hours over 40 by 0.5 the hourly rate. Compare this gross pay to the gross pay found in Exercise 1.

3. Explain why the methods for calculating gross pay in Exercises 1 and 2 are mathematically equivalent.

4. Most businesses prefer to use the method used in Exercise 1 to calculate gross pay. Discuss reasons for this preference.

Assume that the taxpayers in Questions 5–7 claim zero withholding allowances.

5. If a person is paid weekly and is married, use Figure 10-5 to find the annual salary range that causes a portion of the person's salary to fall in the "28% bracket" for withholding purposes.

6. Compare the annual salary range found in Exercise 5 with the annual salary range for a person who is paid biweekly, is married, and whose salary is in the "28% bracket."

7. Find the annual salary range a married person who is paid semi-monthly would need to earn to fall in the "28% bracket." Use Table 3b of Figure 10-5. Compare the ranges for weekly, biweekly, and semimonthly.

8. Use Exercises 5, 6, and 7 to make a general statement about the amount of withholding tax on an annual salary for the various types of pay periods. To what can you attribute any differences you noted?

9. Many people think that if an increase in earnings moves their salary to a higher tax bracket, their entire salary will be taxed at the higher rate. Is this true? Give an example to justify your answer.

10. Shameka Jones earns $112,820 and is paid semimonthly. Her last pay stub for the year shows $197.43 is deducted for Social Security and $68.16 is deducted for Medicare. Should she call her payroll office for a correction? If so, what would that correction be?

Challenge Problem

Complete the following time card for Janice Anderson in Figure 10-6. She earns time and a half overtime when she works more than eight hours on a weekday or on Saturday. She earns double time on Sundays and holidays. Calculate Janice's net pay if she earns $19.75 per hour, is married, and claims one withholding allowance.

WEEKLY TIME CARD
CHD Company

Name: Janice Anderson   SS#: 000-00-0000

Pay for period ending

DATE	IN	OUT	IN	OUT	Total Regular Hours	Total Overtime Hours
M 8/4	7:00	11:00	11:30	7:30		
Tu 8/5	8:00	12:00	12:30	4:30		
W 8/6	8:00	12:00	12:30	4:30		
Th 8/7	7:00	11:00	12:30	5:30		
F 8/8	8:00	12:00	12:30	4:30		
Sa 8/9	7:00	12:00				
Su 8/10						

	HOURS	RATE	GROSS PAY
Regular			
Overtime (1.5X)			
Overtime (2X)			0.00
Total			

FIGURE 10-6

CASE STUDIES

10-1 Score Skateboard Company

Score Skateboard Company is a small firm that designs and manufactures custom skateboards. Score has two employees that receive $1,100 gross pay per semimonthly pay period and four employees that receive $850 gross pay per semimonthly pay period. The company owner and manager, Christie, needs to determine how much to include in her budget for each employee. Starting in January, Score will be contributing $75 per pay period to each employee's retirement fund. Score is in a state that has a maximum of $7,000 gross pay for SUTA and Score is required to pay 5.4% of the first $7,000 for each employee.

1. Calculate the cost (salary, employer's portion of Social Security and Medicare, pension, etc.) to Score for an employee with $1,100 gross pay in the first period in January.

2. Calculate the cost to Score for an employee with $850 gross pay in the first period in January.

3. Find the total gross semimonthly pay for all six employees and compare this to the total amount Score must include in its budget. How much extra is needed in the budget?

4. Calculate the total amount Score will need for its first quarter FUTA and SUTA deposit. There are six semimonthly pay periods in the first quarter of the year.

10-2 Welcome Care

Welcome Care, a senior citizen day-care center, pays the major portion of its employees' medical insurance—$300 of the $446 monthly premium for an individual employee. An employee who selects coverage for him- or herself and spouse must pay $326 per month. The employee's cost for an employee and family (including spouse) is $512 per month. The center hires three new employees. Calculate their semimonthly take-home pay using the percentage method tables. The company pays time and a half for overtime hours in excess of 40 hours in a given week. Medical insurance premiums are paid with pretax dollars. Withholding taxes, Social Security, and Medicare deductions are calculated on the lower adjusted gross salary.

1. An activities director is hired at an annual salary of $32,000. He is single with two dependent children (three withholding

allowances) and wants family medical insurance coverage. Find his total deductions and his net income. Use the percentage method tables.

2. A dietitian is hired at a monthly salary of $3,500 a month paid semimonthly. She is married with one withholding allowance and wants medical insurance for herself and her spouse. Find her take-home pay if she is subject to an IRS garnishment of $100 per month for back taxes. Use the percentage method of withholding (Table 3b of Figure 10-5).

3. A vehicle driver is hired at $12 per hour to transport seniors to appointments and leisure activities. The driver is single and claims no withholding allowances. He needs medical coverage for himself only. Find his net pay if he worked 77 hours regular time and 8 hours overtime during the semimonthly pay period, and has $200 per month taken out for court-ordered child support payments. Use the percentage method tables.

4. A part-time caregiver comes daily to sit with and talk with senior citizens at Welcome Care. He is paid $12 per hour and works 4 hours each day for 10 days in the pay period. He is single and claims one withholding allowance. He has medical insurance coverage through another job. Find his net pay for a semimonthly paycheck using the percentage method of withholding.

10-3 First Foreign Auto Parts

Ryan Larson, owner of First Foreign Auto Parts, is considering expanding his operation for the new year by rebuilding shock absorbers. This will require two additional full-time employees. Because of a tight labor market, Ryan presumes he will have to pay $13 per hour, along with health insurance, to attract quality employees. He decides he will contribute 50% towards the $460 monthly health insurance individual premium, in addition to the federal and state

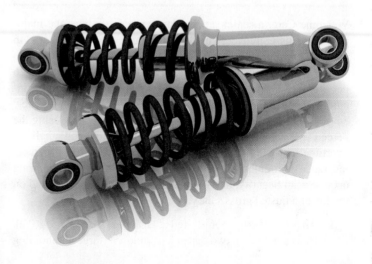

unemployment taxes and Medicare and Social Security taxes that he must pay on the employees' behalf. Ryan needs to decide how much to include in his budget for each employee.

1. Based on a 40-hour work week, calculate the cost to First Foreign Auto Parts for each employee in the first month in January.

2. Ryan hires a new employee at $13 per hour to rebuild shock absorbers. The employee is married, claims no withholding allowances, and needs the individual health coverage. Calculate his weekly take-home pay, assuming he works 40 regular hours and 10 overtime hours, and pays 29% of his gross earnings for court-ordered child support. His health insurance premiums can be paid with pre-tax dollars. Use Figure 10-3 to determine the federal tax to be withheld.

3. Ryan is considering a differential piecework rate to give his new employees incentive to produce more and increase their wages. Ryan came up with the following schedule:

Shocks assembled per week	Pay per shock
First 40 shocks	$6.50
Next 40 shocks	$7.50
Over 80 shocks	$8.50

How much would each employee make for completing 75 shocks per week? How much more would each employee make by completing just 15 additional shocks per week beyond the first 75 shocks?

CHAPTER
11

Simple Interest
and Simple Discount

18 Months Same as Cash Financing on New TVs*

Radhika had just received mail for the first time in her new apartment, and there it was in big bold letters: 18 MONTHS SAME AS CASH FINANCING*. The ad read: "The minimum monthly payment for this purchase does not include interest charges during the promotional period. You'll pay no interest for 18 months. Simply pay at least the total minimum monthly payment due as indicated on your billing statement. There's no prepayment penalty, and this offer provides you with the flexibility you need to meet your specific budget and purchasing requirements."

It sounded like a great deal. She really wanted to buy a flat-panel TV and was short on cash. But Radhika had some concerns. First, she didn't know much about financing or how interest was computed; and second, she knew that the asterisk would probably mean trouble. After reading further, she found the following:

*The 18-month promotion is for televisions with a minimum value of $499.99. The 12-month promotion requires a minimum purchase of $299.99. These are "same as cash" promotions. If the balance on these purchases is paid in full before the expiration of the promotional period indicated on your billing statement and your account is kept current, then accrued finance charges will not be imposed on these purchases. If the balance on these purchases is not paid in full, finance charges will be assessed from the purchase date at the annual simple interest rate of 24.99%. For accounts not kept current, the default simple interest rate of 27.99% will be applied to all balances on your account. Minimum monthly payments are required. The minimum finance charge is $2.00. Certain rules apply to the allocation of payments and finance charges on your promotional purchase if you make more than one purchase on your account.

Wow! That was a lot to digest. Radhika had her heart set on a TV that cost about $800, and she was hoping to keep her payments under $20 per month. Would that be enough to pay the account in full in 18 months? And if she came up short by a few hundred dollars, would she still be charged all of that interest? If so, how much would 24.99% cost her during that time? What was simple interest, anyway? None of this sounded simple to her. And the late penalties—she didn't even want to think about those.

Radhika took a deep breath. Maybe this wasn't such a good idea, she thought as she reached for her keys. But she really wanted that TV.

LEARNING OUTCOMES

11-1 The Simple Interest Formula
1. Find simple interest using the simple interest formula.
2. Find the maturity value of a loan.
3. Convert months to a fractional or decimal part of a year.
4. Find the principal, rate, or time using the simple interest formula.

11-2 Ordinary and Exact Interest
1. Find the exact time.
2. Find the due date.
3. Find the ordinary interest and the exact interest.
4. Make a partial payment before the maturity date.

11-3 Promissory Notes
1. Find the bank discount and proceeds for a simple discount note.
2. Find the true or effective interest rate of a simple discount note.
3. Find the third-party discount and proceeds for a third-party discount note.

Interest: an amount paid or earned for the use of money.

Simple interest: interest when a loan or investment is repaid in a lump sum.

Principal: the amount of money borrowed or invested.

Rate: the percent of the principal paid as interest per time period.

Time: the number of days, months, or years that the money is borrowed or invested.

Every business and every person at some time borrows or invests money. A person (or business) who borrows money must pay for the use of the money. A person who invests money must be paid by the person or firm who uses the money. The price paid for using money is called **interest.**

In the business world, we encounter two basic kinds of interest, *simple* and *compound.* **Simple interest** applies when a loan or investment is repaid in a lump sum. The person using the money has use of the full amount of money for the entire time of the loan or investment. Compound interest, which is explained in Chapter 13, most often applies to savings accounts, annuities, and long-term investments.

Both types of interest take into account three factors: the principal, the interest rate, and the time period involved. **Principal** is the amount of money borrowed or invested. **Rate** is the percent of the principal paid as interest per time period. **Time** is the number of days, months, or years that the money is borrowed or invested.

11-1 THE SIMPLE INTEREST FORMULA

LEARNING OUTCOMES

1. Find simple interest using the simple interest formula.
2. Find the maturity value of a loan.
3. Convert months to a fractional or decimal part of a year.
4. Find the principal, rate, or time using the simple interest formula.

1 Find simple interest using the simple interest formula.

The interest formula $I = PRT$ shows how interest, principal, rate, and time are related and gives us a way of finding one of these values if the other three values are known.

> ## HOW TO Find simple interest using the simple interest formula
>
> 1. Identify the principal, rate, and time.
> 2. Multiply the principal by the rate and time.
>
> $$\text{Interest} = \text{principal} \times \text{rate} \times \text{time} \qquad I = PRT$$

The rate of interest is a percent for a given time period, usually one year. The time in the interest formula must be expressed in the same unit of time as the rate. If the rate is a percent per year, the time must be expressed in years or a decimal or fractional part of a year. Similarly, if the rate is a percent per month, the time must be expressed in months.

EXAMPLE 1
Find the interest paid on a loan of $1,500 for one year at a simple interest rate of 9% per year.

$I = PRT$	Use the simple interest formula. Principal P is $1,500, rate R is 9% per year, and time T is one year.
$I = (\$1,500)(9\%)(1)$	Write 9% as a decimal. Multiply.
$I = (\$1,500)(0.09)(1)$	
$I = \$135$	

The interest on the loan is $135.

EXAMPLE 2
Kanette's Salon borrowed $5,000 at $8\frac{1}{2}\%$ per year simple interest for two years to buy new hair dryers. How much interest must be paid?

$I = PRT$	Use the simple interest formula. Principal P is $5,000, rate R is $8\frac{1}{2}\%$ per year, and time T is two years.
$I = (\$5,000)(8\frac{1}{2}\%)(2)$	
$I = (\$5,000)(0.085)(2)$	Write $8\frac{1}{2}\%$ as a decimal. Multiply.
$I = \$850$	

Kanette's Salon will pay $850 interest.

A loan that is made using simple interest is to be repaid in a lump sum at the end of the time of the loan. Banks and lending institutions make loans at a variety of different rates based on factors such as prime interest rate and the amount of risk that the loan will be repaid. The **prime interest rate** is the lowest rate of interest charged by banks for short-term loans to their most creditworthy customers. Banks establish the rate of a loan based on the current prime rate and the likelihood that it will not change significantly over the time of the loan. Some banks may refer to the prime lending rate as the **reference rate** or the **base lending rate.**

Loans are made at the prime rate or higher, often significantly higher. Investments such as savings accounts and certificates of deposit earn interest at a rate less than prime. Lending institutions make a profit based on the difference between the rate of interest charged for loans and the rate of interest given for investments.

Prime interest rate (prime), reference rate, or base lending rate: the lowest rate of interest charged by banks for short-term loans to their most creditworthy customers.

DID YOU KNOW?

Banks Lend Money to Other Banks?

Yes, these loans are short term (usually overnight) and made through the Federal Reserve at a rate that is lower than prime. This rate is referred to as the **federal funds rate**. Each bank establishes its own prime rate, but this rate is almost always the same among the major banks. Changes to the prime rate are usually made at the same time as a change in the federal funds rate is made. There is no scheduled time that these changes occur.

Federal funds rate: the interest rate which banks actively trade balances held at the Federal Reserve, with each other, usually overnight. Banks with surplus balances in their accounts lend those balances to banks in need of larger balances on a short term basis.

STOP AND CHECK

See Example 1.

1. Find the interest paid on a loan of $38,000 for one year at a simple interest rate of 10.5%.

2. A loan of $17,500 for six years has a simple interest rate of 7.75%. Find the interest.

See Example 2.

3. The 7th Inning borrowed $6,700 at 9.5% simple interest for three years. How much interest is paid?

4. Find the interest on a $38,500 loan at a simple interest rate of 12.3% for five years.

---

2 Find the maturity value of a loan.

The *total* amount of money due at the end of a loan period—the amount of the loan *and* the interest—is called the **maturity value** of the loan. When the principal and interest of a loan are known, the maturity value is found by adding the principal and the interest. The maturity value can also be found directly from the principal, rate, and time.

Maturity value: the total amount of money due at the end of a loan period—the amount of the loan and the interest.

HOW TO   Find the maturity value of a loan

1. If the principal and interest are known, add them.

$$\text{Maturity value} = \text{principal} + \text{interest}$$
$$MV = P + I$$

2. If the principal, rate, and time are known, use either of the formulas:
   (a) Maturity value = principal + (principal × rate × time)
$$MV = P + PRT$$

   (b) Maturity value = principal (1 + rate × time)
$$MV = P(1 + RT)$$

Both variations of the formula for finding the maturity value when the principal, rate, and time are known require that the operations be performed according to the standard order of operations. To review briefly, when more than one operation is to be performed, perform operations within parentheses first. Perform multiplications and divisions before additions and subtractions. Perform additions and subtractions last. For a more detailed discussion of the order of operations, review Chapter 1, Section 3, Learning Outcome 2.

EXAMPLE 3

In Example 2 on page 388, we found that Kanette's Salon would pay $850 interest on a $5,000 loan. How much money will Kanette's Salon pay at the end of two years?

Maturity value = principal + interest P and I are known.

$MV = P + I$ Substitute known values.

$\quad\quad = \$5,000 + \$850 = \$5,850$

Kanette's Salon will pay $5,850 at the end of the loan period.

EXAMPLE 4

Marcus Logan can purchase furniture with a two-year simple interest loan at 9% interest per year. What is the maturity value for a $2,500 loan?

Maturity value = principal (1 + rate × time) P, R, and T are known.
$MV = P(1 + RT)$ Substitute $P = \$2,500$,
                                    $R = 9\%$ or 0.09,
                                    $T = 2$ years.
$MV = \$2,500(1 + 0.09 \times 2)$ Multiply in parentheses.
$MV = \$2,500(1 + 0.18)$ Add in parentheses.
$MV = \$2,500(1.18)$ Multiply.
$MV = \$2,950$

Marcus will pay $2,950 at the end of two years.

TIP

Does a Calculator Know the Proper Order of Operations? Some Do, Some Don't.

Using a basic calculator, you enter calculations as they should be performed according to the standard order of operations.

AC .09 × 2 = + 1 = × 2500 = ⟹ 2950

Using a business or scientific calculator with parentheses keys allows you to enter values for the maturity value formula as they appear. The calculator is programmed to perform the operations in the standard order. The calculator has special keys for entering parentheses, (and).

AC 2500 × (1 + .09 × 2) = ⟹ 2950

STOP AND CHECK

1. How much is paid at the end of two years for a loan of $8,000 if the total interest is $660? *See Example 3.*

2. A loan of $7,250 is to be repaid in three years and has a simple interest rate of 12%. How much is paid after the three years? *See Example 4.*

3. Find the maturity value of a $1,800 loan made for two years at $9\frac{3}{4}\%$ simple interest per year.

4. Find the maturity value of a three-year, simple interest loan at 11% per year in the amount of $7,275.

3   Convert months to a fractional or decimal part of a year.

Not all loans or investments are made for a whole number of years; but, as the interest rate is most often given per year, the time must also be expressed in the same unit of time as the rate.

HOW TO   Convert months to a fractional or decimal part of a year

1. Write the number of months as the numerator of a fraction.
2. Write 12 as the denominator of the fraction.
3. Reduce the fraction to lowest terms if using the fractional equivalent.
4. Divide the numerator by the denominator to get the decimal equivalent of the fraction.

EXAMPLE 5 Convert (a) 5 months and (b) 15 months to years, expressed in both fraction or mixed-number and decimal form.

(a) 5 months $= \dfrac{5}{12}$ year

5 months equal $\frac{5}{12}$ year.

$$12\overline{)5.0000000} \quad 0.4166666 \text{ year} = 0.42 \text{ year}$$

To write the fraction as a decimal, divide the number of months (the numerator) by the number of months in a year (the denominator).

5 months $= \frac{5}{12}$ year or 0.42 year (rounded)

(b) 15 months $= \dfrac{15}{12}$ years $= \dfrac{5}{4}$ or $1\dfrac{1}{4}$ years

15 months equal $\frac{15}{12}$ years.

$$
\begin{array}{r}
1.25 \text{ years} \\
12\overline{)15.00} \\
\underline{12.00} \\
3\,0 \\
\underline{2\,4} \\
60 \\
\underline{60} \\
0
\end{array}
$$

To write the fraction as a decimal, divide the number of months (the numerator) by the number of months in a year (the denominator).

15 months $= 1\frac{1}{4}$ years or 1.25 years

EXAMPLE 6 To save money for a shoe repair shop, Stan Wright invested $2,500 for 45 months at $3\frac{1}{2}\%$ simple interest per year. How much interest did he earn?

$T = 45$ months $= \dfrac{45}{12}$ years $= 3\dfrac{3}{4}$ or 3.75 years

Write the time in terms of years.

$I = PRT$

Use the simple interest formula.

$I = \$2,500\,(0.035)(3.75)$

Principal P is $2,500, rate R is 0.035, and time T is $\frac{45}{12}$ or 3.75. Multiply. Round to the nearest cent.

$I = \$328.13$

Stan Wright earned $328.13 in interest.

Check Calculations by Estimating

As careful as we are, there will always be times that we hit an incorrect key or use an improper sequence of steps and produce an incorrect solution. You can catch most of these mistakes by first anticipating what a reasonable answer should be.

In Example 6, 1% interest for one year would be $25. At that rate the interest for four years would be $100. The actual rate is $3\frac{1}{2}$ times one percent and the time is less than four years, so a reasonable estimate would be $350.

So Many Choices!

When time is expressed in months, the calculator sequence is the same as when time is expressed in years, except that you do not enter a whole number for the time. Months can be changed to years in the sequence rather than as a separate calculation. All other steps are the same.

To solve the equation in Example 6 using a calculator without the percent key, use the decimal equivalent of $3\frac{1}{2}\%$ and the fraction for the time.

$$\boxed{\text{AC}}\ 2500\ \boxed{\times}\ .035\ \boxed{\times}\ 45\ \boxed{\div}\ 12\ \boxed{=} \Rightarrow 328.125$$

It is not necessary to find the decimal equivalent of $\frac{45}{12}$ or to reduce $\frac{45}{12}$. However, you will get the same result if you use 3.75 or $\frac{15}{4}$.

$$\boxed{\text{AC}}\ 2500\ \boxed{\times}\ .035\ \boxed{\times}\ 3.75\ \boxed{=} \Rightarrow 328.125$$

$$\boxed{\text{AC}}\ 2500\ \boxed{\times}\ .035\ \boxed{\times}\ 15\ \boxed{\div}\ 4\ \boxed{=} \Rightarrow 328.125$$

STOP AND CHECK

See Example 5.

1. Change eight months to years, expressed in fraction and decimal form. Round to the nearest millionth.

2. Change 18 months to years, expressed in both fraction and decimal form.

See Example 6.

3. Carrie made a $1,200 loan for 18 months at 9.5% simple interest. How much interest was paid?

4. Find the maturity value of a loan of $1,750 for 28 months at 9.8% simple interest.

4 Find the principal, rate, or time using the simple interest formula.

So far in this chapter, we have used the formula $I = PRT$ to find the simple interest on a loan. However, sometimes you need to find the principal or the rate or the time instead of the interest. You can remember the different forms of this formula with a circle diagram (see Figure 11-1) like the one used for the percentage formula. Cover the unknown term to see the form of the simple interest formula needed to find the missing value.

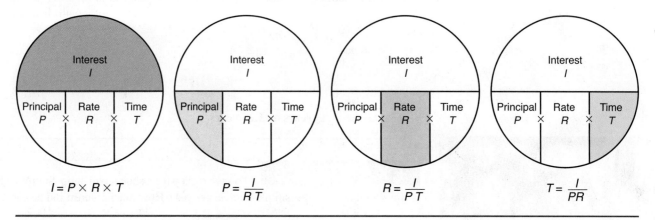

FIGURE 11-1
Various Forms of the Simple Interest Formula

HOW TO   Find the principal, rate, or time using the simple interest formula

1. Select the appropriate form of the formula.
    (a) To find the principal, use

$$P = \frac{I}{RT}$$

    (b) To find the rate, use

$$R = \frac{I}{PT}$$

    (c) To find the time, use

$$T = \frac{I}{PR}$$

2. Replace letters with known values and perform the indicated operations.

EXAMPLE 7   To buy a food preparation table for his restaurant, the owner of the 7th Inning borrowed $1,800 for $1\frac{1}{2}$ years and paid $202.50 simple interest on the loan. What rate of interest did he pay?

$R = \dfrac{I}{PT}$ *R* is unknown. Select the correct form of the simple interest formula. Replace letters with known values: *I* is $202.50, *P* is $1,800, *T* is 1.5 years. Perform the operations.

$R = \dfrac{\$202.50}{(\$1,800)(1.5)}$

$R = 0.075$ Write the rate in percent form by moving the decimal point two places to the right and attaching a % symbol.

$R = 7.5\%$

The owner paid 7.5% interest.

EXAMPLE 8

Phyllis Cox wanted to borrow some money to expand her photography business. She was told she could borrow a sum of money for 18 months at 6% simple interest per year. She thinks she can afford to pay as much as $540 in interest charges. How much money could she borrow?

$$P = \frac{I}{RT}$$

$I = \$540$

$R = 6\% = 0.06$

$T = 18 \text{ months} = \frac{18}{12}$

$\qquad\qquad\quad = 1.5 \text{ years}$

$$P = \frac{\$540}{0.06(1.5)}$$

$P = \$6,000$

P is unknown. Select the correct form of the simple interest formula.

Write the percent as a decimal equivalent.

The interest rate is per year, so write 18 months as 1.5 years.

Replace letters with known values: *I* is $540, *R* is 0.06, *T* is 1.5.

Perform the operations. $0.06(1.5) = 0.09$; $\$540 \div 0.09 = \$6,000$

The principal is $6,000.

TIP

Numerator Divided by Denominator

When a series of calculations has fractions and a calculation in the denominator, the numerator must be divided by the entire denominator. You can do this three ways:

1. With a basic calculator and using memory, multiply 0.06×1.5, store the result in memory and clear the display, and divide 540 by the stored product:

$$\boxed{\text{AC}}\ .06\ \boxed{\times}\ 1.5\ \boxed{=}\ \boxed{\text{M}^+}\ \text{CE/C}\ 540\ \boxed{\div}\ \boxed{\text{MRC}}\ \boxed{=}\ \Rightarrow 6000$$

2. Using repeated division, divide 540 by both .06 and 1.5:

$$\boxed{\text{AC}}\ 540\ \boxed{\div}\ .06\ \boxed{\div}\ 1.5\ \boxed{=}\ \Rightarrow 6000$$

3. With a business or scientific calculator and parentheses, group the calculation in the denominator using parentheses:

$$\boxed{\text{AC}}\ 540\ \boxed{\div}\ \boxed{(}\ (.06\ \boxed{\times}\ 1.5\ \boxed{)}\ \boxed{=}\ \Rightarrow 6000$$

EXAMPLE 9

The 7th Inning borrowed $2,400 at 7% simple interest per year to buy new tables for Brubaker's Restaurant. If it paid $420 interest, what was the duration of the loan?

$$T = \frac{I}{PR}$$

$$T = \frac{\$420}{\$2,400(0.07)} = 2.5 \text{ years}$$

T is unknown. Select the correct form of the simple interest formula. Replace letters with known values: $I = \$420$, $P = \$2,400$, $R = 0.07$.

Perform the operations.

The duration of the loan is 2.5 years.

TIP

Is the Answer Reasonable?

Suppose in the previous example we had mistakenly made the following calculations:

$$420 \div 2400 \times 0.07 = \Rightarrow 0.01225$$

Is it reasonable to think that $420 in interest would be paid on a $2,400 loan that is made for such a small portion of a year? The interest on a 10% loan for one year would be $240. The interest on a 10% loan for two years would be $480. This type of reasoning draws attention to an unreasonable answer.

You can reexamine your steps to discover that you should have used your memory function, repeated division, or your parentheses keys.

STOP AND CHECK

See Example 7.

1. What is the simple interest rate of a loan of $2,680 for $2\frac{1}{2}$ years if $636.50 interest is paid?

2. Find the simple interest rate of a loan of $5,000 that is made for three years and requires $1,762.50 in interest.

3. How much money is borrowed if the interest rate is $9\frac{1}{4}\%$ simple interest and the loan is made for 3.5 years and has $904.88 interest? *See Example 8.*

4. A loan of $16,840 is borrowed at 9% simple interest and is repaid with $4,167.90 interest. What is the duration of the loan? *See Example 9.*

11-1 SECTION EXERCISES

SKILL BUILDERS

1. Find the interest paid on a loan of $2,400 for one year at a simple interest rate of 11% per year. *See Example 1.*

2. Find the interest paid on a loan of $800 at $8\frac{1}{2}\%$ annual simple interest for two years. *See Example 2.*

See Example 4.

3. Find the maturity value for the loan in Exercise 2. *See Example 3.*

4. Find the total amount of money (maturity value) that the borrower will pay back on a loan of $1,400 at $12\frac{1}{2}\%$ annual simple interest for three years.

5. Find the maturity value of a loan of $2,800 after three years. The loan carries a simple interest rate of 7.5% per year.

6. Susan Duke borrowed $20,000 for four years to purchase a car. The simple interest loan has a rate of 8.2% per year. What is the maturity value of the loan?

Convert to years, expressed in decimal form to the nearest hundredth. See Example 5.

7. 9 months

8. 40 months

9. A loan is made for 18 months. Convert the time to years.

10. Express 28 months as years in decimal form.

APPLICATIONS

11. Alexa May took out a $42,000 construction loan to remodel a house. The loan rate is 8.3% simple interest per year and will be repaid in six months. How much is paid back? *See Example 6.*

12. Madison Duke needed start-up money for her bakery. She borrowed $1,200 for 30 months and paid $360 simple interest on the loan. What interest rate did she pay? *See Example 7.*

13. Raul Fletes needed money to buy lawn equipment. He borrowed $500 for seven months and paid $53.96 in interest. What was the rate of interest?

14. Linda Davis agreed to lend money to Alex Luciano at a special interest rate of 9% per year, on the condition that he borrow enough that he would pay her $500 in interest over a two-year period. What was the minimum amount Alex could borrow? *See Example 8.*

15. Jake McAnally needed money for college. He borrowed $6,000 at 12% simple interest per year. If he paid $360 interest, what was the duration of the loan? *See Example 9.*

16. Keaton Smith borrowed $25,000 to purchase stock for his baseball card shop. He repaid the simple interest loan after three years. He paid interest of $6,750. What was the interest rate?

11-2 ORDINARY AND EXACT INTEREST

LEARNING OUTCOMES

1 Find the exact time.
2 Find the due date.
3 Find the ordinary interest and the exact interest.
4 Make a partial payment before the maturity date.

Sometimes the time period of a loan is indicated by the beginning date and the due date of the loan rather than by a specific number of months or days. In such cases, you must first determine the time period of the loan.

1 Find the exact time.

Exact time: time that is based on counting the exact number of days in a time period.

In Chapter 8, Section 3, Learning Outcome 1 we found the exact days in each month of a year. The exact number of days in a time period is called **exact time**.

EXAMPLE 1 Find the exact time of a loan made on July 12 and due on September 12.

Days in July	$31 - 12 = 19$	July has 31 days.
Days in August	$= 31$	August has 31 days.
Days in September	$= 12$	
Total days	$\overline{62}$	

The exact time from July 12 to September 12 is 62 days.

Another way to calculate exact time is by using a table or calendar that assigns each day of the year a numerical value. See Table 11-1.

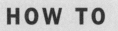

HOW TO

Find the exact time of a loan using the sequential numbers table (Table 11-1)

1. If the beginning and due dates of the loan fall within the same year, subtract the beginning date's sequential number from the due date's sequential number.

From May 15 to Oct. 15
$288 - 135 = 153$ days

2. If the beginning and due dates of the loan do not fall within the same year:
   (a) Subtract the beginning date's sequential number from 365.
   (b) Add the due date's sequential number to the difference from step 2a.

From May 15 to March 15

$365 - 135 = 230$

$230 + 74 = 304$ days
(non–leap year)

3. If February 29 is between the beginning and due dates, add 1 to the difference from step 1 or the sum from step 2b.

$304 + 1 = 305$ days
(leap year)

EXAMPLE 2

Find the exact time of a loan from July 12 to September 12.

$$\begin{array}{r} 255 \\ -\ 193 \\ \hline 62 \text{ days} \end{array}$$

Sequence number for September 12
Sequence number for July 12

TABLE 11-1
Sequential Numbers for Dates of the Year

Day of Month	Jan.	Feb.	Mar.	Apr.	May	June	July	Aug.	Sept.	Oct.	Nov.	Dec.
1	1	32	60	91	121	152	182	213	244	274	305	335
2	2	33	61	92	122	153	183	214	245	275	306	336
3	3	34	62	93	123	154	184	215	246	276	307	337
4	4	35	63	94	124	155	185	216	247	277	308	338
5	5	36	64	95	125	156	186	217	248	278	309	339
6	6	37	65	96	126	157	187	218	249	279	310	340
7	7	38	66	97	127	158	188	219	250	280	311	341
8	8	39	67	98	128	159	189	220	251	281	312	342
9	9	40	68	99	129	160	190	221	252	282	313	343
10	10	41	69	100	130	161	191	222	253	283	314	344
11	11	42	70	101	131	162	192	223	254	284	315	345
12	12	43	71	102	132	163	193	224	255	285	316	346
13	13	44	72	103	133	164	194	225	256	286	317	347
14	14	45	73	104	134	165	195	226	257	287	318	348
15	15	46	74	105	135	166	196	227	258	288	319	349
16	16	47	75	106	136	167	197	228	259	289	320	350
17	17	48	76	107	137	168	198	229	260	290	321	351
18	18	49	77	108	138	169	199	230	261	291	322	352
19	19	50	78	109	139	170	200	231	262	292	323	353
20	20	51	79	110	140	171	201	232	263	293	324	354
21	21	52	80	111	141	172	202	233	264	294	325	355
22	22	53	81	112	142	173	203	234	265	295	326	356
23	23	54	82	113	143	174	204	235	266	296	327	357
24	24	55	83	114	144	175	205	236	267	297	328	358
25	25	56	84	115	145	176	206	237	268	298	329	359
26	26	57	85	116	146	177	207	238	269	299	330	360
27	27	58	86	117	147	178	208	239	270	300	331	361
28	28	59	87	118	148	179	209	240	271	301	332	362
29	29	*	88	119	149	180	210	241	272	302	333	363
30	30		89	120	150	181	211	242	273	303	334	364
31	31		90		151		212	243		304		365

*For centennial years (those at the turn of the century), leap years occur only when the number of the year is evenly divisible by 400. Thus, 2000 was a leap year (2000/400 divides exactly), but 1700, 1800, and 1900 were not leap years.

EXAMPLE 3

A loan made on September 5 is due July 5 of the *following year*. Find (a) the exact time for the loan in a non–leap year and (b) the exact time in a leap year.

(a) *Exact time in a non–leap year*

From Table 11-1, September 5 is the 248th day.

$$\begin{array}{r} 365 \\ -248 \\ \hline 117 \text{ days} \end{array}$$ Subtract 248 from 365.
Days from September 5 through December 31

July 5 is the 186th day.

$117 + 186 = 303$ days   Add 117 and 186 to find the exact time of the loan.

(b) *Exact time in a leap year*

$303 + 1 = 304$ days   Because Feb. 29 is between the beginning and due dates, add 1 to the non–leap year total.

Exact time is 303 days in a non-leap year and 304 days in a leap year.

STOP AND CHECK

1. Find the exact time of a loan made on March 20 and due on September 20 by adding the exact days in each month. *See Example 1.*

2. Find the exact time of a loan made on April 15 and due on October 15 by using Table 11-1. *See Example 2.*

3. Find the exact number of days of a loan made on October 14 and due on December 21. *See Example 2.*

4. A loan made on November 1 is due on March 1 of the following year. How many days are in the loan using exact time? *See Example 3.*

2 Find the due date.

Sometimes the beginning date of a loan and the time period of the loan are known and the due date must be determined.

DID YOU KNOW?

Adjusting for February 29 in this period of the loan requires that you subtract one day. Because the process using Table 11-1 does not include February 29, when this date is actually included in the time period, it uses one of the days of the loan period. Thus, there will be one day less in advancing the given number of days to the due date.

HOW TO

Find the due date of a loan given the beginning date and the time period in days

1. Add the sequential number of the beginning date to the number of days in the time period.
2. If the sum is less than or equal to 365, find the date (Table 11-1) corresponding to the sum.
3. If the sum is more than 365, subtract 365 from the sum. Then find the date (Table 11-1) in the following year corresponding to the difference.
4. Adjust for February 29 in a leap year if appropriate by *subtracting* 1 from the result in step 2 or 3. See Tip regarding one exception.

60-day loan beginning on July 1:
July 1 = Day 182
$182 + 60 = 242$
242nd day = August 30

TIP

Exception Regarding Leap Day

In the previous How To box, if the result from Step 2 or 3 is *exactly* 60, then the 60th day on a leap year is February 29. You *do not* subtract one and move back to the 59th day.

EXAMPLE 4

Find the due date for a 90-day loan made on November 15.

From Table 11-1, November 15 is the 319th day.

$$\begin{array}{r} 319 \\ + 90 \\ \hline 409 \end{array}$$ Add 319 to 90 days in the time period.

409 is greater than 365, so the loan is due in the following year.

$$\begin{array}{r} 409 \\ - 365 \\ \hline 44 \end{array}$$ Subtract 365 from 409.

In Table 11-1, day 44 corresponds to February 13.

The loan is due February 13 of the following year.

See Example 4.

1. Find the due date for a 120-day loan made on June 12.

2. What is the due date for a loan made on July 17 for 150 days?

3. Use exact time and find the due date of a $3,200 loan made on January 29 for 90 days.

4. Use exact time and find the due date of a $2,582 loan made on November 22 for 120 days.

3 Find the ordinary interest and the exact interest.

An interest rate is normally given as a rate *per year*. But if the time period of the loan is in days, then using the simple interest formula requires that the rate *also* be expressed as a rate *per day*. We convert a rate per year to a rate per day in two different ways, depending on whether the rate per day is to be an **ordinary interest** or an **exact interest**. Ordinary interest assumes 360 days per year; exact interest assumes 365 days per year.

Ordinary interest: assumes 360 days per year.

Exact interest: assumes 365 days per year.

HOW TO   Find the ordinary interest and the exact interest

1. To find the ordinary interest, use 360 as the number of days in a year.
2. To find the exact interest, use 365 as the number of days in a year.

EXAMPLE 5
Find the ordinary interest for a loan of $500 at a 7% annual interest rate. The loan was made on March 15 and is due May 15.

Exact time $= 135 - 74 = 61$ days	Find each date's sequential number in Table 11-1 and subtract.
$I = PRT$	Replace with known values.
$I = \$500(0.07)\left(\dfrac{61}{360}\right)$	Perform the operations.
$I = \$5.93$	Round to the nearest cent.

The interest is $5.93.

EXAMPLE 6
Find the exact interest on the loan in Example 5.

Exact time $= 61$ days	
$I = PRT$	Replace with known values.
$I = \$500(0.07)\left(\dfrac{61}{365}\right)$	Perform the operations.
$I = \$5.85$	Round to the nearest cent.

The interest is $5.85.

TIP

Make Comparisons Quickly by Storing Common Portions of Problems

The two preceding examples can be calculated and compared using the memory function of a calculator.

Be sure memory is clear or equal to 0 before you begin. Store the first calculation (500×0.07) in memory.

$\boxed{\text{AC}}$ 500 $\boxed{\times}$ .07 $\boxed{=}$ M$^+$

$\boxed{\text{AC}}$ $\boxed{\text{MR}}$ $\boxed{\times}$ 61 $\boxed{\div}$ 360 $\boxed{=}$ $\Rightarrow$ 5.930555556

$\boxed{\text{AC}}$ $\boxed{\text{MR}}$ $\boxed{\times}$ 61 $\boxed{\div}$ 365 $\boxed{=}$ $\Rightarrow$ 5.849315068

Note that the interest varies in the two cases. The first method illustrated, *ordinary interest,* is most often used by bankers when they are *lending* money because it yields a slightly higher amount of interest. It is sometimes called the **banker's rule**. On the other hand, when bankers *pay* interest on savings accounts, they normally use a 365-day year—exact interest—which yields the most accurate amount of interest but is less than the amount yielded by the banker's rule.

EXAMPLE 7

Borrowing money to pay cash for large purchases is sometimes profitable when a cash discount is allowed on the purchases. For her consulting firm, Joann Jimanez purchased a computer, printer, copier, and fax machine that regularly sold for $5,999. A special promotion offered the equipment for $5,890, with cash terms of 3/10, n/30. She does not have the cash to pay the bill now, but she will within the next three months. She finds a bank that will loan her the money for the equipment at 10% (using ordinary interest) for 90 days. Should she take out the loan to take advantage of the special promotion and cash discount?

What You Know	What You Are Looking For	Solution Plan
Regular price: $5,999 Special price: $5,890 Cash discount rate: 3% Exact term of loan: 90 days Ordinary interest uses 360 days.	Should Joann Jimanez take out the loan? Cash discount on special price, compared with interest on loan	Cash discount = special price $\times$ discount rate Ordinary interest on loan = principal $\times$ rate $\times$ time The principal of the loan is the net amount Joann would pay, once the cash discount is allowed on the special price, or 97% of the cash price.

Solution

$$\text{Cash discount} = \$5{,}890(0.03) = \$176.70$$
$$\text{Principal} = \$5{,}890(0.97) = \$5{,}713.30$$
$$\text{Interest on loan} = \$5{,}713.30(0.1)\left(\frac{90}{360}\right) = \$142.83$$
$$\text{Difference} = \$176.70 - \$142.83 = \$33.87$$

Conclusion

The interest on the loan is $142.83, which is $33.87 less than the cash discount of $176.70. Because the cash discount is more than the interest on the loan, Joann will not lose money by borrowing to take advantage of the discount terms of the sale. But other factors—the time she spends to take out the loan, for example—should be considered.

STOP AND CHECK

1. Find the ordinary interest on a loan of $1,350 at 6.5% annual interest rate if the loan is made on March 3 and due on September 3. *See Example 5.*

2. Find the exact interest for the loan in Exercise 1. *See Example 6.*

3. Compare the interest amounts from the two methods. Which method would you guess bankers offer to borrowers?

4. Use the banker's rule to find the maturity value of a loan of $4,250 made on April 12 and repaid on October 12. The interest rate is 7.2% simple interest.

5. The loan in Exercise 4 was made to take advantage of a special offer on equipment that normally costs $4,500. The equipment is needed now, but the money to pay for the equipment will not be available until the first of October. Is it advisable to borrow the money to get the equipment now? *See Example 7.*

4 Make a partial payment before the maturity date.

U.S. rule: any partial loan payment first covers any interest that has accumulated. The remainder of the partial payment reduces the loan principal.

Simple interest loans are intended to be paid with a lump sum payment at the maturity date. To save some interest, a borrower may decide to make one or more partial payments before the maturity date. The most common method for properly crediting a partial payment is to first apply the loan payment to the accumulated interest. The remainder of the partial payment is applied to the principal. This process is called the **U.S. rule.**

Some states have passed legislation that forbids a lender from charging interest on interest. That means if the partial payment does not cover the accumulated interest, the principal for calculating the interest cannot be increased by the unpaid interest.

Adjusted principal: the remaining principal after a partial payment has been properly credited.

Adjusted balance due at maturity: the remaining balance due at maturity after one or more partial payments have been made.

HOW TO   Find the adjusted principal and adjusted balance due at maturity for a partial payment made before the maturity date

1. Determine the exact time from the date of the loan to the first partial payment.
2. Calculate the interest using the time found in step 1.
3. Subtract the amount of interest found in step 2 from the partial payment.
4. Subtract the remainder of the partial payment (step 3) from the original principal. This is the **adjusted principal.**
5. Repeat the process with the adjusted principal if additional partial payments are made.
6. At maturity, calculate the interest from the last partial payment. Add this interest to the adjusted principal from the last partial payment. This is the **adjusted balance due at maturity.**

EXAMPLE 8

Tony Powers borrows $5,000 on a 10%, 90-day note. On the 30th day, Tony pays $1,500 on the note. If ordinary interest is applied, what is Tony's adjusted principal after the partial payment? What is the adjusted balance due at maturity?

$$\$5,000(0.1)\left(\frac{30}{360}\right) = \$41.67$$ Calculate the ordinary interest on 30 days.

$\$1,500 - \$41.67 = \$1,458.33$ Amount of partial payment applied to principal

$\$5,000 - \$1,458.33 = \$3,541.67$ Adjusted principal

$$\$3,541.67(0.1)\left(\frac{60}{360}\right) = \$59.03$$ Interest on adjusted principal

$\$3,541.67 + \$59.03 = \$3,600.70$ Adjusted balance due at maturity

The adjusted principal after 30 days is $3,541.67 and the adjusted balance due at maturity is $3,600.70.

EXAMPLE 9

How much interest was saved by making the partial payment in Example 8?

$\$41.67 + \$59.03 = \$100.70$ Total interest paid with partial payment

$$\$5,000(0.1)\left(\frac{90}{360}\right) = \$125$$ Interest if no partial payment is made

$\$125 - \$100.70 = \$24.30$ Interest saved

The interest saved by making a partial payment is $24.30.

STOP AND CHECK

1. James Ligon borrowed $10,000 at 9% for 270 days with ordinary interest applied. On the 60th day he paid $3,000 on the note. What is the adjusted balance due at maturity? *See Example 8.*

2. Jennifer Raymond borrowed $5,800 on a 120-day note that required ordinary interest at 7.5%. Jennifer paid $2,500 on the note on the 30th day. How much interest did she save by making the partial payment? *See Example 9.*

3. Tatiana Jacobs borrowed $8,500 on a 9%, 180-day note. On the 60th day, Tatiana paid $3,000 on the note. If ordinary interest is applied, find Tatiana's adjusted principal on the loan after the partial payment.

4. Find the adjusted balance due at maturity on Tatiana's loan (Exercise 3).

SKILL BUILDERS

See Example 6.

1. Find the exact interest on a loan of $32,400 at 8% annually for 30 days.

2. Find the exact interest on a loan of $12,500 at 7.75% annually for 45 days.

3. Find the exact interest on a loan of $6,000 at 8.25% annually for 50 days.

4. Find the exact interest on a loan of $9,580 at 8.5% annually for 40 days.

5. A loan made on March 10 is due September 10 of the *following year*. Find the exact time for the loan in a non–leap year and a leap year. *See Example 3.*

6. Find the exact time of a loan made on March 25 and due on November 15 of the same year by adding the exact days in each month. *See Example 1.*

See Example 4.

7. A loan is made on January 15 and has a due date of October 20 during a leap year. Find the exact time of the loan using Table 11-1.

8. Find the due date for a loan made on October 15 for 120 days.

9. A loan is made on March 20 for 180 days. Find the due date.

10. Find the due date of a loan that is made on February 10 of a leap year and is due in 60 days.

APPLICATIONS

Exercises 11 and 12: A loan for $3,000 with a simple annual interest rate of 15% was made on June 15 and was due on August 15.

11. Find the exact interest. *See Example 6.*

12. Find the ordinary interest. *See Example 5.*

13. The loan in Exercise 11 was made to avoid a $100 price increase that will take place on June 20. The equipment is needed now but the money to pay for the equipment will not be available until the middle of August. Is it advisable to borrow the money to get the equipment now? *See Example 7.*

14. Find the adjusted balance due at maturity for a 90-day note of $15,000 at 13.8% ordinary interest if a partial payment of $5,000 is made on the 60th day of the loan. *See Example 8.*

15. Raul Fletes borrowed $8,500 on a 300-day note that required ordinary interest at 11.76%. Raul paid $4,250 on the note on the 60th day. How much interest did he save by making the partial payment? *See Example 9.*

11-3 PROMISSORY NOTES

LEARNING OUTCOMES
1 Find the bank discount and proceeds for a simple discount note.
2 Find the true or effective interest rate of a simple discount note.
3 Find the third-party discount and proceeds for a third-party discount note.

Promissory note: a legal document promising to repay a loan.

Maker: the person or business that borrows the money.

Payee: the person or business loaning the money.

Term: the length of time for which the money is borrowed.

Maturity date: the date on which the loan is due to be repaid.

Face value: the amount borrowed.

Bank discount: the interest or fee on a discounted note that is subtracted from the amount borrowed at the time the loan is made.

Proceeds: the face value of the loan minus the bank discount.

Simple discount note: a loan made by a bank at a simple interest rate with interest collected at the time the loan is made.

When a business or individual borrows money, it is customary for the borrower to sign a legal document promising to repay the loan. The document is called a **promissory note.** The note includes all necessary information about the loan. The **maker** is the person borrowing the money. The **payee** is the person loaning the money. The **term** of the note is the length of time for which the money is borrowed; the **maturity date** is the date on which the loan is due to be repaid. The **face value** of the note is the amount borrowed.

1 Find the bank discount and proceeds for a simple discount note.

If money is borrowed from a bank at a simple interest rate, the bank sometimes collects the interest, which is also called the **bank discount,** at the time the loan is made. Thus, the maker receives the face value of the loan minus the bank discount. This difference is called the **proceeds.** Such a loan is called a **simple discount note.** Loans of this type allow the bank or payee of the loan to receive all fees and interest at the time the loan is made. This increases the yield on the loan because the interest and fees can be reinvested immediately. Besides increased yields, a bank may require this type of loan when the maker of the loan has an inadequate or poor credit history. This decreases the amount of risk to the bank or lender.

HOW TO   Find the bank discount and proceeds for a simple discount note

1. For the bank discount, use:

$$\text{Bank discount} = \text{face value} \times \text{discount rate} \times \text{time}$$
$$I = PRT$$

2. For the proceeds, use:

$$\text{Proceeds} = \text{face value} - \text{bank discount}$$
$$A = P - I$$

New Formulas Related to Previously Learned Formulas

In the How To box for finding the bank discount and proceeds for a simple discount note, a new formula,

$$\text{Bank discount} = \text{face value} \times \text{discount rate} \times \text{time}$$

is related to a previously learned formula, $I = PRT$.

Similarly,

$$\text{Proceeds} = \text{face value} - \text{bank discount}$$

relates to $A = P - I$.

This allows you to connect back to previously learned concepts. If you prefer to let the letters of the formula relate to the terminology of the new formula, you might use:

$$B = FDT \text{ and } P = F - B$$

Just remember, P refers to Principal in the simple interest formula and to *Proceeds* in the simple discount formula.

EXAMPLE 1 Find the (a) bank discount and (b) proceeds using ordinary interest on a promissory note to Mary Fisher for $4,000 at 8% annual simple interest from June 5 to September 5.

(a) Exact days $= 248 - 156 = 92$ Subtract sequential numbers (Table 11-1).

Bank discount $= FDT$

Bank discount $= \$4,000(0.08)\left(\dfrac{92}{360}\right)$ Multiply.

Bank discount $= \$81.78$ Rounded to the nearest cent.

The bank discount is $81.78.

(b) Proceeds $= F - B$

Proceeds $= \$4,000 - \$81.78$ Subtract the bank discount from the face

Proceeds $= \$3,918.22$ value of the note.

The proceeds are $3,918.22.

Undiscounted note: another term for a simple interest note.

The difference between the simple interest note—which is also called an **undiscounted note**—and the simple discount note is the amount of money the borrower has use of for the length of the loan, and the maturity value of the loan—the amount owed at the end of the loan term. Interest is paid on the same amount for the same period of time in both cases. In the simple interest note, the borrower has use of the full principal of the loan, but the maturity value is principal plus interest. In the simple discount note, the borrower has use of only the proceeds (face value $-$ discount), but the maturity value is just the face value, as the interest (the discount) was paid "in advance."

Suppose Bill borrows $5,000 with a discount (interest) rate of 10%. The discount is 10% ($5,000), or $500, so he gets the use of only $4,500, although the bank charges interest on the full $5,000. The maturity value is $5,000.

Here is a comparison of simple interest notes versus simple discount notes:

	Simple interest note	Simple discount note
Principal or face value	$5,000	$5,000
Interest or discount	500	500
Amount available to borrower or proceeds	5,000	4,500
Amount to be repaid or maturity value	5,500	5,000

1. Find the bank discount and proceeds using ordinary interest for a loan to Michelle Anders for $7,200 at 8.25% annual simple interest from August 8 to November 8.

2. Find the bank discount and proceeds using ordinary interest for a loan to Andre Peters for $9,250 at 7.75% annual simple interest from January 17 to July 17.

3. Find the bank discount and proceeds using ordinary interest for a loan to Megan Anders for $3,250 at 8.75% annual simple interest from February 23 to November 23.

4. Frances Johnson is making a bank loan for $32,800 at 7.5% annual simple interest from May 10 to July 10. Find the bank discount and proceeds using ordinary interest.

2 Find the true or effective interest rate of a simple discount note.

Effective interest rate of a simple discount note: the actual interest rate based on the proceeds of the loan.

For a simple interest note, the borrower uses the full face value of the loan for the entire period of the loan. In a simple discount note, the borrower only uses the proceeds of the loan for the period of the loan. Because the proceeds are less than the face value of the loan, the stated discount rate is not the true or effective rate of interest of the note. To find the **effective interest rate of a simple discount note,** the proceeds of the loan are used as the principal in the interest formula.

HOW TO   Find the true or effective interest rate of a simple discount note

1. Find the bank discount (interest).

$$I = PRT$$

2. Find the proceeds.

$$\text{Proceeds} = \text{principal} - \text{bank discount}$$

3. Find the effective interest rate.

$$R = \frac{I}{PT} \text{ using the proceeds as the principal.}$$

EXAMPLE 2   What is the effective interest rate of a simple discount note for $5,000, at an ordinary bank discount rate of 12%, for 90 days? Round to the nearest tenth of a percent.

Find the bank discount:

$$I = PRT$$

$$I = \$5,000(0.12)\left(\frac{90}{360}\right)$$

$$I = \$150 \qquad\qquad \text{Bank discount}$$

Find the proceeds:

$$\text{Proceeds} = \text{principal} - \text{bank discount}$$
$$\text{Proceeds} = \$5,000 - \$150$$
$$\text{Proceeds} = \$4,850$$

Find the effective interest rate:

$$R = \frac{I}{PT} \qquad\qquad \text{Substitute proceeds for principal.}$$

$$R = \frac{\$150}{\$4,850\left(\dfrac{90}{360}\right)}$$

$$R = \frac{\$150}{\$1,212.50}$$

$$R = 0.1237113402$$

$$R = 12.4\% \qquad\qquad \text{Effective interest rate}$$

The effective interest rate for a simple discount note of $5,000 for 90 days is 12.4%.

1. What is the effective interest rate of a simple discount note for $8,000, at an ordinary bank discount rate of 11%, for 120 days? Round to the nearest tenth of a percent.

2. What is the effective interest rate of a simple discount note for $22,000, at an ordinary bank discount rate of 8.36%, for 90 days? Round to the nearest tenth of a percent.

3. Ebbe Wojtek needs to calculate the effective interest rate of a simple discount note for $18,000, at an ordinary bank discount rate of 9.6%, for 270 days. Find the effective rate rounded to the nearest tenth.

4. Ole Christian Borgesen needs to calculate the effective interest rate of a simple discount note for $16,000, at an ordinary bank discount rate of 8.4%, for 210 days. Find the effective rate rounded to the nearest tenth.

3 Find the third-party discount and proceeds for a third-party discount note.

Third party: an investment group or individual that assumes a note that was made between two other parties.

Third-party discount note: a note that is sold to a third party (usually a bank) so that the original payee gets the proceeds immediately and the maker pays the third party the original amount at maturity.

Discount period: the amount of time that the third party owns the third-party discounted note.

Many businesses agree to be the payee for a promissory note as payment for the sale of goods. If these businesses in turn need cash, they may sell such a note to an investment group or person who is the **third party** of the note. Selling a note to a third party in return for cash is called *discounting* a note. The note is called a **third-party discount note.**

When the third party discounts a note, it gives the business owning the note the maturity value of the note minus a third-party discount. The discount is based on how long the third party holds the note, called the **discount period.** The third party receives the full maturity value of the note from the maker when it comes due. From the standpoint of the note maker (the borrower), the term of the note is the same because the maturity (due) date is the same, and the maturity value is the same.

The following diagram shows how the discount period is determined.

Original date of loan		Date loan is discounted		Maturity date
July 14		Aug. 3		Sept. 12
		Discount period		

DID YOU KNOW?

If a business sells a note to a third party, the customer pays the same amount as originally agreed. The business will get less money, but it will get the money sooner. Also, the responsibility for collecting the note is shifted to the third party.

HOW TO Find the third-party discount and proceeds for a third-party discount note

1. For the third-party discount, use:

Third-party discount = maturity value of original note × discount rate × discount period
$$I = PRT$$

2. For the proceeds to the original payee, use:

Proceeds = maturity value of original note − third-party discount
$$A = P - I$$

EXAMPLE 3 Alpine Pleasures, Inc., delivers ski equipment to retailers in July but does not expect payment until mid-September, so the retailers agree to sign promissory notes for the equipment. These notes are based on exact interest, with a 10% annual simple interest rate. One promissory note held by Alpine is for $8,000, was made on July 14, and is due September 12. Alpine needs cash, so it takes the note to an investment group. On August 3, the group agrees to buy the note at a 12% discount rate using the banker's rule (ordinary interest). Find the proceeds for the note.

A table can help you organize the facts:

Date of original note	Principal of note	Simple interest rate	Date of discount note	Third-party discount rate	Maturity date
July 14	$8,000	10%	Aug. 3	12%	Sept. 12

Calculate the time and maturity value of the original note.

255	September 12 (Table 11-1)
− 195	July 14 (Table 11-1)
60 days	Exact days of the original loan

$I = PRT$ Use the simple interest formula to find exact interest.

$I = \$8,000(0.1)\left(\dfrac{60}{365}\right)$ Use 365 days in a year.

$I = \$131.51$ (rounded)

The simple interest for the original loan is \$131.51.

To find the maturity value, add the principal and interest.

Maturity value = principal + interest
Maturity value = \$8,000 + \$131.51
Maturity value = \$8,131.51

The maturity value of the original loan is \$8,131.51.

Now calculate the discount period.

Discount period = number of days from August 3 to September 12
August 3 is the 215th day.

255	September 12
− 215	August 3
40 days	Exact days of discount period

The discount period for the discount note is 40 days.

Now calculate the third-party discount based on the banker's rule (ordinary interest).
Third-party discount = maturity value × third-party discount rate × discount period

Third-party discount = $\$8,131.51(0.12)\left(\dfrac{40}{360}\right)$ Use 360 days in a year.

Third-party discount = \$108.42

The third-party discount is \$108.42.

Now calculate the proceeds that will be received by Alpine.

Proceeds = maturity value − third-party discount
Proceeds = \$8,131.51 − \$108.42
Proceeds = \$8,023.09

The proceeds to Alpine are \$8,023.09.

TIP

Interest-Free Money

A non-interest-bearing note is very uncommon but sometimes available. This means that you borrow a certain amount and pay that same amount back later. The note itself carries no interest, and the maturity value of the note is the same as the face value or principal. The payee or person loaning the money only wants the original amount of money at the maturity date.

What happens if a non-interest-bearing note is discounted? Use the information from Example 1, without the simple interest on the original loan.

Third-party discount = maturity value × discount rate × discount period

Third-party discount = $\$8,000(0.12)\left(\dfrac{40}{360}\right)$ The maturity value is the face value, or \$8,000, rather than \$8,131.51, which

Third-party discount = \$106.67   included interest.

The third-party discount is \$106.67.

Proceeds = maturity value − third-party discount

Proceeds = $8,000 − $106.67   The maturity value is $8,000.

Proceeds = $7,893.33

The proceeds are $7,893.33.

The original payee or lender loans $8,000 and receives $7,893.33 in cash from the third party.

That is, the original payee loses money.

STOP AND CHECK

See Example 3.

1. Hugh's Trailers delivers trailers to retailers in February and expects payment in July. The retailers sign promissory notes based on exact interest with 8.25% annual simple interest. One promissory note held by Hugh's for $19,500 was made on February 15 and is due July 20. On May 5 a third party buys the note at a 10% discount using the banker's rule. Find the number of days until maturity using exact time of the original note.

2. Find the maturity value of the original note in Exercise 1.

3. Find the third-party discount for the note in Exercise 1.

4. Find the proceeds to Hugh's Trailers for the discounted note in Exercise 1.

11-3 SECTION EXERCISES

SKILL BUILDERS

Use the banker's rule unless otherwise specified. See Example 1.

1. José makes a simple discount note with a face value of $2,500, a term of 120 days, and a 9% discount rate. Find the discount.

2. Find the proceeds for Exercise 1.

3. Find the discount and proceeds on a $3,250 face-value note for six months if the discount rate is 9.2%.

4. Find the maturity value of the undiscounted promissory note shown in Figure 11-2.

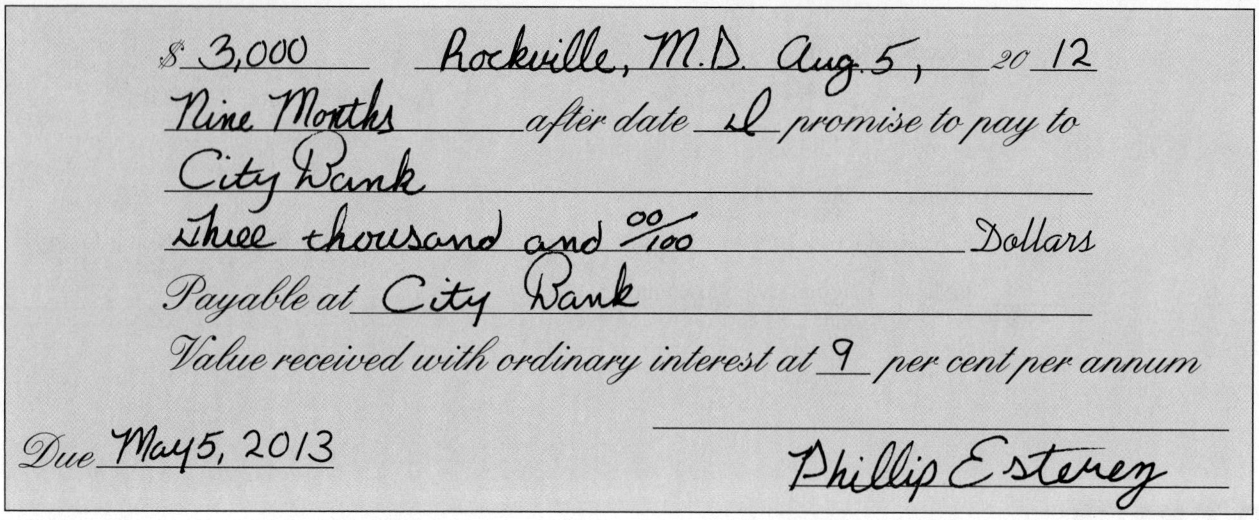
$ 3,000 Rockville, M.D. Aug. 5, 20 12

Nine Months after date I promise to pay to

City Bank

three thousand and 00/100 Dollars

Payable at City Bank

Value received with ordinary interest at 9 per cent per annum

Due May 5, 2013

Phillip Esterez

FIGURE 11-2
Promissory Note

See Example 2.

5. Roland Clark has a simple discount note for $6,500, at an ordinary bank discount rate of 8.74%, for 60 days. What is the effective interest rate? Round to the nearest tenth of a percent.

6. What is the effective interest rate of a simple discount note for $30,800, at an ordinary bank discount rate of 14%, for 20 days? Round to the nearest tenth of a percent.

7. Shanquayle Jenkins needs to calculate the effective interest rate of a simple discount note for $19,750, at an ordinary bank discount rate of 7.82%, for 90 days. Find the effective rate rounded to the nearest hundredth of a percent.

8. Matt Crouse needs to calculate the effective interest rate of a simple discount note for $12,800, at an ordinary bank discount rate of 8.75%, for 150 days. Find the effective rate rounded to the nearest tenth of a percent.

See Example 3.

9. Carter Manufacturing holds a note of $5,000 that has an interest rate of 11% annually. The note was made on March 18 and is due November 13. Carter sells the note to a bank on June 13 at a discount rate of 10% annually. Find the proceeds on the third-party discount note.

10. Discuss reasons a payee might agree to a non-interest-bearing note.

11. Discuss reasons a payee would sell a note to a third party and lose money in the process.

Learning Outcomes

Section 11-1

1 Find simple interest using the simple interest formula. (p. 388)

What to Remember with Examples

1. Identify the principal, rate, and time.
2. Multiply the principal by the rate and time.

$$\text{Interest} = \text{principal} \times \text{rate} \times \text{time}$$
$$I = PRT$$

Find the interest paid on a loan of $8,400 for one year at $9\frac{1}{2}\%$ annual simple interest rate.	Find the interest paid on a loan of $4,500 for two years at a simple interest rate of 12% per year.
Interest = principal × rate × time = $8,400(0.095)(1)$ = 798	Interest = principal × rate × time = $4,500(0.12)(2)$ = $1,080$

2 Find the maturity value of a loan. (p. 389)

1. If the principal and interest are known, add them.

$$\text{Maturity value} = \text{principal} + \text{interest}$$
$$MV = P + I$$

2. If the principal, rate, and time are known, use either of the formulas:

    (a) Maturity value = principal + (principal × rate × time)
$$MV = P + PRT$$

    (b) Maturity value = principal (1 + rate × time)
$$MV = P(1 + RT)$$

Find the maturity value of a loan of $8,400 with $798 interest. $MV = P + I$ $MV = \$8,400 + \$798$ $MV = \$9,198$	Find the maturity value of a loan of $4,500 for two years at a simple interest rate of 12% per year. $MV = P(1 + RT)$ $MV = \$4,500[1 + 0.12(2)]$ $MV = \$4,500(1.24)$ $MV = \$5,580$

3 Convert months to a fractional or decimal part of a year. (p. 390)

1. Write the number of months as the numerator of a fraction.
2. Write 12 as the denominator of the fraction.
3. Reduce the fraction to lowest terms if using the fractional equivalent.
4. Divide the numerator by the denominator to get the decimal equivalent of the fraction.

Convert 42 months to years. $\dfrac{42}{12} = \dfrac{7}{2} = 3.5$ years	Convert 3 months to years. $\dfrac{3}{12} = \dfrac{1}{4} = 0.25$ years

4 Find the principal, rate, or time using the simple interest formula. (p. 392)

1. Select the appropriate form of the formula.

    (a) To find the principal, use $P = \dfrac{I}{RT}$ **(b)** To find the rate, use $R = \dfrac{I}{PT}$

    (c) To find the time, use $T = \dfrac{I}{PR}$

2. Replace letters with known values and perform the indicated operations.

Nancy Jeggle borrowed $6,000 for $3\frac{1}{2}$ years and paid $2,800 simple interest. What was the annual interest rate?	R is unknown. $R = \dfrac{I}{PT}$ $R = \dfrac{\$2,800}{(\$6,000)(3.5)}$ $R = 0.1333333333$ $R = 13.3\%$ annually (rounded)

Donna Ruscitti paid $675 interest on an 18-month loan at 10% annual simple interest. What was the principal?	P is unknown. $P = \dfrac{I}{RT}$ $\qquad \dfrac{18}{12} = \dfrac{3}{2} = 1.5$ $P = \dfrac{\$675}{0.10(1.5)}$ $P = \$4,500$

Ashish Paranjape borrowed $1,500 at 8% annual simple interest. If he paid $866.25 interest, what was the time period of the loan?	T is unknown. $T = \dfrac{I}{PR}$ $T = \dfrac{\$866.25}{\$1,500(0.08)}$ $T = 7.2 \text{ years (rounded)}$

Section 11-2

1 Find the exact time. (p. 395)

Change months and years to exact time in days.

1 month = exact number of days in the month; 1 year = 365 days (or 366 days in a leap year)

Find the exact time of a loan made October 1 and due May 1 (non-leap year).

October, December, January, and March have 31 days. November and April have 30 days. February has 28 days.

4(31) + 2(30) + 28 = 212 days

Find the exact time of a loan using the sequential numbers table (Table 11-1).

1. If the beginning and due dates of the loan fall within the same year, subtract the beginning date's sequential number from the due date's sequential number.
2. If the beginning and due dates of the loan do not fall within the same year:
   (a) Subtract the beginning date's sequential number from 365.
   (b) Add the due date's sequential number to the difference from step 2a.
3. If February 29 is between the beginning and due dates, add 1 to the difference from step 1 or to the sum from step 2b.

Find the exact time of a loan made on March 25 and due on October 10. October 10 = day 283 March 25 = day 84 199 days The loan is made for 199 days.	Find the exact time of a loan made on June 7 and due the following March 7 in a non-leap year. December 31 = day 365 June 7 = day 158 207 days March 7 = + 66 days 273 days The loan is made for 273 days in all.

2 Find the due date. (p. 397)

Find the due date of a loan given the beginning date and the time period in days.

1. Add the sequential number of the beginning date to the number of days in the time period.
2. If the sum is less than or equal to 365, find the date (Table 11-1) corresponding to the sum.
3. If the sum is more than 365, subtract 365 from the sum. Then find the date (Table 11-1) in the following year corresponding to the difference.
4. Adjust for February 29 in a leap year if appropriate by subtracting 1 from the result in step 2 or 3. Note exception in Tip on p. 397.

Figure the due date for a 60-day loan made on August 12.

August 12 = day 224

    + 60
    284   Day 284 is October 11.

3 Find the ordinary interest and the exact interest. (p. 398)

1. To find the ordinary interest, use 360 as the number of days in a year.
2. To find the exact interest, use 365 as the number of days in a year.

On May 15, Roberta Krech borrowed $6,000 at 12.5% annual simple interest. The loan was due on November 15. Find the ordinary interest due on the loan.

Use Table 11-1 to find exact time. November 15 is day 319. May 15 is day 135. So time is $319 - 135 = 184$ days.

$$I = PRT$$
$$I = (\$6,000)(0.125)\left(\frac{184}{360}\right)$$
$$I = \$383.33$$

Find the exact interest due on Roberta's loan (see above).

$$I = PRT$$
$$I = (\$6,000)(0.125)\left(\frac{184}{365}\right)$$
$$I = \$378.08$$

4 Make a partial payment before the maturity date. (p. 400)

1. Determine the exact time from the date of the loan to the first partial payment.
2. Calculate the interest using the time found in step 1.
3. Subtract the amount of interest found in step 2 from the partial payment.
4. Subtract the remainder of the partial payment (step 3) from the original principal. This is the adjusted principal.
5. Repeat the process with the adjusted principal if additional partial payments are made.
6. At maturity, calculate the interest from the last partial payment. Add this interest to the adjusted principal from the last partial payment. This is the adjusted balance due at maturity.

Kate Sebastian borrows $7,000 on a 12%, 90-day note. On the 60th day, Kate pays $1,500 on the note. If ordinary interest is applied, what is Kate's adjusted principal after the partial payment? What is the adjusted balance due at maturity?

$\$7,000(0.12)\left(\dfrac{60}{360}\right) = \$140$	Calculate the ordinary interest on 60 days.
$\$1,500 - \$140 = \$1,360$	Amount of partial payment applied to principal
$\$7,000 - \$1,360 = \$5,640$	Adjusted principal
$\$5,640(0.12)\left(\dfrac{30}{360}\right) = \$56.40$	Interest on adjusted principal
$\$5,640 + \$56.40 = \$5,696.40$	Adjusted balance due at maturity

The adjusted principal after 90 days is $5,640 and the adjusted balance due at maturity is $5,696.40.

Section 11-3

1 Find the bank discount and proceeds for a simple discount note. (p. 402)

1. For the bank discount, use:

$$\text{Bank discount} = \text{face value} \times \text{discount rate} \times \text{time}$$
$$I = PRT$$

2. For the proceeds, use:

$$\text{Proceeds} = \text{face value} - \text{bank discount}$$
$$A = P - I$$

The bank charged Robert Milewsky a 11.5% annual discount rate on a bank note of $1,500 for 120 days. Find the proceeds of the note using the banker's rule.

First find the discount, and then subtract the discount from the face value of $1,500.

$$\text{Discount} = I = PRT$$
$$\text{Discount} = \$1,500(0.115)\left(\frac{120}{360}\right) \quad \text{Ordinary interest}$$
$$\text{Discount} = \$57.50$$
$$\text{Proceeds} = A = P - I$$
$$\text{Proceeds} = \$1,500 - \$57.50$$
$$\text{Proceeds} = \$1,442.50$$

2 Find the true or effective interest rate of a simple discount note. (p. 404)

1. Find the bank discount (interest).
$$I = PRT$$

2. Find the proceeds.
$$\text{Proceeds} = \text{principal} - \text{bank discount}$$

3. Find the effective interest rate.
$$R = \frac{I}{PT} \qquad \text{Use the proceeds as the principal.}$$

Larinda Temple has a simple discount note for $5,000, at an ordinary bank discount rate of 8%, for 90 days. What is the effective interest rate? Round to the nearest tenth of a percent.

Find the bank discount:

$$I = PRT$$
$$I = \$5{,}000(0.08)\left(\frac{90}{360}\right)$$
$$I = \$100$$

$$\text{Proceeds} = \text{principal} - \text{bank discount}$$
$$\text{Proceeds} = \$5{,}000 - \$100$$
$$\text{Proceeds} = \$4{,}900$$

$$R = \frac{I}{PT}$$
$$R = \frac{\$100}{\$4{,}900\left(\dfrac{90}{360}\right)}$$
$$R = \frac{\$100}{\$1{,}225}$$
$$R = 0.0816326531$$
$$R = 8.2\%$$

The effective interest rate for a simple discount note of $5,000 for 90 days is 8.2%.

3 Find the third-party discount and proceeds for a third-party discount note. (p. 405)

1. For the third-party discount, use:

Third-party discount = maturity value of original note × discount rate × discount period
$$I = PRT$$

2. For the proceeds to the original payee, use:

Proceeds = maturity value of original note − third-party discount
$$A = P - I$$

Mihoc Trailer Sales made a note of $10,000 with Darcy Mihoc, company owner, at 9% simple interest based on exact interest. The note is made on August 12 and due on November 10. However, Mihoc Trailer Sales needs cash, so the note is taken to a third party on September 5. The third party agrees to accept the note with a 13% annual discount rate using the banker's rule. Find the proceeds of the note to the original payee.

To find the proceeds, we find the maturity value of the original note and then find the third-party discount. Exact time is 90 days (314 − 224).

$$\text{Maturity value} = P(1 + RT)$$
$$\text{Maturity value} = \$10{,}000\left(1 + 0.09\left(\frac{90}{365}\right)\right) \quad \text{Exact interest}$$
$$\text{Maturity value} = \$10{,}221.92$$

Exact time of the discount period is 66 days (314 − 248). Use the banker's rule.

$$\text{Third-party discount} = I = PRT$$
$$\text{Third-party discount} = \$10{,}221.92(0.13)\left(\frac{66}{360}\right) \quad \text{Ordinary interest}$$
$$\text{Third-party discount} = \$243.62$$
$$\text{Proceeds} = A = P - I$$
$$\text{Proceeds} = \$10{,}221.92 - \$243.62$$
$$\text{Proceeds} = \$9{,}978.30$$

EXERCISES SET A

SKILL BUILDERS

Find the simple interest. Round to the nearest cent when necessary.

Principal	Annual rate	Time	Interest
1. $500 Excel	12%	2 years	____
2. $3,575 Excel	11%	3 years	____

3. Capco, Inc., borrowed $4,275 for three years at 12% interest. (a) How much simple interest did the company pay? (b) What is the maturity value?

Find the rate of annual simple interest in each of the following problems.

Principal	Interest	Time	Rate
4. $800	$124	1 year	____
5. $175	$ 31.50	2 years	____

Find the time period of the loan using the formula for simple interest.

Principal	Annual rate	Interest	Time
6. $450	10%	$135	____
7. $1,500	$8\frac{1}{2}$%	$478.13	____

In each of the following problems, find the principal, based on simple interest.

Interest	Annual rate	Time	Principal
8. $300	3%	2 years	____
9. $90	3.2%	1 year	____

10. A loan for three years with an annual simple interest rate of 9% costs $486 interest. Find the principal.

Write a fraction expressing each amount of time as a part of a year (12 months = 1 year).

11. 7 months

12. 16 months

APPLICATIONS

13. Carol Stoy invested $500 at 2% annually for six months. How much interest did she receive?

14. Use the banker's rule to find the interest paid on a loan of $1,200 for 60 days at a simple interest rate of 6% annually.

15. Use the banker's rule to find the interest paid on a loan of $800 for 120 days at a simple interest rate of 6% annually.

16. Interest figured using 360 days per year is called what kind of interest?

Use Table 11-1 to find the exact time from the first date to the second date for non–leap years unless a leap year is identified.

17. March 15 to July 10

18. January 27, 2008, to September 30, 2008

If a loan is made on the given date, find the date it is due.

19. January 10 for 210 days

20. August 12 for 60 days

For Exercise 21, find (a) the exact interest and (b) the ordinary interest. Round answers to the nearest cent.

21. A loan of $1,200 at 10% annually made on October 15 and due on March 20 of the following non–leap year

22. Find the discount (ordinary interest) and proceeds on a promissory note for $2,000 made by Barbara Jones on February 10, 2011, and payable to First State Bank on August 10, 2011, with a discount rate of 9%.

23. MAK, Inc., accepted an interest-bearing note for $10,000 with 9% annual ordinary interest. The note was made on April 10 and was due December 6. MAK needed cash and took the note to First United Bank, which offered to buy the note at a discount rate of $12\frac{1}{2}$%. The transaction was made on July 7. How much cash did MAK receive for the note?

24. Malinda Levi borrows $12,000 on a 9.5%, 90-day note. On the 30th day, Malinda pays $4,000 on the note. If ordinary interest is applied, what is Malinda's adjusted principal after the partial payment? What is the adjusted balance due at maturity? What is the amount of interest saved by making the partial payment?

25. Shameka Bonner has a simple discount note for $11,000, at an ordinary bank discount rate of 11%, for 120 days. What is the effective interest rate? Round to the nearest tenth of a percent.

26. Bennett Sales holds a 180-day note of $7,500 that has an interest rate of 8% annually. After 60 days, the note is sold to a bank at a discount rate of 7% annually. Find the proceeds on the third-party discount note.

EXERCISES SET B

SKILL BUILDERS

Find the simple interest. Round to the nearest cent when necessary.

Principal	Annual rate	Time	Interest
1. 1,000 Excel	$9\frac{1}{2}\%$	3 years	_____
2. $2,975 Excel	$12\frac{1}{2}\%$	2 years	_____

3. Legan Company borrowed $15,280 at $10\frac{1}{2}\%$ for 12 years. How much simple interest did the company pay? What was the total amount paid back?

Find the rate of annual simple interest in each of the following problems.

Principal	Interest	Time	Rate
4. $1,280	$256	2 years	_____
5. $40,000	$32,000	10 years	_____

Find the time period of the loan using the formula for simple interest.

Principal	Annual rate	Interest	Time
6. $700	6%	$84	_____
7. $3,549	9.2%	$979.52	_____

In each of the following problems, find the principal, based on simple interest.

Interest	Annual rate	Time	Principal
8. $56.25	$2\frac{1}{2}\%$	3 years	_____
9. $20	1.25%	2 years	_____

10. An investor earned $1,170 interest on funds invested at $9\frac{3}{4}\%$ annual simple interest for four years. How much was invested?

Write a fraction expressing each amount of time as a part of a year (12 months = 1 year).

11. 18 months

12. 9 months

APPLICATIONS

13. Alpha Hodge borrowed $500 for three months and paid $12.50 interest. What was the annual rate of interest?

14. Find the ordinary interest paid on a loan of $2,100 for 90 days at a simple interest rate of 4% annually.

15. Find the ordinary interest paid on a loan of $15,835 for 45 days at a simple interest rate of 8.1% annually.

16. When the exact number of days in a year is used to figure time, it is called what kind of interest?

Use Table 11-1 to find the exact time from the first date to the second date for non-leap years unless a leap year is identified.

17. April 12 to November 15

18. November 12 to April 15 of the next year

19. February 3, 2012 to August 12, 2012

If a loan is made on the given date, find the date it is due.

20. May 30 for 240 days

21. June 13 for 90 days

22. A loan of $8,900 at 7.75% annually is made on September 10 and due on December 10. Find (a) the exact interest and (b) the ordinary interest. Round answers to the nearest cent.

23. Find the discount and proceeds using the banker's rule on a promissory note for $1,980 at 8% made by Alexa Green on January 30, 2012, and payable to Enterprise Bank on July 30, 2012.

24. Find the exact interest on a loan of $2,100 at 7.75% annual interest for 40 days.

25. Allan Stojanovich can purchase an office desk for $1,500 with cash terms of 2/10, n/30. If he can borrow the money at 12% annual simple ordinary interest for 20 days, will he save money by taking advantage of the cash discount offered?

26. Shaunda Sanders borrows $16,000 on a 10.8%, 120-day note. On the 60th day, Shaunda pays $10,000 on the note. If ordinary interest is applied, what is Shaunda's adjusted principal after the partial payment? What is the adjusted balance due at maturity? What is the amount of interest saved by making the partial payment?

27. Bam Doyen has a simple discount note for $6,250, at an ordinary bank discount rate of 9%, for 90 days. What is the effective interest rate? Round to the nearest tenth of a percent.

28. Custom Computers holds a 120-day note of $8,000 that has an interest rate of 6% annually. After 60 days, the note is sold to a bank at a discount rate of 5% annually. Find the proceeds on the third-party discount note.

PRACTICE TEST

1. Find the simple interest on $500 invested at 4% annually for three years.

2. How much money was borrowed at 12% annually for 6 months if the interest was $90?

3. A loan of $3,000 was made for 210 days. If ordinary interest is $218.75, find the rate.

4. A loan of $5,000 at 12% annually requires $1,200 interest. For how long is the money borrowed?

5. Find the exact time from February 13 to November 27 in a non–leap year.

6. Find the exact time from October 12 to March 28 of the following year (a leap year).

7. Find the exact time from January 28, 2012, to July 5, 2012.

8. Sondra Davis borrows $6,000 on a 10%, 120-day note. On the 60th day, Sondra pays $2,000 on the note. If ordinary interest is applied, what is Sondra's adjusted principal after the partial payment? What is the adjusted balance due at maturity? What is the amount of interest saved by making the partial payment?

9. Find the ordinary interest on a loan of $2,800 at 10% annually made on March 15 for 270 days.

10. A bread machine with a cash price of $188 can be purchased with a one-year loan at 10% annual simple interest. Find the total amount to be repaid.

11. A copier that originally cost $3,000 was purchased with a loan for 12 months at 15% annual simple interest. What was the *total* cost of the copier?

12. Find the exact interest on a loan of $850 at 11% annually. The loan was made January 15 and was due March 15.

13. Michael Denton has a simple discount note for $2,000, at an ordinary bank discount rate of 12%, for 240 days. What is the effective interest rate? Round to the nearest tenth of a percent.

14. Find the duration of a loan of $3,000 if the loan required interest of $213.75 and was at a rate of $9\frac{1}{2}\%$ annual simple interest.

15. Find the rate of simple interest on a $1,200 loan that requires the borrower to repay a total of $1,302 after one year.

16. A promissory note using the banker's rule has a face value of $5,000 and is discounted by the bank at the rate of 14%. If the note is made for 180 days, find the amount of the discount.

17. Find the ordinary interest paid on a loan of $1,600 for 90 days at a simple interest rate of 13% annually.

18. Jerry Brooks purchases office supplies totaling $1,890. He can take advantage of cash terms of 2/10, n/30 if he obtains a short-term loan. If he can borrow the money at $10\frac{1}{2}\%$ annual simple ordinary interest for 20 days, will he save money if he borrows to take advantage of the cash discount? How much will he save?

19. Find the exact interest on a loan of $25,000 at $8\frac{1}{2}\%$ annually for 21 days.

20. Find the exact interest on a loan of $1,510 at $7\frac{3}{4}\%$ annual interest for 27 days.

21. Jackson Manufacturing holds a 150-day note of $10,000 that has an interest rate of 7% annually. After 90 days, the note is sold to a bank at a discount rate of 6% annually. Find the proceeds on the third-party discount note.

1. In applying most formulas involving a rate, a fractional or decimal equivalent of the rate is used. Explain how a rate can be mentally changed to a decimal equivalent.

2. When solving problems, one should devise a method to estimate the solution. Describe a strategy for estimating the interest in the first example of Section 11-1 on page 388.

3. Explain how the rate can be estimated in Example 7 on page 392.

4. Use the formula $I = P\left(R \times \dfrac{D}{365}\right)$ to find the exact interest on $100 for 30 days and 7.50%. D is the exact number of days.

5. Find the exact interest on $1,000 for 60 days at 5.3% annual interest rate.

6. The ordinary interest using exact time (banker's rule) will always be higher than exact interest using exact time. Explain why this is true.

7. Show how the formulas $I = PRT$ and $MV = P + I$ lead to the formula $MV = P(I + RT)$.

8. The maturity value for a loan of $2,000 at 9% interest for two years was found to be $4,360. Examine the solution to identify the incorrect mathematical process. Explain the correct process and rework the problem correctly.

$$MV = P(1 + RT)$$
$$MV = \$2,000(1 + 0.09 \times 2)$$
$$MV = \$2,000(1.09 \times 2)$$
$$MV = \$2,000(2.18)$$
$$MV = \$4,360$$

Challenge Problem

A simple interest loan with a final "balloon payment" can be a good deal for both the consumer and the banker. For the banker, this loan reduces the rate risk, because the loan rate is locked in for a short period of time. For the consumer, this loan allows lower monthly payments.

You borrow $5,000 at 13% simple interest rate for a year.

For 12 monthly payments:

$$\$5,000(13\%)(1) = \$650 \text{ interest per year}$$

$$\frac{\$5,000 + \$650}{12} = \frac{\$5,650}{12} = \$470.83 \text{ monthly payment}$$

Your banker offers to make the loan as if it is to be extended over five years but with interest for only one year, or 60 monthly payments, but with a final balloon payment on the 12th payment. This means a much lower monthly payment.

For 60 monthly payments:

$$\frac{\$5,650}{60} = \$94.17 \text{ monthly payment}$$

The lower monthly payment is tempting! The banker will expect you to make these lower payments for *one* year. You will actually make 11 payments of $94.17: $94.17(11) = $1,035.87$, which is the amount paid during the first 11 months.

The 12th and final payment, the *balloon payment,* is the *remainder* of the loan.

$$\$5,650 - \$1,035.87 = \$4,614.13$$

At this time you are expected to pay the balance of the loan in the balloon payment shown above. Don't panic! Usually the loan is refinanced for another year. But beware—you may have to pay a higher interest rate for the next year.

a. Find the monthly payment for a $2,500 loan at 12% interest for one year, extended over a three-year period with a balloon payment at the end of the first year.

b. What is the amount of the final balloon payment for a $1,000 loan at 10% interest for one year, extended over five years?

c. You need a loan of $5,000 at 10% interest for one year. What is the amount of the monthly payment?

d. Compare the monthly payment and final balloon payment of the loan in part c if the loan is extended over two years.

11-1 90 Days Same as Cash!

Sara had just rented her first apartment starting December 1 before beginning college in January. The apartment had washer and dryer hook-ups, so Sara wanted to buy the appliances to avoid trips to the laundromat. The Saturday newspaper had an advertisement for a local appliance store offering "90 days, same as cash!" financing. Sara asked how the financing worked and learned that she could pay for the washer and dryer any time during the first 90 days for the purchase price plus sales tax. If she waited longer, she would have to pay the purchase price, plus sales tax, plus 26.8% annual simple interest for the first 90 days, plus 3% simple interest per month (or any part of a month) on the unpaid balance after 90 days. Together, the washer and dryer cost $699 plus the 8.25% sales tax. Sara knew that her tax refund from the IRS would be $1,000, so she bought the washer and dryer confident that she could pay off the balance within the 90 days.

1. If Sara pays off the balance within 90 days, how much will she pay?

2. If Sara bought the washer and dryer on December 15, using the exact interest, what is her deadline for paying no interest in a non–leap year? In a leap year? Is the finance company likely to use exact or ordinary interest and why?

3. If Sara's IRS refund does not come until April 1, what is her payoff amount? (Assume ordinary interest and a non–leap year.)

4. How much did it cost her to pay off this loan 17 days late? What annual simple interest rate does this amount to?

11-2 The Price of Money

James wants to buy a 50-inch flat-screen television, and the model he wants costs $1,200. So far, he has saved $700, but still needs $500 more. The bank where he has a checking and savings account will loan him $500 at 12% annual interest using a 90-day promissory note. James also visited a loan store for a "pay day" loan to compare the cost of borrowing. The manager told James that he could borrow $500 at 12% for two weeks. If James needed more time to repay the loan, he would be charged 16% on the balance due for each additional week. He wondered how much it would cost to pay the loan back in 12 weeks so he could compare the cost to the bank's lending rate. James recognized that 12 weeks is a few days less than 90 days.

1. Calculate the total cost (principal plus interest) for the 90-day promissory note from the bank.

2. How much will James pay if he gets the money from the loan store and pays the balance back in two weeks?

3. How much will it cost if James gets the money from the loan store and pays it back in 12 weeks (nearly 90 days)?

4. James wondered how the loan store can stay in business unless its customers neglect to determine how much they owe before agreeing to borrow. What do you think? When would a pay day loan be an appropriate choice?

11-3 Quality Photo Printing

As a professional photographer, Jillian had seen a significant shift in customer demand for digital technologies in photography. Many customers, attempting to save a few dollars, had invested in low-end digital cameras (and even lower-end printers) to avoid processing fees typically associated with printing photographs. The end result, for most customers, was a bounty of digital photographic images but with limited options for creating quality printed digital photographs. Jillian was hoping to tap into this underserved market by offering customers superior quality digital printing using advanced pigment inks to produce exquisite color prints. To provide this service, Jillian needs to purchase a state-of-the-art photo printer she found listed through a photography supply company for $8,725, plus sales tax of 5.5%. The supply company is offering cash terms of 3/15, n/30, with a 1.5% service charge on late payments, or 90 days same as cash financing if Jillian will apply and is approved for a company credit card. If she is unable to pay within 90 days under the second option, she would have to pay 24.9% annual simple interest for the first 90 days, plus 2% simple interest per month on the unpaid balance after 90 days. Jillian has an excellent credit rating, but is not sure what to do.

1. If Jillian took the cash option and was able to pay off the printer within the 15-day discount period, how much would she save? How much would she owe?

2. If Jillian takes the 90 days same as cash option and purchases the printer on December 30 to get a current-year tax deduction, using exact time, what is her deadline for paying no interest in a non–leap year? In a leap year? Is the finance company likely to use exact or ordinary interest and why?

3. If Jillian takes the 90 days same as cash and pays within 90 days, what is her payoff amount? If she can't pay until April 30, how much additional money would she owe? (Assume ordinary interest and exact time and a non–leap year.)

4. Jillian finds financing available through a local bank. Find the bank discount and proceeds using ordinary interest for a 90-day promissory note for $9,200 at 8% annual simple interest. Is this enough money for Jillian to cover the purchase price of the printer? Is this a better option for Jillian to pursue, and why or why not?

Consumer Credit

Get Out of Debt Diet

Having trouble paying your bills? Constantly making minimum payments each month? Don't know how much you owe? Worried about getting a bad credit report? According to CreditCards.com, the average credit card debt per U.S. household that has credit card debt is nearly $16,000 with an average APR of 12.78%. Unfortunately, credit card companies have made running up that balance deceptively easy.

However, there are a number of steps you can take to pay off the debt and get back on track. Of course, this will require you to adjust your spending habits and become more careful about your spending.

1. **Determine what you owe.** Make a list of all the debts you have including the name of the creditor, your total balance, your minimum monthly payment, and your interest rate. This will help you determine in which order you should pay down your debts.

2. **Pay it down.** Work overtime or take on a second job and devote that income to paying down debt. Cash in CDs, pay down home equity loans, and pay down loans against retirement. Have a garage sale. Do whatever you can to earn extra money and devote that money to paying down your debt.

3. **Reduce expenses.** Eliminate any unnecessary expenses such as eating out and expensive entertainment. Clip coupons, shop at sales, and avoid impulse purchases. Brown bag it at work and be creative about gifts. Above all, stop using credit cards. Just giving up that expensive cup of coffee each morning can save you more than $750 a year.

4. **Record your spending.** This is actually your key to getting out of debt. You're in debt because you spent money you didn't have. Avoiding more debt starts with knowing what you are spending your money on. Each day for at least one month, write down every amount you spend, no matter how small. Reviewing how you spend your money allows you to set priorities.

5. **Make a budget based on your spending record.** Write down the amount you spent in each category of spending last month as you budget for spending for the next month. Categorize your monthly expenses into logical groups such as *necessities* (food, rent, medicine, pet food, and so on), *should have* (things you need but not immediately, such as new workout gear), and *like to have* (things you don't need but enjoy, such as magazines and cable television). One expense should be paying off your debt. Did you know that making a minimum payment of $26 on a single credit card with a $1,000 balance and 19% interest will take more than five years to pay off?

6. **Pay cash.** This results in a significant savings in terms of what you purchase and not having to pay interest on those purchases. When you don't have the cash, you don't buy.

7. **Resolve to spend less than you make.** Realize once and for all that if you can't pay for it today then you can't afford it.

Managing your credit and knowing exactly how much you are paying for using credit are important concepts that you will learn in this chapter.

LEARNING OUTCOMES

12-1 Installment Loans and Closed-End Credit

1. Find the amount financed, the installment price, and the finance charge of an installment loan.
2. Find the installment payment of an installment loan.
3. Find the estimated annual percentage rate (APR) using a table.

12-2 Paying a Loan Before It Is Due: The Rule of 78

1. Find the interest refund using the rule of 78.

12-3 Open-End Credit

1. Find the finance charge and new balance using the average daily balance method.
2. Find the finance charge and new balance using the unpaid or previous month's balance.

Consumer credit: a type of credit or loan that is available to individuals or businesses. The loan is repaid in regular payments.

Installment loan: a loan that is repaid in regular payments.

Closed-end credit: a type of installment loan in which the amount borrowed and the interest are repaid in a specified number of equal payments.

Open-end credit: a type of installment loan in which there is no fixed amount borrowed or fixed number of payments. Payments are made until the loan is paid off.

Many individuals and businesses make purchases for which they do not pay the full amount at the time of purchase. These purchases are paid for by paying a portion of the amount owed in regular payments until the loan is completely paid. This type of loan or credit is often referred to as **consumer credit.**

In the preceding chapters we discussed the interest to be paid on loans that are paid in full on the date of maturity of the loan. Many times, loans are made so that the maker (the borrower) pays a given amount in regular payments. Loans with regular payments are called **installment loans.**

There are two kinds of installment loans. **Closed-end credit** is a type of loan in which the amount borrowed plus interest is repaid in a specified number of equal payments. Examples include bank loans and loans for large purchases such as cars and appliances. **Open-end credit** is a type of loan in which there is no fixed number of payments—the person keeps making payments until the amount is paid off, and the interest is computed on the unpaid balance at the end of each payment period. Credit card accounts, retail store accounts, and line-of-credit accounts are types of open-end credit.

12-1 INSTALLMENT LOANS AND CLOSED-END CREDIT

LEARNING OUTCOMES

1 Find the amount financed, the installment price, and the finance charge of an installment loan.
2 Find the installment payment of an installment loan.
3 Find the estimated annual percentage rate (APR) using a table.

Should you or your business take out an installment loan? That depends on the interest you will pay and how it is computed. The interest associated with an installment loan is part of the charges referred to as **finance charges** or **carrying charges.** In addition to accrued interest charges, installment loans often include charges for insurance, credit-report fees, or loan fees. Under the truth-in-lending law, all of these charges must be disclosed in writing to the consumer.

Finance charges or carrying charges: the interest and any fee associated with an installment loan.

1 Find the amount financed, the installment price, and the finance charge of an installment loan.

Cash price: the price if all charges are paid at once at the time of the purchase.

Down payment: a partial payment that is paid at the time of the purchase.

Amount financed: the cash price minus the down payment.

Installment payment: the amount that is paid (including interest) in each regular payment.

Installment price: the total amount paid for a purchase, including all payments, the finance charges, and the down payment.

The **cash price** is the price you pay if you pay all at once at the time of the purchase. If you pay on an installment basis instead, the **down payment** is a partial payment of the cash price at the time of the purchase. The **amount financed** is the cash price minus the down payment. The **installment payment** is the amount you pay each period, including interest, to pay off the loan. The **installment price** is the total paid, including all of the installment payments, the finance charges, and the down payment.

HOW TO Find the amount financed and the installment price

1. Find the amount financed: Subtract the down payment from the cash price.

$$\text{Amount financed} = \text{cash price} - \text{down payment}$$

2. Find the installment price: Add the down payment to the total of the installment payments.

$$\text{Installment price} = \text{total of installment payments} + \text{down payment}$$

EXAMPLE 1 The 7th Inning purchased a mat cutter for the framing department on the installment plan with a $600 down payment and 12 payments of $145.58. Find the installment price of the mat cutter.

$$\begin{pmatrix}\text{Total of}\\\text{installment}\\\text{payments}\end{pmatrix} = \begin{pmatrix}\text{number of}\\\text{installments}\end{pmatrix} \times \begin{pmatrix}\text{installment}\\\text{payment}\end{pmatrix}$$

$$= \quad 12 \quad \times \quad \$145.58$$

$$= \$1,746.96$$

$$\text{Installment price} = \text{total of installment payments} + \text{down payment}$$
$$= \$1{,}746.96 + \$600$$
$$= \$2{,}346.96$$

The installment price is $2,346.96.

HOW TO   Find the finance charge of an installment loan

1. Determine the cash price of the item.
2. Find the installment price of the item.
3. Subtract the result found in step 2 from the result of step 1.

Finance charge = installment price − cash price

EXAMPLE 2   If the cash price of the mat cutter in Example 1 was $2,200, find the finance charge and the amount financed.

Finance charge = installment price − cash price	Installment price = $2,346.96
$\quad = \$2{,}346.96 - \$2{,}200.00$	Cash price = $2,200.00
$\quad = \$146.96$	Down payment = $600

$$\text{Amount financed} = \text{cash price} - \text{down payment.}$$
$$= \$2{,}200 - \$600$$
$$= \$1{,}600$$

The finance charge is $146.96 and the amount financed is $1,600.

STOP AND CHECK

See Examples 1 and 2.

1. An ice machine with a cash price of $1,095 is purchased on the installment plan with a $100 down payment and 18 monthly payments of $62.50. Find the amount financed, installment price, and finance charge for the machine.

2. A copy machine is purchased on the installment plan with a $200 down payment and 24 monthly payments of $118.50. The cash price is $2,695. Find the amount financed, installment price, and finance charge for the machine.

3. An industrial freezer with a cash price of $2,295 is purchased on the installment plan with a $275 down payment and 30 monthly installment payments of $78.98. Find the amount financed, installment price, and finance charge for the freezer.

4. The cash price of a music system is $2,859 and the installment price is $3,115.35. How much is the finance charge?

---

2   Find the installment payment of an installment loan.

Since the installment price is the total of the installment payments plus the down payment, we can find the installment payment if we know the installment price, the down payment, and the number of payments.

HOW TO   Find the installment payment, given the installment price, the down payment, and the number of payments

1. Find the total of the installment payments: Subtract the down payment from the installment price.

$$\text{Total of installment payments} = \text{installment price} - \text{down payment}$$

2. Divide the total of the installment payments by the number of installment payments.

$$\text{Installment payment} = \frac{\text{total of installment payments}}{\text{number of payments}}$$

TIP

Protect Your Credit Rating

Your credit reputation is just as important as your personal reputation. Three different agencies track credit records. They are Equifax, Experian, and TransUnion. You are entitled to a free annual credit report from each of these three nationwide consumer reporting agencies.

EXAMPLE 3 The installment price of a drafting table was $1,627 for a 12-month loan. If a $175 down payment had been made, find the installment payment.

Total of installment payments = installment price − down payment

$$= \$1,627 - \$175 = \$1,452 \qquad \text{Subtract.}$$

$$\text{Installment payment} = \frac{\text{total of installment payments}}{\text{number of payments}}$$

$$= \frac{\$1,452}{12} = \$121 \qquad \text{Divide.}$$

The installment payment is $121.

STOP AND CHECK

See Example 3.

1. The installment price of a refrigerator is $2,087 for a 24-month loan. If a down payment of $150 had been made, what is the installment payment?

2. The installment price of a piano is $8,997.40 and a down payment of $1,000 is made. What is the monthly installment payment if the piano is financed for 36 months?

3. The installment price of a tire machine is $2,795.28. A down payment of $600 is made. What is the installment payment if the machine is financed for 36 months?

4. Find the installment payment for a trailer if its installment price is $3,296.96 over 30 months and an $800 down payment is made.

3 Find the estimated annual percentage rate (APR) using a table.

In 1969 the federal government passed the Consumer Credit Protection Act, Regulation Z, also known as the Truth-in-Lending Act. Several amendments have been made to this original legislation. It requires that a lending institution tell the borrower, in writing, what the actual annual rate of interest is as it applies to the balance due on the loan each period. This interest rate tells the borrower the true cost of the loan.

If you borrowed $1,500 for a year and paid an interest charge of $165, you would be paying an interest rate of 11% annually on the entire $1,500 (165 ÷ $1,500 = 0.11 = 11%). But if you paid the money back in 12 monthly installments of $138.75 ([$1,500 + $165] ÷ 12 =$138.75), you would not have the use of the $1,500 for a full year. Instead, you would be paying it back in 12 payments of $138.75 each. Thus, you are losing the use of some of the money every month but are still paying interest at the rate of 11% of *the entire amount*. This means that you are actually paying *more than* 11% interest. The equivalent rate is the **annual percentage rate (APR)**. Applied to installment loans, the APR is the *annual simple interest rate equivalent* that is actually being paid on the unpaid balances. The APR can be determined using a government-issued table.

The federal government issues annual percentage rate tables, which are used to find APR rates (within $\frac{1}{4}$%, which is the federal standard). A portion of one of these tables, based on the number of monthly payments, is shown in Table 12-1.

Annual percentage rate (APR): the rate of an installment loan that is equivalent to a comparable annual simple interest rate.

TIP

Don't Forget Up-Front Charges

When computing the APR using the rate table, be sure to compute the total finance charge. The *total finance charge amount* should include all charges the customer had to pay to obtain the loan, even if some of the charges were paid for with cash at the beginning of the loan.

HOW TO Find the estimated annual percentage rate using a per $100 of amount financed table

1. Find the interest per $100 of amount financed: Divide the finance charge including interest by the amount financed and multiply by $100.

$$\text{Interest per }\$100 = \frac{\text{finance charge}}{\text{amount financed}} \times \$100$$

2. Find the row corresponding to the number of monthly payments. Move across the row to find the number closest to the value from step 1. Read up the column to find the annual percentage rate for that column. If the result in step 1 is exactly halfway between two table values, a rate halfway between the two rates can be used.

TABLE 12-1
Interest per $100 of Amount Financed

Number of monthly payments	APR (Annual Percentage Rate) for Selected Rates															
	10.75%	11.00%	11.25%	11.50%	11.75%	12.00%	12.25%	12.50%	12.75%	13.00%	13.25%	13.50%	13.75%	14.00%	14.25%	15.00%
1	0.90	0.92	0.94	0.96	0.98	1.00	1.02	1.04	1.06	1.08	1.10	1.12	1.15	1.17	1.19	1.25
2	1.35	1.38	1.41	1.44	1.47	1.50	1.53	1.57	1.60	1.63	1.66	1.69	1.72	1.75	1.78	1.88
3	1.80	1.84	1.88	1.92	1.96	2.01	2.05	2.09	2.13	2.17	2.22	2.26	2.30	2.34	2.38	2.51
4	2.25	2.30	2.35	2.41	2.46	2.51	2.57	2.62	2.67	2.72	2.78	2.83	2.88	2.93	2.99	3.14
5	2.70	2.77	2.83	2.89	2.96	3.02	3.08	3.15	3.21	3.27	3.34	3.40	3.46	3.53	3.59	3.78
6	3.16	3.23	3.31	3.38	3.45	3.53	3.60	3.68	3.75	3.83	3.90	3.97	4.05	4.12	4.20	4.42
7	3.62	3.70	3.78	3.87	3.95	4.04	4.12	4.21	4.29	4.38	4.47	4.55	4.64	4.72	4.81	5.06
8	4.07	4.17	4.26	4.36	4.46	4.55	4.65	4.74	4.84	4.94	5.03	5.13	5.22	5.32	5.42	5.71
9	4.53	4.64	4.75	4.85	4.96	5.07	5.17	5.28	5.39	5.49	5.60	5.71	5.82	5.92	6.03	6.35
10	4.99	5.11	5.23	5.35	5.46	5.58	5.70	5.82	5.94	6.05	6.17	6.29	6.41	6.53	6.65	7.00
11	5.45	5.58	5.71	5.84	5.97	6.10	6.23	6.36	6.49	6.62	6.75	6.88	7.01	7.14	7.27	7.66
12	5.92	6.06	6.20	6.34	6.48	6.62	6.76	6.90	7.04	7.18	7.32	7.46	7.60	7.74	7.89	8.31
13	6.38	6.53	6.68	6.84	6.99	7.14	7.29	7.44	7.59	7.75	7.90	8.05	8.20	8.36	8.51	8.97
14	6.85	7.01	7.17	7.34	7.50	7.66	7.82	7.99	8.15	8.31	8.48	8.64	8.81	8.97	9.13	9.63
15	7.32	7.49	7.66	7.84	8.01	8.19	8.36	8.53	8.71	8.88	9.06	9.23	9.41	9.59	9.76	10.29
16	7.78	7.97	8.15	8.34	8.53	8.71	8.90	9.08	9.27	9.46	9.64	9.83	10.02	10.20	10.39	10.95
17	8.25	8.45	8.65	8.84	9.04	9.24	9.44	9.63	9.83	10.03	10.23	10.43	10.63	10.82	11.02	11.62
18	8.73	8.93	9.14	9.35	9.56	9.77	9.98	10.19	10.40	10.61	10.82	11.03	11.24	11.45	11.66	12.29
19	9.20	9.42	9.64	9.86	10.08	10.30	10.52	10.74	10.96	11.18	11.41	11.63	11.85	12.07	12.30	12.97
20	9.67	9.90	10.13	10.37	10.60	10.83	11.06	11.30	11.53	11.76	12.00	12.23	12.46	12.70	12.93	13.64
21	10.15	10.39	10.63	10.88	11.12	11.36	11.61	11.85	12.10	12.34	12.59	12.84	13.08	13.33	13.58	14.32
22	10.62	10.88	11.13	11.39	11.64	11.90	12.16	12.41	12.67	12.93	13.19	13.44	13.70	13.96	14.22	15.00
23	11.10	11.37	11.63	11.90	12.17	12.44	12.71	12.97	13.24	13.51	13.78	14.05	14.32	14.59	14.87	15.68
24	11.58	11.86	12.14	12.42	12.70	12.98	13.26	13.54	13.82	14.10	14.38	14.66	14.95	15.23	15.51	16.37
25	12.06	12.35	12.64	12.93	13.22	13.52	13.81	14.10	14.40	14.69	14.98	15.28	15.57	15.87	16.17	17.06
26	12.54	12.85	13.15	13.45	13.75	14.06	14.36	14.67	14.97	15.28	15.59	15.89	16.20	16.51	16.82	17.75
27	13.03	13.34	13.66	13.97	14.29	14.60	14.92	15.24	15.56	15.87	16.19	16.51	16.83	17.15	17.47	18.44
28	13.51	13.84	14.16	14.49	14.82	15.15	15.48	15.81	16.14	16.47	16.80	17.13	17.46	17.80	18.13	19.14
29	14.00	14.33	14.67	15.01	15.35	15.70	16.04	16.38	16.72	17.07	17.41	17.75	18.10	18.45	18.79	19.83
30	14.48	14.83	15.19	15.54	15.89	16.24	16.60	16.95	17.31	17.66	18.02	18.38	18.74	19.10	19.45	20.54
31	14.97	15.33	15.70	16.06	16.43	16.79	17.16	17.53	17.90	18.27	18.63	19.00	19.38	19.75	20.12	21.24
32	15.46	15.84	16.21	16.59	16.97	17.35	17.73	18.11	18.49	18.87	19.25	19.63	20.02	20.40	20.79	21.95
33	15.95	16.34	16.73	17.12	17.51	17.90	18.29	18.69	19.08	19.47	19.87	20.26	20.66	21.06	21.46	22.65
34	16.44	16.85	17.25	17.65	18.05	18.46	18.86	19.27	19.67	20.08	20.49	20.90	21.31	21.72	22.13	23.37
35	16.94	17.35	17.77	18.18	18.60	19.01	19.43	19.85	20.27	20.69	21.11	21.53	21.95	22.38	22.80	24.08
36	17.43	17.86	18.29	18.71	19.14	19.57	20.00	20.43	20.87	21.30	21.73	22.17	22.60	23.04	23.48	24.80
37	17.93	18.37	18.81	19.25	19.69	20.13	20.58	21.02	21.46	21.91	22.36	22.81	23.25	23.70	24.16	25.51
38	18.43	18.88	19.33	19.78	20.24	20.69	21.15	21.61	22.07	22.52	22.99	23.45	23.91	24.37	24.84	26.24
39	18.93	19.39	19.86	20.32	20.79	21.26	21.73	22.20	22.67	23.14	23.61	24.09	24.56	25.04	25.52	26.96
40	19.43	19.90	20.38	20.86	21.34	21.82	22.30	22.79	23.27	23.76	24.25	24.73	25.22	25.71	26.20	27.69
41	19.93	20.42	20.91	21.40	21.89	22.39	22.88	23.38	23.88	24.38	24.88	25.38	25.88	26.39	26.89	28.41
42	20.43	20.93	21.44	21.94	22.45	22.96	23.47	23.98	24.49	25.00	25.51	26.03	26.55	27.06	27.58	29.15
43	20.94	21.45	21.97	22.49	23.01	23.53	24.05	24.57	25.10	25.62	26.15	26.68	27.21	27.74	28.27	29.88
44	21.44	21.97	22.50	23.03	23.57	24.10	24.64	25.17	25.71	26.25	26.79	27.33	27.88	28.42	28.97	30.62
45	21.95	22.49	23.03	23.58	24.12	24.67	25.22	25.77	26.32	26.88	27.43	27.99	28.55	29.11	29.67	31.36
46	22.46	23.01	23.57	24.13	24.69	25.25	25.81	26.37	26.94	27.51	28.08	28.65	29.22	29.79	30.36	32.10
47	22.97	23.53	24.10	24.68	25.25	25.82	26.40	26.98	27.56	28.14	28.72	29.31	29.89	30.48	31.07	32.84
48	23.48	24.06	24.64	25.23	25.81	26.40	26.99	27.58	28.18	28.77	29.37	29.97	30.57	31.17	31.77	33.59
49	23.99	24.58	25.18	25.78	26.38	26.98	27.59	28.19	28.80	29.41	30.02	30.63	31.24	31.86	32.48	34.34
50	24.50	25.11	25.72	26.33	26.95	27.56	28.18	28.80	29.42	30.04	30.67	31.29	31.92	32.55	33.18	35.09
51	25.02	25.64	26.26	26.89	27.52	28.15	28.78	29.41	30.05	30.68	31.32	31.96	32.60	33.25	33.89	35.84
52	25.53	26.17	26.81	27.45	28.09	28.73	29.38	30.02	30.67	31.32	31.98	32.63	33.29	33.95	34.61	36.60
53	26.05	26.70	27.35	28.00	28.66	29.32	29.98	30.64	31.30	31.97	32.63	33.30	33.97	34.65	35.32	37.36
54	26.57	27.23	27.90	28.56	29.23	29.91	30.58	31.25	31.93	32.61	33.29	33.98	34.66	35.35	36.04	38.12
55	27.09	27.77	28.44	29.13	29.81	30.50	31.18	31.87	32.56	33.26	33.95	34.65	35.35	36.05	36.76	38.88
56	27.61	28.30	28.99	29.69	30.39	31.09	31.79	32.49	33.20	33.91	34.62	35.33	36.04	36.76	37.48	39.65
57	28.13	28.84	29.54	30.25	30.97	31.68	32.39	33.11	33.83	34.56	35.28	36.01	36.74	37.47	38.20	40.42
58	28.66	29.37	30.10	30.82	31.55	32.27	33.00	33.74	34.47	35.21	35.95	36.69	37.43	38.18	38.93	41.19
59	29.18	29.91	30.65	31.39	32.13	32.87	33.61	34.36	35.11	35.86	36.62	37.37	38.13	38.89	39.66	41.96
60	29.71	30.45	31.20	31.96	32.71	33.47	34.23	34.99	35.75	36.52	37.29	38.06	38.83	39.61	40.39	42.74

TABLE 12-1
Interest per $100 of Amount Financed—*Continued*

Number of monthly payments	APR (Annual Percentage Rate) for Selected Rates															
	15.50%	15.75%	16.00%	16.25%	16.50%	16.75%	17.00%	19.50%	19.75%	20.00%	20.25%	20.50%	20.75%	21.00%	21.25%	21.50%
1	1.29	1.31	1.33	1.35	1.37	1.40	1.42	1.62	1.65	1.67	1.69	1.71	1.73	1.75	1.77	1.79
2	1.94	1.97	2.00	2.04	2.07	2.10	2.13	2.44	2.48	2.51	2.54	2.57	2.60	2.63	2.66	2.70
3	2.59	2.64	2.68	2.72	2.76	2.80	2.85	3.27	3.31	3.35	3.39	3.44	3.48	3.52	3.56	3.60
4	3.25	3.30	3.36	3.41	3.46	3.51	3.57	4.10	4.15	4.20	4.25	4.31	4.36	4.41	4.47	4.52
5	3.91	3.97	4.04	4.10	4.16	4.23	4.29	4.93	4.99	5.06	5.12	5.18	5.25	5.31	5.37	5.44
6	4.57	4.64	4.72	4.79	4.87	4.94	5.02	5.76	5.84	5.91	5.99	6.06	6.14	6.21	6.29	6.36
7	5.23	5.32	5.40	5.49	5.58	5.66	5.75	6.60	6.69	6.78	6.86	6.95	7.04	7.12	7.21	7.29
8	5.90	6.00	6.09	6.19	6.29	6.38	6.48	7.45	7.55	7.64	7.74	7.84	7.94	8.03	8.13	8.23
9	6.57	6.68	6.78	6.89	7.00	7.11	7.22	8.30	8.41	8.52	8.63	8.73	8.84	8.95	9.06	9.17
10	7.24	7.36	7.48	7.60	7.72	7.84	7.96	9.15	9.27	9.39	9.51	9.63	9.75	9.88	10.00	10.12
11	7.92	8.05	8.18	8.31	8.44	8.57	8.70	10.01	10.14	10.28	10.41	10.54	10.67	10.80	10.94	11.07
12	8.59	8.74	8.88	9.02	9.16	9.30	9.45	10.87	11.02	11.16	11.31	11.45	11.59	11.74	11.88	12.02
13	9.27	9.43	9.58	9.73	9.89	10.04	10.20	11.74	11.90	12.05	12.21	12.36	12.52	12.67	12.83	12.99
14	9.96	10.12	10.29	10.45	10.67	10.78	10.95	12.61	12.78	12.95	13.11	13.28	13.45	13.62	13.79	13.95
15	10.64	10.82	11.00	11.17	11.35	11.53	11.71	13.49	13.67	13.85	14.03	14.21	14.39	14.57	14.75	14.93
16	11.33	11.52	11.71	11.90	12.09	12.28	12.46	14.37	14.56	14.75	14.94	15.13	15.33	15.52	15.71	15.90
17	12.02	12.22	12.42	12.62	12.83	13.03	13.23	15.25	15.46	15.66	15.86	16.07	16.27	16.48	16.68	16.89
18	12.72	12.93	13.14	13.35	13.57	13.78	13.99	16.14	16.36	16.57	16.79	17.01	17.22	17.44	17.66	17.88
19	13.41	13.64	13.86	14.09	14.31	14.54	14.76	17.03	17.26	17.49	17.72	17.95	18.18	18.41	18.64	18.87
20	14.11	14.35	14.59	14.82	15.06	15.30	15.54	17.93	18.17	18.41	18.66	18.90	19.14	19.38	19.63	19.87
21	14.82	15.06	15.31	15.56	15.81	16.06	16.31	18.83	19.09	19.34	19.60	19.85	20.11	20.36	20.62	20.87
22	15.52	15.78	16.04	16.30	16.57	16.83	17.09	19.74	20.01	20.27	20.54	20.81	21.08	21.34	21.61	21.88
23	16.23	16.50	16.78	17.05	17.32	17.60	17.88	20.65	20.93	21.21	21.49	21.77	22.05	22.33	22.61	22.90
24	16.94	17.22	17.51	17.80	18.09	18.37	18.66	21.56	21.86	22.15	22.44	22.74	23.03	23.33	23.62	23.92
25	17.65	17.95	18.25	18.55	18.85	19.15	19.45	22.48	22.79	23.10	23.40	23.71	24.02	24.32	24.63	24.94
26	18.37	18.68	18.99	19.30	19.62	19.93	20.24	23.41	23.73	24.04	24.36	24.68	25.01	25.33	25.65	25.97
27	19.09	19.41	19.74	20.06	20.39	20.71	21.04	24.33	24.67	25.00	25.33	25.67	26.00	26.34	26.67	27.01
28	19.81	20.15	20.48	20.82	21.16	21.50	21.84	25.27	25.61	25.96	26.30	26.65	27.00	27.35	27.70	28.05
29	20.53	20.88	21.23	21.58	21.94	22.29	22.64	26.20	26.56	26.92	27.28	27.64	28.00	28.37	28.73	29.09
30	21.26	21.62	21.99	22.35	22.72	23.08	23.45	27.14	27.52	27.89	28.26	28.64	29.01	29.39	29.77	30.14
31	21.99	22.37	22.74	23.12	23.50	23.88	24.26	28.09	28.47	28.86	29.25	29.64	30.03	30.42	30.81	31.20
32	22.72	23.11	23.50	23.89	24.28	24.68	25.07	29.04	29.44	29.84	30.24	30.64	31.05	31.45	31.85	32.26
33	23.46	23.86	24.26	24.67	25.07	25.48	25.88	29.99	30.40	30.82	31.23	31.65	32.07	32.49	32.91	33.33
34	24.19	24.61	25.03	25.44	25.86	26.28	26.70	30.95	31.37	31.80	32.23	32.67	33.10	33.53	33.96	34.40
35	24.94	25.36	25.79	26.23	26.66	27.09	27.52	31.91	32.35	32.79	33.24	33.68	34.13	34.58	35.03	35.47
36	25.68	26.12	26.57	27.01	27.46	27.90	28.35	32.87	33.33	33.79	34.25	34.71	35.17	35.63	36.09	36.56
37	26.42	26.88	27.34	27.80	28.26	28.72	29.18	33.84	34.32	34.79	35.26	35.74	36.21	36.69	37.16	37.64
38	27.17	27.64	28.11	28.59	29.06	29.53	30.01	34.82	35.30	35.79	36.28	36.77	37.26	37.75	38.24	38.73
39	27.92	28.41	28.89	29.38	29.87	30.36	30.85	35.80	36.30	36.80	37.30	37.81	38.31	38.82	39.32	39.83
40	28.68	29.18	29.68	30.18	30.68	31.18	31.68	36.78	37.29	37.81	38.33	38.85	39.37	39.89	40.41	40.93
41	29.44	29.95	30.46	30.97	31.49	32.01	32.52	37.77	38.30	38.83	39.36	39.89	40.43	40.96	41.50	42.04
42	30.19	30.72	31.25	31.78	32.31	32.84	33.37	38.76	39.30	39.85	40.40	40.95	41.50	42.05	42.60	43.15
43	30.96	31.50	32.04	32.58	33.13	33.67	34.22	39.75	40.31	40.87	41.44	42.00	42.57	43.13	43.70	44.27
44	31.72	32.28	32.83	33.39	33.95	34.51	35.07	40.75	41.33	41.90	42.48	43.06	43.64	44.22	44.81	45.39
45	32.49	33.06	33.63	34.20	34.77	35.35	35.92	41.75	42.35	42.94	43.53	44.13	44.72	45.32	45.92	46.52
46	33.26	33.84	34.43	35.01	35.60	36.19	36.78	42.76	43.37	43.98	44.58	45.20	45.81	46.42	47.03	47.65
47	34.03	34.63	35.23	35.83	36.43	37.04	37.64	43.77	44.40	45.02	45.64	46.27	46.90	47.53	48.16	48.79
48	34.81	35.42	36.03	36.65	37.27	37.88	38.50	44.79	45.43	46.07	46.71	47.35	47.99	48.64	49.28	49.93
49	35.59	36.21	36.84	37.47	38.10	38.74	39.37	45.81	46.46	47.12	47.77	48.43	49.09	49.75	50.41	51.08
50	36.37	37.01	37.65	38.30	38.94	39.59	40.24	46.83	47.50	48.17	48.84	49.52	50.19	50.87	51.55	52.23
51	37.15	37.81	38.46	39.12	39.79	40.45	41.11	47.86	48.55	49.23	49.92	50.61	51.30	51.99	52.69	53.38
52	37.94	38.61	39.28	39.96	40.63	41.31	41.99	48.89	49.59	50.30	51.00	51.71	52.41	53.12	53.83	54.55
53	38.72	39.41	40.10	40.79	41.48	42.17	42.87	49.93	50.65	51.37	52.09	52.81	53.53	54.26	54.98	55.71
54	39.52	40.22	40.92	41.63	42.33	43.04	43.75	50.97	51.70	52.44	53.17	53.91	54.65	55.39	56.14	56.88
55	40.31	41.03	41.74	42.47	43.19	43.91	44.64	52.02	52.76	53.52	54.27	55.02	55.78	56.54	57.30	58.06
56	41.11	41.84	42.57	43.31	44.05	44.79	45.53	53.06	53.83	54.60	55.37	56.14	56.91	57.68	58.46	59.24
57	41.91	42.65	43.40	44.15	44.91	45.66	46.42	54.12	54.90	55.68	56.47	57.25	58.04	58.84	59.63	60.43
58	42.71	43.47	44.23	45.00	45.77	46.54	47.32	55.17	55.97	56.77	57.57	58.38	59.18	59.99	60.80	61.62
59	43.51	44.29	45.07	45.85	46.64	47.42	48.21	56.23	57.05	57.87	58.68	59.51	60.33	61.15	61.98	62.81
60	44.32	45.11	45.91	46.71	47.51	48.31	49.12	57.30	58.13	58.96	59.80	60.64	61.48	62.32	63.17	64.01

EXAMPLE 4 Lewis Strang bought a motorcycle for $3,500, which was financed at $142 per month for 24 months. The down payment was $500. Find the APR.

Installment price = 24($142) + $500 = $3,408 + $500 = $3,908

Finance charge = $3,908 − $3,500 = $408

Amount financed = $3,500 − $500 = $3,000

$$\text{Interest per } \$100 = \frac{\text{finance charge}}{\text{amount financed}} \times \$100 = \frac{\$408}{\$3,000}(\$100) = \$13.60$$

Find the row for 24 monthly payments. Move across to find the number nearest to $13.60.

$$\begin{array}{c} \$13.60 \\ -\ \$13.54 \\ \hline \$\ 0.06 \\ \text{Closest} \\ \text{value} \end{array} \qquad \begin{array}{c} \$13.82 \\ -\ \$13.60 \\ \hline \$\ 0.22 \end{array}$$ Find the table value closest to $13.60.

Move up to the top of that column to find the **annual percentage rate, which is 12.5%.**

TIP

Finding the Closest Table Value

Another way to find the closest table value to the interest per $100 is to compare the interest to the amount halfway between two table values. The halfway amount is the average of the two table values.

$$\text{Halfway} = \frac{\text{larger value} + \text{smaller value}}{2}$$

In the previous example, $13.60 is between $13.54 and $13.82.

$$\text{Halfway} = \frac{\$13.54 + \$13.82}{2} = \frac{\$27.36}{2}$$
$$= \$13.68$$

Because $13.60 is less than the halfway amount ($13.68), it is closer to the lower table value ($13.54).

DID YOU KNOW?

Not All Quoted APRs Are the Same!

The APR quoted on a loan *may or may not* include other fees and charges associated with a loan such as private mortgage insurance, processing fees, and discount points. Some do, some don't. Look closely at the details.

STOP AND CHECK

See Example 4.

1. Jaime Lopez purchased a preowned car that listed for $11,935. After making a down payment of $1,500, he financed the balance over 36 months with payments of $347.49 per month. Use Table 12-1 to find the annual percentage rate (APR) of the loan.

2. Peggy Portzen purchased new kitchen appliances with a cash price of $6,800. After making a down payment of $900, she financed the balance over 24 months with payments of $279.65. Find the annual percentage rate (APR) of the loan.

3. Alan Dan could purchase a jet ski for $9,995 cash. He paid $2,000 down and financed the balance with 36 monthly payments of $295.34. Find the APR of the loan.

4. Nellie Chapman bought a Harley-Davidson motorcycle that had a cash price of $12,799 with a $2,500 down payment. She paid for the motorcycle in 48 monthly payments of $296.37. Find the APR for the loan.

12-1 SECTION EXERCISES

SKILL BUILDERS

1. Find the installment price of a recliner bought on the installment plan with a down payment of $100 and six payments of $108.20. *See Example 1.*

2. Find the amount financed if a $125 down payment is made on a TV with a cash price of $579. *See Example 2.*

See Example 1.

3. Stephen Helba purchased a TV with surround sound and remote control on an installment plan with $100 down and 12 payments of $106.32. Find the installment price of the TV.

4. A queen-size bedroom suite can be purchased on an installment plan with 18 payments of $97.42 if an $80 down payment is made. What is the installment price of the suite?

5. Zack's Trailer Sales will finance a 16-foot utility trailer with ramps and electric brakes. If a down payment of $100 and eight monthly payments of $82.56 are required, what is the installment price of the trailer?

6. A forklift is purchased for $10,000. The forklift is used as collateral and no down payment is required. Twenty-four monthly payments of $503 are required to repay the loan. What is the installment price of the forklift?

See Example 3.

7. A computer with software costs $2,987, and Docie Johnson has agreed to pay a 19% per year finance charge on the cash price. If she contracts to pay the loan in 18 months, how much will she pay each month?

8. The cash price of a bedroom suite is $2,590. There is a 24% finance charge on the cash price and 12 monthly payments. Find the monthly payment.

9. Find the monthly payment on a HD LED television with an installment price of $929, 12 monthly payments, and a down payment of $100.

10. The installment price of a teakwood extension table and four chairs is $625 with 18 monthly payments and a down payment of $75. What is the monthly payment?

APPLICATIONS

11. An entertainment center is financed at a total cost of $2,357 including a down payment of $250. If the center is financed over 24 months, find the monthly payment.

12. A Hepplewhite sofa costs $3,780 in cash. Jaquanna Wilson will purchase the sofa in 36 monthly installment payments. A 13% per year finance charge will be assessed on the amount financed. Find the finance charge, the installment price, and the monthly payment.

See Example 4.

13. A fishing boat is purchased for $5,600 and financed for 36 months. If the total finance charge is $1,025, find the annual percentage rate using Table 12-1.

14. An air compressor costs $780 and is financed with monthly payments for 12 months. The total finance charge is $90. Find the annual percentage rate using Table 12-1.

15. Jim Meriweather purchased an engraving machine for $28,000 and financed it for 36 months. The total finance charge was $5,036. Use Table 12-1 to find the annual percentage rate.

12-2 PAYING A LOAN BEFORE IT IS DUE: THE RULE OF 78

LEARNING OUTCOME

1 Find the interest refund using the rule of 78.

If a closed-end installment loan is paid entirely before the last payment is actually due, is part of the interest refundable? In most cases it is, but not always at the rate you might hope. If you paid a 12-month loan in 6 months, you might expect a refund of half the total interest. However, this is not the case because the portion of the monthly payment that is interest is not the same from month to month. In some cases, interest or finance charge refunds are made according to the **rule of 78.** Some states allow this method to be used for short-term loans, generally 60 months or less. Laws and court rulings protect and inform the consumer in matters involving interest.

Rule of 78: method for determining the amount of refund of the finance charge for an installment loan that is paid before it is due.

1 Find the interest refund using the rule of 78.

The rule of 78 is not based on the actual unpaid balance after a payment is made. Instead, it is an approximation that assumes the amount financed (which includes the interest) of a one-year loan is paid in 12 equal parts. For the first payment, the interest is based on the total amount financed, or $\frac{12}{12}$ of the loan. The interest for the second payment is based on $\frac{11}{12}$ of the amount financed because $\frac{1}{12}$ of this amount has already been paid. The interest for the third payment is $\frac{10}{12}$ of the amount financed, and so on. The interest on the last payment is based on $\frac{1}{12}$ of the amount financed.

The sum of all the parts accruing interest for a 12-month loan is $12 + 11 + 10 + 9 + 8 + 7 + 6 + 5 + 4 + 3 + 2 + 1$, or 78.

Thus, 78 equal parts accrue interest. The interest each part accrues is the same because the rate is the same and the parts are the same (each is $\frac{1}{12}$ of the principal). Because 78 equal parts each accrue equal interest, the interest each part accrues must be $\frac{1}{78}$ of the total interest for the one-year loan. So if the loan is paid in full with three months remaining, then the interest that would have accrued in the 10th, 11th, and 12th months is refunded. In the 10th month, three parts each accrue $\frac{1}{78}$ of the total interest; in the 11th month, two parts each accrue $\frac{1}{78}$ of the total interest; and in the 12th month, one part accrues $\frac{1}{78}$ of the total interest. So each of the $3 + 2 + 1$ parts, or 6 parts, accrues $\frac{1}{78}$ of the total interest. Thus $\frac{6}{78}$ of the total interest is refunded. The fraction $\frac{6}{78}$ is called the **refund fraction.**

Refund fraction: the fractional part of the total interest that is refunded when a loan is paid early using the rule of 78.

Not all installment loans are for 12 months, but the rule of 78 gives us a pattern that we can apply to loans of any allowable length.

HOW TO Find the refund fraction for the interest refund

1. The numerator is the sum of the digits from 1 through the number of months remaining of a loan paid off before it was due.
2. The denominator is the sum of the digits from 1 through the original number of months of the loan.
3. The original fraction, the reduced fraction, or the decimal equivalent of the fraction can be used.

The sum-of-digits table in Table 12-2 can be used to find the numerator and denominator of the refund fraction.

TABLE 12-2
Sum-of-Digits

Months	Sum of digits	Months	Sum of digits	Months	Sum of digits
1	1	21	231	41	861
2	3	22	253	42	903
3	6	23	276	43	946
4	10	24	300	44	990
5	15	25	325	45	1,035
6	21	26	351	46	1,081
7	28	27	378	47	1,128
8	36	28	406	48	1,176
9	45	29	435	49	1,225
10	55	30	465	50	1,275
11	66	31	496	51	1,326
12	78	32	528	52	1,378
13	91	33	561	53	1,431
14	105	34	595	54	1,485
15	120	35	630	55	1,540
16	136	36	666	56	1,596
17	153	37	703	57	1,653
18	171	38	741	58	1,711
19	190	39	780	59	1,770
20	210	40	820	60	1,830

There is a shortcut for finding the sum of consecutive numbers beginning with 1. You may be interested to know that a young boy in elementary school discovered this shortcut in the late 18th century. He later went on to be one of the greatest mathematicians of all time. His name was Carl Friedrich Gauss (1777–1855).

TIP

The Sum of Consecutive Numbers Beginning with 1

Multiply the largest number by 1 more than the largest number and divide the product by 2.

Sum of consecutive numbers beginning with 1
$$= \frac{\text{largest number} \times (\text{largest number} + 1)}{2}$$

Sum of consecutive numbers from 1 through 4
$$= \frac{4(5)}{2} = \frac{20}{2} = 10$$

Sum of consecutive numbers from 1 through 12
$$= \frac{12(13)}{2} = \frac{156}{2} = 78$$

HOW TO   Find the interest refund using the rule of 78

1. Find the refund fraction.
2. Multiply the total interest by the refund fraction.

$$\text{Interest refund} = \text{total interest} \times \text{refund fraction}$$

EXAMPLE 1

A loan for 12 months with interest of $117 is paid in full with four payments remaining. Find the refund fraction for the interest refund.

$$\text{Refund fraction} = \frac{\text{sum of the digits for number of payments remaining}}{\text{sum of the digits for total number of payments}}$$

$$= \frac{1 + 2 + 3 + 4}{1 + 2 + 3 + 4 + 5 + 6 + 7 + 8 + 9 + 10 + 11 + 12}$$

$$= \frac{10}{78} = \frac{5}{39} \text{ or } 0.1282051282 \qquad 10 \div 78 = 0.1282051282$$

The refund fraction is $\frac{10}{78}$ or $\frac{5}{39}$ or 0.1282051282.

EXAMPLE 2

Find the interest refund for the installment loan in Example 1.

Interest refund = total interest × refund fraction   Total interest = $117

$$\text{Refund fraction} = \frac{10}{78} \text{ or } \frac{5}{39} \text{ or } 0.1282051282$$

$$= \$117(0.1282051282) \qquad \text{Multiply.}$$
$$= \$15$$

The interest refund is $15.

TIP

Continuous Sequence of Steps Using a Calculator

It is advisable in making calculations as in Example 2 that you use a continuous sequence of steps in a calculator. It is time-consuming and more mistakes are made if you reenter the result of a previous calculation to make another calculation.

For Example 2, the continuous sequence of steps is:

$\boxed{\text{CLEAR}}\ 117\ \boxed{\times}\ 10\ \boxed{\div}\ 78\ \boxed{=}\ \Rightarrow 15$

When using a calculator, there is no need to reduce fractions first.

EXAMPLE 3

A loan for 36 months, with a finance charge of $1,276.50, is paid in full with 15 payments remaining. Find the finance charge to be refunded.

$$\text{Refund fraction} = \frac{\text{sum of the digits for number of payments remaining}}{\text{sum of the digits for total number of payments}}$$

$$= \frac{\text{sum of digits from 1 through 15}}{\text{sum of digits from 1 through 36}} \qquad \begin{array}{l} \boxed{15} \times \boxed{16} \div \boxed{2} = \Rightarrow 120 \\ \boxed{36} \times \boxed{37} \div \boxed{2} = \Rightarrow 666 \end{array}$$

$$\text{Refund fraction} = \frac{120}{666}$$

Finance charge refund = finance charge × refund fraction

$$= \$1,276.50\left(\frac{120}{666}\right)$$

$$= \$230$$

Calculator sequence: 1276.50 $\boxed{\times}$ 120 $\boxed{\div}$ 666 $\boxed{=}$

The finance charge refund is $230.

STOP AND CHECK

See Example 1.

1. A loan for 12 months with interest of $397.85 is paid in full with five payments remaining. What is the refund fraction for the interest refund?

2. A loan for 48 months has interest of $2,896 and is paid in full with 18 months remaining. What is the refund fraction for the interest refund?

3. A loan for 36 months requires $1,798 interest. The loan is paid in full with 6 months remaining. How much interest is refunded? *See Example 2.*

4. Ruth Brechner borrowed money to purchase a retail business. The 60-month loan had $4,917 interest. Ruth's business flourished and she repaid the loan after 50 months. How much interest refund did she receive? *See Example 3.*

12-2 SECTION EXERCISES

SKILL BUILDERS

See Example 1.

1. Calculate the refund fraction for a 60-month loan that is paid off with 18 months remaining.

2. Find the refund fraction on an 18-month loan if it is paid off with 8 months remaining.

See Examples 2 and 3.

3. Find the interest refund on a 36-month loan with interest of $2,817 if the loan is paid in full with 9 months remaining.

4. Stephen Helba took out a loan to purchase a computer. He originally agreed to pay off the loan in 18 months with a finance charge of $205. He paid the loan in full after 12 payments. How much finance charge refund should he get?

APPLICATIONS

5. John Paszel took out a loan for 48 months but paid it in full after 28 months. Find the refund fraction he should use to calculate the amount of his refund. *See Example 1.*

6. If the finance charge on a loan made by Marjorie Young is $1,645 and the loan is to be paid in 48 monthly payments, find the finance charge refund if the loan is paid in full with 28 months remaining. *See Examples 2 and 3.*

See Examples 2 and 3.

7. Phillamone Berry has a car loan with a company that refunds interest using the rule of 78 when loans are paid in full ahead of schedule. He is using an employee bonus to pay off his Traverse, which is on a 42-month loan. The total interest for the loan is $2,397, and he has 15 more payments to make. How much finance charge will he get credit for if he pays the loan in full immediately?

8. Dwayne Moody purchased a four-wheel drive vehicle and is using severance pay from his current job to pay off the vehicle loan before moving to his new job. The total interest on the 36-month loan is $3,227. How much finance charge refund will he receive if he pays the loan in full with 10 more payments left?

12-3 OPEN-END CREDIT

LEARNING OUTCOMES

1 Find the finance charge and new balance using the average daily balance method.
2 Find the finance charge and new balance using the unpaid or previous month's balance.

Line-of-credit accounts: a type of open-end loan.

Open-end loans are often called **line-of-credit accounts.** While a person or company is paying off loans, that person or company may also be adding to the total loan account by making a new purchase or otherwise borrowing money on the account.

For example, you may want to use your Visa card to buy new textbooks even though you still owe for clothes bought last winter. Likewise, a business may use an open-end credit account to buy a new machine this month even though it still owes the bank for funds used to pay a major supplier six months ago.

Nearly all open-end accounts are billed monthly. Interest rates are most often stated as annual rates. The Fair Credit and Charge Card Disclosure Act of 1988 and updates passed since that time specify the required details that must be disclosed for charge cards and line-of-credit accounts. These details include all fees, grace period, how finance charges are calculated, how late fees are assessed, and so on. While this act addresses the disclosure of fees and charges, the Credit Card Act of 2009 (effective February 22, 2010) imposes regulations on credit card issuers in an attempt to stop them from unfairly taking advantage of consumers.

1 Find the finance charge and new balance using the average daily balance method.

Average daily balance: the average of the daily balances for each day of the billing cycle.

Many lenders determine the finance charge using the **average daily balance** method. In this method, the daily balances of the account are determined, and then the sum of these balances is divided by the number of days in the billing cycle. This average daily balance is next multiplied by the monthly interest rate to find the finance charge for the month.

Billing cycle: the days that are included on a statement or bill.

Even though open-end credit accounts are billed monthly, the monthly period may not coincide with the first and last days of a calendar month. To spread out the workload for the billing department, each account is given a monthly billing cycle. The **billing cycle** is the days that are included on a statement or bill. This cycle can start on any day of a month. For example, a billing cycle may start on the 22nd of one month and end on the 21st of the next month. This means that the number of days of a billing cycle will vary from month to month based on the number of days in the months involved.

HOW TO Find the average daily balance

1. Find the daily unpaid balance for each day in the billing cycle.
   (a) Find the total purchases and cash advances charged to the account during the day.
   (b) Find the total credits (payments and adjustments) credited to the account during the day.
   (c) To the previous daily unpaid balance, add the total purchases and cash advances for the day (from step 1a). Then subtract the total credits for the day (from step 1b).

   Daily unpaid balance = previous daily unpaid balance + total purchases and cash advances for the day − total credits for the day

2. Add the unpaid balances from step 1 for each day of the billing cycle, and divide the sum by the number of days in the cycle.

$$\text{Average daily balance} = \frac{\text{sum of daily unpaid balances}}{\text{number of days in billing cycle}}$$

HOW TO   Find the finance charge using the average daily balance

1. Determine the decimal equivalent of the rate per period.
2. Multiply the average daily balance by the decimal equivalent of the rate per period.

EXAMPLE 1   Use the chart showing May activity in the Hodge's Tax Service charge account to determine the average daily balance and finance charge for the month. The bank's finance charge is 1.5% per month on the average daily balance.

Date transaction posted	Transaction	Transaction amount
May 1	Billing date	Balance $122.70
May 7	Payment	25.00
May 10	Purchase (pencils)	12.00
May 13	Purchase (envelopes)	20.00
May 20	Cash advance	50.00
May 23	Purchase (business forms)	100.00

To find the average daily balance, we must find the unpaid balance for each day, add these balances, and divide by the number of days.

Day	Balance		Day	Balance		Day	Balance	
1	122.70		11	109.70		21	179.70	
2	122.70		12	109.70		22	179.70	
3	122.70		13	129.70	(109.70 + 20)	23	279.70	(179.70 + 100)
4	122.70		14	129.70		24	279.70	
5	122.70		15	129.70		25	279.70	
6	122.70		16	129.70		26	279.70	
7	97.70	(122.70 − 25)	17	129.70		27	279.70	
8	97.70		18	129.70		28	279.70	
9	97.70		19	129.70		29	279.70	
10	109.70	(97.70 + 12)	20	179.70	(129.70 + 50)	30	279.70	
						31	279.70	

Total: $5,322.70   Average Daily Balance: $171.70

The average daily balance can also be determined by grouping days that have the same balance.

For the first six days, May 1–May 6, there is no activity, so the daily unpaid balance is the previous unpaid balance of $122.70. The sum of daily unpaid balances for these six days, then, is 122.70(6).

$$\$122.70(6) = \$736.20$$

On May 7 there is a payment of $25, which reduces the daily unpaid balance.

$$\$122.70 - \$25 = \$97.70$$

The new balance of $97.70 holds for the three days (May 7, 8, and 9) until May 10.

$$\$97.70(3) = \$293.10$$

Continue doing this until you get to the end of the cycle. The calculations can be organized in a chart.

Date	Change	Daily unpaid balance	Number of days	Partial sum
May 1–May 6		$122.70	6	$ 736.20
May 7–May 9	−$25.00	97.70	3	293.10
May 10–May 12	+10.00	109.70	3	329.10
May 13–May 19	+20.00	129.70	7	907.90
May 20–May 22	+50.00	179.70	3	539.10
May 23–May 31	+100.00	279.70	9	2,517.30
			Total 31	$5,322.70

Divide the sum of $5,322.70 by the 31 days.

$$\text{Average daily balance} = \frac{\text{sum of daily unpaid balances}}{\text{number of days}}$$

$$= \frac{\$5,322.70}{31} = \$171.70$$

To find the interest, multiply the average daily balance by the monthly interest rate of 1.5%.

$$\text{Finance charge} = \$171.70(0.015)$$

$$= \$2.58$$

The average daily balance is $171.70 and the finance charge is $2.58.

STOP AND CHECK

Account Number	Credit Limit	Available Credit	Billing Period	
xxxx-xxxx-xxxx-xxxx	$5,000	$4,212.28	9/24/12 to 10/23/12	

Posting Date	Transaction Date	Description	Amount CR–Credit PY–Payment	
9/26	9/24	The Store Oxford MS	$11.93	CR
10/6	10/02	Chili's Oxford MS	$15.24	CR
10/8	10/06	Durall St Cloud FL	$86.98	CR
10/10	10/10	Payment Received–Thank You	$927.86	PY
10/14	10/12	Foley's Knitwear San Antonio TX	$113.19	CR
10/20	10/16	Red Lobster Tupelo MS	$22.88	CR
10/20	10/19	JC Penny Co Oxford MS	$47.36	CR

Finance Charge					Balance		
Average Daily Balance	Monthly Periodic Rate	Corresponding Annual Percentage Rate	Finance Charge		Previous Balance	$	1,406.54
					Purchases	+	297.58
					Other Charges	+	.00
Purchases		Variable			Cash Advances	+	0.00
	1.0750%	12.90%			Credits	−	.00
					Payments	−	927.86
Cash Advances		Variable			Late Charges	+	.00
$0.00	1.0750%	12.90%			Finance Charges	+	11.46
					New Balance	$	787.72

FIGURE 12-1

Use the statement in Figure 12-1 for Exercises 1–4. See Example 1.

1. Make a table showing the unpaid balance for each day in the billing period.

2. Find the average daily balance for the month.

3. Find the finance charge for the month.

4. Find the new balance for the month.

2 Find the finance charge and new balance using the unpaid or previous month's balance.

Not all open-end credit accounts use the average daily balance method for determining the monthly finance charge. Another method uses the unpaid or previous month's balance as the basis for determining the finance charge. In this method, the new purchases or payments made during a month do not affect the finance charge for that month. Some businesses such as used car dealerships or independent retail stores provide the financing for purchases made and use this method for applying finance charges.

> **HOW TO** Find the finance charge and new balance using the unpaid or previous month's balance
>
> Finance charge:
>
> 1. Find the monthly rate.
>
> $$\text{Monthly rate} = \frac{\text{Annual percentage rate}}{12}$$
>
> 2. Multiply the unpaid or previous month's balance by the monthly rate.
>
> Finance charge = Unpaid balance × Monthly rate
>
> New balance:
>
> 1. Total the purchases and cash advances for the billing cycle.
> 2. Total the payments and credits for the billing cycle.
> 3. Adjust the unpaid balance of the previous month using the totals in steps 1 and 2.
>
> New balance = Previous balance + Finance charge + Purchases and cash advances − Payments and credits

EXAMPLE 2 Hanna Stein has a department store revolving credit account with an annual percentage rate of 21%. Her unpaid balance for her March billing cycle is $285.45. During the billing cycle she purchased shoes for $62.58 and a handbag for $35.18. She returned a blouse that she had purchased in the previous billing cycle, received a credit of $22.79, and she made a payment of $75. If the store uses the unpaid balance method, what are the finance charge and the new balance?

Monthly rate:

$$\text{Monthly rate} = \frac{\text{Annual percentage rate}}{12}$$

$$\text{Monthly rate} = \frac{21\%}{12} = \frac{0.21}{12} = 0.0175$$

Finance charge:

Finance charge = Unpaid balance × Monthly rate

Finance charge = $285.45(0.0175) = $5.00   Rounded from $4.995375

New balance:

Total purchases and cash advances = $62.58 + $35.18 = $97.76

Total payments and credits = $75 + $22.79 = $97.79

New balance = Previous balance + Finance charge + Purchases and cash advances − Payments and credits

New balance = $285.45 + $5 + $97.76 − $97.79 = $290.42

STOP AND CHECK

See Example 2.

1. Shakina Brewster has a Target revolving credit account that has an annual percentage rate of 18% on the unpaid balance. Her unpaid balance for the July billing cycle is $1,285.96. During the billing cycle, Shakina purchased groceries for $98.76 and received $50 in cash. She purchased linens for $46.98. Shakina made a payment of $135. Find the finance charge and new balance if Target uses the unpaid balance method.

2. Shameka Brown has a Best Buy Stores revolving credit account that has an annual percentage rate of 15% on the unpaid balance. Her unpaid balance for the October billing cycle is $2,531.77. During the billing cycle, Shameka purchased movies for $58.63 and received $70 in cash. She purchased a camera for $562.78 and returned a printer purchased in September for credit of $85.46. Shameka made a payment of $455. Find the finance charge and new balance if Best Buy uses the unpaid balance method.

3. Dallas Hunsucker has a Master Card account with an annual percentage rate of 24%. The unpaid balance for his January billing cycle is $2,094.54. During the billing cycle he made grocery purchases of $65.82, $83.92, $12.73, and gasoline purchases of $29.12 and $28.87. He made a payment of $400. If the account applies the unpaid balance method, what were the finance charge and the new balance?

4. Ryan Bradley has a Visa Card with an introductory annual percentage rate of 9%. The unpaid balance for his February billing cycle is $245.18. During the billing cycle he purchased fresh flowers for $45.00, candy for $22.38, and gasoline for $36.53. He made a payment of $100 and had a return for credit of $74.93. If the account applies the unpaid balance method, what are the finance charge and the new balance?

12-3 SECTION EXERCISES

SKILL BUILDERS

See Example 1.

1. What is the monthly interest rate if an annual rate is 13.8%?

2. Find the monthly interest rate if the annual rate is 15.6%.

See Example 2.

3. A credit card has an average daily balance of $2,817.48 and the monthly periodic rate is 1.325%. What is the finance charge for the month?

4. What is the finance charge on a credit card account that has an average daily balance of $5,826.42 and the monthly interest rate is 1.55%?

APPLICATIONS

See Examples 1 and 2.

5. Suppose the charge account of Strong's Mailing Service at the local supply store had a 1.8% interest rate per month on the average daily balance. Find the average daily balance if Strong's had an unpaid balance on March 1 of $128.50, a payment of $20 posted on March 6, and a purchase of $25.60 posted on March 20. The billing cycle ends March 31.

6. Jim Riddle has a credit card that charges 10% annual interest on the monthly average daily balance for the billing cycle. The current billing cycle has 29 days. For 15 days his balance was $2,534.95. For 7 days the balance was $1,534.95. And for 7 days the balance was $1,892.57. Find the average daily balance. Find the amount of interest.

7. Using Exercise 5, find Strong's finance charge on April 1.

8. Make a chart to show the transactions for Rick Schiendler's credit card account in which interest is charged on the average daily balance. The cycle begins on May 4, and the cycle ends on June 3. The beginning balance is $283.57. A payment of $200 is posted on May 18. A charge of $19.73 is posted on May 7. A charge of $53.82 is posted on May 12. A charge of $115.18 is posted on May 29. How many days are in the cycle? What is the average daily balance?

9. In Exercise 8, Rick is charged 1.42% per period. What is the finance charge for the cycle?

10. Using Exercise 9, what is the beginning balance for the next cycle of Rick's credit card account?

11. Jamel Cisco has a Visa Card with an annual percentage rate of 16.8%. The unpaid balance for his June billing cycle is $1,300.84. During the billing cycle he purchased a printer cartridge for $42.39, books for $286.50 and gasoline for $16.71. He made a payment of $1,200. If the account applies the unpaid balance method, what are the finance charge and the new balance?

12. Chaundra Mixon has a Master Card with an annual percentage rate of 19.8%. The unpaid balance for her August billing cycle is $675.21. During the billing cycle she purchased shoes for $87.52, a suit for $132.48, and a wallet for $28.94. She made a payment of $225. If the account applies the unpaid balance method, what are the finance charge and the new balance?

Learning Outcomes

Section 12-1

1 Find the amount financed, the installment price, and the finance charge of an installment loan. (p. 428)

What to Remember with Examples

1. Find the amount financed: Subtract the down payment from the cash price.

$$\text{Amount financed} = \text{cash price} - \text{down payment}$$

2. Find the installment price: Add the down payment to the total of the installment payments.

$$\text{Installment price} = \text{total of installment payments} + \text{down payment}$$

Find the installment price of a computer that is paid for in 24 monthly payments of $113 if a down payment of $50 is made.

$$(24)(\$113) + \$50 = \$2{,}712 + \$50 = \$2{,}762$$

Find the finance charge of an installment loan:

Subtract the cash price from the installment price.

$$\text{Finance charge} = \text{installment price} - \text{cash price}$$

If the cash price of the computer in the previous example was $2,499, how much is the finance charge?

$$\$2{,}762 - \$2{,}499 = \$263$$

---

2 Find the installment payment of an installment loan. (p. 429)

1. Find the total of the installment payments: Subtract the down payment from the installment price.

$$\text{Total of installment payments} = \text{installment price} - \text{down payment}$$

2. Divide the total of installment payments by the number of installment payments.

$$\text{Installment payment} = \frac{\text{total of installment payments}}{\text{number of payments}}$$

Find the monthly payment on a computer if the cash price is $3,285. A 14% interest rate is charged on the cash price, and there are 12 monthly payments.

$$\$3{,}285(0.14)(1) = \$459.90$$
$$\text{Installment price} = \$3{,}285 + \$459.90 = \$3{,}744.90$$
$$\text{Monthly payment} = \frac{\$3{,}744.90}{12} = \$312.08$$

A computer has an installment price of $2,187.25 when financed over 18 months. If a $100 down payment is made, find the monthly payment.

$$\$2{,}187.25 - \$100 = \$2{,}087.25$$
$$\text{Monthly payment} = \frac{\$2{,}087.25}{18} = \$115.96$$

---

3 Find the estimated annual percentage rate (APR) using a table. (p. 430)

1. Find the interest per $100 of amount financed: Divide the finance charge by the amount financed and multiply by $100.

$$\text{Interest per }\$100 = \frac{\text{total finance charge}}{\text{amount financed}} \times \$100$$

2. Find the row corresponding to the number of monthly payments. Move across the row to find the number closest to the value from step 1. Read up the column to find the annual percentage rate for that column. If the result in step 1 is exactly halfway between two table values, use the higher rate or a rate halfway between the two rates can be used.

Find the annual percentage rate on a loan of $500 that is repaid in 36 monthly installments. The interest for the loan is $95.

$$\text{Interest per } \$100 = \frac{\$95}{\$500}(\$100) = \$19$$

In the row for 36 months, move across to 19.14 (nearest to 19). APR is at the top of the column, 11.75%.

Section 12-2

1 Find the interest refund using the rule of 78. (p. 435)

Find the refund fraction.

1. The numerator is the sum of the digits from 1 through the number of months remaining of a loan paid off before it was due.
2. The denominator is the sum of the digits from 1 through the original number of months of the loan.
3. The original fraction, the reduced fraction or the decimal equivalent of the fraction can be used.

Find the refund fraction on a loan that has a total finance charge of $892 and was made for 24 months. The loan is paid in full with 10 months (payments) remaining.

$$\text{Refund fraction} = \frac{\text{sum of digits from 1 to the number of periods remaining}}{\text{sum of digits from 1 through original number of periods}}$$

$$= \frac{\text{sum of 1 to 10}}{\text{sum of 1 to 24}}$$

$$= \frac{55}{300} \text{ or } \frac{11}{60} \text{ or } 0.1833333333$$

Find the interest refund using the rule of 78.

1. Find the refund fraction.
2. Multiply the total interest by the refund fraction.

$$\text{Interest refund} = \text{total interest} \times \text{refund fraction}$$

Find the interest refund for the previous example.

$$\text{Interest refund} = \$892\left(\frac{11}{60}\right) = \$163.53 \quad 892 \;\boxed{\times}\; 11 \;\boxed{\div}\; 60 \;\boxed{=}\; \Rightarrow 163.5333333$$

Section 12-3

1 Find the finance charge and new balance using the average daily balance method. (p. 439)

1. Find the daily unpaid balance for each day in the billing cycle.
   (a) Find the total purchases and cash advances charged to the account during the day.
   (b) Find the total credits (payments and adjustments) credited to the account during the day.
   (c) To the previous daily unpaid balance, add the total purchases and cash advances for the day (from step 1a). Then subtract the total payments for the day (from step 1b).

$$\text{Daily unpaid balance} = \text{previous daily unpaid balance} + \text{total purchases}$$
$$\text{and cash advances for the day} - \text{total credits for the day}$$

2. Add the unpaid balances from step 1 for each day of the billing cycle, and divide the sum by the number of days in the cycle.

$$\text{Average daily balance} = \frac{\text{sum of daily unpaid balances}}{\text{number of days in billing cycle}}$$

A credit card has a balance of $398.42 on September 14, the first day of the billing cycle. A charge of $182.37 is posted to the account on September 16. Another charge of $82.21 is posted to the account on September 25. The amount of a returned item ($19.98) is posted to the account on October 10 and a payment of $500 is made on October 12. The billing period ends on October 13. Find the average daily balance.

Date	Change	Daily Unpaid Balance	Number of Days	Partial Sum
September 14–15		$398.42	2 days	$ 796.84
September 16–24	+$182.37	580.79	9 days	5,227.11
September 25–October 9	+82.21	663.00	15 days	9,945.00
October 10–11	−19.98	643.02	2 days	1,286.04
October 12–13	−500.00	143.02	2 days	286.04
			Total 30 days	$17,541.03

Average daily balance = $17,541.03 ÷ 30 = $584.70

Find the finance charge using the average daily balance:

1. Determine the decimal equivalent of the rate per period.
2. Multiply the average daily balance by the decimal equivalent of the rate per period.

Find the finance charge for the average daily balance in the preceding example if the monthly rate is 1.3%.

$$\text{Finance charge} = \$584.70(0.013) = \$7.60$$

2 Find the finance charge and new balance using the unpaid or previous month's balance. (p. 442)

Finance charge:

1. Find the monthly rate.

$$\text{Monthly rate} = \frac{\text{Annual percentage rate}}{12}$$

2. Multiply the unpaid or previous month's balance by the monthly rate.

$$\text{Finance charge} = \text{Unpaid balance} \times \text{Monthly rate}$$

New balance:

1. Total the purchases and cash advances for the billing cycle.
2. Total the payments and credits for the billing cycle.
3. Adjust the unpaid balance of the previous month using the totals in steps 1 and 2.

$$\text{New balance} = \text{previous balance} + \text{finance charge} + \text{purchases and cash advances} - \text{payments and credits}$$

Dakota Beasley has a Visa account with an annual percentage rate of 24%. Her unpaid balance for her September billing cycle is $381.15. During the billing cycle she made purchases of $25.18, $18.29, $22.75, and $19.12. She made a payment of $100. If the account applies the unpaid balance method, what is the finance charge and the new balance?

$$\text{Monthly rate} = \frac{\text{Annual percentage rate}}{12}$$

$$\text{Monthly rate} = \frac{24\%}{12} = \frac{0.24}{12} = 0.02 = 2\%$$

Finance charge = Unpaid balance × Monthly rate
Finance charge = $381.15(0.02) = $7.62   Rounded from $7.623
Total purchases = $25.18 + $18.29 + $22.75 + $19.12
　　　　　　　= $85.34
　　　Payments = $100
　New balance = $381.15 + $7.62 + $85.34 − $100
　　　　　　　= $374.11

EXERCISES SET A

1. Find the installment price of a notebook computer system bought on the installment plan with $250 down and 12 payments of $111.33.

2. Find the monthly payment on a water bed if the installment price is $1,050, the down payment is $200, and there are 10 monthly payments.

3. If the cash price of a refrigerator is $879 and a down payment of $150 is made, how much is to be financed?

4. Find the refund fraction for a 60-month loan if it is paid in full with 22 months remaining.

Use the rule of 78 to find the finance charge (interest) refund in each of the following.

	Finance charge	Number of monthly payments	Remaining payments	Interest refund
EXCEL 5.	$238	12	4	
EXCEL 6.	$2,175	24	10	
EXCEL 7.	$896	18	4	

8. The finance charge on a copier was $1,778. The loan for the copier was to be paid in 18 monthly payments. Find the finance charge refund if it is paid off in eight months.

9. Becky Whitehead has a loan with $1,115 in finance charges, which she paid in full after 10 of the 24 monthly payments. What is her finance charge refund?

10. Alice Dubois was charged $455 in finance charges on a loan for 15 months. Find the finance charge refund if she pays off the loan in full after 10 payments.

11. Find the finance charge refund on a 24-month loan with monthly payments of $103.50 if you decide to pay off the loan with 10 months remaining. The finance charge is $215.55.

12. If you purchase a fishing boat for 18 monthly payments of $106 and an interest charge of $238, how much is the refund after 10 payments?

13. Find the interest on an average daily balance of $265 with an interest rate of $1\frac{1}{2}\%$.

14. Find the finance charge on a credit card with an average daily balance of $465 if the rate charged is 1.25%.

15. Use the following activity chart for a credit card to find the unpaid balance on November 1. The billing cycle ended on October 31, and the finance charge is 1.5% of the average daily balance.

Date posted	Activity	Amount
October 1	Billing date	Previous balance $426.40
October 8	Purchase	41.60
October 11	Payment	70.00
October 16	Purchase	31.25
October 21	Purchase	26.80

Use Table 12-1 to find the annual percentage rate (APR) for the following exercises.

16. Find the annual percentage rate on a loan of $1,500 for 18 months if the loan requires $190 interest and is repaid monthly.

17. Find the annual percentage rate on a loan of $3,820 if the monthly payment is $130 for 36 months.

18. A vacuum cleaner was purchased on the installment plan with 12 monthly payments of $36.98 each. If the cash price was $415 and there was no down payment, find the annual percentage rate.

19. A merchant charged $420 in cash for a dining room set that could be bought for $50 down and $40.75 per month for 10 months. What is the annual percentage rate?

20. An electric mixer was purchased on the installment plan for a down payment of $60 and 11 monthly payments of $11.05 each. The cash price was $170. Find the annual percentage rate.

21. A computer was purchased by paying $50 down and 24 monthly payments of $65 each. The cash price was $1,400. Find the annual percentage rate to the nearest tenth of a percent.

EXERCISES SET B

1. A television set has been purchased on the installment plan with a down payment of $120 and six monthly payments of $98.50. Find the installment price of the television set.

2. A dishwasher sold for a $983 installment price with a down payment of $150 and 12 monthly payments. How much is each payment?

3. What is the cash price of a chair if the installment price is $679, the finance charge is $102, and there was no down payment?

4. Find the refund fraction for a 42-month loan if it is paid in full with 16 months remaining.

Use the rule of 78 to find the finance charge refund in each of the following.

	Finance charge	Number of monthly payments	Remaining payments	Interest refund
EXCEL 5.	$1,076	18	6	
EXCEL 6.	$476	12	5	
EXCEL 7.	$683	15	11	

8. Find the refund fraction on a 48-month loan if it is paid off after 20 months.

9. Lanny Jacobs made a loan to purchase a computer. Find the refund due on this loan with interest charges of $657 if it is paid off after paying 7 of the 12 monthly payments.

10. Suppose you have borrowed money that is being repaid at $45 a month for 12 months. What is the finance charge refund after making eight payments if the finance charge is $105?

11. You have purchased a new stereo on the installment plan. The plan calls for 12 monthly payments of $45 and a $115 finance charge. After nine months you decide to pay off the loan. How much is the refund?

12. The interest for an automobile loan is $2,843. The automobile is financed for 36 monthly payments, and interest refunds are made using the rule of 78. How much interest should be refunded if the loan is paid in full with 22 months still remaining?

13. Find the finance charge on $371 if the interest charge is 1.4% of the average daily balance.

14. A new desk for an office has a cash price of $1,500 and can be purchased on the installment plan with a 12.5% finance charge. The desk will be paid for in 12 monthly payments. Find the amount of the finance charge, the total price, and the amount of each monthly payment, if there was no down payment.

15. On January 1 the previous balance for Lynn's charge account was $569.80. On the following days, purchases were posted:

January 13 $38.50   jewelry
January 21 $44.56   clothing

On January 16 a $50 payment was posted. Using the average daily balance method, find the finance charge and unpaid balance on February 1 if the bank charges interest of 1.5% per month.

Use Table 12-1 to find the annual percentage rate for the following exercises.

16. Find the annual percentage rate on a loan for 25 months if the amount of the loan without interest is $300. The loan requires $40 interest.

17. Find the annual percentage rate on a loan of $700 without interest with 12 monthly payments. The loan requires $50 interest.

18. A queen-size brass bed costs $1,155 and is financed with monthly payments for three years. The total finance charge is $415.80. Find the annual percentage rate.

19. John Edmonds borrowed $500. He repaid the loan in 22 monthly payments of $26.30 each. Find the annual percentage rate.

20. A loan of $3,380 was paid back in 30 monthly payments with an interest charge of $620. Find the annual percentage rate.

21. A 6 × 6 color enlarger costs $1,295 and is financed with monthly payments for two years. The total finance charge is $310.80. Find the annual percentage rate.

PRACTICE TEST

1. Find the finance charge on an item with a cash price of $469 if the installment price is $503 and no down payment was made.

2. An item with a cash price of $578 can be purchased on the installment plan in 15 monthly payments of $46. Find the installment price if no down payment was made. Find the finance charge.

3. The installment price of a Bosch stainless steel refrigerator is $2,199.99 for an 18-month loan. If a $300 down payment has been made, find the installment payment.

4. The installment price of an Electrolux front-load washer is $1,299.90. What is the installment payment if a down payment of $295 is made and the loan is for 12 months?

5. A copier that originally cost $300 was sold on the installment plan at $28 per month for 12 months. Find the installment price if no down payment was made. Find the finance charge.

6. Use Table 12-1 to find the annual percentage rate for the loan in Exercise 3.

7. Use Table 12-1 to find the APR on a loan of $3,000 for three years if the loan had $810 interest and was repaid monthly.

8. Find the interest on an average daily balance of $165 if the monthly interest rate is $1\frac{3}{4}\%$.

9. Find the yearly rate of interest on a loan if the monthly rate is 2%.

10. Find the interest refunded on a 15-month loan with total interest of $72 if the loan is paid in full with six months remaining.

11. Find the annual percentage rate on a loan of $1,600 for 24 months if $200 interest is charged and the loan is repaid in monthly payments. Use Table 12-1.

12. Find the annual interest rate on a loan that is repaid monthly for 26 months if the amount of the loan is $1,075. The interest charged is $134.85.

13. Office equipment was purchased on the installment plan with 12 monthly payments of $11.20 each. If the cash price was $120 and there was no down payment, find the annual percentage rate.

14. A canoe has been purchased on the installment plan with a down payment of $75 and 10 monthly payments of $80 each. Find the installment price of the canoe.

15. Find the monthly payment when the installment price is $2,300, a down payment of $400 is made, and there are 12 monthly payments.

16. How much is to be financed on a cash price of $729 if a down payment of $75 is made?

17. Maurice Van Norman made a 48-month loan that has interest of $1,987. He paid the loan in full with 11 months remaining. The interest is refunded based on the rule of 78. Find the amount of interest to be refunded.

18. Larry Williams made a 60-month loan that has interest of $2,518. He paid the loan in full with 21 months remaining. The interest is refunded based on the rule of 78. Find the amount of interest to be refunded.

19. A 30-month loan that has interest of $3,987 is paid in full with 7 months remaining. Find the amount of interest to be refunded using the rule of 78.

20. Use the following activity chart to find the average daily balance, finance charge, and unpaid balance for July. The monthly interest rate is 1.75%. The billing cycle has 31 days.

Date Posted	Activity	Amount
July 1	Billing date	Previous balance $441.05
July 5	Payment	$75.00
July 16	Purchase	23.50
July 26	Purchase	31.40

21. Mary Lawson has a credit card account with an annual percentage rate of 18.24%. The unpaid balance for her November billing cycle is $783.56. During the billing cycle she purchased a desk chair for $134.77 and a floor mat for $82.36. Mary returned a grill purchased in the previous month for a credit of $186.21 and she made a payment of $80. If the account applies the unpaid balance method, what are the finance charge and the new balance?

22. Leslie Joiner has a credit card with an annual percentage rate of 17.4%. The unpaid balance for his June billing cycle is $2,156.28. During the billing cycle he purchased a refrigerator for $989.21 and a computer for $873.52. Leslie returned clothing purchased in May for a credit of $215.77 and made a payment of $425. If the account applies the unpaid balance method, what are the finance charge and the new balance?

1. Explain the mistake in the solution of the problem and correct the solution.

    Dawn Mayhall financed a car and the loan of 42 months required $3,827 interest. She paid the loan off after making 20 payments. How much interest should be refunded if the rule of 78 is used?

    Solution:

    Refund fraction $= \dfrac{210}{903}$

    $\dfrac{210}{903}(\$3,827) = \$890$

    Thus, $890 should be refunded.

2. Explain the mistake in the solution and correct the solution.

    Ava Landry agreed to pay $2,847 interest for a 36-month loan to redecorate her greeting card shop. However, business was better than expected and she repaid the loan with 16 months remaining. If the rule of 78 was used, how much interest should she get back?

    Solution:

    $\dfrac{16}{36}(\$2,847) = \$1,265.33$

    Thus, $1,265.33 should be refunded.

3. Arrange the consecutive numbers from 1 to 10 in ascending order, then in descending order, so that 1 and 10, 2 and 9, 3 and 8, and so on, align vertically. Add vertically. Find the grand total. Finally divide the grand total by 2. Compare the result to the sum of digits 1 through 10.

    $1 + 2 + 3 + 4 + 5 + 6 + 7 + 8 + 9 + 10$
    $10 + 9 + 8 + 7 + 6 + 5 + 4 + 3 + 2 + 1$

4. Explain why finding the sum of consecutive numbers by using the process in Exercise 3 requires that the product be divided by 2.

5. Explain why the formula for finding the sum of consecutive numbers requires the product of the largest number and one *more* than the largest number rather than one *less* than the largest number.

6. Give three examples of finding the sum of consecutive *odd* numbers beginning with 1.

Challenge Problem

It pays to read the details! Bank One Delaware offers a Platinum Visa Credit Card to qualifying persons with an introductory 0% fixed APR on all purchases and balance transfers and, after the 12-month introductory period, a low variable APR on purchases and balance transfers at a current annual rate of 8.99%. However, the default rate is 24.99% APR. A default occurs if the minimum payment is not received by the due date on the billing statement or if your balance ever exceeds your credit limit. Find the difference in just one month's interest on an average daily balance of $1,000 if the payment is not received by the due date.

CASE STUDIES

12-1 Know What You Owe

Nancy Tai has recently opened a revolving charge account with MasterCard. Her credit limit is $1,000, but she has not charged that much since opening the account. Nancy hasn't had the time to review her monthly statements promptly as she should, but over the upcoming weekend she plans to catch up on her work. She has been putting it off because she can't tell how much interest she paid or the unpaid balance in November. She spilled watercolor paint on that portion of the statement.

In reviewing November's statement she notices that her beginning balance was $600 and that she made a $200 payment on November 10. She also charged purchases of $80 on November 5, $100 on November 15, and $50 on November 30. She paid $5.27 in interest the month before. She does remember, though, seeing the letters APR and the number 16%. Also, the back of her statement indicates that interest was charged using the average daily balance method, including current purchases, which considers the day of a charge or credit.

1. Find the unpaid balance on November 30 before the interest is charged.

2. Assuming a 30-day period in November, find the average daily balance.

3. Calculate the interest for November.

4. What was the unpaid balance for November after interest is charged?

5. If Nancy's account instead used the unpaid balance method, calculate the finance charge and new balance for the month of November.

Source: Adapted from Winger and Frasca, *Personal Finance: An Integrated Approach*, 6th edition, Upper Saddle River, NJ: Prentice Hall, p. 162.

12-2 Massage Therapy

It was time to expand her massage therapy business, and Arminte had finally found a commercial space that met her needs. With room for herself and the two new massage therapists she planned to hire, and adjacent to a chiropractor's office, the space was everything that she had hoped for. Now all she needed was to finalize purchases for three massage rooms, furniture for the reception area, various artwork, and miscellaneous supplies. Arminte started to make a list of massage equipment: 3 tables at $1,695 each; 3 stools at $189 each; a portable massage chair for $399; and the list went on—bolsters, pillows, sheets, table warmers, and music. By the time Arminte was finished, her massage equipment alone totaled $7,644.25, including sales tax. The supplier offered in-house financing of 24 monthly payments at $325.33 per month, with a 10% down payment.

1. Find the amount financed, installment price, and the finance charge presuming Arminte goes with the financing available through her supplier.

2. Use Table 12-1 to find the annual percentage rate (APR) of the financing.

3. If Arminte takes the financing but pays the balance in full with 9 months remaining, what is the amount of the finance charge to be refunded using the rule of 78?

4. Arminte had recently opened a revolving charge account with MasterCard to pick up some miscellaneous supplies for her business. Her credit limit is $1,500, with 18% APR. Her beginning balance for the month of April was $440, and she made a payment of $60, which was received on April 10. She purchased massage oil for $240 on April 6, office supplies for $68.45 on April 14, a CD player for $129.44 on April 20, and $25 in gas on April 27. Arminte's statement indicates that interest is charged using the average daily balance method, including current purchases, which considers the day of a charge or credit. Assuming a 30-day period in April, find the average daily balance and the interest for April.

5. If Arminte's account instead used the unpaid balance method, calculate the finance charge and new balance for the month of April.

6. Which method is Arminte's credit card company more likely to use, the average daily balance method or the unpaid or previous month's balance method?

Compound Interest, Future Value, and Present Value

Auto Loans: When Is 4% APR Better Than 0% APR?

What could possibly be wrong with a zero percent auto loan? Nothing could be more enticing than free money, and that's exactly what zero-percent finance deals seem to offer. With an auto loan, zero-percent financing may cost more than you think. Before taking on any loan, there are many things to consider. Compound interest—one of the topics you'll learn about in this chapter—is of special concern. With compound interest, you will actually pay more interest than you expect. Look for the annual percentage rate (APR) on your loan information. The APR tells you the effective interest rate that you will actually pay for the term of your loan. Does that mean a lower interest rate is the best deal? Not always. Here are a few things you should know about this special financing arrangement.

Anyone who purchases a vehicle with a cash rebate gets the rebate. But only about 5 percent of all consumers qualify for zero percent financing. You must have an excellent credit rating and a certain amount of income to qualify. Most zero-percent loans have short payback terms, which mean higher monthly payments. You may have to make a large down payment and be subject to prepayment penalties. Also, most zero percent financing applies only to certain makes and models of vehicles or those already on the lot.

Want to make the best deal? Consider rebates instead of special financing. Rebates are simply a form of discount, or savings, which may be greater than the amount you would save with even zero percent financing. The table below shows a comparison of a lower percent financing rate versus a higher rate with a rebate. In both cases, the rebate deals saved money compared to a lower financing rate—more than $800 savings over the life of the loan! So make sure you do the math ahead of time to find out whether the rebate or the special financing would save you more money when buying your next car.

Financing a $20,000 New Car				
Loan terms	**36 Months**		**60 Months**	
APR	0%	4.0%	2.9%	5.6%
Price of new car	$20,000.00	$20,000.00	$20,000.00	$20,000.00
Less dealer rebate	$0	$2,000.00	$0	$2,000.00
Amount to finance	$20,000.00	$18,000.00	$20,000.00	$18,000.00
Monthly payment	$555.56	$531.43	$358.49	$344.65
Total financing cost	$20,000.00	$19,131.48	$21,509.40	$20,679.00
Savings		**$868.52**		**$830.40**

LEARNING OUTCOMES

13-1 Compound Interest and Future Value

1. Find the future value and compound interest by compounding manually.
2. Find the future value and compound interest using a $1.00 future value table.
3. Find the future value and compound interest using a formula or a calculator application (optional).
4. Find the effective interest rate.
5. Find the interest compounded daily using a table.

13-2 Present Value

1. Find the present value based on annual compounding for one year.
2. Find the present value using a $1.00 present value table.
3. Find the present value using a formula or a calculator application (optional).

For some loans made on a short-term basis, interest is computed once, using the simple interest formula. For other loans, interest may be *compounded:* Interest is calculated more than once during the term of the loan or investment and this interest is added to the principal. This sum (principal + interest) then becomes the principal for the next calculation of interest, and interest is charged or paid on this new amount. This process of adding interest to the principal before interest is calculated for the next period is called *compounding interest.*

13-1 COMPOUND INTEREST AND FUTURE VALUE

LEARNING OUTCOMES

1 Find the future value and compound interest by compounding manually.
2 Find the future value and compound interest using a $1.00 future value table.
3 Find the future value and compound interest using a formula or a calculator application (optional).
4 Find the effective interest rate.
5 Find the interest compounded daily using a table.

Interest period: the amount of time after which interest is calculated and added to the principal.

Compound interest: the total interest that accumulated after more than one interest period.

Future value, maturity value, compound amount: the accumulated principal and interest after one or more interest periods.

Whether the interest rate is simple or compound, interest is calculated for each **interest period.** When simple interest is calculated, the entire period of the loan or investment is the interest period. When the interest is compounded, there are two or more interest periods, each of the same duration. The interest period may be one day, one week, one month, one quarter, one year, or some other designated period of time. The greater the number of interest periods in the time period of the loan or investment, the greater the total interest that accumulates during the time period. The total interest that accumulates is the **compound interest.** The sum of the compound interest and the original principal is the **future value** or **maturity value** or **compound amount** in the case of an investment, or the compound amount in the case of a loan. In this chapter we use the term *future value* to mean future value *or* compound amount, depending on whether the principal is an investment or a loan.

1 Find the future value and compound interest by compounding manually.

We can calculate the future value of the principal using the simple interest formula method. The terms of a loan or investment indicate the annual number of interest periods and the annual interest rate. Dividing the annual interest rate by the annual number of interest periods gives us the **period interest rate** or interest rate per period. We can use the period interest rate to calculate the interest that accumulates for each period using the familiar simple interest formula: $I = PRT$. I is the interest for the period, P is the principal at the beginning of the period, R is the period interest rate, and T is one period. As the value of T in the formula is one period, the formula is simplified to $I = PR(1)$, or $I = PR$. The value of P is different for each period in turn because the principal at the beginning of each period includes the original principal and all the interest so far accumulated. We can find the end-of-period principal directly by using $1 + R$ for the rate.

Period interest rate: the rate for calculating interest for one interest period—the annual interest rate divided by the number of interest periods per year.

HOW TO   Find the period interest rate

Divide the annual interest rate by the number of interest periods per year.

$$\text{Period interest rate} = \frac{\text{annual interest rate}}{\text{number of interest periods per year}}$$

HOW TO   Find the future value using the simple interest formula method

1. Find the first end-of-period principal: Multiply the original principal by the sum of 1 and the period interest rate.

First end-of-period principal = original principal × (1 + period interest rate)

$$A = P(1 + R)$$

2. For each remaining period in turn, find the next end-of-period principal: Multiply the previous end-of-period principal by the sum of 1 and the period interest rate.

End-of-period principal = previous end-of-period principal × (1 + period interest rate)

3. Identify the last end-of-period principal as the future value.

$$\text{Future value} = \text{last end-of-period principal}$$

The future value is calculated before the amount of the compound interest can be calculated.

HOW TO Find the compound interest

Subtract the original principal from the future value.

$$\text{Compound interest} = \text{future value} - \text{original principal}$$
$$I = A - P$$

EXAMPLE 1

Susan Riddle Duke's Photography secured a small business loan of $8,000 for three years, compounded annually. If the interest rate was 9%, find (a) the compound amount and (b) the compound interest paid on the loan. (c) Compare the compound interest with simple interest for the same loan period, original principal, and annual interest rate.

$$\text{Period interest rate} = \frac{\text{rate per year}}{\text{number of interest periods per year}}$$

(a) Because the loan is compounded annually, there is one interest period per year. So the period interest rate is 0.09. There are three interest periods, one for each of the three years.

First end-of-period principal $= \$8,000(1 + 0.09)$ $8,000(1.09) = 8,720$

$$= \$8,720$$

Next end-of-period principal $= \$8,720(1 + 0.09)$ $8,720(1.09) = 9,504.8$

$$= \$9,504.80$$

Third end-of-period principal $= \$9,504.80(1 + 0.09)$ $9,504.80(1.09) = 10,360.232$

$$= \$10,360.23$$

The compound amount is $10,360.23.

(b) Compound interest is the future value (compound amount) minus the original principal.

$10,360.23	Future value
$-8,000.00$	Original principal
$\$ 2,360.23$	Compound interest

The compound interest is $2,360.23.

(c) Use the simple interest formula to find the simple interest on $8,000 at 9% annually for three years.

$$I = PRT$$
$$I = \$8,000(0.09)(3)$$
$$I = \$2,160.00 \qquad \text{Simple interest}$$

Difference: $\$2,360.23 - \$2,160.00 = \$200.23$

The simple interest is $2,160.00, which is $200.23 less than the compound interest.

EXAMPLE 2

Find the future value of a $10,000 investment at 2% annual interest compounded semiannually for three years.

$$\text{Period interest rate} = \frac{2\% \text{ annually}}{2 \text{ periods annually}} = \frac{0.02}{2} = 0.01 \text{ or } 1\%$$

Number of periods $=$ years$(2) = 3(2) = 6$

First end-of-period principal $= \$10,000(1 + 0.01)$ $10,000(1.01) = 10,100$

$$= \$10,100$$

Second end-of-period principal $= \$10,100(1 + 0.01)$ $10,100(1.01) = 10,201$

$$= \$10,201$$

Third end-of-period principal $= \$10,303.01$ $10,201(1.01) = 10,303.01$

Fourth end-of-period principal $= \$10,406.04$ $10,303.01(1.01) = 10,406.04$

Fifth end-of-period principal = $10,510.10   10,406.04(1.01) = 10,510.10
Sixth end-of-period principal = $10,615.20   10,510.10(1.01) = 10,615.20

The future value is $10,615.20.

TIP

Calculator Shortcut for Compounding

Many calculators keep the result of a calculation in the calculator and allow the next calculation to begin with this amount.

Examine the calculator steps that can be used for Example 2.

10000 $\times$ 1.01 $=$ $\Rightarrow$ 10100   Record display as first end-of-period principal.

Do not clear the calculator.

$\times$ 1.01 $=$ $\Rightarrow$ 10,201   Record display as second end-of-period principal.

Continue without clearing the calculator.

$\times$ 1.01 $=$ $\Rightarrow$ 10,303.01   Record display as third end-of-period principal.

$\times$ 1.01 $=$ $\Rightarrow$ 10,406.0401   Record display as fourth end-of-period principal.

$\times$ 1.01 $=$ $\Rightarrow$ 10,510.1005   Record display as fifth end-of-period principal.

$\times$ 1.01 $=$ $\Rightarrow$ 10,615.20151   Record display as sixth end-of-period principal.

STOP AND CHECK

See Example 1.

1. Find the monthly interest rate on a loan that has an annual interest rate of 9.2%. Round to thousandths.

2. A loan of $2,950 at 8% is made for two years compounded annually. Find the future value (compound amount) of the loan. Find the amount of interest paid on the loan.

See Example 2.

3. Find the future value of a $20,000 investment at 3.5% annual interest compounded semiannually for two years.

4. Find the future value of a $15,000 money market investment at 2.8% annual interest compounded semiannually for three years.

2 Find the future value and compound interest using a $1.00 future value table.

As you may have guessed from the previous examples, compounding interest for a large number of periods is very time-consuming. This task is done more quickly by using other methods. One method is to use a compound interest table, as shown in Table 13-1.

Table 13-1 gives the future value of $1.00, depending on the number of interest periods per year and the interest rate per period.

HOW TO   Find the future value and compound interest using a $1.00 future value table

1. Find the number of interest periods: Multiply the number of years by the number of interest periods per year.

   Interest periods = number of years $\times$ number of interest periods per year

2. Find the period interest rate: Divide the annual interest rate by the number of interest periods per year.

$$\text{Period interest rate} = \frac{\text{annual interest rate}}{\text{number of interest periods per year}}$$

3. Using Table 13-1, select the periods row corresponding to the number of interest periods.
4. Select the rate-per-period column corresponding to the period interest rate.
5. Locate the value in the cell where the periods row intersects the rate-per-period column. This value is sometimes called the *i-factor*.
6. Multiply the original principal by the value from step 5 to find the future value or compound amount.

   Future value = principal $\times$ table value

7. To find the compound interest,

   Compound interest = future value $-$ original principal

TABLE 13-1
Future Value or Compound Amount of $1.00

Rate per period

Periods	0.50%	1.00%	1.50%	2.00%	2.50%	3.00%	3.50%	4.00%	4.50%	5.00%	5.50%
1	1.00500	1.01000	1.01500	1.02000	1.02500	1.03000	1.03500	1.04000	1.04500	1.05000	1.05500
2	1.01003	1.02010	1.03023	1.04040	1.05063	1.06090	1.07123	1.08160	1.09203	1.10250	1.11303
3	1.01508	1.03030	1.04568	1.06121	1.07689	1.09273	1.10872	1.12486	1.14117	1.15763	1.17424
4	1.02015	1.04060	1.06136	1.08243	1.10381	1.12551	1.14752	1.16986	1.19252	1.21551	1.23882
5	1.02525	1.05101	1.07728	1.10408	1.13141	1.15927	1.18769	1.21665	1.24618	1.27628	1.30696
6	1.03038	1.06152	1.09344	1.12616	1.15969	1.19405	1.22926	1.26532	1.30226	1.34010	1.37884
7	1.03553	1.07214	1.10984	1.14869	1.18869	1.22987	1.27228	1.31593	1.36086	1.40710	1.45468
8	1.04071	1.08286	1.12649	1.17166	1.21840	1.26677	1.31681	1.36857	1.42210	1.47746	1.53469
9	1.04591	1.09369	1.14339	1.19509	1.24886	1.30477	1.36290	1.42331	1.48610	1.55133	1.61909
10	1.05114	1.10462	1.16054	1.21899	1.28008	1.34392	1.41060	1.48024	1.55297	1.62889	1.70814
11	1.05640	1.11567	1.17795	1.24337	1.31209	1.38423	1.45997	1.53945	1.62285	1.71034	1.80209
12	1.06168	1.12683	1.19562	1.26824	1.34489	1.42576	1.51107	1.60103	1.69588	1.79586	1.90121
13	1.06699	1.13809	1.21355	1.29361	1.37851	1.46853	1.56396	1.66507	1.77220	1.88565	2.00577
14	1.07232	1.14947	1.23176	1.31948	1.41297	1.51259	1.61869	1.73168	1.85194	1.97993	2.11609
15	1.07768	1.16097	1.25023	1.34587	1.44830	1.55797	1.67535	1.80094	1.93528	2.07893	2.23248
16	1.08307	1.17258	1.26899	1.37279	1.48451	1.60471	1.73399	1.87298	2.02237	2.18287	2.35526
17	1.08849	1.18430	1.28802	1.40024	1.52162	1.65285	1.79468	1.94790	2.11338	2.29202	2.48480
18	1.09393	1.19615	1.30734	1.42825	1.55966	1.70243	1.85749	2.02582	2.20848	2.40662	2.62147
19	1.09940	1.20811	1.32695	1.45681	1.59865	1.75351	1.92250	2.10685	2.30786	2.52695	2.76565
20	1.10490	1.22019	1.34686	1.48595	1.63862	1.80611	1.98979	2.19112	2.41171	2.65330	2.91776
21	1.11042	1.23239	1.36706	1.51567	1.67958	1.86029	2.05943	2.27877	2.52024	2.78596	3.07823
22	1.11597	1.24472	1.38756	1.54598	1.72157	1.91610	2.13151	2.36992	2.63365	2.92526	3.24754
23	1.12155	1.25716	1.40838	1.57690	1.76461	1.97359	2.20611	2.46472	2.75217	3.07152	3.42615
24	1.12716	1.26973	1.42950	1.60844	1.80873	2.03279	2.28333	2.56330	2.87601	3.22510	3.61459
25	1.13280	1.28243	1.45095	1.64061	1.85394	2.09378	2.36324	2.66584	3.00543	3.38635	3.81339
26	1.13846	1.29526	1.47271	1.67342	1.90029	2.15659	2.44596	2.77247	3.14068	3.55567	4.02313
27	1.14415	1.30821	1.49480	1.70689	1.94780	2.22129	2.53157	2.88337	3.28201	3.73346	4.24440
28	1.14987	1.32129	1.51722	1.74102	1.99650	2.28793	2.62017	2.99870	3.42970	3.92013	4.47784
29	1.15562	1.33450	1.53998	1.77584	2.04641	2.35657	2.71188	3.11865	3.58404	4.11614	4.72412
30	1.16140	1.34785	1.56308	1.81136	2.09757	2.42726	2.80679	3.24340	3.74532	4.32194	4.98395

Periods	6.00%	6.50%	7.00%	7.50%	8.00%	8.50%	9.00%	9.50%	10.00%	11.00%	12.00%
1	1.06000	1.06500	1.07000	1.07500	1.08000	1.08500	1.09000	1.09500	1.10000	1.11000	1.12000
2	1.12360	1.13423	1.14490	1.15563	1.16640	1.17723	1.18810	1.19903	1.21000	1.23210	1.25440
3	1.19102	1.20795	1.22504	1.24230	1.25971	1.27729	1.29503	1.31293	1.33100	1.36763	1.40493
4	1.26248	1.28647	1.31080	1.33547	1.36049	1.38586	1.41158	1.43766	1.46410	1.51807	1.57352
5	1.33823	1.37009	1.40255	1.43563	1.46933	1.50366	1.53862	1.57424	1.61051	1.68506	1.76234
6	1.41852	1.45914	1.50073	1.54330	1.58687	1.63147	1.67710	1.72379	1.77156	1.87041	1.97382
7	1.50363	1.55399	1.60578	1.65905	1.71382	1.77014	1.82804	1.88755	1.94872	2.07616	2.21068
8	1.59385	1.65500	1.71819	1.78348	1.85093	1.92060	1.99253	2.06687	2.14359	2.30454	2.47596
9	1.68948	1.76257	1.83846	1.91724	1.99900	2.08386	2.17189	2.26322	2.35795	2.55804	2.77308
10	1.79085	1.87714	1.96715	2.06103	2.15892	2.26098	2.36736	2.47823	2.59374	2.83942	3.10585
11	1.89830	1.99915	2.10485	2.21561	2.33164	2.45317	2.58043	2.71366	2.85312	3.15176	3.47855
12	2.01220	2.12910	2.25219	2.38178	2.51817	2.66169	2.81266	2.97146	3.13843	3.49845	3.89598
13	2.13293	2.26749	2.40985	2.56041	2.71962	2.88793	3.06580	3.25375	3.45227	3.88328	4.36349
14	2.26090	2.41487	2.57853	2.75244	2.93719	3.13340	3.34173	3.56285	3.79750	4.31044	4.88711
15	2.39656	2.57184	2.75903	2.95888	3.17217	3.39974	3.64248	3.90132	4.17725	4.78459	5.47357
16	2.54035	2.73901	2.95216	3.18079	3.42594	3.68872	3.97031	4.27195	4.59497	5.31089	6.13039
17	2.69277	2.91705	3.15882	3.41935	3.70002	4.00226	4.32763	4.67778	5.05447	5.89509	6.86604
18	2.85434	3.10665	3.37993	3.67580	3.99602	4.34245	4.71712	5.12217	5.55992	6.54355	7.68997
19	3.02560	3.30859	3.61653	3.95149	4.31570	4.71156	5.14166	5.60878	6.11591	7.26334	8.61276
20	3.20714	3.52365	3.86968	4.24785	4.66096	5.11205	5.60441	6.14161	6.72750	8.06231	9.64629
21	3.39956	3.75268	4.14056	4.56644	5.03383	5.54657	6.10881	6.72507	7.40025	8.94917	10.80385
22	3.60354	3.99661	4.43040	4.90892	5.43654	6.01803	6.65860	7.36395	8.14027	9.93357	12.10031
23	3.81975	4.25639	4.74053	5.27709	5.87146	6.52956	7.25787	8.06352	8.95430	11.02627	13.55235
24	4.04893	4.53305	5.07237	5.67287	6.34118	7.08457	7.91108	8.82956	9.84973	12.23916	15.17863
25	4.29187	4.82770	5.42743	6.09834	6.84848	7.68676	8.62308	9.66836	10.83471	13.58546	17.00006
26	4.54938	5.14150	5.80735	6.55572	7.39635	8.34014	9.39916	10.58686	11.91818	15.07986	19.04007
27	4.82235	5.47570	6.21387	7.04739	7.98806	9.04905	10.24508	11.59261	13.10999	16.73865	21.32488
28	5.11169	5.83162	6.64884	7.57595	8.62711	9.81822	11.16714	12.69391	14.42099	18.57990	23.88387
29	5.41839	6.21067	7.11426	8.14414	9.31727	10.65277	12.17218	13.89983	15.86309	20.62369	26.74993
30	5.74349	6.61437	7.61226	8.75496	10.06266	11.55825	13.26768	15.22031	17.44940	22.89230	29.95992

Table shows future value (*FV*) of $1.00 compounded for *N* periods at *R* rate per period.
Table values can be generated using the formula $FV = \$1(1 + R)^N$.

EXAMPLE 3

Use Table 13-1 to compute the compound interest on a $5,000 loan for six years compounded annually at 8%.

Interest periods = number of years × interest periods per year

= 6(1) = 6 periods

Period interest rate = $\dfrac{\text{annual interest rate}}{\text{interest periods per year}}$ $\dfrac{4}{24}$

= $\dfrac{8\%}{1}$ = 8%

Find period row 6 of the table and the 8% rate column. The value in the intersecting cell is 1.58687. This means that $1 would be worth $1.58687, or $1.59 rounded, compounded annually at the end of six years.

$5,000(1.58687) = $7,934.35   The loan is for $5,000, so multiply $5,000 by 1.58687 to find the compound amount of the loan.

The compound amount is $7,934.35.

$7,934.35 − $5,000 = $2,934.35   The compound amount minus the principal is the compound interest.

The compound interest on $5,000 for six years compounded annually at 8% is $2,934.35.

EXAMPLE 4

An investment of $3,000 at 4% annually is compounded *quarterly* (four times a year) for three years. Find the future value and the compound interest.

Interest periods = number of years × number of interest periods per year

= 3(4) = 12   The investment is compounded four times a year for three years.

Period interest rate = $\dfrac{\text{annual interest rate}}{\text{number of interest periods per year}}$

= $\dfrac{4\%}{4}$ = 1%

Future value of $1 = 1.12683

$3,000(1.12683) = $3,380.49

$3,380.49 is the future value.

Divide the annual rate of 8% by the number of periods per year to find the period interest rate.

Find the 12 periods row in Table 13-1. Move across to the 1% column.

The principal times the future value per dollar equals the total future value. Round to the nearest cent.

Compound interest = future value − original principal

= $3,380.49 − $3,000

= $380.49

The compound interest is $380.49.

STOP AND CHECK

See Example 3.

1. Use Table 13-1 to compute the compound interest on $2,890 for five years compounded annually at 4%.

2. A loan of $2,982 is repaid in three years. Find the amount of interest paid on the loan if it is compounded quarterly at 10%.

See Example 4.

3. Andre Castello owns a savings account that is paying 2.5% interest compounded annually. His current balance is $7,598.42. How much interest will he earn over five years if the rate remains constant?

4. Natalie Bradley invested $25,000 at 2% for three years compounded semiannually. Find the future value at the end of three years using Table 13-1.

3 Find the future value and compound interest using a formula or a calculator application (optional).

Table values are most often generated with a formula. When the table does not include the rate you need or does not have as many periods as you need, the equivalent table value can be found by using the formula. The formula for finding the future value or the compound interest will require a calculator or electronic spreadsheet that has a power function. A business or scientific calculator or an electronic spreadsheet, such as Excel, is normally used.

HOW TO Find the future value and the compound interest using formulas

The future value formula is

$$FV = P(1 + R)^N$$

where FV is the future value, P is the principal, R is the period interest rate, and N is the number of periods.

The compound interest formula is

$$I = P(1 + R)^N - P$$

where I is the amount of compound interest, P is the principal, R is the period rate, and N is the number of periods.

Business calculators, scientific calculators, and electronic spreadsheets impose a standard order of operations when making calculations. However, it is helpful to make some of the calculations in a formula mentally or before you begin the evaluation of the formula. For instance, in the future value formula you can find the period interest rate and the number of periods first. Also, you can change the period interest rate to a decimal equivalent and add 1.00 mentally.

EXAMPLE 5

Find the future value of a three-year investment of $5,000 that earns 6% compounded monthly.

Find the period interest rate:

$$R = \frac{6\%}{12} = \frac{0.06}{12} = 0.005$$

Change the annual rate to a decimal equivalent and divide by 12.

Find the number of periods:

$$N = 3(12) = 36$$

Multiply the number of years by 12.

Evaluate the future value formula:

$$FV = P(1 + R)^N$$ Substitute known values.
$$FV = 5,000(1 + 0.005)^{36}$$ Mentally add inside parentheses.
$$FV = 5,000(1.005)^{36}$$ Evaluate using a calculator or spreadsheet.

5000 $\boxed{(}$ 1.005 $\boxed{)}$ $\boxed{\wedge}$ 36 $\boxed{=}$ ⟹ 5983.402624

$$FV = \$5,983.40$$ Rounded

EXAMPLE 6

Find the compound interest earned on a four-year investment of $3,500 at 4.5% compounded monthly.

Find the period interest rate:

$$R = \frac{4.5\%}{12} = \frac{0.045}{12} = 0.00375$$

Change the annual rate to a decimal equivalent and divide by 12.

Find the number of periods:

$$N = 4(12) = 48$$

Multiply the number of years by 12.

Evaluate the compound interest formula:

$I = P(1 + R)^N - P$ 　　　　　　　　　　Substitute known values.

$I = 3,500(1 + 0.00375)^{48} - 3,500$ 　　　Mentally add inside parentheses.

$I = 3,500(1.00375)^{48} - 3,500$ 　　　　Evaluate using a calculator or spreadsheet.

3500 $\boxed{(}$ 1.00375 $\boxed{)}$ $\boxed{\wedge}$ 48 $\boxed{=}$ $\boxed{-}$ 3500 $\boxed{=}$ $\Rightarrow$ 　　688.850321

$I = \$688.85$ 　　　　　　　　　　　　Rounded

Business and graphing calculators have financial applications that already have the formulas entered. To use these applications, you enter amounts for the known variables and solve for the unknown variables. For our illustrations we will use the BA II Plus™, the TI-84 Plus™ by Texas Instruments, and the Casio fx-CG10.

Let's rework Example 5 using calculator applications.

EXAMPLE 7

Rework Example 5 using the calculator applications of the BA II Plus, the TI-84 Plus, and the Casio fx-CG10 calculators.

BA II Plus:

	Keys to press	Display shows
Set decimals to two places if necessary.	$\boxed{\text{2nd}}$ [FORMAT] 2 $\boxed{\text{ENTER}}$	DEC= 2.00
Set all variables to defaults.	$\boxed{\text{2nd}}$ [RESET] $\boxed{\text{ENTER}}$	RST 0.00 ◁
Enter number of periods/payments.	36 $\boxed{\text{N}}$	N= 36.00 ◁
Enter interest rate per period (as a %).	$\boxed{.}$ 5 $\boxed{\text{I/Y}}$	I/Y= 0.50 ◁
Enter beginning amount as a negative.	5000 $\boxed{+/-}$ $\boxed{\text{PV}}$	PV=−5,000.00
Compute future value.	$\boxed{\text{CPT}}$ $\boxed{\text{FV}}$	FV= 5,983.40 *
Set the calculator back to normal mode.	$\boxed{\text{2nd}}$ $\boxed{\text{QUIT}}$	

The symbol ◁ shown above a number indicates that the value in the display has been assigned to the indicated variable.

The symbol * shown above the number indicates that the value in the display is the result of a calculation.

TI-84:

Change to 2 fixed decimal places.	$\boxed{\text{MODE}}$ ↓ → → → $\boxed{\text{ENTER}}$
Select Finance Application.	Press $\boxed{\text{APPS}}$ 1:Finance $\boxed{\text{ENTER}}$
Select TVM Solver, which is already highlighted.	$\boxed{\text{ENTER}}$

Use the arrow keys to move cursor to appropriate variables and enter amounts. Enter 0 for unknowns.

Press 36 $\boxed{\text{ENTER}}$ to store 36 months to N. Press 6 $\boxed{\text{ENTER}}$ to store 6% per year to 1%.

Press $\boxed{(-)}$ 5000 $\boxed{\text{ENTER}}$ to store 5,000 to PV. Press 0 $\boxed{\text{ENTER}}$ to leave PMT unassigned. When you are *making payments* the present value (PV) is negative, so it is important to enter the negative sign in front of 5000. When you are *receiving* payments, as in an annuity, the present value will be positive.

Press 0 $\boxed{\text{ENTER}}$ to leave FV unassigned.

Press 12 $\boxed{\text{ENTER}}$ to store 12 payments/periods per year to P/Y and C/Y will automatically change to 12 also.

PMT at the bottom of the screen should have END highlighted.

Use up arrow to move cursor up to FV. Press $\boxed{\text{ALPHA}}$ [SOLVE] to solve for future value. The future value is calculated and replaces the 0 at the blinking cursor.

```
N=        36.00
I%=        6.00
PV=−5000.00
PMT=       0.00
▪FV=   5983.40
P/Y=     12.00
C/Y=     12.00
PMT:END BEGIN
```

Casio fx-CG10

Select **Financial** mode from the main menu. This will display the financial screen. Press

$\boxed{\text{SHIFT}}\,\boxed{\text{MENU}}$ to set up items.

Payment   : END

Date Mode   : 365

Periods/Yr   : Annual

Graph Color   : Blue

Background   : None

Label   : On

Display   : Fix (set to 2)

Press $\boxed{\text{EXIT}}$ to leave the set-up menu.

Press $\boxed{\text{F2}}$ to select compound interest.

Press 36 $\boxed{\text{EXE}}$ to store 36 months (total number of interest payments) to n.

Press 6 $\boxed{\text{EXE}}$ to store 6% to I%.

Press $\boxed{-}$ 5000 $\boxed{\text{EXE}}$ to store the present value in PV.

Press the down cursor to leave PMT unassigned.

Press the down cursor to leave FV unassigned.

Press 12 $\boxed{\text{EXE}}$ to store 12 payments/periods per year to P/Y and C/Y will automatically change to 12 also.

Press $\boxed{\text{F5}}$ to display future value.

EXAMPLE 8   Joe Gallegos can invest $10,000 at 8% compounded quarterly for two years. Or he can invest the same $10,000 at 8.2% compounded annually for the same two years. If all other conditions (such as early withdrawal penalty, and so on) are the same, which deal should he take?

What You Know	What You Are Looking For
Principal: $10,000 Time period: 2 years Deal 1 annual rate: 8% Deal 1 interest periods per year: 4 Deal 2 annual rate: 8.2% Deal 2 interest periods per year: 1	Which deal should Joe take? Future value for each investment

Solution Plan

Number of interest periods = number of years × number of interest periods per year

Deal 1 interest periods = 2(4) = 8   Deal 2 interest periods = 2(1) = 2

$$\text{Period interest rate} = \frac{\text{annual interest rate}}{\text{number of interest periods per year}}$$

Deal 1 period interest rate $= \dfrac{8\%}{4} = 2\%$ Deal 2 period interest rate $= \dfrac{8.2\%}{1} = 8.2\%$

Solution

Deal 1: Using the future value formula for $10,000 at 2% per period for 8 periods

$FV = P(1 + R)^N$	Substitute known values.
$FV = \$10,000(1 + 0.02)^8$	Mentally add inside parentheses.
$FV = 10,000(1.02)^8$	Evaluate using a calculator or spreadsheet.
$10000\,\boxed{(}\,1.02\,\boxed{)}\,\boxed{\wedge}\,8\,\boxed{=} \Rightarrow$	11716.59381
$FV = \$11,716.59$	Future value for Deal 1

Deal 2: Using the future value formula for $10,000 at 8.2% per period for 2 periods

$FV = P(1 + R)^N$ Substitute known values.

$FV = \$10{,}000(1 + 0.082)^2$ Mentally add inside parentheses.

$FV = 10{,}000(1.082)^2$ Evaluate using a calculator or spreadsheet.

10000 (1.082) ^ 2 = ⟹   11707.24

$FV = \$11{,}707.24$ Future value for Deal 2

Conclusion

Deal 1, the lower interest rate of 8% compounded more frequently (quarterly), is a slightly better deal because it yields the greater future value.

TIP

Using Calculator Applications for Example 8.

TI BA II Plus:

Set decimal to two places if necessary.

Deal 1	Deal 2
2nd [RESET] ENTER	2nd [RESET] ENTER
8 N	2 N
2 I/Y	2.05 I/Y
10000 +/− PV	10000 +/− PV
CPT FV	CPT FV
$11,716.59	**$11,707.24**

TI-84

APPS 1:Finance ENTER 1:TVM Solver ENTER

Enter the appropriate amounts.

Deal 1	Deal 2
N=8.00	N=2.00
I%=8.00	I%=8.20
PV=−10000.00	PV=−10000.00
PMT=0.00	PMT=0.00
FV=0.00	FV=0.00
P/Y=4.00	P/Y=1.00
C/Y=4.00	C/Y=1.00
PMT:**END** BEGIN	PMT:**END** BEGIN

Move cursor up to FV.   ALPHA [SOLVE]

The future value is calculated and replaces the 0 at the blinking cursor.

$11,716.59   **$11,707.24**

Casio fx-CG10

MENU Financial EXE F2

Enter the appropriate amounts.

Deal 1	Deal 2
n=8	n=2
I%=8	I%=8.2
PV= −10000	PV= −10000
PMT=0	PMT=0
FV=0	FV=0
P/Y=4	P/Y=1
C/Y=4	C/Y=1
Press F5 **$11,716.59**	Press F5 **$11,707.24**

STOP AND CHECK

1. Kellen Davis invested $20,000 that earns 2.4% compounded monthly for four years. Find the future value of Kellen's investment. *See Example 5.*

2. Jonathan Vergues invested $17,500 that earns 1.2% compounded semiannually for 2 years. What is the future value of the investment after 2 years? *See Example 6.*

3. Lunetha Pryor has a $18,200 certificate of deposit (CD) that earns 2.25% interest compounded quarterly for 5 years. Find the compound interest after 5 years. *See Example 7.*

4. Susan Bertrees can invest $12,000 at 2% interest compounded twice a year or compounded quarterly. If either investment is for five years, which investment results in more interest? How much more interest is yielded by the better investment? *See Example 8.*

4 Find the effective interest rate.

If the investment in Example 4 on page 460 is compounded annually instead of quarterly for three years—three periods at 4% per period—the future value is $3,374.58 using table value 1.12486, and the compound interest is $374.58. The simple interest at the end of three years is $3,000 × 4% × 3, or $360. $3,000 at 4% for 3 years:

| $360 | $374.58 | $380.49 |
| Simple interest | Compounded annually using table value | Compounded quarterly using table value |

You can see from these comparisons that a loan or investment with an interest rate of 4% compounded quarterly carries higher interest than a loan with an interest rate of 4% compounded annually or a loan with an annual simple interest rate of 4%. When you compare interest rates, you need to know the actual or **effective rate** of interest. The effective rate of interest equates compound interest rates to equivalent simple interest rates so that comparisons can be made.

The effective rate of interest is also referred to as the **annual percentage yield** (APY) when identifying the rate of earnings on an investment. It is referred to as the **annual percentage rate** (APR) when identifying the rate of interest on a loan.

HOW TO   Find the effective interest rate of a compound interest rate

Using the manual compound interest method: Divide the compound interest for the first year by the principal.

$$\text{Effective annual interest rate} = \frac{\text{compound interest for first year}}{\text{principal}} \times 100\%$$

Using the table method: Find the future value of $1.00 by using the future value table, Table 13-1. Subtract $1.00 from the future value of $1.00 after one year and divide by $1.00 to remove the dollar sign.

$$\text{Effective annual interest rate} = \frac{\text{future value of \$1.00 after 1 year} - \$1.00}{\$1.00} \times 100\%$$

EXAMPLE 9   Marcia borrowed $6,000 at 10% compounded semiannually. What is the effective interest rate?

Using the manual compound interest method:

$$\text{Period interest rate} = \frac{10\%}{2} = 5\% = 0.05$$

First end-of-period principal $= \$6,000(1 + 0.05)$
$$= \$6,300$$

Second end-of-period principal $= \$6,300(1 + 0.05)$
$$= \$6,615$$

Compound interest after first year $= \$6,615 - \$6,000 = \$615$

$$\text{Effective annual interest rate} = \frac{\$615}{\$6,000}(100\%)$$
$$= 0.1025(100\%)$$
$$= 10.25\%$$

Using the table method:

10% compounded semiannually means two periods in the first (and every) year and a period interest rate of 5%. The Table 13-1 value is 1.10250. Subtract 1.00.

Effective annual interest rate $= (1.10250 - 1.00)(100\%)$
$$= 0.10250(100\%)$$
$$= 10.25\%$$

The effective interest rate is 10.25%.

1. Willy Spears borrowed $2,800 at 8% compounded semiannually. Use the manual compound interest method to find the effective interest rate.

2. Use Table 13-1 to find the effective interest rate on Willy Spears's loan in Exercise 1. Compare the rate using the table with the rate found manually.

3. Mindi Lancaster invested $82,500 at 2% compounded semi-annually. Use Table 13-1 to find the APY for her investment.

4. Una Sircy invested $5,000 at 3% compounded semiannually. Use Table 13-1 to find the APY for her investment.

5 Find the interest compounded daily using a table.

Some banks compound interest daily and others use continuous compounding to compute interest on savings accounts. There is no significant difference in the interest earned on money using interest compounded daily and interest compounded continuously. A computer is generally used in calculating interest if either daily or continuous compounding is used.

Table 13-2 gives compound interest for $100 compounded daily (using 365 days as a year). Notice that this table gives the *compound interest* rather than the future value of the principal, as is given in Table 13-1.

Using Table 13-2 is exactly like using Table 12-1, which gives the *simple* interest on $100.

HOW TO   Find the compounded daily interest using a table

1. Determine the amount of money the table uses as the principal ($1, $100, or $1,000).
2. Divide the loan principal by the table principal.
3. Using Table 13-2, select the days row corresponding to the time period (in days) of the loan.
4. Select the interest rate column corresponding to the interest rate of the loan.
5. Locate the value in the cell where the interest column intersects the days row.
6. Multiply the quotient from step 2 by the value from step 5.

TIP

Examine Table Title and Footnote Carefully!

All tables are not alike! Different reference sources may approach finding the same information using different methods.

In working with compound interest, you may more frequently want to know the accumulated amount than the accumulated interest, or vice versa. A table can be designed to give a factor for finding either amount directly.

- Determine whether the table will help you find the compound amount or the compound interest. Table 13-1 finds the compound amount and Table 13-2 finds the compound interest. Also, the principal that is used to determine the table value may be $1, $10, $100, or some other amount.
- Determine the principal amount used in calculating table values. Table 13-1 uses $1 as the principal and Table 13-2 uses $100 as the principal.

TABLE 13-2
Compound Interest on $100, Compounded Daily (365 Days) (Exact Time, Exact Interest Basis)

Annual rate for selected rates

Days	0.50%	0.75%	1.00%	1.25%	1.50%	1.75%	2.00%	2.25%	2.50%
1	0.001370	0.002055	0.002740	0.003425	0.004110	0.004795	0.005479	0.006164	0.006849
2	0.002740	0.004110	0.005480	0.006849	0.008219	0.009589	0.010959	0.012329	0.013699
3	0.004110	0.006165	0.008219	0.010274	0.012329	0.014384	0.016439	0.018494	0.020549
4	0.005480	0.008219	0.010959	0.013699	0.016439	0.019179	0.021920	0.024660	0.027400
5	0.006850	0.010274	0.013699	0.017124	0.020550	0.023975	0.027400	0.030826	0.034251
6	0.008219	0.012329	0.016439	0.020550	0.024660	0.028771	0.032881	0.036992	0.041103
7	0.009589	0.014384	0.019180	0.023975	0.028771	0.033566	0.038362	0.043159	0.047955
8	0.010959	0.016440	0.021920	0.027401	0.032881	0.038363	0.043844	0.049326	0.054808
9	0.012329	0.018495	0.024660	0.030826	0.036992	0.043159	0.049326	0.055493	0.061661
10	0.013699	0.020550	0.027401	0.034252	0.041103	0.047956	0.054808	0.061661	0.068514
11	0.015070	0.022605	0.030141	0.037678	0.045215	0.052752	0.060290	0.067829	0.075368
12	0.016440	0.024660	0.032882	0.041104	0.049326	0.057549	0.065773	0.073998	0.082223
13	0.017810	0.026716	0.035622	0.044530	0.053438	0.062347	0.071256	0.080167	0.089078
14	0.019180	0.028771	0.038363	0.047956	0.057550	0.067144	0.076740	0.086336	0.095933
15	0.020550	0.030826	0.041104	0.051382	0.061662	0.071942	0.082223	0.092506	0.102789
16	0.021920	0.032882	0.043845	0.054809	0.065774	0.076740	0.087707	0.098676	0.109645
17	0.023290	0.034937	0.046586	0.058235	0.069886	0.081538	0.093192	0.104846	0.116502
18	0.024660	0.036993	0.049327	0.061662	0.073998	0.086337	0.098676	0.111017	0.123359
19	0.026031	0.039048	0.052068	0.065089	0.078111	0.091135	0.104161	0.117188	0.130217
20	0.027401	0.041104	0.054809	0.068515	0.082224	0.095934	0.109646	0.123360	0.137075
21	0.028771	0.043160	0.057550	0.071942	0.086337	0.100733	0.115132	0.129532	0.143934
22	0.030141	0.045215	0.060291	0.075370	0.090450	0.105533	0.120617	0.135704	0.150793
23	0.031512	0.047271	0.063033	0.078797	0.094563	0.110332	0.126103	0.141877	0.157653
24	0.032882	0.049327	0.065774	0.082224	0.098677	0.115132	0.131590	0.148050	0.164513
25	0.034252	0.051383	0.068516	0.085652	0.102790	0.119932	0.137076	0.154224	0.171374
26	0.035623	0.053438	0.071257	0.089079	0.106904	0.124732	0.142563	0.160398	0.178235
27	0.036993	0.055494	0.073999	0.092507	0.111018	0.129533	0.148051	0.166572	0.185096
28	0.038363	0.057550	0.076741	0.095935	0.115132	0.134334	0.153538	0.172746	0.191958
29	0.039734	0.059606	0.079483	0.099363	0.119247	0.139134	0.159026	0.178921	0.198821
30	0.041104	0.061662	0.082224	0.102791	0.123361	0.143936	0.164514	0.185097	0.205684
31	0.042474	0.063718	0.084966	0.106219	0.127476	0.148737	0.170003	0.191273	0.212547
32	0.043845	0.065774	0.087708	0.109647	0.131591	0.153539	0.175491	0.197449	0.219411
33	0.045215	0.067831	0.090451	0.113076	0.135706	0.158341	0.180981	0.203625	0.226275
34	0.046586	0.069887	0.093193	0.116504	0.139821	0.163143	0.186470	0.209802	0.233140
35	0.047956	0.071943	0.095935	0.119933	0.143936	0.167945	0.191960	0.215980	0.240005
40	0.054809	0.082225	0.109648	0.137078	0.164515	0.191960	0.219412	0.246872	0.274339
45	0.061662	0.092508	0.123362	0.154226	0.185099	0.215981	0.246873	0.277774	0.308684
50	0.068516	0.102791	0.137078	0.171377	0.205686	0.240008	0.274341	0.308685	0.343041
55	0.075370	0.113076	0.150796	0.188530	0.226278	0.264040	0.301816	0.339606	0.377410
60	0.082225	0.123362	0.164516	0.205687	0.246875	0.288078	0.329299	0.370536	0.411790
90	0.123363	0.185101	0.246876	0.308689	0.370540	0.432429	0.494355	0.556319	0.618321
120	0.164518	0.246877	0.329304	0.411797	0.494358	0.576987	0.659683	0.742446	0.825276
150	0.205689	0.308691	0.411799	0.515011	0.618330	0.721753	0.825282	0.928917	1.032658
180	0.246878	0.370544	0.494362	0.618332	0.742453	0.866728	0.991154	1.115733	1.240465
240	0.329306	0.494364	0.659692	0.825291	0.991161	1.157303	1.323717	1.490404	1.657364
360	0.494365	0.742461	0.991168	1.240487	1.490419	1.740967	1.992132	2.243915	2.496318
365	0.501249	0.752812	1.005003	1.257823	1.511275	1.765360	2.020078	2.275432	2.531424
730	1.005010	1.511291	2.020106	2.531468	3.045390	3.561884	4.080963	4.602641	5.126930
1095	1.511296	2.275480	3.045411	3.821133	4.602689	5.390124	6.183480	6.982803	7.788138
1825	2.531494	3.821160	5.127038	6.449332	7.788249	9.143998	10.516789	11.906838	13.314360
3650	5.127074	7.788332	10.516940	13.314603	16.183066	19.124122	22.139607	25.231403	28.401442

Table shows interest (I) on $100 compounded daily for N days at an annual rate of R. Table values can be generated using the formula $I = 100(1 + R/365)^N - 100$.

TABLE 13-2

Compound Interest on $100, Compounded Daily (365 Days) (Exact Time, Exact Interest Basis)—Continued

Annual rate for selected rates

Days	5.00%	5.25%	5.75%	6.00%	6.75%	7.25%	7.50%	8.00%	8.25%	8.50%	9.00%
1	0.013699	0.014384	0.015753	0.016438	0.018493	0.019863	0.020548	0.021918	0.022603	0.023288	0.024658
2	0.027399	0.028769	0.031509	0.032879	0.036990	0.039730	0.041100	0.043840	0.045211	0.046581	0.049321
3	0.041102	0.043157	0.047268	0.049323	0.055490	0.059601	0.061657	0.065768	0.067824	0.069879	0.073991
4	0.054806	0.057547	0.063029	0.065770	0.073993	0.079476	0.082217	0.087700	0.090442	0.093183	0.098667
5	0.068512	0.071938	0.078792	0.082219	0.092500	0.099355	0.102782	0.109637	0.113065	0.116493	0.123348
6	0.082220	0.086332	0.094558	0.098671	0.111010	0.119237	0.123351	0.131579	0.135693	0.139807	0.148036
7	0.095930	0.100728	0.110326	0.115125	0.129524	0.139124	0.143924	0.153526	0.158327	0.163128	0.172730
8	0.109642	0.115126	0.126097	0.131583	0.148041	0.159015	0.164502	0.175477	0.180965	0.186453	0.197431
9	0.123355	0.129527	0.141870	0.148043	0.166562	0.178909	0.185084	0.197433	0.203609	0.209784	0.222137
10	0.137071	0.143929	0.157646	0.164505	0.185085	0.198808	0.205670	0.219394	0.226257	0.233121	0.246849
11	0.150788	0.158333	0.173424	0.180971	0.203613	0.218710	0.226260	0.241360	0.248911	0.256463	0.271568
12	0.164507	0.172739	0.189205	0.197439	0.222144	0.238617	0.246854	0.263331	0.271570	0.279810	0.296292
13	0.178229	0.187148	0.204988	0.213910	0.240678	0.258527	0.267453	0.285307	0.294234	0.303163	0.321023
14	0.191952	0.201558	0.220774	0.230383	0.259216	0.278442	0.288056	0.307287	0.316904	0.326521	0.345759
15	0.205677	0.215971	0.236562	0.246859	0.277757	0.298360	0.308663	0.329272	0.339578	0.349885	0.370502
16	0.219403	0.230385	0.252353	0.263338	0.296301	0.318282	0.329274	0.351262	0.362258	0.373254	0.395251
17	0.233132	0.244802	0.268146	0.279820	0.314849	0.338208	0.349890	0.373257	0.384942	0.396629	0.420006
18	0.246863	0.259221	0.283942	0.296304	0.333400	0.358139	0.370510	0.395256	0.407632	0.420009	0.444767
19	0.260595	0.273642	0.299740	0.312791	0.351955	0.378073	0.391134	0.417261	0.430327	0.443394	0.469534
20	0.274329	0.288065	0.315540	0.329281	0.370514	0.398011	0.411762	0.439270	0.453027	0.466785	0.494308
21	0.288066	0.302490	0.331344	0.345774	0.389075	0.417953	0.432395	0.461284	0.475732	0.490182	0.519087
22	0.301804	0.316917	0.347149	0.362269	0.407640	0.437899	0.453031	0.483303	0.498442	0.513583	0.543873
23	0.315544	0.331346	0.362957	0.378767	0.426209	0.457849	0.473672	0.505327	0.521158	0.536991	0.568664
24	0.329286	0.345777	0.378768	0.395267	0.444781	0.477803	0.494318	0.527355	0.543878	0.560403	0.593462
25	0.343029	0.360210	0.394581	0.411771	0.463356	0.497761	0.514967	0.549389	0.566604	0.583822	0.618266
26	0.356775	0.374646	0.410397	0.428277	0.481935	0.517723	0.535621	0.571427	0.589335	0.607245	0.643076
27	0.370522	0.389083	0.426215	0.444785	0.500517	0.537688	0.556279	0.593470	0.612071	0.630674	0.667892
28	0.384272	0.403523	0.442035	0.461297	0.519103	0.557658	0.576941	0.615518	0.634812	0.654109	0.692714
29	0.398023	0.417964	0.457858	0.477811	0.537692	0.577632	0.597608	0.637571	0.657558	0.677549	0.717542
30	0.411776	0.432408	0.473684	0.494328	0.556285	0.597610	0.618279	0.659628	0.680309	0.700994	0.742377
31	0.425531	0.446854	0.489512	0.510848	0.574881	0.617592	0.638954	0.681691	0.703066	0.724445	0.767217
32	0.439288	0.461302	0.505342	0.527370	0.593480	0.637577	0.659633	0.703758	0.725827	0.747902	0.792064
33	0.453047	0.475752	0.521175	0.543895	0.612083	0.657567	0.680316	0.725830	0.748594	0.771363	0.816917
34	0.127683	0.134071	0.146849	0.153238	0.630690	0.677561	0.701004	0.204368	0.771366	0.794831	0.841776
35	0.131441	0.138017	0.151171	0.157749	0.649299	0.697558	0.721696	0.210385	0.794143	0.818304	0.866641
40	0.549411	0.576959	0.632077	0.659646	0.742400	0.797606	0.825220	0.880470	0.908106	0.935749	0.991059
45	0.618300	0.649313	0.711367	0.742408	0.835587	0.897753	0.928850	0.991072	1.022197	1.053332	1.115630
50	0.687235	0.721718	0.790719	0.825237	0.928859	0.997999	1.032586	1.101796	1.136418	1.171052	1.240354
55	0.756218	0.794176	0.870134	0.908134	1.022219	1.098345	1.136430	1.212641	1.250768	1.288909	1.365233
60	0.825248	0.866686	0.949612	0.991099	1.115664	1.198791	1.240380	1.323608	1.365247	1.406903	1.490265
90	1.240422	1.302841	1.427794	1.490327	1.678155	1.803565	1.866327	1.991967	2.054844	2.117759	2.243705
120	1.657306	1.740883	1.908241	1.992022	2.243775	2.411953	2.496145	2.664734	2.749132	2.833599	3.002739
150	2.075907	2.180819	2.390964	2.496197	2.812542	3.023977	3.129857	3.341940	3.448144	3.554457	3.767407
180	2.496231	2.622657	2.875973	3.002864	3.384472	3.639658	3.767486	4.023613	4.151911	4.280368	4.537753
240	3.342080	3.512073	3.852895	4.023725	4.537896	4.882081	5.054597	5.400477	5.573842	5.747491	6.095642
360	5.054775	5.314097	5.834658	6.095900	6.883491	7.411788	7.676912	8.209120	8.476207	8.743951	9.281418
365	5.126750	5.389858	5.918047	6.183131	6.982358	7.518507	7.787585	8.327757	8.598855	8.870629	9.416214
730	10.516335	11.070222	12.186328	12.748573	14.452250	15.602292	16.181634	17.349030	17.937113	18.528139	19.719080
1095	16.182231	17.056750	18.825568	19.719965	22.443716	24.293858	25.229377	27.121572	28.078354	29.042331	30.992085
1825	28.400343	30.015193	33.306041	34.982553	40.139588	43.686550	45.493537	49.175931	51.051913	52.951474	56.822519
3650	64.866481	69.039503	77.705005	82.202895	96.391041	106.458246	111.683692	122.534585	128.166805	133.941534	145.933026

Table shows interest (*I*) on $100 compounded daily for *N* days at an annual rate of *R*. Table values can be generated using the formula $I = 100(1 + R/365)^N - 100$.

| EXAMPLE 10 | Find the interest on $800 at 7.5% annually, compounded daily, for 28 days. |

$800 ÷ $100 = 8   Find the number of $100 units in the principal.
                         Find the 28 days row in Table 13-2. Move across to the
                         7.5% column and find the interest for $100.

8($0.576941) = $4.615528   Multiply the table value by 8, the number of $100 units.

The interest is $4.62.

STOP AND CHECK

See Example 10.

1. Find the interest on $1,850 at 7.25% annually, compounded daily for 60 days.

2. Find the interest on $3,050 at 6% annually, compounded daily for 365 days.

3. Find the interest on $10,000 at 6.75% annually, compounded daily for 730 days.

4. Bob Weaver has $20,000 invested for three years at a 5.25% annual rate compounded daily. How much interest will he earn?

13-1 SECTION EXERCISES

SKILL BUILDERS

Find the future value (compound amount) and compound interest. Use Table 13-1 or the future value and compound interest formula. See Examples 3 and 4.

1. A loan of $5,000 at 6% compounded semiannually for two years

2. A loan of $18,500 at 6% compounded quarterly for four years

3. An investment of $7,000 at 2% compounded semiannually for six years

4. A loan of $500 at 5% compounded semiannually for five years

5. A loan of $1,000 at 12% compounded monthly for two years

6. An investment of $2,000 at 1.5% compounded annually for ten years

APPLICATIONS

Use the simple interest formula method for Exercises 7 to 10. See Examples 1 and 2.

7. Thayer Farm Trust made a farmer a loan of $1,200 at 16% for three years compounded annually. Find the future value and the compound interest paid on the loan. Compare the compound interest with simple interest for the same period.

8. Maeola Killebrew invests $3,800 at 2% compounded semiannually for two years. What is the future value of the investment, and how much interest will she earn over the two-year period?

9. Carolyn Smith borrowed $6,300 at $8\frac{1}{2}$% for three years compounded annually. What is the compound amount of the loan and how much interest will she pay on the loan?

10. Margaret Hillman invested $5,000 at 1.8% compounded quarterly for one year. Find the future value and the interest earned for the year.

Use Table 13-1 or the appropriate formula for Exercises 11–16. See Examples 3 and 4 for table or Examples 5 through 7 for formulas.

11. First State Bank loaned Doug Morgan $2,000 for four years compounded annually at 8%. How much interest was Doug required to pay on the loan?

12. A loan of $8,000 for two acres of woodland is compounded quarterly at an annual rate of 6% for five years. Find the compound amount and the compound interest.

13. Compute the compound amount and the interest on a loan of $10,500 compounded annually for four years at 10%.

14. Find the future value of an investment of $10,500 if it is invested for four years and compounded semiannually at an annual rate of 2%.

15. You have $8,000 that you plan to invest in a compound-interest-bearing instrument. Your investment agent advises you that you can invest the $8,000 at 8% compounded quarterly for three years or you can invest the $8,000 at $8\frac{1}{4}$% compounded annually for three years. Which investment should you choose to receive the most interest? *See Example 8.*

16. Find the future value of $50,000 at 6% compounded semiannually for ten years.

See Example 9.

17. Find the effective interest rate for a loan for four years compounded semiannually at an annual rate of 2%. Use the table method.

18. What is the effective interest rate for a loan of $5,000 at 10% compounded semiannually for three years? Use the simple interest formula method.

19. Ross Land has a loan of $8,500 compounded quarterly for four years at 6%. What is the effective interest rate for the loan? Use the table method.

20. What is the effective interest rate for a loan of $20,000 for three years if the interest is compounded quarterly at a rate of 12%?

Use Table 13-2 for Exercises 21 to 24. See Example 10.

21. Find the compound interest on $2,500 at 0.75% compounded daily by Leader Financial Bank for 20 days.

22. How much compound interest is earned on a deposit of $1,500 at 0.5% compounded daily for 30 days?

23. John McCormick has found a short-term investment opportunity. He can invest $8,000 at 0.5% interest for 15 days. How much interest will he earn on this investment if the interest is compounded daily?

24. What is the compound interest on $8,000 invested at 1.25% for 180 days if it is compounded daily?

13-2 PRESENT VALUE

LEARNING OUTCOMES

1 Find the present value based on annual compounding for one year.
2 Find the present value using a $1.00 present value table.
3 Find the present value using a formula or a calculator application (optional).

In Section 1 of this chapter we learned how to find the future value of money invested at the present time. Sometimes businesses and individuals need to know how much to invest at the present time to yield a certain amount at some specified future date. For example, a business may want to set aside a lump sum of money to provide pensions for employees in years to come. Individuals may want to set aside a lump sum of money now to pay for a child's college education or for a vacation. You can use the concepts of compound interest to determine the amount of money that must be set aside at present and compounded periodically to yield a certain amount of money at some specific time in the future. The amount of money set aside now is called *present value*. See Figure 13-1.

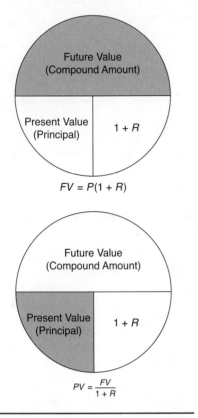

FIGURE 13-1
Relationship Between Future Value and Present Value

1 Find the present value based on annual compounding for one year.

Finding the present value of $100 means finding the *principal* that we must invest today so that $100 is its future value. We know that the future value of principal depends on the period interest rate and the number of interest periods. Just as calculating future value by hand is time-consuming when there are many interest periods, so is calculating **present value** by hand. A present value table is more efficient. For now, we find present value based on the simplest case—annual compounding for one year. In this case, the number of interest periods is 1, and the period interest rate is the annual interest rate. In this case,

$$\text{Future value} = \text{principal}(1 + \text{annual interest rate}) \text{ or } FV = P(1 + R)$$

If we know the future value and want to know the present value,

$$\text{Principal(present value)} = \frac{\text{future value}}{1 + \text{annual interest rate}} \text{ or } PV = \frac{FV}{1 + R}$$

HOW TO   Find the present value based on annual compounding for one year

Divide the future value by the sum of 1 and the decimal equivalent of the annual interest rate.

$$\text{Present value(principal)} = \frac{\text{future value}}{1 + \text{annual interest rate}} \text{ or } PV = \frac{FV}{1 + R}$$

EXAMPLE 1   Find the amount of money that Brienne and Greg Jackson need to set aside today to ensure that $10,000 will be available to buy a new large-screen plasma television in one year if the annual interest rate is 4% compounded annually.

$1 + 0.04 = \boxed{1.04}$ Convert the annual interest rate to a decimal and add to 1.

$\dfrac{\$10,000}{\boxed{1.04}} = \$9,615.38$ Divide the future value by 1.04 to get the present value.

An investment of $9,615.38 at 4% would have a value of $10,000 in one year.

STOP AND CHECK

See Example 1.

1. How much money needs to be set aside today to have $15,000 in one year if the annual interest rate is 2% compounded annually?

2. How much should be set aside today to have $15,000 in one year if the annual interest rate is 4% compounded annually?

3. Greg Karrass should set aside how much money today to have $30,000 in one year if the annual interest rate is 2.8% compounded annually?

4. Jamie Puckett plans to purchase real estate in one year that costs $148,000. How much should be set aside today at an annual interest rate of 3.46% compounded annually?

2 Find the present value using a $1.00 present value table.

If the interest in the preceding example had been compounded more than once a year, you would have to make calculations for each time the money was compounded. One method for finding the present value when the principal is compounded for more than one period is to use Table 13-3, which shows the present value of $1.00 at different interest rates for different periods. Table 13-3 is used like Table 13-1, which gives the future value of $1.00.

TABLE 13-3
Present Value of $1.00

Periods						Rate per period						
	0.5%	1%	1.5%	2%	2.5%	3%	4%	5%	6%	8%	10%	12%
1	0.99502	0.99010	0.98522	0.98039	0.97561	0.97087	0.96154	0.95238	0.94340	0.92593	0.90909	0.89286
2	0.99007	0.98030	0.97066	0.96117	0.95181	0.94260	0.92456	0.90703	0.89000	0.85734	0.82645	0.79719
3	0.98515	0.97059	0.95632	0.94232	0.92860	0.91514	0.88900	0.86384	0.83962	0.79383	0.75131	0.71178
4	0.98025	0.96098	0.94218	0.92385	0.90595	0.88849	0.85480	0.82270	0.79209	0.73503	0.68301	0.63552
5	0.97537	0.95147	0.92826	0.90573	0.88385	0.86261	0.82193	0.78353	0.74726	0.68058	0.62092	0.56743
6	0.97052	0.94205	0.91454	0.88797	0.86230	0.83748	0.79031	0.74622	0.70496	0.63017	0.56447	0.50663
7	0.96569	0.93272	0.90103	0.87056	0.84127	0.81309	0.75992	0.71068	0.66506	0.58349	0.51316	0.45235
8	0.96089	0.92348	0.88771	0.85349	0.82075	0.78941	0.73069	0.67684	0.62741	0.54027	0.46651	0.40388
9	0.95610	0.91434	0.87459	0.83676	0.80073	0.76642	0.70259	0.64461	0.59190	0.50025	0.42410	0.36061
10	0.95135	0.90529	0.86167	0.82035	0.78120	0.74409	0.67556	0.61391	0.55839	0.46319	0.38554	0.32197
11	0.94661	0.89632	0.84893	0.80426	0.76214	0.72242	0.64958	0.58468	0.52679	0.42888	0.35049	0.28748
12	0.94191	0.88745	0.83639	0.78849	0.74356	0.70138	0.62460	0.55684	0.49697	0.39711	0.31863	0.25668
13	0.93722	0.87866	0.82403	0.77303	0.72542	0.68095	0.60057	0.53032	0.46884	0.36770	0.28966	0.22917
14	0.93256	0.86996	0.81185	0.75788	0.70773	0.66112	0.57748	0.50507	0.44230	0.34046	0.26333	0.20462
15	0.92792	0.86135	0.79985	0.74301	0.69047	0.64186	0.55526	0.48102	0.41727	0.31524	0.23939	0.18270
16	0.92330	0.85282	0.78803	0.72845	0.67362	0.62317	0.53391	0.45811	0.39365	0.29189	0.21763	0.16312
17	0.91871	0.84438	0.77639	0.71416	0.65720	0.60502	0.51337	0.43630	0.37136	0.27027	0.19784	0.14564
18	0.91414	0.83602	0.76491	0.70016	0.64117	0.58739	0.49363	0.41552	0.35034	0.25025	0.17986	0.13004
19	0.90959	0.82774	0.75361	0.68643	0.62553	0.57029	0.47464	0.39573	0.33051	0.23171	0.16351	0.11611
20	0.90506	0.81954	0.74247	0.67297	0.61027	0.55368	0.45639	0.37689	0.31180	0.21455	0.14864	0.10367
21	0.90056	0.81143	0.73150	0.65978	0.59539	0.53755	0.43883	0.35894	0.29416	0.19866	0.13513	0.09256
22	0.89608	0.80340	0.72069	0.64684	0.58086	0.52189	0.42196	0.34185	0.27751	0.18394	0.12285	0.08264
23	0.89162	0.79544	0.71004	0.63416	0.56670	0.50669	0.40573	0.32557	0.26180	0.17032	0.11168	0.07379
24	0.88719	0.78757	0.69954	0.62172	0.55288	0.49193	0.39012	0.31007	0.24698	0.15770	0.10153	0.06588
25	0.88277	0.77977	0.68921	0.60953	0.53939	0.47761	0.37512	0.29530	0.23300	0.14602	0.09230	0.05882
26	0.87838	0.77205	0.67902	0.59758	0.52623	0.46369	0.36069	0.28124	0.21981	0.13520	0.08391	0.05252
27	0.87401	0.76440	0.66899	0.58586	0.51340	0.45019	0.34682	0.26785	0.20737	0.12519	0.07628	0.04689
28	0.86966	0.75684	0.65910	0.57437	0.50088	0.43708	0.33348	0.25509	0.19563	0.11591	0.06934	0.04187
29	0.86533	0.74934	0.64936	0.56311	0.48866	0.42435	0.32065	0.24295	0.18456	0.10733	0.06304	0.03738
30	0.86103	0.74192	0.63976	0.55207	0.47674	0.41199	0.30832	0.23138	0.17411	0.09938	0.05731	0.03338

The table shows the lump sum amount of money, present value (*PV*), that should be invested now so that the accumulated amount will be $1.00 after a specified number of periods, *N*, at a specified rate per period, *R*. Table values can be generated using the formula $PV = \dfrac{\$1.00}{(1 + R)^N}$.

HOW TO   Find the present value using a $1.00 present value table

1. Find the number of interest periods: Multiply the time period, in years, by the number of interest periods per year.

   Interest periods = number of years × number of interest periods per year

2. Find the period interest rate: Divide the annual interest rate by the number of interest periods per year.

   $$\text{Period interest rate} = \frac{\text{annual interest rate}}{\text{number of interest periods per year}}$$

3. Using Table 13-3, select the periods row corresponding to the number of interest periods.
4. Select the rate-per-period column corresponding to the period interest rate.
5. Locate the value in the cell where the periods row intersects the rate-per-period column.
6. Multiply the future value by the value from step 5.

EXAMPLE 2   The Absorbent Diaper Company needs $20,000 in five years to buy a new diaper edging machine. How much must the firm invest at the present if it receives 5% interest compounded annually?

R = 5% and *N* = 5 years

Table value = 0.78353

$20,000(0.78353) = \$15,670.60

The money is to be compounded for 5 periods, so we find periods row 5 in Table 13-3 and the 5% rate column to find the present value of $1.00.

Multiply the present value factor times the desired future value to find the amount that must be invested at the present.

The Absorbent Diaper Company should invest \$15,670.60 today to have \$20,000 in five years.

TIP

Which Table Do I Use?

Tables 13-1 and 13-3 have entries that are reciprocals. Except for minor rounding discrepancies, the product of corresponding entries is 1. And 1 divided by a table value equals its comparable table value in the other table.

Look at period row 1 at 1% on each table.

Table 13-1: 1.01000 $1 \div 1.01000 = 0.99010$ (rounded)   Table 13-3: 0.99010

Look at period row 16 at 4% on each table.

Table 13-1: 1.87298 $1 \div 1.87298 = 0.53391$ (rounded)   Table 13-3: 0.53391

One way to select the appropriate table is to anticipate whether you expect a larger or smaller amount. You expect a future value to be larger than what you start with. All entries in Table 13-1 are greater than 1 and produce a larger product.

You expect a present value to require a smaller investment to reach a desired amount. All entries in Table 13-3 are less than 1 and produce a smaller product.

FV table factors > 1
PV table factors < 1

STOP AND CHECK

See Example 2.

1. The 7th Inning needs $35,000 in four years to buy new framing equipment. How much should be invested at 4% interest compounded annually?

2. How much should be invested now to have $15,000 in two years if interest is 4% compounded quarterly?

3. How much should be invested now to have $15,000 in four years if interest is 4% compounded quarterly?

4. How much should be invested now to have $15,000 in six years if interest is 4% compounded quarterly? Compare your results for Exercises 2–4.

3   Find the present value using a formula or a calculator application (optional).

A formula for finding the present value can be found by solving the future value formula for the (original) principal.

$FV = P(1 + R)^N$

Divide both sides of the equations by $(1 + R)^N$.

$$\frac{FV}{(1 + R)^N} = \frac{P(1 + R)^N}{(1 + R)^N}$$

Reduce.

$$\frac{FV}{(1 + R)^N} = P$$

Rewrite with P on the left side of the equation.

$$P = \frac{FV}{(1 + R)^N}$$

Original principal is present value.

$$PV = \frac{FV}{(1 + R)^N}$$

Now use *PV* for *P*.

HOW TO Find the present value using a formula.

The present value formula is

$$PV = \frac{FV}{(1 + R)^N}$$

where PV is the present value, FV is the future value, R is the interest rate per period, and N is the number of periods.

EXAMPLE 3

The Holiday Boutique would like to put away some of the holiday profits to save for a planned expansion. A total of $8,000 is needed in three years. How much money in a 5.2% three-year certificate of deposit that is compounded monthly must be invested now to have the $8,000 in three years?

Period interest rate $= \dfrac{5.2\%}{12} = \dfrac{0.052}{12} = 0.0043333333$

Number of periods $= 3(12) = 36$

$PV = \dfrac{FV}{(1 + R)^N}$ Substitute known values.

$PV = \dfrac{8,000}{(1 + 0.0043333333)^{36}}$ Mentally add inside parentheses.

$PV = \dfrac{8,000}{(1.0043333333)^{36}}$ Evaluate using a calculator.

$8000 \boxed{\div} \boxed{(} \boxed{(} 1.0043333333 \boxed{)} \boxed{\wedge} 36 \boxed{=} \Rightarrow 6846.78069$

$PV = \$6,846.78$ Rounded

The Holiday Boutique must invest $6,846.78 now at 5.2% interest for three years, compounded monthly to have $8,000 at the end of the three years.

EXAMPLE 4

Rework Example 3 using the calculator applications of the BA II Plus, the TI-84 Plus and the Casio fx-CG10 calculators. See pp. 466–467 for more detailed instruction.

BA II Plus:

2nd [FORMAT] 2 ENTER
2nd [RESET] ENTER
36 N
. 43333333 I/Y
8000 +/− FV
CPT PV
⇒ **6846.78**

TI-84:

APPS ENTER ENTER
36 ENTER 5.2 ENTER
0 ENTER 0 ENTER
(−) 8000 ENTER
12 ENTER
Be sure PMT has **END** highlighted. Use up arrow to move cursor up to PV. Press ALPHA [SOLVE].
PV = 6846.78

Casio fx-CG10:

Menu [Financial] EXE
F2 36 EXE 5.2 EXE 0
EXE 0 EXE (−) 8000
EXE 12 EXE F3 ⇒
6846.78
PV = 6846.78

STOP AND CHECK

Use the present value formula or a calculator application. See Examples 3 and 4.

1. Mary Kaye Keller needs $30,000 in seven years. How much must she set aside today at 4.8% compounded monthly?

2. How much should a family invest now at $2\frac{3}{4}\%$ compounded annually to have a $7,000 house down payment in four years?

3. If you were offered $700 today or $800 in two years, which would you accept if the $700 can be invested at 2.4% annual interest compounded monthly?

4. Bridgett Smith inherited some money and needs $45,000 in 15 years for her child's college fund. How much of the inheritance should she invest now at 2.8% compounded quarterly?

SKILL BUILDERS

Find the amount that should be set aside today to yield the desired future amount; use Table 13-3 (see Example 2) or the appropriate formula (see Examples 3 and 4).

	Future amount needed	Interest rate	Compounding period	Investment time
1.	$4,000	3%	semiannually	2 years
2.	$7,000	2.5%	annually	20 years
3.	$10,000	4%	quarterly	4 years
4.	$5,000	3%	semiannually	6 years

APPLICATIONS

See Example 1.

5. Compute the amount of money to be set aside today to ensure a future value of $2,500 in one year if the interest rate is 2.5% annually, compounded annually.

6. How much should Linda Bryan set aside now to buy equipment that costs $8,500 in one year? The current interest rate is 0.95% annually, compounded annually.

7. Ronnie Cox has just inherited $27,000. How much of this money should he set aside today to have $21,000 to pay cash for a Ventura Van, which he plans to purchase in one year? He can invest at 1.9% annually, compounded annually.

8. Shirley Riddle received a $10,000 gift from her mother and plans a minor renovation to her home. She also plans to make an investment for one year, at which time she plans to take a trip projected to cost $6,999. The current interest rate is 2.3% annually, compounded annually. How much should be set aside today for her trip?

See Example 2.

9. Rosa Burnett needs $2,000 in three years to make the down payment on a new car. How much must she invest today if she receives 1.5% interest annually, compounded annually? Use Table 13-3.

10. Use Table 13-3 to calculate the amount of money that must be invested now at 4% annually, compounded quarterly, to obtain $1,500 in three years.

11. Dewey Sykes plans to open a business in four years when he retires. How much must he invest today to have $10,000 when he retires if the bank pays 2% annually, compounded quarterly?

12. Charlie Bryant has a child who will be college age in five years. How much must he set aside today to have $20,000 for college tuition in five years if he gets 1.5% annually, compounded annually?

Learning Outcomes

Section 13-1

1 Find the future value and compound interest by compounding manually. (p. 460)

What to Remember with Examples

Find the period interest rate: Divide the annual interest rate by the number of interest periods per year.

$$\text{Period interest rate} = \frac{\text{annual interest rate}}{\text{number of interest periods per year}}$$

Find the future value using the simple interest formula method:

1. Find the first end-of-period principal: Multiply the original principal by the sum of 1 and the period interest rate.

   First end-of-period principal = original principal $\times$ (1 + period interest rate)

2. For each remaining period in turn, find the next end-of-period principal: Multiply the previous end-of-period principal by the sum of 1 and the period interest rate.

   End-of-period principal = previous end-of-period principal $\times$ (1 + period interest rate)

3. Identify the last end-of-period principal as the future value.

   Future value = last end-of-period principal

Find the compound interest: Subtract the original principal from the future value.

   Compound interest = future value − original principal

Find the compound amount and compound interest on $5,000 at 7% compounded annually for two years.

($5,000)(1 + 0.07) = $5,350 end-of-first-period principal
($5,350)(1 + 0.07) = $5,724.50 end-of-last-period principal (future value)
 Compound amount = $5,724.50
 Compound interest = $5,724.50 − $5,000 = $724.50

Find the compound amount (future value) and compound interest on $1,500 at 8% compounded semiannually for two years.

Number of interest periods = 2(2) = 4 periods

$$\text{Period interest rate} = \frac{8\%}{2} = 4\% \text{ or } 0.04 \text{ per period}$$

$1,500(1 + 0.04) = $1,560 (first period)
$1,560(1 + 0.04) = $1,622.40 (second period)
$1,622.40(1 + 0.04) = $1,687.30 (third period)
$1,687.30(1 + 0.04) = $1,754.79 (fourth period)
Compound amount = $1,754.79
Compound interest = $1,754.79 − $1,500 = $254.79

---

2 Find the future value and compound interest using a $1.00 future value table. (p. 462)

1. Find the number of interest periods: Multiply the number of years by the number of interest periods per year.

   Interest periods = number of years $\times$ number of interest periods per year

2. Find the period interest rate: Divide the annual interest rate by the number of interest periods per year.

$$\text{Period interest rate} = \frac{\text{annual interest rate}}{\text{number of interest periods per year}}$$

3. Using Table 13-1, select the periods row corresponding to the number of interest periods.
4. Select the rate-per-period column corresponding to the period interest rate.
5. Locate the value in the cell where the periods row intersects the rate-per-period column.
6. Multiply the original principal by the value from step 5 to find future value or compound amount.

   Future value = principal $\times$ table value

7. To find the compound interest:

$$\text{Compound interest} = \text{future value} - \text{original principal}$$

Find the future value of $2,000 at 12% compounded semiannually for four years.	Find the compound interest on $800 at 8% compounded annually for four years for 4 periods.
$4(2) = 8$ periods	Annually indicates one period per year. Period interest rate is 8%.
$\dfrac{12\%}{2} = 6\%$ period interest rate.	Find periods row 4 in Table 13-1.
Find periods row 8 in Table 13-1 and move across to the 6% rate column: 1.59385.	Move across to the 8% rate column and find the compound amount per dollar of principal: 1.36049.
$2,000(1.59385) = \$3,187.70$ future value or compound amount	$800(1.36049) = \$1,088.39$ compound amount
	$\$1,088.39$ compound amount or future value
	$\underline{-800.00}$ principal
	$\$288.39$ compound interest

---

3 Find the future value and compound interest using a formula or a calculator application (optional). (p. 465)

The future value formula is

$$FV = P(1 + R)^N$$

where FV is the future value, P is the principal, R is the period interest rate, and N is the number of periods.

Find the future value of a three-year investment of $3,500 that earns 5.4% compounded monthly.	
Find the period interest rate:	
$R = \dfrac{5.4\%}{12} = \dfrac{0.054}{12} = 0.0045$	Change the annual rate to a decimal equivalent and divide by 12.
Find the number of periods:	
$N = (3)(12) = 36$	Multiply the number of years by 12.
Evaluate the future value formula:	
$FV = P(1 + R)^N$	Substitute known values.
$FV = 3,500(1 + 0.0045)^{36}$	Mentally add inside parentheses.
$FV = 3,500(1.0045)^{36}$	Evaluate using a calculator or spreadsheet.
$3500\ \boxed{(}\ 1.0045\ \boxed{)}\ \boxed{\wedge}\ 36\ \boxed{=}\ \Rightarrow\ 4114.015498$	
$FV = \$4,114.02$	Rounded

To solve using a calculator application with the TI BA II Plus or TI-84, see Example 7 on pp. 466–467 and in the Tip following Example 8 on pp. 467–468.

The compound interest formula is

$$I = P(1 + R)^N - P$$

where I is the amount of compound interest, P is the principal, R is the period rate, and N is the number of periods.

Find the compound interest earned on a four-year investment of $6,500 at 5.5% compounded monthly.	
Find the period interest rate:	
$R = \dfrac{5.5\%}{12} = \dfrac{0.055}{12} = 0.0045833333$	Change the annual rate to a decimal equivalent and divide by 12.
Find the number of periods:	
$N = (4)(12) = 48$	Multiply the number of years by 12.

Evaluate the compound interest formula:

$I = P(1 + R)^N - P$ Substitute known values.

$I = 6{,}500(1 + 0.0045833333)^{48} - 6{,}500$ Mentally add inside parentheses.

$I = 6{,}500(1.0045833333)^{48} - 6{,}500$ Evaluate using a calculator or spreadsheet.

$6500 \boxed{(} 1.0045833333 \boxed{)} \boxed{\wedge} 48 \boxed{=} \boxed{-} 6500 \boxed{=} \Rightarrow 1{,}595.428696$

$I = \$1{,}595.43$ Rounded

4 Find the effective interest rate. (p. 469)

Using the manual compound interest method: Divide the compound interest for the *first year* by the principal.

$$\text{Effective annual interest rate} = \frac{\text{compound interest for first year}}{\text{principal}} \times 100\%$$

Using the table method: Use Table 13-1 to find the future value of $1.00 of the investment. Subtract $1.00 from the future value of $1.00 after one year and divide by $1.00 to remove the dollar sign.

$$\text{Effective interest rate} = \frac{\text{future value of \$1.00 after 1 year} - \$1.00}{\$1.00} \times 100\%$$

Betty Padgett earned $247.29 interest on a one-year investment of $3,000 at 8% annually, compounded quarterly. Find the effective interest rate.

Using the simple interest formula method:

$$\text{Effective interest} = \frac{\$247.29}{\$3{,}000} (100\%) = 0.08243\,(100\%) = 8.24\%$$

Using Table 13-1: Periods per year $= 4$

$$\text{Rate per period} = \frac{8\%}{4} = 2\%$$

$$\text{Table value} = 1.08243 \text{ (from Table 13-1)}$$

$$\text{Effective interest rate} = 1.08243 - 1.00 = 0.08243 = 8.24\%$$

5 Find the interest compounded daily using a table. (p. 470)

1. Determine the amount of money the table uses as the principal. (A typical table principal is $1, $100, or $1,000.)
2. Divide the loan principal by the table principal.
3. Using Table 13-2, select the days row corresponding to the time period (in days) of the loan.
4. Select the interest rate column corresponding to the interest rate of the loan.
5. Locate the value in the cell where the interest column intersects the days row.
6. Multiply the quotient from step 2 by the value from step 5.

Find the interest on a $300 loan borrowed at 9% compounded daily for 21 days.
Select the 21 days row of Table 13-2; then move across to the 9% rate column. The table value is 0.519087.

$$\frac{\$300}{100} (0.519087) = \$1.56$$

The interest on $300 is $1.56.

Section 13-2

1 Find the present value based on annual compounding for one year. (p. 476)

Divide the future value by the sum of 1 and the decimal equivalent of the annual interest rate.

$$\text{Present value (principal)} = \frac{\text{future value}}{1 + \text{annual interest rate}}$$

Find the amount of money that must be invested to produce $4,000 in one year if the interest rate is 7% annually, compounded annually.

$$\text{Present value} = \frac{\$4{,}000}{1 + 0.07} = \frac{\$4{,}000}{1.07} = \$3{,}738.32$$

How much must be invested to produce $30,000 in one year if the interest rate is 6% annually, compounded annually?

$$\text{Present value} = \frac{\$30{,}000}{1 + 0.06} = \frac{\$30{,}000}{1.06} = \$28{,}301.89$$

2 Find the present value using a $1.00 present value table. (p. 476)

1. Find the number of interest periods: Multiply the time period, in years, by the number of interest periods per year.

$$\text{Interest periods} = \text{number of years} \times \text{number of interest periods per year}$$

2. Find the period interest rate: Divide the annual interest rate by the number of interest periods per year.

$$\text{Period interest rate} = \frac{\text{annual interest rate}}{\text{number of interest periods per year}}$$

3. Using Table 13-3, select the periods row corresponding to the number of interest periods.
4. Select the rate-per-period column corresponding to the period interest rate.
5. Locate the value in the cell where the periods row intersects the rate-per-period column.
6. Multiply the future value by the value from step 5.

Find the amount of money that must be deposited to ensure $3,000 at the end of three years if the investment earns 6% compounded semiannually.

$(3)(2) = 6$ periods

$\dfrac{6\%}{2} = 3\%$ rate per period

Find periods row 6 in Table 13-3 and move across to the 3% rate column: 0.83748.

$3,000(0.83748) = \$2,512.44$

The amount that must be invested now to have $3,000 in three years is $2,512.44.

3 Find the present value using a formula or a calculator application (optional). (p. 478)

Present Value Formula:

$PV = \dfrac{FV}{(1 + R)^N}$ where PV is the present value, FV is the future value, R is the interest rate per period, and N is the number of periods.

Ezell Allen has saved some money that he wants to put away for a down payment on a home in five years. He can invest the money in a 5.4% five-year certificate of deposit that is compounded monthly. How much of his money should he set aside now for a down payment of $10,000 in 5 years?

$$\text{Period interest rate} = \frac{5.4\%}{12} = \frac{0.054}{12} = 0.0045$$

Number of periods $= 5(12) = 60$

$PV = \dfrac{FV}{(1 + R)^N}$ Substitute known values.

$PV = \dfrac{10,000}{(1 + 0.0045)^{60}}$ Mentally add inside parentheses.

$PV = \dfrac{10,000}{(1.0045)^{60}}$ Evaluate using a calculator.

$10000 \boxed{\div} \boxed{(} 1.0045 \boxed{)} \boxed{\wedge} 60 \boxed{=} \Rightarrow 7638.420009$

$PV = \$7,638.42$ Rounded

Ezell must invest $7,638.42 now at 5.4% interest for five years, compounded monthly to have $10,000 at the end of the five years.

To solve using a calculator application with the TI BA II Plus, TI-84 or Casio fx-CG10, see Example 4 on p. 479.

EXERCISES SET A

Use Table 13-1 or the appropriate formula for Exercises 1–4.

Principal	Term (years)	Rate of compound interest	Compounded	Compound amount	Compound interest
1. $2,000	3	3%	semiannually	_____	_____
2. $5,000	4	4%	quarterly	_____	_____
3. $10,000	2	2.5%	annually	_____	_____
4. $8,000	4	1%	semiannually	_____	_____

Find the amount that should be set aside today to yield the desired future amount. Use Table 13-3 or the present value formula.

	Future amount needed	Interest rate	Compounding	Investment time (years)		Future amount needed	Interest rate	Compounding	Investment time (years)
EXCEL 5.	$20,000	4%	semiannually	5	**EXCEL 6.**	$8,000	6%	quarterly	6
EXCEL 7.	$9,800	2%	semiannually	12	**EXCEL 8.**	$14,700	3%	annually	20

9. Manually calculate the compound interest on a loan of $1,000 at 8%, compounded annually for two years.

10. Manually calculate the compound interest on a 13% loan of $1,600 for three years if the interest is compounded annually.

11. Use Table 13-1 or the appropriate formula to find the future value of an investment of $3,000 made by Ling Lee for five years at 3% annual interest compounded semiannually.

12. Use Table 13-1 or the appropriate formula to find the interest on a certificate of deposit (CD) of $10,000 for five years at 4% compounded semiannually.

13. Find the future value of an investment of $8,000 compounded quarterly for seven years at 2%.

14. Find the compound interest on a loan of $5,000 for two years if the interest is compounded quarterly at 12%.

15. Mario Piazza was offered $900 now for one of his salon photographs or $1,100 in one year for the same photograph. Which would give Mr. Piazza a greater yield if he could invest the $900 for one year at 4% compounded quarterly? Use Table 13-1.

16. Lauren McAnally invests $2,000 at 2% compounded semiannually for two years, and Inez Everett invests an equal amount at 2% compounded quarterly for 18 months. Use Table 13-1 to determine which investment yields the greater interest.

17. Use Table 13-2 to find the compound interest and the future value on an investment of $2,000 if it is invested for 21 days at 0.75% compounded daily.

18. Use Table 13-2 to find the amount of interest on $100 invested for 10 days at 8.5% compounded daily.

19. Find the effective interest rate for a loan of $3,500 at 10% interest compounded quarterly.

20. Find the amount of money that Keaton and Jana Smith must set aside today so that they will have $5,000 available to buy a home security system in one year if the annual interest rate is 5% compounded annually.

In Exercises 21–26, find the amount of money that should be invested (present value) at the stated interest rate to yield the given amount (future value) after the indicated amount of time. Use Table 13-3 or the appropriate formula.

21. $1,500 in three years at 2.5% compounded annually

22. $1,000 in seven years at 8% compounded quarterly

23. $4,000 in two years at 2% annual interest compounded quarterly

24. $500 in 15 years at 4% annual interest compounded semiannually

25. Find the amount that should be invested today to have $1,800 in one year at 6% annual interest compounded monthly.

26. Myrna Lewis wishes to have $4,000 in four years to tour Europe. How much must she invest today at 6% annual interest compounded quarterly to have $4,000 in four years?

EXERCISES SET B

Use Table 13-1 for Exercises 1–4.

Principal	Term (years)	Rate of compound interest	Compounded	Compound amount	Compound interest
1. $5,000	5	5%	semiannually	_____	_____
2. $12,000	7	4%	quarterly	_____	_____
3. $7,000	10	2%	semiannually	_____	_____
4. $2,985	8	3%	annually	_____	_____

Find the amount that should be set aside today to yield the desired future amount. Use Table 13-3 or the present value formula.

	Future amount needed	Interest rate	Compounding	Investment time (years)		Future amount needed	Interest rate	Compounding	Investment time (years)
EXCEL 5.	$3,000	6%	quarterly	5	EXCEL 6.	$46,000	2.5%	annually	25
EXCEL 7.	$17,000	3%	semiannually	8	EXCEL 8.	$11,200	4%	quarterly	3

9. Manually calculate the compound interest on a loan of $200 at 6% compounded annually for four years.

10. Manually calculate the compound interest on a loan of $6,150 at $11\frac{1}{2}$% annual interest compounded annually for three years.

11. EZ Loan Company loaned $500 at 8% annual interest compounded quarterly for one year. Use Table 13-1 or the appropriate formula to calculate the amount the loan company will earn in interest.

12. Use Table 13-2 to find the daily interest on $2,500 invested for 21 days at 2.25% compounded daily.

13. Find the factor for compounding an amount for 25 periods at 8% per period.

14. Find the compound interest on a loan of $5,000 for two years if the interest is compounded semiannually at 12%.

15. An investment of $1,000 is made for two years and is compounded semiannually at 5%. Find the future value and compound interest at the end of the two years.

16. Carlee McNally invests $5,000 at 6% compounded semiannually for one year, and Jake McNally invests an equal amount at 6% compounded quarterly for one year. Use Table 13-1 to determine the interest for each investment. Find the effective rate to the nearest hundredth percent for each investment.

17. Use Table 13-2 to find the compound interest and the future value on an investment of $24,982 if it is invested for 28 days at 2.25% compounded daily.

18. Use Table 13-2 to find the accumulated daily interest on an investment of $5,000 invested for 120 days at 2.5%.

In Exercises 19–24, find the amount of money that should be invested (present value) at the stated interest rate to yield the given amount (future value) after the indicated amount of time. Use Table 13-3 or the appropriate formula.

19. $2,000 in five years at 3% compounded semiannually

20. $3,500 in 12 years at 2% compounded annually

21. $10,000 in seven years at 4% annual interest compounded quarterly

22. $800 in four years at 3% annual interest compounded annually

23. Find the amount that should be invested today to have $700 in six years at 6% annual interest compounded quarterly.

24. Louis Banks was offered $25,000 cash now or $29,500 to be paid after two years for a resort cabin. If money can be invested in today's market for 4% annual interest compounded quarterly, which offer should Louis accept?

25. Find the effective interest rate for a loan of $8,500 at 12% interest compounded monthly.

PRACTICE TEST

CHAPTER 13

1. Manually calculate the compound interest on a loan of $2,000 at 7% compounded annually for three years.

2. Manually calculate the compound interest on a 6.25% annual interest loan of $3,000 for four years if interest is compounded annually.

3. Use Table 13-1 or the appropriate formula to find the interest on a loan of $5,000 for six years at 10% annual interest if interest is compounded semiannually.

4. Use Table 13-1 or the appropriate formula to find the future value on an investment of $12,000 for seven years at 6% annual interest compounded quarterly.

5. An investment of $1,500 is made for two years at 2% annual interest compounded semiannually. Find the compound amount and the compound interest at the end of two years.

6. Use Table 13-1 to find the compound interest on a loan of $3,000 for one year at 12% annual interest if the interest is compounded quarterly.

7. Find the effective interest rate for the loan described in Exercise 6.

8. Use Table 13-2 to find the interest compounded on an investment of $2,000 invested at 5.75% for 28 days compounded daily.

9. Use Tables 13-1 and 13-2 to compare the interest on an investment of $3,000 that is invested at 8% annual interest compounded quarterly and daily, respectively, for one year.

Find the amount that should be invested today (present value) at the stated interest rate to yield the given amount (future value) after the indicated amount of time for Exercises 10–13.

10. $3,400 in four years at 4% annual interest compounded annually

11. $5,000 in eight years at 3% annual interest compounded semiannually

12. $8,000 in 12 years at 5% annual interest compounded annually

13. $6,000 in six years at 4% annual interest compounded quarterly

14. Jamie Juarez needs $12,000 in 10 years for her daughter's college education. How much must be invested today at 2% annual interest compounded semiannually to have the needed funds?

15. If you were offered $600 today or $680 in one year, which would you accept if money can be invested at 2% annual interest compounded semiannually?

16. Derek Anderson plans to buy a house in four years. He will make an $8,000 down payment on the property. How much should he invest today at 6% annual interest compounded quarterly to have the required amount in four years?

17. Which of the two options yields the greatest return on your investment of $2,000?
    Option 1: 8% annual interest compounded quarterly for four years
    Option 2: $8\frac{1}{4}$% annual interest compounded annually for four years

18. If you invest $2,000 today at 6% annual interest compounded quarterly, how much will you have after three years? (Table 13-1 or appropriate formula or calculator application)

19. If you invest $1,000 today at 5% annual interest compounded daily, how much will you have after 20 days? (Table 13-2 or appropriate formula or calculator application)

20. How much money should Bryan Trailer Sales set aside today to have $15,000 in one year to purchase a forklift if the interest rate is 2.95% compounded annually?

1. The compound amount or future value can be found using two formulas: $I = PR$ (assuming $T = 1$) and $A = P + I$. Show how these two formulas relate to the single formula $A = P(1 + R)$.

2. Because the entries in the present value table (Table 13-3) are reciprocals of the corresponding entries in the future value table (Table 13-1), how can Table 13-3 be used to find the future value of an investment?

3. In finding a future value, how will your result compare in size to your original investment?

4. In finding a present value, how will your result compare in size to your desired goal (future value)?

5. How can the future value table (Table 13-1) be used to find the present value of a desired goal?

6. Banking regulations require that the effective interest rate (APR or APY) be stated on all loan or investment contracts. Why?

7. Illustrate the procedure described in Exercise 5 to find the present value of an investment if you want to have $500 at the end of two years. The investment earns 8% compounded quarterly. Check your result using the present value table.

8. How does the effective interest rate compare with the compounded rate on a loan or investment? Illustrate your answer with an example that shows the compounded rate and the effective rate.

Challenge Problem

One real estate sales technique is to encourage customers or clients to buy today because the value of the property will probably increase during the next few years. "Buy this lot today for $28,000. In two years, I project it will sell for $32,500." The buyer has a CD worth $30,000 now, which earns 4% compounded annually and will mature in 2 years. Cashing in the CD now requires the buyer to pay an early withdrawal penalty of $600.

a. Should the buyer purchase the land now or in two years?

b. What are some of the problems with waiting to buy land?

c. What are some of the advantages of waiting?

d. Lots in a new subdivision sell for $15,600. Assuming that the price of the lot does not increase, how much would you need to invest today at 8% compounded quarterly to buy the lot in one year?

e. 1. You have inherited $60,000 and plan to buy a home. If you invest the $60,000 today at 5%, compounded annually, how much could you spend on the house in one year?

    2. If you intend to spend $60,000 on a house in one year, how much of your inheritance should you invest today at 5%, compounded annually? How much do you have left to spend on a car?

CASE STUDIES

13-1 How Fast Does Your Money Grow?

Barry learned in an online investment course that he should start investing as soon as possible. He had always thought that it would be smart to start investing after he finishes college and when his salary is high enough to pay the bills and to have money left over. He projects that will be 5–10 years from now. Barry wants to compare the difference between investing now and investing later. A financial advisor who spoke to Barry suggested that a Roth IRA (Individual Retirement Account) would be a good investment for him to start.

(Note: When table values do not include the information you need, use the formula $FV = \$1(1 + R)^N$ where R is the period rate and N is the number of periods.)

1. If Barry purchases a $2,000 Roth IRA when he is 25 years old and expects to earn an average of 6% per year compounded annually over 35 years (until he is 60), how much will accumulate in the investment?

2. If Barry doesn't put the money in the IRA until he is 35 years old, how much money will accumulate in the account by the time he is 60 years old using the same return of 6%? How much less will he earn because he invested 10 years later?

3. Barry knows that the interest rate is critical to the speed at which your investment grows. For instance, if $1 is invested at 2% compounded annually, it takes approximately 34.9 years to double. If $1 is invested at 5% compounded annually, it takes approximately 14.2 years to double. Use Table 13-1 to determine how many years it takes $1 to double if invested at 10% compounded annually; at 12% compounded annually.

4. At what interest rate would you need to invest to have your money double in 10 years if it is compounded annually?

13-2 Planning: The Key to Wealth

Abdol Akhim has just come from a Personal Finance class where he learned that he can determine how much his savings will be worth in the future. Abdol is completing his two-year business administration degree this semester and has been repairing computers in his spare time to pay for his tuition and books. Abdol got out his savings records and decided to apply what he had learned. He has a balance of $1,000 in a money market account at First Savings Bank, and he considers this to be an emergency fund. His instructor says that he should have 3–6 months of his total bills in an emergency fund. His bills are currently $700 a month. He also has a checking account and a regular savings account at First Savings Bank, and he will shift some of his funds from those accounts into the emergency fund. One of Abdol's future goals is to buy a house. He wants to start another account to save the $8,000 he needs for a down payment.

1. How much interest will Abdol receive on $1,000 in a 365-day year if he keeps it in the money market account earning 1.00% compounded daily?

2. How much money must Abdol shift from his other accounts to his emergency fund to have four times his monthly bills in the account by the end of the year?

3. Abdol realizes he needs to earn more interest than his current money market can provide. Using annual compounding on an account that pays 5.5% interest annually, find the amount Abdol needs to invest to have the $8,000 down payment for his house in 5 years.

4. Is 5.5% a realistic rate for Abdol to earn in a relatively short-term investment of 5 years, particularly at his bank?

13-3 Future Value/Present Value

At 45 years of age, Seth figured he wanted to work only 10 more years. Being a full-time landlord had a lot of advantages: cash flow, free time, being his own boss—but it was time to start thinking toward retirement. The real estate investments that he had made over the last 15 years had paid off handsomely. After selling a duplex and a four-unit and paying the associated taxes, Seth had $350,000 in the bank and was debt-free. With only 10 years before retirement, Seth wanted to make solid financial decisions that would limit his risk exposure. Fortunately, he had located another property that seemed to meet his needs—an older, but well maintained four-unit apartment. The price tag was $250,000, well within his range, and the apartment would require no remodeling. Seth figured he could invest the other $100,000, and between the two hoped to have $1 million to retire on by age 55.

1. Seth read an article in the local newspaper stating the real estate in the area had appreciated by 5% per year over the last 30 years. Assuming the article is correct, what would the future value of the $250,000 apartment be in 10 years?

2. Seth's current bank offers a 1-year certificate of deposit account paying 2% compounded semiannually. A competitor bank is also offering 2%, but compounded daily. If Seth invests the $100,000, how much more money will he have in the second bank after one year, due to the daily compounding?

3. After looking at the results from questions 1. and 2. Seth realizes that a 2% return in a certificate of deposit will never allow him to reach his goal of $1 million in 10 years. Presuming his apartment will indeed be worth $400,000 in 10 years, compute the future value of Seth's $100,000 investment using a 10%, 15%, and 20% return compounded semiannually for 10 years. Will any of these rates of return allow him to accomplish his goal of reaching $1 million by age 55?

4. A friend of Seth's who is a real estate developer needs to borrow $80,000 to finish a development project. He is desperate for cash and offers Seth 18%, compounded monthly, for $2\frac{1}{2}$ years. Find the future value of the loan using the future value table. Does this loan meet Seth's goals of low risk? How could he reduce the risk associated with this loan?

5. After purchasing the apartment, Seth receives a street, sewer, and gutter assessment for $12,500 due in 2 years. How much would he have to invest today in a CD paying 2%, compounded semiannually, to fully pay the assessment in 2 years?

Annuities and Sinking Funds

Is Social Security in Crisis?

Will Social Security be there when you need it? A summary of the 2012 annual reports by the Social Security and Medicare boards of trustees states that Social Security's expenditures exceeded noninterest income in 2010 and 2011, the first such occurrences since 1983. Social Security projections are that benefits will continue to exceed revenues and by 2033, the trust fund will be exhausted, and will be unable to pay the full benefits that have been promised to older Americans.

So continues the formal Social Security debate, which has dominated most of the past decade, and has since become largely a political fight. But what was the original purpose of Social Security? And what are the implications for you today?

Social Security provided a critical foundation of income for retired and disabled workers. For one-third of Americans over 65, Social Security benefits represent 90% of their total income. It was originally structured to resemble private-sector pensions (retirement plans). The retirement benefit was based on a worker's wages and years of service. In most plans, the monthly lifetime benefit after 35 years of service would be at least half of the income earned in the final working year.

Congress expected that company pensions would eventually replace Social Security benefits. But pension coverage peaked at 40% in the 1960s. Today, approximately only 15% of private-sector workers are covered by defined-benefit pensions.

So how can you avoid relying on Social Security when you retire? One of the best things you can do is start a supplemental retirement program right now with an annuity. Annuities may be single- or flexible-payment; fixed or variable; deferred or immediate. No matter the type, annuities are financial contracts with an insurance company that are designed to be a source of retirement income. The very best plans are systematic and enable the investor to make regular and consistent payments into the annuity fund, which compounds interest. And these plans are not expensive; many require as little as $25 a month, or $300 annually to get started. Let's say you're age 25. By investing $300 annually for 40 years at 7%, you would end up with $59,890.50 at age 65. Not a bad investment for $25 a month—about the same price as dinner and a movie.

Will Social Security still be there when you retire? It's impossible to say. Better to get started investing with an annuity now (or soon), rather than find out later when it's too late.

LEARNING OUTCOMES

14-1 Future Value of an Annuity

1. Find the future value of an ordinary annuity using the simple interest formula method.
2. Find the future value of an ordinary annuity with periodic payments using a $1.00 ordinary annuity future value table.
3. Find the future value of an annuity due with periodic payments using the simple interest formula method.
4. Find the future value of an annuity due with periodic payments using a $1.00 ordinary annuity future value table.
5. Find the future value of a retirement plan annuity.
6. Find the future value of an ordinary annuity or an annuity due using a formula or a calculator application.

14-2 Sinking Funds and the Present Value of an Annuity

1. Find the sinking fund payment using a $1.00 sinking fund payment table.
2. Find the present value of an ordinary annuity using a $1.00 ordinary annuity present value table.
3. Find the sinking fund payment or the present value of an annuity using a formula or a calculator application.

Annuity: a contract between a person (the annuitant) and an insurance company (the insurer) for receiving and disbursing money for the annuitant or the beneficiary of the annuitant.

Accumulation phase of an annuity: the time when money is being paid into the fund and earnings are being added to the fund.

Liquidation or payout phase of an annuity: the time when the annuitant or beneficiary is receiving money from the fund.

So far we have discussed interest accumulated from one *lump-sum* amount of money. Another type of investment option is an annuity. An **annuity** is a contract between you (the *annuitant*) and an insurance company (the *insurer*) for receiving and disbursing money for the annuitant or the beneficiary of the annuitant. An annuity has two phases—the accumulation phase and the liquidation phase. The **accumulation phase of an annuity** is the period during which you are paying money into the fund. The **liquidation or payout phase of an annuity** is the period during which you are receiving money from the fund. During both phases of the annuity, the fund balance may earn compound interest. An annuity is purchased by making either a single lump-sum payment or a series of periodic payments. Under the terms of the contract, the insurer agrees to make a lump-sum payment or periodic payments to you beginning at some future date. This investment option is a long-term investment option that is commonly used for retirement planning or as a college fund for small children. Penalties are normally applied if funds are withdrawn before a time specified in the agreement.

There are many options to consider when purchasing an annuity. You can choose how the money is invested (stocks, bonds, money market instruments, or a combination of these) and the level of risk of the investment. High-risk options have the potential to earn a high rate of return but the investment may be at risk. Low-risk options normally earn a lower rate of interest but the risk is also lower. A guaranteed rate of interest has no risk at all on the principal and guarantees a specific interest rate.

You can choose to invest with pre-taxed money or with taxed money. If pre-taxed money is invested, the tax on the entire fund is deferred until you begin receiving payments. If taxed money is invested, only the tax on the earnings is deferred until you begin receiving payments. In our study of annuities, we will examine only some basic interest-based options. Other options can be investigated by contacting insurance agencies or brokers or the Office of Investor Education and Assistance with the U.S. Securities and Exchange Commission (*http://www.sec.gov/investor/pubs/varannty.htm*).

14-1 FUTURE VALUE OF AN ANNUITY

LEARNING OUTCOMES

1. Find the future value of an ordinary annuity using the simple interest formula method.
2. Find the future value of an ordinary annuity with periodic payments using a $1.00 ordinary annuity future value table.
3. Find the future value of an annuity due with periodic payments using the simple interest formula method.
4. Find the future value of an annuity due with periodic payments using a $1.00 ordinary annuity future value table.
5. Find the future value of a retirement plan annuity.
6. Find the future value of an ordinary annuity or an annuity due using a formula or a calculator application.

Annuity certain: an annuity paid over a guaranteed number of periods.

Contingent annuity: an annuity paid over an uncertain number of periods.

Ordinary annuity: an annuity for which payments are made at the end of each period.

Annuity due: an annuity for which payments are made at the beginning of each period.

An annuity paid out over a guaranteed number of periods is an **annuity certain.** An annuity paid out over an uncertain number of periods is a **contingent annuity.**

We can also categorize annuities according to when payment is made into the fund. For an **ordinary annuity,** payment is made at the *end* of the period. For an **annuity due,** payment is made at the *beginning* of the period.

1 Find the future value of an ordinary annuity using the simple interest formula method.

Finding the future value of an annuity into which periodic payments are made means finding the amount of the annuity at the end of the accumulation phase. This is similar to finding the future value of a lump sum. The significant difference is that for each interest period, more principal—the annuity payment—is added to the amount on which interest is earned. The simple interest formula $I = PRT$ is still the basis of calculating interest for each period of the annuity.

HOW TO Find the future value of an ordinary annuity in the accumulation phase with periodic payments using the simple interest formula method

1. Find the first end-of-period principal.

$$\text{First end-of-period principal} = \text{annuity payment}$$

2. For each remaining period in turn, find the next end-of-period principal.
   (a) Multiply the previous end-of-period principal by the sum of 1 and the decimal equivalent of the period interest rate.

(b) Add the product from step 2a and the annuity payment.

$$\text{End-of-period principal} = \text{previous end-of-period principal} \times (1 + \text{period interest rate}) + \text{annuity payment}$$

3. Identify the last end-of-period principal as the future value.

$$\text{Future value} = \text{last end-of-period principal}$$

For an ordinary annuity, no interest accumulates on the annuity payment during the period in which it is paid because the payment is made at the *end* of the period. For the first period, this means no interest accumulates at all.

EXAMPLE 1

What is the future value of an ordinary annuity with annual payments of $1,000 after three years at 4% annual interest?

The decimal equivalent of the period interest rate is 0.04. The annuity is $1,000.
End-of-year value = (previous end-of-year value)(1 + 0.04) + $1,000

End-of-year 1 = $1,000.00   No interest is earned the first year.
End-of-year 2 = $1,000.00(1.04) + $1,000.00
      = $1,040.00 + $1,000.00
      = $2,040.00

End-of-year 3 = $2,040.00(1.04) + $1,000.00
      = $2,121.60 + $1,000.00
      = $3,121.60

The future value is $3,121.60.

HOW TO   Find the total interest earned on an annuity

1. Find the total amount invested:

$$\text{Total invested} = \text{payment amount} \times \text{number of payments}$$

2. Find the total interest:

$$\text{Total interest} = \text{future value of annuity} - \text{total invested}$$

EXAMPLE 2

Find the total interest earned on the annuity in the preceding example.

Total invested = $1,000(3)   Payment = $1,000
                            Number of payments = 3
      = $3,000
Total interest = $3,121.60 − $3,000   Future value = $3,121.60
      = $121.60

The total interest earned is $121.60.

A lump-sum investment earns more interest than an annuity. Compare the earnings of a $3,000 lump-sum investment (Figure 14-1) and an annuity of the same accumulated investment (Figure 14-2).

FIGURE 14-1
Lump-Sum Investment of $3,000 at 4% Annually

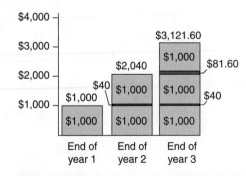

FIGURE 14-2
Three-Year Ordinary Annuity of $1,000 per Year at 4% Annually

The advantages of the lump-sum annuity are obvious, but an annuity with periodic payments also offers some advantages. When a lump sum is not available, an annuity with periodic payments provides an alternative investment strategy.

STOP AND CHECK

See Examples 1 and 2.

1. Find the future value and total interest of an ordinary annuity with annual payments of $5,000 at 2.9% annual interest after four years.

2. Find the future value and total interest of an ordinary annuity with annual payments of $3,500 at 3.42% annual interest after three years.

3. Find the value of an ordinary annuity after two years of $1,500 invested semiannually at 4% annual interest.

4. What is the value after 2 years of an ordinary annuity of $300 paid semiannually at 3% annual interest?

2 Find the future value of an ordinary annuity with periodic payments using a $1.00 ordinary annuity future value table.

Calculating the future value of an ordinary annuity with periodic payments can become quite tedious if the number of periods is large. For example, a monthly annuity such as a monthly savings plan running for five years has 60 periods and 60 calculation sequences. For this reason, most businesspeople rely on prepared tables, calculators, or computers.

HOW TO Find the future value of an ordinary annuity with periodic payments using a $1.00 ordinary annuity future value table

Using Table 14-1:

1. Select the periods row corresponding to the number of interest periods.
2. Select the rate-per-period column corresponding to the period interest rate.
3. Locate the value in the cell where the periods row intersects the rate-per-period column.
4. Multiply the annuity payment by the table value from step 3.

$$\text{Future value} = \text{annuity payment} \times \text{table value}$$

EXAMPLE 3 Use Table 14-1 to find the future value of a semiannual ordinary annuity of $6,000 for five years at 6% annual interest compounded semiannually.

$$5 \text{ years} \times 2 \text{ periods per year} = 10 \text{ periods}$$

$$\frac{6\% \text{ annual interest rate}}{2 \text{ periods per year}} = 3\% \text{ period interest rate}$$

The Table 14-1 value for 10 periods at 3% is 11.464.

$$
\begin{aligned}
\text{Future value of annuity} &= \text{annuity payment} \times \text{table value} \\
&= \$6,000(11.464) \\
&= \$68,784
\end{aligned}
$$

The future value of the ordinary annuity is $68,784.

EXAMPLE 4 Find the total interest earned on the annuity in Example 1.

Total invested = $6,000(10)   Payment = $6,000
                                               Number of payments = 10

              = $60,000
Total interest = $68,784 − $60,000   Future value = $68,784
              = $8,784

The total interest earned is $8,784.

TABLE 14-1
Future Value of $1.00 Ordinary Annuity

Periods	\multicolumn{10}{c}{Rate per period}
	0.25%	0.50%	0.75%	1.00%	1.50%	2.00%	2.50%	3.00%	3.50%	4.00%
1	1.000	1.000	1.000	1.000	1.000	1.000	1.000	1.000	1.000	1.000
2	2.002	2.005	2.008	2.010	2.015	2.020	2.025	2.030	2.035	2.040
3	3.008	3.015	3.023	3.030	3.045	3.060	3.076	3.091	3.106	3.122
4	4.015	4.030	4.045	4.060	4.091	4.122	4.153	4.184	4.215	4.246
5	5.025	5.050	5.076	5.101	5.152	5.204	5.256	5.309	5.362	5.416
6	6.038	6.076	6.114	6.152	6.230	6.308	6.388	6.468	6.550	6.633
7	7.053	7.106	7.159	7.214	7.323	7.434	7.547	7.662	7.779	7.898
8	8.070	8.141	8.213	8.286	8.433	8.583	8.736	8.892	9.052	9.214
9	9.091	9.182	9.275	9.369	9.559	9.755	9.955	10.159	10.368	10.583
10	10.113	10.228	10.344	10.462	10.703	10.950	11.203	11.464	11.731	12.006
11	11.139	11.279	11.422	11.567	11.863	12.169	12.483	12.808	13.142	13.486
12	12.166	12.336	12.508	12.683	13.041	13.412	13.796	14.192	14.602	15.026
13	13.197	13.397	13.601	13.809	14.237	14.680	15.140	15.618	16.113	16.627
14	14.230	14.464	14.703	14.947	15.450	15.974	16.519	17.086	17.677	18.292
15	15.265	15.537	15.814	16.097	16.682	17.293	17.932	18.599	19.296	20.024
16	16.304	16.614	16.932	17.258	17.932	18.639	19.380	20.157	20.971	21.825
17	17.344	17.697	18.059	18.430	19.201	20.012	20.865	21.762	22.705	23.698
18	18.388	18.786	19.195	19.615	20.489	21.412	22.386	23.414	24.500	25.645
19	19.434	19.880	20.339	20.811	21.797	22.841	23.946	25.117	26.357	27.671
20	20.482	20.979	21.491	22.019	23.124	24.297	25.545	26.870	28.280	29.778
21	21.533	22.084	22.652	23.239	24.471	25.783	27.183	28.676	30.269	31.969
22	22.587	23.194	23.822	24.472	25.838	27.299	28.863	30.537	32.329	34.248
23	23.644	24.310	25.001	25.716	27.225	28.845	30.584	32.453	34.460	36.618
24	24.703	25.432	26.188	26.973	28.634	30.422	32.349	34.426	36.667	39.083
25	25.765	26.559	27.385	28.243	30.063	32.030	34.158	36.459	38.950	41.646
26	26.829	27.692	28.590	29.526	31.514	33.671	36.012	38.553	41.313	44.312
27	27.896	28.830	29.805	30.821	32.987	35.344	37.912	40.710	43.759	47.084
28	28.966	29.975	31.028	32.129	34.481	37.051	39.860	42.931	46.291	49.968
29	30.038	31.124	32.261	33.450	35.999	38.792	41.856	45.219	48.911	52.966
30	31.113	32.280	33.503	34.785	37.539	40.568	43.903	47.575	51.623	56.085
35	36.529	38.145	39.854	41.660	45.592	49.994	54.928	60.462	66.674	73.652
36	37.621	39.336	41.153	43.077	47.276	51.994	57.301	63.276	70.008	77.598
40	42.013	44.159	46.446	48.886	54.268	60.402	67.403	75.401	84.550	95.026
42	44.226	46.607	49.153	51.879	57.923	64.862	72.840	82.023	92.607	104.820
48	50.931	54.098	57.521	61.223	69.565	79.354	90.860	104.408	120.388	139.263
54	57.738	61.817	66.272	71.141	82.295	95.673	111.757	131.137	154.538	182.845
60	64.647	69.770	75.424	81.670	96.215	114.052	135.992	163.053	196.517	237.991
66	71.660	77.965	84.996	92.846	111.435	134.749	164.096	201.163	248.120	307.767
72	78.779	86.409	95.007	104.710	128.077	158.057	196.689	246.667	311.552	396.057
78	86.006	95.109	105.477	117.304	146.275	184.306	234.487	301.002	389.528	507.771
84	93.342	104.074	116.427	130.672	166.173	213.867	278.321	365.881	485.379	649.125
90	100.788	113.311	127.879	144.863	187.930	247.157	329.154	443.349	603.205	827.983
96	108.347	122.829	139.856	159.927	211.720	284.647	388.106	535.850	748.043	1054.296
100	113.450	129.334	148.145	170.481	228.803	312.232	432.549	607.288	862.612	1237.624
102	116.020	132.635	152.383	175.918	237.734	326.866	456.471	646.302	926.086	1340.654
108	123.809	142.740	165.483	192.893	266.178	374.413	535.755	778.186	1144.947	1702.988
114	131.716	153.151	179.185	210.911	297.280	427.958	627.699	935.664	1413.982	2161.456
120	139.741	163.879	193.514	230.039	331.288	488.258	734.326	1123.700	1744.695	2741.564
126	147.888	174.933	208.501	250.343	368.474	556.166	857.981	1348.224	2151.225	3475.586
132	156.158	186.323	224.175	271.896	409.135	632.641	1001.382	1616.319	2650.956	4404.358

Table values show the future value, or accumulated amount of the investment and interest, of a $1.00 investment for a given number of periods at a given rate per period.

Table values can be generated using the formula FV of $1.00 per period $= \dfrac{(1 + R)^N - 1}{R}$, where FV is the future value, R is the interest rate per period, and N is the number of periods.

TABLE 14-1
Future Value of $1.00 Ordinary Annuity—Continued

Periods	4.50%	5.00%	5.50%	6.00%	6.50%	7.00%	8.00%	9.00%	10.00%	12.00%
1	1.000	1.000	1.000	1.000	1.000	1.000	1.000	1.000	1.000	1.000
2	2.045	2.050	2.055	2.060	2.065	2.070	2.080	2.090	2.100	2.120
3	3.137	3.153	3.168	3.184	3.199	3.215	3.246	3.278	3.310	3.374
4	4.278	4.310	4.342	4.375	4.407	4.440	4.506	4.573	4.641	4.779
5	5.471	5.526	5.581	5.637	5.694	5.751	5.867	5.985	6.105	6.353
6	6.717	6.802	6.888	6.975	7.064	7.153	7.336	7.523	7.716	8.115
7	8.019	8.142	8.267	8.394	8.523	8.654	8.923	9.200	9.487	10.089
8	9.380	9.549	9.722	9.897	10.077	10.260	10.637	11.028	11.436	12.300
9	10.802	11.027	11.256	11.491	11.732	11.978	12.488	13.021	13.579	14.776
10	12.288	12.578	12.875	13.181	13.494	13.816	14.487	15.193	15.937	17.549
11	13.841	14.207	14.583	14.972	15.372	15.784	16.645	17.560	18.531	20.655
12	15.464	15.917	16.386	16.870	17.371	17.888	18.977	20.141	21.384	24.133
13	17.160	17.713	18.287	18.882	19.500	20.141	21.495	22.953	24.523	28.029
14	18.932	19.599	20.293	21.015	21.767	22.550	24.215	26.019	27.975	32.393
15	20.784	21.579	22.409	23.276	24.182	25.129	27.152	29.361	31.772	37.280
16	22.719	23.657	24.641	25.673	26.754	27.888	30.324	33.003	35.950	42.753
17	24.742	25.840	26.996	28.213	29.493	30.840	33.750	36.974	40.545	48.884
18	26.855	28.132	29.481	30.906	32.410	33.999	37.450	41.301	45.599	55.750
19	29.064	30.539	32.103	33.760	35.517	37.379	41.446	46.018	51.159	63.440
20	31.371	33.066	34.868	36.786	38.825	40.995	45.762	51.160	57.275	72.052
21	33.783	35.719	37.786	39.993	42.349	44.865	50.423	56.765	64.002	81.699
22	36.303	38.505	40.864	43.392	46.102	49.006	55.457	62.873	71.403	92.503
23	38.937	41.430	44.112	46.996	50.098	53.436	60.893	69.532	79.543	104.603
24	41.689	44.502	47.538	50.816	54.355	58.177	66.765	76.790	88.497	118.155
25	44.565	47.727	51.153	54.865	58.888	63.249	73.106	84.701	98.347	133.334
26	47.571	51.113	54.966	59.156	63.715	68.676	79.954	93.324	109.182	150.334
27	50.711	54.669	58.989	63.706	68.857	74.484	87.351	102.723	121.100	169.374
28	53.993	58.403	63.234	68.528	74.333	80.698	95.339	112.968	134.210	190.699
29	57.423	62.323	67.711	73.640	80.164	87.347	103.966	124.135	148.631	214.583
30	61.007	66.439	72.435	79.058	86.375	94.461	113.283	136.308	164.494	241.333
35	81.497	90.320	100.251	111.435	124.035	138.237	172.317	215.711	271.024	431.663
36	86.164	95.836	106.765	119.121	133.097	148.913	187.102	236.125	299.127	484.463
40	107.030	120.800	136.606	154.762	175.632	199.635	259.057	337.882	442.593	767.091
42	118.925	135.232	154.100	175.951	201.271	230.632	304.244	403.528	537.637	964.359
48	161.588	188.025	219.368	256.565	300.747	353.270	490.132	684.280	960.172	1911.590
54	217.146	258.774	309.363	370.917	445.896	537.316	785.114	1155.130	1708.719	3781.255
60	289.498	353.584	433.450	533.128	657.690	813.520	1253.213	1944.792	3034.816	7471.641
66	383.719	480.638	604.548	763.228	966.727	1228.028	1996.028	3269.134	5384.078	14755.810
72	506.418	650.903	840.465	1089.629	1417.656	1850.092	3174.781	5490.189	9545.938	29133.468
78	666.205	879.074	1165.757	1552.634	2075.625	2783.643	5045.315	9215.120	16918.927	57512.414
84	874.289	1184.845	1614.283	2209.417	3035.696	4184.651	8013.617	15462.202	29980.628	113527.423
90	1145.269	1594.607	2232.731	3141.075	4436.576	6287.185	12723.939	25939.184	53120.226	224091.119
96	1498.155	2143.728	3085.473	4462.651	6480.660	9442.523	20198.627	43510.132	94113.437	442324.248
100	1790.856	2610.025	3826.702	5638.368	8341.558	12381.662	27484.516	61422.675	137796.123	696010.548
102	1957.704	2879.603	4261.271	6337.330	9463.269	14177.835	32060.019	72978.371	166735.409	873077.751
108	2556.157	3865.745	5882.510	8996.600	13815.319	21284.260	50882.557	122399.557	295389.664	1723308.786
114	3335.499	5187.270	8117.945	12768.824	20165.580	31949.088	80751.559	205283.834	523308.524	3401514.091
120	4350.404	6958.240	11200.258	18119.796	29431.515	47954.120	128149.912	344289.064	927080.688	6713993.792
126	5672.074	9331.509	15450.283	25710.252	42951.832	71973.356	203365.140	577414.751	1642387.707	13252241.370
132	7393.233	12511.916	21310.400	36477.459	62679.899	108019.754	322722.255	968389.865	2909597.724	26157582.760

Table values show the future value, or accumulated amount of the investment and interest, of a $1.00 investment for a given number of periods at a given rate per period.

Table values can be generated using the formula $FV \text{ of } \$1.00 \text{ per period} = \dfrac{(1 + R)^N - 1}{R}$, where FV is the future value, R is the interest rate per period, and N is the number of periods.

STOP AND CHECK

See Examples 3 and 4.

1. Use Table 14-1 to find the accumulation phase future value and total interest of an ordinary annuity of $4,000 for eight years at 2% annual interest.

2. Use Table 14-1 to find the accumulated amount and total interest of an ordinary annuity with semiannual payments of $6,000 for five years at 4% annual interest.

3. John Crampton put $1,200 in an ordinary annuity account every quarter of the accumulation phase for five years at a 2% annual rate compounded quarterly. What is the future value of the annuity?

4. Tiffany Evans created an ordinary annuity with $2,500 payments made semiannually at 6% annually. Find her annuity value at the end of six years.

3 Find the future value of an annuity due with periodic payments using the simple interest formula method.

Because an annuity due is paid at the *beginning* of each period rather than at the end, the annuity due payment earns interest throughout the period in which it is paid. The future value of an annuity due, then, is greater than the future value of the corresponding ordinary annuity, given the same number of periods, the same period interest rate, and the same annuity payment. The difference in the future value of an ordinary annuity and an annuity due is exactly one additional period's worth of interest.

> **HOW TO** Find the future value of an annuity due with periodic payments using the simple interest formula method
>
> 1. Find the first end-of-period principal: Multiply the annuity payment by the sum of 1 and the decimal equivalent of the period interest rate.
>
> First end-of-period principal = annuity payment × (1 + period interest rate)
>
> 2. For each remaining period in turn, find the next end-of-period principal:
>   (a) Add the previous end-of-period principal and the annuity payment.
>   (b) Multiply the sum from step 2a by the sum of 1 and the period interest rate.
>
> End-of-period principal = (previous end-of-period principal + annuity payment) ×
> (1 + period interest rate)
>
> 3. Identify the last end-of-period principal as the future value.
>
> Future value = last end-of-period principal

EXAMPLE 5 What is the future value of an annuity due with an annual payment of $1,000 for three years at 4% annual interest? Find the total investment and the total interest earned.

The annuity payment is $1,000; the period interest rate is 4%.

End-of-year value = (previous end-of-year + $1,000)(1 + 0.04)
  End-of-year 1 = $1,000(1.04)   The annuity due earns interest
         = $1,040   during the first period.
  End-of-year 2 = ($1,040 + $1,000)(1.04) Second payment is made.
         = ($2,040)(1.04)
         = $2,121.60
  End-of-year 3 = ($2,121.60 + $1,000)(1.04) Third payment is made.
         = ($3,121.60)(1.04)
         = $3,246.46   Future value of annuity due
  Total investment = investment per period × total periods
         = $1,000(3)
         = $3,000
  Total interest earned = future value − total investment
         = $3,246.46 − $3,000
         = $246.46

The future value of the annuity due is $3,246.46, the total investment is $3,000, and the total interest earned is $246.46.

TIP

Ordinary Annuity versus Annuity Due

The difference between an ordinary annuity and an annuity due is whether you make the first payment immediately or at the end of the first period.

If you are establishing your own annuity plan through a savings account, you begin your annuity with your first payment or deposit (annuity due).

If you are entering a payroll deduction plan, a 401(k) plan, or an annuity plan with an insurance company, you may complete the paperwork to establish the plan, and the first payment will be made at a later time.

In the three-year ordinary annuity (Figure 14-3, repeated from Figure 14-2 for comparison purposes) the total interest earned is $121.60. In the annuity due (Figure 14-4) the first $1,000 payment earns interest during the first period and then interest is earned on that interest throughout the duration of the annuity. The total interest earned is $246.46 or $124.86 more than an ordinary annuity.

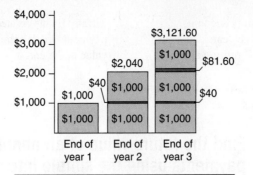

FIGURE 14-3
Three-Year Ordinary Annuity of $1,000 per Year
at 4% Annually

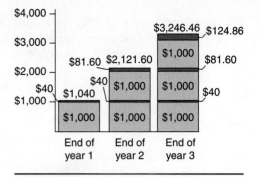

FIGURE 14-4
Three-Year Annuity Due of $1,000 per Year
at 4% Annually

STOP AND CHECK

See Example 5.

1. Manually calculate the future value of an annuity due that sets aside $1,500 annually for four years at 3.75% annual interest compounded annually. How much interest is earned?

2. Manually calculate the value of an annuity due after two years of $4,000 payments at 4.25% compounded annually.

3. DeMarco receives $5,000 semiannually from his grandmother's estate. He invests the money at 3.8% compounded semiannually. How much will he have after two years investing as an annuity due?

4. If you make six monthly payments of $50 to an annuity due and receive 3% annual interest compounded monthly, how much will you accumulate?

4 Find the future value of an annuity due with periodic payments using a $1.00 ordinary annuity future value table.

Because the future value of an annuity due is so closely related to the future value of the corresponding ordinary annuity, we can also use Table 14-1 to find the future value of an annuity due. An annuity due accumulates interest one period more than does the ordinary annuity, but has the same number of payments. Thus, we adjust Table 14-1 values by multiplying by the sum of 1 and the period interest rate. This applies interest for the first payment, which is made at the beginning of the first period, for the entire time of the annuity.

HOW TO Find the future value of an annuity due with a periodic payment using a $1.00 ordinary annuity future value table

Use Table 14-1:

1. Select the periods row corresponding to the number of interest periods.
2. Select the rate-per-period column corresponding to the period interest rate.
3. Locate the value in the cell where the periods row intersects the rate-per-period column.
4. Multiply the annuity payment by the table value from step 3. This is equivalent to an *ordinary annuity.*
5. Multiply the amount that is equivalent to an ordinary annuity by the sum of 1 and the period interest rate to adjust for the extra interest that is earned on an annuity due.

Future value = annuity payment × table value × (1 + period interest rate)

EXAMPLE 6 Use Table 14-1 to find the future value of a quarterly annuity due of $2,800 for four years at 4% annual interest compounded quarterly.

$$4 \text{ years} \times 4 \text{ periods per year} = 16 \text{ periods}$$

$$\frac{4\% \text{ annual interest rate}}{4 \text{ periods per year}} = 1\% \text{ period interest rate}$$

The Table 14-1 value for 16 periods at 1% is 17.258.

Future value = annuity payment × table value × (1 + period interest rate)
          = $2,800(17.258)(1.01)   Future value for ordinary annuity
          = $48,322.40(1.01)   Adjustment for annuity due
          = $48,805.62   Future value for annuity due

The future value is $48,805.62.

EXAMPLE 7

What is the total interest earned on the annuity due in Example 6?

Total invested = $2,800(16)   Payment = $2,800
            = $44,800   Number of payments = 16
Total interest = $48,805.62 − $44,800
            = $4,005.62

The total interest earned is $4,005.62.

EXAMPLE 8

Sarah Smith wants to select the best annuity plan. She plans to invest a total of $40,000 over ten years' time at 8% annual interest. Annuity 1 is a quarterly ordinary annuity of $1,000; interest is compounded quarterly. Annuity 2 is a semiannual ordinary annuity of $2,000; interest is compounded semiannually. Annuity 3 is a quarterly annuity due of $1,000; interest is compounded quarterly. Annuity 4 is a semiannual annuity due of $2,000; interest is compounded semiannually. Which annuity yields the greatest future value?

What You Know	What You Are Looking For	Solution Plan
Annuity 1: Ordinary annuity of $1,000 quarterly for ten years at 8% annual interest compounded quarterly	Which annuity yields the greatest future value? Future value of each annuity	Number of periods = years × periods per year $$\text{Period interest rate} = \frac{\text{annual interest rate}}{\text{periods per year}}$$
Annuity 2: Ordinary annuity of $2,000 semiannually for ten years at 8% annual interest compounded semiannually		Future value of ordinary annuity = annuity payment × Table 14-1 value
Annuity 3: Annuity due of $1,000 quarterly for ten years at 8% annual interest compounded quarterly		Future value of annuity due = annuity payment × Table 14-1 value × (1 + period interest rate)
Annuity 4: Annuity due of $2,000 semiannually for ten years at 8% annual interest compounded semiannually.		

Solution

Annuity 1   *Annuity 2*
Number of periods = years × periods per year
              = 10(4) = 40   = 10(2) = 20

Period interest rate = $\dfrac{\text{annual interest rate}}{\text{periods per year}}$

              = $\dfrac{8\%}{4}$ = 2%   = $\dfrac{8\%}{2}$ = 4%

Table value = 60.402   = 29.778
Future value = annuity payment × table value
Future value = ($1,000)(60.402)   = $2,000(29.778)
          = $60,402   = $59,556

Annuity 3
The number of periods and period interest rate are the same as those for annuity 1.
Future value = annuity payment × table value × (1 + period interest rate)
          = $1,000(60.402)(1.02)
          = $61,610.04

ANNUITIES AND SINKING FUNDS

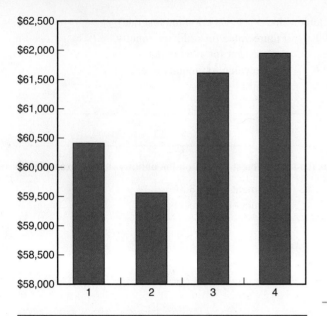

Annuity 4
The number of periods and period interest rate are the same as those for annuity 2.

Future value = annuity payment × table value × (1 + period interest rate)
$$= \$2,000(29.778)(1.04)$$
$$= \$61,938.24$$

Conclusion

Annuity 4, with the larger annuity due payment, yields the greatest future value. Notice that the ordinary annuity with fewer periods per year yields the least future value of all four annuities. If the total investment is the same, the number of years is the same, and the annual rate of interest is the same, any annuity due yields a larger future value than any corresponding ordinary annuity. The annuity due with the largest payment is the most profitable, while the ordinary annuity paid most frequently is the most profitable ordinary annuity. See Figure 14-5.

FIGURE 14-5
Four Two-Year Annuities at 8% Annual Interest

STOP AND CHECK

See Example 6.

1. Use Table 14-1 to find the future value of an annual annuity due of $3,000 for ten years at 2%.

2. Use Table 14-1 to find the future value of a semiannual annuity due of $1,000 for five years at 6% annually compounded semiannually.

3. Use Table 14-1 to find the future value and total interest of a quarterly annuity due of $500 invested at 2% annually compounded quarterly for five years. *See Example 7.*

4. Use Table 14-1 to find the future value of a semiannual annuity due of $1,000 for five years invested at 2% annually compounded semiannually. Compare the interest earned on this annuity with the interest earned on the annuity in Exercise 3. *See Example 8.*

5   Find the future value of a retirement plan annuity.

Pension: an arrangement to provide people with an income when they are no longer earning a regular income from employment, typically provided by an employer.

Defined benefit plan: a plan that guarantees a certain payout at retirement, according to a fixed formula that usually depends on the member's salary and the number of years' membership in the plan.

Defined contribution plan: a plan that provides a payout at retirement that is dependent on the amount of money contributed and the performance of the investment vehicles utilized.

401(k) plan: a defined contribution retirement plan for individuals working for private-sector companies.

403(b) plan: a defined contribution retirement plan designed for employees of public education entities and most other nonprofit organizations.

Traditional IRA: an individual retirement arrangement is a personal savings plan that allows you to set aside money for retirement. Contributions are typically tax-deductible in the year of the contribution, and taxes are deferred until contributions are withdrawn.

A retirement plan is an arrangement to provide people with an income during retirement when they are no longer earning a steady income from employment. Employment-based retirement plans or **pensions** may be classified as **defined benefit** or **defined contribution,** according to how the benefits are determined. A defined benefit plan guarantees a certain payout at retirement, according to a fixed formula that usually depends on the member's salary and the number of years' membership in the plan. A defined contribution plan will provide a payout at retirement that is dependent on the amount of money contributed and the performance of the investment vehicles utilized.

Over the last 20 years, there has been a notable shift in corporate America away from pensions and defined benefit plans. Defined contribution plans have gained in popularity, mostly because they are governed by fewer rules, are simpler to administer, and unlike defined benefit plans, do not require firms to pay for pension insurance to protect them. They also reflect a movement toward the individual choice and responsibility of the employee. The version that corporations offer to their employees, **401(k) plans,** are the most common type of defined contribution plan, followed by **403(b) plans,** designed for employees of public education entities and most other nonprofit organizations. Both are named for sections of the Internal Revenue Service code that defines these plans.

All defined contribution plans work basically the same way. You decide what percentage of your salary or a specified amount you would like to contribute, and your employer makes regular contributions into your individual account on your behalf, through payroll deduction. Your contributions are deducted *before* taxes are calculated. Your employer's plan will have a limited selection of investment options from which to choose, and you decide in which option to invest your money. When you leave your job, you still maintain ownership over your account. Many employers also match all or part of an employee's contribution.

Beyond the retirement plan options available through your employer, individuals who receive taxable compensation during the year are also eligible to set up an **individual retirement arrangement (IRA).** Contributions to a **traditional IRA** are often tax-deductible—money is deposited *before tax*, that is, contributions are made *with pre-tax assets* and withdrawals at retirement are taxed as income. Currently, the most that can be contributed to your traditional IRA generally is the smaller of $5,000 ($6,000 if you are age 50 or older) or your taxable compensation for the year. If neither you nor your spouse was covered for any part of the year by an employer retirement plan, you can take an income tax deduction for total contributions to one or more of your traditional IRAs for those same amounts. For example, a 45-year-old individual making $35,000 who is not covered by an employer-sponsored plan would be eligible to contribute (and deduct from taxable income) $5,000 to a traditional IRA. You can withdraw or use your traditional IRA assets at any time. However, a 10% additional tax (in addition to regular income tax) generally applies if you withdraw or use IRA assets before you are age $59\frac{1}{2}$—unless the funds are used toward significant medical expenses, costs for higher education, and first-time home expenses, among others. See IRS Publications for additional details.

Another popular type of IRA is a **Roth IRA,** which is generally subject to the same rules that apply to a traditional IRA. One notable exception is that, unlike a traditional IRA, you do not get an income tax deduction for contributions to a Roth IRA. However, a major advantage to a Roth IRA is that if you satisfy all requirements, qualified distributions (defined in IRS Publication 590) will be tax free.

Regular contributions made to either form of IRA or to a defined contribution retirement plan constitute an annuity. The future value of the annuity is determined using the same methods found earlier in this chapter. Payments made at the end of each period signify an ordinary annuity, while payments made at the beginning of each period signify an annuity due.

DID YOU KNOW?

Generally, retirement plans that are payroll deducted like 401(k) or 403(b) plans are *ordinary annuities.* The plan is set up and the first payment is deducted at the end of the pay period. On the other hand, an IRA or Roth IRA is generally an *annuity due.* The payment is made as soon as the plan is established.

EXAMPLE 9

Ethan Thomas, who is currently 20 years old, wants to plan for retirement by contributing $5,000 each year to a Roth IRA. He has an option that earns 4% per year. How much will he have in his retirement fund at age 60 when he can withdraw funds without a penalty? He will not make a contribution at age 60, so he will have made 40 payments.

A Roth IRA contribution is made as the fund is established, so it is an annuity due.

Number of periods = 40
Rate per period = 4%
Annuity payment = $5,000
Table 14-1 value = 95.026

$$\text{Future value of annuity due} = \text{annuity payment} \times \text{table value} \times 1.04$$
$$= \$5,000(95.026)(1.04)$$
$$= \$494,135.20$$

Ethan will have $494,135.20 in a 4% Roth IRA fund at age 60.

EXAMPLE 10

Tyson Smithey has the opportunity to contribute to a payroll deduction 401(k) plan at work. He selects an option that averages 3% per year compounded monthly and contributes $500 per month. How much should he have in the account in 5 years?

A payroll-deduction plan is considered to be an ordinary annuity.

Number of periods = 5(12) = 60   Rate per period = $\frac{3\%}{12}$ = 0.25%

Annuity payment = $500   Table 14-1 value = 64.647

Future value of the ordinary annuity = annuity payment × table value
$$= \$500(64.647) = \$32,323.50$$

Tyson will have $32,323.50 in his 401(k) plan after 5 years.

EXAMPLE 11

In Example 10, if Tyson's employer will match the first $100 per month of his contribution, how much will this increase his fund after 5 years?

Number of periods = 5(12) = 60   Rate per period = $\frac{3\%}{12}$ = 0.25%

Annuity payment = $500 + $100 match = $600   Table 14-1 value = 64.647

Future value of the ordinary annuity = annuity payment × table value
$$= \$600(64.647) = \$38,788.20$$

Tyson will have $38,788.20 in his 401(k) plan with his employer's matching funds, which is an increase of $6,464.70 over what he contributes.

TIP

Employer Match

Some employers will match an individual's contribution to a retirement plan up to a certain amount. This match adds to the individual's contribution, and interest is calculated on the sum of the two amounts.

STOP AND CHECK

See Example 9.

1. Alexandra May plans to contribute $3,500 each year to a Roth IRA. Her investment is projected to earn 6% per year. How much should she expect to have when she retires in 10 years?

2. Karen Paul is contributing $800 each year to a Roth IRA that is projected to earn 5.5% per year. How much can Karen expect to have in 25 years?

3. Laura Pipkin contributes $135 per month to a payroll deduction 401(k) plan at work. She averages 9% per year compounded monthly. How much should she have in the account in 10 years? *See Example 10.*

4. April Morrison contributes $350 per month to a payroll deduction 401(k) plan at work, and her employer matches $100 of her contribution. How much should Laura have in 7.5 years if the investment is expected to average 3% per year, compounded monthly? *See Example 11.*

6 Find the future value of an ordinary annuity or an annuity due using a formula or a calculator application.

Using tables to find the future value of an annuity can be limiting. Annuity rates may not be stated as whole number percents. Evaluating an annuity formula requires a business, scientific, or graphing calculator or computer software like Excel. Many of the calculator or software features can be used to facilitate these calculations. Be sure to apply the *order of operations*. For more details, review Chapter 5, Section 1, Learning Outcome 5.

HOW TO Find the future value of an ordinary annuity or an annuity due using a formula:

1. Identify the period rate R as a decimal equivalent, the number of periods N, and the amount of the annuity payment PMT.
2. Substitute the values from step 1 into the appropriate formula.

$$FV_{\text{ordinary annuity}} = PMT\left(\frac{(1 + R)^N - 1}{R}\right)$$

$$FV_{\text{annuity due}} = PMT\left(\frac{(1 + R)^N - 1}{R}\right)(1 + R)$$

3. Evaluate the formula.

EXAMPLE 12 Find the future value of an ordinary annuity of $100 paid monthly at 5.25% compounded monthly for 10 years.

$$R = \frac{5.25\%}{12} = \frac{0.0525}{12} = 0.004375$$ Periodic interest rate

$$N = 10(12) = 120$$ Number of payments

$$PMT = \$100$$

$$FV_{\text{ordinary annuity}} = \$100\left(\frac{(1 + 0.004375)^{120} - 1}{0.004375}\right)$$ Mentally add within the innermost parentheses.

$$FV_{\text{ordinary annuity}} = \$100\left(\frac{(1.004375)^{120} - 1}{0.004375}\right)$$

Calculator sequence: 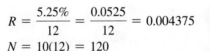 $\Rightarrow 15737.69632$

The future value of the ordinary annuity is $15,737.70.

EXAMPLE 13 Find the future value of an annuity due of $50 monthly at 5.75% compounded monthly for 5 years.

$$R = \frac{5.75\%}{12} = \frac{0.0575}{12} = 0.0047916667$$ Periodic interest rate

$$N = 5(12) = 60$$ Number of payments

$$PMT = \$50$$

$$FV_{\text{annuity due}} = \$50\left(\frac{(1 + 0.0047916667)^{60} - 1}{0.0047916667}\right)(1 + 0.0047916667)$$

Mentally add within the parentheses.

$$FV_{\text{annuity due}} = \$50\left(\frac{(1.0047916667)^{60} - 1}{0.0047916667}\right)(1.0047916667)$$

Calculator sequence: 50 $\boxed{(}$ 1.0047916667 $\boxed{\wedge}$ 60 $\boxed{-}$ 1 $\boxed{)}$ $\boxed{\div}$ 0.0047916667 $\boxed{=}$ $\boxed{\text{ANS}}$ $\boxed{(}$
1.0047916667 $\boxed{)}$ $\boxed{=}$ $\Rightarrow$ 3482.788889

The future value of the annuity due is \$3,482.79.

Calculator applications are also available for calculating annuities. The steps are similar to those used in calculating future value of a lump sum. You key in different known and unknown values. The default setting on most calculators is for an ordinary annuity.

EXAMPLE 14
Rework Example 12 using a TI BA II Plus, a TI-84 calculator, and a Casio fx-CG10.

BA II Plus:

	Keys to press	Display shows
Set decimals to two places if necessary.	$\boxed{\text{2ND}}$ $\boxed{\text{FORMAT}}$ 2 $\boxed{\text{ENTER}}$	DEC= 2.00
Set all variables to defaults.	$\boxed{\text{2ND}}$ $\boxed{\text{RESET}}$ $\boxed{\text{ENTER}}$	RST 0.00
Enter number of periods/payments.	120 $\boxed{\text{N}}$	N= 120.00 ◁
Enter interest rate per period (as a %).	$\boxed{.}$ 4375 $\boxed{\text{I/Y}}$	I/Y= 0.44 ◁
Enter payment amount as a negative.	100 $\boxed{+/-}$ $\boxed{\text{PMT}}$	PMT=−100.00 ◁
Compute future value.	$\boxed{\text{CPT}}$ $\boxed{\text{FV}}$	FV= 15,737.70*

TI-84:

Change to 2 fixed decimal places.	$\boxed{\text{MODE}}$ ↓ → → → $\boxed{\text{ENTER}}$
Select Finance Application.	Press $\boxed{\text{APPS}}$ 1:Finance $\boxed{\text{ENTER}}$
Select TVM Solver.	1:TVM Solver $\boxed{\text{ENTER}}$

Use the arrow keys to move the cursor to appropriate variables and enter amounts. Enter 0 for unknowns.

Press 120 $\boxed{\text{ENTER}}$ to store 120 months to N. Press 5.25 $\boxed{\text{ENTER}}$ to store 5.25% per year to I%. Press 0 $\boxed{\text{ENTER}}$ to leave PV unassigned. Press $\boxed{(-)}$ 100 $\boxed{\text{ENTER}}$ to store \$100 to PMT. Press 0 $\boxed{\text{ENTER}}$ to leave FV unassigned. Press 12 $\boxed{\text{ENTER}}$ to store 12 payments/periods per year to P/Y and C/Y (number of compounding periods per year) will automatically change to 12 also. PMT: END should be highlighted.

Use the up arrow to move the cursor up to FV. Press $\boxed{\text{ALPHA}}$ [SOLVE] to solve for future value.

Your calculator screen should look like the one below with a ■ beside FV=15737.70 showing the calculated future value.

```
N=        120.00
I%=         5.25
PV=         0.00
PMT=     -100.00
■FV=    15737.70
P/Y=       12.00
C/Y=       12.00
PMT:END BEGIN
```

Casio fx-CG10

Select **Financial** mode from the main menu. This will display the financial screen. Press $\boxed{\text{SHIFT}}$ $\boxed{\text{MENU}}$ to set up items.

Payment	: END
Date Mode	: 365
Periods/Yr	: Annual
Graph Color	: Blue
Background	: None
Label	: On
Display	: Fix (set to 2)

Press [EXIT] to leave the set-up menu. Press [F2] to select compound interest. Press 120 [EXE] to store 120 months (total number of interest payments) to n. Press 5.25 [EXE] to store 5.25% to I%. Press the down cursor to leave PV unassigned. Press [−] 100 [EXE] to store $100 in PMT. Press the down cursor to leave PMT unassigned. Press the down cursor to leave FV unassigned. Press 12 [EXE] to store 12 payments/periods per year to P/Y and C/Y will automatically change to 12 also. Press [F5] to display future value.

The future value, $15,737.70, is the same result that was found in Example 12.

For an annuity due on the TI BA II Plus, change the setting by pressing [2nd] [BGN] [2nd] [SET]. Then return to calculator mode by pressing [2nd] [QUIT]. On the TI-84, at the bottom of the TMV Solver screen, change PMT to BEGIN.

EXAMPLE 15

Rework Example 13 using a TI BA II Plus, a TI-84 calculator, and a Casio fx-CG10.

BA II Plus:

[2ND] [FORMAT] 2 [ENTER]
[2ND] [RESET] [ENTER] 60 [N]
[.] 47916667 [I/Y]
50 [+/−] [PMT]
[2ND] [BGN] [2ND] [SET]
[2ND] [QUIT]
CPT FV ⇒ 3,482.79

TI-84:

[APPS] [ENTER] [ENTER]
Use the arrows keys to move the cursor to appropriate variables and enter amounts. Enter 0 for unknowns.
60 [ENTER] 5.75 [ENTER]
0 [ENTER] [(−)] 50 [ENTER]
0 [ENTER]
12 [ENTER] [↓] highlight
BEGIN [ENTER] [↑][↑][↑]
[ALPHA] [SOLVE]
⇒ 3,482.79

Casio fx-CG10

Select **Financial** Mode from the main menu. Use [SHIFT] [MENU] to set Payment to **Begin** and Display to Fix2 for two decimal places. Then press [F2] to select Compound Interest. Use the arrow keys to move the cursor to appropriate variables and enter amounts.
60 [EXE] 5.75 [EXE] 0 [EXE] [(−)] 50 [EXE] 0 [EXE] 12 [EXE] [F5]

The future value, $3,482.79, is the same result that was found in Example 13.

STOP AND CHECK

See Example 12.

1. Use the formula to find the future value of an ordinary annuity of $250 paid monthly at 4.62% for 25 years.

2. Use the formula to find the future value of an ordinary annuity of $30 paid weekly at 5.2% for 15 years.

See Example 13.

3. Use the formula to find the future value of an annuity due of $200 monthly at 1.35% for 14 years.

4. Marquita is creating an annuity due of $25 every two weeks at 6% for 35 years. Find the future value of her annuity due.

5. Doris Pallandino contributes $3,500 each year to a Roth IRA that earns 3% per year. Use a calculator to determine how much she will have at the end of 35 years. *See Example 14.*

6. Ernie Prather contributes $400 per month to a 401(k) retirement plan at work. The plan averages 5% per year. Use a calculator to find the amount he can expect to have in 10 years. *See Example 15.*

SKILL BUILDERS

Use Table 14-1 to find the future value and total interest of the annuities. See Examples 3, 4, 6, and 7.

	Annuity type	Periodic payment	Annual interest rate	Payment paid	Years
1.	Ordinary annuity	$1,000	5%	Annually	8
2.	Ordinary annuity	$ 500	4%	Semiannually	4
3.	Ordinary annuity	$2,000	8%	Quarterly	3
4.	Annuity due	$3,000	6%	Semiannually	3
5.	Annuity due	$5,000	3%	Annually	4
6.	Annuity due	$ 800	7%	Annually	5

7. Manually find the future value of an ordinary annuity of $300 paid annually at 5% for three years. Verify your result by using the table method. *See Examples 1 and 3.*

8. Manually find the future value of an annuity due of $500 paid semiannually for two years at 6% annual interest compounded semiannually. Verify your result by using the table method. *See Examples 5 and 6.*

APPLICATIONS

Use the simple interest formula method for Exercises 9–12. See Examples 1 and 2.

9. Find the future value of an ordinary annuity of $3,000 annually after two years at 3.8% annual interest. Find the total interest earned.

10. Len and Sharron Smith are saving money for their daughter Heather to attend college. They set aside an ordinary annuity of $4,000 annually for ten years at 7% annual interest. How much will Heather have for college after two years? Find the total interest earned.

11. Harry Taylor plans to pay an ordinary annuity of $5,000 annually for ten years. The annual rate of interest is 3.8%. How much will Harry have at the end of three years? How much interest will he earn on the investment after three years?

12. Scott Martin is planning to establish a retirement annuity. He is committed to an ordinary annuity of $3,000 annually at 3.6% annual interest. How much will Scott have accumulated after three years? How much interest will he earn?

Use Table 14-1 or the appropriate formula or calculator application for Exercises 13–17. See Examples 3, 12, and 14.

13. Find the future value of an ordinary annuity of $6,500 semiannually for seven years at 6% annual interest compounded semiannually. How much was invested? How much interest was earned?

14. Pat Lechleiter pays an ordinary annuity of $2,500 quarterly at 8% annual interest compounded quarterly to establish supplemental income for retirement. How much will Pat have available at the end of five years?

See Examples 5 and 7.

15. Latanya Brown established an ordinary annuity of $1,000 annually at 7% annual interest. What is the future value of the annuity after 15 years? How much of her own money will Latanya have invested during this time period? By how much will her investment have grown?

16. You invest in an ordinary annuity of $500 annually at 8% annual interest. Find the future value of the annuity at the end of ten years. How much have you invested? How much interest has your annuity earned?

17. You invest in an ordinary annuity of $2,000 annually at 8% annual interest. What is the future value of the annuity at the end of five years? How much have you invested? How much interest has your annuity earned?

18. Make a chart comparing your results for Exercises 16 and 17. Use these headings: Years, Total Investment, Total Interest. What general conclusion might you draw about effective investment strategy?

19. Find the future value of an annuity due of $12,000 annually for three years at 3% annual interest. How much was invested? How much interest was earned?

20. Bernard McGhee has decided to establish an annuity due of $2,500 annually for 15 years at 7.2% annual interest. How much is the annuity due worth after two years? How much was invested? How much interest was earned?

21. Find the future value of an annuity due of $7,800 annually for two years at 8.1% annual interest. Find the total amount invested. Find the interest.

22. Find the future value of an annuity due of $400 annually for two years at 6.8% annual interest compounded annually.

Use Table 14-1 or the appropriate formula or calculator application for Exercises 23–26. See Examples 6, 13, and 15.

23. Find the future value of a quarterly annuity due of $4,400 for three years at 8% annual interest compounded quarterly. How much was invested? How much interest was earned?

24. Find the future value of an annuity due of $750 semiannually for four years at 8% annual interest compounded semiannually. What is the total investment? What is the interest?

25. Which annuity earns more interest: an annuity due of $300 quarterly for one year at 8% annual interest compounded quarterly, or an annuity due of $600 semiannually for one year at 8% annual interest compounded semiannually?

26. You have carefully examined your budget and determined that you can manage to set aside $250 per year. So you set up an annuity due of $250 annually at 7% annual interest. How much will you have contributed after 20 years? What is the future value of your annuity after 20 years? How much interest will you earn?

27. June Watson is contributing $3,000 each year to a Roth IRA. The IRA earns 3.2% per year. How much will she have at the end of 25 years? *See Examples 9 and 15.*

28. Marvin Murphy contributes $400 per month to a payroll deduction 401(k) at work. His employer matches his contribution up to $200 per month. If the fund averages 5.4% per year, how much will be in the account in 10 years? *See Examples 10 and 14.*

29. Dorothy Strawn has plans to invest $30,000 over five years in an annuity at 6%, and she wants the best plan. Annuity 1 is a monthly ordinary annuity of $500 compounded monthly. Annuity 2 is a semiannual ordinary annuity of $3,000 compounded semiannually. Annuity 3 is a quarterly annuity due of $1,500 compounded quarterly. Annuity 4 is a yearly annuity due of $6,000 compounded annually. What annuity yields the greatest future value? *See Example 8.*

30. Robert Shands contributes $200 by monthly payroll deduction to a 401(k) plan at work. If he averages 3% annual interest compounded monthly, how much more should he have in 7 years if his employer contributes $50 per month to his 401(k)? *See Example 11.*

LEARNING OUTCOMES

1 Find the sinking fund payment using a $1.00 sinking fund payment table.
2 Find the present value of an ordinary annuity using a $1.00 ordinary annuity present value table.
3 Find the sinking fund payment or the present value of an annuity using a formula or a calculator application.

Businesses and individuals often use sinking funds to accumulate a desired amount of money by the end of a certain period of time to pay off a financial obligation, to use for a retirement or college fund, or to reach a specific goal such as retiring a bond issue or paying for equipment replacement and modernization. Essentially, a **sinking fund** is payment into an ordinary annuity to yield a desired future value. That is, the future value is known and the payment amount is unknown.

Sinking fund: payment into an ordinary annuity to yield a desired future value.

	Payment	**Future Value**
Sinking Fund	Unknown	Known
Accumulation Phase of an Annuity	Known	Unknown

1 Find the sinking fund payment using a $1.00 sinking fund payment table.

A sinking fund payment is made at the *end* of each period, so a sinking fund payment is an ordinary annuity payment. These payments, along with the interest, accumulate over a period of time to provide the desired future value.

To calculate the *payment* required to yield a desired future value, use Table 14-2. The procedure for locating a value in Table 14-2 is similar to the procedure used for Table 14-1.

TABLE 14-2
$1.00 Sinking Fund Payments

				Rate per period			
Periods	**1%**	**2%**	**3%**	**4%**	**6%**	**8%**	**12%**
1	1.0000000	1.0000000	1.0000000	1.0000000	1.0000000	1.0000000	1.0000000
2	0.4975124	0.4950495	0.4926108	0.4901961	0.4854369	0.4807692	0.4716981
3	0.3300221	0.3267547	0.3235304	0.3203485	0.3141098	0.3080335	0.2963490
4	0.2462811	0.2426238	0.2390270	0.2354900	0.2285915	0.2219208	0.2092344
5	0.1960398	0.1921584	0.1883546	0.1846271	0.1773964	0.1704565	0.1574097
6	0.1625484	0.1585258	0.1545975	0.1507619	0.1433626	0.1363154	0.1232257
7	0.1386283	0.1345120	0.1305064	0.1266096	0.1191350	0.1120724	0.0991177
8	0.1206903	0.1165098	0.1124564	0.1085278	0.1010359	0.0940148	0.0813028
9	0.1067404	0.1025154	0.0984339	0.0944930	0.0870222	0.0800797	0.0676789
10	0.0955821	0.0913265	0.0872305	0.0832909	0.0758680	0.0690295	0.0569842
11	0.0864541	0.0821779	0.0780774	0.0741490	0.0667929	0.0600763	0.0484154
12	0.0788488	0.0745596	0.0704621	0.0665522	0.0592770	0.0526950	0.0414368
13	0.0724148	0.0681184	0.0670295	0.0601437	0.0529601	0.0465218	0.0356772
14	0.0669012	0.0626020	0.0585263	0.0546690	0.0475849	0.0412969	0.0308712
15	0.0621238	0.0578255	0.0537666	0.0499411	0.0429628	0.0368295	0.0268242
16	0.0579446	0.0536501	0.0496108	0.0458200	0.0389521	0.0329769	0.0233900
17	0.0542581	0.0499698	0.0459525	0.0421985	0.0354448	0.0296294	0.0204567
18	0.0509820	0.0467021	0.0427087	0.0389933	0.0323565	0.0267021	0.0179373
19	0.0480518	0.0437818	0.0398139	0.0361386	0.0296209	0.0241276	0.0157630
20	0.0454153	0.0411567	0.0372157	0.0335818	0.0271846	0.0218522	0.0138788
25	0.0354068	0.0312204	0.0274279	0.0240120	0.0182267	0.0136788	0.0075000
30	0.0287481	0.0246499	0.0210193	0.0178301	0.0126489	0.0088274	0.0041437
40	0.0204556	0.0165558	0.0132624	0.0105235	0.0064615	0.0038602	0.0013036
50	0.0155127	0.0118232	0.0088655	0.0065502	0.0034443	0.0017429	0.0004167

Table values show the sinking fund payment earning a given rate for a given number of periods so that the accumulated amount at the end of the time will be $1.00. The formula for generating the table values is $TV = \dfrac{R}{(1 + R)^N - 1}$, where *TV* is the table value, *R* is the rate per period, and *N* is the number of periods or payments.

HOW TO Find the sinking fund payment using a $1.00 sinking fund payment table

Use Table 14-2:

1. Select the periods row corresponding to the number of interest periods.
2. Select the rate-per-period column corresponding to the period interest rate.
3. Locate the value in the cell where the periods row intersects the rate-per-period column.
4. Multiply the table value from step 3 by the desired future value.

$$\text{Sinking fund payment} = \text{future value} \times \text{Table 14-2 value}$$

EXAMPLE 1 Use Table 14-2 to find the annual sinking fund payment required to accumulate $140,000 in 12 years at 6% annual interest.

$$12 \text{ years} \times 1 \text{ period per year} = 12 \text{ periods}$$

$$\frac{6\% \text{ annual interest rate}}{1 \text{ period per year}} = 6\% \text{ period interest rate}$$

The Table 14-2 value for 12 periods at 6% is 0.0592770

$$
\begin{aligned}
\text{Sinking fund payment (PMT)} &= \text{desired future value} \times \text{table factor}\\
&= \$140,000(0.0592770)\\
&= \$8,298.78
\end{aligned}
$$

A sinking fund payment of $8,298.78 is required at the end of each year for 12 years at 6% to yield the desired $140,000.

EXAMPLE 2 Find the total interest earned on the sinking fund in the previous example.

$FV = \$140,000$ Number of payments $= 12$

$$
\begin{aligned}
\text{Total investment} &= \text{amount of payment} \times 12\\
&= \$8,298.78(12)\\
&= \$99,585.36
\end{aligned}
$$

$$
\begin{aligned}
\text{Total interest earned} &= \$140,000 - \$99,585.36\\
&= \mathbf{\$40,414.64}
\end{aligned}
$$

STOP AND CHECK

See Example 1.

1. Use Table 14-2 to find the annual sinking fund payment needed to accumulate $12,000 in six years at 4% annual interest.

2. Use Table 14-2 to find the quarterly sinking fund payment needed to accumulate $25,000 in ten years at 4% annual interest compounded quarterly.

See Example 2.

3. What is the total amount paid and the interest on the sinking fund in Exercise 1?

4. What is the amount paid and the interest on the sinking fund in Exercise 2?

2 Find the present value of an ordinary annuity using a $1.00 ordinary annuity present value table.

In the liquidation or payout phase of an annuity, a common option is for periodic payments to be made to the annuitant or beneficiary for a certain period of time. The future value of the *accumulation phase* of the annuity becomes the present value of the *liquidated or payout phase*

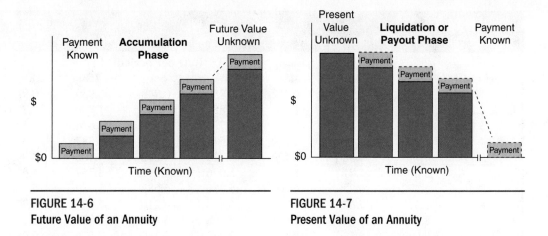

FIGURE 14-6
Future Value of an Annuity

FIGURE 14-7
Present Value of an Annuity

of the annuity. Figure 14-6 shows the accumulation phase or future value growth of an annuity. The **present value of an annuity** is the amount needed in a fund to pay out a specific periodic payment over a specified period of time during the liquidation or payout phase. The balance that is in the fund continues to earn interest while payouts are being made, but the balance is steadily declining. At the end of the specified time of the liquidation phase, the balance will be zero. See Figure 14-7.

Present value of an annuity: the amount needed in a fund so that the fund can pay out a specified regular payment for a specified amount of time.

HOW TO Find the present value of an annuity using a table value

Use Table 14-3:

1. Locate the table value for the given number of payout periods and the given rate per period.
2. Multiply the table value times the periodic annuity payment.

$$\text{Present value of annuity} = \text{periodic annuity payment} \times \text{table value}$$

DID YOU KNOW?

When you set your calculator to *display* two decimal places as you did in finding annuities, the calculator retains calculated values that have as many decimal places as the capacity of the calculator, so the internal calculations are often more accurate than calculations made with table values rounded to as few as three decimal places. For example, if you use a calculator (the **BA II Plus, TI-84** or **Casio Fx–CG 10**) to find the present value of the annuity in Example 3, the present value would be $33,888.22—which is $0.22 more than the result using the table value.

EXAMPLE 3   Use Table 14-3 to find the present value of an ordinary annuity in the payout phase with semiannual payments of $3,000 for seven years at 6% annual interest compounded semiannually.

$$7 \text{ years} \times 2 \text{ periods per year} = 14 \text{ periods}$$

$$\frac{6\% \text{ annual interest}}{2 \text{ periods per year}} = 3\% \text{ period interest rate}$$

The Table 14-3 value for 14 periods at 3% is 11.296.

$$\begin{aligned}
\text{Present value of annuity} &= \text{annuity payment} \times \text{table factor} \\
&= \$3,000(11.296) \\
&= \$33,888
\end{aligned}$$

A fund of $33,888 is needed now at 6% interest compounded semiannually to receive an annuity payment of $3,000 twice a year for seven years.

TABLE 14-3
Present Value of a $1.00 Ordinary Annuity

| | | | | | Rate per period | | | | | |
Periods	2%	3%	4%	5%	6%	7%	8%	9%	10%	12%
1	0.980	0.971	0.962	0.952	0.943	0.935	0.926	0.917	0.909	0.893
2	1.942	1.913	1.886	1.859	1.833	1.808	1.783	1.759	1.736	1.690
3	2.884	2.829	2.775	2.723	2.673	2.624	2.577	2.531	2.487	2.402
4	3.808	3.717	3.630	3.546	3.465	3.387	3.312	3.240	3.170	3.037
5	4.713	4.580	4.452	4.329	4.212	4.100	3.993	3.890	3.791	3.605
6	5.601	5.417	5.242	5.076	4.917	4.767	4.623	4.486	4.355	4.111
7	6.472	6.230	6.002	5.786	5.582	5.389	5.206	5.033	4.868	4.564
8	7.325	7.020	6.733	6.463	6.210	5.971	5.747	5.535	5.335	4.968
9	8.162	7.786	7.435	7.108	6.802	6.515	6.247	5.995	5.759	5.328
10	8.983	8.530	8.111	7.722	7.360	7.024	6.710	6.418	6.145	5.650
11	9.787	9.253	8.760	8.306	7.887	7.499	7.139	6.805	6.495	5.938
12	10.575	9.954	9.385	8.863	8.384	7.943	7.536	7.161	6.814	6.194
13	11.348	10.635	9.986	9.394	8.853	8.358	7.904	7.487	7.103	6.424
14	12.106	11.296	10.563	9.899	9.295	8.745	8.244	7.786	7.367	6.628
15	12.849	11.938	11.118	10.380	9.712	9.108	8.559	8.061	7.606	6.811
16	13.578	12.561	11.652	10.838	10.106	9.447	8.851	8.313	7.824	6.974
17	14.292	13.166	12.166	11.274	10.477	9.763	9.122	8.544	8.022	7.120
18	14.992	13.754	12.659	11.690	10.828	10.059	9.372	8.756	8.201	7.250
19	15.678	14.324	13.134	12.085	11.158	10.336	9.604	8.950	8.365	7.366
20	16.351	14.877	13.590	12.462	11.470	10.594	9.818	9.129	8.514	7.469
25	19.523	17.413	15.622	14.094	12.783	11.654	10.675	9.823	9.077	7.843
30	22.396	19.600	17.292	15.372	13.765	12.409	11.258	10.274	9.427	8.055
40	27.355	23.115	19.793	17.159	15.046	13.332	11.925	10.757	9.779	8.244
50	31.424	25.730	21.482	18.256	15.762	13.801	12.233	10.962	9.915	8.304

Table values show the present value of a $1.00 ordinary annuity, or the lump sum amount that, invested now, yields the same compounded amount as an annuity of $1.00 at a given rate per period for a given number of periods. The formula for generating the table values is $TV = \dfrac{(1 + R)^N - 1}{R(1 + R)^N}$, where TV is the table value, R is the rate per period, and N is the number of periods.

STOP AND CHECK

See Example 3.

1. Use Table 14-3 to find the present value of an ordinary annuity with an annual payout of $5,000 for five years at 4% interest compounded annually.

2. What is the present value of an ordinary annuity with an annual payout of $20,000 at 7% annual interest for 20 years?

3. What lump sum must be set aside today at 8% annual interest compounded quarterly to provide quarterly payments of $7,000 to Demetrius Ball for the next ten years?

4. Tim Warren is setting up an ordinary annuity and wants to receive $10,000 semiannually for the next 20 years. How much should he set aside at 6% annual interest compounded semiannually?

3 **Find the sinking fund payment or the present value of an annuity using a formula or a calculator application.**

As with future value, tables do not always have the values that you need to find a sinking fund payment or a present value of an annuity. A formula allows you the flexibility of using any interest rate or any number of periods.

HOW TO
Find the sinking fund payment or present value of an ordinary annuity using a formula

1. Identify the period rate R as a decimal equivalent, the number of periods N, and the future value FV of the annuity.
2. Substitute the values from step 1 in the appropriate formula.

$$PMT_{\text{ordinary annuity}} = FV\left(\frac{R}{(1 + R)^N - 1}\right)$$

$$PV_{\text{ordinary annuity}} = PMT\left(\frac{(1 + R)^N - 1}{R(1 + R)^N}\right)$$

3. Evaluate the formula.

EXAMPLE 4

Debbie Bennett wants to have $100,000 in a retirement fund to supplement her retirement. She plans to work for 20 more years and has found an annuity fund that earns 5.5% annual interest compounded monthly. How much does she need to contribute to the fund each month to reach her goal?

$R = \dfrac{5.5\%}{12} = \dfrac{0.055}{12} = 0.0045833333$ Periodic interest rate

$N = 20(12) = 240$ Number of payments

$FV = \$100,000$

Formula:

$$PMT_{\text{ordinary annuity}} = \$100,000\left(\frac{0.0045833333}{(1 + 0.0045833333)^{240} - 1}\right)$$

$100000 \boxed{\times} .0045833333 \boxed{\div} \boxed{(} \boxed{(} 1.0045833333 \boxed{\wedge} 240 \boxed{-} 1 \boxed{)} \boxed{)} \boxed{=} \Rightarrow$

$PMT = 229.5539756$ (round to nearest cent)

BA II Plus:

$\boxed{\text{2ND}}$ [FORMAT] 2 $\boxed{\text{ENTER}}$
$\boxed{\text{2ND}}$ [RESET] $\boxed{\text{ENTER}}$
240 $\boxed{\text{N}}$
$\boxed{.}$ 45833333 $\boxed{\text{I/Y}}$
100000 $\boxed{\text{FV}}$
$\boxed{\text{CPT}}$ $\boxed{\text{PMT}}$ $\Rightarrow -229.55$

TI-84:

$\boxed{\text{APPS}}$ $\boxed{\text{ENTER}}$ $\boxed{\text{ENTER}}$
240 $\boxed{\text{ENTER}}$ 5.5 $\boxed{\text{ENTER}}$
0 $\boxed{\text{ENTER}}$ 0 $\boxed{\text{ENTER}}$
100000 $\boxed{\text{ENTER}}$
12 $\boxed{\text{ENTER}}$ highlight END $\boxed{\text{ENTER}}$ $\boxed{\uparrow}\boxed{\uparrow}\boxed{\uparrow}\boxed{\uparrow}$
$\boxed{\text{ALPHA}}$ [SOLVE] $\Rightarrow -229.55$

Casio fx-CG10:

Select **Financial** Mode from the main menu. Use $\boxed{\text{SHIFT}}$ $\boxed{\text{MENU}}$ to set Payment to **End** and Display to **Fix2** for two decimal places. Then press $\boxed{\text{F2}}$ to select **Compound Interest**. Use the arrow keys to move the cursor to appropriate variables and enter amounts.

240 $\boxed{\text{EXE}}$ 5.5 $\boxed{\text{EXE}}$ 0 $\boxed{\text{EXE}}$ 0 $\boxed{\text{EXE}}$ 100000 $\boxed{\text{EXE}}$ 12 $\boxed{\text{EXE}}$ $\boxed{\text{F4}}$ $\Rightarrow -229.55$

The payment that Debbie should make into the sinking fund each month is $229.55.

EXAMPLE 5

At retirement Debbie Bennett will begin drawing a payment each month from her retirement fund. How much does she need in a fund that pays 5.5% annual interest compounded monthly to receive a $700 per month payment for 20 years?

$R = \dfrac{5.5\%}{12} = \dfrac{0.055}{12} = 0.0045833333$ Periodic interest rate

$N = 20(12) = 240$ Number of payments

$PMT = \$700$

Formula:

$$PV_{\text{ordinary annuity}} = \$700\left(\frac{(1 + 0.0045833333)^{240} - 1}{0.0045833333(1 + 0.0045833333)^{240}}\right)$$

$700 \boxed{(} 1.0045833333 \boxed{\wedge} 240 \boxed{-} 1 \boxed{)} \boxed{\div}$
$\boxed{(} .0045833333 \boxed{\times} 1.0045833333 \boxed{\wedge} 240 \boxed{)} \boxed{=} \Rightarrow$

$PV = 101760.8545$ Round to nearest cent.

BA II Plus:

2ND [FORMAT] 2 ENTER
2ND [RESET] ENTER
240 N
. 45833333 I/Y
700 +/− PMT
CPT PV ⇒ 101,760.85

TI-84:

APPS ENTER ENTER
240 ENTER 5.5 ENTER
0 ENTER (−) 700 ENTER
0 ENTER 12 ENTER ENTER
↓ highlight END ENTER
↑↑↑↑↑ ALPHA [SOLVE] ⇒ 101760.85

Casio fx-CG10:

Select **Financial** Mode from the main menu. Use SHIFT MENU to set Payment to **End** and Display to **Fix2** for two decimal places. Then press F2 to select **Compound Interest**. Use the arrow keys to move the cursor to appropriate variables and enter amounts.

240 EXE 5.5 EXE 0 EXE (−) 700 EXE 0 EXE 12 EXE F3 ⇒ 101760.85

Debbie needs to have $101,760.85 in the fund to receive an annuity payment of $700 each month for 20 years.

STOP AND CHECK

1. Shameka plans to have $350,000 in a retirement fund at her retirement. She plans to work for 26 years and has found a sinking fund that earns 4.85% annual interest compounded monthly. How much does she need to contribute to the fund each month to reach her goal? *See Example 4.*

2. At retirement Mekisha will begin drawing a payment each month from her retirement fund. Use the formula to determine the amount she needs in a fund that pays 5.25% interest to receive a $2,000 per month payment for 25 years. *See Example 5.*

14-2 SECTION EXERCISES

SKILL BUILDERS

See Example 1.

1. What semiannual sinking fund payment would be required to yield $48,000 nine years from now? The annual interest rate is 6% compounded semiannually.

2. The Bamboo Furniture Company manufactures rattan patio furniture. It has just purchased a machine for $13,500 to cut and glue the pieces of wood. The machine is expected to last five years. If the company establishes a sinking fund to replace this machine, what annual payments must be made if the annual interest rate is 8%?

See Examples 1 and 4.

3. Tristin and Kim Denley are establishing a college fund for their 1-year-old daughter, Chloe. They want to save enough now to pay college tuition at the time she enters college (17 years from now). If her tuition is projected to be $35,000 for a two-year degree, what annual sinking fund payment should they establish if the annual interest is 8%? Use Table 14-2, the formula, or a calculator application.

4. Kathy and Patrick Mowers have a 12-year-old daughter and are now in a financial position to begin saving for her college education. What annual sinking fund payment should they make to have her entire college expenses paid at the time she enters college six years from now? Her college expenses are projected to be $30,000 and the annual interest rate is 6%. Use Table 14-2, the formula, or a calculator application.

5. Matthew Bennett recognizes the value of saving part of his income. He has set a goal to have $25,000 in cash available for emergencies. How much should he invest semiannually to have $25,000 in ten years if the sinking fund he has selected pays 8% annually, compounded semiannually?

6. Stein and Company has established a sinking fund to retire a bond issue of $500,000, which is due in ten years. How much is the quarterly sinking fund payment if the account pays 8% annual interest compounded quarterly?

See Example 2.

7. Find the total interest earned on the sinking fund in Exercise 5.

See Example 2.

8. Find the total interest earned on the sinking fund in Exercise 6.

9. Find the present value of an ordinary annuity with annual payments of $680 at 9% annual interest for 25 years?

10. Erin Calipari plans to have a stream of $2,500 payments each year for two years at 8% annual interest. How much should she set aside today?

11. Emily Bennett is setting up an annuity for a memorial scholarship. What lump sum does she need to set aside today at 7% annual interest to have the scholarship pay $3,000 annually for 10 years?

12. Kristin Bennett, a nationally recognized philanthropist, set up an ordinary annuity of $1,600 for ten years at 9% annual interest. How much does Bennett have to deposit today to pay the stream of annual payments?

See Examples 2 and 5.

13. Ken and Debbie Bennett have agreed to pay for their granddaughter's college education and need to know how much to set aside so annual payments of $15,000 can be made for five years at 3% annual interest. Use Table 14-2, the formula, or a calculator application.

14. Janice and Terry Van Dyke have decided to establish a quarterly ordinary annuity of $3,000 for the next ten years at 8% annual interest compounded quarterly. How much should they invest in a lump sum now to provide the stream of payments? Use Table 14-2, the formula, or a calculator application.

Learning Outcomes

Section 14-1

1 Find the future value of an ordinary annuity using the simple interest formula method. (p. 498)

What to Remember with Examples

1. Find the first end-of-period principal.

$$\text{First end-of-period principal} = \text{annuity payment}$$

2. For each remaining period in turn, find the next end-of-period principal:
   (a) Multiply the previous end-of-period principal by the sum of 1 and the decimal equivalent of the period interest rate.
   (b) Add the product from step 2a and the annuity payment.

$$\text{End-of-period principal} = \text{previous end-of-period principal} \times$$
$$(1 + \text{period interest rate}) + \text{annuity payment}$$

3. Identify the last end-of-period principal as the future value.

$$\text{Future value} = \text{last end-of-period principal}$$

Find the future value of an annual ordinary annuity of $2,000 for two years at 4% annual interest.

$$\text{End-of-year 1} = \$2,000$$
$$\text{End-of-year 2} = \$2,000(1.04) + \$2,000$$
$$= \$2,080 + \$2,000$$
$$= \$4,080$$

The future value is $4,080.

Find the future value of a semiannual ordinary annuity of $300 for one year at 5% annual interest, compounded semiannually.

$$\frac{5\% \text{ annual interest rate}}{2 \text{ periods per year}} = 2.5\% = 0.025 \text{ period interest rate}$$
$$\text{End-of-period 1} = \$300$$
$$\text{End-of-period 2} = \$300(1.025) + \$300$$
$$= \$307.50 + \$300$$
$$= \$607.50$$

The future value is $607.50.

Find the total interest earned on an annuity:

1. Find the total amount invested:

$$\text{Total invested} = \text{payment amount} \times \text{number of payments}$$

2. Find the total interest:

$$\text{Total interest} = \text{future value of annuity} - \text{total invested}$$

Find the total interest earned on the semiannual ordinary annuity in the previous example.

Total invested = $300(2)	Payment = $300
= $600	Number of payments = 2
Total interest = $607.50 − $600	Future value = $607.50
= $7.50	

2 Find the future value of an ordinary annuity with periodic payments using a $1.00 ordinary annuity future value table. (p. 500)

Using Table 14-1:

1. Select the periods row corresponding to the number of interest periods.
2. Select the rate-per-period column corresponding to the period interest rate.
3. Locate the value in the cell where the periods row intersects the rate-per-period column.
4. Multiply the annuity payment by the table value from step 3.

$$\text{Future value} = \text{annuity payment} \times \text{table value}$$

Find the future value of an ordinary annuity of $5,000 semiannually for four years at 4% annual interest compounded semiannually.

$$4 \text{ years} \times 2 \text{ periods per year} = 8 \text{ periods}$$

$$\frac{4\% \text{ annual interest rate}}{2 \text{ periods per year}} = 2\% \text{ period interest rate}$$

The Table 14-1 value for eight periods at 2% is 8.583.

$$\text{Future value} = \$5,000(8.583)$$
$$= \$42,915$$

The future value is $42,915.

3 Find the future value of an annuity due with periodic payments using the simple interest formula method. (p. 503)

1. Find the first end-of-period principal: Multiply the annuity payment by the sum of 1 and the decimal equivalent of the period interest rate.

$$\text{First end-of-period principal} = \text{annuity payment} \times (1 + \text{period interest rate})$$

2. For each remaining period in turn, find the next end-of-period principal:
   (a) Add the previous end-of-period principal and the annuity payment.
   (b) Multiply the sum from step 2a by the sum of 1 and the period interest rate.

$$\text{End-of-period principal} = (\text{previous end-of-period principal} + \text{annuity payment}) \times (1 + \text{period interest rate})$$

3. Identify the last end-of-period principal as the future value.

$$\text{Future value} = \text{last end-of-period principal}$$

Find the future value of an annual annuity due of $3,000 for two years at 5% annual interest.

$$\text{End-of-year 1} = \$3,000(1.05)$$
$$= \$3,150$$
$$\text{End-of-year 2} = (\$3,150 + \$3,000)(1.05)$$
$$= \$6,150(1.05)$$
$$= \$6,457.50$$

The future value is $6,457.50.

Find the future value and the total interest earned of a semiannual annuity due of $400 for one year at 4% annual interest compounded semiannually.

$$\frac{4\% \text{ annual interest rate}}{2 \text{ periods per year}} = 2\% = 0.02 \text{ period interest rate in decimal form}$$

$$\text{End-of-period 1} = \$400(1.02)$$
$$= \$408$$
$$\text{End-of-period 2} = (\$408 + \$400)(1.02)$$
$$= (\$808)(1.02)$$
$$= \$824.16$$

The future value is $824.16.

Find the total interest earned on the semiannual annuity:

Total invested = $400(2)	Payment = $400
= $800	Number of payments = 2
Total interest = $824.16 − $800	Future value = $824.16
= $24.16	

The total interest is $24.16.

4 Find the future value of an annuity due with periodic payments using a $1.00 ordinary annuity future value table. (p. 504)

Use Table 14-1:

1. Select the periods row corresponding to the number of interest periods.
2. Select the rate-per-period column corresponding to the period interest rate.
3. Locate the value in the cell where the periods row intersects the rate-per-period column.

4. Multiply the annuity payment by the table value from step 3. This is equivalent to an ordinary annuity.
5. Multiply the product from step 4 by the sum of 1 and the period interest rate to adjust for the extra interest that is earned on an annuity due.

Future value = annuity payment × table value × (1 + period interest rate)

Find the future value of a quarterly annuity due of $1,500 for three years at 8% annual interest compounded quarterly.

$$3 \text{ years} \times 4 \text{ periods per year} = 12 \text{ periods}$$

$$\frac{8\% \text{ annual interest rate}}{4 \text{ periods per year}} = 2\% \text{ period interest rate}$$

The Table 14-1 value for 12 periods at 2% is 13.412.

$$\text{Future value} = \$1,500(13.412)(1.02)$$
$$= \$20,520.36$$

The future value is $20,520.36.

5 Find the future value of a retirement plan annuity. (p. 506)

Various retirement plan options are available from employers or from individual retirement arrangements. Retirement plans are generally annuities. In most instances, individual retirement arrangements are annuity due plans and employment-based plans (through payroll deductions) are ordinary annuities.

Campbell Johnson has the opportunity to contribute to a payroll deduction 401(k) plan at work. She selects an option that averages 3% per year and contributes $200 per month. How much should she have in the account in 5 years?

A payroll-deduction plan is considered to be an ordinary annuity.

$$\text{Number of periods} = 5(12) = 60$$

$$\text{Rate per period} = \frac{3\%}{12} = 0.25\%$$

$$\text{Annuity payment} = \$200$$

$$\text{Table 14-1 value} = 64.647$$

$$\text{Future value of ordinary annuity} = \text{annuity payment} \times \text{table value}$$
$$= \$200(64.647)$$
$$= \$12,929.40$$

Campbell will have $12,929.40 in her 401(k) plan after 5 years.

6 Find the future value of an ordinary annuity or an annuity due using a formula or a calculator application. (p. 508)

Find the future value of an ordinary annuity or an annuity due using the formula.

1. Identify the period rate R as a decimal equivalent, the number of periods N, and the amount of the annuity payment PMT.
2. Substitute the values from step 1 into the appropriate formula.

$$FV_{\text{ordinary annuity}} = PMT\left(\frac{(1 + R)^N - 1}{R}\right)$$

$$FV_{\text{annuity due}} = PMT\left(\frac{(1 + R)^N - 1}{R}\right)(1 + R)$$

3. Evaluate the formula.

Use the formula to find the future value of an ordinary annuity of $50 paid monthly at 5% for 20 years.

$$R = \frac{5\%}{12} = \frac{0.05}{12} = 0.0041666667 \qquad \text{Periodic interest rate}$$

$$N = 20(12) = 240 \qquad\qquad\qquad \text{Number of payments}$$

$$PMT = \$50$$

$$FV_{\text{ordinary annuity}} = \$50\left(\frac{(1 + 0.0041666667)^{240} - 1}{0.0041666667}\right) \qquad \begin{array}{l}\text{Mentally add within innermost} \\ \text{parentheses.}\end{array}$$

$$FV_{\text{ordinary annuity}} = \$50\left(\frac{(1.0041666667)^{240} - 1}{0.0041666667}\right)$$

Calculator sequence:

50 (1.0041666667 ^ 240 − 1) ÷ 0.0041666667 = ⟹ 20551.68352

The future value of the ordinary annuity is $20,551.68.

Refer to Example 14 (p. 509) and Example 15 (p. 510) for using calculator applications on the TI BA II Plus, TI-84 and Casio fx-CG10.

Section 14-2

1 Find the sinking fund payment using a $1.00 sinking fund payment table. (p. 515)

Use Table 14-2:

1. Select the periods row corresponding to the number of interest periods.
2. Select the rate-per-period column corresponding to the period interest rate.
3. Locate the value in the cell where the periods row intersects the rate-per-period column.
4. Multiply the table value from step 3 by the desired future value.

$$\text{Sinking fund payment} = \text{future value} \times \text{table value}$$

Find the quarterly sinking fund payment required to yield $15,000 in five years if interest is 8% compounded quarterly.

$$5 \text{ years} \times 4 \text{ periods per year} = 20 \text{ periods}$$

$$\frac{8\% \text{ annual interest rate}}{4 \text{ periods per year}} = 2\% \text{ period interest rate}$$

The Table 14-2 value for 20 periods at 2% is 0.0411567.

$$\begin{aligned}\text{Sinking fund payment} &= \$15{,}000(0.0411567) \\ &= \$617.35\end{aligned}$$

The required quarterly payment is $617.35.

2 Find the present value of an ordinary annuity using a $1.00 ordinary annuity present value table. (p. 516)

Use Table 14-3:

1. Locate the table value for the given number of payout periods and the given rate per period.
2. Multiply the table value by the periodic annuity payment.

$$\text{Present value of annuity} = \text{periodic annuity payment} \times \text{table value}$$

Find the lump sum required today earning 6% annual interest compounded semiannually to yield the same as a semiannual ordinary annuity payment of $2,500 for 15 years.

$$15 \text{ years} \times 2 \text{ periods per year} = 30 \text{ periods}$$

$$\frac{6\% \text{ annual interest rate}}{2 \text{ periods per year}} = 3\% \text{ period interest rate}$$

The Table 14-3 value for 30 periods at 3% is 19.600.

$$\begin{aligned}\text{Present value} &= \$2{,}500(19.600) \\ &= \$49{,}000\end{aligned}$$

The lump sum required for deposit today is $49,000.

3 Find the sinking fund payment or the present value of an annuity using a formula or a calculator application. (p. 518)

Find the sinking fund payment or present value of an ordinary annuity using a formula:

1. Identify the period rate R as a decimal equivalent, the number of periods N, and the future value FV of the annuity.
2. Substitute the values from step 1 in the appropriate formula.

$$PMT_{\text{ordinary annuity}} = FV\left(\frac{R}{(1 + R)^N - 1}\right)$$

$$PV_{\text{ordinary annuity}} = PMT\left(\frac{(1 + R)^N - 1}{R(1 + R)^N}\right)$$

3. Evaluate the formula.

Camesa plans to have $500,000 in her retirement fund when she retires in 23 years. She is investigating a sinking fund that earns 4.75% annual interest. How much does she need to contribute to the fund each month to reach her goal?

$$R = \frac{4.75\%}{12} = \frac{0.0475}{12} = 0.0039583333 \qquad \text{Periodic interest rate in decimal form}$$

$$N = 23(12) = 276 \qquad\qquad\qquad\qquad\qquad \text{Number of payments}$$

$$FV = \$500,000$$

$$PMT_{\text{ordinary annuity}} = \$500,000\left(\frac{0.0039583333}{(1 + 0.0039583333)^{276} - 1}\right)$$

500000 ⊠ 0.0039583333 ÷ ⎛ 1.0039583333 ^ 276 − 1 ⎞ =

$PMT - 1{,}001.959664$ (round to next cent)

Camesa should make monthly payments of $1,001.96 into the sinking fund.

Refer to Example 4 (p. 519) and Example 5 (p. 519) for using calculator applications on the TI BA II Plus, TI-84 and Casio fx-CG10.

EXERCISES SET A

Use Table 14-1 to complete the following table.

Annuity payment	Annual rate	Annual interest	Years	Type of annuity	Future value of annuity	Total interest
1. $1,400	3%	Compounded annually	5	Ordinary	_____	_____
2. $2,900	8%	Compounded quarterly	10	Ordinary	_____	_____
3. $1,250	6%	Compounded semiannually	$1\frac{1}{2}$	Annuity due	_____	_____
4. $800	5%	Compounded annually	15	Annuity due	_____	_____

Use Table 14-2 to find the sinking fund payment.

	Desired future value	Annual interest rate	Years	Frequency of payments
EXCEL **5.**	$240,000	6%	15	Annually
EXCEL **6.**	$3,000	4%	10	Semiannually
EXCEL **7.**	$50,000	4%	5	Quarterly
EXCEL **8.**	$45,000	3%	8	Annually

Use Table 14-3 to find the amount that needs to be invested today to provide a stream of payments in the annuity liquidation phase.

	Payment amount	Annual interest rate	Years	Frequency of payments
9.	$10,000	4%	20	Annually
10.	$12,000	4%	10	Semiannually
11.	$5,000	8%	4	Quarterly
12.	$1,000	3%	15	Annually

13. Roni Sue deposited $1,500 at the beginning of each year for three years at an annual interest rate of 9%. Find the future value and total interest manually.

Use Table 14-1.

14. Barry Michael plans to deposit $2,000 at the end of every six months for the next five years to save up for a boat. If the interest rate is 6% annually, compounded semiannually, how much money will Barry have in his boat fund after five years?

15. Bob Paris opens a retirement income account paying 5% annually. He deposits $3,000 at the beginning of each year.
  (a) How much will be in the account after ten years?
  (b) When Bob retires at age 65, in 19 years, how much will be in the account?

16. The Shari Joy Corporation decided to set aside $3,200 at the beginning of every six months to provide donation funds for a new Little League baseball field scheduled to be built in 18 months. If money earns 4% annual interest compounded semiannually, how much will be available as a donation for the field?

Use Table 14-2 for Exercises 17 and 18.

17. How much must be set aside at the end of each six months by the Fabulous Toy Company to replace a $155,000 piece of equipment at the end of eight years if the account pays 6% annual interest compounded semiannually?

18. Lausanne Private School System needs to set aside funds for a new computer system. What quarterly sinking fund payment would be required to amount to $45,000, the approximate cost of the system, in $1\frac{1}{2}$ years at 4% annual interest compounded quarterly?

19. Ernie Wroten contributes $1,750 each year to a Roth IRA. The IRA earns 2.67% per year. How much will he have at the end of 15 years? Use the formula or a calculator application.

EXERCISES SET B

Use Table 14-1 to complete the table below.

Annuity payment	Annual rate	Annual interest	Years	Type of annuity	Future value of annuity	Total interest
1. $1,900	8%	Compounded quarterly	3	Ordinary	_____	_____
2. $5,000	5%	Compounded annually	20	Ordinary	_____	_____
3. $2,150	7%	Compounded annually	8	Annuity due	_____	_____
4. $600	6%	Compounded semiannually	5	Annuity due	_____	_____

Use Table 14-2 to find the sinking fund payment.

	Desired future value	Annual interest rate	Years	Frequency of payments	Sinking fund payment
EXCEL 5.	$24,000	6%	10	Semiannually	_____
EXCEL 6.	$45,000	8%	4	Quarterly	_____
EXCEL 7.	$8,000	6%	17	Annually	_____
EXCEL 8.	$10,000	4%	19	Annually	_____

Use Table 14-3 to find the amount that needs to be invested today to receive payments for the specified length of time.

Payment amount	Annual interest rate	Years	Frequency of payments
9. $7,000	2%	30	Annually
10. $20,000	6%	15	Semiannually
11. $10,000	8%	5	Quarterly
12. $6,000	5%	10	Annually

13. Manually find the future value and total interest of an annuity due of $1,100 deposited annually for three years at 5% interest.

14. Sam and Jane Crawford had a baby in 1998. At the end of that year they began putting away $2,000 a year at 10% annual interest for a college fund. How much money will be in the account when the child is 18 years old?

15. A business deposits $4,500 at the end of each quarter in an account that earns 8% annual interest compounded quarterly. What is the value of the annuity in five years?

16. University Trailers is setting aside $800 at the beginning of every quarter to purchase a forklift in 30 months. The annual interest will be 8% compounded quarterly. How much will be available for the purchase?

Use Table 14-2 for Exercises 17 and 20.

17. Tasty Food Manufacturers, Inc., has a bond issue of $1,400,000 due in 30 years. If it wants to establish a sinking fund to meet this obligation, how much must be set aside at the end of each year if the annual interest rate is 6%?

18. Zachary Alexander owns a limousine that will need to be replaced in four years at a cost of $65,000. How much must he put aside each year in a sinking fund at 8% annual interest to purchase the new limousine?

19. Randy Tolar contributes $250 each year to a Roth IRA. The IRA earns 2.45% per year. How much will he have at the end of 10 years? Use the formula or a calculator application.

20. Jennifer Guyton contributes $75 per month to a payroll deduction 401(k) at work. Her employer contributes $25 per month. If the fund averages 4.8% per year, how much will be in the account in 17 years? Use the formula or a computer application.

PRACTICE TEST

CHAPTER 14

1. Manually find the future value of an ordinary annuity of $9,000 per year for two years at 3.25% annual interest.

2. Manually find the future value of an annuity due of $2,700 per year for three years at 4.5% annual interest.

3. What is the future value of an annuity due of $5,645 paid every six months for three years at 6% annual interest compounded semiannually? What is the interest?

4. What is the future value of an ordinary annuity of $300 every three months for four years at 8% annual interest compounded quarterly?

5. What is the sinking fund payment required at the end of each year to accumulate $125,000 in 16 years at 4% annual interest?

6. What is the present value of an ordinary annuity of $985 paid out every six months for eight years at 8% annual interest compounded semiannually?

7. Mike's Sport Shop deposited $3,400 at the end of each year for 12 years at 7% annual interest. How much will Mike have in the account at the end of the time period?

8. How much would the annuity amount to in Exercise 7 if Mike had deposited the money at the beginning of each year instead of at the end of each year?

9. How much must be set aside at the end of each year by the Caroline Cab Company to replace four taxicabs at a cost of $90,000? The current interest rate is 6% annually. The existing cabs will wear out in three years.

10. How much must Johnny Williams invest today to have an amount equivalent to investing $2,800 at the end of every six months for the next 15 years if interest is earned at 8% annually compounded semiannually?

11. Maurice Eftink owns a lawn design business. His lawnmower cost $7,800 and should last for six years. How much must he set aside each year at 6% annual interest to have enough money to buy a new mower?

12. Reed and Sondra Davis want to know how much they must deposit in a retirement savings account today to have payments of $1,500 every six months for 15 years. The retirement account is paying 8% annual interest compounded semiannually.

13. Morris Stocks has a Roth IRA with $2,200 payments each year for 11 years in an account paying 7% annual interest. What is the future value of the annuity due at the end of this period of time?

14. Maura Helba is saving for her college expenses. She sets aside $175 at the beginning of each three months in an account paying 8% annual interest compounded quarterly. How much will Maura have accumulated in the account at the end of four years?

15. What is the present value of a semiannual ordinary annuity of $2,500 for seven years at 6% annual interest compounded semiannually?

16. How much will you need to invest today to have quarterly payments of $800 for ten years? The interest rate is 8% annually, compounded quarterly.

17. Goldie's Department Store has a fleet of delivery trucks that will last for three years of heavy use and then need to be replaced at a cost of $75,000. How much must they set aside every three months in a sinking fund at 8% annual interest, compounded quarterly, to have enough money to replace the trucks?

18. Linda Zuk wants to save $25,000 for a new boat in six years. How much must be put aside in equal payments each year in an account earning 6% annual interest for Linda to be able to purchase the boat?

19. What is the present value of an ordinary annuity of $3,400 at 5% annual interest for seven years?

20. An annual ordinary annuity of $2,500 for five years at 5% annual interest requires what lump-sum payment now?

21. Danny Lawrence Properties, Inc., has a bond issue that will mature in 25 years for $1 million. How much must the company set aside each year in a sinking fund at 8% annual interest to meet this future obligation?

22. How much money needs to be set aside today at 10% annual interest compounded semiannually to pay $500 for five years?

23. You are starting an ordinary annuity of $680 for 25 years at 5% annual interest. What lump-sum amount would have to be set aside today for this annuity?

24. Your parents are retiring and want to set aside a lump sum earning 8% annual interest compounded quarterly to pay out $5,000 quarterly for ten years. What lump sum should your parents set aside today?

25. Ted Davis has set the goal of accumulating $80,000 for his son's college fund, which will be needed 18 years in the future. How much should he deposit each year in a sinking fund that earns 8% annual interest? How much should he deposit each year if he waits until his son starts school (at age six) to begin saving? Compare the two payment amounts.

1. Select three table values from Table 14-1 and verify them using the formula

$$FV = \frac{(1 + R)^N - 1}{R}$$

2. To find the future value of an annuity due, you multiply the future value of an ordinary annuity by the sum of 1 + the period interest rate. Explain why this is the same as adding the simple interest earned on the first payment for the entire length of the annuity.

3. In Example 8 on page 505, we found that the annuity due with semiannual payments had the greater future value. Also, the ordinary annuity with the quarterly payments was more than the ordinary annuity with semiannual payments. Why?

4. How are future value of a lump sum and future value of an annuity similar?

5. How are future value of a lump sum and future value of an annuity different?

6. How are the present value of a lump sum and the periodic payment of a sinking fund similar? How are they different?

7. How are annuities and sinking funds similar? How are they different?

8. Explain the difference in an ordinary annuity and an annuity due.

9. Select three table values from Table 14-3 and verify them using the formula

$$TV = \frac{(1 + R)^N - 1}{R(1 + R)^N}$$

10. Select three table values from Table 14-2 and verify them using the formula

$$TV = \frac{R}{(1 + R)^N - 1}$$

Challenge Problem

Carolyn Ellis is setting up an annuity for her retirement. She can set aside $2,000 at the end of each year for the next 20 years and it will earn 6% annual interest. What lump sum will she need to set aside today at 6% annual interest to have the same retirement fund available 20 years from now? How much more will Carolyn need to invest in periodic payments than she will if she makes a lump sum payment if she intends to accumulate the same retirement balance?

CASE STUDIES

14-1 Annuities for Retirement

Naomi Dexter is 20 years old and attends Southwest Tennessee Community College. Her Business English instructor asked her to write a report detailing her plans for retirement. Naomi decided she would investigate several ways to accumulate $1 million by the time she retires. She also thinks she would like to retire early when she is 50 years old so she can travel around the world. She is considering a long-term certificate of deposit (CD) that pays 3% annually and an annuity that returns 6% annually. She also did a little research and learned that the average long-term return from stock market investments is between 10% and 12%. Now she needs to calculate how much money she will need to deposit each year to accumulate $1 million.

1. If Naomi wants to accumulate $1,000,000 by investing money every year into her CD at 3% for 30 years until retirement, how much does she need to deposit each year?

2. If she decides to invest in an annuity that returns at 6% interest, how much will she need to deposit annually to accumulate the $1,000,000?

3. If Naomi invests in a stock portfolio she hopes her returns for 10 or more years will average 10%–12%. Naomi realizes that the stock market has higher returns because it is a more risky investment than a savings account or a CD. She wants her calculations to be conservative, so she decides to use 8% to calculate possible stock market earnings. How much will she need to invest annually to accumulate $1,000,000 in the stock market?

4. After looking at the results of her calculations, Naomi has decided to aim for $500,000 savings by the time she retires. She expects to have a starting salary after college of $25,000 to $35,000 and she has taken into account all of the living expenses that will come out of her salary. What will Naomi's annual deposits need to be to accumulate $500,000 in an investment at 6%?

5. If Naomi decides that she will invest $3,000 per year in a 6% annuity for the first ten years, $6,000 for the next ten years, and $9,000 for the next ten years, how much will she accumulate? Treat each ten-year period as a separate annuity. After the ten years of an annuity, then it will continue to grow at compound interest for the remaining years of the 30 years.

14-2 Accumulating Money

Joseph reads a lot about people who are success oriented. He loves to learn about courage, risk taking, and as he describes it, "the road less traveled." His local bookstore has a large business section where he has found biographies of entrepreneurs and maverick corporate leaders. He also finds fascinating some of the books he has seen on financial planning and ways to accumulate wealth. One interesting savings plan he read about challenges the reader to put aside one full paycheck at the end of the year as a "holiday present to yourself." Joseph had never thought about saving in that way, and wondered if it would really accumulate much savings.

1. He decided to test the numbers by seeing how much money he would accumulate by a retirement age of 65 if he put one paycheck away at the end of each year. Right now that would mean depositing $1,000 at year-end for the next 35 years. Assuming he makes one yearly deposit of $1,000 at 5% compounded annually, how much interest would he earn?

2. Joseph was surprised at how large the sum would be and then realized that he would be able to put more money away in future years because most likely, his salary would go up. He also thought that he could invest the money over the long term at a higher interest rate, so he redid the calculations with a $1,500 annual year-end deposit at 8% for 35 years. What was his result?

3. Joseph was amazed at how much he could save in this manner and decided to design a detailed savings plan based on projected yearly increases. He realized that he could not start depositing $1,500 now, but that he would be able to deposit more than that in the future. If he were able to deposit $1,000 at the end of each year for the next 5 years at 8% compounded annually, $1,500 at the end of years 6–10 at 8% compounded annually, and $2,000 at the end of years 11–35 at 5% compounded annually, how much would he accumulate at the end of 35 years? Assume that any balances from earlier depositing periods would continue to earn the same rate of annual interest. Use the tables for future value of annuities and compound amount.

4. By how much do the results differ for the accumulated values calculated in Exercises 2 and 3. What accounts for the difference?

5. If Joseph decided that he wanted to have $300,000 accumulated in 30 years by making an annual payment at the end of each year that would earn 12% compounded annually, what would his sinking fund payment be? Use the appropriate table to determine the answer.

14-3 Certified Financial Planner

After completing his Certified Financial Planner designation (CFP), Andre was excited about the prospects of working with small business owners and their employees regarding retirement planning. Andre wanted to show the value of an annuity program as one of the viable investment options in a salary reduction retirement plan. In addition, he wanted to demonstrate the substantial tax benefits that annuities can provide. For instance, qualified annuities (by definition) not only reduce your current taxable salary, they also accumulate earnings on a tax-deferred basis—meaning you don't pay taxes on the earnings until they are withdrawn. Andre was developing a spreadsheet to show the way that annuities could grow using various rates of return.

1. If an individual put the equivalent of $50 per month, or $600 annually into an ordinary annuity, how much money would accumulate in 20 years at 3% compounded annually? How much at 5%?

2. Using the same information from Exercise 1 and assuming a 25% tax bracket, what would be the net effect of investing at 8% for 20 years if taxes on the earnings were paid from the investment fund each year? How would this compare if no taxes had to be paid, such as in a tax-deferred annuity at 8% for 20 years?

3. Jessica, a 25-year-old client of Andre's, wants to retire by age 65 with $1,000,000. How much would she have to invest annually assuming a 6% rate of return?

4. Jessica decides that 40 years is just too long to work, and she thinks that she can do much better than 6%. She decides that she wants to accumulate $1,000,000 by age 55 using a variable annuity earning 12%. How much will she have to invest annually to achieve this goal? Do you think that 12% is a reasonable interest rate to use? Why or why not?

5. Andre suggests that Jessica consider a more balanced approach to spread out her risk by investing $1,000 per year in each of five different subaccounts in a variable annuity. Andre shows Jessica a spreadsheet detailing the following rates of return for each of the five subaccounts for 30 years: 0%; 3%; 5%; 8%; and 12%. Use Table 14-1 to compute the total value for investing $1,000 annually in each of the five subaccounts for 30 years.

6. Andre assures Jessica that investing in the five different subaccounts is a more sensible approach and will still yield a composite rate of return of approximately 7.25%. Do you agree with Andre? How would you check his math to verify the rate of return?

Building Wealth Through Investments

Getting Started Investing

Have you been putting off investing because you don't know where to start? Getting started can be the most difficult step. Let's face it, there is an incredible amount of investment information available, and just beginning your research can be overwhelming. Fortunately, there are tools available that can point you in the right direction. One of the most valuable is the investment pyramid.

The investment pyramid is very similar to the food pyramid. At the base of the pyramid are low-risk investments with lower returns. These investments should make up a foundation percentage of your portfolio. As you move up the pyramid, the risk and possible returns increase.

The basic principle of the investment pyramid is to build a solid foundation in lower-risk investments such as money markets, before moving to higher-risk investments such as stocks. That way, your investment choices will be able to withstand the ups and downs in the marketplace.

This chapter covers stocks, bonds, and mutual funds. In what section of the investment pyramid would each of these fit? Would a corporate bond be more risky than a treasury bond that is backed by the government? Which is more risky,

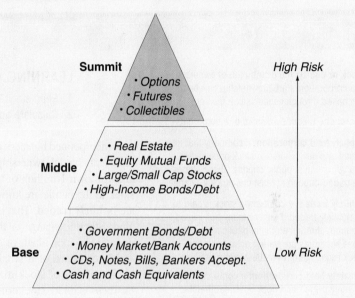

an individual stock or a mutual fund? And if you could pick only one investment to get started with, what would it be? What would your investment pyramid look like? Read on; your investment in studying Chapter 15 will answer many of these important questions.

LEARNING OUTCOMES

15-1 Stocks

1. Read stock listings.
2. Calculate and distribute dividends.

15-2 Bonds

1. Read bond listings.
2. Calculate the price of bonds.
3. Calculate the current bond yield.

15-3 Mutual Funds

1. Read mutual fund listings.
2. Calculate return on investment.

The concept of building wealth has appeal to most individuals, but the challenge of investing appropriately given the vast array of investment options can indeed be overwhelming. In fact, when it comes to investing money, studies done by a leading human resources firm show that most Americans don't feel comfortable managing their own money. In fact, investing is a subject that a lot of people don't even want to think about. Investing seems scary. It either sounds like something only the rich do or something that only a skilled professional can do. But the truth is that investing is something that everyone can and should do—as soon as possible.

Although most people are convinced that investing is the right thing to do, they are often confused by the terminology of the investment industry. Terms like *publicly traded, municipal bonds, mutual funds, indexes,* or *preferred stock* can be intimidating. But you don't need to be intimidated by a bunch of words—in the end they are just words. Just like you probably didn't know what APR was before you got your first credit card (or studied Chapter 12, "Consumer Credit"), you can learn what these words mean. And you will find that they aren't so hard to learn. The focus of this chapter is to present investment terminology in a straightforward way that not only helps you to learn the meaning of these terms, but to become familiar with their mathematical applications as well.

15-1 STOCKS

Stock or equity: the distribution of ownership of a corporation. Partial ownership can be purchased through various stock markets.

Share: one unit of ownership of a corporation.

Publicly held corporation: a company that has issued and sells shares of stock or securities through an initial public offering. These shares are traded through at least one stock exchange.

Publicly traded: a company's stock is said to be publicly traded if the company has issued securities through an initial public offering and these securities are traded on at least one stock exchange or over-the-counter market.

Privately held corporation: a company that is privately owned and does not meet the strict Securities and Exchange Commission filing required of publicly held corporations. Private corporations may issue stock and the owners are shareholders.

Face value (par value): the value of one share of stock.

Stock certificate: a certificate of ownership of stock issued to the buyer.

Dividend: a portion of the profit of a company that is periodically distributed to the stockholders of a company.

Preferred stock: a type of nonvoting stock that provides for a specific dividend that is paid before any dividends are paid to common stockholders and which takes precedence over common stock in the event of a company liquidation.

Common stock: a type of stock that gives the stockholder voting rights. After dividends are paid to preferred stockholders, the remaining dividends are distributed among the common stockholders.

Stock market: the structure for buying and selling stock.

Trade: either the buying or the selling of a stock.

Stockbroker: the person who handles the trading of stock. A stockbroker receives a commission for these services.

Stock listings: information about the price of a share of stock and some historical information that is published in some newspapers and on the Internet.

LEARNING OUTCOMES

1 Read stock listings.
2 Calculate and distribute dividends.

Any incorporated business can issue **stocks,** also known as **equities** or securities. Each **share** of stock represents partial ownership of the corporation. Thus, if a company issues 2 million shares of stock and you own 1 million of them, you own one-half of the company. Corporations that sell shares of stock to the public are known as **publicly held corporations.** Shares of stock in these corporations are **publicly traded.** That is, the stock is bought and sold through a stock exchange such as the New York Stock Exchange or the American Stock Exchange. Companies in which all the stock is held privately by individuals or groups of individuals are called **privately held corporations.**

Each share of a stock has a specific value, called the **face value (par value).** A person buying shares of stock may receive a certificate of ownership, called a **stock certificate.** If the business is good, stockholders may receive a portion of the company profits in the form of a **dividend** for each share they hold. Some stockholders also have voting rights in corporate affairs.

There are two basic types of stock: **preferred stock** and **common stock.** Holders of preferred stock receive certain preferential financial benefits over common stockholders. But common stockholders have voting rights in the company—one vote per share—that preferred stockholders do not have.

After the stock is issued, people buy and sell their shares in the **stock market** for prices that vary from day to day and within a day. The price of a given company's shares is affected by supply and demand: When more people want to buy than want to sell, the price tends to rise; when more people want to sell than want to buy, the price tends to fall. Keep in mind that for each sale (called a **trade**) there is both a buyer and a seller at a given price, but supply and demand exert a pressure on the price to go up or down. Factors that affect demand include good news about a company's product, bad news of higher-than-expected business expenses, international events, or what people think the trend of the national economy or of the business is.

The actual buying and selling of shares is done by a person called a **stockbroker,** who specializes in work in the stock market. Usually a person who wishes to buy or sell stock contacts a broker in person, by phone or fax, or on the Internet. The broker's representative at the actual trading location (such as at the New York Stock Exchange on Wall Street in New York or at the American Stock Exchange in Chicago) performs the transaction. The broker receives a *commission* for the services of both buying and selling stocks.

1 Read stock listings.

The daily prices of stocks, along with other information about the companies, are reported on the Internet and in some newspapers. Most print media are migrating to the Internet. Some of the best sources that still provide both are *The New York Times, Barron's Weekly,* and *The Wall Street Journal.* In Table 15-1, we look at listings from *The Wall Street Journal Online* to see how to read **stock listings.** Stock prices are listed in dollars and cents. Positive and negative signs show the direction of change. Thus +0.13 is read "up thirteen cents" and means the price of each share has gone up by 13 cents over the previous day's price. Similarly, −1.75 means the price of one share of stock has gone down by $1.75.

TABLE 15-1
Portion of New York Stock Exchange Listing

(1) Name	(2) Symbol	(3) Open	(4) High	(5) Low	(6) Close	(7) Net Chg	(8) % Chg	(9) Vol.	(10) 52 Wk High	(11) 52 Wk Low	(12) Div	(13) Yield	(14) P/E	(15) YTD % Chg
AAR CORP.	AIR	24.57	25.91	24.57	25.90	1.52	6.23	288,242	26.08	14.14	—	—	16	12.7
ABM INDUSTRIES INC.	ABM	21.63	22.04	21.44	22.03	0.54	2.51	103,122	23.32	15.75	0.54	2.5	22	6.6
ACCO BRANDS CORP.	ABD	9.19	9.30	9.05	9.20	0.07	0.77	385,238	9.47	2.01	—	—	dd	26.4
ACE LTD.	ACE	53.21	53.34	52.71	52.87	−0.32	−0.60	2,397,964	55.64	40.00	1.24	2.3	7	4.9
AES CORP.	AES	11.64	12.10	11.53	12.06	0.52	4.51	9,168,210	15.44	6.80	—	—	11	−9.4
AFLAC INC.	AFL	51.40	51.74	50.84	51.43	0.47	0.92	2,960,158	56.56	28.17	1.12	2.2	15	11.2
AGL RESOURCES INC.	AGL	39.75	40.08	39.43	39.98	0.47	1.19	234,938	40.00	28.12	1.76	4.4	13	9.6
AGRIA CORP. ADS	GRO	1.85	1.94	1.84	1.86	0.03	1.64	352,284	4.53	1.58	—	—	dd	−40.6
AK STEEL HOLDING CORP.	AKS	17.02	17.14	16.25	16.51	−0.24	−1.43	13,327,793	26.75	10.62	0.20	1.2	—	−22.7
AMB PROPERTY CORP.	AMB	28.13	29.00	28.13	28.88	1.02	3.66	1,386,460	29.60	15.91	1.12	3.9	dd	13.0
AMCOL INTERNATIONAL CORP.	ACO	28.82	29.93	28.82	29.84	1.10	3.83	123,371	32.60	18.24	0.72	2.4	25	5.0
AMR CORP.	AMR	7.57	7.70	7.30	7.59	0.21	2.85	14,781,378	10.50	3.79	—	—	dd	−1.8
AT&T INC.	T	26.24	26.43	26.07	26.28	0.22	0.84	23,382,357	28.73	23.19	1.68e	6.4	13	−6.2
AVX CORP.	AVX	15.56	15.72	15.34	15.56	0.11	0.71	261,592	15.69	9.07	0.16	1.0	19	22.8
AZZ INCORPORATED	AZZ	40.71	41.65	39.62	41.52	0.90	2.22	120,768	43.01	27.90	.50e	—	14	27.0
A.H. BELO CORP. SERIES A	AHC	8.45	8.89	8.30	8.71	0.21	2.47	140,111	9.16	0.92	—	—	dd	51.2
AARON RENTS INC.	AAN	22.66	22.79	22.41	22.68	0.11	0.49	576,684	24.32	16.40	0.05	0.2	16	22.7
AARON RENTS INC. CL A	AANA	18.64	18.66	18.32	18.42	−0.34	−1.81	900	20.30	9.56	0.05	0.3	—	22.8
ABB LTD. ADS	ABB	19.28	19.58	19.22	19.45	0.29	1.51	2,568,085	22.61	14.04	.44e	2.3	16	1.8
ABBOTT LABORATORIES	ABT	51.45	51.59	50.55	50.87	−0.29	−0.57	8,149,823	56.79	41.27	1.76f	3.5	15	−5.8
ABERCROMBIE & FITCH CO. CL A	ANF	44.33	45.32	43.45	44.68	0.95	2.17	2,625,958	51.12	22.70	0.70	1.6	50	28.2
ABOVENET INC.	ABVT	50.54	52.10	50.20	50.80	0.26	0.51	88,833	67.00	27.30	—	—	5	−21.9
ACADIA REALTY TRUST SBI	AKR	19.15	19.76	19.15	19.71	0.63	3.30	278,437	19.80	11.55	0.72	3.7	33	16.8
ACCENTURE LTD. CL A	ACN	43.44	43.82	43.26	43.75	0.11	0.25	2,329,886	44.67	28.39	0.75	1.7	19	5.4

Source: *Wall Street Journal Online:* http://online.wsj.com

a—Extra dividend or extras in addition to the regular dividend.

b—Indicates annual rate of the cash dividend and that a stock dividend was paid.

dd—Loss in the most recent four quarters.

e—Indicates a dividend was declared in the preceding 12 months, but that there isn't a regular dividend rate. Amount shown may have been adjusted to reflect stock split, spinoff, or other distribution.

f—Annual rate, increased on latest declaration.

g—Indicates the dividend and earnings are expressed in Canadian currency. The stock trades in U.S. dollars. No yield or P/E ratio is shown.

i—Indicates amount declared or paid after a stock dividend or split.

j—Indicates dividend was paid this year, and that at the last dividend meeting a dividend was omitted or deferred.

m—Annual rate, reduced on latest declaration.

p—Initial dividend; no yield calculated.

r—Indicates a cash dividend declared in the preceding 12 months, plus a stock dividend.

stk—Paid in stock in the last 12 months. Company doesn't pay cash dividend.

x—Ex-dividend, ex-distribution, ex-rights or without warrants.

The How To box below lists the steps for reading each column of a stock listing. To illustrate these steps, we use the listing in Table 15-2.

TABLE 15-2
New York Stock Exchange Listing for AT&T

① Name	② Symbol	③ Open	④ High	⑤ Low	⑥ Close	⑦ Net Chg	⑧ % Chg	⑨ Vol.	⑩ 52 Wk High	⑪ 52 Wk Low	⑫ Div	⑬ Yield	⑭ P/E	⑮ Year-to-Date % Chg
AT&T	T	26.24	26.43	26.07	26.28	0.22	0.84	23,382,357	28.73	23.19	1.68e	6.4	13	−6.2

HOW TO   Read stock listings

1. Column 1 (Name) shows the name of the corporation in abbreviated form.
2. Column 2 (Symbol) shows the company symbol used in stock listings.
3. Column 3 (Open) shows the share price when the market opened for this day.
4. Columns 4 (High), 5 (Low), and 6 (Close) show the highest and lowest prices at which the stock sold this day and the price of the stock at market closing time.
5. Column 7 (Net Chg) shows how much this day's closing price per share differs from the previous day's closing price per share for that stock.
6. Column 8 (% Chg) shows the percentage of increase or decrease of the day's closing price over the day's opening price of a stock.
7. Column 9 (Volume) shows the total number of shares of the stock that are traded on this day.
8. Columns 10 (52 Wk High) and 11 (52 Wk Low) show the highest and lowest prices at which the stock has sold in the last year (52 weeks), not including this day.
9. Column 12 (Div) shows the dividend paid per share of stock the previous year. An *e* following the dividend indicates that the dividend is an irregular cash dividend.
10. Column 13 (Yield) shows the previous year's dividend as a percent of the current price per share. If no dividend was paid the previous year, the entry is "…"
11. Column 14 (P/E) shows the stock's price/earnings ratio.
12. Column 15 (YTD% Chg) shows the percentage by which this day's closing price per share differs from the closing price per share on the first day of business of the current year.

Read the stock listing in Table 15-2 for **AT&T.**
Stock symbol is T.

Open price is $26.24.

High is $26.43; low is $26.07; close is $26.28.

Net change is $0.22 higher.

Percent change is 0.84%.

Number of shares sold on this day is 23,382,357.
52 Wk High is $28.73; 52 Wk Low is $23.19.

This stock paid an irregular cash dividend of $1.68 per share in the previous year.

Yield is 6.4%.

The P/E ratio is 13.

The price per share fell −6.2% from the beginning of the year.

TIP
Explanation of Additional Symbols

Additional symbols in the stock listings are defined or explained in most stock listings. For example, in the *Wall Street Journal Online,* colored type marks stocks that have gained (green) or lost (red) value from close of the previous day to close of this day. An <u>underscore</u> means the stock traded more than 1 percent of its total shares outstanding. An *n* following the name of a stock indicates a new issue. An *e* following the dividend payment indicates the sum of dividends paid per share during the last year. This may also be called an *irregular dividend.* An *f* following the dividend payment indicates the annual dividend rate increased over the previous year.

EXAMPLE 1   Refer to Table 15-1.

(a) How many shares of AFLAC, Inc., or AFL were traded this day?

(b) What is the difference between the high price and low price of the day?

(c) What was the closing price the previous day?

(a) From column 9, we see that the day's traded shares are 2,960,158 shares.

(b) From columns 4 and 5, we see the difference in high and low is

$$\begin{array}{r} \text{High } 51.74 \\ -\text{ Low } 50.84 \\ \hline \text{\$0.90 difference per share} \end{array}$$

(c) Column 6 shows the closing price of $51.43. From column 7, we see the change in price is +$0.47. Because the change is up, the price the previous day was less.

$$\text{Previous day's closing price} = \text{this day's closing price} - \text{change}$$
$$= \$51.43 - \$0.47$$
$$= \$50.96$$

Thus, 2,960,158 shares were traded, with a difference between the high and low of $0.90 and a closing price the previous day of $50.96.

There is no tried and true way to select the most likely stocks that will increase in value. However, two important measurements that investors often consider before selecting an individual stock are the **current yield** and **price-earnings (P/E) ratio.** Current yield is a measurement that tells you the percentage return a company pays out to shareholders in the form of dividends. Although the current yield of a stock is represented by Yield in column 13 of Table 15-1, it is important to understand the math used to compute this ratio.

Current yield: the ratio of the annual dividend per share of stock to the closing price per share.

Price-earnings (P/E) ratio: the ratio of the closing price of a share of stock to the annual earnings per share.

HOW TO Calculate the current yield on a stock

1. Divide the annual dividend per share by the closing price per share, then multiply by 100% to express as a percent.

$$\text{Current Yield} = \frac{\text{Annual dividend per share}}{\text{closing price per share}} \times 100\%$$

2. Round the quotient to the nearest tenth of a percent.

EXAMPLE 2 Find the current yield of AT&T's stock that reported a dividend of $1.68 and a closing price of $26.28.

$$\text{Current Yield} = \frac{\text{Annual dividend per share}}{\text{closing price per share}} \times 100\%$$
$$= \frac{\$1.68}{\$26.28}(100\%)$$
$$= 0.064(100\%)$$

Current Yield = 6.4% (Note: this is consistent with the Yield for AT&T in Table 15-2.)

Trailing earnings: a company's earnings-per-share for the past 12 months; found by dividing the company's after-tax profit by the number of outstanding shares.

Trailing P/E ratio: a company's P/E ratio calculated using the company's trailing earnings per share as the net income per share.

Leading earnings: a company's projected earnings-per-share for the upcoming 12-month period.

Leading P/E ratio: a company's P/E ratio calculated using the company's leading earnings per share as the net income per share.

Important historical information is given by the percent yield of a stock. A large yield would ordinarily be more desirable than a small one, but if a company is putting its profits into redevelopment instead of dividends, there may be a small yield now. However, if the company becomes a stronger business, the stock price itself might rise. If an investor sold the stock at that later time, the return on the investment then could be high, even though the yield figure now is low.

A company's P/E ratio is the current market price (at the close of business) of one share of stock divided by the company's annual per-share earnings (net income). The company's earnings-per-share is found by dividing the company's after-tax profit by the number of outstanding shares. P/E ratios are usually expressed as whole numbers and are usually computed with trailing earnings. **Trailing earnings** are earnings for the past 12 months. This is called the **trailing P/E ratio.** If the P/E ratio is computed with **leading earnings,** earnings that are projected for the upcoming 12-month period, the ratio is called a **leading P/E ratio.**

HOW TO Calculate the P/E ratio of a stock

1. Divide the current stock price by the annual net income per share for the past 12 months.

$$\text{P/E ratio} = \frac{\text{current price per share}}{\text{net income per share (past 12 months)}}$$

2. Round the quotient to the nearest whole number.

EXAMPLE 3 Find the P/E ratio of a corporation that reported last year's net income as $6.16 per share if the company's stock sells for $58 per share.

Current price per share = $58

Net income per share = $6.16

$$\text{P/E ratio} = \frac{\text{current price per share}}{\text{net income per share (past 12 months)}}$$

$$\text{P/E ratio} = \frac{\$58}{\$6.16} \qquad \text{Divide.}$$

P/E ratio = 9.415584416   Round to the nearest whole number.

The P/E ratio is 9. Stated differently, investors are willing to pay $9 for every $1 of last year's earnings for this stock at the price of $58.

While P/E ratios change every day as the stock price fluctuates, the P/E ratio for a company is best viewed over time. Companies with steadily increasing P/E ratios may be viewed by the investment community as becoming increasingly speculative. Companies that are expected to grow and have higher future earnings should have a higher P/E than companies in decline. The P/E ratio is a better indicator of the value of a stock than its share price. As a general rule, the P/E ratio of a company should be comparable to the company's growth rate. It is also important to consider the P/E ratio in comparison with other companies for the industry sector. If a P/E ratio is not given in the stock listings, the company probably has lost money during the past year.

Stocks cannot be judged on any one aspect. One stock may have a high dividend, a high yield, yet a high P/E ratio. A cautious investor "follows the stock market" and seeks advice from knowledgeable persons, such as stockbrokers, to determine if a particular company meets his or her investment needs.

STOP AND CHECK

See Example 1.

1. How many shares of AMR stock traded on the day shown in Table 15-1?

2. What is the difference in the high price and low price for AMR on the day shown in Table 15-1?

3. AMR closed at $7.59. What was its closing price on the previous day shown in Table 15-1?

4. Which stock listed in Table 15-1 had the highest percentage year-to-date change?

5. Find the current yield for a stock that has an annual dividend per share of $1.56 and a closing price per share of $27.98. *See Example 2.*

6. Find the P/E ratio of a corporation that reported last year's net income as $4.32 per share if the company's stock sells for $54 per share. *See Example 3.*

2   Calculate and distribute dividends.

A corporation's board of directors can vote to reinvest any profits into the business or can declare a dividend with some or all of the profits. The dividend is expressed as a dollar amount per share. It is usually declared quarterly (every three months), but if a business is in poor financial condition or if the directors so decide, there may be no dividends at all.

Sometimes dividends vary according to whether the stock is preferred stock or common stock. Holders of preferred stock (which has the letters "pf" after its name in a stock listing) are entitled to first claim on the corporation's profits and assets. Thus, if a company has limited profits, it must pay all its preferred shareholders dividends before it can pay any of its common stock shareholders. Similarly, in case of bankruptcy, preferred stockholders must be paid before common stockholders. However, only holders of common stock are entitled to a vote in corporate affairs (one vote per share).

Dividends on various kinds of preferred stock are usually fixed, although owners of **participating preferred stock** can receive additional dividends if the company decides to do so. This sometimes occurs after a hostile takeover attempt. **Convertible preferred stock** allows the stock to be exchanged for a certain number of shares of common stock later. And with **cumulative preferred stock,** dividends are earned every year. If no dividends are paid one year, the amounts not paid are recorded. These **dividends in arrears** must be paid when money becomes available before other preferred or common stock dividends are paid.

Participating preferred stock: a type of preferred stock that allows stockholders to receive additional dividends if the company decides to do so.

Convertible preferred stock: a stock option that allows the stockholder to exchange the stock for a certain number of shares of common stock.

Cumulative preferred stock: preferred stock that earns dividends every year.

Dividends in arrears: dividends that were not paid in a previous year and must be paid to cumulative preferred stockholders before dividends can be distributed to other stockholders.

1. First pay dividends in arrears:
   (a) Multiply the number of shares held by preferred stockholders by the given dividend rate, expressed as dollars per share.
   (b) Subtract these dividends in arrears from the available amount of money.
2. Pay the present year's preferred stock dividends:
   (a) Multiply the number of preferred shares held by stockholders by the given dividend rate.
   (b) Subtract these preferred stock dividends from the difference from step 1b.
3. Pay the common stock dividend: Divide the difference from step 2b by the number of common shares held by stockholders. This is the dividend per share paid to common stockholders.

EXAMPLE 4   A company has issued 20,000 shares of cumulative preferred stock that will earn dividends at $0.60 per share and has issued 100,000 shares of common stock. Last year the company paid no dividends. This year $250,000 is available for dividends. How are the dividends to be distributed?

Preferred stockholders received no dividends last year, so this year's dividends in arrears must be paid:

Dividends in arrears: $20,000(\$0.60) = \$12,000$ To preferred stockholders

The remaining money ($\$250,000 - \$12,000 = \$238,000$) is distributed to the preferred and common stockholders for this year as follows:

$$\text{To preferred stockholders: } 20,000(\$0.60) = \$12,000$$

The amount left for common stockholders ($\$238,000 - \$12,000 = \$226,000$) is divided among all the common stockholders:

$$\text{To common stockholders: } \frac{\$226,000}{100,000} = \$2.26 \text{ per share}$$

Preferred stockholders receive $24,000 and common stockholders receive $226,000.

Notice that the $0.60 dividend per share for the preferred stock is a guaranteed but fixed rate, whereas the dividend per share of common stock has the *potential* to be higher (or lower) than that, but with no guarantee. Last year's common stock owners received no dividends, but this year they received more than did the preferred stockholders in two years. Because dividends are income to the stockholder and now receive preferential income tax treatement, they are one measure of the desirability of owning a particular stock.

STOP AND CHECK

See Example 4.

1. American Transit Company has 100,000 shares of common stock held by stockholders and paid $0.32 per share in dividends. How much was paid out in dividends?

2. A publicly traded corporation has issued 10,000 shares of cumulative preferred stock that will earn $0.73 per share and 1,000,000 shares of common stock. No dividends were paid last year. This year the corporation's board of directors has voted to pay out $2,800,000 in dividends. How are the dividends distributed?

3. What is the dividend per share of the common stock for the corporation in Exercise 2?

4. AVX, a stock in Table 15-1, has 6,684,582 outstanding shares of common stock. How much was paid in dividends for last year?

15-1 SECTION EXERCISES

Use information about the common stock for AK Steel (Table 15-1) for Exercises 1–5. See Example 1.

1. What was the closing price in dollars and cents?

2. During the previous year, what was its high price? Its low price?

3. What is the difference between this day's high price and low price?

4. What was the previous day's closing price?

5. How many shares of AK Steel stock were sold?

6. AFL stock had what P/E ratio?

See Example 2.

7. Find the current yield of American Water Works Co. that reported a dividend of $0.84 and a closing price of $21.38.

8. Find the current yield of Baxter International, Inc., that reported a dividend of $1.16 and a closing price of $43.53.

See Example 3.

9. Find the P/E ratio of a corporation that reported last year's net income of $3.18 per share if the company's stock sells for $43.16 per share.

10. Find the P/E ratio of Amcol International Corp. that reported last year's net income of $1.19 per share if the company's stock sells for $29.84 per share.

See Example 4.

11. If AFL (Table 15-1) had 989,532,000 shares of common stock outstanding when it paid dividends last year, how much did it pay in dividends?

12. What was the market value of AFL's stock that was traded on this day of business according to the stock listing in Table 15-1 using the stock's closing price?

A company has $200,000 to distribute in dividends. There are 20,000 shares of preferred stock that earn dividends at $0.50 per share and 80,000 shares of common stock.

13. How much money goes to preferred stockholders?

14. How much money goes to common stockholders?

15. How much per share does a common stockholder receive in dividends to the nearest cent?

The ARMMO Corporation has $1,550,000 to distribute in dividends and did not distribute dividends the previous year. There are 100,000 shares of cumulative preferred stock that earn dividends at $0.78 per share and 800,000 shares of common stock.

16. How much money goes to preferred stockholders?

17. How much money goes to common stockholders?

18. How much per share does a common stockholder receive in dividends to the nearest cent?

Bond: a type of loan to the issuer to raise money for a company, state, or municipality. The investor or bondholder will be paid a specified rate of interest each year and will be paid the entire value of the bond at maturity.

Issuer: a company, state, or municipality that issues bonds to raise money.

Coupon: the annual interest paid by the issuer to the lender on a bond.

Coupon rate: the annual payout percentage based on the bond's par value (original value of the bond).

Face value (par value): the original value of a bond, usually $1,000.

Maturity date: the date at which the face value of the bond is paid to the bondholder.

Credit risk: the possibility that a bond issuer will default by failing to repay principal and interest in a timely manner.

Investment grade bond: a bond with a high probability of being paid with few speculative risks.

Junk bonds: high-risk bonds that are usually from companies in bankruptcy or in financial difficulty.

Corporate bonds: bonds issued by businesses.

Municipal bonds: bonds issued by local and state governments.

Treasury bonds: bonds issued by the federal government.

Registered bonds: bonds for which investors receive interest automatically by being listed with the company.

Convertible bonds: bonds with a provision for being converted to stock.

Recallable bonds: bonds that can be repurchased by the company before the maturity date.

Bond market: the structure for buying and selling bonds.

Premium bond: a bond that sells for more than the face value.

Discount bond: a bond that sells for less than the face value.

TIP

How Much Do I Get at Maturity of a Bond?

Keep in mind that no matter what the market price of a bond, the corporation pays interest on the face value of $1,000 per bond and repays the face or par value of the bond at maturity.

LEARNING OUTCOMES

1 Read bond listings.
2 Calculate the price of bonds.
3 Calculate the current bond yield.

After time passes, a corporation may need to raise more money than its initial offering of stock produced. It can then issue more stock, thereby creating more shares of ownership. However, the company management may be reluctant to do so because additional shares lessen the ownership power (dilute the rights) of the existing stockholders. To raise the needed money, the company may decide to borrow it for a short term from a bank or for a longer term (five years or more) from the public, by selling bonds. In exchange for money from the sale, the company issues a **bond,** a promise to repay the money at a specific later date and in the meantime to pay interest annually. The company, state, or municipality that issues the bond is called the **issuer.** The annual interest paid by the issuer to the lender (bondholder) on the bond is referred to as the **coupon**. The **coupon rate** is the annual payout as a percentage of the bond's par value.

A bond has a **face value (par value),** usually $1,000 or a multiple of $1,000, a date of repayment **(maturity date),** and a fixed *rate of interest* per year. Because a bond obligates the company to future repayment, the public's judgment of the company's future will affect sales of a bond. Investors also look closely at the interest to be paid.

Just like stocks, bond prices fluctuate according to market conditions. Even though bonds generally carry less risk and volatility than stocks, they are by no means risk and volatility free. Every bond carries with it some **credit risk,** the possibility that a bond issuer will default by failing to repay principal and interest in a timely manner. There are a number of different rating agencies including Moody's, Standard & Poor's, and Fitch that assess how great this risk is with any given bond issuer, similar to a credit rating for an individual.

Bonds issued by the federal government, for the most part, are immune from default (if the government needs money it can just print more) and therefore have the highest credit rating. The bonds of issuers that have a high probability of being paid, and few, if any, speculative risks are often referred to as **investment grade bonds.** A bond issuer's rating can have significant impact on the interest rates that it will have to pay to borrow money, just like an individual with good credit ratings can borrow more easily at more favorable rates than those with poor ratings.

Because bonds are a legal debt of the corporation, if the company goes bankrupt, the bondholder's claims have priority over those of the stockholders. Bonds of businesses that are bankrupt or in financial difficulty also have the lowest ratings (below BBB/Baa) and are referred to as **junk bonds.** They can yield a high return—or be next to worthless—making them a risky and speculative investment.

In addition to these **corporate bonds** issued by businesses, state and local governments sell **municipal bonds** and the federal government sells **Treasury bonds.** Government bonds are often attractive to investors because the interest payments on them may be exempt from federal income tax. In this text, however, we deal only with corporate bonds.

Corporate bonds come in various types. **Registered bonds** allow the investor to receive interest automatically by being listed with the corporation. **Convertible bonds** have a provision that allows them to be converted to stock. **Recallable bonds** allow the corporation to repurchase the bonds before the maturity date.

Once bonds are issued, they may be bought and sold at varying prices in the **bond market.** Here, as in the stock market, "market conditions" prevail: A bond with high interest payments may be attractive to investors, so its price may rise, causing the bond to *sell at a premium* (a **premium bond**). Or, if interest payments are low, a bond price may tend to drop to attract investors, causing the bond to *sell at a discount* (a **discount bond**).

1 Read bond listings.

Table 15-3 shows how bonds are listed in the *Wall Street Journal Online (WSJ Online).* While bond prices, like stock prices, change during business hours, the listing information provided by *WSJ Online* is updated after each trading day. In this table, bonds are listed by the category of most active investment grade bonds. The discount bonds have a listing less than 100%; the premium bonds have a listing greater than 100%. A quick look at the closing price in column 8 (Last) in Table 15-3 reveals only one bond, GOLDMAN SACHS GP: 96.642, selling at a discount. Can you give some reasons for this bond selling at a discount?

TABLE 15-3
Bond Listing from *Wall Street Journal Online*

① Issuer Name	② Symbol	③ Coupon	④ Maturity	⑤ Rating Moody's/S&P/ Fitch	⑥ High	⑦ Low	⑧ Last	⑨ Change	⑩ Yield %
CITIGROUP	C.HRY	8.500%	May 2019	A3/A/A+	119.268	116.615	117.733	0.448	5.940
GENERAL ELECTRIC CAPITAL	GE.HMX	5.500%	Jan 2020	Aa2/AA+/– –	105.307	102.374	103.097	−0.028	5.090
KRAFT FOODS	KFT.GX	5.375%	Feb 2020	Baa2/BBB−/ BBB−	106.081	101.999	103.411	0.687	4.930
BANK OF AMERICA	BAC.ICB	7.625%	Jun 2019	A2/A/A+	113.172	111.839	112.847	0.283	5.786
ANHEUSER-BUSCH	BUD.ID	5.375%	Jan 2020	Baa2/BBB+/– –	104.693	104.061	104.526	−0.466	4.784
COMCAST CORP	CMCD.GC	5.150%	Mar 2020	Baa1/BBB+/ BBB+	104.832	100.923	101.225	0.441	N/A
GOLDMAN SACHS GP	GS.IAR	5.375%	Mar 2020	A1/A/A+	99.750	95.636	96.642	−0.592	5.826
BANK OF AMERICA	BAC.IOP	4.500%	Apr 2015	A2/A/A+	101.750	99.288	100.231	0.518	4.445
BARCLAYS BANK PLC	BCS.GYR	5.000%	Sep 2016	Aa3/AA−/AA−	107.104	102.680	103.584	0.595	4.351
AT&T	T.KM	5.800%	Feb 2019	A2/A/A	109.969	106.736	109.931	2.440	4.423

HOW TO   Read bond listings

1. Columns 1 and 2 give the name of the issuing company and its corresponding symbol.
2. Column 3 gives the annual interest rate, expressed as a percent of face value.
3. Column 4 gives the maturity, the month/year when the bond will mature.
4. Column 5 provides the issuer's bond rating from the three primary rating services.
5. Columns 6 and 7 provide the high and low values for the trading day.
6. Column 8 shows the last or closing price per bond as a percent of face value; an entry of 101.225 (COMCAST CORP) means the bond sold for 101.225% of $1,000 per bond, or 1.01225 times $1,000, or $1,012.25 per bond.
7. Column 9 shows the change in price from the previous day's closing price per bond, as a percent of the face value per bond.
8. Column 10 gives the yield to maturity, which is the annual rate of return over the life of the bond.

EXAMPLE 1   Refer to Table 15-3.

(a) What are the interest rate and the date of maturity for BAC.ICB?

(b) What is the rating for this bond provided by Fitch?
(c) What are the change and yield % for this bond issue?

(a) From column 3, we see the interest rate is 7.625%, and from column 4 the maturity is Jun 2019.

(b) From column 5, the rating provided by Fitch is A+.
(c) From columns 9 and 10, the change is 0.283 and the yield is 5.786%.

TIP

What Does *Maturity Date* Mean?

This is the date on which the principal amount of a bond becomes due and is repaid to the investor and interest payments stop. However, it is important to note that some bonds are "callable," which means that the issuer of the debt is able to pay back the principal at any time. Thus, before buying any fixed-income securities, investors should inquire whether the bond is callable or not.

STOP AND CHECK

See Example 1.

1. From Table 15-3 find the interest rate and the date of maturity for Kraft Foods.

2. What is the Moody's rating for the Kraft Foods bond?

3. What was the net change in the Kraft Foods bond price?

4. What is the current yield for the Kraft Foods bond?

2   Calculate the price of bonds.

Even though a bond has a face value of $1,000, bonds on the bond market are bought and sold for more or less than $1,000. Column 8 in Table 15-3 gives the closing price per bond as a percent of $1,000.

HOW TO   Calculate the price of a bond

1. Locate the percent of $1,000 that the bond was selling for at the close of the day (column 8).
2. Multiply the decimal equivalent of the percent by $1,000.
3. Round the product to the nearest cent.

EXAMPLE 2   Calculate the closing price of the C.HRY bond.

From column 8, the closing price as a percent of face value was 117.733%.

$$117.733\% = 1.17733$$

$$\text{Closing bond price} = \$1.000 \times \text{percent in column 8}$$
$$= \$1,000\,(1.17733)$$
$$= \$1,177.33$$

The closing bond price is $1,177.33

DID YOU KNOW?

The change from a percent to a decimal equivalent moves the decimal two places to the left. Multiplying by 1,000 moves the decimal three places to the right. Therefore, finding a percent of $1,000 moves the decimal point one place to the right.

EXAMPLE 3   Calculate the previous day's closing price per bond for T.KM (Table 15-3).

The bond closed at 109.931% of its face value, up 2.440% of its face value from the previous day's closing price. The previous day's closing price was this day's closing price minus 2.440% of the face value.

$$\text{Previous day's closing listing} = 109.931\% - 2.440\% = 107.491\%$$
$$107.491\% = 1.07491$$
$$\text{Previous day's bond price} = \$1,000(1.07491) = \$1,074.91$$

The previous day's bond closing price is $1,074.91.

STOP AND CHECK

See Example 2.

1. What was the closing price of the GE.HMX bond?

2. Find the closing price of the KFT.GX bond.

See Example 3.

3. What was the closing price of the BUD.ID bond in the previous day?

4. Find the closing price of the BAC.IOP bond in the previous day.

Yield: a measure of the profitability of the investment.

Yield to maturity: measures profitability over the life of an investment.

Current bond yield or average annual yield: the ratio of the annual interest per bond to the current price per bond.

3 Calculate the current bond yield.

Investors in bonds, like investors in stocks, want to know the **yield** of their investments. In Table 15-3, the yield % column (10) provides a measure of how profitable the investment is for the life of the investment, often referred to as **yield to maturity.** **Current bond yield** compares annual earnings (interest) with the closing price of a bond. It is expressed as a percent of face value.

TIP

Discounted Bonds Versus Premium Bonds

A discounted bond always has a higher current yield than its stated interest rate, and a premium bond always has a lower current yield than its stated interest rate.

HOW TO   Calculate the current yield of a bond

1. Calculate the current price of a bond.
2. Locate the stated interest rate or coupon in column 3.
3. Multiply the stated interest rate by $1,000, the face value of the bond.
4. Divide the result by the current price of the bond.

$$\text{Current yield} = \frac{\text{stated interest rate (as a decimal)} \times \$1,000}{\text{current price of bond}} \times 100\%$$

EXAMPLE 4   Calculate the current bond yield for KFT.GX (Table 15-3).

$$\text{Current yield} = \frac{0.05375(\$1,000)}{\$1,034.11}(100\%)$$

Current price of the bond is 103.411% of $1,000, or $1,034.11. Stated interest rate or coupon in column 3 is 5.375%, or 0.05375.

$$= \frac{\$53.75}{\$1,034.11}(100\%)$$

$$= 0.0519770624(100\%)$$

Current yield = 5.198% (rounded to three decimal places)

STOP AND CHECK

See Example 4.

1. Calculate the current bond yield for GS.IAR.

2. Calculate the current bond yield for C.HRY.

15-2 SECTION EXERCISES

SKILL BUILDERS

See Example 1.

1. Refer to Table 15-3 to determine the coupon rate and maturity of a bond issued by General Electric Capital.

2. What is the yield to maturity for the bond issue of Citigroup?

3. Use Table 15-3 to find the Fitch bond rating for Goldman Sachs GP.

4. BUD.ID closed at 104.526 in Table 15-3. What does this mean?

5. Which of the two bonds, BAC.IOP or BCS.GYR, (Table 15-3) is producing the greater yield to maturity?

6. What is the S&P rating for the BCS.GYR bond?

See Example 2.

7. Use Table 15-3 to find the selling price at the close of the selling day of the bond issue for BAC.ICB that matures in 2019.

8. Give the closing price of the Comcast Corp. bond that matures in 2020.

9. What is the daily high of the AT&T bond? *See Example 1.*

10. From Table 15-3, what was the previous day's closing bond price for a Kraft Foods bond? *See Example 3.*

11. What is the closing bond price for GE.HMX (Table 15-3)? *See Example 2.*

12. Calculate the previous day's closing price for BAC.ICB (Table 15-3). *See Example 3.*

See Example 4.

13. Calculate the current bond yield for BCS.GYR (Table 15-3).

14. Calculate the current bond yield for a bond that has a current bond price of 98.431% and a stated interest rate of 6.375%.

15-3 MUTUAL FUNDS

LEARNING OUTCOMES

1 Read mutual fund listings.
2 Calculate return on investment.

1 Read mutual fund listings.

Now that you've learned more about individual securities (stocks and bonds, and so on), which security would you choose if you had $1,000 to invest? That, frankly, is a very difficult question to answer. With literally thousands of options to choose from, knowing which individual **security** is likely to outperform all others would be like trying to find a needle in the proverbial haystack. No matter how solid a company looks when you first decide to invest in it, there is always the very real possibility or risk that it could fall on hard economic times, causing your investment to decline in value—or worse yet, become worthless. We tend to think of this type of risk in predominantly negative terms, as something to be avoided or a threat that we hope won't materialize. In the investment world, however, risk is inseparable from performance and, rather than being desirable or undesirable, is simply necessary.

Understanding this **investment risk** is one of the most important parts of a financial education. A common definition for investment risk is deviation from an expected outcome, such as comparison to a market **benchmark.** This deviation can be positive or negative, and relates to the idea of "no pain, no gain"—and that to achieve higher returns in the long run you have to

Securities: investments such as stocks, bonds, notes, debentures, limited partnership interests, oil and gas interests, or other investment contracts.

Investment risk: the potential for fluctuation in the value of an investment, which could result in total loss or a decrease in value.

Benchmark: a standard against which the performance of a security can be measured.

Volatility: refers to the amount of uncertainty or risk about the changes in a security's value. A higher volatility means that a security's value can change dramatically over a short time period in either direction.

Portfolio: a collection of different types of investments, normally owned by an individual.

Diversification: dividing your assets on a percentage basis among different broad categories of investments, or asset classes.

Asset classes: different categories of investments that provide returns in different ways are described as asset classes. Stocks, bonds, cash and cash equivalents, real estate, collectibles, and precious metals are among the primary asset classes.

Mutual fund: a collection of stocks, bonds, and other securities that is managed by a mutual fund company.

Net asset value (NAV): the value of one share of a mutual fund.

Prospectus: for mutual funds, it is the official document that describes the fund's investment objectives, policies, services and fees; you should read it carefully before you invest.

Administrative fee or management fee: A fee that is periodically applied to a mutual fund account that is in addition to the fees charged for buying or selling mutual funds.

accept more short-term **volatility,** or change. How much volatility you will accept depends on your risk tolerance—taking into account your psychological comfort with uncertainty and the possibility of incurring short-term losses in your investments.

But what are some of the ways to reduce risk in your investment **portfolio?** One of the best is through **diversification.** Diversification is the process of investing a portfolio across different **asset classes** (stocks, bonds, bank accounts, and so forth) in varying proportions that are unlikely to all have the same volatility. Volatility is typically limited by the fact that not all asset classes or industries or individual companies move up and down in value at the same time or at the same rate. Depending on an investor's time horizon, risk tolerance, and goals, diversification helps reduce both the upside and downside potential and allows for more consistent performance under a wide range of economic conditions. Although diversification does not assure or guarantee better performance and cannot eliminate the risk of investment losses, this disciplined approach does help alleviate some of the speculation often involved with investing.

Most individual investors, however, do not have the time nor expertise to research all of the many investments available to create a diversified portfolio.

To accomplish these goals, many investors choose a **mutual fund.** A mutual fund or investment trust is a collection of stocks, bonds, or other securities that is managed by a mutual fund company. Individual investors purchase shares in the mutual fund and own a small portion of each holding in the fund. The value of one share of the fund is called the **net asset value.** The net asset value is the amount of money you would get per share if you sold shares of your mutual fund stock. This value fluctuates just as the value of stocks and bonds fluctuates.

What are the key advantages of mutual fund investing? There are a number of different reasons that investors choose mutual funds, including:

1. **Diversification.** As discussed above, when investing in a single mutual fund, an investor is actually investing in numerous securities—which can help reduce risk.
2. **Professional Management.** Mutual funds are managed and supervised by investment professionals. Per the stated objectives set forth in the **prospectus,** along with prevailing market conditions and other factors, the mutual fund manager decides when to buy or sell securities in the mutual fund.
3. **Convenience.** With most mutual funds, buying and selling shares, changing distribution options, and obtaining information can be accomplished conveniently by telephone, by mail, or online.
4. **Liquidity.** Shares of a mutual fund are liquid, meaning they are characterized by the ability to buy and sell with relative ease.
5. **Minimum Initial Investment.** Many funds have a minimum initial purchase of as little as $1,000 and you can buy some funds for as little as $50, if you agree to invest a certain dollar amount each month or quarter.

TABLE 15-4
Portion of Mutual Fund Listing

Family/ Fund ①	Symbol ②	NAV ③	Chg ④	YTD % return ⑤	3-yr % chg ⑥
AARP Funds					
Aggr	AAGSX	10.25	0.08	6.2	−1.6
Consrv	AACNX	10.55	0.02	4.0	4.0
Mod p	AAMDX	10.50	0.05	4.9	1.3
AMF Funds					
IntMtg	ASCPX	4.81	−0.01	0.1	−14.3
LgCpEq	IICAX	8.16	0.08	7.5	−2.1
ShtUSGv	ASITX	9.36	−0.01	0.2	0.7
UltraShrt p	AULTX	5.45	−0.02	3.2	−12.2
UltShrtMtg	ASARX	7.39	—	2.4	−4.4
USGvMtg	ASMTX	8.64	−0.02	0.2	−0.7
APIEffFrtGrPrim fp					
APIEffFrtGrPrim fp	APITX	8.13	0.10	9.0	−6.5
APIMultIdxPrim					
APIMultIdxPrim	AFMMX	10.98	0.09	4.4	−9.6
AVS LPE Ptf					
AVS LPE Ptf	LPEVX	5.82	−0.01	11.3	NS
Aberdeen Fds					
EqLS A t	MLSAX	11.16	0.05	1.5	0.7

Source: *Wall Street Journal Online*

Of course there are disadvantages associated with mutual funds as well. Changing market conditions can create fluctuations in the value of a mutual fund investment, so there are no guarantees. Fees and expenses that do not usually occur when purchasing individual securities directly are usually associated with investing in mutual funds.

Mutual fund listings can be found on the Internet just like listings for stocks and bonds. The information given varies with the source of the listing. Table 15-4 is a portion of a listing from the *Wall Street Journal Online.* A mutual fund corporation may offer more than one type of fund to satisfy a variety of investors. Some funds may be high-risk aggressive funds while others have a moderate risk. The mutual fund company is listed as the **fund family** and the various funds that are offered are listed under the fund family.

HOW TO   Read mutual fund listings

In Table 15-4,

1. Find the appropriate fund family (bold entry in column 1).
2. Find the appropriate fund name (indented entry in column 1).
3. Find the mutual fund symbol in column 2.
4. Find the net asset value (NAV) in column 3.
5. Identify the one-day total change (Chg) from column 4.
6. Identify the total return for the year to date (YTD % return) from column 5 and the three-year total return (3-yr. % chg) from column 6.

EXAMPLE 1   (a) Find the current price per share of AFMMX fund. (b) What was the price per share yesterday?

(a) Current price per share (NAV) = $10.98
(b) Change = +0.09
　　Yesterday's price = $10.98 − $0.09
　　Yesterday's price = $10.89

The selling price of a share of a mutual fund usually includes a sales charge. The sales charge is found by subtracting the net asset value from the selling price of a share of stock in a mutual fund. The load is paid either when purchasing the shares, in a **front-end load,** or when selling the shares, in a **back-end load.** Some mutual funds do not charge a load and are known as **no-load mutual funds.**

HOW TO   Find the mutual fund sales charge and the sales charge percent

1. Subtract net asset value from selling (offer) price.

$$\text{Mutual fund sales charge} = \text{selling (offer) price} - \text{net asset value}$$

2. Sales charge percent $= \dfrac{\text{sales charge}}{\text{net asset value}} \times 100\%$

EXAMPLE 2   Find the sales charge and the sales charge percent for one share of MLSAX mutual fund stock if the stock was offered at $11.59. Use Table 15-4.

The NAV is $11.16 and the offering (selling) price of the stock is $11.59.

Mutual fund sales charge = offer price − net asset value

Mutual fund sales charge = $11.59 − $11.16 = $0.43

Sales charge percent $= \dfrac{\text{sales charge}}{\text{net asset value}} \times 100\%$

Sales charge percent $= \left(\dfrac{\$0.43}{\$11.16}\right)(100\%)$

Sales charge percent = 0.0385304659(100%) ≈ 3.85%.

Find the net asset value (NAV) at the beginning of the year for one share of a mutual fund

1. Divide the Current NAV by the sum of 100% and YTD % return

$$\text{Beginning of year NAV} = \frac{\text{current NAV}}{100\% + \text{YTD \% return}}$$

2. Round the quotient to the nearest cent.

EXAMPLE 3 Find the beginning of year NAV for IICAX.

$$\text{Beginning of year NAV} = \frac{\text{current NAV}}{100\% + \text{YTD \% return}}$$

$$\text{Beginning of year NAV} = \frac{\$8.16}{100\% + 7.5\%} = \frac{\$8.16}{1 + 0.075} = \frac{\$8.16}{1.075} = \$7.590697674$$

The beginning of year NAV = \$7.59.

TIP

Use Previously Learned Procedures as a Pattern

Columns 5 and 6 of the mutual fund listing represent a percent increase or decrease. The amount in column 3 is the new amount *after* the increase or decrease. To find the amount before the increase or decrease, use the procedure that is appropriate.

$$\text{Amount before increase} = \frac{\text{current amount}}{100\% + \text{increase\%}}$$

$$\text{Amount before decrease} = \frac{\text{current amount}}{100\% - \text{decrease\%}}$$

The previous example applied the *before increase* procedure.

HOW TO Calculate the number of shares purchased of a mutual fund

1. Calculate the number of shares purchased by dividing the total amount of the investment by the offer price of the fund. With a no load fund, use the NAV as the denominator.

$$\text{Number of shares purchased} = \frac{\text{Total investment}}{\text{Offer price}}$$

2. Round the quotient to the nearest thousandth, or three decimal places.

EXAMPLE 4 Calculate the number of shares purchased with a \$1,000 investment in a no-load mutual fund with a NAV of \$4.82. Round to the nearest thousandth.

$$\text{Number of shares purchased} = \frac{\text{Total investment}}{\text{Offer price}}$$

$$\text{Number of shares purchased} = \frac{\$1,000}{\$4.82} = 207.4688797 \text{ or } 207.469 \text{ shares}$$

STOP AND CHECK

See Example 1.

1. Find the current price per share of AAMDX fund.

2. What was yesterday's price per share of AAMDX fund?

See Example 3.

3. What was the price per share (NAV) of AAMDX at the beginning of the year?

4. What was the price per share (NAV) of MLSAX at the beginning of the year?

See Example 2.

5. Use Table 15-4 to find the sales charge and the sales charge percent for one share of AFMMX mutual fund stock if the stock was offered at $11.52.

6. Use Table 15-4 to find the sales charge and the sales charge percent for one share of LPEVX mutual fund stock if the stock was offered at $6.05.

See Example 4.

7. If $1,500 is invested in a no-load mutual fund with a NAV of $9.23, how many shares (to the nearest thousandth) are purchased?

8. How many shares can be purchased in a no-load mutual fund if $2,000 is invested in a fund with a NAV of $7.84? Round to the nearest thousandth.

2 Calculate return on investment.

One of the most important tools for measuring the performance of an investment is known as the **return on investment, or (ROI).** It is used to make a comparison between different investments like stocks, bonds, mutual funds, and so on over a given period of time, and is expressed as a percentage or ratio.

Return on investment (ROI): a performance measure used to evaluate the efficiency of an investment, expressed as a percentage or a ratio.

HOW TO Calculate the return on investment

1. Calculate the amount of gain or loss on the sale or value of the investment by subtracting the total cost from the proceeds of the sale, including any additions from dividends or interest.

$$\text{Gain or loss on investment} = (\text{proceeds of sale} + \text{additions}) - \text{total cost}$$

2. Calculate the return on investment by dividing the total gain or loss of the investment by the total cost of the investment.

$$\text{ROI} = \frac{\text{total gain (or loss)}}{\text{total cost of investment}}$$

EXAMPLE 5 Calculate return on investment for 1,000 shares of a mutual fund purchased with an offer price of $8.16, which were sold with an NAV of $9.36, and had paid a dividend during ownership of $0.27 per share. Round to the nearest hundredth of a percent.

$$\text{Total proceeds from sale} = 1,000 \text{ shares } (\$9.36) = \$9,360$$
$$\text{Additions} = 1,000 \text{ shares } (\$0.27) = \$270$$
$$\text{Total cost of purchase} = 1,000 \text{ shares } (\$8.16) = \$8,160$$
$$\text{Gain (or loss) on investment} = (\$9,360 + \$270) - \$8,160 = \$1,470$$
$$\text{ROI} = \frac{\$1,470}{\$8,160} = 0.1801470588 \approx 18.01\%$$

Although there is no secret formula for building wealth, finding the right mix of investments depends on your age, assets, financial objectives, and risk tolerance. Building a solid base in lower-risk investments, similar to the approach of the investment pyramid, will allow you to create a foundation from which you can create a more diversified portfolio of additional investments—and hopefully allow you to participate more intelligently in the market.

STOP AND CHECK

See Example 5.

1. Calculate the ROI for 1,000 shares of a mutual fund purchased with an offer price of $12.73 per share if the shares were sold with a net asset value (NAV) of $14.52 per share and had paid a dividend of $0.83 per share during ownership.

2. Calculate the ROI for 1,500 shares of a mutual fund purchased with an offer price of $22.84 per share if the shares were sold with a net asset value (NAV) of $21.97 and had paid a dividend of $0.21 per share during ownership.

3. Calculate the ROI for 2,322.341 shares of a mutual fund purchased with an offer price of $21.53 if the shares were sold with a net asset value (NAV) of $23.89 and had paid a dividend of $1.78 per share during ownership.

4. Mary Wingard invested $20,000 in mutual funds with an offer price of $17.54 per share. The shares were sold with a net asset value of $22.35 and had paid a dividend of $1.06 per share during ownership. Calculate the ROI for this investment. (Hint: Divide the total invested by the offer price to get the number of shares in the investment.)

15-3 SECTION EXERCISES

SKILL BUILDERS

See Example 1.

1. What is the current price per share of the IICAX mutual fund (Table 15-4)?

2. What is the current price per share of the AAGSX mutual fund (Table 15-4)?

See Example 2.

3. Find the sales charge and sales charge percent for one share of LPEVX mutual fund stock if the stock was offered at $6.01 per share.

4. Find the sales charge and sales charge percent for one share of APITX mutual fund stock if the stock was offered at $8.51 per share.

See Example 1.

5. Find the price per share of ASITX for the previous day (Table 15-4).

6. Find the price per share of ASMTX for the previous day (Table 15-4).

APPLICATIONS

See Example 3.

7. Find the beginning of year NAV for AAGSX (Table 15-4).

8. Find the beginning of year NAV for ASARX (Table 15-4).

See Example 4.

9. Calculate the number of shares purchased with a $5,000 investment in a no load mutual fund with a net asset value of $7.93.

10. How many shares of mutual fund stock can be purchased with a $12,000 investment if the fund net asset value is $11.17 per share and it is a no load mutual fund?

See Example 5.

11. Calculate the return on investment for 2,000 shares of a mutual fund purchased with an offer price of $15.83 if the shares were sold with a NAV of $18.72. The shares paid a dividend of $0.87 per share during ownership. Round percent to hundredths.

12. Find the return on investment for 1,800 shares of a mutual fund purchased with an offer price of $28.47 if the shares were sold with a NAV of $26.99. The shares paid a dividend of $0.12 per share during ownership. Round percent to hundredths.

Learning Outcomes

Section 15-1

1 Read stock listings. (p. 542)

What to Remember with Examples

1. Column 1 (Name) shows the name of the corporation in abbreviated form.
2. Column 2 (Symbol) shows the company symbol used in stock listings.
3. Column 3 (Open) shows the share price when the market opens for this day.
4. Columns 4 (High), 5 (Low), and 6 (Close) show the highest and lowest prices at which the stock sold this day and the price of the stock at market closing time.
5. Column 7 (Net Chg) shows how much this day's closing price per share differs from the previous day's closing price per share for that stock.
6. Column 8 (% Chg) shows the percentage of increase or decrease of the day's closing price over the day's opening price of a stock.
7. Column 9 (Volume) shows the total number of shares of the stock that are traded on this day.
8. Columns 10 (52 Wk High) and 11 (52 Wk Low) show the highest and lowest prices at which the stock has sold in the last year (52 weeks), not including this day.
9. Column 12 (Div) shows the dividend paid per share of stock the previous year. An *e* following the dividend indicates that the dividend is an irregular cash dividend.
10. Column 13 (Yield) shows the previous year's dividend as a percent of the current price per share. If no dividend was paid the previous year, the entry is "…"
11. Column 14 (P/E) shows the stock's price/earnings ratio.
12. Column 15 (YTD% Chg) shows the percentage by which this day's closing price per share differs from the closing price per share on the first day of business of the current year.

Refer to Table 15-1:

How many shares of ACO were traded this day?

From column 9:
123,371 shares traded this day

What is the difference between the highest and lowest prices of ACO stock for the year?

From columns 10 and 11:
$32.60 - $18.24 = $14.36

Calculate the current yield on a stock.

1. Divide the annual dividend per share by the closing price per share then multiply by 100% to express as a percent.

$$\text{Current Yield} = \frac{\text{Annual dividend per share}}{\text{closing price per share}} \times 100\%$$

2. Round the quotient to the nearest tenth of a percent.

Find the current yield of AMB stock that reported a dividend of $1.12 and a closing price of $28.88.

$$\text{Current Yield} = \frac{\text{annual dividend per share}}{\text{closing price per share}} \times 100\%$$

$$= \frac{\$1.12}{\$28.88}(100\%)$$

$$= 0.038781163 (100\%)$$

Current Yield = 3.9% (Note: this is consistent with the Yield for AMB in Table 15-1.)

Calculate the price-earnings ratio of a stock.

1. Divide the current stock price by the annual net income per share for the past 12 months.

$$\text{Price-earnings (P/E) ratio} = \frac{\text{current price per share}}{\text{net income per share (past 12 months)}}$$

2. Round the quotient to the nearest whole number.

Find the P/E ratio of a corporation that reported last year's net income as $7.32 per share if the company's stock currently sells for $58.32 per share.

$$P/E \text{ ratio} = \frac{\text{current price per share}}{\text{net income per share (past 12 months)}}$$

$$= \frac{\$58.32}{\$7.32}$$

$$= 7.967213115$$

P/E ratio = 8 (round to the nearest whole number)

2 Calculate and distribute dividends. (p. 546)

1. First pay dividends in arrears:
   (a) Multiply the number of shares held by preferred stockholders by the given dividend rate, expressed as dollars per share.
   (b) Subtract the dividends in arrears from the available amount of money.
2. Pay the present year's preferred stock dividends:
   (a) Multiply the number of preferred shares held by stockholders by the given dividend rate.
   (b) Subtract these preferred stock dividends from the difference from step 1b.
3. Pay the common stock dividend: Divide the difference from step 2b by the number of common shares held by stockholders. This is the dividend per share for common stockholders.

$500,000 is available for dividends, including $20,000 for dividends in arrears and $20,000 for current preferred stock dividends. How much will be given for common stock dividends?

$$\$500,000 - \$40,000 = \$460,000$$

$460,000 is available for common stock dividends. There are 300,000 shares of common stock. What is the dividend per share?

$$\frac{\$460,000}{300,000} = \$1.533333333 = \$1.53 \text{ per share}$$

Section 15-2

1 Read bond listings. (p. 549)

1. Columns 1 and 2 give the name of the issuing company and its corresponding symbol.
2. Column 3 gives the annual interest rate, expressed as a percent of face value.
3. Column 4 gives the maturity, the month/year when the bond will mature.
4. Column 5 provides the issuer's bond rating from the three primary rating services.
5. Columns 6 and 7 provide the high and low values for the trading day.
6. Column 8 shows the last or closing price per bond as a percent of face value; an entry of 101.225 (COMCAST CORP) means the bond sold for 101.225% of $1,000 per bond, or 1.01225 times $1,000, or $1,012.25 per bond.
7. Column 9 shows the change in price from the previous day's closing price per bond, as a percent of the face value per bond.
8. Column 10 gives the yield to maturity, which is the rate of return over the life of the bond.

Refer to Table 15-3.

(a) What are the interest rate and the date of maturity for BCS.GYR?
(b) What is the rating for this bond provided by Moody's?
(c) What are the change and yield % for this bond issue?

(a) **From column 3, we see the interest rate is 5.000%, and from column 4, the maturity date is Sep 2016.**
(b) **From column 5, the rating provided by Moody's is Aa3.**
(c) **From columns 9 and 10, the change is 0.595 and the yield is 4.351%.**

2 Calculate the price of bonds. (p. 551)

1. Locate the percent of $1,000 that the bond was selling for at the close of the day (column 8).
2. Multiply the decimal equivalent of the percent by $1,000.
3. Round the product to the nearest cent.

You purchase five bonds listed at 98.500. What is the cost of one bond? five bonds?

For one bond: 98.500% of $1,000 = 0.985($1,000) = $985

For five bonds: 5($985) = $4,925
Cost of bonds: $4,925

---

3 Calculate the current bond yield. (p. 552)

1. Calculate the current price of a bond.
2. Locate the stated interest rate or coupon in column 3.
3. Multiply the stated interest rate by $1,000, the face value of the bond.
4. Divide the result by the current price of the bond.

$$\text{Current yield} = \frac{\text{stated interest rate (as a decimal)} \times \$1,000}{\text{current price of bond}} \times 100\%$$

Calculate the current bond yield for CMCD.GC (Table 15-3).

$$\text{Current yield} = \frac{\text{Stated interest rate (as a decimal)} \times \$1,000}{\text{Price of bond}} \times 100\%$$

$$\text{Current yield} = \frac{0.0515(\$1,000)}{\$1,012.25}(100\%)$$

Current price of the bond is 101.225% of $1,000, or $1,012.25.

$$= \frac{\$51.50}{\$1,012.25}(100\%)$$

Stated interest rate or coupon in column 3 is 5.150%, or 0.0515.

$$= 0.0508767597(100\%)$$

Current yield = 5.088% (rounded to three decimal places)

Section 15-3

1 Read mutual fund listings. (p. 553)

1. Find the appropriate fund family (bold entry in column 1, Table 15-4).
2. Find the appropriate fund name (indented entry in column 1).
3. Find the mutual fund symbol in column 2.
4. Find the net asset value (NAV) in column 3.
5. Identify the one-day total change (Chg) from column 4.
6. Identify the total return for the year to date (YTD % return) from column 5 and the three-year total return (3-yr. % Chg) from column 6.

Use Table 15-4 to find the current price per share (NAV), the percent change from yesterday's NAV (Chg), and the percent change in the NAV from the beginning of the year (YTD % return) for ASCPX.

NAV = $4.81   Current price per share
Chg = −0.01   Percent change from yesterday's price per share

YTD % return = 0.1%   Percent change from the price per share at the beginning of the year

---

Find the mutual fund sales charge and the sales charge percent:

1. Subtract net asset value from selling (offer) price.

$$\text{Mutual fund sales charge} = \text{selling (offer) price} - \text{net asset value}$$

2. $\text{Sales charge percent} = \dfrac{\text{sales charge}}{\text{net asset value}} \times 100\%$

Find the sales charge and the sales charge percent for one share of a mutual fund stock that is offered at $17.43 if its net asset value is $16.97.

$$\text{Mutual fund sales charge} = \$17.43 - \$16.97 = \$0.46$$

$$\text{Sales charge percent} = \left(\frac{\$0.46}{\$16.97}\right)100\% = 2.71\%$$

Find the net asset value at the beginning of the year for one share of a mutual fund.

1. Divide the Current NAV by the sum of 100% and the YTD% return.

$$\text{Beginning of year NAV} = \frac{\text{current NAV}}{100\% + \text{YTD\% return}}$$

2. Round the quotient to the nearest cent.

Find the beginning of year NAV for ASMTX (Table 15-4).

$$\begin{aligned}
\text{Beginning of year NAV} &= \frac{\text{current NAV}}{100\% + \text{YTD\% return}} \\
&= \frac{\$8.64}{1 + 0.002} \\
&= \frac{\$8.64}{1.002} \\
&= \$8.622754491
\end{aligned}$$

The beginning of year NAV = 8.62 (round to hundredths)

Calculate the number of shares purchased of a mutual fund.

1. Calculate the number of shares purchased by dividing the total amount of the investment by the offer price of the fund. With a no-load fund, use the NAV as the denominator.

$$\text{Number of shares purchased} = \frac{\text{total investment}}{\text{offer price}}$$

2. Round the quotient to the nearest thousandth, or three decimal places.

Calculate the number of shares purchased with a $2,000 investment in a no load mutual fund with a NAV of $9.47.

$$\text{Number of shares purchased} = \frac{\text{total investment}}{\text{offer price}}$$

$$\text{Number of shares purchased} = \frac{\$2,000}{\$9.47} = 211.1932418 \text{ or } 211.193 \text{ shares}$$

2 Calculate return on investment (ROI). (p. 557)

1. Calculate the amount of gain or loss on the sale or value of the investment by subtracting the total cost from the proceeds of the sale, including any additions from dividends or interest.

$$\text{Gain or loss on investment} = (\text{proceeds of sale} + \text{additions}) - \text{total cost}$$

2. Calculate the ROI by dividing the total gain of the investment by the total cost of the investment.

$$\text{ROI} = \frac{\text{total gain (or loss)}}{\text{total cost of investment}}$$

Calculate return on investment for 1,800 shares of a mutual fund purchased with an offer price of $10.65, which were sold with a NAV of $12.58, and had paid a dividend during ownership of $0.23 per share.

$$\begin{aligned}
\text{Total proceeds from sale} &= 1,800 \text{ shares } (\$12.58) = \$22,644 \\
\text{Additions} &= 1,800 \text{ shares } (\$0.23) = \$414 \\
\text{Total cost of investment} &= 1,800 \text{ shares } (\$10.65) = \$19,170 \\
\text{Gain (or loss) on investment} &= (\$22,644 + \$414) - \$19,170 = \$3,888 \\
\text{ROI} &= \frac{\$3,888}{\$19,170} = 0.202816901 = 20.28\%
\end{aligned}$$

EXERCISES SET A

For Exercises 1–6, refer to Table 15-1.

1. How many shares of ACE LTD. stock were traded?

2. What is the difference between the high and low prices of ACE LTD. for the last 52 weeks?

3. What was the difference between the day's high and low trading prices for one share of ACE LTD. stock?

4. What was the previous day's closing price of ACE LTD. stock?

5. How much money was paid in dividends for one share of Abercrombie stock? For 50 shares? For 100 shares?

6. What is this day's closing price for one share of AFLAC Inc. stock?

7. Find the current yield of Oil-Dri Corp. of America (ODC) that reported a dividend of $0.60 and a closing price of $21.19.

8. Find the current yield of Penn Virginia Partners (PVR) that reported a dividend of $1.88 and a closing price of $21.82.

9. Find the P/E ratio of a corporation that reported last year's net income of $7.71 per share if the company's stock sells for $67.95 per share.

10. Find the P/E ratio of a corporation that reported last year's net income of $2.59 per share if the company's stock sells for $41.44 per share.

Your company has 120,000 shares of cumulative preferred stock that pays dividends at $0.25 per share and 200,000 shares of common stock. This year, $500,000 is to be distributed. The preferred stockholders are also due to receive dividends in arrears for one year.

11. What is the amount of the dividends in arrears?

12. How much will go to the preferred stockholders for this year's dividends?

13. How much money will be distributed in all to common stockholders?

14. What is the dividend per share for the common stockholders?

For Exercises 15–22, refer to Table 15-3.

15. What was the closing price of the GS.IAR bond?

16. What is the yield to maturity for the GS.IAR bond?

17. What is the date of maturity of the GS.IAR bond?

18. Find the previous day's closing price for a GS.IAR bond.

19. Calculate the previous day's closing price for a T.KM bond.

20. What is the S&P rating for the T.KM bond?

21. Calculate the current yield of a BAC.ICB bond.

22. Calculate the current bond yield for a bond that has a close of 108.633 and a coupon of 6.800%.

23. Use Table 15-4 to find yesterday's NAV for the AAMDX mutual fund.

EXCEL 24. Find the beginning-of-the-year NAV for the AACNX mutual fund.

25. Find the beginning-of-the-year NAV for a mutual fund that has a current NAV of 15.06 and a YTD% return of 7.9.

26. Find the beginning-of-the-year NAV for a mutual fund that has a current NAV of 10.76 and a YTD% return of 1.7.

27. Find the current price per share of the AULTX mutual fund. What was the price per share yesterday? Use Table 15-4.

28. Find the sales charge and the sales charge percent for one share of the ASCPX mutual fund stock if the stock was offered at $4.94. Use Table 15-4. Round to the nearest hundredth of a percent.

29. Calculate the number of shares purchased with a $5,000 investment in a no-load mutual fund with a NAV of $21.47. Round to the nearest thousandth of a share.

30. Calculate the return on investment for 5,000 shares of a mutual fund purchased with an offer price of $32.16 if the shares were sold with a NAV of $34.72. The shares paid a dividend of $0.26 per share during ownership. Round percent to hundredths.

EXERCISES SET B

For Exercises 1–6, refer to Table 15-1.

1. What was the annual dividend paid for one share of AT&T INC. stock?

2. What is this day's closing price of AT&T INC. stock?

3. What is the current yield on AT&T INC. stock?

4. Find the current yield for ABBOT Laboratories.

5. Which of the two companies, AMB Property or AT&T INC., has the greater dividend per share?

6. Which of the two companies, AT&T INC. or AVX CORP, has the greater yield?

7. Find the current yield of New York Community Bancorp (NYB) that reported a dividend of $1.00 and a closing price of $15.99.

8. Find the current yield of National Semiconductor Corp. (NSM) that reported a dividend of $0.32 and a closing price of $14.05.

9. Find the P/E ratio of a corporation that reported last year's net income of $4.85 per share if the company's stock sells for $33.65 per share.

10. Find the P/E ratio of Murphy Oil Corp. (MUR) that reported last year's net income of $4.34 per share if the company's stock sells for $56.47 per share.

Aetna has 400,000 shares of cumulative preferred stock that pays dividends at $2.13 per share and 1,500,000 shares of common stock. This year, $4,250,000 is to be distributed, and preferred stockholders are due to receive dividends in arrears for one year.

11. What is the amount of dividends in arrears?

12. What are this year's preferred stockholder dividends?

13. Find the dividends distributed to common stockholders.

14. What is the dividend per share for common stockholders?

For Exercises 15–22, refer to Table 15-3.

15. What is the coupon rate of the Bank of America bond that is listed at closing at 100.231%?

16. What is the dollar price of a Barclays Bank PLC bond listed at closing?

17. Which of the bonds GS.IAR or BUD.ID is selling at a discount? At a premium?

18. Find the previous day's closing price for a BAC.ICB bond.

19. Find the previous day's closing price for a KFT.GX bond.

20. What is the S&P rating for the KFT.GX bond?

21. Calculate the current yield of a C.HRY bond (Table 15-3).

22. Calculate the current bond yield for a bond that has a close of 113.461 and a coupon of 7.875%.

23. Find the closing NAV for the IICAX mutual fund in Table 15-4.

24. Find the beginning-of-the-year NAV for the AULTX mutual fund in Table 15-4.

25. Find the beginning-of-the-year NAV for a mutual fund that has a current NAV of 9.72 and a YTD% return of 2.6.

26. Find the beginning-of-the-year NAV for a mutual fund that has a current NAV of 12.42 and a YTD% return of 0.9.

27. Find the current price per share of the MLSAX mutual fund. What was the price per share yesterday? Use Table 15-4.

28. Find the sales charge and the sales charge percent for one share of the AACNX mutual fund stock if the stock was offered at $10.66. Use Table 15-4. Round to the nearest hundredth of a percent.

29. Calculate the number of shares purchased with a $8,000 investment in a no-load mutual fund with a NAV of $17.84. Round to the nearest thousandth of a share.

30. Calculate the return on investment for 12,500 shares of a mutual fund purchased with an offer price of $16.23 if the shares were sold with a NAV of $16.08. The shares paid a dividend of $0.11 per share during ownership. Round percent to hundredths.

PRACTICE TEST

CHAPTER 15

Use the following stock listing for McDonaldsCorp for Exercises 1–7.

52 Weeks				Yld								YTD%
High	Low	Symbol	Div	%	P/E	Volume	High	Low	Close	Chg	Chg	
71.84	53.03	MCD	2.2	3.2	16	8,429,746	70.45	69.10	69.59	−0.91	11.5	

1. What is the difference between this day's high and low?

2. What is the current yield?

3. What is this day's closing price, in dollars?

4. What was the previous day's closing price, in dollars?

5. How many shares were traded this day?

6. Last year you bought 120 shares of McDonaldsCorp at $54.86. Calculate the amount the shares cost when purchased.

7. Calculate the value of your stock at the close of business this day.

Use the following information to answer Exercises 8–11.

Your company has $200,000 to distribute in dividends to three groups:
A: One year's dividends in arrears for 5,000 shares of cumulative preferred stock ($0.40 per share)
B: The current year's dividends for those 5,000 shares of cumulative preferred stock ($0.40 per share)
C: Dividends on 75,000 shares of common stock

8. How much is distributed to group A?

9. How much is distributed to group B?

10. How much is distributed to group C?

11. What is the dividend per share of common stock?

Use the following stock listing for Exercises 12 and 13.

52 Weeks				Yld		Sales				
High	Low	Stock	Div	%	P/E	100s	High	Low	Last	Chg
$9.75	$6.63	PennAM	0.21	2.7	dd	11	7.69	7.56	7.69	+0.13
$34.31	$20.00	PennEMA	0.56	1.9	12	5	29.81	21.81	29.81	−0.06

12. What is the P/E ratio of PennEMA?

13. You own 1,000 shares of PennAM. How much do you receive in annual dividends?

Use the following bond listing for Exercises 14–17.

12 Mo				Cur		Daily				
Hi	Lo	Name	Maturity	Yld	Vol	Hi	Lo	Cls	Chg	
106.875	60	Polaroid	May 2019	18.0	2211	73.875	60	64	−8.375	

14. What is the date of maturity of the bond?

15. What is the closing price of the bond, in dollars?

16. What was the previous day's closing price, in dollars?

17. Is the Polaroid bond selling at a premium or a discount?

18. Use Table 15-4 to find the current price per share of the ASARX mutual fund.

19. Find yesterday's price per share of the AACNX mutual fund in Table 15-4.

20. What is the price per share of the LPEVX mutual fund at the beginning of the year from Table 15-4?

21. Find the current yield of Medtronic, Inc., stock that reported a dividend of $0.82 and a closing price of $42.39.

22. Find the current yield of McDonalds' Corp (MCD) stock that reported a dividend of $2.20 and a closing price of $69.59.

23. Find the P/E ratio of Massey Energy Co. (MEE) that reported last year's net income of $1.23 per share if the company's stock sells for $37.00 per share.

24. Calculate the current bond yield for a bond that has a close of 107.632 and a coupon of 6.625%.

25. Find the beginning-of-the-year NAV for a mutual fund that has a current NAV of 11.15 and YTD% return of 3.8.

26. Find the current price per share of the APITX mutual fund. What was the price per share yesterday? Use Table 15-4.

27. Find the current price per share of the ASARX mutual fund. What was the price per share yesterday? Use Table 15-4.

28. Find the sales charge and the sales charge percent for one share of the AACNX mutual fund stock if the stock was offered at $10.60275. Use Table 15-4. Round to the nearest hundredth of a percent.

29. Calculate the number of shares purchased with a $12,375 investment in a no-load mutual fund with a NAV of $19.12. Round to the nearest thousandth of a share.

30. Calculate the return on investment for 6,100 shares of a mutual fund purchased with an offer price of $18.39 if the shares were sold with a NAV of $19.01. The shares paid a dividend of $0.55 per share during ownership. Round percent to hundredths.

1. In the columns for listing stock information, some columns give necessary information for finding additional information, and other columns give convenience information that could have been generated by information in other columns. Give an example of a column giving convenience information.

2. To find the previous day's price of a stock, you use the current day's price and the amount of change. When do you add and when do you subtract? Give a strategy for predicting the result that will help you to avoid performing the wrong operation.

3. Using the formula

$$\text{P/E ratio} = \frac{\text{closing price per share}}{\text{annual earnings per share}}$$

write a formula and explain your rationale for finding the annual earnings per share for the stock listing information.

4. How are bonds different from stocks?

5. How are bonds different from certificates of deposit or savings accounts?

6. Does column 13 in Table 15-1 give convenience information or new information that could not be calculated from other table information? Explain your answer.

7. In Table 15-3, select the bond that is discounted. How can you tell the difference?

8. When are premium bonds a wise investment? When are discounted bonds a wise investment?

Challenge Problem

Column 13 of Table 15-1 shows the Yield in percent form. The notes on reading stock listings indicate the yield is the previous year's dividends as a percent of the current price per share. Use this explanation to verify the yield of ABM stock that has a closing price of $22.03 and paid dividends of $0.54 last year.

CASE STUDIES

15-1 Dynamic Thermoforming, Inc.

With the upcoming annual shareholders' meeting only a week away, Chief Executive Officer Christopher Lee had a great deal of information to prepare. There was some very good news to communicate: Profits for the five-year-old plastics company were at record levels and $275,000 was available for dividends to be paid, unlike last year when no dividends were paid. But the business was at a crossroads as well. Technological advancements in the thermoforming industry were forcing individual companies to make substantial investments in advanced production capacity to remain viable. Christopher would be recommending to the board of directors a $2.4 million corporate bond issue to pay for the improved production capabilities. In addition, employee retention was also a major goal for the company. Feedback from the employees had focused on the need for a company-sanctioned retirement program. In response, Dynamic Thermoforming, Inc., would be offering a 401(k) retirement program complete with a number of different investment choices, including some of the top mutual fund families. In addition, the first 3% of an employee's salary contributed would be fully matched by the company. Together, these three topics would set the tone for continued success in the marketplace, and surely give a boost to the already favorable employee morale.

1. Dynamic Thermoforming, Inc., has previously issued 25,000 shares of cumulative preferred stock that will earn dividends at $0.70 per share and 75,000 shares of common stock. Because no dividends were paid last year, how will the $275,000 declared for dividends be distributed?

2. A Dynamic Thermoforming $1,000 corporate bond is issued and has a stated interest rate of 5.375% with a current price of 95.50. What is the current yield? Round your answer to the nearest 0.01%.

3. Quentin Avery, a sales manager with Dynamic Thermoforming, decides to put 3% of his $72,000 salary into an international growth fund offered through the new 401(k) plan. The current net asset value is 17.94 and the year-to-date return is +4.9%. How many shares will Quentin be able to purchase each month, and what was the net asset value of the fund at the beginning of the year?

4. Nicole Wagner, a new employee, decides to roll over her existing 401(k) plan, worth $27,081, into a fund with a net asset value of 13.50. Calculate the number of shares that Nicole purchased with this initial investment. Also, calculate the return on investment if Nicole's shares grew to $14.58 per share with a dividend paid of $0.21 per share during ownership, before she moved it to a different fund. Ignore the 3% matching on all calculations.

15-2 Corporate Dividends and Investments

Jason is the supervisor of his company's accounting department and reports to the company's assistant controller. Jason's duties vary, but two things he is responsible for include determining how much money must be on hand to pay dividends when the board of directors declares them, and recommending investments when his company has extra cash to invest.

Earnings have been strong and recently the board of directors declared a dividend. The 500,000 shares of cumulative preferred stock are entitled to 30 cents a share each year and the 1,000,000 common shares are to be given 40 cents a share. Because earnings were less than expected for the last two years, dividends were not paid to any of the shareholders last year. Because the preferred shares are cumulative, Jason knows the preferred shareholders must be paid their contractual amount along with this year's dividend.

1. How much money should Jason plan to have available for the dividend distribution that is to occur in two weeks?

Jason knows the amount of cash needed to distribute dividends. In fact, in addition to this amount, he feels that the company could invest another $1,000,000 in the stock and bond market. He feels that it would be appropriate to put half in the bond market and half in the stock market and intends to make that suggestion to the assistant controller. He would also like to make some specific recommendations for the assistant controller to consider. He only suggests investments that are actively traded, do not fluctuate widely in their prices, and have moderate yields.

Jason has been scanning the financial market data online. In the bond market data he studied the differences between the bonds' high and low prices, their current yields, and the volume traded. In the stock data, he focused on high and low prices, volume, and yield. He has identified the following three bonds and three stocks with their respective closing prices and PE ratios as possible candidates for his company to buy:

Bonds		Stocks		
TRICOR	97.75	AGCO	9.25	PE = 5
COMCAST	103	RADIAN GROUP	12.5	PE = 15
CITI GROUP	92.5	BUCKEYE TECH	14.75	PE = 10

2. Based on the above information, at what price is each bond currently selling?

3. Based on the stock prices listed above, how much would 100 shares of each stock cost? Ignore commission costs. What were the earnings per share over the last year for each stock?

4. Based on upcoming cash needs, the assistant controller feels that the company should invest only $750,000 and should put the full amount into stocks. If she distributes the money evenly among the three stocks, how much money will she spend on each purchase? How many shares will she be able to buy of each stock?

5. A year after the company invests $250,000 into shares of RADIAN GROUP at a price of $12.50 per share, the stock climbs to $13.46; in addition, a dividend of $0.20 per share was distributed during the year. Compute the ROI for this investment.

Real Estate Tax Benefits

For most individuals, owning an affordable home is the American dream, but did you know that borrowing to pay for one is a taxpayer's dream? Home mortgage interest is deductible on your income taxes if you itemize deductions. You can deduct the interest on up to $1 million of home mortgage debt, whether it is used to purchase a first or a second home. You can also deduct the interest on up to $100,000 of home equity debt, even if you don't use the money for home improvements. What could the home mortgage deduction mean to you? What follows is an example of the potential tax savings for Devin, age 27.

Devin rents a home at a cost of $1,200 per month. He is single with no children and takes the standard deduction on his income taxes. His adjusted gross income is $50,000. He has $3,500 in state income tax withheld from his paychecks throughout the year, but doesn't qualify for any other itemized deductions. Devin's federal income tax liability for 2012 will look something like this:

Adjusted gross income:	$50,000
Less standard deduction (single):	$5,950
Less personal exemption:	$3,800
Taxable income	$40,250

Devin's 2012 federal income tax is $6,093

However, if Devin purchases a home with a monthly mortgage payment of $1,200, his tax liability is lowered. At the end of the year Devin will receive a Form 1098 from his mortgage company that shows how much of his mortgage payments for the year went to mortgage interest. In this case, Devin's 1098 for the year 2012 shows that he paid $11,400 in mortgage interest. Devin also paid $2,500 in real estate taxes on his home in 2012. His federal income tax liability for 2012 will look something like this:

Adjusted gross income:	$50,000
Less itemized deduction (state taxes):	$3,500
Less itemized deduction (real estate taxes):	$2,500
Less itemized deduction (mortgage interest):	$11,400
Less personal exemption:	$3,800
Taxable income	$28,880

Devin's 2012 federal income tax is $3,885.

In this example, Devin saves $2,208 in federal income taxes, nearly enough to pay for his real estate taxes of $2,500. In addition, his monthly housing cost stays the same and he owns his home rather than renting. Good deal, Devin!

LEARNING OUTCOMES

16-1 Mortgage Payments

1. Find the monthly mortgage payment.
2. Find the total interest on a mortgage and the PITI.

16-2 Amortization Schedules and Qualifying Ratios

1. Prepare a partial amortization schedule of a mortgage.
2. Calculate qualifying ratios.

LEARNING OUTCOMES

1 Find the monthly mortgage payment.
2 Find the total interest on a mortgage and the PITI.

Real estate or real property: land plus any permanent improvements to the land.

Mortgage: a loan in which real property is used to secure the debt.

Collateral: the property that is held as security on a mortgage.

Equity: the difference between the expected selling price and the balance owed on property.

Market value: the expected selling price of a property.

First mortgage: the primary mortgage on a property.

Conventional mortgage: mortgage that is not insured by a government program.

Fixed-rate mortgage: the interest rate for the mortgage remains the same for the entire loan.

Biweekly mortgage: payment is made every two weeks for 26 payments per year.

Graduated payments mortgage: payments at the beginning of the loan are smaller and they increase during the loan.

Adjustable-rate mortgage: the interest rate may change during the time of the loan.

Federal Housing Administration (FHA): a governmental agency within the U.S. Department of Housing and Urban Development (HUD) that insures residential mortgage loans. To receive an FHA loan, specific construction standards must be met and the lender must be approved.

Veterans Administration (VA): a governmental agency that guarantees the repayment of a loan made to an eligible veteran. The loans are also called GI loans.

Second mortgage: a mortgage in addition to the first mortgage that is secured by the real property.

Equity line of credit: a revolving, open-end account that is secured by real property.

The purchase of a home is one of the most costly purchases individuals or families make in a lifetime. A home is a type of "real" property. **Real estate** or **real property** is land plus any permanent improvements to the land. The improvements can be water or sewage systems, homes, commercial buildings, or any type of structure. Most individuals must borrow money to pay for the real property. These loans are referred to as **mortgages** because the lending agency requires that the real property be held as **collateral.** If the payments are not made as scheduled, the lending agency can take possession of the property and sell it to pay against the loan.

As a home buyer makes payments on a mortgage, the home buyer builds equity in the home. The home buyer's **equity** is the difference between the expected selling price of a home or **market value** and the balance owed on the home. A home may increase or decrease in value as a result of economic changes and average prices of other homes in the neighborhood. This change in value also changes the owner's equity in the home.

A home buyer may select from several types of first mortgages. A **first mortgage** is the primary mortgage on a home and is ordinarily made at the time of purchase of the home. The agency holding the first mortgage has the first right to the proceeds up to the amount of the mortgage and settlement fees from the sale of the home if the homeowner fails to make required payments.

One type of first mortgage is the **conventional mortgage.** Money for a conventional mortgage is usually obtained through a mortgage lender or a bank. These loans are not insured by a government program. Two types of conventional mortgages are the *fixed-rate mortgage* (FRM) and the *adjustable-rate mortgage* (ARM). The rate of interest on the loan for a **fixed-rate mortgage** remains the same for the entire time of the loan. Fixed-rate mortgages have several payment options. The number of years of the loan may vary, but 15- and 30-year loans are the most common. The home buyer makes the same payment (principal plus interest) each month of the loan. Another option is the **biweekly mortgage**. The home buyer makes 26 equal payments each year rather than 12. This method builds equity more quickly than the monthly payment method.

Another option for fixed-rate loans is the **graduated payments mortgage**. The home buyer makes small payments at the beginning of the loan and larger payments at the end. Home buyers who expect their income to rise may choose this option.

The rate of interest on a loan for an **adjustable-rate mortgage** may escalate (increase) or de-escalate (decrease) during the time of the loan. The rate of an adjustable-rate mortgage depends on the prime lending rate of most banks.

Several government agencies insure the repayment of first mortgage loans. Loans with this insurance include those made under the **Federal Housing Administration (FHA)** and the **Veterans Administration (VA).** These loans may be obtained through a savings and loan institution, a bank, or a mortgage lending company and are insured by a government program.

Interest paid on home loans is an allowable deduction on personal federal income tax under certain conditions. For this reason, many homeowners choose to borrow money for home improvements, college education, and the like by making an additional loan using the real property as collateral. This type of loan is a **second mortgage** or an **equity line of credit** and is made against the equity in the home. In the case of a loan default, the second mortgage lender has rights to the proceeds of the sale of the home *after* the first mortgage has been paid.

1 Find the monthly mortgage payment.

Amortization: the process for repaying a loan through equal payments at a specified rate for a specific length of time.

Monthly mortgage payment: the amount of the equal monthly payment that includes interest and principal.

The repayment of a loan in equal installments that are applied to principal and interest over a specific period of time is called the **amortization** of the loan. To calculate the **monthly mortgage payment,** it is customary to use a table, a formula, a business or financial calculator that has the formula programmed into the calculator, or computer software. The monthly payment table gives the factor that is multiplied by the dollar amount of the loan in thousands to give the total monthly payment, including principal and interest. A portion of a monthly payment table is shown in Table 16-1.

The interest rate for first mortgages has fluctuated between 3% and 8% for the past few years. Second mortgage rates are generally higher than first mortgage rates.

TABLE 16-1
Monthly Payment of Principal and Interest per $1,000 of Amount Financed

Years financed	Annual interest rate															
	3.00%	3.25%	3.50%	3.75%	4.00%	4.25%	4.50%	4.75%	5.00%	5.25%	5.50%	5.75%	6.00%	6.25%	6.50%	6.75%
10	9.66	9.77	9.89	10.01	10.12	10.24	10.36	10.48	10.61	10.73	10.85	10.98	11.10	11.23	11.35	11.48
12	8.28	8.40	8.51	8.63	8.76	8.88	9.00	9.12	9.25	9.37	9.50	9.63	9.76	9.89	10.02	10.15
15	6.91	7.03	7.15	7.27	7.40	7.52	7.65	7.78	7.91	8.04	8.17	8.30	8.44	8.57	8.71	8.85
17	6.26	6.39	6.51	6.64	6.76	6.89	7.02	7.15	7.29	7.42	7.56	7.69	7.83	7.97	8.11	8.25
20	5.55	5.67	5.80	5.93	6.06	6.19	6.33	6.46	6.60	6.74	6.88	7.02	7.16	7.31	7.46	7.60
22	5.18	5.31	5.44	5.57	5.70	5.84	5.97	6.11	6.25	6.39	6.54	6.68	6.83	6.98	7.13	7.28
25	4.74	4.87	5.01	5.14	5.28	5.42	5.56	5.70	5.85	5.99	6.14	6.29	6.44	6.60	6.75	6.91
30	4.22	4.35	4.49	4.63	4.77	4.92	5.07	5.22	5.37	5.52	5.68	5.84	6.00	6.16	6.32	6.49
35	3.85	3.99	4.13	4.28	4.43	4.58	4.73	4.89	5.05	5.21	5.37	5.54	5.70	5.87	6.04	6.21

Table values show the monthly payment of a $1,000 mortgage for the given number of years at the given annual interest rate if the interest is compounded monthly. Table values can be generated by using the formula: $M = (\$1,000R)/(1 - (1 + R)^{\wedge}(-N))$, where M = monthly payment, R = the monthly interest rate, and N = total number of payments of the loan.

HOW TO   Find the monthly mortgage payment of principal and interest using a per-$1,000 monthly payment table

1. Find the amount financed: Subtract the down payment from the purchase price.
2. Find the number of $1,000 units in the amount financed: Divide the amount financed (from step 1) by $1,000.
3. Locate the table value for the number of years financed and the annual interest rate.
4. Multiply the table value from step 3 by the number of $1,000 units from step 2.

$$\text{Monthly mortgage payment} = \frac{\text{amount financed}}{\$1,000} \times \text{table value}$$

EXAMPLE 1   Lunelle Miller is purchasing a home for $212,000. Home Federal Savings and Loan has approved her loan application for a 30-year fixed-rate loan at 6% annual interest. If Lunelle agrees to pay 20% of the purchase price as a down payment, calculate the monthly payment.

$212,000(0.20) = $42,400	Down payment
$212,000 - $42,400 = $169,600	Amount to be financed
$169,600 ÷ $1,000 = 169.6	$1,000 units

Use Table 16-1 to find the factor for financing a loan for 30 years with a 6% annual interest rate. This factor is 6.00.
Multiply the number of thousands times the factor.

$$169.6(6.00) = \$1,017.60$$

The monthly payment of $1,017.60 includes the principal and interest.

HOW TO   Find the monthly mortgage payment of principal and interest using a formula

1. Identify the monthly rate (R) as a decimal equivalent, the number of months (N), and the loan principal (P).
2. Substitute the values from step 1 in the formula.

$$M = P\left(\frac{R}{1 - (1 + R)^{-N}}\right)$$

3. Evaluate the formula.

EXAMPLE 2
Use the monthly payment of principal and interest formula to find the monthly payment for Lunelle Miller's loan from Example 1.

$R = \dfrac{6\%}{12} = \dfrac{0.06}{12} = 0.005$ Monthly interest rate

$N = 30(12) = 360$ Total number of payments

$P = \$169{,}600$ Amount financed

$M = P\left(\dfrac{R}{1 - (1 + R)^{-N}}\right)$ Substitute known values.

$M = \$169{,}600\left(\dfrac{0.005}{1 - (1 + 0.005)^{-360}}\right)$

$M = \$169{,}600\left(\dfrac{0.005}{1 - (1.005)^{-360}}\right)$

$M = \$169{,}600\left(\dfrac{0.005}{1 - (0.166041928)}\right)$

$M = \$169{,}600\left(\dfrac{0.005}{0.833958072}\right)$

$M = \$169{,}600(0.0059955053)$

$M = \$1016.837691$

$M = \$1{,}016.84$

Calculator sequence:

169600 $\boxed{(}$ .005 $\boxed{)}$ $\boxed{\div}$ $\boxed{(}$ $\boxed{(}$ 1 $\boxed{-}$ $\boxed{(}$ 1 $\boxed{+}$ .005 $\boxed{)}$ $\boxed{\wedge}$ $\boxed{(}$ $\boxed{(}$ $\boxed{(-)}$ 360 $\boxed{)}$ $\boxed{)}$ $\boxed{)}$

$\boxed{\text{ENTER}} \Rightarrow 1016.837691$

On many calculators entering a negative number like -360 requires using a special key $\boxed{(-)}$.

The monthly payment of \$1,016.84 includes the principal and interest.

Note that the monthly payment using the table value of 6.00 compared to the formula calculation of 0.0059955053 times 1,000 or 5.9955053 causes a variation in the monthly payment.

HOW TO
Find the monthly payment of principal and interest using a calculator application

Values for Example 1 are used for illustration.

TI BA II Plus:

	Keys:	Display:	
Set decimals to two places if necessary.	2nd [FORMAT] 2 ENTER	DEC=	2.00
Reset TMV variables.	2nd [RESET] ENTER	RST	0.00
Set payments per year to 12.	2nd [P/Y] 12 ENTER	P/Y=	12.00
Return to standard calculator mode.	2nd [QUIT]		0.00
Enter number of years. using payment multiplier.	30 2nd [xP/Y] N	N=	360.00
Enter interest rate.	6 I/Y	I/Y=	6.00
Enter loan amount.	169600 PV	PV=	169,600.00
Compute payment.	CPT PMT	PMT=	−1,016.84

The monthly payment is \$1,016.84. Recall that *amounts paid out* are given as negative amounts.

The discrepancy in the table calculations and the calculator calculations is from table values being rounded to the nearest cent.

TI-84:

Change to 2 fixed decimal places.	MODE ↓ → → → ENTER
Select Finance Application.	APPS 1:Finance ENTER
Select TVM Solver.	ENTER

Use the arrows keys to move cursor to appropriate variables and enter amounts. Enter 0 for unknowns.

Press 360 ENTER to store 360 months to N.
Press 6 ENTER to store 6% per year to I%.
Press 169600 ENTER to store $169,600 to PV.
Press 0 ENTER to leave PMT unassigned.
Press 0 ENTER to leave FV unassigned.
Press 12 ENTER to store 12 payments/periods per year to P/Y and C/Y will automatically change to 12.
PMT: **END** should be highlighted.

Use the up arrow to move the cursor up to PMT in the middle of the screen. Press ALPHA [SOLVE] to solve for the monthly payment.

```
N=            360.00
I%=             6.00
PV=        169600.00
∎PMT=        −1016.84
FV=             0.00
P/Y=           12.00
C/Y=           12.00
PMT:END BEGIN
```

Casio fx-CG10
Select Financial Mode and set default to End and Display to Fix2.
Then press F2 to select Compound Interest. Use the arrow keys to move the cursor to appropriate variables and enter amounts.
360 EXE 6 EXE 0 EXE 169600 EXE 0 EXE 12 EXE F4 ⟹ −1016.837691

STOP AND CHECK

Use Table 16-1, the formula, or a calculator application. See Example 1.

1. Natalie Bradley is purchasing a home for $148,500 and has been preapproved for a 30-year fixed-rate loan of 5.75% annual interest. If Natalie pays 20% of the purchase price as a down payment, what will her principal-plus-interest payment be?

2. Find the monthly payment for a home loan of $160,000 using a 20-year fixed-rate mortgage at 5.5%.

See Example 2.

3. Find the monthly payment for a home loan of $160,000 using a 25-year fixed-rate mortgage at 5.5%.

4. Find the monthly payment for a home loan of $160,000 using a 30-year fixed-rate mortgage at 5.5%.

2   Find the total interest on a mortgage and the PITI.

Often, a buyer wants to know the total amount of interest that will be paid during the entire loan.

HOW TO   Find the total interest on a mortgage

1. Find the total of the payments: Multiply the number of payments by the amount of the payment (principal + interest).
2. Subtract the amount financed from the total of the payments.

Total interest = number of payments × amount of payment − amount financed

EXAMPLE 3

Calculate the total interest paid on the fixed-rate loan of $169,600 for 30 years at 6% interest rate using the payment amount found in Example 1.

Total interest = number of payments × amount of payment − amount financed
$$= 30(12)(\$1,017.60) - \$169,600$$
$$= \$366,336.00 - \$169,600$$
$$= \$196,736.00$$

The total interest is $196,736.00.

The three preceding examples show how to calculate the monthly payment and the total interest for a mortgage loan. There are other costs associated with purchasing a home. Lending companies may require the borrower to pay **points** at the time the loan is made or closed. Payment of points is a one-time payment of a percentage of the loan that is an additional cost of making the mortgage. One point is 1%, two points is 2%, and so on.

Fees charged for services that must be performed to process and close a home mortgage loan are called **mortgage closing costs.** Examples of these costs include credit reports, surveys, inspections, appraisals, legal fees, title insurance, and taxes. Even though these fees are paid when the loan is closed, lenders are required by law to disclose to the buyer in writing the estimated mortgage closing costs prior to the closing date. This estimate is known as the **good faith estimate.** Some fees are paid by the buyer and some by the seller. Average closing costs for most home purchases are about 6% of the loan amount.

Because the lending agency must be assured that the property taxes and insurance are paid on the property, the annual costs of these items may be prorated each year and added to the monthly payment for that year. These funds are held in **escrow** until the taxes or insurance payment is due, at which time the lending agency makes the payment for the homeowner. These additional costs make the monthly payment more than just the principal and interest payment we found in the preceding examples. The adjusted monthly payment that includes the principal, interest, taxes, and insurance is abbreviated as **PITI.**

Points: a one-time payment to the lender made at closing that is a percentage of the total loan.

Mortgage closing costs: fees charged for services that must be performed to process and close a home mortgage loan.

Good faith estimate: an estimate of the mortgage closing costs that lenders are required to provide to the buyer in writing prior to the loan closing date.

Escrow: an account for holding the part of a monthly payment that is to be used to pay taxes and insurance. The amount accumulates and the lender pays the taxes and insurance from this account as they are due.

PITI: the adjusted monthly payment that includes the principal, interest, taxes, and insurance.

HOW TO   Find the total PITI payment

1. Find the principal and interest portion of the monthly payment.
2. Find the monthly taxes by dividing the annual taxes by 12.
3. Find the monthly insurance by dividing the annual insurance by 12.
4. Find the sum of the monthly principal, interest, taxes, and insurance.

EXAMPLE 4

Find the total PITI payment for Lunelle Miller's loan from Example 1 if her annual taxes are $1,985 and her annual homeowner's insurance is $960.

$1,017.60	Monthly principal and interest found in Example 1
$1,985 ÷ 12 = $165.4166667	Monthly taxes
$960 ÷ 12 = $80.00	Monthly insurance

PITI = $1,017.60 + $165.42 + $80.00
= $1,263.02

The total PITI payment is $1,263.02.

EXAMPLE 5

Qua Wau is trying to determine whether to accept a 25-year 6.5% mortgage or a 20-year 6% mortgage on the house he is planning to buy. He needs to finance $125,700 and has planned to budget $1,000 monthly for his payment of principal and interest. Which mortgage should Qua choose?

What You Know	What You Are Looking For
Amount financed: $125,700 Annual interest rate: 6.5% for 25 years and 6% for 20 years Monthly budget allowance for payment: $1,000	Monthly payment and total cost for 25-year mortgage and monthly payment and total cost for 20-year mortgage. Which mortgage should Qua choose?

Solution Plan

Number of $1,000 units of amount financed = amount financed ÷ $1,000
Monthly payment = number of $1,000 units of amount financed × table value
Total cost = monthly payment × 12 × number of years financed

Solution

Number of $1,000 units financed = $125,700 ÷ $1,000
$$= 125.7$$

25-Year Mortgage
The Table 16-1 value for 25 years and 6.5% is $6.75.

Monthly payment = number of $1,000 units financed × table value
$$= 125.7 (\$6.75)$$
$$= \$848.48$$

Total cost = monthly payment × 12 × number of years financed
$$= \$848.48(12)(25)$$
$$= \$254,544.00$$

20-Year Mortgage
The Table 16-1 value for 20 years and 6% is $7.16.

Monthly payment = number of $1,000 units financed × table value
$$= 125.7 (\$7.16)$$
$$= \$900.01$$

Total cost = monthly payment × 12 × years financed
$$= \$900.01(12)(20)$$
$$= \$216,002.40$$

The monthly payment for the 25-year mortgage is $848.48 for a total cost of $254,544.00. The monthly payment for the 20-year mortgage is $900.01 for a total cost of $216,002.40.

Conclusion

Qua's budget of $1,000 monthly can cover either monthly payment. He would save $38,541.60 over the 20-year period if he chooses the 20-year plan. That is the plan he should choose. Other considerations that could impact his decision would be the return on an investment of the difference in the monthly payments ($51.53) if an annuity were started with the difference. Also, will the addition of the taxes and insurance to the monthly payment (PITI) be more than he can manage?

STOP AND CHECK

See Example 1.

1. Find the monthly payment on a home mortgage of $195,000 at 4.25% annual interest for 17 years.

See Example 3.

2. How much interest is paid on the mortgage in Exercise 1?

See Example 4.

3. The annual insurance premium on the home in Exercise 1 is $1,080 and the annual property tax is $1,252. Find the adjusted monthly payment including principal, interest, taxes, and insurance (PITI).

See Example 5.

4. Marcella Cannon can budget $1,200 monthly for a house note (not including taxes and insurance). The home she has fallen in love with would have a $185,400 mortgage. She can finance the loan for 15 years at 5.75% or 30 years at 6.25%. Which terms should she choose to best fit her budget?

SKILL BUILDERS

Find the indicated amounts for the fixed-rate mortgages. See Examples 1–3.

Purchase price of home	Down payment	Mortgage amount	Interest rate	Years	Monthly payment per $1,000	Mortgage payment	Total paid for mortgage	Interest paid
1. $100,000	$0		4.75%	30				
2. $183,000	$13,000		5.50%	30				
3. $95,000	$8,000		5.75%	25				
4. $125,500	20%		4.25%	20				
5. $495,750	18%		5.00%	35				
6. $83,750	15%		6%	22				

APPLICATIONS

See Example 5 for Exercises 7–10.

7. Stephen Black purchased a home for $155,000. Northridge Mortgage Inc. has approved his loan application for a 30-year fixed-rate loan at 5.00%. Stephen will pay 25% of the purchase price as a down payment. Find the down payment, amount of mortgage, and monthly payment.

8. Find the total interest Stephen will pay if he pays the loan on schedule.

9. If Stephen made the same loan for 20 years, how much interest would he save?

10. How much would Stephen's monthly payment increase for a 20-year mortgage over a 30-year mortgage?

See Example 4 for Exercises 11–12.

11. The annual insurance premium on Maria Snyder's home is $2,074 and the annual property tax is $1,403. If her monthly principal and interest payment is $1,603, find the adjusted monthly payment including principal, interest, taxes, and insurance (PITI).

12. Susan Blair has a 25-year home mortgage of $208,917 at 4.75% interest and will pay $1,798 annual insurance premium. Her annual property tax will be $2,106. Find her monthly PITI payment.

13. Use the formula or a calculator application to find the monthly payment on a home mortgage of $276,834 at 4.776% interest for 25 years.

14. Use the formula or a calculator application to find the monthly payment on a home mortgage of $192,050 at 5.125% interest for 30 years.

16-2 AMORTIZATION SCHEDULES AND QUALIFYING RATIOS

LEARNING OUTCOMES

1 Prepare a partial amortization schedule of a mortgage.
2 Calculate qualifying ratios.

1 Prepare a partial amortization schedule of a mortgage.

Amortization schedule: a table that shows the balance of principal and interest for each payment of the mortgage.

Homeowners are sometimes given an **amortization schedule** that shows the amount of principal and interest for each payment of the loan. With some loan arrangements, extra amounts paid with the monthly payment are credited against the principal, allowing for the mortgage to be paid sooner.

EXAMPLE 1 Complete the first two rows of the amortization schedule for Lunelle's mortgage of $69,600 at 7% annual interest for 30 years. The monthly payment for interest and principal was found to be $462.84.

First month

$$\text{Interest portion of monthly payment} = \text{original principal} \times \text{monthly rate}$$

$$= \$69{,}600\left(\frac{0.07}{12}\right)$$

$$= \$406.00$$

Principal portion of monthly payment = monthly payment (without insurance and taxes) − interest portion of monthly payment
$$= \$462.84 - \$406.00 = \$56.84$$

End-of-month principal = previous end-of-month principal − principal portion of monthly payment
$$= \$69{,}600 - \$56.84 = \$69{,}543.16$$

Second month

$$\text{Interest portion of monthly payment} = \$69{,}543.16\left(\frac{0.07}{12}\right) = \$405.67$$

$$\text{Principal portion of monthly payment} = \$462.84 - \$405.67 = \$57.17$$

$$\text{End-of-month principal} = \$69{,}543.16 - \$57.17 = \$69{,}485.99$$

The first two rows of an amortization schedule for this loan are shown in the following chart.

Portion of payment applied to:

Month	Monthly payment	Interest [previous end-of-month principal × monthly rate]	Principal [monthly payment − interest portion]	End-of-month principal [previous end-of-month principal − principal portion]
1	$462.84	$406.00	$56.84	$69,543.16
2	$462.84	$405.67	$57.17	$69,485.99

STOP AND CHECK

See Example 1.

1. Complete two rows of an amortization schedule for Natalie's home mortgage of $118,800 at 5.75% for 30 years if the monthly payment is $693.79.

2. Complete two rows of an amortization schedule for a home mortgage of $160,000 for 20 years at 5.5% with a monthly payment of $1,100.80.

3. Complete three rows of an amortization schedule for a home mortgage of $160,000 at 5.5% for 25 years if the monthly payment is $982.40.

4. Complete rows 4–6 of an amortization schedule for a home mortgage of $160,000 at 5.5% for 30 years if the year 4 beginning principal owed is $159,471.18 and the monthly payment is $908.80.

Qualifying ratio: a ratio that lenders use to determine an applicant's capacity to repay a loan.

Loan-to-value (LTV) ratio: the amount mortgaged divided by the appraised value of the property.

Housing or front-end ratio: monthly housing expenses (PITI) divided by the gross monthly income.

Debt-to-income (DTI) or back-end ratio: total fixed monthly expenses divided by the gross monthly income.

2 Calculate qualifying ratios.

Mortgage **qualifying ratios** are the most important factors, after your credit report, that lending institutions examine to determine loan applicants' capacity to repay a loan. The **loan-to-value ratio (LTV)** is found by dividing the amount mortgaged by the appraised value of the property. If this ratio, when expressed as a percent, is more than 80%, the borrower may be required to purchase private mortgage insurance (PMI). The **housing ratio** or **front-end ratio** is found by dividing the monthly housing expenses (PITI) by your gross monthly income. In most cases the housing ratio should not exceed 28%.

The **debt-to-income ratio (DTI)** or **back-end ratio** is found by dividing your fixed monthly expenses by your gross monthly income. The debt-to-income ratio should be no more than 36%. Fixed monthly expenses are monthly housing expenses (PITI plus any other expenses directly associated with home ownership), monthly installment loan payments, monthly revolving credit line payments, alimony and child support, and other fixed monthly expenses. Monthly income includes income from employment, including overtime and commissions, self-employment income, alimony, child support, Social Security, retirement or VA benefits, interest and dividend income, income from trusts, partnerships, and so on.

HOW TO Find the qualifying ratio for a mortgage

1. Select the formula for the desired qualifying ratio.

$$\text{Loan-to-value ratio} = \frac{\text{amount mortgaged}}{\text{appraised value of property}}$$

$$\text{Housing ratio} = \frac{\text{total mortgage payment (PITI)}}{\text{gross monthly income}}$$

$$\text{Debt-to-income ratio} = \frac{\text{total fixed monthly expenses}}{\text{gross monthly income}}$$

2. Evaluate the formula.

EXAMPLE 2 Find the loan-to-value ratio for a home appraised at $250,000 that the buyer will purchase for $248,000. The buyer plans to make a down payment of $68,000.

Amount mortgaged = $248,000 − $68,000 = $180,000
Appraised value = $250,000

$$\text{Loan-to-value ratio} = \frac{\text{Amount mortgaged}}{\text{Appraised value of property}}$$

Substitute values in the formula.

$$\text{Loan-to-value ratio} = \frac{\$180,000}{\$250,000}$$

Divide.

$$\text{Loan-to-value ratio} = 0.72 \text{ or } 72\%$$

The loan-to-value ratio is 72%.

STOP AND CHECK

See Example 2.

1. Reed Davis has $84,000 for a down payment on a home and has identified a property that can be purchased for $386,000. The appraised value of the property is $395,000. What is the loan-to-value ratio?

2. If Sheri Rieth has total gross monthly earnings of $5,893 and the total PITI for the loan she wants is $1,482, what is the housing ratio? How does this ratio compare with the desired acceptable ratio?

3. Emily Harrington has $1,675 total fixed monthly expenses and gross monthly income of $4,975. What is the debt-to-income ratio she would use in purchasing a home?

4. Pam Cox expects to pay monthly $1,845 in principal and interest, $74 in homeowner's insurance, and $104 in real estate tax for her home mortgage. Her gross monthly salary is $5,798 and she receives alimony of $200 per month. Find the housing ratio she would have when purchasing the home. Is her ratio favorable?

16-2 SECTION EXERCISES

SKILL BUILDERS

Make an amortization table to show the first two payments for the mortgages in Exercises 1–6. See Example 1.

	Amount of mortgage	Annual interest rate	Years	Monthly payment		Amount of mortgage	Annual interest rate	Years	Monthly payment
1.	$100,000	5.75%	30	$584	2.	$180,000	5.5%	30	$1,022.40

Amount of mortgage	Annual interest rate	Years	Monthly payment	Amount of mortgage	Annual interest rate	Years	Monthly payment
3. $87,000	5.75%	25	$547.23	**4.** $100,400	4.25%	20	$621.48

Amount of mortgage	Annual interest rate	Years	Monthly payment	Amount of mortgage	Annual interest rate	Years	Monthly payment
5. $406,515	5%	35	$2,052.90	**6.** $71,187.50	6%	22	$486.21

APPLICATIONS

See Example 1 for Exercises 7–10.

7. Justin Wimmer is financing $169,700 for a home at 5.25% interest with a 20-year fixed-rate loan. Find the interest paid and principal paid for each of the first two months of the loan and find the principal owed at the end of the second month.

8. Heike Drechsler is financing $84,700 for a home in the mountains. The 17-year fixed-rate loan has an interest rate of 6%. Create an amortization schedule for the first two months of the loan.

9. Conchita Martinez has made a $210,300 loan for a home near Albany, New York. Her 20-year fixed-rate loan has an interest rate of 5.50%. Create an amortization schedule for the first two payments.

10. Jake Drewrey is financing $142,500 for a ten-year fixed-rate mortgage at 5.75%. Create an amortization schedule for the first two payments.

See Example 2.

11. Conchita Martinez will have a monthly interest and principal payment of $1,825.40. Her monthly real estate taxes will be $58.93 and her monthly homeowner's payments will be $84.15. If her gross monthly income is $6,793, find the housing ratio.

See Example 2.

12. Jake Drewrey has total fixed monthly expenses of $1,340 and his gross monthly income is $3,875. What is his debt-to-income ratio? How does his ratio compare to the desired ratio?

Learning Outcomes

Section 16-1

1 Find the monthly mortgage payment. (p. 576)

What to Remember with Examples

Find the monthly mortgage payment of principal and interest using a per-$1,000 monthly payment table.

1. Find the amount financed: Subtract the down payment from the purchase price.
2. Find the number of $1,000 units in the amount financed: Divide the amount financed (from step 1) by $1,000.
3. Locate the table value in Table 16-1 for the number of years financed and the annual interest rate.
4. Multiply the table value from step 3 by the number of $1,000 units from step 2.

$$\text{Monthly mortgage payment} = \frac{\text{amount financed}}{\$1,000} \times \text{table value}$$

Find the monthly payment for a home selling for $90,000 if a 10% down payment is made, payments are made for 30 years, and the annual interest rate is 5.5%.

$$\$90,000(0.1) = \$9,000 \text{ down payment}$$
$$\$90,000 - \$9,000 = \$81,000 \text{ mortgage amount}$$
$$\$81,000 \div \$1,000 = 81 \text{ units of } \$1,000$$

The table value for 30 years and 5.5% is $5.68.
Payment = 81($5.68) = $460.08

Find the monthly mortgage payment of principal and interest using a formula.

1. Identify the monthly rate (R) as a decimal equivalent, the number of months (N), and the loan principal (P).
2. Substitute the values from step 1 in the formula.

$$M = P\left(\frac{R}{1 - (1 + R)^{-N}}\right)$$

3. Evaluate the formula.

Find the monthly payment for the loan in the previous example.

$R = 0.055/12 = 0.0045833333; N = 360; P = \$81,000$

$$M = P\left(\frac{R}{1 - (1 + R)^{-N}}\right)$$

$$M = 81,000\left(\frac{0.0045833333}{1 - (1 + 0.0045833333)^{-360}}\right)$$

Calculator sequence:

81000 $($ .0045833333 $)$ $\div$ $($ 1 $-$ $($ 1 $+$ .0045833333 $)$ $\wedge$ $($ $(-)$ 360 $)$ $)$ $)$
ENTER

Display: 459.9090891
The monthly payment is $459.91.

See pp. 578–579 for instructions for the TI BAII Plus, TI-84 and Casio fx-CG10.

2 Find the total interest on a mortgage and the PITI. (p. 579)

1. Find the total of the payments: Multiply the number of payments by the amount of the payment (principal + interest).
2. Subtract the amount financed from the total of the payments.

$$\text{Total interest} = \text{number of payments} \times \text{amount of payment} - \text{amount financed}$$

Find the total interest on the mortgage in the preceding example.

$$\text{Total interest} = 30(12)(\$459.91) - \$81,000$$
$$= \$165,567.60 - \$81,000$$
$$= \$84,567.60$$

To find the total PITI payment:

1. Find the principal and interest portion of the monthly payment.
2. Find the monthly taxes by dividing the annual taxes by 12.
3. Find the monthly insurance by dividing the annual insurance by 12.
4. Find the sum of the monthly principal, interest, taxes, and insurance.

Find the total PITI payment for a loan that has monthly principal and interest payments of $2,134, annual taxes of $1,085, and annual homeowners insurance of $1,062.

$2,134	Monthly principal and interest
$1,085 ÷ 12 = $90.41666667	Monthly taxes
$1,062 ÷ 12 = $88.50	Monthly insurance

PITI = $2,134 + $90.42 + $88.50 = $2,312.92

The total PITI payment is $2,312.92.

Section 16-2

1 Prepare a partial amortization schedule of a mortgage. (p. 583)

1. For the first month:
   (a) Find the interest portion of the first monthly payment (principal and interest only):

   Interest portion of the first monthly payment = original principal ×
   monthly interest rate

   (b) Find the principal portion of the monthly payment:

   Principal portion of the first monthly payment = monthly payment −
   interest portion of first monthly payment

   (c) Find the first end-of-month principal:

   First end-of-month principal = original principal −
   principal portion of the first monthly payment

2. For each remaining month in turn:
   (a) Find the interest portion of the monthly payment:

   Interest portion of the monthly payment = previous end-of-month principal ×
   monthly interest rate

   (b) Find the principal portion of the monthly payment:

   Principal portion of the monthly payment = monthly payment −
   interest portion of the monthly payment

   (c) Find the end-of-month principal:

   End-of-month principal = previous end-of-month principal −
   principal portion of the monthly payment

Complete an amortization schedule for three months of payments on a $90,000 mortgage at 4.25% for 30 years.

$$\text{Monthly payment} = \frac{\$90,000}{\$1,000} \times \text{table value}$$
$$= 90(\$4.92)$$
$$= \$442.80$$

Month 1

$$\text{Interest portion} = \$90{,}000\left(\frac{0.0425}{12}\right)$$
$$= \$318.75$$

$$\text{Principal portion} = \$442.80 - \$318.75$$
$$= \$124.05$$

$$\text{End-of-month principal} = \$90{,}000 - \$124.05$$
$$= \$89{,}875.95$$

Month 2

$$\text{Interest portion} = \$89{,}875.95\left(\frac{0.0425}{12}\right)$$
$$= \$318.31$$

$$\text{Principal portion} = \$442.80 - \$318.31$$
$$= \$124.49$$

$$\text{End-of-month principal} = \$89{,}875.95 - \$124.49$$
$$= \$89{,}751.46$$

Month 3

$$\text{Interest portion} = \$89{,}751.46\left(\frac{0.0425}{12}\right)$$
$$= \$317.87$$

$$\text{Principal portion} = \$442.80 - \$317.87$$
$$= \$124.93$$

$$\text{End-of-month principal} = \$89{,}751.46 - \$124.93$$
$$= \$89{,}626.53$$

Portion of payment applied to:

Month	Monthly payment	Interest	Principal	End-of-month principal
1	$442.80	$318.75	$124.05	$89,875.95
2	$442.80	318.31	124.49	89,751.46
3	$442.80	317.87	124.93	89,626.53

2 Calculate qualifying ratios. (p. 585)

Find the qualifying ratio for a mortgage.

1. Select the formula for the desired qualifying ratio.

$$\text{Loan-to-value ratio} = \frac{\text{amount mortgaged}}{\text{appraised value of property}}$$

$$\text{Housing ratio} = \frac{\text{total mortgage payment (PITI)}}{\text{gross monthly income}}$$

$$\text{Debt-to-income ratio} = \frac{\text{total fixed monthly expenses}}{\text{gross monthly income}}$$

2. Evaluate the formula.

Find the loan-to-value ratio for a home appraised at $398,400 that the buyer will purchase for $398,000. The buyer plans to make a down payment of $100,000.

Amount mortgaged = $398,000 − $100,000 = $298,000

Appraised value = $398,400

$$\text{Loan-to-value ratio} = \frac{\text{amount mortgaged}}{\text{appraised value of property}} \qquad \text{Substitute values in the formula.}$$

$$\text{Loan-to-value ratio} = \frac{\$298{,}000}{\$398{,}400} \qquad \text{Divide.}$$

Loan-to-value ratio = 0.7479919679 or 75%

EXERCISES SET A

Find the monthly payment.

Mortgage amount	Annual percentage rate	Years
1. $287,500	5.75%	20
2. $146,800	5.25%	30
3. $152,300	6.25%	25
4. $113,400	5%	15

EXCEL 5. Find the total interest paid for the mortgage in Exercise 1.

EXCEL 6. Find the total interest paid for the mortgage in Exercise 2.

EXCEL 7. Find the total interest paid for the mortgage in Exercise 3.

EXCEL 8. Find the total interest paid for the mortgage in Exercise 4.

9. Create an amortization schedule for the first two months' payments on a mortgage of $487,700 with an interest rate of 6% and monthly payment of $2,926.20.

10. Louise Grantham is buying a home for $198,500 with a 20% down payment. She has a 5.75% loan for 25 years. Create an amortization schedule for the first two months of her loan.

11. James Author's monthly principal plus interest payment is $1,565.74 and his annual homeowner's insurance premium is $1,100. His annual real estate taxes total $1,035. Find his PITI payment.

12. Find the loan-to-value ratio for a home appraised at $583,620 that the buyer will purchase for $585,000. The buyer plans to make a down payment of $175,000.

13. Find James Author's housing ratio if his PITI is $1,743.66 and his gross monthly income is $6,310.

14. Find Julia Rholes' debt-to-income ratio if her fixed monthly expenses are $1,836 and her gross monthly income is $4,934.

15. Use the formula or a calculator application to find the monthly payment on a home mortgage of $645,730 at 4.862% interest for 20 years.

16. Use the formula or a calculator application to find the monthly payment on a home mortgage of $219,275 at 5.265% interest for 30 years.

EXERCISES SET B

Find the monthly payment.

Mortgage amount	Annual percentage rate	Years
1. $487,700	6%	30
2. $212,983	6.75%	15
3. $82,900	4.5%	35
4. $179,500	4.0%	17

5. Find the total interest paid for the mortgage in Exercise 1.

6. Find the total interest paid for the mortgage in Exercise 2.

7. Find the total interest paid for the mortgage in Exercise 3.

8. Find the total interest paid for the mortgage in Exercise 4.

9. Create a partial amortization schedule for the first two payments on a mortgage of $152,300 at 6.25% that has a monthly payment of $1,005.18 and is financed for 25 years.

10. Mary Starnes is paying $14,000 down on a house that costs $138,200 and she has a 6% loan for 30 years. Create a partial amortization table for the first two months of her mortgage.

11. Jerry Corless's monthly principal plus interest payment is $2,665.45 and his annual homeowner's insurance premium is $1,320. His annual real estate taxes total $1,325. Find his PITI payment.

12. Find the loan-to-value ratio for a home appraised at $135,230 that the buyer will purchase for $135,000. The buyer plans to make a down payment of $25,000.

13. Find Jerry Corless's housing ratio if his PITI is $2,885.87 and his gross monthly income is $8,310.

14. Find Elizabeth Herrington's debt-to-income ratio if her fixed monthly expenses are $1,236 and her gross monthly income is $4,194.

15. Use the formula or a calculator application to find the monthly payment on a home mortgage of $315,200 at 4.658% interest for 25 years.

16. Use the formula or a calculator application to find the monthly payment on a home mortgage of $327,790 at 5.402% interest for 35 years.

PRACTICE TEST

1. Find the table value for a 25-year mortgage at 6%.

2. Find the monthly payment on a mortgage of $230,000 for 30 years at 6.5%.

3. Find the total amount of interest that will be paid on the mortgage in Exercise 2.

4. What percent of the mortgage in Exercise 2 is the interest paid?

Hullett Houpt is purchasing a home for $197,000. He will finance the mortgage for 15 years and pay 4% interest on the loan. He makes a down payment that is 20% of the purchase price. Use Table 16-1 as needed. Houpt's annual taxes are $2,364 and his annual homeowner's insurance is $1,758.

5. Find the down payment.

6. Find the amount of the mortgage.

7. Find the monthly payment that includes principal and interest only.

8. Find the total interest Hullett will pay over the 15-year period.

9. Find the PITI payment.

10. Calculate the monthly payment and the total interest Hullett would have to pay if he decided to make the loan for 30 years instead of 15 years.

11. How much interest can be saved by paying for the home in 15 years rather than 30 years?

12. Find the interest portion and principal portion for the first payment of Hullett's 15-year loan.

13. Make an amortization schedule for the first three payments of the 15-year loan Hullett could make.

14. Make an amortization schedule for the first three payments of the 30-year loan Hullett could make.

15. Find Leshaundra's debt-to-income ratio if her fixed monthly expenses are $1,972 and her gross monthly income is $5,305.

16. Use the formula or a calculator application to find the monthly payment on a home mortgage of $249,500 at 5.389% interest for 30 years.

1. How does a mortgage relate to a sinking fund?

2. For a mortgage of a given amount and rate, what happens to the total amount of interest paid if the number of years in the mortgage increases?

3. How can you reduce your monthly payment on a home mortgage?

4. Describe the process for finding the monthly payment for a mortgage of a given amount at a given rate for a given period.

Challenge Problem

Bob Owen is closing a real estate transaction on a farm in Yocona, Mississippi, for $385,900. His mortgage holder requires a 25% down payment and he also must pay $60.00 to record the deed, $100 in attorney's fees for document preparation, and $350 for an appraisal report. Bob will also have to pay a 1.5% loan origination fee. Bob chooses a 35-year mortgage at 3.75%. (a) How much cash will Bob need to close on the property? (b) How much will Bob's mortgage be? (c) What is Bob's monthly payment on the property?

16-1 Home Buying: A 30-Year Commitment?

Shantel and Kwamie are planning to buy their first home. Although they are excited about the prospect of being homeowners, they are also a little frightened. A mortgage payment for the next 30 years sounds like a huge commitment. They visited a few new developments and scanned the real estate listings of preowned homes, but they really have no idea how much a mortgage payment would be on a $150,000, $175,000, or $200,000 loan. They have come to you for advice.

1. After you explain to them that they can borrow money at different rates and for different amounts of time, Shantel and Kwamie ask you to complete a chart indicating what the monthly mortgage payment would be under some possible interest rates and borrowing periods. They also want to know what their total interest would be on each if they chose a 25-year loan at 4% interest. Complete the chart.

Amount borrowed	3.25% 15 year	3.75% 20 year	4.0% 25 year	4.25% 30 year	Total interest paid on 25-year loan
$150,000					
$175,000					
$200,000					

2. If Shantel and Kwamie made a down payment of $20,000 on a $175,000 home, what would be their monthly mortgage payment assuming they finance for 25 years at 4.0%? How much would they save on each monthly payment by making the down payment? How much interest would they save over the life of the loan?

3. Using your answer from question 2 with the down payment of $20,000 on a $175,000 loan financed for 25 years at 4.0%, find the total PITI payment for Shantel and Kwamie's home if their annual taxes are $3,840 and their annual homeowner's insurance premium is $1,140.

4. Shantel and Kwamie have a gross monthly income of $5,800 and total fixed monthly expenses of $2,420, including the home ownership–related expenses. Using your answers from question 3, calculate the loan-to-value ratio, housing ratio, and debt-to-income ratio if the home they wish to purchase appraises for $185,000. How might your answers affect Shantel and Kwamie's ability to purchase this home?

16-2 Investing in Real Estate

Jacob had finally found the house that he was looking for, and he was anxious to make an offer. He knew that one of the keys to successful real estate investing was to purchase properties for at least 30% below market value. He had done his research, and with an asking price of only $124,500, this 2-bedroom starter home was a bargain and well within his price range. The house, though, needed a number of repairs including paint, carpet, appliances, and a new wall to turn an open area into another bedroom. After contacting several contractors, he felt confident that the work could be completed for $12,000. With that figure in mind, Jacob decided that the total cost of the house would be $140,000 or less, including any settlement charges. He just needed to finalize some of the payment details to make sure the house was right for him.

1. By putting 20% down on the house, Jacob can get a 30-year fixed-rate mortgage for 4.25%. Based on a purchase price of $140,000, compute the down payment, and the principal and interest payment for the loan.

2. Although Jacob hopes to have the house sold within a few months, he knows there is a possibility that it will not sell quickly. In that case, he would likely end up keeping it as a rental property. Using the information from Exercise 1, find the total amount of interest that Jacob will pay on the mortgage if he keeps it for the full 30 years.

3. Jacob finds a lender that will offer him 100% financing using an adjustable-rate mortgage based on a 30-year amortization, with a 5-year interest lock at 5.0%. The loan, however, would include a prepayment penalty, which is applied as follows: prepayment penalty is 80% of the balance of the first mortgage, times the interest rate, divided by 2. Compute the new mortgage payment, along with the maximum prepayment penalty. Is it a good idea for Jacob to take this loan? Why or why not?

4. Jacob decides that the 30-year fixed-rate mortgage in Exercise 1 is the best for him. Construct an amortization table for the first three payments of the mortgage. The monthly payment will be $551.04.

5. Jacob has a gross monthly income of $3,660 and total fixed monthly expenses of $1,320 including the home ownership-related expenses. His annual real estate taxes will be $2,856 and his annual homeowner's insurance will be $840. Using a monthly principal and interest payment of $551.04, calculate the total PITI payment, loan-to-value ratio, housing ratio, and debt-to-income ratio if the home appraises for $145,000. Are your answers within an acceptable range? What are the implications for Jacob?

CHAPTER 17 | Depreciation

Is There a Benefit to Depreciation?

It is the end of a very profitable year for Kristoff's vegetable produce business. After expenses, his business shows a net profit of almost $50,000. The business is growing, so he is considering purchasing a new 4-wheel-drive tractor for $42,000 before the end of the year. Kristoff knows that he can use depreciation to his benefit, though he does not know how it applies to this particular purchase.

Depreciation is an income tax deduction that allows a taxpayer to recover the cost or other basis of certain property. It is an annual allowance or "paper loss" for the wear and tear, deterioration, or obsolescence of the property. Most types of tangible property (except land) such as buildings, machinery, vehicles, furniture, and equipment are depreciable. Likewise, certain intangible property, such as patents, copyrights, and computer software, is depreciable.

After some research, Kristoff consults IRS Publication 946, How to Depreciate Property. There he sees that the modified accelerated cost-recovery system (MACRS) is the proper depreciation method for *most* property. In the MACRS, he sees that agricultural machinery and equipment is listed as 7-year property. Using the formula presented in the publication, he figures that he can write off (*depreciate*) $6,000 in the year of purchase.

The tractor manufacturer is offering a financing plan with 0% for 36 months, or 2.9% for 60 months with 20% down. Kristoff has enough money available to make the down payment, but he is not sure if the $8,400 would also be depreciable, not to mention the annual interest—so more research is required. Although he realizes he needs to learn more about depreciation, the one thing that Kristoff knows for sure is that he could really use the new tractor in his operation. The amount of the purchase would certainly reduce his profit for the year and could significantly reduce his income tax liability. This purchase seems like a really good idea, but he isn't sure. What would you recommend?

LEARNING OUTCOMES

17-1 Depreciation Methods for Financial Statement Reporting

1. Depreciate an asset and prepare a depreciation schedule using the straight-line method.
2. Depreciate an asset and prepare a depreciation schedule using the units-of-production method.
3. Depreciate an asset and prepare a depreciation schedule using the sum-of-the-years'-digits method.
4. Depreciate an asset and prepare a depreciation schedule using the declining-balance method.

17-2 Depreciation Methods for IRS Reporting

1. Depreciate an asset and prepare a depreciation schedule using the modified accelerated cost-recovery system (MACRS).

Assets: properties owned by the business, including anything of monetary value and anything that can be exchanged for cash or other property.

Estimated life or useful life: the number of years an asset is expected to be useable.

Salvage value or scrap value or residual value: an estimated dollar value of an asset at the end of the asset's estimated useful life.

Depreciation: the amount an asset decreases in value from its original cost.

Buildings, machinery, equipment, furniture, and other items bought for the operation of a business are included among the **assets** of that business. The dollar value of each asset is used in figuring the value and profitability of the business and in figuring the taxable income for the business. The expense of running a business, including the purchase of assets, can be deducted from the company's taxable income before taxes are calculated, so it is important to have a way of keeping track of the value of assets.

Some assets have a useful life of one year or less, and the cost of acquiring them can be deducted from the business's income in the year they are purchased. The cost of items that are expected to last more than a year can be prorated (spread out) and deducted over a period of years, called the **estimated life,** or **useful life,** of the item. During this time period, the asset *depreciates*, or decreases in value. At the end of an asset's estimated life, it may still have a dollar value, called the **salvage value, scrap value,** or **residual value.** The amount an asset decreases in value from its original cost is called its **depreciation.**

This chapter examines five widely used depreciation methods: straight-line, units-of-production, sum-of-the-years'-digits, declining-balance, and the modified accelerated cost-recovery system (MACRS) method. The Internal Revenue Service (IRS) regulates the methods of depreciation that are allowed for income tax purposes. In general, the same depreciation method must be used throughout the useful life of any particular asset. The IRS requires the use of the modified accelerated cost-recovery system of depreciation unless special circumstances are approved by the IRS. The IRS limits the use of many methods of depreciation, so you should consult IRS publications or an accountant before choosing a depreciation method for IRS reporting.

17-1 DEPRECIATION METHODS FOR FINANCIAL STATEMENT REPORTING

LEARNING OUTCOMES

1 Depreciate an asset and prepare a depreciation schedule using the straight-line method.
2 Depreciate an asset and prepare a depreciation schedule using the units-of-production method.
3 Depreciate an asset and prepare a depreciation schedule using the sum-of-the-years'-digits method.
4 Depreciate an asset and prepare a depreciation schedule using the declining-balance method.

1 Depreciate an asset and prepare a depreciation schedule using the straight-line method.

Straight-line depreciation: a method of depreciation in which the amount of depreciation of an asset is spread equally over the number of years of useful life of the asset.

Total cost: the cost of an asset including shipping and installation charges.

Depreciable value: the cost of an asset minus the salvage value.

A commonly used method of depreciation for internal business purposes is the **straight-line depreciation** method. It is easy to use because the depreciation is the same for each full year the equipment is used.

If you know the original cost of an asset, its estimated useful life, and its salvage value, you can find the yearly depreciation amount. In calculating depreciation, by whatever method, the cost of an asset means the **total cost,** including shipping and installation charges if the asset is a piece of equipment. The **depreciable value** is the cost minus the salvage value.

HOW TO Find the yearly depreciation using the straight-line method

1. Find the *total cost* of the asset:

$$\text{Total cost} = \text{cost} + \text{shipping} + \text{installation}$$

2. Find the *depreciable value:*

$$\text{Depreciable value} = \text{total cost} - \text{salvage value}$$

3. Find the *yearly depreciation:*

$$\text{Yearly depreciation} = \frac{\text{depreciable value}}{\text{number of years of expected life}}$$

EXAMPLE 1
Use the straight-line method to find the yearly depreciation for a plating machine that has an expected useful life of five years. The plating machine costs $27,300, its shipping costs totaled $250, its installation charges came to $450, and its salvage value is $1,000.

$$\text{Total cost} = \text{cost of asset} + \text{shipping} + \text{installation}$$
$$= \$27,300 + \$250 + \$450 = \boxed{\$28,000}$$

$$\text{Depreciable value} = \text{total cost} - \text{salvage value}$$
$$= \$28,000 - \$1,000$$
$$= \$27,000$$

$$\text{Yearly depreciation} = \frac{\text{depreciable value}}{\text{years of expected life}}$$
$$= \frac{\$27,000}{5} = \$5,400$$

The depreciation is $5,400 per year.

TIP

Total Cost Versus Depreciable Value

A common mistake in figuring yearly depreciation using the straight-line method is to divide the total cost rather than the depreciable value by the expected life. See what happens when this is done with the preceding example:

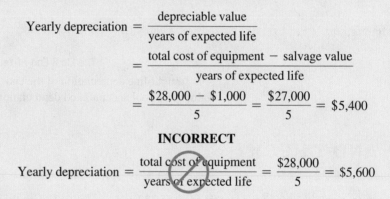

CORRECT

$$\text{Yearly depreciation} = \frac{\text{depreciable value}}{\text{years of expected life}}$$
$$= \frac{\text{total cost of equipment} - \text{salvage value}}{\text{years of expected life}}$$
$$= \frac{\$28,000 - \$1,000}{5} = \frac{\$27,000}{5} = \$5,400$$

INCORRECT

$$\text{Yearly depreciation} = \frac{\text{total cost of equipment}}{\text{years of expected life}} = \frac{\$28,000}{5} = \$5,600$$

Depreciation schedule: a table showing the year's depreciation, the accumulated depreciation, and the end-of-year book value.

Accumulated depreciation: the current year's depreciation plus all previous years' depreciation of an asset.

End-of-year book value: total cost minus accumulated depreciation. Thereafter, it is the previous year's end-of-year book value minus the current year's depreciation.

Book value: the total cost of an asset minus the accumulated depreciation.

A **depreciation schedule** is often the best way to record the depreciation of an asset over time. The depreciation schedule shows consistent information for any depreciation method. For each year of depreciation, the following values are recorded: the year's depreciation, the accumulated depreciation and the year's end-of-year book value. **Accumulated depreciation** is the year's depreciation plus the sum of all previous years' depreciation. The first year's **end-of-year book value** is the total cost minus the year's depreciation. For all other years, the year's end-of-year book value is the previous end-of-year book value minus the year's depreciation. The **book value** is an accounting concept that is not necessarily the same as the worth or market value of the property.

HOW TO   Prepare a Depreciation Schedule

1. For the first year of expected life:
   (a) Find the yearly or annual depreciation.
   (b) Find the first end-of-year book value:

   $$\text{First end-of-year book value} = \text{total cost} - \text{first year's depreciation}$$

2. For each remaining year of expected life:
   (a) Find the year's annual depreciation.
   (b) Find the year's accumulated depreciation:

   $$\text{Year's accumulated depreciation} = \text{annual depreciation} + \text{sum of all the previous years' depreciation}$$

   (c) Find the year's end-of-year book value:

   $$\text{Year's end-of-year book value} = \text{previous end-of-year book value} - \text{annual depreciation}$$

3. Make a table with the following column headings and fill in the data: year, annual depreciation, accumulated depreciation, end-of-year book value.

EXAMPLE 2 Prepare a depreciation schedule for the plating machine in Example 1. Calculate the accumulated depreciation and end-of-year book value for each year.

Year 1: $28,000 − $5,400 = $22,600
Year 2: $22,600 − $5,400 = $17,200
Year 3: $17,200 − $5,400 = $11,800
Year 4: $11,800 − $5,400 = $6,400
Year 5: $ 6,400 − $5,400 = $1,000

The completed schedule is shown in Table 17-1.

TABLE 17-1
Straight-Line Depreciation Schedule for Plating Machine

Total cost: $28,000	Year	Annual depreciation	Accumulated depreciation	End-of-year book value
Depreciable	1	$5,400	$ 5,400	$22,600
value:	2	5,400	10,800	17,200
$27,000	3	5,400	16,200	11,800
	4	5,400	21,600	6,400
	5	$5,400	$27,000	$ 1,000

TIP

The Final End-of-Year Book Value Is the Salvage Value

The straight-line depreciation of the end-of-year book value cannot be less than the salvage value. The final accumulated depreciation plus the salvage value must equal the total cost.

STOP AND CHECK

See Example 1.

1. Find the depreciable value of an asset that costs $5,323 and has a scrap value of $500.

2. Use the straight-line method to find the yearly depreciation for a van that costs $18,000, has an expected life of three years, and has a residual value of $3,000.

3. Find the yearly depreciation for a computer network system that costs $21,500, has an expected life of four years, and has a salvage value of $4,000. Use straight-line depreciation.

4. Find the straight-line depreciation for a security system that costs $5,800, has an expected life of three years, and has a residual value of $1,500.

5. Prepare a depreciation schedule for the computer network system in Exercise 3.

2 Depreciate an asset and prepare a depreciation schedule using the units-of-production method.

Units-of-production depreciation: a method of depreciation that is based on the expected number of units produced by an asset.

Machines and other types of equipment that are used heavily for a period of time and then left to sit idle for another period of time, sometimes months, are often depreciated using the **units-of-production depreciation** method. For example, earth-moving equipment and farm equipment are often idle during the winter months. Instead of basing depreciation on the expected lifetime of a piece of equipment in years, this method takes into account how the equipment is used—for

example, how many items it has produced, how many miles it has been driven, how many hours it has operated, or how many times it has performed some particular operation.

The units-of-production method of depreciation is used for internal accounting purposes. Special written permission from the IRS is required for this method to be used on tax returns. Companies that use this method internally often adjust to a method acceptable by the IRS for tax-reporting purposes.

To use the units-of-production method, you must find the **unit depreciation**—how much the asset depreciates with each unit produced, each mile driven, or each hour of operation.

HOW TO   Find the depreciation for units produced using the units-of-production method

1. Find the *unit depreciation.*

$$\text{Unit depreciation} = \frac{\text{depreciable value}}{\text{number of units produced during expected life}}$$

Keep the full calculator value of the quotient.

2. Multiply the unit depreciation by the number of units produced.

$$\text{Depreciation for units produced} = \text{unit depreciation} \times \text{number of units produced}$$

EXAMPLE 3   A label-making machine that costs $28,000 after shipping and installation is expected to print 50,000,000 labels during its useful life. If the salvage value of the machine is $1,000, find the unit depreciation and depreciation for printing 2,125,000 labels.

$$\text{Unit depreciation} = \frac{\text{depreciable value}}{\text{unit produced during expected life}}$$
$$= \frac{\$28,000 - \$1,000}{50,000,000}$$
$$= \$0.00054$$

Use the full calculator value of the unit depreciation.

Depreciation = unit depreciation × units produced
$$= \$0.00054(2,125,000) = \$1,147.50$$

Continuous calculator keystokes: $(28000 - 1000) \div 500\ 00\ 00\ 0 =$ (*Stop and record the unit depreciation*) $\times 2125000 \times = \Rightarrow 1147.5$

The unit depreciation is $0.00054 and the depreciation is $1,147.50.

Equipment such as the label-making machine in Example 3 will most likely make a different number of labels from year to year. The units-of-production method of depreciation is most often used in a situation such as this.

EXAMPLE 4   The label-making machine in Example 3 was used to print the following number of labels each year for the five years of useful life: 2,125,000, 11,830,000, 12,765,000, 12,210,000, and 11,070,000. Make a depreciation schedule using the units-of-production method.

Find the annual depreciation for each year by multiplying the number of labels printed by the unit depreciation. Complete the schedule by calculating the accumulated depreciation and the end-of-year book value for each year.

Year 1:   2,125,000 ($0.00054) = $1,147.50   annual and accumulated depreciation
          $28,000 − $1,147.50 = $26,852.50   end-of-year book value
Year 2:   11,830,000 ($0.00054) = $6,388.20   annual depreciation
          $1,147.50 + $6,388.20 = $7,535.70   accumulated depreciation
          $26,852.50 − $7,535.70 = $20,464.30   end-of-year book value
Continue with years 3–5.

The completed depreciation schedule is given in Table 17-2.

TABLE 17-2
Units-of-Production Depreciation Schedule for the Label Maker

Total cost $28,000 Depreciable value: $27,000 Unit depreciation: $0.00054	Year	Labels printed	Annual depreciation	Accumulated depreciation	End-of-year book value
	1	2,125,000	$ 1,147.50	$ 1,147.50	$26,852.50
	2	11,830,000	6,388.20	7,535.70	20,464.30
	3	12,765,000	6,893.10	14,428.80	13,571.20
	4	12,210,000	6,593.40	21,022.20	6,977.80
	5	11,070,000	$ 5,977.80	$27,000.00	$ 1,000.00
Totals		50,000,000	$27,000.00		

TIP

Check Your Schedule Calculations

One way to check your schedule calculations is to find the totals of the labels printed and the yearly depreciation amounts. The total labels printed should equal the useful life. The total of the yearly depreciations should equal the depreciable value and the last entry in the accumulated depreciation column.

STOP AND CHECK

Use full calculator value of the unit depreciation. See Examples 3 and 4.

1. A van that costs $18,000 is expected to be driven 75,000 miles during its useful life. If the salvage value of the van is $3,000, find the unit depreciation and the depreciation for 56,000 miles.

2. A company car is purchased for $23,580 and is expected to be driven 95,000 miles before being sold. The expected salvage value for the car is $2,300. Find the unit depreciation for the car.

3. An engraving machine that costs $28,700 is being set up on a unit depreciation schedule. The scrap value of the machine is anticipated to be $2,500. If the machine will engrave 300,000 objects during its useful life, find the unit depreciation. What is the first year's depreciation if 28,452 objects are engraved?

4. Chou's Meat Processing Company purchased a meat cutting machine for $7,500. Its expected life is 60,000 hours, and it will have a salvage value of $600. Use units-of-production depreciation to find the year's depreciation on the machine if it is used 8,500 hours during the first year.

3 Depreciate an asset and prepare a depreciation schedule using the sum-of-the-years'-digits method.

Sum-of-the-years'-digits depreciation: a depreciation method that allows the greatest depreciation the first year and a decreasing amount each year thereafter.

Year's depreciation rate: the depreciation rate for any given year of a depreciation schedule.

The straight-line depreciation method of depreciating an asset is the simplest way to depreciate the asset, but it is not always the most realistic method of depreciation to use. Most equipment depreciates more during its first year of operation than during any subsequent year. Many businesses prefer to use a method that shows the largest depreciation during the first year or two. One such method is the **sum-of-the-years'-digits depreciation** method.

To find the depreciation for a year, we find the **year's depreciation rate** for that year and multiply it by the depreciable value. The numerator of the year's depreciation rate is the number of years of expected life *remaining*. The denominator of the year's depreciation rate is the sum of the numbers from 1 through the number of years of expected life. We can use the shortcut formula for finding such a sum. If, for example, the expected life is five years, the sum from 1 to 5 is

$$\frac{n(n + 1)}{2} = \frac{5(5 + 1)}{2} = \frac{5(6)}{2} = \frac{30}{2} = 15$$

If the number of years of expected life is five years, the denominator of the depreciation rate is always 15.

Year	1	2	3	4	5
Year's depreciation rate	$\frac{5}{15}$	$\frac{4}{15}$	$\frac{3}{15}$	$\frac{2}{15}$	$\frac{1}{15}$

HOW TO Find the year's depreciation using the sum-of-the-years'-digits method

1. Find the year's depreciation rate:
   (a) Use the $\dfrac{n(n + 1)}{2}$ shortcut formula to find the sum from 1 through the number of years of expected life.

   Sum from 1 through the number of years of expected life

   $$= \frac{(\text{number of years of expected life})(1 + \text{number of years of expected life})}{2}$$

   (b) Divide the number of years remaining of expected life by the value from step 1a.

   $$\text{Year's sum-of-the-years' depreciation rate} = \frac{\text{number of years remaining of expected life}}{\text{sum from 1 through the years of expected life}}$$

2. Find the depreciable value:

   $$\text{Depreciable value} = \text{total cost} - \text{salvage value}$$

3. Multiply the depreciable value by the year's depreciation rate:

   $$\text{Depreciation for the year} = \text{depreciable value} \times \text{depreciation rate for the year}$$

EXAMPLE 5
Find the depreciation using the sum-of-the-years'-digits method for each of the five years of expected life of a bottle-capping machine that costs $27,300 and has a shipping cost of $250, an installation cost of $450, and a salvage value of $1,000. Make a depreciation schedule.

$$\text{Denominator of depreciation rate} = \frac{5(6)}{2} = \boxed{15} \quad \text{Sum of 1 to 5}$$

Find the depreciation rates for all five years.

Depreciation rate for each year $\quad \dfrac{5}{15}, \dfrac{4}{15}, \dfrac{3}{15}, \dfrac{2}{15}, \dfrac{1}{15}, \quad$ Years remaining

$$\begin{array}{cccccc} \uparrow & & \uparrow & \uparrow & \uparrow & \uparrow & \uparrow \\ \text{Year} & 1 & 2 & 3 & 4 & 5 \end{array}$$

Depreciable value = total cost − salvage value
($27,300 + $250 + $450) − $1,000 = $\boxed{27,000}$

Year 1 depreciation = depreciable value × depreciation rate

$$= \frac{\$27,000}{1}\left(\frac{5}{15}\right)$$

$$= \$9,000$$

Year 1 end-of-year book value = total cost − depreciation
$$= \$28,000 - \boxed{\$9,000}$$
$$= \$19,000$$

The results of the calculations for the remaining years can be organized in a depreciation schedule (Table 17-3).

TIP

Built-In Checks

One way to check your calculations in the depreciation schedule in Table 17-3 is to add the columns for the depreciation rate and annual depreciation.

- The sum of the depreciation rates should equal 1.
- The sum of the annual depreciation amounts should equal the depreciable value.
- The last entry in the accumulated depreciation column is the depreciable value.
- The last entry in the end-of-year book-value column is the salvage value.

TABLE 17-3

Sum-of-the-Years'-Digits Depreciation Schedule for Bottle-Capping Machine

Total cost $28,000 Depreciable value: $27,000	Year	Depreciation rate	Annual depreciation	Accumulated depreciation	End-of-year book value
	1	$\frac{5}{15}$	$ 9,000	$ 9,000	$19,000
	2	$\frac{4}{15}$	7,200	16,200	11,800
	3	$\frac{3}{15}$	5,400	21,600	6,400
	4	$\frac{2}{15}$	3,600	25,200	2,800
	5	$\frac{1}{15}$	$ 1,800	$27,000	$ 1,000
Check:		$\frac{15}{15} = 1$	$27,000		

TIP

Fractions Versus Decimal Equivalents

Rates can be written as fractions or decimal equivalents. For example, $\frac{5}{15} = 0.33\overline{3}$, $\frac{4}{15} = 0.26\overline{6}$, $\frac{3}{15} = 0.2$, $\frac{2}{15} = 0.13\overline{3}$, and $\frac{1}{15} = 0.06\overline{6}$. When decimals are repeating decimals as indicated by the bar over the last digit, using the fraction form gives the most accurate result.

$$5 \div 15 = \times 27000 = \Rightarrow 9000$$
$$0.333333333 \times 27000 = \Rightarrow 8999.999991$$

TIP

Which Fraction Goes First?

A common mistake is to list the smallest fraction rather than the largest fraction for the first year's depreciation fraction. In the preceding example, the smallest fraction is $\frac{1}{15}$ and the largest is $\frac{5}{15}$. The confusion often occurs because the smallest fraction goes with the largest year; that is, year 5 uses $\frac{1}{15}$, and year 1 uses $\frac{5}{15}$. Remember that in this method the largest depreciation happens during the first year.

Let's look at how to figure the depreciation for year 1 from the example again, showing both the correct and the incorrect ways to do it.

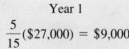 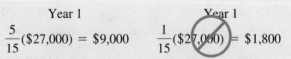

Year 1

$$\frac{5}{15}(\$27,000) = \$9,000 \qquad \frac{1}{15}(\$27,000) = \$1,800$$

CORRECT   **INCORRECT**

An easy way to check yourself is to remember when using the sum-of-the-years'-digits method, the *first* year's depreciation should be the *largest*. This shows you that $9,000 is correct and $1,800 is incorrect for the first year's depreciation.

STOP AND CHECK

See Example 5.

1. Find the denominator of the depreciation rate if the expected life is (a) 8 years and (b) 12 years.

2. Use the sum-of-the-years'-digits method to find the depreciation for each of the three years of the expected life of a van that has a total cost of $18,000 and a salvage value of $3,000.

3. Use the sum-of-the-years'-digits method to make a depreciation schedule for an asset that has a total cost of $9,000 and a scrap value of $1,500 after four years.

4. Brown Shipping Company is making a depreciation schedule for one of its new tractor/trailer rigs by using the sum-of-the-years'-digits method of depreciation. The rig has a total cost of $45,000 and is expected to be in service for ten years. The scrap value is approximated to be $3,500. Find the depreciation rate for each of the ten years. Make a sum-of-the-years'-digits depreciation schedule for the first four years' depreciation of the rig.

4 Depreciate an asset and prepare a depreciation schedule using the declining-balance method.

Declining-balance method: a depreciation method that provides for greater depreciation in the early years of the life of an asset.

Double-declining rate: a declining-balance depreciation rate that is twice the straight-line depreciation rate.

200%-declining-balance method: another name for the double-declining-balance method of depreciation.

150%-declining rate: a common declining-balance rate that is one and one-half times the straight-line rate.

Another way to calculate depreciation so that the depreciation is greater in the early years of the asset's life and becomes less in the later years is by using the **declining-balance method.**

The *straight-line rate* of depreciation is a fraction with a numerator of 1 and a denominator equal to the number of useful years of an asset. The **double-declining rate** is twice the straight-line rate. The double-declining-balance method is also referred to as the **200%-declining-balance method.** Other declining-balance rates are possible, too, and each rate is some factor times the straight-line rate. The **150%-declining rate** is a common declining-balance rate.

> **HOW TO** Find the year's depreciation using the declining-balance method
>
> 1. Find the yearly depreciation rate.
>   (a) Using *straight-line declining balance:* Divide 1 by the number of years of expected life.
>
> $$\text{Yearly straight-line depreciation rate} = \frac{1}{\text{number of years of expected life}}$$
>
>   (b) Using other declining-balance depreciation rates, such as *double-declining-balance* or *150%-declining-balance:* Multiply the yearly straight-line depreciation rate by the appropriate factor.
>
>   Yearly double-declining depreciation rate = yearly straight-line depreciation rate $\times$ 2
>
>   Yearly 150%-declining depreciation rate = yearly straight-line depreciation rate $\times$ 1.5
>
> 2. Find the depreciation for the first year.
>
>   First year's depreciation = total cost $\times$ yearly depreciation rate
>
> 3. Find the depreciation for all other years. Do not depreciate below the salvage value.
>
>   Year's depreciation = previous end-of-year book value $\times$ yearly depreciation rate

EXAMPLE 6 An ice cream freezer has a useful life of six years. Find the yearly (a) straight-line rate expressed as a decimal and percent, (b) double-declining rate expressed as a decimal and percent, and (c) 150%-declining rate expressed as a decimal and percent.

(a) Yearly straight-line rate $= \dfrac{1}{\text{number of years of expected life}} = \dfrac{1}{6}$

$$\dfrac{1}{6} = 0.1666666667 \text{ (decimal equivalent)}$$

$$= 16.67\% \text{ (percent equivalent)}$$

The yearly straight-line rate is 0.1666666667 or 16.67%.

(b) Yearly double-declining rate $=$ straight-line rate $\times 2 = \dfrac{1}{6}(2) = \dfrac{2}{6} = \dfrac{1}{3}$

$$\dfrac{1}{3} = 0.3333333333 \text{ (decimal equivalent)}$$

$$= 33.33\% \text{ (percent equivalent)}$$

The yearly double-declining rate is 0.3333333333 or 33.33%.

(c) 150%-declining rate $=$ straight-line rate $\times 1.5$

$$= \dfrac{1}{6}(1.5) = 0.1666666667(1.5)$$

$$= 0.2500000001 \text{ (decimal equivalent)}$$

$$= 25\% \text{ (percent equivalent)}$$

The yearly 150%-declining rate is 0.25 or 25%.

TIP

Declining-Balance Methods and the Salvage Value

In declining-balance depreciation, the depreciation for the first year **is based on the total cost of the asset.** Do *not* subtract the salvage value from the total cost to find the depreciation for the first year. At the end of the year, subtract the year's depreciation from the total cost of the asset, not the depreciable value, to get the end-of-year book value.

The end-of-year book value for any year *cannot* drop below the salvage value of the asset. In such cases when calculations would cause the end-of-year book value to be less than the salvage value, the year's ending value will be the salvage value, and the year's depreciation is adjusted. There will then be no further depreciation in future years.

EXAMPLE 7 A packaging machine costing \$28,000 with an expected life of five years and a resale value of \$1,000 is depreciated by the declining-balance method at twice the straight-line rate. Prepare a depreciation schedule.

$$\text{Double-declining rate} = \text{straight-line rate} \times 2$$

$$= \dfrac{1}{\text{number of years of expected life}} \times 2$$

$$= \dfrac{1}{5}(2) = \dfrac{2}{5} = 0.4 = 40\%$$

$$\text{Year 1 depreciation} = \text{total cost} \times \text{double-declining rate}$$
$$= \$28,000(0.4)$$
$$= \$11,200$$

$$\text{End-of-year 1 book value} = \text{total cost} - \text{depreciation}$$
$$= \$28,000 - \$11,200$$
$$= \$16,800$$

$$\text{Year 2 depreciation} = \text{previous end-of-year book value} \times \text{double-declining rate}$$
$$= \$16,800(0.4)$$
$$= \$6,720$$

$$\text{End-of-year 2 book value} = \text{previous end-of-year book value} - \text{depreciation}$$
$$= \$16,800 - \$6,720$$
$$= \$10,080$$

$$\text{Year 3 depreciation} = \$10,080(0.4)$$
$$= \$4,032$$

$$\text{End-of-year 3 book value} = \$10{,}080 - \$4{,}032$$
$$= \$6{,}048$$

$$\text{Year 4 depreciation} = \$6{,}048(0.4)$$
$$= \$2{,}419.20$$

$$\text{End-of-year 4 book value} = \$6{,}048 - \$2{,}419.20$$
$$= \$3{,}628.80$$

$$\text{Year 5 depreciation} = \$3{,}628.80(0.4)$$
$$= \$1{,}451.52$$

$$\text{End-of-year 5 book value} = \$3{,}628.80 - \$1{,}451.52$$
$$= \$2{,}177.28$$

Table 17-4 shows the depreciation schedule for the packaging machine.

TABLE 17-4
Double-Declining Balance Depreciation Schedule for Packaging Machine

Total cost: $28,000	Year	Annual depreciation	Accumulated depreciation	End-of-year book value
	1	$11,200.00	$11,200.00	$16,800.00
	2	6,720.00	17,920.00	10,080.00
	3	4,032.00	21,952.00	6,048.00
	4	2,419.20	24,371.20	3,628.80
	5	1,451.52	25,822.72	2,177.28

TIP

Which Amount Do I Start With?

Be sure to *start with the total cost of the asset* when using the declining-balance method. A common error is to use total cost minus salvage value, rather than total cost. That is, in the previous example:

$$\text{Depreciation for year 1} = \text{total cost} \times \text{declining balance rate}$$
$$\$28{,}000(0.4) = \$11{,}200$$

CORRECT

$$\text{Total cost} - \text{salvage value} = \$28{,}000 - \$1{,}000 = \$27{,}000$$
$$\text{Depreciation for year 1} = \$27{,}000(0.4) = \$10{,}800$$

INCORRECT

STOP AND CHECK

See Example 6.

1. An acid disposal tank has a useful life of three years. Find (a) the straight-line rate of depreciation expressed as a decimal and percent and (b) the double-declining rate expressed as a decimal and percent. Round to hundredths.

2. A van costing $18,000 with an expected life of four years and a salvage value of $1,000 is depreciated by the declining-balance method at twice the straight-line rate. Determine the depreciation and the year-end book value for each of the four years.

See Example 7.

3. Use the double-declining-balance method to make a depreciation schedule for equipment that cost $4,500 and has a salvage value of $300. The equipment is expected to last five years.

4. A robot designed to paint cars costs $25,000 and is expected to last eight years. It will have a scrap value of $2,500. Use the 200%-declining-balance method to make a depreciation schedule for the robot.

SKILL BUILDERS

Use the straight-line method to complete the depreciation table for an SUV that costs $44,000, has a residual value of $8,000, and has an estimated life of six years. See Examples 1 and 2.

Total cost = $44,000	Year	Annual depreciation	Accumulated depreciation	End-of-year book value
1.				
2.				
3.				
4.				
5.				
6.				

Make a partial depreciation schedule for the first three years using the units-of-production depreciation for a laser engraver that costs $38,000 and has a scrap value of $2,000. The engraver has an expected life of 500,000 hours and is expected to last 15 years. See Examples 3 and 4.

Total cost $38,000	Year	Hours used	Annual depreciation	Accumulated depreciation	End-of-year book value
7.	1	24,848			
8.	2	20,040			
9.	3	20,860			

Use the sum-of-the-years'-digits depreciation method to make a depreciation schedule (first three years) for a forklift that cost $28,000, has an expected useful life of ten years, and has a residual value of $2,500. See Example 5.

Total cost $28,000	Year	Depreciation rate	Annual depreciation	Accumulated depreciation	End-of-year book value
10.	1				
11.	2				
12.	3				

A printing press that costs $285,900 is depreciated using the 1.5 declining-balance method. The scrap value of the press is estimated to be $3,000 and the press has an expected life of 20 years. Prepare the first four years of a depreciation schedule. See Examples 6 and 7.

Total cost $285,900	Year	Annual depreciation	Accumulated depreciation	End-of-year book value
13.	1	_____	_____	_____
14.	2	_____	_____	_____
15.	3	_____	_____	_____
16.	4	_____	_____	_____

APPLICATIONS

See Examples 1 and 2.

17. A tractor costs $25,000, has an expected life of 12 years, and has a salvage value of $2,500. Use straight-line depreciation to find the yearly depreciation. Make a depreciation schedule for the first three years' depreciation.

18. Prepare a straight-line depreciation schedule for the first four years of depreciation of a forklift that costs $9,450, is expected to be used for 12 years, and is projected to be scrapped for $500.

19. Find the yearly straight-line depreciation of a notebook computer system including the computer and monitor, the networking equipment, and a postscript printer that costs $6,300 and has a scrap value of $600 after an expected life of five years in a college engineering lab.

20. Make a straight-line depreciation schedule for an asset that costs $7,500 and has a scrap value of $1,200. The useful life of the asset is eight years.

21. A printing machine is expected to be operational for 90,000 hours. If the machine costs $84,500 and has a projected salvage value of $2,900, find the unit depreciation. The machine is used for 3,853 hours the first year. What is the first year's depreciation? Use the full calculator value of the unit depreciation. *See Example 3.*

22. Stuart Dybeck purchased an asphalt packing machine for $56,900 and is using sum-of-the-years' digits depreciation to schedule depreciation over six years. If the residual value is $4,000, make the depreciation schedule. *See Example 5.*

23. Ron Tibbett is depreciating a panel truck purchased for $37,290. He will use double-declining-balance and depreciate over seven years. What is the yearly double-declining-balance rate rounded to the nearest ten-thousandth and the first year's depreciation? *See Example 6.*

17-2 DEPRECIATION METHODS FOR IRS REPORTING

LEARNING OUTCOME

1 Depreciate an asset and prepare a depreciation schedule using the modified accelerated cost-recovery system (MACRS).

1 Depreciate an asset and prepare a depreciation schedule using the modified accelerated cost-recovery system (MACRS).

Modified accelerated cost-recovery system (MACRS): a modified depreciation method implemented by the IRS for property placed in service after 1986.

Recovery period: the length of time over which an asset can be depreciated. The recovery period is determined by the property class.

The Tax Reform Act of 1986 introduced some changes in the depreciation rates for property put in use after 1986 (but not affecting property in use before 1986). These changes comprise the **modified accelerated cost-recovery system** or **MACRS.** MACRS consists of two systems that determine how you depreciate your property—the General Depreciation System (GDS) and the Alternative Depreciation System (ADS). Your use of either the GDS or the ADS to depreciate property under MACRS determines what depreciation method and **recovery period** you use. You should use GDS unless you are specifically required by law to use ADS or you elect to use ADS. To figure your MACRS deduction, you need to know the recovery period, placed-in-service date, and depreciable basis for the property. This method of depreciation, which is used in figuring depreciation for federal income tax purposes, allows businesses to write off the cost of assets more quickly than in the past. The other methods of depreciation are used for accounting purposes. The faster depreciation was meant to encourage businesses to invest in more assets despite an economic slowdown at the time. The following is a list of property classes with examples that can be depreciated under the MACRS. The list is provided by an IRS publication.

1. 3-year property.
   a. Tractor units for over-the-road use.
   b. Any race horse over 2 years old when placed in service.
   c. Any other 0 over 12 years old when placed in service.
   d. Qualified rent-to-own property (defined later).
2. 5-year property.
   a. Automobiles, taxis, buses, and trucks.
   b. Computers and peripheral equipment.
   c. Office machinery (such as typewriters, calculators, and copiers).
   d. Any property used in research and experimentation.
   e. Breeding cattle and dairy cattle.
   f. Appliances, carpets, furniture, etc., used in a residential rental real estate activity.
   g. Any qualified Liberty Zone leasehold improvement property (see *Qualified New York Liberty Zone leasehold improvement property* under *Excepted Property* in Chapter 3 of IRS Publication 946).
3. 7-year property.
   a. Office furniture and fixtures (such as desks, files, and safes).
   b. Agricultural machinery and equipment.
   c. Any property that does not have a class life and has not been designated by law as being in any other class.
4. 10-year property.
   a. Vessels, barges, tugs, and similar water transportation equipment.
   b. Any single purpose agricultural or horticultural structure.
   c. Any tree or vine bearing fruits or nuts.
5. 15-year property.
   a. Certain improvements made directly to land or added to it (such as shrubbery, fences, roads, and bridges).
   b. Any retail motor fuels outlet (defined in IRS publication), such as a convenience store.
   c. Any municipal wastewater treatment plant.
6. 20-year property. This class includes farm buildings (other than single-purpose agricultural or horticultural structures).
7. 25-year property. This class is water utility property, which is either of the following.
   a. Property that is an integral part of the gathering, treatment, or commercial distribution of water, and that, without regard to this provision, would be 20-year property.
   b. Any municipal sewer.
8. Residential rental property. This is any building or structure, such as a rental home (including a mobile home), if 80% or more of its gross rental income for the tax year is from dwelling units. A dwelling unit is a house or apartment used to provide living accommodations in a building or structure. It does not include a unit in a hotel, motel, or other establishment where more than half the units are used on a transient basis. If you occupy any part of the building or structure for personal use, its gross rental income includes the fair rental value of the part you occupy.
9. Nonresidential real property. This is section 1250 property, such as an office building, store, or warehouse, that is neither residential rental property nor property with a class life of less than 27.5 years.

IRS publications outline all the options that may be used in calculating depreciation with MACRS. Some of the options involve placing properties in service at various times during the year. Several tables of rates are provided in IRS publications. MACRS rates when property is placed in service midyear are shown in Table 17-5.

In Table 17-5 each recovery period has a depreciation rate for one year more than the recovery period indicates. The first and last years in the recovery period are partial years because the property is placed in service at midyear. The largest amount of depreciation is realized in the second year, which is the first full year.

TABLE 17-5
MACRS Cost-Recovery Rates, Half-Year Convention, in Percents

Year	Depreciation rate for recovery period					
	3-Year	**5-Year**	**7-Year**	**10-Year**	**15-Year**	**20-Year**
1	33.33%	20.00%	14.29%	10.00%	5.00%	3.750%
2	44.45	32.00	24.49	18.00	9.50	7.219
3	14.81	19.20	17.49	14.40	8.55	6.677
4	7.41	11.52	12.49	11.52	7.70	6.177
5		11.52	8.93	9.22	6.93	5.713
6		5.76	8.92	7.37	6.23	5.285
7			8.93	6.55	5.90	4.888
8			4.46	6.55	5.90	4.522
9				6.56	5.91	4.462
10				6.55	5.90	4.461
11				3.28	5.91	4.462
12					5.90	4.461
13					5.91	4.462
14					5.90	4.461
15					5.91	4.462
16					2.95	4.461
17						4.462
18						4.461
19						4.462
20						4.461
21						2.231

Source: IRS Publication 946 (www.irs.gov/publications).

HOW TO Find the year's depreciation using the MACRS method

1. According to IRS publications, determine the asset's recovery period (expected life) and the appropriate table based on the time of year the property is placed in service.
2. Find the year's MACRS rate: Using Table 17-5, locate the MACRS rate for the year and recovery period.
3. Multiply the year's MACRS rate by the total cost of the asset.

$$\text{Year's depreciation} = \text{year's MACRS rate} \times \text{total cost}$$

TIP

What Makes MACRS Easier?

Three major differences in the MACRS method of depreciation from the other methods are:

1. You do not have to find a depreciable value.
2. You do not have to determine a salvage value.
3. The useful life is determined by the property classes.

EXAMPLE 1 Find the depreciation for each year and prepare a depreciation schedule for a boiler that was purchased for $28,000 and placed in service at midyear under the MACRS method of depreciation as a five-year property.

Year 1 depreciation = MACRS rate × total cost
= 20%($28,000)
= 0.2($28,000)
= $5,600

Year 2 depreciation = 0.32($28,000) = $8,960

Year 3 depreciation = 0.192($28,000) = $5,376

Year 4 depreciation = 0.1152($28,000) = $3,225.60

Year 5 depreciation = 0.1152($28,000) = $3,225.60

Year 6 depreciation = 0.0576($28,000) = $1,612.80

The sum of the yearly depreciations should equal the total cost.

$5,600 + $8,960 + $5,376 + $3,225.60 + $3,225.60 + $1,612.80 = $28,000

These calculations are most useful if they are organized into a depreciation schedule such as the one shown in Table 17-6.

TABLE 17-6
MACRS Depreciation Schedule for Boiler

Total cost: $28,000	Year	MACRS rate	Depreciation	Accumulated depreciation	End-of-year book value
	1	20.00%	$5,600.00	$ 5,600.00	$22,400.00
	2	32.00%	$8,960.00	$14,560.00	$13,440.00
	3	19.20%	$5,376.00	$19,936.00	$ 8,064.00
	4	11.52%	$3,225.60	$23,161.60	$ 4,838.40
	5	11.52%	$3,225.60	$26,387.20	$ 1,612.80
	6	5.76%	$1,612.80	$28,000.00	$ 0

As changes to the laws regarding depreciation are made, updates are posted to IRS Publication 946. These changes can be found online at www.irs.gov/pub946.

STOP AND CHECK

Assume all property is placed in service using the midyear convention. See Example 1.

1. Find the depreciation for the ninth year for a vineyard that was purchased for $58,000 and placed in service under the MACRS method of depreciation as a 10-year property.

2. Use the MACRS table to find the 8th year's depreciation for a property that cost $45,000 and is depreciated over a 10-year period.

3. Find the depreciation for the 14th year of a property that cost $83,500 and is placed in service as a 15-year property under the MACRS method of depreciation.

4. Complete a depreciation schedule for the vineyard in Exercise 1.

17-2 SECTION EXERCISES

SKILL BUILDERS

Find the depreciation for the indicated year using MACRS cost-recovery rates for the properties placed in service at midyear. See Example 1.

	Property class	Depreciation year	Cost of property
1.	3-year	2	$ 82,500
2.	5-year	4	$ 46,250
3.	10-year	1	$127,900
4.	20-year	8	$ 42,500

See Example 1.

5. Find the depreciation each year for a tractor that was purchased for $18,000 and placed in service midyear under the MACRS method of depreciation as a 3-year property.

6. Use the MACRS method to find the depreciation for the 17th year of a municipal sewer that is placed in service at midyear as a 20-year property with a cost of $385,400.

7. A barn that cost $45,000 to construct is placed in service midyear as a 20-year property. What is the MACRS depreciation for year 7?

8. Kentucky Thoroughbred Farms has a racehorse that is just over 2-years old. The racehorse, a 3-year property, is being placed in service midyear with a total cost of $83,500. Use the MACRS to find the depreciation that can be taken for the horse for each year of its service.

9. Jones' Automotive purchased equipment for $70,000. What is the first year's depreciation on the 7-year property if the property is placed in service in July 2011?

10. Find the third-year depreciation using MACRS for a fleet of taxis (5-year property) that is purchased and placed in service at midyear. The price of the fleet is $154,971.

APPLICATIONS

See Example 1.

11. A Western Star over-the-road tractor is purchased for $132,895 and placed in service in July 2010. The owner elects to depreciate this 3-year property using MACRS. Make a depreciation schedule showing each year's depreciation, accumulated depreciation, and end-of-year book value for the property.

12. Use the MACRS method to make a depreciation schedule for property that cost $4,800 and was placed in service midyear with a 3-year recovery period.

13. A 5-year property costing $286,000 is placed in service at midyear in 2011. The property is depreciated using MACRS. Prepare a depreciation schedule for the property.

Learning Outcomes

Section 17-1

1 Depreciate an asset and prepare a depreciation schedule using the straight-line method (p. 604)

What to Remember with Examples

Find the yearly depreciation using the straight-line method.

1. Find the *total cost* of the asset.

$$\text{Total cost} = \text{cost} + \text{shipping} + \text{installation}$$

2. Find the *depreciable value.*

$$\text{Depreciable value} = \text{total cost} - \text{salvage value}$$

3. Find the yearly depreciation.

$$\text{Yearly depreciation} = \frac{\text{depreciable value}}{\text{number of years of expected life}}$$

Prepare a depreciation schedule.

1. For the first year of expected life:
   (a) Find the yearly or annual depreciation.
   (b) Find the *first end-of-year book value.*

   $$\text{First end-of-year book value} = \text{total cost} - \text{first year's depreciation}$$

2. For each remaining year of expected life:
   (a) Find the year's annual depreciation.
   (b) Find the *year's accumulated depreciation.*

   $$\text{Year's accumulated depreciation} = \text{annual depreciation} + \text{sum of all the previous years' depreciation}$$

   (c) Find the *year's end-of-year book value.*

   $$\text{Year's end-of-year book value} = \text{previous end-of-year book value} - \text{annual depreciation}$$

3. Make a table with the following column headings and fill in the data: year, annual depreciation, accumulated depreciation, end-of-year book value.

Make a straight-line depreciation schedule for a property that costs $3,700 and has a salvage value of $400 at the end of three years.

$$\text{Depreciable value} = \$3,700 - \$400 = \$3,300$$

$$\text{Yearly depreciation} = \frac{\$3,300}{3} = \$1,100$$

Total cost: $3,700	Year	Depreciation	Accumulated depreciation	End-of-year book value
Depreciable	1	$1,100	$1,100	$2,600
value: $3,300	2	1,100	2,200	1,500
	3	1,100	3,300	400

2 Depreciate an asset and prepare a depreciation schedule using the units-of-production method. (p. 606)

Find the depreciation for units produced using the units-of-production method.

1. Find the *unit depreciation.*

$$\text{Unit depreciation} = \frac{\text{depreciable value}}{\text{number of units produced during expected life}}$$

Keep the full calculator value of the quotient.

2. Multiply the unit depreciation by the number of units produced.

$$\text{Depreciation for units produced} = \text{unit depreciation} \times \text{number of units produced}$$

Make a units-of-production depreciation schedule for a vehicle that costs $18,900 and has a resale value of $3,000 after 150,000 miles. The vehicle is driven 39,270 miles the first year, 37,960 miles the second year, 38,520 miles the third year, and 34,250 miles the fourth year.

$$\text{Depreciable value} = \$18,900 - \$3,000 = \$15,900$$

$$\text{Unit depreciation} = \frac{\$15,900}{150,000} = \$0.106 \text{ per mile}$$

Total cost: $18,900	Year	Miles driven	Depreciation	Accumulated depreciation	End-of-year book value
Depreciable	1	39,270	$4,162.62	$4,162.62	$14,737.38
value:	2	37,960	4,023.76	8,186.38	10,713.62
$15,900	3	38,520	4,083.12	12,269.50	6,630.50
	4	34,250	3,630.50	15,900.00	3,000.00

---

3 Depreciate an asset and prepare a depreciation schedule using the sum-of-the-years'-digits method. (p. 608)

Find the year's depreciation using the sum-of-the-years'-digits method.

1. Find the *year's depreciation rate:*

   (a) Use the $\dfrac{n(n+1)}{2}$ shortcut to find the sum from 1 through the number of years of expected life.

   Sum from 1 through the number of years of expected life
   $$= \frac{(\text{number of years of expected life})(1 + \text{number of years of expected life})}{2}$$

   (b) Divide the number of years remaining of expected life by the sum from step 1a.

   $$\text{Year's sum-of-the-years' depreciation rate} = \frac{\text{number of years remaining of expected life}}{\text{sum from 1 through the years of expected life}}$$

2. Find the depreciable value:

   $$\text{Depreciable value} = \text{total cost} - \text{salvage value}$$

3. Multiply the year's depreciable value by the year's depreciation rate.

   $$\text{Depreciation for the year} = \text{depreciable value} \times \text{depreciation rate for the year}$$

Make a sum-of-the-years'-digits schedule for a property that costs $3,700 and has a salvage value of $400 at the end of three years.

$$\text{Depreciable value} = \text{cost} - \text{salvage value} = \$3,700 - \$400 = \$3,300$$

$$\text{Sum of the years' digits} = \frac{n(n+1)}{2} = \frac{3(3+1)}{2} = 6$$

$$\text{Depreciation rate} = \frac{\text{number of years remaining}}{\text{sum of the years of expected life}} = \frac{\text{number of years remaining}}{6}$$

Total cost:	Year	Depreciation rate	Depreciation	Accumulated depreciation	End-of-year book value
$3,700	1	$\frac{3}{6}$	$1,650	$1,650	$2,050
Depreciable value:	2	$\frac{2}{6}$	1,100	2,750	950
$3,300	3	$\frac{1}{6}$	550	3,300	400

---

4 Depreciate an asset and prepare a depreciation schedule using the declining-balance method. (p. 611)

Find the year's depreciation using the declining-balance method.

1. Find the yearly depreciation rate:

   (a) Using *straight-line declining balance*, divide 1 by the number of years of expected life.

   $$\text{Yearly straight-line depreciation rate} = \frac{1}{\text{number of years of expected life}}$$

   (b) Using other declining-balance depreciation rates, such as *double-declining-balance* or *150%-declining-balance*: Multiply the yearly straight-line depreciation rate by the appropriate factor.

   Yearly double-declining depreciation rate = yearly straight-line depreciation rate $\times$ 2
   Yearly 150%-declining depreciation rate = yearly straight-line depreciation rate $\times$ 1.5

2. Find the depreciation for the first year.

$$\text{First year's depreciation} = \text{total cost} \times \text{yearly depreciation rate}$$

3. Find the depreciation for all other years.

$$\text{Year's depreciation} = \text{previous end-of-year book value} \times \text{yearly depreciation rate}$$

Make a double-declining-balance schedule of depreciation for a property that costs $3,700 and has a salvage value of $400 after three years' use.

$$\text{Yearly double-declining rate} = \frac{1}{3}(2) = \frac{2}{3} = 0.6666666667$$

Total cost: $3,700	Year	Depreciation	Accumulated depreciation	End-of-year book value
	1	$2,466.67	$2,466.67	$1,233.33
	2	822.22	3,288.89	411.11
	3	11.11*	3,300.00	400.00

*An asset *cannot* be depreciated below its salvage value. So the depreciation for year 3 is $411.11 − $400 = $11.11.

Section 17-2

1 Depreciate an asset and prepare a depreciation schedule using the modified accelerated cost-recovery system (MACRS). (p. 616)

Find the year's depreciation using the MACRS method.

1. According to IRS publications, determine the asset's recovery period (expected life) and the appropriate table.
2. Find the year's MACRS rate: Using Table 17-5, locate the MACRS rate for the year and recovery period.
3. Multiply the year's MACRS rate by the total cost of the asset. (*Note:* 100% of the asset's value is depreciated.)

$$\text{Year's depreciation} = \text{year's MACRS rate} \times \text{total cost}$$

Make a MACRS depreciation schedule for a property that costs $3,700, is put into service at midyear, and is to be depreciated over a three-year recovery period. The salvage value is $200.

Total cost: $3,700	Year	MACRS rate	Depreciation	Accumulated depreciation	End-of-year book value
	1	33.33%	$1,233.21	$1,233.21	$2,466.79
	2	44.45%	1,644.65	2,877.86	822.14
	3	14.81%	547.97	3,425.83	274.17
	4	7.41%	274.17	3,700.00	0

EXERCISES SET A

Use straight-line depreciation to complete the yearly depreciation column of a depreciation schedule. Round answers to the nearest cent.

	Total cost	Salvage value	Expected life	Yearly depreciation
1.	$7,200	$300	3 years	
2.	$12,000	$2,500	5 years	
3.	$100,000	$10,000	20 years	

4. A machine was purchased by the Wabash Company for $5,900. Its normal life expectancy is four years. If it can be traded in for $900 at the end of this time, determine the yearly depreciation by the straight-line method.

5. Station WMAT spent $5,000 for a new television camera. This camera will be replaced in five years. If the scrap value will be $500, determine the annual depreciation by the straight-line method.

6. The Acme Management Corporation purchased a computer for $5,400. Its life expectancy is projected to be four years, and the salvage value will be $800. Make a straight-line depreciation schedule like Table 17-1.

Find the unit depreciation and year's depreciation columns.

	Cost	Scrap value	Expected life	Hours operated this year
7.	$42,000	$2,000	80,000 (hours)	6,700
8.	$4,340	$340	16,000	2,580
9.	$2,370	$420	7,800	1,520

10. A tractor for trailers was purchased for $58,000 and has a resale value of $8,000. The tractor is expected to be used for 250,000 miles and is driven 19,740 miles the first year. Find the depreciation for the year.

11. Find the unit depreciation for an air conditioning–heating unit that costs $7,800 and has a scrap value of $600 if it is expected to operate 40,000 hours.

12. Make a depreciation schedule for the first two years like Table 17-2 for a truck driven 28,580 miles the first year, 32,140 miles the second year, 29,760 miles the third year, 31,810 miles the fourth year, and 27,710 miles the fifth year. The expected life of the truck is 150,000 miles and it costs $18,500. The salvage value is $2,000.

EXCEL

13. Using the sum-of-the-years'-digits method, make a depreciation schedule for the first two years for a machine that costs $4,200 and will be worth $750 at the end of five years.

14. Make a depreciation schedule using the double-declining rate for three years for a computer system costing $21,000 with an estimated life of three years and a resale value of $1,000.

Round answers to the nearest cent.

15. Find the depreciation for the tenth year for a theme park structure that was purchased for $14,489 and placed in service under the MACRS as a ten-year property.

16. Find the depreciation for the ninth year for a property that was purchased for $302,588 and placed in service under the MACRS as a ten-year property.

17. Find the depreciation for the first three years for a laser printer that costs $5,800 and was placed in service midyear under the MACRS as a five-year property.

18. Find the MACRS depreciation for year 4 for office furniture that costs $6,000 and is placed in service at midyear as a seven-year property.

19. Make a depreciation schedule like Table 17-6 for an asset that costs $3,270 and was placed in service midyear under the MACRS as a three-year property.

EXERCISES SET B

Use straight-line depreciation to fill in the yearly depreciation column. Round answers to the nearest cent.

	Total cost	Salvage value	Expected life	Yearly depreciation
1.	$6,000	$50	11 years	
2.	$50,000	$5,000	10 years	
3.	$82,500	$12,000	12 years	

4. A stamping machine was purchased by Deskin Glass Company for $8,595. Freight and installation costs were $405. If it will be worth $2,000 after seven years, find the annual depreciation using the straight-line method.

5. A dress factory paid $14,000 for an assembly-line system. If the used equipment will be worth $2,000 at the end of 15 years, find the annual depreciation by the straight-line method.

6. Make a depreciation schedule for Exercise 5 showing the first four years.

Total cost: $14,000	Year	Depreciation	Accumulated depreciation	End-of-year book value

Fill in the unit depreciation and year's depreciation columns.

	Cost	Scrap value	Expected life	Hours operated this year	Unit depreciation	Year's depreciation
7.	$25,000	$2,500	90,000 hours	7,000	$0.25	$1,750
8.	$19,000	$1,000	45,000	8,000		

9. SERV-U Computer Service Company bought a laser printer for $15,000. The machine is expected to operate for 28,000 hours, after which its trade-in value will be $1,000. Find the unit depreciation for the printer. The first year the machine was operated 4,160 hours. Find the depreciation for the year.

10. BEST Delivery Service purchased a delivery truck for $18,500 and expected to resell it for $2,000 after driving it 150,000 miles. Find the unit depreciation for the truck.

11. Make a depreciation schedule for the printer in Exercise 9 to show the depreciation for three years if it was operated 3,140 hours the second year and 6,820 hours the third year.

Total cost: $15,000	Year	Hours used	Depreciation	Accumulated depreciation	End-of-year book value

12. If the asset in Exercise 7 operates 6,190 hours the second year, what is the depreciation for the year?

13. Wee-Kare purchased a van for $21,500 and will drive it 75,000 miles. If the resale value of the van is projected to be $6,500, find the unit depreciation. Wee-Kare drove the van 2,584 miles the second year. Find the year's depreciation.

14. Make a sum-of-the-years'-digits depreciation schedule for the first two years for an asset that costs $21,500 and will be worth $5,000 at the end of four years.

Total cost: $21,500	Year	Depreciation rate	Depreciation	Accumulated depreciation	End-of-year book value

15. Concon Corp. bought office equipment for $6,000. At the end of three years, its scrap value is $750. Use a double-declining rate to make a depreciation schedule. Note that an asset *cannot* be depreciated below its scrap value.

Total cost: $6,000	Year	Depreciation	Accumulated depreciation	End-of-year book value

16. Make a depreciation schedule using a 150%-declining-balance for three years for furniture that costs $15,000 and has a salvage value of $500.

Total cost: $15,000	Year	Depreciation	Accumulated depreciation	End-of-year book value

17. Find the depreciation for each of the final two years for property purchased for $113,984 and placed in service under the MACRS as a 15-year property.

18. Find the depreciation for the 15th year of a 15-year rental property purchased for $182,500 and placed in service before March 15, 2011, under the MACRS.

19. Make a depreciation schedule like Table 17-6 for the first three years for an asset that costs $141,250 and was placed in service midyear under the MACRS as a five-year property.

PRACTICE TEST

1. Using the sum-of-the-years'-digits method, find the denominator of the depreciation rates for assets with an expected life of seven years.

2. Find the depreciable value of an asset that costs $38,490 and has a scrap value of $4,800 if the straight-line method of depreciation is used.

3. Make a depreciation schedule to show the annual straight-line depreciation, accumulated depreciation, and end-of-year book value for furniture that costs $4,500 and has a scrap value of $700. The useful life of the furniture is five years.

Total cost: $4,500	Year	Depreciation	Accumulated depreciation	End-of-year book value

4. A pizza delivery car was purchased for $19,580. The car is expected to be driven 125,000 miles before being sold for $500. What is the unit depreciation on the car (depreciation per mile)?

5. Using the sum-of-the-years'-digits method, find the denominator of the depreciation rates for an asset with an expected life of 24 years.

6. Use the sum-of-the-years'-digits method to make a depreciation schedule for an asset that costs $7,500 and has a salvage value of $1,500. The asset is to be used for three years.

Total cost: $7,500	Year	Depreciation rate	Depreciation	Accumulated depreciation	End-of-year book value

7. Use the double-declining-balance method to make a depreciation schedule for a piece of equipment that costs $2,780 and has a salvage value of $300. The equipment is expected to be used for four years.

Total cost: $2,780	Year	Depreciation	Accumulated depreciation	End-of-year book value

8. Use the MACRS to make a depreciation schedule for a vehicle that was placed in service at midyear and cost $13,580. The vehicle is to be depreciated over a three-year period.

Total cost: $13,580	Year	MACRS rate	Depreciation	Accumulated depreciation	End-of-year book value

9. Use the MACRS to find the first year's depreciation on an asset that costs $8,580 if the asset is placed in service at midyear to be depreciated over a three-year period.

10. Use the MACRS to find the depreciation for the fourth year for office furniture that costs $17,872. A recovery period of seven years is used.

11. Capital equipment for a marine biological research lab costing $227,800 is placed in service at midyear as a five-year property under the MACRS. What is the first-year depreciation?

12. Dabney Wholesale Plant Nursery placed a new greenhouse into service at midyear as a 20-year property under the MACRS depreciation method. Find the depreciation for the greenhouse for year 7 if it has a cost basis of $85,800.

1. Using the three formulas in the How To on page 604, find the yearly depreciation using the straight-line method to write one formula to find the yearly depreciation.

2. Observing patterns in business formulas and calculations enables the businessperson to better estimate or predict results and trends. Examine Table 17-3 on page 610 and explain the pattern found in the Annual Depreciation column. Explain how each subsequent year's depreciation can be found without using the depreciation rate fraction.

3. In Table 17-3, compare the pattern identified in the Accumulated Depreciation column with the pattern formed by the data in the End-of-Year Book Value column.

4. Examine Table 17-5 and explain why the second year's depreciation percent is larger than any of the other years' percents.

5. Make a chart that shows the depreciation method and the value that is used as the basis for depreciation for the five depreciation methods described in this chapter.

6. Both declining-balance depreciation and MACRS depreciation use the total cost of an asset as the basis for depreciation. Explain the difference in the way the ending book value is handled in the two methods.

7. Explain how you could use only the data in Table 17-5 to verify that any asset depreciated using the MACRS method can be depreciated for its entire cost.

Challenge Problem

A new minivan was purchased for $24,400 and currently has an end-of-year book value of $20,081.20 after one year of operation. Find the year's rate of depreciation. What will be the end-of-year book value of this minivan after two years if the rate of depreciation remains the same and depreciation is based on the purchase price?

CASE STUDIES

17-1 O'Brien Nursery

"With the Luck of the Irish, May All of Your Plants Stay Green." So reads the slogan of O'Brien Nursery, a family-owned nursery business located in west-central Illinois. Started as a small greenhouse, the business has evolved into a full-scale nursery, including landscape services. The primary assets of the business include the following: 54 acres of land including a 4-acre active vineyard of grape vines; 4 trucks, 2 vans, and 4 tractors; a greenhouse, a storage building, a building housing the retail space and offices; and office equipment. Because of substantial residential growth in the area, there is more demand than ever for landscaping services and nursery stock. One of the hottest selling items has been small ornamental trees, which are typically priced from $40 to $200 each. To meet this demand, the nursery is considering the purchase of additional land and a state-of-the-art tree planter, which sells for $17,500.

1. Using the MACRS classification guide, determine the property classification for all of the current assets owned by the nursery.

2. After one of the cargo vans breaks down, Mike O'Brien purchases a used van to replace it, though it requires some paint detailing to be done. The cost of the van is $21,400, and the custom painting costs $350. Find the depreciation for year three using MACRS.

3. Create a depreciation schedule for the tree planter costing $17,500 using the MACRS method of depreciation as a 7-year property, and placed in service at midyear.

4. The tree planter is expected to plant 92,000 trees during its useful life. If the salvage value is $1,500, find the unit depreciation and depreciation for planting 8,700 trees in a year. Would this be a better depreciation method than the MACRS? Why or why not?

17-2 The Life of a Mower

Carla has decided to fund her college expenses by mowing lawns and doing landscape maintenance during her free time. She already has some of the equipment she will need, but still needs to purchase a riding mower. Because she will be mowing primarily residential lots, she decides that a John Deere mower with a hydrostatic drive would be her best choice. The mower will cost $2,800. Carla lives in an area where grass needs to be mowed year-round, and she hopes to have 25 to 30 weekly clients. Carla thinks the estimated useful life of the mower will be four years, at which time she thinks she will be able to sell it for $800.

1. If Carla uses the straight-line method of depreciation, how much depreciation will she record for each of the next four years? Complete the following chart.

Total cost: $2,800   Depreciable value. $2,000 Annual depreciation:
$$\frac{\$2,000}{4} = \$500$$

Year	Annual depreciation	Accumulated depreciation	End-of-year book value

2. If Carla uses the sum-of-the-years'-digits method, how much depreciation will she record for each of the next four years? Complete the following chart:

Total cost: $2,800   Depreciable value: $2,000

Year	Depreciation rate	Annual depreciation	Accumulated depreciation	End-of-year book value
1				
2				
3				
4				

3. Carla thinks that her riding mower will fall under the 7-year agricultural machinery and equipment category for MACRS tax depreciation purposes. How much depreciation will she record each year on her tax return? Complete the chart for the full 7 years.

Total cost: $2,800

Year	MACRS rate	Depreciation	Accumulated depreciation	End-of-year book value
1				
2				
3				
4				
5				
6				
7				
8				

Controlling Employee Theft

Employees and customers in almost every type of business steal goods worth nearly a billion dollars a week. Theft of goods is on the rise in retail establishments nationwide. The National Retail Security Survey is produced annually in a collaborative effort between the National Retail Federation and the University of Florida. The most recent survey reported that total inventory shrinkage (the reduction in physical inventory) approached $37.1 billion. Amazingly, the number one cause was employee theft, which totaled $16.2 billion, while shoplifting was $12.1 billion. Administrative errors totaled $4.8 billion and vendor fraud $2 billion. Retailers said that the cause of the remaining shrinkage was unknown.

In the retail industry, businesses recover approximately $1,000 from each employee apprehended for stealing, compared to $150 recovered from shoplifters. So who pays for this reduction in physical inventory through employee theft and shoplifting? Unfortunately, we all do—through higher prices.

There are proven ways to detect and prevent theft-related losses within your business. A comprehensive program to eliminate employee theft can be simple and inexpensive, or elaborate and expensive.

1. **Keep a closer eye.** It is possible to install physical obstacles to theft, such as alarm systems and secured, restricted areas. Electronic security systems can protect your building when it is unoccupied. These systems include window and door monitors, movement sensors, alarms, and video cameras. However, be aware that while these devices deter theft and help prevent losses, they also convey clearly to employees that they are not trusted.

2. **Hire people you can trust.** Perform thorough background checks on all new hire prospects, particularly for sensitive positions involving the flow of money. Call previous employers to verify resume and application information. Make sure applicants do not have a history of stealing from previous employers and that all credentials and references are valid. Personal interviews, drug screening, reference checks, and criminal background reviews all have merit—and should be used prior to hiring employees.

3. **Occasionally inspect or audit inventory.** Monitoring activities, especially in receiving, can prevent theft. Keep records of any problems such as overages, shortages, and damage discrepancies. Cycle counting and periodic inventories are essential to verify the physical inventory levels on hand. Try to have a management-level supervisor oversee inventory.

Although there are many different ways to value inventory, as you will see in Chapter 18, inventory has no value to a business if it has been stolen. By paying attention to the basics of inventory management, you can help ensure that your inventory leaves in the hands of paying customers, not with employees or shoplifters.

LEARNING OUTCOMES

18-1 Inventory

1. Use the specific identification inventory method to find the ending inventory and the cost of goods sold.
2. Use the weighted-average inventory method to find the ending inventory and the cost of goods sold.
3. Use the first-in, first-out (FIFO) inventory method to find the ending inventory and the cost of goods sold.
4. Use the last-in, first-out (LIFO) inventory method to find the ending inventory and the cost of goods sold.
5. Use the retail inventory method to estimate the ending inventory and the cost of goods sold.
6. Use the gross profit inventory method to estimate the ending inventory and the cost of goods sold.

18-2 Turnover and Overhead

1. Find the inventory turnover rate.
2. Find the department overhead based on sales or floor space.

Any business needs to know the value of goods on hand that are available for sale or for use in manufacturing items for sale. Any business also needs to know how often all merchandise is sold or used and replaced with new merchandise. The expenses incurred in operating the business are other critical pieces of information needed to run a successful business. A knowledge of these concepts—inventory, turnover, and overhead—is important for making wise business decisions and for preparing required tax documents.

18-1 INVENTORY

LEARNING OUTCOMES

1 Use the specific identification inventory method to find the ending inventory and the cost of goods sold.
2 Use the weighted-average inventory method to find the ending inventory and the cost of goods sold.
3 Use the first-in, first-out (FIFO) inventory method to find the ending inventory and the cost of goods sold.
4 Use the last-in, first-out (LIFO) inventory method to find the ending inventory and the cost of goods sold.
5 Use the retail inventory method to estimate the ending inventory and the cost of goods sold.
6 Use the gross profit inventory method to estimate the ending inventory and the cost of goods sold.

Inventory: merchandise available for sale or goods available for the production of products.

Periodic or physical inventory: a physical count of goods or merchandise made at a specific time.

Perpetual inventory: an inventory process that adjusts the inventory count after each sale or purchase of goods.

Generally accepted accounting principles (GAAP): accounting principles that are accepted by industry standards and the IRS for reporting purposes and tax determination.

Cost of goods sold (COGS): the difference between the cost of goods available for sale and the cost of the ending inventory. COGS may also be referred to a **net sales at cost.**

Merchandise available for sale or goods available for the production of products on a certain date are called **inventory.** The value of inventory is important for a number of reasons. Two of the financial statements covered in Chapter 21 require inventory values, as do various tax documents. Inventory may be taken weekly, monthly, quarterly, semiannually, annually, or at any other specific interval of time. At the end of the specified time, a physical count is made of the merchandise on hand. This type of inventory is called a **periodic inventory** or **physical inventory.**

Many stores have computerized the inventory process so that the inventory is adjusted with each sale or purchase of additional goods. That is, a count of merchandise on hand is available at any time. This continual inventory method is called **perpetual inventory.** Even with a perpetual inventory system, a physical count is made periodically to verify and adjust the inventory records. A discrepancy between the perpetual inventory and the actual inventory is sometimes a result of theft or loss from damage.

Once a count of merchandise has been made, the merchandise is given a value according to **generally accepted accounting principles (GAAP).** What makes this process time-consuming is that the cost of the goods purchased during a specific period often varies. For example, at one point in a month, coffee may be purchased at $2.79 a pound. The next time coffee is ordered, the cost may be $2.93 a pound. This section discusses six methods commonly used by accountants to assign a value to an inventory: specific identification; weighted-average; first-in, first-out (FIFO); last-in, first-out (LIFO); retail; and gross profit.

For the purpose of examining the various methods of assigning the value to inventory, we use an overly simplified set of circumstances. In actual practice, the process involves many different items. For our example we use the inventory records for 12-inch battery clocks. Table 18-1 gives these records.

Throughout this discussion, the same formula is used. It shows how to find the **cost of goods sold (COGS)** during the period:

Cost of goods sold = cost of goods available for sale − cost of ending inventory

The data in Table 18-1 are used to find the cost of goods available for sale. This amount remains the same throughout the discussion. The cost of the ending inventory and the cost of goods sold vary with each method.

TABLE 18-1
Inventory Report for Battery Wall Clocks

Date of purchase	Units purchased	Cost per unit
Beginning inventory	29	$ 8
January 15	18	7
February 4	9	10
March 3	14	8

1 Use the specific identification inventory method to find the ending inventory and the cost of goods sold.

Many companies code their incoming merchandise with the purchase price or cost. Their inventory values are based on the actual cost of each item available for sale. This system of evaluating inventory is the **specific identification inventory method.** This method is best for low-volume, high-cost items, such as automobiles or fine jewelry, because a company must be able to identify the actual cost of the specific individual items bought. The name of this method is derived from the fact that in each case, when calculating the cost of goods available for sale and the cost of ending inventory, an *exact price per unit* is available.

Specific identification inventory method: an inventory valuation method that is based on the actual cost of each item available for sale.

HOW TO   Find the ending inventory and the cost of goods sold (COGS) using the specific identification inventory method

1. Find the cost of goods available for sale:

   Cost of goods available for sale = number of units purchased × cost per unit

2. Find the cost of ending inventory:

   Cost of ending inventory = number of units in ending inventory × cost per unit

3. Find the cost of goods sold (COGS):

   Cost of goods sold = cost of goods available for sale − cost of ending inventory

EXAMPLE 1

Use the ending inventory information for the wall clocks in Table 18-2 to calculate the cost of goods available for sale using the specific identification method. Then determine the cost of goods sold.

Find the cost of goods available for sale:

$$29(\$8) + 18(\$7) + 9(\$10) + 14(\$8) = \$232 + \$126 + \$90 + \$112 = \$560$$

$$\text{Ending inventory} = 14 + 5 + 3 = \textbf{22 items}$$

Find the cost of ending inventory:

$$14(\$8) + 5(\$7) + 3(\$10) = \$112 + \$35 + \$30 = \$177$$

$$\text{Cost of goods sold} = \text{cost of goods available for sale} - \text{cost of ending inventory}$$
$$= \$560 - \$177 = \$383$$

The cost of goods sold is $383.

TABLE 18-2

Cost of Goods Available for Sale and the Ending Inventory for 12-inch Battery Clocks

Date of purchase	Units purchased	Cost per unit	Total cost	Ending inventory
Beginning inventory	29	$8	$232	14
January 15	18	7	126	5
February 4	9	10	90	3
March 3	+14	8	112	—
Goods available for sale	70		$560	22

STOP AND CHECK

See Example 1.

1. Complete the inventory table and find the total cost of goods available for sale, cost of ending inventory, and cost of goods sold using the specific identification inventory method.

Inventory Table for Gadgets by Marqueta

Date of purchase	Number of bottle coolers purchased	Cost per unit	Total cost	Ending inventory
January 1 inventory	314	$9		128
February 1	200	$8		79
March 1	300	$11		183

2. Complete the inventory table and find the cost of goods available for sale, cost of ending inventory, and cost of goods sold.

Date of purchase	Number of plate stands purchased	Cost per unit	Total cost	Ending inventory
January 1 inventory	538	$2		317
April 1	400	$1.90		17
July 1	200	$2.10		123
October 1	500	$1.90		47

3. Use the specific identification inventory method to find the cost of goods available for sale, cost of ending inventory, and cost of goods sold.

Date of purchase	Number of book bags purchased	Cost per unit	Total cost	Ending inventory
February 1	389	$7		117
February 12	400	$6		89
February 25	200	$9		36

4. Find the cost of ending inventory, cost of goods available for sale, and cost of goods sold using the specific identification inventory method.

Date of purchase	Number of pencils purchased	Cost per unit	Total cost	Ending inventory
January 1	538	$0.86		115
April 1	576	$0.93		219
July 1	360	$0.95		28
October 1	624	$0.90		107

2 Use the weighted-average inventory method to find the ending inventory and the cost of goods sold.

Weighted-average inventory method: an inventory valuation method that is based on the average unit cost of the goods available for sale.

Another way to place a value on the ending inventory is the **weighted-average inventory method.** The cost of goods available for sale is divided by the number of units available for sale to get the average unit cost. This method takes less time than finding the exact price for each unit. It often is used with goods that are similar in cost and have a relatively stable cost.

HOW TO Find the ending inventory and the cost of goods sold (COGS) using the weighted-average inventory method

1. Find the cost of goods available for sale:

   Cost of goods available for sale = number of units purchased × cost per unit

2. Find the average unit cost:

   $$\text{Average unit cost} = \frac{\text{cost of goods available for sale}}{\text{number of units available for sale}}$$

3. Find the cost of ending inventory:

   Cost of ending inventory = number of units in ending inventory × average unit cost

4. Find the cost of goods sold (COGS):

   COGS = cost of goods available for sale − cost of ending inventory

 **EXAMPLE 2** Calculate the cost of ending inventory and the COGS using the weighted-average method and the data in Table 18-2.

$$\text{Average unit cost} = \frac{\text{cost of goods available for sale}}{\text{units of goods available for sale}} = \frac{\$560}{70} = \$8$$

$$\text{Cost of ending inventory} = \text{units of ending inventory} \times \text{average unit cost}$$
$$= 22(\$8)$$
$$= \$176$$

$$\text{Cost of goods sold} = \text{cost of goods available for sale} - \text{cost of ending inventory}$$
$$= \$560 - \$176$$
$$= \$384$$

The cost of goods sold is $384.

STOP AND CHECK

See Example 2.

1. Use the weighted-average method to complete the inventory table and find the average unit cost, cost of ending inventory, and cost of goods sold.

   Inventory Table for Gadgets by Marqueta

Date of purchase	Number of bottle coolers purchased	Cost per unit	Total cost	Ending inventory
January 1 inventory	314	$9		128
February 1	200	$8		79
March 1	300	$11		183

2. Use the weighted-average method to complete the inventory table and find the average unit cost, cost of ending inventory, and cost of goods sold.

Date of purchase	Number of plate stands purchased	Cost per unit	Total cost	Ending inventory
January 1 inventory	538	$2		317
April 1	400	$1.90		17
July 1	200	$2.10		123
October 1	500	$1.90		47

3. Use the weighted-average method to find the average unit cost, cost of ending inventory, and cost of goods sold.

Date of purchase	Number of book bags purchased	Cost per unit	Total cost	Ending inventory
February 1	389	$7		117
February 12	400	$6		89
February 25	200	$9		36

4. Find the average unit cost, cost of ending inventory, and cost of goods sold using the weighted-average method.

Date of purchase	Number of pencils purchased	Cost per unit	Total cost	Ending inventory
January 1	538	$0.86		115
April 1	576	$0.93		219
July 1	360	$0.95		28
October 1	624	$0.90		107

3 Use the first-in, first-out (FIFO) inventory method to find the ending inventory and the cost of goods sold.

FIFO (first-in, first-out) inventory method: an inventory valuation method in which the first items sold are assumed to be the first items purchased. The items remaining in the ending inventory are assumed to be the ones most recently purchased.

Many companies, especially those who want the cost of inventory to match replacement costs as closely as possible, use the **FIFO (first-in, first-out) inventory method.** In the FIFO method, the earliest units purchased (the first in) are assumed to be the first units sold (the first out). In this method, the ending inventory is assumed to consist of the latest units purchased. Thus, the cost of the goods available for sale is relatively close to the current cost for purchasing additional items.

HOW TO
Find the ending inventory and the cost of goods sold (COGS) using the first-in, first-out (FIFO) inventory method

1. Find the cost of goods available for sale:

    Cost of goods available for sale = number of units purchased × cost per unit

2. Find the assigned cost per unit: Assign a cost per unit in the ending inventory by assuming these units were the *latest* units purchased.
3. Find the cost of ending inventory:

    Cost of ending inventory = number of units in ending inventory × assigned cost per unit

4. Find the cost of goods sold (COGS):

    Cost of goods sold = cost of goods available for sale − cost of ending inventory

EXAMPLE 3

using the FIFO method. Use the information from Table 18-2 to find the cost of goods sold

Assign a cost per unit in the ending inventory by assuming that these units were the latest units purchased.

There are 22 units in the ending inventory, and by this method they must be the latest units purchased. Count back in the table from the most recently purchased units until you have 22 units.

March 3   14 units at $8 per unit

22 − 14 = 8 units left to be assigned

Multiply the cost per unit by the number of units. Add to get the cost of ending inventory.

March 3	14 units ($8)	= $112
February 4	8 units ($10) =	$80
	22 units	$192

Cost of goods sold = cost of goods available for sale − cost of ending inventory

= $560 − $192 = $368

The cost of goods sold is $368.

STOP AND CHECK

See Example 3.

1. Use the FIFO inventory method to complete the inventory table and find the total cost of goods available for sale, cost of ending inventory, and cost of goods sold.

Inventory Table for Gadgets by Marqueta

Date of purchase	Number of bottle coolers purchased	Cost per unit	Total cost	Ending inventory
January 1 inventory	314	$9		128
February 1	200	$8		79
March 1	300	$11		183

2. Use the FIFO inventory method to complete the inventory table and find the cost of goods available for sale, cost of ending inventory, and cost of goods sold.

Date of purchase	Number of plate stands purchased	Cost per unit	Total cost	Ending inventory
January 1 inventory	538	$2		317
April 1	400	$1.90		17
July 1	200	$2.10		123
October 1	500	$1.90		47

3. Use the FIFO inventory method to find the cost of goods available for sale, cost of ending inventory, and cost of goods sold.

Date of purchase	Number of book bags purchased	Cost per unit	Total cost	Ending inventory
February 1	389	$7		117
February 12	400	$6		89
February 25	200	$9		36

4. Find the cost of ending inventory, cost of goods available for sale, and cost of goods sold using the FIFO inventory method.

Date of purchase	Number of pencils purchased	Cost per unit	Total cost	Ending inventory
January 1	538	$0.86		115
April 1	576	$0.93		219
July 1	360	$0.95		28
October 1	624	$0.90		107

4 Use the last-in, first-out (LIFO) inventory method to find the ending inventory and the cost of goods sold.

LIFO (last-in, first-out) inventory method: an inventory valuation method in which the first items sold are assumed to be the most recent purchases. The goods remaining in the ending inventory are assumed to be earliest purchased.

A fourth method for determining the cost of the ending inventory and the cost of goods sold is the **LIFO (last-in, first-out) inventory method.** In this method, the latest units purchased (the last in) are assumed to be the first units sold (the first out). The ending inventory is assumed to consist of the earliest units purchased. The cost of the ending inventory is figured on the cost of the oldest stock. Thus, the difference between the cost of the goods available for sale and the replacement cost for new goods could be significant. Also, the short-term profit on goods sold would be less because the newer, higher-priced goods were sold first. At some later point, when the lower-priced goods are sold, the profits will be high.

Even though this method does not follow natural business practices of rotating stock to maintain freshness or quality, there are some economic advantages to using this method under certain conditions.

HOW TO   Find the ending inventory and the cost of goods sold (COGS) using the last-in, first-out (LIFO) inventory method

1. Find the cost of goods available for sale:

   Cost of goods available for sale = number of units purchased × cost per unit

2. Find the assigned cost per unit: Assign a cost per unit in the ending inventory by assuming these units were the *earliest* units purchased.
3. Find the cost of ending inventory:

   Cost of ending inventory = number of units in ending inventory × assigned cost per unit

4. Find the COGS:

   COGS = cost of goods available for sale − cost of ending inventory

EXAMPLE 4 Use the information from Table 18-2 to find the cost of goods sold using the LIFO method.

Assign a cost for each unit in the ending inventory by assuming these units were the earliest units purchased.

There are 22 items in the ending inventory, and by this method they must be the earliest units purchased. Count from the top of the table until you have 22 items. These items are all from beginning inventory.

Beginning inventory: 22 items at $8 per unit

Multiply the cost per unit by the number of units.

Cost of ending inventory: $8(22)$ items $= \$176$

$$\text{Cost of goods sold} = \text{cost of goods available for sale} - \text{cost of ending inventory}$$
$$= \$560 - \$176$$
$$= \$384$$

The cost of goods sold is $384.

Certain types of businesses may experience a severe decline in the value of inventory based on market conditions. For example, over the past decade in some parts of the country, the market value of sports trading cards has declined. In cases such as this, companies that use the weighted average, FIFO, or LIFO methods for valuing inventory may use a method known as the **lower-of-cost-or-market (LCM) rule** to evaluate inventory. The LCM rule compares the market value (current replacement cost) with the cost of each item on hand and the lower amount is used as the inventory value of that item.

Lower-of-cost-or-market (LCM) rule: compares market value with the cost of each item on hand and uses the lower amount as the inventory value of the item.

STOP AND CHECK

See Example 4.

1. Use the LIFO method to complete the inventory table and find the total cost of goods available for sale, cost of ending inventory, and cost of goods sold.

Inventory Table for Gadgets by Marqueta

Date of purchase	Number of bottle coolers purchased	Cost per unit	Total cost	Ending inventory
January 1 inventory	314	$9		128
February 1	200	$8		79
March 1	300	$11		183

2. Use the LIFO method to complete the inventory table and find the cost of goods available for sale, cost of ending inventory, and cost of goods sold.

Date of purchase	Number of plate stands purchased	Cost per unit	Total cost	Ending inventory
January 1 inventory	538	$2		317
April 1	400	$1.90		17
July 1	200	$2.10		123
October 1	500	$1.90		47

3. Use the LIFO method to find the cost of goods available for sale, cost of ending inventory, and cost of goods sold.

Date of purchase	Number of book bags purchased	Cost per unit	Total cost	Ending inventory
February 1	389	$7		117
February 12	400	$6		89
February 25	200	$9		36

4. Find the cost of ending inventory, cost of goods available for sale, and cost of goods sold using the LIFO method.

Date of purchase	Number of pencils purchased	Cost per unit	Total cost	Ending inventory
January 1	538	$0.86		115
April 1	576	$0.93		219
July 1	360	$0.95		28
October 1	624	$0.90		107

5 Use the retail inventory method to estimate the ending inventory and the cost of goods sold.

Sometimes businesses do not make monthly or periodic inventories. Instead, they *estimate* the cost of inventory rather than counting goods individually. One method used to estimate inventory is called the **retail inventory method.**

The retail inventory method uses a ratio that compares the cost of goods available for sale to the retail value of those goods. That is, it compares what it costs to buy the goods with what the goods sell for. To use this method to find the cost of goods sold, you also need to know the dollar value of sales. Take note that we refer to the cost of ending inventory as the **ending inventory at cost**, and we refer to the retail value of ending inventory as the **ending inventory at retail.**

HOW TO Estimate the ending inventory and the cost of goods sold (COGS) using the retail inventory method

1. Find the cost of goods available for sale:

$$\text{Cost of goods available for sale} = \text{number of units purchased} \times \text{cost per unit}$$

2. Find the retail value of goods available for sale.
3. Find the cost ratio:

$$\text{Cost ratio} = \frac{\text{cost of goods available for sale}}{\text{retail value of goods available for sale}}$$

4. Find the ending inventory at retail:

$$\text{Ending inventory at retail} = \text{retail value of goods available for sale} - \text{sales}$$

5. Find the ending inventory at cost:

$$\text{Ending inventory at cost} = \text{ending inventory at retail} \times \text{cost ratio}$$

6. Find the COGS:

$$\text{COGS} = \text{cost of goods available for sale} - \text{ending inventory at cost}$$

or

$$\text{COGS} = \text{dollar value of sales} \times \text{cost ratio}$$

The retail inventory method is popular among small businesses, especially businesses that have limited human resources and technology for handling the more complex methods. Another reason for the popularity of this method is that it uses information already being collected for other purposes and does not greatly increase the inventory maintenance workload.

EXAMPLE 5 Use the information from Table 18-2 and the following retail value information to find the cost of the ending inventory and the cost of goods sold using the retail method.

Date of purchase	Retail value
Beginning inventory	$331
January 15	180
February 4	129
March 3	160
Goods available for sale	$800
Sales	$487

According to Table 18-2, the cost of goods available for sale is $560. Their retail price is $800.

$$\text{Cost ratio} = \frac{\text{cost of goods available for sale}}{\text{retail value of goods available for sale}} = \frac{\$560}{\$800} = 0.7$$

$$\text{Ending inventory at retail} = \text{retail value of goods available for sale} - \text{retail value of sales}$$
$$= \$800 - \$487 = \$313$$

$$\text{Ending inventory at cost} = \text{ending inventory at retail} \times \text{cost ratio}$$
$$= \$313(0.7) = \$219.10$$

$$COGS = \text{dollar value of sales} \times \text{cost ratio}$$
$$= \$487(0.7) = \$340.90$$

or

$$= \text{cost of goods available for sale} - \text{ending inventory at cost}$$
$$= \$560.00 - \$219.10$$
$$= \$340.90$$

The ending inventory at cost is \$219.10 and the COGS is \$340.90.

STOP AND CHECK

See Example 5.

1. Use the information in the table to find the cost of ending inventory and the cost of goods sold using the retail inventory method if sales total \$5,029.12.

Inventory Table for Gadgets by Marqueta

Date of purchase	Number of bottle coolers purchased	Cost per unit	Total cost	Ending inventory	Retail value of goods available for sale
January 1 inventory	314	\$9		128	\$3,617.28
February 1	200	\$8		79	\$2,048
March 1	300	\$11		183	\$4,224

2. Use the retail inventory method to find the cost of ending inventory and the cost of goods sold for the inventory data in the table if sales for the period total \$3,171.32.

Date of purchase	Number of plate stands purchased	Cost per unit	Total cost	Ending inventory	Retail value of goods available for sale
January 1 inventory	538	\$2		317	\$1,554.37
April 1	400	\$1.90		17	\$1,100
July 1	200	\$2.10		123	\$608
October 1	500	\$1.90		47	\$1,375

3. Use the retail inventory method to find the cost of ending inventory and the cost of goods sold for the inventory data in the table if sales for the period total \$7,606.70.

Date of purchase	Book bags purchased	Cost per unit	Total cost	Ending inventory	Retail value of goods available for sale
February 1 inventory	389	\$7		117	\$3,948.35
February 12	400	\$6		89	\$3,480
February 25	200	\$9		36	\$2,610

4. Use the retail inventory method to find the cost of ending inventory and the cost of goods sold for the inventory data in the table if retail sales total \$2,436.22.

Date of purchase	Pencils purchased	Cost per unit	Total cost	Ending inventory	Retail value of goods available for sale
January 1 inventory	538	\$0.86		115	\$763.42
April 1	576	\$0.93		219	\$883.87
July 1	360	\$0.95		28	\$564.30
October 1	624	\$0.90		107	\$926.64

6 Use the gross profit inventory method to estimate the ending inventory and the cost of goods sold.

Gross profit (margin) inventory method: a method for estimating the value of inventory that is based on a constant gross profit (margin) rate and net sales.

Another method for estimating inventory for interim reports or for insurance claims is the **gross profit (margin) inventory method.** This method assumes that a company maintains approximately the same gross profit rate from year to year. This method is not used for preparing annual financial statements or calculating income taxes.

EXAMPLE 6 Use the inventory report in Table 18-1 and net sales of $487 to estimate inventory with the gross profit method if gross profit on sales is 28%.

$$\text{Cost of beginning inventory} = 29(\$8) = \$232$$

$$\text{Net purchases} = 18(\$7) + 9(\$10) + 14(\$8) = \$328$$

$$\text{Cost of goods available for sale} = \$232 + \$328 = \$560$$

$$\begin{aligned}\text{Estimated cost of goods sold} &= \$487(1 - 0.28)\\ &= \$487(0.72)\\ &= \$350.64\end{aligned}$$

$$\begin{aligned}\text{Estimated cost of ending inventory} &= \$560 - \$350.64\\ &= \$209.36\end{aligned}$$

Each of the different methods of figuring the value of inventory has advantages and disadvantages, depending on current economic conditions, tax regulations, and so on. However, it is important to know that once a business has selected a method, it must get approval from the IRS to change methods.

This section shows the result of calculating the value of the same inventory by each of the six different methods. Table 18-3 compares the six methods and their results.

TABLE 18-3
Summary of Inventory Methods Based on Table 18-2 Data

Method	Cost of ending inventory	Cost of goods sold	Comment
Specific identification	$177	$383	The most accurate method, but also the most time-consuming.
Weighted-average	$176	$384	Perhaps the easiest to use, but appropriate only when the economy is relatively stable. Radical changes in prices may result in a distorted inventory value.
First-in, first-out (FIFO)	$192	$368	The value of ending inventory is closely related to the current market price of the goods. During high inflation, this method produces the highest income.
Last-in, first-out (LIFO)	$176	$384	The value of ending inventory may vary significantly from the current market price of the goods. During high inflation, this method produces lower income, which results in a lower income tax for the company.
Retail	$219.10	$340.90	Cost of ending inventory is based on the retail value and the net sales. Because the information needed for using this method is easily accessible, this is one of the most efficient methods.
Gross profit	$209.36	$350.64	Cost of ending inventory is based on estimating the cost of goods sold using the gross profit percent.

EXAMPLE 7 The Sports Card Department of The 7th Inning bases its prices for vintage cards on the most recent edition of an appropriate pricing guide, such as *Beckett's Almanac of Baseball Cards and Collectibles*. These guides are distributed annually and prices vary significantly from year to year. What method of inventory valuation should be used?

What You Know	What You Are Looking For	Solution Plan
Prices change as a new pricing guide is available	An appropriate method for determining the value of inventory	Examine the advantages and disadvantages of each method

Solution

Specific identification:	too many individual cards to keep up with
Weighted-average:	cost of cards very unstable
FIFO and LIFO:	decrease in quality not an issue, some cards increase in value while others decrease, inflation not an issue
Retail inventory:	a good choice for annual financial statements
Gross profit:	not acceptable for official reporting, but a good choice for interim reports and insurance claims

Conclusion

The retail inventory method is the most practical for the official records of the business.

TIP

Let the Title Be Your Guide

The title of each method for finding the *cost of goods sold* contains key words to help you remember the procedures.

Method	Clue
• Specific identification	*Specific* cost to be determined.
• Weighted-average	Varying costs to be *averaged.*
• FIFO	Cost of *oldest* merchandise is used.
• LIFO	Cost of *most recently purchased* merchandise is used.
• Retail inventory	COGS is calculated from *retail value,* and the ratio of retail value to cost is shown.
• Gross profit	Percent of *profit* is used.

STOP AND CHECK

See Example 6.

1. Use the information in the table to estimate ending inventory value using the gross profit method if gross profit on sales is 36% and net sales are $5,815.

Inventory Table for Gadgets by Marqueta

Date of purchase	Number of bottle coolers purchased	Cost per unit
January 1 inventory	314	$9
February 1	200	$8
March 1	300	$11

2. Use the gross profit method to estimate the ending inventory for the inventory data in the table if gross profit on sales is 42% and net sales are $2,058.

Date of purchase	Number of plate stands purchased	Cost per unit
January 1 inventory	538	$2
April 1	400	$1.90
July 1	200	$2.10
October 1	500	$1.90

3. Use the gross profit method to estimate the cost of ending inventory for the inventory data in the table if the gross profit is 40% on sales and net sales is $4,283.

Date of purchase	Number of book bags purchased	Cost per unit
February 1 inventory	389	$7
February 12	400	$6
February 25	200	$9

4. Use the gross profit method to estimate the cost of ending inventory for the inventory data in the table if gross profit is 56% on sales and net sales is $2,048.

Date of purchase	Number of pencils purchased	Cost per unit
January 1 inventory	538	$0.86
April 1	576	$0.93
July 1	360	$0.95
October 1	624	$0.90

5. Majestic Sweets, Inc. bases its prices for cookies, cupcakes, candies, and other specialty treats on the cost of the merchandise, which can vary, especially when inflation is high. What method of inventory valuation should be used? Explain your choice.

18-1 SECTION EXERCISES

SKILL BUILDERS

Use the specific identification inventory method for Exercises 1–6. See Example 1.

1. Complete Inventory Table A for total cost of purchases, goods available for sale, cost of goods available for sale, and ending inventory using the specific inventory method. Total retail value is calculated in Exercise 21.

Inventory Table A

Date of purchase	Units purchased	Cost per unit	Total cost	Retail price per unit	Total retail value
Beginning inventory	42	$850		$975	
February 5	21	$1,760		$2,115	
February 19	17	$965		$1,206	
March 3	28	$480		$600	
Goods available for sale					
Units sold	74				
Ending inventory					

2. Cost Table A shows a breakdown of the ending inventory from Inventory Table A according to various costs per unit. Complete Cost Table A.

Cost Table A

Cost per unit	Number of units on hand	Total cost
$850	9	
$1,760	11	
$965	8	
$480	6	
Ending inventory	34	

3. Use Inventory Table A and Cost Table A to calculate the cost of goods sold.

4. Complete Inventory Table B for total cost of purchases, goods available for sale, cost of goods available for sale, and ending inventory. Total retail value is calculated in Exercise 24.

Inventory Table B

Date of purchase	Units purchased	Cost per unit	Total cost	Retail price per unit	Total retail value
Beginning inventory	96	$12		$18	
April 12	23	$9		$13	
May 8	15	$11		$17	
June 2	37	$15		$21	
Goods available for sale					
Units sold	89				
Ending inventory					

5. Cost Table B breaks down the ending inventory from Inventory Table B. Complete Cost Table B.

Cost Table B

Cost per unit	Number of units on hand	Total cost
$12	43	
$9	11	
$11	7	
$15	21	
Ending inventory		

6. Use Inventory Table B and Cost Table B to calculate the cost of goods sold.

Use the weighted-average inventory method for Exercises 7–12. See Example 2.

7. Calculate the average unit cost for Inventory Table A.

8. Calculate the cost of ending inventory for Inventory Table A.

9. Calculate the cost of goods sold for Inventory Table A.

10. Calculate the average unit cost for Inventory Table B.

11. Calculate the cost of ending inventory for Inventory Table B.

12. Calculate the cost of goods sold for Inventory Table B.

Use the first-in, first-out inventory method for Exercises 13–16. See Example 3.

13. Determine the unit cost and cost of ending inventory for units in ending inventory for Inventory Table A.

14. Find the cost of goods sold for Inventory Table A.

15. Determine the unit costs for units in ending inventory for Inventory Table B.

16. Find the cost of goods sold for Inventory Table B.

Use the last-in, first-out inventory method for Exercises 17–20. See Example 4.

17. Determine the unit costs for units in ending inventory for Inventory Table A.

18. Find the cost of goods sold for Inventory Table A.

19. Determine the unit cost for units in ending inventory for Inventory Table B.

20. Find the cost of goods sold for Inventory Table B

APPLICATIONS

Use the retail inventory method for Exercises 21–26. See Example 5.

21. Complete Inventory Table A for the total retail value.

22. Find the cost ratio to the nearest thousandth for Inventory Table A.

23. Find the cost of goods sold if sales total $78,982 for Table A.

24. Complete Inventory Table B for the total retail value.

25. Find the cost ratio for Inventory Table B.

26. Find the cost of goods sold if sales total $1,691 for Table B.

See Example 6.

27. Use Inventory Table A and the gross profit inventory method to estimate the ending inventory and cost of goods sold if a 30% gross profit is realized on sales and net sales are $115,440.

28. Use Inventory Table B and the gross profit inventory method to estimate the ending inventory and cost of goods sold if a 54% gross profit on sales is realized and net sales are $1,644.72.

29. Aspen Lakes Extreme, an outdoor adventure shop specializing in extreme mountain sports, keeps track of its inventory records using an accounting system that tracks the cost and selling price of each individual item. The system also records sales and merchandise returns. The owner maintains inventory records electronically. What method of inventory valuation should be used? Explain your choice.

LEARNING OUTCOMES

1 Find the inventory turnover rate.
2 Find the department overhead based on sales or floor space.

Inventory turnover: the frequency with which the inventory is sold and replaced.

Businesses keep careful records of their **inventory turnover,** which is how often the inventory of merchandise is sold and replaced. The rate of inventory turnover varies greatly according to the type of business. A restaurant, for example, should have a high turnover rate but probably carries a small inventory of goods. A furniture company, on the other hand, normally keeps a larger inventory but has a relatively low turnover. Another term that retailers use is *sell through* to discuss the rate inventory is turned over.

Knowing the turnover of a business can be useful in making future decisions and in analyzing business practices. For example, a low turnover rate may indicate some or all of the following:

1. Too much capital (company's money) is tied up in inventory.
2. Customers are dissatisfied with merchandise choice, quality, or price.
3. Merchandise is not properly marketed.

On the other hand, a high turnover rate may indicate some or all of the following:

1. Inventory is too small for the demand, resulting in a loss in sales because merchandise is "out of stock."
2. Merchandise is highly desirable.
3. Merchandise prices may be significantly lower than the competition's prices.

1 Find the inventory turnover rate.

Lending institutions use the turnover rate as one of the factors considered in making business loans. There are two ways to calculate turnover rate: *at cost* and *at retail.* Cost means the price at which the company buys the merchandise. Retail means the price at which the company sells the merchandise. Turnover rate can cover any period of time, but is usually calculated monthly, semiannually (twice a year), or yearly.

> **HOW TO**   Find the turnover rate at cost
>
> 1. Find the average inventory at cost:
>
> $$\text{Average inventory at cost} = \frac{\text{beginning inventory at cost} + \text{ending inventory at cost}}{2}$$
>
> 2. Divide the cost of goods sold by the average inventory at cost:
>
> $$\text{Turnover rate at cost} = \frac{\text{cost of goods sold}}{\text{average inventory at cost}}$$

Inventory turnover ratio: another term for the inventory turnover rate.

The formula for finding inventory turnover rate is often referred to as the **inventory turnover ratio.** The ratio shows the number of times a business's inventory has been sold during a specified period. For example, an inventory turnover of 3 to 1 for one year means that a store sold three times the value of the average inventory during the year. Its "sell through" rate is 3 to 1. Another way of saying this is that the merchandise has been sold and replaced three times during the year.

> **EXAMPLE 1**   Ann's Dress Shop had net sales of $52,500 at cost for the month of September. The cost of inventory at the beginning of September was $15,980 and at the end of September was $18,000. Find the average inventory at cost and the turnover rate at cost for September.
>
> $$\text{Average inventory at cost} = \frac{\text{beginning inventory at cost} + \text{ending inventory at cost}}{2}$$
> $$= \frac{\$15,980 + \$18,000}{2}$$
> $$= \frac{\$33,980}{2}$$
> $$= \boxed{\$16,990}$$

$$\text{Turnover rate at cost} = \frac{\text{cost of goods sold}}{\text{average inventory at cost}}$$

$$= \frac{\$52{,}500}{\$16{,}990}$$

$$\text{Turnover rate at cost} = 3 \text{ (rounded)}$$

The average inventory at cost is \$16,990 and the turnover rate at cost is three times.

HOW TO   Find the turnover rate at retail

1. Find the average inventory at retail:

$$\text{Average inventory at retail} = \frac{\text{beginning inventory at retail} + \text{ending inventory at retail}}{2}$$

2. Divide the sales by the average inventory at retail:

$$\text{Turnover rate at retail} = \frac{\text{sales}}{\text{average inventory at retail}}$$

EXAMPLE 2   A local Hungarian restaurant had net sales of \$32,000 for the month of June. The retail price of inventory at the beginning of June was \$7,000, and at the end of June was \$9,000. Find the average inventory at retail and the turnover rate at retail for June.

Average inventory at retail

$$= \frac{\text{beginning inventory at retail} + \text{ending inventory at retail}}{2}$$

$$= \frac{\$7{,}000 + \$9{,}000}{2} = \frac{\$16{,}000}{2} = \$8{,}000$$

$$\text{Turnover rate at retail} = \frac{\text{sales}}{\text{average inventory at retail}}$$

$$= \frac{\$32{,}000}{\$8{,}000}$$

$$= 4$$

The turnover rate at retail is four times in the month of June.

Lending institutions examine the turnover rate when determining the risk of a business repaying a loan. An acceptable turnover rate varies based on the type of merchandise and whether the business is expanding. A high turnover rate indicates a good cash flow and is desirable unless sales are lost because of out-of-stock merchandise.

In general, a rate of less than two to three times per year is a reason for concern unless the company is undergoing extensive expansion that involves expanding its inventory. Three to four times per year is usually judged to be a good turnover rate for nonperishable or nonseasonal inventory goods unless the average turnover for the particular industry is higher.

TIP

What Does the Inventory Turnover Ratio Really Mean?

The ratio has little meaning if it is not compared to another ratio. Most companies compare it to industry figures for similar businesses. Using this comparison, a business can determine how well it is doing. Comparing a company's inventory turnover ratio with industry ratios is sometimes called **benchmarking.**

Benchmarking: comparing a company's performance, such as inventory turnover ratio, with industry standards or with a similar company's performance.

STOP AND CHECK

See Example 1. Round rates to the nearest hundredth.

1. Brubaker's in the 7th Inning had net sales of $71,817 at cost for November. The cost of inventory on November 1 was $13,217, and on November 30, the inventory was $14,067. Find the average inventory at cost and the turnover rate at cost for September.

2. The Frame Shop in the 7th Inning had net sales of $48,206 at cost for June. The cost of inventory on June 1 was $8,915, and on June 30, the inventory was $9,205. Find the average inventory at cost and the turnover rate at cost for June.

See Example 2.

3. The Indian Restaurant had net sales of $74,508 for June. The retail inventory on June 1 was $5,972, and on June 30, the retail inventory was $7,291. Find the average inventory at retail and the turnover rate at retail for June.

4. Square Books Jr had net sales of $107,582 for August. On August 1, the inventory at retail was $35,169, and on August 31, the inventory at retail was $28,437. Find the average inventory at retail and the turnover rate at retail for August.

2 Find the department overhead based on sales or floor space.

A business encounters many expenses other than buying stock (merchandise to sell) and equipment. It must pay salaries, rent or mortgages, utilities, taxes, and insurance fees. It must buy office supplies and keep up equipment. These expenses, along with depreciation, are called **overhead.** The ratio between overhead and sales can say much about a firm's efficiency. Overhead is another factor that lending institutions use in making decisions about business loans.

In addition, companies sometimes need to know not only how much total overhead expenses are but also the overhead expense of each department so that excessive overhead expenses of certain departments can be reduced to increase profits. There are many methods of calculating overhead by department. Two of the most widely used methods are according to sales and according to floor space. Other ways of calculating overhead are similar to these and apply a similar problem-solving approach.

Using the sales method, the company determines what fraction of the total sales was made by each department. This department sales fraction is multiplied by the total overhead to find the overhead for each department.

> **Overhead:** depreciation and expenses required for the operation of a business, such as salaries, rent or mortgages, utilities, office supplies, taxes, insurance, and maintenance of equipment.

HOW TO   Find the department overhead based on sales

1. Find the total sales: Add the sales of individual departments.
2. Find the department sales rate:

$$\text{Department sales rate} = \frac{\text{department sales}}{\text{total sales}}$$

3. Find the overhead assigned to the department by sales:

$$\text{Department overhead} = \text{department sales rate} \times \text{total overhead}$$

EXAMPLE 3   Just For Fun's overhead totaled $8,000 during one month. Find the overhead for each department, based on total sales, if the store had the following monthly sales by department: cameras, $5,000; jewelry, $8,200; sporting goods, $6,700; silver, $9,200; and toys, $12,000.

Organize the facts and results of calculations in a table.

Department	Sales	Sales rate[*]	Overhead[*]
Cameras	$5,000	$\dfrac{\$5,000}{\$41,100}$ or 0.1216545	0.1216545($8,000) or $ 973.24
Jewelry	$8,200	$\dfrac{\$8,200}{\$41,100}$ or 0.1995134	0.1995134($8,000) or $1,596.11
Sporting goods	$6,700	$\dfrac{\$6,700}{\$41,100}$ or 0.1630170	0.1630170($8,000) or $1,304.14
Silver	$9,200	$\dfrac{\$9,200}{\$41,100}$ or 0.2238443	0.2238443($8,000) or $1,790.75
Toys	$12,000	$\dfrac{\$12,000}{\$41,100}$ or 0.2919708	0.2919708($8,000) or $2,335.77
Total	$41,100	$\dfrac{\$41,100}{\$41,100}$ or 1.000000	$8,000.01

[*]Full calculator values are not shown but are used for all calculations.

TIP

Making Periodic Checks of Calculations

When an example requires several calculations, it is helpful to periodically check your work rather than checking only the final result.

Interim Check: The total of the sales rates should be 1 or very close to 1.
Final Check: The sum of the amounts of overhead for each department should be the total overhead or very close to the total overhead.

In the preceding example, the interim check is exactly 1 and the final check is 1 cent more than the total overhead as a result of rounding.

TIP

Using Conversion Factors

In both methods for allocating overhead by department, a value by department is divided by a total value and multiplied by the total overhead. A conversion factor can be determined by making the calculations with the values that stay the same. The total sales and overhead are the same for all departments.

$$\frac{\text{Department sales}}{\text{Total sales}} = \text{department sales} \times \frac{1}{\text{total sales}}$$

In the series of calculations,

$$\text{Department sales} \times \frac{1}{\text{total sales}} \times \text{overhead}$$

the one value that changes is department sales. A conversion factor can be made by finding

$$\frac{1}{\text{total sales}} \times \text{overhead}$$

In Example 3, the conversion factor would be

$$\frac{1}{\$41,100}(\$8,000) = \frac{\$8,000}{\$41,100} = 0.1946472019$$

Use this conversion factor and the calculator memory function to recalculate the overhead by department in the example.

A computer spreadsheet can also be used to generate the table.

Department	Sales	Conversion factor	Overhead
Cameras	$5,000	0.1946472019	$973.24
Jewelry	$8,200	0.1946472019	$1,596.11
Sporting goods	$6,700	0.1946472019	$1,304.14
Silver	$9,200	0.1946472019	$1,790.75
Toys	$12,000	0.1946472019	$2,335.77
Total	$41,100		$8,000.01

Another way to distribute overhead is according to the amount of floor space each department occupies. This method is similar to the sales method. A rate for each department is calculated, this time by dividing the department's floor space by the total floor space. To find the overhead for the department, multiply the department floor-space rate by the total overhead.

HOW TO   Find department overhead based on floor space

1. Find the total floor space: Add the square feet of floor space in each department.
2. Find the department floor space rate:

$$\text{Department floor space rate} = \frac{\text{floor space in department}}{\text{total floor space}}$$

3. Find the overhead assigned to the department by floor space:

$$\text{Department overhead by floor space} = \text{department floor space rate} \times \text{total overhead}$$

EXAMPLE 4

The Super Store assigns overhead to its various departments according to the floor space used by each department. The store's total overhead is $25,000. Find the overhead for each department if each department occupies the following square feet: junior department, 3,000; women's wear, 4,000; men's wear, 3,500; children's wear, 3,000; china and silver, 2,500; housewares, 2,500; linens, 2,000; toys, 1,500; carpets, 3,500; and cosmetics, 500. Round the *final* answers to the nearest cent if necessary.

Calculator steps for Junior department:

3000 ÷ 26000 × 25000 ⇒ 2884.615385

Use similar calculator steps for all departments.

Organize the information and results in a table. This table could also be generated using a spreadsheet.

Department	Floor space in square feet	Floor space rate*	Overhead*
Junior Department	3,000	$\frac{3,000}{26,000}$ or 0.115385	0.115385($25,000) or $2,884.62
Women's Wear	4,000	$\frac{4,000}{26,000}$ or 0.153846	0.153846($25,000) or $3,846.15
Men's Wear	3,500	$\frac{3,500}{26,000}$ or 0.134615	0.134615($25,000) or $3,365.38
Children's Wear	3,000	$\frac{3,000}{26,000}$ or 0.115385	0.115385($25,000) or $2,884.62
China and Silver	2,500	$\frac{2,500}{26,000}$ or 0.096154	0.096154($25,000) or $2,403.85
Housewares	2,500	$\frac{2,500}{26,000}$ or 0.096154	0.096154($25,000) or $2,403.85
Linens	2,000	$\frac{2,000}{26,000}$ or 0.076923	0.076923($25,000) or $1,923.08
Toys	1,500	$\frac{1,500}{26,000}$ or 0.057692	0.057692($25,000) or $1,442.31

Carpets	3,500	$\frac{3,500}{26,000}$ or 0.134615	0.134615($25,000) or $3,365.38
Cosmetics	500	$\frac{500}{26,000}$ or 0.019231	0.019231($25,000) or $480.77
Total	26,000	$\frac{26,000}{26,000}$ or 1.000000	$25,000.01

*Full calculator values are not shown but are used for all calculations.

The conversion-factor method could also be used in the preceding example. The conversion factor would be

$$\frac{1}{26,000}\,(\$25,000) = \frac{\$25,000}{26,000} = \$0.9615384615$$

STOP AND CHECK

See Example 3.

1. The 7th Inning paid $12,516 in total overhead for May. Find the overhead for each department based on each department's sales: Memorabilia, $3,816; Brubaker's Restaurant, $32,167; Engraving, $67,015; and Frame Shop, $17,816.

2. Home Depot had $25,116 in total overhead for March. Find the overhead for each department based on sales: Paint, $17,815; Lighting, $19,583; Lumber, $58,982; Plumbing, $38,917; Tiles and Flooring, $27,895; Chemicals, $32,518; Home and Garden, $62,906.

See Example 4.

3. Square Books assigned overhead of $12,196 based on floor space. Textbooks uses 100 square feet, casebound travel and fiction uses 120 square feet, paperbacks uses 80 square feet, children's books uses 130 square feet, electronic media uses 140 square feet, and the coffee shop uses 300 square feet. Allocate the overhead by floor space.

4. Oxford Floral allocated overhead of $7,815 by floor space. What is the overhead for each department? Floor space: fresh flowers, 1,000 square feet; pottery, 300 square feet; fine china, 700 square feet; gifts, 800 square feet.

18-2 SECTION EXERCISES

SKILL BUILDERS

Round rates to the nearest hundredth.

1. University Trailer Sales had a beginning inventory cost of $38,440. The ending inventory cost was $52,833. The cost of merchandise sold during the period was $184,302. Find the turnover rate based on cost. *See Example 1.*

2. The 7th Inning Baseball Card Shop had a beginning inventory cost of $59,800. The ending inventory cost was $48,500. If the cost of the goods sold during the period was $117,500, find the turnover rate at cost. *See Example 1.*

3. Rutledge Equipment Company had net sales of $335,000. The beginning inventory at retail was $122,000 and the ending inventory at retail was $155,000. Find the turnover rate at retail. *See Example 2.*

4. Jeremiah Williams, owner of The Lamb Shop, needed to calculate the turnover rate based on retail prices. Net sales of $225,294 were recorded for a recent year. The retail price of inventory at the beginning of the year was $89,023 and was $68,392 at the end of the year. Find the turnover rate at retail for the year. *See Example 2.*

APPLICATIONS

5. Overhead for one month at the Allimore Department Store totaled $6,000. Find the overhead for each department, based on sales, if the store had the following monthly sales by department: toys, $4,000; appliances, $6,600; children's clothing, $6,800; books, $4,600; and furniture, $8,400. Round overhead to the nearest cent. *See Example 3.*

6. Carlisle's Stock Trailer Sales had overhead expenses that totaled $4,932 during one month. The business had the following departmental sales for the month: cattle trailers, $8,523; utility trailers, $6,201; boat trailers, $2,932; parts, $1,392. Find the overhead for each department, based on sales. Round overhead to the nearest cent. *See Example 3.*

7. Dale Crosby's Gift Shop had overhead expenses totaling $2,732 during the month of August. The business recorded departmental sales for the month of August as follows: china, $3,923; silver, $8,923; crystal, $2,932; linens, $1,923; new gifts, $6,291; antiques, $8,923. Use this information to find the overhead to the nearest cent for each department based on sales. *See Example 3.*

8. Savemore Discount Clothing Store assigns overhead to its various departments according to the floor space used by each department. The store's total monthly overhead is $15,800. Find the overhead for each department using the following square feet for each department: women's clothing, 2,000; men's clothing, 1,200; children's clothing, 2,500. Round *final* answers to the nearest cent if necessary. *See Example 4.*

9. Hughes' Trailer Manufacturer assigns overhead to its departments according to the floor space used by each department. The company's total monthly overhead for the month of April is $7,832. Find the overhead for each department using the following square feet for each department: welding bay, 2,100; paint shop, 1,950; axles and steel storage, 780; flooring lumber, 380; office space, 500. *See Example 4.*

10. Make a conversion factor for the data in Example 4 (p. 654) and use the conversion factor to calculate the overhead for each department.

Learning Outcomes

Section 18-1

1 Use the specific identification inventory method to find the ending inventory and the cost of goods sold. (p. 637)

What to Remember with Examples

1. Find the cost of goods available for sale:

Cost of goods available for sale = number of units purchased × cost per unit

2. Find the cost of ending inventory:

Cost of ending inventory = number of units in ending inventory × cost per unit

3. Find the cost of goods sold (COGS):

Cost of goods sold = cost of goods available for sale − cost of ending inventory

Use the specific identification method to find the cost of goods available for sale, the cost of ending inventory, and the cost of goods sold.

Date of purchase	Units purchased	Cost per unit	Total cost
Beginning inventory	17	$10	$170
January 8	25	$8	$200
February 3	22	$12	$264
March 5	20	$8	$160
Goods available for sale			$794

Cost per unit	Units	Total cost
$10	12	$120
$8	19	$152
$12	11	$132
$8	16	$128
Ending inventory		$532

Cost of goods sold = cost of goods available for sale

− cost of ending inventory = $794 − $532 = $262

2 Use the weighted-average inventory method to find the ending inventory and the cost of goods sold. (p. 638)

1. Find the cost of goods available for sale:

Cost of goods available for sale = number of units purchased × cost per unit

2. Find the average unit cost:

$$\text{Average unit cost} = \frac{\text{cost of goods available for sale}}{\text{number of units available for sale}}$$

3. Find the cost of ending inventory:

Cost of ending inventory = number of units in ending inventory × average unit cost

4. Find the cost of goods sold:

Cost of goods sold = cost of goods available for sale − cost of ending inventory

Find the average unit cost using the following table:

Date of purchase	Units purchased	Cost per unit	Total cost
Beginning inventory	18	$18	$324
April 6	25	$19	$475
May 4	26	$12	$312
June 9	22	$8	$176
Goods available for sale	91		$1,287

$$\text{Average unit cost} = \frac{\$1,287}{91} = \$14.14$$

Now find the cost of ending inventory and the cost of goods sold if the ending inventory is 50 units.

$$\text{Cost of ending inventory} = 50(\$14.14) = \$707$$
$$\text{Cost of goods sold} = \$1,287 - \$707 = \$580$$

3 Use the first-in, first-out (FIFO) inventory method to find the ending inventory and the cost of goods sold. (p. 640)

1. Find the cost of goods available for sale:

   Cost of goods available for sale = number of units purchased × cost per unit

2. Find the assigned cost per unit: Assign a cost per unit in the ending inventory by assuming these units were the *latest* units purchased.

3. Find the cost of ending inventory:

   Cost of ending inventory = number of units in ending inventory × assigned cost per unit

4. Find the cost of goods sold.

   Cost of goods sold = cost of goods available for sale − cost of ending inventory

Find the cost of goods sold and the cost of ending inventory if 465 units are in ending inventory.

Date of purchase	Units purchased	Cost per unit	Total cost
Beginning inventory	222	$10	$2,220
January 15	142	$12	$1,704
February 5	134	$15	$2,010
March 2	141	$24	$3,384
Goods available for sale	639		$9,318

Units sold = 639 − 465 = 174

Date of purchase	Number of units in ending inventory	Cost per unit	Total cost
Beginning inventory	48 (222 − 174)	$10	$480
January 15	142	$12	$1,704
February 5	134	$15	$2,010
March 2	141	$24	$3,384
Ending inventory	465		$7,578

Cost of goods sold = $9,318 − $7,578 = $1,740

4 Use the last-in, first-out (LIFO) inventory method to find the ending inventory and the cost of goods sold. (p. 641)

1. Find the cost of goods available for sale:

   Cost of goods available for sale = number of units purchased × cost per unit

2. Find the assigned cost per unit: Assign a cost per unit in the ending inventory by assuming these units were the *earliest* units purchased.

3. Find the cost of ending inventory:

   Cost of ending inventory = number of units in ending inventory × assigned cost per unit

4. Find the cost of goods sold:

   Cost of goods sold = cost of goods available for sale − cost of ending inventory

Find the cost of goods sold and the cost of ending inventory if 282 units are in ending inventory.

Date of purchase	Units purchased	Cost per unit	Total cost
Beginning inventory	111	$10	$1,110
April 12	343	$12	$4,116
May 8	191	$9	$1,719
June 10	106	$24	$2,544
Goods available for sale	751		$9,489

Units sold = 751 − 282 = 469

Date of purchase	Units in ending inventory	Cost per unit	Total cost
Beginning inventory	111	$10	$1,110
April 12	<u>171</u> (282 − 111)	$12	<u>$2,052</u>
Ending inventory	282		$3,162

Cost of goods sold = $9,489 − $3,162 = $6,327

5 Use the retail inventory method to estimate the ending inventory and the cost of goods sold. (p. 643)

1. Find the cost of goods available for sale:

   Cost of goods available for sale = number of units purchased × cost per unit

2. Find the retail value of goods available for sale.
3. Find the cost ratio:

$$\text{Cost ratio} = \frac{\text{cost of goods available for sale}}{\text{retail value of goods available for sale}}$$

4. Find the ending inventory at retail:

   Ending inventory at retail = retail value of goods available for sale − sales

5. Find the ending inventory at cost:

   Ending inventory at cost = ending inventory at retail × cost ratio

6. Find the cost of goods sold:

   Cost of goods sold = cost of goods available for sale − ending inventory at cost

   OR

   Cost of goods sold = dollar value of sales × cost ratio

Find the cost of goods sold and the cost of ending inventory.

	Cost	Retail
Beginning inventory	$4,824	$6,030
Purchases	<u>$872</u>	<u>$1,090</u>
Goods available for sale	$5,696	$7,120
Sales		<u>$2,464</u>
Ending inventory		$4,656

$$\text{Cost ratio} = \frac{\$5,696}{\$7,120} = 0.8$$

Ending inventory at cost = $4,656(0.8) = $3,724.80
Cost of goods sold = $5,696 − $3,724.80 = $1,971.20

6 Use the gross profit inventory method to estimate the ending inventory and the cost of goods sold. (p. 644)

1. Find the cost of goods available for sale:

   Cost of goods available for sale = cost of beginning inventory + net purchases

2. Find the estimated cost of goods sold:

   Estimated cost of goods sold = net sales × complement of percent of gross profit

3. Find the estimated cost of ending inventory:

   Estimated cost of ending inventory = cost of goods available for sale −

   estimated cost of goods sold

Estimate the cost of goods sold and the cost of ending inventory. Net sales for the period are $4,395 and gross profit on sales is 30%.

Date of purchase	Units purchased	Cost per unit
Beginning inventory	47	$12
March 1	216	$12
March 12	288	$10
March 31	360	$9

Cost of beginning inventory = 47($12) = $564
Net purchases = 216($12) + 288($10) + 360($9) = $8,712
Cost of goods available for sale = $564 + $8,712 = $9,276

$$\text{Estimated cost of goods sold} = \$4,395(1 - 0.30)$$
$$= \$4,395(0.7)$$
$$= \$3,076.50$$

$$\text{Estimated cost of ending inventory} = \$9,276 - \$3,076.50$$
$$= \$6,199.50$$

Section 18-2

1 Find the inventory turnover rate. (p. 650)

Find the turnover rate at cost:

1. Find the average inventory at cost:

$$\text{Average inventory at cost} = \frac{\text{beginning inventory at cost} + \text{ending inventory at cost}}{2}$$

2. Divide the cost of goods sold by the average inventory at cost:

$$\text{Turnover rate at cost} = \frac{\text{cost of goods sold}}{\text{average inventory at cost}}$$

Find the turnover rate at retail:

1. Find the average inventory at retail:

$$\text{Average inventory at retail} = \frac{\text{beginning inventory at retail} + \text{ending inventory at retail}}{2}$$

2. Divide the sales by the average inventory at retail:

$$\text{Turnover rate at retail} = \frac{\text{sales}}{\text{average inventory at retail}}$$

A store had net sales of $10,000 ($5,000 cost) with a beginning inventory of $5,000 retail ($2,500 cost) and an ending inventory of $6,000 retail ($3,000 cost). Find the turnover rate at cost and at retail.

$$\text{Average inventory at cost} = \frac{\$2,500 + \$3,000}{2} = \$2,750$$

$$\text{Turnover rate at cost} = \frac{\$5,000}{\$2,750} = 1.818181818$$

$$\text{Average inventory at retail} = \frac{\$5,000 + \$6,000}{2} = \$5,500$$

$$\text{Turnover at retail} = \frac{\$10,000}{\$5,500} = 1.818181818$$

2 Find the department overhead based on sales or floor space. (p. 652)

Find the department overhead based on sales:

1. Find the total sales: Add the sales of individual departments.
2. Find the department sales rate:

$$\text{Department sales rate} = \frac{\text{department sales}}{\text{total sales}}$$

3. Find the overhead assigned to the department by sales:

$$\text{Department overhead} = \text{department sales rate} \times \text{total overhead}$$

Make a table to show the overhead by departments if overhead is assigned based on total sales and the store had the following monthly sales by department: paint, $5,000; lumber, $6,200; wall coverings, $3,200; plumbing, $3,200; and electrical, $1,500. Overhead expenses during the month are $1,780.

Multiply each department's sales rate by the total overhead to find the overhead for each department.

Department	Sales	Sales rate	Overhead
Paint	$ 5,000	$\frac{\$5,000}{\$19,100}$ or 0.2617801047	0.2617801047($1,780) = $465.97
Lumber	$ 6,200	$\frac{\$6,200}{\$19,100}$ or 0.3246073298	0.3246073298($1,780) = $577.80
Wall coverings	$ 3,200	$\frac{\$3,200}{\$19,100}$ or 0.167539267	0.167539267($1,780) = $298.22
Plumbing	$ 3,200	$\frac{\$3,200}{\$19,100}$ or 0.167539267	0.167539267($1,780) = $298.22
Electrical	$ 1,500	$\frac{\$1,500}{\$19,100}$ or 0.0785340314	0.0785340314($1,780) = $139.79
Total	$19,100	$\frac{\$19,100}{\$19,100}$ or 0.9999999999*	$1,780.00

*Sum of rounded decimal equivalents.

Find department overhead based on floor space:

1. Find the total floor space: Add the square feet of floor space in each department.
2. Find the department floor space rate:

$$\text{Department floor space rate} = \frac{\text{floor space in department}}{\text{total floor space}}$$

3. Find the overhead assigned to the department by floor space:

$$\text{Department overhead by floor space} = \text{department floor space rate} \times \text{total overhead}$$

Make a table to show the overhead for a store that had $25,000 in overhead if overhead is calculated based on number of square feet a department uses: department 1: 5,100; department 2: 4,120; department 3: 1,200; department 4: 2,500.

Department	Floor space in square feet	Floor space rate	Overhead
1	5,100	$\frac{5,100}{12,920}$ or 0.3947368421	0.3947368421($25,000) = $9,868.42
2	4,120	$\frac{4,120}{12,920}$ or 0.3188854489	0.3188854489($25,000) = $7,972.14
3	1,200	$\frac{1,200}{12,920}$ or 0.092879257	0.092879257($25,000) = $2,321.98
4	2,500	$\frac{2,500}{12,920}$ or 0.193498452	0.193498452($25,000) = $4,837.46
Total	12,920	$\frac{12,920}{12,920}$ or 1	$25,000.00

*Sum of rounded decimal equivalents.

EXERCISES SET A

Use the specific identification method for Exercises 2–3.

1. Find the cost of goods available for sale using the following table:

Date of purchase	Units purchased	Cost per unit	Total cost
Beginning inventory	182	$21	
August 20	78	$27	
September 12	39	$28	
October 2	52	$21	
Cost of goods available for sale			

2. Find the cost of ending inventory using the following table showing a breakdown of unit costs for ending inventory:

Cost per unit	Units	Total cost
$21	13	
$27	64	
$28	29	
$21	48	

3. Find the cost of goods sold using the tables in Exercises 1 and 2.

Use the weighted-average method for Exercises 4–5.

4. Find the average unit cost using the table in Exercise 1.

5. Find the cost of ending inventory and the cost of goods sold using the tables in Exercises 1 and 2.

6. Use the first-in, first-out method to find the cost of goods sold and the cost of ending inventory using the table from Exercise 1 and the fact that the ending inventory is 96 units.

7. Use the last-in, first-out method to find the cost of goods sold and the cost of ending inventory using the table from Exercise 1 and the fact that the ending inventory is 200 units.

8. Use the retail method to find the cost of goods sold and the cost of ending inventory using the table in Exercise 1, the following table, and the fact that sales are $5,000:

Date of purchase	Retail price per unit
Beginning inventory	$26
August 20	$32
September 12	$35
October 2	$26

9. Find the turnover rate at cost for Phones and More, Inc. if it has a beginning inventory at cost of $51,266; an ending inventory at cost of $42,780; and cost of goods sold is $25,000.

10. Find the turnover rate at retail for a pottery shop if the beginning inventory at retail is $486,923 and the ending inventory at retail is $326,843. Sales for the period are $935,830.

11. Use the inventory table for Evanger's Canned Dog Food and net sales of $3,982 to estimate the cost of ending inventory with the gross profit method if gross profit on sales is 45%.

Inventory Report for Evanger's Canned Dog Food		
Date of purchase	Units (cases) purchased	Cost per unit (case)
Beginning inventory	148	$12.88
January 15	144	$14.27
February 13	152	$13.56
March 16	215	$12.38

12. PetMeds® usually calculates the cost of goods sold from the retail value of its merchandise and shows the ratio of retail value to cost. Which method of inventory valuation are they most likely to use?

13. Find the turnover rate at retail for a business with sales of $75,000 and an average inventory at retail of $15,000.

The entire calculator value should be used to calculate the overhead in Exercises 14–15.

14. Department 1 had $5,200 in sales for the month, department 2 had $4,700, department 3 had $6,520, department 4 had $4,870, and department 5 had $2,010. The total overhead was $10,000. Find each department's overhead based on sales.

EXCEL

15. Tyson's Fixit Store has a monthly overhead of $9,200. Find each department's monthly overhead based on floor space using the following square feet for each department: hardware, 800; plumbing, 600; tools, 400; supplies, 600.

EXERCISES SET B

Use the specific identification method for Exercises 2–3.

1. Find the cost of goods available for sale using the following table:

Date of purchase	Units purchased	Cost per unit
Beginning inventory	25	$18
June 8	10	$19
July 7	18	$20
August 3	22	$17

2. Find the cost of ending inventory using the following table showing a breakdown of unit costs for ending inventory:

Date of purchase	Cost per unit	Unit
January 1	$18	17
February 9	$19	12
March 5	$20	7
April 7	$17	14

3. Use the weighted-average method to find the average unit cost using the following table:

Date of purchase	Units purchased	Cost per unit
Beginning inventory	21	$12
May 12	10	$10
June 9	16	$11
July 5	20	$13
Units sold	46	

4. Find the cost of goods sold using the tables in Exercises 1 and 2.

5. Find the cost of ending inventory and the cost of goods sold using the results of Exercises 3 and 4.

6. Use the first-in, first-out method to find the cost of goods sold and the cost of ending inventory using the following table and the fact that the ending inventory is 500 units:

Date of purchase	Number of units purchased	Cost per unit
Beginning inventory	221	$16
April 15	328	$15
May 12	167	$12
June 5	201	$9

7. Use the last-in, first-out method to find the cost of goods sold and the cost of ending inventory using the following table:

Date of purchase	Number of units purchased	Number of units in ending inventory	Cost per unit
Beginning inventory	221	221	$16
April 15	328	279	$15
May 12	167	0	$12
June 5	201	0	$9
		500	

8. Use the retail method of inventory to find the cost of goods sold and the cost of ending inventory using the table in Exercise 1, the following table, and the fact that sales are $987.

Date of purchases	Retail price per unit
Beginning inventory	$32
June 8	$33
July 7	$35
August 3	$30

9. Find the turnover rate at cost for Ole Tyme Pictures if it has a beginning inventory at cost of $26,108; an ending inventory at cost of $5,892; and the cost of goods sold is $73,600.

10. Find the turnover rate at retail for a cupcake shop that has a beginning inventory at retail of $8,920; an ending inventory at retail of $7,460; and sales of $19,270.

11. At Best Buy Hardware, the nuts and bolts department had $1,500 in sales for the month, the electrical department had $4,000, and the paint department had $2,300. The total overhead was $3,800. Find each department's overhead based on sales.

12. A corner grocery store has a monthly overhead of $1,500. Find each department's monthly overhead based on sales if department sales were as follows: meats, $1,200; groceries, $2,400; dairy, $600; and housewares, $800.

1. Find the cost of goods available for sale using the following table:

Date of purchase	Units purchased	Cost per unit
Beginning inventory	26	$10
March 12	32	$13
April 3	29	$9
May 5	25	$12

2. Find the cost of ending inventory using the specific identification method and the following table showing a breakdown of unit costs for ending inventory:

Cost per unit	Units
$10	17
$13	12
$9	15
$12	25

3. Find the cost of goods sold using the specific identification method and the tables in Exercises 1 and 2.

4. Find the average unit cost using the table in Exercise 1.

5. Find the cost of ending inventory and the cost of goods sold using the weighted-average method and the tables in Exercises 1 and 2.

6. Find the cost of goods sold and the cost of ending inventory using the FIFO method, the table in Exercise 1, and the fact that the ending inventory is 32 units.

7. Find the cost of goods sold and the cost of ending inventory using the LIFO method, the table in Exercise 1, and the fact that the ending inventory is 82 units.

8. AMX Department Store's overhead totaled $12,000 during one month. The sales by department for the month were as follows: cameras, $12,000; toys, $14,000; hardware, $13,500; garden supplies, $8,400; sporting goods, $9,500; and clothing, $28,600. Find the monthly overhead for all departments. Use the full calculator value of the decimal equivalent to find overhead.

9. Office Supply World assigns overhead to a department based on the square feet of office space it occupies. The overhead for a month totaled $9,000 and each department occupies the following number of square feet: furniture, 2,000; computer supplies, 1,600; consumable office supplies, 2,500; leather goods, 1,200; and administrative services, 800. Find each department's overhead. Use the full calculator value of the decimal equivalent to find overhead.

10. Use the ending inventory information for Evanger's Canned Dog Food in the table to calculate the cost of goods available for sale using the specific identification method. Then determine the cost of goods sold.

Cost of Goods Available for Sale and Ending Inventory for Evanger's Canned Dog Food				
Date of purchase	**Units (cases) purchased**	**Cost per unit (case)**	**Total cost**	**Ending inventory**
Beginning inventory	148	$12.88		23
January 15	144	$14.27		16
February 13	152	$13.56		7
March 16	215	$12.38		9
Goods available for sale	659			55

11. Use the table in Exercise 10 to calculate the cost of ending inventory and the cost of goods sold using the weighted-average method.

12. A restaurant had a beginning inventory at retail of $13,900 and an ending inventory at retail of $10,000. If the net sales were $47,800, find the turnover rate at retail.

13. A retail parts business had an average inventory at retail of $258,968 and net sales of $756,893. Find the rate of turnover at retail to the nearest hundredth.

14. A plant had an average inventory at cost of $13,000 and sales of $26,000. Find the rate of turnover at cost.

15. The office photocopy machine is on the blink again. You are responsible for replacing the photocopier with a more powerful model and equitably charging each department its share of the cost of the new copier. The new copier costs $7,580 and is expected to produce 500,000 copies in its lifetime. You decide that each department's share of the cost should be based on the number of copies the department makes. The following record of use was recorded at the end of the first year. How much do you charge the four departments for the first year?

Department	Number of copies made
Purchasing	8,711
Personnel	30,872
Payroll	32,521
Secretarial pool	52,896

16. Department A uses 5,000 square feet of floor space, department B uses 2,500, department C uses 4,300, and department D uses 2,700. The total overhead is $8,200. Find each department's overhead based on floor space.

1. Combine the formulas in steps 1 and 2 of the How To box: Find the Cost of Goods Sold Using the Specific Identification Inventory Method (p. 637) to rewrite the formula in step 3 to find the cost of goods sold.

2. Combine the formulas in steps 2 and 3 of the How To box: Find the Cost of Goods Sold Using the Weighted-Average Inventory Method (p. 638) to rewrite the formula in step 3 to find the cost of ending inventory.

3. Combine the formulas in steps 1, 3, and 4 of the How To box: Find the Cost of Goods Sold Using the First-In, First-Out Inventory Method (p. 640) to find the cost of goods sold.

4. Explain the difference between a turnover rate at retail and a turnover rate at cost.

5. Discuss the difference in finding the cost of goods sold using the specific inventory method and using the retail method.

6. Explain the difference in the assumptions made in using the FIFO inventory method versus the LIFO inventory method.

7. Combine the formulas in steps 1 and 3 of the How To box: Find the Cost of Goods Sold Using the Retail Inventory Method (p. 643) to find the cost ratio.

8. Combine and simplify the formulas in steps 1 and 2 in the How To box: Find the Turnover Rate at Cost (p. 650) to solve for turnover rate at cost.

Challenge Problem

The 7th Inning Memorabilia Shop has five departments and allocates its monthly overhead by floor space. The Gallery has 4,250 square feet, Engraving has 2,675 square feet, Framing has 3,500 square feet, Brubaker's Restaurant has 5,000 square feet, and Sports Cards and Memorabilia has 4,700 square feet. In June, rent was $2,900, telephone was $289.46, utilities were $512.72, parking lot and grounds maintenance was $195, and salaries were $1,980. How much overhead should Charlie assign to Brubaker's Restaurant? If the shop had a total revenue of $27,984 for June and each department was expected to produce revenue in proportion to its space, how much of the revenue should be produced by Brubaker's Restaurant?

18-1 Decorah Custom Canoes

In the tradition of their Native American ancestors, Decorah Custom Canoes specializes in creating handcrafted canoes using only the finest natural materials. Whether they are from birch bark or cedar, all canoes are custom-built from native wood. Each piece is a work of art, and normal construction time varies from one to two months. Once completed, the canoes are purchased by and sold through a retail outlet under the same name. Only three canoes are offered, the Iroquois, Chippewa, and Winnebago, which cost $1,100, $1,400, and $2,100, respectively. Each canoe also comes as a kit and costs $450, $550, and $800, respectively. Custom paddles are also available and cost $45 and $75, for medium and large sizes. The beginning inventory on April 1 is as follows: Iroquois— 1 canoe/2 kits; Chippewa—2 canoes/2 kits; Winnebago—0 canoes/3 kits; and paddles—6 medium/6 large. The ending inventory on June 30 is as follows: Iroquois—2 canoes/1 kit; Chippewa—0 canoes/1 kit; Winnebago—2 canoes/1 kit; and paddles—6 medium/4 large. The following information is a summary of inventory purchased by the retail outlet during the past three months (April through June):

Date of purchase	Units	Item	Cost per unit
April 5	3	Iroquois canoe	$1,100
	3	Chippewa canoe	$1,400
	3	Winnebago canoe	$2,100
May 1	3	Iroquois kit	$450
	2	Chippewa kit	$550
	1	Winnebago kit	$800
	8	Paddle medium	$45
	6	Paddle large	$75
June 10	2	Chippewa kit	$550
	1	Winnebago kit	$800

1. Find the cost of goods sold using the specific identification inventory method.

2. Find the cost of goods sold using the weighted-average inventory method.

3. Decorah Custom Canoes had net sales of $8,085 at cost for the month of April, and the ending inventory on April 30 was $14,645. Compute the beginning inventory on April 1 (hint: based on what is listed in the case), and then find the average inventory at cost and the turnover rate at cost for April.

18-2 Aspen Lakes Extreme

Aspen Lakes Extreme is an outdoor adventure shop specializing in extreme mountain sports. August is typically their busiest month as summer is in full swing but winter enthusiasts also start gearing up for the snow season, which can come as early as October. Sales in August for the various departments, along with their corresponding square footage, were as follows: climbing, $1,944/1,200 ft^2; water and snow sports, $5,923/2,200 ft^2; footwear and apparel, $2,816/ 1,600 ft^2; camping and hiking, $1,650/1,650 ft^2; fitness, $1,447/ 1,350 ft^2; biking, $2,420/2,000 ft^2. Overhead for August totaled $4,680. The owners have typically allocated overhead by the sales of the various departments but are considering increasing the floor space for their more profitable departments. They want to compare the overhead based on the sales method with the overhead based on the floor space method.

1. Find the overhead to the nearest cent for each department based on sales and organize your results in a table.

2. Find the overhead to the nearest cent for each department based on floor space and organize your results in a table.

Lloyd's of London

Lloyd's is not an insurance company. It is an insurance market of members. The market began in Lloyd's Coffee House, opened by Edward Lloyd around 1688 in Tower Street, London. This establishment was a popular place for sailors, merchants, and shipowners, and Lloyd catered to them with reliable shipping news. Shipowners frequented the place to discuss insurance deals with people who had capital to insure them. Just after Christmas 1691, the coffee shop relocated to Lombard Street (a blue plaque commemorates this location). Long after Lloyd's death in 1713, this arrangement carried on until 1774, when the participating members of the insurance arrangement formed a committee and moved to the Royal Exchange on Cornhill as the Society of Lloyd's.

As the oldest continuously active insurance marketplace in the world, Lloyd's has retained some unusual structures and practices that differ from all other insurance providers today. Lloyd's syndicates—a group of underwriters on the Lloyd's insurance market—write a diverse range of policies, both direct insurance and reinsurance, covering casualty, property, marine, energy, motor, aviation, and many other types of risk. Lloyd's has a unique niche in unusual, specialized business such as kidnap and ransom, fine art, aviation, marine, and other insurances.

The general public knows Lloyd's for some unusual or notable policies it has written. For example, Lloyd's has insured:

- Silent Film comedian Ben Turpin's eyes against uncrossing
- Betty Grable's, Brooke Shields's, and Tina Turner's legs
- Jimmy Durante's nose
- 1932 World Yo-Yo Champion Harvey Lowe's hands

- The Rolling Stones founder/member Keith Richards's fingers
- Food critic and gourmet Egon Ronay's taste buds
- Celine Dion's, Bob Dylan's, and Bruce Springsteen's vocal cords
- *Riverdance* and *Lord of the Dance* star Michael Flatley's legs for $47 million
- The bodies of several professional wrestlers
- Pittsburgh Steelers player/Head and Shoulders spokesman Troy Polamalu's hair for $1 million
- Participating automobiles in the carpools involved in the Montgomery Bus Boycott in 1955–1956
- The development of the new World Trade Center with workers' compensation, general liability, excess liability, and specialty insurance programs

Lloyd's even has a market for space-related commerce. By 2013 around 35 satellites per year will be launched, of which some 25 will be insured, and Lloyd's insurers cover them for physical damage, business interruption, and even third-party liability. Space tourism could also represent a brand-new class of insurance. The FAA has cleared a Virgin Galactic spaceship for test flights with over 500 space tourists already having paid deposits for "missions," which cost $200,000 each. But while Lloyd's has provided coverage for things that are truly out of this world, and space travel is likely not in your budget—the insurance concepts presented in this chapter are certainly more down to earth, and hopefully will all be within your grasp.

LEARNING OUTCOMES

19-1 Life Insurance

1. Estimate life insurance premiums using a rate table.
2. Apply the extended term nonforfeiture option to a cancelled whole-life policy.

19-2 Property Insurance

1. Estimate renters insurance premiums using a rate table.
2. Estimate homeowners insurance premiums using a rate table.
3. Find the compensation with a coinsurance clause.

19-3 Motor Vehicle Insurance

1. Find automobile insurance premiums using rate tables.

Insurance: a form of protection against unexpected financial loss.

Comprehensive policy: insurance policy that protects the insured against several risks.

Insured (policyholder): the individual, organization, or business that carries the insurance or financial protection against loss.

Insurer (underwriter): the insurance company that insures for a specific loss according to contract provisions.

Policy: the contract between the insurer and the insured.

Premium: the amount paid by the insured for the protection provided by the policy.

Face value: the maximum amount of insurance provided by the policy.

Beneficiary: the individual, organization, or business to whom the proceeds of the policy are payable.

Insurance is a form of protection against unexpected financial loss. Businesses and individuals need insurance to help bear the burden of accidents, acts of God that result in large financial losses, and loss of life. Insurance helps distribute the burden of financial loss among those who share the same type of risk. Many types of insurance are available, such as fire, life, homeowners, health, accident, and automobile. Many insurance companies offer a **comprehensive policy** that protects the insured against several risks. The combined rate for a comprehensive policy is usually lower than if each type of protection is purchased separately.

Before we can discuss specific types of insurance, we need to understand some important terms used in the insurance field.

Insured (policyholder)	The individual, organization, or business that carries the insurance or financial protection against loss
Insurer (underwriter)	The insurance company that assures payment for a specific loss according to contract provisions
Policy	The contract between the insurer and the insured
Premium	The amount paid by the insured for the protection provided by the policy
Face value	The maximum amount of insurance provided by the policy
Beneficiary	The individual, organization, or business to whom the proceeds of the policy are payable

19-1 LIFE INSURANCE

LEARNING OUTCOMES

1 Estimate life insurance premiums using a rate table.
2 Apply the extended term nonforfeiture option to a cancelled whole-life policy.

Life insurance: an insurance policy that pays a specified amount to the beneficiary of the policy upon the death of the insured.

Income shortfall: the difference in the total living expenses of a family and the amount of income a family would have after the death of the insured. This shortfall can be used to project the amount of insurance needed by the family.

Life insurance provides financial assistance to the designated beneficiary, surviving spouse, or dependents of the insured in the event of the insured person's death. Knowing the right amount of life insurance to carry is as important as understanding the type of insurance to carry. Life insurance is usually purchased for the purpose of providing income for a family upon the death or disability of the insured person. Some financial planners suggest life insurance coverage should be seven to ten times annual income. Another way to determine the amount of life insurance needed by a family is to determine the difference in the total expenses of a family and the amount of income the family would have after the death of the insured. This difference is sometimes called **income shortfall.**

Although anyone may purchase life insurance, companies often insure the lives of their employees as a fringe benefit of employment. In partnerships, the beneficiary is often the surviving partner. Several types of life insurance policies are available, some of which even function as savings programs. In this section, we look at three types of life insurance policies in common use: *term, whole-life,* and *universal life.*

Term insurance: insurance purchased for a certain period of time. At the end of the time period, the policy has no cash value and the insurance ends. If the premium stays the same for the entire term of the insurance, it is called *level* term.

Term insurance is purchased for a certain period of time such as 5, 10, or 20 years. For example, those insured under a 10-year term policy pay premiums for 10 years or until they die, whichever occurs first. If the insured dies during the 10-year period, the beneficiary of the policy receives the face value of the policy. If the insured is still living at the end of the 10-year period, the insurance ends and the policy has no cash value. The insured would then be required to reapply for a new policy, with no guarantee of insurability under the new contract. Term insurance, however, often provides for convertibility to a policy with permanent protection, such as whole-life or universal life. This convertibility option typically does not last for the entire coverage period. The advantage of conversion is that the new policy would be issued at the same rate class as the original term policy, even after a change in insurability. The major advantage of term insurance is that it is the least expensive type of life insurance.

Whole-life (ordinary life) insurance: the insured pays premiums for his or her entire life. At the death of the insured, the beneficiary receives the face value of the policy. If the policy is cancelled, the insured is paid the cash value of the policy.

People who take out **whole-life (ordinary life) insurance** policies agree to pay premiums for their entire lives. At the time of the insured's death, a beneficiary receives the face value of the policy. This type of policy also builds up a cash value. Policyholders who cancel their policy are entitled to a certain sum of money back, depending on the amount that was paid in.

Universal life: provides permanent insurance coverage with flexibility in premium payment, and death benefit options.

Another popular form of life insurance coverage is **universal life,** often referred to as flexible premium life. Universal life provides permanent insurance coverage with greater flexibility in premium payment and the potential for cash accumulation. A universal life policy includes a cash account, which is increased with each premium payment. Interest is paid within the policy (credited) on the account at a rate specified by the company. Mortality charges and administrative costs are then charged against (reduce) the cash account. The surrender value of the policy is the amount remaining in the cash account less applicable surrender charges, if any.

When compared to whole-life coverage, universal life has two major advantages: (1) The internal rate of return of a universal life policy can be higher because it moves with prevailing interest rates (interest sensitive) or the financial markets (equity indexed universal life and variable universal life); and (2) universal life policies provide for greater flexibility, because the owner can discontinue or adjust premiums if the cash value allows it; and death benefits can be increased/decreased, subject to the limitations of the policy.

1 Estimate life insurance premiums using a rate table.

Life insurance rates are typically determined by the age, gender, and health of the insured and the type of policy. Therefore, rate quotes are generally made on an individual basis. Many rate calculators are available on the Internet that can be used for personalized rate quotes. Table 19-1 gives some typical annual premiums for fixed-rate term, whole-life, and universal life insurance that can be used to estimate an annual premium.

TABLE 19-1
Estimated Annual Life Insurance Premium Rates per $1,000 of Face Value

10-Year Level Term

Age	Male PREF	NT	T	Female PREF	NT	T
20	0.87	1.27	2.28	0.75	1.10	1.88
25	0.87	1.27	2.28	0.75	1.10	1.88
30	0.87	1.36	2.49	0.75	1.16	2.06
35	0.87	1.44	2.73	0.75	1.26	2.23
40	1.13	1.96	3.78	1.00	1.57	2.93
45	1.51	2.69	5.33	1.38	2.12	4.08
50	2.03	3.76	8.08	1.72	2.98	5.78
55	2.95	5.61	12.48	2.27	4.44	8.33
60	4.61	9.07	20.07	3.46	6.95	12.57

20-Year Level Term

Age	Male PREF	NT	T	Female PREF	NT	T
20	1.09	1.50	2.86	0.91	1.31	2.56
25	1.09	1.50	2.86	0.91	1.31	2.56
30	1.12	1.61	3.24	0.96	1.42	2.67
35	1.17	1.73	3.62	1.02	1.53	2.78
40	1.49	2.36	5.38	1.26	2.00	3.77
45	2.23	3.73	8.42	1.75	2.92	5.57
50	3.45	5.99	12.90	2.59	4.40	8.02
55	5.38	9.52	19.15	3.96	6.66	11.45
60	8.46	15.15	29.14	6.17	10.36	16.74

Whole Life

Age	Male PREF	NT	T	Female PREF	NT	T
20	8.39	9.02	10.55	7.55	8.12	9.95
25	9.51	10.22	12.70	8.65	9.30	11.59
30	10.86	11.68	14.77	9.82	10.56	13.48
35	12.37	13.30	16.59	10.97	11.80	14.85
40	14.42	15.50	19.31	12.54	13.48	16.69
45	17.65	18.98	24.03	15.14	16.28	20.43
50	22.45	24.14	30.65	19.09	20.53	25.39
55	28.67	30.82	39.00	24.11	25.92	30.97
60	36.06	38.77	49.39	29.75	31.99	37.25

Universal Life

Age	Male PREF	NT	T	Female PREF	NT	T
20	5.25	5.78	7.17	4.53	4.65	5.97
25	6.21	6.69	8.61	5.37	5.61	7.17
30	7.41	8.13	10.29	6.45	6.81	8.73
35	9.09	9.93	12.69	7.89	8.25	10.77
40	11.25	12.33	15.69	9.69	10.17	13.41
45	14.01	15.45	19.65	12.09	12.69	16.77
50	17.61	19.17	24.45	15.09	16.05	21.33
55	22.41	24.57	31.41	18.93	20.25	26.97
60	28.77	34.53	43.65	23.97	28.29	37.53

PREF = preferred; NT = non-tobacco; T = tobacco usage

HOW TO — Estimate an annual life insurance premium using a rate table

1. Locate the estimated annual rate in Table 19-1 according to type of policy, age, sex, and rate class.
2. Divide the policy face value by $1,000 and multiply the quotient by the rate from step 1.

$$\text{Estimated annual premium} = \frac{\text{face value}}{\$1,000} \times \text{rate}$$

EXAMPLE 1

Estimate the annual premium of an insurance policy with a preferred rate class and a face value of $100,000 for a 30-year-old male for (a) a 10-year level term policy; (b) 20-year level term policy; (c) a whole-life policy; (d) a universal life policy.

$$\text{Estimated annual premium} = \frac{\text{face value}}{\$1,000} \times \text{rate}$$

$$= \frac{\$100,000}{\$1,000} \times \text{rate} \qquad \text{The face value is } \$100,000.$$

$$= 100 \times \text{rate}$$

Look at Table 19-1 to find the rate for each type of policy.

(a) A 10-year level term policy: $100(\$0.87) = \$87$
(b) 20-year level term policy: $100(\$1.12) = \$112$
(c) A whole-life policy: $100(\$10.86) = \$1,086$
(d) A universal life policy: $100(\$7.41) = \$741$

The estimated annual premium for a $100,000 10-year level term policy is $87; for a 20-year level term policy is $112; for a whole-life policy is $1,086; and for a universal life policy is $741.

Since it is often inconvenient to make lump-sum annual payments, most companies allow payments to be made semiannually (twice a year), quarterly (every three months), or monthly for slightly higher rates than would apply on an annual basis. Table 19-2 shows some typical rates for periods of less than one year.

EXAMPLE 2

Use Tables 19-1 and 19-2 to estimate the (a) semiannual, (b) quarterly, and (c) monthly premiums for a $250,000 whole-life policy on a 40-year-old female, using a non-tobacco rate.

$$\text{Annual premium} = \frac{\text{amount of coverage}}{\$1,000} \times \text{rate}$$

$$= \left(\frac{\$250,000}{\$1,000} \right)(\$13.48) \qquad \text{The face value is } \$250,000. \text{ The annual rate, according to Table 19-1, is } \$13.48.$$

$$= 250(\$13.48) = \$3,370$$

Find the period rates using Table 19-2.

(a) Semiannual premium: $\qquad$ Annual premium $\times$ semiannual rate = semiannual premium
$3,370 (51%)
$= \$3,370 (0.51) = \$1,718.70$

(b) Quarterly premium: $\qquad$ Annual premium $\times$ quarterly rate = quarterly premium
$3,370 (26%)
$= \$3,370 (0.26) = \$876.20$

(c) Monthly premium $\qquad$ Annual premium $\times$ monthly rate = monthly premium
$3,370 (8.75%)
$= \$3,370 (0.0875) = \$294.88$

The semiannual premium is $1,718.70, quarterly is $876.20, and monthly is $294.88.

Other types of life insurance are fixed-time payment insurance, fixed-time endowment, and variable life policies. A **fixed-time payment insurance** policy gives a specified face value for the insured's entire life, but premium payments are made only for a fixed period of time. At

TABLE 19-2
Premium Rates for Periods Less than One Year

Period	Percent of Annual Premium
Semiannually	51.00
Quarterly	26.00
Monthly	8.75

Fixed-time payment insurance: a policy with a specified face value for the insured's entire life with premium payment made for a fixed period of time.

Paid-up insurance: insurance that continues after premiums are no longer paid.

Fixed-time endowment insurance: a policy that is a combination insurance and savings plan that is paid for a fixed period of time.

Variable life: a policy that builds up a cash reserve that you can invest in any of the choices offered by the insurance company, based on how well those investments are doing.

the end of the fixed time, the insured has **paid-up insurance,** that is, the insurance continues after premiums are no longer paid. A **fixed-time endowment insurance** policy is a combination insurance and savings plan. The insured has term insurance protection for the face value of the policy for the fixed time of the policy. At the end of the fixed time, the insured receives the face value of the policy and the insurance ends. The premiums for fixed-term payment and fixed-term endowment policies are significantly higher than the premiums for term or straight-life policies.

Another popular form of permanent life insurance protection is **variable life.** This type of life insurance is "variable" because it allows you to allocate a portion of your premium dollars to a separate account comprised of various investment funds within the insurance company's portfolio, such as an equity fund, a money market fund, a bond fund, or some combination thereof. Hence, the value of the death benefit and the cash value may fluctuate up or down, depending on the performance of the investment portion of the policy.

Which life insurance policy you choose depends on a number of factors, among the most important being the level of coverage needed and affordability. It's difficult to apply a rule of thumb because the amount of life insurance you need depends on factors such as your other sources of income, how many dependents you have, your debts, and your lifestyle. As mentioned at the beginning of this chapter, the general guideline is between seven and ten times your annual salary. What you can afford is based largely on your budget. If you are on a limited budget, then term insurance is probably the best choice for you. If you would like to build cash value but need flexibility, universal life would be best. If you are concerned with guaranteed coverage and can afford the premiums, then whole life is an excellent option. If your salary is important to supporting your family, paying the mortgage or other recurring bills, or sending your kids to college, then purchasing adequate life insurance coverage is an important means to ensure that these financial obligations are covered in the event of your death.

STOP AND CHECK

See Example 1.

1. Estimate the annual premium of a 10-year level term insurance policy with a face value of $200,000 for a 20-year-old female using a non-tobacco rate.

See Example 2.

2. Use Tables 19-1 and 19-2 to estimate the (a) semiannual, (b) quarterly, and (c) monthly premiums for a $500,000 whole-life insurance policy on a 50-year-old male using a non-tobacco rate.

See Example 2.

3. Estimate the monthly premium on a 20-year level term insurance policy of $300,000 for a 60-year-old male who uses tobacco.

See Example 2.

4. Estimate the quarterly premium on a universal-life insurance policy for a 30-year-old female who gets a preferred rate. The face value of the policy is $600,000.

2 Apply the extended term nonforfeiture option to a cancelled whole-life policy.

Lapse: the loss of insurance coverage due to nonpayment of premiums.

Nonforfeiture options: the options that are available to a policyholder when payments are discontinued.

Most types of life insurance policies except term insurance build up cash value. If a policyholder decides to cancel a policy or to allow it to **lapse** by not making the required payments, the insured normally has three choices, called **nonforfeiture options:**

1. **Cash Value or Surrender Option.** A policyholder can choose to surrender (give up) a policy and receive its cash value. If the insured wants to maintain the insurance coverage but use the cash value, a loan can be made for the amount of the cash value. The loan must be repaid with interest, or the amount of the loan and interest is deducted from the face value of the policy.

2. **Paid-Up Insurance.** The cash value of the policy is applied to a reduced amount of paid-up insurance. The reduced insurance continues for the entire life of the insured and no additional premiums are paid.

3. **Extended Term Insurance.** The cash value of the policy is applied to a term policy for the same face value as the original policy. The term policy will last as long a time period as the cash value will purchase. If the insured stops paying a policy and does not choose a nonforfeiture option, in most cases this option will be automatically implemented.

Apply the extended term nonforfeiture option to a cancelled whole-life policy.

1. Identify the cash value of the cancelled policy.
2. Estimate the annual premium for a term policy of the same face value. Use a fixed rate in Table 19-1.
3. Determine the number of years of paid-up term insurance.

$$\text{Years of paid-up term insurance} = \frac{\text{cash value of surrendered policy}}{\text{annual premium of term policy}}$$

EXAMPLE 3

Eleanor McLeod, a smoker, started a $100,000 whole-life insurance policy when she was 30 years old. At age 50, she determines that her policy has a cash value of $20,200 and wants to convert to extended term for the same face value. Using the 20-year level term rates, estimate how long her extended term insurance will last.

Estimated annual term premium: $8.02 per $1,000   50-year-old female; 20-year level term rate

$$\frac{\$100,000}{\$1,000} = 100 \text{ units} \quad \text{Number of insurance units}$$

$$\$8.02(100) = \$802 \qquad \text{Annual term rate}$$

$$\text{Years of paid-up term insurance:} \frac{\text{cash value of surrendered policy}}{\text{annual premium of term policy}}$$

$$\frac{\$20,200}{\$802} = 25.18703242 \text{ years}$$

The paid-up term insurance will extend for 25 years.

STOP AND CHECK

See Example 3.

1. Juanna Makhloufi started a whole-life insurance policy for $300,000 when she was 20 years old. At age 50, the policy has a cash value of $19,340 and Juanna decides to convert the policy to extended term for the same face value. Using 20-year level term non-tobacco rates, estimate the number of years her extended term insurance will last.

2. Byron Johnson, who gets a preferred rate, started a whole-life insurance policy for $500,000 when he was 38 years old. At age 60, the policy has a cash value of $13,208 and Bryon plans to convert the policy to extended term for the same face value. Use 10-year level term rates to estimate the number of years of extended coverage he will have.

3. Frances Johnson, who smokes, started a $250,000 whole-life insurance policy at age 32. Her policy has a cash value of $20,915 at age 50. Use 10-year level term rates to estimate the number of years of extended term coverage she can expect.

4. At age 60, Norman McLeod, who uses tobacco, wants to convert a $300,000 whole-life insurance policy to extended term with the same face value. Use 20-year level term rates to estimate the number of years of extended term coverage his cash value of $31,390 will buy.

19-1 SECTION EXERCISES

SKILL BUILDERS

Use Tables 19-1 and 19-2.

See Example 1.

1. Find the annual premium for a 10-year level term insurance policy with a face value of $45,000 for a 35-year-old female using a non-tobacco rate.

2. Find the annual premium for a whole-life insurance policy with a face value of $75,000 for a 45-year-old female who smokes.

3. What are the quarterly payments on a $100,000 whole-life insurance policy for a 30-year-old male with a preferred rate?

4. What are the monthly payments on a $200,000 universal-life insurance policy for a 50-year-old male using a non-tobacco rate?

5. Compare the premiums for a 10-year level term policy for $75,000 for a 40-year-old male to the same policy for a 40-year-old female. Use a non-tobacco rate.

6. Compare the premiums for a 20-year level term policy for $500,000 for a 60-year-old male to the same policy for a 60-year-old female. Both use tobacco.

APPLICATIONS

7. Compare the annual life insurance premium of Jenny Davis who is 35 years old, and purchases a $250,000, 20-year level term policy using a non-tobacco rate to the premium paid by Chloe Levine, her friend who is the same age as Jenny and purchases exactly the same policy. Chloe is a smoker.

8. Compare the annual life insurance premium of Garrett Townse who is 30 years old, and purchases a $100,000, 10-year level term policy using a non-tobacco rate to the premium paid by Edward Collins, his business partner who is the same age as Garrett and purchases exactly the same policy and uses tobacco.

9. Cindy Franklin started a whole-life insurance policy for $250,000 when she was 23 years old. At age 50, the policy has a cash value of $12,606 and Cindy converts the policy to extended term insurance for the same face value. Use 20-year level term rates to estimate the number of years of extended term insurance she has using a non-tobacco rate.

10. Parker Water's $200,000 whole-life insurance policy has a cash value of $11,288. Parker is 60 years old, smokes, and is converting to an extended term policy for the same face value. Use 10-year level term rates to estimate the number of years of extended term insurance she has.

19-2 PROPERTY INSURANCE

LEARNING OUTCOMES

1 Estimate renters insurance premiums using a rate table.
2 Estimate homeowners insurance premiums using a rate table.
3 Find the compensation with a coinsurance clause.

Businesses, homeowners, and renters need insurance to protect them from financial loss if their property is damaged or destroyed. Some types of perils that might cause damage or loss to property are fire, storms, burglary, and vandalism. Many types of comprehensive policies are available to cover property damage or loss, medical expenses for injuries on the property, loss of income when damage/peril causes a business to be closed for a period of time, rental expense when a peril causes a home to be unlivable, and injury or damage to the property of others. Because premiums for a comprehensive business insurance policy are based on numerous factors specific to the nature of an individual business, we will illustrate property insurance by focusing on renters and homeowners insurance.

1 Estimate renters insurance premiums using a rate table.

Take a good look around your home or apartment. If everything you own was destroyed by a natural disaster, would you be able to afford to replace it all? If any of your valuable personal property was stolen or vandalized, would you be able to afford to pay for it out of your own pocket? Do you have the cash on hand to replace your computer, laptop, iPod, DVD player, TV, stereo, jewelry, clothing, furniture, or appliances? If the answer to any of those questions was no, then **renters insurance** would be a wise investment. Renters insurance is a necessity for anyone renting or subletting a home or apartment. Whether you live in a single-family home, duplex, townhome, condo, loft, studio, or apartment, you need to have renters insurance to protect your belongings and personal liability.

Renters insurance: provides both property and liability protection for the covered policyholder, as well as certain additional benefits.

Property owners or landlords are required to carry property coverage, which protects the actual structure of the house or apartment. Most renters, however, aren't aware that all their personal property inside the dwelling will be covered only if they have renters insurance. In fact, today many landlords throughout America require tenants to purchase renters insurance when they sign a lease. The good news is that a renters insurance policy is typically very affordable and easy to obtain.

Rates for renters insurance vary according to a few factors, including the coverage and liability limits. One of the most important determinants, though, is your credit score. A poor credit score not only affects your ability to borrow money, it also increases your renters insurance premium! Even an occasional late payment past 30 days will have an effect, so make sure that all of your bills are always paid in a timely manner.

As you can see from Table 19-3, renters insurance rates are expressed in annual premiums, depending on the property coverage limit, the amount of liability coverage, the deductible selected, and the credit rating category of the applicant. In addition to the base coverage, options can be added including: identity theft/fraud protection—$20/year; sewer/sump pump backup protection (for property located in a basement)—$75/year. Extended coverage endorsements beyond the maximum coverage amounts can also be added for specific personal property: jewelry, watches, and furs—$0.85/$100/year; camera equipment—$1.35/$100/year; computer equipment—$0.95/$100/year; fine art and collectibles—$1.10/$100/year; firearms and accessories—$1.45/$100/year; and portable tools—$3.25/$100/year.

TABLE 19-3
Estimated Annual Renters Insurance Premium Rates

Liability	$20,000 Policy Limit						$40,000 Policy Limit					
	$500 Deductible			$1,000 Deductible			$500 Deductible			$1,000 Deductible		
	GOOD	OCC	BAD	GOOD	OCC	BAD	GOOD	OCC	BAD	GOOD	OCC	BAD
$300,000	141	226	253	126	203	227	195	312	349	174	280	313
$500,000	149	239	268	134	215	241	206	330	370	185	297	333
$1,000,000	169	270	303	154	246	276	233	373	418	213	339	381

GOOD = good credit; OCC = occasional payments past 30 days; BAD = judgments, collection, bankruptcy

HOW TO   Estimate an annual renters insurance premium using a rate table

1. Locate the base annual premium in Table 19-3 according to maximum policy coverage limit, liability limit, deductible, and credit score rating for the applicant.
2. Add the additional cost for any options selected.
3. Compute the annual cost for extended coverage endorsements.

$$\text{Cost} = \left(\frac{\text{coverage desired}}{\$100} \right)(\text{rate for endorsement})$$

4. Add the premiums from *steps 1 to 3*.

Total annual premium = base annual premium + cost for each option + cost for each extended coverage endorsement

EXAMPLE 1
Kirsten Lewen wants to buy renters insurance for her new apartment. She has excellent credit, and wants to find the most affordable policy. She also decides to add the identity theft/fraud protection, and an additional $2,000 of computer equipment coverage. Find the annual premium for a $20,000 policy, with the minimum liability offered, using a $1,000 deductible.

The annual base premium for a $20,000 policy, $300,000 liability, and $1,000 deductible is $126.

The cost for the identity theft/fraud protection is $20.

$$\text{Cost for additional computer coverage} = \frac{\$2,000}{\$100}(\$0.95) = \$19$$

Total annual premium $= \$126 + \$20 + \$19 = \$165$

The annual premium for the renters insurance policy is $165.

STOP AND CHECK

See Example 1.

1. Lars Pacheco needs a $40,000 renters insurance policy and has selected the $500,000 liability with $1,000 deductible. The insurance company has determined his credit is excellent and given him the "good" credit rate. If he adds an endorsement to insure $7,000 of jewelry and the option of identity theft, find his annual premium.

2. Fred Rayburn is a renter who has a renters insurance policy for $20,000 of household goods and has selected the maximum liability with $500 deductible. His credit is rated as occasional payments after 30 days. If Fred also adds an endorsement of $2,500 for firearms he keeps at his condo, how much is his annual premium?

3. Beth Grubbs rents an apartment in New York and has renters insurance to cover $20,000 of her personal belongings. She selects the minimum liability with a deductible of $500 for each claim. Beth's credit is rated as bad as she has a recent bankruptcy on her record. Find her annual premium.

4. Barbara Hensley is moving into a loft apartment and is required to have renters insurance to protect her personal property. She has an excellent credit rating and elects to purchase a policy that will cover $40,000 in personal property and $500,000 in liability. She will have a deductible of $1,000. Barbara also selects an endorsement for her $8,500 engagement ring and $2,000 for her camera equipment. Find her annual renters insurance premium.

2 Estimate homeowners insurance premiums using a rate table.

As the old adage goes—home is where your heart is—along with a healthy chunk of your net worth. For most individuals, the purchase of a home will be one the most significant investments of their life. And let's face it, disasters happen. Fires, hurricanes, earthquakes, tornadoes, and floods are all too often a part of life today. Natural disasters and man-made accidents are not just a possibility, but an eventuality—so be sure to protect the investment in your home with a homeowners insurance policy. A **homeowners insurance** policy covers both property and liability. It protects your home, personal property, and other structures on your property in case of damage or total loss. It is designed to pay homeowners for damages to their home and its contents, but can also protect them from financial liability if someone is injured on their property, or elsewhere.

Homeowners insurance: provides property coverage for both the covered dwelling and additional structures, and liability protection for the covered policyholder, as well as certain additional benefits.

What Does Homeowners Insurance Protect? Each home insurance policy is different, but standard policies usually provide the following:

- Broad coverage for damage to your house and any permanent structures on your property (unless the cause of the damage is specifically excluded in your policy).

- Damage to your personal property from causes specified in your policy.

- Limited coverage, which is available for items like stolen jewelry or cash. Coverage amounts vary depending on your state of residence.

- Additional coverage for valuable items and additional supplementary liability coverage, which can be purchased through endorsements to your homeowners policy.

Typical exclusions to a homeowners policy include damage from flooding, earthquake, normal wear and tear, war, intentional damage, or buildings used for business. Flood and earthquake coverage generally must be purchased separately. Make sure you recognize what your needs are, what is covered, and what is excluded in any policy before you buy.

Rates for homeowners insurance vary according to several factors, such as type of dwelling, location, proximity to the fire station, rating of the fire department, water supply, and fire hazards. Most states have developed a system for classifying rates according to these factors. In addition, the credit rating category of the policyholder and/or spouse has a major impact on homeowners insurance rates. In the case of spouses with different credit ratings, the lower credit classification will determine the rate category. Table 19-4 shows a sample classification system for two of the primary home construction styles—frame regular, and masonry—along with different zone ratings representing access to fire protection.

TABLE 19-4
Estimated Annual Homeowners Insurance Premium Rates per $100 of Face Value

	Frame Regular						Masonry					
	Zone 1			Zone 2			Zone 1			Zone 2		
Deductible	GOOD	OCC	BAD	GOOD	OCC	BAD	GOOD	OCC	BAD	GOOD	OCC	BAD
$1,000	0.29	0.38	0.75	0.34	0.46	0.92	0.27	0.36	0.71	0.32	0.43	0.86
$1,500	0.27	0.36	0.71	0.32	0.44	0.87	0.25	0.34	0.67	0.30	0.41	0.81

GOOD = good credit; OCC = occasional payments past 30 days; BAD = judgments, collection, bankruptcy

As you can see from Table 19-4, homeowners insurance rates are expressed as an annual amount per $100 of coverage, based on the construction type, fire protection zone, credit rating category, and deductible selected. To find the annual premium, divide the amount of coverage by $100 and multiply the result by the rate in the table. In addition, options can be added to the base coverage including the following: identity theft/fraud protection—$20/year; sewer/sump pump backup protection—$75/year. Extended coverage endorsements beyond the maximum coverage amounts can also be added for specific personal property. Endorsements can be added for: jewelry, watches, and furs—$0.85/$100/year; camera equipment—$1.35/$100/year; computer equipment—$0.95/$100/year; fine art and collectibles—$1.10/$100/year; firearms and accessories—$1.45/$100/year; and portable tools—$3.25/$100/year.

HOW TO   Estimate an annual homeowners insurance premium using a rate table

1. Locate the base annual rate in Table 19-4 according to construction type, zone, deductible, and credit score rating for the applicant(s).

$$\text{Base annual premium} = \left(\frac{\text{dwelling coverage}}{\$100}\right)(\text{rate from table})$$

2. Add the additional cost for any options selected.
3. Compute the annual cost for extended coverage endorsements.

$$\text{Cost} = \left(\frac{\text{coverage desired}}{\$100}\right)(\text{rate for endorsement})$$

4. Add the premiums from steps 1 to 3.

$$\begin{aligned}\text{Total annual premium} =\ & \text{base annual premium} \\ & + \text{cost for each option} \\ & + \text{cost for each extended coverage endorsement}\end{aligned}$$

EXAMPLE 2   Eric and Angela are in the process of buying a new home and need homeowners insurance. Their credit history, as provided by the bank, shows that they both occasionally make payments past 30 days, but with no other major problems. They need to insure their masonry home for $150,000, which is located in fire protection zone 1, and decide to go with a $1,000 deductible. They also decide to add the identity theft/fraud protection and the sewer/sump pump backup coverage, and an additional $3,000 of protection for jewelry, watches, and furs. Find the annual premium for their homeowners policy.

$$\text{Annual premium for dwelling} = \left(\frac{\text{dwelling amount}}{\$100}\right)(\text{rate}) \quad \text{rate for dwelling is } \$0.36 \text{ per } \$100$$

$$= \frac{\$150,000}{\$100}(\$0.36) = \$540$$

The cost for the identity theft/fraud protection is $20 and the cost for sewer backup is $75.

$$\text{Cost for additional coverage for jewelry, watches, and furs} = \frac{\$3,000}{\$100}(\$0.85) = \$25.50$$

Total annual premium = $540 + $20 + $75 + $25.50 = $660.50

The annual premium for the homeowners insurance policy is $660.50.

STOP AND CHECK

See Example 2.

1. Paul and Vanessa Herndon have their masonry home insured for $600,000. The home is in zone 1. Find the annual premium for the home if they have a good credit rating and select a $1,000 deductible.

2. Stewart Ungo insures his frame home for $350,000 and chooses a $1,500 deductible. The home is located in zone 1. Find the annual homeowners premium if his credit rating is good.

3. Larry Byrd insures his frame home for $265,000 and includes an endorsement for jewelry worth $5,000. What is the annual premium for his home located in zone 2 if his credit is OCC and his deductible is $1,000?

4. Kim Kiser's masonry home is insured for $328,000 with a $1,500 deductible. The home is located in zone 1. Find the annual premium if Kim's credit is rated BAD.

3 Find the compensation with a coinsurance clause.

One of the most important protection considerations with your homeowners insurance has to do with replacement cost. Most homeowners policies issued by quality insurance carriers today provide personal property replacement coverage; if not as standard coverage, it is typically available as an endorsement to your policy. Without this important protection, your policy would provide only actual cash value coverage. Actual cash value is the replacement cost of your property minus depreciation. For example, using actual cash value, a three-year-old television stolen from your home that originally sold for $1,000 might result in a settlement of only 40% of the original purchase price. That's a $600 difference! Full replacement cost coverage on personal property would compensate you for the full replacement of the television, even if it cost more to purchase today.

The concept of replacement cost applies to your dwelling as well, not just the contents. Most of today's standardized homeowners policies provide replacement cost coverage for your dwelling, up to your policy's dollar limits. Replacement cost is what you would pay to rebuild or repair your home, based on current construction costs. Replacement cost is different from market value. It does not include the value of your land. To assist you in determining the amount it would cost to rebuild your home, your company or agent usually has construction cost tables to help you figure the cost. To encourage homeowners to take out full replacement coverage, insurance companies offer plans that include a **coinsurance clause.** Such a clause means that to receive full protection or compensation up to the value of the policy for a partial loss, such as a storm-damaged roof, you must insure your dwelling for at least 80% of its replacement cost. If you insure your dwelling for less than 80% of the full replacement cost, the insurance company will pay only part of the expense of a partial loss.

Coinsurance clause: property must be insured for at least 80% of the replacement cost for full compensation for a loss.

HOW TO Find the compensation with a coinsurance clause

1. Find the face value required by the 80% coinsurance clause for full compensation: Multiply 0.8 by the replacement value of the property.
2. Find the compensation for the loss if the insurance is less than 80% of the replacement value:

Compensation (up to amount of loss)
= amount of loss (up to the face value)

$$\times \frac{\text{face value of policy}}{80\% \text{ of replacement value of property}}$$

EXAMPLE 3 Cassandra Brighton owns a home with a replacement value of $200,000. She has a homeowners insurance policy with an 80% coinsurance clause and a face value of $130,000. There is a fire, and the building damage is figured to be $50,000. What will the insurance company pay as compensation?

Does Cassandra carry as much insurance as its coinsurance clause requires for full protection?

Face value required for full compensation = 0.8($200,000) = $160,000

Cassandra has a policy worth only $130,000, so she does *not* get full compensation for the loss. Find the compensation:

$$\text{Compensation} = \text{loss} \times \frac{\text{face value of policy}}{80\% \text{ of replacement value}}$$

$$\text{Compensation} = \$50,000\left(\frac{\$130,000}{\$160,000}\right) = \$40,625$$

Cassandra receives $40,625 compensation for her loss of $50,000.

If Cassandra had carried a policy for 80% of the replacement value of her property, she would have gotten the full $50,000 compensation for the loss.

EXAMPLE 4

John Worthy's home is insured for 80% of the replacement value. The replacement value of the home is $105,000. A fire causes $90,000 worth of damage to the property. How much compensation will John receive from the insurance company?

Face value of policy = 0.8($105,000) = $84,000   Compensation cannot exceed the face value of the policy.

Compensation = $84,000

The loss compensation is $84,000.

In the preceding example, the $90,000 loss can only be compensated at $84,000 because the face value of the policy is only $84,000.

STOP AND CHECK

See Example 3.

1. Audrey Boles owns a home with a replacement value of $650,000. Its homeowners insurance policy has an 80% coinsurance clause and a face value of $400,000. Damage from a fire is estimated to be $82,000. What compensation will the insurance company pay?

See Example 3.

2. Maggie Mallette owns a home with a replacement value of $492,000. The homeowners insurance policy has an 80% coinsurance clause and a face value of $350,000. Damage caused by a storm costs $43,790 to repair. What compensation will the insurance company pay?

See Example 4.

3. Max McLeod owns a home with a replacement value of $798,500. His homeowners insurance policy has an 80% coinsurance clause and a face value of $638,800. Damage caused by a hurricane costs $590,000. How much will Max's insurance company pay?

See Example 4.

4. Tim Akers has insured his home for $552,000. The replacement value of the home is $690,000 with an 80% coinsurance clause. Repairs from a fire cost $38,588. How much will the insurance company pay?

19-2 SECTION EXERCISES

SKILL BUILDERS

Use Table 19-3 and the information on page 680 to find the total annual renters insurance premiums in Exercises 1–4.

See Example 1.

1. Tim Navholtz needs a $20,000 renters insurance policy and has selected the $1,000,000 liability with $1,000 deductible. The insurance company has determined his credit is excellent and has given him the "good" credit rate. If he adds an endorsement to ensure $12,000 of jewelry and the options of identity theft/protection and sewer/sump pump backup protection for his basement, find his annual premium.

See Example 1.

2. Margaret Davis has a renters insurance policy for $40,000 of household goods and has selected $500,000 liability with $1,000 deductible. Her credit is rated as occasional payments after 30 days. If Margaret also adds an endorsement of $18,500 to insure her collectible antiques and $5,000 to insure the jewelry she keeps at her condo, how much is her annual premium?

See Example 1.

3. Shay Manning rents an apartment in Chicago and carries $20,000 insurance on her personal belongings. She selects the minimum liability with a deductible of $1,000 for each claim and carries identity theft/fraud protection. Shay's credit is rated as bad as she has a recent bankruptcy on her record. Find her annual premium.

See Example 1.

4. Nevelyn Smith is moving into a loft apartment and is required to have renters insurance to protect her personal property. She has an excellent credit rating and elects to purchase a policy that will cover $20,000 in personal property, cover $300,000 in liability, and have a deductible of $1,000. Nevelyn also selects an endorsement for her $8,500 engagement ring and $2,000 for her camera equipment. Find her annual renters insurance premium.

See Example 2.

5. Find the annual homeowners insurance premium on a masonry home located in zone 2 if the home is insured for $275,000. The owner chooses a $1,500 deductible and has good credit.

See Example 2.

6. A frame home and its contents are located in zone 1 and are insured for $150,000. Find the total annual insurance premium if the insured has a credit rating of OCC and chooses a deductible of $1,000.

See Example 2.

7. If a 2% charge is added to the annual premium of $1,021.80 when payments are made semiannually, how much would semiannual payments be?

See Example 2.

8. Chandler Burford owns a masonry home located in zone 2. What is the annual homeowners insurance premium if the home is insured for $350,000, the owner has an OCC credit rating and chooses a deductible of $1,000. The homeowner also has endorsements for a $2,000 watch and portable tools valued at $3,500.

See Example 2.

9. Alice Lee owns a masony home in zone 1. The home is insured for $200,000 and the computer equipment endorsement is added for $8,000. Alice has excellent credit and her deductible is $1,500. A 3% charge is added to the annual premium because she pays quarterly. Find her quarterly payment.

APPLICATIONS

See Example 4.

10. The replacement cost of a home is $255,000. It has been insured for $204,000 in a homeowners insurance policy with an 80% coinsurance clause. What part of a loss due to fire will the insurance company pay?

See Example 4.

11. If a fire causes damage valued at $75,000, what is the amount of compensation to the owner of the home in Exercise 10?

See Example 3.

12. A home valued at $295,000 is insured in a policy that contains an 80% coinsurance clause. The face value of the policy is $100,000. If the home is a total loss, what is the amount of compensation?

See Example 3.

13. Marjorie Mays owns a home that has a replacement value of $395,000. How much insurance is required on the property for coverage up to the face value of the policy if an 80% coinsurance clause exists?

See Example 3.

14. Marjorie (Exercise 13) had a fire that resulted in a loss valued at $83,000. How much compensation is the insurance company obligated to pay if the home is insured for $220,000?

See Example 3.

15. How much compensation is the insurance company obligated to pay Marjorie if she has the $83,000 loss shown in Exercise 14 but the property is insured for $300,000?

19-3 MOTOR VEHICLE INSURANCE

LEARNING OUTCOME

1 Find automobile insurance premiums using rate tables.

Motor vehicle insurance: liability, comprehensive, and collision insurance for a motor vehicle.

Liability insurance: protection for the owner of a vehicle if an accident causes personal injury or damage to someone else's property and is the fault of the driver of the insured vehicle.

Comprehensive insurance: protection for the owner of a vehicle for damage to the vehicle typically caused by a nonaccident incident such as fire, water, theft, vandalism, or other risks.

Collision insurance: protection for the owner of a vehicle for damages (both personal and property) from an accident that is the insured driver's fault.

No-fault insurance: protection for the owner of a vehicle for damage to the insured vehicle when the amount of damage is within the no-fault limits imposed by state law.

Deductible: the dollar amount the insured pays for each automobile insurance claim. The insurance company pays the remainder of the cost of each covered loss up to the limits of the policy.

Motor vehicle insurance is a major expense item for individuals and businesses because of the high risk of personal injury or death and damage to property. Insurance for motor vehicles may be purchased to protect the individual or business from several risks. These include liability for personal injury and property damage; damage to or loss of the insured vehicle and its occupants caused by a collision; and damage or loss to the insured vehicle caused by theft, fire, flood, storms, and other incidents that may not be related to a collision. These types of insurance generally fall into three types: liability, comprehensive, and collision.

Liability insurance protects the insured from losses incurred in a vehicle accident resulting in personal injury or damage to someone else's property if the accident is the fault of the insured or a designated driver.

Comprehensive insurance protects the insured's vehicle from damage caused by fire, theft, vandalism, wildlife, and other risks, such as falling debris, storm damage, or road hazards such as rocks.

Collision insurance protects the insured's vehicle from damage (both personal and property) caused by an automobile accident in which the driver of the insured vehicle is *also* at fault. This type of insurance is also used when the driver of another vehicle who is at fault does not have insurance coverage.

Some states have **no-fault insurance** programs. In these states, all parties involved in an accident submit a claim for personal and property damages to their own insurance company if the amount is under a certain stated maximum. However, a person can still pursue legal action for additional compensation if the damage is above the stated maximum.

All auto insurance policies have a deductible. The **deductible** is the portion of the policy the policyholder is responsible for paying if a claim is filed. The amount the insured is required to pay for damages depends on the policy. Deductibles vary, but they are most often amounts of $100, $250, $500, or $1,000. For example, if you are at fault in a vehicle crash that causes $3,500 worth of damage to your vehicle and your deductible is $1,000, you are required to pay the first $1,000 and the insurance company will pay the remaining amount up to the amount of the policy, or $2,500 in this example. Deductibles are paid each and every time the insured requires the insurance company to cover damages. The insurance premium you pay, or the price of your total annual coverage, can be reduced by choosing a higher deductible. In other words, if you are willing to pay a larger amount of each and every claim, you can reduce the total cost of your insurance.

1 Find automobile insurance premiums using rate tables.

Factors that affect the cost of automobile insurance include the primary location of the vehicle (large city, small town, rural area); the total distance traveled per year and the distance traveled to work each day; the types of use (such as pleasure, traveling to and from work, strictly business);

TABLE 19-5
Annual Automobile Liability Insurance Premiums

Liability Limits[*]	Territory 1			Territory 2		
	GOOD	OCC	BAD	GOOD	OCC	BAD
50/100/50	385	600	846	354	552	778
100/300/100	425	682	961	391	627	884
250/500/250	460	750	1036	423	690	953
500/1000/500	530	843	1208	488	776	1111

GOOD = good credit; OCC = occasional payments past 30 days; BAD = judgments, collection, bankruptcy
[*]Bodily injury maximum for one person/Total bodily injury coverage per accident/Property damage

Uninsured or under insured motorist coverage: protection for the owner of a vehicle when damages are incurred in an accident that is not the owner's fault but the other driver has no or insufficient insurance.

Medical expenses: provides payment to the driver and each passenger in the insured's vehicle of 100% of any medical bills up to the coverage limit arising from a collision.

Liability limits: the maximum amount that an insurance company will pay for a single accident based on coverage selected by the insured.

Bodily injury: personal injury of a person other than the insured or members of the insured's household that is sustained in an accident.

Property damage: damage to the property of others in an accident.

Territory: the type of area in which the car is kept and driven.

the driving record and training of the insured driver(s); the academic grades of drivers who are still in school; the age, sex, and marital status of the insured driver(s); the type and age of the vehicle; and the amount of coverage desired. Similar to both renters and homeowners insurance, the credit rating category of the policyholder has a major impact on automobile insurance rates. Accident statistics and probabilities involving these factors are also used in determining appropriate insurance rates. Many companies offer **uninsured or under insured motorist coverage,** which compensates the insured person when the accident is the fault of a motorist who has no or insufficient insurance.

Table 19-5 shows a hypothetical annual rate schedule for liability insurance, including uninsured/underinsured motorist bodily injury and property damage protection, as well as $10,000 of **medical expense** coverage. Using **liability limits** of 50/100/50 as an example, the first number is the maximum dollar limit (expressed in thousands) the company will pay for the **bodily injury** per person in an accident—in this case $50,000. The second number, 100, is the maximum dollar limit the company will pay for *all* bodily injuries combined in any one accident—in this case $100,000. The third number, 50, refers to the maximum dollar limit the company will pay others for **property damage,** including other vehicles or property such as fences, buildings, utility poles, etc.—in this case $50,000.

The uninsured/underinsured motorist protection included in Table 19-5 includes the same coverage maximums provided by the bodily injury/total bodily injury/property damage liability limits chosen by the insured, in this example 50/100/50. This means that in the event an at-fault driver has no or insufficient coverage, the coverage limits provided by one's own uninsured/underinsured motorist protection per accident would be $50,000 per bodily injury/$100,000 bodily injury maximum/$50,000 property damage.

Notice that there are several columns of information. The **territory** refers to the type of area in which the car is kept and driven. Under each territory are three credit rating categories which refer to the credit rating of the insured. In fact, credit history is becoming one of the major factors in determining auto insurance rates. In the case of spouses with different credit ratings and one vehicle, the lower credit classification will determine the rate category. If there are two vehicles covered under one auto policy, then each spouse (and their individual credit rating classifications) will be assigned to the vehicle they each primarily drive.

Two other components of the motor vehicle insurance premium are premiums for comprehensive and collision coverage. Comprehensive and collision premiums are based on the *model class* (compact, luxury, SUV, truck, etc.), the *vehicle age*, the *credit rating*, and the amount of the *deductible*. Table 19-6 gives sample rates for comprehensive and collision premiums.

In addition to the base premiums for liability, comprehensive, and collision coverage, several discounts and surcharges may apply to your automobile insurance coverage, including: 25% good student discount for full-time students between the ages of 16 and 24 with at least a "B" average or 3.0 grade point average; 5% accident free for 3 years discount; 10% multivehicle discount; $60/year ticket surcharge for any moving violation issued during the past 3 years (maximum $120/year); and a $150 accident surcharge for each at-fault accident during the past 3 years (maximum $300/year).

HOW TO   Find an annual automobile insurance premium using table values

1. Locate the bodily injury and property damage premium according to territory, credit rating, and per person/per accident bodily injury and property damage coverage (Table 19-5).
2. Locate the comprehensive premium in Table 19-6 according to model class, vehicle age, territory, credit rating, and deductible.
3. Locate the collision premium in Table 19-6 according to model class, vehicle age, territory, credit rating, and deductible.
4. Add the premiums from steps 1 to 3 to find the base annual premium.

5. Multiply any applicable discounts by the base premium and subtract.
6. Add any ticket or accident surcharges.

Total annual premium = bodily injury/property damage premium +
comprehensive premium + collision premium − discounts + surcharges

TABLE 19-6
Annual Auto Insurance Premium Rates for Comprehensive and Collision

Territory 1

Model Class	Vehicle Age	Comprehensive $0 Deductible			$250 Deductible			Collision $500 Deductible			$1,000 Deductible		
		GOOD	OCC	BAD	GOOD	OCC	BAD	GOOD	OCC	BAD	GOOD	OCC	BAD
1	0–1	584	934	1129	393	628	759	535	855	1279	471	753	1126
	2–3	520	831	1005	350	559	676	449	718	1074	396	633	946
	4–5	397	635	768	267	427	516	396	633	946	349	557	833
	6+	374	598	723	252	402	486	332	530	793	292	467	698
2	0–1	502	803	971	338	540	653	503	804	1202	443	708	1058
	2–3	447	715	864	301	481	581	417	667	998	367	587	879
	4–5	342	546	660	230	367	444	367	587	878	323	517	773
	6+	321	514	621	216	346	418	297	474	709	261	418	624
3	0–1	472	755	913	318	508	614	478	764	1142	421	672	1006
	2–3	420	672	812	283	452	546	392	627	938	345	552	826
	4–5	321	513	621	216	345	417	342	547	818	301	481	720
	6+	302	483	584	203	325	393	277	442	661	244	389	582

Territory 2

Model Class	Vehicle Age	Comprehensive $0 Deductible			$250 Deductible			Collision $500 Deductible			$1,000 Deductible		
		GOOD	OCC	BAD	GOOD	OCC	BAD	GOOD	OCC	BAD	GOOD	OCC	BAD
1	0–1	514	822	994	346	553	668	492	787	1177	433	693	1036
	2–3	457	732	884	308	492	594	413	661	988	364	582	870
	4–5	349	559	676	235	376	454	364	582	871	321	513	767
	6+	329	526	636	221	354	427	305	488	730	269	430	642
2	0–1	442	707	854	297	475	574	463	739	1106	407	651	974
	2–3	393	629	760	265	423	511	384	614	918	338	540	808
	4–5	301	481	581	202	323	391	338	540	807	297	475	711
	6+	283	452	547	190	304	368	273	436	653	240	384	575
3	0–1	415	664	803	280	447	540	440	702	1051	387	619	925
	2–3	370	591	715	249	398	481	361	577	863	318	508	760
	4–5	283	452	546	190	304	367	315	503	752	277	443	662
	6+	266	425	514	179	286	346	255	407	608	224	358	536

GOOD = good credit; OCC = occasional payments past 30 days; BAD = judgments, collection, bankruptcy

EXAMPLE 1

Use Tables 19-5 and 19-6 to find the annual premium for an automobile insurance policy in which the insured lives in territory 1, has good credit, and selects 50/100/50 coverage. The vehicle is three years old, model class 2 with a deductible for comprehensive of $250 and $500 for collision. The insured has been accident and ticket free for the last three years.

Liability premium = $385 — Territory 1, good credit, 50/100/50. (Table 19-5)

Comprehensive premium = $301 — Model class 2, age 3, $250 deductible, good credit. (Table 19-6)

Collision premium = $417 — Model class 2, age 3, $500 deductible, good credit.

Base annual premium =
$385 + $301 + $417 = $1,103 — Sum.

$1,103 × 0.05 = $55.15 — 5% accident-free discount

Total annual premium = $1,103 − $55.15 = $1,047.85

Book value: the value of a specific model and year of a used vehicle that is based on the estimated resale value of the vehicle.

Totaled: when damages to a vehicle exceed the book value, the insurance covers the damages up to the book value.

Claim compensation: money paid by the insurance company to persons as a result of an automobile crash when the insured is at fault. The money may be for bodily injury or for property damage. The insured must pay any amounts that exceed the amount of coverage of the policy.

While the insured pays insurance premiums, the insurance company must pay when the insured is involved in an automobile crash or if something happens to the insured automobile. These payments are called **claim compensation.**

EXAMPLE 2   Margo Mahler has 50/100/50 vehicle insurance. She has $500 deductible collision and $250 deductible comprehensive. Margo crashed into a vehicle (failed to yield so was at fault). Three persons, Leslie, Jim, and Ursala, were injured. Leslie's medical care was $21,000, Jim's medical care was $68,754, Ursala had no injuries, and their car required $3,895 to repair. Margo's vehicle damage amounted to $5,093, but she had no injuries. How much will the insurance company be responsible for paying and to whom? Will Margo be responsible for paying anything? If so, how much?

Liability: Margo's insurance is responsible for paying up to $50,000 per person. Leslie's $21,000 medical care will be the responsibility of the insurance company. The insurance company is responsible for paying the limit, $50,000, for Jim's medical care. Margo is responsible for paying the difference $68,754 − $50,000 = $18,754. The insurance company is responsible for paying $3,895 to Ursala for vehicle repair and $5,093 − $500 = $4,593 to Margo for vehicle repairs.

STOP AND CHECK

See Example 1.

1. Use Tables 19-5 and 19-6 to find the annual premium for an automobile insurance policy in which the insured lives in territory 1, has good credit, and buys 100/300/100 coverage. The vehicle is a 5-year-old, model class 3 vehicle and both comprehensive and collision are carried with a $500 deductible on collision and a $250 deductible on comprehensive.

See Example 1.

3. Margaret Davis has an automobile insurance policy with OCC credit rating and she lives in territory 2. She buys 100/300/100 coverage. Her vehicle is new, in model class 1, and she elects a $250 deductible on comprehensive and a $1,000 deductible on collision. What is her annual premium?

See Example 2.

5. Logan Cox has 100/300/100 vehicle insurance. He has a $250 deductible on comprehensive and a $1,000 deductible on collision. Logan had an at-fault crash with another vehicle (failed to stop at a stop sign). Lynn and Cameron, the driver and passenger in the other car, were injured. Lynn's medical care was $85,000 and Cameron's medical care was $145,000. Their car required $18,980 to repair. Logan's vehicle had $12,815 in damages but he had no injuries. How much will the insurance company be responsible for paying and to whom? How much, if any, is Logan responsible for paying?

See Example 1.

2. Use Tables 19-5 and 19-6 to find the annual premium for an automobile insurance policy for Megan Anders, who lives in territory 2, has good credit, and buys 50/100/50 coverage. The vehicle is 7 years old, model class 2, and both comprehensive and collision are carried with a $250 deductible on comprehensive and a $1,000 deductible on collision.

See Example 1.

4. Find the annual auto insurance premium for Reed Davis if he has a good credit rating and lives in territory 1. Reed buys 50/100/50 liability coverage and $250 deductible comprehensive and $1,000 deductible collision coverage. Reed's truck is 2 years old and falls in model class 2.

6. Rusty Cox has 100/250/100 vehicle insurance. He has a $250 deductible on comprehensive and a $500 deductible on collision. Rusty crashed into another vehicle (he followed too closely and was at fault). Rodger, Ryan, and Tina, the driver and passengers in the other vehicle, were injured. Rodger's medical care was $17,650 and Tina's medical care was $107,760. Ryan did not seek medical care. Their car required $21,750 to repair. Rusty's vehicle had $8,438 in damages but he had no injuries. How much will the insurance company pay and to whom? How much, if any, is Rusty responsible for paying?

19-3 SECTION EXERCISES

SKILL BUILDERS

Find the total annual automobile insurance premium. See Example 1.

	Territory	Credit rating	Model class	Vehicle age	Liability coverage	Comprehensive deductible	Collision deductible
1.	1	GOOD	1	New	50/100/50	$250	$500
2.	1	OCC	2	3 years	250/500/250	$0	$500
3.	2	BAD	3	4 years	100/300/100	$0	$500
4.	2	GOOD	2	6 years	100/300/100	$250	$1,000
5.	1	OCC	1	1 year	50/100/50	$250	$1,000
6.	2	BAD	3	2 years	50/100/50	$0	$1,000

7. Find the annual auto insurance premium for Dontae Knight if he has good credit and lives in territory 2. Dontae has 50/100/50 liability coverage and a $250 comprehensive deductible and a $500 collision deductible. His vehicle is new and is in model class 1.

8. What is the annual vehicle insurance premium for Shanté Banks if she has good credit and lives in territory 1? Shanté has 100/300/100 liability coverage and a $250 deductible on comprehensive coverage and $1,000 deductible on collision. Her vehicle is 30 months old and is in model class 1.

APPLICATIONS

See Example 1.

9. Find the annual premium for an automobile insurance policy if the insured lives in territory 2 and is classified OCC. The policy contains 250/500/250 liability coverage. The vehicle is 3 years old and in model class 3, the deductible for collision is $500, and the deductible for comprehensive is $250.

10. Find the annual premium on a 50/100/50 liability policy for a driver in territory 1 if the vehicle is 4.5 years old and in model class 2. The insured selects a comprehensive deductible of $250 and a collision deductible of $500. The insured's credit is good.

11. What are the monthly payments on an automobile insurance policy for a driver in territory 1 with 50/100/50 liability coverage? The 8-year-old vehicle is in model class 1; the comprehensive deductible is $250 and the collision deductible is $1,000. The insured has a recent bankruptcy on his credit report. Assume no additional fee is required for the monthly payment option.

12. How much will the liability portion of the automobile insurance policy pay an injured person with medical expenses of $8,362 if the insured has a policy with 50/100/50 coverage and is liable for his or her injuries?

See Example 2.

13. Jamie Loden has 100/500/100 vehicle insurance. He has a $250 deductible on comprehensive and a $1,000 deductible on collision. Jamie had an at-fault crash into another vehicle while texting. Carolyn, Larry, and Maria, the driver and passengers in the other vehicle, were injured. Carolyn's medical care was $34,580 and Maria's medical care was $57,840. Larry was not injured. Their car required $12,350 to repair. Jamie's vehicle had $11,540 in damages but he had no injuries. How much will the insurance company be responsible for paying and to whom? How much, if any, will Jamie be responsible for paying?

14. Judy Atwood has 100/500/100 vehicle insurance. She has a $0 deductible on comprehensive and a $1,000 deductible on collision. Judy crashed into another vehicle while speeding and was at fault. Sheila, Kathy, and Bob, the driver and passengers in the other vehicle, were injured. Sheila's medical care was $25,940, Kathy's medical care was $88,760, and Bob's medical expenses were $66,890. Their car required $26,380 to repair. Judy's vehicle had $6,620 in damages but she had no injuries. How much will the insurance company be responsible for paying and to whom? How much, if any, will Judy be responsible for paying?

Learning Outcomes

Section 19-1

1 Estimate life insurance premiums using a rate table. (p. 675)

What to Remember with Examples

1. Locate the estimated annual rate in Table 19-1 according to type of policy, age, sex and rate class.
2. Divide the policy face value by $1,000 and multiply the quotient by the rate from step 1.

$$\text{Estimated annual premium} = \frac{\text{face value}}{\$1,000} \times \text{rate}$$

Use Table 19-1 to find the annual premium for a 40-year-old male who uses tobacco for a $50,000 (a) 10-year level term policy and (b) whole-life policy.

(a) 10-year level term policy: $\left(\dfrac{\$50,000}{\$1,000}\right)(\$3.78) = \$189$

(b) Whole-life policy: $\left(\dfrac{\$50,000}{\$1,000}\right)(\$19.31) = \$965.50$

Use Tables 19-1 and 19-2 to find the quarterly premium for a $50,000 whole-life policy on a 30-year-old female using a preferred rate classification.

$$\begin{pmatrix} \text{Monthly, quarterly,} \\ \text{or semiannual} \\ \text{premium} \end{pmatrix} = \begin{pmatrix} \text{annual} \\ \text{premium} \end{pmatrix} \times \begin{pmatrix} \text{rate from} \\ \text{Table 19-2} \end{pmatrix}$$

$$\text{Annual premium} = \left(\frac{\$50,000}{\$1,000}\right)(\$9.82) = \$491$$

$$\text{Quarterly premium} = (\$491)(0.26) = \$127.66$$

2 Apply the extended term nonforfeiture option to a cancelled whole-life policy. (p. 677)

1. Identify the cash value of the cancelled policy.
2. Estimate the annual premium for a term policy of the same face value. Use a fixed rate in Table 19-1.
3. Determine the number of years of paid-up term insurance.

$$\text{Years of paid-up term insurance} = \frac{\text{cash value of surrendered policy}}{\text{annual premium of term policy}}$$

Craig Schmaling got a non-tobacco rate and started a $200,000 whole-life insurance policy at age 45. At age 60, he decides to use the $13,278 cash value for paid-up 10-year term insurance for the same face value. How many years of paid-up insurance will he have?

$9.07 per $1,000 from Table 19-1

$$\frac{\$200,000}{\$1,000} = 200 \text{ units}$$

$$\text{Estimated annual term premium} = 200(\$9.07) = \$1,814$$

$$\text{Years of paid-up term insurance} = \frac{\text{cash value of surrendered policy}}{\text{annual premium of term policy}}$$

$$= \frac{\$13,278}{\$1,814} = 7.32 \text{ years}$$

Section 19-2

1 Estimate renters insurance premiums using a rate table. (p. 680)

1. Locate the base annual premium in Table 19-3 according to maximum policy coverage limit, liability limit, deductible, and credit score rating for the applicant.
2. Add the additional cost for any options selected.
3. Compute the annual cost for extended coverage endorsements.

$$\text{Cost} = \left(\frac{\text{coverage desired}}{\$100}\right)(\text{rate for endorsement})$$

4. Add the premiums from steps 1 through 3.

$$\text{Total annual premium} = \text{base annual premium} + \text{cost for each option} + \text{cost for each extended coverage endorsement}$$

Suzette Cannon wants to buy renters insurance for her new condominium. She has excellent credit, and decides she needs a $40,000 policy with $500,000 liability and $1,000 deductible. She also decides to add the identity theft/fraud protection and an additional $4,000 of coverage for her engagement ring. Find Suzette's total annual premium for her renters insurance if she has a good credit rating.

The base annual premium for a $40,000 policy, $500,000 liability, and $1,000 deductible with good credit is $185.

The cost for the identity theft/fraud protection is $20.

$$\text{Cost for additional jewelry coverage} = \left(\frac{\$4,000}{\$100}\right)(\$0.85) = \$34$$

$$\text{Total annual premium} = \$185 + \$20 + \$34 = \$239$$

The annual premium for the renters insurance policy is $239.

2 Estimate homeowners insurance premiums using a rate table. (p. 681)

1. Locate the base annual rate in Table 19-4 according to construction type, zone, deductible, and credit score rating for the applicant(s).

$$\text{Base annual premium} = \left(\frac{\text{dwelling coverage}}{\$100}\right)(\text{rate from table})$$

2. Add the additional cost for any options selected.
3. Compute the annual cost for extended coverage endorsements.

$$\text{Cost} = \left(\frac{\text{coverage desired}}{\$100}\right)(\text{rate for endorsement})$$

4. Add the premiums from steps 1 through 3.

$$\text{Total annual premium} = \text{base annual premium} + \text{cost for each option} + \text{cost for each extended coverage endorsement}$$

Use Table 19-4 to find the annual premium for a masonry home if it is insured for $350,000. The building is in zone 2 and the owner's credit rating is BAD. A $1,000 deductible is selected. The owner also adds an endorsement for $8,000 in firearms.

$$\text{Annual premium for dwelling} = \left(\frac{\$350,000}{\$100}\right)(\$0.86) = \$3,010$$

$$\text{Cost of additional firearms coverage} = \left(\frac{\$8,000}{\$100}\right)(\$1.45) = \$116$$

$$\text{Total annual premium} = \$3,010 + \$116 = \$3,126$$

3 Find the compensation with a coinsurance clause. (p. 683)

1. Find the face value required by the 80% coinsurance clause for full compensation: Multiply 0.8 by the replacement value of the property.
2. Find the compensation for the loss if the insurance is less than 80% of the replacement value.

$$\begin{array}{c}\text{Compensation (up to} \\ \text{amount of loss)}\end{array} = \begin{array}{c}\text{amount of loss} \\ \text{(up to face value)}\end{array} \times \frac{\text{face value of policy}}{80\% \text{ of replacement value of property}}$$

A property valued at $325,000 is insured with a policy that contains an 80% coinsurance clause. The face value of the policy is $200,000. What is the amount of compensation if a fire results in a total loss of the property?

$$\text{Compensation} = \$200,000\left(\frac{\$200,000}{0.8 \times \$325,000}\right)$$

$$= \$200,000\left(\frac{\$200,000}{\$260,000}\right)$$

$$\text{Compensation} = \$200,000(0.7692307692) = \$153,846.15$$

Even though the fire caused damages valued at $325,000, the insured receives only $153,846.15 in compensation.

Section 19-3

1 Find automobile insurance premiums using rate tables. (p. 686)

1. Locate the bodily injury and property damage premium according to territory, credit rating, and per person/per accident bodily injury and property damage coverage (Table 19-5).
2. Locate the comprehensive premium according to model class, vehicle age, territory, credit rating, and deductible.
3. Locate the collision premium according to model class, vehicle age, territory, credit rating, and deductible.
4. Add the premiums from steps 1 to 3 to find the base annual premium.
5. Multiply any applicable discounts by the base premium and subtract.
6. Add any ticket or accident surcharges.

$$\text{Total annual premium} = \text{bodily injury/property damage premium}$$
$$+ \text{ comprehensive premium } + \text{ collision premium}$$
$$- \text{ discounts } + \text{ surcharges}$$

Use Tables 19-5 and 19-6 to find the annual premium for an automobile policy in which the insured lives in territory 2, makes occasional payments over 30 days, has a 4-year-old model class 2 vehicle, and wishes to have 100/300/100 liability coverage, a comprehensive deductible of $0, and a collision deductible of $1,000. The insured was accident free for the last three years, but received one moving violation during that time.

The cost of 100/300/100 bodily injury and property damage coverage for territory 2, OCC credit is $627 (Table 19-5).

The cost of comprehensive coverage with a $0 deductible is $481.

The cost of collision coverage with a $1,000 deductible is $475.

Base annual premium = $627 + $481 + $475 = $1,583

The 5% accident-free discount = $1,583(0.05) = $79.15

The surcharge for one ticket during the last three years is $60.

Total annual premium = $627 + $481 + $475 − $79.15 + $60 = $1,563.85.

EXERCISES SET A

CHAPTER 19

Using Table 19-3 and the option/endorsement rates on p. 680, find the annual renters insurance premium for each of the following.

	Policy limit	Deductible	Credit rating	Liability	Endorsement or option	Base Premium	Endorsement or option premium	Total annual premium
EXCEL 1.	$20,000	$500	GOOD	$300,000	$18,500 (computer)			
2.	$40,000	$1,000	OCC	$500,000	$25,000 (art and collectibles)			
3.	$40,000	$1,000	BAD	$300,000	none			

Use Table 19-4 and the information that foillows it to solve the following problems.

4. Linda Kodama owns a frame home in zone 2 valued at $95,000. The building is insured for $60,000 and the policy has an 80% coinsurance clause. How much will Linda receive from her policy if a fire causes $38,000 in damages?

5. Robyn Presley insures her masonry home located in zone 2 for $260,000 and adds an endorsement for $16,000 in antique collectibles. She has excellent credit and selects a deductible of $1,000. Find the total annual insurance premium.

6. Frank Hopkins's home is insured for 80% of the replacement value of $528,900. A storm causes $435,800 worth of damage to the structure. Find the compensation Frank will receive.

Use Tables 19-5 and 19-6 and the information that follows the tables to find the total annual premium for each of the following automobile liability insurance policies.

	Territory	Credit rating	Liability coverage	Model class	Vehicle age	Comprehensive deductible	Collision deductible
7.	1	GOOD	250/500/250	3	New	$250	$500
8.	1	OCC	100/300/100	2	4 years	$0	$500
9.	2	BAD	50/100/50	1	3 years	$250	$1,000

10. The company car for the Greenwood Rental Agency in territory 2 for a driver is insured with 50/100/50 coverage. The car is model class 1, is 3 years old, and has a comprehensive deductible of $0 and a collision deductible of $500. What is the annual insurance premium if the credit rating is good?

11. Sally Greenspan has 100/300/100 liability coverage and lives in territory 2. She has a good credit rating and carries a comprehensive deductible of $250 and a collision deductible of $500. Her 4-year-old vehicle falls in model class 3. Find her annual insurance premium.

12. A driver in territory 1, Laura Jansky is buying an auto insurance policy with 100/300/100 liability coverage. She has a comprehensive deductible of $250 and a collision deductible of $1,000. Her new vehicle is in model class 2. Find her annual premium if her credit rating is OCC.

13. Cheuk Nam Lam lives in territory 1. He has auto liability insurance with 50/100/50 coverage. He has a $250 deductible for comprehensive and $500 for collision. His 8-year-old vehicle is in model class 2. Find his annual premium if his credit is BAD.

Use Table 19-1 to find the annual premium of each of the following life insurance policies:

	Sex	Age	Policy type	Rate classification	Face value	Annual premium
14.	Male	25	20-year level term	T	$150,000	
15.	Female	30	Whole-life	NT	$200,000	

Use Tables 19-1 and 19-2 to find the following premiums:

	Sex	Age	Policy type	Rate classification	Face value	Annual premium	Monthly premium	Quarterly premium
16.	Female	60	Whole-life	NT	$350,000			
17.	Female	35	10-year level term	PREF	$480,000			

18. a. Find the annual premium paid by Sara Cushion, age 45, on a universal-life insurance policy for $500,000 if Sara smokes.

    b. Find the semiannual premium Sara would pay on the universal-life policy.

19. A whole-life policy purchased at age 50 by Thomas Wimberly costs how much more per $1,000 than the same policy for a male age 60? Use a non-tobacco rate.

20. How much are the total quarterly payments paid by Erich Shultz, age 40, and his wife Demetria, age 35, if each has a 20-year level term insurance policy for $300,000 and both use tobacco?

21. Marguerite Jones is 40 years old, uses tobacco, and decides to convert her $500,000 whole-life insurance policy to extended term insurance. Use 20-year level term rates to estimate the number of years of extended term life insurance her cash value of $27,879 will buy.

22. Pam Murray has 100/250/100 vehicle insurance. She has a $0 deductible on comprehensive and a $1,000 deductible on collision. Pam had an at-fault crash into another vehicle (she was distracted while using her cell phone). Tom and Rodney, the driver and passenger in the other vehicle, were injured. Tom's medical expenses were $155,400 and Rodney's medical expenses were $48,690. Their car required $15,810 to repair. Pam's vehicle had $16,450 in damages but she had no injuries. How much will the insurance company be responsible for paying and to whom? How much, if any, will Pam be responsible for paying?

EXERCISES SET B

Using Table 19-3 and the option/endorsement rates on p. 680, find the annual renters insurance premium for each of the following:

	Policy limit	Deductible	Credit rating	Liability	Endorsement or option	Base premium	Endorsement or option premium	Total annual premium
1.	40,000	$500	OCC	$500,000	$4,200 camera equipment			
2.	20,000	$500	GOOD	$300,000	identity theft protection			
3.	20,000	1,000	BAD	$300,000	$5,000 portable tools			

Use Table 19-4 and the information that follows the table when necessary to solve the following.

4. What part of the damages will Hampton Insurance Company pay on a home with $18,000 damage by fire if the replacement cost is $86,000 and it is insured for $65,000? The policy contains an 80% coinsurance clause.

5. In zone 1, a frame dwelling is insured for $305,000 and the insured has good credit and selects a $1,500 deductible. If no extra charge is added for semiannual payments, find the premium paid every six months.

6. Shaniqua Dunlap has a homeowners policy for his brick (masonry) home located in zone 1 for its appraised value of $248,500 and selects a deductible of $1,000. If Shaniqua has excellent credit, find her total annual homeowners premium.

Use Tables 19-5 and 19-6 and the information that follows the tables to find the total annual premium for each of the following automobile liability insurance policies.

	Territory	Credit rating	Total coverage	Model class	Vehicle age	Comprehensive deductible	Collision deductible
7.	2	OCC	50/100/50	1	1 year	$0	$500
8.	2	BAD	50/100/50	3	4 years	$0	$500
9.	1	GOOD	100/300/100	2	New	$250	$1,000

10. Aggawal Montoya has a good credit rating and lives in territory 1. He has automobile insurance on his 3-year-old vehicle with 100/300/100 coverage. The vehicle is in model class 1 and has a $250 deductible for comprehensive and $1,000 for collision. Find his annual premium.

11. Larry Tremont has an insurance policy with a $1,000 deductible clause for collision and a $250 deductible clause for comprehensive. Larry's liability coverage on his 5-year-old, model class 2 vehicle is 50/100/50. Find his annual premium if he lives in territory 2 and has an OCC credit rating.

12. Fred Case has an auto insurance policy with 500/1000/500 liability coverage. He lives in territory 2 and has good credit. His vehicle is in model class 3 and is 26 months old. His deductible for comprehensive is $250 and for collision is $500. Find his annual premium.

13. John Malinowsky has auto insurance with 100/300/100 liability coverage. His vehicle is 12 years old and is in model class 2. John lives in territory 1. Find his annual premium if he has a $250 deductible on comprehensive and a $500 deductible on collision and has good credit.

Use Table 19-1 to find the annual premium of the following life insurance policies:

	Sex	Age	Policy type	Rate classification	Face value	Annual premium
14.	Male	30	10-year level term	NT	$300,000	
15.	Female	50	Whole-life	T	$100,000	

Use Tables 19-1 and 19-2 to find the premiums.

	Sex	Age	Policy type	Rate classification	Face value	Annual premium	Monthly premium	Quarterly premium
16.	Female	20	Universal-life	PREF	$350,000		$138.73	$412.23
17.	Male	40	20-year level term	T	$100,000		$47.08	$139.88

18. Sam Molla has a 10-year level term life insurance policy with a value of $250,000. How much is his semiannual premium if he is 40 years old with a non-tobacco rate?

19. Find the annual premium paid on a whole-life insurance policy for $375,000 taken out at age 30 by a male who has the preferred rate.

20. Find the monthly premium of a $450,000 universal-life insurance policy purchased by a 25-year-old female, who gets the preferred rate.

21. At 30 years old, Jaime Dawson finds the need to convert his whole-life insurance policy of $500,000 to extended term coverage with the same face value. Use 10-year level term rates to estimate the number of years of extended term coverage his cash value of $1,095 will provide using a non-tobacco rate.

22. Tancia Brown is 55 years old, has a non-tobacco rate, and is converting her $450,000 whole-life insurance policy to extended term insurance with the same face value. Use 10-year level term rates to estimate the number of years of coverage her cash value of $13,826 will buy.

23. Cathy Worley has 100/300/100 vehicle insurance. She has a $250 deductible on comprehensive and a $1,000 deductible on collision. Cathy was at fault when she crashed into two bicyclists, injuring both (she was distracted by a deer in the right of way). One of the bicyclists had $83,000 in medical expenses and the other had $167,500 in medical expenses. Both bicycles were totaled. One bicycle was valued at $895 and the other was valued at $1,215. Cathy's vehicle had $1,988 in damages but she had no injuries associated with the crash. How much will the insurance company be responsible for paying and to whom? How much, if any, will Cathy be responsible for paying?

PRACTICE TEST

1. Find the annual premium on a $300,000 whole-life insurance policy for a 40-year-old male using a non-tobacco rate.

2. Find the annual premium on an automobile insurance policy with liability limits of 50/100/50 in territory 2 for a person who has a 2-year-old car in model class 2. The comprehensive deductible is $250 and the collision deductible is $1,000. The insured person has good credit.

3. Find the annual premium for a homeowners policy on a masonry home insured at $287,500 in zone 2. The owner has excellent credit, chooses a $1,500 deductible, and insures $3,000 in jewelry.

4. Find the annual premium on a 100/300/100 liability limits automobile insurance policy for a driver in territory 2. The vehicle is 5 years old, in model class 2. The comprehensive deductible is $250 and the collision deductible is $1,000. The insured has good credit.

5. Find the annual premium on a 10-year level term life insurance policy for $150,000 for a 30-year-old male who uses tobacco.

6. Find the annual premium on an automobile insurance policy for a driver in territory 1 with 100/300/100 liability limits. The new car is in model class 3 and has a $500 collision deductible and a $250 comprehensive deductible. The insured has OCC credit rating.

7. A frame home is insured for $178,000. Find the total annual premium if the home is in zone 1 and the owner chooses $1,000 deductible and the optional identity theft protection. The owner also adds an endorsement to insure camera equipment valued at $3,700 and has an OCC credit rating.

8. Compare the cost per year of a whole-life insurance policy for $200,000 to a 20-year level term policy for a 60-year-old male using a non-tobacco rate.

9. How much does a 45-year-old female using a non-tobacco rate pay in monthly premiums for a $250,000 whole-life insurance policy?

10. Find the quarterly payments on a 10-year level term life insurance policy for $150,000 on a 40-year-old male with a non-tobacco rate.

11. The replacement cost of a home is $72,500. It is insured for $50,000 with an 80% coinsurance clause. If a fire causes $62,000 in damages, how much of the damages will the policy cover?

12. Find the annual premium for a 50/100/50 automobile liability insurance policy for a driver in territory 2 with a 12-year-old car in model class 3. Collision has a $500 deductible and comprehensive has a $250 deductible. The insured has an OCC credit rating.

13. Mary Lynne Winston is 55 years old, has a non-tobacco rate, and decides to convert her $100,000 whole-life insurance policy to extended term coverage with the same face value. How many years of 10-year level term insurance will she have if her cash value is $1,856?

Use Table 19-3 and the information on page 680 to find the total annual renters insurance premiums in Exercises 14–18.

14. Brett Smyly needs a $40,000 renters insurance policy and has selected the $500,000 liability with $1,000 deductible. The insurance company has determined his credit is excellent and has given him the "good" credit rate. If he adds an endorsement to ensure $6,500 of jewelry and the option of identity theft/protection coverage, find his annual premium.

15. Duke Schmidt has a renters insurance policy for $20,000 of household goods, has selected $300,000 liability with $1,000 deductible, and his credit is rated as occasional payments past 30 days. If Duke also adds an endorsement of $12,500 to insure his gun collection and $3,500 to insure the jewelry he keeps at his condo, how much is his annual premium?

16. Tashundra Bolsinger rents an apartment in St. Louis and carries $40,000 insurance on her personal belongings. She selects the maximum liability with a deductible of $1,000 for each claim and carries identity theft/fraud protection. Tashundra's credit is rated as OCC because she has a couple of late payments on her record. Find her annual premium.

17. Laquita Marbut lives in a condo and is required to have renters insurance to protect her personal property. She has an excellent credit rating and elects to purchase a policy that will cover $20,000 in personal property and $300,000 in liability. She will have a deductible of $1,000. Laquita also selects an endorsement of $3,800 for her computer and $1,500 for her camera equipment and the identity theft protection option. Find her annual renters insurance premium.

18. Laura Bains lives in an apartment in San Francisco and her landlord requires her to have renters insurance to protect her personal property. She has an OCC credit rating and elects to purchase a policy that will cover $40,000 in personal property and $500,000 in liability. She will have a deductible of $1,000. Laura also selects an endorsement of $3,000 for jewelry and $2,500 for her collectibles. Find her annual renters insurance premium.

19. Tasville Furukawa's property is insured for 80% of the replacement value of $315,500. A fire caused $257,000 damage to the property. How much compensation will Tasville receive from the insurance company?

20. Brandi Dulin has 500/1000/500 vehicle insurance. She has a $250 deductible on comprehensive and a $1,000 deductible on collision. Brandi had an at-fault crash into two motorcycles in a heavy downpour. Damion and Keisha, drivers of the motorcycles, were injured. Damion's medical expenses were $198,500 and Keisha's medical expenses were $375,840. Their motorcycles required $4,987 and $7,515, respectively, to repair. Brandi's vehicle had $2,875 in damages but she had no injuries. How much will the insurance company be responsible for paying and to whom? How much, if any, will Brandi be responsible for paying?

1. The formula for finding the estimated annual life insurance premium rate using a table with rates per $1,000 of face value (Table 19-1) is given on page 675. Another source may have a table giving rates per $100 of face value. How will the formula change when using the rate per $100 of face value?

2. Examine Table 19-1 and compare the annual life insurance premium rates per $1,000 of face value for non-tobacco users with the rate for persons who use tobacco.

3. If Claudia McLeod had a homeowners policy insurance to cover 60% of the property's value, and fire damages were 40% of the property value, what percent will the insurance company with an 80% coinsurance clause pay for the loss?

4. If Payten Pastner had homeowners insurance to cover 80% of the property's value, and fire damages were 90% of the total value, what percent will the insurance company with an 80% coinsurance clause pay for the loss?

5. If a car rental agency charges $15.50 per day for a liability, comprehensive, and collision waiver, this would be equivalent to what annual premium? Why do you suppose no difference is made for territory or driver class?

6. Why is whole-life insurance more expensive than level term life insurance?

7. Justify why life insurance premiums are higher for males than for females who are in the same age category.

8. The formula given for using Table 19-1 is

$$\text{Annual premium} = \frac{\text{face value}}{\$1,000} \times \text{rate.}$$

Is the formula

$$\text{Annual premium} = \text{face value} \times \frac{\text{rate}}{\$1,000}$$

equivalent? Why or why not?

Challenge Problem

Manny Bober has a homeowners insurance policy with a value of $500,000. His masonry home is located in zone 2. Use the rates in Table 19-4 to compare the cost of his annual premium based on which deductible he selects if his credit rating is GOOD.

19-1 How Much Is Enough?

Alex and Christa are married and have two teenage children. Alex works full-time as an electrical engineer and Christa works part-time as a floral designer. They own a modest 3-bedroom, 2-bath home on a ¼-acre lot and have two cars, and both have excellent credit. They recently attended a financial planning seminar that highlighted a number of issues, such as saving, investing, insuring, and tax and estate planning. Alex and Christa have decided to reassess their insurance needs to determine what portion of their budget should be designated for insurance premiums.

They decide to review their auto insurance first. According to the literature they picked up, they live in territory 1. They own two cars, one of which is 2 years old and considered model class 1; the other is 6 years old and considered model class 2. They feel they should have $100/$300 bodily injury coverage, and $100,000 of property damage coverage. They decide to purchase comprehensive coverage with $0 deductible and collision coverage with a $1,000 deductible on their newer vehicle, but they decide to forego comprehensive and collision coverage on their older vehicle. They both have excellent driving records, with no moving violations or at-fault accidents during the past 3 years. Their insurance company allows a 5% discount for being accident free for 3 years and a 10% discount for insuring multiple vehicles.

1. What amount should Alex and Christa plan to spend annually on their automobile insurance? Use the tables provided in this chapter.

Coverage	Car 1: 2 years old	Car 2: 6 years old
Body injury/property damage		
Comprehensive		
Collision		

2. Christa remembers seeing an article on the Internet stating that wrongful death claim settlements have been increasing in their home state, with a median claim settlement value of nearly $1 million. How much would it cost to increase the auto liability coverage to 250/500/250 for both vehicles? How much to increase to 500/1000/500? Is increasing their liability coverage a wise decision?

3. The replacement value of their home is $180,000. Their insurance policy contains a coinsurance clause. How much insurance should Alex and Christa carry to meet the coinsurance requirement and how much should they anticipate for an annual insurance premium for that level of coverage if their home is in zone 1, is masonry construction, and they choose a $1,000 deductible? How much would it cost to fully insure their home?

4. Alex is also thinking about purchasing additional life insurance. His employer provides some life insurance coverage, but the financial planner at the seminar they attended suggested he carry insurance to represent an amount 5 to 15 times his annual earnings. Alex earns $75,000 a year and his employer provides $75,000 of life insurance. If Alex decides to purchase enough insurance to cover 10 times his earnings, how much more insurance should he purchase? If he is a 40-year-old male, preferred rate class, and selects 20-year level term insurance, how much should he plan to spend annually on life insurance?

5. Considering the auto insurance with 250/500/250 liability coverage, the property insurance with a fully insured dwelling, and the additional life insurance, how much should Alex and Christa plan to pay each year in premiums? What percentage of Alex's gross pay does the total premium represent?

19-2 Soul Food Catering

Amaya left the doctor's office with a strange feeling that seemed to be a combination of euphoria and apprehension. As if moving her catering business to a new location wasn't enough, her family was also moving into a new home. Now she felt apprehension at being a first-time mom at age 30 while running a successful business. But she also felt euphoria about the new addition to the family. Amaya couldn't wait to tell her husband that they were expecting a baby. This was going to mean big changes. Her first thought was child care—but for now, that could wait. Her most pressing concern was insurance. With the move to a new home valued at $250,000, certainly the cost for property insurance was going up. By adding two brand-new delivery vans for her catering business at $17,500 each, the cost for automobile insurance would, at minimum, double. And now with a baby on the way, life insurance was more important than ever. After her husband, the next call was going to be to their insurance agent. Thank goodness she and her husband had maintained their excellent credit ratings, but there was a lot of planning to do.

1. Amaya's agent states that a good rule of thumb for life insurance is to purchase 5 to 7 times your annual income. Amaya's income averages $50,000 annually, but she would like to have the house paid off as well in the event of her death, so she decides $600,000 is the face amount she would like to have. Using the life insurance table, make a comparison of 10-year, 20-year, whole-life, and universal life annual rates for $600,000 of face amount using a preferred rate class.

2. Given your answers to question 1, which coverage would you recommend that Amaya take? What incentive does she have to take a higher-priced premium? Explain.

3. Because of the higher replacement cost, Amaya's agent recommends insuring the new home at $275,000. The dwelling is a regular frame home located in zone 2. Using homeowners insurance rates per $100 of face value in Table 19-4, find the annual premium for the dwelling using a $1,500 deductible.

4. Even though there have been no accidents or tickets during the past 3 years, Amaya is very concerned about the liability on the new vans, so she decides to go with 500/1000/500 liability coverage. Use Table 19-5 to find the annual premium for automobile liability insurance using territory 2, and Table 19-6 to find the comprehensive and collision rates using territory 2, model class 1, with a $250 deductible for comprehensive and a $1,000 deductible for collision. Allow discounts of 5% for being accident free for three years and 10% for insuring multiple vehicles.

Taxes

Preparing Your Own Tax Return

Preparing your own tax return for the first time can be intimidating, but it has several advantages. You are in full control of your tax return, you can work on your taxes at your own pace, and you get to see firsthand how various parts of your financial situation come together to impact your tax bill. Software packages for preparing your own tax return have improved, and it is often just as easy to use tax software as it is to go to a professional tax preparer.

Before preparing your taxes, take the time to organize all the documents you will need. These documents include all W-2 forms sent from your employers and tax statements relating to your bank accounts and investment holdings. You can find Web-based versions of powerful tax software, such as Secure Tax or TurboTax, that help you prepare and file your taxes. These sites are still best suited to simple returns, but they are becoming more sophisticated. And most individuals preparing their returns for the first time qualify for IRS Form 1040-EZ (EZ stands for easy), the simplest of the IRS returns.

You qualify to use the 1040-EZ[*] if:

1. Your filing status is single or married filing jointly. If you were a nonresident alien at any time in 2011, your filing status must be married filing jointly.
2. You (and your spouse if married filing a joint return) were under age 65 and not blind at the end of 2011.
3. You do not claim any dependents.
4. Your taxable income is less than $100,000.

[*]Always check with the IRS at www.irs.gov for the current tax year requirements.

5. You had only wages, salaries, tips, unemployment compensation, Alaska Permanent Fund dividends, taxable scholarship or fellowship grants, and your taxable interest was not over $1,500.
6. If you earned tips, they are included in boxes 5 and 7 on your form W-2.
7. You do not claim any adjustments to income.
8. You claim only the earned income credit.
9. You do not owe any household employment taxes on wages you paid to a household employee.
10. You are not a debtor in a Chapter 11 bankruptcy case filed after October 16, 2005.

If you plan to prepare your taxes, you may want to file electronically instead of sending your tax documents via U.S. Mail. E-filing or electronic filing is a quick, easy, and accurate alternative to traditional paper returns with many advantages:

- You receive your refund in about 3 weeks instead of the usual 10 weeks.
- Your chance of getting an error notice from the IRS is decreased because it is more accurate than mailing a paper return. The error rate for electronic returns is less than 1 percent versus approximately 20 percent for paper returns.
- You get proof that the IRS has accepted your return within 48 hours.
- Your privacy and security are assured.
- You help the environment, use less paper, and save taxpayer money.

LEARNING OUTCOMES

20-1 Sales Tax and Excise Tax

1. Use the percent method to find the sales tax and excise tax.
2. Find the marked price and the sales tax from the total price.

20-2 Property Tax

1. Find the assessed value.
2. Calculate property tax.
3. Determine the property tax rate.

20-3 Income Taxes

1. Find taxable income.
2. Use the tax tables to calculate income tax.
3. Use the tax computation worksheet to calculate income tax.

Tax: money collected by a government for its support and for providing services to the populace.

Taxes affect everyone in one way or another. A **tax** is money collected by a government for its support and for providing services to the populace. Governments use tax money to pay the salaries of government officials and employees. Tax monies run and staff public schools, parks, and playgrounds; build and maintain roads and highways; and provide police and fire protection, health services, unemployment compensation, and numerous other benefits.

To meet these many needs, governments have a variety of tax types from which to choose. Among the most common are sales taxes, property taxes, and income taxes.

20-1 SALES TAX AND EXCISE TAX

LEARNING OUTCOMES

1 Use the percent method to find the sales tax and excise tax.
2 Find the marked price and the sales tax from the total price.

Sales tax: a tax that is based on the price of a purchase. The tax is collected at the time of purchase and the business periodically sends the collected tax to a governmental agency.

The sales tax is probably the first type of tax that most people encounter because most states have sales taxes. Sales taxes are determined by state and local governments. At the time of a purchase, a store collects an extra amount, called a **sales tax,** and later pays it to the state. In some states, county or city governments charge a local sales tax in addition to the state sales tax. Many states charge no sales tax on food nor medicine, and some states make other exceptions. New Jersey, for example, does not charge sales tax on clothing. By a recent count, eighteen states and Washington, DC, have sales tax holidays. These are days when the shoppers get a tax break on some items. For example, Tennessee has a sales tax holiday on the first weekend in August on clothes, school supplies, and computers that are less than $1,500 each. Alabama, Louisiana, and Virginia have a tax holiday week for hurricane preparedness items. Missouri had a tax holiday week called Green Holiday. Certain energy-efficient new appliances were tax exempt for the first $1,500 of the cost of each item.

In some areas a sales tax is charged only on purchases made and delivered within the tax area. For instance, if an item is purchased in one state and delivered to another, the sales tax is not always charged. This also applies to many catalog and Internet purchases. State laws vary and change often, and it is the responsibility of the seller to determine if tax is exempt on a sale. However, the state to which large purchases are delivered may impose its sales tax. For instance, if an automobile is purchased in one state and delivered to another, the state into which it is delivered may require that sales tax be paid before the automobile can be registered.

1 Use the percent method to find the sales tax and excise tax.

In most states the sales tax is a specified percent of the selling price. Most businesses use computerized cash registers that allow the current tax rate to be programmed into the cash register. Then the register automatically figures sales tax.

Excise tax: a tax or duty levied on the sale or importation of goods for the purpose of raising revenue or discouraging a particular behavior.

Excise tax is usually a tax or duty levied on the sale or importation of particular goods. These taxes usually are included in the price to consumers and imposed to raise revenue or to discourage a particular behavior. Most states impose excise tax on sales of fuel, alcohol, and tobacco to accomplish both aims. Portions of excise tax from alcohol and tobacco are used to pay for the treatment of diseases caused by these substances. Excise tax on motor fuel ranges from a low of $0.08 per gallon on gasoline in Alaska to a high of $0.486 per gallon on gasoline in California. In a recent year excise tax rates for cigarettes ranged from a low of $0.07 per pack in South Carolina to a high of $3.46 per pack in Rhode Island.

HOW TO   Use the percent method to find the sales tax or excise tax

1. Write the given percent as a decimal.
2. Find the sales tax or excise tax:

$$\text{Tax} = \text{purchase price} \times \text{tax rate}$$

where tax rate = tax per $1.00 of the purchase price or a percent of the purchase price.

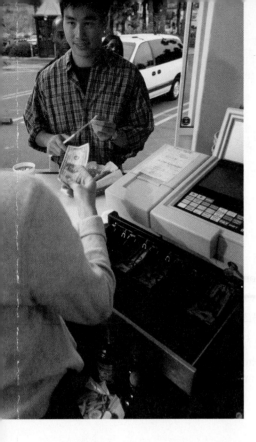

EXAMPLE 1

Kentucky has a state sales tax rate of 6%. Find the Kentucky state sales tax on $128.72 at six cents per $1.00, or 6%.

$128.72(6\%) = \$128.72(0.06)$ Multiply the purchase price by 6%.
Change the percent to a decimal (0.06).

$= \$7.72$ (rounded)   Round the answer to the nearest cent.

The state sales tax is $7.72.

EXAMPLE 2

Find the excise tax on a purchase of $45.93 in gasoline (before tax is added) in Washington if the excise tax rate is 37.5%.

$\$45.93(37.5\%) =$ Multiply the price before taxes by the excise tax rate.
Change the percent to a decimal.

$\$45.93(0.375) = \$17.22375$ Round to the nearest cent.

The excise tax on the purchase is $17.22.

STOP AND CHECK

See Example 1.

1. California's state sales tax rate is 6.25%. What is the sales tax on a CD that costs $19.95 and is purchased in California?

2. Colorado's state sales tax rate is 2.9%. Find the sales tax on a DVD player purchased in Colorado for $298.99.

3. The state sales tax rate in Utah is 4.7%. How much sales tax is paid on a skateboard that costs $49.99?

4. Maine has a 5% state sales tax rate. How much tax is paid on a pair of boots purchased in Maine for $149.95?

See Example 2.

5. Alaska has one of the lowest excise tax rates on gasoline at 8.0%. Find the excise tax on gasoline that cost $38.96 before the excise tax is added.

6. North Carolina has the highest excise tax rate on gasoline with a rate of 38.9%. Find the excise tax on gasoline in North Carolina that cost $82.34 before excise tax is added.

2   Find the marked price and the sales tax from the total price.

Some circumstances make it more convenient to include the sales tax in the quoted price. These circumstances may include sporting events, amusement parks, flea markets, or other places where making change can be difficult and time-consuming. In these instances, the sales tax eventually must be calculated so that the proper tax is turned over to the tax agency. When the sales tax is not itemized, you may want to know how much the sales tax was or what the *marked price* of the item was. The **marked price** is the purchase price or the price before sales tax is added. The **total price** is the marked price plus the sales tax.

Marked price: the purchase price before sales tax is added.

Total price: the marked price plus the sales tax.

HOW TO   Find the marked price and the sales tax from the total price

1. Find the marked price:
   (a) Write the sales tax rate as a decimal equivalent.
   (b) Add 1 to the decimal equivalent of the sales tax rate from step 1a.
   (c) Divide the total price by the sum from step 1b.

$$\text{Marked price} = \frac{\text{total price}}{1 + \text{sales tax rate}}$$

2. Find the sales tax:

$$\text{Sales tax} = \text{total price} - \text{marked price}$$

EXAMPLE 3 At an amusement park concession, the items are priced to include tax. Find the marked price and the sales tax. The sales tax rate is 7%.

Popcorn: $3.00; soft drink: $3.50; hot dog: $4.00

$$\text{Marked price} = \frac{\text{total price}}{1 + \text{sales tax rate (as a decimal)}}$$

$$\text{Popcorn marked price} = \frac{\$3.00}{1 + 0.07} = \frac{\$3.00}{1.07} = \$2.80$$

$$\text{Soft drink marked price} = \frac{\$3.50}{1 + 0.07} = \frac{\$3.50}{1.07} = \$3.27$$

$$\text{Hot dog marked price} = \frac{\$4.00}{1 + 0.07} = \frac{\$4.00}{1.07} = \$3.74$$

Sales tax = total price − marked price

Popcorn sales tax = $3.00 − $2.80 = $0.20

Soft drink sales tax = $3.50 − $3.27 = $0.23

Hot dog sales tax = $4.00 − $3.74 = $0.26

The marked prices for the popcorn, soft drink, and hot dog are $2.80, $3.27, and $3.74. The sales taxes for the popcorn, soft drink, and hot dog are $0.20, $0.23, and $0.26.

TIP

Why Not Just Multiply the Sales Tax Rate Times the Total Price and Subtract?

A common mistake when determining the marked price from the total price is to apply the sales tax rate to the total price and then subtract. Let's try that with the $3 popcorn.

$$\text{Popcorn} = \frac{\$3.00}{1 + 0.07}$$
$$= \frac{\$3.00}{1.07}$$
$$= \$2.80 \text{ (marked price)}$$

CORRECT

Popcorn = $3.00 × 0.07
= 0.21
$3.00 − $0.21 = $2.79 (marked price)

INCORRECT

What happened? Sales tax is applied to the marked or purchase price. That is, the marked price is the base. To find a percent of the total price, the total price is the base.

As the marked price increases, the difference would be more dramatic. Look at a painting sold at a flea market for $200 with a sales tax rate of 7%.

$$\text{Marked price} = \frac{\$200}{1 + 0.07}$$
$$= \frac{\$200}{1.07}$$
$$= \$186.92 \text{ (rounded)}$$

Sales tax = $200 − $186.92
= $13.08

CORRECT

Sales tax = $200 × 0.07
= $14
Marked price = $200 − $14
= $186

INCORRECT

Here the correct sales tax is $0.92 less than the incorrect calculations.

STOP AND CHECK

See Example 3.

1. Susan Riddle includes state sales tax in the cost of her photos. One client paid a total of $790 for family photos. Susan lives in Tennessee where the state sales tax rate is 7%. How much sales tax does Susan send to the state for this sale?

2. First Serve Vending had $5,852.25 in sales from its vending machines. These sales include taxes at 6.25%. Find the marked price and the sales tax for these items.

3. A sports team sold $380,926 in admission tickets, all including a 5.75% state sales tax. Find the total marked price of admission tickets and the sales tax.

4. A flea market vendor who sells all his items "including tax" reported a total of $12,583 in weekend sales. Find the marked price total and the sales tax if the tax rate is 7%.

20-1 SECTION EXERCISES

SKILL BUILDERS

Find the sales tax and total sale.

	Item marked price	Sales tax rate
1.	$592.36	5.125%

	Item marked price	Sales tax rate
2.	$38.56	4.225%

3.	$3,296	4.5%

4.	$738.47	6%

See Example 2.

5. Massachusetts has a gasoline excise tax rate of 21.0%. How much excise tax is paid on a gasoline purchase of $54.19 if the purchase is before excise tax is added?

6. The gasoline excise tax rate in Maryland is 23.5%. How much excise tax is paid on gasoline that costs $47.83 before the excise tax is added?

Find the marked price and sales tax. See Example 3.

	Total price	Sales tax rate
7.	$681.42	4%

	Total price	Sales tax rate
8.	$48.97	1.225%

9.	$395.17	6.5%

10.	$1,382.56	5.2%

See Example 1.

11. Find the sales tax on an appliance costing $288.63 purchased in Ohio where the state tax rate is 5.5%.

12. Find the state sales tax on a ring that costs $2,860 in Washington with a 6.5% sales tax rate.

13. Parker Waters purchased 100 azaleas at a cost of $283. Find the sales tax on the purchase if the rate is 7.25%.

14. Bianca Schwimmer paid $195.95 for a new television. She paid sales tax at a rate of 6.75%. How much tax did she pay?

15. What is the marked price if a total bill is $182.38 and the sales tax rate is 6%?

16. Clifford Shropshire has a flea market booth and marks all his items so that the price includes state sales tax at a rate of 6.5%. He sold a set of china for $285. How much sales tax should he send to the state?

17. You have agreed to pay $850 for a used utility trailer. The price includes sales tax at a rate of 7.75%. What was the marked price of the trailer and how much tax was paid?

18. You have a receipt for a purchase that shows the total amount of the purchase to be $318.97. The sales tax rate is 8.25%. How much of the $318.97 is the cost of the item and how much is sales tax?

LEARNING OUTCOMES

1 Find the assessed value.
2 Calculate property tax.
3 Determine the property tax rate.

Property tax: tax collected by county, municipality, or local governments from property owners. The tax is based on the type of property and the value of the property.

Most states allow cities and counties to collect money by charging a **property tax** on land, houses, buildings, and improvements and on such personal property as automobiles, jewelry, and furniture.

1 Find the assessed value.

Market value: the expected selling price of a property.

Assessed value: a specified percent of the estimated market value of the property.

Property tax is usually calculated using the assessed value of the property rather than using the **market value** (the expected selling price of the property). The **assessed value** is a specified percent of the estimated market value of the property. This percent, which may vary according to the type of property, is set by the city or county that charges the tax. For example, your city or county may assess farm property and single-family dwellings at 25% of the market value, businesses and multifamily dwellings (duplexes, apartments) at 40% of the market value, and utilities (power companies, telephone companies) at 50% of the market value.

DID YOU KNOW?

Real estate property taxes are a type of *ad valorem* taxes. Ad valorem taxes are assessed based on the dollar value of the item, which can be real estate property, personal property such as vehicles, or even duty on imported items.

HOW TO   Find the assessed value

1. Write the assessment rate as the decimal equivalent of the percent.
2. Find the assessed value:

$$\text{Assessed value} = \text{market value} \times \text{assessment rate}$$

EXAMPLE 1   Find the assessed value of a farm with a market value of $175,000 if the assessed valuation is 25% of the market value.

$175,000(0.25) = $43,750   Find 25% of $175,000.

The assessed value is $43,750.

STOP AND CHECK

See Example 1

1. Find the assessed value of a single-family dwelling with a market value of $338,500 if the assessed valuation is 25% of the market value.

2. What is the assessed value of an apartment building with a market value of $2,580,000 if the assessed valuation is 40% of market value?

3. Lafayette Water Company has a market value of $2,839,800 and utilities are assessed at 50% of market value. Find the assessed value of the utility company.

4. The 7th Inning Sports Memorabilia Shop has a market value of $1,800,000 and is assessed at 40% of its market value. Find the assessed value of the shop.

2 Calculate property tax.

Property tax rate: the rate of tax that is paid for owning property.

Mill: one-thousandth of a dollar.

The city or county government imposes a property tax that might express the **property tax rate,** the rate of tax that must be paid on a piece of property, in one of several ways. The rate could be stated as a percent of the assessed value, as an amount of tax per $1.00 of assessed value, as an amount of tax per $100 of assessed value, as an amount of tax per $1,000 of assessed value, or in mills. A **mill** is one-thousandth ($\frac{1}{1,000}$, or 0.001) of a dollar.

Calculate the property tax

1. Express the given property tax rate as tax per $1.00 of assessed value:
   (a) If the given rate is a percent of assessed value, write the percent in decimal form.

   $$\text{Tax per } \$1.00 = \text{decimal form of the percent of assessed value}$$

   (b) If the given rate is tax per $100 of assessed value, divide the tax on $100 by $100.

   $$\text{Tax per } \$1.00 = \frac{\text{tax on } \$100}{\$100}$$

   (c) If the given rate is tax per $1,000 of assessed value, divide the tax on $1,000 by $1,000.

   $$\text{Tax per } \$1.00 = \frac{\text{tax on } \$1,000}{\$1,000}$$

   (d) If the given rate is a number of mills per $1.00 of assessed value, divide the number of mills by 1,000.

   $$\text{Tax per } \$1.00 = \frac{\text{mills per } \$1.00}{1,000}$$

2. Find the property tax:

   $$\text{Property tax} = \text{assessed value} \times \text{property tax rate per } \$1.00$$

EXAMPLE 2 Find the property tax on a home with an assessed value of $90,000 if the property tax rate is (a) 11.08% of the assessed value, (b) $11.08 per $100 of the assessed value, (c) $110.80 per $1,000 of the assessed value, (d) 110.8 mills per $1.00 of assessed value.

(a) Property tax = assessed value × tax rate | Write the percent in decimal form as a tax per $1.00 of assessed value.
= $90,000 (0.1108) = $9,972 | Multiply.

The property tax is $9,972.

(b) Property tax = assessed value × $\dfrac{\text{tax on } \$100}{\$100}$ | Write the tax rate as an equivalent amount per $1.00 of assessed value.

= $90,000\left(\dfrac{\$11.08}{\$100}\right)$ | Divide.

= $90,000 (0.1108) = $9,972 | Multiply the assessed value by the property tax rate per $1.00.

The property tax is $9,972.

(c) Property tax = assessed value × $\dfrac{\text{tax on } \$1,000}{\$1,000}$ | Write the tax rate as an equivalent amount per $1.00 of assessed value.

= $90,000\left(\dfrac{\$110.80}{\$1,000}\right)$ | Divide.

= $90,000 (0.1108) = $9,972 | Multiply the assessed value by the property tax rate per $1.00.

The property tax is $9,972.

(d) Property tax = assessed value × $\dfrac{\text{mills per } \$1.00}{1,000}$ | Write the tax rate as an equivalent amount per $1.00 of assessed value.

= $90,000\left(\dfrac{110.8 \text{ mills}}{1,000}\right)$ | Divide.

= $90,000 (0.1108) = $9,972 | Multiply the assessed value by the property tax rate per $1.00.

The property tax is $9,972.

STOP AND CHECK

See Example 2.

1. Find the property tax on a home with an assessed value of $85,250 if the property tax rate is 9.58% of the assessed value.

2. What is the property tax on The 7th Inning Sports Memorabilia Shop, which has an assessed value of $720,000, if the property tax rate is $3.45 per $100 of assessed value?

3. Reggie Howard owns property assessed at $125,300 and the property tax rate is $78.45 per $1,000 of assessed value. How much tax does Reggie pay?

4. Antonio Burks's home has an assessed value of $72,520. The property tax rate is 72.5 mills per $1.00 of assessed value. How much tax does Antonio pay?

3 Determine the property tax rate.

How does the city or county decide what the tax rate should be? The local government uses its estimated budget to determine how much money it will need in the year ahead. That amount is then divided by the **total assessed value** of *all* the property in its area. This calculation tells how much tax must be collected for each dollar of assessed property value. The tax rate can be written as a tax per $100 or $1,000 of assessed value by multiplying the tax on $1.00 by 100 or 1,000. Whenever you calculate the tax rate, if the division does not come out even, *round* the digit in the hundredths position *up* to the next digit.

TIP

Why Is the Tax Rate Always Rounded Up?

Find the tax rate per $1.00 if the total estimated budget is $18,000,000 and the total assessed property value is $118,400,000. Round using ordinary methods.

$$\text{Tax per } \$1.00 = \frac{\$18,000,000}{\$118,400,000} = \$0.152027027 = \$0.15$$

Now, calculate the amount of tax that will be collected.

Total tax = assessed value × tax rate per $1.00 = $118,400,000($0.15) = $17,760,000

The amount of money needed for the estimated budget would be short by $240,000. ($18,000,000 − $17,760,000 = $240,000)

HOW TO   Determine a property tax rate

1. Select the appropriate formula according to the desired tax rate type.

$$(\text{Tax per } \$1.00 \text{ of assessed value}) = \frac{\text{total estimated budget}}{\text{total assessed property value}}$$

$$(\text{Tax per } \$100 \text{ of assessed value}) = \frac{\text{total estimated budget}}{\text{total assessed property value}} \times \$100$$

$$(\text{Tax per } \$1,000 \text{ of assessed value}) = \frac{\text{total estimated budget}}{\text{total assessed property value}} \times \$1,000$$

$$(\text{Tax, in mills, per } \$1.00 \text{ of assessed value}) = \frac{\text{total estimated budget}}{\text{total assessed property value}} \times 1,000$$

2. Make calculations using the selected formula. Always round up.

EXAMPLE 3   Find the tax rate expressed as tax per $100 of assessed value for Harbortown, which anticipates expenses of $95,590,000 and has property assessed at $3,868,758,500.

$$\begin{aligned}(\text{Tax per } \$100 \text{ of assessed value}) &= \left(\frac{\$95,590,000}{\$3,868,758,500}\right)(\$100)\\ &= \$0.024708184(\$100)\\ &= \$2.4708184\\ &= \$2.48 \text{ (rounded up)}\end{aligned}$$

The tax rate is $2.48 per $100 of assessed value.

EXAMPLE 4 Harbortown (see the previous example) expects an increase in expenses of $5,000,000. To cover these expenses, the city has to increase the tax rate or to reassess property values. The city assessor's office predicts that the reassessment would cost $100,000 and increase the city's assessment value of property to $4,300,000,000. The city leaders prefer the reassessment choice but do not want to reassess property value and increase the tax rate in the same year. Which choice should the city leaders make?

What You Know

Current expenses: $95,590,000	Expected reassessment
Expected increase in expenses: $5,000,000	value: $4,300,000,000
Current assessed property: $3,868,758,500	Cost of reassessment:
Current tax rate: $2.48 per $100 of	$100,000
assessed value	

What You Are Looking For

Total revenue from property taxes if property is reassessed
Should property be reassessed or should the tax rate be increased?

Solution Plan

Total property taxes from reassessed property values = expected reassessed values $\times \dfrac{\$2.48}{\$100}$

Expected total expenses if property is reassessed =
current expenses + expected increase + cost of reassessment

Solution

Total property taxes revenue from reassessment = $\$4,300,000,000\left(\dfrac{\$2.48}{\$100}\right)$

$= \$106,640,000$

Expected total expenses = $\$95,590,000 + \$5,000,000 + \$100,000$
$= \$100,690,000$

Conclusion

Property taxes from the reassessment ($106,640,000) are more than expected total expenses ($100,690,000). Because a reassessment will cover the increase in expenses without a tax increase, property will be reassessed.

STOP AND CHECK

See Example 3.

1. Find the tax rate expressed as tax per $100 of assessed value for Suffolk County, which anticipates tax-funded expenses of $109,047,773 and has property assessed at $4,098,530,000.

2. Find the tax per $1.00 of assessed value for the town of Tuxedo, which anticipates property tax funded expenses of $5,347,364 and has property assessed at $218,560,000.

3. Ithaca has property tax-funded expenses of $6,344,549.65 and assessed real property valued at $544,029,090. Find the tax rate in mills.

4. Northhaven anticipates expenses of $68,914,808 and has real estate with a total assessed value of $2,856,919,000. Find the tax rate per $1,000 for the year.

See Example 4.

5. Ithaca (see Exercise 3) expects an increase in expenses of $135,000. The city must increase the tax rate or reassess property values. A reassessment would cost the city $22,000 and would increase the assessed value of property in the city to $568,193,000. The city council must make a choice based on whether the reassessed property will increase the revenue from taxes enough to cover the increase in expenses. Which should they choose?

6. Northhaven (see Exercise 4) expects an increase in expenses of $1,345,000. The city must increase the tax rate or reassess property values. A reassessment would cost the city $54,000 and would increase the assessed value of property in the city to $2,857,590,000. Should the city increase the tax rate or reassess property?

SKILL BUILDERS

Find the property tax for each property. See Example 2.

	Assessed value	Tax rate		Assessed value	Tax rate
1.	$78,920	5.75%	2.	$125,035	$3.07 per $100
3.	$682,500	$19.86 per $1,000	4.	$12,800	15.46 mills

Determine the tax rate for each city or county. For Exercises 5–10, an equal number of zeros in the numerator and denominator can be reduced to facilitate calculator entry. See Example 3.

	Assessed Property value	Expenses to be funded by property tax	Tax per amount of assessed value		Assessed Property value	Expenses to be funded by property tax	Tax per amount of assessed value
5.	$1,549,465,000	$125,807,560	$1.00	6.	$2,252,136,000	$86,987,037	$100
7.	$7,063,274,000	$188,942,580	$1,000	8.	$17,881,455,000	$376,583,460	mill
9.	$2,412,500,000	$86,529,807	$100	10.	$1,950,000,000	$48,957,840	$1,000

See Example 1.

11. Find the assessed value of a store with a market value of $150,000 if the rate for assessed value is 35% of market value.

See Example 1.

12. Donna McAnally owns an apartment building that has a market value of $583,000. If apartments are assessed at 40% of market value, find the assessed value of Donna's apartment building.

13. Tim Warner's farm has a market value of $385,000. Find the assessed value of the farm if farms are assessed at 25% of the market value.

14. Rebecca Drewrey owns a small telephone company that has a market value of $1,895,000. If the phone company is assessed at 50% of market value, what is the assessed value of the property?

15. What is the tax on a property with an assessed value of $88,500 if the tax rate is 4.5% of the assessed value?

16. Find the property tax on a vacant lot with an assessed value of $32,350 and a tax rate of $4.37 per $100 of assessed value.

17. Find the property tax on a home with an assessed value of $75,000 in a community with a tax rate of $12.75 per $1,000 of assessed value.

18. Calculate the property tax on a store with an assessed value of $150,250 if the tax rate is 58 mills per $1.00 of assessed value.

19. Find the tax rate expressed as tax per $1.00 of assessed value in a municipality that has budgeted expenses of $5,985,500 and has property assessed at $230,211,500.

20. Find the tax rate expressed as tax per $100 of assessed value for a town that anticipates expenses of $55,800 and has property assessed at $9,830,000.

21. What is the tax rate expressed as tax per $1,000 of assessed property value in a county that has property assessed at $185,910,000 and has budgeted expenses of $5,810,000?

22. What is the tax rate expressed in mills per $1.00 of assessed value if an incorporated town has a budget of $497,000 and has property assessed at $11,045,000?

See Example 2.

23. New Jersey has an excise tax rate on wine of $0.875 per gallon. In a year, 119,282,000 gallons of wine were sold. What was the revenue generated from wine sales?

24. Idaho has a wine excise tax rate of $0.45 per gallon. If 18,048,800 gallons of wine were sold in a year, what revenue was generated?

20-3 INCOME TAXES

LEARNING OUTCOMES

1 Find taxable income.
2 Use the tax tables to calculate income tax.
3 Use the tax computation worksheet to calculate income tax.

Income tax: a tax collected by the federal government, many states, and some cities that is based on a person's income.

Gross income: all income received in the form of money, goods, property, and services that is not exempt from tax.

Adjusted gross income: total or gross income minus certain employee expenses and allowable deductions such as IRAs, student loan interest, tuition and fees, alimony paid, and so on.

Taxable income: adjusted gross income minus exemptions and either the standard or the itemized deductions.

Exemption or allowance: an amount of money that a taxpayer is allowed to subtract from the adjusted gross income for himself or herself, a spouse, and each dependent.

Deductions: certain expenses the taxpayer is allowed to subtract from income to reduce the amount of taxable income.

Itemized deductions: a listing of deductions that can be used by certain taxpayers to reduce taxable income. Normally, taxpayers use itemized deductions when the total of their itemized deductions is greater than the standard deduction.

Standard deduction: a specified reduction of taxable income. The standard deduction amount is based on filing status and is adjusted yearly for inflation. Normally, taxpayers who do not use the standard deduction have eligible itemized deductions that exceed the standard deduction.

Filing status: category of taxpayer: single, married filing jointly, married filing separately, or head of household.

Many state governments and the federal government collect much of their revenue through individual and business **income taxes.** Federal income tax regulations are enacted by the Congress of the United States, and the tax laws change frequently.

Although the laws and forms change from year to year, the *procedures* for computing income tax remain basically the same. Each year an instruction booklet accompanies the current income tax forms. This booklet explains any recent changes in the tax laws, provides instructions for computing tax and filling out the forms, and contains various tax tables needed for filing an income tax return.

To calculate income tax owed, begin with a business's or individual's **gross income,** which is the money, goods, and property received during the year. From this subtract any adjustments allowed, such as credit for employee expenses that are not reimbursed by the employer; this gives you the **adjusted gross income.** Next, arrive at the **taxable income,** which is the adjusted gross income minus exemptions and deductions. The taxable income is the amount that is used to calculate the taxes owed.

Exemptions provide one of the ways of reducing taxable income. One personal **exemption** or **allowance** is allowed for the taxpayer, and additional exemptions are allowed for the taxpayer's spouse and other dependents if the adjusted gross income is below a certain level. Other exemptions are allowed if the taxpayer or the spouse is over 65 or blind. The deduction for personal exemptions was $3,700 in 2011.

A taxpayer is allowed to take **deductions,** or to deduct certain expenses such as charitable contributions, interest paid on certain loans, certain taxes, certain losses, excessive medical expenses, and certain miscellaneous expenses, to name a few. Rather than listing these expenses (called **itemized deductions**), the taxpayer may choose to take the **standard deduction.** The standard deduction changes from year to year, but in a recent year for most people it was $11,600 for married taxpayers filing jointly (if both were under 65) or a qualifying widow (widower) with a dependent child; $5,800 for married taxpayers filing separately or for single taxpayers; and $8,500 for taxpayers who were the head of a household.

The tax due on taxable personal income also depends on the **filing status** of the taxpayer. Filing status is the marital status of the taxpayer. The individual taxpayer must select the filing status from four categories. The *single* category is for a person who has never married, is legally separated, is widowed, or is divorced. A husband and wife filing a return together, even if only one had income, are classified as *married filing jointly*. This filing status sometimes results in married persons paying a different tax than single persons with a comparable income. When a husband and wife each file a separate return, they are classified as *married filing separately*, and this status may result in a different tax liability than the married filing jointly status. The filing status *head of household* should be selected by individuals who provide a home for certain other persons.

1 Find taxable income.

W-2 form: a form an employer must provide each employee that shows the earned income, income tax withheld, and Social Security and Medicare taxes withheld.

Whether you choose to itemize deductions or use the standard deduction, you must determine your *taxable income* before you can compute the tax. An employer is required to issue each employee a **W-2 form,** which shows the income earned, income tax withheld, Social Security tax withheld, and Medicare tax withheld for the employee for the calendar year. If a person works for more than one employer in a year, he or she will receive a W-2 form from each employer. Under some circumstances a form 1099 is used to report income to an individual.

DID YOU KNOW?

The allowable *deductions* that are subtracted from total income to get the adjusted gross income are different from the itemized or standard *deductions* that are used to find the taxable income. Both of these deductions are defined by the IRS and are subject to change.

TIP

When Do You Expect Your W-2 Form?

The IRS requires employers to deliver or have postmarked W-2 forms by midnight on January 31 following the year the income was earned. Employees who do not receive a W-2 from an employer because of address changes or other changes should contact the employer soon after January 31.

HOW TO Find the taxable income

1. Find the adjusted gross income:

   Adjusted gross income = total income − allowable expenses and deductions

2. Total the deductions or choose the standard deduction and total the exemptions.
3. Find the taxable income:

   Taxable income = adjusted gross income
   − itemized or standard deductions − exemptions

EXAMPLE 1
Find the taxable income for a family of four (husband, wife, two children) if their adjusted gross income is $67,754 and their itemized deductions are $11,345. Use $3,700 as the amount of each personal exemption.

Taxable income = adjusted gross income
− itemized or standard deductions − exemptions
= $67,754 − $11,345 − ($3,700)(4)
= $67,754 − $11,345 − $14,800 = $41,609

The taxable income is $41,609.

STOP AND CHECK

See Example 1.

1. Find the taxable income for a married couple filing a joint return with one additional dependent if their adjusted gross income is $62,596 and itemized deductions are $10,109. Use $3,700 for each personal exemption.

2. Find the taxable income for a single person if her adjusted gross income is $105,896 and her itemized deductions are $12,057. Use $3,700 for her personal exemption.

3. Corey Wells's family of five has an adjusted gross income of $115,993 and $18,930 in itemized deductions. Use $3,700 for each personal exemption and find the Wells's taxable income.

4. Bonzi McFagdon files as head of a household, has an adjusted gross income of $68,929, and takes the standard deduction of $8,480. He claims only one personal exemption of $3,700. Find his taxable income.

2 Use the tax tables to calculate income tax.

Income tax tables: tax tables found in the IRS 1040 instructions publication for finding the amount of tax liability.

Once you know your taxable income and filing status, you can determine the taxes owed. **Income tax tables** like those in Table 20-1 are used to find the tax liability for taxable incomes of *less than* $100,000.

TIP

Other Tax Tables

If a taxpayer files a 1040 or 1040EZ form, the instructions and corresponding tax tables reference lines 43 and 6 respectively for taxable income.

HOW TO   Use the tax tables to calculate income tax

1. Locate the taxable income under the column headed "If line 43 (taxable income) is—."
2. Move across to the column headed "And you are—," which has the four filing status categories listed under it. The tax owed appears under the appropriate category.

EXAMPLE 2   Find the tax owed by a married taxpayer (a) filing separately on a taxable income of $39,478; (b) filing jointly on a taxable income of $39,478.

First, use Table 20-1 and locate the income range in which $39,478 falls. Because $39,478 is *at least* $39,450 *but less than* $39,500, it falls within the range of $39,450–$39,500.

(a) Locate the tax in the column to the right headed *married filing separately*. **The tax is $5,994.**
(b) For the taxable income range $39,450–$39,500, the tax for a taxpayer *married filing jointly* is **$5,071.**

TIP

Settling Up on Income Tax

Most taxpayers have taxes withheld from their paychecks throughout the year. By April 15 of the following year, taxpayers are required to file a return that will determine if additional taxes are owed or if a refund is due.

The taxpayer refers to his or her W-2 or 1099 form to determine the income tax that has been withheld during the year. This tax withheld is subtracted from the tax owed to determine the remaining tax that must be paid. If more tax has been withheld than the taxpayer owes, subtraction will show the tax refund due the taxpayer.

STOP AND CHECK

See Example 2.

1. Find the tax owed by a married taxpayer filing jointly on a total taxable income of $37,519.

2. Find the tax for a single taxpayer who has a taxable income of $31,795.

3. Find the tax for a married person filing separately if her taxable income is $30,650.

4. Find the tax owed by Grayson Lee, whose taxable income is $38,456, if his filing status is "Head of a household."

TABLE 20-1
Portion of Income Tax Table

23,000 – 25,950

If line 43 (taxable income) is— At least	But less than	Single	Married filing jointly*	Married filing separately	Head of a household
23,000					
23,000	23,050	3,029	2,604	3,029	2,846
23,050	23,100	3,036	2,611	3,036	2,854
23,100	23,150	3,044	2,619	3,044	2,861
23,150	23,200	3,051	2,626	3,051	2,869
23,200	23,250	3,059	2,634	3,059	2,876
23,250	23,300	3,066	2,641	3,066	2,884
23,300	23,350	3,074	2,649	3,074	2,891
23,350	23,400	3,081	2,656	3,081	2,899
23,400	23,450	3,089	2,664	3,089	2,906
23,450	23,500	3,096	2,671	3,096	2,914
23,500	23,550	3,104	2,679	3,104	2,921
23,550	23,600	3,111	2,686	3,111	2,929
23,600	23,650	3,119	2,694	3,119	2,936
23,650	23,700	3,126	2,701	3,126	2,944
23,700	23,750	3,134	2,709	3,134	2,951
23,750	23,800	3,141	2,716	3,141	2,959
23,800	23,850	3,149	2,724	3,149	2,966
23,850	23,900	3,156	2,731	3,156	2,974
23,900	23,950	3,164	2,739	3,164	2,981
23,950	24,000	3,171	2,746	3,171	2,989
24,000					
24,000	24,050	3,179	2,754	3,179	2,996
24,050	24,100	3,186	2,761	3,186	3,004
24,100	24,150	3,194	2,769	3,194	3,011
24,150	24,200	3,201	2,776	3,201	3,019
24,200	24,250	3,209	2,784	3,209	3,026
24,250	24,300	3,216	2,791	3,216	3,034
24,300	24,350	3,224	2,799	3,224	3,041
24,350	24,400	3,231	2,806	3,231	3,049
24,400	24,450	3,239	2,814	3,239	3,056
24,450	24,500	3,246	2,821	3,246	3,064
24,500	24,550	3,254	2,829	3,254	3,071
24,550	24,600	3,261	2,836	3,261	3,079
24,600	24,650	3,269	2,844	3,269	3,086
24,650	24,700	3,276	2,851	3,276	3,094
24,700	24,750	3,284	2,859	3,284	3,101
24,750	24,800	3,291	2,866	3,291	3,109
24,800	24,850	3,299	2,874	3,299	3,116
24,850	24,900	3,306	2,881	3,306	3,124
24,900	24,950	3,314	2,889	3,314	3,131
24,950	25,000	3,321	2,896	3,321	3,139
25,000					
25,000	25,050	3,329	2,904	3,329	3,146
25,050	25,100	3,336	2,911	3,336	3,154
25,100	25,150	3,344	2,919	3,344	3,161
25,150	25,200	3,351	2,926	3,351	3,169
25,200	25,250	3,359	2,934	3,359	3,176
25,250	25,300	3,366	2,941	3,366	3,184
25,300	25,350	3,374	2,949	3,374	3,191
25,350	25,400	3,381	2,956	3,381	3,199
25,400	25,450	3,389	2,964	3,389	3,206
25,450	25,500	3,396	2,971	3,396	3,214
25,500	25,550	3,404	2,979	3,404	3,221
25,550	25,600	3,411	2,986	3,411	3,229
25,600	25,650	3,419	2,994	3,419	3,236
25,650	25,700	3,426	3,001	3,426	3,244
25,700	25,750	3,434	3,009	3,434	3,251
25,750	25,800	3,441	3,016	3,441	3,259
25,800	25,850	3,449	3,024	3,449	3,266
25,850	25,900	3,456	3,031	3,456	3,274
25,900	25,950	3,464	3,039	3,464	3,281
25,950	26,000	3,471	3,046	3,471	3,289

26,000 – 28,950

If line 43 (taxable income) is— At least	But less than	Single	Married filing jointly*	Married filing separately	Head of a household
26,000					
26,000	26,050	3,479	3,054	3,479	3,296
26,050	26,100	3,486	3,061	3,486	3,304
26,100	26,150	3,494	3,069	3,494	3,311
26,150	26,200	3,501	3,076	3,501	3,319
26,200	26,250	3,509	3,084	3,509	3,326
26,250	26,300	3,516	3,091	3,516	3,334
26,300	26,350	3,524	3,099	3,524	3,341
26,350	26,400	3,531	3,106	3,531	3,349
26,400	26,450	3,539	3,114	3,539	3,356
26,450	26,500	3,546	3,121	3,546	3,364
26,500	26,550	3,554	3,129	3,554	3,371
26,550	26,600	3,561	3,136	3,561	3,379
26,600	26,650	3,569	3,144	3,569	3,386
26,650	26,700	3,576	3,151	3,576	3,394
26,700	26,750	3,584	3,159	3,584	3,401
26,750	26,800	3,591	3,166	3,591	3,409
26,800	26,850	3,599	3,174	3,599	3,416
26,850	26,900	3,606	3,181	3,606	3,424
26,900	26,950	3,614	3,189	3,614	3,431
26,950	27,000	3,621	3,196	3,621	3,439
27,000					
27,000	27,050	3,629	3,204	3,629	3,446
27,050	27,100	3,636	3,211	3,636	3,454
27,100	27,150	3,644	3,219	3,644	3,461
27,150	27,200	3,651	3,226	3,651	3,469
27,200	27,250	3,659	3,234	3,659	3,476
27,250	27,300	3,666	3,241	3,666	3,484
27,300	27,350	3,674	3,249	3,674	3,491
27,350	27,400	3,681	3,256	3,681	3,499
27,400	27,450	3,689	3,264	3,689	3,506
27,450	27,500	3,696	3,271	3,696	3,514
27,500	27,550	3,704	3,279	3,704	3,521
27,550	27,600	3,711	3,286	3,711	3,529
27,600	27,650	3,719	3,294	3,719	3,536
27,650	27,700	3,726	3,301	3,726	3,544
27,700	27,750	3,734	3,309	3,734	3,551
27,750	27,800	3,741	3,316	3,741	3,559
27,800	27,850	3,749	3,324	3,749	3,566
27,850	27,900	3,756	3,331	3,756	3,574
27,900	27,950	3,764	3,339	3,764	3,581
27,950	28,000	3,771	3,346	3,771	3,589
28,000					
28,000	28,050	3,779	3,354	3,779	3,596
28,050	28,100	3,786	3,361	3,786	3,604
28,100	28,150	3,794	3,369	3,794	3,611
28,150	28,200	3,801	3,376	3,801	3,619
28,200	28,250	3,809	3,384	3,809	3,626
28,250	28,300	3,816	3,391	3,816	3,634
28,300	28,350	3,824	3,399	3,824	3,641
28,350	28,400	3,831	3,406	3,831	3,649
28,400	28,450	3,839	3,414	3,839	3,656
28,450	28,500	3,846	3,421	3,846	3,664
28,500	28,550	3,854	3,429	3,854	3,671
28,550	28,600	3,861	3,436	3,861	3,679
28,600	28,650	3,869	3,444	3,869	3,686
28,650	28,700	3,876	3,451	3,876	3,694
28,700	28,750	3,884	3,459	3,884	3,701
28,750	28,800	3,891	3,466	3,891	3,709
28,800	28,850	3,899	3,474	3,899	3,716
28,850	28,900	3,906	3,481	3,906	3,724
28,900	28,950	3,914	3,489	3,914	3,731
28,950	29,000	3,921	3,496	3,921	3,739

29,000 – 31,950

If line 43 (taxable income) is— At least	But less than	Single	Married filing jointly*	Married filing separately	Head of a household
29,000					
29,000	29,050	3,929	3,504	3,929	3,746
29,050	29,100	3,936	3,511	3,936	3,754
29,100	29,150	3,944	3,519	3,944	3,761
29,150	29,200	3,951	3,526	3,951	3,769
29,200	29,250	3,959	3,534	3,959	3,776
29,250	29,300	3,966	3,541	3,966	3,784
29,300	29,350	3,974	3,549	3,974	3,791
29,350	29,400	3,981	3,556	3,981	3,799
29,400	29,450	3,989	3,564	3,989	3,806
29,450	29,500	3,996	3,571	3,996	3,814
29,500	29,550	4,004	3,579	4,004	3,821
29,550	29,600	4,011	3,586	4,011	3,829
29,600	29,650	4,019	3,594	4,019	3,836
29,650	29,700	4,026	3,601	4,026	3,844
29,700	29,750	4,034	3,609	4,034	3,851
29,750	29,800	4,041	3,616	4,041	3,859
29,800	29,850	4,049	3,624	4,049	3,866
29,850	29,900	4,056	3,631	4,056	3,874
29,900	29,950	4,064	3,639	4,064	3,881
29,950	30,000	4,071	3,646	4,071	3,889
30,000					
30,000	30,050	4,079	3,654	4,079	3,896
30,050	30,100	4,086	3,661	4,086	3,904
30,100	30,150	4,094	3,669	4,094	3,911
30,150	30,200	4,101	3,676	4,101	3,919
30,200	30,250	4,109	3,684	4,109	3,926
30,250	30,300	4,116	3,691	4,116	3,934
30,300	30,350	4,124	3,699	4,124	3,941
30,350	30,400	4,131	3,706	4,131	3,949
30,400	30,450	4,139	3,714	4,139	3,956
30,450	30,500	4,146	3,721	4,146	3,964
30,500	30,550	4,154	3,729	4,154	3,971
30,550	30,600	4,161	3,736	4,161	3,979
30,600	30,650	4,169	3,744	4,169	3,986
30,650	30,700	4,176	3,751	4,176	3,994
30,700	30,750	4,184	3,759	4,184	4,001
30,750	30,800	4,191	3,766	4,191	4,009
30,800	30,850	4,199	3,774	4,199	4,016
30,850	30,900	4,206	3,781	4,206	4,024
30,900	30,950	4,214	3,789	4,214	4,031
30,950	31,000	4,221	3,796	4,221	4,039
31,000					
31,000	31,050	4,229	3,804	4,229	4,046
31,050	31,100	4,236	3,811	4,236	4,054
31,100	31,150	4,244	3,819	4,244	4,061
31,150	31,200	4,251	3,826	4,251	4,069
31,200	31,250	4,259	3,834	4,259	4,076
31,250	31,300	4,266	3,841	4,266	4,084
31,300	31,350	4,274	3,849	4,274	4,091
31,350	31,400	4,281	3,856	4,281	4,099
31,400	31,450	4,289	3,864	4,289	4,106
31,450	31,500	4,296	3,871	4,296	4,114
31,500	31,550	4,304	3,879	4,304	4,121
31,550	31,600	4,311	3,886	4,311	4,129
31,600	31,650	4,319	3,894	4,319	4,136
31,650	31,700	4,326	3,901	4,326	4,144
31,700	31,750	4,334	3,909	4,334	4,151
31,750	31,800	4,341	3,916	4,341	4,159
31,800	31,850	4,349	3,924	4,349	4,166
31,850	31,900	4,356	3,931	4,356	4,174
31,900	31,950	4,364	3,939	4,364	4,181
31,950	32,000	4,371	3,946	4,371	4,189

*This column must also be used by a qualifying widow(er).

Source: IRS Publication 2011 1040 Instructions.

TABLE 20-1
Portion of Income Tax Table—*Continued*

2011 Tax Table–*Continued*

If line 43 (taxable income) is—		And you are—			
At least	But less than	Single	Married filing jointly *	Married filing separately	Head of a household
		Your tax is—			

32,000

At least	But less than	Single	Married filing jointly	Married filing separately	Head of a household
32,000	32,050	4,379	3,954	4,379	4,196
32,050	32,100	4,386	3,961	4,386	4,204
32,100	32,150	4,394	3,969	4,394	4,211
32,150	32,200	4,401	3,976	4,401	4,219
32,200	32,250	4,409	3,984	4,409	4,226
32,250	32,300	4,416	3,991	4,416	4,234
32,300	32,350	4,424	3,999	4,424	4,241
32,350	32,400	4,431	4,006	4,431	4,249
32,400	32,450	4,439	4,014	4,439	4,256
32,450	32,500	4,446	4,021	4,446	4,264
32,500	32,550	4,454	4,029	4,454	4,271
32,550	32,600	4,461	4,036	4,461	4,279
32,600	32,650	4,469	4,044	4,469	4,286
32,650	32,700	4,476	4,051	4,476	4,294
32,700	32,750	4,484	4,059	4,484	4,301
32,750	32,800	4,491	4,066	4,491	4,309
32,800	32,850	4,499	4,074	4,499	4,316
32,850	32,900	4,506	4,081	4,506	4,324
32,900	32,950	4,514	4,089	4,514	4,331
32,950	33,000	4,521	4,096	4,521	4,339

33,000

At least	But less than	Single	Married filing jointly	Married filing separately	Head of a household
33,000	33,050	4,529	4,104	4,529	4,346
33,050	33,100	4,536	4,111	4,536	4,354
33,100	33,150	4,544	4,119	4,544	4,361
33,150	33,200	4,551	4,126	4,551	4,369
33,200	33,250	4,559	4,134	4,559	4,376
33,250	33,300	4,566	4,141	4,566	4,384
33,300	33,350	4,574	4,149	4,574	4,391
33,350	33,400	4,581	4,156	4,581	4,399
33,400	33,450	4,589	4,164	4,589	4,406
33,450	33,500	4,596	4,171	4,596	4,414
33,500	33,550	4,604	4,179	4,604	4,421
33,550	33,600	4,611	4,186	4,611	4,429
33,600	33,650	4,619	4,194	4,619	4,436
33,650	33,700	4,626	4,201	4,626	4,444
33,700	33,750	4,634	4,209	4,634	4,451
33,750	33,800	4,641	4,216	4,641	4,459
33,800	33,850	4,649	4,224	4,649	4,466
33,850	33,900	4,656	4,231	4,656	4,474
33,900	33,950	4,664	4,239	4,664	4,481
33,950	34,000	4,671	4,246	4,671	4,489

34,000

At least	But less than	Single	Married filing jointly	Married filing separately	Head of a household
34,000	34,050	4,679	4,254	4,679	4,496
34,050	34,100	4,686	4,261	4,686	4,504
34,100	34,150	4,694	4,269	4,694	4,511
34,150	34,200	4,701	4,276	4,701	4,519
34,200	34,250	4,709	4,284	4,709	4,526
34,250	34,300	4,716	4,291	4,716	4,534
34,300	34,350	4,724	4,299	4,724	4,541
34,350	34,400	4,731	4,306	4,731	4,549
34,400	34,450	4,739	4,314	4,739	4,556
34,450	34,500	4,746	4,321	4,746	4,564
34,500	34,550	4,756	4,329	4,756	4,571
34,550	34,600	4,769	4,336	4,769	4,579
34,600	34,650	4,781	4,344	4,781	4,586
34,650	34,700	4,794	4,351	4,794	4,594
34,700	34,750	4,806	4,359	4,806	4,601
34,750	34,800	4,819	4,366	4,819	4,609
34,800	34,850	4,831	4,374	4,831	4,616
34,850	34,900	4,844	4,381	4,844	4,624
34,900	34,950	4,856	4,389	4,856	4,631
34,950	35,000	4,869	4,396	4,869	4,639

35,000

At least	But less than	Single	Married filing jointly	Married filing separately	Head of a household
35,000	35,050	4,881	4,404	4,881	4,646
35,050	35,100	4,894	4,411	4,894	4,654
35,100	35,150	4,906	4,419	4,906	4,661
35,150	35,200	4,919	4,426	4,919	4,669
35,200	35,250	4,931	4,434	4,931	4,676
35,250	35,300	4,944	4,441	4,944	4,684
35,300	35,350	4,956	4,449	4,956	4,691
35,350	35,400	4,969	4,456	4,969	4,699
35,400	35,450	4,981	4,464	4,981	4,706
35,450	35,500	4,994	4,471	4,994	4,714
35,500	35,550	5,006	4,479	5,006	4,721
35,550	35,600	5,019	4,486	5,019	4,729
35,600	35,650	5,031	4,494	5,031	4,736
35,650	35,700	5,044	4,501	5,044	4,744
35,700	35,750	5,056	4,509	5,056	4,751
35,750	35,800	5,069	4,516	5,069	4,759
35,800	35,850	5,081	4,524	5,081	4,766
35,850	35,900	5,094	4,531	5,094	4,774
35,900	35,950	5,106	4,539	5,106	4,781
35,950	36,000	5,119	4,546	5,119	4,789

36,000

At least	But less than	Single	Married filing jointly	Married filing separately	Head of a household
36,000	36,050	5,131	4,554	5,131	4,796
36,050	36,100	5,144	4,561	5,144	4,804
36,100	36,150	5,156	4,569	5,156	4,811
36,150	36,200	5,169	4,576	5,169	4,819
36,200	36,250	5,181	4,584	5,181	4,826
36,250	36,300	5,194	4,591	5,194	4,834
36,300	36,350	5,206	4,599	5,206	4,841
36,350	36,400	5,219	4,606	5,219	4,849
36,400	36,450	5,231	4,614	5,231	4,856
36,450	36,500	5,244	4,621	5,244	4,864
36,500	36,550	5,256	4,629	5,256	4,871
36,550	36,600	5,269	4,636	5,269	4,879
36,600	36,650	5,281	4,644	5,281	4,886
36,650	36,700	5,294	4,651	5,294	4,894
36,700	36,750	5,306	4,659	5,306	4,901
36,750	36,800	5,319	4,666	5,319	4,909
36,800	36,850	5,331	4,674	5,331	4,916
36,850	36,900	5,344	4,681	5,344	4,924
36,900	36,950	5,356	4,689	5,356	4,931
36,950	37,000	5,369	4,696	5,369	4,939

37,000

At least	But less than	Single	Married filing jointly	Married filing separately	Head of a household
37,000	37,050	5,381	4,704	5,381	4,946
37,050	37,100	5,394	4,711	5,394	4,954
37,100	37,150	5,406	4,719	5,406	4,961
37,150	37,200	5,419	4,726	5,419	4,969
37,200	37,250	5,431	4,734	5,431	4,976
37,250	37,300	5,444	4,741	5,444	4,984
37,300	37,350	5,456	4,749	5,456	4,991
37,350	37,400	5,469	4,756	5,469	4,999
37,400	37,450	5,481	4,764	5,481	5,006
37,450	37,500	5,494	4,771	5,494	5,014
37,500	37,550	5,506	4,779	5,506	5,021
37,550	37,600	5,519	4,786	5,519	5,029
37,600	37,650	5,531	4,794	5,531	5,036
37,650	37,700	5,544	4,801	5,544	5,044
37,700	37,750	5,556	4,809	5,556	5,051
37,750	37,800	5,569	4,816	5,569	5,059
37,800	37,850	5,581	4,824	5,581	5,066
37,850	37,900	5,594	4,831	5,594	5,074
37,900	37,950	5,606	4,839	5,606	5,081
37,950	38,000	5,619	4,846	5,619	5,089

38,000

At least	But less than	Single	Married filing jointly	Married filing separately	Head of a household
38,000	38,050	5,631	4,854	5,631	5,096
38,050	38,100	5,644	4,861	5,644	5,104
38,100	38,150	5,656	4,869	5,656	5,111
38,150	38,200	5,669	4,876	5,669	5,119
38,200	38,250	5,681	4,884	5,681	5,126
38,250	38,300	5,694	4,891	5,694	5,134
38,300	38,350	5,706	4,899	5,706	5,141
38,350	38,400	5,719	4,906	5,719	5,149
38,400	38,450	5,731	4,914	5,731	5,156
38,450	38,500	5,744	4,921	5,744	5,164
38,500	38,550	5,756	4,929	5,756	5,171
38,550	38,600	5,769	4,936	5,769	5,179
38,600	38,650	5,781	4,944	5,781	5,186
38,650	38,700	5,794	4,951	5,794	5,194
38,700	38,750	5,806	4,959	5,806	5,201
38,750	38,800	5,819	4,966	5,819	5,209
38,800	38,850	5,831	4,974	5,831	5,216
38,850	38,900	5,844	4,981	5,844	5,224
38,900	38,950	5,856	4,989	5,856	5,231
38,950	39,000	5,869	4,996	5,869	5,239

39,000

At least	But less than	Single	Married filing jointly	Married filing separately	Head of a household
39,000	39,050	5,881	5,004	5,881	5,246
39,050	39,100	5,894	5,011	5,894	5,254
39,100	39,150	5,906	5,019	5,906	5,261
39,150	39,200	5,919	5,026	5,919	5,269
39,200	39,250	5,931	5,034	5,931	5,276
39,250	39,300	5,944	5,041	5,944	5,284
39,300	39,350	5,956	5,049	5,956	5,291
39,350	39,400	5,969	5,056	5,969	5,299
39,400	39,450	5,981	5,064	5,981	5,306
39,450	39,500	5,994	5,071	5,994	5,314
39,500	39,550	6,006	5,079	6,006	5,321
39,550	39,600	6,019	5,086	6,019	5,329
39,600	39,650	6,031	5,094	6,031	5,336
39,650	39,700	6,044	5,101	6,044	5,344
39,700	39,750	6,056	5,109	6,056	5,351
39,750	39,800	6,069	5,116	6,069	5,359
39,800	39,850	6,081	5,124	6,081	5,366
39,850	39,900	6,094	5,131	6,094	5,374
39,900	39,950	6,106	5,139	6,106	5,381
39,950	40,000	6,119	5,146	6,119	5,389

40,000

At least	But less than	Single	Married filing jointly	Married filing separately	Head of a household
40,000	40,050	6,131	5,154	6,131	5,396
40,050	40,100	6,144	5,161	6,144	5,404
40,100	40,150	6,156	5,169	6,156	5,411
40,150	40,200	6,169	5,176	6,169	5,419
40,200	40,250	6,181	5,184	6,181	5,426
40,250	40,300	6,194	5,191	6,194	5,434
40,300	40,350	6,206	5,199	6,206	5,441
40,350	40,400	6,219	5,206	6,219	5,449
40,400	40,450	6,231	5,214	6,231	5,456
40,450	40,500	6,244	5,221	6,244	5,464
40,500	40,550	6,256	5,229	6,256	5,471
40,550	40,600	6,269	5,236	6,269	5,479
40,600	40,650	6,281	5,244	6,281	5,486
40,650	40,700	6,294	5,251	6,294	5,494
40,700	40,750	6,306	5,259	6,306	5,501
40,750	40,800	6,319	5,266	6,319	5,509
40,800	40,850	6,331	5,274	6,331	5,516
40,850	40,900	6,344	5,281	6,344	5,524
40,900	40,950	6,356	5,289	6,356	5,531
40,950	41,000	6,369	5,296	6,369	5,539

*This column must also be used by a qualifying widow(er).
Source: IRS Publication 2011 1040 Instructions.

TABLE 20-1
Portion of Income Tax Table—*Continued*

2011 Tax Table–*Continued*

If line 43 (taxable income) is—		And you are—				If line 43 (taxable income) is—		And you are—				If line 43 (taxable income) is—		And you are—			
At least	But less than	Single	Married filing jointly *	Married filing separately	Head of a household	At least	But less than	Single	Married filing jointly *	Married filing separately	Head of a household	At least	But less than	Single	Married filing jointly *	Married filing separately	Head of a household
		Your tax is—						Your tax is—						Your tax is—			
41,000						**44,000**						**47,000**					
41,000	41,050	6,381	5,304	6,381	5,546	44,000	44,050	7,131	5,754	7,131	5,996	47,000	47,050	7,881	6,204	7,881	6,524
41,050	41,100	6,394	5,311	6,394	5,554	44,050	44,100	7,144	5,761	7,144	6,004	47,050	47,100	7,894	6,211	7,894	6,536
41,100	41,150	6,406	5,319	6,406	5,561	44,100	44,150	7,156	5,769	7,156	6,011	47,100	47,150	7,906	6,219	7,906	6,549
41,150	41,200	6,419	5,326	6,419	5,569	44,150	44,200	7,169	5,776	7,169	6,019	47,150	47,200	7,919	6,226	7,919	6,561
41,200	41,250	6,431	5,334	6,431	5,576	44,200	44,250	7,181	5,784	7,181	6,026	47,200	47,250	7,931	6,234	7,931	6,574
41,250	41,300	6,444	5,341	6,444	5,584	44,250	44,300	7,194	5,791	7,194	6,034	47,250	47,300	7,944	6,241	7,944	6,586
41,300	41,350	6,456	5,349	6,456	5,591	44,300	44,350	7,206	5,799	7,206	6,041	47,300	47,350	7,956	6,249	7,956	6,599
41,350	41,400	6,469	5,356	6,469	5,599	44,350	44,400	7,219	5,806	7,219	6,049	47,350	47,400	7,969	6,256	7,969	6,611
41,400	41,450	6,481	5,364	6,481	5,606	44,400	44,450	7,231	5,814	7,231	6,056	47,400	47,450	7,981	6,264	7,981	6,624
41,450	41,500	6,494	5,371	6,494	5,614	44,450	44,500	7,244	5,821	7,244	6,064	47,450	47,500	7,994	6,271	7,994	6,636
41,500	41,550	6,506	5,379	6,506	5,621	44,500	44,550	7,256	5,829	7,256	6,071	47,500	47,550	8,006	6,279	8,006	6,649
41,550	41,600	6,519	5,386	6,519	5,629	44,550	44,600	7,269	5,836	7,269	6,079	47,550	47,600	8,019	6,286	8,019	6,661
41,600	41,650	6,531	5,394	6,531	5,636	44,600	44,650	7,281	5,844	7,281	6,086	47,600	47,650	8,031	6,294	8,031	6,674
41,650	41,700	6,544	5,401	6,544	5,644	44,650	44,700	7,294	5,851	7,294	6,094	47,650	47,700	8,044	6,301	8,044	6,686
41,700	41,750	6,556	5,409	6,556	5,651	44,700	44,750	7,306	5,859	7,306	6,101	47,700	47,750	8,056	6,309	8,056	6,699
41,750	41,800	6,569	5,416	6,569	5,659	44,750	44,800	7,319	5,866	7,319	6,109	47,750	47,800	8,069	6,316	8,069	6,711
41,800	41,850	6,581	5,424	6,581	5,666	44,800	44,850	7,331	5,874	7,331	6,116	47,800	47,850	8,081	6,324	8,081	6,724
41,850	41,900	6,594	5,431	6,594	5,674	44,850	44,900	7,344	5,881	7,344	6,124	47,850	47,900	8,094	6,331	8,094	6,736
41,900	41,950	6,606	5,439	6,606	5,681	44,900	44,950	7,356	5,889	7,356	6,131	47,900	47,950	8,106	6,339	8,106	6,749
41,950	42,000	6,619	5,446	6,619	5,689	44,950	45,000	7,369	5,896	7,369	6,139	47,950	48,000	8,119	6,346	8,119	6,761
42,000						**45,000**						**48,000**					
42,000	42,050	6,631	5,454	6,631	5,696	45,000	45,050	7,381	5,904	7,381	6,146	48,000	48,050	8,131	6,354	8,131	6,774
42,050	42,100	6,644	5,461	6,644	5,704	45,050	45,100	7,394	5,911	7,394	6,154	48,050	48,100	8,144	6,361	8,144	6,786
42,100	42,150	6,656	5,469	6,656	5,711	45,100	45,150	7,406	5,919	7,406	6,161	48,100	48,150	8,156	6,369	8,156	6,799
42,150	42,200	6,669	5,476	6,669	5,719	45,150	45,200	7,419	5,926	7,419	6,169	48,150	48,200	8,169	6,376	8,169	6,811
42,200	42,250	6,681	5,484	6,681	5,726	45,200	45,250	7,431	5,934	7,431	6,176	48,200	48,250	8,181	6,384	8,181	6,824
42,250	42,300	6,694	5,491	6,694	5,734	45,250	45,300	7,444	5,941	7,444	6,184	48,250	48,300	8,194	6,391	8,194	6,836
42,300	42,350	6,706	5,499	6,706	5,741	45,300	45,350	7,456	5,949	7,456	6,191	48,300	48,350	8,206	6,399	8,206	6,849
42,350	42,400	6,719	5,506	6,719	5,749	45,350	45,400	7,469	5,956	7,469	6,199	48,350	48,400	8,219	6,406	8,219	6,861
42,400	42,450	6,731	5,514	6,731	5,756	45,400	45,450	7,481	5,964	7,481	6,206	48,400	48,450	8,231	6,414	8,231	6,874
42,450	42,500	6,744	5,521	6,744	5,764	45,450	45,500	7,494	5,971	7,494	6,214	48,450	48,500	8,244	6,421	8,244	6,886
42,500	42,550	6,756	5,529	6,756	5,771	45,500	45,550	7,506	5,979	7,506	6,221	48,500	48,550	8,256	6,429	8,256	6,899
42,550	42,600	6,769	5,536	6,769	5,779	45,550	45,600	7,519	5,986	7,519	6,229	48,550	48,600	8,269	6,436	8,269	6,911
42,600	42,650	6,781	5,544	6,781	5,786	45,600	45,650	7,531	5,994	7,531	6,236	48,600	48,650	8,281	6,444	8,281	6,924
42,650	42,700	6,794	5,551	6,794	5,794	45,650	45,700	7,544	6,001	7,544	6,244	48,650	48,700	8,294	6,451	8,294	6,936
42,700	42,750	6,806	5,559	6,806	5,801	45,700	45,750	7,556	6,009	7,556	6,251	48,700	48,750	8,306	6,459	8,306	6,949
42,750	42,800	6,819	5,566	6,819	5,809	45,750	45,800	7,569	6,016	7,569	6,259	48,750	48,800	8,319	6,466	8,319	6,961
42,800	42,850	6,831	5,574	6,831	5,816	45,800	45,850	7,581	6,024	7,581	6,266	48,800	48,850	8,331	6,474	8,331	6,974
42,850	42,900	6,844	5,581	6,844	5,824	45,850	45,900	7,594	6,031	7,594	6,274	48,850	48,900	8,344	6,481	8,344	6,986
42,900	42,950	6,856	5,589	6,856	5,831	45,900	45,950	7,606	6,039	7,606	6,281	48,900	48,950	8,356	6,489	8,356	6,999
42,950	43,000	6,869	5,596	6,869	5,839	45,950	46,000	7,619	6,046	7,619	6,289	48,950	49,000	8,369	6,496	8,369	7,011
43,000						**46,000**						**49,000**					
43,000	43,050	6,881	5,604	6,881	5,846	46,000	46,050	7,631	6,054	7,631	6,296	49,000	49,050	8,381	6,504	8,381	7,024
43,050	43,100	6,894	5,611	6,894	5,854	46,050	46,100	7,644	6,061	7,644	6,304	49,050	49,100	8,394	6,511	8,394	7,036
43,100	43,150	6,906	5,619	6,906	5,861	46,100	46,150	7,656	6,069	7,656	6,311	49,100	49,150	8,406	6,519	8,406	7,049
43,150	43,200	6,919	5,626	6,919	5,869	46,150	46,200	7,669	6,076	7,669	6,319	49,150	49,200	8,419	6,526	8,419	7,061
43,200	43,250	6,931	5,634	6,931	5,876	46,200	46,250	7,681	6,084	7,681	6,326	49,200	49,250	8,431	6,534	8,431	7,074
43,250	43,300	6,944	5,641	6,944	5,884	46,250	46,300	7,694	6,091	7,694	6,336	49,250	49,300	8,444	6,541	8,444	7,086
43,300	43,350	6,956	5,649	6,956	5,891	46,300	46,350	7,706	6,099	7,706	6,349	49,300	49,350	8,456	6,549	8,456	7,099
43,350	43,400	6,969	5,656	6,969	5,899	46,350	46,400	7,719	6,106	7,719	6,361	49,350	49,400	8,469	6,556	8,469	7,111
43,400	43,450	6,981	5,664	6,981	5,906	46,400	46,450	7,731	6,114	7,731	6,374	49,400	49,450	8,481	6,564	8,481	7,124
43,450	43,500	6,994	5,671	6,994	5,914	46,450	46,500	7,744	6,121	7,744	6,386	49,450	49,500	8,494	6,571	8,494	7,136
43,500	43,550	7,006	5,679	7,006	5,921	46,500	46,550	7,756	6,129	7,756	6,399	49,500	49,550	8,506	6,579	8,506	7,149
43,550	43,600	7,019	5,686	7,019	5,929	46,550	46,600	7,769	6,136	7,769	6,411	49,550	49,600	8,519	6,586	8,519	7,161
43,600	43,650	7,031	5,694	7,031	5,936	46,600	46,650	7,781	6,144	7,781	6,424	49,600	49,650	8,531	6,594	8,531	7,174
43,650	43,700	7,044	5,701	7,044	5,944	46,650	46,700	7,794	6,151	7,794	6,436	49,650	49,700	8,544	6,601	8,544	7,186
43,700	43,750	7,056	5,709	7,056	5,951	46,700	46,750	7,806	6,159	7,806	6,449	49,700	49,750	8,556	6,609	8,556	7,199
43,750	43,800	7,069	5,716	7,069	5,959	46,750	46,800	7,819	6,166	7,819	6,461	49,750	49,800	8,569	6,616	8,569	7,211
43,800	43,850	7,081	5,724	7,081	5,966	46,800	46,850	7,831	6,174	7,831	6,474	49,800	49,850	8,581	6,624	8,581	7,224
43,850	43,900	7,094	5,731	7,094	5,974	46,850	46,900	7,844	6,181	7,844	6,486	49,850	49,900	8,594	6,631	8,594	7,236
43,900	43,950	7,106	5,739	7,106	5,981	46,900	46,950	7,856	6,189	7,856	6,499	49,900	49,950	8,606	6,639	8,606	7,249
43,950	44,000	7,119	5,746	7,119	5,989	46,950	47,000	7,869	6,196	7,869	6,511	49,950	50,000	8,619	6,646	8,619	7,261

*This column must also be used by a qualifying widow(er).

Source: IRS Publication 2011 1040 Instructions.

TABLE 20-1
Portion of Income Tax Table—Continued

2011 Tax Table–Continued

If line 43 (taxable income) is—		And you are—			
At least	But less than	Single	Married filing jointly *	Married filing separately	Head of a household
		Your tax is—			

50,000

At least	But less than	Single	MFJ *	MFS	HoH
50,000	50,050	8,631	6,654	8,631	7,274
50,050	50,100	8,644	6,661	8,644	7,286
50,100	50,150	8,656	6,669	8,656	7,299
50,150	50,200	8,669	6,676	8,669	7,311
50,200	50,250	8,681	6,684	8,681	7,324
50,250	50,300	8,694	6,691	8,694	7,336
50,300	50,350	8,706	6,699	8,706	7,349
50,350	50,400	8,719	6,706	8,719	7,361
50,400	50,450	8,731	6,714	8,731	7,374
50,450	50,500	8,744	6,721	8,744	7,386
50,500	50,550	8,756	6,729	8,756	7,399
50,550	50,600	8,769	6,736	8,769	7,411
50,600	50,650	8,781	6,744	8,781	7,424
50,650	50,700	8,794	6,751	8,794	7,436
50,700	50,750	8,806	6,759	8,806	7,449
50,750	50,800	8,819	6,766	8,819	7,461
50,800	50,850	8,831	6,774	8,831	7,474
50,850	50,900	8,844	6,781	8,844	7,486
50,900	50,950	8,856	6,789	8,856	7,499
50,950	51,000	8,869	6,796	8,869	7,511

51,000

At least	But less than	Single	MFJ *	MFS	HoH
51,000	51,050	8,881	6,804	8,881	7,524
51,050	51,100	8,894	6,811	8,894	7,536
51,100	51,150	8,906	6,819	8,906	7,549
51,150	51,200	8,919	6,826	8,919	7,561
51,200	51,250	8,931	6,834	8,931	7,574
51,250	51,300	8,944	6,841	8,944	7,586
51,300	51,350	8,956	6,849	8,956	7,599
51,350	51,400	8,969	6,856	8,969	7,611
51,400	51,450	8,981	6,864	8,981	7,624
51,450	51,500	8,994	6,871	8,994	7,636
51,500	51,550	9,006	6,879	9,006	7,649
51,550	51,600	9,019	6,886	9,019	7,661
51,600	51,650	9,031	6,894	9,031	7,674
51,650	51,700	9,044	6,901	9,044	7,686
51,700	51,750	9,056	6,909	9,056	7,699
51,750	51,800	9,069	6,916	9,069	7,711
51,800	51,850	9,081	6,924	9,081	7,724
51,850	51,900	9,094	6,931	9,094	7,736
51,900	51,950	9,106	6,939	9,106	7,749
51,950	52,000	9,119	6,946	9,119	7,761

52,000

At least	But less than	Single	MFJ *	MFS	HoH
52,000	52,050	9,131	6,954	9,131	7,774
52,050	52,100	9,144	6,961	9,144	7,786
52,100	52,150	9,156	6,969	9,156	7,799
52,150	52,200	9,169	6,976	9,169	7,811
52,200	52,250	9,181	6,984	9,181	7,824
52,250	52,300	9,194	6,991	9,194	7,836
52,300	52,350	9,206	6,999	9,206	7,849
52,350	52,400	9,219	7,006	9,219	7,861
52,400	52,450	9,231	7,014	9,231	7,874
52,450	52,500	9,244	7,021	9,244	7,886
52,500	52,550	9,256	7,029	9,256	7,899
52,550	52,600	9,269	7,036	9,269	7,911
52,600	52,650	9,281	7,044	9,281	7,924
52,650	52,700	9,294	7,051	9,294	7,936
52,700	52,750	9,306	7,059	9,306	7,949
52,750	52,800	9,319	7,066	9,319	7,961
52,800	52,850	9,331	7,074	9,331	7,974
52,850	52,900	9,344	7,081	9,344	7,986
52,900	52,950	9,356	7,089	9,356	7,999
52,950	53,000	9,369	7,096	9,369	8,011

53,000

At least	But less than	Single	MFJ *	MFS	HoH
53,000	53,050	9,381	7,104	9,381	8,024
53,050	53,100	9,394	7,111	9,394	8,036
53,100	53,150	9,406	7,119	9,406	8,049
53,150	53,200	9,419	7,126	9,419	8,061
53,200	53,250	9,431	7,134	9,431	8,074
53,250	53,300	9,444	7,141	9,444	8,086
53,300	53,350	9,456	7,149	9,456	8,099
53,350	53,400	9,469	7,156	9,469	8,111
53,400	53,450	9,481	7,164	9,481	8,124
53,450	53,500	9,494	7,171	9,494	8,136
53,500	53,550	9,506	7,179	9,506	8,149
53,550	53,600	9,519	7,186	9,519	8,161
53,600	53,650	9,531	7,194	9,531	8,174
53,650	53,700	9,544	7,201	9,544	8,186
53,700	53,750	9,556	7,209	9,556	8,199
53,750	53,800	9,569	7,216	9,569	8,211
53,800	53,850	9,581	7,224	9,581	8,224
53,850	53,900	9,594	7,231	9,594	8,236
53,900	53,950	9,606	7,239	9,606	8,249
53,950	54,000	9,619	7,246	9,619	8,261

54,000

At least	But less than	Single	MFJ *	MFS	HoH
54,000	54,050	9,631	7,254	9,631	8,274
54,050	54,100	9,644	7,261	9,644	8,286
54,100	54,150	9,656	7,269	9,656	8,299
54,150	54,200	9,669	7,276	9,669	8,311
54,200	54,250	9,681	7,284	9,681	8,324
54,250	54,300	9,694	7,291	9,694	8,336
54,300	54,350	9,706	7,299	9,706	8,349
54,350	54,400	9,719	7,306	9,719	8,361
54,400	54,450	9,731	7,314	9,731	8,374
54,450	54,500	9,744	7,321	9,744	8,386
54,500	54,550	9,756	7,329	9,756	8,399
54,550	54,600	9,769	7,336	9,769	8,411
54,600	54,650	9,781	7,344	9,781	8,424
54,650	54,700	9,794	7,351	9,794	8,436
54,700	54,750	9,806	7,359	9,806	8,449
54,750	54,800	9,819	7,366	9,819	8,461
54,800	54,850	9,831	7,374	9,831	8,474
54,850	54,900	9,844	7,381	9,844	8,486
54,900	54,950	9,856	7,389	9,856	8,499
54,950	55,000	9,869	7,396	9,869	8,511

55,000

At least	But less than	Single	MFJ *	MFS	HoH
55,000	55,050	9,881	7,404	9,881	8,524
55,050	55,100	9,894	7,411	9,894	8,536
55,100	55,150	9,906	7,419	9,906	8,549
55,150	55,200	9,919	7,426	9,919	8,561
55,200	55,250	9,931	7,434	9,931	8,574
55,250	55,300	9,944	7,441	9,944	8,586
55,300	55,350	9,956	7,449	9,956	8,599
55,350	55,400	9,969	7,456	9,969	8,611
55,400	55,450	9,981	7,464	9,981	8,624
55,450	55,500	9,994	7,471	9,994	8,636
55,500	55,550	10,006	7,479	10,006	8,649
55,550	55,600	10,019	7,486	10,019	8,661
55,600	55,650	10,031	7,494	10,031	8,674
55,650	55,700	10,044	7,501	10,044	8,686
55,700	55,750	10,056	7,509	10,056	8,699
55,750	55,800	10,069	7,516	10,069	8,711
55,800	55,850	10,081	7,524	10,081	8,724
55,850	55,900	10,094	7,531	10,094	8,736
55,900	55,950	10,106	7,539	10,106	8,749
55,950	56,000	10,119	7,546	10,119	8,761

56,000

At least	But less than	Single	MFJ *	MFS	HoH
56,000	56,050	10,131	7,554	10,131	8,774
56,050	56,100	10,144	7,561	10,144	8,786
56,100	56,150	10,156	7,569	10,156	8,799
56,150	56,200	10,169	7,576	10,169	8,811
56,200	56,250	10,181	7,584	10,181	8,824
56,250	56,300	10,194	7,591	10,194	8,836
56,300	56,350	10,206	7,599	10,206	8,849
56,350	56,400	10,219	7,606	10,219	8,861
56,400	56,450	10,231	7,614	10,231	8,874
56,450	56,500	10,244	7,621	10,244	8,886
56,500	56,550	10,256	7,629	10,256	8,899
56,550	56,600	10,269	7,636	10,269	8,911
56,600	56,650	10,281	7,644	10,281	8,924
56,650	56,700	10,294	7,651	10,294	8,936
56,700	56,750	10,306	7,659	10,306	8,949
56,750	56,800	10,319	7,666	10,319	8,961
56,800	56,850	10,331	7,674	10,331	8,974
56,850	56,900	10,344	7,681	10,344	8,986
56,900	56,950	10,356	7,689	10,356	8,999
56,950	57,000	10,369	7,696	10,369	9,011

57,000

At least	But less than	Single	MFJ *	MFS	HoH
57,000	57,050	10,381	7,704	10,381	9,024
57,050	57,100	10,394	7,711	10,394	9,036
57,100	57,150	10,406	7,719	10,406	9,049
57,150	57,200	10,419	7,726	10,419	9,061
57,200	57,250	10,431	7,734	10,431	9,074
57,250	57,300	10,444	7,741	10,444	9,086
57,300	57,350	10,456	7,749	10,456	9,099
57,350	57,400	10,469	7,756	10,469	9,111
57,400	57,450	10,481	7,764	10,481	9,124
57,450	57,500	10,494	7,771	10,494	9,136
57,500	57,550	10,506	7,779	10,506	9,149
57,550	57,600	10,519	7,786	10,519	9,161
57,600	57,650	10,531	7,794	10,531	9,174
57,650	57,700	10,544	7,801	10,544	9,186
57,700	57,750	10,556	7,809	10,556	9,199
57,750	57,800	10,569	7,816	10,569	9,211
57,800	57,850	10,581	7,824	10,581	9,224
57,850	57,900	10,594	7,831	10,594	9,236
57,900	57,950	10,606	7,839	10,606	9,249
57,950	58,000	10,619	7,846	10,619	9,261

58,000

At least	But less than	Single	MFJ *	MFS	HoH
58,000	58,050	10,631	7,854	10,631	9,274
58,050	58,100	10,644	7,861	10,644	9,286
58,100	58,150	10,656	7,869	10,656	9,299
58,150	58,200	10,669	7,876	10,669	9,311
58,200	58,250	10,681	7,884	10,681	9,324
58,250	58,300	10,694	7,891	10,694	9,336
58,300	58,350	10,706	7,899	10,706	9,349
58,350	58,400	10,719	7,906	10,719	9,361
58,400	58,450	10,731	7,914	10,731	9,374
58,450	58,500	10,744	7,921	10,744	9,386
58,500	58,550	10,756	7,929	10,756	9,399
58,550	58,600	10,769	7,936	10,769	9,411
58,600	58,650	10,781	7,944	10,781	9,424
58,650	58,700	10,794	7,951	10,794	9,436
58,700	58,750	10,806	7,959	10,806	9,449
58,750	58,800	10,819	7,966	10,819	9,461
58,800	58,850	10,831	7,974	10,831	9,474
58,850	58,900	10,844	7,981	10,844	9,486
58,900	58,950	10,856	7,989	10,856	9,499
58,950	59,000	10,869	7,996	10,869	9,511

*This column must also be used by a qualifying widow(er).

Source: IRS Publication 2011 1040 Instructions.

3 Use the tax computation worksheet to calculate income tax.

Tax computation worksheet: directions for calculating the tax on taxable incomes of $100,000 or more.

The **tax computation worksheet** is used to compute tax on taxable incomes of $100,000 *or more*. There are separate sections for single taxpayers, heads of households, and married taxpayers (and certain qualifying widows and widowers).

TABLE 20-2
2011 Tax Computation Worksheet

2011 Tax Computation Worksheet—Line 44

 See the instructions for line 44 to see if you must use the worksheet below to figure your tax.

Note. If you are required to use this worksheet to figure the tax on an amount from another form or worksheet, such as the Qualified Dividends and Capital Gain Tax Worksheet, the Schedule D Tax Worksheet, Schedule J, Form 8615, or the Foreign Earned Income Tax Worksheet, enter the amount from that form or worksheet in column (a) of the row that applies to the amount you are looking up. Enter the result on the appropriate line of the form or worksheet that you are completing.

Section A—Use if your filing status is **Single.** Complete the row below that applies to you.

Taxable income. If line 43 is—	(a) Enter the amount from line 43	(b) Multiplication amount	(c) Multiply (a) by (b)	(d) Subtraction amount	Tax. Subtract (d) from (c). Enter the result here and on Form 1040, line 44
At least $100,000 but not over $174,400	$	× 28% (.28)	$	$ 6,383.00	$
Over $174,400 but not over $379,150	$	× 33% (.33)	$	$ 15,103.00	$
Over $379,150	$	× 35% (.35)	$	$22,686.00	$

Section B—Use if your filing status is **Married filing jointly** or **Qualifying widow(er).** Complete the row below that applies to you.

Taxable income. If line 43 is—	(a) Enter the amount from line 43	(b) Multiplication amount	(c) Multiply (a) by (b)	(d) Subtraction amount	Tax. Subtract (d) from (c). Enter the result here and on Form 1040, line 44
At least $100,000 but not over $139,350	$	× 25% (.25)	$	$ 7,750.00	$
Over $139,350 but not over $212,300	$	× 28% (.28)	$	$ 11,930.50	$
Over $212,300 but not over $379,150	$	× 33% (.33)	$	$ 22,545.50	$
Over $379,150	$	× 35% (.35)	$	$ 30,128.50	$

Section C—Use if your filing status is **Married filing separately.** Complete the row below that applies to you.

Taxable income. If line 43 is—	(a) Enter the amount from line 43	(b) Multiplication amount	(c) Multiply (a) by (b)	(d) Subtraction amount	Tax. Subtract (d) from (c). Enter the result here and on Form 1040, line 44
At least $100,000 but not over $106,150	$	× 28% (.28)	$	$ 5,965.25	$
Over $106,150 but not over $189,575	$	× 33% (.33)	$	$ 11,272.75	$
Over $189,575	$	× 35% (.35)	$	$ 15,064.25	$

Section D—Use if your filing status is **Head of household.** Complete the row below that applies to you.

Taxable income. If line 43 is—	(a) Enter the amount from line 43	(b) Multiplication amount	(c) Multiply (a) by (b)	(d) Subtraction amount	Tax. Subtract (d) from (c). Enter the result here and on Form 1040, line 44
At least $100,000 but not over $119,400	$	× 25% (.25)	$	$ 5,232.50	$
Over $119,400 but not over $193,350	$	× 28% (.28)	$	$ 8,814.50	$
Over $193,350 but not over $379,150	$	× 33% (.33)	$	$ 18,482.00	$
Over $379,150	$	× 35% (.35)	$	$ 26,065.00	$

Need more information or forms? Visit IRS.gov.

An individual's income is taxed at different rates depending on how much of his or her income falls into each of various income brackets. Table 20-2 shows the tax rates for 2011.

HOW TO   Use the tax computation worksheet to calculate income tax

1. Locate the correct section according to filing status.
2. Locate the range in which the taxable income falls.
3. Enter the taxable income (line 43 of Form 1040) on the appropriate line of Column a.
4. Multiply the amount in Column a by the amount in Column b and enter the result in Column c.
5. Subtract the amount in Column d from the amount in Column c and enter the result in the Tax column. This is the amount that will be entered on line 44 on Form 1040.

EXAMPLE 3   Use Table 20-2 to find the tax on a taxable income of (a) $112,418 for a married taxpayer filing jointly; (b) $148,382 for a married taxpayer filing separately.

(a) The taxpayer would use Section B. Section B shows that the taxable income falls in the range. "At least $100,000 but not over $139,350."

Column a	Column b	Column c	Column d	Tax
$112,418	× 25% (.25)	$28,104.50	$7,750.00	$20,354.50

112418 $\boxed{\times}$ .25 $\boxed{-}$ 7750 $\boxed{=}$ ⟹ 20354.5

The tax is $20,354.50.

(b) The taxpayer is married filing separately, so use Section C. The taxable income, $148,382, falls in the range. "Over $106,150 but not over $189,575."

Column a	Column b	Column c	Column d	Tax
$148,382	× 33% (.33)	$48,966.06	$11,272.75	$37,693.31

148382 $\boxed{\times}$ .33 $\boxed{-}$ 11272.75 $\boxed{=}$ ⟹ 37693.31

The tax is $37,693.31.

Tax credit: an amount that is subtracted from the *tax owed*, in contrast to a deduction, which is subtracted from the gross income.

Tax refund: the amount of income tax a taxpayer gets back when filing an income tax return. It is the difference in the amount of tax the taxpayer has paid during the year and the amount of tax owed for a tax year.

Tax owed: the amount of income tax a taxpayer must pay when filing an income tax return. It is the difference in the amount of tax already paid and the total amount of tax that should be paid.

Electronic filing: a paperless way to file income tax with the IRS. The tax forms are submitted electronically to the IRS.

Taxpayers can take a **tax credit** in certain cases. A tax credit is an amount that is subtracted from the amount of tax owed rather than the gross income. The subtraction is made after the amount of tax owed has been calculated.

If a taxpayer pays in more income tax during the year than is owed when the income tax is filed, the difference is a **tax refund.** If the taxpayer has not paid as much income tax during the year as is owed when the income tax is filed, the taxpayer must pay the difference, which is called **tax owed.**

Taxpayers may file their income tax return electronically, known as **electronic filing.** The IRS web site, www.irs.gov/efile, provides all the details and latest information. Taxpayers who elect to *e-file* receive refunds in half the time as paper filers. The IRS provides electronic proof of receipt of all electronically filed tax returns within 48 hours after the IRS receives the return. Persons who file electronically can also authorize an electronic funds withdrawal from a bank account or pay by credit card. Computer software programs such as TurboTax can be used to calculate income tax and make electronic filing easier than ever before.

Taxpayers can also use TeleTax to receive recorded tax information about many tax return preparation topics. This service is available 24 hours a day, seven days a week. The toll-free number is 1-800-829-4477.

STOP AND CHECK

See Example 3.

1. Find the tax on a taxable income of $152,783 for a married taxpayer filing jointly.

2. Find the tax on a taxable income of $172,500 for a married taxpayer filing separately.

3. What is the tax on a taxable income of $117,832 for a single taxpayer?

4. Rodney Carney has a taxable income of $456,987 and his filing status is head of household. What is his tax?

20-3 SECTION EXERCISES

SKILL BUILDERS

Find the taxable income. Use $3,700 for each exemption. See Example 1.

Use Table 20-1 to find the federal income tax. See Example 2.

	Number of exemptions	Adjusted gross income	Itemized deductions		Taxable income	Filing status
1.	4	$49,071	$12,019	5.	$40,317	Single
2.	1	$138,503	$32,167	6.	$32,417	Married, filing jointly
3.	5	$167,413	$27,534	7.	$45,307	Married, filing separately
4.	2	$75,013	$16,532	8.	$49,553	Head of household

Use Table 20-2 to find the federal income tax. See Example 3.

	Taxable income	Filing status
9.	$179,518	Single

	Taxable income	Filing status
10.	$198,846	Married, filing jointly

11. Find the taxable income for a family of six (husband, wife, four children) whose adjusted gross income is $43,873 and itemized deductions are $9,582. (One exemption = $3,700.)

12. Find the taxable income for a single person whose adjusted gross income is $28,932 and itemized deductions are $4,915. (One exemption = $3,700.)

13. Canty O'Neal has an adjusted gross income of $68,917 and itemized deductions that total $18,473. Canty can claim three exemptions. What is her taxable income? (One exemption = $3,700.)

14. Noel Womack is single and calculates his taxable income to be $30,175. How much tax does he owe? Use Table 20-1.

15. Tommy and Michelle Fernandez have a combined taxable income of $23,300. How much tax should they pay if they file jointly? Use Table 20-1.

16. Vladimir Bozin is a head of household and has a taxable income of $26,873. Use Table 20-1 to find his tax.

17. Donna Shroyer is single and has a taxable income of $29,897. If her W-2 form shows that she has already paid $5,647 in income taxes for the year, use Table 20-1 to determine if she is due a refund or if she must pay more taxes. How much is the refund or how much more must she pay?

18. Paul Smith is married and filing his tax jointly with his wife, Anna. Their combined taxable income is $167,983. Use the tax computation worksheet (Table 20-2) to calculate the tax they must pay.

19. Dr. Steven Katz is single and has a taxable income of $160,842. Use the tax computation worksheet (Table 20-2) to calculate his income tax liability.

20. Jack Falcinelli is filing his tax as a head of household. His taxable income is $133,896 and his W-2 form shows he has already paid $34,197.00. Calculate his tax refund or payment.

Learning Outcomes

What to Remember with Examples

Section 20-1

1 Use the percent method to find the sales tax and excise tax. (p. 706)

1. Write the given percent as a decimal.
2. Find the sales tax or excise tax:

$$\text{Tax} = \text{purchase price} \times \text{tax rate}$$

where tax rate = tax per $1.00 of purchase price or a percent of the purchase price.

Use the percent method to find the sales tax on a $685 fax machine taxed at 6.6%.

$$6.6\% = 0.066$$
$$\text{Tax} = \$685(0.066)$$
$$= \$45.21$$

2 Find the marked price and the sales tax from the total price. (p. 707)

1. Find the marked price:
   (a) Write the sales tax rate as a decimal equivalent.
   (b) Add 1 to the decimal equivalent of the sales tax rate from step 1a.
   (c) Divide the total price by the sum from step 1b.

$$\text{Marked price} = \frac{\text{total price}}{1 + \text{sales tax rate (in decimal form)}}$$

2. Find the sales tax:

$$\text{Sales tax} = \text{total price} - \text{marked price}$$

Homer Ray sells handcrafted furniture at prices that include the state sales tax. One inlaid table sold for $3,950. Calculate the marked price and the sales tax Homer must send to the state if the tax rate is 8%.

$$\text{Marked price} = \frac{\text{total price}}{1 + \text{sales tax rate}}$$
$$= \frac{\$3,950}{1 + 0.08}$$
$$= \frac{\$3,950}{1.08}$$
$$= \$3,657.41$$

$$\text{Sales tax} = \text{total price} - \text{marked price}$$
$$= \$3,950 - \$3,657.41$$
$$= \$292.59$$

or

$$\$3,657.41(0.08)$$
$$= \$292.59$$

Section 20-2

1 Find the assessed value. (p. 710)

1. Write the assessment rate as the decimal equivalent of the percent.
2. Find the assessed value:

$$\text{Assessed value} = \text{market value} \times \text{assessment rate}$$

Find the assessed value of a home with a market value of $106,000 if the assessed value is 30% of the market value.

$$30\% = 0.3$$
$$\$106,000(0.3) = \$31,800$$

2 Calculate property tax. (p. 710)

1. Express the given property tax rate as tax per $1.00 of assessed value:
   (a) If the given rate is a percent of assessed value, write the percent in decimal form:

$$\text{Tax per } \$1.00 = \text{decimal form of the percent of assessed value}$$

   (b) If the given rate is tax per $100 of assessed value, divide the tax on $100 by $100:

$$\text{Tax per } \$1.00 = \frac{\text{tax on } \$100}{\$100}$$

(c) If the given rate is tax per $1,000 of assessed value, divide the tax on $1,000 by $1,000:

$$\text{Tax per } \$1.00 = \frac{\text{tax on } \$1,000}{\$1,000}$$

(d) If the given rate is a number of mills per $1.00 of assessed value, divide the number of mills by 1,000:

$$\text{Tax per } \$1.00 = \frac{\text{mills per } \$1.00}{\$1,000}$$

2. Find the property tax:

$$\text{Property tax} = \text{assessed value} \times \text{property tax rate per } \$1.00$$

Find the property tax on a farm with an assessed value of $430,000 for each given tax rate.

The tax rate is 8.05% of the assessed value:

$$\begin{aligned} \text{Property tax} &= \$430,000(0.0805) \\ &= \$34,615 \end{aligned}$$

The tax rate is $8.05 per $100 of assessed value:

$$\text{Property tax} = \$430,000\left(\frac{\$8.05}{\$100}\right) = \$34,615$$

The tax rate is $80.50 per $1,000 of assessed value:

$$\text{Property tax} = \$430,000\left(\frac{\$80.50}{\$1,000}\right) = \$34,615$$

The tax rate is 80.5 mills per $1.00 of assessed value:

$$80.5 \text{ mills} = \frac{80.5}{1,000}$$

$$\text{Property tax} = \$430,000\left(\frac{80.5}{1,000}\right) = \$34,615$$

3 Determine the property tax rate. (p. 712)

1. Select the appropriate formula according to the desired tax rate type.

$$\text{Tax per } \$1.00 \text{ of assessed value} = \frac{\text{total estimated budget}}{\text{total assessed property value}}$$

$$\text{Tax per } \$100 \text{ of assessed value} = \frac{\text{total estimated budget}}{\text{total assessed property value}} \times \$100$$

$$\text{Tax per } \$1,000 \text{ of assessed value} = \frac{\text{total estimated budget}}{\text{total assessed property value}} \times \$1,000$$

$$\text{Tax, in mills, per } \$1.00 \text{ of assessed value} = \frac{\text{total estimated budget}}{\text{total assessed property value}} \times 1,000$$

2. Make calculations using the selected formula. Always round up.

Find the tax expressed as tax per $1,000 of assessed value for Piperton if $15,872,000 is anticipated for expenses and the town has property assessed at $651,375,000.

$$\begin{aligned} \text{Tax per } \$1,000 \text{ of assessed value} &= \left(\frac{\$15,872,000}{\$651,375,000}\right)(\$1,000) \\ &= \$24.36691614 = \$24.37 \end{aligned}$$

Section 20-3

1 Find taxable income. (p. 716)

1. Find the adjusted gross income:

$$\text{Adjusted gross income} = \text{total income} - \text{allowable expenses and deductions}$$

2. Total the deductions or choose the standard deduction and total the exemptions.
3. Find the taxable income:

$$\text{Taxable income} = \text{adjusted gross income} - \text{itemized or standard deductions} - \text{exemptions}$$

Toni Wilson and her spouse earned $53,950 gross income and had itemized deductions of $10,700. They have a seven-year-old daughter. Find the taxable income, using $3,700 for each exemption.

$$\text{Taxable income} = \$53,950 - \$10,700 - (3)(\$3,700)$$
$$= \$53,950 - \$10,700 - \$11,100 = \$32,150$$

2 Use the tax tables to calculate income tax. (p. 717)

1. Locate the taxable income under the column headed "If line 43 (taxable income) is—."
2. Move across to the column headed "And you are—," which has the four filing status categories listed under it. The tax owed appears under the appropriate category.

Use Table 20-1 to find Toni's tax (previous example) if she and her husband file jointly.

Find the range of $32,150–$32,200. Move across to the tax in the column "Married filing jointly," which is $3,976.

3 Use the tax computation worksheet to calculate income tax. (p. 722)

1. Locate the correct schedule according to filing status.
2. Locate the range in which the taxable income falls.
3. Enter the taxable income (line 43 of Form 1040) on the appropriate line of Column a.
4. Multiple the amount in Column a by the amount in Column b and enter the result in Column c.
5. Subtract the amount in Column d from the amount in Column c and enter the result in the Tax column. This is the amount that will be entered on line 44 on Form 1040.

Sue Wilson has a taxable income of $153,897. Her filing status is single. Find the income tax she owes.

Using Section A in Table 20-2. $153,897 falls in the range. "At least $100,000 but not over $174,400."

Column a	Column b	Column c	Column d	Tax
$153,897	$\times$ 28% (.28)	$43,091.16	$6,383.00	$36,708.16

$153897 \boxed{\times} .28 \boxed{-} 6383 \boxed{=} \Rightarrow 36708.16$

The tax is $36,708.16.

EXERCISES SET A

Calculate the sales tax on the given purchase using the given sales tax rate. (Round to the nearest cent.)

1. $237.42; 6%

2. $1,294.26; 4.5%

3. $675.93; 5%

4. Delaware has a diesel fuel excise tax rate of 22.0%. How much excise tax is paid on a diesel fuel purchase of $219.83 if the purchase is before excise tax is added?

5. The diesel fuel excise tax rate in Connecticut is 46.2%, the highest in the nation. How much excise tax is paid on diesel fuel that costs $78.47 before the excise tax is added?

Find the marked price if the given total bill includes sales tax at the given rate. (Round to the nearest cent.)

6. $27.45; 5%

7. $347.28; 4.5%

8. $87.26; 3.5%

Find the assessed value of each property using the following rates. Farm property or single-family dwellings: 25% of market value Commercial property or multifamily dwellings: 40% of market value Utilities: 50% of market value

9. Single-family dwelling with market value of $55,000

10. Grocery store with market value of $115,000

11. Power company with market value of $5,175,000

Find the property tax on the given assessed value using the given rate.

12. $37,000; 1.5% of assessed value

13. $12,500; 2% of assessed value

14. If the county tax rate is $3.74 per $100 of assessed value, find the tax on a property that is assessed at $35,000.

15. The tax rate for a city is $3.25 per $100 of assessed value. Find the tax on a property that is assessed at $125,000.

16. A home has a market value of $50,000 (assessed value = 25% of market value). Find the amount of county taxes to be paid on the home if the county tax rate is $4.00 per $100 of assessed value.

17. $37,000; $14.25 per $1,000 of assessed value

18. $172,500; $16.23 per $1,000 of assessed value

19. $87,500; $12.67 per $1,000 of assessed value

Express the mills as dollars to the nearest thousandth.

20. 63 mills

21. 72 mills

Find the tax on each property at the given assessed valuation using the given tax rate.

22. $23,275; 55 mills per $1.00 of assessed value

23. $28,750; 64 mills per $1.00 of assessed value

Complete the following table. (Express the tax on the given assessed valuation in cents or dollars and cents. Round up any remainder.)

EXCEL	Total assessed value	Total expenses	Tax on $1.00	$100	$1,000
24.	$87,460,000	$4,348,800			
25.	$528,739,000	$17,205,160			

26. Acworth expects an increase in expenses of $215,000 over the currently budgeted $1,996,801. The town must increase the tax rate or reassess property values. A reassessment would cost the town $27,500 and would increase the assessed value of property in the town to $28,500,000. The town council must make a choice based on whether the reassessed property will increase the revenue from taxes enough to cover the increase in expenses. Which should they choose if the town property currently has an assessed evaluation of $23,678,300 and the current town property tax rate is $6.83 per $100?

27. Bartlett has a property tax rate of $4.21 per $100 and expects an increase in expenses of $185,000 over the current commitment of $9,868,910. The town must increase the tax rate or reassess property values. A reassessment would cost the town $62,500 and would increase the assessed value of property in the town to $251,500,000. Should the town increase the tax rate or reassess property if the town currently has an assessed valuation of $227,768,000?

Use $3,700 for each allowed personal exemption in Exercises 28–30.

28. Find the taxable income for the Zuckmans, a family of four (husband, wife, two children), if the adjusted gross income is $34,728, and the itemized deductions are $10,246.

29. Find the taxable income for Mario Gravez, a single person whose adjusted gross income is $37,486 and whose itemized deductions are $5,412.

30. Find the taxable income for Lorenda and James Atlas, a husband and wife with no children who have an adjusted gross income of $56,000 and are filing jointly. Their total itemized deductions are $13,589.

Use Table 20-1 (pp. 718–721) to find the tax owed by taxpayers with the following taxable incomes:

31. $39,678 (single)

32. $40,876 (single)

33. $38,979 (married, filing jointly)

34. $40,987 (married, filing separately)

Use Table 20-2 (p. 722) to find the tax on the following taxable incomes:

35. $172,478 (married, filing separately)

36. $188,342 (single)

EXERCISES SET B

Calculate the sales tax on the given purchase using the given sales tax rate. (Round to the nearest cent.)

1. $523.85; 5%

2. $482.12; 6%

3. $2,998.97; 4.5%

4. Oklahoma has a gasoline excise tax rate of 16.0%. How much excise tax is paid on a gasoline purchase of $62.53 if the purchase is before excise tax is added?

5. The diesel fuel excise tax rate in Oklahoma is 13.0%. How much excise tax is paid on diesel fuel that costs $257.88 before the excise tax is added?

Find the marked price if the given total bill includes sales tax at the given rate. (Round to the nearest cent.)

6. $139.53; 6%

7. $53.92; 5%

8. $3,580.53; 7.25%

Find the assessed value of each property using the following rates: Farm property or single-family dwellings: 25% of market value; Commercial property or multifamily dwellings: 40% of market value; Utilities: 50% of market value

9. Apartment with market value of $235,000

10. Farmland with market value of $150,000

11. Thomas Richardson owns a home on 2 acres of land. The property has a market value of $215,000. What is the assessed value?

Find the property tax on the given assessed value using the given rate.

12. $45,000; 1.75% of assessed value

13. $575,000; 1.8% of assessed value

14. If the county tax rate is increased to $4.25 from $3.74 per $100 of assessed value, how much is the tax increase on a $35,000 piece of property?

15. Vicki Froehlich lives in a city where the tax rate is $21.50 per $1,000 of assessed value. Vicki's home has an assessed value of $31,820. How much city tax must Vicki pay?

16. What is the city property tax on a house assessed at $12,500 if the city tax rate is $3.06 per $100 of assessed valuation?

17. $150,000; $15.50 per $1,000 of assessed value

18. $32,250; $13.78 per $1,000 of assessed value

Express the mills as dollars to the nearest thousandth.

19. 34 mills

20. 51 mills

Find the tax on each property at the given assessed valuation using the given tax rate.

21. $12,500; 65 mills per $1.00 of assessed value

22. $52,575; 71 mills per $1.00 of assessed value

Complete the following table. (Express the tax on the given assessed valuation in cents or dollars and cents. Round up any remainder.)

Total assessed value	Total expenses	Tax on			Total assessed value	Total expenses	Tax on		
		$1.00	$100	$1,000			$1.00	$100	$1,000
23. $11,370,000	$386,450				**24.** $5,718,000	$374,740			

25. Clarksdale has a property tax rate of $17.20 per $1,000 of assessed valuation and expects an increase in expenses of $197,500 over the current commitment of $6,985,000. The city must increase the tax rate or reassess property values. A reassessment would cost the city $45,000 and would increase the assessed value of property in the city to $416,830,000. The city council must make a choice based on whether the reassessed property will increase the revenue from taxes enough to cover the increase in expenses. Which should they choose?

26. Lancaster has a property tax rate of $0.0162 per $1 of assessed property valuation and expects an increase in expenses of $85,000 over the current budget of $1,206,000. The city must increase the tax rate or reassess property values. A reassessment would cost the city $28,500 and would increase the assessed value of property in the city to $85,443,000. Should the city increase the tax rate or reassess property?

Use $3,700 for each allowed personal exemption in Exercises 27–29.

27. Find the taxable income for Sam and Delois Johns, a husband and wife without children, whose adjusted gross income is $48,378 and itemized deductions are $10,023.

28. Find the taxable income for the Shotwells, a family of three (husband, wife, one child), if their adjusted gross income is $72,376 and itemized deductions are $24,375.

29. Find the taxable income for the Thungs, a family of three (husband, wife, one child), if their adjusted gross income is $66,833 and itemized deductions are $12,583.

Use Table 20-1 (pp. 718–721) to find the tax owed by taxpayers with the following taxable incomes:

30. $36,057 (single)

31. $39,512 (single)

32. $40,095 (married, filing jointly)

33. $40,002 (head of household)

Use Table 20-2 (p. 722) to find the tax on the following taxable incomes:

34. $154,456 (married, filing jointly)

35. $161,200 (head of household)

36. $458,919 (single)

PRACTICE TEST

Find the sales tax on the given marked price using the given sales tax rate.

1. $15.17; 5%

2. $18.26; 6.25%

3. $287.52; 7.75%

4. $2.98; 6.5%

5. Kentucky has a gasoline excise tax rate of 26.4%. How much excise tax is paid on a gasoline purchase of $39.17 if the purchase is before excise tax is added?

6. The diesel fuel excise tax rate in Kentucky is 23.4%. How much excise tax is paid on diesel fuel that costs $87.89 before the excise tax is added?

What is the total price if the given sales tax rate is applied to the given marked price?

7. $187.21; 6%

8. $4.25; 5.25%

Find the marked price if the given total price includes sales tax at the given rate.

9. $18.84; 7%

10. $7.87; 6.5%

11. $52.63; 5.25%

12. A telephone bill of $84.15 is assessed state sales tax at a rate of 6%. Find the tax on the telephone bill.

13. Find the total telephone bill in Exercise 12.

14. Find the assessed value of an apartment building (assessed at 40% of the market value) if the market value is $485,298.

15. Find the tax on a business property if the assessed value of the property is $176,297 and the tax rate is $7.56 per $100 of assessed value.

16. Find the tax on a home if the assessed value is $24,375 and the tax rate is $43.97 per $1,000.

17. A property has an assessed value of $72,000. The city property tax rate for this property is $4.12 per $100 of assessed valuation. Find the city tax on the property.

18. The property in Exercise 17 is located in a county that has set a property tax rate of $2.57 per $100 of assessed value. What is the county tax on the property?

19. Find the property tax rate per $100 of assessed value that a county should set if the total assessed property value in the county is $31,800,000 and the total expenses are $957,300.

20. Use Table 20-2 (p. 722) to calculate the amount of tax owed by Erma Thornton Braddy if her taxable income is $182,817 and her filing status is single.

21. Charles Wossum and his wife Ruby are filing their income tax jointly. Their combined taxable income is $39,872. How much tax must they pay? Use Table 20-1 (pp. 718–721).

22. Juanita and Robert Gray have a gross income of $68,521, all of which is subject to income tax. They have two children and plan to file a joint income tax return. If each exemption is $3,700 and they have itemized deductions of $14,521, what is their taxable income?

1. Explain why the following formulas are equivalent.

$$\text{Tax per } \$1.00 = \frac{\text{tax on } \$100}{\$100}$$

$$\text{Tax per } \$1.00 = \frac{\text{tax on } \$1,000}{\$1,000}$$

2. Examine Table 20-1 to find the relationship between income tax for a single person and a married person filing jointly for incomes more than $23,000 and less than $41,000.

3. Examine Table 20-1 to identify the tax relationship between single persons and married persons filing separately.

4. Compare Sections A, B, C, and D in Table 20-2 to determine which type of taxpayer that earns $112,000 would pay the most income tax. Which pays the least?

5. Using Section A from the 2011 Tax Computation Work Sheet, we see that the tax on $140,000 for a single person is $32,817. Compare this tax to the amount of tax required for a married person filing separately and earning $140,000 in the tax worksheet (Table 20-2, Section C).

6. Use Table 20-1 to compare tax amounts for each of the four filing categories to determine which category pays the least amount of taxes for any given taxable income amount.

7. Section A in Table 20-2 indicates that the maximum percent of income tax is 35% of the taxable income. Calculate the income tax for a single person whose taxable income is $400,000. Calculate the tax rate across the entire $400,000. Explain why the overall rate is less than 35%.

Challenge Problem

Before purchasing investment property, an interested buyer can go to the tax assessor's office to find the taxes to be paid on the property. Using a computer provided for this purpose, the assessor can find the assessed value of the property, the tax rate, and the tax. If the property is purchased before the end of the tax year, the seller will pay the taxes only for the number of days the seller owns the land. This amount is called the seller's *pro rata* share of the annual taxes and can be found by dividing the annual taxes by 365 days to get the taxes due per day and then multiplying by the number of days the land is owned during that tax year by the seller. The buyer also pays a *pro rata* share.

Dan is interested in buying a piece of investment property. The market value is $30,500 and the assessment rate is 18% of the market value. Dan found the city tax rate to be 92.7 mills per $1.00 of assessed value and the county rate to be 138.4 mills per $1.00 of assessed value. Dan buys the land on April 13. What is Dan's *pro rata* share of the property taxes? The tax years for both the city and the county start and stop at the same time.

CASE STUDIES

20-1 Computing Taxes Due

It was the end of a very busy and successful year for Casim Walker's environmental consulting business, and the paperwork had been piling up. Most of it seemingly had to do with taxes. Casim had an inquiry from his home state of Colorado regarding sales tax due on some environmental testing equipment he had purchased out of state. The equipment totaled $11,884.76, and the 2.9% sales tax apparently had not been paid. Casim made a mental note to send in payment with the return envelope. The sales tax inquiry reminded him that he still hadn't calculated the sales tax for the radon testing units that he was going to market online. Each unit sold for $9.95, but he knew a portion would have to be paid to the state for sales tax. Another letter contained the new assessment from the county for his small office building. The letter indicated that the market value of the building had increased to $350,000, and the assessed valuation had increased to 60%. And finally, Casim received his last outstanding 1099 form (which shows income for independent contractors) and was finally able to calculate the adjusted gross income for his family of five (husband, wife, three children) as $152,214. Casim knew that he would end up paying a lot of money in taxes, but at least he had all of the information he needed to do so.

1. Based on Casim's equipment purchase of $11,884.76, how much does he owe the state of Colorado in sales tax? Is state sales tax the only sales tax that Casim needs to be concerned with?

2. Casim plans to sell radon testing units for $9.95 each, or at $9.00 apiece for quantities of 20 or more, sales tax included. Find the marked price and the sales tax for each unit price using a sales tax rate of 2.9%.

3. Calculate the property tax due on Casim's building if the property tax rate is $3.57 per $100 of assessed value.

4. Using the Walkers' adjusted gross income, find the taxable income and income tax due as a married couple filing a joint return. The Walkers have itemized deductions totaling $26,457. Use $3,700 for each personal exemption.

20-2 A Tax Dilemma

Rita recently completed her educational requirements to become a dental hygienist. She has been offered jobs in two different cities and is close to determining which one she should accept. Both employers offer similar benefits and working conditions, but the jobs are in two different states. Rita will move to the state in which she accepts a position.

The first position is in Pennsylvania. Rita would earn $50,000 a year, and she could purchase a starter duplex in the older part of the city for about $75,000. Property taxes equal about 3.5% of assessed value. Assessed value is normally 85% of market value. The state sales tax rate is 6% but does not apply to clothing or food among other items. State income taxes average 3%.

The other position is in Maryland. Rita would earn $65,000 a year, but a starter duplex would cost her at least $135,000. In that area, property taxes average about 4% of assessed value, and values are typically assessed at 60% of market value. The state sales tax is generally considered to be about 1% higher than in Pennsylvania because it applies to clothing as well as other purchases. Additionally, state income taxes average 1.75% higher in Maryland than in Pennsylvania.

1. What would be the difference in cost of living between the two locations based only on the differences in sales tax, income tax, and property tax? Assume $24,000 of taxable purchases for this exercise.

Tax	Pennsylvania	Maryland	Difference
Property			
State Sales			
State Income			

2. Using your answers from Exercise 1, what percentage of the difference in annual salaries does this additional cost represent? In addition, which of these different taxes would be tax deductible if Rita itemizes deductions on her federal tax return?

3. Rita receives a new job offer from the clinic in Pennsylvania that includes a 10% signing bonus, based on her expected first-year income. Compute the federal income taxes due for both states. In Pennsylvania, use her new total income along with a standard deduction of $5,800; in Maryland, use her income of $65,000 but with itemized deductions totaling $8,100.

4. Based on the new job offer in Pennsylvania that includes the signing bonus and your answers to Exercises 1–3, which job would you recommend that Rita accept, and why?

Financial Statements

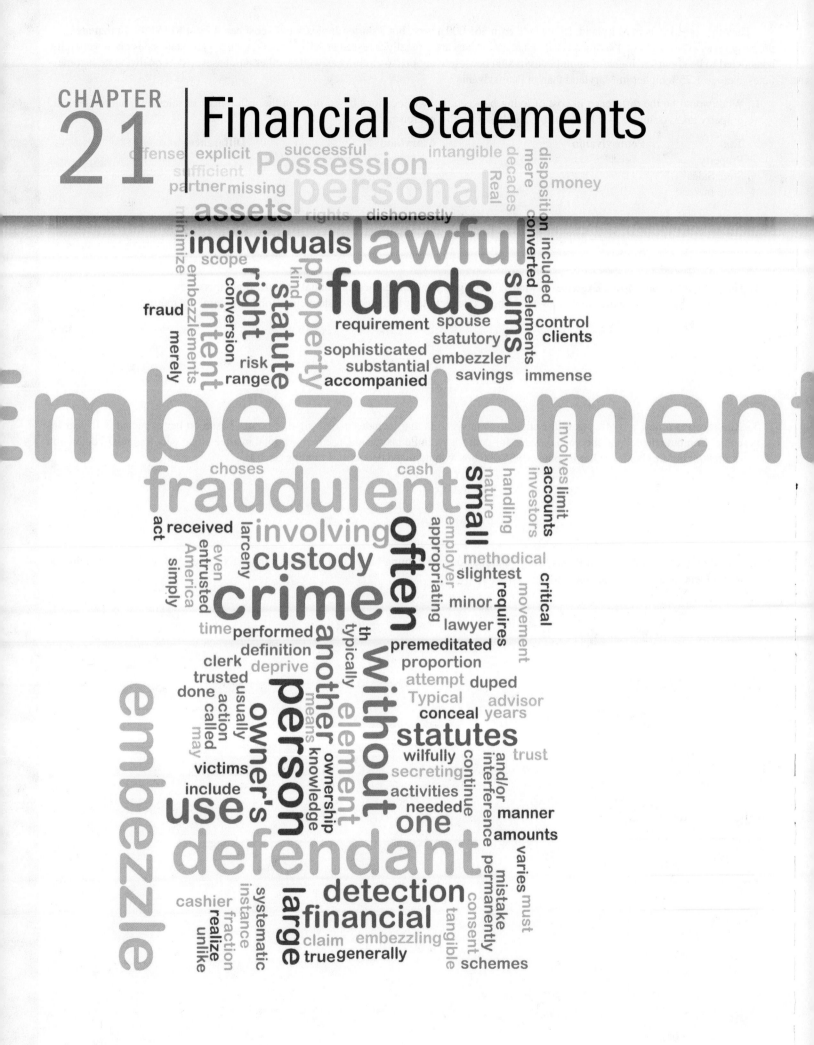

Financial Statement Fraud

A financial statement (or **financial report**) is a formal record of the financial activities of a business, person, or other entity. Financial statements are *extremely* important reports. They show how a business is doing and are very useful internally for a company's stockholders and to its board of directors, its managers, and some employees, including labor unions. Externally, they are important to prospective investors, to government agencies responsible for taxing and regulating, to lenders such as banks and credit rating agencies, and to investment analysts and stockbrokers. For a business enterprise, all the relevant financial information, presented in a structured and easy to understand manner, will be included in the financial statements. These statements show the financial wealth of a company (how much it owes and owns), but unfortunately, they can be manipulated.

According to a recent study by the Committee of Sponsoring Organizations of the Treadway Commission (COSO), fraudulent financial reporting by U.S. public companies has significant negative consequences for investors and executives. The study examined nearly 350 alleged accounting fraud cases investigated by the Securities and Exchange Commission (SEC) over a 10-year period. It showed the following:

- Financial fraud affects companies of all sizes, with the median company having assets and revenues just under $100 million.
- The median fraud was $12.1 million. More than 30 of the fraud cases each involved misstatements/ misappropriations of $500 million or more.
- The SEC named the chief executive officer (CEO) and/ or chief financial officer (CFO) as being involved in 89 percent of the fraud cases. Within two years of the completion of the SEC investigation, about 20 percent of CEOs/CFOs had been indicted. Over 60 percent of those indicted were convicted.
- Twenty-six percent of the firms engaged in fraud changed auditors during the period examined compared to a 12 percent rate for no-fraud firms.
- Initial news in the press of an alleged fraud resulted in an average 16.7 percent abnormal stock price decline for the fraudulent company in the two days surrounding the announcement.
- News of an SEC or Department of Justice investigation resulted in an average 7.3 percent abnormal stock price decline.
- Companies engaged in fraud often experienced bankruptcy, delisting from a stock exchange, or material asset sales at rates much higher than those experienced by other firms.

The message is clear. The impact of fraudulent financial reporting is devastating to both investors and the financial markets in general. And unfortunately, not only do the company, its employees, and executives pay dearly for the practice of fraudulent financial reporting—but society as a whole pays as well.

LEARNING OUTCOMES

21-1 The Balance Sheet

1. Prepare a balance sheet.
2. Prepare a vertical analysis of a balance sheet.
3. Prepare a horizontal analysis of a balance sheet.

21-2 Income Statements

1. Prepare an income statement.
2. Prepare a vertical analysis of an income statement.
3. Prepare a horizontal analysis of an income statement.

21-3 Financial Statement Ratios

1. Find and use financial ratios.

The financial condition of a business must be monitored at all times. The owner of a business, investors, and creditors need to know the financial condition of the business before they can make decisions and plans. Lending institutions consider the overall financial health of a business before lending money. The stockholders of incorporated businesses expect to receive periodic reports on the financial condition of the corporation. Many companies or organizations hire an auditor once a year to determine this condition. Two financial statements, the *balance sheet* and the *income statement,* are normally prepared as part of this analysis. The balance sheet describes the condition of a business at some exact point in time, whereas the income statement shows what the business did over a period of time.

21-1 THE BALANCE SHEET

LEARNING OUTCOMES

1 Prepare a balance sheet.
2 Prepare a vertical analysis of a balance sheet.
3 Prepare a horizontal analysis of a balance sheet.

1 Prepare a balance sheet.

Balance sheet: financial statement that indicates the worth or financial condition of a business as of a certain date.

Assets: properties or anything of monetary value owned by the business.

Current assets: assets that are normally turned into cash within a year.

Plant and equipment: assets used in transacting business.

Cash: a current asset of money in the bank or cash on hand.

Accounts receivable: a current asset that is the money owed by customers.

Notes receivable: a current asset that is a promissory note owed to the business.

Merchandise inventory: a current asset that is the value of merchandise on hand.

Business equipment: value of equipment such as tools, display cases, and machinery owned by the business.

Office furniture and equipment: value of office furniture and equipment such as computers, printers, and copiers owned by the business.

Buildings: value of buildings and structures owned by the business.

Land: value of the grounds or land owned by the business.

Liabilities: amounts that the business owes.

Current liabilities: debts that must be paid within a short amount of time.

Long-term liabilities: debts that are paid over a long period of time.

Accounts payable: a current liability for merchandise or services that have not been paid for.

Notes payable: promissory notes that are owed.

Wages payable: salaries a business owes its employees.

Mortgage payable: a long-term liability for the building and land the business owns.

The **balance sheet** is a type of financial statement that indicates the worth or financial condition of a business *as of a certain date*. It does not give any historical background about the company or make future projections, but rather shows the status of the company on a given date. On that date, it answers these questions:

How much does the business own? What are its *assets*?
How much does the business owe? What are its *liabilities*?
How much is the business worth? What is its *equity*?

Assets are properties owned by the business. They include anything of monetary value and things that could be exchanged for cash or other property. **Current assets** are assets that are normally turned into cash within a year. **Plant and equipment** are assets that are used in transacting business and are more long-term in nature. These types of assets can be further subdivided as follows:

Current assets

Cash	Money in the bank as well as cash on hand
Accounts receivable	Money that customers owe the business for merchandise or services they have received but have not yet paid for
Notes receivable	Promissory notes owed to the business
Merchandise inventory	Value of merchandise on hand
Office supplies	Value of supplies such as stationery, pens, file folders, and computer storage devices

Plant and equipment

Business equipment	Value of equipment (tools, display cases, machinery, and so on) that the business owns
Office furniture and equipment	Value of office furniture (desks, chairs, filing cabinets, and so on) and equipment (computers, printers, copiers, calculators, postage meters, fax machines, and the like) that the business owns
Buildings	Value of the buildings the business owns
Land	Value of the property and grounds on which the buildings stand and other land the business owns

Liabilities are amounts that the business owes. **Current liabilities** are those that must be paid shortly. **Long-term liabilities** are those that will be paid over a long period of time—a year or more. These types of liabilities can be further subdivided as follows:

Current liabilities

Accounts payable	Money owed for merchandise or services that the business has received but has not yet paid for
Notes payable	Promissory notes that the business owes
Wages payable	Salaries that a business owes its employees

Long-term liabilities

Mortgage payable	The debt owed on buildings and land that the business owns

Owner's equity or stockholder's equity: the difference between the company's assets and the liabilities.

Capital, proprietorship, or net worth: other terms for owner's equity.

In addition to its debts to creditors, a firm is considered to owe its investors. This "debt," expressed as **owner's equity,** also called **stockholder's equity,** is the amount of clear ownership or the owner's rights to the properties. It is the difference between assets and liabilities. For instance, if a business has assets of $175,000 and liabilities of $100,000, the owner's equity is $175,000 − $100,000, or $75,000. Other words used to mean the same thing as owner's equity are **capital, proprietorship,** and **net worth.**

The money amounts used in this chapter are for illustrative purposes and are unrealistically low and simplistic. Real-life examples will have much larger amounts and situations will be much more complex. We will focus on the concepts that are being presented.

A balance sheet (see Figure 21-1) lists the assets, liabilities, and owner's equity of a business on a specific date, using the basic accounting equation of business:

Basic Accounting Equation

$$\text{Assets} = \text{liabilities} + \text{owner's equity}$$
$$A = L + OE$$

| Move It Fitness |
| Balance Sheet |
| December 31, 2012 |

Assets

Current assets
Cash
Accounts receivable
Merchandise inventory
Total current assets

Plant and equipment
Equipment
Total plant and equipment
Total assets

Liabilities

Current liabilities
Accounts payable
Wages payable
Total current liabilities

Long-term liabilities
Mortgage note payable
Total long-term liabilities
Total liabilities

Owner's Equity
B. Pierson, capital
Total liabilities and owner's equity

FIGURE 21-1
Move It Fitness Balance Sheet Template

HOW TO Prepare a balance sheet

1. Find and record the *total assets,* working by asset category.
   (a) List the *current assets* and draw a single line underneath the last entry.
   (b) Add the entries and record the *total current assets,* drawing a single line underneath the total.
   (c) Repeat step 1a for *plant and equipment assets* and step 1b for *total plant and equipment assets.*
   (d) Add the category totals and draw a double line underneath the grand total.

   Total assets = total current assets + total plant and equipment

2. Find and record the *total liabilities*, working by liability category.
   (a) Repeat step 1a for *current liabilities* and step 1b for *total current liabilities*.
   (b) Repeat step 1a for *long-term liabilities* and step 1b for *total long-term liabilities*.
   (c) Add the category totals and draw a single line underneath the total.

   Total liabilities = total current liabilities + total long-term liabilities

3. Find and record the *total owner's equity*.
   (a) List the equity entries and draw a single line underneath the last entry.
   (b) Add the entries and draw a single line underneath the total.
4. Find and record the *total liabilities and owner's equity:* Add the total liabilities to the total owner's equity and draw a double line underneath the grand total.

   Total liabilities and owner's equity = total liabilities + total owner's equity

5. Confirm that the double line grand totals from step 1 and step 4 are the same.

   Total Assets = total liabilities + owner's equity

EXAMPLE 1 Prepare a balance sheet, using Figure 21-1 as a guide, for Move It Fitness for December 31, 2012. The company assets are: cash, $1,973; accounts receivable, $2,118; merchandise inventory, $18,476; equipment, $18,591. The liabilities are: accounts payable, $2,317; wages payable, $684; mortgage note payable, $15,286. The owner's capital is $22,871.

The completed balance sheet is shown in Figure 21-2.

Move It Fitness
Balance Sheet
December 31, 2012

Assets

Current assets
Cash	$1,973
Accounts receivable	2,118
Merchandise inventory	18,476
Total current assets	22,567 ← Subtotal

Plant and equipment
Equipment	18,591
Total plant and equipment	18,591
Total assets	$41,158 ← Total

Liabilities

Current liabilities
Accounts payable	$2,317
Wages payable	684
Total current liabilities	3,001 ← Subtotal

Long-term liabilities
Mortgage note payable	15,286
Total long-term liabilities	15,286 ← Subtotal
Total liabilities	18,287 ← Subtotal

Owner's Equity
B. Pierson, capital	22,871
Total liabilities and owner's equity	$41,158 ← Total

FIGURE 21-2
Completed Balance Sheet

STOP AND CHECK

1. Find total current assets if The 7th Inning has $43,518 in cash; $3,988 in accounts receivable; and $96,532 in merchandise inventory.

2. Datatech, Inc., has $15,817 in accounts payable; $9,892 in wages payable; and $418,250 for its mortgage note. If owner's equity totals $45,986, find total liabilities and owner's equity.

See Example 1.

3. Prepare a balance sheet for Rayco, Inc., for December 31, 2012. The company assets are: cash, $105,095; accounts receivable, $6,503; merchandise inventory, $190,014; equipment, $32,507. The liabilities are: accounts payable, $6,007; wages payable, $4,761; mortgage note payable, $281,017. The owner's capital is $42,334.

4. Prepare a balance sheet for Rayco, Inc., for December 31, 2013. The company assets are: cash, $114,975; accounts receivable, $8,918; merchandise inventory, $187,915; equipment, $29,719. The liabilities are: accounts payable, $6,832; wages payable, $5,215; mortgage note payable, $279,409. The owner's capital is $50,071.

2   Prepare a vertical analysis of a balance sheet.

Vertical analysis: the ratio of each item on the balance sheet to total assets.

A **vertical analysis** of a balance sheet shows the ratio of each item on the balance sheet to the *total assets*. To find these ratios, we use the percentage formula $R = \frac{P}{B}$. Each item on the balance sheet is a portion P and the total assets amount is the base B. Their ratio R is expressed as a percent.

For instance, if total assets are $50,000, a liability of $5,000 is 10% of total assets.

$$R = \frac{P}{B} = \frac{\text{liability}}{\text{total assets}} = \frac{\$5,000}{\$50,000} = 0.1 = 10\%$$

HOW TO   Prepare a vertical analysis of a balance sheet

1. Prepare a balance sheet of assets, liabilities, and owner's equity.
2. Create an additional column labeled *percent*: For each item, divide the amount of the item by the total assets then multiply by 100% to record the result as a percent.

$$\text{Percent of total assets} = \frac{\text{amount of item}}{\text{total assets}} \times 100\%$$

EXAMPLE 2   Prepare a vertical analysis of the balance sheet for Move It Fitness shown in Figure 21-2.

For each item, divide the amount of the item by the total assets.

Cash: $\dfrac{\$1,973}{\$41,158}(100\%) = 0.0479372176(100\%) = $ 4.8% (nearest tenth of a percent)

Accounts receivable: $\dfrac{\$2,118}{\$41,158}(100\%) = 0.0514602264(100\%) = $ 5.1%

Merchandise inventory: $\dfrac{\$18,476}{\$41,158}(100\%) = 0.4489042228(100\%) = $ 44.9%

Total current assets: $\dfrac{\$22{,}567}{\$41{,}158}(100\%) = 0.5483016667(100\%) = $ 54.8%

Equipment: $\dfrac{\$18{,}591}{\$41{,}158}(100\%) = 0.4516983333(100\%) = $ 45.2%

Total assets: $\dfrac{\$41{,}158}{\$41{,}158}(100\%) = 1(100\%) = $ 100%

Accounts payable: $\dfrac{\$2{,}317}{\$41{,}158}(100\%) = 0.0562952524(100\%) = $ 5.6%

Wages payable: $\dfrac{\$684}{\$41{,}158}(100\%) = 0.0166188833(100\%) = $ 1.7%

Total current liabilities: $\dfrac{\$3{,}001}{\$41{,}158}(100\%) = 0.0729141358(100\%) = $ 7.3%

Mortgage note payable: $\dfrac{\$15{,}286}{\$41{,}158}(100\%) = 0.3713980271(100\%) = $ 37.1%

Total liabilities: $\dfrac{\$18{,}287}{\$41{,}158}(100\%) = 0.4443121629(100\%) = $ 44.4%

B. Pierson's capital: $\dfrac{\$22{,}871}{\$41{,}158}(100\%) = 0.5556878371(100\%) = $ 55.6%

Total liabilities and owner's equity: $\dfrac{\$41{,}158}{\$41{,}158}(100\%) = 1(100\%) = $ 100%

The percent both for total assets and for total liabilities and owner's equity is 100%. Minor discrepancies may occur because of rounding. The completed balance sheet is shown in Figure 21-3.

Move It Fitness Balance Sheet December 31, 2012		
	Amount	**Percent**
Assets		
Current assets		
Cash	$1,973	4.8
Accounts receivable	2,118	5.1
Merchandise inventory	18,476	44.9
Total current assets	22,567	54.8
Plant and equipment		
Equipment	18,591	45.2
Total plant and equipment	18,591	45.2
Total assets	$41,158 ←—Total—→	100.0
Liabilities		
Current liabilities		
Accounts payable	$ 2,317	5.6
Wages payable	684	1.7
Total current liabilities	3,001	7.3
Long-term liabilities		
Mortgage note payable	15,286	37.1
Total long-term liabilities	15,286	37.1
Total liabilities	18,287	44.4
Owner's Equity		
B. Pierson, capital	22,871	55.6
Total liabilities and owner's equity	$41,158 ←—Total—→	100.0

FIGURE 21-3
Vertical Analysis of Move It Fitness Balance Sheet

TIP

Checking Calculations

The percent values for all the assets should add up to 100%. The percent values for all the liabilities plus the percent value for the owner's equity should add up to 100%. Minor discrepancies may occur due to rounding.

Watch the Base!

Be careful to use the total assets as the base when figuring each percent. Look what happens to the percent for *Wages payable* in Figure 21-3 if the total liabilities is used for the base instead of total assets:

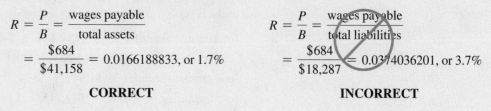

$$R = \frac{P}{B} = \frac{\text{wages payable}}{\text{total assets}}$$

$$= \frac{\$684}{\$41,158} = 0.0166188833, \text{ or } 1.7\%$$

CORRECT

$$R = \frac{P}{B} = \frac{\text{wages payable}}{\text{total liabilities}}$$

$$= \frac{\$684}{\$18,287} = 0.0374036201, \text{ or } 3.7\%$$

INCORRECT

Comparing balance sheets from two years may reveal important trends in a business's operations. A **comparative balance sheet** is shown in Figure 21-4. Note that data for the most recent year are entered in the first columns.

Comparative balance sheet: a balance sheet that includes data from two or more years.

Move It Fitness Comparative Balance Sheet December 31, 2012 and 2013	2013		2012	
Most recent year first	Amount	Percent	Amount	Percent
Assets				
Current assets				
Cash	$2,184	5.7	$1,973	4.8
Accounts receivable	4,308	11.3	2,118	5.1
Merchandise inventory	17,317	45.6	18,476	44.9
Total current assets	23,809	62.6	22,567	54.8
Plant and equipment				
Equipment	14,203	37.4	18,591	45.2
Total plant and equipment	14,203	37.4	18,591	45.2
Total assets	$38,012	100.0	$41,158	100.0
Liabilities				
Current liabilities				
Accounts payable	$ 1,647	4.3	$ 2,317	5.6
Wages payable	894	2.4	684	1.7
Total current liabilities	2,541	6.7	3,001	7.3
Long-term liabilities				
Mortgage note payable	12,715	33.4	15,286	37.1
Total long-term liabilities	12,715	33.4	15,286	37.1
Total liabilities	15,256	40.1	18,287	44.4
Owner's Equity				
B. Pierson, capital	22,756	59.9	22,871	55.6
Total liabilities and owner's equity	$38,012	100.0	$41,158	100.0

FIGURE 21-4
Vertical Analysis of Move It Fitness Comparative Balance Sheet

HOW TO   Prepare a comparative balance sheet

1. Prepare a vertical analysis of the balance sheet for a company for two comparable business periods such as years.
2. Represent both sets of data on the same statement by showing the data for the most current period to the left of the data for the earlier period.

EXAMPLE 3 Move It Fitness reported the following assets for 2013: cash, $2,184; accounts receivable, $4,308; merchandise inventory, $17,317; equipment, $14,203. Liabilities for the same period are: accounts payable, $1,647; wages payable, $894; mortgage note payable, $12,715. The owner's capital is $22,756. Complete a comparable balance sheet for Move It Fitness for 2012 and 2013.

Use the balance sheet in Figure 21-3 as the data for 2012. Complete the balance sheet and vertical analysis for 2013. Then show both sets of data on the same statement.

Total current assets for 2013 = $2,184 + $4,308 + $17,317 = $23,809

Total assets = $23,809 + $14,203 = $38,012

Total current liabilities = $1,647 + $894 = $2,541

Total liabilities = $2,541 + $12,715 = $15,256

Total liabilities and owner's equity = $15,256 + $22,756 = $38,012

For each item, divide the amount of the item by the total assets.

Cash: $\dfrac{\$2,184}{\$38,012}(100\%) = 0.05745554036(100\%) = 5.7\%$ (nearest tenth of a percent)

Accounts receivable: $\dfrac{\$4,308}{\$38,012}(100\%) = 0.1133589393(100\%) = 11.3\%$

Merchandise inventory: $\dfrac{\$17,317}{\$38,012}(100\%) = 0.4555666632(100\%) = 45.6\%$

Total current assets: $\dfrac{\$23,809}{\$38,012}(100\%) = 0.6263548353(100\%) = 62.6\%$

Equipment: $\dfrac{\$14,203}{\$38,012}(100\%) = 0.3736451647(100\%) = 37.4\%$

Total assets: $\dfrac{\$38,012}{\$38,012}(100\%) = 1(100\%) = 100\%$

Accounts payable: $\dfrac{\$1,647}{\$38,012}(100\%) = 0.0433284226(100\%) = 4.3\%$

Wages payable: $\dfrac{\$894}{\$38,012}(100\%) = 0.02351888877(100\%) = 2.4\%$

Total current liabilities: $\dfrac{\$2,541}{\$38,012}(100\%) = 0.06684731138(100\%) = 6.7\%$

Mortgage note payable: $\dfrac{\$12,715}{\$38,012}(100\%) = 0.3344996317(100\%) = 33.4\%$

Total liabilities: $\dfrac{\$15,256}{\$38,012}(100\%) = 0.4013469431(100\%) = 40.1\%$

B. Pierson's capital: $\dfrac{\$22,756}{\$38,012}(100\%) = 0.5986530569(100\%) = 59.9\%$

Total liabilities and owner's equity: $\dfrac{\$38,012}{\$38,012}(100\%) = 1(100\%) = 100\%$

The completed comparative balance sheet is shown in Figure 21-4.

STOP AND CHECK

See Example 2.

1. Prepare a vertical analysis of the Rayco, Inc., balance sheet for December 31, 2012, from Exercise 3 in the Stop and Check on page 743.

2. Prepare a vertical analysis of the Rayco, Inc., balance sheet for December 31, 2013, from Exercise 4 in the Stop and Check on page 743.

See Example 3.

3. Prepare a comparative balance sheet for Rayco for December 2012 and 2013 using information from Exercises 3 and 4 on page 743.

4. From the comparative balance sheet for Rayco, Inc., in Exercise 3, in which year did Rayco have the greater total assets?

3   Prepare a horizontal analysis of a balance sheet.

Horizontal analysis: a balance sheet analysis that compares the same item for two different years.

Another way to analyze information on a comparative balance sheet is to compare item by item in a **horizontal analysis.** While a vertical analysis compares each item to total assets, a horizontal analysis compares the same item for two different years, recording both the amount of increase (or decrease) and the increase (or decrease) as a percent of the earlier year's amount.

HOW TO   Prepare a horizontal analysis of a comparative balance sheet

1. Prepare a balance sheet for two or more years: Record each year's amounts in separate columns.
2. Create an additional column labeled *amount of increase (decrease)*: For each yearly item,
   (a) Subtract the smaller amount from the larger amount and record the difference.
   (b) If the earlier year's amount is larger than the more recent year's amount, record the difference from step 2a as a decrease by using parentheses or a negative (minus) sign.
3. Create an additional column labeled *percent increase (decrease)*: For each yearly item, divide the amount of increase (decrease) by the earlier year's amount, multiply by 100%, and record the difference as a percent.

$$\text{Percent increase (decrease)} = \frac{\text{amount of increase (decrease)}}{\text{earlier year's amount}} \times 100\%$$

EXAMPLE 4   Prepare a horizontal analysis for Move It Fitness using the yearly amounts in Figure 21-5.

Cash: $2,184 − $1,973 = $211 (increase)
$211 ÷ $1,973 = 0.1069437405(100%) = 10.7% (increase)

Accounts receivable: $4,308 − $2,118 = $2,190 (increase)
$2,190 ÷ $2,118 = 1.033994334 = 103.4% (increase)

Inventory: $18,476 − $17,317 = $1,159 (decrease)
1,159 ÷ $18,476 = 0.0627300281 = 6.3% (decrease)

Equipment: $18,591 − $14,203 = $4,388 (decrease)
$4,388 ÷ $18,591 = 0.2360281857 = 23.6% (decrease)

Total assets: $41,158 − $38,012 = $3,146 (decrease)
$3,146 ÷ $41,158 = 0.0764371447 = 7.6% (decrease)

Accounts payable: $2,317 − $1,647 = $670 (decrease)
$670 ÷ $2,317 = 0.2891670262 = 28.9% (decrease)

Wages payable: $894 − $684 = $210 (increase)
$210 ÷ $684 = 0.3070175439 = 30.7% (increase)

Mortgage note payable: $15,286 − $12,715 = $2,571 (decrease)
$2,571 ÷ $15,286 = 0.1681931179 = 16.8% (decrease)

Total liabilities: $18,287 − $15,256 = $3,031 (decrease)
$3,031 ÷ $18,287 = 0.1657461585 = 16.6% (decrease)

B. Pierson, capital: $22,871 − $22,756 = $115 (decrease)
$115 ÷ $22,871 = 0.0050282017 = 0.5% (decrease)

Total liabilities and owner's equity:

$41,158 − $38,012 = $3,146 (decrease)
$3,146 ÷ $41,158 = 0.0764371447 = 7.6% (decrease)

If the horizontal analysis has been made properly, the amount of change for any *total* should equal the sum of the increases minus all decreases in the category. Also, the total liabilities and owner's equity amount of change should equal the total assets amount of change. The percent of change for the total is *not* the sum of the percents of increases and the difference of percents of decreases. This is because the base is different for each entry.

Move It Fitness Comparative Balance Sheet December 31, 2012 and 2013				
			Increase (Decrease)*	
	2013	**2012**	**Amount**	**Percent**
Assets				
Cash	$2,184	$1,973	$ 211	10.7
Accounts receivable	4,308	2,118	2,190	103.4
Inventory	17,317	18,476	(1,159)	(6.3)
Equipment	14,203	18,591	(4,388)	(23.6)
Total assets	$38,012	$41,158	($3,146)	(7.6)
Liabilities				
Accounts payable	$ 1,647	$ 2,317	$ (670)	(28.9)
Salaries payable	894	684	210	30.7
Mortgage note payable	12,715	15,286	(2,571)	(16.8)
Total liabilities	15,256	18,287	(3,031)	(16.6)
Owner's Equity				
B. Pierson, capital	22,756	22,871	(115)	(0.5)
Total liabilities and owner's equity	$38,012	$41,158	($3,146)	(7.6)

*Parentheses indicate decrease.

FIGURE 21-5

Horizontal Analysis of Move It Fitness Comparative Balance Sheet

TIP

Which Year Is the Base in the Percent of Increase?

In a horizontal analysis, the *earlier* year is always the base year in calculating percent increase or decrease. It is possible to have a 0% change if there is no dollar change in the amounts.

TIP

Working with Decreases and Negative Values

If the most recent year is *always* entered first, a decrease is indicated in the calculator display with a minus sign.

$$17317 \boxed{-} 18476 \boxed{=} \Rightarrow -1159$$

To find percent decrease, do not clear the calculator. The percent decrease will also be a negative value.

$$\boxed{\div} 18476 \boxed{=} \boxed{\times} 100 \boxed{=} \Rightarrow -6.2730 \text{ or } -6.3\%$$

STOP AND CHECK

1. Use the 2012 and 2013 data on the comparative balance sheet prepared for Rayco, Inc., in Stop and Check Exercise 3 on p. 746 and calculate the amount of increase (or decrease) for each category in the sheet.

2. Use the 2012 and 2013 increases or decreases in Exercise 1 to compute the percent of increase (or decrease) based on total assets.

See Exercise 4.

3. Use the information for Rayco from Exercises 2 and 3 on page 746 to prepare a horizontal analysis of the balance sheet for 2012 and 2013.

4. What was Rayco's percentage growth in total assets from 2012 to 2013?

21-1 SECTION EXERCISES

SKILL BUILDERS

See Example 1.

1. Prepare a balance sheet for Miss Muffins' Bakery for December 31, 2014. The company assets are: cash, $1,985; accounts receivable, $4,219; merchandise inventory, $2,512. The liabilities are: accounts payable, $3,483; wages payable, $1,696. The owner's capital is $3,537.

2. Expand the balance sheet for Exercise 1 to include figures for 2013. The company assets are: cash, $1,762; accounts receivable, $3,785; merchandise inventory, $2,036. The liabilities are: accounts payable, $3,631; wages payable, $1,421. The owner's capital is $2,531.

3. Prepare the balance sheet for O'Dell's Nursery for December 31, 2014. The company assets are: cash, $8,917; accounts receivable, $7,521; merchandise inventory, $17,826. The liabilities are: accounts payable, $10,215; wages payable, $3,716. The owner's capital is $20,333.

4. Expand the balance sheet for Exercise 3 for 2013. The company assets are: cash, $12,842; accounts receivable, $5,836; merchandise inventory, $18,917. The liabilities are: accounts payable, $8,968; wages payable, $2,582. The owner's capital is $26,045.

See Examples 2 and 3.

5. Complete the vertical analyses on the comparative balance sheet for Miss Muffins' Bakery for 2014. (Use parentheses to indicate decreases.) Use Exercise 1.

6. Use Exercises 1 and 2 to complete the vertical analyses on the comparative balance sheet for Miss Muffins' Bakery for 2013.

7. Complete the vertical analyses on the comparative balance sheet for O'Dell's Nursery for 2014.

8. Complete the vertical analyses on the comparative balance sheet for O'Dell's Nursery for 2013.

See Example 4.

9. Use Exercises 1 and 2 to complete the horizontal analyses showing differences in dollar amounts and percents on the comparative balance sheet for Miss Muffins' Bakery.

10. Complete the horizontal analyses showing differences in dollar amounts and percent increases (decreases) on the comparative balance sheet for O'Dell's Nursery.

11. To find the percent of total debt compared to total assets, divide the total liabilities by the total assets and write in percent form. Find the total debt to total assets for Miss Muffins' Bakery for 2014. Use Exercise 1.

12. Use the formula in Exercise 11 to find the percent of total debt compared to total assets for Miss Muffins' Bakery for 2013. Use Exercise 2.

21-2 INCOME STATEMENTS

LEARNING OUTCOMES

1 Prepare an income statement.
2 Prepare a vertical analysis of an income statement.
3 Prepare a horizontal analysis of an income statement.

Income statement: a financial statement of the net income of a business over a period of time.

Total sales: earnings from the sale of goods or the performance of services.

Sales returns or allowances: refunds or adjustments for unsatisfactory merchandise or services.

Net sales: total sales minus sales returns or allowances.

Cost of goods sold (COGS): cost to the business for merchandise or goods sold.

Gross profit or gross margin: net sales minus the cost of goods sold.

Operating expenses: overhead or cost incurred in operating a business.

Net income or net profit: gross profit or gross margin minus the operating expenses.

Another important financial statement, the **income statement,** shows the net income of a business *over a period of time.* (Remember, the balance sheet shows the financial condition of a business at a specific time.)

Among the many terms on an income statement are the following:

Total sales	Earnings from the sale of goods or the performance of services
Sales returns or allowances	Refunds or adjustments for unsatisfactory merchandise or services
Net sales	The difference between the total sales and the sales returns or allowances
Cost of goods sold	Cost to the business for merchandise or goods sold (COGS)
Gross profit or gross margin	The difference between the net sales and the cost of goods sold
Operating expenses	The overhead or cost incurred in operating the business; examples of operating expenses are utilities, rent, insurance, permits, taxes, and employees' salaries
Net income or net profit	The difference between the gross profit (gross margin) and the operating expenses

1 Prepare an income statement.

Calculating the cost of goods sold is an important part of preparing an income statement. Reviewing some of the concepts in Chapter 18, the cost of goods sold is the difference between the cost of goods available for sale and the cost of ending inventory. The cost of goods available for sale is the cost of the beginning inventory plus the cost of purchases. There are various ways to find the cost of ending inventory.

HOW TO   Prepare an income statement

1. Find and record *net sales.*
   (a) Record *gross sales.*
   (b) Record *sales returns and allowances.*
   (c) Subtract sales returns and allowances from gross sales.

   Net sales = gross sales − sales returns and allowances

2. Find and record *cost of goods sold.*
   (a) Record cost of beginning inventory.
   (b) Record cost of purchases.
   (c) Record cost of ending inventory.
   (d) Add cost of beginning inventory and cost of purchases and subtract cost of ending inventory.

   Cost of goods sold = cost of beginning inventory + cost of purchases − cost of ending inventory

3. Find and record *gross profit from sales.*

   Gross profit from sales = net sales − cost of goods sold

4. Find and record *total operating expenses*. List the operating expenses and add the entries.
5. Find and record *net income*.

Net income = gross profit from sales − operating expenses

EXAMPLE 1   Complete the portion of the income statement shown for Green Zone Organics using the information given.

Gross sales: $25,283; returns and allowances: $492; cost of beginning inventory: $5,384; cost of purchases: $18,923; cost of ending inventory: $5,557; total operating expenses: $3,750

Net sales = gross sales − returns and allowances
= $25,283 − $492 = $24,791

Cost of goods sold = cost of beginning inventory + cost of purchases − cost of ending inventory
= $5,384 + $18,923 − $5,557 = $18,750

Gross profit = net sales − cost of goods sold
= $24,791 − $18,750 = $6,041

Net income = gross profit − operating expenses
= $6,041 − $3,750 = $2,291

The completed income statement is shown in Figure 21-6.

Green Zone Organics Income Statement For the Month Ending June 30, 2013		
Revenue:		
Gross sales		$25,283
Less: Sales returns and allowances		492
Net sales		24,791
Cost of goods sold:		
Cost of beginning inventory	$ 5,384	
Add: Purchases	18,923	
	24,307	
Less: ending inventory	5,557	
Cost of goods sold		18,750
Gross profit (loss)		6,041
Expenses:		
Operating expenses	3,750	
Total expenses		3,750
Net income (loss)		$ 2,291

FIGURE 21-6
Income Statement for Green Zone Organics

STOP AND CHECK

See Example 1.

1. Find the gross profit and net income for Cedar Rapids American Auto for the year ending December 31, 2013, if the company had net sales of $5,385,920; cost of goods sold of $2,073,587; and operating expenses of $498,507.

2. Prepare an income statement for Cedar Rapids American Auto for 2013.

3. For 2013 Amaya's Soul Food Catering had gross sales of $597,341; sales returns and allowances of $10,514; beginning inventory cost of $38,917; cost of purchases, $261,053; and year-end inventory of $42,013. Find the net sales, cost of goods sold, and gross profit from sales.

4. Amaya's Soul Food Catering had the following 2013 operating expenses: salary, $90,500; insurance, $12,200; utilities, $7,582; maintenance, $1,077; rent, $18,400; and depreciation, $2,700. Find the total operating expenses and net income using the data from Exercise 3. Prepare an income statement to show financial information for 2011.

2 Prepare a vertical analysis of an income statement.

Vertical analysis of an income statement: comparison of each entry in an income statement to net sales.

Just as you do with a vertical analysis of a balance sheet, to make a **vertical analysis of an income statement** you use the percentage formula $R = \frac{P}{B}$, in which each entry on the income statement is a portion or percentage P, net sales is the base B, and their ratio R is expressed as a percent.

HOW TO Prepare a vertical analysis of an income statement

1. Prepare an income statement.
2. Create an additional column labeled *percent of net sales*: For each item, divide the amount of the item by the net sales and record the result as a percent.

$$\text{Percent of net sales} = \frac{\text{amount of item}}{\text{net sales}} \times 100\%$$

EXAMPLE 2 Figure 21-7 is an income statement for The 7th Inning. Complete a vertical analysis of the statement.

The 7th Inning Income Statement For the Year Ending December 31, 2013	
Revenue:	
Gross sales	$846,891
Sales returns and allowances	7,835
Net sales	839,056
Cost of goods sold:	
Beginning inventory, January 1, 2013	28,527
Purchases	521,054
Less: ending inventory, December 31, 2013	33,562
Cost of goods sold	516,019
Operating expenses:	
Gross profit from sales	323,037
Salary	64,607
Insurance	10,137
Utilities	11,712
Maintenance	3,839
Rent	30,976
Depreciation	5,034
Total operating expenses	126,305
Net income	$196,732

FIGURE 21-7
The 7th Inning Income Statement

For each item, divide the amount by the net sales and record the result as a percent. For instance,

$$\text{Gross sales: } \frac{\text{gross sales}}{\text{net sales}} \times 100\% = \frac{\$846{,}891}{\$839{,}056}(100\%) = 1.009337875(100\%) = 100.9\%$$

The completed vertical analysis is shown in Figure 21-8.

TIP

What Is the Base on a Vertical Analysis of an Income Statement?

As with balance sheets, each item on the income statement is expressed as a percent of a base figure. For income statements, *net sales is the base.*

The 7th Inning
Vertical Analysis Income Statement
For the Year Ending December 31, 2013

	Amount	Percent of Net Sales
Revenue:		
Gross sales	$846,891	100.9
Sales returns and allowances	7,835	0.9
Net sales	839,056	100.0
Cost of goods sold:		
Beginning inventory, January 1, 2013	28,527	3.4
Purchases	521,054	62.1
Less: ending inventory, December 31, 2013	33,562	4.0
Cost of goods sold	516,019	61.5
Gross profit from sales	323,037	38.5
Operating expenses:		
Salary	64,607	7.7
Insurance	10,137	1.2
Utilities	11,712	1.4
Maintenance	3,839	0.5
Rent	30,976	3.7
Depreciation	5,034	0.6
Total operating expenses	126,305	15.1
Net income	$196,732	23.4

FIGURE 21-8
Vertical Analysis of The 7th Inning's Income Statement

TIP

Use the Memory Function and the Percent Key.

On a 4-function or basic calculator:

Enter the net sales into memory.

[AC] 839056 [M+]

Divide each entry by net sales and use the percent key.

[CE/C] 846891 [÷] [MRC] [%] ⇒ 100.9337875

[CE/C] 7835 [÷] [MRC] [%] ⇒ 0.93378749

Continue by dividing each item by the net sales, which is stored in memory.

On the TI BA II Plus there are 10 memory locations for storing numbers. To store a number that is in your calculator display, press [STO], then assign a location by pressing a number from 0 to 9. Then you can clear the calculator to begin a different calculation. To recall the stored number, press [RCL] and the assigned number location.

On the TI-84, there is also a storage key labeled [STO]. In assigning a memory location, assign a letter by using the [ALPHA] key and a letter. The letters are written in green, above and to the right of certain keys. The [RCL] function is located as a second function above the [STO] key.

Comparative income statement: an income statement showing two or more years of data and a horizontal analysis of the data.

An income statement can also contain information for more than one year. These statements are called **comparative income statements** and show a horizontal analysis of the two years' data.

	2014		2013	
	Amount	**Percent of Net Sales**	**Amount**	**Percent of Net Sales**
Aspen Lakes Extreme Comparative Income Statement for the Years Ending June 30, 2013 and 2014				
Net sales	$242,897	100.0	$239,528	100.0
Cost of goods sold	116,582	48.0	115,351	48.2
Gross profit	126,315	52.0	124,177	51.8
Operating expenses	38,725	15.9	37,982	15.9
Net income	$87,590	36.1	$86,195	36.0

FIGURE 21-9
Vertical Analysis of the Aspen Lakes Extreme Comparative Income Statement

STOP AND CHECK

See Example 2.

1. Complete a vertical analysis of the income statement for Cedar Rapids American Auto found in Exercise 2 on page 753.

3. Complete a vertical analysis of the income statement for Amaya's Soul Food Catering found in Exercises 3 and 4 on page 754.

See Example 3.

2. In 2012, Cedar Rapids American Auto had net sales of $4,103,370; cost of goods sold totaled $1,992,500; and total operating expenses were $503,719. Prepare a comparative income statement with a vertical analysis of 2012 and 2013.

4. In 2012, Amaya's Soul Food Catering had gross sales of $435,913; sales returns and allowances of $8,019; beginning inventory cost of $36,992; cost of purchases of $248,504; and ending inventory of $41,007. Expenses were salaries, $82,450; insurance, $12,200; utilities, $6,097; maintenance, $817; rent, $17,800; and depreciation, $2,300. Prepare a comparative income statement with a vertical analysis of 2012 and 2013.

Comparative income statement: an income statement that includes data from two or more years.

Horizontal analysis of an income statement: comparison of like entries for two years. The amount of increase or decrease and the percent of increase or decrease are determined.

3 Prepare a horizontal analysis of an income statement.

The horizontal analysis of an income statement is similar to the horizontal analysis of a balance sheet. Items on the statement are compared for more than one period. A **comparative income statement** is used for displaying more than one income period. The **horizontal analysis of an income statement** examines the increase or decrease of an item from one period to another.

HOW TO Prepare a horizontal analysis of a comparative income statement

1. Prepare an income statement for two or more years: Record each year's amounts in separate columns.
2. Create an additional column labeled *amount of increase (decrease).*
   For each yearly item,
   (a) Subtract the smaller amount from the larger amount and record the difference.
   (b) If the earlier year's amount is larger than the later year's amount, record the difference from step 2a as a decrease by using parentheses.
3. Create an additional column labeled *percent increase (decrease).* For each yearly item:

$$\text{Percent increase (decrease)} = \frac{\text{amount of increase (decrease)}}{\text{earlier year's amount}} \times 100\%$$

EXAMPLE 3 Prepare a horizontal analysis for the Comparative Income Statement for Aspen Lakes Extreme using the yearly amounts in Figure 21-9.

For each item, find the amount of increase or decrease by subtracting the smaller amount from the larger amount. For Aspen Lakes Extreme, the later year's amounts are all larger than the earlier year's amounts, so the difference of each amount is recorded as an increase in every case.

Next, find the percent increase by dividing the amount of increase by the earlier year's amount. For instance,

$$\text{Percent increase in net sales} = \frac{\text{amount of increase}}{\text{2013 amount}} \times 100\%$$

$$= \frac{\$242,897 - \$239,528}{\$239,528}(100\%)$$

$$= \frac{\$3,369}{\$239,528}(100\%)$$

$$= 1.4\%$$

The completed analysis is shown in Figure 21-10.

Aspen Lakes Extreme
Comparative Income Statement
for the Years Ending June 30, 2013 and 2014

			Increase (Decrease)	
	2014	2013	Amount	Percent of net sales
Net sales	$242,897	$239,528	$3,369	1.4
Cost of goods sold	116,582	115,351	1,231	1.1
Gross profit	126,315	124,177	2,138	1.7
Operating expenses	38,725	37,982	743	2.0
Net income	$87,590	$86,195	$1,395	1.6

FIGURE 21-10
Horizontal Analysis of the Aspen Lakes Extreme Comparative Income Statement

STOP AND CHECK

See Example 3.

1. Prepare a horizontal analysis of Cedar Rapids American Auto's comparative income statement for 2012 and 2013. See pages 753 and 756.

2. Prepare a horizontal analysis of Amaya's Soul Food Catering comparative income statement for 2012 and 2013. See pages 754 and 756.

3. What number is used as the base when calculating percentages on a vertical analysis of an income statement?

4. What number is used as the base when calculating percentages on a horizontal analysis of an income statement?

21-2 SECTION EXERCISES

SKILL BUILDERS

See Example 1.

1. Complete the income statement for Sitha Ros's Oriental Groceries for the years 2013 and 2014.

Sitha Ros's Oriental Groceries
Income Statement
for the Years Ending June 30, 2013 and 2014

	2014	2013
Net sales	$97,384	$92,196
Cost of goods sold	82,157	72,894
Gross profit		
Operating expenses	4,783	3,951
Net income		

2. Complete the portion for July 31, 2012, of the income statement shown for Miss Muffins' Bakery using the given information: gross sales, $32,596; returns and allowances, $296; cost of beginning inventory, $16,872; cost of purchases, $33,596; cost of ending inventory, $21,843; total operating expenses, $1,894. Compute net sales, cost of goods sold, gross profit, and net income.

3. Use the information recorded for Miss Muffins' Bakery for the month ending July 31, 2013, to extend the income statement for Exercise 2: gross sales, $35,403; returns and allowances, $342; cost of beginning inventory, $17,403; cost of purchases, $27,983; cost of ending inventory, $22,583; total operating expenses, $3,053. Compute net sales, cost of goods sold, gross profit, and net income.

Miss Muffins' Bakery
Comparative Income Statement for the Months Ending
July 31, 2012 and July 31, 2013

	2013	2012
Gross sales		
Returns and allowances		
Net sales	___	___
Cost of beginning inventory		
Cost of purchases		
Cost of ending inventory	___	___
Cost of goods sold	___	___
Gross profit		
Total operating expenses	___	___
Net income	═══	═══

APPLICATIONS

See Example 2.

4. Extend the income statement for Sitha Ros's Oriental Groceries to include a vertical analysis for 2013 and for 2014.

Sitha Ros's Oriental Groceries
Income Statement for Years Ending
June 30, 2013 and 2014

	2014	Percent of Net Sales	2013	Percent of Net Sales
Net sales				
Cost of goods sold	___		___	
Gross profit				
Operating expenses	___		___	
Net income	═══		═══	

5. Extend the income statement for Miss Muffins' Bakery to include a vertical analysis for 2012 and 2013.

	2013	Percent of Net Sales	2012	Percent of Net Sales
Gross sales				
Returns and allowances				
Net sales	_____		_____	
Cost of beginning inventory				
Cost of purchases				
Cost of ending inventory				
Cost of goods sold	_____		_____	
Gross profit	_____		_____	
Total operating expenses				
Net income	_____		_____	

Miss Muffins' Bakery
Vertical Analysis of Income Statement for the Months Ending
July 31, 2012 and July 31, 2013

6. *See Example 3.* Extend the income statements for Sitha Ros's Oriental Groceries to include the amounts of increase or decrease and the percents of increase or decrease for a horizontal analysis.

7. *See Example 3.* Extend the income statement for Miss Muffins' Bakery to include the amounts of increase or decrease and the percents of increase or decrease for a horizontal analysis.

Miss Muffins' Bakery
Comparative Income Statement for the Months Ending
July 31, 2012 and July 31, 2013

	2013	2012	Increase (Decrease) Amount	Percent
Gross sales				
Returns and allowances	_____	_____		
Net sales	_____	_____		
Cost of beginning inventory				
Cost of purchases				
Cost of ending inventory	_____	_____		
Cost of goods sold	_____	_____		
Gross profit				
Total operating expenses	_____	_____		
Net income	_____	_____		

21-3 FINANCIAL STATEMENT RATIOS

LEARNING OUTCOME

1 Find and use financial ratios.

Financial ratio: an analysis of financial data to compare a business's performance with past performance or with other similar businesses.

Financial statements organize and summarize information about the financial condition of a business. Using data from financial statements, **financial ratios** give businesses a way to evaluate their business compared to its past performance and compared to other similar businesses. Financial ratios are used by lending institutions and stockholders to determine the financial well-being of a business.

1 Find and use financial ratios.

Cash flow is an aspect of a business's operation. A business must know if it has enough cash on hand or cash coming in to pay its bills as they come due. Financial ratios that show a comparison between a business's cash on hand to its financial obligations that are due within the next few months are called **liquidity ratios.** These ratios are of interest to short-term creditors.

Liquidity ratio: a financial ratio that shows how well a business can be expected to meet its short-term financial obligations.

Working capital: current assets minus current liabilities.

Current Ratio It is important to know whether a business has enough assets to cover its liabilities. The **working capital** of a business is the current assets minus current liabilities. But that amount alone does not tell much about the relative financial condition of the business. Look at the following information about Aaron's Air Conditioning and Zelda's Zeppelins:

	Aaron's Air Conditioning	Zelda's Zeppelins
Current assets	$11,000	$615,000
Current liabilities	− 5,000	− 609,000
Working capital	$6,000	$6,000

Working capital = current assets − current liabilities

Both companies have the same working capital, but Zelda's *owes* almost as much as it *owns*. To compare these companies, we need to use ratios. A commonly used ratio in business is the **current ratio** (also called the **working capital ratio**), which is the ratio of current assets to current liabilities.

$$\text{Current ratio} = \frac{\text{current assets}}{\text{current liabilities}}$$

The current ratio for Aaron's Air Conditioning, for example, is the ratio of $11,000 to $5,000.

$$\text{Aaron's current ratio} = \frac{\text{Aaron's current assets}}{\text{Aaron's current liabilities}} = \frac{\$11,000}{\$5,000}$$

This ratio expresses the fact that Aaron's has $11,000 in current assets for $5,000 of current liabilities. If we write this ratio in decimal form, we have an equivalent ratio whose denominator is 1:

$$\frac{\$11,000}{\$5,000} = 2.2 = \frac{2.2}{1}$$

Thus, Aaron's current ratio is 2.2 to 1, telling us that Aaron's has $2.20 in current assets for every $1 in current liabilities.

The current ratio for Zelda's Zeppelins is the ratio of $615,000 to $609,000. Writing Zelda's current ratio in decimal form, we are able to see the usefulness of current ratio as a way of comparing businesses.

$$\text{Zelda's current ratio} = \frac{\text{Zelda's current assets}}{\text{Zelda's current liabilities}} = \frac{\$615,000}{\$609,000} = 1.01 = \frac{1.01}{1}$$

This ratio tells us that Zelda's has $1.01 in current assets for every $1 in current liabilities. Because Aaron's ratio is 2.2 to 1, we see that for every $1 of current liability, Aaron's has more than twice as much in current assets as does Zelda's. There are many financial ratios we might calculate, but the basic process is the same for all.

HOW TO   Calculate a financial ratio

1. Write one amount as the numerator of a fraction and a second amount as the denominator.
2. Write the fraction in decimal form (or, for some ratios, in percent form).

EXAMPLE 1
Find the current ratio of a business whose current assets are $18,000 and whose current liabilities are $12,000.

Write the ratio of current assets to current liabilities in decimal form.

$$\text{Current ratio} = \frac{\text{current assets}}{\text{current liabilities}} = \frac{\$18,000}{\$12,000} = 1.5$$

The current ratio is 1.5, or 1.5 to 1.

Many lending companies consider a current ratio of 2 to 1 $\left(\frac{2}{1}\right)$ to be the minimum acceptable current ratio for approving a loan to a business. The business in the preceding example, for instance, may find it difficult to get a loan because its current ratio is 1.5 to 1.

Acid-Test Ratio   Another ratio used to evaluate the financial condition of a business is the **acid-test ratio,** sometimes called the **quick ratio.** Instead of using all of the current assets of a business, the acid-test ratio uses only the **quick current assets,** those assets that can be readily exchanged for cash: marketable securities, accounts receivable, and notes receivable. Merchandise inventory is a current asset, but it is not included because a loss would probably occur if a business were to make a quick sale of all merchandise.

$$\text{Acid-test ratio (quick ratio)} = \frac{\text{quick current assets}}{\text{current liabilities}}$$

Ratios to net sales: ratios that make comparisons to net sales.

Operating ratio: the cost of goods sold plus the operating expenses divided by net sales.

Profitability ratio: a ratio comparing profits and sales.

Gross profit margin ratio: the ratio of the gross profit from sales to the net sales.

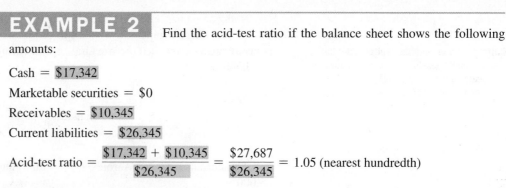

EXAMPLE 2   Find the acid-test ratio if the balance sheet shows the following amounts:

Cash = $17,342

Marketable securities = $0

Receivables = $10,345

Current liabilities = $26,345

$$\text{Acid-test ratio} = \frac{\$17,342 + \$10,345}{\$26,345} = \frac{\$27,687}{\$26,345} = 1.05 \text{ (nearest hundredth)}$$

The acid-test ratio is 1.05 to 1.

Ratios to Net Sales   Other useful ratios can be determined from an income statement. Two of the most important are the *operating ratio* and the *gross profit margin ratio*. These two are also called **ratios to net sales.** These ratios make comparisons possible between the major elements of the statement and net sales. These ratios are usually expressed in percent form, rather than decimal form, and they usually (but do not necessarily) cover one year.

Remember, the first amount in a ratio appears in the numerator and the second amount appears in the denominator. In both of the ratios to net sales, the denominator is the net sales.

The **operating ratio** indicates the amount of sales dollars that are used to pay for the cost of goods and operating expenses. A ratio of *less* than 1:1 is desirable. The lower the operating ratio, the more income there is to meet financial obligations.

$$\text{Operating ratio} = \frac{\text{cost of goods sold} + \text{operating expenses}}{\text{net sales}}$$

Another important category of financial ratios is **profitability ratios.** A profitability ratio shows the relationship between the sales and the gross and net profit. Stockholders and investors have a keen interest in these ratios.

The **gross profit margin ratio** shows the average spread between cost of goods sold and the selling price. The desirable gross profit margin ratio varies with the type of business. For example, a jewelry store might expect to have a ratio of 0.6 to 1 because there is a high rate of markup in jewelry. An auto parts store may, however, have a ratio of 0.25 to 1.

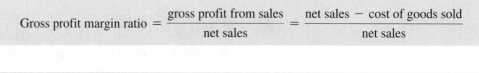

$$\text{Gross profit margin ratio} = \frac{\text{gross profit from sales}}{\text{net sales}} = \frac{\text{net sales} - \text{cost of goods sold}}{\text{net sales}}$$

EXAMPLE 3   Based on the income statement in Figure 21-11, find the operating ratio and the gross profit margin ratio for Vincent's Gift Shop. Express results in percent form, rounded to the nearest tenth of a percent.

Vincent's Gift Shop Income Statement for the Year Ending December 31, 2012	
Net sales	$173,157
Cost of beginning inventory	37,376
Cost of purchases	123,574
Cost of goods available for sale	160,950
Less: Cost of ending inventory	34,579
Cost of goods sold	126,371
Gross profit	46,786
Operating expenses	17,643
Net income	$29,143

FIGURE 21-11
Income Statement for Vincent's Gift Shop

$$\text{Operating ratio} = \frac{\text{cost of goods sold} + \text{operating expenses}}{\text{net sales}}$$

$$= \frac{\$126{,}371 + \$17{,}643}{\$173{,}157} = 0.831696 \text{ or } 83.2\%$$

The operating ratio is 0.832 to 1 or 83.2%.

$$\text{Gross profit margin ratio} = \frac{\text{net sales} - \text{cost of goods sold}}{\text{net sales}}$$

$$= \frac{\$173{,}157 - \$126{,}371}{\$173{,}157} = 0.2701941301 \text{ or } 27.0\%.$$

The gross profit margin ratio is 0.270 to 1 or 27.0%.

Other Financial Ratios Many other comparisons can be made using data found on the balance sheet, income statement, and other financial documents that are useful in analyzing various aspects of the business. For instance, the **asset turnover ratio** compares the net sales to the average total assets. This comparison shows the average return in sales for each $1 invested in assets. The asset turnover ratio and the inventory turnover ratios that were introduced in Chapter 18 are examples of **efficiency ratios.** An efficiency ratio is a measure of how effectively a business uses its assets to generate sales. The **total debt to total assets ratio** compares the total liabilities to the total assets. This comparison shows total indebtedness of the company for each $1 in assets and is an example of a **leverage ratio.** A leverage ratio examines the debts of a business.

The calculations for determining these ratios are the same as for determining any ratio. The amount in the numerator is divided by the amount in the denominator to give a decimal equivalent. This decimal equivalent can be interpreted as a comparison of the decimal equivalent to 1, or it can be interpreted as a percent by multiplying the decimal equivalent by 100%.

Asset turnover ratio: the ratio of the net sales to the average total assets.

Efficiency ratio: a financial ratio that measures a business's ability to effectively use its assets to generate sales.

Total debt to total assets ratio: the ratio of the total liabilities to the total assets.

Leverage ratio: a financial ratio that examines a business's indebtedness.

$$\text{Asset turnover ratio} = \frac{\text{net sales}}{\text{average total assets}}$$

$$\text{Total debt to total assets ratio} = \frac{\text{total liabilities}}{\text{total assets}}$$

Interpreting Financial Ratios A business needs to track its own progress over several periods of time to make sound business decisions and to compare its results to industry standards. A business uses financial ratios to make internal decisions or to distribute to stockholders, lenders, and prospective investors or buyers to show the financial status of the business. In Table 21-1 you will see some possible interpretations of financial ratios. Keep in mind, just as one statistic does not give a total picture, one ratio does not give a complete profile of a business's financial status.

TABLE 21-1
Financial Ratio Analysis

Ratio	Value Less Than 1	Value = 1	Value More Than 1
$\text{Current ratio} = \dfrac{\text{current assets}}{\text{current liabilities}}$	Debts greater than assets; potentially major problems	Debts and assets are equal	Assets greater than debts; current ratio of 2 is desirable
$\text{Acid-test ratio} = \dfrac{\text{quick current assets}}{\text{current liabilities}}$	Cash flow could be a problem	Business is in satisfactory condition	Business is in good financial condition
$\text{Operating ratio} = \dfrac{\text{COGS} + \text{operating expenses}}{\text{net sales}}$	Desirable	Marginal	Undesirable
$\text{Gross profit margin ratio} = \dfrac{\text{gross profit from sales}}{\text{net sales}}$	0.25 to 0.40 is industry average	Uncommon except for businesses with low turnover and high investment	Undesirable
$\text{Asset turnover ratio} = \dfrac{\text{net sales}}{\text{average total assets}}$	0.40 to 1.0 is industry average	Uncommon	Uncommon
$\text{Total debt to total assets ratio} = \dfrac{\text{total liabilities}}{\text{total assets}}$	0.05 to 0.75 is industry average	Debt ratio is too high	Debt ratio is dangerously high

EXAMPLE 4

Arsella would like to apply for a loan to expand Vincent's Gift Shop. The business's current assets are $58,482, its average total assets are $210,580, and total (current) liabilities are $32,289. Other information about the business can be found in Example 3. Analyze the financial condition of the business using information given in Table 21-1. Should Arsella plan to expand the business at this time?

What You Know	What You Are Looking For	Solution Plan
Current assets: $58,482 Average total assets: $210,580 Total (current) liabilities: $32,289 Ending inventory: $34,579 Net sales: $173,157 Operating expenses: $17,643 Cost of goods sold: $126,371	Current ratio Acid-test ratio Operating ratio Gross profit margin ratio Asset turnover ratio Total debt to total assets ratio Should Arsella expand the business at this time?	Find the financial ratios and use Table 21-1 to analyze the results.

Solution

$$\text{Current ratio} = \frac{\text{current assets}}{\text{current liabilities}} = \frac{\$58,482}{\$32,289} = 1.81$$

$$\text{Acid-test ratio} = \frac{\text{quick current assets}}{\text{current liabilities}} = \frac{\$58,482 - \$34,579}{\$32,289} = 0.74$$

$$\text{Operating ratio} = \frac{\text{COGS + operating expenses}}{\text{net sales}} = \frac{\$126,371 + \$17,643}{\$173,157} = 0.83$$

$$\text{Gross profit margin ratio} = \frac{\text{gross profit from sales}}{\text{net sales}} = \frac{\text{net sales} - \text{COGS}}{\text{net sales}}$$
$$= \frac{\$173,157 - \$126,371}{\$173,157} = 0.27$$

$$\text{Asset turnover ratio} = \frac{\text{net sales}}{\text{average total assets}} = \frac{\$173,157}{\$210,580} = 0.82$$

$$\text{Total debt to total assets ratio} = \frac{\text{total liabilities}}{\text{total assets}} = \frac{\$32,289}{\$210,580} = 0.15$$

TIP

Total Assets and Average Total Assets

In the asset turnover ratio, the divisor is average total assets. This is not necessarily the same as the total assets. In many cases it is the average of the total assets of two or more years.

Conclusion

The current ratio, operating ratio, gross profit margin ratio, and total debt to total assets ratio demonstrate a business with a healthy financial status. The acid-test ratio may indicate a potential cash flow problem, and the asset turnover ratio shows that inventory turnover is within the industry average.

Arsella should proceed cautiously in making a decision to expand. This decision should include an analysis of the local economic forecast and the cost of making a loan including repayment terms.

Shareholder ratio: translates the overall results of business operations so that they can be compared in terms of a share of stock.

Earnings per share: the amount of income earned during a period per share of common stock.

Book value per share: the amount of equity attributable to each share of common stock.

Price-to-earnings (P/E) ratio: the amount that someone buying the company stock is paying for each dollar of annual earnings.

Shareholder Ratios The financial ratios that we have examined to this point deal with the performance and financial condition of the company. These ratios provide information for managers and creditors, but an investor evaluating a company as a potential investment needs to be able to determine whether the price of a company's stock is reasonable from the basis of its financial position. **Shareholder ratios** translate the overall results of business operations so that they can be compared in terms of a share of stock. A company's earnings per share and book value per share are used to calculate shareholder ratios. **Earnings per share** is the amount of income earned during a period per share of common stock. **Book value per share** is the amount of equity attributable to each share of common stock. The **price-to-earnings (P/E) ratio** is the amount that someone buying the company stock is paying for each dollar of annual earnings. You may recall from Chapter 15 that while P/E ratios change every day as the stock price fluctuates, they are best viewed over time. As a general rule, the P/E ratio of a company should be comparable to a company's growth rate and with P/E ratios of other companies in the industry sector. The **price-to-book ratio**, by comparison, is a measure of how much someone buying the company stock is paying for each dollar's worth of equity.

$$\text{Earnings per share} = \frac{\text{net income for a period}}{\text{number of shares outstanding}}$$

$$\text{Book value per share} = \frac{\text{owner's equity for a period}}{\text{number of shares outstanding}}$$

$$\text{Price-earnings ratio} = \frac{\text{stock price per share}}{\text{earnings per share}}$$

$$\text{Price-to book ratio} = \frac{\text{stock price per share}}{\text{book value per share}}$$

EXAMPLE 5

Progeny Plastics Inc. is a public company with 1,000,000 shares of stock outstanding. As of the year's end the stock was selling for $36.12 per share and had total net income of $1,854,180 and total owner's equity of $8,241,100. Calculate the earnings per share and book value per share, then use them to calculate the P/E ratio and price-to-book ratio for Progeny Plastics. What will these two ratios tell you about investing in the company?

$$\text{Earnings per share} = \frac{\text{net income for a period}}{\text{number of shares outstanding}} = \frac{\$1,854,180}{1,000,000} = \$1.85$$

$$\text{Book value per share} = \frac{\text{owner's equity for a period}}{\text{number of shares outstanding}} = \frac{\$8,241,100}{1,000,000} = \$8.24$$

$$\text{Price-earnings ratio} = \frac{\text{stock price per share}}{\text{earnings per share}} = \frac{\$36.12}{\$1.85} = 19.52$$

$$\text{Price-to-book ratio} = \frac{\text{stock price per share}}{\text{book value per share}} = \frac{\$36.12}{\$8.24} = 4.38$$

An investor buying stock in Progeny Plastics would be paying $19.52 for each $1 of earnings. Similarly, an investor would pay $4.38 for each dollar of equity in the company. While there is no absolute way of determining the ideal price-to-earnings (P/E) ratio or price-to-book ratio, investors often look to these ratios as a guide to investing, relative to a similarly situated company within the overall context of the market sector.

It is important to both internal and external decisions for a business to look at business trends over an extended period of time. The most common type of analysis is to examine the percent of change for several successive operating time periods (normally years). This process is often referred to as a **trend analysis.** One way to analyze trends is to select one particular period (year) to be the reference or base in the percentage formula. The selected year (base year) is considered to be 100%. All other years are a percent of the base year. These percents are referred to as **index numbers.**

HOW TO   Prepare a trend analysis

1. Select a base year to be represented by 100%.
2. Calculate the index number for each successive year using the variation of the percentage formula.

$$\text{Index number (rate)} = \frac{\text{yearly amount (portion)}}{\text{base year amount (base)}}$$

3. Express the index number to the nearest tenth of a percent.
4. Prepare a table of the base and index numbers.
5. Prepare a graph of the base and index numbers.

EXAMPLE 6 The following data were collected by Stein Enterprises, Inc. Prepare a trend analysis of the net sales, the net income, and the total assets.

Stein Enterprises, Inc.
Financial Data for 2009–2013

	2013	2012	2011	2010	2009
Net Sales	594,398	507,287	572,103	550,524	512,854
Net Income	84,312	65,214	78,513	72,998	68,415
Total Assets	218,345	215,997	205,143	201,445	195,295

Index	2013	2012	2011	2010	2009
Net Sales	115.9	98.9	111.6	107.3	100.0
Net Income	123.2	95.3	114.8	106.7	100.0
Total Assets	111.8	110.6	105.0	103.1	100.0

Figure 21-12 plots the trend analysis of net sales, net income, and total assets.

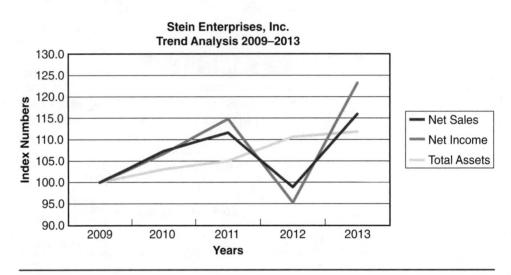

FIGURE 21-12
Trend Analysis of Net Sales, Net Income, and Total Assets.

STOP AND CHECK

See Example 1.

1. Find the current ratio for Cannon Motors if the current assets are $897,584 and current liabilities are $683,777. Round to tenths.

See Example 2.

2. Calculate the acid-test ratio for Johnson's Furniture if the balance sheet shows: cash, $297,518; marketable securities, $10,000; receivables, $143,812; and current liabilities, $86,950. Round to tenths.

See Example 3.

3. Find the operating ratio for Cedar Rapids American Auto, Inc., for 2013. This income statement was prepared as Exercise 2 on page 756.

4. Interpret the ratio found for Cedar Rapids American Auto, Inc.

5. Find the debt ratio at the end of 2012 for Rayco, Inc. This balance sheet was prepared as Exercise 3 on page 743.

6. Interpret the debt ratio found for Rayco, Inc.

See Example 4.

7. Kelli Drewery plans to apply for a loan to renovate Sugaree's Specialty Cakes. The business has current assets of $62,415, its average total assets are $174,400, and its total (current) liabilities are $43,717. Sugaree's ending inventory for the year was $12,592 and net sales for the year were $215,413. Operating expenses were $23,897 and cost of goods sold was $62,518. Should Kelli plan to renovate at this time?

See Example 5.

Thermaldine Corp. is a public company with 2,500,000 shares of stock outstanding. As of the year's end the stock was selling for $48.97 per share, and had total net income of $3,579,840 and total owner's equity of $15,398,500.

8. Calculate the shareholder earnings per share and book value per share, for Thermaldine Corp.

9. Calculate the PE ratio and the price-to-book ratio for Thermaldine Corp.

See Example 6.

10. Use the data for Ancor International, Inc. to prepare a trend analysis of net sales, net income, and total assets. Excel® should be used to prepare the analysis.

Ancor International, Inc.
Financial Data for 2010–2014

	2014	2013	2012	2011	2010
Net Sales	892,513	847,580	805,613	792,500	615,390
Net Income	149,432	105,324	87,513	96,873	75,830
Total Assets	297,583	253,840	239,500	238,900	215,103
Index	**2014**	**2013**	**2012**	**2011**	**2010**
Net Sales	145.0	137.7	130.9	128.8	100.0
Net Income	197.1	138.9	115.4	127.8	100.0
Total Assets	138.3	118.0	111.3	111.1	100.0

21-3 SECTION EXERCISES

SKILL BUILDERS

1. What is the current ratio for Denmark, Inc., which has current assets of $148,947 and current liabilities of $103,537?

2. Find the operating ratio for Chaney's Pharmacy if the annual cost of goods sold is $315,842, the operating expenses are $62,917, and net sales are $597,064.

3. Find the gross profit margin ratio if The Premier Eatery had net sales of $392,054 and its cost of goods sold was $179,515.

4. Proud Larry's Grill reported net sales of $289,512 and had average total assets of $145,753. Find its asset turnover ratio.

APPLICATIONS

5. Find the current ratio for George's business and the current ratio for José's business, given the following information:

	George	José
Current assets	$28,000	$840,000
Current liabilities	− 7,000	−819,000
Working capital	$21,000	$21,000

6. Find the acid-test ratio for Carley's business if the balance sheet shows the following amounts: cash, $32,981; receivables, $12,045; marketable securities, $0; current liabilities, $22,178.

7. Find the operating ratio for Sol's Dry Goods if the income statement for the month shows net sales, $15,500; cost of goods sold, $7,500; gross profit, $8,000; operating expenses, $3,500; net income, $4,500. Express results to the nearest tenth of a percent.

8. Find the gross profit margin ratio for Sol's Dry Goods in Exercise 7 to the nearest tenth of a percent.

Blaw's Knifeworks, Inc. is a public company with 1,650,000 shares of stock outstanding. At year's end, the stock price was $23.17 per share and the company had total net income of $2,118,534. Total owner's equity at end of year was $9,524,000.

9. Calculate the shareholder ratios of earnings per share and book value per share for Blaw's Knifeworks.

10. Calculate the P/E ratio and the price-to-book ratio for Blaw's Knifeworks.

Learning Outcomes

Section 21-1

1 Prepare a balance sheet. (p. 740)

What to Remember with Examples

1. Find and record the *total assets*. Balance sheets may be prepared by asset category.
  (a) List the *current assets* and draw a single line underneath the last entry.
  (b) Add the entries and record the *total current assets*, drawing a single line underneath the total.
  (c) Repeat step 1a for *plant and equipment assets* and step 1b for *total plant and equipment assets*.
  (d) Add the category totals and draw a double line underneath the grand total.

Total assets = total current assets + total plant and equipment

2. Find and record the *total liabilities*. Balance sheets may be prepared by liability category.
  (a) Repeat step 1a for *current liabilities* and step 1b for *total current liabilities*.
  (b) Repeat step 1a for *long-term liabilities* and step 1b for *total long-term liabilities*.
  (c) Add the category totals and draw a single line underneath the total.

Total liabilities = total current liabilities + total long-term liabilities

3. Find and record the *total owner's equity*.
  (a) List the equity entries and draw a single line underneath the last entry.
  (b) Add the entries and draw a single line underneath the total.
4. Find and record the *total liabilities and owner's equity*: Add the total liabilities to the total owner's equity and draw a double line underneath the grand total.

Total liabilities and owner's equity = total liabilities + total owner's equity

5. Confirm that the double line grand total from step 1 and step 4 are the same.

Total assets = total liabilities + owner's equity

Roy Russell's Security Service
Balance Sheet

		2013
Assets		
Cash		$8,000
Accounts receivable		4,860
Inventory		19,823
Equipment		8,925
Total assets		$41,608
Liabilities		
Accounts payable		$11,281
Wages payable		11,185
Total liabilities		22,466
Owner's equity		19,142
Total liabilities and owner's equity		$41,608

2 Prepare a vertical analysis of a balance sheet. (p. 743)

1. Prepare a balance sheet of assets, liabilities, and owner's equity.
2. Create an additional column labeled *percent*: For each item, divide the amount of the item by the total assets then multiply by 100% to record the result as a percent.

$$\text{Percent of total assets} = \frac{\text{amount of item}}{\text{total assets}} \times 100\%$$

Following is a vertical analysis of the balance sheet above. Each entry in the percent column is a percent of total assets. For example, for the item *cash*, the percent is

$$\frac{\text{Cash}}{\text{Total assets}} = \frac{\$8,000}{\$41,608}(100\%) = 0.1922707172(100\%) = 19.2\%$$

Roy Russell's Security Service
Balance Sheet

	2013	Percent of total assets
Assets		
Cash	$8,000	19.2
Accounts receivable	4,860	11.7
Inventory	19,823	47.6
Equipment	8,925	21.5
Total assets	$41,608	100.0
Liabilities		
Accounts payable	$11,281	27.1
Wages payable	11,185	26.9
Total liabilities	22,466	54.0
Owner's equity	19,142	46.0
Total liabilities and owner's equity	$41,608	100.0

3 Prepare a horizontal analysis of a balance sheet. (p. 747)

1. Prepare a balance sheet for two or more years: Record each year's amounts in separate columns.
2. Create an additional column labeled *amount of increase (decrease)*: For each yearly item,
   (a) Subtract the smaller amount from the larger amount and record the difference.
   (b) If the earlier year's amount is larger than the later year's amount, record the difference from step 2a as a decrease by using parentheses or a negative (minus) sign.
3. Create an additional column labeled *percent increase (decrease)*: For each yearly item, divide the amount of increase (decrease) by the earlier year's amount and record the difference as a percent.

$$\text{Percent increase (decrease)} = \frac{\text{amount of increase (decrease)}}{\text{earlier year's amount}} \times 100\%$$

Following is a horizontal analysis of the corporation balance sheet that extends the balance sheet for Russell's Security Service. Notice that an additional year's data are given and two *increase (decrease)* columns, one for *amount* and one for *percent*, are given as well. Notice that parentheses indicate that an item decreased from the earlier year to the later year.

Roy Russell's Security Service
Balance Sheet

	2014	2013	Increase (decrease)	Percent increase (decrease)
Assets				
Cash	$8,983	$8,000	$983	12.3
Accounts receivable	3,952	4,860	(908)	(18.7)
Inventory	22,507	19,823	2,684	13.5
Equipment	12,784	8,925	3,859	43.2
Total assets	$48,226	$41,608	6,618	15.9
Liabilities				
Accounts payable	$12,197	$11,281	$916	8.1
Wages payable	5,872	11,185	(5,313)	(47.5)
Total liabilities	18,069	22,466	(4,397)	(19.6)
Owner's equity	30,157	19,142	11,015	57.5
Total liabilities and owner's equity	$48,226	$41,608	$6,618	15.9

Section 21-2

1 Prepare an income statement. (p. 752)

1. Find and record *net sales*.
   (a) Record *gross sales*.
   (b) Record *sales returns and allowances*.
   (c) Subtract sales returns and allowances from gross sales.

$$\text{Net sales} = \text{gross sales} - \text{sales returns and allowances}$$

2. Find and record *cost of goods sold*.
   (a) Record cost of beginning inventory.
   (b) Record cost of purchases.
   (c) Record cost of ending inventory.
   (d) Add cost of beginning inventory and cost of purchases and subtract cost of ending inventory.

$$\text{Cost of goods sold} = \text{cost of beginning inventory} + \text{cost of purchases} - \text{cost of ending inventory}$$

3. Find and record *gross profit from sales*.

$$\text{Gross profit from sales} = \text{net sales} - \text{cost of goods sold}$$

4. Find and record *total operating expenses*. List the operating expenses and add the entries.
5. Find and record *net income*.

$$\text{Net income} = \text{gross profit from sales} - \text{operating expenses}$$

The Cyprien Corporation records the following data for the year 2013: gross sales, $187,700; sales returns and allowances, $8,200; cost of beginning inventory, $83,540; cost of purchases, $127,386; cost of ending inventory, $64,126; operating expenses, $18,500. Using this data, prepare an income statement.

$$\begin{aligned}
\text{Net sales} &= \text{gross sales} - \text{sales returns and allowances} \\
&= \$187,700 - \$8,200 \\
&= \$179,500
\end{aligned}$$

$$\begin{aligned}
\text{Cost of goods sold} &= \text{cost of beginning inventory} + \text{cost of purchases} \\
&\qquad - \text{cost of ending inventory} \\
&= \$83,540 + \$127,386 - \$64,126 \\
&= \$146,800
\end{aligned}$$

$$\begin{aligned}
\text{Gross profit from sales} &= \text{net sales} - \text{cost of goods sold} \\
&= \$179,500 - \$146,800 \\
&= \$32,700
\end{aligned}$$

$$\begin{aligned}
\text{Net income} &= \text{gross profit from sales} - \text{operating expenses} \\
&= \$32,700 - \$18,500 \\
&= \$14,200
\end{aligned}$$

Cyprien Corporation
Income Statement for 2013

Gross sales	$187,700	
Sales returns and allowances	8,200	
Net sales	179,500	
Cost of goods sold		
Beginning inventory	83,540	
Purchases	127,386	Add.
Goods available for sale	210,926	
Less: ending inventory	64,126	Subtract.
Cost of goods sold	146,800	
Gross profit from sales	32,700	Net sales − COGS
Operating expenses	18,500	Subtract.
Net income	$14,200	

---

2 Prepare a vertical analysis of an income statement. (p. 754)

1. Prepare an income statement.
2. Create an additional column labeled *percent of net sales*: For each item, divide the amount of the item by the net sales and record the result as a percent.

$$\text{Percent of net sales} = \frac{\text{amount of item}}{\text{net sales}} \times 100\%$$

Following is a vertical analysis of the income statement for Cyprien Corporation. Each entry in the percent column is a percent of net sales. For example, for the item *net income*, the percent is:

$$\frac{\text{Net income}}{\text{Net sales}} = \frac{\$14,200}{\$179,500}(100\%) = 0.0791086351(100\%) = 7.9\%$$

Cyprien Corporation
Income Statement

	2013	Percent of net sales
Net sales	$179,500	100.0
Cost of goods sold		
Beginning inventory	83,540	46.5
Purchases	127,386	71.0
Goods available for sale	210,926	117.5
Less: ending inventory	64,126	35.7
Cost of goods sold	146,800	81.8
Gross profit from sales	32,700	18.2
Operating expenses	18,500	10.3
Net income	$14,200	7.9

3 Prepare a horizontal analysis of an income statement. (p. 756)

1. Prepare an income statement for two or more years: Record each year's amounts in separate columns.
2. Create an additional column labeled *amount of increase (decrease).*
   For each yearly item,
   (a) Subtract the smaller amount from the larger amount and record the difference.
   (b) If the earlier year's amount is larger than the later year's amount, record the difference from step 2a as a decrease by using parentheses.
3. Create an additional column labeled *percent increase (decrease).* For each yearly item,

$$\text{Percent increase (decrease)} = \frac{\text{amount of increase (decrease)}}{\text{earlier year's amount}} \times 100\%$$

Following is a horizontal analysis of the Cyprien Corporation income statement that extends the income statement in the previous section. Notice that an additional year's data are given and two *increase (decrease)* columns, one for *amount* and one for *percent,* are given as well. Notice that parentheses indicate that an item decreased from the earlier year to the later year.

Cyprien Corporation
Comparative
Income Statement

	2014	2013	Increase (decrease)	Percent increase (decrease)
Net sales	$215,832	$179,500	$36,332	20.2
Cost of goods sold				
Beginning inventory	95,843	83,540	12,303	14.7
Purchases	107,395	127,386	(19,991)	(15.7)
Goods available for sale	203,238	210,926	(7,688)	(3.6)
Less: ending inventory	79,583	64,126	15,457	24.1
Cost of goods sold	123,655	146,800	(23,145)	(15.8)
Gross profit from sales	92,177	32,700	59,477	181.9
Operating expenses	25,713	18,500	7,213	39.0
Net income	$66,464	$14,200	$52,264	368.1

Section 21-3

1 Find and use financial ratios.
(p. 760)

1. Write one amount as the numerator of a fraction and a second amount as the denominator.
2. Write the fraction in decimal form (or, for some ratios, in percent form).

$$\text{Working capital} = \text{current assets} - \text{current liabilities}$$

$$\text{Current ratio} = \frac{\text{current assets}}{\text{current liabilities}}$$

$$\text{Acid-test ratio (quick ratio)} = \frac{\text{quick current assets}}{\text{current liabilities}}$$

$$\text{Operating ratio} = \frac{\text{cost of goods sold} + \text{operating expenses}}{\text{net sales}}$$

$$\text{Gross profit margin ratio} = \frac{\text{gross profit from sales}}{\text{net sales}} = \frac{\text{net sales} - \text{cost of goods sold}}{\text{net sales}}$$

$$\text{Asset turnover ratio} = \frac{\text{net sales}}{\text{average total assets}}$$

$$\text{Total debt to total assets ratio} = \frac{\text{total liabilities}}{\text{total assets}}$$

Use the income statement amounts for 2013 for the Cyprien Corporation (p. 771) to find the financial ratios. Additional information needed from the balance sheet is total assets, $108,000; current assets, $40,000; quick current assets: cash, $15,892; marketable securities, $10,000; and receivables, $7,486; total liabilities, $57,000; current liabilities, $28,000.

$$\text{Working capital} = \text{current assets} - \text{current liabilities}$$
$$= \$40,000 - \$28,000 = \$12,000$$

$$\text{Current ratio} = \frac{\text{current assets}}{\text{current liabilities}} = \frac{\$40,000}{\$28,000} = 1.43 \text{ to } 1$$

$$\text{Acid-test ratio} = \frac{\text{quick current assets}}{\text{current liabilities}}$$
$$= \frac{\$15,892 + \$10,000 + \$7,486}{\$28,000} = 1.19 \text{ to } 1$$

$$\text{Operating ratio} = \frac{\text{cost of goods sold} + \text{operating expenses}}{\text{net sales}}$$
$$= \frac{\$146,800 + \$18,500}{\$179,500} = 0.921 \text{ or } 92.1\%$$

$$\text{Gross profit margin ratio} = \frac{\text{gross profit from sales}}{\text{net sales}} = \frac{\text{net sales} - \text{cost of goods sold}}{\text{net sales}}$$
$$= \frac{\$179,500 - \$146,800}{\$179,500}$$
$$= 0.182 \text{ or } 18.2\%$$

$$\text{Asset turnover ratio} = \frac{\text{net sales}}{\text{average total assets}} = \frac{\$179,500}{\$108,000^*} = 1.66 \text{ to } 1$$

$$\text{Total debt to total assets ratio} = \frac{\text{total liabilities}}{\text{total assets}} = \frac{\$57,000}{\$108,000} = 0.528 \text{ to } 1$$

*Since only one value is given for total assets, it is also used for average total assets.

Durham Corp. is a public company with 500,000 shares of stock outstanding. As of the year's end the stock was selling for $27.12 per share and had total net income of $857,000 and total owner's equity of $3,214,000. Calculate the shareholder ratios of earnings per share, book value per share, P/E ratio, and price-to-book ratio for Durham Corp.

$$\text{Earnings per share} = \frac{\text{net income}}{\text{number of shares outstanding}} = \frac{\$857,000}{500,000} = \$1.71$$

$$\text{Book value per share} = \frac{\text{owner's equity}}{\text{number of shares outstanding}} = \frac{\$3,214,000}{500,000} = \$6.43$$

$$\text{Price-earnings ratio} = \frac{\text{price per share}}{\text{earnings per share}} = \frac{\$27.12}{\$1.71} = 15.86$$

$$\text{Price-to-book ratio} = \frac{\text{price per share}}{\text{book value per share}} = \frac{\$27.12}{\$6.43} = 4.22$$

Prepare a trend analysis:

1. Select a base year to be represented by 100%.
2. Calculate the index number for each successive year using the variation of the percentage formula.

$$\text{Index number(rate)} = \frac{\text{yearly amount(portion)}}{\text{base year amount(base)}}$$

3. Express the index number to the nearest tenth of a percent.
4. Prepare a table of the base and index numbers.
5. Prepare a graph of the base and index numbers.

See Example 6 on page 766 for an illustration of a trend analysis.

EXERCISES SET A

1. Complete the following balance sheet for Fawcett's Plumbing Supplies.

Fawcett's Plumbing Supplies
Balance Sheet
March 31, 2013

Assets
Current assets
Cash	$1,724.00
Office supplies	173.00
Accounts receivable	9,374.00
Total current assets	

Plant and equipment
Equipment	12,187.00
Total plant and equipment	12,187.00
Total assets	

Liabilities
Current liabilities
Accounts payable	$2,174.00
Wages payable	674.00
Property and taxes payable	250.00
Total current liabilities	
Total liabilities	

Owner's equity
D. W. Fawcett, capital	20,360.00
Total liabilities and owner's equity	

EXCEL 2. Complete the vertical analysis and horizontal analysis of the comparative balance sheet for Seymour's Organics, LLC. Express percents to the nearest tenth of a percent.

Seymour's Organics, LLC.
Comparative Balance Sheet
December 31, 2012 and 2013

	2013	2012	Increase (decrease) Amount	Increase (decrease) Percent	Percent of total assets 2013	Percent of total assets 2012
Assets						
Current assets						
Cash	$2,374	$2,184				
Accounts receivable	5,374	4,286				
Merchandise inventory	15,589	16,107				
Total assets						
Liabilities						
Current liabilities						
Accounts payable	$7,384	$6,118				
Wages payable	1,024	964				
Total liabilities						
Owner's equity						
James Seymour, capital	14,929	15,495				
Total liabilities and owner's equity						

3. Complete the following income statement and vertical analysis.

Marten's Family Store
Income Statement
For Year Ending December 31, 2013

		Percent of net sales
Revenue:		
Gross sales	$238,923	
Sales returns and allowances	13,815	
Net sales		
Cost of goods sold:		
Beginning inventory, January 1, 2013	25,814	
Purchases	109,838	
Ending inventory, December 31, 2013	23,423	
Cost of goods sold		
Gross profit from sales		
Operating expenses:		
Salary	42,523	
Rent	8,640	
Utilities	1,484	
Insurance	2,842	
Fees	860	
Depreciation	1,920	
Miscellaneous	3,420	
Total operating expenses	61,689	
Net income		

4. Complete the following horizontal analysis of a comparative income statement.

Alonzo's Auto Parts
Comparative Income Statement
For years ending June 30, 2013 and 2014

	2014	2013	Increase (decrease) Amount	Percent
Revenue:				
Gross sales	$291,707	$275,873		
Sales returns and allowances	5,895	6,821		
Net sales				
Cost of goods sold:				
Beginning inventory, July 1	35,892	32,587		
Purchases	157,213	146,999		
Ending inventory, June 30	32,516	30,013		
Cost of goods sold				
Gross profit from sales				
Operating expenses:				
Salary	42,000	40,000		
Insurance	3,800	3,800		
Utilities	1,986	2,097		
Rent	3,600	3,300		
Depreciation	4,000	4,500		
Total operating expenses				
Net income				

Find the current ratio for each of the following businesses. Round answers to the nearest hundredth.

	Current assets	Current liabilities			Current assets	Current liabilities
5.	$1,231,704	$784,184		**6.**	$174,316	$125,342

7. Stevens Gift Shop: cash, $2,345; accounts receivable, $5,450; government securities, $4,500; accounts payable, $6,748; notes payable, $7,457. Find the acid-test ratio. Round to the nearest hundredth.

8. Find the acid-test ratio for Edna Nunez and Company if the balance sheet shows cash, $23,500; marketable securities, $0; receivables, $12,300; current liabilities, $27,800. Round to the nearest hundredth.

9. Find the operating ratio and gross profit margin ratio for the following income statement:

Green Zone Organics
Income Statement
For the Month Ending June 30, 2013

Net sales	$25,000
Cost of goods sold	$18,750
Gross profit	$6,250
Operating expenses	$3,750
Net income	$2,500

10. Find the operating ratio for A to Z Sales if the income statement for the month shows net sales, $173,200; cost of goods sold, $138,400; gross profit, $34,800; operating expenses, $16,300; net income, $18,500. Express answer to the nearest tenth of a percent.

11. Find the gross profit margin ratio for the business in Exercise 10 to the nearest tenth of a percent.

12. Find the operating ratio and the gross profit margin ratio for Molene Internet Store if the month's income statement shows net sales, $285,832; cost of goods sold, $198,530; gross profit, $87,302; operating expenses, $36,593; net income, $50,709. Round to the nearest tenth.

Buffalo Outback Outfitters is a public company with 37,360,000 shares of stock outstanding. As of the year's end the stock was selling for $26.18 per share, and had total net income of $51,710,000 and total owner's equity of $416,850,000.

13. Calculate the shareholder ratios of earnings per share and book value per share for Buffalo Outback Outfitters.

14. Calculate the P/E ratio and the price-to-book ratio for Buffalo Outback Outfitters.

EXERCISES SET B

1. Complete the following balance sheet for Rooter Green Construction Company.

Rooter Green Construction Company
Balance Sheet
June 30, 2014

Assets
Current assets
Cash	$2,350.00
Supplies	175.00
Accounts receivable	8,956.00
Total current assets	

Plant and equipment
Equipment	11,375.00
Total plant and equipment	11,375.00
Total assets	

Liabilities
Current liabilities
Accounts payable	$1,940.00
Wages payable	855.00
Rent payable	775.00
Total current liabilities	
Total liabilities	

Owner's equity
Wilson Rooter, capital	19,286.00
Total liabilities and owner's equity	

2. Complete the vertical analysis and the horizontal analysis of the comparative balance sheet for Miller's Life Coaching. Express percents to the nearest tenth of a percent.

Miller's Life Coaching
Comparative Balance Sheet
December 31, 2012 and 2013

	2013	2012	Increase (decrease) Amount	Increase (decrease) Percent	Percent of total assets 2013	Percent of total assets 2012
Assets						
Current assets						
Cash	$2,176	$1,948				
Accounts receivable	2,789	1,742				
Merchandise inventory	4,985	5,450				
Total assets						
Liabilities						
Current liabilities						
Accounts payable	$901	$872				
Wages payable	1,342	1,224				
Insurance payable	690	680				
Total liabilities						
Owner's equity						
Kathy Miller, capital	7,017	6,364				
Total liabilities and owner's equity						

3. Complete the following income statement and vertical analysis. Express percents to the nearest tenth of a percent.

Serpa's Gifts
Income Statement
For Year Ending December 31, 2012

		Percent of net sales
Revenue:		
Gross sales	$148,645	
Sales returns and allowances	8,892	
Net sales		
Cost of goods sold:		
Beginning inventory, January 1, 2012	12,100	
Purchases	47,800	
Ending inventory, December 31, 2012	11,950	
Cost of goods sold	_____	
Gross profit from sales	_____	
Operating expenses:		
Salary	25,500	
Rent	4,500	
Utilities	1,445	
Insurance	2,100	
Fees	225	
Depreciation	1,240	
Miscellaneous	750	
Total operating expenses	_____	
Net income	_____	

4. Complete the following horizontal analysis of a comparative income statement. Express percents to the nearest tenth of a percent.

Designer Crafts
Comparative Income Statement
For Years Ending December 31, 2013 and 2014

	2014	2013	Increase (decrease) Amount	Percent
Revenue:				
Gross sales	$239,873	$236,941		
Sales returns and allowances	12,815	13,895		
Net sales				
Cost of goods sold:				
Beginning inventory, January 1	27,814	25,887		
Purchases	123,213	112,604		
Ending inventory, December 31	24,482	23,838		
Cost of goods sold				
Gross profit from sales				
Operating expenses:				
Salary	44,772	42,640		
Insurance	3,006	2,863		
Utilities	1,597	1,521		
Rent	3,600	3,600		
Depreciation	4,100	3,400		
Total operating expenses				
Net income				

Find the current ratio for each of the following businesses. Round answers to the nearest hundredth.

	Current assets	**Current liabilities**		**Current assets**	**Current liabilities**
5.	$32,194	$38,714	**6.**	$724,987	$334,169

7. Find the acid-test ratio for Central Office Supply: cash, $5,745; accounts receivable, $12,496; accounts payable, $10,475. Round to the nearest hundredth.

8. Find the acid-test ratio for Jefferson's Photo if the balance sheet shows cash, $6,700; marketable securities, $0; receivables, $12,756; current liabilities, $18,345.

9. Find the operating ratio for M. Ng's Grocery if the income statement for the month shows net sales, $23,500; cost of goods sold, $16,435; gross profit, $7,065; operating expenses, $3,100; net income, $3,965. Round to the nearest tenth of a percent.

10. Find the gross profit margin ratio for the business in Exercise 9 to the nearest tenth of a percent.

Fresh Fruit Organics is a public company with 2,350,000 shares of stock outstanding. As of the year's end the stock was selling for $16.38 per share and had total net income of $4,200,000 and total owner's equity of $12,160,000.

11. Calculate the shareholder ratios of earnings per share and the book value per share for Fresh Fruit Organics.

12. Calculate the P/E ratio and the price-to-book ratio for Fresh Fruit Organics.

PRACTICE TEST

CHAPTER 21

1. Complete the horizontal analysis of the following comparative balance sheet. Express percents to the nearest tenth of a percent.

O'Toole's Hardware Store
Comparative Balance Sheet
December 31, 2013 and 2014

	2014	2013	Increase (Decrease) Amount	Percent
Assets				
Current assets				
Cash	$7,318	$5,283		
Accounts receivable	3,147	3,008		
Merchandise inventory	63,594	60,187		
Total current assets				
Plant and equipment				
Building	36,561	37,531		
Equipment	8,256	4,386		
Total plant and equipment				
Total assets				
Liabilities				
Current liabilities				
Accounts payable	$5,174	$4,563		
Wages payable	780	624		
Total current liabilities				
Long-term liabilities				
Mortgage note payable	34,917	36,510		
Total long-term liabilities				
Total liabilities				
Owner's Equity				
James O'Toole, capital	78,005	68,698		
Total liabilities and owner's equity				

2. Find the current ratio to the nearest hundredth for 2014 for O'Toole's Hardware Store.

3. Find the acid-test ratio to the nearest hundredth for 2014 for O'Toole's Hardware Store.

4. Find the current ratio to the nearest hundredth for 2013 for O'Toole's Hardware Store.

5. Find the acid-test ratio to the nearest hundredth for 2013 for O'Toole's Hardware Store.

6. Complete the horizontal analysis of the following comparative income statement.

Mile Wide Organic Woolens, Inc.
Comparative Income Statement
For Years Ending December 31, 2012 and 2013

	2013	2012	Increase (decrease) Amount	Percent
Revenue				
Gross sales	$219,827	$205,852		
Sales returns and allowances	8,512	7,983		
Net sales				
Cost of goods sold				
Beginning inventory, January 1	42,816	40,512		
Purchases	97,523	94,812		
Ending inventory, December 31	43,182	42,521		
Cost of goods sold				
Gross profit from sales				
Operating expenses				
Salary	28,940	27,000		
Insurance	800	750		
Utilities	1,700	1,580		
Rent	3,600	3,000		
Depreciation	2,000	2,400		
Total operating expenses				
Net income				

7. Find the operating ratio for Mile Wide for 2012 and 2013.

8. Find the gross profit margin ratio for Mile Wide for 2012 and 2013.

9. Find the asset turnover ratio for Mile Wide for 2012 if its average total assets were $126,432.

10. Find the asset turnover ratio for Mile Wide for 2013 if its average total assets were $138,057.

Houston Technology, Inc. is a public company with 2,350,000 shares of stock outstanding. As of the year's end the stock was selling for $9.83 per share and had total net income of $1,290,000 and total owner's equity of $9,600,000.

11. Calculate the shareholder earnings per share and book value per share for Houston Technology, Inc.

12. Calculate the P/E ratio and the price-to-book ratio for Houston Technology, Inc.

1. Use the formulas in the How To box: Prepare a Balance Sheet (p. 741) to explain the formula: Total current assets + total plant and equipment = total liabilities + total owner's equity.

2. Explain how the formula
Gross profit = net sales − cost of goods sold can be rearranged to find net sales.

3. If you have the formula:
Net profit = gross profit − operating expenses,
and the net profit is $25,982 and operating expenses are $150,986, write an equation to find gross profit.

4. Explain how the formula
$$\text{Percent of net sales} = \frac{\text{amount of item}}{\text{net sales}}$$
can be rearranged to find the amount of the item.

5. Compare the formula in step 3 of the How To box: Prepare a Horizontal Analysis of a Comparative Income Statement (p. 756) with the formula you would use to find the percent of sales tax if you know the amount of tax and the amount (price) of the item.

6. How do the two formulas in Exercise 5 compare to the basic percentage formula $P = RB$?

7. Explain why the same formula $P = RB$ can be used to calculate an increase or a decrease.

8. If a current ratio for a company equals 1, what is the relationship of the current assets to the current liabilities?

9. If the current ratio is less than 1, what is the relationship of the current assets to the current liabilities?

10. If a company has an acid-test ratio that is greater than 1, what is the relationship of the quick current assets to current liabilities?

Challenge Problem

Cedar-Crest Greeting Card Company ended the year 2012 with assets that totaled $120,000. The assets for 2013 increased to $580,000. What was the rate of growth for Cedar-Crest?

21-1 Contemporary Wood Furniture

Charles Royston was checking the year-end balances for his wood furniture manufacturing and retail business and was concerned about the numbers. From what he remembered, his debts and accounts receivable were higher than the previous year. Rather than get worked up over nothing, he decided he would gather the information and make a comparison. For December 31, 2013, the business had current assets of: $1,844 cash, $11,807 accounts receivable, and $9,628 inventory. Plant and equipment totaled $158,700. Current liabilities were: accounts payable $13,446; wages payable $650; and property and taxes payable $4,124. Long-term debt totaled $92,800 and owner's equity $70,959. By comparison, for December 31, 2012, the business had current assets of: $3,278 cash; $6,954 accounts receivable; $17,417 inventory. Plant and equipment totaled $144,500. Current liabilities were: accounts payable $9,250; wages payable $1,110; property and taxes payable $3,650. Long-term debt totaled $75,800; and owner's equity $82,339.

1. Construct a comparative balance sheet for Contemporary Wood Furniture for year-end 2012 and 2013, including a vertical and horizontal analysis of the comparative balance sheet. Express percents to the nearest tenth of a percent.

2. Calculate the current ratio and the total debt to total assets ratio for 2012 and 2013.

3. Overall, what does your analysis mean? Is Charles correct to be concerned about these numbers? Explain.

21-2 Balanced Books Bookkeeping

Jessica and David are student interns at Balanced Books Bookkeeping. They have taken several business math and accounting classes and are now applying what they have learned to real-life situations. They enjoy their internship, but they are sometimes surprised by the assignments they are given. Luckily, they work together, so they share the assignments and learn from each other. Their most recent assignment is to take a listing of accounts provided by one of Balanced Books' clients and turn them into a balance sheet and income statement. David suggests that their client might appreciate it if they also performed a vertical analysis of each statement. Jessica suggests that they should also compute the current ratio and the acid-test ratio.

1. Create the financial statements for December 31, 2013, depict them in vertical format, and compute the current and acid test ratios.

Account title	Amount	Account title	Amount
Cash	$4,000	Accounts payable	$3,500
Depreciation	2,000	Merchandise inventory	15,000
Carlton, equity	34,500	Accounts receivable	6,000
Cost of goods sold	85,000	Net sales	120,000
Rent expense	15,000	Insurance payable	500
Wages payable	1,500	Equipment	15,000
Utilities	6,500	Wages	8,000
Miscellaneous expenses	1,500		

CHAPTER 1

SECTION 1-1

1, p. 5

1. Seven million, three hundred fifty-two thousand, four hundred ninety-six
2. Four million, twenty-three thousand, five hundred eight
3. Sixty-two billion, eight hundred five million, nine hundred twenty-seven
4. Five hundred eighty-seven billion, nine hundred twelve

2, p. 6

1. $18,078,397,203   2. $36,017   3. $932,806   4. 52,896

3, p. 7

1. 3,785,000   2. 6,100   3. 53,000   4. 20,000   5. 600,000 tickets   6. $57,000

4, p. 9

1. Negative ninety-four billion, two million, fifty-two thousand, one hundred fifty-seven dollars   2. Negative nineteen billion, eight hundred twelve million, four hundred eighty-six thousand, one hundred eighty-seven dollars   3. −$20,000   4. −$9,000

SECTION 1-2

1, p. 13

1.				2.				3.				4.		
372	400	372		9,823	10,000	9,823		$618	$600	$618		$1,809	$2,000	$1,809
583	600	583		7,516	8,000	7,516		736	700	736		3,521	4,000	3,521
697	700	697		8,205	8,000	8,205		107	100	107			$6,000	$5,330
	1,700	1,652			26,000	25,544			$1,400	$1,461				

5.			6.				7.				8.		
138	100	138		1,352	1,000	1,352		$3,807	$4,000	$3,807		10,523	10,000	10,523
− 96	−100	− 96		− 787	− 800	− 787		− 2,689	− 3,000	− 2,689		− 5,897	− 6,000	− 5,897
	0	42			200	565			$1,000	$1,118			4,000	4,626

9.

What You Know	What You Are Looking For	Solution Plan
Projected total revenue = $1,200,000 Revenue from 10 largest = $789,000 Revenue from others = $342,000	Total revenue Did the company reach its projection?	Add and compare total revenue with projected revenue.

Solution

$ 789,000	revenue from 10 largest clients
342,000	revenue from other clients total
$1,131,000	revenue

Conclusion

The total revenue of **$1,131,000 is less than $1,200,000, so the company did not reach its projection.**

10.

What You Know	What You Are Looking For	Solution Plan
Projected total revenue = $2,500,000 Revenue from Quarter 1 = $492,568 Revenue from Quarter 2 = $648,942 Revenue from Quarter 3 = $703,840 Revenue from Quarter 4 = $683,491	Total revenue Did the shop reach its projected revenue?	Add and compare total revenue with projected revenue.

Solution

492568 $\boxed{+}$ 648942 $\boxed{+}$ 703840 $\boxed{+}$ 683491 $\Rightarrow$ 2528841
Calculator steps for the sum.

Conclusion

The shop exceeded its **revenue goal of $2,500,000 since $2,528,841 is more than $2,500,000.**

11.

What You Know	What You Are Looking For	Solution Plan
Jet Blue sold 2,196,512 tickets. Southwest sold 1,993,813 tickets.	Difference in number of tickets sold by two airlines	Difference = Jet Blue tickets minus Southwest tickets

Solution

$$\begin{array}{r} 2{,}196{,}512 \\ -\ 1{,}993{,}813 \\ \hline 202{,}699 \end{array}$$ Jet Blue tickets
Southwest tickets
difference

Conclusion

Jet Blue sold 202,699 more tickets than Southwest.

12.

What You Know	What You Are Looking For	Solution Plan
Number of firms with 1 to 4 employees = 2,734,133. Number of firms with 5 to 9 employees = 1,025,497.	Difference in number of firms by size of firm.	Difference = number of firms with 1 to 4 employees minus number of firms with 5 to 9 employees.

Solution

2734133 $\boxed{-}$ 1025497 $\Rightarrow$ 1708636   Calculator steps for the difference.

Conclusion

There are 1,708,636 more firms with 1 to 4 employees than there are firms with 5 to 9 employees.

2, p. 16

1. $-\$7{,}217 + (-\$2{,}314) = -\$9{,}531$ **2.** $-\$137{,}942 + (-\$38{,}457) = -\$176{,}399$ **3.** $\$118{,}298 \text{ million} - (-\$1{,}131 \text{ million}) = \$119{,}429 \text{ million}$

4. $-\$4{,}815 + \$928 = -\$3{,}887$ **5.** $48 - (-21) = 48 + 21 = 69$ **6.** $-18 - 14 = -18 + (-14) = -32$

3, p. 19

1.
$$\begin{array}{r} 317 \\ \times\ 52 \\ \hline 15{,}000 \end{array} \qquad \begin{array}{r} 300 \\ \times\ 50 \\ \hline \end{array} \qquad \begin{array}{r} 317 \\ \times\ 52 \\ \hline 634 \\ 15\ 85 \\ \hline 16{,}484 \end{array}$$

2.
$$\begin{array}{r} 6{,}723 \\ \times\ 87 \\ \hline \end{array} \qquad \begin{array}{r} 7{,}000 \\ \times\ 9\,0 \\ \hline 63\,0{,}000 \end{array} \qquad \begin{array}{r} 6{,}723 \\ \times\ 87 \\ \hline 47\ 061 \\ 537\ 84 \\ \hline 584{,}901 \end{array}$$

3.
$$\begin{array}{r} 4{,}600 \\ \times\ 70 \\ \hline \end{array} \qquad \begin{array}{r} 5{,}000 \\ \times\ 70 \\ \hline 350{,}000 \end{array} \qquad \begin{array}{r} 4{,}600 \\ \times\ 70 \\ \hline 322{,}000 \end{array}$$

4.
$$\begin{array}{r} 538{,}000 \\ \times\ 420 \\ \hline \end{array} \qquad \begin{array}{r} 5\,00{,}000 \\ \times\ 4\,00 \\ \hline 020\,0{,}000{,}000 \end{array} \qquad \begin{array}{r} 538\,{,}000 \\ \times\ 42\,0 \\ \hline \times010\ 76\ 0\ 000 \\ 215\ 2 \\ \hline 225{,}96\ 0{,}000 \end{array}$$

5. $(-21)(-15) = 315$ **6.** $(-8)(-12)(-9) = -864$

7.

What You Know	What You Are Looking For	Solution Plan
One machine produces 75 rolls per hour. There are 15 machines.	Number of rolls produced in 24 hours by 1 machine; by 15 machines.	Multiply production per hour times number of hours times number of machines.

Solution

75 rolls $\times$ 24 hours = 1,800 rolls per machine
1,800 rolls $\times$ 15 machines = 27,000 rolls

Conclusion

1,800 rolls can be produced by 1 machine in 24 hours. 27,000 rolls can be produced by 15 machines in 24 hours.

9. $456(-\$4) = -\$1{,}824$ **10.** $976(-\$9) = -\$8{,}784$

8.

What You Know	What You Are Looking For	Solution Plan
Number of coffee cups produced in a day = 48. Number of bowls produced in a day = 72. Number of coffee cups (809) and number of bowls (1,242) sold in the 22-day month.	Number of coffee cups and number of bowls that can be produced in a 22-day month and number of each item left in inventory at the end of the month.	Multiply the number of items produced in one day by the number of days of production, which is 22 days. Subtract the number of each item sold from the number produced in the month.

Solution

48 $\boxed{\times}$ 22 $\Rightarrow$ 1056   Calculator steps for the product.
72 $\boxed{\times}$ 22 $\Rightarrow$ 1584
1056 $\boxed{-}$ 809 $\Rightarrow$ 247   Calculator steps for the difference.
1584 $\boxed{-}$ 1242 $\Rightarrow$ 342

Conclusion

1,056 coffee cups and 1,584 bowls were produced in a month. At the end of the month 247 coffee cups and 342 bowls remained in inventory.

4, p. 23

1.
$$\begin{array}{r} 462 \\ 6\overline{)2{,}772} \\ 2\ 4 \\ \hline 37 \\ 36 \\ \hline 12 \\ 12 \end{array}$$

2.
$$\begin{array}{r} 281 \\ 24\overline{)6{,}744} \\ 4\ 8 \\ \hline 1\ 94 \\ 1\ 92 \\ \hline 24 \\ 24 \end{array}$$

3.
$$\begin{array}{r} 304\ \text{R}17 \\ 47\overline{)14{,}305} \\ 14\ 1 \\ \hline 205 \\ 188 \\ \hline 17 \end{array}$$

4.
$$\begin{array}{r} 84\ \text{R}3 \\ 15\overline{)1{,}263} \\ 1{,}20 \\ \hline 63 \\ 60 \\ \hline 3 \end{array}$$

5.

What You Know	What You Are Looking For	Solution Plan
The Gap purchases 5,184 pairs of jeans and divides them among 324 stores.	How many pairs are sent to each store?	Divide the number of pairs of jeans by the number of stores.

Solution

$$
\begin{array}{r}
16 \\
324\overline{)5{,}184} \\
3\ 24 \\
\hline
1\ 944 \\
1\ 944 \\
\hline
\end{array}
$$

Conclusion

Each store should be sent 16 pairs of jeans.

6.

What You Know	What You Are Looking For	Solution Plan
Auto Zone purchases 26,560 cans of car wax in cases of 64 cans per case.	How many stores can get 1 case of the wax?	Divide the total number of cans purchased by the number of cans sent to each store.

Solution

$$
\begin{array}{r}
415 \\
64\overline{)26{,}560} \\
25\ 6 \\
\hline
96 \\
64 \\
\hline
320 \\
320 \\
\hline
\end{array}
$$

Conclusion

One case of 64 cans of wax can be shipped to each of 415 stores.

7. $-\$27{,}684 \div 12 = -\$2{,}307$ million   **8.** $-\$16{,}998{,}000{,}000 \div 12 = -\$1{,}416{,}500{,}000$ **9.** $834{,}000 \div 600 = 8{,}340 \div 6 = 1{,}390$

10. $14{,}560{,}000 \div 7{,}000 = 14{,}560 \div 7 = 2{,}080$

5, p. 24

1. $38 - (5 + 12) =$
$38 - 17 = 21$

2. $(42 + 38 + 26 + 86) \div 12 =$
$192 \div 12 = 16$

3. $42 - 26 + 13 \times 3 =$
$42 - 26 + 39 =$
$16 + 39 = 55$

4. $38 + 12 \div (-3) =$
$38 + (-4) = 34$

CHAPTER 2

SECTION 2-1

1, p. 45

1. $\frac{3}{7}$; the numerator is less than the denominator, so the fraction is proper.

2. $\frac{4}{3}$; the numerator is greater than the denominator, so the fraction is improper.

3. $\frac{3}{7}$ is a proper fraction because the numerator is smaller than the denominator.

4. $\frac{12}{5}$ is an improper fraction because the numerator is larger than the denominator.

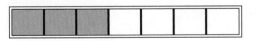

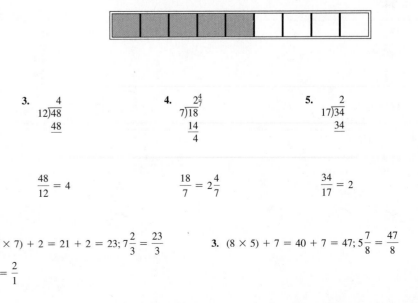

5. $\frac{16}{16}$ is an improper fraction because the numerator is equal to the denominator.

6. $\frac{5}{9}$ is a proper fraction because the numerator is smaller than the denominator.

2, p. 46

1.
$$
\begin{array}{r}
5\frac{5}{28} \\
28\overline{)145} \\
140 \\
\hline
5 \\
\end{array}
$$
$\frac{145}{28} = 5\frac{5}{28}$

2.
$$
\begin{array}{r}
11 \\
12\overline{)132} \\
12 \\
\hline
12 \\
12 \\
\hline
\end{array}
$$
$\frac{132}{12} = 11$

3.
$$
\begin{array}{r}
4 \\
12\overline{)48} \\
48 \\
\hline
\end{array}
$$
$\frac{48}{12} = 4$

4.
$$
\begin{array}{r}
2\frac{4}{7} \\
7\overline{)18} \\
14 \\
\hline
4 \\
\end{array}
$$
$\frac{18}{7} = 2\frac{4}{7}$

5.
$$
\begin{array}{r}
2 \\
17\overline{)34} \\
34 \\
\hline
\end{array}
$$
$\frac{34}{17} = 2$

3, p. 47

1. $(4 \times 3) + 1 = 12 + 1 = 13;\ 3\frac{1}{4} = \frac{13}{4}$

2. $(3 \times 7) + 2 = 21 + 2 = 23;\ 7\frac{2}{3} = \frac{23}{3}$

3. $(8 \times 5) + 7 = 40 + 7 = 47;\ 5\frac{7}{8} = \frac{47}{8}$

4. $3 = \frac{3}{1}$

5. $2 = \frac{2}{1}$

4, p. 48

1. $\dfrac{18 \div 6}{24 \div 6} = \dfrac{3}{4}$

2. $\dfrac{12 \div 12}{36 \div 12} = \dfrac{1}{3}$

3. $\dfrac{932 \div 4}{1{,}000 \div 4} = \dfrac{233}{250}$

4. $\dfrac{850 \div 50}{1{,}000 \div 50} = \dfrac{17}{20}$

5.
$$16\overline{)24} \quad 8\overline{)16}$$
$$\underline{16} \qquad \underline{16}$$
$$8 \qquad\; 0$$

8 is the GCD.

$\dfrac{16 \div 8}{24 \div 8} = \dfrac{2}{3}$

6.
$$39\overline{)51} \quad 12\overline{)39} \quad 3\overline{)12}$$
$$\underline{39} \qquad \underline{36} \qquad \underline{12}$$
$$12 \qquad\; 3 \qquad\; 0$$

3 is the GCD.

$\dfrac{39 \div 3}{51 \div 3} = \dfrac{13}{17}$

7.
$$12\overline{)28} \quad 4\overline{)12}$$
$$\underline{24} \qquad \underline{12}$$
$$4 \qquad\; 0$$

4 is the GCD.

$\dfrac{12 \div 4}{28 \div 4} = \dfrac{3}{7}$

8.
$$21\overline{)24} \quad 3\overline{)21}$$
$$\underline{21} \qquad \underline{21}$$
$$3 \qquad\; 0$$

3 is the GCD.

$\dfrac{21 \div 3}{24 \div 3} = \dfrac{7}{8}$

5, p. 49

1. $36 \div 12 = 3;$
$\dfrac{7}{12} = \dfrac{7 \times 3}{12 \times 3} = \dfrac{21}{36}$

2. $32 \div 4 = 8;$
$\dfrac{3}{4} = \dfrac{3 \times 8}{4 \times 8} = \dfrac{24}{32}$

3. $18 \div 2 = 9;$
$\dfrac{1}{2} = \dfrac{1 \times 9}{2 \times 9} = \dfrac{9}{18}$

4. $25 \div 5 = 5;$
$\dfrac{3}{5} = \dfrac{3 \times 5}{5 \times 5} = \dfrac{15}{25}$

5. $36 \div 12 = 3;$
$\dfrac{5}{12} = \dfrac{5 \times 3}{12 \times 3} = \dfrac{15}{36}$

6. $24 \div 8 = 3;$
$\dfrac{7}{8} = \dfrac{7 \times 3}{8 \times 3} = \dfrac{21}{24}$

SECTION 2-2

1, p. 51

1.
$\dfrac{3}{4}$
$\dfrac{1}{4}$
$\dfrac{1}{4}$
$\dfrac{5}{4} = 1\dfrac{1}{4}$

2.
$\dfrac{3}{8}$
$\dfrac{7}{8}$
$\dfrac{1}{8}$
$\dfrac{11}{8} = 1\dfrac{3}{8}$

3.
$\dfrac{1}{5}$
$\dfrac{2}{5}$
$\dfrac{2}{5}$
$\dfrac{5}{5} = 1$

4.
$\dfrac{5}{8}$
$\dfrac{3}{8}$
$\dfrac{1}{8}$
$\dfrac{9}{8} = 1\dfrac{1}{8}$

5.
$\dfrac{5}{12}$
$\dfrac{7}{12}$
$\dfrac{11}{12}$
$\dfrac{23}{12} = 1\dfrac{11}{12}$

2, p. 52

1.
$$2\overline{)6}\;\;12$$
$$2\overline{)3}\;\;\;\;6$$
$$3\overline{)3}\;\;\;\;3$$
$$\;\;\,1\;\;\;\;1$$

LCD =
$2 \times 2 \times 3 = 12$

2.
$$2\overline{)24}\;\;48$$
$$2\overline{)12}\;\;24$$
$$2\overline{)6}\;\;12$$
$$2\overline{)3}\;\;\;\;6$$
$$3\overline{)3}\;\;\;\;3$$
$$\;\;\,1\;\;\;\;1$$

LCD =
$2 \times 2 \times 2 \times 2 \times 3 = 48$

3.
$$2\overline{)2}\;\;8$$
$$2\overline{)1}\;\;4$$
$$2\overline{)1}\;\;2$$
$$\;\;\,1\;\;1$$

LCD =
$2 \times 2 \times 2 = 8$

4.
$$7\overline{)11}\;\;7$$
$$11\overline{)11}\;\;1$$
$$\;\;\;\;1\;\;\;1$$

LCD = $7 \times 11 = 77$

5.
$$2\overline{)42}\;\;30\;\;35$$
$$3\overline{)21}\;\;15\;\;35$$
$$5\overline{)7}\;\;\;\;5\;\;35$$
$$7\overline{)7}\;\;\;\;1\;\;\;\;7$$
$$\;\;\,1\;\;\;\;1\;\;\;\;1$$

LCD =
$2 \times 3 \times 5 \times 7 = 210$

3, p. 54

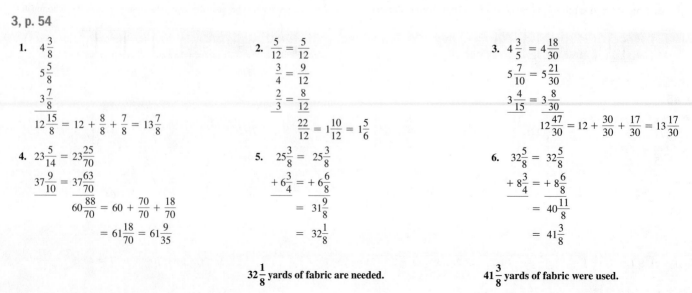

1.
$4\dfrac{3}{8}$
$5\dfrac{5}{8}$
$3\dfrac{7}{8}$
$12\dfrac{15}{8} = 12 + \dfrac{8}{8} + \dfrac{7}{8} = 13\dfrac{7}{8}$

2.
$\dfrac{5}{12} = \dfrac{5}{12}$
$\dfrac{3}{4} = \dfrac{9}{12}$
$\dfrac{2}{3} = \dfrac{8}{12}$
$\dfrac{22}{12} = 1\dfrac{10}{12} = 1\dfrac{5}{6}$

3.
$4\dfrac{3}{5} = 4\dfrac{18}{30}$
$5\dfrac{7}{10} = 5\dfrac{21}{30}$
$3\dfrac{4}{15} = 3\dfrac{8}{30}$
$12\dfrac{47}{30} = 12 + \dfrac{30}{30} + \dfrac{17}{30} = 13\dfrac{17}{30}$

4.
$23\dfrac{5}{14} = 23\dfrac{25}{70}$
$37\dfrac{9}{10} = 37\dfrac{63}{70}$
$60\dfrac{88}{70} = 60 + \dfrac{70}{70} + \dfrac{18}{70}$
$= 61\dfrac{18}{70} = 61\dfrac{9}{35}$

5.
$25\dfrac{3}{8} = 25\dfrac{3}{8}$
$+6\dfrac{3}{4} = +6\dfrac{6}{8}$
$= 31\dfrac{9}{8}$
$= 32\dfrac{1}{8}$

$32\dfrac{1}{8}$ yards of fabric are needed.

6.
$32\dfrac{5}{8} = 32\dfrac{5}{8}$
$+8\dfrac{3}{4} = +8\dfrac{6}{8}$
$= 40\dfrac{11}{8}$
$= 41\dfrac{3}{8}$

$41\dfrac{3}{8}$ yards of fabric were used.

1.
$$\frac{7}{8}$$
$$-\frac{3}{8}$$
$$\frac{4}{8} = \frac{1}{2}$$

2.
$$\frac{5}{8} = \frac{5 \times 3}{8 \times 3} = \frac{15}{24}$$
$$-\frac{1}{12} = -\frac{1 \times 2}{12 \times 2} = -\frac{2}{24}$$
$$\frac{13}{24}$$

3.
$$12\frac{5}{8} = 11 + \frac{8}{8} + \frac{5}{8} = 11\frac{13}{8}$$
$$-3\frac{7}{8} = -3\frac{7}{8}$$
$$8\frac{6}{8} = 8\frac{3}{4}$$

4.
$$15\frac{11}{12} = 15\frac{11 \times 3}{12 \times 3} = 15\frac{33}{36}$$
$$-7\frac{5}{18} = -7\frac{5 \times 2}{18 \times 2} = -7\frac{10}{36}$$
$$8\frac{23}{36}$$

$$2)\underline{12\ \ 18}$$
$$2)\underline{\ 6\ \ \ 9}$$
$$3)\underline{\ 3\ \ \ 9}$$
$$3)\underline{\ 1\ \ \ 3}$$
$$\ \ \ \ 1\ \ \ 1$$

LCD = $2 \times 2 \times 3 \times 3 = 36$

5.
$$32 = 31\frac{12}{12}$$
$$-14\frac{5}{12} = -14\frac{5}{12}$$
$$17\frac{7}{12}$$

6.
$$27\frac{4}{15} = 27\frac{4 \times 4}{15 \times 4} = 27\frac{16}{60} = 26\frac{60}{60} + \frac{16}{60} = 26\frac{76}{60}$$
$$-14\frac{7}{12} = -14\frac{7 \times 5}{12 \times 5} = -14\frac{35}{60} = -14\frac{35}{60} = -14\frac{35}{60}$$
$$12\frac{41}{60}$$

$$2)\underline{15\ \ 12}$$
$$2)\underline{15\ \ \ 6}$$
$$3)\underline{15\ \ \ 3}$$
$$5)\underline{\ 5\ \ \ 1}$$
$$\ \ \ \ 1\ \ \ 1$$

LCD = $2 \times 2 \times 3 \times 5 = 60$

7. $50 - 38\frac{3}{4} = 49\frac{4}{4} - 38\frac{3}{4} = 11\frac{1}{4}$ pounds

Chef Simmons has $11\frac{1}{4}$ pounds of cheese left for other uses.

8. $9\frac{1}{4} - 3\frac{3}{4} =$
$$8\frac{5}{4} - 3\frac{3}{4} = 5\frac{2}{4}$$
$$5\frac{2}{4} = 5\frac{1}{2}\text{ feet}$$

The leftover granite slab measures $5\frac{1}{2}$ feet long.

9.

What You Know	What You Are Looking For	Solution Plan
Amount of land originally owned = 100 acres	Total acres purchased	Acreage originally owned plus acreage purchased minus acreage sold equals acreage still owned.
Acreage of 3 additional purchases = $12\frac{3}{4} + 23\frac{2}{3} + 5\frac{1}{8}$ acres	Acres that Marcus still owns	
Acreage that was sold during the year = $65\frac{2}{3}$ acres		

Solution

$$100 = 100$$ LCD = 24
$$12\frac{3}{4} = 12\frac{18}{24}$$
$$23\frac{2}{3} = 23\frac{16}{24}$$
$$5\frac{1}{8} = 5\frac{3}{24}$$
$$140\frac{37}{24} =$$
$$141\frac{13}{24}$$ Acres owned before sale.

$$141\frac{13}{24} = 141\frac{13}{24} = 140\frac{37}{24}$$
$$-65\frac{2}{3} = -65\frac{16}{24} = -65\frac{16}{24}$$
$$= 75\frac{21}{24}$$
$$= 75\frac{7}{8}$$ Acres owned after sale.

Conclusion

There are $75\frac{7}{8}$ **acres remaining after the purchases and sale.**

10.

What You Know	What You Are Looking For	Solution Plan
Amount of frame material = 60 inches.	Length of frame material remaining.	Total frame length minus amount used equals frame material remaining.
Frame material needed = $10\frac{3}{4} + 10\frac{3}{4} + 12\frac{5}{8} + 12\frac{5}{8}$		

Solution

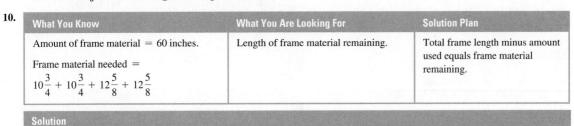

$$10\frac{3}{4} + 10\frac{3}{4} + 12\frac{5}{8} + 12\frac{5}{8} =$$
$$10\frac{6}{8} + 10\frac{6}{8} + 12\frac{5}{8} + 12\frac{5}{8} =$$
$$44\frac{22}{8} = 46\frac{3}{4}\text{ inches used}$$
$$60 - 46\frac{3}{4} = 59\frac{4}{4} - 46\frac{3}{4} = 13\frac{1}{4}$$

Conclusion

There are $13\frac{1}{4}$ **inches of frame material remaining.**

SECTION 2-3

1, p. 61

1. $\dfrac{3}{7} \times \dfrac{5}{8} = \dfrac{15}{56}$

2. $\dfrac{\overset{1}{\cancel{4}}}{\underset{3}{\cancel{9}}} \times \dfrac{\overset{1}{\cancel{3}}}{\underset{2}{\cancel{8}}} = \dfrac{1}{6}$

3. $3\dfrac{1}{4} \times 1\dfrac{5}{13} = \dfrac{13}{\underset{2}{\cancel{4}}} \times \dfrac{\overset{9}{\cancel{18}}}{\cancel{13}} = \dfrac{9}{2} = 4\dfrac{1}{2}$

4. $1\dfrac{1}{9} \times 3 = \dfrac{10}{\underset{3}{\cancel{9}}} \times \dfrac{\overset{1}{\cancel{3}}}{1} = \dfrac{10}{3} = 3\dfrac{1}{3}$

5. $2\dfrac{2}{5} \times \dfrac{15}{21} = \dfrac{\overset{4}{\cancel{12}}}{\underset{1}{\cancel{5}}} \times \dfrac{\overset{3}{\cancel{15}}}{\underset{7}{\cancel{21}}} = \dfrac{12}{7} = 1\dfrac{5}{7}$

6. $2\dfrac{3}{8} \times 16 = \dfrac{19}{\underset{1}{\cancel{8}}} \times \dfrac{\overset{2}{\cancel{16}}}{1} = 38 \text{ feet}$

7. $2\dfrac{1}{3} \times 14 = \dfrac{7}{3} \times \dfrac{14}{1} = \dfrac{98}{3} = 32\dfrac{2}{3} \text{ feet}$

2, p. 63

1. $\dfrac{5}{12}$; reciprocal $\dfrac{12}{5}$ or $2\dfrac{2}{5}$

2. $32 = \dfrac{32}{1}$; reciprocal $\dfrac{1}{32}$

3. $7\dfrac{1}{8} = \dfrac{57}{8}$; reciprocal $\dfrac{8}{57}$

4. $\dfrac{7}{8} \div \dfrac{3}{4} = \dfrac{7}{\underset{2}{\cancel{8}}} \times \dfrac{\overset{1}{\cancel{4}}}{3} = \dfrac{7}{6} = 1\dfrac{1}{6}$

5. $2\dfrac{2}{5} \div 2\dfrac{1}{10} = \dfrac{12}{5} \div \dfrac{21}{10} = \dfrac{\overset{4}{\cancel{12}}}{\underset{1}{\cancel{5}}} \times \dfrac{\overset{2}{\cancel{10}}}{\underset{7}{\cancel{21}}} = \dfrac{8}{7} = 1\dfrac{1}{7}$

6. $3\dfrac{3}{8} \div 9 = \dfrac{27}{8} \div \dfrac{9}{1} = \dfrac{\overset{3}{\cancel{27}}}{8} \cdot \dfrac{1}{\underset{1}{\cancel{9}}} = \dfrac{3}{8}$

7. $72 \div \dfrac{3}{4} = \dfrac{\overset{24}{\cancel{72}}}{1} \times \dfrac{4}{\underset{1}{\cancel{3}}} = 96 \text{ sheets of plywood}$

CHAPTER 3

SECTION 3-1

1, p. 83

1. Five and eight-tenths

2. Seven hundred twenty-one thousandths

3. Seven hundred eighty-nine and forty-eight hundredths phones per 1,000 people

4. One thousand, three hundred forty-one and four hundred sixty-six thousandths phones per 1,000 people

5. 0.3548

6. $4.87

2, p. 84

1. 14.342   3 is in the tenths place and 4 is less than 5. Round down by leaving 3 as it is and dropping the 4 and 2.

14.3

2. 48.7965   9 is in the hundredths place and 6 is 5 or more. Round up by adding 1 to 9.

48.80

3. $768.57   Round to the ones place. 5 is in the tenths place and is 5 or more. Round up by adding 1 to 8.

$769

4. $54.834   Round to the hundredths place. 4 is in the thousandths place and is less than 5. Round down.

$54.83

SECTION 3-2

1, p. 86

1.
$$\begin{array}{r} 67. \\ 4.38 \\ + 0.291 \\ \hline 71.671 \end{array}$$

2.
$$\begin{array}{r} 57.5 \\ 13.4 \\ + 5.238 \\ \hline 76.138 \end{array}$$

3.
$$\begin{array}{r} 17.53 \\ - 12.17 \\ \hline 5.36 \end{array}$$

4.
$$\begin{array}{r} 542.830 \\ - 219.593 \\ \hline 323.237 \end{array}$$

5.
$$\begin{array}{r} \$20.00 \\ - 18.97 \\ \hline \$1.03 \end{array}$$

6. $120.01 - $95.79 = $24.22

2, p. 87

1.
$$\begin{array}{r} 4.35 \\ \times 0.27 \\ \hline 30\,45 \\ 87\,0 \\ \hline 1.17\,45 \end{array}$$

2.
$$\begin{array}{r} 7.03 \\ \times 0.0\,35 \\ \hline 3515 \\ 2109 \\ \hline 0.24605 \end{array}$$

3.
$$\begin{array}{r} 5.32 \\ \times 15 \\ \hline 26\,60 \text{ or } 79.8 \\ 53\,2 \\ \hline 79.80 \end{array}$$

4.
$$\begin{array}{r} \$8.31 \\ \times 4 \\ \hline \$33.24 \end{array}$$

5. Move the decimal one place to the right; 183.8

6. Move the decimal two places to the right; 524.1

7. Add two zeros, then move the decimal three places to the right; 125,600

8.
$$\begin{array}{r} \$27.42 \\ \times \quad 500 \\ \hline \$13,710.00 \end{array}$$

The dinner costs $13,710.

9. $94.05 \times 1,000 = $94,050

10. Amount of tip = taxi fare times rate of tip. Amount of tip = $38.50(0.20) = $7.70.

1.
$$\begin{array}{r} 6.72 \\ 15\overline{)100.80} \\ \underline{90} \\ 10\ 8 \\ \underline{10\ 5} \\ 30 \\ \underline{30} \end{array}$$

$$\begin{array}{r} 15.57 \approx 15.6 \\ 23\overline{)358.26} \\ \underline{23} \\ 128 \\ \underline{115} \\ 132 \\ \underline{115} \\ 176 \\ \underline{161} \\ 15 \end{array}$$

2.
$$\begin{array}{r} 17.06 \\ 21\overline{)358.26} \\ \underline{21} \\ 148 \\ \underline{147} \\ 1\ 2 \\ \underline{0} \\ 1\ 26 \\ \underline{1\ 26} \end{array}$$

3. Move the decimal two places to the left; 0.78

4.
$$\begin{array}{r} 3.41 \approx 3.4 \\ 3.8\overline{)12.970} \\ \underline{114} \\ 15\ 7 \\ \underline{15\ 2} \\ 50 \\ \underline{38} \\ 12 \end{array}$$

5.
$$\begin{array}{r} 1\ 7.469 \approx 17.47 \\ 5,9\overline{)103,0.700} \\ \underline{59} \\ 44\ 0 \\ \underline{41\ 3} \\ 2\ 77 \\ \underline{2\ 36} \\ 4\ 10 \\ \underline{3\ 54} \\ 560 \\ \underline{531} \\ 29 \end{array}$$

6.
$$\begin{array}{r} 37 \\ 19.36\overline{)716.32} \\ \underline{580\ 8} \\ 135\ 52 \\ \underline{135\ 52} \end{array}$$

Gwen worked 37 hours.

7. $648,000,000 ÷ 1,000,000 = $648

SECTION 3-3

1, p. 93

1. $\dfrac{7}{10}$

2. $\dfrac{32}{100} = \dfrac{8}{25}$

3. $\dfrac{7}{100}$

4. $2\dfrac{87}{1,000}$

5. $23\dfrac{41}{100}$

2, p. 94

1. $\dfrac{3}{5} = 0.6$ $\quad\begin{array}{r}0.6\\5\overline{)3.0}\end{array}$

2. $\dfrac{7}{8} = 0.88$

3. $\dfrac{5}{12} = 0.42$

4. $0.83\dfrac{2}{6} = 0.83\dfrac{1}{3}$

5. $7\dfrac{4}{5} = 7.8$

6. $8\dfrac{4}{7} = 8.57$

2.
$$\begin{array}{r} 0.875 \approx 0.88 \\ 8\overline{)7.000} \\ \underline{6\ 4} \\ 60 \\ \underline{56} \\ 40 \\ \underline{40} \end{array}$$

3.
$$\begin{array}{r} 0.416 \approx 0.42 \\ 12\overline{)5.000} \\ \underline{4\ 8} \\ 20 \\ \underline{12} \\ 80 \\ \underline{72} \\ 8 \end{array}$$

4.
$$\begin{array}{r} 6\overline{)5.00} \\ \underline{48} \\ 20 \\ \underline{18} \\ 2 \end{array}$$

5.
$$\begin{array}{r} 0.8 \\ 5\overline{)4.0} \end{array}$$

6.
$$\begin{array}{r} 0.571 \approx 0.57 \\ 7\overline{)4.000} \\ \underline{3\ 5} \\ 50 \\ \underline{49} \\ 10 \\ \underline{7} \\ 3 \end{array}$$

CHAPTER 4

SECTION 4-1

1, p. 114

1.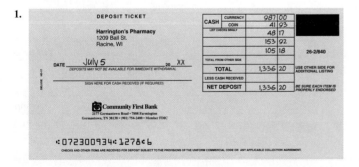

2.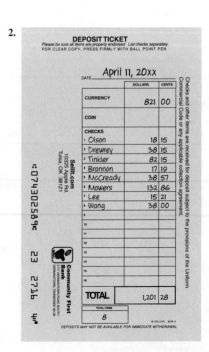

3.

ABC Plumbing						**4359**
408 Jefferson						
Rexburg, ID 00000				October 18 20 XX		07-278/840
PAY TO THE ORDER OF Frances Johnson					$ 583.17	
Five hundred eighty-three and $^{17}/_{100}$					DOLLARS	
First National Bank						
400 Washington						
Rexburg, ID 00000						
MEMO tool chest				Albert Adkins		
⑈044503279⑈						

4.

Max's Motorcycle Shop						**5887**
1280 State Street						
Tulsa, OK 00000				August 18 20 XX		07-278/840
PAY TO THE ORDER OF Harley Davidson, Inc.					$ 2,872.15	
Two thousand eight hundred seventy-two and $^{15}/_{100}$					DOLLARS	
Tulsa State Bank						
295 Adams Street						
Tulsa, OK 00000						
MEMO motorcycle parts				Max Murphy		
⑈584325911⑈						

5. Answers will vary. Bank statements are available online. Bills can be paid online. Accounts are accessible 24 hours a day. Bank statements can be reconciled online. Bank records can be stored electronically.

2, p. 118

1. (a) $152.87

(b) $2,896.15

(c) $3,543.28

2.

4359		Date Oct 18 20 XX
Amount 583.17		
To Frances Johnson		
For tool chest		
Balance Forward	5,902	08
Deposits		
Total	5,902	08
Amount This Check	583	17
Balance	5,318	91

3.

		RECORD ALL TRANSACTIONS THAT AFFECT YOUR ACCOUNT							
NUMBER	DATE	DESCRIPTION OF TRANSACTION	DEBIT (–)		√ T	FEE (IF ANY) (–)	CREDIT (+)	BALANCE	
								6,007	82
5887	8/18	Harley Davidson, Inc.	2,872	15				–2,872	15
		motorcycle parts						3,135	67
Debit	8/20	Remmie Raynor	498	31				–498	31
		pool services						2,637	36

4.

		RECORD ALL TRANSACTIONS THAT AFFECT YOUR ACCOUNT							
NUMBER	DATE	DESCRIPTION OF TRANSACTION	DEBIT (–)		√ T	FEE (IF ANY) (–)	CREDIT (+)	BALANCE	
								5,108	31
4358	10/6	Quesha Blunt	49	80				–49	80
		Cleaning Service						5,058	51
Dep	10/6	Deposit					843 57	+843	57
		travel reimb.						5,902	08
4359	10/8	Frances Johnson	583	17				–583	17
		tool chest						5,318	91
ATM	10/8	Cash	250	00				–250	00
								5,068	91

SECTION 4-2

1, p. 125

1. four   **2.** $5.00   **3.** $8,218.00   **4.** five   **5.** $700.81   **6.** $3,485.73   **7.** $490.00   **8.** 6/20

9. Answers will vary. Yes, provided the amount requested does not exceed the limit set by the Kroger Company nor the limit set by Lindy's bank.

10.

		RECORD ALL TRANSACTIONS THAT AFFECT YOUR ACCOUNT							
NUMBER	DATE	DESCRIPTION OF TRANSACTION	DEBIT (–)		√ T	FEE (IF ANY) (–)	CREDIT (+)	BALANCE	
								700	81
8213	5/28	Lands End	647	93	√			–647	93
								52	88
Deposit	6/1	Receipts			√		1,830 00	+1,830	00
								1,882	88
8214	6/1	Colliee Management Co.	490	00	√			–490	00
								1,392	88
8215	6/3	Jinkins Wholesale	728	32	√			–728	32
								664	56
Deposit	6/5	Receipts			√		2583 00	+2,583	00
								3,247	56
8216	6/5	Minneapolis Utility Co.	257	13				–257	13
								2,990	43
8217	6/10	State of MN	416	83	√			–416	83
								2573	60
Deposit	6/15	Receipts			√		3,800 00	+3,800	00
								6,373	60
8218	6/15	Tracie Burke Salary	2,000	00				–2,000	00
								4,373	60
8219	6/20	Brown's Wholesale	3,150	00	√			–3,150	00
								1,223	60
Deposit	7/2	Receipts					1,720 00	+1,720	00
								2943	60
	6/30	Interest Earned			√		5 00	+5	00
								2948	60
	6/30	Statement Reconciled							

$		
3,485 73	BALANCE AS SHOWN ON BANK STATEMENT	
+1,720 00	TOTAL OF OUTSTANDING DEPOSITS	
5,205 73	NEW TOTAL	
–2,257 13	SUBTRACT TOTAL OF OUTSTANDING CHECKS	
$2,948 60	YOUR ADJUSTED STATEMENT BALANCE	

SHOULD		
EQUAL		

	$
BALANCE AS SHOWN IN YOUR REGISTER	2,943 60
SUBTRACT AMOUNT OF SERVICE CHARGE	0
NEW TOTAL	2,943 60
ADJUSTMENTS IF ANY Interest	+ 5 00
YOUR ADJUSTED REGISTER BALANCE	$2,948 60

Outstanding Deposits (Credits)		
Date	Amount	
7/2	$ 1,720 00	
Total	$ 1,720 00	

Outstanding Checks (Debits)		
Check Number	Date	Amount
8216	6/5	$ 257 13
8218	6/20	2,000 00
	Total	$ 2,257 13

CHAPTER 5

SECTION 5-1

1, p. 151

1. $3A = 24$
$\dfrac{3A}{3} = \dfrac{24}{3}$
$A = 8$

2. $5N = 30$
$\dfrac{5N}{5} = \dfrac{30}{5}$
$N = 6$

3. $8 = \dfrac{B}{6}$
$(6)8 = \dfrac{B}{6}(6)$
$48 = B$
or
$B = 48$

4. $\dfrac{M}{5} = 7$
$5\left(\dfrac{M}{5}\right) = 7(5)$
$M = 35$

5. $\dfrac{K}{2} = 3$
$(2)\dfrac{K}{2} = 3(2)$
$K = 6$

6. $7 = \dfrac{A}{3}$
$(3)7 = \dfrac{A}{3}(3)$
$21 = A$
or
$A = 21$

2, p. 152

1. $A + 12 = 20$
$\underline{\quad -12 \quad -12}$
$A \qquad = \quad 8$

2. $A + 5 = 28$
$\underline{\quad -5 \quad -5}$
$A \qquad = \quad 23$

3. $15 = A + 3$
$\underline{-3 \qquad -3}$
$12 = A$
or
$A = 12$

4. $N - 5 = 11$
$\underline{\quad +5 \quad +5}$
$N \qquad = \quad 16$

5. $N - 7 = 10$
$\underline{\quad +7 \quad +7}$
$N \qquad = \quad 17$

6. $28 = M - 5$
$\underline{+5 \qquad +5}$
$33 = M$
or
$M = 33$

3, p. 154

1. $3N + 4 = 16$
$\underline{\quad -4 \quad -4}$
$3N \qquad = 12$
$\dfrac{3N}{3} = \dfrac{12}{3}$
$N = 4$

2. $5N - 7 = 13$
$\underline{\quad +7 \quad +7}$
$5N \qquad = 20$
$\dfrac{5N}{5} = \dfrac{20}{5}$
$N = 4$

3. $\dfrac{B}{8} - 2 = 2$
$\underline{\quad +2 \quad +2}$
$\dfrac{B}{8} \qquad = 4$
$(8)\dfrac{B}{8} = 4(8)$
$B = 32$

4. $\dfrac{M}{3} + 2 = 5$
$\underline{\quad -2 \quad -2}$
$\dfrac{M}{3} \qquad = 3$
$(3)\dfrac{M}{3} = 3(3)$
$M = 9$

5. $\dfrac{S}{6} - 3 = 4$
$\underline{\quad +3 \quad +3}$
$\dfrac{S}{6} \qquad = 7$
$(6)\dfrac{S}{6} = 7(6)$
$S = 42$

6. $12 = \dfrac{A}{5} - 8$
$\underline{+8 = \qquad +8}$
$20 = \dfrac{A}{5}$
$(5)20 = \dfrac{A}{5}(5)$
$100 = A$
or
$A = 100$

4, p. 155

1. $B + 3B - 5 = 19$
$4B - 5 = 19$
$\underline{\quad +5 \quad +5}$
$4B \qquad = 24$
$\dfrac{4B}{4} = \dfrac{24}{4}$
$B = 6$

2. $6B - 2B - 7 = 13$
$4B - 7 = 13$
$\underline{\quad +7 \quad +7}$
$4B \qquad = 20$
$\dfrac{4B}{4} = \dfrac{20}{4}$
$B = 5$

3. $7 + 3B + 2B = 17$
$7 + 5B = 17$
$\underline{-7 \qquad -7}$
$5B = 10$
$\dfrac{5B}{5} = \dfrac{10}{5}$
$B = 2$

4. $5A - 3 + 2A = 18$
$7A - 3 = 18$
$\underline{\quad +3 \quad +3}$
$7A \qquad = 21$
$\dfrac{7A}{7} = \dfrac{21}{7}$
$A = 3$

5. $3C - C = 16$
$2C = 16$
$\dfrac{2C}{2} = \dfrac{16}{2}$
$C = 8$

6. $12 = 8C - 5C$
$12 = 3C$
$\dfrac{12}{3} = \dfrac{3C}{3}$
$4 = C$
or
$C = 4$

5, p. 156

1. $2(N + 4) = 26$
$2N + 2(4) = 26$
$2N + 8 = 26$
$\underline{\quad -8 \quad -8}$
$2N = 18$
$\dfrac{2N}{2} = \dfrac{18}{2}$
$N = 9$

2. $3(N - 30) = 45$
$3N - 90 = 45$
$\underline{\quad +90 \quad +90}$
$3N \qquad = 135$
$\dfrac{3N}{3} = \dfrac{135}{3}$
$N = 45$

3. $4(R - 3) = 8$
$4R - 12 = 8$
$\underline{\quad +12 \quad +12}$
$4R \qquad = 20$
$\dfrac{4R}{4} = \dfrac{20}{4}$
$R = 5$

4. $7(2R - 3) = 21$
$14R - 21 = 21$
$\underline{\quad +21 \quad +21}$
$14R \qquad = 42$
$\dfrac{14R}{14} = \dfrac{42}{14}$
$R = 3$

5. $5(3R + 2) = 40$
$15R + 10 = 40$
$\underline{\quad -10 \quad -10}$
$15R \qquad = 30$
$\dfrac{15R}{15} = \dfrac{30}{15}$
$R = 2$

6. $30 = 6(2A + 3)$
$30 = 12A + 18$
$\underline{-18 = \qquad -18}$
$12 = 12A$
$\dfrac{12}{12} = \dfrac{12A}{12}$
$1 = A$
or
$A = 1$

6, p. 157

1.
$$\frac{5}{7} \overset{?}{=} \frac{20}{28}$$
$$5(28) = 7(20)$$
$$140 = 140$$
$\frac{5}{7}$ is proportional to $\frac{20}{28}$.

$$\frac{3}{4} \overset{?}{=} \frac{20}{28}$$
$$3(28) \overset{?}{=} 4(20)$$
$$84 \overset{?}{=} 80$$
$\frac{3}{4}$ is not proportional to $\frac{20}{28}$.

2.
$$\frac{1}{2} \overset{?}{=} \frac{12}{18}$$
$$1(18) \overset{?}{=} 2(12)$$
$$18 \overset{?}{=} 24$$
$\frac{1}{2}$ is not proportional to $\frac{12}{18}$.

$$\frac{2}{3} \overset{?}{=} \frac{12}{18}$$
$$2(18) = 3(12)$$
$$36 = 36$$
$\frac{2}{3}$ is proportional to $\frac{12}{18}$.

3.
$$\frac{3}{4} = \frac{N}{8}$$
$$4N = 3(8)$$
$$4N = 24$$
$$\left(\frac{1}{4}\right)4N = 24\left(\frac{1}{4}\right)$$
$$N = \frac{24}{4} = 6$$

4.
$$\frac{5}{N} = \frac{4}{12}$$
$$4N = 5(12)$$
$$4N = 60$$
$$\frac{4N}{4} = \frac{60}{4}$$
$$N = 15$$

5.
$$\frac{N}{4} = \frac{9}{6}$$
$$6N = 4(9)$$
$$6N = 36$$
$$\frac{6N}{6} = \frac{36}{6}$$
$$N = 6$$

6.
$$\frac{5}{12} = \frac{15}{N}$$
$$5N = 12(15)$$
$$5N = 180$$
$$\frac{5N}{5} = \frac{180}{5}$$
$$N = 36$$

SECTION 5-2

1, p. 164

1.

What You Know	What You Are Looking For	Solution Plan
Total pounds of produce = 2,500 pounds potatoes = 800 pounds broccoli = 150 pounds tomatoes = 390 pounds	Number of pounds of apples = N	Number of pounds of potatoes + pounds of broccoli + pounds of tomatoes + pounds of apples = 2,500 pounds

Solution

$$800 + 150 + 390 + N = 2,500$$
$$1,340 + N = 2,500$$
$$-1,340 = -1,340$$
$$N = 1,160$$

Conclusion

Marcus purchased 1,160 pounds of apples.

2.

What You Know	What You Are Looking For	Solution Plan
$\frac{1}{6}$ of earnings spent on groceries $117.50 spent on groceries each week	The amount of weekly earnings = N	One sixth times weekly earnings = amount spent on groceries

Solution

$$\frac{1}{6}N = \$117.50$$
$$(6)\frac{N}{6} = 117.50(6)$$
$$N = \$705$$

Conclusion

Carrie earns $705 weekly.

3.

What You Know	What You Are Looking For	Solution Plan
Total rooms = 873 8 times as many nonsmoking as there are smoking rooms.	Number of smoking rooms = N Number of nonsmoking rooms = 8N	The number of smoking rooms plus the number of nonsmoking rooms = 873.

Solution

$$N + 8N = 873$$
$$9N = 873$$
$$\frac{9N}{9} = \frac{873}{9}$$
$$N = 97$$

Conclusion

The hotel has 97 rooms designated as smoking rooms.

4.

What You Know	What You Are Looking For	Solution Plan
480 notebooks cost $1,656.	The number of notebooks that can be purchased for $2,242.50 = N	Pair 1: 480 notebooks; $1,656 Pair 2: N notebooks; $2,242.50

Solution

$$\frac{480}{\$1,656} = \frac{N}{\$2,242.50}$$
$$\text{Pair 1} \qquad \text{Pair 2}$$
$$1,656N = 480(2,242.50)$$
$$1,656N = 1,076,400$$
$$\frac{1,656N}{1,656} = \frac{1,076,400}{1,656}$$
$$N = 650$$

Conclusion

650 notebooks can be purchased for $2,242.50.

5.

What You Know	What You Are Looking For	Solution Plan
Total cost of beauty products: $131,263 Cost of face cream: $18.20 Cost of perfume: $32.10 Total number of units of beauty products: 5,280	There are two unknown facts: N = number of units of perfume $5,280 - N$ = number of units of face cream	Total cost = (cost per unit of cream)(number of units of cream) + (cost per unit of perfume)(number of units of perfume)

Solution

$$\$131,263 = \$18.20(5,280 - N) + \$32.10(N)$$
$$131,263 = 32.10N + 18.20(5,280) - 18.50N$$
$$131,263 = 32.1N + 96,096 - 18.2N$$
$$131,263 = 13.9N + 96,096$$
$$131,263 - 96,096 = 13.9N$$
$$35,167 = 13.9N$$
$$\frac{35,167}{13.9} = \frac{13.9N}{13.9}$$
$$N - 2,530$$
$$5,280 - N = 5,280 - 2,530 = 2,750$$

Conclusion

DFS ordered 2,530 units of perfume and 2,750 units of face cream.

SECTION 5-3

1, p. 168

1. $S = C + M$
$S = \$317 + \$250$
$S = \$567$

2. $S = \quad C + M$
$\$629 = \quad \$463 + M$
$\underline{- \$463 \quad - \$463}$
$166 = M$
$M = \$166$

3. $P = RH$
$P = \$19.26(40)$
$P = \$770.40$

4. $P = RH$
$\$612 = R(40)$
$\dfrac{\$612}{40} = \dfrac{R(40)}{40}$
$\$15.30 = R$
$R = \$15.30$

2, p. 169

1. $S = \quad C + M$
$\underline{- C = - C}$
$S - C = \quad M$
$M = \quad S - C$

2. $M = S - N$
$\underline{+ N = \quad + N}$
$M + N = S$
$S = M + N$

3. $U = \dfrac{P}{N}$

$(N)U = \dfrac{P}{N}(N)$

$NU = P$

$\dfrac{NU}{U} = \dfrac{P}{U}$

$N = \dfrac{P}{U}$

4. $U = \dfrac{V}{P}$

$U(P) = \dfrac{V}{P}(P)$

$UP = V$

$V = UP$

CHAPTER 6

SECTION 6-1

1, p. 187

1. $0.82 = 0.82(100\%) = 082.\% = 82\%$

2. $3.45 = 3.45(100\%) = 345.\% = 345\%$

3. $0.0007 = 0.0007(100\%) = 000.07\% = 0.07\%$

4. $5 = 5(100\%) = 500\%$

5. $0.273(100\%) = 27.3\%$

6. $0.752(100\%) = 75.2\%$

7. $\dfrac{43}{100} = \dfrac{43}{\underset{1}{\cancel{100}}}\left(\dfrac{\overset{1}{\cancel{100\%}}}{1}\right) = 43\%$

8. $\dfrac{3}{10} = \dfrac{3}{\underset{1}{\cancel{10}}}\left(\dfrac{\overset{10}{\cancel{100\%}}}{1}\right) = 30\%$

9. $8\dfrac{1}{4} = 8\dfrac{1}{4}(100\%) = \dfrac{33}{\underset{1}{\cancel{4}}}\left(\dfrac{\overset{25}{\cancel{100\%}}}{1}\right) = 825\%$

10. $\dfrac{1}{6} = \dfrac{1}{\underset{3}{\cancel{6}}}\left(\dfrac{\overset{25}{\cancel{100\%}}}{1}\right) = \dfrac{50}{3}\% = 16\dfrac{2}{3}\%$

11. $\dfrac{2}{5}\left(\dfrac{100\%}{1}\right) = 40\%$

12. $\dfrac{9}{10}\left(\dfrac{100\%}{1}\right) = 90\%$

2, p. 189

1. $52\% = 52\% \div 100\% = 0.52 = 0.52$

2. $38.5\% = 38.5\% \div 100\% = 0.385 = 0.385$

3. $143\% = 143\% \div 100\% = 1.43 = 1.43$

4. $0.72\% = 0.72\% \div 100\% = 0.0072 = 0.0072$

5. $54.8\% \div 100\% = 0.548$

6. $25.7\% \div 100\% = 0.257$ under 18 years old
$0.4\% \div 100\% = 0.004$ Native Hawaiian or Other Pacific Islander

7. $72\% = 72\% \div 100\% = \dfrac{\overset{18}{\cancel{72\%}}}{1}\left(\dfrac{1}{\underset{25}{\cancel{100\%}}}\right) = \dfrac{18}{25}$

8. $\dfrac{1}{8}\% = \dfrac{1}{8}\% \div 100\% = \dfrac{1}{8}\%\left(\dfrac{1}{100\%}\right) = \dfrac{1}{800}$

9. $325\% = 325\% \div 100\% = \dfrac{325\%}{1}\left(\dfrac{1}{100\%}\right) = \dfrac{325}{100} = 3\dfrac{1}{4}$

10. $16\dfrac{2}{3}\% = 16\dfrac{2}{3}\% \div 100\% = \dfrac{\overset{50}{\cancel{50}}\%}{3}\left(\dfrac{1}{\cancel{100}\%}\right) = \dfrac{1}{6}$

11. $30\% \div 100\% = \dfrac{30\%}{100\%} = \dfrac{3}{10}$ women ownership;

$15\% \div 100\% = \dfrac{15\%}{100\%} = \dfrac{3}{20}$ Hispanic ownership

12. $0.5\% \div 100\% = \dfrac{0.5\%}{100\%}\left(\dfrac{10}{10}\right) = \dfrac{5}{1,000} = \dfrac{1}{200}$ American Indian or Alaskan Native

SECTION 6-2

1, p. 192

1. Base (of), 85; rate (%), 42%; portion (part), not known
3. Base (of), 80; rate (%), not known; portion (part), 20
5. Base (of), 72; rate (%), 125%; portion (part), not known
7. Base, 1,195; rate, not known; portion (part), 987

2. Base (of), not known; rate (%), 15%; portion (part) 50
4. Base (of), not known; rate (%), 20%; portion (part), 17
6. Base (of), 160; rate (%), not known; portion (part), 32
8. Base, 1,195; rate, 2.6%; portion (part), not known

2, p. 195

1. $P = RB$ $R = 15\% = 0.15$
$P = 0.15(200)$ $B = 200$
$P = 30$

2. $B = \dfrac{P}{R}$ $P = 120$

$B = \dfrac{120}{0.25}$ $R = 25\% = 0.25$

$B = 480$

3. $R = \dfrac{P}{B}$ $P = 150$

$R = \dfrac{150}{750}$ $B = 750$

$R = 0.2$

$R = 20\%$

4. $P = RB$ $R = 33\dfrac{1}{3}\% = \dfrac{100}{3}\% = \dfrac{100}{3}\left(\dfrac{1}{100}\right) = \dfrac{1}{3}$

$P = \dfrac{1}{3}(72)$ $B = 72$

$P = 24$

5. $P = RB$

$P = \left(16\dfrac{2}{3}\%\right)(81)$

$P = \left(\dfrac{50}{3}\right)\left(\dfrac{1}{100}\right)(81)$

$P = \left(\dfrac{1}{6}\right)(81)$

$P = 13\dfrac{1}{2}$ or 13.5

6. $R = \dfrac{P}{B}$

$R = \dfrac{180}{45}$

$R = 4(100\%)$

$R = 400\%$

7.

What You Know	What You Are Looking For	Solution Plan
Total students or the base: 40	Number of students who passed	$P = RB$, where $R = 0.75$ and $B = 40$
Percent of students who passed: 75%		

Solution

$P = RB$
$P = 0.75(40)$
$P = 30$

Conclusion

30 students passed the test.

8. $R = \dfrac{P}{B}$

$R = \dfrac{33,588,320}{419,854,000}$

$R = 0.08$

$R = 0.08(100\%)$

$R = 8\%$

Eight percent of the U.S. population in 2050 is expected to be Asians alone.

9. $B = \dfrac{P}{R}$

$B = \dfrac{877}{10\%}$

$B = \dfrac{877}{0.10}$

$B = 8,770$

8,770 people paid the entry fee.

SECTION 6-3

1, p. 199

1.

What You Know	What You Are Looking For	Solution Plan
New Lexus = $53,444	Amount of increase	Amount of increase = new price − previous price
Previous year's model = $51,989		

Solution

$53,444 − $51,989 = $1,455

Conclusion

The Lexus increased by $1,455.

2.

What You Know	What You Are Looking For	Solution Plan
Ending price of $73.57	Amount of decrease	Amount of decrease = beginning price − ending price
Beginning price $81.99		

Solution

$81.99 − $73.57 = $8.42

Conclusion

The stock price fell $8.42.

3.

What You Know	What You Are Looking For	Solution Plan
Current earnings: $62,870 4.3% raise	Amount of her raise	Amount of raise = current earnings × percent raise

Solution

$62,870 × 4.3% = $62,870(0.043) = $2,703.41

Conclusion

Her raise was $2,703.41.

4.

What You Know	What You Are Looking For	Solution Plan
Original cost of stock = $145 million Percent of decrease = 16%	Amount of decrease of stock	$P = RB$ Decrease = percent of decrease × original earnings

Solution

Decrease = 16%($145) = 0.16($145)
= $23.2 million or $23,200,000

Conclusion

The earnings decreased $23.2 million, or $23,200,000.

5.

What You Know	What You Are Looking For	Solution Plan
Zack's original weight = 230 pounds Zack's percent of weight loss = 12%	The number of pounds Zack lost	$P = RB$ Decrease = percent weight loss × original weight

Solution

Decrease = 0.12(230)
Decrease = 27.6

Conclusion

Zack lost 27.6 pounds.

6.

What You Know	What You Are Looking For	Solution Plan
Number of active nurses = 2,249,000 Percent of nurses added by 2020 = 20.3%	Number of new nurses to be added by 2020	$P = RB$ Increase = percent of nurses needed × original number of nurses

Solution

Increase = 20.3%(2,249,000)
= 0.203(2,249,000)
= 456,547

Conclusion

The number of additional nurses needed by 2020 is 456,547.

2, p. 200

1. 100% + 4.3% = 104.3%
   $62,870(1.043) = $65,573.41
3. 100% − 12% = 88%
   230(0.88) = 202.4 pounds
5. 100% + 51% = 151%
   $24.25(1.51) = $36.62 (rounded)

2. 100% − 16% = 84%
   $145 million (0.84) = $121.8 million, or $121,800,000
4. 100% + 250% = 350%
   $9,500(3.5) = $33,250
6. 100% + 20.3% = 120.3%
   2,249,000(1.203) = 2,705,547 nurses needed by 2020

3, p. 202

1.

What You Know	What You Are Looking For	Solution Plan
Third quarter sales (original amount) = $23,583,000 Fourth quarter sales (new amount) = $38,792,000	Percent of increase	Amount of increase = new amount − original amount Percent of increase = $\dfrac{\text{amount of increase}}{\text{original amount}}$

Solution

Amount of increase = $38,792,000 − $23,583,000
= $15,209,000

Percent of increase = $\dfrac{\$15,209,000}{\$23,583,000}$
= 0.644913709
= 64.5% (rounded)

Conclusion

The percent of increase in sales is 64.5%.

2.

What You Know	What You Are Looking For	Solution Plan
Fall semester spending = $9,524 (original amount) Spring semester spending = $8,756 (new amount)	Percent of decrease in spending	Amount of decrease = original amount − new amount Percent of decrease = $\dfrac{\text{amount of decrease}}{\text{original amount}}$

Solution

Amount of decrease = $9,524 − $8,756 = $768

$$\text{Percent of decrease} = \frac{\$768}{\$9,524}$$
$$= 0.08063838723$$
$$= 8\% \text{ (rounded)}$$

Conclusion

Ken's spending decreased 8%.

3.

What You Know	What You Are Looking For	Solution Plan
Sale (reduced) price = $148,500 Percent decrease = 10%	Original price	Percent representing sale price = 100% − percent decrease $$B = \frac{P}{R}$$ Original price = $\dfrac{\text{sale price}}{\text{percent representing sale price}}$

Solution

Percent representing sale price = 100% − 10% = 90%

$$\text{Original price} = \frac{\$148,500}{0.9}$$

Original price = $165,000

Conclusion

The house was originally priced at $165,000.

4.

What You Know	What You Are Looking For	Solution Plan
Amount DVD is reduced = $6.25 Percent DVD is reduced = 25%	Original price of DVD Discounted price of DVD	$B = \dfrac{P}{R}$; Original price = $\dfrac{\text{amount of reduction}}{\text{percent of reduction}}$ Discounted price = original price − amount of reduction

Solution

$$\text{Original price} = \frac{\$6.25}{0.25}$$
$$= \$25$$
$$\text{Discounted price} = \$25 − \$6.25$$
$$= \$18.75$$

Conclusion

The DVD originally cost $25 and was reduced to sell for $18.75.

5.

What You Know	What You Are Looking For	Solution Plan
Used price (reduced price) = $14,799 Percent of reduction = 48%	"New" price (original price)	Percent representing the used or reduced price = 100% − percent of reduction "New" price (original price) = $\dfrac{\text{used price}}{\text{percent representing used price}}$

Solution

Percent representing the used or reduced price = 100% − 48% = 52%

$$\text{"New" price} = \frac{\$14,799}{0.52} = \$28,459.61538$$
$$= \$28,460 \text{ rounded to the nearest dollar}$$

Conclusion

The "new" price is $28,460.

6.

What You Know	What You Are Looking For	Solution Plan
Average ticket price for 2011 = $113.17	Percent of increase in ticket price	Increase in ticket price = 2011 ticket price − 2007 ticket price
Average ticket price for 2007 = $72.20		Percent increase in ticket price $= \dfrac{\text{Amount of increase}}{\text{Original amount}}$

Solution

Increase = $113.17 − $72.20
       = $40.97

Percent of increase $= \dfrac{\$40.97}{\$72.20}$ 40.97 ÷ 72.20 = ⇒ .5674515235

Percent of increase = 0.567(100%)   rounded

Percent of increase = 56.7%

Conclusion

The average NFL ticket price increased by 56.7%.

CHAPTER 7

SECTION 7-1

1, p. 220

1. 5 students

2. 5 + 15 + 15 = 35 students

3. $\dfrac{35}{50}(100\%) = 0.7(100\%) = 70\%$

5. 20–39 interval

4.

2, p. 222

1. Fluctuating

2. $\dfrac{100 + 250 + 150 + 200 + 200 + 300}{6} = \dfrac{1,200}{6} = 200$ CDs

4. Increasing

5. December 2009

3.

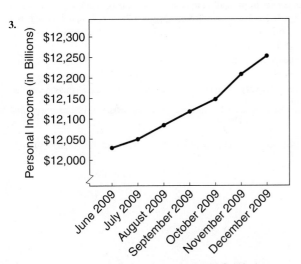

Personal Income for U.S. Workers

3, p. 224

1. $0.35(360°) = 126°$
   $0.32(360°) = 115.2°$
   $0.05(360°) = 18°$
   $0.04(360°) = 14.4°$
   $0.04(360°) = 14.4°$
   $0.2(360°) = 72°$

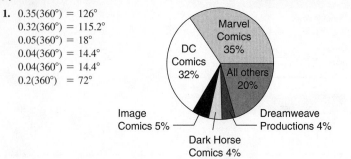

2. $35\% + 32\% + 5\% = 72\%$
3. $\$80,000,000(0.35) = \$28,000,000$
4. $\$80,000,000(0.05) = \$4,000,000$

SECTION 7-2

1, p. 228

1. $\dfrac{\$37,500 + \$32,000 + \$28,800 + \$35,750 + \$29,500 + \$47,300}{6} = \dfrac{\$210,850}{6} = \$35,141.66667 \approx \$35,142$

2. $\dfrac{2,400 + 2,100 + 1,800 + 2,800 + 3,450}{5} = \dfrac{12,550}{5} = 2,510 \text{ hours}$

3. $\dfrac{2 + 15 + 7 + 3 + 1 + 3 + 5 + 2 + 4 + 1 + 2 + 6 + 4 + 2}{14} = \dfrac{57}{14} = 4.071428571 \text{ or 4 whole days}$

4. $\dfrac{12 + 7 + 5 + 2 + 1 + 8 + 0 + 3 + 1 + 2 + 7 + 5 + 30 + 5 + 2}{15} = \dfrac{90}{15} = 6 \text{ CDs per month}$

5. $\dfrac{\$23,627,320,000 + \$25,289,663,000 + \$25,532,186,000 + \$25,618,377,000 + \$20,887,883,000 + \$24,130,143,000 + \$23,565,164,000 + \$26,717,493,000 + \$24,557,815,000 + \$26,543,433,000}{10}$

$= \dfrac{246,469,477,000}{10} = 24,646,947,700$

6. $\dfrac{\$4,758,287,000 + \$4,103,243,000 + \$3,958,253,000 + \$1,709,329,000 + \$1,939,025,000 + \$1,449,319,000 + \$2,040,367,000 + \$1,970,032,000 + \$2,420,138,000 + \$3,280,502,000}{10}$

$= \dfrac{\$27,628,495,000}{10} = \$2,762,849,500$

2, p. 229

1. Arrange in order by size: $28,800; $29,500; $32,000; $35,750; $37,500; $47,300. Since the number of scores is even, average the two middle scores.

   $\text{Median} = \dfrac{\$32,000 + \$35,750}{2} = \dfrac{\$67,750}{2} = \$33,875$

2. Arrange in order by size: 1,800; 2,100; 2,400; 2,800; 3,450. Since the number of scores is odd, select the middle score.

   $\text{Median} = 2,400 \text{ hours}$

3. Arrange in order by size: 1 day, 1 day, 2 days, 2 days, 2 days, 2 days, 3 days, 3 days, 4 days, 4 days, 5 days, 6 days, 7 days, 15 days. The number of scores is even so average the middle 2.

   $\text{Median} = \dfrac{3 \text{ days} + 3 \text{ days}}{2} = \dfrac{6 \text{ days}}{2} = 3 \text{ days}$

4. Arrange in order from smallest to largest: 0, 1, 1, 2, 2, 2, 3, 5, 5, 5, 7, 7, 8, 12, 30.

   $\text{Median} = \text{middle scores} = 5 \text{ CDs per month}$

5. Arrange in order by size then average the two middle scores. $\dfrac{\$24,557,815,000 + \$25,289,663,000}{10} = \dfrac{49,847,478,000}{2} = 24,923,739,000$

6. Arrange in order by size then average the two middle scores. $\dfrac{\$2,040,367,000 + \$2,420,138,000}{2} = \dfrac{\$4,460,505,000}{2} = \$2,230,252,500$

3, p. 231

1. Arrange scores from smallest to largest: 0, 2, 6, 7, 9, 12, 17, 17, 18, 18, 19, 21, 23, 23, 32, 32, 32, 32, 32, 32, 32, 32, 38, 48, 48, 48, 48, 56, 62, 62, 66, 73, 74, 83, 86, 92. The mode is 32 because it is listed 8 times, more than any other score.

2. Arrange rates from smallest to largest: 0, 0, 0, 0, 0, 2.9, 4, 4, 4, 4, 4, 4, 4, 4.225, 4.5, 4.7, 5, 5, 5, 5, 5.3, 5.5, 5.5, 5.6, 5.75, 6, 6, 6, 6, 6, 6, 6, 6, 6, 6, 6, 6, 6.25, 6.25, 6.25, 6.5, 6.85, 6.875, 7, 7, 7, 7, 7, 8.25. The mode is 6% since 12 states have a rate of 6%.

3. Arrange scores from smallest to largest: 42, 48, 76, 79, 83, 86, 92, 97, 98, 100. There is no mode as no score is reported more than once.

4. Arrange the scores from smallest to largest: 0, 2, 7, 8, 11, 11, 12, 22. The mode is 11.

5. Mean $= (148 + 172 + 158 + 160 + 170 + 158 + 170 + 165 + 162 + 173 + 155 + 161)/12 = 1,952/12 = 162.67$ rounded to the nearest hundredth. Arrange the scores from smallest to largest: 148, 155, 158, 158, 160, 161, 162, 165, 170, 170, 172, 173.

   $\text{Median} = \dfrac{161 + 162}{2} = \dfrac{323}{2} = 161.5$ The modes are 158 and 170. Each mode is listed twice.

6. Answers may vary. Both the mean and median give a realistic view of the average of the data set.

4, p. 233

1.

Class intervals	Tally	Class frequency
0–19	𝐼𝐼𝐼𝐼 𝐼𝐼𝐼𝐼 𝐼	11
20–39	𝐼𝐼𝐼𝐼 𝐼𝐼𝐼𝐼 𝐼𝐼	12
40–59	𝐼𝐼𝐼𝐼	5
60–79	𝐼𝐼𝐼𝐼	5
80–99	𝐼𝐼𝐼	3
		36

2. $5 + 5 + 3 = 13$ staff have more than 39 days vacation.

3. $11 + 12 = 23$ staff have fewer than 40 days vacation.

4. $\dfrac{3}{36}(100\%) = 8.3\%$

5. $\dfrac{(12 + 5)}{36}(100\%) = \dfrac{17}{36}(100\%) = 47.2\%$

6.

Class interval	Class frequency	Calculations	Relative frequency
0–19	11	$\dfrac{11}{36}(100\%) = \dfrac{1100\%}{36} = 30.6\%$	30.6%
20–39	12	$\dfrac{12}{36}(100\%) = \dfrac{1200\%}{36} = 33.3\%$	33.3%
40–59	5	$\dfrac{5}{36}(100\%) = \dfrac{500\%}{36} = 13.9\%$	13.9%
60–79	5	$\dfrac{5}{36}(100\%) = \dfrac{500\%}{36} = 13.9\%$	13.9%
80–99	3	$\dfrac{3}{36}(100\%) = \dfrac{300\%}{36} = 8.3\%$	8.3%
Total	36		100%

5, p. 235

1. Find the midpoint of each class interval:

$\dfrac{0 + 19}{2} = \dfrac{19}{2} = 9.5$ $\dfrac{20 + 39}{2} = \dfrac{59}{2} = 29.5$ $\dfrac{40 + 59}{2} = \dfrac{99}{2} = 49.5$

$\dfrac{60 + 79}{2} = \dfrac{139}{2} = 69.5$ $\dfrac{80 + 99}{2} = \dfrac{179}{2} = 89.5$

Class interval	Class frequency	Midpoint	Product of midpoint and frequency
0–19	11	9.5	104.5
20–39	12	29.5	354
40–59	5	49.5	247.5
60–79	5	69.5	347.5
80–99	3	89.5	268.5
Total	36		1,322

Mean of grouped data $= \dfrac{1,322}{36} = 36.7$ days

2. $\dfrac{60 + 64}{2} = \dfrac{124}{2} = 62$ $\dfrac{65 + 69}{2} = \dfrac{134}{2} = 67$ $\dfrac{70 + 74}{2} = \dfrac{144}{2} = 72$

$\dfrac{75 + 79}{2} = \dfrac{154}{2} = 77$ $\dfrac{80 + 84}{2} = \dfrac{164}{2} = 82$ $\dfrac{85 + 89}{2} = \dfrac{174}{2} = 87$

3. $\dfrac{0 + 4}{2} = \dfrac{4}{2} = 2$ $\dfrac{5 + 9}{2} = \dfrac{14}{2} = 7$ $\dfrac{10 + 14}{2} = \dfrac{24}{2} = 12$

$\dfrac{15 + 19}{2} = \dfrac{34}{2} = 17$

Class interval	Class frequency	Midpoint	Product of midpoint and frequency
60–64	6	62	372
65–69	8	67	536
70–74	12	72	864
75–79	22	77	1,694
80–84	18	82	1,476
85–89	9	87	783
Total	75		5,725

Class interval	Class frequency	Midpoint	Product of midpoint and frequency
0–4	3	2	6
5–9	7	7	49
10–14	4	12	48
15–19	2	17	34
Total	16		137

Mean of grouped data $= \dfrac{5,725}{75} = 76.33333333$ or 76.33 rounded

Mean of grouped data $= \dfrac{137}{16} = 8.5625$ or 8.56 rounded

SECTION 7-3

1, p. 238

1. $\$47,300 - \$28,800 = \$18,500$

2. $3,450 \text{ hours} - 1,800 \text{ hours} = 1,650 \text{ hours}$

3. $15 \text{ days} - 1 \text{ days} = 14 \text{ days}$

4. $30 \text{ CDs} - 0 \text{ CDs} = 30 \text{ CDs}$

5. Range $= \$26,717,493,000 - \$20,887,883,000 = \$5,829,610,000$

6. Range $= 4,758,287,000 - 1,449,319,000 = 3,308,968,000$

2, p. 241

1. Mean $= \dfrac{72 + 75 + 68 + 73 + 69}{5} = \dfrac{357}{5} = 71.4$

Value	Mean	Deviation from the mean
72	71.4	0.6
75	71.4	3.6
68	71.4	−3.4
73	71.4	1.6
69	71.4	−2.4

2. $0.6 + 3.6 + 1.6 = 5.8$
$(-3.4) + (-2.4) = -5.8$
$5.8 + (-5.8) = 0$

3.

Deviation from the mean	Square of deviation
0.6	0.36
3.6	12.96
−3.4	11.56
1.6	2.56
−2.4	5.76

$0.36 + 12.96 + 11.56 + 2.56 + 5.76 = 33.2$

4. $\dfrac{33.2}{5 - 1} = \dfrac{33.2}{4} = 8.3$

5. $\sqrt{8.3} = 2.880972058$ or 2.88 (rounded)

6.

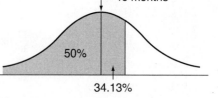

46 months

50%

34.13%

50 months − 46 months = 4 months above the mean

$\dfrac{4 \text{ months above the mean}}{4 \text{ months per standard deviation}} = 1$ standard deviation above the mean

$50\% + 34.13\% = 84.13\%$

$0.8413(100) = 84.13$ batteries or 84 batteries should last less than 50 months

CHAPTER 8

SECTION 8-1

1, p. 265

1. a. Trade discount $= 12\%(\$89{,}765) = 0.12(\$89{,}765)$
$= \$10{,}771.80$

b. Net price $= \$89{,}765 - \$10{,}771.80$
Net price $= \$78{,}993.20$

3. Trade discount $= 8\%(\$425) = 0.08(\$425) = \$34$
Net price $= \$425 - \$34 = \$391$

5. Trade discount $= 24\%(\$21) = 0.24(\$21) = \$5.04$
Net price $= \$21 - \$5.04 = \$15.96$

2. Trade discount $= 32\%(\$124) = 0.32(\$124)$
$= \$39.68$
Net price $= \$124 - \$39.68 = \$84.32$

4. Trade discount $= 18\%(\$395) = 0.18(\$395) = \$71.10$
Net price $= \$395 - \$71.10 = \$323.90$

6. Trade discount $= 15\%(\$20{,}588.24)$
$= 0.15(\$20{,}588.24)$
$= \$3{,}088.24$
Net price $= \$20{,}588.24 - \$3{,}088.24$
$= \$17{,}500.00$

2, p. 267

1. Net percent $= 100\% - 12\% = 88\%$
Net price $= 88\%(\$70)$
$= 0.88(\$70)$
$= \$61.60$

3. Net percent $= 100\% - 18\% = 82\%$
Net price $= 82\%(\$1{,}299)$
$= 0.82(\$1{,}299)$
$= \$1{,}065.18$

2. Net percent $= 100\% - 15\% = 85\%$
Net price $= 85\%(\$3{,}200)$
$= 0.85(\$3{,}200)$
$= \$2{,}720$

4. Total list price $= 100(\$3.99) + 40(\$1.89) + 20(\$3.99)$
$= \$399 + \$75.60 + \$79.80$
$= \$554.40$
Net percent $= 100\% - 22\% = 78\%$
Net price $= 78\%(\$554.40)$
$= 0.78(\$554.40)$
$= \$432.43$

SECTION 8-2

1, p. 270

1. Discount complements: $100\% - 10\% = 90\% = 0.9$
$100\% - 5\% = 95\% = 0.95$
Net decimal equivalent $= 0.9(0.95)$
$= 0.855$
Net price $= 0.855(\$4{,}800) = \$4{,}104$

3. Discount complements: $100\% - 15\% = 85\% = 0.85$
$100\% - 10\% = 90\% = 0.9$
Net decimal equivalent $= 0.85(0.9) = 0.765$
Net price $= 0.765(\$600) = \$459$

2. Discount complements: $100\% - 12\% = 88\% = 0.88$
$100\% - 6\% = 94\% = 0.94$
Net decimal equivalent $= 0.88(0.94) = 0.8272$
Net price $= 0.8272(\$535) = \$442.55$

4. Discount complements: $100\% - 10\% = 90\% = 0.9$
$100\% - 6\% = 94\% = 0.94$
$100\% - 5\% = 95\% = 0.95$
Net decimal equivalent $= 0.9(0.94)(0.95) = 0.8037$
Net price $= 0.8037(\$219) = \$176.01$

5. *First manufacturer:*

Discount complements: 100% − 10% = 90% = 0.9
100% − 6% = 94% = 0.94
100% − 4% = 96% = 0.96

Net decimal equivalent = 0.9(0.94)(0.96) = 0.81216

Net price = 0.81216($448) = $363.85

Second manufacturer:

Discount complements: 100% − 15% = 85% = 0.85
100% − 10% = 90% = 0.9
100% − 10% = 90% = 0.9

Net decimal equivalent = 0.85(0.9)(0.9) = 0.6885

Net price = 0.6885($550) = $378.68

The first manufacturer has the lower price (better deal).

6. *First manufacturer:*

Discount complements: 100% − 5% = 95% = 0.95
100% − 10% = 90% = 0.9
100% − 10% = 90% = 0.9

Net decimal equivalent = 0.95(0.9)(0.9) = 0.7695

Net price = 0.7695($695) = $534.80

Second manufacturer:

Discount complements: 100% − 6% = 94% = 0.94
100% − 10% = 90% = 0.9
100% − 12% = 88% = 0.88

Net decimal equivalent = 0.94(0.9)(0.88) = 0.74448

Net price = 0.74448($705) = $524.86

The second manufacturer has the lower net price (better deal).

2, p. 272

1. Complements of discounts: 100% − 12% = 88% = 0.88
100% − 10% = 90% = 0.9
100% − 5% = 95% = 0.95

Net decimal equivalent = 0.88(0.9)(0.95) = 0.7524

Single discount equivalent = 1 − 0.7524 = 0.2476

Trade discount = 0.2476($504) = $124.79

3. Complements of discounts: 100% − 10% = 90% = 0.9
100% − 5% = 95% = 0.95
100% − 3% = 97% = 0.97

Net decimal equivalent = 0.9(0.95)(0.97) = 0.82935

Single discount equivalent = 1 − 0.82935 = 0.17065

Trade discount = 0.17065($24) = $4.10

5. Complements of discounts: 100% − 8% = 92% = 0.92
100% − 6% = 94% = 0.94
100% − 5% = 95% = 0.95

Net decimal equivalent = 0.92(0.94)(0.95) = 0.82156

Single discount equivalent = 1 − 0.82156 = 0.17844

Trade discount = 0.17844($289.95) = $51.74

2. Complements of discounts: 100% − 10% = 90% = 0.9
100% − 5% = 95% = 0.95

Net decimal equivalent = 0.9(0.95) = 0.855

Single discount equivalent = 1 − 0.855 = 0.145

Trade discount = 0.145($317) = $45.97

4. Complements of discounts: 100% − 12% = 88% = 0.88
100% − 8% = 92% = 0.92
100% − 6% = 94% = 0.94

Net decimal equivalent = 0.88(0.92)(0.94) = 0.761024

Single discount equivalent = 1 − 0.761024 = 0.238976

Trade discount = 0.238976($74) = $17.68

6. Answers will vary. The single discount equivalent, when multiplied by the list price, gives the discount amount directly and would normally be the preferred method.

SECTION 8-3

1, p. 277

1. August has 31 days.

August + 20
+ 15 days
―――――
"August 35"
− 31
―――――
September 4

The invoice must be paid by September 4 to get the discount.

3. Latest day to pay and get discount: March 15 + 15 days = March 30.

Cash discount = 0.02($985) = $19.70

Net amount = $985 − $19.70 = $965.30

5. a. 3% discount; 0.97($3,814) = $3,699.58

b. No discount because payment date is after the discount period. Amount due is $3,814.

c. Since May has 31 days, June 7 is 30 days from billing, so invoice amount of $3,814 must be paid.

d. A penalty of 1% is assessed.

0.01($3,814) = $38.14

Amount to be paid = $3,814 + $38.14 = $3,852.14

2. Invoice must be paid by October 22 to receive a 2% discount. A discount of $2,869.17 should be applied to the invoice payment on October 25.

4. Cash discount = 0.01($3,848.96) = $38.49

Net amount = $3,848.96 − $38.49 = $3,810.47

2, p. 278

1. The discount applies because the invoice was paid before December 15.

Amount paid = 0.97($2,697) = $2,616.09

3. The invoice must be paid by June 10.

100% − 2% = 98% of the invoice amount must be paid.

2. The invoice must be paid by January 10 to get a discount of $11.97.

0.02($598.46) = $11.97

4. The discount applies:

100% − 1% = 99%
99% = 0.99
0.99($1,096.82) = $1,085.85

5. The entire amount of the invoice, $187.17, must be paid because the discount terms require the invoice to be paid within the first 10 days of the next month.

6. The discount applies:
$100\% - 3\% = 97\%$
$97\% = 0.97$
$0.97(\$84,896) = \$82,349.12$

3, p. 279

1. The invoice must be paid by September 27 for the discount.
September 12 + 15 = September 27.
$0.97(\$3,097.15) = \$3,004.24$ must be paid.

2. The invoice must be paid within 10 days of receipt of goods to get a 2% discount. The full invoice amount must be paid after 10 days and within 30 days of receipt of goods.

March 20 is within 10 days of receipt of goods so the discount applies.
Amount to be paid = $0.98(\$8,917.48) = \$8,739.13$

3. Pay on May 28, $0.98(\$1,215) = \$1,190.70$; pay on June 14, $1,215

4. The full invoice amount of $797 must be paid because July 12 is more than 15 days from June 17, the date the dryers arrived.

4, p. 280

1. Amount credited $= \dfrac{\$200,000}{0.97} = \$206,185.57$

2. Amount credited $= \dfrac{\$1,900,000}{0.98} = \$1,938,775.51$

3. Amount credited $= \dfrac{\$50,000}{0.98} = \$51,020.41$

4. Amount credited $= \dfrac{\$400,000}{0.97} = \$412,371.13$

Amount of invoice (no discount) = $6,000(\$79) = \$474,000$

Amount still to be paid: $\$474,000 - \$412,371.13 = \$61,628.87$

5, p. 281

1. Cash discount = $0.02(\$2,896) = \$57.92$
Net amount = $0.98(\$2,896) = \$2,838.08$
Total amount = $\$2,838.08 + \$72 = \$2,910.08$

3. Net amount = $0.98(\$7,925) = \$7,766.50$
Total amount = $\$7,766.50 + \$215 = \$7,981.50$

2. Nortex Mills

4. Cost of teak boards = $10(\$26.50) = \$265.00$
Cost of mahogany boards = $25(\$7.95) = \$198.75$
Total cost of merchandise = $\$265 + \$198.75 = \$463.75$
Net amount = $0.97(\$463.75) = \$449.84$
Total = $\$449.84 + \$65 = \$514.84$

CHAPTER 9

SECTION 9-1

1, p. 302

1. $\$32 + \$40 = \$72$

2. $\$12.95 - \$7 = \$5.95$

3. $\$34.95 - \$18 = \$16.95$

4. Markup = $\$5.25 - \$3 = \$2.25$

2, p. 305

1. Markup = $\$599 - \$220 = \$379$
$M\% = \dfrac{\$379}{\$220}(100\%) = 172.3\%$

2. Markup = $\$197.20 - \$145 = \$52.20$
$M\% = \dfrac{\$52.20}{\$145}(100\%) = 36\%$

3. Markup = $\$395 - \$245 = \$150$
$M\% = \dfrac{\$150}{\$245}(100\%) = 61.2\%$

4. Markup = $\$1,420 - \$690 = \$730$
$M\% = \dfrac{\$730}{\$690}(100\%) = 105.8\%$

5. Markup = $\$249 - \$89 = \$160$
$M\% = \dfrac{\$160}{\$89}(100\%) = 179.8\%$

6. Markup = $\$1,048 - \$738$
Markup = $\$310$
$M\% = \dfrac{\$310}{\$738}(100\%)$
$M\% = 42.0\%$
Calculator steps: (1048 − 738) ÷ 738 × 100 = ⇒ 42.00542005

7. $S\% = 100\% + 78\%$
$S\% = 178\%$
$S = 178\%(\$218)$
$S = 1.78(\$218)$
$S = \$388.04$

8. $S\% = 100\% + 95\%$
$S\% = 195\%$
$S = 195\%(\$87.50)$
$S = 1.95(\$87.50)$
$S = \$170.63$

9. $S\% = 100\% + 80\%$
$S\% = 180\%$
$S = 180\%(\$465)$
$S = 1.8(\$465)$
$S = \$837$

10. $S\% = 100\% + 365\%$
$S\% = 465\%$
$S = 465\%(\$0.86)$
$S = 4.65(\$0.86)$
$S = \$4.00$

11. $S\% = 100\% + 110\%$
$S\% = 210\%$
$S = 210\%(\$0.45)$
$S = 2.1(\$0.45)$
$S = \$0.95$

12. $S\% = 100\% + C\%$
$S\% = 100\% + 70\%$
$S\% = 170\%$
$S = 170\%(\$58.82)$
$S = 1.7(\$58.82)$
$S = \$99.99$

13. $C = \dfrac{M}{M\%}$
$C = \dfrac{\$38}{62\%}$
$C = \dfrac{\$38}{0.62}$
$C = \$61.29$

14. $C = \dfrac{M}{M\%}$
$C = \dfrac{\$650}{92\%}$
$C = \dfrac{\$650}{0.92}$
$C = \$706.52$

15. $C = \dfrac{M}{M\%}$
$C = \dfrac{\$358}{65\%}$
$C = \dfrac{\$358}{0.65}$
$C = \$550.77$

16. $C = \dfrac{M}{M\%}$
$C = \dfrac{\$4.14}{125\%}$
$C = \dfrac{\$4.14}{1.25}$
$C = \$3.31$

17. $C = \dfrac{M}{M\%}$

$C = \dfrac{\$7.82}{80\%}$

$C = \dfrac{\$7.82}{0.8}$

$C = \$9.78$

18. $C = \dfrac{M}{M\%}$

$C = \dfrac{0.24}{32\%}$

$C = \dfrac{0.24}{0.32}$

$C = \$0.75$

19. $S\% = 100\% + M\%$
$S\% = 100\% + 60\%$
$S\% = 160\%$

$C = \dfrac{S}{S\%}$

$C = \dfrac{\$39}{160\%}$

$C = \dfrac{\$39}{1.6}$

$C = \$24.38$
$M = S - C$
$M = \$39 - \$24.38$
$M = \$14.62$

20. $S\% = 100\% + M\%$
$S\% = 100\% + 110\%$
$S\% = 210\%$

$C = \dfrac{S}{S\%}$

$C = \dfrac{\$149}{210\%}$

$C = \dfrac{\$149}{2.1}$

$C = \$70.95$
$M = S - C$
$M = \$149 - \$70.95$
$M = \$78.05$

21. $S\% = 100\% + M\%$
$S\% = 100\% + 85\%$
$S\% = 185\%$

$C = \dfrac{\$4.65}{185\%}$

$C = \dfrac{\$4.65}{1.85}$

$C = \$2.51$
$M = S - C$
$M = \$4.65 - \$2.51$
$M = \$2.14$

22. $S\% = 100\% + 165\%$
$S\% = 265\%$

$C = \dfrac{\$595}{265\%}$

$C = \dfrac{\$595}{2.65}$

$C = \$224.53$
$M = S - C$
$M = \$595 - \$224.53$
$M = \$370.47$

23. $S\% = 100\% + 45\%$
$S\% = 145\%$

$C = \dfrac{\$65}{145\%}$

$C = \dfrac{\$65}{1.45}$

$C = \$44.83$
$M = S - C$
$M = \$65 - \$44.83$
$M = \$20.17$

24. $S\% = 100 + M\%$
$S\% = 100\% + 62\%$
$S\% = 162\%$

$C = \dfrac{S}{S\%}$

$C = \dfrac{\$9.99}{162\%}$

$C = \dfrac{\$9.99}{1.62}$

$C = \$6.17$
$M = S - C$
$M = \$9.99 - \$6.17$
$M = \$3.82$

SECTION 9-2

1, p. 313

1. $M = \$70 - \$58$
$M = \$12$
$M\% = \dfrac{\$12}{\$70}(100\%)$
$M\% = 17.1\%$

2. $M = \$1,499 - \$385$
$M = \$1,114$
$M\% = \dfrac{\$1,114}{\$1,499}(100\%)$
$M\% = 74.3\%$

3. $M = \$795 - \$395$
$M = \$400$
$M\% = \dfrac{\$400}{\$795}(100\%)$
$M\% = 50.3\%$

4. $M = \$6.00 - \$2.40$
$M = \$3.60$
$M\% = \dfrac{\$3.60}{\$6.00}(100\%)$
$M\% = 60\%$

5. $M = \$2.39 - \$0.84$
$M = \$1.55$
$M\% = \dfrac{\$1.55}{\$2.39}(100\%)$
$M\% = 64.9\%$

6. $M = \$229 - \$132$
$M = \$97$
$M\% = \dfrac{\$97}{\$229}(100\%)$
$M\% = 42.4\%$

7. $S = \dfrac{\$195}{60\%}$

$S = \dfrac{\$195}{0.6}$

$S = \$325$
$C = \$325 - \$195$
$C = \$130$

8. $S = \dfrac{\$21}{80\%}$

$S = \dfrac{\$21}{0.8}$

$S = \$26.25$
$C = \$26.25 - \$21$
$C = \$5.25$

9. $S = \dfrac{\$14}{75\%}$

$S = \dfrac{\$14}{0.75}$

$S = \$18.67$
$C = \$18.67 - \$14$
$C = \$4.67$

10. $S = \dfrac{\$145}{25\%}$

$S = \dfrac{\$145}{0.25}$

$S = \$580$
$C = \$580 - \$145$
$C = \$435$

11. $S = \dfrac{\$38}{70\%}$

$S = \dfrac{\$38}{0.7}$

$S = \$54.29$
$C = \$54.29 - \$38$
$C = \$16.29$

12. $S = \dfrac{\$70.08}{32\%}$

$S = \dfrac{\$70.08}{0.32}$

$S = \$219$
$C = \$219 - \$70.08$
$C = \$148.92$

13. $C\% = 100\% - 25\%$
$C\% = 75\%$

$S = \dfrac{\$2.99}{75\%}$

$S = \$3.99$
$M = \$3.99 - \$2.99$
$M = \$1.00$

14. $C\% = 100\% - 38\%$
$C\% = 62\%$

$S = \dfrac{\$187}{62\%}$

$S = \$301.61$
$M = \$301.61 - \$187$
$M = \$114.61$

15. $C\% = 100\% - 27\%$
$C\% = 73\%$

$S = \dfrac{\$3.84}{73\%}$

$S = \$5.26$
$M = \$5.26 - \$3.84$
$M = \$1.42$

16. $C\% = 100\% - 23\%$
$C\% = 77\%$

$S = \dfrac{\$127.59}{77\%}$

$S = \$165.70$
$M = \$165.70 - \$127.59$
$M = \$38.11$

17. $C\% = 100\% - 65\%$
$C\% = 35\%$

$S = \dfrac{\$1.92}{35\%}$

$S = \$5.49$
$M = \$5.49 - \$1.92$
$M = \$3.57$

18. $C\% = 100\% - 35\%$
$C\% = 65\%$

$S = \dfrac{\$32.49}{65\%}$

$S = \$49.98$
$M = \$49.98 - \$32.49$
$M = \$17.49$

19. $C\% = 100\% - M\%$
$C\% = 100\% - 38\%$
$C\% = 62\%$
$C = 62\%(\$18.99)$
$C = 0.62(\$18.99)$
$C = \$11.77$
$M = \$18.99 - \$11.77$
$M = \$7.22$

20. $C\% = 100\%$
$M\% = 60\%$
$S\% = C\% + M\%$
$S\% = 100\% + 60\%$
$S\% = 160\%$

$C = \dfrac{M}{M\%}$

$C = \dfrac{\$135}{0.6}$

$C = \$225$
$S = C + M$
$S = \$225 + \$135$
$S = \$360$

21. $C\% = 100\% - 58\%$
$C\% = 42\%$
$C = 42\%(\$349)$
$C = \$146.58$
$M = \$349 - \$146.58$
$M = \$202.42$

22. $C\% = 100\% - 80\%$
$C\% = 20\%$
$C = 20\%(\$49)$
$C = \$9.80$
$M = \$49 - \$9.80$
$M = \$39.20$

23. $C\% = 100\% - 46\%$
$C\% = 54\%$
$C = 54\%(\$675)$
$C = \$364.50$
$M = \$675 - \$364.50$
$M = \$310.50$

24. $C\% = 100\% - M\%$
$C\% = 100\% - 38\%$
$C\% = 62\%$

$S = \dfrac{\$3,034.90}{62\%}$

$S = \dfrac{\$3,034.90}{0.62}$

$S = \$4,895$
$M = \$4,895 - \$3,034.90$
$M = \$1,860.10$

2, p. 316

1. $M = S - C$

$M = \$38 - \$12.50$

$M = \$25.50$

$M\%_{cost} = \dfrac{M}{C} \times 100\%$

$M\%_{cost} = \dfrac{\$25.50}{\$12.50}(100\%)$

$M\%_{cost} = 204\%$

$M\%_{selling\ price} = \dfrac{M}{S} \times 100\%$

$M\%_{selling\ price} = \dfrac{\$25.50}{\$38}(100\%)$

$M\%_{selling\ price} = 67.1\%$

4. $M\%_{cost} = \dfrac{M\%_{selling\ price}}{100 - M\%_{selling\ price}} \times 100\%$

$M\%_{cost} = \dfrac{40\%}{100\% - 40\%}(100\%)$

$M\%_{cost} = 66.7\%$

2. $M = S - C$

$M = \$18,900 - \$12.500$

$M = \$6,400$

$M\%_{cost} = \dfrac{M}{C} \times 100\%$

$M\%_{cost} = \dfrac{\$6,400}{\$12,500}(100\%)$

$M\%_{cost} = 51.2\%$

$M\%_{selling\ price} = \dfrac{M}{S} \times 100\%$

$M\%_{selling\ price} = \dfrac{\$6,400}{\$18,900}(100\%)$

$M\%_{selling\ price} = 33.9\%$

5. $M\%_{selling\ price} = \dfrac{M\%_{cost}}{100\% + M\%_{cost}} \times 100\%$

$M\%_{selling\ price} = \dfrac{120\%}{100\% + 120\%}(100\%)$

$M\%_{selling\ price} = \dfrac{120\%}{220\%}(100\%)$

$M\%_{selling\ price} = 54.5\%$

3. $M\%_{cost} = \dfrac{M\%_{selling\ price}}{100\% - M\%_{selling\ price}} \times 100\%$

$M\%_{cost} = \dfrac{75\%}{100\% - 75\%}(100\%)$

$M\%_{cost} = \dfrac{75\%}{25\%}(100\%)$

$M\%_{cost} = 3(100\%)$

$M\%_{cost} = 300\%$

6. $M\%_{selling\ price} = \dfrac{M\%_{cost}}{100\% + M\%_{cost}}$

$M\%_{selling\ price} = \dfrac{60\%}{100\% + 60\%}$

$M\%_{selling\ price} = \dfrac{60\%}{160\%}$

$M\%_{selling\ price} = \dfrac{0.6}{1.6}$

$M\%_{selling\ price} = 37.5\%$

SECTION 9-3

1, p. 320

1. Markdown $= \$135 - \$75$

Markdown $= \$60$

$M\% = \dfrac{\$60}{\$135}(100\%)$

$M\% = 44.4\%$

4. Markdown $= \$38.99(25\%)$

Markdown $= \$38.99(0.25)$

Markdown $= \$9.75$

Reduced price $= \$38.99 - \$9.75$

Reduced price $= \$29.24$

2. Markdown $= \$15 - \$8$

Markdown $= \$7$

$M\% = \dfrac{\$7}{\$15}(100\%)$

$M\% = 46.7\%$

5. Markdown $= \$85(40\%)$

Markdown $= \$85(0.4)$

Markdown $= \$34$

Sale price $= \$85 - \$34$

Sale price $= \$51$

3. Markdown $= \$249(35\%)$

Markdown $= \$249(0.35)$

Markdown $= \$87.15$

New price $= \$249 - \$87.15$

New price $= \$161.85$

6. Markdown $= 12.563\%(\$398)$

Markdown $= 0.12563(\$398)$

Markdown $= \$50.00$

Reduced price $= \$398.00 - \$50.00$

Reduced price $= \$348.00$

2, p. 322

1.
$S\% = C\% + M\%$
$S\% = 100\% + 60\%$
$S\% = 160\%$
$S = 160\%(\$189)$
$S = \$302.40$
$N\% = 100\% - 30\%$
$N\% = 70\%$
$N = 70\%(\$302.40)$
$N = \$211.68$
Final$\% = 100\% - 40\%$
Final$\% = 60\%$
Final price $= 60\%(\$211.68)$
Final price $= \$127.01$

4. Net decimal equivalent $= 0.85(0.6) = 0.51$
Final reduced price $= 0.51(\$249) = \$126.99$
Final rate of reduction $= 1 - 0.51 = 0.49$
Percent equivalent $= 0.49(100\%) = 49\%$

2.
$S\% = 100\% + 85\%$
$S\% = 185\%$
$S = 185\%(\$262)$
$S = \$484.70$
$N\% = 100\% - 25\%$
$N\% = 75\%$
$N = 75\%(\$484.70)$
$N = \$363.53$
Final$\% = 100\% - 30\%$
Final$\% = 70\%$
Final price $= 70\%(\$363.53)$
Final price $= \$254.47$

3. Net decimal equivalent $= 0.9(0.7) = 0.63$
Final reduced price $= 0.63(\$128) = \$80.64$
Final rate of reduction $= 1 - 0.63 = 0.37$
Percent equivalent $= 0.37(100\%) = 37\%$

3, p. 324

1. $C = \$0.30(300) = \$90$
$M = 1.8(\$90) = \$162$
$S = C + M = \$90 + \$162 = \$252$
$100\% - 5\% = 95\%$ will sell
$0.95(300) = 285$ pounds will sell
Selling price per pound $= \dfrac{\$252}{285} = \$0.88$

4. $C = \$0.92(1,000) = \$920$
$M = 1.8(\$920) = \$1,656$
$S = C + M = \$920 + \$1,656 = \$2,576$
Pounds that will sell $= 0.9(1,000) = 900$ pounds
Selling price per pound $= \dfrac{2,576}{900} = \$2.86$

2. $C = \$0.35(500) = \$175$
$M = 1.75(\$175) = \$306.25$
$S = C + M = \$175 + \$306.25$
$S = \$481.25$
Pounds that will sell $= 0.92(500)$
$= 460$ pounds
Selling price per pound $= \dfrac{\$481.25}{460}$
Selling price per pound $= \$1.05$

3. $C = \$0.27(2,000) = \$540$
$M = 1.6(\$540) = \$864$
$S = C + M = \$540 + \$864 = \$1,404$
Pounds that will sell $= 0.96(2,000)$
$= 1,920$ pounds
Selling price per pound $= \dfrac{\$1,404}{1,920}$
Selling price per pound $= \$0.73$

CHAPTER 10

SECTION 10-1

1, p. 345

1. $42,822 ÷ 26 = $1,647   **2.** $32,928 ÷ 24 = $1,372   **3.** $1,872(52) = $97,344   **4.** $3,315(12) = $39,780

2, p. 346

1. 48 − 40 = 8 hours overtime
40($15.83) = $633.20
8($15.83)(1.5) = $189.96
Gross pay = $633.20 + $189.96 = $823.16

2. 52 − 40 = 12 hours overtime
40($13.56) = $542.40
12($13.56)(1.5) = $244.08
Gross pay = $542.40 + $244.08 = $786.48

3. 55 − 40 = 15 hours overtime
40($14.27) = $570.80
15($14.27)(1.5) = $321.08
Gross pay = $570.80 + $321.08 = $891.88

4. 62 − 40 = 22 hours overtime
22 − 8 = 14 hours overtime at time and a half
40($22.75) = $910
14($22.75)(1.5) = $477.75
8($22.75)(2) = $364
Gross pay = $910 + $477.75 + $364
     = $1,751.75

5. $3,224(12) = $38,688
$38,688 ÷ 52 = $744.00
$744.00 ÷ 40 = $18.60
$18.60(1.5) = $27.90
61 − 40 = 21
21($27.90) = $585.90

6. $4,472(12) = $53,664
$53,664 ÷ 52 = $1,032.00
$1,032.00 ÷ 40 = $25.80
$25.80(1.5) = $38.70
48 − 40 = 8
8($38.70) = $309.60

3, p. 347

1. 12($70) = $840

2. 21 + 27 + 18 + 29 + 24 = 119 tires
119($5.50) = $654.50

3. First 200 units: 200($1.18) = $236
Next 200 units: 200($1.35) = $270
Next 135 units: 135($1.55) = $209.25
Gross pay = $236 + $270 + $209.25
     = $715.25

4. Total units = 37 + 42 + 40 + 46 + 52 = 217
First 50 units = 50($2.95) = $147.50
Units 51–150 = 100($3.10) = $310.00
Last 67 units = 67($3.35) = $224.45
Gross pay = $147.50 + $310.00 + $224.45 = $681.95

4, p. 349

1. Gross earnings = 0.06($17,945) =
$1,076.70

2. Earnings for listings = $4.00(547) =
$2,188
Earnings for commission =
0.01($30,248) = $302.48
Gross earnings = $2,188 + $302.48 =
$2,490.48

3. Amount on which commission is paid =
$26,572 − $3,000 = $23,572
Commission = 0.02($23,572) = $471.44
Gross earnings = $471.44 + $200 =
$671.44
Annual gross earnings = $671.44(52) =
$34,914.88

4. Commission = 0.04($32,017) = $1,280.68
Gross earnings = $1,280.68 + $275 = $1,555.68
Annual gross earnings = $1,555.68(26) = $40,447.68

SECTION 10-2

1, p. 357

1. Use Figure 10-2. Select row for interval "At least 1,680 but less than 1,700." Move across to the column for two withholding allowances. The withholding tax is $174.

2. Use Figure 10-2. Select row for interval "At least 2,020 but less than 2,040." Move across to the column for one withholding allowance. The withholding tax is $280.

3. Use Figure 10-3. Select row for interval "At least 700 but less than 710." Move across to the column for four withholding allowances. The withholding tax is $26.

4. Find taxable earnings: $1,128 − $20 = $1,108.
Use Figure 10-3. Select row for interval "At least 1,100 but less than 1,110." Move across to the column for seven withholding allowances. The withholding tax is $49.

2, p. 360

1. 3($73.08) = $219.24   **2.** $850 − $219.24 = $630.76

3. Use Table 1a in Figure 10-5.
$630.76 − $209 = $421.76
$421.76(0.15) = $63.26
Total withholding tax =
$16.80 + $63.26 = $80.06

4. Withholding allowance = 4($158.33) = $633.32
Adjusted gross income = $4,700 − $633.32
     = $4,066.68
Use Table 3b in Figure 10-5.
$4,066.68 − $3,283 = $783.68
$783.68(0.25) = $195.92
Total withholding tax = $405.50 + $195.92 = $601.42

3, p. 361

1. Maximum annual income = $1,730(26) = $44,980
All earnings will be taxed.
Social Security tax = $1,730(0.042) = $72.66
Medicare tax = $1,730(0.0145) = $25.09

2. Maximum annual income = $6,230(12) = $74,760
All earnings will be taxed.
Social Security tax = $6,230(0.042) = $261.66
Medicare tax = $6,230(0.0145) = $90.34

3. Accumulated pay for 23 pay periods = \$4,675(23) = \$107,525
Maximum amount subject to Social Security = \$110,100.
\$110,100 − \$107,525 = \$2,575
Social Security tax = \$2,575(0.042) = \$108.15
Medicare tax = \$4,675(0.0145) = \$67.79

4. Accumulated pay for 46 weeks = \$2,156(46) = \$99,176
\$110,100 − \$99,176 = \$10,924 earnings subject to Social Security tax in the 47th week. All earnings in the 47th week are subject to Social Security tax.
Social security tax = \$2,156(0.042) = \$90.55
Medicare tax = \$2,156(0.0145) = \$31.26

4, p. 362

1. Retirement = \$1,032(0.06) = \$61.92
Social Security tax = \$1,032(0.042) = \$43.34
Medicare tax = \$1,032(0.0145) = \$14.96

3. Total deductions = \$110.15 + \$61.92 + \$43.34 + \$14.96 + \$82 = \$312.37

2. Use the table in Figure 10-3. Use the "At least 1,030 but less than 1,040" row and move across to the column with three deductions. The amount is \$82.

4. Net pay = \$1,032 − \$312.37 = \$719.63

SECTION 10-3

1, p. 365

1. \$61 + \$90 + \$33 + \$53 = \$237

3. \$10.73 + \$12.57 + \$9.14 + \$10.08 = \$42.52

2. \$31.08 + \$36.41 + \$26.46 + \$29.19 = \$123.14

4. Employer's share Medicare taxes = \$42.52
Employer's share of Social Security taxes = (\$740 + \$867 + \$630 + \$695)(0.062) = \$2,932 (0.062) = \$181.78
Employer's deposit = \$237 + \$123.14 + \$42.52 + \$42.52 + \$181.78 = \$626.96

2, p. 367

1. SUTA = 5.4%(\$7,000) = 0.054(\$7,000) = \$378

2. FUTA = 0.8%(\$7,000) = 0.008(\$7,000) = \$56

3.

Pay period	Employee 1 salary	Accumulated salary subject to FUTA tax	FUTA tax	Employee 2 salary	Accumulated salary subject to FUTA tax	FUTA tax
Jan 15	\$1,320	\$1,320	\$10.56	\$1,275	\$1,275	\$10.20
Jan 31	\$1,320	\$2,640	\$10.56	\$1,275	\$2,550	\$10.20
Feb 15	\$1,320	\$3,960	\$10.56	\$1,275	\$3,825	\$10.20
Feb 28	\$1,320	\$5,280	\$10.56	\$1,275	\$5,100	\$10.20
Mar 15	\$1,320	\$6,600	\$10.56	\$1,275	\$6,375	\$10.20
Mar 31	\$1,320	\$7,000	\$3.20	\$1,275	\$7,000	\$5.00

For Employee 1 on March 31: \$7,000 − \$6,600 = \$400
FUTA = \$400(0.008) = \$3.20
For Employee 2 on March 31: \$7,000 − \$6,375 = \$625
FUTA = \$625(0.008) = \$5.00
First quarter FUTA tax = (\$10.56(5) + \$3.20) + (\$10.20(5) + \$5.00) = \$56 + \$56 = \$112
The deposit should be made at the end of the fourth quarter as the total is less than \$500.

4. The fourth quarter payment of FUTA tax is \$112.
The total FUTA tax for the first \$7,000 for each employee is \$7,000(0.008)(2) = \$112. This is less than \$500.

CHAPTER 11

SECTION 11-1

1, p. 389

1. \$38,000(0.105)(1) = \$3,990

2. \$17,500(0.0775)(6) = \$8,137.50

3. \$6,700(0.095)(3) = \$1,909.50

4. \$38,500(0.123)(5) = \$23,677.50

2, p. 390

1. MV = \$8,000 + \$660 = \$8,660

2. I = \$7,250(0.12)(3) = \$2,610
MV = \$7,250 + \$2,610 = \$9,860

3. $MV = P(I + RT)$
MV = \$1,800(1 + 0.0975(2))
MV = \$1,800(1 + 0.195)
MV = \$1,800(1.195)
MV = \$2,151

4. $MV = P(I + RT)$
MV = \$7,275(1 + 0.11(3))
MV = \$7,275(1 + 0.33)
MV = \$7,275(1.33)
MV = \$9,675.75

3, p. 391

1. $\frac{8}{12} = \frac{2}{3}$; 8 ÷ 12 = 0.666667

2. $\frac{18}{12} = 1\frac{6}{12} = 1\frac{1}{2}$; 18 ÷ 12 = 1.5

3. 18 months = 18 ÷ 12 = 1.5 years
I = \$1,200(0.095)(1.5)
I = \$171

4. 28 ÷ 12 = 2.333333333
MV = \$1,750(1 + 0.098(2.333333333))
MV = \$1,750(1.228666667)
MV = \$2,150.17

4, p. 394

1. $\dfrac{\$636.50}{\$2,680(2.5)} = \dfrac{\$636.50}{\$6,700} = 0.095 = 9.5\%$

2. $\dfrac{\$1,762.50}{\$5,000(3)} = \dfrac{\$1,762.50}{\$15,000} = 0.1175 = 11.75\%$

3. $\dfrac{\$904.88}{3.5(0.0925)} = \dfrac{\$904.88}{0.32375} = \$2,795$

4. $\dfrac{\$4,167.90}{\$16,840(0.09)} = \dfrac{\$4,167.90}{\$1,515.60} = 2.75$ years, or $2\dfrac{3}{4}$ years

SECTION 11-2

1, p. 397

1. Days in March: $31 - 20 = 11$
   Days in April: $= 30$
   Days in May: $= 31$
   Days in June: $= 30$
   Days in July: $= 31$
   Days in August: $= 31$
   Days in September: $= 20$
   $ \overline{ 184}$ days
   or $263 - 79 = 184$ days

2. April 15: 105th day
   October 15: 288th day
   $288 - 105 = 183$ days

3. December 21: 355th day
   October 14: 287th day
   $355 - 287 = 68$ days

4. December 31: 365th day
   November 1: 305th day
   $365 - 305 = 60$ days
   March 1: 60th day
   $60 + 60 = 120$ days
   In a leap year: $120 + 1 = 121$ days

2, p. 398

1. June 12 is day number 163.
   $163 + 120 = 283$
   October 10 is day number 283.

2. July 17 is day number 198.
   $198 + 150 = 348$
   December 14 is day number 348.

3. January 29 is the 29th day of the year.
   $29 + 90 = 119$
   The 119th day of the year is April 29.

4. November 22 is day number 326.
   $326 + 120 = 446$
   $446 - 365 = 81$ days in the next year.
   March 22 is the 81st day in the next year.

3, p. 399

1. March 3: 62nd day
   September 3: 246th day
   $246 - 62 = 184$ days
   $I = \$1,350(0.065)\left(\dfrac{184}{360}\right) = \$44.85$

2. $I = \$1,350(0.065)\left(\dfrac{184}{365}\right) = \$44.24$

3. $\$44.85 - \$44.24 = \$0.61$
   Ordinary interest is $0.61 more than exact interest. Bankers offer borrowers ordinary interest.

4. April 12: 102nd day
   October 12: 285th day
   $285 - 102 = 183$ days
   $I = \$4,250(0.072)\left(\dfrac{183}{360}\right) = \$155.55$
   $MV = \$4,250 + \$155.55 = \$4,405.55$

Answers will vary. The equipment can be purchased now at a $250 savings and the cost of the loan (interest) is only $155.55. Since the equipment is needed now and the loan will allow a savings of $94.45, it is advisable to borrow the money to make the purchase.

4, p. 400

1. $\$10,000(0.09)\left(\dfrac{60}{360}\right) = \$150.00$
   $\$3,000 - \$150 = \$2,850$
   $\$10,000 - \$2,850 = \$7,150$
   $\$7,150(0.09)\left(\dfrac{210}{360}\right) = \$375.38$
   $\$7,150 + \$375.38 = \$7,525.38$

2. $\$5,800(0.075)\left(\dfrac{30}{360}\right) = \$36.25$
   $\$2,500 - \$36.25 = \$2,463.75$
   $\$5,800 - \$2,463.75 = \$3,336.25$
   $\$3,336.25(0.075)\left(\dfrac{90}{360}\right) = \$62.55$
   $\$3,336.25 + \$62.55 = \$3,398.80$
   Total interest $= \$36.25 + \$62.55 = \$98.80$
   $\$5,800(0.075)\left(\dfrac{120}{360}\right) = \$145$
   $\$145 - \$98.80 = \$46.20$

3. $\$8,500(0.09)\left(\dfrac{60}{360}\right) = \$127.50$
   $\$3,000 - \$127.50 = \$2,872.50$
   $\$8,500 - \$2,872.50 = \$5,627.50$

4. $\$5,627.50(0.09)\left(\dfrac{120}{360}\right) = \$168.83$
   $\$5,627.50 + \$168.83 = \$5,796.33$

SECTION 11-3

1, p. 404

1. Exact days $= 312 - 220 = 92$ days
   Bank discount $= \$7,200(0.0825)\left(\dfrac{92}{360}\right) = \$151.80$
   Proceeds $= \$7,200 - \$151.80 = \$7,048.20$

2. Exact days $= 198 - 17 = 181$ days
   Bank discount $= \$9,250(0.0775)\left(\dfrac{181}{360}\right) = \$360.43$
   Proceeds $= \$9,250 - \$360.43 = \$8,889.57$

3. Exact days $= 327 - 54 = 273$ days

Bank discount $= \$3{,}250(0.0875)\left(\dfrac{273}{360}\right) = \$215.65$

Proceeds $= \$3{,}250 - \$215.65 = \$3{,}034.35$

4. Exact days $= 191 - 130 = 61$ days

Bank discount $= \$32{,}800(0.075)\left(\dfrac{61}{360}\right) = \$416.83$

Proceeds $= \$32{,}800 - \$416.83 = \$32{,}383.17$

2, p. 405

1. $I = PRT$

$I = \$8{,}000(0.11)\left(\dfrac{120}{360}\right)$

$I = \$293.33$

Proceeds $=$ principal $-$ bank discount

Proceeds $= \$8{,}000 - \$293.33$

Proceeds $= \$7{,}706.67$

Find the effective interest rate:

$R = \dfrac{I}{PT}$

$R = \dfrac{\$293.33}{\$7{,}706.67\left(\dfrac{120}{360}\right)}$

$R = \dfrac{\$293.33}{\$2{,}568.89}$

$R = 0.1141855042$

$R = 11.4\%$

The effective interest rate for a simple discount note of $8,000 for 120 days is approximately 11.4%.

2. $I = PRT$

$I = \$22{,}000(0.0836)\left(\dfrac{90}{360}\right)$

$I = \$459.80$

Proceeds $=$ principal $-$ bank discount

Proceeds $= \$22{,}000 - \$459.80$

Proceeds $= \$21{,}540.20$

Find the effective interest rate:

$R = \dfrac{I}{PT}$ Substitute proceeds for principal.

$R = \dfrac{\$459.80}{\$21{,}540.20\left(\dfrac{90}{360}\right)}$

$R = \dfrac{\$459.80}{\$5{,}385.05}$

$R = 0.0853845368$

$R = 8.5\%$ Effective interest rate

The effective interest rate for a simple discount note of $22,000 for 120 days is approximately 8.5%.

3. Bank discount:

$I = PRT$

$I = \$18{,}000(0.096)\left(\dfrac{270}{360}\right)$

$I = \$1{,}296$

Proceeds $= \$18{,}000 - \$1{,}296$

Proceeds $= \$16{,}704$

Effective rate:

$R = \dfrac{I}{PT}$

$R = \dfrac{\$1{,}296}{\$16{,}704\left(\dfrac{270}{360}\right)}$

$R = 0.1034482759$

$R = 10.3\%$

4. $I = PRT$

$I = \$16{,}000(0.084)\left(\dfrac{210}{360}\right)$

$I = \$784$

Proceeds $= \$16{,}000 - \$784$

Proceeds $= \$15{,}216$

$R = \dfrac{I}{PT}$

$R = \dfrac{\$784}{\$15{,}216\left(\dfrac{210}{360}\right)}$

$R = 0.0883280757$

$R = 8.8\%$

3, p. 407

1.
$\begin{array}{ll} 201 & \text{July 20} \\ -\,46 & \text{February 15} \\ \hline 155 & \text{days} \end{array}$

3.
$\begin{array}{ll} 201 & \text{July 20} \\ -\,125 & \text{May 5} \\ \hline 76 & \text{days} \end{array}$

Third-party discount $= \$20{,}183.17(0.1)\left(\dfrac{76}{360}\right) = \$426.09$

2. Interest $= \$19{,}500(0.0825)\left(\dfrac{155}{365}\right)$

$= \$683.17$

Maturity value $= \$19{,}500 + \$683.17$

$= \$20{,}183.17$

4. Proceeds to Hugh's Trailers $= \$20{,}183.17 - \$426.09$

$= \$19{,}757.08$

CHAPTER 12

SECTION 12-1

1, p. 429

1. Amount financed $= \$1{,}095 - \$100 = \$995$
Total of payments $= 18(\$62.50) = \$1{,}125$
Installment price $= \$1{,}125 + \$100 = \$1{,}225$
Finance charge $= \$1{,}225 - \$1{,}095 = \$130$

3. Amount financed $= \$2{,}295 - \$275 = \$2{,}020$
Total of payments $= 30(\$78.98) = \$2{,}369.40$
Installment price $= \$2{,}369.40 + \$275 = \$2{,}644.40$
Finance charge $= \$2{,}644.40 - \$2{,}295 = \$349.40$

2. Amount financed $= \$2{,}695 - \$200 = \$2{,}495$
Total of payments $= 24(\$118.50) = \$2{,}844$
Installment price $= \$2{,}844 + \$200 = \$3{,}044$
Finance charge $= \$3{,}044 - \$2{,}695 = \$349$

4. Finance charge $= \$3{,}115.35 - \$2{,}859 = \$256.35$

2, p. 430

1. Total of installment payments $= \$2{,}087 - \$150 = \$1{,}937$

Installment payment $= \dfrac{\$1{,}937}{24} = \$80.71$

2. Total of installment payments $= \$8{,}997.40 - \$1{,}000 = \$7{,}997.40$

Installment payment $= \dfrac{\$7{,}997.40}{36} = \$222.15$

3. Total of installment payments = $2,795.28 − $600 = $2,195.28

$$\text{Installment payment} = \frac{\$2,195.28}{36} = \$60.98$$

4. Total of installment payments = $3,296.96 − $800 = $2,496.96

$$\text{Installment payment} = \frac{\$2,496.96}{30} = \$83.23$$

3, p. 433

1. Installment price = $347.49(36) + $1,500
= $12,509.64 + $1,500 = $14,009.64
Amount financed = $11,935 − $1,500 = $10,435
Finance charge (Interest) = $14,009.64 − $11,935 = $2,074.64

$$\text{Interest per } \$100 = \frac{\$2,074.64}{\$10,435}(\$100) = \$19.88$$

In Table 12-1, move down the Monthly Payments column to 36. Move across to 20.00 (nearest to 19.88). Move to the top of the column to find 12.25%. APR = 12.25%.

3. Installment price = $295.34(36) + $2,000
= $10,632.24 + $2,000 = $12,632.24
Amount financed = $9,995 − $2,000 = $7,995
Finance charge = $12,632.24 − $9,995 = $2,637.24

$$\text{Interest per } \$100 = \frac{\$2,637.24}{\$7,995}(\$100) = \$32.99$$

In Table 12-1, move down the Monthly Payments column to 36. Move across to 32.87 (nearest to 32.99). Move to the top of the column to find 19.5% APR.

2. Installment price = $279.65(24) + $900
= $6,711.60 + $900 = $7,611.60
Amount financed = $6,800 − $900 = $5,900
Finance charge (interest) = $7,611.60 − $6,800 = $811.60

$$\text{Interest per } \$100 = \frac{\$811.60}{\$5,900}(\$100) = \$13.76$$

In Table 12-1, move down the Monthly Payments column to 24. Move across to 13.82 (nearest to 13.76). Move to the top of the column to find 12.75%. APR = 12.75%.

4. Installment price = $296.37(48) + $2,500
= $14,225.76 + $2,500 = $16,725.76
Amount financed = $12,799 − $2,500 = $10,299
Finance charge = $16,725.76 − $12,799 = $3,926.76

$$\text{Interest per } \$100 = \frac{\$3,926.76}{\$10,299}(\$100) = \$38.13$$

In Table 12-1, move down the Monthly Payments column to 48. Move across to 37.88 (nearest to 38.13). Move to the top of the column to find 16.75% APR.

SECTION 12-2

1, p. 438

1. $\text{numerator} = \dfrac{5(6)}{2} = 15$

$\text{denominator} = \dfrac{12(13)}{2} = 78$

$\text{refund fraction} = \dfrac{15}{78} = \dfrac{5}{26}$

2. $\text{numerator} = \dfrac{18(19)}{2} = 171$

$\text{denominator} = \dfrac{48(49)}{2} = 1,176$

$\text{refund fraction} = \dfrac{171}{1,176} = \dfrac{57}{392}$

3. $\text{refund fraction} = \dfrac{21}{666}$

$\text{refund} = \dfrac{21}{666}(\$1,798) = \$56.69$

4. number of months remaining is 10 months

$\text{refund fraction} = \dfrac{55}{1,830} = \dfrac{11}{366}$

$\text{refund} = \dfrac{11}{366}(\$4,917) = \$147.78$

SECTION 12-3

1, p. 441

1.

Day	Balance	Day	Balance	Day	Balance
25	$1,406.54	5	$1,418.47	15	$706.02
26	$1,418.47	6	$1,433.71	16	$706.02
27	$1,418.47	7	$1,433.71	17	$706.02
28	$1,418.47	8	$1,520.69	18	$706.02
29	$1,418.47	9	$1,520.69	19	$706.02
30	$1,418.47	10	$592.83	20	$776.26
1	$1,418.47	11	$592.83	21	$776.26
2	$1,418.47	12	$592.83	22	$776.26
3	$1,418.47	13	$592.83	23	$776.26
4	$1,418.47	14	$706.02	24	$776.26

2. [$1,406.54 + 10($1,418.47) + 2($1,433.71) + 2($1,520.69) + 4($592.83) + 6($706.02) + 5($776.26)] ÷ 30 =
($1,406.54 + $14,184.70 + $2,867.42 + $3,041.38 + $2,371.32 + $4,236.12 + $3,881.30) ÷ 30 = $31,988.78 ÷ 30 = $1,066.29

3. $1,066.29(0.01075) = $11.46

4. $1,406.54 + $297.58 − $927.86 + $11.46 = $787.72

2, p. 443

1. $\text{Monthly rate} = \dfrac{18\%}{12} = \dfrac{0.18}{12} = 0.015$

Finance charge = $1,285.96(0.015) = $19.29
Total purchases and cash advances = $98.76 + $50 + $46.98 = $195.74
Total payments and credits = $135
New balance = $1,285.96 + $19.29 + $195.74 − $135 = $1,365.99

3. $\text{Monthly rate} = \dfrac{24\%}{12} = 2\% = 0.02$

Finance charge = $2,094.54(0.02)
= $41.89
Total purchases = $65.82 + $83.92 + $12.73 + $29.12 + $28.87
= $220.46
Payments = $400
New balance = $2,094.54 + $41.89 + $220.46 − $400
= $1,956.89

2. $\text{Monthly rate} = \dfrac{15\%}{12} = \dfrac{0.15}{12} = 0.0125$

Finance charge = $2,531.77(0.0125) = $31.65
Total purchases and cash advances = $58.63 + $70 + $562.78 = $691.41
Total payments and credits = $455 + $85.46 = $540.46
New balance = $2,531.77 + $31.65 + $691.41 − $540.46 = $2,714.37

4. $\text{Monthly rate} = \dfrac{9\%}{12} = 0.75\% = 0.0075$

Finance charge = $245.18(0.0075) = $1.84
Total purchases = $45.00 + $22.38 + $36.53 = $103.91
Total payments and credits = $100 + $74.93 = $174.93
New balance = $245.18 + $1.84 + $103.91 − $174.93 = $176.00

CHAPTER 13

SECTION 13-1

1, p. 462

1. Monthly rate $= \dfrac{9.2}{12} = 0.767\%$

2. Period interest rate $= 8\% = 0.08$
First end-of-period principal $= \$2,950(1 + 0.08)$
$= \$3,186$
Second end-of-period principal $= \$3,186(1 + 0.08)$
$= \$3,440.88$
The future value is $3,440.88.
Compound interest $= \$3,440.88 - \$2,950$
$= \$490.88$

3. Period interest rate $= \dfrac{3.5\%}{2 \text{ periods annually}} = 1.75\%$
Number of periods $= 2$ periods annually(2 years) $= 4$ periods
First end-of-period principal $= \$20,000(1 + 0.0175) = \$20,350$
Second end-of-period principal $= \$20,350(1 + 0.0175) = \$20,706.13$
Third end-of-period principal $= \$20,706.13(1 + 0.0175) = \$21,068.49$
Fourth end-of-period principal $= \$21,068.49(1 + 0.0175) = \$21,437.19$
The future value is $21,437.19.

4. Period interest rate $= \dfrac{2.8\%}{2 \text{ periods annually}} = 1.4\%$
Number of periods $= 2$ periods annually(3 years) $= 6$ periods
First end-of-period principal $= \$15,000(1 + 0.014) = \$15,210$
Second end-of-period principal $= \$15,210(1 + 0.014) = \$15,422.94$
Third end-of-period principal $= \$15,422.94(1 + 0.014) = \$15,638.86$
Fourth end-of-period principal $= \$15,638.86(1 + 0.014) = \$15,857.80$
Fifth end-of-period principal $= \$15,857.80(1 + 0.014) = \$16,079.81$
Sixth end-of-period principal $= \$16,079.81(1 + 0.014) = \$16,304.93$
The future value is $16,304.93.

2, p. 464

1. Number of interest periods $= 5(1) = 5$ periods
Period interest rate $= \dfrac{4\%}{1} = 4\%$
Using Table 13-1, move down the Periods column to row 5.
Move across to the column with 4% at the top. Read 1.21665.
$\$2,890(1.21665) = \$3,516.12$
The compound amount is $3,516.12.
The compound interest $= \$3,516.12 - \$2,890 = \$626.12$

2. Number of interest periods $= 3(4) = 12$ periods
Period interest rate $= \dfrac{10\%}{4} = 2.5\%$
From Table 13-1, find the intersection of 12 periods and 2.5%. The future value of $1.00 is 1.34489.
Compound amount $= \$2,982(1.34489) = \$4,010.46$
Compound interest $= \$4,010.46 - \$2,982 = \$1,028.46$

3. Number of periods $= 5(1) = 5$ periods
Period interest rate $= \dfrac{2.5\%}{1} = 2.5\%$
From Table 13-1, find the intersection of the 5-periods row and the 2.5% column. The future value of $1.00 is 1.13141.
Compound amount $= \$7,598.42(1.13141) = \$8,596.93$
Compound interest $= \$8,596.93 - \$7,598.42 = \$998.51$

4. Number of interest periods $= 3(2) = 6$
Period interest rate $= \dfrac{1\%}{2} = 1\%$
From Table 13-1, find the intersection of the 6-periods row and the 1% column. The future value of $1.00 is 1.06152.
Compound amount $= \$25,000(1.06152) = \$26,538.00$

3, p. 468

1. Number of interest periods $= 4(12) = 48$
Period interest rate $= \dfrac{2.4\%}{12} = 0.2\% = 0.002$
$FV = P(1 + R)^N$
$FV = \$20,000(1 + 0.002)^{48}$
$FV = \$22,013.07$

3. Number of interest periods $= 5(4) = 20$
Period interest rate $= \dfrac{2.25\%}{4} = 0.5625\% = 0.005625$
$FV = P(1 + R)^N$
$FV = \$18,200(1 + 0.005625)^{20}$
$FV = \$20,360.70$
Compound interest $= \$20,360.70 - \$18,200 = \$2,160.70$

TI BAII Plus

2nd [RESET] [ENTER] 20 [N] .5625 [I/Y] 18,200 [+/−] [PV] [CPT] [FV]
$FV = \$20,360.70$
Compound interest $= \$20,360.70 - \$18,200 = \$2,160.70$

TI - 84

N = 20
I% = 2.25
PV = −18200
PMT = 0
FV = 0
P/Y = 4
C/Y = 4
PMT : **END** BEGIN
Move Cursor to FV. [Alpha] [Solve]
$FV = \$20,360.70$
Compound interest $= \$20,360.70 - \$18,200 = \$2,160.70$

2. Number of interest periods $= 2(2) = 4$
Period interest rate $= \dfrac{1.2\%}{2} = 0.6\% = 0.006$
$FV = P(1 + R)^N$
$FV = \$17,500(1 + 0.006)^4$
$FV = \$17,923.80$

Casio fx-CG10

n = 20
I% = 2.25
PV = −18200
PMT = 0
FV = 0
P/Y = 4
C/Y = 4
Press [F5]
$FV = \$20,360.70$
Compound interest $= \$20,360.70 - \$18,200 = \$2,160.70$

4. For twice a year compounding:

Number of periods = 5(2) = 10 periods

Period interest rate = $\dfrac{2\%}{2} = 1\%$

Compound amount = $12,000(1.01)^{10}$ = $13,255.47

Compound interest = $13,255.47 − $12,000 = $1,255.47

For quarterly compounding:

Number of periods = 5(4) = 20 periods

Period interest rate = $\dfrac{2\%}{4} = 0.5\%$

Compound amount = $12,000(1.005)^{20}$ = $13,258.75

Compound interest = $13,258.75 − $12,000 = $1,258.75

Compounding quarterly yields more interest than compounding semiannually.

$1,258.75 − $1,255.47 = $3.28

The quarterly compounding yields $3.28 more interest than semiannual compounding.

4, p. 470

1. Period interest rate = $\dfrac{8\%}{2} = 4\%$

First end-of-period principal = $2,800(1 + 0.04) = $2,912

Second end-of-period principal = $2,912(1 + 0.04) = $3,028.48

Compound interest after first year = $3,028.48 − $2,800 = $228.48

Effective annual interest rate = $\dfrac{\$228.48}{\$2,800}(100\%) = 8.16\%$

2. Number of periods per year = 2 (semiannually)

Period interest rate = $\dfrac{8\%}{2} = 4\%$

From Table 13-1, find the intersection of the 2-period row and the 4% column. The table value is 1.08160.

Effective annual interest rate = (1.08160 − 1.00)(100%)

= 0.08160(100%) = 8.16%

The manual rate is the same as the table rate.

3. Number of periods per year = 2

Period interest rate = $\dfrac{2\%}{2} = 1\%$

From Table 13-1, find the intersection of the 2-period row and the 1% column. The table value is 1.02010.

Effective annual interest rate = (1.02010 − 1.00)(100%)

= 0.02010(100%)

= 2.01%

4. Number of periods per year = 2

Period interest rate = $\dfrac{3\%}{2} = 1.5\%$

From Table 13-1, find the intersection of the 2-period row and the 1.5% column. The table value is 1.03023.

Effective annual interest rate = (1.03023 − 1.00)(100%)

= 0.03023(100%)

= 3.023%

5, p. 473

1. $1,850 ÷ $100 = 18.5

Find the table value at the intersection of the 60-day row and the 7.25% column.

Table value = 1.198791

Compound interest = 18.5($1.198791)

= $22.18

2. $3,050 ÷ $100 = 30.5

Find the table value at the intersection of the 365-day row and the 6% column.

Table value = 6.183131

Compound interest = 30.5($6.183131)

= $188.59

3. $10,000 ÷ $100 = 100

Find the table value at the intersection of the 730-day row and the 6.75% column. Table value = 14.452250.

Compound interest = 100($14.452250)

= $1,445.23

4. $20,000 ÷ $100 = 200

3 years = 365(3) = 1,095 days

Find the table value at the intersection of the 1,095-day row and the 5.25% column. Table value = 17.056750.

Compound interest = 200($17.056750)

= $3,411.35

SECTION 13-2

1, p. 476

1. Present value = $\dfrac{\$15,000}{1 + 0.02} = \$14,705.88$

2. Present value = $\dfrac{\$15,000}{1 + 0.04} = \$14,423.08$

3. Present value = $\dfrac{\$30,000}{1 + 0.028} = \$29,182.88$

4. Present value = $\dfrac{\$148,000}{1 + 0.0346} = \$143,050.45$

2, p. 478

1. Number of periods = 4(1) = 4 periods

Period interest rate = $\dfrac{4\%}{1} = 4\%$

Table value = 0.85480

Present value = $35,000(0.8548) = $29,918

2. Number of periods = 2(4) = 8 periods

Period interest rate = $\dfrac{4\%}{4} = 1\%$ per period

Table value = 0.92348

Present value = $15,000(0.92348) = $13,852.20

3. Number of periods = 4(4) = 16 periods

Period interest rate = $\dfrac{4\%}{4} = 1\%$

Table value = 0.85282

Present value = $15,000(0.85282) = $12,792.30

4. Number of periods = 6(4) = 24 periods

Period interest rate = $\dfrac{4\%}{4} = 1\%$

Table value = 0.78757

Present value = $15,000(0.78757) = $11,813.55

3, p. 479

1. Number of interest periods = 7(12) = 84

   Period interest rate = $\dfrac{4.8\%}{12}$ = 0.4% = 0.004

   $PV = \dfrac{FV}{(1 + R)^N}$

   $PV = \dfrac{\$30,000}{(1 + 0.004)^{84}}$

   $PV = \dfrac{\$30,000}{(1.004)^{84}}$

   $PV = \$21,453.07$

   Calculator steps:

   30000 $\div$ $($ 1.004 $)$ $^\wedge$ 84 $\Rightarrow$ 21453.06649

3. Number of interest periods = 2(12) = 24

   Period interest rate = $\dfrac{2.4\%}{12}$ = 0.2% = 0.002

   $PV = \dfrac{FV}{(1 + R)^N}$

   $PV = \dfrac{\$800}{(1 + 0.002)^{24}}$

   $PV = \dfrac{\$800}{(1.002)^{24}}$

   $PV = \$762.54$

   $800 in two years is worth $762.54 now. $800 in two years is better than $700 today.

2. Number of interest periods = 4(1) = 4

   Period interest rate = $\dfrac{2.75\%}{1}$ = 2.75% = 0.0275

   $PV = \dfrac{FV}{(1 + R)^N}$

   $PV = \dfrac{\$7,000}{(1 + 0.0275)^{4}}$

   $PV = \dfrac{\$7,000}{(1.0275)^{4}}$

   $PV = \$6,280.16$

   Calculator steps:

   7000 $\div$ $($ 1.0275 $)$ $^\wedge$ 4 $\Rightarrow$ 6280.160136

4. Number of interest periods = 15(4) = 60

   Period interest rate = $\dfrac{2.8\%}{4}$ = 0.7% = 0.007

   $PV = \dfrac{FV}{(1 + R)^N}$

   $PV = \dfrac{\$45,000}{(1 + 0.007)^{60}}$

   $PV = \dfrac{\$45,000}{(1.007)^{60}}$

   $PV = \$29,610.40$

CHAPTER 14

SECTION 14-1

1, p. 500

1. Periodic interest rate = 2.9%. Number of periods = 4
   Annuity payment = $5,000
   End-of-year 1 = $5,000
   End-of-year 2 = $5,000(1.029) + $5,000
        = $5,145 + $5,000 = $10,145
   End-of-year 3 = $10,145(1.029) + $5,000
        = $10,439.21 + $5,000 = $15,439.21
   End-of-year 4 = $15,439.21(1.029) + $5,000
        = $15,886.95 + $5,000 = $20,886.95 future value
   Total investment = $5,000(4) = $20,000
     Total interest = $20,886.95 − $20,000 = $886.95

2. Periodic interest rate = 3.42%. Number of periods = 3
   Annuity payment = $3,500
   End-of-year 1 = $3,500
   End-of-year 2 = $3,500(1.0342) + $3,500
        = $3,619.70 + $3,500 = $7,119.70
   End-of-year 3 = $7,119.70(1.0342) + $3,500
        = $7,363.19 + $3,500 = $10,863.19 future value
   Total investment = $3,500(3) = $10,500
     Total interest = $10,863.19 − $10,500 = $363.19

3. Periodic interest rate = $\dfrac{4\%}{2}$ = 2%
   Number of payments = 2(2) = 4 periods
   Annuity payment = $1,500
   End-of-period 1 = $1,500
   End-of-period 2 = $1,500(1.02) + $1,500
        = $1,530 + $1,500 = $3,030
   End-of-period 3 = $3,030(1.02) + $1,500
        = $3,090.60 + $1,500 = $4,590.60
   End-of-period 4 = $4,590.60(1.02) + $1,500
        = $4,682.41 + $1,500 = $6,182.41

4. Periodic interest rate = $\dfrac{3\%}{2}$ = 1.5%
   Number of payments = 2(2) = 4 periods
   Annuity payment = $300
   End-of-period 1 = $300
   End-of-period 2 = $300(1.015) + $300
        = $304.50 + $300 = $604.50
   End-of-period 3 = $604.50(1.015) + $300
        = $613.57 + $300 = $913.57
   End-of-period 4 = $913.57(1.015) + $300
        = $927.27 + $300 = $1,227.27

2, p. 502

1. Number of periods = 8
   Period rate = 2%
   Table value at intersection of 8-periods row and 2% column = 8.583
   Future value = $4,000(8.583) = $34,332
   Total interest = $34,332 − ($4,000)(8)
       = $34,332 − $32,000 = $2,332

2. Number of periods = 5(2) = 10
   Period rate = $\dfrac{4\%}{2}$ = 2%
   Table value at intersection of 10-periods row and 2% column = 10.950
   Future value = $6,000(10.950) = $65,700
   Total interest = $65,700 − ($6,000)(10)
       = $65,700 − $60,000 = $5,700

3. Number of periods = 5(4) = 20
   Period rate = $\dfrac{2\%}{4}$ = 0.5%
   Table value at intersection of 20-periods row and 0.5% column = 20.979
   Future value = $1,200(20.979) = $25,174.80

4. Number of periods = 6(2) = 12
   Period rate = $\dfrac{6\%}{2}$ = 3%
   Table value at intersection of 12-periods row and 3% column = 14.192
   Future value = $2,500(14.192) = $35,480

3, p. 504

1. Number of periods = 4
Period rate = 3.75%
End-of-year 1 = $1,500(1 + 0.0375)
= $1,500(1.0375) = $1,556.25
End-of-year 2 = ($1,556.25 + $1,500)(1.0375)
= ($3,056.25)(1.0375) = $3,170.86
End-of-year 3 = ($3,170.86 + $1,500)(1.0375)
= ($4,670.86)(1.0375) = $4,846.02
End-of-year 4 = ($4,846.02 + $1,500)(1.0375)
= ($6,346.02)(1.0375) = $6,584.00
Total paid in = $1,500(4) = $6,000
Interest = $6,584 − $6,000 = $584

3. Number of periods = 2(2) = 4
Period rate = $\frac{3.8\%}{2}$ = 1.9%
End-of-period 1 = $5,000(1.019) = $5,095
End-of-period 2 = ($5,095 + $5,000)(1.019)
= $10,095(1.019) = $10,286.81
End-of-period 3 = ($10,286.81 + $5,000)(1.019)
= $15,286.81(1.019) = $15,577.26
End-of-period 4 = ($15,577.26 + $5,000)(1.019)
= $20,577.26(1.019) = $20,968.23

2. Number of periods = 2
Period rate = 4.25%
End-of-year 1 = $4,000(1.0425) = $4,170
End-of-year 2 = ($4,170 + $4,000)(1.0425)
= $8,170(1.0425) = $8,517.23

4. Number of periods = 6
Period rate = $\frac{3\%}{12}$ = 0.25% = 0.0025
End-of-period 1 value = ($50)(1.0025) = $50.13
End-of-period 2 value = ($50.13 + $50)(1.0025) = $100.38
End-of-period 3 value = ($100.38 + $50)(1.0025) = $150.76
End-of-period 4 value = ($150.76 + $50)(1.0025) = $201.26
End-of-period 5 value = ($201.26 + $50)(1.0025) = $251.89
End-of-period 6 value = ($251.89 + $50)(1.0025) = $302.64

4, p. 506

1. Number of periods = 10
Period rate = 2%
Table value for 10-periods row and 5% column = 12.578
Future value = $3,000(12.578)(1.05) = $39,620.70

3. Number of periods = 5(4) = 20
Period rate = $\frac{2\%}{4}$ = 0.5%
Table value for 20-periods row and 0.5% column = 20.979
Future value = $500(20.979)(1.005)
= $10,541.95
Total interest = $541.95

2. Number of periods = 5(2) = 10
Period rate = $\frac{6\%}{2}$ = 3%
Table value for 10-periods row and 3% column = 11.464
Future value = $1,000(11.464)1.03 = $11,807.92

4. Number of periods = 5(2) = 10
Period rate = $\frac{2\%}{2}$ = 1%
Table value for 10-periods row and 1% column = 10.462
Future value = $1,000(10.462)(1.01) = $10,566.62
For both exercises, the amount paid is $10,000 over the term of the investment.
Interest in #3 = $541.95
Interest in #4 = $566.62
The interest is slightly higher for payments of $1,000 because a larger amount earns interest from the very beginning.

5, p. 508

1. A Roth IRA is an annuity due.
Number of periods = 10
Rate per period = 6%
Annuity payment = $3,500
Table 14-1 value = 13.181
Future value of annuity due = $3,500(13.181)(1.06) = $48,901.51

3. A payroll deduction is an ordinary annuity.
Number of periods = 10(12) = 120
Rate per period = $\frac{9\%}{12}$ = 0.75%
Annuity payment = $135
Table 14-1 value = 193.514
Future value of annuity due = $135(193.514) = $26,124.39

2. A Roth IRA is an annuity due.
Number of periods = 25
Rate per period = 5.5%
Annuity payment = $800
Table 14-1 value = 51.153
Future value of annuity due = $800(51.153)(1.055) = $43,173.13

4. A payroll deduction is an ordinary annuity.
Number of periods = 7.5(12) = 90
Rate per period = $\frac{3\%}{12}$ = 0.25%
Annuity payment = $450 (including employer match)
Table 14-1 value = 100.788
Future value of annuity due = $450(100.788) = $45,354.60

6, p. 510

1. $R = \frac{4.62\%}{12} = \frac{0.0462}{12} = 0.00385$ Periodic interest rate
$N = 25(12) = 300$ Number of payments
$PMT = \$250$
$FV_{\text{ordinary annuity}} = \$250\left(\frac{(1 + 0.00385)^{300} - 1}{0.00385}\right)$
          Mentally add within innermost parentheses.
$FV_{\text{ordinary annuity}} = \$250\left(\frac{(1.00385)^{300} - 1}{0.00385}\right)$
Calculator sequence:
250 1.00385 ∧ 300 − 1) ÷ 0.00385 = ⟹ 140713.7814
The future value of the ordinary annuity is $140,713.78.

2. $R = \frac{5.2\%}{52} = \frac{0.052}{52} = 0.001$ Periodic interest rate
$N = 15(52) = 780$ Number of payments
$PMT = \$30$
$FV_{\text{ordinary annuity}} = \$30\left(\frac{(1 + 0.001)^{780} - 1}{0.001}\right)$
          Mentally add within innermost parentheses.
$FV_{\text{ordinary annuity}} = \$30\left(\frac{(1.001)^{780} - 1}{0.001}\right)$
Calculator sequence:
30 (1.001 ∧ 780 − 1) ÷ 0.001 = ⟹ 35418.66671
The future value of the ordinary annuity is $35,418.67.

3. $R = \dfrac{1.35\%}{12} = \dfrac{0.0135}{12} = 0.001125$ Periodic interest rate

$N = 14(12) = 168$ Number of payments

$PMT = \$200$

$FV_{\text{annuity due}} = \$200\left(\dfrac{(1 + 0.001125)^{168} - 1}{0.001125}\right)(1 + 0.001125)$

                                      Mentally add within parentheses.

$FV_{\text{annuity due}} = \$200\left(\dfrac{(1.001125)^{168} - 1}{0.001125}\right)(1.001125)$

Calculator sequence:

200 $($ 1.001125 $\wedge$ 168 $-$ 1 $)$ $\div$ 0.001125 $=$

ANS $($ 1.001125 $)$ $=$ $\Rightarrow$ 37003.82709

The future value of the annuity due is \$37,003.83.

4. $R = \dfrac{6\%}{26} = \dfrac{0.06}{26} = 0.0023076923$ Periodic interest rate

$N = 35(26) = 910$ Number of payments

$PMT = \$25$

$FV_{\text{annuity due}} = \$25\left(\dfrac{(1 + 0.0023076923)^{910} - 1}{0.0023076923}\right) \times$

               $(1 + 0.0023076923)$ Mentally add within parentheses.

$FV_{\text{annuity due}} = \$25\left(\dfrac{(1.0023076923)^{910} - 1}{0.0023076923}\right)(1.0023076923)$

Calculator sequence:

25 $($ 1.0023076923 $\wedge$ 910 $-$ 1 $)$ $\div$ 0.0023076923 $=$

ANS $($ 1.0023076923 $)$ $=$ $\Rightarrow$ 77598.39391

The future value of the annuity due is \$77,598.39.

5. A Roth IRA is an annuity due instrument.

BA II Plus: 2ND [FORMAT] 2 ENTER 2ND [RESET] ENTER 35 N 3 I/Y 3500 +/− PMT 2ND [BGN] 2ND [SET] 2ND [QUIT] CPT FV $\Rightarrow$ 217,965.80

TI-84: APPS ENTER ENTER 35 ENTER 3 ENTER 0 ENTER (−) 3500 ENTER 0 ENTER 1 ENTER ENTER highlight **BEGIN** ENTER ↑ ↑ ↑ ALPHA [SOLVE] $\Rightarrow$ 217965.8049

The future value is \$217,965.80.

6. A 401(k) is an ordinary annuity. $10(12) = 120$ payments; $\dfrac{5\%}{12} = 0.416666667$ rate per period

BA II Plus: 2ND [FORMAT] 2 ENTER 2ND [RESET] ENTER 120 N . 416666667 I/Y 400 +/− PMT CPT FV $\Rightarrow$ 62,112.91

TI-84: MODE ↓ → → → ENTER APPS ENTER ENTER 120 ENTER 5 ENTER 0 ENTER (−) 400 ENTER 0 ENTER 12 ENTER ENTER highlight **END** ↑ ↑ ↑ ALPHA [SOLVE] $\Rightarrow$ 62112.91

The future value of the annuity is \$62,112.91.

SECTION 14-2

1, p. 516

1. Number of periods $= 6$
Period rate $= 4\%$
Table value $= 0.1507619$
Sinking fund payment $= \$12,000(0.1507619)$
                   $= \$1,809.14$

3. Total paid $= \$1,809.14(6)$
           $= \$10,854.84$
Interest $= \$12,000 - \$10,854.84$
       $= \$1,145.16$

2. Number of periods $= 10(4) = 40$
Period rate $= \dfrac{4\%}{4} = 1\%$
Table value $= 0.0204556$
Sinking fund payment $= \$25,000(0.0204556)$
                   $= \$511.39$

4. Total paid $= \$511.39(40)$
          $= \$20,455.60$
Interest $= \$25,000 - \$20,455.60$
       $= \$4,544.40$

2, p. 518

1. Number of periods $= 5$
Period rate $= 4\%$
Table 14-3 value $= 4.452$
Present value $= \$5,000(4.452)$
              $= \$22,260$

3. Number of periods $= 10(4) = 40$
Period rate $= \dfrac{8\%}{4} = 2\%$
Table value $= 27.355$
Present value $= \$7,000(27.355)$
              $= \$191,485$

2. Number of periods $= 20$
Period rate $= 7\%$
Table value $= 10.594$
Present value $= \$20,000(10.594)$
              $= \$211,880$

4. Number of periods $= 20(2) = 40$
Period rate $= \dfrac{6\%}{2} = 3\%$
Table value $= 23.115$
Present value $= \$10,000(23.115)$
              $= \$231,150$

3, p. 520

1. $R = \dfrac{4.85\%}{12} = \dfrac{0.0485}{12} = 0.0040416667$ Periodic interest rate

$N = 26(12) = 312$ Number of payments

$FV = \$350,000$

$PMT_{\text{ordinary annuity}} = \$350,000\left(\dfrac{0.0040416667}{(1 + 0.0040416667)^{312} - 1}\right)$

350000 $\times$ 0.0040416667 $\div$ $($ 1.0040416667 $\wedge$

312 $-$ 1 $)$ $=$ $\Rightarrow$ PMT $= 561.3444827$ (round to nearest cent)

Shameka should pay \$561.34 into the sinking fund each month.

2. $R = \dfrac{5.25\%}{12} = \dfrac{0.0525}{12} = 0.004375$ Periodic interest rate

$N = 25(12) = 300$ Number of payments

$P = \$2,000$

$PV_{\text{ordinary annuity}} = \$2,000\left(\dfrac{(1 + 0.004375)^{300} - 1}{0.004375(1 + 0.004375)^{300}}\right)$

2,000 $($ $($ 1.004375 $\wedge$ 300 $-$ 1 $)$ $\div$

$($ 0.004375 $\times$ 1.004375 $\wedge$ 300 $)$ $)$ $=$ $\Rightarrow$

$PV = 333751.794$ Round to nearest cent.

Mekisha needs to have \$333,751.79 in the fund to receive an annuity payment of \$2,000 each month for 25 years.

CHAPTER 15

SECTION 15-1

1, p. 546

1. 14,781,378 shares

2. $7.70 - $7.30 = $0.40

3. A change of $+$0.21 means the closing price the previous day was $0.21 less than today's closing price. $7.59 - $0.21 = $7.38

4. Examine column 15 to find A.H. BELO has a YTD% Chg of 51.2%.

5. $\text{Current Yield} = \dfrac{\text{annual dividend per share}}{\text{closing price per share}} \times 100\%$

$\text{Current Yield} = \dfrac{\$1.56}{\$27.98}(100\%)$

$\text{Current Yield} = 0.056(100\%)$

$\text{Current Yield} = 5.6\%$

6. Current price per share = $54
   Net income per share = $4.32

$\text{P/E ratio} = \dfrac{\text{current price per share}}{\text{net income per share (past 12 months)}}$

$\text{P/E ratio} = \dfrac{\$54}{\$4.32} = 12.5 \text{ or } 13 \text{ rounded}$

2, p. 547

1. 100,000($0.32) = $32,000

2. Dividends in arrears: 10,000($0.73) = $7,300
   Current dividends to preferred stockholders = 10,000($0.73)
   $= \$7,300$
   Remaining dividends = $2,800,000 - $14,600
   $= \$2,785,400$

3. $\text{Dividends per share paid to common stockholders} = \dfrac{\$2,785,400}{1,000,000}$
   $= \$2.7854$
   $= \$2.79$

4. $0.16(6,684,582) = $1,069,533.12

SECTION 15-2

1, p. 551

1. Column 3 shows 5.375% and a maturity date of Feb 2020.

2. Column 5 shows the Moody's rating of Baa 2.

3. The net change (column 9) of 0.687% indicates a net change = (0.687%)($1,000) = 0.00687($1,000) = $6.87

4. Column 10 is current yield. For Kraft Foods the current yield is 4.930%.

2, p. 552

1. From column 8 in Table 15-3, the closing price as a percent of the face value is 103.097%. Convert 103.097% to a decimal.
   103.097% ÷ 100% = 1.03097
   Closing bond price = $1,000(1.03097) = $1,030.97

2. From column 8 in Table 15-3, the closing price as a percent of the face value is 103.411%. Convert 103.411% to a decimal.
   103.411% ÷ 100% = 1.03411
   Closing bond price = $1,000(1.03411) = $1,034.11

3. The bond closed at 104.526% of its face value, down −0.466% of its face value from the previous day's closing price.
   Previous day's closing price = 104.526% − (−0.466%)
   $\qquad = 104.526\% + 0.466\%$
   $\qquad = 104.992\%$
   $\qquad = 1.04992$
   Previous day's bond price = $1,000(1.04992)
   $\qquad = \$1,049.92$

4. The bond closed at 100.231% of its face value, up 0.518% of its face value from the previous day's closing price.
   Previous day's closing price = 100.231% − 0.518%
   $\qquad = 99.713\%$
   $\qquad = 0.99713$
   Previous day's bond price = $1,000(0.99713)
   $\qquad = \$997.13$

3, p. 552

1. $\text{Current Yield} = \dfrac{0.05375(\$1,000)}{\$966.42}(100\%)$

   $= \dfrac{\$53.75}{\$966.42}(100\%)$

   $= 0.0556176404(100\%)$

   $= 5.562\%$ (rounded to three decimal places)

   Current price of the bond is 96.642% of $1,000, which is $966.42.
   Stated interest rate or coupon in column 3 is 5.375%, which is 0.05375.

2. $\text{Current Yield} = \dfrac{0.085(\$1,000)}{\$1,177.33}(100\%)$

   $= \dfrac{\$85}{\$1,177.33}(100\%)$

   $= 0.0721972599(100\%)$

   $= 7.220\%$ (rounded to three decimal places)

   Current price of the bond is 117.733% of $1,000, which is $1,177.33.
   Stated interest rate or coupon in column 3 is 8.500%, which is 0.085.

SECTION 15-3

1, p. 556

1. Current price per share (NAV) = $10.50 from column 3 of Table 15-4.

2. Change = +0.05
   Yesterday's price = $10.50 − $0.05
   $\qquad = \$10.45$

3. $\text{Beginning of year NAV} = \dfrac{\text{Current NAV}}{100\% + \text{YTD\% return}}$

$\qquad\qquad\qquad\qquad = \dfrac{\$10.50}{1 + 0.049}$

$\qquad\qquad\qquad\qquad = \dfrac{\$10.50}{1.049}$

$\qquad\qquad\qquad\qquad = \$10.00953289$

$\qquad\qquad\qquad\qquad = \$10.01$

5. $\text{Mutual fund sales charge} = \text{offer price} - \text{net asset value}$

$\qquad\qquad\qquad\qquad\quad = \$11.52 - \$10.98$

$\qquad\qquad\qquad\qquad\quad = \$0.54$

$\text{Mutual fund sales charge percent} = \dfrac{\text{Sales charge}}{\text{Net asset value}} \times 100\%$

$\qquad\qquad\qquad\qquad\qquad\quad = \dfrac{\$0.54}{\$10.98}(100\%)$

$\qquad\qquad\qquad\qquad\qquad\quad = 0.0491803279(100\%)$ or 4.92%
(rounded)

7. $\text{Number of shares purchased} = \dfrac{\$1,500}{\$9.23} = 162.5135428 \approx 162.514$ shares

4. $\text{Beginning of year NAV} = \dfrac{\text{Current NAV}}{100\% + \text{YTD\% return}}$

$\qquad\qquad\qquad\qquad = \dfrac{\$11.16}{1 + 0.015}$

$\text{Beginning of year NAV} = \dfrac{\$11.16}{1.015}$

$\qquad\qquad\qquad\qquad = \$10.99507389$

$\qquad\qquad\qquad\qquad = \$11.00$

6. $\text{Mutual fund sales charge} = \text{offer price} - \text{net asset value}$

$\qquad\qquad\qquad\qquad\quad = \$6.05 - \$5.82$

$\qquad\qquad\qquad\qquad\quad = \$0.23$

$\text{Mutual fund sales charge percent} = \dfrac{\text{Sales charge}}{\text{Net asset value}} \times 100\%$

$\qquad\qquad\qquad\qquad\qquad\quad = \dfrac{\$0.23}{\$5.82}(100\%)$

$\qquad\qquad\qquad\qquad\qquad\quad = 3.951890034\%$ or 3.95%
(rounded)

8. $\text{Number of shares purchased} = \dfrac{\$2,000}{\$7.84} = 255.1020408 \approx 255.102$ shares

2, p. 558

1. Total proceeds from sale = 1,000 shares ($14.52) = $14,520
Additions = 1,000 shares ($0.83) = $830
Total cost of purchase = 1,000 shares ($12.73) = $12,730
Gain on investment = ($14,520 + $830) − $12,730 = $2,620

$\text{Return on investment (ROI)} = \dfrac{\$2,620}{\$12,730} = 0.2058130401 = 20.6\%$

3. Total proceeds from sale = 2,322.341 shares ($23.89) = $55,480.73
Additions = 2,322.341 shares ($1.78) = $4,133.77
Total cost of purchase = 2,322.341 shares ($21.53) = $50,000
Gain on investment = ($55,480.73 + $4,133.77) − $50,000
$\qquad\qquad\qquad\quad = \$9,614.50$

$\text{ROI} = \dfrac{\$9,614.50}{\$50,000} = 0.19229 = 19.2\%$

2. Total proceeds from sale = 1,500 shares ($21.97) = $32,955
Additions = 1,500 shares ($0.21) = $315
Total cost of purchase = 1,500 shares ($22.84) = $34,260
Loss on investment = ($32,955 + $315) − $34,260 = −$990

$\text{ROI} = \dfrac{-\$990}{\$34,260} = -0.0288966725 = -2.9\%$ (a loss)

4. $\text{Number of shares purchased} = \dfrac{\$20,000}{\$17.54} = 1,140.251$ shares

Total proceeds from sale = 1,140.251 shares ($22.35) = $25,484.61
Additions = 1,140.251 shares ($1.06) = $1,208.67
Total cost of purchase = 1,140.251 shares ($17.54) = $20,000
Gain on investment = ($25,484.61 + $1,208.67) − $20,000
$\qquad\qquad\qquad\quad = \$6,693.28$

$\text{ROI} = \dfrac{\$6,693.28}{\$20,000.00} = 0.334664 = 33.5\%$

CHAPTER 16

SECTION 16-1

1, p. 579

1. $148,500(0.20) = $29,700
Amount financed = $148,500 − $29,700 = $118,800
Number of $1,000 units = $118,800 ÷ $1,000 = 118.8
Table 16-1 value for 30 years and 5.75% interest rate = 5.84
Monthly payment = 118.8($5.84) = $693.79

3. Number of $1,000 units = $160,000 ÷ $1,000 = 160
Table 16-1 value for 25 years and 5.5% interest rate = 6.14
Monthly payment = 160($6.14) = $982.40

2. Number of $1,000 units = $160,000 ÷ $1,000 = 160
Table 16-1 value for 20 years and 5.5% interest rate = 6.88
Monthly payment = 160($6.88) = $1,100.80

4. Number of units = $160,000 ÷ $1,000 = 160
Table 16-1 value for 30 years and 5.5% interest rate = 5.68
Monthly payment = 160($5.68) = $908.80

2, p. 581

1. Number of $1,000 units = $195,000 ÷ $1,000 = 195
Table 16-1 value for 17 years and 4.25% interest rate = $6.89
Monthly payment = 195($6.89) = $1,343.55

3. Monthly insurance payment = $1,080 ÷ 12 = $90
Monthly taxes payment = $1,252 ÷ 12 = $104.33
Adjusted monthly payment = $1,343.55 + $90 + $104.33 = $1,537.88

2. Total paid = $1,343.55(17)(12) = $274,084.20
Interest = $274,084.20 − $195,000 = $79,084.20

4. Monthly payment for loan of 15 years at 5.75%
Interest = 185.4($8.30) = $1,538.82
Monthly payment for loan of 30 years at 6.25%
Interest = 185.4($6.16) = $1,142.06
Marcella should finance for 30 years at 6.25%.

1, p. 585

1. Month 1 interest $= \$118,800\left(\dfrac{0.0575}{12}\right) = \$569.25$

   Principal portion of 1st payment $= \$693.79 - \$569.25 = \$124.54$
   End-of-month principal $= \$118,800 - \$124.54 = \$118,675.46$

   Month 2 interest $= \$118,675.46\left(\dfrac{0.0575}{12}\right) = \$568.65$

   Principal portion of 2nd payment $= \$693.79 - \$568.65 = \$125.14$
   End-of-month principal $= \$118,675.46 - \$125.14 = \$118,550.32$

Month	Monthly payment	Interest	Principal	End-of-month principal
1	$693.79	$569.25	$124.54	$118,675.46
2	$693.79	$568.65	$125.14	$118,550.32

3. Month 1 interest $= \$160,000\left(\dfrac{0.055}{12}\right) = \$733.33$

   Principal portion of 1st payment $= \$982.40 - \$733.33 = \$249.07$
   End-of-month principal $= \$160,000 - \$249.07 = \$159,750.93$

   Month 2 interest $= \$159,750.93\left(\dfrac{0.055}{12}\right) = \$732.19$

   Principal portion of 2nd payment $= \$982.40 - \$732.19 = \$250.21$
   End-of-month principal $= \$159,750.93 - \$250.21 = \$159,500.72$

   Month 3 interest $= \$159,500.72\left(\dfrac{0.055}{12}\right) = \$731.04$

   Principal portion of 3rd payment $= \$982.40 - \$731.04 = \$251.36$
   End-of-month principal $= \$159,500.72 - \$251.36 = \$159,249.36$

Month	Monthly payment	Interest	Principal	End-of-month principal
1	$982.40	$733.33	$249.07	$159,750.93
2	$982.40	$732.19	$250.21	$159,500.72
3	$982.40	$731.04	$251.36	$159,249.36

2. Month 1 interest $= \$160,000\left(\dfrac{0.055}{12}\right) = \$733.33$

   Principal portion of 1st payment $= \$1,100.80 - \$733.33 = \$367.47$
   End-of-month principal $= \$160,000 - \$367.47 = \$159,632.53$

   Month 2 interest $= \$159,632.53\left(\dfrac{0.055}{12}\right) = \$731.65$

   Principal portion of 2nd payment $= \$1,100.80 - \$731.65 = \$369.15$
   End-of-month principal $= \$159,632.53 - \$369.15 = \$159,263.38$

Month	Monthly payment	Interest	Principal	End-of-month principal
1	$1,100.80	$733.33	$367.47	$159,632.53
2	$1,100.80	$731.65	$369.15	$159,263.38

4. Month 4 interest $= \$159,471.18\left(\dfrac{0.055}{12}\right) = \$730.91$

   Principal portion of 4th payment $= \$908.80 - \$730.91 = \$177.89$
   End-of-month principal $= \$159,471.18 - \$177.89 = \$159,293.29$

   Month 5 interest $= \$159,293.29\left(\dfrac{0.055}{12}\right) = \$730.09$

   Principal portion $= \$908.80 - \$730.09 = \$178.71$
   End-of-month principal $= \$159,293.29 - \$178.71 = \$159,114.58$

   Month 6 interest $= \$159,114.58\left(\dfrac{0.055}{12}\right) = \$729.28$

   Principal portion $= \$908.80 - \$729.28 = \$179.52$
   End-of-month principal $= \$159,114.58 - \$179.52 = \$158,935.06$

Month	Monthly payment	Interest	Principal	End-of-month principal
4	$908.80	$730.91	$177.89	$159,293.29
5	$908.80	$730.09	$178.71	$159,114.58
6	$908.80	$729.28	$179.52	$158,935.06

2, p. 586

1. Amount mortgaged $= \$386,000 - \$84,000 = \$302,000$

   Loan-to-value ratio $= \dfrac{\text{Amount mortgaged}}{\text{Appraised value of property}}$

   Loan-to-value ratio $= \dfrac{\$302,000}{\$395,000}$

   Loan-to-value ratio $= 0.764556962$ or 76%

3. Debt-to-income ratio $= \dfrac{\text{total fixed monthly expenses}}{\text{gross monthly income}}$

   Debt-to-income ratio $= \dfrac{\$1,675}{\$4,975}$

   Debt-to-income ratio $= 0.3366834171$ or 34%

2. Housing ratio $= \dfrac{\text{total mortgage payment (PITI)}}{\text{gross monthly income}}$

   Housing ratio $= \dfrac{\$1,482}{\$5,893}$

   Housing ratio $= 0.2514848125$ or 25%, which is below the desirable maximum percentage.

4. Housing ratio $= \dfrac{\text{total mortgage payment (PITI)}}{\text{gross monthly income}}$

   PITI $= \$1,845 + \$74 + \$104 = \$2,023$
   Gross monthly income $= \$5,798 + \$200 = \$5,998$

   Housing ratio $= \dfrac{\$2,023}{\$5,998}$

   Housing ratio $= 0.337279073$ or 34%, which is above the maximum desired percentage, so her ratio is not favorable.

CHAPTER 17

SECTION 17-1

1, p. 606

1. Depreciable value $= \$5,323 - \$500 = \$4,823$

3. Yearly depreciation $= \dfrac{\text{cost} - \text{salvage value}}{\text{years of expected life}}$

   $= \dfrac{\$21,500 - \$4,000}{4} = \dfrac{\$17,500}{4} = \$4,375$

2. Yearly depreciation $= \dfrac{\text{cost of equipment} - \text{salvage value}}{\text{years of expected life}}$

   $= \dfrac{\$18,000 - \$3,000}{3} = \dfrac{\$15,000}{3} = \$5,000$

4. Yearly depreciation $= \dfrac{\text{cost} - \text{salvage value}}{\text{years of expected life}}$

   $= \dfrac{\$5,800 - \$1,500}{3} = \dfrac{\$4,300}{3} = \$1,433.33$

5.

Total cost: $21,500	Year	Annual depreciation	Accumulated depreciation	End-of-year book value
	1	$4,375	$4,375	$17,125
Depreciable	2	4,375	8,750	12,750
value:	3	4,375	13,125	8,375
$17,500	4	$4,375	$17,500	4,000

2, p. 608

1. Unit depreciation $= \dfrac{\$18,000 - \$3,000}{75,000} = \$0.20$ per mile

   Depreciation after 56,000 miles $= \$0.20(56,000) = \$11,200$

3. Unit depreciation $= \dfrac{\$28,700 - \$2,500}{300,000} = \$0.0873333$

   Depreciation for 28,452 objects $= \$0.0873333(28,452) = \$2,484.81$

2. Unit depreciation $= \dfrac{\$23,580 - \$2,300}{95,000} = \$0.224$ per mile

4. Unit depreciation $= \dfrac{\$7,500 - \$600}{60,000} = \dfrac{\$6,900}{60,000} = \$0.115$ per hour

   Year's depreciation $= \$0.115(8,500) = \$977.50$

3, p. 610

1. (a) $\dfrac{8(8 + 1)}{2} = \dfrac{8(9)}{2} = 36$

   (b) $\dfrac{12(12 + 1)}{2} = \dfrac{12(13)}{2} = 78$

3. Year 1 depreciation $= \frac{4}{10}(\$7,500) = \$3,000$
   End-of-year 1 book value $= \$9,000 - \$3,000 = \$6,000$
   Year 2 depreciation $= \frac{3}{10}(\$7,500) = \$2,250$
   Accumulated depreciation $= \$3,000 + \$2,250 = \$5,250$
   End-of-year 2 book value $= \$6,000 - \$2,250 = \$3,750$
   Year 3 depreciation $= \frac{2}{10}(\$7,500) = \$1,500$
   Accumulated depreciation $= \$5,250 + \$1,500 = \$6,750$
   End-of-year 3 book value $= \$3,750 - \$1,500 = \$2,250$
   Year 4 depreciation $= \frac{1}{10}(\$7,500) = \$750$
   Accumulated depreciation $= \$6,750 + \$750 = \$7,500$
   End-of-year 4 book value $= \$2,250 - \$750 = \$1,500$

2. Denominator of depreciation rate $= \dfrac{3(3 + 1)}{2} = 6$

   Depreciation rate for each year: $\dfrac{3}{6}, \dfrac{2}{6}, \dfrac{1}{6}$

   Original cost $-$ salvage value $= \$18,000 - \$3,000 = \$15,000$

   Year 1 depreciation $= \$15,000\left(\dfrac{3}{6}\right) = \$7,500$

   Year 2 depreciation $= \$15,000\left(\dfrac{2}{6}\right) = \$5,000$

   Year 3 depreciation $= \$15,000\left(\dfrac{1}{6}\right) = \$2,500$

Total cost: $9,000	Year	Depreciation rate	Depreciation	Accumulated depreciation	End-of-year book value
Depreciable value:	1	$\frac{4}{10}$	$3,000	$3,000	$6,000
$9,000 − $1,500 = $7,500	2	$\frac{3}{10}$	$2,250	$5,250	$3,750
	3	$\frac{2}{10}$	$1,500	$6,750	$2,250
	4	$\frac{1}{10}$	$750	$7,500	$1,500

4. Sum of the years' digits $= \dfrac{10(10 + 1)}{2} = \dfrac{10(11)}{2} = 55$

Year	1	2	3	4	5	6	7	8	9	10
Rate	$\frac{10}{55}$,	$\frac{9}{55}$,	$\frac{8}{55}$,	$\frac{7}{55}$,	$\frac{6}{55}$,	$\frac{5}{55}$,	$\frac{4}{55}$,	$\frac{3}{55}$,	$\frac{2}{55}$,	$\frac{1}{55}$

Total cost: $45,000	Year	Depreciation rate	Depreciation	Accumulated depreciation	End-of-year book value
Depreciable	1	$\frac{10}{55}$	$7,545.45	$ 7,545.45	$37,454.55
	2	$\frac{9}{55}$	6,790.91	14,336.36	30,663.64
	3	$\frac{8}{55}$	6,036.36	20,372.72	24,627.28
	4	$\frac{7}{55}$	5,281.82	25,654.54	19,345.46

4, p. 613

1. (a) $\dfrac{1}{3} = 0.33333 = 33.33\%$

   (b) $\dfrac{1}{3}(2) = \dfrac{2}{3} = 0.66667 = 66.67\%$

2. Double-declining rate $= \dfrac{1}{4}(2) = \dfrac{2}{4} = \dfrac{1}{2} = 0.5 = 50\%$

   Year 1 depreciation $= \$18,000(0.5) = \$9,000$
   End-of-year 1 book value $= \$18,000 - \$9,000 = \$9,000$
   Year 2 depreciation $= \$9,000(0.5) = \$4,500$
   End-of-year 2 book value $= \$9,000 - \$4,500 = \$4,500$
   Year 3 depreciation $= \$4,500(0.5) = \$2,250$
   End-of-year 3 book value $= \$4,500 - \$2,250 = \$2,250$
   Year 4 depreciation $= \$2,250(0.5) = \$1,125$
   End-of-year 4 book value $= \$2,250 - \$1,125 = \$1,125$

3. Double-declining rate $= \dfrac{1}{5}(2) = \dfrac{2}{5} = 0.4 = 40\%$

Total cost: $4,500	Year	Depreciation	Accumulated depreciation	End-of-year book value
	1	$1,800.00	$1,800.00	$2,700.00
	2	1,080.00	2,880.00	1,620.00
	3	648.00	3,528.00	972.00
	4	388.80	3,916.80	583.20
	5	233.28	4,150.08	349.92

4. 200%-declining rate $= \dfrac{1}{8}(2) = \dfrac{2}{8} = \dfrac{1}{4} = 0.25 = 25\%$

Total cost: $25,000	Year	Depreciation	Accumulated depreciation	End-of-year book value
	1	$6,250.00	$ 6,250.00	$18,750.00
	2	4,687.50	10,937.50	14,062.50
	3	3,515.63	14,453.13	10,546.87
	4	2,636.72	17,089.85	7,910.15
	5	1,977.54	19,067.39	5,932.61
	6	1,483.15	20,550.54	4,449.46
	7	1,112.37	21,662.91	3,337.09
	8	834.27	22,497.18	2,502.82

1, p. 619

1. Year 9 depreciation = 6.56% × total cost = 0.0656($58,000) = $3,804.80

2. Year 8 depreciation = 6.55% × total cost = 0.0655($45,000) = $2,947.50

3. Year 14 depreciation = 5.90% × total cost = 0.059($83,500) = $4,926.50

4.
Total cost: $58,000		MACRS		Accumulated	End-of-year
	Year	rate	Depreciation	depreciation	book value
	1	10.00	$ 5,800	$ 5,800	$52,200
	2	18.00	10,440	16,240	41,760
	3	14.40	8,352	24,592	33,408
	4	11.52	6,681.60	31,273.60	26,726.40
	5	9.22	5,347.60	36,621.20	21,378.80
	6	7.37	4,274.60	40,895.80	17,104.20
	7	6.55	3,799	44,694.80	13,305.20
	8	6.55	3,799	48,493.80	9,506.20
	9	6.56	3,804.80	52,298.60	5,701.40
	10	6.55	3,799	56,097.60	1,902.40
	11	3.28	1,902.40	58,000	0

CHAPTER 18

SECTION 18-1

1, p. 638

1. Cost of ending inventory = $9(128) + $8(79) + $11(183) = $3,797
   Cost of goods available for sale = $9(314) + $8(200) + $11(300) = $2,826 + $1,600 + $3,300 = $7,726
   Cost of good sold = $7,726 − $3,797 = $3,929

2. Cost of ending inventory = $2(317) + $1.90(17) + $2.10(123) + $1.90(47) = $634 + $32.30 + $258.30 + $89.30 = $1,013.90
   Cost of goods available for sale = $2(538) + $1.90(400) + $2.10(200) + $1.90(500) = $1,076 + $760 + $420 + $950 = $3,206
   Cost of goods sold = $3,206 − $1,013.90 = $2,192.10

3. Cost of ending inventory = $7(117) + $6(89) + $9(36) = $819 + $534 + $324 = $1,677
   Cost of goods available for sale = $7(389) + $6(400) + $9(200) = $2,723 + $2,400 + $1,800 = $6,923
   Cost of goods sold = $6,923 − $1,677 = $5,246

4. Cost of ending inventory = $0.86(115) + $0.93(219) + $0.95(28) + $0.90(107) = $98.90 + $203.67 + $26.60 + $96.30 = $425.47
   Cost of goods available for sale = $0.86(538) + $0.93(576) + $0.95(360) + $0.90(624) = $462.68 + $535.68 + $342 + $561.60 = $1,901.96
   Cost of goods sold = $1,901.96 − $425.47 = $1,476.49

2, p. 639

1. Units available for sale = 314 + 200 + 300 = 814
   Cost of goods available for sale = 314($9) + 200($8) + 300($11) = $2,826 + $1,600 + $3,300 = $7,726

   Average unit cost = $\dfrac{\$7,726}{814}$ = $9.49

   Ending inventory = 128 + 79 + 183 = 390
   Cost of ending inventory = 390($9.49) = $3,701.10
   Cost of goods sold = $7,726 − $3,701.10 = $4,024.90

2. Units available for sale = 538 + 400 + 200 + 500 = 1,638
   Cost of goods available for sale = 538($2) + 400($1.90) + 200($2.10) + 500($1.90) = $1,076 + $760 + $420 + $950 = $3,206

   Average unit cost = $\dfrac{\$3,206}{1,638}$ = $1.96

   Ending inventory = 317 + 17 + 123 + 47 = 504
   Cost of ending inventory = 504($1.96) = $987.84
   Cost of goods sold = $3,206 − $987.84 = $2,218.16

3. Units available for sale = 389 + 400 + 200 = 989
   Cost of goods available for sale = 389($7) + 400($6) + 200($9) = $2,723 + $2,400 + $1,800 = $6,923

   Average unit cost = $\dfrac{\$6,923}{989}$ = $7

   Ending inventory = 117 + 89 + 36 = 242
   Cost of ending inventory = 242($7) = $1,694
   Cost of goods sold = $6,923 − $1,694 = $5,229

4. Units available for sale = 538 + 576 + 360 + 624 = 2,098
   Cost of goods available for sale = 538($0.86) + 576($0.93) + 360($0.95) + 624($0.90) = $462.68 + $535.68 + $342 + $561.60 = $1,901.96

   Average unit cost = $\dfrac{\$1,901.96}{2,098}$ = $0.91

   Ending inventory = 115 + 219 + 28 + 107 = 469
   Cost of ending inventory = 469($0.91) = $426.79
   Cost of goods sold = $1,901.96 − $426.79 = $1,475.17

3, p. 640

1. Ending inventory = 128 + 79 + 183 = 390

Most recent units purchased March 1 = 300 units

Units from February 1 purchase = 390 − 300 = 90

Cost of ending inventory = 300($11) + 90($8) = $3,300 + $720 = $4,020

Cost of goods available for sale = 314($9) + 200($8) + 300($11) = $2,826 + $1,600 + $3,300 = $7,726

Cost of goods sold = $7,726 − $4,020 = $3,706

2. Ending inventory = 317 + 17 + 123 + 47 = 504 units

Most recent units purchased October 1 = 500 units

Units purchased on July 1 = 504 − 500 = 4 units

Cost of ending inventory = 500($1.90) + 4($2.10) = $958.40

Cost of goods available for sale = 538($2) + 400($1.90) + 200($2.10) + 500($1.90) = $1,076 + $760 + $420 + $950 = $3,206

Cost of goods sold = $3,206 − $958.40 = $2,247.60

3. Ending inventory = 117 + 89 + 36 = 242

Most recent units purchased February 25 = 200

Units purchased on February 12 = 242 − 200 = 42

Cost of ending inventory = 200($9) + 42($6) = $1,800 + $252 = $2,052

Cost of goods available for sale = 389($7) + 400($6) + 200($9) = $2,723 + $2,400 + $1,800 = $6,923

Cost of goods sold = $6,923 − $2,052 = $4,871

4. Ending inventory = 115 + 219 + 28 + 107 = 469

Most recent units purchased October 1 = 469

Cost of ending inventory = 469($0.90) = $422.10

Cost of goods available for sale = 538($0.86) + 576($0.93) + 360($0.95) + 624($0.90) = $462.68 + $535.68 + $342 + $561.60 = $1,901.96

Cost of goods sold = $1,901.96 − $422.10 = $1,479.86

4, p. 642

1. Ending inventory = 128 + 79 + 183 = 390

Units in ending inventory from January 1 inventory = 314

Units in ending inventory from February 1 purchase = 390 − 314 = 76

Cost of goods available for sale = 314($9) + 200($8) + 300($11) = $2,826 + $1,600 + $3,300 = $7,726

Cost of ending inventory = $9(314) + $8(76) = $2,826 + $608 = $3,434

Cost of goods sold = $7,726 − $3,434 = $4,292

2. Ending inventory = 317 + 17 + 123 + 47 = 504

Units in ending inventory from January 1 inventory = 504

Cost of goods available for sale = 538($2) + 400($1.90) + 200($2.10) + 500($1.90) = $1,076 + $760 + $420 + $950 = $3,206

Cost of ending inventory = 504($2) = $1,008

Cost of goods sold = $3,206 − $1,008 = $2,198

3. Ending inventory = 117 + 89 + 36 = 242

Units in ending inventory from February 1 purchase = 242

Cost of goods available for sale = $7(389) + $6(400) + $9(200) = $2,723 + $2,400 + $1,800 = $6,923

Cost of ending inventory = 242($7) = $1,694

Cost of goods sold = $6,923 − $1,694 = $5,229

4. Ending inventory = 115 + 219 + 28 + 107 = 469

Units in ending inventory from January 1 = 469

Cost of ending inventory = 469($0.86) = $403.34

Cost of goods available for sale = 538($0.86) + 576($0.93) + 360($0.95) + 624($0.90) = $462.68 + $535.68 + $342 + $561.60 = $1,901.96

Cost of goods sold = $1,901.96 − $403.34 = $1,498.62

5, p. 644

1. Cost of goods available for sale = 314($9) + 200($8) + 300($11) = $2,826 + $1,600 + $3,300 = $7,726

Retail value of goods available for sale = $3,617.28 + $2,048 + $4,224 = $9,889.28

Cost ratio $= \dfrac{\$7,726}{\$9,889.28} = 0.78125$

Ending inventory at retail = $9,889.28 − $5,029.12 = $4,860.16

Ending inventory at cost = $4,860.16(0.78125) = $3,797

Cost of goods sold = $5,029.12(0.78125) = $3,929 or $7,726 − $3,797 = $3,929

2. Cost of goods available for sale = $1,076 + $760 + $420 + $950 = $3,206

Retail value of goods available for sale = $1,554.37 + $1,100 + $608 + $1,375 = $4,637.37

Cost ratio $= \dfrac{\$3,206}{\$4,637.37} = 0.6913401346$

Ending inventory at retail = $4,637.37 − $3,171.32 = $1,466.05

Ending inventory at cost = $1,466.05(0.6913401346) = $1,013.54

Cost of goods sold = $3,171.32(0.6913401346) = $2,192.46 or $3,206 − $1,013.54 = $2,192.46

3. Cost of goods available for sale = $2,723 + $2,400 + $1,800 = $6,923

Retail value of goods available for sale = $3,948.35 + $3,480 + $2,610 = $10,038.35

Cost ratio $= \dfrac{\$6,923}{\$10,038.35} = 0.6896551724$

Ending inventory at retail = $10,038.35 − $7,606.70 = $2,431.65

Ending inventory at cost = $2,431.65(0.6896551724) = $1,677.00

Cost of goods sold = $7,606.70(0.6896551724) = $5,246

4. Cost of goods available for sale = \$462.68 + \$535.68 + \$342 + \$561.60 = \$1,901.96

Retail value of goods available for sale = \$763.42 + \$883.87 + \$564.30 + \$926.64 = \$3,138.23

Cost ratio $= \dfrac{\$1,901.96}{\$3,138.23} = 0.6060613785$

Ending inventory at retail = \$3,138.23 − \$2,436.22 = \$702.01

Ending inventory at cost = \$702.01(0.6060613785) = \$425.46

Cost of goods sold = \$2,436.22 (0.6060613785) = \$1,476.50 or \$1,901.96 − \$425.46 = \$1,476.50

6, p. 646

1. Beginning inventory = 314(\$9) = \$2,826

Net purchases = 200(\$8) + 300(\$11) = \$1,600 + \$3,300 = \$4,900

Cost of goods available for sale = \$2,826 + \$4,900 = \$7,726

Estimated cost of goods sold = \$5,815(1 − 0.36)

$\qquad\qquad$ = \$5,815(0.64) = \$3,721.60

Estimated ending inventory = \$7,726 − \$3,721.60 = \$4,004.40

3. Beginning inventory = 389(\$7) = \$2,723

Net purchases = 400(\$6) + 200(\$9) = \$2,400 + \$1,800 = \$4,200

Cost of goods available for sale = \$2,723 + \$4,200 = \$6,923

Estimated cost of goods sold = \$4,283(1 − 0.4)

$\qquad\qquad$ = \$4,283(0.6) = \$2,569.80

Estimated ending inventory = \$6,923 − \$2,569.80 = \$4,353.20

5. Since the cost of goods varies, especially during inflation, the first-in, first-out (FIFO) method of inventory valuation is the most practical method to use. Also, since the merchandise is perishable, FIFO is a practical method to use.

2. Beginning inventory = 538(\$2) = \$1,076

Net purchase = 400(\$1.90) + 200(\$2.10) + 500(\$1.90)

$\qquad\qquad$ = \$760 + \$420 + \$950 = \$2,130

Cost of goods available for sale = \$1,076 + \$2,130 = \$3,206

Estimated cost of goods sold = \$2,058(1 − 0.42)

$\qquad\qquad$ = \$2,058(0.58) = \$1,193.64

Estimated ending inventory = \$3,206 − \$1,193.64 = \$2,012.36

4. Beginning inventory = 538(\$0.86) = \$462.68

Net purchases = 576(\$0.93) + 360(\$0.95) + 624(\$0.90)

$\qquad\qquad$ = \$535.68 + \$342 + \$561.60 = \$1,439.28

Cost of goods available for sale = \$462.68 + \$1,439.28 = \$1,901.96

Estimated cost of goods sold = \$2,048(1 − 0.56) = \$2,048(0.44)

Estimated ending inventory = \$1,901.96 − \$901.12 = \$1,000.84

SECTION 18-2

1, p. 652

1. Average inventory at cost $= \dfrac{\$13,217 + \$14,067}{2} = \dfrac{\$27,284}{2} = \$13,642$

Turnover rate at cost $= \dfrac{\$71,817}{\$13,642} = 5.26$

3. Average inventory at retail $= \dfrac{\$5,972 + \$7,291}{2} = \$6,631.50$

Turnover rate at retail $= \dfrac{\$74,508}{\$6,631.50} = 11.24$

2. Average inventory at cost $= \dfrac{\$8,915 + \$9,205}{2} = \dfrac{\$18,120}{2} = \$9,060$

Turnover rate at cost $= \dfrac{\$48,206}{\$9,060} = 5.32$

4. Average inventory at retail $= \dfrac{\$35,169 + \$28,437}{2} = \dfrac{\$63,606}{2} = \$31,803$

Turnover rate at retail $= \dfrac{\$107,582}{\$31,803} = 3.38$

2, p. 655

1. Total sales = \$3,816 + \$32,167 + \$67,015 + \$17,816 = \$120,814

Overhead: Memorabilia $= \dfrac{\$3,816}{\$120,814}(\$12,516) = \$395.33$

Brubaker's Restaurant $= \dfrac{\$32,167}{\$120,814}(\$12,516) = \$3,332.41$

Engraving $= \dfrac{\$67,015}{\$120,814}(\$12,516) = \$6,942.57$

Frame Shop $= \dfrac{\$17,816}{\$120,814}(\$12,516) = \$1,845.69$

2. Total sales = \$17,815 + \$19,583 + \$58,982 + \$38,917 + \$27,895 + \$32,518 + \$62,906 = \$258,616

Overhead: Paint $= \dfrac{\$17,815}{\$258,616}(\$25,116) = \$1,730.14$

Lighting $= \dfrac{\$19,583}{\$258,616}(\$25,116) = \$1,901.84$

Lumber $= \dfrac{\$58,982}{\$258,616}(\$25,116) = \$5,728.15$

Plumbing $= \dfrac{\$38,917}{\$258,616}(\$25,116) = \$3,779.50$

Tiles and Flooring $= \dfrac{\$27,895}{\$258,616}(\$25,116) = \$2,709.08$

Chemicals $= \dfrac{\$32,518}{\$258,616}(\$25,116) = \$3,158.05$

Home and Garden $= \dfrac{\$62,906}{\$258,616}(\$25,116) = \$6,109.24$

3. Total floor space = 100 ft² + 120 ft² + 80 ft² + 130 ft² + 140 ft² + 300 ft² = 870 ft²

Overhead: text books $= \dfrac{100 \text{ ft}^2}{870 \text{ ft}^2}(\$12,196) = \$1,401.84$

Casebound books $= \dfrac{120 \text{ ft}^2}{870 \text{ ft}^2}(\$12,196) = \$1,682.21$

Paperbacks $= \dfrac{80 \text{ ft}^2}{870 \text{ ft}^2}(\$12,196) = \$1,121.47$

Children's books $= \dfrac{130 \text{ ft}^2}{870 \text{ ft}^2}(\$12,196) = \$1,822.39$

Electronic media $= \dfrac{140 \text{ ft}^2}{870 \text{ ft}^2}(\$12,196) = \$1,962.57$

Coffee shop $= \dfrac{300 \text{ ft}^2}{870 \text{ ft}^2}(\$12,196) = \$4,205.52$

4. Total floor space = 1,000 ft² + 300 ft² + 700 ft² + 800 ft² = 2,800 ft²

Overhead: Fresh flowers $= \dfrac{1,000 \text{ ft}^2}{2,800 \text{ ft}^2}(\$7,815) = \$2,791.07$

Pottery $= \dfrac{300 \text{ ft}^2}{2,800 \text{ ft}^2}(\$7,815) = \$837.32$

Fine china $= \dfrac{700 \text{ ft}^2}{2,800 \text{ ft}^2}(\$7,815) = \$1,953.75$

Gifts $= \dfrac{800 \text{ ft}^2}{2,800 \text{ ft}^2}(\$7,815) = \$2,232.86$

SECTION 19-1

1, p. 677

1. Estimated annual premium $= \left(\dfrac{\$200,000}{\$1,000}\right)(\$1.10)$

$= \$220$

3. Estimated annual premium $= \left(\dfrac{\$300,000}{\$1,000}\right)(\$29.14) = \$8,742$

Monthly premium $= \$8,742(0.0875) = \$764.93$

2. Estimated annual premium $= \left(\dfrac{\$500,000}{\$1,000}\right)(\$24.14) = \$12,070$

  a. Semiannual premium $= \$12,070(0.51) = \$6,155.70$
  b. Quarterly premium $= \$12,070(0.26) = \$3,138.20$
  c. Monthly premium $= \$12,070(0.0875) = \$1,056.13$

4. Estimated annual premium $= \left(\dfrac{\$600,000}{\$1,000}\right)(\$6.45) = \$3,870$

Quarterly premium $= \$3,870(0.26) = \$1,006.20$

2, p. 678

1. Estimated annual term premium $= \left(\dfrac{\$300,000}{\$1,000}\right)(\$4.40) = \$1,320$

Years of term insurance $= \dfrac{\$19,340}{\$1,320} = 14.65151515$ years $= 14.65$ years

3. Estimated annual term premium $= \left(\dfrac{\$250,000}{\$1,000}\right)(\$5.78) = \$1,445$

Years of term insurance $= \dfrac{\$20,915}{\$1,445} = 14.47404844$ years $= 14.47$ years

2. Estimated annual term premium $= \left(\dfrac{\$500,000}{\$1,000}\right)(\$4.61) = \$2,305$

Years of term insurance $= \dfrac{\$13,208}{\$2,305} = 5.730151844 = 5.73$ years

4. Estimated annual term premium $= \left(\dfrac{\$300,000}{\$1,000}\right)(\$29.14)$

$= \$8,742$

$= \dfrac{\$31,390}{\$8,742} = 3.590711508$ or 3.59 years

SECTION 19-2

1, p. 681

1. Base annual renters insurance premium $= \$185$ (from Table 19-3)

Jewelry endorsement premium $= \dfrac{\$7,000}{\$100}(\$0.85) = \$59.50$

Identity theft option $= \$20$

Total annual renters insurance premium $= \$185 + \$59.50 + \$20$
$= \$264.50$

3. Base annual renters insurance premium $= \$253$ (from Table 19-3)

Beth has no options or endorsements so her annual renters insurance premium is $253.

2. Base annual renters insurance premium $= \$270$ (from Table 19-3)

Firearms endorsement premium $= \dfrac{\$2,500}{\$100}(\$1.45) = \$36.25$

Total annual renters insurance premium $= \$270 + \$36.25$
$= \$306.25$

4. Base annual renters insurance premium $= \$185$ (from Table 19-3)
Jewelry and camera endorsement premium

$= \dfrac{\$8,500}{\$100}(\$0.85) + \dfrac{\$2,000}{\$100}(\$1.35)$

$= \$72.25 + \$27 = \$99.25$

Total annual renters insurance premium $= \$185 + \$99.25 = \$284.25$

2, p. 683

1. Base annual homeowners insurance premium $= \dfrac{\$600,000}{\$100}(\$0.27) = \$1,620$

3. Base annual homeowners insurance premium $= \dfrac{\$265,000}{\$100}(\$0.46) = \$1,219$

Jewelry endorsement $= \dfrac{\$5,000}{\$100}(\$0.85) = \$42.50$

Total annual homeowners insurance premium $= \$1,219 + \$42.50$
$= \$1,261.50$

2. Base annual homeowners insurance premium $= \dfrac{\$350,000}{\$100}(\$0.27) = \$945$

4. Base annual homeowners insurance premium $= \dfrac{\$328,000}{\$100}(\$0.67)$

$= \$2,197.60$

3, p. 684

1. Full protection: $\$650,000(0.8) = \$520,000$

Compensation $= \left(\dfrac{\$400,000}{\$520,000}\right)(\$82,000) = \$63,076.92$

3. Full protection $= \$798,500(0.8) = \$638,800$

Compensation $= \left(\dfrac{\$638,800}{\$638,800}\right)(\$590,000) = \$590,000$

2. Full protection $= \$492,000(0.8) = \$393,600$

Compensation $= \left(\dfrac{\$350,000}{\$393,600}\right)(\$43,790) = \$38,939.28$

4. Full protection $= \$690,000(0.8) = \$552,000$

Compensation $= \left(\dfrac{\$552,000}{\$552,000}\right)(\$38,588) = \$38,588$

SECTION 19-3

1, p. 689

1. Liability premium $= \$425$
Comprehensive premium $= \$216$
Collision premium $= \$342$
Total premium $= \$425 + \$216 + \$342 = \$983$

2. Liability premium $= \$354$
Comprehensive premium $= \$190$
Collision premium $= \$240$
Total premium $= \$354 + \$190 + \$240 = \$784$

3. Liability premium = $627
Comprehensive premium = $553
Collision premium = $693
Total premium = $627 + $553 + $693 = $1,873

5. Logan's insurance is responsible for paying up to $100,000 per person and up to $300,000 per crash for liability. Logan's insurance company is responsible for paying $85,000 for Lynn's medical care and $100,000 for Cameron's medical care since each single claim is allowed $100,000 and the combined claims are within the $300,000 limit. The insurance company is responsible for paying $18,980 to repair Lynn's car and $12,815 − $1,000 = $11,815 to Logan for vehicle repairs. Logan is responsible for paying the $1,000 deductible for collision plus the $45,000 balance of Cameron's medical expenses.

4. Liability premium = $385
Comprehensive premium = $301
Collision premium = $367
Total premium = $385 + $301 + $367 = $1,053

6. Rusty's insurance company is responsible for paying up to $100,000 per person for personal injury. The maximum for all personal injury is $250,000. So, the company is responsible for paying $17,650 for Rodger's medical care and $100,000 for Tina's medical care. Rusty will be responsible for paying $7,760 for Tina's medical care that is not covered by the insurance company. The insurance company will be responsible for paying $21,750 to repair Rodger's car and $8,438 − $500 = $7,938 to repair Rusty's vehicle. Rusty is responsible for $500 deductible for his car repair.

CHAPTER 20

SECTION 20-1

1, p. 707

1. Sales tax = $19.95(0.0625) = $1.25

2. Sales tax = $298.99(0.029) = $8.67

3. Sales tax = $49.99(0.047) = $2.35

4. Sales tax = $149.95(0.05) = $7.50

5. $38.96(80\%) = $38.96(0.8) = $3.12

6. $82.34(38.9\%) = $82.34(0.389) = $32.03

2, p. 708

1. Marked price $= \dfrac{\$790}{1 + 0.07} = \dfrac{\$790}{1.07} = \$738.32$

Sales tax = $790 − $738.32 = $51.68

3. Marked price $= \dfrac{\$380,926}{1 + 0.0575} = \dfrac{\$380,926}{1.0575} = \$360,213.71$

Sales tax = $380,926 − $360,213.71 = $20,712.29

2. Marked price $= \dfrac{\$5,852.25}{1 + 0.0625} = \dfrac{\$5,852.25}{1.0625} = \$5,508$

Sales tax = $5,852.25 − $5,508 = $344.25

4. Marked price $= \dfrac{\$12,583}{1 + 0.07} = \dfrac{\$12,583}{1.07} = \$11,759.81$

Sales tax = $12,583 − $11,759.81 = $823.19

SECTION 20-2

1, p. 710

1. Assessed value = $338,500(0.25) = $84,625

2. Assessed value = $2,580,000(0.4) = $1,032,000

3. Assessed value = $2,839,800(0.5) = $1,419,900

4. Assessed value = $1,800,000(0.4) = $720,000

2, p. 711

1. Property tax = $85,250(0.0958) = $8,166.95

2. Property tax $= \$720,000\left(\dfrac{\$3.45}{\$100}\right) = \$24,840$

3. Property tax $= \$125,300\left(\dfrac{\$78.45}{\$1,000}\right) = \$9,829.79$

4. Property tax $= \$72,520\left(\dfrac{72.5\text{ mills}}{\$1,000}\right) = \$5,257.70$

3, p. 713

1. Tax per $100 of assessed value $= \left(\dfrac{\$109,047,773}{\$4,098,530,000}\right)(\$100) = 0.02660655723(\$100) = \$2.660655723 = \$2.67$ per $100

2. Tax per $1.00 of assessed value $= \left(\dfrac{\$5,347,364}{\$218,560,000}\right)(\$1.00) = \$0.0244634334 = \$0.03$ per $1.00

3. Tax in mills per $1.00 of assessed value $= \left(\dfrac{\$6,344,549.65}{\$544,029,090}\right)(1,000) = 11.66215147$ mills $= 11.67$ mills

4. Tax per $1,000 $= \left(\dfrac{\$68,914,808}{\$2,856,919,000}\right)(\$1,000) = \$24.12207276 = \$24.13$ per $1,000

5. Total property tax revenue with projected reassessed property values =
$\$568,193,000\left(\dfrac{11.67}{1,000}\right) = \$6,630,812.31$
Total expected expenses = $6,344,549.65 + $135,000 + $22,000 = $6,501,549.65
Property tax revenue from the reassessment exceeds the expected total expenses plus cost of reassessment. The city should reassess property to raise the needed revenue.

6. Total property tax revenue with projected reassessed property values =
$\$2,857,590,000\left(\dfrac{\$24.13}{\$1,000}\right) = \$68,953,646.70$
Total expected expenses = $68,914,808 + $1,345,000 + $54,000 = $70,313,808
Since the total expenses with the reassessment plan exceeds the end-of-year projected tax collection, the city should increase the tax rate to raise the needed revenue.

SECTION 20-3

1, p. 716

1. Taxable income = $62,596 − $10,109 − ($3,700)(3) = $62,596 − $10,109 − $11,100 = $41,387

2. Taxable income = $105,896 − $12,057 − $3,700 = $90,139

3. Taxable income = $115,993 − $18,930 − ($3,700)(5) = $115,993 − $18,930 − $18,500 = $78,563

4. Taxable income = $68,929 − $8,400 − $3,700 = $56,829

2, p. 717

1. Locate range for $37,519 in Table 20-1. Range is $37,500–$37,550. Move across two columns to $4,779, the tax for "Married filing jointly" column.

3. Locate the range for $30,650 in Table 20-1. Range is $30,650–$30,700. Move three columns to the right to $4,176, the tax for "Married filing separately" column.

2. Locate the range for $31,795 in Table 20-1. Range is $31,750–$31,800. Move one column to the right to $4,341, the tax for "Single" column.

4. Locate the range for $38,456 in Table 20-1. Range is $38,450–$38,500. Move four columns to the right to $5,164, the tax for "Head of a household" column.

3, p. 724

1. Use Section B from Table 20-2. "Over $139,350 but not over $212,300."

Column a	Column b	Column c	Column d	Tax
$152,783	× 28% (.28)	$42,779.24	$11,930.50	$30,848.74

152783 ×.28 − 11930.5 = ⇒ 30848.74

2. Use Section C from Table 20-2. "Over $106,150 but not over $189,575."

Column a	Column b	Column c	Column d	Tax
$172,500	× 33% (.33)	$56,925	$11,272.75	$45,652.25

172500 ×.33 − 11272.75 = ⇒ 45652.25

3. Use Section A from Table 20-2. "At least $100,000 but not over $171,400."

Column a	Column b	Column c	Column d	Tax
$117,832	× 28% (.28)	$32,992.96	$6,383.00	$26,609.96

117832 ×.28 − 6383 = ⇒ 26609.96

4. Use Section D from Table 20-2. "Over $379,150."

Column a	Column b	Column c	Column d	Tax
$456,987	× 35% (.35)	$159,945.45	$26,065.00	$133,880.45

456987 ×.35 − 26065 = ⇒ 133880.45

CHAPTER 21

SECTION 21-1

1, p. 743

1. Total assets = $43,518 + $3,988 + $96,532 = $144,038

2. Total liabilities and owner's equity = $15,817 + $9,892 + $418,250 + $45,986 = $489,945

3. $105,095 + $6,503 + $190,014 = $301,612
$301,612 + $32,507 = $334,119
$6,007 + $4,761 = $10,768
$10,768 + $281,017 = $291,785
$291,785 + $42,334 = $334,119

4. $114,975 + $8,918 + $187,915 = $311,808
$311,808 + $29,719 = $341,527
$6,832 + $5,215 = $12,047
$12,047 + $279,409 = $291,456
$291,456 + $50,071 = $341,527

Rayco, Inc.
Balance Sheet
December 31, 2012

Assets
Current assets
Cash	$105,095
Accounts receivable	6,503
Merchandise inventory	190,014
Total current assets	301,612

Plant and equipment
Equipment	32,507
Total plant and equipment	32,507
Total assets	$334,119

Liabilities
Current liabilities
Accounts payable	$6,007
Wages payable	4,761
Total current liabilities	10,768

Long-term liabilities
Mortgage note payable	281,017
Total long-term liabilities	281,017
Total liabilities	291,785

Owner's Equity
Frank Rayco, capital	42,334
Total liabilities and owner's equity	$334,119

Rayco, Inc.
Balance Sheet
December 31, 2013

Assets
Current assets
Cash	$114,975
Accounts receivable	8,918
Merchandise inventory	187,915
Total current assets	311,808

Plant and equipment
Equipment	29,719
Total plant and equipment	29,719
Total assets	$341,527

Liabilities
Current liabilities
Accounts payable	$6,832
Wages payable	5,215
Total current liabilities	12,047

Long-term liabilities
Mortgage note payable	279,409
Total long-term liabilities	279,409
Total liabilities	291,456

Owner's Equity
Frank Rayco, capital	50,071
Total liabilities and owner's equity	$341,527

1. $105,095 ÷ $334,119 = 0.315 = 31.5%
   $6,503 ÷ $334,119 = 0.019 = 1.9%
   $190,014 ÷ $334,119 = 0.569 = 56.9%
   $301,612 ÷ $334,119 = 0.903 = 90.3%
   $32,507 ÷ $334,119 = 0.097 = 9.7%
   $334,119 ÷ $334,119 = 1 = 100%
   $6,007 ÷ $334,119 = 0.018 = 1.8%
   $4,761 ÷ $334,119 = 0.014 = 1.4%
   $10,768 ÷ $334,119 = 0.032 = 3.2%
   $281,017 ÷ $334,119 = 0.841 = 84.1%
   $291,785 ÷ $334,119 = 0.873 = 87.3%
   $42,334 ÷ $334,119 = 0.127 = 12.7%

2. $114,975 ÷ $341,527 = 0.337 = 33.7%
   $8,918 ÷ $341,527 = 0.026 = 2.6%
   $187,915 ÷ $341,527 = 0.550 = 55.0%
   $311,808 ÷ $341,527 = 0.913 = 91.3%
   $29,719 ÷ $341,527 = 0.087 = 8.7%
   $341,527 ÷ $341,527 = 1 = 100%
   $6,832 ÷ $341,527 = 0.020 = 2.0%
   $5,215 ÷ $341,527 = 0.015 = 1.5%
   $12,047 ÷ $341,527 = 0.035 = 3.5%
   $279,409 ÷ $341,527 = 0.818 = 81.8%
   $291,456 ÷ $341,527 = 0.853 = 85.3%
   $50,071 ÷ $341,527 = 0.147 = 14.7%

Rayco, Inc.
Balance Sheet
December 31, 2012

	Amount	Percent
Assets		
Current assets		
Cash	$105,095	31.5%
Accounts receivable	6,503	1.9%
Merchandise inventory	190,014	56.9%
Total current assets	301,612	90.3%
Plant and equipment		
Equipment	32,507	9.7%
Total plant and equipment	32,507	9.7%
Total assets	$334,119	100.0%
Liabilities		
Current liabilities		
Accounts payable	$6,007	1.8%
Wages payable	4,761	1.4%
Total current liabilities	10,768	3.2%
Long-term liabilities		
Mortgage note payable	281,017	84.1%
Total long-term liabilities	281,017	84.1%
Total liabilities	291,785	87.3%
Owner's Equity		
Frank Rayco, capital	42,334	12.7%
Total liabilities and owner's equity	$334,119	100.0%

Rayco, Inc.
Balance Sheet
December 31, 2013

	Amount	Percent
Assets		
Current assets		
Cash	$114,975	33.7%
Accounts receivable	8,918	2.6%
Merchandise inventory	187,915	55.0%
Total current assets	311,808	91.3%
Plant and equipment		
Equipment	29,719	8.7%
Total plant and equipment	29,719	8.7%
Total assets	$341,527	100.0%
Liabilities		
Current liabilities		
Accounts payable	$6,832	2.0%
Wages payable	5,215	1.5%
Total current liabilities	12,047	3.5%
Long-term liabilities		
Mortgage note payable	279,409	81.8%
Total long-term liabilities	279,409	81.8%
Total liabilities	291,456	85.3%
Owner's Equity		
Frank Rayco, capital	50,071	14.7%
Total liabilities and owner's equity	$341,527	100.0%

3. Show the vertical analysis for 2012 and 2013 on the same balance sheet. Use same calculations from Exercises 1 and 2.

4. In 2013 Rayco, Inc., had total assets of $341,527, which is more than the $334,119 reported as total assets for 2012.

Rayco, Inc.
Comparative Balance Sheet
December 31, 2012 and December 31, 2013

	2013	Percent	2012	Percent
Assets				
Current assets				
Cash	$114,975	33.7%	$105,095	31.5%
Accounts receivable	8,918	2.6%	6,503	1.9%
Merchandise inventory	187,915	55.0%	190,014	56.9%
Total current assets	311,808	91.3%	301,612	90.3%
Plant and equipment				
Equipment	29,719	8.7%	32,507	9.7%
Total plant and equipment	29,719	8.7%	32,507	9.7%
Total assets	$341,527	100.0%	$334,119	100.0%
Liabilities				
Current liabilities				
Accounts payable	$6,832	2.0%	$6,007	1.8%
Wages payable	5,215	1.5%	4,761	1.4%
Total current liabilities	12,047	3.5%	10,768	3.2%
Long-term liabilities				
Mortgage note payable	279,409	81.8%	281,017	84.1%
Total long-term liabilities	279,409	81.8%	281,017	84.1%
Total liabilities	291,456	85.3%	291,785	87.3%
Owner's Equity				
Frank Rayco, capital	50,071	14.7%	42,334	12.7%
Total liabilities and owner's equity	$341,527	100.0%	$334,119	100.0%

3, p. 748

1. Cash: $114,975 - $105,095 = $9,880
   Accounts receivable: $8,918 - $6,503 = $2,415
   Inventory: $187,915 - $190,014 = ($2,099)
   Total current assets: $311,808 - $301,612 = $10,196
   Equipment: $29,719 - $32,507 = ($2,788)
   Total assets: $341,527 - $334,119 = $7,408
   Accounts payable: $6,832 - $6,007 = $825
   Wages payable: $5,215 - $4,761 = $454
   Total current liabilities: $12,047 - $10,768 = $1,279
   Mortgage note payable: $279,409 - $281,017 = ($1,608)
   Total liabilities: $291,456 - $291,785 = ($329)
   Rayco capital: $50,071 - $42,334 = $7,737
   Total liabilities and owner's equity = $341,527 - $334,119 = $7,408

2. Cash: $\frac{\$9,880}{\$105,095}(100\%) = 9.4\%$

   Accounts receivable: $\frac{\$2,415}{\$6,503}(100\%) = 37.1\%$

   Inventory: $\frac{(\$2,099)}{\$190,014}(100\%) = (1.1\%)$

   Total current assets: $\frac{\$10,196}{\$301,612}(100\%) = 3.4\%$

   Equipment: $\frac{(\$2,788)}{\$32,507}(100\%) = (8.6\%)$

   Total assets: $\frac{\$7,408}{\$334,119}(100\%) = 2.2\%$

   Accounts payable: $\frac{\$825}{\$6,007}(100\%) = 13.7\%$

   Wages payable: $\frac{\$454}{\$4,761}(100\%) = 9.5\%$

   Total current liabilities: $\frac{\$1,279}{\$10,768}(100\%) = 11.9\%$

   Mortgage note payable: $\frac{(\$1,608)}{\$281,017}(100\%) = (0.6\%)$

   Total liabilities: $\frac{(\$329)}{\$291,785}(100\%) = (0.1\%)$

   Rayco capital: $\frac{\$7,737}{\$42,334}(100\%) = 18.3\%$

   Total liabilities and owner's equity: $\frac{\$7,408}{\$334,119}(100\%) = 2.2\%$

3.

Rayco, Inc.
Horizontal Analysis of Comparative Balance Sheet
December 31, 2012 and December 31, 2013

	2013	2012	Increase or (Decrease)	Percent of increase or (Decrease)
Assets				
Current assets				
Cash	$114,975	$105,095	$9,880	9.4
Accounts receivable	8,918	6,503	$2,415	37.1
Merchandise inventory	187,915	190,014	($2,099)	(1.1)
Total current assets	311,808	301,612	$10,196	3.4
Plant and equipment				
Equipment	29,719	32,507	($2,788)	(8.6)
Total plant and equipment	29,719	32,507	($2,788)	(8.6)
Total assets	$341,527	$334,119	$7,408	2.2
Liabilities				
Current liabilities				
Accounts payable	$6,832	$6,007	$825	13.7
Wages payable	5,215	4,761	$454	9.5
Total current liabilities	12,047	10,768	$1,279	11.9
Long-term liabilities				
Mortgage note payable	279,409	281,017	($1,608)	(0.6)
Total long-term liabilities	279,409	281,017	($1,608)	(0.6)
Total liabilities	291,456	291,785	($329)	(0.1)
Owner's Equity				
Frank Rayco, capital	50,071	42,334	$7,737	18.3
Total liabilities and owner's equity	$341,527	$334,119	$7,408	2.2

4. Read from the statement prepared in Exercise 3. The percentage of increase in total assets is 2.2%.

SECTION 21-2

1, p. 753

1. Gross profit = $5,385,920 - $2,073,587 = $3,312,333
   Net income = $3,312,333 - $498,507 = $2,813,826

2.

Cedar Rapids American Auto, Inc.
Income Statement for
December 31, 2013

Net sales	$5,385,920
Cost of goods sold	2,073,587
Gross profit	$3,312,333
Operating expenses	498,507
Net income	$2,813,826

3. Net sales $= \$597{,}341 - \$10{,}514 = \$586{,}827$

Cost of goods sold $= \$38{,}917 + \$261{,}053 - \$42{,}013 = \$257{,}957$

Gross profit from sales $= \$586{,}827 - \$257{,}957 = \$328{,}870$

4. Total operating expenses $= \$90{,}500 + \$12{,}200 + \$7{,}582 + \$1{,}077 + \$18{,}400 + \$2{,}700 = \$132{,}459$

Net income $= \$328{,}870 - \$132{,}459 = \$196{,}411$

Amaya's Soul Food Catering Income Statement for December 31, 2013	
Gross sales	$597,341
Sales returns and allowances	10,514
Net sales	586,827
Beginning inventory cost	38,917
Cost of purchases	261,053
Ending inventory	42,013
Cost of goods sold	257,957
Gross profit from sales	$328,870
Salary	90,500
Insurance	12,200
Utilities	7,582
Maintenance	1,077
Rent	18,400
Depreciation	2,700
Total operating expenses	132,459
Net income	$196,411

2, p. 756

1.

Cedar Rapids American Auto, Inc. Income Statement for December 31, 2013		Percent of Net Sales
Net sales	$5,385,920	100.0
Cost of goods sold	2,073,587	38.5
Gross profit	3,312,333	61.5
Operating expenses	498,507	9.3
Net income	$2,813,826	52.2

2.

Cedar Rapids American Auto, Inc. Comparative Income Statement for December 31, 2012 and December 31, 2013	2013	Percent of Net Sales	2012	Percent of Net Sales
Net sales	$5,385,920	100.0	$4,103,370	100.0
Cost of goods sold	2,073,587	38.5	1,992,500	48.6
Gross profit	3,312,333	61.5	2,110,870	51.4
Operating expenses	498,507	9.3	503,719	12.3
Net income	$2,813,826	52.2	$1,607,151	39.2

3.

Amaya's Soul Food Catering Income Statement for December 31, 2013		Percent of Net Sales
Gross sales	$597,341	101.8
Sales returns and allowances	10,514	1.8
Net sales	586,827	100.0
Beginning inventory cost	38,917	6.6
Cost of purchases	261,053	44.5
Ending inventory	42,013	7.2
Cost of goods sold	257,957	44.0
Gross profit from sales	$328,870	56.0
Salary	90,500	15.4
Insurance	12,200	2.1
Utilities	7,582	1.3
Maintenance	1,077	0.2
Rent	18,400	3.1
Depreciation	2,700	0.5
Total operating expenses	132,459	22.6
Net income	$196,411	33.5

4.

Amaya's Soul Food Catering Income Statement for December 31, 2013	2013	Percent of Net Sales	2012	Percent of Net Sales
Gross sales	$597,341	101.8	$435,913	101.9
Sales returns and allowances	10,514	1.8	8,019	1.9
Net sales	586,827	100.0	427,894	100.0
Beginning inventory cost	38,917	6.6	36,992	8.6
Cost of purchases	261,053	44.5	248,504	58.1
Ending inventory	42,013	7.2	41,007	9.6
Cost of goods sold	257,957	44.0	244,489	57.1
Gross profit from sales	$328,870	56.0	$183,405	42.9
Salary	90,500	15.4	82,450	19.3
Insurance	12,200	2.1	12,200	2.9
Utilities	7,582	1.3	6,097	1.4
Maintenance	1,077	0.2	817	0.2
Rent	18,400	3.1	17,800	4.2
Depreciation	2,700	0.1	2,300	0.5
Total operating expenses	132,459	22.6	121,664	28.4
Net income	$196,411	33.5	$61,741	14.4

3, p. 757

1. Net sales increase = $5,385,920 − $4,103,370 = $1,282,550

   Percent increase = $\dfrac{\$1,282,550}{\$4,103,370}(100\%) = 31.3\%$

   Cost of goods sold increase = $2,073,587 − $1,992,500 = $81,087

   Percent increase = $\dfrac{\$81,087}{\$1,992,500}(100\%) = 4.1\%$

   Gross profit increase = $3,312,333 − $2,110,870 = $1,201,463

   Percent increase = $\dfrac{\$1,201,463}{\$2,110,870}(100\%) = 56.9\%$

   Operating expenses decrease = $498,507 − $503,719 = ($5,212)

   Percent decrease = $\dfrac{(\$5,212)}{\$503,719}(100\%) = (1.0)\%$

   Net income increase = $2,813,826 − $1,607,151 = $1,206,675

   Percent increase = $\dfrac{\$1,206,675}{\$1,607,151}(100\%) = 75.1\%$

Cedar Rapids American Auto, Inc. Comparative Income Statement for December 31, 2012 and December 31, 2013				
	2013	2012	Increase or (Decrease)	Percent of increase or (Decrease)
Net sales	$5,385,920	$4,103,370	$1,282,550	31.3
Cost of goods sold	2,073,587	1,992,500	$81,087	4.1
Gross profit	3,312,333	2,110,870	$1,201,463	56.9
Operating expenses	498,507	503,719	($5,212)	(1.0)
Net income	$2,813,826	$1,607,151	$1,206,675	75.1

2. Gross sales increase = $597,341 − $435,913 = $161,428

   Percent increase = $\dfrac{\$161,428}{\$435,913}(100\%) = 37.0\%$

   Sales returns and allowances increase = $10,514 − $8,019 = $2,495

   Percent increase = $\dfrac{\$2,495}{\$8,019}(100\%) = 31.1\%$

   Remaining increases and decreases and percents are calculated similarly.

Amaya's Soul Food Catering Income Statement for December 31, 2013				
	2013	2012	Increase or (Decrease)	Percent of increase or (Decrease)
Gross sales	$597,341	$435,913	$161,428	37.0
Sales returns and allowances	10,514	8,019	2,495	31.1
Net sales	586,827	427,894	158,933	37.1
Beginning inventory cost	38,917	36,992	1,925	5.2
Cost of purchases	261,053	248,504	12,549	5.0
Ending inventory	42,013	41,007	1,006	2.5
Cost of goods sold	257,957	244,489	13,468	5.5
Gross profit from sales	$328,870	$183,405	145,465	79.3
Salary	90,500	82,450	8,050	9.8
Insurance	12,200	12,200	0	0.0
Utilities	7,582	6,097	1,485	24.4
Maintenance	1,077	817	260	31.8
Rent	18,400	17,800	600	3.4
Depreciation	2,700	2,300	400	17.4
Total operating expenses	132,459	121,664	10,795	8.9
Net income	$196,411	$61,741	134,670	218.1

3. Net sales is the base when calculating percentages for a vertical analysis.

4. The dollar amount for the earliest year is used as the base.

SECTION 21-3

1, p. 766

1. Current ratio = $\dfrac{\$897,584}{\$683,888} = 1.3$

3. Operating ratio = $\dfrac{\$2,073,587 + \$498,507}{\$5,385,920}$

   $= \dfrac{\$2,572,094}{\$5,385,920}$

   $= 0.478$ to 1

5. Debt ratio = $\dfrac{\$291,785}{\$334,119} = 0.873$ to 1

7. Current ratio = $\dfrac{\$62,415}{\$43,717} = 1.43$

   Acid test ratio = $\dfrac{\$62,415 - \$12,592}{\$43,717} = 1.14$

   Operating ratio = $\dfrac{\$62,518 + \$23,897}{\$215,413} = 0.40$

   Gross profit margin ratio = $\dfrac{\$215,413 - \$62,518}{\$215,413} = 0.71$

   Asset turnover ratio = $\dfrac{\$215,413}{\$174,400} = 1.24$

   Total debt to total assets ratio = $\dfrac{\$43,717}{\$174,400} = 0.25$

   The gross profit margin ratio is unusually high and the asset turnover rate is uncommonly high. Both these ratios indicate the company is profitable. The other ratios are in the desirable range. This is a good time for Kelli to renovate her business.

9. Price-earnings ratio = $\dfrac{\text{price per share}}{\text{earnings per share}} = \dfrac{\$48.97}{\$1.43} = 34.24$

   Price-to-book ratio = $\dfrac{\text{price per share}}{\text{book value per share}} = \dfrac{\$48.97}{\$6.16} = 7.95$

2. Acid test ratio = $\dfrac{\$297,518 + \$10,000 + \$143,812}{\$86,950} = 5.2$

4. The ratio is desirable because it is less than 1.

6. This debt ratio is slightly high. The industry average for this ratio is generally from 0.05 to 0.75.

8. Earnings per share = $\dfrac{\text{net income}}{\text{number of shares outstanding}} = \dfrac{\$3,579,840}{2,500,000} = \$1.43$

   Book value per share = $\dfrac{\text{owner's equity}}{\text{number of shares outstanding}} = \dfrac{\$15,398,500}{2,500,000} = \$6.16$

10.

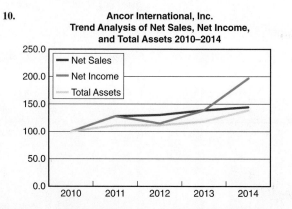

Ancor International, Inc. Trend Analysis of Net Sales, Net Income, and Total Assets 2010–2014

ANSWERS TO ODD-NUMBERED EXERCISES

CHAPTER 1

SECTION EXERCISES

1-1, P. 9

1. Twenty-two million, three hundred fifty-six thousand, twenty-seven **3.** Seven hundred thirty million, five hundred thirty-one thousand, nine hundred sixty-eight
5. Five hundred twenty-three billion, eight hundred million, seven thousand, one hundred ninety
7. 14,985   **9.** 17,000,803,075   **11.** 306,541   **13.** 480   **15.** 300,000   **17.** Three billion, five hundred eighty-five million dollars
19. 86,000,000   **21.** Negative fifteen thousand, three hundred fourteen dollars   **23.** Negative eight thousand, six hundred thirty-six dollars
25. −$520,000,000

1-2, P. 24

1. 1,600; 1,637   **3.** 1,850; 1,843   **5.** −6   **7.** −8,188   **9.** 33   **11.** 21   **13.** 12   **15.** 43,800   **17.** 89,445   **19.** −480
21. −$580,412   **23.** 407   **25.** −8   **27.** −42   **29.** 4   **31.** 26   **33.** 59   **35.** 28,900

37.

Region	W	Th	F	S	Su	Region Totals
Eastern	$ 72,492	$ 81,948	$ 32,307	$ 24,301	$ 32,589	$243,637
Southern	81,897	59,421	48,598	61,025	21,897	272,838
Central	71,708	22,096	23,222	21,507	42,801	181,334
Western	61,723	71,687	52,196	41,737	22,186	249,529
Daily Sales Total	$287,820	$235,152	$156,323	$148,570	$119,473	$947,338

Difference = $436,662 Goal was not reached.

39. Nearly $923   **41.** Wages = $567; Gross profit = $273   **43.** 29 boxes   **45.** $199,500,000   **47.** $1,680,000   **49.** −$63,069   **51.** −$873
53. She needs to order more paper.

EXERCISES SET A, P. 33

1. $7,000,000,000   **3.** Negative fourteen billion, six hundred seventy-two million dollars   **5.** 400   **7.** −830   **9.** 300,000; 6,300,000
11. 5,000   **13.** 63,601   **15.** 22,000; 21,335   **17.** 240; 230 items   **19.** 4,000; 4,072   **21.** 50,000; 55,632   **23.** 244 fan belts
25. −$26   **27.** −18   **29.** 782,878   **31.** 47,220,000   **33.** 1,550,000; 1,495,184   **35.** 336 radios per thousand   **37.** 8,000; 8,805 R6
39. 7,346   **41.** $16 per hour   **43.** −$5,809   **45.** $8

EXERCISES SET B, P. 35

1. 26   **3.** Negative twenty-seven billion, six hundred eighty-four million dollars   **5.** 8,200   **7.** 30,000   **9.** 2,000 radios
11. 20,000,000,000   **13.** 59,882   **15.** 8,400; 8,759   **17.** 723 cards   **19.** 200,000; 182,902   **21.** 60,000; 74,385   **23.** 13 pounds
25. −$17   **27.** 114   **29.** 6,840,462   **31.** 162,000   **33.** 200,000; 206,388   **35.** Approximately 88 TVs per thousand people
37. 600; 505 R161   **39.** 6,865   **41.** 77 coins   **43.** −$657   **45.** $363

PRACTICE TEST, P. 37

1. five hundred three   **2.** twelve million, fifty-six thousand, thirty-nine   **3.** 84,300   **4.** 59,000   **5.** 80,000   **6.** 600,000
7. 5,017,135,632   **8.** 17,500,608   **9.** Twenty-two billion, six hundred ninety-seven million dollars   **10.** Eighty-seven billion, four
hundred seventy-one million, nine hundred thousand dollars   **11.** Negative nine hundred forty-nine million, seven hundred thousand dollars
12. Negative four billion, eight hundred three million dollars   **13.** 2,200; 2,117   **14.** 700; 641   **15.** 45,000; 41,032   **16.** 80; 75 R46
17. 1,153 items were counted.   **18.** Only 15 boxes can be stacked.   **19.** 249 packages   **20.** 20 pairs of shoes   **21.** $17 per hour
22. 280 pieces of fruit   **23.** 48 pages   **24.** 37 novels   **25.** $19,209,200,000   **26.** $34,757,100,000   **27.** −$2,046   **28.** −$2,178
29. −50   **30.** $729Answers to Odd-Numbered Exercises

CHAPTER 2

SECTION EXERCISES

2-1, P. 49

1. proper   **3.** improper   **5.** proper   **7.** $1\frac{5}{7}$ **9.** 1   **11.** 2   **13.** $1\frac{3}{10}$ phones per person   **15.** $\frac{25}{4}$ **17.** $\frac{7}{3}$

19. $\frac{13}{8}$ **21.** $\frac{4}{5}$ **23.** $\frac{5}{6}$ **25.** $\frac{2}{3}$ **27.** $\frac{2}{45}$ **29.** $3; \frac{7}{12}$ **31.** $6; \frac{3}{8}$ **33.** $\frac{6}{16}$ **35.** $\frac{12}{32}$ **37.** $\frac{5}{15}$

2-2, P. 57

1. $\frac{8}{9}$ **3.** $1\frac{3}{10}$ **5.** $12\frac{1}{3}$ **7.** $137\frac{47}{72}$ **9.** $9\frac{1}{6}$ **11.** $\frac{1}{2}$ **13.** $\frac{1}{28}$ **15.** $2\frac{2}{9}$ **17.** $8\frac{7}{60}$ **19.** $3\frac{1}{3}$

21. $42\frac{1}{8}$ yards   **23.** 89 feet   **25.** She can use the fabric.   **27.** $1\frac{5}{16}$ feet; $1\frac{1}{2}$ feet; $1\frac{3}{8}$ feet; $1\frac{3}{16}$ feet

2-3, P. 64

1. $\frac{3}{10}$ **3.** $22\frac{13}{36}$ **5.** $\frac{12}{7}$ **7.** $\frac{1}{9}$ **9.** $\frac{7}{39}$ **11.** $\frac{5}{6}$ **13.** $2\frac{1}{10}$ **15.** $\frac{3}{20}$ **17.** $20\frac{20}{39}$ rooms   **19.** 6

21. $16\frac{1}{2}$ feet; yes

EXERCISES SET A, P. 71

1. $\frac{3}{5}, \frac{7}{9}, \frac{5}{8}, \frac{100}{301}, \frac{41}{53}$; proper fractions   **3.** $20\frac{2}{3}$ **5.** $8\frac{1}{2}$ **7.** $\frac{13}{3}$ **9.** $\frac{5}{6}$ **11.** $\frac{5}{8}$ **13.** $\frac{20}{32}$ **15.** $\frac{1}{7}$ of the employees

17. 168   **19.** $1\frac{2}{5}$ **21.** $11\frac{7}{8}$ **23.** 29 yards   **25.** $3\frac{3}{10}$ **27.** $1\frac{1}{2}$ **29.** $\frac{5}{18}$ **31.** 28   **33.** 4   **35.** 3

37. $\frac{4}{7}$ **39.** $1\frac{1}{4}$ inches   **41.** $192

EXERCISES SET B, P. 73

1. $3\frac{7}{15}$ **3.** 7   **5.** $\frac{59}{8}$ **7.** $\frac{9}{10}$ **9.** $\frac{2}{7}$ **11.** $\frac{63}{81}$ **13.** $\frac{4}{15}$ of the class   **15.** 72   **17.** 1   **19.** $9\frac{5}{12}$

21. $\frac{1}{2}$ **23.** $7\frac{7}{8}$ **25.** Maxine Ford worked $2\frac{1}{2}$ hours more than George.   **27.** $3\frac{3}{7}$ **29.** 18   **31.** $\frac{3}{2}$ **33.** $\frac{8}{19}$

35. $6\frac{2}{3}$ **37.** $4\frac{1}{2}$ **39.** $5\frac{9}{20}$ feet   **41.** 13 feet

PRACTICE TEST, P. 75

1. $\frac{1}{5}$ **2.** $\frac{5}{3}$ **3.** $\frac{5}{8}$ **4.** $\frac{4}{5}$ **5.** $\frac{3}{7}$ **6.** $\frac{7}{17}$ **7.** $\frac{21}{8}$ **8.** $\frac{37}{12}$ **9.** $2\frac{1}{3}$ **10.** $4\frac{4}{13}$ **11.** $\frac{1}{6}$

12. $1\frac{21}{40}$ **13.** $\frac{7}{16}$ **14.** $1\frac{1}{9}$ **15.** $1\frac{19}{23}$ **16.** 1,840   **17.** $5\frac{5}{6}$ **18.** $47\frac{1}{5}$

19. $\frac{1}{2}$ of the truckload remains to be unloaded   **20.** $\frac{3}{20}$ **21.** 100 sheets   **22.** $7\frac{3}{4}\%$ **23.** $\frac{2}{5}$ of total budget

24. $31\frac{1}{4}$ cups of sugar

CHAPTER 3

SECTION EXERCISES

3-1, P. 84

1. Five hundred eighty-two thousandths   **3.** One and nine ten-thousandths   **5.** Seven hundred eighty-two and seven hundredths
7. 0.312   **9.** 5.03   **11.** $785   **13.** $1,823   **15.** $0.40   **17.** $32,048.87   **19.** 17.0
21. Nineteen dollars and eighty-nine cents   **23.** Eight hundred thirty-nine and eighteen hundredths in millions of dollars

3-2, P. 90

1. 933.935   **3.** $80.30   **5.** 109.57   **7.** $244.85   **9.** $7,270.48   **11.** 78.8   **13.** 1.474   **15.** 0.36719
17. 10.31   **19.** ≈ 0.02 **21.** 3.273   **23.** 48.3   **25.** $85.81   **27.** $7.52 in change   **29.** $236.04   **31.**$2,470.00
33. Yes, each person will pay $6.18.

3-3, P. 94

1. $\frac{3}{5}$ **3.** $\frac{5}{8}$ **5.** $7\frac{5}{16}$ **7.** 0.7   **9.** $0.16\frac{2}{3}$ **11.** ≈ 0.58 **13.** ≈ 2.13

EXERCISES SET A, P. 99

1. five-tenths   **3.** two hundred seventy-five hundred-thousandths   **5.** one hundred twenty-eight and twenty-three hundredths
7. 0.078   **9.** 0.135   **11.** 1,700   **13.** 1.246   **15.** $28.82   **17.** 376.74   **19.** 135.6   **21.** 193.41

23. 21.2352   **25.** ≈ 8.57 **27.** $\approx 1,559.79$ **29.** $\frac{11}{20}$ **31.** 0.85   **33.** $20.93   **35.** $88.96   **37.** $19.20

EXERCISES SET B, P. 101

1. twenty-seven hundredths   **3.** one hundred twenty thousand seven hundred four millionths   **5.** three thousand and three thousandths

7. 0.02017   **9.** 384.7   **11.** 33   **13.** 41.233   **15.** $34.93   **17.** 479.41   **19.** 277.59   **21.** 1,347.84

23. 1,101.15   **25.** 13.52   **27.** ≈ 1,706.45   **29.** $\frac{3}{4}$ **31.** 0.05   **33.** 183.4 square meters   **35.** $555.00

37. 212.14 inches

PRACTICE TEST, P. 103

1. 42.9   **2.** 30   **3.** twenty-four and one thousand seven ten-thousandths   **4.** 3.028   **5.** 24.092   **6.** 2,741.8

7. 224.857   **8.** 0.566 ≈ 0.57   **9.** 447.12   **10.** 0.0138   **11.** 89.82   **12.** 5.76875   **13.** 34.366   **14.** 7.3

15. 179.24   **16.** 37,417   **17.** 1.7 degrees   **18.** $7,980.00   **19.** $11,043.50   **20.** $31.55

CHAPTER 4

SECTION EXERCISES

4-1, P. 119

1.

DEPOSIT TICKET			
Park's Oriental Shop	CASH	CURRENCY	850 00
1428 Central Ave.		COIN	9 63
Germantown, TN 38138	LIST CHECKS SINGLY		157 38
			32 49
DATE 4/29 20 XX		26-2/840	
	TOTAL FROM OTHER SIDE		
	TOTAL		
	LESS CASH RECEIVED		
	NET DEPOSIT		1,048 50

Community First Bank

:084000063: 1579 5

3.

Park's Oriental Shop
1428 Central Ave.
Germantown, TN 38138   456

April 29 20XX   87-278/840

PAY TO THE ORDER OF   Green Harvest   155.30

One hundred fifty-five and 30/100 —— DOLLARS

Community First Bank
2177 Germantown Rd. South
Germantown, Tennessee 38138

MEMO fresh vegetables   Yan Yu

:084002781:

5.

456	Date 4/29 20 XX
Amount $155.30	
To Green Harvest	
For fresh vegetables	
Balance Forward	7,869 40
Deposits	1,048 50
Total	8,917 90
Amount This Check	155 30
Balance	8,762 60

7. $8,762.60;

RECORD ALL TRANSACTIONS THAT AFFECT YOUR ACCOUNT							
NUMBER	DATE	DESCRIPTION OF TRANSACTION	DEBIT	√	FEE (IF ANY)	CREDIT	BALANCE
							7,869 40
Dep	4/29	Deposit Payroll	$			$ 1,048 50	+1,048 50
							8,917 90
456	4/29	Green Harvest	155 30				−155 30
							8,762 60

9. For Deposit to acct 26-8224021; Ronald H. Cox Realty; restricted endorsement

11. Answers will vary. Deposits can be made to checking or savings accounts. Withdrawals can be made from checking or savings accounts. Loan payments can be made on bank loans. Checking and savings account information can be accessed. Funds can be transferred from savings accounts to checking accounts and from checking accounts to savings accounts. All these transaction options must be arranged between the account holder and the bank and mutually agreed upon by both. Banks may charge from some or all of these transactions. An ATM/debit card also can be used to get checking account information.

4-2, P. 126

1. Leader Federal: $942.18; LG&W: $217.17   **3.** lowest: $2,403.55; highest: $4,804.87

5.

RECORD ALL TRANSACTIONS THAT AFFECT YOUR ACCOUNT							
NUMBER	DATE	DESCRIPTION OF TRANSACTION	DEBIT (−)	√	FEE (IF ANY)	CREDIT (+)	BALANCE
							2,472 86
1094	8/28	K-mart	42 37	√			−42 37
							2,430 49
1095	8/28	Walgreen's	12 96	√			−12 96
							2,417 53
Deposit	9/1	Payroll Schering-Plough		√		2,401 32	+2,401 32
							4,818 85
AW	9/1	Leader Federal	942 18	√			−942 18
							3,876 67
AW	9/1	LG & W	217 17	√			−217 17
							3,659 50
1096	9/1	Kroger	36 01	√			−36 01
							3,623 49
1097	9/1	Texaco	178 13	√			−178 13
							3,445 36
1098	9/1	Univ. of Memphis	458 60	√			−458 60
							2,986 76
1099	9/4	GMAC Credit Corp	583 21	√			−583 21
							2,403 55
1100	9/8	Visa	283 21	√			−283 21
							2,120 34
1101	9/10	Radio Shack	189 57	√			−189 57
							1,930 97
1102	9/10	Auto Zone	48 23	√			−48 23
							1,882 74
Deposit	9/15	Payroll - Schering Plough		√		2,401 32	+2,401 32
							4,284 06

REMEMBER TO RECORD AUTOMATIC PAYMENTS/DEPOSITS ON DATE AUTHORIZED

RECORD ALL TRANSACTIONS THAT AFFECT YOUR ACCOUNT							
NUMBER	DATE	DESCRIPTION OF TRANSACTION	DEBIT (−)	√	FEE (IF ANY)	CREDIT	BALANCE
							4,284 06
1103	9/15	Geoffrey Beane	71 16	√			−71 16
							4,212 90
1104	9/14	Heaven Scent Flowers	12 75	√			−12 75
							4,200 15
1105	9/20	Kroger	87 75	√			−87 75
							4,112 40
ATM	9/20	Kirby Woods	60 00	√			−60 00
							4,052 40
1106	9/21	Traveler's Insurance	1,238 42	√			−1,238 42
							2,813 98
1107	9/23	Nation's Bank - Savings	500 00	√			−500 00
							2,313 98
	9/27	Interest earned		√		9 48	+9 48
							2,323 46
	9/29	Statement reconciled					—

$ 2,600 58	BALANCE AS SHOWN ON BANK STATEMENT
0	TOTAL OF OUTSTANDING DEPOSITS
2,600 58	NEW TOTAL
−277 12	SUBTRACT TOTAL OF OUTSTANDING CHECKS
$2,323 46	YOUR ADJUSTED STATEMENT BALANCE

BALANCE AS SHOWN IN YOUR REGISTER	$ 2,313 98
SUBTRACT AMOUNT OF SERVICE CHARGE	0
NEW TOTAL	2,313 98
ADJUSTMENTS IF ANY Interest	+9 48
YOUR ADJUSTED REGISTER BALANCE	$2,323 46

Outstanding Deposits (Credits)		
Date	Amount	
	$	
Total	$ 0	

Outstanding Checks (Debits)		
Check Number	Date	Amount
1101	9/10	$ 189 37
1105	9/20	87 75
Total	$	277 12

1.

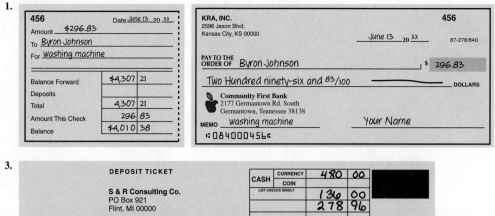

456	Date June 13 20 XX
Amount $296.83	
To Byron Johnson	
For Washing machine	

Balance Forward	$4,307	21
Deposits		
Total	4,307	21
Amount This Check	296	83
Balance	$4,010	38

KRA, INC.
2596 Jason Blvd.
Kansas City, KS 00000

456

June 13 20 XX   87-278/840

PAY TO THE
ORDER OF Byron Johnson $ 296.83

Two Hundred ninety-six and 83/100 ———————— DOLLARS

Community First Bank
2177 Germantown Rd. South
Germantown, Tennessee 38138

MEMO Washing machine   Your Name

⑈084000456⑈

3.

DEPOSIT TICKET

S & R Consulting Co.
PO Box 921
Flint, MI 00000

DATE May 8   20 XX

DEPOSITS MAY NOT BE AVAILABLE FOR IMMEDIATE WITHDRAWAL

SIGN HERE FOR CASH RECEIVED (IF REQUIRED)

CASH	CURRENCY	480	00
	COIN		
LIST CHECKS SINGLY		136	00
		278	96
TOTAL FROM OTHER SIDE			
TOTAL			
LESS CASH RECEIVED			
NET DEPOSIT		894	96

26-2/840

USE OTHER SIDE FOR
ADDITIONAL LISTING

BE SURE EACH ITEM IS
PROPERLY ENDORSED

Community First Bank
2177 Germantown Road • 7808 Farmington
Germantown, TN 38138 • (901) 754-2400 • Member FDIC

⑈084000026⑈9998

CHECKS AND OTHER ITEMS ARE RECEIVED FOR DEPOSIT SUBJECT TO THE PROVISIONS OF THE UNIFORM COMMERCIAL CODE OR ANY APPLICABLE COLLECTION AGREEMENT.

5. three   **7.** $238.00   **9.** $4,782.96   **11.** $29.36

13.

RECORD ALL TRANSACTIONS THAT AFFECT YOUR ACCOUNT

NUMBER	DATE	DESCRIPTION OF TRANSACTION	DEBIT (-)	√ T	FEE (IF ANY) (-)	CREDIT (+)	BALANCE
							4,782 96
716	7/1	Dabney Nursery	90 23	✓			4,692 73
717	7/1	Office Max	42 78	✓			4,649 95
Deposit	7/3	Lonis Lechlefter		✓		200 00	4,849 95
Deposit	7/5	Tony Trim		✓		175 00	5,024 95
Deposit	7/9	Dale Crosby		✓		50 00	5,074 95
718	7/10	Texaco Gas	29 36	✓			5,045 59
719	7/10	Nation's Bank	238 00	✓			4,807 59
Deposit	7/15	Bobby Cornelius				300 00	5,107 59
ATM	7/20	Withdrawl Branch	80 00	✓			5,027 59
Debit card	7/20	AT&T	30 92	✓			4,996 67
720	7/20	Visa	172 83				4,823 84
	7/25	Check Order	21 17	✓			4,802 67
	8/2	Statement Reconciled ✓					———

REMEMBER TO RECORD AUTOMATIC PAYMENTS/DEPOSITS ON DATE AUTHORIZED.

$ 4,675 50	BALANCE AS SHOWN ON BANK STATEMENT
+300 00	TOTAL OF OUTSTANDING DEPOSITS
4,975 50	NEW TOTAL
-172 83	SUBTRACT TOTAL OF OUTSTANDING CHECKS
$4,802 67	YOUR ADJUSTED STATEMENT BALANCE

SHOULD EQUAL

$ 4,823 84	BALANCE AS SHOWN IN YOUR REGISTER
0	SUBTRACT AMOUNT OF SERVICE CHARGE
4,823 84	NEW TOTAL
-21 17	ADJUSTMENTS IF ANY Check Order
$4,802 67	YOUR ADJUSTED REGISTER BALANCE

Outstanding Deposits (Credits)

Date	Amount
7/15	$ 300 00
Total	$ 300 00

Outstanding Checks (Debits)

Check Number	Date	Amount
720		$ 172 83
Total		$ 172 83

15.

$ 275 25	BALANCE AS SHOWN ON BANK STATEMENT
+745 99	TOTAL OF OUTSTANDING DEPOSITS
1,021 24	NEW TOTAL
-441 11	SUBTRACT TOTAL OF OUTSTANDING CHECKS
$580 13	YOUR ADJUSTED STATEMENT BALANCE

SHOULD EQUAL

$ 587 63	BALANCE AS SHOWN IN YOUR REGISTER
-7 50	SUBTRACT AMOUNT OF SERVICE CHARGE
580 13	NEW TOTAL
0	ADJUSTMENTS IF ANY
$580 13	YOUR ADJUSTED REGISTER BALANCE

Outstanding Deposits (Credits)

Date	Amount
	$ 120 43
	625 56
Total	$ 745 99

Outstanding Checks (Debits)

Check Number	Date	Amount
		$ 144 24
		154 48
		24 17
		18 22
ATM		100 00
Total		$ 441 11

1.

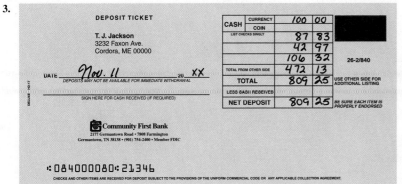

789	Date Aug. 18 20 XX
Amount	$189.32
To	Valley Electric Co-op
For	Utilities

Balance Forward	1,037	15
Deposits	—	
Total	1,037	15
Amount This Check	189	32
Balance	847	83

Fileclip, Co.
10003 Lapolma Av.
Radcliff, NH 00000

789

Aug. 18 20 XX   87-278/840

PAY TO THE ORDER OF Valley Electric Co-op $ 189.32

One hundred eighty-nine and 32/100   DOLLARS

Neshoba Bank
1518 S. Bramlett
Radcliff, NH 00000

MEMO Utilities   Your Name

⑆084000789⑆

3.

DEPOSIT TICKET

T. J. Jackson
3232 Faxon Ave.
Cordora, ME 00000

DATE Nov. 11 20 XX

DEPOSITS MAY NOT BE AVAILABLE FOR IMMEDIATE WITHDRAWAL

SIGN HERE FOR CASH RECEIVED (IF REQUIRED)

Community First Bank
2177 Germantown Road • 7808 Farmington
Germantown, TN 38138 • (901) 754-2400 • Member FDIC

⑆084000080⑆ 21346

CHECKS AND OTHER ITEMS ARE RECEIVED FOR DEPOSIT SUBJECT TO THE PROVISIONS OF THE UNIFORM COMMERCIAL CODE OR ANY APPLICABLE COLLECTION AGREEMENT.

CASH	CURRENCY	100	00
	COIN		
LIST CHECKS SINGLY		87	83
		42	97
		106	32
TOTAL FROM OTHER SIDE		472	13
TOTAL		809	25
LESS CASH RECEIVED			
NET DEPOSIT		809	25

26-2/840

USE OTHER SIDE FOR ADDITIONAL LISTING

BE SURE EACH ITEM IS PROPERLY ENDORSED

5. three   **7.** $82.75   **9.** $1,034.10   **11.** $82.75

13.

RECORD ALL TRANSACTIONS THAT AFFECT YOUR ACCOUNT

NUMBER	DATE	DESCRIPTION OF TRANSACTION	DEBIT (-)	√ T	FEE (IF ANY) (-)	CREDIT (+)	BALANCE
							1,034 10
Deposit	4/1	Payroll		√		850 00	+850 00
							1,884 10
Deposit	4/3	Payroll - Bonus		√		800 00	+800 00
							2,684 10
5374	4/3	First Union Mortgage Co.	647 53	√			-647 53
							2,036 57
5375	4/3	South Florida Utility	82 75	√			-82 75
							1,953 82
5376	4/5	First Federal Credit Union	219 95	√			-219 95
							1,733 87
5377	4/15	Banc Boston	510 48				-510 48
							1,223 39
Deposit	4/15	Payroll		√		850 00	+850 00
							2,073 39
5378	4/20	Northwest Air lines	403 21				-403 21
							1,670 18
5379	4/26	Auto Zone	18 97				-18 97
							1,651 21
ATM	5/4	Cordova Branch	100 00				-100 00
							1,551 21
	4/30	Service Fee		√	12 50		-12 50
							1,538 71
	4/30	Statement Reconciled					

REMEMBER TO RECORD AUTOMATIC PAYMENTS/DEPOSITS ON DATE AUTHORIZED

$ 2,571 37	BALANCE AS SHOWN ON BANK STATEMENT
0	TOTAL OF OUTSTANDING DEPOSITS
2,571 37	NEW TOTAL
-1,032 66	SUBTRACT TOTAL OF OUTSTANDING CHECKS
$1,538 71	YOUR ADJUSTED STATEMENT BALANCE

SHOULD EQUAL

BALANCE AS SHOWN IN YOUR REGISTER	$ 1,551 21
SUBTRACT AMOUNT OF SERVICE CHARGE	-12 50
NEW TOTAL	1,538 71
ADJUSTMENTS IF ANY	0
YOUR ADJUSTED REGISTER BALANCE	$1,538 71

Outstanding Deposits (Credits)

Date	Amount
	$
Total	$ 0

Outstanding Checks (Debits)

Check Number	Date	Amount
5377		$ 510 48
5378		403 21
5379		18 97
ATM		100 00
Total		$ 1,032 66

15.

$ 1,102 35	BALANCE AS SHOWN ON BANK STATEMENT
+265 49	TOTAL OF OUTSTANDING DEPOSITS
1,367 84	NEW TOTAL
-1,073 83	SUBTRACT TOTAL OF OUTSTANDING CHECKS
$294 01	YOUR ADJUSTED STATEMENT BALANCE

SHOULD EQUAL

BALANCE AS SHOWN IN YOUR REGISTER	$ 336 51
SUBTRACT AMOUNT OF SERVICE CHARGE	-6 50
NEW TOTAL	330 01
ADJUSTMENTS IF ANY	-36 00
YOUR ADJUSTED REGISTER BALANCE	$294 01

Outstanding Deposits (Credits)

Date	Amount
	$ 265 49
Total	$ 265 49

Outstanding Checks (Debits)

Check Number	Date	Amount
		$ 617 23
		456 60
Total		$ 1,073 83

1.

195	Date 5/25 20 XX
Amount $152.50	
To Lon Associates	
For Supplies	

Balance Forward	2,301	42
Deposits	283	17
Total	2,584	59
Amount This Check	152	50
Balance	2,432	09

Khayat Cleaners
2438 Broad St.
Oklahoma City, OK 00000   195

May 25 20 XX   87-278/840

PAY TO THE
ORDER OF   Lon Associates $ 152.50

One hundred fifty-two and 50/100 ———— DOLLARS

First State Bank
1543 S. Main
Oklahoma City, OK 00000

MEMO supplies   Lonnie Branch

⑈074200195⑈

2. $5,283.17   **3.** five   **4.** $0   **5.** $142.38   **6.** 3/15   **7.** $3,600   **8.** $6,982.68   **9.** $1,881.49

10.

RECORD ALL TRANSACTIONS THAT AFFECT YOUR ACCOUNT

NUMBER	DATE	DESCRIPTION OF TRANSACTION	DEBIT (−)		√ T	FEE (IF ANY) (−)	CREDIT (+)	BALANCE
							5,283 17
3784	2/27		96	03	√			−96 03 / 5,187 14
3785	3/5		346	18				−346 18 / 4840 96
3786	3/5		142	38	√			−142 38 / 4698 58
3787	3/11		487	93	√			−487 93 / 4,210 65
3788	3/11		973	12	√			−973 12 / 3237 53
3789	3/15		72	83				−72 83 / 3,164 70
Dep.	3/15				√		1,600 00	+1,600 00 / 4,764 70
3790	3/17		146	17				−146 17 / 4,618 53
3791	3/20		152	03				−152 03 / 4466 50
3792	3/31	*	182	08	√			−182 08 / 4,284 42
Deposit	3/31				√		2,000 00	+2,000 00 / 6,284 42
	3/31	Adjust for check # 3792 add 0.05 back			√		05	+.05 / 6,284 47
	3/17	Return check charge	19	00	√			−19 00 / 6,265 47
	3/31	Statement Reconciled						

REMEMBER TO RECORD AUTOMATIC PAYMENTS/DEPOSITS ON DATE AUTHORIZED.

$ 6,982 68	BALANCE AS SHOWN ON BANK STATEMENT		BALANCE AS SHOWN IN YOUR REGISTER	$ 6,284 42
0	TOTAL OF OUTSTANDING DEPOSITS		SUBTRACT AMOUNT OF SERVICE CHARGE	−19 00
6,982 68	NEW TOTAL		NEW TOTAL	6,265 42
−717 21	SUBTRACT TOTAL OF OUTSTANDING CHECKS		ADJUSTMENTS IF ANY	+0 05
$6,265 47	YOUR ADJUSTED STATEMENT BALANCE	SHOULD EQUAL	YOUR ADJUSTED REGISTER BALANCE	$6,265 47

Outstanding Deposits (Credits)

Date	Amount
	$ 0
Total	$ 0

Outstanding Checks (Debits)

Check Number	Date	Amount
3785	3/5	$ 346 18
3789	3/15	72 83
3790	3/17	146 17
3791	3/17	152 03
Total		$ 717 21

11.

$ 860 21	BALANCE AS SHOWN ON BANK STATEMENT		BALANCE AS SHOWN IN YOUR REGISTER	$ 1,817 93
+1,212 13	TOTAL OF OUTSTANDING DEPOSITS		SUBTRACT AMOUNT OF SERVICE CHARGE	−15 00
2,072 34	NEW TOTAL		NEW TOTAL	1,802 93
−483 24	SUBTRACT TOTAL OF OUTSTANDING CHECKS		ADJUSTMENTS IF ANY	−213 83
$1,589 10	YOUR ADJUSTED STATEMENT BALANCE	SHOULD EQUAL	YOUR ADJUSTED REGISTER BALANCE	$1,589 10

Outstanding Deposits (Credits)

Date	Amount
	$ 800 00
	412 13
Total	$ 1,212 13

Outstanding Checks (Debits)

Check Number	Date	Amount
		$ 243 17
		167 18
		13 97
		42 12
		16 80
Total		$ 483 24

CHAPTER 5

SECTION EXERCISES

5-1, P. 158

1. $A = 4$ **3.** $C = 8$ **5.** $R = 36$ **7.** $B = 5$ **9.** $C = 16$ **11.** $A = 19$ **13.** $A = 6$ **15.** $B = 1$ **17.** $B = 15$

19. $K = 4$ **21.** $A = 5$ **23.** $K = 20$ **25.** $J = 7$ **27.** $B = 3$ **29.** $X = 6$ **31.** $B = 8$ **33.** $N = 3$ **35.** $N = 8$ **37.** $\frac{3}{5}$

5-2, P. 165

1. The number of full-time hours is 9.   **3.** 132 tie-dyed shirts were sold.   **5.** 4 boxes of felt-tip pens and 8 boxes of ballpoint pens   **7.** 131,304,347.8 shares of stock

9. $\frac{5}{6}$ cup of milk   **11.** The seller pays $1,740.75 and the buyer pays $580.25.   **13.** Charris's salary is $17,155.20 and Chloe's is $11,436.80.

15. $N = 1,527.6$ yuan

5-3, P. 169

1. $S = \$39.99$ **3.** $C = \$33.87$ **5.** $5,580$ **7.** $C = T - S - I$ **9.** $V = LY$ **11.** $D = C - A$

EXERCISES SET A, P. 175

1. $N = 7$ **3.** $N = 17$ **5.** $A = 24$ **7.** $x = 11$ **9.** $X = 7$ **11.** $N = 84$ **13.** The number of cars sold is 9.   **15.** $96

17. $8.75 each hour   **19.** 280 headlights were purchased at a total cost of $3,906. 720 taillights were purchased at a total cost of $5,436.

21. $T = \$4{,}258.72$ **23.** $T = Np$

EXERCISES SET B, P. 177

1. $N = 9$ **3.** $N = 12$ **5.** $A = 12$ **7.** $B = 5$ **9.** $X = 3$ **11.** $N = 3$ **13.** 18 cookbooks   **15.** 27 hours   **17.** The purse sells for $43.49.

19. 1,897 imprints in 1 hour.   **21.** $C = \$137{,}509$ **23.** $A = LC$

PRACTICE TEST, P. 179

1. $N = 11$ **2.** $A = 18$ **3.** $A = 5$ **4.** $N = 6$ **5.** $A = 12$ **6.** $R = 1$ **7.** $N = 9$ **8.** $B = 15$

9. $A = 5$ **10.** $A = 5$ **11.** The new salary is $285.   **12.** 130 containers are needed.   **13.** 116 ceramic cups and 284 plastic cups were sold. The value of the ceramic cups was $464. The value of the plastic cups was $994.   **14.** The cost of 200 suits is $27,200.   **15.** The cost of 2,000 pounds of chemicals is $1,940.   **16.** $N = 3{,}406.92$ EUR   **17.** $N = 2.7815$ JPY   **18.** $I = \$27{,}346.38$ **19.** $D = \$3{,}173.50$ **20.** $D = I - T$

CHAPTER 6

SECTION EXERCISES

6-1, P. 189

1. 39%   **3.** 75%   **5.** 292%   **7.** 7.21%   **9.** 39%   **11.** 340%   **13.** 225%   **15.** $\frac{2}{3}\%$ **17.** 80%   **19.** 90%   **21.** 0.00125   **23.** 1.5

25. 0.004 (rounded)   **27.** 0.086   **29.** $\frac{3}{5}$ **31.** $1\frac{4}{5}$ **33.** $\frac{1}{3}$ **35.** $\frac{1}{8}$ or 1 of every 8 residents is uninsured.

6-2, P. 195

1. rate (%) = 48%   **3.** rate (%) = unknown number   **5.** rate (%) = 15%   **7.** $P = 75$ **9.** $P = 46.2$
base (of) = 12   base (of) = 158   base (of) = unknown number
portion (is) = unknown number   portion (is) = 47.4   portion (is) = 80

11. $B = 54$ **13.** $P = 12$ **15.** $B = 70$ **17.** $R = 25\%$ **19.** $P = 86$ **21.** $R = 83.55\%$ (rounded)   **23.** $R = 125\%$ **25.** $51.66 saved

27. 74 gallons (rounded)   **29.** $75,000 annual salary   **31.** $6,373.91 original cost   **33.** 92% correct   **35.** 6% tax rate (rounded)

6-3, P. 203

1. 2,309   **3.** $P = 108$ **5.** 33.75   **7.** 50%   **9.** 875   **11.** 7% (rounded)   **13.** $1,752.75   **15.** $14.72   **17.** 12.5%

EXERCISES SET A, P. 207

1. 23%   **3.** 3%   **5.** 60.1%   **7.** 300%   **9.** 20%   **11.** 17%   **13.** 52%   **15.** 125%   **17.** 0.0025   **19.** 2.56   **21.** 0.005   **23.** $\frac{1}{10}$

25. $\frac{89}{100}$ **27.** $2\frac{1}{4}$ **29.** 12.5%; $\frac{1}{8}$ **31.** $P = 81$ **33.** $B = \$12{,}000$ **35.** $R = 250\%$ **37.** $B = 30$ **39.** $169.26   **41.** 2,270 people

43. 26% (rounded) is *not* within the budgeted 25%   **45.** $145

EXERCISES SET B, P. 209

1. 67.5%   **3.** 0.7%   **5.** 0.04%   **7.** 24.2%   **9.** 99%   **11.** 65%   **13.** 40%   **15.** 3.284   **17.** 0.52   **19.** 0.0002   **21.** $\frac{1}{5}$ **23.** $3\frac{61}{100}$

25. $\frac{1}{8}$ **27.** $\frac{1}{2}$; 0.5   **29.** 45%; $\frac{9}{20}$ **31.** $R = 200\%$ **33.** $R = 80\%$ **35.** $B = 305.88$ **37.** 115   **39.** $54   **41.** 540 fuses

43. $2,754.70   **45.** $56

PRACTICE TEST, P. 211

1. 24%   **2.** 92.5%   **3.** 60%   **4.** 93%   **5.** 43%   **6.** 21%   **7.** 37.5%   **8.** $\frac{1}{400}$ **9.** 2.764   **10.** $\frac{51}{125}$ **11.** $72   **12.** 250%

13. 87.5%, or $87\frac{1}{2}\%$ **14.** $2.52   **15.** 22 rooms   **16.** 3%   **17.** 90 employees   **18.** $2.92 tip; Total bill = $22.39   **19.** 56,600 automobiles

20. 31.5%   **21.** 18.3%   **22.** 65%   **23.** $92,287.80   **24.** $140,790   **25.** $486   **26.** $271.19

SECTION EXERCISES

7-1, P. 225

1.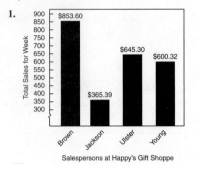

Salespersons at Happy's Gift Shoppe

3. Highest: Saturday ($611.77); lowest: Monday ($233.94)   **5.** April–June   **7.** 50%   **9.** 40 mph
11. 20 mph; compact car   **13.** Take-home pay = $1,600; Transportation percent = 10%
15. Percent of take-home pay allocated for food = 25%   **17.** 20%   **19.** $1,000; 2.5%
21. Yes, the salary percent of increase was 13.9%, and it exceeded the rate of inflation.

7-2, P. 235

1. 5,470   **3.** $15,679   **5.** 79.5   **7.** No score is reported more than once, so there is no mode.   **9.** $14,978   **11.** a. $34,746;   b. $34,991;   c. There is no mode.
d. Answers will vary. The mean and median are very close, so they give a realistic view of the average of the data.

13. $29,840   **15.**

Class intervals	Tally	Class frequency
60–69	//	2
70–79	///	3
80–89	LH1 ///	8
90–99	LH1 //	7

17.

Class intervals	Tally	Class frequency	Relative frequency
$0–$9.99	LH1 LH1	10	33.3%
$10–$19.99	LH1 ////	9	30.0%
$20–$29.99	LH1	5	16.7%
$30–$39.99	///	3	10.0%
$40–$49.99	///	3	10.0%

19. 10%

7-3, P. 242

1. 13   **3.** 1, 7, −6, −1, −1   **5.** 22   **7.** a. 15.87 scores (approximately 16 scores);   b. 97.72 scores (approximately 98 scores)   **9.** 12   **11.** 90
13. 4.242640687 or 4.24 (rounded)

EXERCISES SET A, P. 249

1. Range = 14; Mean = 22; Median = 22; There is no mode.   **3.** Range = $9.27; Mean = $8.42 (rounded); Median = $5.53 (rounded); Mode = $13.95
Statements about the data set may vary. The median is significantly lower than the mean. The mode is the highest three values. There are two data clusters. These clusters are around the high and the low values.

5. 1 = 291   2 = 624
    3 = 799   4 = 790
    5 = 801   6 = 640
    7 = 639   8 = 584
    9 = 293   10 = 123

7. Period 10

9. Early morning and late afternoon classes have lower enrollment than midmorning classes.

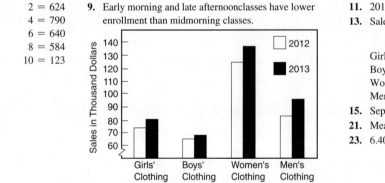

The Family Store Sales by Department for 2012-2013

11. 2012: $125,115; 2013: $137,340
13. Sales for The Family Store, 2012–2013

	2012	2013
Girls' clothing	$ 74,675	$ 81,534
Boys' clothing	65,153	68,324
Women's clothing	125,115	137,340
Men's clothing	83,895	96,315

15. September   **17.** 20%   **19.** $306
21. Mean = 87.1; Median = 88; Mode—no mode
23. 6.402256547 or 6.4

25.

Class interval	Tally	Class frequency	Calculations	Relative frequency
91–95	/	1	$\frac{1}{24}(100\%) = \frac{100\%}{24}$	4.2%
86–90	///	3	$\frac{3}{24}(100\%) = \frac{300\%}{24}$	12.5%
81–85	////	4	$\frac{4}{24}(100\%) = \frac{400\%}{24}$	16.7%
76–80	LH1 /	6	$\frac{6}{24}(100\%) = \frac{600\%}{24}$	25%
71–75	//	2	$\frac{2}{24}(100\%) = \frac{200\%}{24}$	8.3%
66–70	///	3	$\frac{3}{24}(100\%) = \frac{300\%}{24}$	12.5%
61–65				
56–60	LH1	5	$\frac{5}{24}(100\%) = \frac{500\%}{24}$	20.8%
Total		24		100%

EXERCISES SET B, P. 253

1. Range = 32; Mean = 74.33; Median = 71; No mode   **3.** Range = 0.17 kg; Mean = 1.145 kg; Median = 1.125 kg; Mode = 1.1 kg   Statements about the data set may vary. The mean, median, and mode are very similar. The data clusters about the mean and there are no outliers.   **5.** misc. expenses and general government

7. education costs   **9.** 90°   **11.**

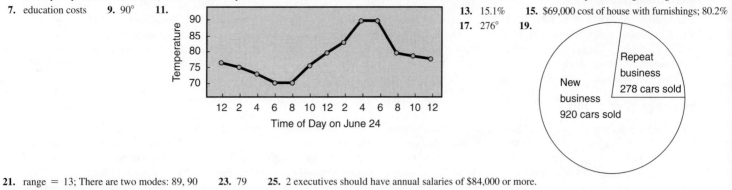

13. 15.1%   **15.** $69,000 cost of house with furnishings; 80.2%

17. 276°   **19.**

21. range = 13; There are two modes: 89, 90   **23.** 79   **25.** 2 executives should have annual salaries of $84,000 or more.

PRACTICE TEST, P. 257

1. a. 77;   b. 41.8;   c. 29.5;   d. 15   **2.** $120   **3.** 37.5%   **4.** 33.3%   **5.** 29.2%   **6.** labor: 135°; materials: 120°; overhead: 105°   **7.**

8. fresh flowers: $23,712; silk flowers: $17,892   **9.** fresh flowers: $10,380; silk flowers: $5,829

10. c. $5,000; other interval sizes would provide too many or too few intervals.

11.

12. smallest; 250; greatest; 1,117

13.

Sales of Laser Printers by
Smart Brothers Computer Store

14. mean = $65.08; variance = 60.67664; standard deviation = 7.79 (rounded to hundredths)

15. 11.4 bulbs or 11 bulbs (rounded)

CHAPTER 8

SECTION EXERCISES

8-1, P. 267

1. $120   **3.** $58.68 trade discount   **5.** $234.72 net price   **7.** $234.72 net price   **9.** Answers will vary.   **11.** Notebooks: $22.50; Loose leaf paper: $8.90; Ballpoint pens: $23.70; Total list price = $55.10; 40% trade discount = $22.04; Net price = $33.06   **13.** Net price rate = 72%; Net price = $106,766.64

8-2, P. 272

1. $64,804.73 total net price of TVs   **3.** $595.58   **5.** $72.90 trade discount; $196.10 net price   **7.** The better deal is $189.97 with discounts of 5/5/10.
9. The better deal is $1,899 with discounts of 5/10/10.   **11.** The better deal is $410 with a discount series of 10/10/5.

8-3, P. 282

1. $10.80 cash discount   **3.** $432 net amount   **5.** No cash is discount allowed. $450 is due.   **7.** $641.52 net amount   **9.** $667.44 total bill
11. $1,257.56 net amount   **13.** $1,225 net amount   **15.** $478.21 net amount   **17.** No cash discount is allowed. $900 is due.
19. No cash discount is allowed. $392.34 is due.   **21.** $2,061.86 amount credited to account; $1,920.62 outstanding balance
23. Better Bilt Bicycles paid the freight to the freight company.   **25.** The vendor pays the shipping company and adds the charge to Charlotte's invoice.

EXERCISES SET A, P. 287

1. $45.00   **3.** $6.00   **5.** $307.23   **7.** Trade discount = $4.00; Net price = $195.95   **9.** Net price rate = 96%; Net price = $315.84
11. Net price rate = 89%; Net price = $1,419.55   **13.** Decimal equivalents of complements = 0.9, 0.85, and 0.9; Net decimal equivalent = 0.6885;
Net price = $963.89   **15.** % form = 76.5%; Single discount equivalent = 23.5%   **17.** % form = 74.34%; Single discount equivalent = 25.66%

19. 16.21% single discount equivalent **21.** $102.50 **23.** $94.50 **25.** $3.42 net price **27.** $60 − $9.45 = $50.55; better deal **29.** $5.40
31. $5,139.06

EXERCISES SET B, P. 289

1. $4.80 **3.** $63.75 **5.** $0.77 **7.** Trade discount = $0.83; Net price = $26.67 **9.** Complement = 95%; Net price = $399.95
11. Complement = 92%; Net price = $3,664.36 **13.** Decimal equivalents of complements: 0.8(0.85)(0.95); Net decimal equivalent: 0.646; Net price: $22.61
15. Net decimal equivalent in percent form: 82%; Single discount equivalent in percent form: 18% **17.** Net decimal equivalent in percent form: 75.8%;
Single discount equivalent in percent form: 24.2% **19.** 23.05% **21.** $0.375 or $0.38 **23.** $1,179 **25.** $513 net price **27.** $190 less 10% or
$171 = better deal **29.** $0.50 cash discount **31.** $515.46 amount credited; $310.54 outstanding balance

PRACTICE TEST, P. 291

1. $110 trade discount **2.** $532.50 net price **3.** $29.24 net price **4.** $250 less 20% is the better deal. **5.** $47.88 net price **6.** 42.4%
7. 0.684 net decimal equivalent **8.** 85% **9.** $42 trade discount **10.** $1,080 net price **11.** $2 cash discount **12.** 3% discount if she pays on or
before September 11. **13.** $392 net amount **14.** $294.00 net amount **15.** $400; no discount if not paid on or after December 21.
16. $31 less 10%, 10%, 5% is the better deal. **17.** $201.60 net price for dartboards; $288 net price for bowling balls; $489.60 total net price
18. Amount credited = $306.12; Outstanding balance = $438.88 **19.** Amount credited = $3,571.43; Outstanding balance = $2,321.78 **20.** Manufacturer

CHAPTER 9

SECTION EXERCISES

9-1, P. 306

1. $50 **3.** $24 **5.** a. $84.34 b. $154.34 **7.** a. $90 b. 150% **9.** $4 **11.** $214 **13.** $8 **15.** $1.75 **17.** a. 80% b. $318.40
19. 125% **21.** 101.5% **23.** $268.57 **25.** $15 **27.** Cost = $235.81; Markup 5 $113.19

9-2, P. 316

1. 20% **3.** 59.8% **5.** $1,666.67; $1,416.67 **7.** $S\% = 132\%$; $C = \$206.25$; $S = \$272.25$ **9.** 42.8% **11.** a. $333.33 b. $233.33
13. 150% **15.** 49.6% **17.** a. $935.94 b. $336.94 **19.** a. $7.80 b. $7.20 **21.** 170.3%

9-3, P. 324

1. $M = \$18$; $M\% = 37.5\%$ **3.** $M = \$350$; $M\% = 41.2\%$ **5.** 49%; $38.25 **7.** $0.38 (rounded) **9.** $191.95 sale price **11.** $101.25 first sale price;
$86.06 second sale price; Final selling price = $33.75 **13.** $0.72 **15.** $4,632

EXERCISES SET A, P. 333

1. $21.99 **3.** $30.77 **5.** $71.50 **7.** $24; $36 **9.** $813.37; $585.63 **11.** $280; $98 **13.** $51.00; $30.60 **15.** $225; $355.50; 158%
17. 25% **19.** a. $38 b. 10% **21.** First markdown = $9.90; Sale price = $39.60; Second markdown = $11.88; Second sale price = $27.72
23. $0.54

EXERCISES SET B, P. 335

1. $126.65 **3.** $76.40 **5.** $279.64 **7.** $170.95; $188.05 **9.** $499.98; $219.99 **11.** a. $14.35 b. $14.35 **13.** 90.3%; 47.4% **15.** 525%
17. $M = \$4.58$; $M\% = 15.3\%$ **19.** $201.59; 28%

PRACTICE TEST, P. 337

1. $7.16 **2.** $73.80 **3.** $15.50; $20.77 **4.** $173.25; $211.75 **5.** $16.80; $5.88 **6.** $91.65 **7.** $26.07 **8.** 30% **9.** $798.15
10. $589.99 **11.** 28.5% **12.** $15; $34.99 **13.** $160; $72 **14.** 40% **15.** $331.31 **16.** $0.35 **17.** $49.70; 44.75%
18. $M\%_{\text{selling price}} = 40\%$ **19.** 185.7% **20.** $M\%_{\text{cost}} = 25.2\%$; $M\%_{\text{selling price}} = 20.1\%$ **21.** $M = \$217.72$; $S = \$563.30$
22. $M = \$18.80$; $C = \$21.19$ **23.** $M = \$313.49$; $C = \$236.50$ **24.** $M\%_{\text{selling price}} = 45.1\%$ **25.** $400; $180 **26.** $181.25; $268.25; 148%

CHAPTER 10

SECTION EXERCISES

10-1, P. 349

1. $677.00 **3.** $4,415.00 **5.** $383.80 **7.** $802.95 **9.** $429.30 **11.** $581.12 **13.** $538.32 **15.** $1,008.39 **17.** $566.05

10-2, P. 363

1. $31 **3.** $135 **5.** $481.57 **7.** $140.08 **9.** Social Security tax = $108.49; Medicare tax = $37.45 **11.** Social Security tax for December =
$123.40; Medicare tax for December = $141.26 **13.** $1,712.39

10-3, P. 368

1. Employer's share of Social Security and Medicare taxes = $354; Employer's tax deposit = $2,263 **3.** Total withholding = $407; Total Employee's Social
Security tax = $207.23; Total Employee's Medicare tax = $143.08; Total Employer's Social Security tax = $305.91; Employer's tax deposit = $1,063.22
5. $378.00 **7.** Payment of $122.64 + $45.36 = $168.00 must be deposited by January 31 of the next year since it does not exceed $500.

EXERCISES SET A, P. 375

1. $483.14 **3.** $452.80 **5.** $7,938 **7.** Her gross weekly earnings are still $825, as a salaried job does not normally pay overtime for hours worked over 40.
9. $722.10 **11.** $700 **13.** $1,191.20 **15.** $22 **17.** $121 **19.** $23.36 **21.** Social Security tax = $35.36; Medicare tax = $12.21
23. Social Security tax = $77.95; Medicare tax = $26.91 **25.** Social Security tax = $28.35; Medicare tax = $9.79; Net earnings = $540.66
27. Employer pays $337.98 for Social Security and Medicare taxes and sends $1,352.86 to IRS.

EXERCISES SET B, P. 377

1. $432.85 **3.** $638.40 **5.** $2,648 **7.** She earns $1,896 because salaried employees do not normally receive overtime pay. **9.** $1,076.40 **11.** $763
13. $1,279.32 **15.** $47 **17.** $66 **19.** no withholding tax **21.** Social Security tax = $147; Medicare tax = $50.75 **23.** Social Security tax = $51.49;
Medicare tax = $17.78 **25.** Net pay = $1,475.88 **27.** The employer must send $2,098.91 to the IRS.

PRACTICE TEST, P. 379

1. $1,827 **2.** $910.91 **3.** $1,050 **4.** $1,374.75 **5.** $1,092 **6.** $875 **7.** $706.68 **8.** Social Security tax = $21.58; Medicare tax = $7.45
9. Social Security tax = $36.17; Medicare tax = $12.49 **10.** $41 **11.** $33 **12.** $1,138.90 **13.** $219.24 **14.** $584.60 **15.** $90 **16.** $235
17. Social Security tax = $30.87; Medicare tax = $10.66; Withholding tax = $70.00; Other deductions = $25.12; Net earnings = $598.35
18. Social Security tax = $28.30; Medicare tax = $9.77; Withholding tax = $50.00; Other deductions = $12.87; Net earnings = $572.86
19. Social Security tax = $37.47; Medicare tax = $12.94; Withholding tax = $72.00; Net earnings = $769.76 **20.** Social Security tax = $24.24;
Medicare tax = $8.37; Withholding tax = $20.00; Other deductions = $4.88; Net earnings = $519.66 **21.** Social Security tax = $25.63;
Medicare tax = $8.85; Withholding tax = $17.00; Net earnings = $558.65 **22.** $285.66 **23.** $378 **24.** $56 **25.** $237.23

CHAPTER 11

SECTION EXERCISES

11-1, P. 394

1. $I = \$264$ **3.** $MV = \$936$ **5.** $MV = \$3,430$ **7.** 0.75 year **9.** 1.5 years **11.** $MV = \$43,743$ **13.** $R = 0.185$, or 18.5% per year
15. $T = \frac{1}{2}$ year, or 6 months

11-2, P. 401

1. $213.04 **3.** $67.81 **5.** Non-leap year: 549 days; Leap year: 550 days **7.** Exact time: 279 days **9.** Exact time: September 16 **11.** $75.21
13. Answers will vary. The equipment can be purchased now at a $100 savings and the cost of the loan (interest) is $75.21. Since a modest savings of only $24.79 will
be realized, the most important consideration is how useful it will be to have the equipment two months early. **15.** $320.14

11-3, P. 407

1. $75 **3.** Discount = $149.50; Proceeds = $3,100.50 **5.** 8.9% **7.** 7.98% **9.** $5,138.59 **11.** Answers will vary. The payee may need quick
cash and can sell the note to get the cash needed.

EXERCISES SET A, P. 415

1. $120 **3.** a. $1,539; b. $5,814 **5.** 9% **7.** 3.75 years **9.** $2,812.50 **11.** $\frac{7}{12}$ year **13.** $5 **15.** $16 **17.** 117 days
19. Exact time: August 8 **21.** a. = $51.29 b. = $52 **23.** $10,040.56 **25.** 11.4%

EXERCISES SET B, P. 417

1. $285 **3.** $19,252.80 (interest); $34,532.80 (MV) **5.** 8% **7.** 3 years **9.** $800 **11.** $1\frac{1}{2}$ years **13.** 10% **15.** $160.33 **17.** 217 days
19. 191 days **21.** September 11 **23.** $80.08 (discount); $1,899.92 (proceeds) **25.** He will save $20.20 **27.** 9.2%

PRACTICE TEST, P. 419

1. $60 **2.** $1,500 **3.** 12.5% annually **4.** 2 years **5.** 287 days **6.** 168 days **7.** 159 days **8.** $4,100; $4,168.33; $31.67 **9.** $210
10. $206.80 **11.** $3,450 **12.** $15.11 **13.** 13.0% **14.** 0.75 or $\frac{3}{4}$ year or 9 months **15.** 8.5% annually **16.** $350 **17.** $52
18. Yes, he saves $27. **19.** $122.26 **20.** $8.66 **21.** $10,188.75

CHAPTER 12

SECTION EXERCISES

12-1, P. 434

1. $749.20 **3.** $1,375.84 **5.** $760.48 **7.** $213.24 **9.** $69.08 **11.** $87.79 **13.** 11.25% **15.** 11.00%

12-2, P. 438

1. $\frac{171}{1,830}$ or 0.093442623 **3.** $190.34 **5.** $\frac{5}{28}$ **7.** $318.54

1. 1.15%   **3.** $37.33   **5.** Average daily balance = $121.64   **7.** $2.19   **9.** $3.61   **11.** Finance charge = $18.21; New balance = $464.65

EXERCISES SET A, P. 449

1. $1,585.96   **3.** $729   **5.** $30.51   **7.** $52.40   **9.** $390.25   **11.** $39.52   **13.** $3.98   **15.** $462.60   **17.** 13.75%   **19.** 21.5%
21. 14.25%

EXERCISES SET B, P. 451

1. $711   **3.** $577   **5.** $132.14   **7.** $375.65   **9.** $126.35   **11.** $8.85   **13.** $5.19   **15.** $8.75 finance charge; $611.61 unpaid balance
17. 13%   **19.** 15.75%   **21.** 21.5%

PRACTICE TEST, P. 453

1. $34   **2.** $690 installment price; Finance charge = $112   **3.** $105.56   **4.** $83.74   **5.** Installment price = $336; Finance charge = $36
6. 21.5%   **7.** 16.25%   **8.** $2.89   **9.** 24%   **10.** $12.60   **11.** 11.5%   **12.** 10.75%   **13.** 21.5%   **14.** $875   **15.** $158.33   **16.** $654
17. $111.52   **18.** $317.85   **19.** $240.08   **20.** $393.93 average daily balance; $6.89 finance charge; $427.84 unpaid balance
21. Finance charge = $11.91; New balance = $746.39   **22.** Finance charge = $31.27; New balance = $3,409.51

CHAPTER 13

SECTION EXERCISES

13-1, P. 473

1. Compound amount = $5,627.55; Compound interest = $627.55   **3.** Compound amount = $7,887.81; Compound interest = $887.81
5. Compound amount = $1,269.73; Compound interest = $269.73   **7.** $1,873.08 (third year) future value; Compound interest = $673.08;
Simple interest = $576; Compound interest is $97.08 more than simple interest.   **9.** Compound amount = $8,046.92; Compound interest = $1,746.92
11. $720.98   **13.** $15,373.05 Compound amount; Interest = $4,873.05   **15.** $8\frac{1}{4}$% annually is the slightly better deal   **17.** Effective rate = 2.01%
19. Effective rate = 6.14%   **21.** Compound interest = $1.03   **23.** $1.64

13-2, P. 480

1. $3,768.72   **3.** $8,528.20   **5.** $2,439.02   **7.** $20,608.44   **9.** $1,912.64   **11.** $9,233.00

EXERCISES SET A, P. 487

1. Compound amount = $2,186.88; Compound interest = $186.88   **3.** Compound amount = $10,506.30; Compound interest = $506.30   **5.** $16,407
7. $7,718.19   **9.** Interest = $166.40   **11.** Future value = $3,481.62   **13.** Future value = $9,198.96   **15.** Compound amount = $936.54; $1,100
in one year would have a greater yield than $900 invested today   **17.** Compound interest = $0.86; Future value = $2,000.86   **19.** 10.38%   **21.** $1,392.90
23. $3,843.56   **25.** $1,695.44

EXERCISES SET B, P. 489

1. Compound amount = $6,400.40; Compound interest = $1,400.40   **3.** Compound amount = $8,541.33; Compound interest = $1,541.33
5. $2,227.41   **7.** $13,396.51   **9.** $52.50   **11.** $41.22   **13.** 6.84848   **15.** Compound interest = $103.81; Future value = $1,103.81
17. Compound interest = $43.16; Future value = $25,025.16   **19.** $1,723.34   **21.** $7,568.40   **23.** $489.68   **25.** 12.68%

PRACTICE TEST, P. 491

1. $450.09   **2.** $823.29   **3.** $3,979.30   **4.** $18,206.64   **5.** $1,560.90 Compound amount; $60.90 Compound interest   **6.** $376.53 Compound interest
7. 12.55%   **8.** $8.84   **9.** Compounding daily yields slightly higher interest.   **10.** $2,906.32   **11.** $3,940.15   **12.** $4,454.72   **13.** $4,725.42
14. $9,834.48   **15.** $680 in one year is better.   **16.** $6,304.24   **17.** Option 2 yields the greater return by $0.68   **18.** $2,391.24   **19.** $1,002.74
20. $14,570.18

CHAPTER 14

SECTION EXERCISES

14-1, P. 511

1. Future value = $9,549; Total interest = $1,549   **3.** Future value = $26,824; Total interest = $2,824   **5.** Future value = $21,547.60;
Total interest = $1,547.60   **7.** $945.75   **9.** $114   **11.** Harry will have $15,577.22 at the end of three years. Interest = $577.22
13. Amount invested = $91,000; Interest = $20,059   **15.** The future value is $25,129. Latanya will have invested 15($1,000) or $15,000 of her own money and
will have received $10,129 in interest.   **17.** The future value of the annuity is $11,734; Your investment = $10,000; Your interest = $1,734
19. The future value is $38,203.52; Investment = $36,000; Interest = $2,203.52   **21.** The future value is $17,546.58; Investment = $15,600;
Interest = $1,946.58   **23.** Future value = $60,193.06; Investment = $52,800; Interest = $7,393.06   **25.** The semiannual annuity yields more interest.
27. $115,889.24   **29.** Annuity 4 at $35,851.32

14-2, P. 520

1. $2,050.02   **3.** $1,037.03   **5.** $839.55   **7.** $8,209   **9.** $6,679.64   **11.** $21,072   **13.** $68,700 or $68,695.31 formula/calculator

1. $7,432.60; $432.60   **3.** $3,979.66; $229.66   **5.** $10,311.07   **7.** $2,270.77   **9.** $135,900   **11.** $67,890   **13.** $5,359.69; $859.69
15. (a) $39,620.70   (b) $96,197.85   **17.** $7,689.67   **19.** $32,620.34

EXERCISES SET B, P. 531

1. $25,482.80; $2,682.80   **3.** $23,603.13; $6,403.13   **5.** $893.18   **7.** $283.56   **9.** $156,772   **11.** $163,510   **13.** $3,641.14; $341.14
15. $109,336.50   **17.** $17,708.46   **19.** $2,862.89

PRACTICE TEST, P. 533

1. $18,292.50   **2.** $8,851.12   **3.** $37,607.22; $3,737.22   **4.** $5,591.70   **5.** $5,727.50   **6.** $11,477.22   **7.** $60,819.20   **8.** $65,076.54
9. $28,269.88   **10.** $48,417.60   **11.** $1,118.23   **12.** $25,938   **13.** $37,155.54   **14.** $3,327.06   **15.** $28,240   **16.** $21,884
17. $5,591.97   **18.** $3,584.07   **19.** $19,672.40   **20.** $10,822.50   **21.** $13,678.80   **22.** $3,861   **23.** $9,583.92   **24.** $136,775
25. $2,136.17 for payment starting at birth; $4,215.60 for payment starting at six years of age; $2,079.43 difference in payment.

CHAPTER 15

SECTION EXERCISES

15-1, p. 548

1. $16.51   **3.** $0.89   **5.** 13,327,793   **7.** 3.9%   **9.** 14   **11.** $1,108,275,840   **13.** $10,000   **15.** $2.38   **17.** $1,394,000

15-2, p. 552

1. 5.500% interest rate and a maturity date of Jan 2020   **3.** A+   **5.** BAC.IOP (4.445%)   **7.** $1,128.47   **9.** 109.969%   **11.** $1,030.97   **13.** 4.827%

15-3, p. 558

1. $8.16   **3.** 3.265%   **5.** $9.37   **7.** $9.65   **9.** 630.517 shares   **11.** 23.75%

EXERCISES SET A, P. 565

1. 2,397,964 shares   **3.** $0.63   **5.** $0.70; $35.00; $70.00   **7.** 2.8%   **9.** 9   **11.** $30,000   **13.** $440,000   **15.** $966.42   **17.** Mar 2020
19. $1,074.91   **21.** 6.757%   **23.** $10.45   **25.** 13.96   **27.** $5.45; $5.47   **29.** 232.833 shares

EXERCISES SET B, P. 567

1. $1.68   **3.** 6.4%   **5.** AT&T at 1.68 per share   **7.** 6.3%   **9.** 7   **11.** $852,000   **13.** $2,546,000   **15.** 4.500%
17. GS.IAR is selling at a discount. BUD.ID is selling at a premium.   **19.** $1,027.24   **21.** 7.220%   **23.** $8.16   **25.** $9.47
27. $11.16; $11.11   **29.** 448.430 shares

PRACTICE TEST, P. 569

1. $1.35   **2.** 3.2%   **3.** $69.59 per share   **4.** $70.50 per share   **5.** 8,429,746 shares   **6.** $6,583.20   **7.** $8,350.80   **8.** $2,000   **9.** $2,000
10. $196,000   **11.** $2.61   **12.** 12   **13.** $210   **14.** May 2019   **15.** $640 per bond   **16.** $723.75   **17.** Discount   **18.** $7.39   **19.** $10.53
20. $5.23   **21.** 1.9%   **22.** 3.2%   **23.** 30   **24.** 6.155%   **25.** 10.74   **26.** $8.03   **27.** $7.39; $7.39   **28.** 0.5%   **29.** 647.228 shares
30. 6.36%

CHAPTER 16

SECTION EXERCISES

16-1, P. 582

	Purchase price of home	Down payment	Mortgage amount	Annual interest rate	Years	Monthly Payment per $1,000	Monthly mortgage payment	Total paid for mortgage	Interest paid
1.	$100,000	$0	$100,000	4.75%	30	$5.22	$ 522	$187,920	$ 87,920
3.	$ 95,000	$8,000	$ 87,000	5.75%	25	$6.29	$ 547.23	$164,169	$ 77,169
5.	$495,750	18%	$406,515	5.00%	35	$5.05	$2,052.90	$862,218	$455,703

7. Down payment = $38,750; Mortgage amount = $116,250; Monthly payment = $624.26   **9.** $40,593.60   **11.** $1,892.75   **13.** $1,582.42

16-2, P. 586

1.

Month	Monthly payment	Interest	Principal	End-of-month principal
1	$584	$479.17	$104.83	$99,895.17
2	$584	$478.66	$105.34	$99,789.83

3.

Month	Monthly payment	Interest	Principal	End-of-month principal
1	$547.23	$416.88	$130.35	$86,869.65
2	$547.23	$416.25	$130.98	$86,738.67

5.

Month	Monthly payment	Interest	Principal	End-of-month principal
1	$2,052.90	$1,693.81	$359.09	$406,155.91
2	$2,052.90	$1,692.32	$360.58	$405,795.33

7. Month 1 interest = $742.44; Principal portion of 1st payment = $401.34; End-of-month principal = $169,298.66;
Month 2 interest = $740.68; Principal portion of 2nd payment = $403.10; End-of-month principal = $168,895.56

9.

Month	Monthly payment	Interest	Principal	End-of-month principal
1	$1,446.86	$963.88	$482.98	$209,817.02
2	$1,446.86	$961.66	$485.20	$209,331.82

11. 29%

EXERCISES SET A, P. 593

1. $2,018.25   **3.** $1,005.18   **5.** $196,880   **7.** $149,254

9.

Month	Monthly payment	Interest	Principal	End-of-month principal
1	$2,926.20	$2,438.50	$487.70	$487,212.30
2	$2,926.20	$2,436.06	$490.14	$486,722.16

11. $1,743.66   **13.** 28%   **15.** $4,212.46

EXERCISES SET B, P. 595

1. $2.926.20   **3.** $392.12   **5.** $565,732   **7.** $81,790.40

9.

Month	Monthly payment	Interest	Principal	End-of-month principal
1	$1,005.18	$793.23	$211.95	$152,088.05
2	$1,005.18	$792.13	$213.05	$151,875.00

11. $2,885.87   **13.** 35%   **15.** $1,780.37

PRACTICE TEST, P. 597

1. 6.44   **2.** $1,453.60   **3.** $348,772   **4.** 151.64%   **5.** $39,400   **6.** $157,600   **7.** $1,166.24   **8.** $52,323.20   **9.** $1,509.74
10. Monthly payment = $751.75; Interest = $113,030   **11.** $60,706.80   **12.** Interest = $525.33; Principal portion = $640.91

13. Portion of payment applied to:

Month	Monthly payment	Interest	Principal	End-of-month Principal
1	$1,166.24	$525.33	$640.91	$156,959.09
2	$1,166.24	$523.20	$642.64	$156,316.05
3	$1,166.24	$521.05	$645.15	$155,670.86

14. Portion of payment applied to:

Month	Monthly payment	Interest	Principal	End-of-month principal
1	$751.75	$525.33	$226.42	$157,373.58
2	$751.75	$524.58	$227.17	$157,146.41
3	$751.75	$523.82	$227.93	$156,918.48

15. 37%   **16.** $1,399.31

CHAPTER 17

SECTION EXERCISES

17-1, P. 614

Total cost $44,000	Year	Annual depreciation	Accumulated depreciation	End-of-year book value
1. Depreciable	1	$6,000	$6,000	$38,000
2. value =	2	$6,000	$12,000	$32,000
3. $36,000	3	$6,000	$18,000	$26,000
4.	4	$6,000	$24,000	$20,000
5.	5	$6,000	$30,000	$14,000
6.	6	$6,000	$36,000	$8,000

Total cost $38,000	Year	Hours used	Annual depreciation	Accumulated depreciation	End-of-year book value
7. Depreciable	1	24,848	$1,789.06	$1,789.06	$36,210.94
8. value =	2	20,040	$1,442.88	$3,231.94	$34,768.06
9. $36,000	3	20,860	$1,501.92	$4,733.86	$33,266.14

Total cost $28,000	Year	Depreciation rate	Annual depreciation	Accumulated depreciation	End-of-year book value
11. Depreciable value = $25,500	2	$\frac{9}{55}$	$4,172.73	$8,809.09	$19,190.91

Total cost $285,900	Year	Annual depreciation	Accumulated depreciation	End-of-year book value
13.	1	$21,442.50	$21,442.50	$264,457.50
15.	3	$18,346.74	$59,623.55	$226,276.45

17. Total cost: $25,000	Year	Depreciation	Accumulated depreciation	End-of-year book value
	1	$1,875	$1,875	$23,125
	2	1,875	3,750	21,250
	3	1,875	5,625	19,375

19. $1,140   **21.** Unit depreciation = $0.9066666667 per hour; First year's depreciation = $3,493.39   **23.** Rate = 0.2857142857 (rounded to the nearest ten-thousandth); First year's depreciation = $10,653.75

17-2, P. 619

1. $36,671.25   **3.** $12,790   **5.** Year 1 depreciation = $5,999.40; Year 2 depreciation = $8,001; Year 3 depreciation = $2,665.80;
Year 4 depreciation = $1,333.80   **7.** Year 7 depreciation = $2,199.60   **9.** Year 1 depreciation = $10,003

11.

Year	MACRS rate	Depreciation	Accumulated depreciation	End-of-year book value
1	33.33%	$44,293.90	$44,293.90	$88,601.10
2	44.45%	$59,071.83	$103,365.73	$29,529.27
3	14.81%	$19,681.75	$123,047.48	$9,847.52
4	7.41%	$9,847.52	$132,895.00	$0

13.

Year	MACRS rate	Depreciation	Accumulated depreciation	End-of-year book value
1	20%	$57,200	$ 57,200	$228,800
2	32%	$91,520	$148,720	$137,280
3	19.2%	$54,912	$203,632	$ 82,368
4	11.52%	$32,947.20	$236,579.20	$ 49,420.80
5	11.52%	$32,947.20	$269,526.40	$ 16,473.60
6	5.76%	$16,473.60	$286,000	$0

EXERCISES SET A, P. 625

1. $2,300 **3.** $4,500 **5.** $900 **7.** Unit depreciation = $0.50; Yearly depreciation = $3,350 **9.** Unit depreciation = $0.25; Yearly depreciation = $380 **11.** $0.18

13. Total cost: **$4,200** Depreciable value: **$4,200 − $750 = $3,450**

Year	Depreciation rate	Depreciation	Accumulated depreciation	End-of-year book value
1	$\frac{5}{15}$	$1,150	$1,150	$3,050
2	$\frac{4}{15}$	$920	$2,070	$2,130

15. $949.03

17. Year 1: $1,160
Year 2: $1,856
Year 3: $1,113.60

19. Depreciable cost: **$3,270**

Year	MACRS rate	Depreciation	Accumulated depreciation	End-of-year book value
1	33.33%	$1,089.89	$1,089.89	$2,180.11
2	44.45%	$1,453.52	$2,543.41	$726.59
3	14.81%	$484.29	$3,027.70	$242.30
4	7.41%	$242.30*	$3,270.00	$0

*adjusted

EXERCISES SET B, P. 627

1. $540.91 **3.** $5,875 **5.** $800 **7.** Unit depreciation = $0.25; Yearly depreciation = $1,750 **9.** Unit depreciation = $0.50; Yearly depreciation = $2,080

11. Total cost: **$15,000**

Year	Hours used	Depreciation	Accumulated depreciation	End-of-year book value
1	4,160	$2,080	$2,080	$12,920
2	3,140	$1,570	$3,650	$11,350
3	6,820	$3,410	$7,060	$7,940

13. Unit depreciation = $0.20; Year's depreciation = $516.80

15. Total cost: **$6,000**

Year	Depreciation	Accumulated depreciation	End-of-year book value
1	$4,000	$4,000	$2,000
2	$1,250	$5,250	$750
3	$0	$5,250	$750

17. Year 15: $6,736.45;
Year 16: $3,362.53

19. Depreciable cost: **$16,250**

Year	MACRS rate	Depreciation	Accumulated depreciation	End-of-year book value
1	20.00%	$28,250	$28,250	$113,000
2	32.00%	$45,200	$73,450	$67,800
3	19.20%	$27,120	$100,570	$40,680

PRACTICE TEST, P. 629

1. 28 **2.** $33,690 **3.** Annual depreciation = $760; Accumulated depreciation: year 1: $760; year 2: $1,520; year 3: $2,280; year 4: $3,040; year 5: $3,800. End-of-year book value: year 1: $3,740; year 2: $2,980; year 3: $2,220; year 4: $1,460; year 5: $700 **4.** $0.15264 **5.** 300

6. Total cost: **$7,500**

Year	Depreciation rate	Depreciation	Accumulated depreciation	End-of-year book value
1	$\frac{3}{6}$	$3,000	$3,000	$4,500
2	$\frac{2}{6}$	$2,000	$5,000	$2,500
3	$\frac{1}{6}$	$1,000	$6,000	$1,500

7. Total cost: **$2,780**

Year	Depreciation	Accumulated depreciation	End-of-year book value
1	$1,390.00	$1,390.00	$1,390.00
2	$695.00	$2,085.00	$695.00
3	$347.50	$2,432.50	$347.50
4	$47.50	$2,480.00	$300.00

8. Total cost: **$13,580**

Year	MACRS rate	Depreciation	Accumulated depreciation	End-of-year book value
1	33.33%	$4,526.21	$4,526.21	$9,053.79
2	44.45%	$6,036.31	$10,562.52	$3,017.48
3	14.81%	$2,011.20	$12,573.72	$1,006.28
4	7.41%	$1,006.28	$13,580.00	$0

9. $2,859.71 **10.** $2,232.21 **11.** $45,560 **12.** $4,193.90

SECTION EXERCISES

18-1, P. 647

1.

Date of purchase	Units purchased	Cost per unit	Total cost	Retail price per unit	Total retail value	Total cost of purchases = $66,805
Beginning inventory	42	$850	$35,700	$975	$40,950	
February 5	21	$1,760	$36,960	$2,115	$44,415	
February 19	17	$965	$16,405	$1,206	$20,502	
March 3	28	$480	$13,440	$600	$16,800	
Goods available for sale	108		$102,505		$122,667	
Units sold	74					
Ending inventory	34					

3. $64,895

5.

Cost per unit	Number of units on hand	Total cost
$12	43	$516
$9	11	$99
$11	7	$77
$15	21	$315
Ending inventory	82	$1,007

7. $949.12   **9.** $70,234.92   **11.** $997.12

13. 28 units @ $480 per unit; 6 units @ $965 per unit; Cost of ending inventory = $19,230

15.
June 2:   37 units @ $15 per unit
May 8:   15 units @ $11 per unit
April 12:   23 units @ $9 per unit
Beginning: 7 units @ $12 per unit
Total   82 items are in the ending inventory

17. 34 units @ $850 per unit   **19.** 82 units @ $12 per unit   **21.** $122,667   **23.** $66,028.95

25. 0.680   **27.** Estimated cost of goods sold = $80,808; Estimated ending inventory = $21,697   **29.** Specific identification method

18-2, P. 655

1. 4.04 times   **3.** 2.42 times

5.

Toys	$789.47
Appliances	$1,302.63
Children's clothing	$1,342.11
Books	$907.89
Furniture	$1,657.89

7.

China	$325.62
Silver	$740.62
Crystal	$243.36
Linens	$159.61
New gifts	$522.16
Antiques	$740.62

9.

Welding bay	$2,880.42
Paint shop	$2,674.68
Axles and steel storage	$1,069.87
Flooring lumber	$521.22
Office space	$685.81

EXERCISES SET A, P. 663

1. $8,112   **3.** $4,291   **5.** Cost of ending inventory = $3,558.94; Cost of goods sold = $4,553.06   **7.** Cost of goods sold = $3,804; Cost of ending inventory = $4,308   **9.** Turnover rate at cost = 0.5 times   **11.** $6,493.84   **13.** 5 times

15.

Hardware	$3,068.67
Plumbing	$2,300.00
Tools	$1,533.33
Supplies	$2,300.33

EXERCISES SET B, P. 665

1. $1,374   **3.** Cost of goods available for sale = $788 Average unit cost = $11.76   **5.** Cost of ending inventory = $246.96; Cost of goods sold = $541.04   **7.** Cost of ending inventory = $7,721; Cost of goods sold = $4,548   **9.** 4.6 times

11.

Nuts and bolts	$730.77
Electrical	$1,948.72
Paint	$1,120.51

PRACTICE TEST, P. 667

1. $1,237   **2.** $761   **3.** $476   **4.** $11.04   **5.** Cost of ending inventory = $761.76; Cost of goods sold = $475.24
6. Cost of ending inventory = $363   **7.** Cost of goods sold = $345; Cost of ending inventory = $892

8.

Cameras	$1,674.42
Toys	$1,953.49
Hardware	$1,883.72
Garden supplies	$1,172.09
Sporting goods	$1,325.58
Clothing	$3,990.70

9.

Furniture	$2,222.22
Computer supplies	$1,777.78
Consumable office supplies	$2,777.78
Leather goods	$1,333.33
Administrative services	$888.89

10. $7,893.04   **11.** $7,959.04   **12.** 4   **13.** 2.92

14. 2

15. Overhead expenses:
Purchasing = $132.06
Personnel = $468.02
Payroll = $493.02
Secretarial = $801.90
Total = $1,895

16.

A	$2,827.59
B	$1,413.79
C	$2,431.72
D	$1,526.90

SECTION EXERCISES

19-1, P. 678

1. $56.70   **3.** $282.36   **5.** The male pays a premium that is $29.25 higher.   **7.** Jenny pays $312.50 less than Chloe.   **9.** 11.46 years

19-2, P. 684

1. $351   **3.** $247   **5.** $825   **7.** $521.12   **9.** $148.32   **11.** $75,000   **13.** $316,000   **15.** $78,797.47

19-3, P. 690

1. $1,313   **3.** $2,182   **5.** $1,981   **7.** $1,192   **9.** $1,665   **11.** $169.17   **13.** Jamie's insurance company is responsible for paying up to $100,000 per person for personal injury. The maximum for all personal injury is $500,000. So, the company is responsible for paying $34,580 for Carolyn's medical care and $57,840 for Maria's medical care. Jamie will not need to pay for any medical care. The insurance company is responsible for paying $12,350 to repair Carolyn's car and $11,540 − $1,000 = $10,540 to repair Jamie's vehicle. Jamie is responsible for $250 deductible for his car repair.

EXERCISES SET A, P. 695

1. Base annual premium = $141; Computer premium = $175.75; Total annual insurance premium = $316.75   **3.** Base annual premium = $313; Total annual insurance premium = $313   **5.** $1,008   **7.** $1,256   **9.** $2,242   **11.** $896   **13.** $1,973   **15.** $2,112
17. Annual premium = $360; Monthly premium = $31.50; Quarterly premium = $93.60   **19.** $14.63   **21.** 14.79 years

EXERCISES SET B, P. 697

1. $386.70   **3.** $389.50   **5.** $411.75   **7.** $2,161   **9.** $1,206   **11.** $1,350   **13.** $938   **15.** $2,539
17. Annual premium = $538; Monthly premium = $47.08; Quarterly premium = $139.88   **19.** $4,072.50   **21.** 1.61 years
23. Cathy's insurance company will be responsible for paying up to $100,000 per person for personal injury. The maximum for all personal injury is $300,000. So, the company will be responsible for paying $83,000 for the first bicyclist's medical expenses and $100,000 for the other cyclist's medical expenses. Cathy will be responsible for paying the $67,000 balance for the medical care of the cyclists since it was over the coverage amount. The insurance company will be responsible for paying $895 and $1,215 to repair the two bicycles. The insurance company will be responsible for paying to Cathy $1,988 − $1,000 = $988 to repair Cathy's vehicle. Cathy is responsible for $1,000 deductible for her car repair in addition to the $67,000 balance in medical expenses.

PRACTICE TEST, P. 699

1. $4,650   **2.** $957   **3.** $888   **4.** $890   **5.** $373.50   **6.** $1,954   **7.** $746.35
8. The whole-life policy is $4,724 more than the 20-year level term policy.   **9.** $356.13   **10.** $76.44   **11.** $53,448.28   **12.** $1,245   **13.** 4.18 years
14. $260.25   **15.** $414   **16.** $359   **17.** $202.35   **18.** $350   **19.** Face value of policy = 0.8($315,500) = $252,400; Compensation = $252,400 The insurance company will not pay more than the face value of the policy. Hence, Tasville will need to pay for the damages in excess of $252,400.
20. Brandi's insurance company is responsible for paying up to $500,000 per person for personal injury. The maximum for all personal injury is $1,000,000 per incident. So, the company is responsible for paying $198,000 for Damion's medical expenses and $375,840 for Keisha's medical expenses. Brandi is not responsible for paying anything for Damion's or Keisha's medical care since each was less than the individual coverage and the total was less than the coverage per incident. The insurance company is responsible for paying $4,987 and $7,515 to repair the motorcycles and $2,875 − $1,000 = $1,875 to repair Brandi's vehicle. Brandi is responsible for paying $1,000 deductible for her vehicle repair.

CHAPTER 20

SECTION EXERCISES

20-1, P. 709

1. Sales tax = $30.36; Total sale = $622.72   **3.** Sales tax = $148.32; Total sale = $3,444.32   **5.** $11.38   **7.** Marked price = $655.21; Sales tax = $26.21   **9.** Marked price = $371.05; Sales tax = $24.12   **11.** $15.87 (rounded)   **13.** $20.52   **15.** $172.06
17. Marked price = $788.86; Sales tax = $61.14

20-2, P. 714

1. $4,537.90   **3.** $13,554.45   **5.** 8.12%   **7.** $26.76 per $1,000   **9.** $3.59 per $100   **11.** $52,500   **13.** $96,250   **15.** $3,982.50
17. $956.25   **19.** 2.7¢ per $1.00 assessed value   **21.** $31.26   **23.** $104,371,750

20-3, P. 724

1. $22,252   **3.** $121,379   **5.** $6,206   **7.** $7,456   **9.** $44,137.94   **11.** $12,091   **13.** $39,344   **15.** $2,649
17. Tax owed is *less* than tax paid so a refund is due. Amount of refund = $1,591   **19.** $38,652.76

EXERCISES SET A, P. 729

1. $14.25   **3.** $33.80   **5.** $36.25   **7.** $332.33   **9.** $13,750   **11.** $2,587,500   **13.** $250   **15.** $4,062.50   **17.** $527.25
19. $1,108.63 (nearest cent)   **21.** $0.072   **23.** $1,840   **25.** $1 tax rate = $0.04; $100 tax rate = $3.26; $1,000 tax rate = $32.54;
27. Reassess property   **29.** $28,374   **31.** $6,044   **33.** $4,996   **35.** $45,644.99

EXERCISES SET B, P. 731

1. $26.19 **3.** $134.95 **5.** $33.52 **7.** $51.35 **9.** $94,000 **11.** $53,750 **13.** $10,350 **15.** $684.13 **17.** $2,325.00 **19.** $0.034
21. $812.50 **23.** $1 tax rate = $0.04; $100 tax rate = $3.40; $1,000 tax rate = $33.99 **25.** Reassess property **27.** $30,955 **29.** $43,150
31. $6,006 **33.** $5,396 **35.** $36,321.50

PRACTICE TEST, P. 733

1. $0.76 (rounded) **2.** $1.14 (rounded) **3.** $22.28 (rounded) **4.** $0.19 (rounded) **5.** $10.34 **6.** $20.57 **7.** $198.44 **8.** $4.47
9. $17.61 (rounded) **10.** $7.39 (rounded) **11.** $50.00 (rounded) **12.** $5.05 (rounded) sales tax **13.** $89.20 **14.** $194,119.20
15. $13,328.05 (rounded) **16.** $1,071.77 (rounded) **17.** $2,966.40 **18.** $1,850.40 **19.** $3.02 (rounded up) **20.** $45,226.61 **21.** $5,131
22. $39,200

CHAPTER 21

SECTION EXERCISES

21-1, P. 749

Answers for 1, 5, 9

Miss Muffin's Bakery
Comparative Balance Sheet
December 31, 2014

	2014	Increase (decrease) Amount	Increase (decrease) Percent	Percent of total assets 2014
Assets				
Current assets				
Cash	$1,985	$223	12.7	22.8
Accounts receivable	4,219	434	11.5	48.4
Merchandise inventory	2,512	476	23.4	28.8
Total assets	$8,716	$1,133	14.9	100.0
Liabilities				
Current liabilities				
Accounts payable	$3,483	$(148)	(4.1)	40.0
Wages payable	1,696	275	19.4	19.5
Total liabilities	5,179	127	2.5	59.4
Owner's Equity				
Mildred Galloway, capital	3,537	1,006	39.7	40.6
Total liabilities and owner's equity	$8,716	$1,133	14.9	100.0

11. 59.4%

Answers for 3, 7

O'Dell's Nursery
Comparative Balance Sheet
December 31, 2014

	2014	Percent of total assets 2014
Assets		
Current assets		
Cash	$8,917	26.0
Accounts receivable	7,521	22.0
Merchandise inventory	17,826	52.0
Total assets	$34,264	100.0
Liabilities		
Current liabilities		
Accounts payable	$10,215	29.8
Wages payable	3,716	10.8
Total liabilities	13,931	40.7
Owner's Equity		
Janelle O'Dell, capital	20,333	59.3
Total liabilities and owner's equity	$34,264	100.0

21-2, P. 757

1.

Sitha Ros's Oriental Groceries
Income Statement
for the Years Ending June 30, 2013 and 2014

	2013	2014
Net sales	$97,384	$92,196
Cost of goods sold	82,157	72,894
Gross profit	15,227	19,302
Operating expenses	4,783	3,951
Net income	$10,444	$15,351

Answers for 3, 5, 7

Miss Muffin's Bakery
Vertical Analysis of Income Statement for the Months Ending
July 31, 2012, and July 31, 2013

	2013	Percent of net sales	2012	Percent of net sales	Increase (decrease) amount	Percent
Gross sales	$35,403	101.0	$32,596	100.9	$2,807	8.6
Returns and allowances	342	1.0	296	0.9	46	15.5
Net sales	35,061	100.0	32,300	100.0	2,761	8.5
Cost of beginning inventory	17,403	49.6	16,872	52.2	531	3.1
Cost of purchases	27,983	79.8	33,596	104.0	(5,613)	(16.7)
Cost of ending inventory	22,583	64.4	21,843	67.6	740	3.4
Cost of goods sold	22,803	65.0	28,625	88.6	(5,822)	(20.3)
Gross profit	12,258	35.0	3,675	11.4	8,583	233.6
Total operating expenses	3,053	8.7	1,894	5.9	1,159	61.2
Net income	$ 9,205	26.3	$ 1,781	5.5	$7,424	416.8

1. 1.44 to 1   **3.** 0.542 to 1   **5.** George's current ratio = 4 or 4 to 1; José's current ratio = 1.03 or 1.03 to 1   **7.** 71.0%   **9.** $1.28; $5.77

EXERCISES SET A, P. 775

1. Total current assets = $11,271; Total assets = $23,458; Total current liabilities = $3,098; Total liabilities and owner's equity = $23,458

3.

Marten's Family Store Income Statement For Year Ending December 31, 2013		Percent of net sales
Revenue:		
Gross sales	$238,923	106.1
Sales returns and allowances	13,815	6.1
Net sales	225,108	100.0
Cost of goods sold:		
Beginning inventory, January 1, 2013	25,814	11.5
Purchases	109,838	48.8
Ending inventory, December 31, 2013	23,423	10.4
Cost of goods sold	112,229	49.9
Gross profit from sales	112,879	50.1
Operating expenses:		
Salary	42,523	18.9
Rent	8,640	3.8
Utilities	1,484	0.7
Insurance	2,842	1.3
Fees	860	0.4
Depreciation	1,920	0.9
Miscellaneous	3,420	1.5
Total operating expenses	61,689	27.4
Net income	$51,190	22.7

5. 1.57 to 1   **7.** 0.87 to 1

9. Operating ratio = 0.9 or 90%; Gross profit margin = 0.25 or 25%

11. 20.1%

13. Earnings per share = $1.38; book value per share = $11.16

EXERCISES SET B, P. 779

1. Total current assets = $11,481;
Total assets = $22,856;
Total current liabilities = $3,570;
Total liabilities and owner's equity = $22,856

3.

Serpa's Gifts Income Statement For Year Ending December 31, 2012		Percent of net sales
Revenue:		
Gross sales	$148,645	106.4
Sales returns and allowances	8,892	6.4
Net sales	139,753	100.0
Cost of goods sold:		
Beginning inventory, January 1, 2012	12,100	8.7
Purchases	47,800	34.2
Ending inventory, December 31, 2012	11,950	8.6
Cost of goods sold	47,950	34.3
Gross profit from sales	91,803	65.7
Operating expenses:		
Salary	25,500	18.2
Rent	4,500	3.2
Utilities	1,445	1.0
Insurance	2,100	1.5
Fees	225	0.2
Depreciation	1,240	0.9
Miscellaneous	750	0.5
Total operating expenses	35,760	25.6
Net income	$56,043	40.1

5. 0.83 to 1   **7.** 1.74 to 1   **9.** 0.8312766, or 83.1%   **11.** Earnings per share = $1.79; book value per share = $5.17

1.

O'Toole's Hardware Store
Comparative Balance Sheet
December 31, 2013 and 2014

	2014	2013	Increase (decrease) Amount	Increase (decrease) Percent
Assets				
Current assets				
Cash	$7,318	$5,283	$2,035	38.5
Accounts receivable	3,147	3,008	139	4.6
Merchandise inventory	63,594	60,187	3,407	5.7
Total current assets	74,059	68,478	5,581	8.2
Plant and equipment				
Building	36,561	37,531	(970)	(2.6)
Equipment	8,256	4,386	3,870	88.2
Total plant and equipment	44,817	41,917	2,900	6.9
Total assets	$118,876	$110,395	$8,481	7.7
Liabilities				
Current liabilities				
Accounts payable	$5,174	$4,563	$611	13.4
Wages payable	780	624	156	25.0
Total current liabilities	5,954	5,187	767	14.8
Long-term liabilities				
Mortgage note payable	34,917	36,510	(1,593)	(4.4)
Total long-term liabilities	34,917	36,510	(1,593)	(4.4)
Total liabilities	40,871	41,697	(826)	(2.0)
Owner's equity				
James O'Toole, capital	78,005	68,698	9,307	13.5
Total liabilities and owner's equity	$118,876	$110,395	$8,481	7.7

2. 12.44 to 1   **3.** 1.76 to 1   **4.** 13.20 to 1   **5.** 1.60 to 1

6.

Mile Wide Organic Woolens, Inc.
Comparative Income Statement
For Years Ending December 31, 2012 and 2013

	2013	2012	Increase (decrease) Amount	Increase (decrease) Percent
Revenue:				
Gross sales	$219,827	$205,852	$13,975	6.8
Sales returns and allowances	8,512	7,983	529	6.6
Net sales	211,315	197,869	13,446	6.8
Cost of goods sold:				
Beginning inventory, January 1	42,816	40,512	2,304	5.7
Purchases	97,523	94,812	2,711	2.9
Ending inventory, December 31	43,182	42,521	661	1.6
Cost of goods sold	97,157	92,803	4,354	4.7
Gross profit from sales	114,158	105,066	9,092	8.7
Operating expenses:				
Salary	28,940	27,000	1,940	7.2
Insurance	800	750	50	6.7
Utilities	1,700	1,580	120	7.6
Rent	3,600	3,000	600	20.0
Depreciation	2,000	2,400	(400)	(16.7)
Total operating expenses	37,040	34,730	2,310	6.7
Net income	$ 77,118	$ 70,336	$6,782	9.6

7. Operating ratio for 2012 = 0.645 or 64.5%; Operating ratio for 2013 = 0.635 or 63.5%

8. Gross profit margin ratio for 2012 = 0.531 or 53.1%; Gross profit margin ratio for 2013 = 0.540 or 54.0%

9. 1.56   **10.** 1.53   **11.** Earnings per share = $0.55; book value per share = $4.09   **12.** Price-earnings ratio = 17.87; price-to-book ratio = 2.40

Glossary/Index

Current yield the ratio of the annual dividend per share of stock to the closing price per share, 545

Data set a collection of values or measurements that have a common characteristic, 218

Dating terms 274

Debit a transaction that decreases an account balance, 112

Debit card a card that can be used like a credit card but the amount of debit (purchase or withdrawal) is deducted immediately from the checking account, 113

Debit memo a notification of an error that decreases the checking account balance, 112

Debt-to-income or back-end ratio fixed monthly expenses divided by the gross monthly income, 585

Decimal convert to fraction, 92

Decimal part the digits to the right of the decimal point, 82

Decimal point the notation that separates the whole-number part of a number from the decimal part, 82

Decimal system a place-value number system based on 10, 82

Decimals adding and subtracting, 85
dividing, 88
multiplying, 86
reading and writing, 82
reading as money amounts, 83
rounding, 83

Declining-balance method a depreciation method that provides for large depreciation in the early years of the life of an asset, 611

Deductible the dollar amount the insured pays for each automobile insurance claim. The insurance company pays the remainder of the cost of each covered loss up to the limits of the policy, 686

Deductions certain expenses the taxpayer is allowed to subtract from income to reduce the amount of taxable income, 715

Defined benefit plan a plan that guarantees a certain payout at retirement, according to a fixed formula that usually depends on the member's salary and the number of years' membership in the plan, 506

Defined contribution plan a plan that provides a payout at retirement that is dependent on the amount of money contributed and the performance of the investment vehicles utilized, 506

Denominator the number of a fraction that shows how many parts one whole quantity is divided into. It is also the divisor of the indicated division, 44

Deposit a transaction that increases a checking account balance; this transaction is also called a credit, 110
of withholding tax, 364–365
payroll, 365

Deposit slip a banking form for recording the details of a deposit, 110

Deposits in transit *See also* Outstanding deposits, 121–122

Depreciable value the cost of an asset minus the salvage value, 604

Depreciation the amount an asset decreases in value from its original cost, 604

modified accelerated cost-recovery system, 616
straight-line method of, 604
sum-of-the-years'-digits method of, 608
units-of-production method of, 604

Depreciation schedule a table showing the year's depreciation, the accumulated depreciation, and the end-of-year book value, 605

Deviation from the mean the difference between a value of a data set and the mean, 239

Difference the answer or the result of subtraction, 11

Differential piece rate (escalating piece rate) piecework rate that increases as more items are produced, 346

Digit one of the ten symbols used in the decimal-number system (0, 1, 2, 3, 4, 5, 6, 7, 8, 9), 4

Direct proportion 163

Discount an amount of money that is deducted from an original price, 264

Discount bond a bond that sells for less than the face value, 549

Discount period the amount of time that the third party owns the third-party discounted note, 405

Discount rate a percent of the list price, 264

Discounted note a promissory note for which the interest or fee is discounted or subtracted at the time the loan is made, 405

Diversification dividing your assets on a percentage basis among different broad categories of investments or asset classes, 554

Divide by integers, 22
by place-value numbers, 88
decimals, 88
whole numbers, 20

Dividend the number being divided or the total quantity, 19; a portion of the profit of a company that is periodically distributed to the stockholders of a company, 542

Dividends in arrears dividends that were not paid in a previous year and must be paid to cumulative preferred stockholders before dividends can be distributed to other stockholders, 546

Dividing fractions, 61
mixed numbers, 61

Divisor the number divided by, 19

Double-declining rate a declining-balance depreciation rate that is twice the straight-line depreciation rate, 611

Double-declining-balance method (200%-declining-balance depreciation) a method of declining-balance depreciation in which the rate of depreciation is twice the straight-line depreciation rate, 611

Down payment a partial payment that is paid at the time of the purchase, 428

Earnings per share the amount of income earned during a period per share of common stock

Effective interest rate the simple interest rate that is equivalent to a compound rate, 469

Effective interest rate for a simple discount note the actual interest rate based on the proceeds of the loan, 404

Efficiency ratio a financial ratio that measures a business's ability to effectively use its assets to generate sales, 763

Electronic deposit a deposit that is made by an electronic transfer of funds, 112

Electronic filing a paperless way to file income tax with the IRS. The tax forms are submitted electronically to the IRS, 723

Electronic funds transfer (EFT) a transaction that transfers funds electronically, 112

Ending inventory at cost the cost of the ending inventory, 643

Ending inventory at retail the retail value of the ending inventory, 643

End-of-month (EOM) terms a discount is applied if the bill is paid within the specified days after the end of the month. An exception occurs when an invoice is dated on or after the 26th of a month, 277

End-of-year book value total cost minus depreciation for the first year. Thereafter, it is the previous year's end-of-year book value minus the current year's depreciation, 605

Endorsement a signature, stamp, or electronic imprint on the back of a check that authorizes payment in cash or directs payment to a third party or account, 117

Equation a mathematical statement in which two quantities are equal, 150
solving containing parentheses, 155
solving using addition or subtraction, 151
solving using multiplication or division, 150
solving with multiple unknowns, 154
using to solve problems, 159

Equity the difference between the expected selling price and the balance owed on property, 576

Equity line of credit a revolving, open-end account that is secured by real property, 576

Equivalent fractions fractions that indicate the same portion of the whole amount, 47

Escalating piece rate *See* Differential piece rate, 346

Escrow an account for holding the part of a monthly payment that is to be used to pay taxes and insurance. The amount accumulates and the lender pays the taxes and insurance from this account as they are due, 580

Estimate to find a reasonable approximate answer for a calculation, 11

Estimated life or useful life the number of years an asset is expected to be usable, 604

Evaluate a formula a process to substitute known values for appropriate letters of the formula and perform the indicated operations to find the unknown value, 167

Exact decimal equivalent a decimal equivalent that is not rounded, 94

Exact interest rate assumes 365 days per year, 398

Exact time time that is based on counting the exact number of days in a time period, 395

Excise tax a tax or duty levied on the sale or importation of goods for the purpose of raising revenue or discouraging a particular behavior, 706

Exemption (withholding allowance) 351

Exemption or allowance an amount of money that a taxpayer is allowed to subtract from the adjusted gross income for himself or herself, a spouse, and each dependent, 715

Extended term insurance 677

Face value the amount borrowed, 402

Face value the amount borrowed; the maximum amount of insurance provided by a policy, 402, 622, 674

Face value (par value) the value of one share of stock at the time the company first issued stock for sale, 542; the original value of a bond, usually $1,000, 549

Factor each number involved in multiplication, 16

Fair Labor Standards Act 345

Federal Housing Administration (FHA) a governmental agency within the U.S. Department of Housing and Urban Development (HUD) that insures residential mortgage loans. To receive an FHA loan, specific construction standards must be met and the lender must be approved, 576

Federal Insurance Contribution Act 360

Federal Reserve Bank 364

Federal tax withholding the amount required to be withheld from a person's pay and paid to the federal government, 351, 365

Federal unemployment (FUTA) tax a federal tax required of most employers. The tax provides for payment of unemployment compensation to certain workers who have lost their jobs, 366

FIFO (first-in, first-out) inventory method an inventory valuation method in which items sold are assumed to be the oldest items in inventory and the most recently purchased goods are those remaining in the ending inventory, 640

Filing status category of taxpayer; single, married filing jointly, married filing separately, or head of household, 715

Finance charges (carrying charges) the interest and any fee associated with an installment loan, 428

Financial ratio an analysis of financial data to compare a business's performance with past performance or with other similar businesses, 760
  acid-test ratio, 761
  asset turnover ratio, 763
  balance sheets, 760
  current ratio, 760
  financial statements, 760
  gross profit margin ratio, 762
  income statement, 762
  operating ratio, 762
  total debt to total assets ratio, 763

First mortgage the primary mortgage on a property, 576

Fixed-rate mortgage the interest rate for the mortgage remains the same for the entire loan, 576

Fixed-time endowment insurance a policy that is a combination insurance and savings plan that is paid for a fixed period of time, 677

Fixed-time payment insurance a policy with a specified face value for the insured's entire life with payment made for a fixed period of time, 676

FOB destination free on board at the destination point. The seller pays the shipping when the merchandise is shipped, 280

FOB shipping point free on board at the shipping point. The buyer pays the shipping when the shipment is received, 280

Formula a procedure that has been used so frequently to solve certain types of problems that it has become the accepted means of solving a problem, 167; a relationship among quantities expressed in words or numbers and letters, 191

Formula evaluate, 167

Fraction a part of a whole amount. It is also a notation for showing division, 44
  write as decimal, 93

Fraction line the line that separates the numerator and denominator. It is also the division symbol, 44

Fractions decimal, 82
  dividing, 62
  equivalent, 47
  identifying types of, 44
  multiplying, 60
  reducing, 47
  refund, 435

Freight collect the buyer pays the shipping when the shipment is received, 280

Freight paid the seller pays the shipping when the merchandise is shipped, 280
  freight payment terms, 280

Front-end load mutual fund a mutual fund for which the sales charge is included in the selling price of the shares, 555

Front-end ratio *See* housing ratio, 585

Fund family the mutual fund company that offers more than one type of fund, 555

Future value table 462–463

Future value, maturity value, compound amount the accumulated principal and interest after one or more interest periods, 460

Generally accepted accounting principles (GAAP) accounting principles that are accepted by industry standards and the IRS for reporting purposes and tax determination, 636

Good faith estimate an estimate of the mortgage closing costs that lenders are required to provide to the buyer in writing prior to the loan closing date, 580

Graduated payments mortgage payments at the beginning of the loan are smaller and they increase during the loan, 576

Graph a symbolic or pictorial display of numerical information, 218

Greatest common divisor (GCD) the greatest number by which both parts of a fraction can be evenly divided, 48

Gross earnings (gross pay) the amount earned before deductions, 344
  based on commission, 348
  based on hourly wage, 345
  based on piecework wage, 347
  based on salary, 344

Gross income all income received in the form of money, goods, property, and services that is not exempt from tax, 715

Gross margin Gross profit, 300
  See Gross profit, 644

Gross profit (margin) inventory method a method for estimating the value of inventory that is based on a constant gross profit (margin) rate and net sales, 644

Gross profit margin ratio the ratio of the gross profit from sales to the net sales, 762

Gross profit or gross margin net sales minus the cost of goods sold, 752; *See also* Markup, 300

Grouped frequency distribution a compilation of class intervals, tallies, and class frequencies of a data set, 232

Guess and check 21

Higher terms a fraction written in an equivalent value, determined by multiplying the numerator and denominator by the same number; the process is used in the addition and subtraction of fractions, 48

Histogram a special type of bar graph that represents the data from a frequency distribution, 219

Homeowners insurance provides property coverage for both the covered dwelling and additional structures, and liability protection for covered policyholder as well as certain additional benefits, 681

Horizontal analysis of an income statement comparison of like entries for two years. The amount of increase or decrease and the percent of increase or decrease are determined, 756

Horizontal analysis of balance sheet a balance sheet analysis that compares the same item for two different years, 747

Horizontal bar graph 219

Hourly rate (hourly wage) the amount of pay per hour worked based on a standard 40-hour work week, 345

Hourly wage *See* Hourly rate, 345

Housing or front-end ratio monthly housing expenses (PITI) divided by the gross monthly income, 585

Improper fraction a fraction with a value that is equal to or greater than 1. The numerator is the same as or greater than the denominator, 44

Income shortfall the difference in the total living expenses of a family and the amount of income a family would have after the death of the insured. This shortfall can be used to project the amount of insurance needed by the family, 674

Income statement a financial statement of the net income of a business over a period of time, 752
  horizontal analysis of, 756
  preparing, 752
  vertical analysis of, 754

Income tax a tax collected by the federal government, many states, and some cities that is based on a person's income, 715
  local, state or federal tax paid on one's income, 351

Income tax tables tax tables found in the IRS 1040 instructions publication for finding the amount of tax liability, 717

Index numbers numbers that represent percent of change for several successive operating time periods (usually years) while keeping one selected year (base year) to represent the base or 100%, 765

Installment loan a loan that is repaid in regular payments, 428

Installment payment the amount that is paid (including interest) in regular payments, 428

Installment price the total amount paid for a purchase, including all payments, the finance charges, and the down payment, 428

Insurance a form of protection against unexpected financial loss, 674
  homeowners, 681
  life, 674
  motor vehicle, 686
  Policy premium, 674
  renters, 680

Insured (policyholder) the individual, organization, or business that carries the insurance or financial protection against loss, 674

Insurer (underwriter) the insurance company that assures payment for a specific loss according to contract provisions, 674

Integers the set of numbers that includes the positive whole numbers, the negative whole numbers, and zero, 8
  add and subtract, 14
  divide by, 22
  divide, 22
  multiply a negative and a positive integer, 18
  multiply two negative or two positive integers, 19
  reading and rounding, 8

Interest an amount paid or earned for the use of money, 388

Interest period the amount of time after which interest is calculated and added to the principal, 460

Internal Revenue Code 360

Interpret financial ratios, 763

Inventory merchandise available for sale or goods available for the production of products, 636
  comparing methods for determining, 645
  first-in, first-out (FIFO) method, 640
  gross profit inventory method, 644
  last-in, first-out (LIFO) method, 641
  retail inventory method, 643
  specific identification method, 637
  turnover and overhead, 650
  weighted-average inventory, 638

Inventory turnover the frequency with which the inventory is sold and replaced, 650

Inventory turnover ratio another term for the inventory turnover rate, 650

Investment grade bond a bond with a high probability of being paid with few speculative risks, 549

Investment risk the potential for fluctuation in the value of an investment which could result in total loss or a decrease in value, 553

IRS Form 941 Employer's Quarterly Federal Tax Return, 365

Isolate unknown or variable perform systematic operations to both sides of the equation so that the unknown or variable is alone on one side of the equation. Its value is given on the other side of the equation, 150

Isolate variable to solve a formula for a designated variable, 168

Issuer a company, state, or municipality that issues bonds to raise money, 549

Itemized deductions a listing of deductions that can be used by certain taxpayers to reduce taxable income. Normally, taxpayers use itemized deductions when the total of their itemized deductions is greater than the standard deduction, 715

Junk bonds high-risk bonds that are usually from companies in bankruptcy or in financial difficulty, 549

Known or (given values) the known amounts or numbers in an equation, 150m 152

Knuckle method 274

Land value of the grounds or land owned by the business, 740

Lapse the loss of insurance coverage due to nonpayment of premiums, 677

Leading earnings a company's projected earnings-per-share for the upcoming 12-month period, 545

Leading P/E ratio a company's P/E ratio calculated using the company's leading earnings per share as the net income per share, 545

Least common denominator (LCD) the smallest number that can be divided evenly by each original denominator, 52

Level term life insurance life insurance, 676

Leverage ratio a financial ratio that examines a business's indebtedness, 763

Liabilities amounts that the business owes, 740

Liability insurance protection for the owner of a vehicle if an accident causes personal injury or damage to someone else's property and is the fault of the driver of the insured vehicle, 686

Liability limits the maximum amount that an insurance company will pay for a single vehicle accident based on coverage selected by the insured, 687

Life insurance an insurance policy that pays a specified amount to the beneficiary of the policy upon the death of the insured, 674

LIFO (last-in, first-out) inventory method an inventory valuation method in which the first items sold are assumed to be from the most recent purchases. The goods remaining in the ending inventory are assumed to be the earliest purchased, 641

Line graph line segments that connect points on a graph to show the rising and falling trends of a data set, 221

Line-of-credit accounts a type of open-end loan, 439

Liquidation or payout phase of an annuity the time when the annuitant or beneficiary is receiving money from the fund, 498

Liquidity 554

Liquidity ratio a financial ratio that shows how well a business can be expected to meet its short-term financial obligations, 760

List price suggested price at which merchandise is sold to consumers, 264

Loan-to-value ratio the amount mortgaged divided by the appraised value of the property, 585

Long-term liabilities liabilities that are paid over a long period of time, 740

Lower-of-cost-or-market (LCM) rule compares market value with the cost of each item on hand and uses the lower amount as the inventory value of the item, 642

Lowest terms the form of a fraction when its numerator and denominator cannot be evenly divided by any whole number except 1, 47

Maker the one who is authorizing the payment of the check; the person or business that borrows the money, 104, 112, 402

Margin markup or gross profit, 300
  See gross profit, 644

Markdown amount the original selling price is reduced, 300, 318

Marked price the purchase price before sales tax is added, 707

Market value the expected selling price of a property, 576, 710

Markup (gross profit or gross margin) the difference between the selling price and the cost, 300
  comparing markup based on cost with markup based on selling price, 314
  finding final selling price for a series of markups, 321
  finding the selling price to achieve a desired profit, 323
  using cost as a base in markup applications, 302
  using selling price as a base in markup applications, 308–310

Mathematical operations calculations with numbers. The four operations that are often called basic operations are addition, subtraction, multiplication, and division, 4

Maturity date the date on which the loan is due to be repaid, 402; the date at which the face value of a bond is paid to the bondholder, 549

Maturity value the total amount of money due at the end of a loan period—the amount of the loan and the interest, 389

Mean the arithmetic average of a set of data or the sum of the values divided by the number of values, 227

Mean of grouped data 234

Measures of central tendency statistical measurements such as the mean, median, or mode that indicate how data group toward the center, 230

Measures of variation or dispersion statistical measurements such as the range and standard deviation that indicate how data are dispersed or spread, 238

Median the middle value of a data set when the values are arranged in order of size, 228

Medical expenses provides for payment of 100% of any medical bills up to the coverage limit resulting from a collision for the driver and each passenger in the insured's vehicle, 687

Medicare tax a federal tax used to provide health-care benefits to retired and disabled workers, 360

Merchandise inventory a current asset that is the value of merchandise on hand, 740

Mill one-thousandth of a dollar, 710

Minuend the beginning amount or the number that a second number is subtracted from, 11

Mixed number an amount that is a combination of a whole number and a fraction, 45
  adding, 53
  dividing, 62
  estimate sum, 53
  multiplying, 59, 60
  subtracting, 54
Mixed percents percents with mixed numbers or mixed decimals, 186
Mode the value or values that occur most frequently in a data set, 229
Model class automobile insurance, 687
Modified accelerated cost-recovery system (MACRS) a modified depreciation method implemented by the IRS for property placed in service after 1986, 616
Monthly once a month or 12 times a year, 344
Monthly mortgage payment the amount of the equal monthly payment that includes interest and principal, 576
Mortgage a loan in which real property is used to secure the debt, 576
  monthly mortgage payment and total interest, 576
  See also individual types, 576
Mortgage closing costs fees charged for services that must be performed to process and close a home mortgage loan, 580
Mortgage payable a long-term liability for the building and land the business owns, 740
Motor vehicle insurance liability, comprehensive, and collision insurance for a motor vehicle, 686
Multiplicand the number being multiplied, 16
Multiplier the number multiplied by, 16
Multiply a negative and a positive integer, 18
  decimals, 86
  numbers that end in zero, 18
  two negative or two positive integers, 19
Multiplying fractions, 59
  mixed numbers, 60
Municipal bonds bonds issued by local and state governments, 549
Mutual fund a collection of stocks, bonds, and other securities that is managed by a mutual fund company, 554
Negative number a number that is less than zero, 8
Negative sign (−) a symbol that is written before a number to show that it is a negative number, 8
Net amount the amount you owe if a cash discount is applied, 275
  calculating using ordinary dating terms, 275
Net asset value the value of one share of a mutual fund, 554
Net decimal equivalent the decimal equivalent of the net price rate for a series of trade discounts, 269
Net earnings (net pay or take-home pay) the amount of your paycheck, 344
Net income or net profit gross profit or gross margin minus the operating expenses, 752
Net pay *See also* Net earnings, 344
Net price the price the wholesaler or retailer pays, or the list price minus the trade discount, 264
  calculating using receipt-of-goods terms, 278
  net decimal equivalent and, 268

single discount equivalent and, 268
  trade discount series and, 268
Net price rate the complement of the trade discount rate, 266
Net profit difference between markup (gross profit or gross margin) and operating expenses and overhead, 300, 752
Net sales total sales minus sales returns or allowances, 752
Net worth *See* Owner's equity, 741
New amount the ending amount after an amount has changed (increased or decreased), 197–198
No load mutual fund a mutual fund that does not charge a sales charge for buying and selling its shares, 555
No-fault insurance protection for the owner of a vehicle for damage to the insured vehicle when the amount of damage is within the no-fault limits imposed by state law, 686
Nonforfeiture options the options that are available to a policyholder when payments are discontinued, 677
Nonsufficient funds (NSF) fee a fee charged to the account holder when a check is written for which there are not sufficient funds, 121
Nonterminating or repeating decimal a quotient that never comes out evenly. The digits will eventually start to repeat, 94
Normal distribution a characteristic of many data sets that shows that data graphs into a bell-shaped curve around the mean, 240
Note payable promissory notes that are owed, 740
Notes receivable a current asset that is a promissory note owed to the business, 740
Numerator the number of a fraction that shows how many parts are considered. It is also the dividend of the indicated division, 44
Office furniture and equipment value of office furniture and equipment such as computers, printers, and copiers owned by the business, 740
Online banking services a variety of services and transaction options that can be made through Internet banking, 113
Open-end credit a type of installment loan in which there is no fixed amount borrowed or fixed number of payments. Payments are made until the loan is paid off, 428
  average daily balance method, 439
Operating expenses overhead or cost incurred in operating a business, 752
Operating ratio the cost of goods sold plus the operating expenses divided by net sales, 762
Opposites a positive and negative number that represent the same distance from 0 but in opposite directions, 239
Order of Operations the specific order in which calculations must be performed to evaluate a series of calculations, 153
Ordinary annuity an annuity for which payments are made at the end of each period, 498
  future value table, 500–501

Ordinary interest rate a rate per day that assumes 360 days per year, 398
Ordinary life insurance *See* Whole-life insurance, 674
Outlier a data point that is outside the overall pattern of the distribution of the data, 239
Outstanding balance the invoice amount minus the amount credited, 279
Outstanding checks checks and debits that have been written and given to the payee but have not been processed at the bank, 121
Outstanding deposits deposits and credits that have been made but have not yet been posted to the maker's account, 121
Overhead depreciation and expenses required for the operation of a business, such as salaries, rent or mortgages, utilities, office supplies, taxes, insurance, and maintenance of equipment, 652
  based on floor space, 654
  based on sales, 652
Overtime pay earnings based on overtime rate of pay, 345
Overtime rate rate of pay for hours worked that are more than 40 hours in a week, 345
Owner's equity or stockholder's equity the difference between the company's assets and the liabilities, 741
Paid-up insurance insurance that continues after premiums are no longer paid, 677
Par value *See* face value of bond, 549
  See face value, 542, 674
Partial cash discount a cash discount applied only to the amount of the partial payment, 279
Partial dividend the part of the dividend that is being considered at a given step of the process, 20
Partial payment a payment that does not equal the full amount of the invoice less any cash discount, 279
Partial product the product of one digit of the multiplier and the entire multiplicand, 16
Partial quotient the quotient of the partial dividend and the divisor, 20
Participating preferred stock a type of preferred stock that allows stockholders to receive additional dividends if the company decides to do so, 546
Payee the one to whom the amount of money written on a check is paid; the person or business loaning the money, 104, 112, 402
Payor the bank or institution that pays the amount of the check to the payee, 112
Payout phase of an annuity *See also* liquidation phase of an annuity, 498
Payroll employer's payroll taxes, 364–365
Payroll gross pay, 345
Pension an arrangement to provide people with an income when they are no longer earning a regular income from employment, typically provided by an employer, 506
Percent a standardized way of expressing quantities in relation to a standard unit of 100 (hundredth, per 100, out of 100, over 100), 186
  of increase or decrease, 200
  mixed, 186–188
  writing as a number, 188
  writing numbers as, 187

Percent of change the percent by which a beginning amount has changed (increased or decreased) 198, 200

Percentage another term for portion, 191 formula, 192

Percentage method income the result of subtracting the appropriate withholding allowances when using the percentage method of withholding, 357 rates and the percentage method, 357

Percentage method of withholding an alternative method to the tax tables for calculating employees' withholding taxes, 357

Period a group of three place values in the decimal-number system, 4

Period interest rate the rate for calculating interest for one interest period—the annual interest rate divided by the number of interest periods per year, 460

Periodic or physical inventory a physical count of goods or merchandise made at a specific time, 636

Perishable an item for sale that has a relatively short time during which the quality of the item is acceptable for sale, 318

Perpetual inventory an inventory process that adjusts the inventory count after each sale or purchase of goods, 636

Personal identification number (PIN) a private code that is used to authorize a transaction on a debit card or ATM card, 113

Piecework rate amount of pay for each acceptable item produced, 346

PITI the adjusted monthly payment that includes the principal, interest, taxes, and insurance, 580

Place-value system a number system that determines the value of a digit by its position in a number, 4

Plant and equipment assets used in transacting business, 740

Point-of-sale transaction electronic transfer of funds when a sale is made, 112

Points a one-time payment to the lender made at closing that is a percentage of the total loan, 580

Policy the contract between the insurer and the insured, 674

Policyholder See Insured, 674

Portfolio a collection of different types of investments, normally owned by an individual, 554

Portion a part of the base, 191

Preferred stock a type of non-voting stock that provides for a specific dividend that is paid before any dividends are paid to common stock holders and which takes precedence over common stock in the event of a company liquidation, 542

Premium the amount paid by the insured for the protection provided by the policy, 674

Premium bond a bond that sells for more than the face value, 549

Prepay and add the seller pays the shipping when the merchandise is shipped, but the shipping costs are added to the invoice for the buyer to pay, 280

Present value based on annual compounding for one year, 476; based on future value using a $1.00 present value table, 476; the amount that must be invested now and

compounded at a specified rate and time to reach a specified value, 476

Present value of an annuity the amount needed in a fund so that the fund can pay out a specified regular payment for a specified amount of time, 516–517

Price-earnings (P/E) ratio the ratio of the closing price of a share of stock to the annual earnings per share, 545

Price-to-book ratio measures how much someone buying the company stock is paying for each dollar's worth of equity.

Price-to-earnings (P/E) ratio the amount that someone buying the company stock is paying for each dollar of annual earnings

Prime interest rate (prime), reference rate, or base lending rate the lowest rate of interest charged by banks for short-term loans to their most creditworthy customers, 389

Prime number a number greater than 1 that can be divided evenly only by itself and 1, 52, 53

Principal the amount of money borrowed or invested, 388

Privately held corporation a company that is privately owned and does not meet the strict Security Exchange Commission filing required of publicly held corporations. Private corporations may issue stock and the owners are shareholders, 542

Problem solving five-step strategy, 12

Problem solving guess and check, 21 using equations, 159 with decimals, 87 with fractions, 60 with percents, 192 with whole numbers, 12

Proceeds the face value of the loan minus the bank discount, 402

Product the answer or result of multiplication, 16

Profitability ratio a ratio comparing profits and sales, 762

Promissory note a legal document promising to repay a loan, 402 simple discount notes, 402 third-party discount notes, 402, 405

Proper fraction a fraction with a value that is less than 1. The numerator is smaller than the denominator, 44

Property damage damage to the property of others in an accident, 687

Property tax tax collected by county, municipality, or local governments from property owners. The tax is based on the type of property and the value of the property, 710

Property tax rate the rate of tax that is paid for owning property, 710

Proportion two fractions or ratios that are equal, 156

Proprietorship See Owner's equity, 741

Prospectus for mutual funds, it is the official document that describes the fund's investment objectives, policies, services and fees; you should read it carefully before you invest, 554

Protractor a measuring device that measures angles, 223

Publicly held corporation a company that has issued and sells shares of stock or

securities through an initial public offering. These shares are traded through at least one stock exchange, 542

Publicly traded a company's stock is said to be publicly traded if the company has issued securities through an initial public offering and these securities are traded on at least one stock exchange or over-the counter market, 542

Qualifying ratio a ratio that lenders use to determine an applicant's capacity to repay a loan, 585

Quick current assets assets that can be readily exchanged for cash, such as marketable securities, accounts receivable, or notes receivable, 761

Quick ratio See Acid-test ratio, 761

Quota a minimum amount of sales that is required before a commission is applicable, 348

Quotient the answer or result of division, 19 convert decimal portion to a remainder, 22

Range the difference between the highest and lowest values in a data set, 238

Rate the relationship between the base and the percentage expressed as a percent, 186, 191; the percent of the principal paid as interest per time period, 388

Ratio the comparison of two numbers through division. Ratios are most often written as fractions, 156

Ratios to net sales ratios to net sales: ratios that make comparisons to new sales, 762

Reading decimals, 83

Real estate or real property land plus any permanent improvements to the land, 576

Recallable bonds bonds that can be repurchased by the company before the maturity date, 549

Receipt-of-goods (ROG) terms a discount applied if the bill is paid within the specified days of the receipt of the goods, 278

Reciprocals two numbers are reciprocals if their product is 1. 4/5 and 5/4 are reciprocals, 62

Reconcile bank records 121

Recovery period the length of time over which an item may be depreciated, 616

Reduce fraction 47

Reference rate 389

Refund fraction the fractional part of the total interest that is refunded when a loan is paid early using the rule of 78, 435

Registered bonds bonds for which investors receive interest automatically by being listed with the company, 549

Regrouping in subtracting 55

Regular pay earnings based on an hourly rate of pay, 345

Relative frequency distribution the percent that each class interval of a frequency distribution relates to the whole, 232

Remainder of quotient a number that is smaller than the divisor that remains after the division is complete, 19

Renters insurance provides both property and liability protection for covered policyholder as well as certain additional benefits, 680

Repeating decimal See Nonterminating decimal, 94

Residual value 604

Restricted endorsement a type of endorsement that reassigns the check to a different payee or directs the check to be deposited to a specified account, 117

Retail inventory method a method for estimating the value of inventory that is based on the cost ratio of the cost of goods available for sale and the retail value of goods available for sale, 643

Retail price 264

Retail price (selling price) price at which a business sells merchandise, 300

Return on investment (ROI) a performance measure used to evaluate the efficiency of an instrument, expressed as a percentage or a ratio, 557

Returned check a deposited check that was returned because the maker's account did not have sufficient funds, 121

Returned check fee a fee the bank charges the depositor for returned checks, 121

Roth IRA an IRA where contributions are not tax-deductible but qualified distributions are tax free, 507

Round, rounding, rounded a procedure to find an estimated or approximate answer, 7

Rounded number an approximate number that is obtained from rounding an exact amount, 7

Rounding decimals, 83

Rule of 78 method for determining the amount of refund of the finance charge for an installment loan that is paid before it is due, 435

Salary an agreed-upon amount of pay that is not based on the number of hours worked, 344

Salary-plus-commission a set amount of pay plus an additional amount based on sales, 348

Sales returns or allowances refunds or adjustments for unsatisfactory merchandise or services, 752

Sales tax a tax that is based on the price of a purchase. The tax is collected at the time of purchase and the business periodically sends the collected tax to a governmental agency, 706

Salvage value or scrap value or residual value an estimated dollar value of an asset at the end of the asset's estimated useful life, 604

Scrap value *See* Salvage value, 604

Second mortgage a mortgage in addition to the first mortgage that is secured by the real property, 576

Sector portion or wedge of a circle identified by two lines from the center to the outer edge of the circle, 223

Securities investments such as stocks, bonds, notes, debentures, limited partnership interests, or and gas interests, or other investment contracts, 553

Self-employment (SE) tax the equivalent of both the employee's and the employer's tax for both Social Security and Medicare. It is two times the employee's rate, 361

Selling price (retail price) price at which a business sells merchandise, 300

Semimonthly twice a month or 24 times a year, 344

Sequential numbers table 396

Service charge a fee the bank charges for maintaining the checking account or for other banking services, 121

Share one unit of ownership of a corporation, 542

Shareholder ratio translates the overall results of business operation so that they can be compared in terms of a share of stock.

Signature card a document that a bank keeps on file to verify the signatures of persons authorized to write checks on an account, 113

Simple discount note a loan made by a bank at a simple interest with interest collected at the time the loan is made, 402

Simple interest finding the principal, rate, or time using the simple interest formula, 392
formula, 388
fractional parts of a year, 390
interest when a loan or investment is repaid in a lump sum, 388
maturity value of a loan, 389
tables, 398

Single discount equivalent the complement of the net decimal equivalent. It is the decimal equivalent of a single discount rate that is equal to the series of discount rates, 270

Single discount rate a term used to indicate that only one discount rate is applied to the list price, 268
complements of, 266
finding the net price using, 266
finding the trade discount using, 268

Sinking fund payment into an ordinary annuity to yield a desired future value, 515
payments, 516
present value of an ordinary annuity, 516–517

Social Security tax a federal tax that goes into a fund that pays monthly benefits to retired and disabled workers, 360–361
calculating employee's contribution to, 360, 361

Solve find the value of the unknown or variable that makes the equation true, 150

Specific identification inventory method an inventory valuation method that is based on the actual cost of each item available for sale, 637

Spread the variation or dispersion of a set of data, 238

Standard bar graph bar graph with just one variable, 219

Standard deduction a specified reduction of taxable income. The standard deduction amount is based on filing status and is adjusted yearly for inflation. Normally, taxpayers who do not use the standard deduction have eligible itemized deductions that exceed the standard deduction, 715

Standard deviation a statistical measurement that shows how data are spread above and below the mean. The square root of the variance is the standard deviation, 239

State unemployment (SUTA) tax a state tax required of most employers. The tax also provides payment of unemployment compensation to certain workers who have lost their jobs, 366

Statistic a standardized, meaningful measure of a set of data that reveals a certain feature or characteristic of the data, 227

Statistic mean, 227
median, 228
mode, 229
range, 238
standard deviation, 239
variance, 239

Stock the distribution of ownership of a corporation. Partial ownership can be purchased through various stock markets, 542
dividends, 542
P/E ratio, 545
price to earnings (P/E) ratio, 545
reading listings, 542

Stock certificate a certificate of ownership of stock issued to the buyer, 542

Stock listings information about the price of a share of stock and some historical information that is published in newspapers and on the Internet, 542

Stock market the structure for buying and selling stock, 542

Stockbroker the person who handles the trading of stock. A stockbroker receives a commission for these services, 542

Straight commission entire pay based on sales, 348

Straight piecework rate piecework rate where the pay is the same per item no matter how many items are produced, 346

Straight-line depreciation a method of depreciation in which the amount of depreciation of an asset is spread equally over the number of years of useful life of the asset, 604

Straight-line rate when used with the declining-balance method of depreciation, the straight-line rate is a fraction with a numerator of 1 and a denominator equal to the number of useful years of an asset. This fraction is usually expressed as a decimal equivalent when making calculations and a percent equivalent when identifying the rate of depreciation, 611

Subtract decimals, 85

Subtracting fractions, 54
mixed numbers, 55

Subtrahend the number being subtracted, 11

Suggested retail price, catalog price, list price Sum or total three common terms for the price at which the manufacturer suggests an item should be sold to the consumer, 264

Sum the answer or result of addition, 10

Sum-of-the-years'-digits depreciation a depreciation method that allows the greatest depreciation the first year and a decreasing amount each year thereafter, 608

Surrender option 677

Symmetrical a figure that if folded at a middle point, the two halves will match, 240

Take-home pay *See* Net earnings (net pay), 344

Tally a mark that is used to count data in class intervals, 232

Tax money collected by a government for its support and for providing services to the populace, 706
excise tax, 706
income, 715
property tax, 710
sales tax, 706
See also income tax tables, 717